KU-644-529

THE PICKERING MASTERS

THE WORKS OF THOMAS DE QUINCEY
VOLUME 16

THE PICKERING MASTERS

THE WORKS OF THOMAS DE QUINCEY

Volumes 8–21

General Editor: Grevel Lindop

Volume Editors: Edmund Baxter
Frederick Burwick
Alina Clej
Grevel Lindop
Robert Morrison
Julian North
Daniel Sanjiv Roberts
Laura Roman
Barry Symonds
John Whale

Consulting Editor: Barry Symonds

Advisory Editors: Thomas McFarland
Robert Woof
Jonathan Wordsworth

The first page of De Quincey's 'The Vision of Sudden Death' (MS VSD E), courtesy of the National Library of Scotland.

THE WORKS OF THOMAS DE QUINCEY

VOLUME 16
ARTICLES FROM
TAIT'S EDINBURGH MAGAZINE,
MACPHAIL'S EDINBURGH ECCLESIASTICAL JOURNAL,
THE *GLASGOW ATHENAEUM ALBUM,*
THE *NORTH BRITISH REVIEW,*
AND *BLACKWOOD'S EDINBURGH MAGAZINE*
1847–9

Edited by
Robert Morrison

LONDON
PICKERING & CHATTO
2003

Published by Pickering & Chatto (Publishers) Ltd

21 Bloomsbury Way, London, WC1A 2TH

2252 Ridge Road, Brookfield, Vermont 05036, USA

www.pickeringchatto.com

All rights reserved.
No part of this publication may be reproduced,
stored in a retrieval system, or transmitted in any form
or by any means, electronic, mechanical, photocopying, recording,
or otherwise without prior permission
of the publisher.

Copyright © Pickering & Chatto (Publishers) Limited 2003

BRITISH LIBRARY CATALOGUING-IN-PUBLICATION DATA
A catalogue record for this title is available from the British Library.

ISBN 1 85196 52 0 3

LIBRARY OF CONGRESS CATALOGING-IN-PUBLICATION DATA
A catalogue record for this title is available from the Library of Congress.

∞
This publication is printed on acid-free paper that
conforms to the American National Standard for the
Permanence of Paper for Printed Library Materials

Typeset by P&C

Printed and bound in Great Britain
by Cromwell Press Ltd., Trowbridge

For my parents,
Glenn and Joyce Morrison

CONTENTS

Articles from *Blackwood's Edinburgh Magazine*, 1849

Manuscript Transcripts

PREFACE

The Social Sciences and Humanities Research Council of Canada has given crucial support at every stage of this project. My work on this edition would not have been possible without the Council's confidence and generosity.

This volume has benefited at every stage from the knowledge and experience of my fellow-editors. I would especially like to thank Grevel Lindop, who gave me the opportunity to participate in this project, and who has led it with such distinction. His advice and support, always generously given, have been invaluable. I have also benefited greatly from the assistance of J. H. Alexander, Tom Archibald, Chris Baldick, Peter Bell, Peter Booth, Kenneth Carpenter, Eileen M. Curran, Bob Freeman, Elizabeth Freeman, Peter Garside, David Higgins, Heather Jackson, J. R. de J. Jackson, Richard Jackson, Larry Krupp, Christopher Mayo, Thomas McFarland, Jon Mee, James Perkin, Robert Perrins, John Richardson, Christopher Ricks, Philip S. Rossi, Roger Savage, Herbert Tucker, Jon Usher, Chris VandenBossche, Uwe Wilhelm, Ian Wilks, and Romira Worvill. In particular, I would like to thank Geoffrey Carnall and Beert Verstraete, who have been enthusiastic supporters of the De Quincey project since its inception, and whose insights and great expertise have improved this volume at many points. I have had the pleasure of working with a series of fine research assistants: thank you to Jana Beasley, Graeme Ching, Anne Chodakowski, Darren Gilmour, Stephanie Johnson, Glenn Parson, Sue Rauth, Tammi Smith, and Katherine Zwicker. I am especially grateful to Sandra Barry. At Pickering and Chatto, Sarah Humbles has provided crucial assistance and support. I completed a good deal of the work on this edition during two stays as a Fellow at the Institute for Advanced Studies in the Humanities at the University of Edinburgh: I would like to thank Cairns Craig, John Frow, Peter Jones, and Anthea Taylor for making my time as a Fellow so stimulating and productive.

I am greatly indebted to several librarians: Ann Hennigar and Darlene Sweet at the Vaughan Library, Acadia University; Jean Archibald, Jill Evans, and Ann Henderson at the University of Edinburgh Library; Jeff Cowton at the Dove Cottage Library, Grasmere; Susan Halpert at Houghton Library, Harvard; Michael Currier, Edward Doctoroff, and Michael Fitzgerald at Widener Library, Harvard; Stephen Crook at the New York Public Library,

Berg Collection; and Iain Brown at the National Library of Scotland. For permission to reproduce manuscript material related to the essays in this volume, I am grateful to the trustees of the following libraries: Boston University Library, Special Collections; British Library, Department of Printed Books; Brown University Library, Department of Rare Books; Buffalo and Erie County Public Library, James Fraser Gluck Collection; University of Chicago Library; Cornell University Library, Wordsworth Collection; University of Edinburgh Library, Special Collections; Dove Cottage Library, Grasmere; Houghton Library, Harvard; Huntington Library; New York Public Library, Berg Collection; Bodleian Library, University of Oxford; Worcester College Library, Oxford; Princeton University, Robert H. Taylor Collection; and the National Library of Scotland.

Finally, I would like to thank Carole, who has supported my work on this project for thirteen years, and whose strength and love are my anchor. Without her, nothing would come to any good.

This edition is for my parents.

Robert Morrison

ABBREVIATIONS

Bacon, *Essayes*	Francis Bacon, *The Essayes or Counsels, Civill and Morall*, ed. Michael Kiernan (Oxford: Clarendon Press, 1985)
Bentley, *Works*	*Richard Bentley: The Works*, ed. Alexander Dyce, 3 vols (London: Macpherson, 1836-8)
Blackwood's	*Blackwood's Edinburgh Magazine* (Edinburgh: William Blackwood, 1817-1980)
Bonner	*De Quincey at Work*, ed. Willard Hallam Bonner (New York: Airport Publishers, 1936)
Boswell	*Life of Johnson*, ed. G. B. Hill, revised L. F. Powell, 6 vols (Oxford: Clarendon Press, 1934-64)
Byron, *PW*	*The Poetical Works of Lord Byron*, ed. Jerome McGann, 7 vols (Oxford: Clarendon Press, 1980-93)
Calvin, *Letters*	*Letters of John Calvin*, trans. David Constable and ed. Jules Bonnet, 2 vols (Edinburgh: Constable, 1855-7)
Carlyle, *Letters*	*The Collected Letters of Thomas and Jane Welsh Carlyle*, eds Charles Richard Sanders, Kenneth J. Fielding, et al., 29 vols (Durham, NC: Duke University Press, 1970-continuing)
Carlyle, *Works*	*The Works of Thomas Carlyle*, ed. H. D. Traill, 30 vols (London: Chapman and Hall, 1896-9)
Coleridge, *PW*	Samuel Taylor Coleridge, *Poetical Works*, ed. J. C. C. Mays, 3 vols (Princeton: Princeton University Press, 2001)
De Quincey as Critic	*De Quincey as Critic*, ed. John E. Jordan (London: Routledge and Kegan Paul, 1973)
Dickens, *Barnaby Rudge*	Charles Dickens, *Barnaby Rudge*, eds Clive Hurst, Jon Mee and Iain McCallam (Oxford: Oxford University Press, 2003)
Dickens, *Dombey and Son*	Charles Dickens, *Dombey and Son*, ed. Alan Horsman (Oxford: Clarendon Press, 1974)

Donaldson	John William Donaldson, *A Vindication of Protestant Principles* (London: John W. Parker, 1847)
Eaton	Horace Eaton, *Thomas De Quincey* (New York: Oxford University Press, 1936)
Emerson, *Essays*	Ralph Waldo Emerson, *Essays: First Series*. New Edition (Boston: James Munroe and Company, 1847)
Emerson, *JMN*	*The Journals and Miscellaneous Notebooks of Ralph Waldo Emerson*, eds William Henry Gilman, Merton M. Sealts, Jr., et al., 16 vols (Cambridge, Mass.: Belknap Press of Harvard University Press, 1960-83)
F	*De Quincey's Writings*, ed. J. T. Fields, 22 vols (Boston: Ticknor and Fields, 1851–9)
Forster	John Forster, *The Life and Adventures of Oliver Goldsmith* (London: Bradbury and Evans, 1848)
Goldman	Albert Goldman, *The Mine and the Mint: Sources for the Writings of Thomas De Quincey* (Carbondale: Southern Illinois University Press, 1965)
Goldsmith, *CW*	*Collected Works of Oliver Goldsmith*, ed. Arthur Friedman, 5 vols (Oxford: Clarendon Press, 1966)
Haydon	*The Diary of Benjamin Robert Haydon*, ed. Willard Bissell Pope, 5 vols (Cambridge, Mass.: Harvard University Press, 1960-3)
HCR	*Henry Crabb Robinson on Books and their Writers*, ed. Edith J. Morley, 3 vols (London: Dent, 1938)
Hogg	James Hogg, *De Quincey and his Friends* (London: Sampson Low, Marston and Company, 1895)
Hunt	*The Selected Writings of Leigh Hunt, Volume 3*, ed. Robert Morrison (London: Pickering and Chatto, 2003)
Japp	Alexander H. Japp, *Thomas De Quincey: His Life and Writings* (London: John Hogg, 1890)
Japp, *PW*	*The Posthumous Works of Thomas De Quincey*, ed. Alexander H. Japp, 2 vols (London: Heinemann, 1891-3)
Jean Paul, *Hesperus*	*Hesperus: or, Forty-five dog-post-days; a biography from the German of Jean Paul Friedrich Richter*, trans. Charles T. Brooks (Boston: Ticknor and Fields, 1865)
Johnson, *Letters*	*The Letters of Samuel Johnson*, ed. Bruce Redford, 5 vols (Princeton: Princeton University Press, 1992-4)

Johnson, *Lives*	Samuel Johnson, *The Lives of the Poets*, ed. G. B. Hill, 3 vols (Oxford: Clarendon Press, 1905)
Jordan	*De Quincey to Wordsworth: A Biography of a Relationship*, ed. John E. Jordan (Berkeley: University of California Press, 1963)
Kant, *CPR*	Immanuel Kant, *Critique of Pure Reason*, eds Paul Guyer and Allen W. Wood (Cambridge: Cambridge University Press, 1998)
Lamb, *Letters*	*The Letters of Charles and Mary Lamb*, ed. E. V. Lucas, 3 vols (London: Dent, 1935)
Lamb, *Works*	*The Works of Charles and Mary Lamb*, ed. E. V. Lucas, 7 vols (London: Methuen, 1903-5)
Landor, *CW*	*The Complete Works of Walter Savage Landor*, eds T. Earle Welby and Stephen Wheeler, 16 vols (London: Chapman and Hall, 1927-36)
Landor, *Works*	*The Works of Walter Savage Landor*, 2 vols (London: Moxon, 1846)
Lindop	Grevel Lindop, *The Opium-Eater: A Life of Thomas De Quincey* (London: Dent, 1981)
Masson	*The Collected Writings of Thomas De Quincey*, ed. David Masson, 14 vols (London: A and C. Black, 1889-90)
Michelet	Jules Michelet, *The History of France*, trans. Walter K. Kelly (London: Chapman and Hall, 1844-6)
Milton, *Works*	*The Works of John Milton*, eds Frank Allen Patterson, et al., 18 vols (New York: Columbia University Press, 1931-8)
Morrison	'Richard Woodhouse's *Cause Book*: The Opium-Eater, the Magazine Wars, and the London Literary Scene in 1821', ed. Robert Morrison, *Harvard Library Bulletin*, NS 9.3 (Fall 1998), pp. 1-43
Proverbs	*The Oxford Dictionary of English Proverbs*, third edition, revised by F. P. Wilson (Oxford: Clarendon Press, 1970)
Roscoe	*The Works of Alexander Pope, Esquire*, ed. W. Roscoe, 8 vols (London: Longman, Brown, 1847)
Schlosser	F. C. Schlosser, *History of the Eighteenth Century and of the Nineteenth till the Overthrow of the French Empire*, trans. D. Davison (London: Chapman and Hall, 1843-52)
Scott, *Mid-Lothian*	Walter Scott, *The Heart of Mid-Lothian*, eds David Hewitt and Alison Lumsden (Edinburgh: Edinburgh University Press, 2003)

Scott, *Old Mortality*	Walter Scott, *The Tale of Old Mortality*, ed. Douglas Mack (Edinburgh: Edinburgh University Press, 1993)
Scott, *Swift*	*The Works of Jonathan Swift*, second edition, ed. Walter Scott, 19 vols (Edinburgh: Constable, 1824)
SGG	*Selections Grave and Grave, from Writings Published and Unpublished, by Thomas De Quincey*, 14 vols (Edinburgh: James Hogg, 1853-60)
Southey, *Letters*	Robert Southey, *Letters from England: by Don Manuel Alvarez Espriella. Translated from the Spanish*, ed. Jack Simmons (London: Cresset Press, 1951)
Southey, *New Letters*	*New Letters of Robert Southey*, ed. Kenneth Curry, 2 vols (New York: Columbia University Press, 1965)
Spectator	Joseph Addison and Richard Steele, *The Spectator*, ed. Donald F. Bond, 5 vols (Oxford: Clarendon Press, 1965)
Stepto	*Lieutenant Nun*, trans. Michele Stepto and Gabriel Stepto (Boston: Deacon Press, 1996)
Super	R. H. Super, *Walter Savage Landor: A Biography* (New York: New York University Press, 1954)
Swift, *Prose*	*The Prose Works of Jonathan Swift*, ed. Herbert Davis, 14 vols (Oxford: Basil Blackwell, 1939-68)
Symonds	Barry Symonds, *De Quincey to His Publishers: The Letters of Thomas De Quincey to His Publishers, and Other Letters, 1819-1832*, (unpublished Ph.D., University of Edinburgh, 1994)
Tait's	*Tait's Edinburgh Magazine* (Edinburgh: William Tait, 1832-61)
Talfourd	Thomas Noon Talfourd, *Final Memorials of Charles Lamb*, 2 vols (London: Moxon, 1848)
Valon	Alex de Valon, 'Catalina de Erauso' in *Revue des Deux Mondes*, 17 (15 February 1847), pp. 589-637
Wordsworth, *Prose*	*The Prose Works of William Wordsworth*, eds W. J. B. Owen and Jane Worthington Smyser, 3 vols (Oxford: Clarendon Press, 1974)

CONVENTIONS FOR MANUSCRIPT TRANSCRIPTION

Where a manuscript is selected for transcription it is given in full, including all holograph deletions. No attempt is made to reproduce the arrangement of text on the page, but the headnote to each manuscript item will indicate the positioning of the text where relevant.

Where possible the headnotes give paper size, colour of ink, watermark details, the nature of any folding, and an indication of which sides are written or left blank.

A folio number and indication of recto (abbreviated as 'r.') or verso (abbreviated as 'v.') is assigned by the editor and given in square brackets at the head of each manuscript page. Thus [1 r.] would indicate the beginning of the recto of the first leaf of a manuscript, and [1 v.] would indicate the verso of the same leaf. Any exceptions to this general principle are explained in the headnotes.

De Quincey's abbreviations are not generally expanded. In the few cases where an abbreviation is expanded to render it intelligible, the expansion is placed in square brackets.

Deleted matter is placed in angle brackets ‹ ›

An illegible character is indicated by **x**

De Quincey's wide range of bracket forms, often hybridized, is normalized to round brackets.

Matter inserted above or between lines is enclosed in curly brackets and preceded by an oblique arrow, thus {↑ }

Matter underlined in the manuscript is given in *italic*

A blank space, stain, tear or other damage completely obliterating text is indicated thus: {stain}

Articles from
Tait's Edinburgh Magazine,
1847–8

NOTES ON WALTER SAVAGE LANDOR*
[Part I]

First published in *Tait's*, XIV, January 1847, pp. 18–23. The essay was printed as 'BY THOMAS DE QUINCEY.' in a centred line following the title and immediately preceding the text.

Reprinted in *F*, IX, *Essays on the Poets, and Other English Writers* (1853), pp. 242–62, 291–3.

Revised text, carrying many accidentals but only four substantive variants from *F*, in *SGG*, IX, *Leaders in Literature, With a Notice of Traditional Errors Affecting Them* (1858), pp. 284–304.

There is one manuscript, as follows:

MS A: Huntington Library, HM 36039. The manuscript is a complete set of *SGG* page proofs. It contains nine significant variants, and these are listed in the textual notes.

Walter Savage Landor (1775–1864; *DNB*), poet and essayist, was the foremost neoclassicist of his age. He was born in Warwick, and as a child was tutored by the famous Whig cleric and controversialist Samuel Parr, who instilled in him a fervent love of liberal politics and Latin literature. Landor attended Rugby and Oxford, but was removed from both schools because of the inflammable temper that caused him throughout his life to quarrel with his father, wife, neighbours, and any form of authority that offended him. His first publication, *The Poems of Walter Savage Landor* (1795), was followed by the exotic poem *Gebir* (1798) and then a collection of verse entitled *Simonidea* (1806), which featured two of his most famous lyrics, 'Rose Aylmer' and 'Mother, I can not mind my wheel'. Like William Wordsworth, Landor journeyed to Paris in 1802 during the Peace of Amiens, and in 1808 he travelled to Corunna to aid the Spanish revolt against Napoleon. That same year he bought an estate, Llanthony Abbey, in Monmouthshire, and began his long friendship with Robert Southey. Landor married Julia Thuillier in 1811, and his best-known tragedy, *Count Julian*, appeared a year later. He left Britain in 1815 and settled in Italy, where he began to produce his famous *Imaginary Conversations*, the first of which, 'Southey and Porson', appeared in the *London Magazine* in 1823. In the years that followed Landor met Wordsworth, Samuel Taylor Coleridge, Charles and Mary Lamb, and Ralph Waldo Emerson. In 1835, he separated from his wife and returned to England, where he drew the attention of a new generation of literary figures, including Robert Browning, Elizabeth

* The Works of Savage Landor. 2 vols. London: Moxon. 1846.

Barrett, Alfred Tennyson, and Charles Dickens, who produced a genial caricature of him as Lawrence Boythorn in *Bleak House* (1852–3). In 1858, Landor went again to live in Italy, where Browning attempted to protect and care for him. Landor died in Florence at the age of eighty-nine. Algernon Swinburne's 'In Memory of Walter Savage Landor' is the most famous tribute.

De Quincey and Landor never met, though each, with qualifications, thought highly of the other. Landor found De Quincey's 1831 *Blackwood's* review of Samuel Parr 'insolent and flippant', but he read a great deal of De Quincey, including his 1834–5 *Tait's* series on Coleridge and several essays in *Selections Grave and Gay*. In 1847, he sent De Quincey an inscribed and 'very prettily bound' copy of his recently published *Poemata et Inscriptiones*, in acknowledgement of the present review and, undoubtedly, of their shared love of classical literature. For his part, De Quincey had admired Landor since 1803, when as a newly arrived eighteen-year-old Oxford undergraduate he bought a copy of *Gebir* and Lamb's tragedy *John Woodvil* on the same December morning, and placed them on his bookshelf beside 'the joint poems of Wordsworth and Coleridge as then associated in the "Lyrical Ballads"'. What especially impressed the young De Quincey about *Gebir* was 'the splendour of its descriptions', for he had 'opened accidentally upon the sea-nymphs marriage with Tamor, the youthful brother of Gebir'. In the *Westmorland Gazette* in 1819 De Quincey described Landor as 'a man of transcendent genius', and in 1823, when he and Landor were fellow contributors to the *London Magazine*, De Quincey told James Hessey that he thought Landor 'one of the most extraordinary men of the Age', and promised to write for the *London* 'a Paper upon Landor's Poetry, with extracts of his finest Passages, and a Character of his Genius &c'. Three years later in *Blackwood's* De Quincey cited Landor as a writer of 'eminent genius' (Vol. 8, pp. 5–6; Super, pp. 251, 422, 378; Vol. 1, p. 189; *The Keats Circle*, ed. H. E. Rollins, 2 vols (Cambridge, Mass.: Harvard University Press, 1965) vol. II, pp. 433–4; Vol. 6, p. 62).

In 1846, Landor published a two-volume edition of his *Works*. To mark the occasion De Quincey published four essays in *Tait's* over the first four months of 1847: 'Notes on Walter Savage Landor' (January and February), 'Orthographic Mutineers' (March), and 'Milton *versus* Southey and Landor' (April). The *Tait's* set was broken, however, when in both *F* and *SGG* the four essays were separated and published in three different volumes. Masson restored the unity of the original, four-part assesment (vol. XI, pp. 394–474), though he published it in its revised form. The present edition reprints the four essays in chronological order, and in the original versions.

De Quincey was hard at work on the series well before the first essay appeared in January 1847. 'The Landor is all but ready', he told William Tait on 10 August 1846, though within a month the project had grown, for he reported on 8 September that he now had 'a long Art. on Landor: which however might be divided. But it needs some alterations that wd. take the rest of the day'. Yet two months later the process was still not complete, and on 6 November De Quincey wrote again to Tait: 'I have just sent a note declining a dinner party for this evening on account of the art. on Landor', he explained: 'so I did last night. And ever since I saw you I have been altering – connecting –

&c. without ceasing. – I sent you the opening part, and will send the rest in the morning' (National Library of Scotland MS 1670, f. 101, f. 104, f. 106).

In the four essays themselves, De Quincey mixes some praise with a good deal of censure, calling Landor 'a man of great genius', but criticizing him for his education, orthography, degrading religious notions, faulty 'sense of discrimination', 'blameable coarseness', and 'Landorian perverseness' (pp. 6, 25, 48). De Quincey partially explains the reasons behind this divided opinion when he confesses that

> I was and am a Tory; and in some remote geological aera, my bones may be dug up...as a specimen of the fossil Tory. Yet, for all that, I loved audacity; and I gazed with some indefinite shade of approbation upon a poet [Landor] whom the attorney-general might have occasion to speak with. (p. 11)

In private correspondence, however, De Quincey was much more forthright in his praise, for when in the autumn of 1847 Landor sent him the inscribed copy of *Poemata et Inscriptiones*, he told his daughter Margaret that there was 'no author from whom I *could* have been more gratified by such a mark of attention' (Japp, p. 262).

NOBODY in this generation reads *The Spectator*.[1] There are, however, several people still surviving who have read No.1. In which No.1. a strange mistake is made. It is there asserted as a general affection of human nature, that it is impossible to read a book with satisfaction until one has ascertained whether the author of it be tall or short, corpulent or thin, and as to complexion, whether he be a 'black' man (which, in the *Spectator*'s time, was the absurd expression for a swarthy man), or a fair man, or a sallow man, or perhaps a green man,[2] which Southey affirmed[*] to be the proper description of many stout artificers in Birmingham, too much given to work in metallic fumes;[4] on which account the name of Southey is an abomination to this day in certain furnaces of Warwickshire. But can anything be more untrue than this Spectatorial doctrine? Did ever the youngest of female novel-readers, on a sultry day, decline to eat a bunch of grapes until she knew whether the fruiterer were a good-looking man? Which of us ever heard a stranger inquiring for a 'Guide to the Trosachs,'[5] but saying, 'I scruple, however, to pay for this book, until I know whether the author is heather-legged?' On this principle, if any such principle prevailed, we authors should be liable to as strict a revision of our physics before having any right to be read, as we all are before having our lives insured from the medical advisers of insurance offices;[6] fellows that examine one with stethescopes, that pinch one, that actually punch one in the ribs, until a man becomes savage, and – in case the insurance should miss fire in consequence of the medical report – speculates on the propriety of pro-

[*] '*Southey affirmed:*' – viz. in the 'Letters of Espriella,' an imaginary Spaniard on a visit to England, about the year 1810.[3]

secuting the medical ruffian for an assault, for a most unprovoked assault and battery, and, if possible, including in the indictment the now odious insurance office as an accomplice before the fact. Meantime the odd thing is, not that Addison should have made a mistake, but that he and his readers should in this mistake have recognised a hidden truth, the sudden illumination of a propensity latent in all people, but now first exposed; for it happens that there really *is* a propensity in all of us very like what Addison describes, very different, and yet, after one correction, the very same. No reader cares about an author's person *before* reading his book: it is *after* reading it, and supposing the book to reveal something of the writer's *moral* nature, as modifying his intellect, it is for his fun, his fancy, his sadness, possibly his craziness, that any reader cares about seeing the author in person. Afflicted with the very satyriasis of curiosity, no man ever wished to see the author of a *Ready Reckoner*, or of a treatise on the *Agistment Tithe*,[7] or on the *Present deplorable Dry-rot in Potatoes*. 'Bundle off, sir, as fast as you can,' the most diligent reader would say to such an author in case he insisted on submitting his charms to inspection. 'I have had quite enough distress of mind from reading your works, without needing the additional dry-rot of your bodily presence.' Neither does any man, on descending from a railway train, turn to look whether the carriage in which he has ridden happens to be a good-looking carriage, or wish for an introduction to the coach-maker. Satisfied that the one has not broken his bones, and that the other has no writ against his person, he dismisses with the same frigid scowl both the carriage and the author of its existence.

But, with respect to Mr Landor, as at all connected with this reformed doctrine of the *Spectator*, a difficulty arises. He is a man of great genius, and, as such, he *ought* to interest the public. More than enough appears of his strong, eccentric nature, through every page of his now extensive writings, to win, amongst those who have read him, a corresponding interest in all that concerns him personally: in his social relations, in his biography, in his manners, in his appearance. Out of two conditions for attracting a *personal* interest, he has powerfully realised one. His moral nature, shining with coloured light through the crystal shrine of his thoughts, will not allow of your forgetting it. A sunset of Claude, or a dying dolphin,[8] *can* be forgotten, and generally *is* forgotten; but not the fiery radiations of a human spirit, built by nature to animate a leader in storms, a martyr, a national reformer, an arch-rebel, as circumstances might dictate, but whom too much wealth,* and the accidents of education, have turned aside into a contemplative recluse. Had Mr Landor,

* '*Too much wealth:*' – Mr Landor, who *should* know best, speaks of himself (once, at least) as 'poor;' but *that* is all nonsense.[9] I have known several people with annual incomes bordering on £20,000, who spoke of themselves, and seemed, seriously to think themselves, unhappy 'paupers.' Lady Hester Stanhope, with £2700 a year (of which about twelve arose from her government pension), and without one solitary dependent in her train, thought herself rich enough to become a queen (an Arabic *maleky*) in the Syrian mountains,[10] but an absolute pauper for London: 'for how, you know,' (as she would say, pathetically) 'could the humblest of spinsters live decently upon that pittance?'

therefore, been read in any extent answering to his merits, he must have become, for the English public, an object of prodigious personal interest. We should have had novels upon him,[11] lampoons upon him, libels upon him; he would have been shown up dramatically on the stage; he would, according to the old joke, have been 'traduced' in French, and also 'overset' in Dutch.[12] Meantime he has *not* been read. It would be an affectation to think it. Many a writer is, by the sycophancy of literature, reputed to be read, whom in all Europe not six eyes settle upon through the revolving year. Literature, with its cowardly falsehoods, exhibits the largest field of conscious Phrygian adulation that human life has ever exposed to the derision of the heavens. Demosthenes, for instance, or Plato,[13] is not read to the extent of twenty pages annually by ten people in Europe. The *sale* of their works would not account for three readers; the six or seven are generously conceded as possibilities furnished by the great public libraries. But, then, Walter Savage Landor, though writing a little in Latin, and a *very* little in Italian, does not write at all in Greek. So far he has some advantage over Plato; and, if he writes chiefly in dialogue, which few people love to read any more than novels in the shape of letters, *that* is a crime common to both. So that he has the d—l's luck and his own, all Plato's chances, and one of his own beside – viz. his English. Still it is no use counting chances; facts are the thing. And printing-presses, whether of Europe or of England, bear witness that neither Plato nor Landor is a marketable commodity. In fact, these two men resemble each other in more particulars than it is at present necessary to say. Especially they were both inclined to be luxurious: both had a hankering after purple and fine linen; both hated 'filthy dowlas' with the hatred of Falstaff,[14] whether in appareling themselves or their diction; and both bestowed pains as elaborately upon the secret *art* of a dialogue as a lapidary would upon the cutting of a sultan's rubies.

But might not a man build a reputation on the basis of *not* being read? To be read is undoubtedly something: to be read by an odd million or so, is a sort of feather in a man's cap; but it is also a distinction that he has been read absolutely by nobody at all. There have been cases, and one or two in modern times, where an author could point to a vast array of his own works, concerning which no evidence existed that so much as one had been opened by human hand, or glanced at by human eye. That was awful: such a sleep of pages by thousands in one eternal darkness, never to be visited by light; such a rare immunity from the villanies of misconstruction; such a Sabbath from the impertinencies of critics! You shuddered to reflect that, for anything known to the contrary, *there* might lurk jewels of truth explored in vain, or treasure for ever intercepted to the interests of man. But such a sublimity supposes *total* defect of readers; whereas it can be proved against Mr Landor, that he has been read by at least a score of people, all wide awake; and if any treason is buried in a page of *his*, thank Heaven, by this time it must have been found out and reported to the authorities. So that neither can Landor plead the unlimited popularity of a novelist, aided by the interest of a tale, and by an artist, nor the total obscuration of a German metaphysician. Neither do mobs read him, as they do M. Sue;[15] nor do all men turn their eyes from him, as they do from Hegel.*

This, however, is true only of Mr Landor's prose works. His first work was a poem, viz. *Gebir;* and it had the sublime distinction, for some time, of having enjoyed only two readers; which two were Southey and myself. It was on first entering at Oxford[17] that I found 'Gebir' printed and (nominally) published; whereas, in fact, all its advertisements of birth and continued existence, were but so many notifications of its intense privacy. Not knowing Southey at that time, I vainly conceited myself to be the one sole purchaser and reader of this poem. I even fancied myself to have been pointed out in the streets of Oxford, where the Landors had been well known in times preceding my own,[18] as the one inexplicable man authentically known to possess 'Gebir,' or even (it might be whispered mysteriously) to have read 'Gebir.' It was not clear but this reputation might stand in lieu of any independent fame, and might raise me to literary distinction. The preceding generation had greatly esteemed the man called '*Single-Speech Hamilton;*'[19] not at all for the speech (which, though good, very few people had read), but entirely for the supposed fact that he had exhausted himself in that one speech, and had become physically incapable of making a second: so that afterwards, when he really *did* make a second, everybody was incredulous; until, the thing being past denial, naturally the world was disgusted, and most people dropped his acquaintance. To be a Mono-Gebirist was quite as good a title to notoriety; and five years after, when I found that I had 'a brother near the throne,'[20] viz. Southey, mortification would have led me willingly to resign altogether in *his* favour. Shall I make the reader acquainted with the story of Gebir?

Gebir is the king of Gibraltar; which, however, it would be an anachronism to call Gibraltar, since it drew that name from this very Gebir;[21] and doubtless, by way of honour to his memory. Mussulmans tell a different story; but who cares for what is said by infidel dogs? King then, let us call him of Calpe; and a very good king he is; young, brave, of upright intention; but being also warlike, and inflamed by popular remembrances of ancient wrongs, he resolves to seek reparation from the children's children of the wrong-doers; and he weighs anchor in search of Mr Pitt's 'indemnity for the past,' though not much regarding that right honourable gentleman's 'security for the future.'[22] Egypt was the land that sheltered the wretches that represented the ancestors that had done the wrong. To Egypt, therefore, does king Gebir steer his expedition, which counted 10,000 picked men:

'Incenst
By meditating on primeval wrongs,

* '*From Hegel:*' – I am not prepared with an affidavit that no man ever read the late Mr Hegel,[16] that great master of the impenetrable. But sufficient evidence of that fact, as I conceive, may be drawn from those who have written commentaries upon him.

He blew his battle-horn; at which uprose
Whole nations; here ten thousand of most might
He called aloud; and soon Charoba saw
His dark helm hover o'er the land of Nile.'[23]

Who is Charoba? As respects the reader, she is the heroine of the poem: as respects Egypt, she is queen by the grace of God, defender of the faith, and so forth. Young and accustomed to unlimited obedience, how could she be otherwise than alarmed by the descent of a host far more martial than her own effeminate people, and assuming a religious character – avengers of wrong in some forgotten age? In her trepidation, she turns for aid and counsel to her nurse Dalica. Dalica, by the way, considered as a word, is a dactyle; that is, you must not lay the accent on the *i,* but on the first syllable. Dalica, considered as a woman, is about as bad a one as even Egypt could furnish. She is a thorough gipsy; a fortune-teller, and something worse, in fact. She is a sorceress, 'stiff in opinion:' and it needs not Pope's authority to infer that – of course she 'is always in the wrong.'[24] By her advice, but for a purpose known best to herself, an interview is arranged between Charoba and the invading monarch. At this interview, the two youthful sovereigns, Charoba, the queen of hearts and Gebir the king of clubs, fall irrevocably in love with each other. There's an end of club law; and Gebir is ever afterwards disarmed. But Dalica, that wicked Dalica, that sad old dactyle, who sees everything clearly that happens to be twenty years distant, cannot see a pike-staff if it is close before her nose; and of course she mistakes Charoba's agitations of love for paroxysms of anger. Charoba is herself partly to blame for this; but you must excuse her. The poor child readily confided her *terrors* to Dalica; but how can she be expected to make a *love* confidante of a tawny old witch like her? Upon this mistake, however, proceeds the whole remaining plot. *Dr* Dalica [which means *doctor* D., and by no means *dear* D.], having totally mistaken the symptoms, the diagnosis, the prognosis, and everything that ends in *osis*, necessarily mistakes also the treatment of the case, and, like some other doctors, failing to make a cure, covers up her blunders by a general slaughter. She visits her sister, a sorceress more potent than herself, living

'Deep in the wilderness of woe, Masar.'[25]

Between them they concert hellish incantations. From these issues a venomous robe, like that of the centaur Nessus.[26] This, at a festal meeting between the two nations and their princes, is given by Charoba to her lover – her lover, but as yet not recognised as such by *her*, nor until the moment of his death, avowed as such by himself. Gebir dies – the accursed robe, dipped in the 'viscous poison' exuding from the gums of the grey cerastes,[27] and tempered by other venomous juices of plant and animal, proves too much for his rocky constitution – Gibraltar is found not impregnable – the blunders of Dalica, the wicked nurse, and the arts of her sister Myrthyr, the wicked witch, are found too potent; and in one moment the union of two nations, with the happiness of two sovereigns, is wrecked for ever. The closing situation of the parties – monarch and monarch, nation and nation, youthful king and youthful queen, dying or despairing – nation and nation that had been reconciled, starting asunder once again amidst festival and flowers – these objects are scenically effective. The conception of the grouping is good; the *mise en scene*[28] is good; but, from want of pains-taking, not sufficiently brought out into strong relief; and the dying words of Gebir, which wind up the whole, are too bookish; they seem to be part of some article which he had been writing for the Gibraltar Quarterly.

There are two episodes, composing jointly about two-sevenths of the poem, and by no means its weakest parts. One describes the descent of Gebir to Hades. His guide is a man – who *is* this man?

'Living – they called him Aroar.'[29]

Is he *not* living, then? No. Is he dead, then? No nor dead either. Poor Aroar cannot live and cannot die – so that he is in an almighty fix. In this disagreeable dilemma, he contrives to amuse himself with politics – and, rather of a jacobinical cast: like the Virgilian Aeneas, Gebir is introduced not to the shades of the past only, but of the future.[30] He sees the pre-existing ghosts of gentlemen who are yet to come, silent as ghosts ought to be, but destined at some far distant time to make a considerable noise in our upper world. Amongst these is our worthy old George III., who (strange to say!) is not foreseen as galloping from Windsor to Kew,[31] surrounded by an escort of dragoons, nor in a scarlet coat riding after a fox, nor taking his morning rounds amongst his sheep and his turnips; but in the likeness of some savage creature, whom really, were it not for his eye-brows and his '*slanting*' forehead, the reader would never recognise:

'Aroar! what wretch that nearest us? what wretch
Is that, with eye-brows white and slanting brow?
———————————————— O king!
Iberia bore him; but the breed accurst
Inclement winds blew blighting from north-east.'[32]

Iberia is spiritual England; and *north-east* is mystical Hanover.[33] But what, then, were the 'wretch's' crimes? The white eye-brows I confess to; those were certainly crimes of considerable magnitude: but what else? Gebir has the same curiosity as myself, and propounds something like the same fishing question:

'He was a warrior then, nor feared the gods?'

To which Aroar answers –

'Gebir! he feared the demons, not the gods;
Though them, indeed, his daily face ador'd,
And was no warrior; yet the thousand lives
Squander'd as if to exercise a sling, &c. &c.'[34]

Really Aroar is too *Tom-Painish*,[35] and seems up to a little treason. He makes the poor king answerable for more than his own share of national offences, if such they were. All of us in the last generation were rather fond of fighting and assisting at fights in the character of mere spectators. I am sure *I* was. But if *that* is any fault, so was Plato, who (though probably inferior as a philosopher to you and me, reader) was much superior to either of us as a cock-fighter. So was Socrates in the preceding age; for, as he notoriously haunted the company of Alcibiades[36] at all hours, he must often have found his pupil diverting himself with those fighting quails which he kept in such numbers. Be assured that the oracle's 'wisest of men'[37] lent a hand very cheerfully to putting on the spurs when a main was to be fought; and, as to betting, probably *that* was the reason that Xantippe[38] was so often down upon him when he went home at night. To come home reeling from a fight, without a drachma left in his pocket, would naturally provoke any woman. Posterity has been very much misinformed about these things; and, no doubt, about Xantippe, poor woman, in particular. If *she* had had a disciple to write books,[39] as her cock-fighting husband had, perhaps we should have read a very different story. By the way, the propensity of *scandalum magnatum*[40] in Aroar was one of the things that fixed my youthful attention, and perhaps my admiration, upon Gebir. For myself, as perhaps the reader may have heard, I was and am a Tory; and in some remote geological aera, my bones may be dug up by some future Buckland[41] as a specimen of the fossil Tory. Yet, for all that, I loved audacity; and I gazed with some indefinite shade of approbation upon a poet whom the attorney-general might have occasion to speak with.

This, however, was a mere condiment to the main attraction of the poem. *That* lay in the picturesqueness of the images, attitudes, groups, dispersed everywhere. The eye seemed to rest everywhere upon festal processions, upon the pannels of Theban gates, or upon sculptured vases. The very first lines that by accident met my eye were those which follow. I cite them in mere obedience to the fact as it really was; else there are more striking illustrations of this sculpturesque faculty in Mr Landor; and for this faculty it was that both Southey and myself separately and independently had named him the English Valerius Flaccus.[42]

GEBIR ON REPAIRING TO HIS FIRST INTERVIEW WITH CHAROBA.

'But Gebir, when he heard of her approach,
Laid by his orbed shield: his vizor helm,
His buckler and his corslet he laid by,
And bade that none attend him: at his side
Two faithful dogs that urge the silent course,
Shaggy, deep-chested, croucht; the crocodile,
Crying, oft made them raise their flaccid ears,
And push their heads within their master's hand.
There was a lightning paleness in his face,
Such as Diana rising o'er the rocks

Showr'd on the lonely Latmian; on his brow
Sorrow there was, but there was nought severe.'[43]

'And the long moonbeam on the hard wet sand
Lay like a jasper column half up-rear'd.'[44]

'The king, who sate before his tent, descried
The dust rise redden'd from the setting sun.'[45]

Now let us pass to the imaginary dialogues: –

Marshal Bugeaud and Arab Chieftain.[46] – This dialogue, which is amongst the shortest, would not challenge a separate notice, were it not for the freshness in the public mind,[47] and the yet uncicatrised rawness of that atrocity which it commemorates. Here is an official account from the commander-in-chief: – 'Of seven hundred refractory and rebellious who took refuge in the caverns, thirty' [says the glory-hunting Marshall], 'and thirty only, are alive; and of these thirty there are only four who are capable of labour, or indeed of motion.'[48] How precious to the Marshal's heart must be that harvest of misery from which he so reluctantly allows the discount of about one-half per cent. Four only out of seven hundred, he is happy to assure Christendom, remain capable of hopping about; as to working, or getting honest bread, or doing any service in this world to themselves or others, it is truly delightful to announce, for public information, that all such practices are put a stop to for ever.

Amongst the fortunate four, who retain the power of hopping, we must reckon the *Arab Chieftain*, who is introduced into the colloquy in the character of respondent. He can hop, of course, *ex hypothesi*,[49] being one of the ever lucky quaternion; he can hop a little also as a rhetorician; indeed, as to *that* he is too much for the Marshal; but on the other hand he cannot see; the cave has cured him of any such impertinence as staring into other people's faces; he is also lame, the cave has shown him the absurdity of rambling about; – and, finally, he is a beggar; or, if he will not allow himself to be called by that name, upon the argument [which seems plausible] that he cannot be a beggar if he never begs, it is not the less certain that, in case of betting a six-pence, the chieftain would find it inconvenient to stake the cash.

The Marshal, who apparently does not pique himself upon politeness, addresses the Arab by the following assortment of names – 'Thief, assassin, traitor! blind greybeard! lame beggar!' The three first titles being probably mistaken for compliments, the Arab pockets in silence; but to the double-barrelled discharges of the two last he replies thus: – 'Cease *there*. Thou canst never make me beg for bread, for water, or for life; my grey beard is from God; my blindness and lameness are from thee.'[50] This is a pleasant way of doing business; rarely does one find little accounts so expeditiously settled and receipted. Beggar? But how if I do not beg? Greybeard? Put that down to the account of God. Cripple? Put that down to your own. Getting sulky under this mode of fencing from the desert-born, the Marshal invites him to enter one of his new-made law courts, where he will hear of something probably *not* to his advantage. Our Arab friend, however, is no connoisseur in courts of law: small wale* of courts in the desert; he does not so much 'do himself the honour to decline' as he turns a deaf ear to this proposal, and on *his* part presents a little counter invitation to the Marshal for a *pic-nic* party to the caves of Dahra. 'Enter' (says the unsparing Sheik) 'and sing and whistle in the cavern where the bones of brave men are never to bleach, are never to decay. Go, where the mother and infant are inseparable for ever – one mass of charcoal; the breasts that gave life, the lips that received it – all, all, save only where two arms, in colour and hardness like corroded iron, cling round a brittle stem, shrunken, warped, and where two heads are calcined. Even this massacre, no doubt, will find defenders in *your* country, for it is the custom of *your* country to cover blood with lies, and lies with blood.' 'And (says the facetious French Marshal) here and there a sprinkling of ashes over both.' ARAB.'Ending in merriment, as befits ye. But *is* it ended?'[53] But *is* it ended? Aye; the wilderness beyond Algiers returns an echo to those ominous words of the blind and mutilated chieftain. No, brave Arab, although the Marshal scoffingly rejoins that at least it is ended for *you*, ended it is not; for the great quarrel by which human nature pleads with such a fiendish spirit of warfare, carried on under the countenance of him who stands first in authority under the nation that stands second in authority amongst the leaders of civilization. A quarrel of that sort, once arising, does not go to sleep again until it is righted for ever. As the English martyr at Oxford said to his fellow martyr – 'Brother, be of good cheer, for we shall this day light up a fire in England that, by the blessing of God, cannot be extinguished for ever'[54] – even so the atrocities of these hybrid campaigns between baffled civilization and barbarism, provoked into frenzy, will, like the horrors of the middle passage rising up from the Atlantic deep, suddenly, at the bar of the British Senate; sooner or later reproduce themselves in strong reactions of the social mind throughout Christendom, upon *all* the horrors of war that are wilful and superfluous. In that case there will be a consolation in reserve for the compatriots of those, the brave men, the women, and the innocent children, who died in that fiery furnace at Dahra.

* *Wale* (Germanice *wahl*) the old ballad word for *choice*. But the motive for using it in this place is in allusion to an excellent old Scottish story[51] (not sufficiently known in the South), of a rustic laird, who profitted by the hospitality of his neighbours, duly to get drunk once (and no more) every lawful night, returning in the happiest frame of mind under the escort of his servant Andrew. In spite of Andrew, however, it sometimes happened that the laird fell off his horse; and on one of these occasions, as he himself was dismounted from his saddle, his wig was dismounted from his cranium. Both fell into a peat-moss, and both were fished out by Andrew. But the laird, in his confusion, putting on the wig wrong side before, reasonably 'jaloused'[52] that this could not be his own wig, but some other man's, which suspicion he communicated to Andrew, who argued *contra* by the memorable reply – 'Hout! laird, there's nae wale o' wigs i' a peat-moss.'

'Their moans
The vales redoubled to the hills, and *they*
To heaven.'*

The caves of Dahra repeated the woe to the hills, and the hills to God. But such a furnace, though fierce, may be viewed as brief indeed if it shall terminate in permanently pointing the wrath of nations (as in this dialogue it has pointed the wrath of genius) to the particular outrage and class of outrages which it concerns. The wrath of nations is a consuming wrath, and the scorn of intellect is a withering scorn, for all abuses upon which either one or the other is led, by strength of circumstances, to settle itself *systematically*. The damage is for the most part that the very violence of public feeling should rock it asleep – the tempest exhausts itself by its own excesses – and the thunder of one or two immediate explosions, by satisfying the first clamours of human justice and indignation, is too apt to intercept that sustained roll of artillery which is requisite for the effectual assault of long-established abuses. Luckily in the present case of the Dahra massacre there is the less danger of such a result, as the bloody scene has happened to fall in with a very awakened state of the public sensibility as to the evils of war generally, and with a state of expectation almost romantically excited as to the possibility of readily or soon exterminating these evils.

Hope meantime, even if unreasonable, becomes wise and holy when it points along a path of purposes that are more than usually beneficent. According to a fine illustration of Sir Philip Sidney's, drawn from the practice of archery, by attempting more than we can possibly accomplish, we shall yet reach farther than ever we *should* have reached with a less ambitious aim;[56] we shall do much for the purification of war, if nothing at all for its abolition;[57] and atrocities of this Algerine order are amongst the earliest that will give way. They will sink before the growing illumination, and (what is equally important) before the growing *combination* of minds acting simultaneously from various centres, in nations otherwise the most at variance. By a rate of motion continually accelerated, the gathering power of the press, falling in with the growing facilities of personal intercourse, is, day by day, bringing Europe more and more into a state of fusion, in which the sublime name of *Christendom*[58] will continually become more significant, and will express a unity of the most awful order, viz., in the midst of strife, long surviving as to inferior interests and subordinate opinions, will express an agreement continually more close, and an agreement continually more operative, upon all capital questions affecting human rights, duties, and the interests of human *progress*. Before that tribunal, which every throb of every steam-engine, in printing-houses and on railroads, is hurrying to establish, all flagrant abuses

* Milton, in uttering his grief (but also his hopes growing out of this grief) upon a similar tragedy, viz., the massacre of the Protestant women and children by 'the bloody Piedmontose.'[55]

of belligerent powers will fall prostrate; and, in particular, no form of pure undisguised murder will be any longer allowed to confound itself with the necessities of honourable warfare.

Much already *has* been accomplished on this path; more than people are aware of; so gradual and silent has been the advance. How noiseless is the growth of corn! Watch it night and day for a week, and you will never see it growing; but return after two months, and you will find it all whitening for the harvest. Such, and so imperceptible in the stages of their motion, are the victories of the press. Here is one instance. Just forty-seven years ago, on the shores of Syria, was celebrated by Napoleon Bonaparte, the most damnable carnival of murder that romance has fabled, or that history has recorded.[59] Rather more than four thousand men – not (like Tyrolese or Spanish guerrillas) even in pretence 'insurgent rustics,'[60] but regular troops, serving the Pacha and the Ottoman Sultan, not old men that might by odd fractions have been thankful for dismissal from a life of care or sorrow, but all young Albanians, in the early morning of manhood, the oldest not twenty-four – were exterminated by successive rolls of musketry, when helpless as infants, having their arms pinioned behind their backs like felons on the scaffold, and having surrendered their muskets (which else would have made so desperate a resistance) on the faith that they were dealing with soldiers and men of honour. I have elsewhere examined, as a question in casuistry,[61] the frivolous pretences for this infamous carnage, but that examination I have here no wish to repeat; for it would draw off the attention from one feature of the case, which I desire to bring before the reader, as giving to this Jaffa tragedy a depth of atrocity wanting in that of Dahra. The four thousand and odd young Albanians had been seduced, trepanned, fraudulently decoyed, from a post of considerable strength, in which they could and would have sold their lives at a bloody rate, by a solemn promise of safety from authorised French officers. 'But,' said Napoleon, in part of excuse, 'these men, my aides-de-camp, were poltroons: to save their own lives, they made promises which they ought *not* to have made.' Suppose it so; and suppose the case one in which the supreme authority has a right to disavow his agents; what then? This entitles that authority to refuse his ratification to the terms agreed on; but this, at the same time, obliges him to replace the hostile parties in the advantages from which his agents had wiled them by these terms. A robber, who even owns himself such, will not pretend that he may refuse the price of the jewel as exorbitant, and yet keep possession of the jewel. And next comes a fraudulent advantage, not obtained by a knavery in the aides-de-camp, but in the leader himself. The surrender of the weapons, and the submission to the fettering of the arms, were not concessions from the Albanians, filched by the representatives of Napoleon, acting (as *he* says) without orders, but by express falsehoods, emanating from himself. The officer commanding at Dahra could not have reached his enemy without the shocking resource which he employed: Napoleon could. The officer at Dahra violated no covenant: Napoleon did. The officer at Dahra had not by lies seduced his victims from their natural advantages: Napoleon had. Such was the atrocity of Jaffa in the year 1799. Now, the relation of that great carnage to the press, the secret argument through which that vast massacre connects itself with the progress of the press, is this – that in 1799, and the two following years, when most it had become important to search the character and acts of Napoleon, excepting Sir Robert Wilson,[62] no writer in Europe, no section of the press, cared much to insist upon this, by so many degrees, the worst deed of modern* military life. From that deed all the waters of the Atlantic would not have cleansed him; and yet, since 1804, we have heard much oftener of the sick men whom he poisoned in his Syrian hospital (an act of merely erroneous humanity), and more of the Duc d'Enguien's execution[68] than of either; though this, savage as it was, admits of such palliations as belong to doubtful provocations in the sufferer, and to extreme personal terror in the inflictor. Here, then, we have a case of wholesale military murder, emanating from Christendom, and not less treacherous than the worst which have been ascribed to the Mahometan Timur,[69] or even to any Hindoo Rajah, which hardly moved a vibration of anger, or a solitary outcry of protestation from the European press (then, perhaps, having the excuse of deadly fear for herself), or even from the press of moral England, having no such excuse. Fifty years have passed; a less enormity is perpetrated, but again by a French leader; and, behold! Europe is *now* convulsed from side to side by unaffected indignation! So travels the press to victory: such is the

* '*Modern military life:*' – by modern I mean since the opening of the thirty years' war. In this war, the sack, or partial sack, of Magdeburg,[63] will occur to the reader as one of the worst amongst martial ruffianisms. But this happens to be a hoax. It is an old experience, that, when once the demure muse of history has allowed herself to tell a lie, she never retracts it. Many are the falsehoods in our own history, which our children read traditionally for truths, merely because our uncritical grandfathers believed them to be such. Magdeburg was *not* sacked. What fault there was in the case belonged to the King of Sweden, who certainly was remiss in this instance, though with excuses more than were hearkened to at that time. Tilly, the Bavarian General, had no reason for severity in this case, and showed none.[64] According to the regular routine of war, Magdeburg had become forfeited to military execution; which, let the reader remember, was not, in those days, a right of the General as against the enemy, and by way of salutary warning to other cities, lest they also should abuse the right of a reasonable defence, but was a right of the soldiery as against their own leaders. A town stormed was then a little perquisite to the ill-fed and ill-paid soldier. So of prisoners. If I made a prisoner of 'Signor Drew' [see Henry V.],[65] it was *my* business to fix his ransom: the General had no business to interfere with that. Magdeburg, therefore, had incurred the common penalty (which she must have foreseen) of obstinacy; and the only difference between *her* case and that of many another brave little town, that quietly submitted to the usual martyrdom, without howling through all the speaking-trumpets of history, was this – that the penalty was, upon Magdeburg, but partially enforced. Harte, the tutor of Lord Chesterfield's son, first published, in his Life of Gustavus Adolphus, an authentic diary of what passed at that time, kept by a Lutheran clergyman.[66] This diary shows sufficiently that no real departures were made from the customary routine, except in the direction of mercy. But it is evident that the people of Magdeburg were a sort of German hogs, of whom, it is notorious, that if you attempt in the kindest way to sheer them, all you get is horrible yelling, and (the proverb asserts) very little wool.[67] The case being a classical one in the annals of military outrages, I have noticed its real features.

light, and so broad, which it diffuses: such is the strength for action by which it combines the hearts of nations.

NOTES ON WALTER SAVAGE LANDOR*
[Part II]

First published in *Tait's*, XIV, February 1847, pp. 96–104. Two centred lines followed the title of the essay and immediately preceded the text. The first stated that the essay was 'BY THOMAS DE QUINCEY.', and the second that it was '*(Concluded from page 23.)*' to denote where in *Tait's* Part I of the essay ended.

Reprinted in *F*, IX, *Essays on the Poets, and Other English Writers* (1853), pp. 262–90, 293–6.

Revised text, carrying many accidentals and eleven substantive variants from *F*, in *SGG*, IX, *Leaders in Literature, With a Notice of Traditional Errors Affecting Them*, (1858), pp. 304–32.

There is one manuscript, as follows:

MS A: Huntington Library, HM 36039. The manuscript is a complete set of *SGG* page proofs. It contains one significant variant, and this is listed in the textual notes.

For the context and occasion of the essay, see headnote, pp. 3–5.

MELANCHTHON AND CALVIN.[1]

OF Mr Landor's notions in religion it would be useless, and without polemic arguments it would be arrogant, to say that they are false. It is sufficient to say that they are degrading. In the dialogue between Melanchthon and Calvin, it is clear that the former represents Mr L. himself, and is not at all the Melanchthon whom we may gather from his writings. Mr Landor has heard that he was gentle and timid in action; and he exhibits him as a mere development of that key-note; as a compromiser of all that is severe in doctrine; and as an effeminate picker and chooser in morals. God, in *his* conception of him, is not a father so much as a benign, but somewhat weak, old grandfather; and we, his grandchildren, being now and then rather naughty, are to be tickled with a rod made of feathers, but upon the whole, may rely upon an eternity of

* The Works of Savage Landor. 2 vols. London: Moxon. 1846.

sugar-plums. For instance, take the puny idea ascribed to Melanchthon upon *Idolatry;* and consider for one moment how little it corresponds to the vast machinery reared up by God himself against this secret poison and dreadful temptation of human nature. Melanchthon cannot mean to question the truth or the importance of the Old Testament; and yet, if *his* view of idolatry (as reported by L.) be sound, the Bible must have been at the root of the worst mischief ever yet produced by idolatry. He begins by describing idolatry as '*Jewish*;'[2] insinuating that it was an irregularity chiefly besetting the Jews. But how perverse a fancy! In the Jews, idolatry was a disease; in Pagan nations, it was the normal state. In a nation (if any such nation could exist) of *crétins* or of *lepers,* nobody would talk of cretinism or leprosy as of any morbid affection; *that* would be the regular and natural condition of man. But where either was spoken of with horror as a ruinous taint in human flesh, it would argue, that naturally (and, perhaps, by a large majority) the people were uninfected. Amongst Pagans, nobody talked of idolatry – no such idea existed – because *that* was the regular form of religious worship. To be named at all, idolatry must be viewed as standing in opposition to some higher worship that is *not* idolatry. But, next, as we are all agreed that in idolatry there is something evil, and differ only as to the propriety of considering it a Jewish evil – in what does this evil lie? It lies, according to the profound Landorian Melanchthon, in this – that different idolaters figure the Deity under different forms: if they could all agree upon one and the same mode of figuring the invisible Being, there need be no quarrelling; and in this case, consequently, there would be no harm in idolatry – none whatever. But, unhappily, it seems each nation, or sometimes section of a nation, has a different fancy: they get to disputing; and from that they get to boxing, in which, it is argued, lies the true evil of idolatry.[3] It is an *extra* cause of broken heads. One tribe of men represent the Deity as a beautiful young man, with a lyre and a golden bow; another as a snake;[4] and a third – Egyptians, for instance, of old – as a beetle or an onion; these last, according to Juvenal's remark, having the happy privilege of growing their own gods in their own kitchen-gardens.[5] In all this there would be no harm, were it not for subsequent polemics and polemical assaults. Such, if we listen to Mr L., is Melanchthon's profound theory* of a false idolatrous religion. Were the police everywhere on an English footing, and the magistrates as unlike as possible to Turkish Cadis,[7] nothing could be less objectionable; but, as things are, the beetle-worshipper despises the onion-worshipper; which breeds ill blood; whence grows a cudgel; and from the cudgel a consta-

* '*Melanchthon's profound theory.*' – That the reader may not suppose me misrepresenting Mr L., I subjoin his words, p. 224, vol. I.:[6] – 'The evil of idolatry is this – rival nations have raised up rival deities; war hath been denounced in the name of heaven; men have been murdered for the love of God; and such impiety hath darkened all the regions of the world, that the Lord of all things hath been mocked by all simultaneously as the Lord of Hosts.' The evil of idolatry is, not that it disfigures the Deity, (in which, it seems, there might be no great harm) but that one man's disfiguration differs from another man's; which leads to quarrelling, and *that* to fighting.

ble; and from the constable an unjust magistrate. Not so, Mr Landor; thus did not Melanchthon speak: and if he *did*, and would defend it for a thousand times, then for a thousand times he would deserve to be trampled by posterity into that German mire which he sought to evade by his Grecian disguise.* The true evil of idolatry is this: there is one sole idea of God, which corresponds adequately and centrally to his total nature. Of this idea, two things may be affirmed: the first being – that it is at the root of all absolute grandeur, of all truth, and of all moral perfection; the second being – that, natural and easy as it seems when once unfolded, it could only have been unfolded by a revelation; and, to all eternity he, that started with a false conception of God, could not, through any effort of his own, have exchanged it for a true one. All idolaters alike, though not all in equal degrees, by intercepting the idea of God through the prism of some representative creature that *partially* resembles God, refract, splinter, and distort that idea. Even the idea of light, of the pure, solar light – the old Persian symbol of God[10] – has that depraving necessity. Light itself, besides being an *imperfect* symbol, is an incarnation for us. However pure itself, or in its original divine manifestation, for us it is incarnated in forms and in matter that are *not* pure: it gravitates towards physical alliances, and therefore towards unspiritual pollutions. And all experience shows that the tendency for man, left to his own imagination, is downwards. The purest symbol, derived from created things, can and will condescend to the grossness of inferior human natures, by submitting to mirror itself in more and more carnal representative symbols, until finally the mixed element of resemblance to God is altogether buried and lost. God, by this succession of imperfect interceptions, falls more and more under the taint and limitation of the *alien* elements associated with all created things; and, for the ruin of all moral grandeur in man, every idolatrous nation left to itself will gradually bring round the idea of God into the idea of a powerful demon. Many things check and disturb this tendency for a time; but finally, and under that intense civilization to which man intellectually is always hurrying under the eternal evolution of physical knowledge, such a degradation of God's idea, ruinous to the *moral* capacities of man, would undoubtedly perfect itself, were it not for the kindling of a purer standard by revelation. Idolatry, therefore, is not merely *an* evil, and one utterly beyond the power of social institutions to redress, but, in fact, it is the fountain of all other evil that seriously menaces the destiny of the human race.

* '*Grecian disguise:*' – The true German name of this learned reformer was *Schwarzerd* (black earth);[8] but the homeliness and pun-provoking quality of such a designation induced Melanchthon to masque it in Greek. By the way, I do not understand how Mr Landor, the arch-purist in orthography, reconciles *his* spelling of the name to Greek orthodoxy: there is no Greek word that *could* be expressed by the English syllable 'cthon.' Such a word as Melancthon would be a hybrid monster – neither fish, flesh, nor good red herring.[9]

PORSON AND SOUTHEY.[11]

THE two dialogues between Southey and Porson relate to Wordsworth;[12] and they connect Mr Landor with a body of groundless criticism, for which vainly he will seek to evade his responsibility by pleading the caution posted up at the head of his Conversations, viz. – 'Avoid a mistake in attributing to the *writer* any opinions in this book but what are spoken under his own name.'[13] If Porson, therefore, should happen to utter villanies that are indictable, *that* (you are to understand) is Porson's affair. Render unto Landor the eloquence of the dialogue, but render unto Porson any kicks which Porson may have merited by his atrocities against a man whom assuredly he never heard of, and probably never saw. Now, unless Wordsworth ran into Porson in the streets of Cambridge on some dark night about the era of the French Revolution, and capsized him into the kennel – a thing which is exceedingly improbable, considering that Wordsworth was never tipsy except once in his life, yet, on the other hand, is exceedingly probable, considering that Porson was very seldom otherwise[14] – barring this one opening for a collision, there is no human possibility or contingency known to insurance offices, through which Porson ever *could* have been brought to trouble his head about Wordsworth. It would have taken three witches, and three broomsticks, clattering about his head, to have extorted from Porson any attention to a contemporary poet that did not give first-rate feeds. And a man that, besides his criminal conduct in respect of dinners, actually made it a principle to drink nothing but water, would have seemed so depraved a character in Porson's eyes that, out of regard to public decency, he would never have mentioned his name, had he even happened to know it. 'Oh no! he never mentioned *him*.' Be assured of *that*. As to Poetry, be it known that Porson read none whatever, unless it were either political or obscene. With no seasoning of either sort, 'wherefore,' he would ask indignantly, 'should I waste my time upon a poem?' Porson had read the Rolliad,[15] because it concerned his political party: he had read the epistle of Obereea, queen of Otaheite, to Sir Joseph Banks,[16] because, if Joseph was rather too demure, the poem was *not*. Else, and with such exceptions, he condescended not to any metrical writer subsequent to the aera of Pope, whose Eloisa to Abelard[17] he could say by heart, and could even sing from beginning to end; which, indeed, he *would* do, whether you chose it or not, after a sufficient charge of brandy, and sometimes even though threatened with a cudgel, in case he persisted in his molestations. Waller[18] he had also read, and occasionally quoted with effect. But as to a critique on Wordsworth, whose name had not begun to mount from the ground when Porson died,* as reasonably and characteristically might it have been put into

* An equal mistake it is in Mr Landor to put into the mouth of Porson any vituperation of Mathias as one that had uttered opinions upon Wordsworth. In the *Pursuits of Literature*,[19]

the mouth of the Hetman Platoff.[24] Instead of Porson's criticisms on writings which he never saw, let us hear Porson's account of a fashionable rout in an aristocratic London mansion: it was the only party of distinction that this hirsute but most learned Theban ever visited; and his history of what passed (comic alike and tragic) is better worth preserving than 'Brantome,' or even than Swift's 'Memoirs of a Parish Clerk.'[25] It was by the hoax of a young Cantab that the Professor was ever decoyed into such a party: the thing was a swindle; but his report of its natural philosophy is not on that account the less picturesque: –

'SOUTHEY. – "Why do you repeat the word *rout* so often?"

'PORSON. – "I was once *at* one by mistake; and really I saw there what you describe: this made me repeat the word and smile. You seem curious."

'SOUTHEY. – "Rather, indeed."

'PORSON. – "I had been dining out; there were some who smoked after dinner: within a few hours, the fumes of their pipes produced such an effect on my head that I was willing to go into the air a little. Still I continued hot and thirsty: and an under-graduate, whose tutor was my old acquaintance, proposed that we should turn into an oyster-cellar, and refresh ourselves with oysters and porter. The rogue, instead of this, conducted me to a fashionable house in the neighbourhood of St James's; and, although I expostulated with him, and insisted that we were going up stairs and not *down*, he appeared to me so ingenuous in his protestations to the contrary that I could well disbelieve him no longer. Nevertheless, receiving on the stairs many shoves and elbowings, I could not help telling him plainly – that, if indeed it *was* the oyster-cellar in Fleet Street, the company was much altered for the worse; and that, in future, I should frequent another. When the fumes of the pipes had left me, I discovered the deceit by the brilliancy and indecency of the dresses; and was resolved not to fall into temptation. Although, to my great satisfaction, no immodest proposal was directly made to me, I looked about anxious that no other man should know me beside *him* whose wantonness had conducted me

---

down to the 15th edition, there is no mention of Wordsworth's name. Southey is mentioned slightingly,[20] and chiefly with reference to his then democratic principles; but not Coleridge, and not Wordsworth. Mathias soon after went to Italy, where he passed the remainder of his life – died,[21] I believe, and was buried – never, perhaps, having heard the name of Wordsworth. As to Porson, it is very true that Mathias took a few liberties with his private habits, such as his writing paragraphs in the little cabinet fitted up for the *gens de plume* at the *Morning Chronicle* Office,[22] and other trifles. But these, though impertinences, were not of a nature seriously to offend. They rather flattered, by the interest which they argued in his movements. And with regard to Porson's main pretension, his exquisite skill in Greek, Mathias was not the man to admire this too little: his weakness, *if in that point he had* a weakness, lay in the opposite direction. His own Greek was not a burthen that could have foundered a camel: he was neither accurate, nor extensive, nor profound. But yet Mr L. is wrong in thinking that he drew it from an Index.[23] In his Italian, he had the advantage probably of Mr Landor himself: at least, he wrote it with more apparent fluency and compass.

thither; and I would have escaped, if I could have found the door, from which every effort I made appeared to remove me farther and farther. # # # A pretty woman said loudly, 'He has no gloves on!' 'What nails the creature has!' replied an older one – 'Piano-forte keys wanting the white.'"'[26]

I pause to say that this, by all accounts which have reached posterity, was really no slander. The Professor's forks had become rather of the dingiest, probably through inveterate habits of scratching up Greek roots from diluvian mould, some of it older than Deucalion's flood,[27] and very good, perhaps, for turnips, but less so for the digits which turn up turnips. What followed, however, if it were of a nature to be circumstantially repeated, must have been more trying to the sensibilities of the Greek oracle, and to the blushes of the Policemen dispersed throughout the rooms, than even the harsh critique upon his nails; which, let the wits say what they would in their malice, were no doubt washed regularly enough once every three years. And, even if they were *not*, I should say that this is not by any means so strong a fact as some that are reported about many a continental professor. Mrs Cl—nt, with the twofold neatness of an Englishwoman and a quaker, told me, that, on visiting Pestalozzi, the celebrated education professor, at Yverdun,[28] about 1820, her first impression, from a distant view of his dilapidated premises, was profound horror at the grimness of his complexion, which struck her as no complexion formed by nature, but as a deposition from half a century of atmospheric rust – a most ancient *aerugo*. She insisted on a radical purification, as a *sine qua non*[29] towards any interview with herself. The meek professor consented. Mrs Cl. hired a stout Swiss charwoman, used to the scouring of staircases, kitchen floors, &c.; the professor, whom on this occasion, one may call 'the prisoner,' was accommodated with a seat (as prisoners at the bar sometimes are with us) in the centre of a mighty washing-tub, and then scoured through a long summer forenoon, by the strength of a brawny Helvetian arm. 'And now, my dear friend' said Mrs Cl. to myself, 'is it thy opinion that this was cruel? Some people say it *was;* and I wish to disguise nothing; – it was not mere soap that I had him scoured with, but soap and sand; so, say honestly, dost thee call *that* cruel?' Laughing no more than the frailty of my human nature compelled me, I replied, 'Far from it; on the contrary, everybody must be charmed with her consideration for the professor, in not having him cleansed on the same principles as her carriage, viz., taken to the stable-yard, mopped severely,' ['*mobbed*, dost thee say?' she exclaimed; 'No, no,' I said, 'not mobbed, but *mopped*, until the gravel should be all gone'], 'then pelted with buckets of water by firemen, and, finally, curry-combed and rubbed down by two grooms, keeping up a sharp *susurrus*[30] between them, so as to soothe his wounded feelings; after all which, a feed of oats might not have been amiss.' The result, however, of this scouring extraordinary was probably as fatal as to Mambrino's helmet in Don Quixote. Pestalozzi issued, indeed, from the washing-tub like Aeson from Medea's kettle;[31] he took his station amongst a younger and fairer generation; and the dispute was now settled whether he belonged to the Caucasian or Mongolian race. But his intellect was thought to have suffered seriously. The tarnish of fifty or sixty years seemed to have acquired powers of re-acting as a stimulant upon the professor's fancy, through the *rete mucosum*,[32] or through – heaven knows what. He was too old to be converted to cleanliness; the Paganism of a neglected person at seventy becomes a sort of religion interwoven with the nervous system – just as the well-known *Plica Polonica* from which the French armies suffered so much in Poland, during 1807–8, though produced by neglect of the hair, will not be cured by extirpation of the hair. The hair becomes matted into Medusa locks, or what look like snakes;[33] and to cut these off is oftentimes to cause nervous frenzy, or other great constitutional disturbance. I never heard, indeed, that Pestalozzi suffered apoplexy from his scouring; but certainly his ideas on education grew bewildered, and will be found essentially damaged, after that great epoch – his baptism by water and sand.

Now, in comparison of an Orson like this man of Yverdun – this great Swiss reformer, who might, perhaps, have bred a pet variety of typhus fever for his own separate use – what signify nails, though worse than Caliban's or Nebuchadnezzar's?[34]

This Greek professor Porson – whose knowledge of English was so limited that his total cargo might have been embarked on board a walnut-shell, on the bosom of a slop bason, and insured for three halfpence – astonishes me, that have been studying English for thirty years and upwards, by the strange discoveries that he announces in this field. One and all, I fear, are mares' nests. He discovered, for instance, on his first and last reception amongst aristocratic people, that in this region of society a female bosom is called her *neck*.[35] But, if it really *had* been so called, I see no objection to the principle concerned in such disguises; and I see the greatest to that savage frankness which virtually is indicated with applause in the Porsonian remark. Let us consider. It is not that we *cannot* speak freely of the female bosom, and we do so daily. In discussing a statue, we do so without reserve; and in the act of suckling an infant, the bosom of every woman is an idea so sheltered by the tenderness and sanctity with which all but ruffians invest that organ of maternity, that no man scruples to name it, if the occasion warrants it. He suppresses it only as he suppresses the name of God; not as an idea that can itself contain any indecorum, but, on the contrary, as making other and more trivial ideas to become indecorous when associated with a conception rising so much above their own standard. Equally, the words, *affliction*, *guilt*, *penitence*, *remorse*, &c., are proscribed from the ordinary current of conversation amongst mere acquaintances; and for the same reason, viz., that they touch chords too impassioned and profound for harmonising with the key in which the mere social civilities of life are exchanged. Meantime, it is not true that any custom ever prevailed in *any* class of calling a woman's bosom her neck. – Porson goes on to say, that, for *his* part, he was born in an age when people had *thighs*.[36] Well, a great many people have thighs still. But in all ages there must have been many of whom it is lawful to suspect such a fact zoologically; and yet, as men honouring our own race, and all its veils of mystery, not too openly to insist upon it, which, luckily, there is seldom any occasion to do.

Mr Landor conceives that we are growing worse in the pedantries of false delicacy. I think not. His own residence in Italy has injured his sense of discrimination. It is not his countrymen that have grown conspicuously more demure and prudish, but he himself that has grown in Italy more tolerant of what is really a blameable coarseness. Various instances occur in these volumes of that faulty compliance with Southern grossness. The tendencies of the age, among ourselves, lie certainly in *one* channel towards excessive refinement. So far, however, they do but balance the opposite tendencies in some other channels. The craving for instant effect in style – as it brings forward many disgusting Germanisms and other barbarisms – as it transplants into literature much slang from the street[37] – as it re-acts painfully upon the grandeurs of the antique scriptural diction, by recalling into *colloquial* use many consecrated words which thus lose their Gothic beauty – also operates daily amongst journalists, by the temptations of apparent strength that lurk in plain-speaking or even in brutality. What other temptation, for instance, can be supposed to govern those who, in speaking of hunger as it affects our paupers, so needlessly offend us by the very coarsest English word for the Latin word *venter?*[38] Surely the word *stomach* would be intelligible to everybody, and yet disgust nobody. It would do for *him* that affects plain-speaking; it would do for you and me that revolt from gross-speaking. Signs from abroad speak the very same language, as to the *liberal* tendencies (in this point) of the nineteenth century. Formerly, it was treason for a Spaniard, even in a laudatory copy of verses, to suppose his own Queen lowered to the level of other females by the possession of legs! Constitutionally, the Queen was incapable of legs. How else her Majesty contrived to walk, or to dance, the Inquisition soon taught the poet was no concern of *his*. Royal legs for females were an inconceivable thing – except amongst Protestant nations; some of whom the Spanish Church affirmed to be even disfigured by tails! Having tails, of course they might have legs. But not *Catholic* Queens. Now-a-days, so changed is all this, that if you should even express your homage to her Most Catholic Majesty, by sending her a pair of embroidered garters – which certainly presuppose legs – there is no doubt that the Spanish Minister of Finance would gratefully carry them to account – on the principle that 'every little helps.'[39] Mr Porson is equally wrong, as I conceive, in another illustration of this matter, drawn from the human toes, and specifically from the great toe. It is true, that, in refined society, upon any rare necessity arising for alluding to so inconsiderable a member of the human statue, generally this is done at present by the French term *doigt-de-pied*[40] – though not always – as may be seen in various honorary certificates granted to chiropodists within the last twenty months. And whereas Mr Porson asks pathetically – What harm has the great toe done that it is never to be named?[41] I answer – The greatest harm; as may be seen in the first act of 'Coriolanus,' where *Menenius* justly complains, that this arrogant subaltern of the crural system,

> '——Being basest, meanest, vilest,
> Still goeth foremost.'[42]

Even in the villany of running away from battle, this unworthy servant still asserts precedency. I repeat, however, that the general tendencies of the age, as to the just limits of *parrhesia* (using the Greek word in a sense wider than of old),[43] are moving at present upon two opposite tacks; which fact it is, as in some other cases, that makes the final judgment difficult.

ROMAN IMPERATOR.

Mr Landor, though really learned, often puts his learning into his pocket.

Thus, with respect to the German Empire, Mr L. asserts that it was a chimaera; that the *Imperium Germanicum*[44] was a mere usage of speech, founded (if I understand him) not even in a legal fiction, but in a blunder; that a German *Imperator* never had a true historical existence; and, finally, that even the Roman title of *Imperator* – which, unquestionably, surmounted in grandeur all titles of honour that ever were or will be – ranged in dignity below the title of *Rex*.[45]

I believe him wrong in every one of these doctrines: let us confine ourselves to the last. The title of Imperator was not *originally* either above or below the title of Rex, or even upon the same level; it was what logicians call *disparate* – it radiated from a different centre, precisely as the modern title of *Decanus*, or *Dean*, which is originally astrological [see the elder Scaliger on Manilius],[46] has no relation, whether of superiority or equality or inferiority, to the title of *Colonel*, nor the title of *Cardinal* any such relation to that of *Field-Marshal;* and not quite as little had *Rex* to *Imperator*. Masters of Ceremonies, or Lord Chamberlains, may certainly *create* a precedency in favour of any title whatever in regard to any other title; but such a precedency for any of the cases before us would be arbitrary, and not growing out of any internal principle, though useful for purposes of convenience. As regarded the Roman *Imperator*, originally like the Roman *Praetor* – this title and the official rank pointed exclusively to military distinctions. In process of time the Praetor came to be a legal officer, and the Imperator to be the supreme political officer. But the motive for assuming the title of *Imperator*, as the badge or cognizance of the sovereign authority, when the great transfiguration of the Republic took place, seems to have been this. An essentially new distribution of political powers had become necessary, and this change masqued itself to Romans, published itself in menaces and muttering thunder to foreign states, through the martial title of

Imperator. A new equilibrium was demanded by the changes which time and luxury and pauperism had silently worked in the composition of Roman society. If Rome was to be saved from herself – if she was to be saved from the eternal flux and reflux – action and re-action – amongst her oligarchy of immense estates [which condition of things it was that forced on the great *sine quâ non* reforms of Caesar, against all the babble of the selfish Cicero, of the wicked Cato,[47] and of the debt-ridden Senate] – then it was indispensable that a new order of powers should be combined for bridling her internal convulsions. To carry her off from her own self-generated vortex, which would, in a very few years, have engulphed her and drawn her down into fragments, some machinery as new as steam power was required: her own native sails filled in the wrong direction. There were already powers in the constitution equal to the work, but distracted and falsely lodged. These must be gathered into one hand. And, yet, as names are all-powerful upon our frail race, this recast must be *verbally* disguised. The title must be such as, whilst flattering the Roman pride, might yet announce to Oriental powers a plenipotentiary of Rome who argued all disputed points, not so much strongly as (in Irish phrase) with 'a strong back' – not so much piquing himself on Aristotelian syllogisms that came within *Barbara* and *Celarent*,[48] as upon thirty legions that stood within call. The Consulship was good for little; *that*, with some reservations, could be safely resigned into subordinate hands. The Consular name, and the name of Senate, which was still suffered to retain an obscure vitality and power of resurrection, continued to throw a popular lustre over the government. Millions were duped. But the essential offices, the offices in which settled the organs of all the life in the administration, were these: – 1, of Military Commander-in-Chief (including such a partition of the provinces as might seal the authority in this officer's hands, and yet flatter the people through the Senate); 2, of Censor, so as to watch the action of morals and social usages upon politics; 3, of Pontifex Maximus; 4, and finally, of Tribune. The tribunitial power, next after the military power, occupied the earliest anxieties of the Caesars. All these powers, and some others belonging to less dignified functions, were made to run through the same central rings (or what in mail-coach harness is called the *turrets*): the 'ribbons' were tossed up to one and the same imperial coachman, looking as amiable as he could, but, in fact, a very truculent personage, having powers more unlimited than was always safe for himself. And now, after all this change of things, what was to be the *name?* By what *title* should men know him? Much depended upon that. The tremendous symbols of S. P. Q. R.[49] still remained; nor had they lost their power. On the contrary, the great idea of the Roman destiny, as of some vast phantom moving under God to some unknown end, was greater than ever: the idea was now *so* great, that it had outgrown all its representative realities. *Consul* and *Proconsul* would no longer answer, because they represented too exclusively the interior or domestic fountains of power, and not the external relations to the terraqueous globe which were beginning to expand with sudden accelerations of velocity. The *central* power could not be forgotten by any who were near enough to have tasted its wrath: but now there was arising a necessity for expressing, by some great unity of denomination, so as no longer to lose the totality in the separate partitions – the enormity of the *circumference*. A necessity for this had repeatedly been found in negotiations, and in contests of ceremonial rank with oriental powers, as between ourselves and China.[50] With Persia, the greatest of these powers, an instinct of inevitable collision* had, for some time, been ripening. It became requisite that there should be a representative officer for the whole Roman grandeur, and one capable of standing on the same level as the Persian king of kings; and this necessity arose at the very same moment that a new organization was required of Roman power for *domestic* purposes. There is no doubt that both purposes were consulted in the choice of the title *Imperator*. The chief alternative title was that of *Dictator*. But to this, as regarded Romans, there were two objections – first, that it was a mere *provisional* title, always commemorating a transitional emergency, and pointing to some happier condition, which the extraordinary powers of the officer ought soon to establish. It was in the nature of a problem, and continually asked for its own solution. The Dictator dictated. He was the greatest *ipse dixit*[52] that ever was heard of. It reminded the people *verbally* of despotic powers and autocracy. Then again, as regarded foreign nations, unacquainted with the Roman constitution, and throughout the servile East incapable of understanding it, the title of *Dictator* had no meaning at all. *The Speaker* is a magnificent title in England, and makes brave men sometimes shake in their shoes. But, yet, if from rustic ignorance it is not understood, even that title means nothing. Of the proudest Speaker that England ever saw, viz., Sir Edward Seymour,[53] it is recorded that his grandeur failed him, sank under him, like the Newgate[54] drop, at the very moment when his boiling anger most relied upon and required it. He was riding near Barnet, when a rustic waggoner a-head of him, by keeping obstinately the middle of the road, prevented him from passing. Sir Edward motioned to him magnificently, that he must turn his horses to the left. The carter, on some fit of the sulks (perhaps from the Jacobinism innate in man), despised this pantomime, and sturdily persisted in his mutinous disrespect. On which Sir Edward shouted – 'Fellow, do you know who I am?' '*Noo-ah*,' replied our rebellious friend, meaning, when faithfully translated, *no*. 'Are you aware, Sirrah,' said Sir Edward, now thoroughly incensed, 'that I am the right honourable the Speaker? At your peril, sir, in the name of the Commons of England, in Parliament assembled, quarter instantly to the left.' This was said in that dreadful voice which sometimes reprimanded penitent offenders, kneeling at the bar of the House. The carter, more struck by the terrific tones than the words, spoke

* Herod the Great, and his father Antipater, owed the favour of Rome, and, finally, the throne of Judaea, to the seasonable election which they made between Rome and Persia;[51] but made not without some doubts, as between forces hardly yet brought to a satisfactory equation.

an aside to 'Dobbin' (his 'thill'[55] horse), which procured an opening to the blazing Speaker, and then replied thus – 'Speaker! Why, if so be as thou can'st speak whoy-y-y-y-y,' (in the tremulous undulation with which he was used to utter his sovereign whoah-h-h-h to his horses), 'Whoy-y-y-y didn't-a speak afore?' The waggoner, it seemed, had presumed Sir Edward, from his mute pantomime, to be a dumb man; and all which the proud Speaker gained, by the proclamation of his style and title, was, to be exonerated from that suspicion, but to the heavy discredit of his sanity. A Roman Dictator stood quite as poor a chance with foreigners, as our Speaker with a rustic. 'Dictator! let him dictate to his wife; but he sha'n't dictate to us.' Any title, to prosper with distant nations, must rest upon the basis of arms. And this fell in admirably with the political exigency for Rome herself. The title of *Imperator* was liable to no jealousy. Being entirely a military title, it clashed with no civil pretensions whatever. Being a military title, that recorded a triumph over external enemies in the field, it was dear to the patriotic heart; whilst it directed the eye to a quarter where all increase of power was concurrent with increase of benefit to the State. And again, as the honour had been hitherto purely titular, accompanied by some *auctoritas*, in the Roman sense [not always honour, for Cicero was an Imperator for Cilician exploits, which he reports with laughter],[56] but no separate authority in our modern sense. Even in military circles it was open to little jealousy: nor apparently could ripen into a shape that ever *would* be so, since, according to all precedent, it would be continually balanced by the extension of the same title, under popular military suffrage, to other fortunate leaders. Who could foresee, at the inauguration of this reform, that this precedent would be abolished? who could guess that henceforwards no more triumphs (but only a sparing distribution of triumphal decorations), henceforwards no more Imperatorial titles for anybody out of the one consecrated family? All this was hidden in the bosom of the earliest Imperator: he seemed, to the great mass of the people, perfectly innocent of civic ambition: he rested upon his truncheon, *i.e.*, upon S. P. Q. R.: like Napoleon, he said, 'I am but the first soldier of the republic,' that is, the most dutiful of her servants; and, like Napoleon, under cover of this martial *paludamentum*,[57] he had soon filched every ensign of authority by which the organs of public power could speak. But, at the beginning, this title of *Imperator* was the one by far the best fitted to masque all this, to disarm suspicion, and to win the confidence of the people.

The title, therefore, began in something like imposture; and it was not certainly at first the gorgeous title into which it afterwards blossomed. The earth did not yet ring with it. The rays of its diadem were not then the first that said *All hail!* to the rising – the last that said *Farewell!* to the setting sun. But still it was already a splendid distinction; and, in a Roman ear, it must have sounded far above all competition from the trivial title (in *that* day) of 'Rex,' unless it were the Persian Rex, viz., 'Rex Regum.'[58] Romans *gave* the title;

they stooped not to accept it.* Even Mark Antony, in the all-magnificent description of him by Shakspere's Cleopatra, could give it in showers – kings waited in his ante-room, 'and from his pocket fell crowns and sceptres.'[66] The title of *Imperator* was indeed reaped in glory that transcended the glory of earth, but it was not, therefore, sown in dishonour.[67]

We are all astonished at Mr Landor – myself and 300 select readers. What *can* he mean by tilting against the *Imperator* – Semper Augustus?[68] Before *him* the sacred fire (that burned from century to century) went pompously in advance – before *him* the children of Europe and Asia – of Africa and the islands, rode as *dorypheroi; his somatophulakes*[69] were princes; and *his* empire, when burning out in Byzantium,[70] furnished from it very ruins the models for our western honours and ceremonial. Had it even begun in circumstances of ignominy, *that* would have been cured easily by its subsequent triumph. Many are the titles of earth that have found a glory in looking back to the humility of their origin as its most memorable feature. The fisherman who sits upon Mount Palatine,[71] in some respects the grandest of all Potentates, as one wielding both earthly and heavenly thunders, is the highest example of this. Some, like the Mamelukes of Egypt and the early janizaries of the Porte,[72] have glorified themselves in being slaves. Others, like the Caliphs,[73] have founded their claims to men's homage in the fact of being *successors* to those who (between ourselves) were knaves. And once it happened to Professor Wilson[74] and myself that we travelled in the same post-chaise with a most agreeable madman, who, amongst a variety of other select facts which he communicated, was kind enough to give us the following etymological account of our much-respected ancestors the Saxons: which furnishes a further illustration [quite unknown to the learned] of the fact – that honour may glory in deducing itself from circumstances of humility. He assured us that

* *Stooped not to accept it.* – The notion that Julius Caesar, who of all men must have held cheapest the title of *Rex*, had seriously intrigued to obtain it, arose (as I conceive) from two mistakes – 1st, From a misinterpretation of a figurative ceremony in the pageant of the Lupercalia.[59] The Romans were ridiculously punctilious in this kind of jealousy. They charged Pompey at one time with a plot for making himself king, because he wore white bandages round his thighs:[60] now *white*, in olden days, was as much the regal colour as *purple*. Think, dear reader, of us – of you and me – being charged with making ourselves kings, because we may choose to wear white cotton drawers. Pompey was very angry, and swore bloody oaths that it was *not* ambition which had cased his thighs in white *fascine*. 'Why, what is it then,' said a grave citizen. 'What is it, man,' replied Pompey, 'it is rheumatism.' Dogberry[61] must have had a hand in this charge: – 'Dost thou bear, thou varlet? Thou are charged with incivism;[62] and it shall go hard with me but I will prove thee to thy face a false knave, and guilty of flat rheumatism.' The other reason which has tended to confirm posterity in the belief that Caesar really coveted the title of *Rex* was the confusion of the truth arising with Greek writers. *Basileus*, the term by which indifferently they designated the mighty Artaxerxes and the pettiest *regulus*,[63] was the original translation used for *Imperator*. Subsequently, and especially after Dioclesian had approximated the aulic[64] pomps to Eastern models, the terms *Autocrator, Kaisar, Augustus, Sebastos,* &c., came more into use. But after Trajan's time, or even to that of Commodus,[65] generally the same terms which expressed *Imperator* and *Imperatorial* viz. *Basileus* and *Basilikos* to a Grecian ear expressed *Rex* and *Regulis*.

these worthy Pagans were a league comprehending every single brave man of German blood; so much so, that on sailing away they left that unhappy land in a state of universal cowardice, which accounts for the licking it subsequently received from Napoleon.[75] The Saxons were very poor, as brave men too often are. In fact, they had no breeches, and, of course, no silk stockings. They had, however, *sacks*, which they mounted on their backs, whence naturally their name *Sax-on*. *Sacks-on!* was the one word of command, and *that* spoken, the army was ready. In reality, it was treason to take them off. But this endorsement of their persons was not assumed on any Jewish principle of humiliation; on the contrary, in the most flagrant spirit of defiance to the whole race of man. For they proclaimed that, having no breeches nor silk stockings of their own, they intended, wind and weather permitting, to fill these same sacks with those of other men. The Welshmen then occupying England were reputed to have a good stock of both, and in quest of this Welsh wardrobe the *Sacks-on* army sailed. With what success it is not requisite to say, since here in one post-chaise, 1430 years after, were three of their posterity, the Professor, the madman, and myself, indorsees (as you may say) of the original indorsers, who were all well equipped with the objects of this great *Sacks-on* exodus.

It is true that the word *emperor* is not in every situation so impressive as the word *king*. But *that* arises in part from the latter word having less of specialty about it; it is more catholic, and to that extent more poetic; and in part from accidents of position which disturb the relations of many other titles beside. The *Proconsul* had a grander sound, as regarded military expeditions, than the principal from whom he emanated. The *Surena* left a more awful remembrance of his title upon the comrades of Julian in his Persian expedition[76] than the Surena's master. And there are many cases extant in which the word *angel* strikes a deeper key, cases where power is contemplated as well as beauty or mysterious existence, than the word archangel, though confessedly higher in the hierarchies of Heaven.

Let me now draw the reader's attention to *Count Julian*,[77] a great conception of Mr Landor's.

The fable of Count Julian (that is, when comprehending all the parties to that web, of which *he* is the centre) may be pronounced the grandest which modern history unfolds. It is, and it is *not*, scenical. In some portions (as the fate so mysterious of Roderick, and in a higher sense of Julian) it rises as much above what the stage could illustrate, as does Thermopylae[78] above the petty details of narration. The man was mad that, instead of breathing from a hurricane of harps some mighty ode over Thermopylae, fancied the little conceit of weaving it into a metrical novel or succession of incidents. Yet, on the other hand, though rising higher, Count Julian sinks lower: though the passions rise far above Troy, above Marathon,[79] above Thermopylae, and are such passions as could not have existed under Paganism; in some respects they condescend and preconform to the stage. The characters are all different, all marked, all *in position;* by which, never assuming fixed attitudes as to purpose and interest, the passions are deliriously complex, and the situations are of corresponding grandeur. Metius Fuffetius,[80] Alban traitor! that wert torn limb from limb by antagonist yet confederate chariots, thy tortures, seen by shuddering armies, were not comparable to the unseen tortures in Count Julian's mind; who – whether his treason prospered or not, whether his dear outraged daughter lived or died, whether his king were trampled in the dust by the horses of infidels, or escaped as a wreck from the fiery struggle, whether his dear native Spain fell for ages under misbelieving hounds, or, combining her strength, tossed off *them*, but then also *himself*, with one loathing from her shores – saw, as he looked out into the mighty darkness, and stretched out his penitential hands vainly for pity or for pardon, nothing but the blackness of ruin, and ruin that was too probably to career through centuries. 'To this pass,' as Caesar said to his soldiers at Pharsalia, 'had his enemies reduced him;'[81] and Count Julian might truly say, as he stretched himself a rueful suppliant before the Cross, listening to the havoc that was driving onwards before the dogs of the Crescent,[82] '*My* enemies, because they would not remember that I was a man, forced *me* to forget that I was a Spaniard: – to forget thee, oh native Spain, – and, alas! thee, oh faith of Christ!'

The story is wrapt in gigantic mists, and looms upon one like the Grecian fable of Oedipus; and there will be great reason for disgust, if the deep Arabic researches now going on in the Escurial,[83] or at Vienna, should succeed in stripping it of its grandeurs. For, as it stands at present, it is the most fearful lesson extant of the great moral, that crime propagates crime, and violence inherits violence; nay, a lesson on the awful *necessity* which exists at times, that one tremendous wrong should blindly reproduce itself in endless retaliatory wrongs. To have resisted the dread temptation, would have needed an angel's nature: to have yielded, is but human; should it, then, plead in vain for pardon? and yet, by some mystery of evil, to have perfected this human vengeance, is, finally, to land all parties alike, oppressor and oppressed, in the passions of hell.

Mr Landor, who always rises with his subject, and dilates like Satan into Teneriffe or Atlas,[84] when he sees before him an antagonist worthy of his powers, is probably the one man in Europe that has adequately conceived the situation, the stern self-dependency and the monumental misery of Count Julian. That sublimity of penitential grief, which cannot accept consolation from man, cannot hear external reproach, cannot condescend to notice insult, cannot so much as see the curiosity of by-standers; that awful carelessness of all but the troubled deeps within his own heart, and of God's spirit brooding upon their surface, and searching their abysses, never was so majestically described as in the following lines; it is the noble Spaniard, Hernando, comprehending and loving Count Julian in the midst of his treasons, who speaks:

– Tarik, the gallant Moor, having said that at last the Count must be happy; for that

> 'Delicious calm
> Follows the fierce enjoyment of revenge.'

Hernando replies thus: –

> 'That calm was never his; no other *will* be,
> Not victory, that o'ershadows him, sees he:
> No airy and light passion stirs abroad
> To ruffle or to soothe him; all are quell'd
> Beneath a mightier, sterner, stress of mind.
> Wakeful he sits, and lonely, and unmov'd,
> Beyond the arrows, shouts, and views of men.
> As oftentimes an eagle, ere the sun
> Throws o'er the varying earth his early ray,
> Stands solitary – stands immovable
> Upon some highest cliff, and rolls his eye,
> Clear, constant, unobservant, unabas'd,
> In the cold light above the dews of morn.'[85]

One change suggests itself to me as possibly for the better, viz., if the magnificent line –

> 'Beyond the arrows, shouts, and views of men' –

were transferred to the secondary object, the eagle, placed after what is *now* the last line, it would give a fuller rhythmus to the close of the entire passage;[86] it would be more *literally* applicable to the majestic and solitary bird, than to the majestic and solitary man; whilst a figurative expression even more impassioned might be found for the utter self-absorption of Count Julian's spirit – too grandly sorrowful to be capable of disdain.

It completes the picture of this ruined prince, that Hernando, the sole friend (except his daughter) still cleaving to him, dwells with yearning desire upon his death, knowing the necessity of this consummation to his own secret desires, knowing the forgiveness which would settle upon his memory after that last penalty should have been paid for his errors, comprehending the peace that would then swallow up the storm: –

> 'For his own sake I could endure his loss,
> Pray for it, and thank God: yet mourn I must
> Him above all, so great, so bountiful,
> So blessed once!'[87]

It is no satisfaction to Hernando that Julian should 'yearn for death with speechless love,' but Julian *does* so: and it is in vain now, amongst these irreparable ruins, to wish it otherwise.

''Tis not my solace that 'tis* *his* desire:
Of all who pass us in life's drear descent
We grieve the most for those who *wish'd* to die.'[89]

How much, then, is in this brief drama of Count Julian, chiseled, as one might think, by the hands of that sculptor who fancied the great idea of chiseling Mount Athos into a demigod,[90] which almost insists on being quoted; which seems to rebuke and frown upon one for *not* quoting it: passages to which, for their solemn grandeur, one raises one's hat as at night in walking under the Coliseum; passages which, for their luxury of loveliness, should be inscribed on the phylactories of brides, or upon the frescoes of Ionia, illustrated by the gorgeous allegories of Rubens.[91]

'Sed fugit interea, fugit irreparabile tempus,
Singula dum capti circumvectamur amore.'[92]

Yet, reader, in spite of time, one word more on the subject we are quitting. Father Time is certainly become very importunate and clamorously shrill since he has been fitted up with that horrid railway whistle;[93] and even old Mother Space is growing rather impertinent, when she speaks out of monthly journals licensed to carry but small quantities of bulky goods; yet one thing I must say in spite of them both.

It is, that although we have had from men of memorable genius, Shelley in particular, both direct and indirect attempts (some of them powerful attempts) to realise the great idea of Prometheus,[94] which idea is *so* great, that (like the primeval majesties of Human Innocence, of avenging Deluges that are past, of fiery visitations yet to come) it has had strength to pass through many climates, and through many religions, without essential loss, but surviving, without tarnish, every furnace of chance and change; so it is that, after all has been done which intellectual power *could* do since Aeschylus (and since, Milton in his Satan),[95] no embodiment of the Promethean situation, none of the Promethean character, fixes the attentive eye upon itself with the same secret feeling of fidelity to the vast archetype, as Mr Landor's 'Count Julian.' There is in this modern aerolithe the same jewelly lustre, which cannot be mistaken; the same '*non imitabile fulgur*,'[96] and the same character of 'fracture,' or *cleavage*, as mineralogists speak, for its beaming iridescent grandeur, redou-

* *''Tis'*: – Scotchmen and Irishmen (for a reason which it may be elsewhere worth while explaining) make the same mistake of supposing *'tis* and *'twas* admissible in prose: which is shocking to an English ear, for since 1740 they have become essentially poetic forms, and cannot, without a sense of painful affectation and sentimentality, be used in conversation or in *any* mode of prose. Mr Landor does not make *that* mistake, but the reduplication of the *'tis* in this line, will he permit me to say? is dreadful. He is wide awake to such blemishes in other men of all nations: so am I. He blazes away all day long against the trespasses of that class, like a man in spring protecting corn-fields against birds. So do I at times. And if ever I publish that work on *Style*,[88] which for years has been in preparation, I fear that, from Mr Landor, it will be necessary to cull some striking flaws in composition, were it only that in *his* works must be sought some of its most striking brilliancies.

bling under the crush of misery. The colour and the coruscation are the same when splintered by violence; the tones of the rocky* harp are the same when swept by sorrow. There is the same spirit of heavenly persecution against his enemy, persecution that would have hung upon his rear, and 'burn'd after him to the bottomless pit,'[99] though it had yawned for both; there is the same gulf fixed between the possibilities of their reconciliation, the same immortality of resistance, the same abysmal anguish. Did Mr Landor *consciously* cherish this Aeschylean ideal in composing 'Count Julian?' I know not: there it is.

* '*Rocky harp:*' – There are now known other cases, beside the ancient one of Memnon's statue,[97] in which the 'deep-grooved'[98] granites, or even the shifting sands of wildernesses, utter mysterious music to ears that watch and wait for the proper combination of circumstances.

ORTHOGRAPHIC MUTINEERS*

First published in *Tait's*, XIV, March 1847, pp. 157–62. The essay was printed as 'BY THOMAS DE QUINCEY.' in a centred line following the title and immediately preceding the text.

Reprinted in *F*, III, *Miscellaneous Essays* (1851), pp. 255–76.

Revised text, carrying several accidentals but only four substantive variants from *F*, in *SGG*, XIV, *Letters to a Young Man whose Education has been Neglected, and Other Papers* (1860), pp. 95–112.

There are no manuscripts.

For the context and occasion of this essay, see headnote, pp. 3–5.

AS we are all of us crazy when the wind sits in some particular quarter, let not Mr Landor be angry with me for suggesting that he is outrageously crazy upon the one solitary subject of spelling. It occurs to me, as a plausible solution of his fury upon this point, that perhaps in his earliest school-days, when it is understood that he was exceedingly pugnacious, he may have detested spelling, and (like Roberte the Deville†) have found it more satisfactory for all parties, that when the presumptuous schoolmaster differed from him on the spelling of a word, the question between them should be settled by a stand-up fight. Both parties would have the victory at times: and if, according to Pope's expression, 'justice rul'd the ball,'[2] the schoolmaster (who is always a villain)[3] would be floored three times out of four; no great matter whether wrong or not upon the immediate point of spelling discussed. It is in this way, viz. from the irregular adjudications upon litigated spelling, which must have arisen

* With a special reference to the Works of Walter Savage Landor.

† *'Roberte the Deville:'* – See the old metrical romance of that name: it belongs to the fourteenth century, and was printed some thirty years ago, with wood engravings of the illuminations. Roberte, however, took the liberty of murdering *his* schoolmaster. But could he well do less? Being a reigning Duke's son, and after the rebellious schoolmaster had said –

> *'Syr, ye bee too bolde:*
> *And therewith tooke a rodde hym for to chaste.'*[1]

Upon which the meek Robin, without using any bad language as the schoolmaster had done, simply took out a long dagger *'hym for to chaste,'* which he did effectually. The schoolmaster gave no bad language after that.

under such a mode of investigating the matter, that we may account for Mr Landor's being sometimes in the right, but too often (with regard to long words) egregiously in the wrong. As he grew stronger and taller, he would be coming more and more amongst polysyllables, and more and more would be getting the upperhand of the schoolmaster; so that at length he would have it all his own way; one round would decide the turn-up; and thenceforwards his spelling would become frightful. Now, I myself detested spelling as much as all people ought to do, except Continental compositors, who have extra fees for doctoring the lame spelling of ladies and gentlemen. But, unhappily, I had no power to thump the schoolmaster into a conviction of his own absurdities; which, however, I greatly desired to do. Still, my nature, powerless at that time for any active recusancy, was strong for passive resistance; and *that* is the hardest to conquer. I took one lesson of this infernal art, and then declined ever to take a second; and, in fact, I never *did*. Well I remember the unique morning's experience. It was the first page of Entick's Dictionary[4] that I had to get by heart; a sweet sentimental task; and not, as may be fancied, the spelling only, but the horrid attempts of this depraved Entick to explain the supposed meaning of words that probably had none; many of these, it is my belief, Entick himself forged. Among the strange, grim-looking words, to whose acquaintance I was introduced on that unhappy morning, were *abalienate* and *ablaqueation*[5] – most respectable words, I am fully persuaded, but so exceedingly retired in their habits, that I never once had the honour of meeting either of them in any book, pamphlet, journal, whether in prose or numerous verse, though haunting such society myself all my life. I also formed the acquaintance, at that time, of the word *abacus*, which, as a Latin word, I have often used, but, as an English one, I really never had occasion to spell, until this very moment. Yet, after all, what harm comes of such obstinate recusancy against orthography? I was an 'occasional conformist;'[6] I conformed for one morning, and never more. But, for all that, I spell as well as my neighbours; and I can spell *ablaqueation* besides, which I suspect that some of them can *not*.

My own spelling, therefore, went right, because I was left to nature, with strict neutrality on the part of the authorities. Mr Landor's too often went wrong, because he was thrown into a perverse channel by his continued triumphs over the prostrate schoolmaster. To toss up, as it were, for the spelling of a word, by the best of nine rounds, inevitably left the impression that chance governed all; and this accounts for the extreme capriciousness of Landor.

It is a work for a separate dictionary in quarto to record *all* the proposed revolutions in spelling, through which our English blood, either at home or in America, has thrown off, at times, the surplus energy that consumed it. I conceive this to be a sort of cutaneous affection, like nettle-rash, or ring-worm, through which the patient gains relief for his own nervous distraction, whilst, in fact, he does no harm to anybody: for usually he forgets his own reforms, and if *he* should not, everybody else *does*. Not to travel back into the seventeenth century, and the noble army of shorthand writers who have all made war upon orthography, for secret purposes of their own, even in the last century, and in the present, what a list of eminent rebels against the spelling-book might be called up to answer for their wickedness at the bar of the Old Bailey,[7] if anybody would be kind enough to make it a felony! Cowper, for instance, too modest and too pensive to raise upon any subject an open standard of rebellion, yet, in quiet Olney, made a small *émeute*[8] as to the word 'Grecian.' Everybody else was content with one '*e*;' but he, recollecting the cornucopia of *e*s, which Providence has thought fit to empty upon the mother word *Greece*, deemed it shocking to disinherit the poor child of its hereditary wealth, and wrote it, therefore, *Greecian* throughout his Homer.[9] Such a modest reform the sternest old Tory could not find in his heart to denounce. But some contagion must have collected about this word *Greece;* for the next man, who had much occasion to use it – viz. Mitford[*] – who wrote that 'History of Greece' so eccentric, and so eccentrically praised by Lord Byron, absolutely took to spelling like a heathen, slashed right and left against decent old English words, until, in fact, the whole of Entick's Dictionary (*ablaqueation* and all) was ready to swear the peace against him. Mitford, in course of time, slept with his fathers; his grave, I trust, not haunted by the injured words whom he had tomahawked; and, at this present moment, the Bishop of St David's reigneth in his stead.[16] His Lordship, bound over to episcopal decorum, has

[*] Mitford, who was the brother of a man better known than himself to the public eye, viz., Lord Redesdale, may be considered a very unfortunate author. His work upon Greece, which Lord Byron celebrated for its 'wrath and its partiality,'[10] really had those merits: choleric it was in excess, and as entirely partial, as nearly perfect in its injustice, as human infirmity would allow. Nothing is truly perfect in this shocking world; absolute injustice, alas! the perfection of wrong, must not be looked for until we reach some high Platonic form of polity. Then shall we revel and bask in a vertical sun of iniquity. Meantime, I *will* say – that to satisfy all bilious and unreasonable men, a better historian of Greece, than Mitford, could not be fancied. And yet, at the very moment when he was stepping into his harvest of popularity, down comes one of those omnivorous Germans that, by reading everything, and a trifle besides, contrive to throw really learned men – and perhaps better thinkers than themselves – into the shade. Ottfried Mueller, with other archaeologists and travellers into Hellas, gave new aspects to the very purposes of Grecian history.[11] Do you hear, reader? not new answers, but new questions. And Mitford, that was gradually displacing the unlearned Gillies,[12] &c., was himself displaced by those who intrigued with Germany. His other work on 'the Harmony of Language,'[13] though one of the many that attempted, and the few that accomplished, the distinction between accent and quantity, or learnedly appreciated the metrical science of Milton, was yet, in my hearing, pronounced utterly unintelligible, by the best *practical* commentator on Milton, viz., the best reproducer of his exquisite effects in blank verse, that any generation since Milton has been able to show.[14] Mr Mitford was one of the many accomplished scholars that are ill-used. Had he possessed the splendid powers of the Landor, he would have raised a clatter on the armour of modern society, such as Samson threatened to the giant Harapha.[15] For, in many respects, he resembled the Landor: he had much of his learning – he had the same extensive access to books and influential circles in great cities – the same gloomy disdain of popular falsehoods or common-places – and the same disposition to run a muck against all nations, languages, and spelling-books.

hitherto been sparing in his assaults upon pure old English words: but one may trace the insurrectionary taint, passing down from Cowper through the word *Grecian*, in many of his Anglo-Hellenic forms. For instance, he insists on our saying – not *Heracleidae* and *Pelopidae*,[17] as we all used to do – but *Heracleids* and *Pelopids*. A list of my Lord's barbarities, in many other cases, upon unprotected words, poor shivering aliens that fall into his power, when thrown upon the coast of his diocese, I had – *had*, I say, for, alas! *fuit Ilium*.[18]

Yet, really, one is ashamed to linger on cases so mild as those, coming, as one does, in the order of atrocity, to Elphinstone, to Noah Webster, a Yankee[19] – which word means, not an American, but that separate order of Americans, growing in Massachussets, Rhode Island, or Connecticut, in fact, a New Englander* – and to the rabid Ritson.[20] Noah would naturally have reduced us all to an antidiluvian simplicity. Shem, Ham, and Japhet,[21] probably separated in consequence of perverse varieties in spelling; so that orthographical unity might seem to him one condition for preventing national schisms. But as to the rabid Ritson, who can describe his vagaries? What great arithmetician can furnish an index to his absurdities, or what great decipherer furnish a key to the principles of these absurdities? In his very title pages, nay, in the most obstinate of ancient technicalities, he showed his cloven foot to the astonished reader. Some of his many works were printed in *Pall-Mall;* now, as the world is pleased to pronounce that word *Pel-Mel*,[22] thus and no otherwise (said Ritson) it shall be spelled for ever. Whereas, on the contrary, some men would have said: The spelling is well enough, it is the public pronunciation which is wrong. This ought to be *Paul-Maul;* or perhaps – agreeably to the sound which we give to the *a* in such words as *what*, *quantity, want* – still better, and with more gallantry, *Poll-Moll*. The word Mr, again, in Ritson's reformation, must have astonished the Post-office. He insisted that this cabalistical-looking form, which might as reasonably be translated into *monster*, was a direct fraud on the national language, quite as bad as clipping the Queen's coinage. How, then, *should* it be written? Reader! reader! that you will ask such a question! *mister*, of course; and mind that you put no capital *m;* unless, indeed, you are speaking of some great gun, some mister of misters, such as Mr Pitt of old,[23] or perhaps a reformer of spelling. The plural, again, of such words as *romance*, *age*, *horse*, he wrote *romanceës*, *ageës*, *horseës;* and upon the following equitable consideration; that, inasmuch as the *e* final in the singular is mute, that is, by a general vote of the nation has been allowed to retire upon a superannuation allowance, it is abominable to call it back upon active service – like the modern Chelsea pensioners[24] – as must be done, if it is to bear the whole weight of a separate syllable like *ces*. Consequently, if the nation and Parliament mean to keep faith, they are

* 'In fact, a New Englander.' This explanation, upon a matter familiar to the well-informed, it is proper to repeat occasionally, because we English exceedingly perplex and confound the Americans by calling, for instance, a Virginian or a Kentuck by the name of Yankee, whilst that term was originally introduced as antithetic to these more southern States.

bound to hire a stout young *e* to run in the traces with the old original *e*, taking the whole work off his aged shoulders. Volumes would not suffice to exhaust the madness of Ritson upon this subject. And there was this peculiarity in his madness, over and above its clamorous ferocity, that being no classical scholar (a meagre self-taught Latinist, and no Grecian at all) though profound as a black-letter scholar,[25] he cared not one straw for ethnographic relations of words, nor for unity of analogy, which are the principles that generally have governed reformers of spelling. He was an attorney, and moved constantly under the *monomaniac* idea that an action lay on behalf of misused letters, mutes, liquids, vowels, and diphthongs, against somebody or other (John Doe, was it, or Richard Roe?) for trespass on any rights of theirs which an attorney might trace, and of course for any direct outrage upon their persons. Yet no man was more systematically an offender in both ways than himself; tying up one leg of a quadruped word, and forcing it to run upon three; cutting off noses and ears, if he fancied that equity required it; and living in eternal hot water with a language which he pretended eternally to protect.

And yet all these fellows were nothing in comparison of Mr* Pinkerton. The most of these men did but ruin the national *spelling*; but Pinkerton – the monster Pinkerton – proposed a revolution which would have left us nothing to spell. It is almost incredible – if a book regularly printed and published, bought and sold, did not remain to attest the fact – that this horrid barbarian seriously proposed, as a glorious discovery for refining our language, the following plan. All people were content with the compass of the English language: its range of expression was equal to anything: but, unfortunately, as compared with the sweet orchestral languages of the south – Spanish the stately, and Italian the lovely – it wanted rhythmus and melody. Clearly, then, the one supplementary grace, which it remained for modern art to give, is that every one should add at discretion *o* and *a*, *ino* and *ano*, to the end of English words. The language, in its old days, should be taught *struttare struttissimamente*.[27] As a specimen, Mr Pinkerton favoured us with his own version of a famous passage in Addison, viz., 'The Vision of Mirza.' The passage, which begins thus, 'As I sat on the top of a rock,'[28] being translated into, 'As I satto on the toppino of a rocko,' &c. But *luckilissime* this *proposalio* of the *absurdissimo Pinkertonio*† was not *adoptado* by *anybody-ini whatever-ano*.

* Pinkerton published one of his earliest volumes, under this title – 'Rimes, by Mr Pinkerton,'[26] not having the fear of Ritson before his eyes. And, for once, we have reason to thank Ritson for his remark – that the form Mr might just as well be read *Monster*. Pinkerton in this point was a perfect monster. As to the word *Rimes*, instead of *Rhymes*, he had something to stand upon: the Greek *rhythmos* was certainly the remote fountain; but the proximate fountain must have been the Italian *rima*.

† This most extravagant of all experiments on language is brought forward in the '*Letters of Literature*, by Robert Heron.'[29] But Robert Heron is a *pseudonyme* for John Pinkerton; and I have

Mr Landor is more learned and probably more consistent in his assaults upon the established spelling than most of these elder reformers.[30] But *that* does not make him either learned enough or consistent enough. He never ascends into Anglo-Saxon, or the many cognate languages of the Teutonic family, which is indispensable to a searching inquest upon our language; he does not put forward in this direction even the slender qualifications of Horne Tooke.[31] But Greek and Latin are quite unequal, when disjoined from the elder wheels in our etymological system, to the working of the total machinery of the English language. Mr Landor proceeds upon no fixed principles in his changes. Sometimes it is on the principle of internal analogy with itself, that he would distort or retrotort the language; sometimes on the principle of external analogy with its roots; sometimes on the principle of euphony, or of metrical convenience. Even within such principles he is not uniform. All well-built English scholars, for instance, know that the word *feâlty* cannot be made into a dissyllable: trissyllabic it ever was* with the elder poets – Spencer,[32] Milton, &c.; and so it is amongst all the modern poets who have taken any pains with their English studies: *e.g.*

> 'The eagle, lord of land and sea,
> Stoop'd down – to pay him fe-al-ty.'[33]

It is dreadful to hear a man say *feal-ty*, in any case; but here it is luckily impossible. Now, Mr Landor generally is correct, and trisects the word; but once, at least, he bisects it.[34] I complain, besides, that Mr Landor, in urging the authority of Milton for orthographic innovations, does not always distinguish as to Milton's motives. It is true, as he contends, that, in some instances, Milton reformed the spelling in obedience to the Italian precedent: and certainly without blame; as in *souran*, *sdeign*, which ought not to be printed (as it is) with an elision before the *s*,[35] as if short for disdain; but in other instances Milton's motive had no reference to etymology. Sometimes it was this. In Milton's day, the modern use of Italics was nearly unknown. Everybody is aware that, in our authorized version of the Bible, published in Milton's infancy,[36] Italics are never once used for the purpose of emphasis – but exclusively to indicate such words or auxiliary forms as, though implied and *virtually* present in the original, are not textually expressed, but must be so in English, from the different genius of the language.† Now, this want of a proper technical

---

been told that Pinkerton's motive for assuming it was – because *Heron* had been the maiden name of his mother. Poor lady, she would have stared to find herself, in old age, transformed into Mistressina Heronilla. What most amuses one in pursuing the steps of such an attempt at refinement, is its reception by 'Jack' in the navy.

* '*It ever was*' – and, of course, being (as there is no need to tell Mr Landor) a form obtained by contraction from *fidelitas*.

† Of this a ludicrous illustration is mentioned by the writer once known to the public as *Trinity Jones*.[37] Some young clergyman, unacquainted with the technical use of italics by the original compositors of James the First's Bible, on coming to the 27th verse, chap. xiii. of 1st

resource amongst the compositors of the age, for indicating a peculiar stress upon a word, evidently drove Milton into some perplexity for a compensatory contrivance. It was unusually requisite for *him*, with his elaborate metrical system and his divine ear, to have an art for throwing attention upon his accents, and upon his muffling of accents. When, for instance, he wishes to direct a bright jet of emphasis upon the possessive pronoun *their*, he writes it as we now write it. But, when he wishes to take off the accent, he writes it *thir*.* Like Ritson, he writes *therefor* and *wherefor* without the final *e;* not regarding the analogy, but singly the metrical quantity: for it was shocking to his classical feeling that a sound so short to the ear should be represented to the eye by so long a combination as *fore;* and the more so, because uneducated people did then, and do now, often equilibrate the accent between the two syllables, or rather make the *quantity* long in both syllables, whilst giving an over-balance of the *accent* to the last. The 'Paradise Lost,' being printed during Milton's blindness, did not receive the full and consistent benefit of his spelling reforms, which (as I have contended) certainly arose partly in the imperfections of typography at that aera; but such changes as had happened most to impress his ear with a sense of their importance, he took a special trouble, even under all the disadvantages of his darkness, to have rigorously adopted. He must have astonished the compositors, though not quite so much as the tiger-cat Ritson or the Mr (viz. monster) Pinkerton – each after *his* kind – astonished *their* compositors.

But the caprice of Mr Landor is shown most of all upon Greek names. *Nous autres* say 'Aristotle,'[38] and are quite content with it, until we migrate into some extra-superfine world; but this title will not do for *him:* 'Aristoteles' it must be. And why so? Because, answers the Landor, if once I consent to say Aristotle, then I am pledged to go the whole hog; and perhaps the next man I meet is Empedocles,[39] whom, in that case, I must call Empedocle. Well, do so. *Call* him Empedocle; it will not break his back, which seems broad enough. But, now, mark the contradictions in which Mr Landor is soon landed. He says, as everybody says, Terence, and not Terentius, Horace[40] and not Horatius; but he must leave off such horrid practices, because he dares not call Lucretius by the analogous name of Lucrece, since *that* would be putting a she instead of a he; nor Propertius[41] by the name of Properce, because *that* would be speaking French instead of English. Next he says, and continually he says, Virgil for Virgilius. But, on that principle, he ought to say Valer for

---

Kings, 'And he' (viz. the old prophet of Bethel) 'spake to his sons, saying, saddle me the ass. And they saddled *him*;' (where the italics *him* simply meant that this word was involved, but not expressed, in the original), read it, 'and they saddled HIM;' as though these undutiful sons, instead of saddling the donkey, had saddled the old prophet. In fact, the old gentleman's directions are not quite without an opening for a filial misconception, if the reader examines them as closely as *I* examine words.

* He uses this and similar artifices, in fact, as the damper in a modern piano-forte, for modifying the swell of the intonation.

Valerius; and yet again he ought *not*; because, as he says Tully and not Tull for Tullius,[42] so also is he bound, in Christian equity, to say Valery for Valer; but he cannot say either Valer or Valery. So here we are in a mess. Thirdly, I charge him with saying Ovid[43] for Ovidius: which *I* do, which everybody does, but which *he* must not do; for, if he means to persist in *that*, then, upon his own argument from analogy, he must call Didius Julianus by the shocking name of *Did*, which is the same thing as Tit – since T is D soft. Did was a very great man indeed, and for a very short time indeed. Probably Did was the only man that ever bade for an empire, and no mistake, at a public auction.[44] Think of Did's bidding for the Roman empire; nay, think also of Did's having the lot actually knocked down to him; and of Did's going home to dinner with the lot in his pocket. It makes one perspire to think that, if the reader or myself had been living at that time, and had been prompted by some whim within us to bid against him, we – that is, he or I – should actually have come down to posterity by the abominable name of Anti-Did. All of us in England say Livy when speaking of the great historian, not Livius. Yet Livius Andronicus[45] it would be impossible to indulge with that brotherly name of Livy. Marcus Antonius is called – not by Shakspere only, but by all the world – Mark Antony; but who is it that ever called Marcus Brutus[46] by the affectionate name of Mark Brute? 'Keep your distance,' we say, to that very doubtful brute, 'and expect no pet names from us.' Finally, apply the principle of abbreviation, involved in the names Pliny,[47] Livy, Tully, all substituting *y* for *ius*, to Marius[48] – that grimmest of grim visions that rises up to us from the phantasmagoria of Roman history. Figure to yourself, reader, that truculent face, trenched and scarred with hostile swords, carrying thunder in its ominous eye-brows, and frightening armies a mile off with its scowl, being saluted by the tenderest of feminine names, as 'My Mary.'

Not only, therefore, is Mr Landor inconsistent in these innovations, but the innovations themselves, supposing them all harmonised and established, would but plough up the landmarks of old hereditary feelings. We learn oftentimes, by a man's bearing a good-natured sobriquet amongst his comrades, that he is a kind-hearted, social creature, popular with them all! And it is an illustration of the same tendency, that the scale of popularity for the classical authors amongst our fathers, is registered tolerably well, in a gross general way, by the difference between having and *not* having a familiar name. If we except the first Caesar, the mighty Caius Julius,[49] who was too majestic to invite familiarity, though too gracious to have repelled it, there is no author whom our forefathers loved, but has won a sort of Christian name in the land. Homer, and Hesiod, and Pindar,[50] we all say; we cancel the alien *us;* but we never say Theocrit for Theocritus. Anacreon[51] remains rigidly Grecian marble; but *that* is only because his name is not of a plastic form – else everybody loves the sad old fellow. The same bar to familiarity existed in the names of the tragic poets, except perhaps for Aeschylus;[52] who, however, like Caesar, is too awful for a caressing name. But Roman names were, generally, more flexible. Livy and Sallust[53] have ever been favourites with men: Livy with everybody; Sallust, in a degree that may be called extravagant, with many celebrated Frenchmen, as the President des Brosses,[54] and in our own days with M. Lerminier, a most eloquent and original writer ('*Etudes Historiques*');[55] and two centuries ago, with the greatest of men, John Milton,[56] in a degree that seems to me absolutely mysterious. These writers are baptized into our society – have gained a settlement in our parish: when you call a man Jack, and not Mr John, it's plain you like him. But, as to the gloomy Tacitus,[57] our fathers liked him not. He was too vinegar a fellow for them; nothing hearty or genial about him; he thought ill of everybody; and we all suspect that, for those times, he was perhaps the worst of the bunch himself. Accordingly, this Tacitus, because he remained so perfectly tacit for our jolly old forefathers' ears, never slipped into the name Tacit for their mouths; nor ever will, I predict, for the mouths of posterity. Coming to the Roman poets, I must grant that three great ones, viz., Lucretius, Statius, and Valerius Flaccus,[58] have not been complimented with the freedom of our city, as they should have been, in a gold box. I regret, also, the ill fortune, in this respect, of Catullus, if he was really the author of that grand headlong dithyrambic, the Atys:[59] he certainly ought to have been ennobled by the title of Catull. Looking to very much of his writings, much more I regret the case of Plautus:[60] and I am sure that if her Majesty would warrant his bearing the name and arms of *Plaut* in all time coming, it would gratify many of us. As to the rest, or those that anybody cares about, Horace, Virgil, Ovid, Lucan, Martial, Claudian,[61] all have been raised to the peerage. Ovid was the great poetic favourite of Milton;[62] and not without a philosophic ground: his festal gaiety, and the brilliant velocity of his *aurora borealis* intellect, forming a deep natural equipoise to the mighty gloom and solemn planetary movement in the mind of the other; like the wedding of male and female counterparts. Ovid was, therefore, rightly Milton's favourite. But the favourite of all the world is Horace. Were there ten peerages, were there three blue ribbons, vacant, he ought to have them all.

Besides, if Mr Landor could issue decrees, and even harmonise his decrees for reforming our Anglo-Grecian spelling – decrees which no Council of Trent could execute, without first rebuilding the Holy office of the Inquisition[63] – still there would be little accomplished. The names of all continental Europe are often in confusion, from different causes, when Anglicised: German names are rarely spelled rightly by the *laity* of our isle: Polish and Hungarian never. Many foreign towns have in England what botanists would call *trivial*[64] names; Leghorn, for instance, Florence, Madrid, Lisbon, Vienna, Munich, Antwerp, Brussels, the Hague – all unintelligible names to the savage Continental native. Then, if Mr Landor reads as much of Anglo-Indian books as I do, he must be aware that, for many years back, they have all been at sixes and sevens;[65] so that now most Hindoo words are in masquerade, and we shall soon require *English* pundits in Leadenhall Street.* How does he like, for instance, *Sipahee* the modern form of *Sepoy?* or *Tepheen* for *Tiffin?*[69] At this rate of metamorphosis, absorbing even the consecrated names of social meals, we shall soon cease to understand what that *disjune* was which his sacred Majesty graciously accepted at Tillietudlem.[70] But even elder forms of oriental speech are as little harmonised in Christendom. A few leagues of travelling make the Hebrew unintelligible to us; and the Bible becomes a Delphic mystery to Englishmen amongst the countrymen of Luther. Solomon is there called Salamo; Sampson is called Simson, though probably he never published an edition of Euclid.[71] Nay, even in this native isle of ours, you may be at cross purposes on the Bible with your own brother. I am, myself, next door neighbour to Westmoreland, being a Lancashire man;[72] and, one day, I was talking with a Westmoreland farmer, whom, of course, I ought to have understood very well; but I had no chance with him: for I could not make out who that *No* was, concerning *whom* or concerning *which*, he persisted in talking. It seemed to me, from the context, that *No* must be a man, and by no means a chair; but so very negative a name, you perceive, furnished no positive hints for solving the problem. I said as much to the farmer, who stared in stupefaction. 'What,' cried he, 'did a far-larn'd man, like you, fresh from Oxford,[73] never hear of *No*, an old gentleman that should have been drowned, but was *not*, when all his folk were drowned?' 'Never, so help me Jupiter,'[74] was my reply: 'never heard of him to this hour, any more than of *Yes*, an old gentleman that should have been hanged, but was *not*, when all his folk were hanged. *Populous No* – I had read of in the Prophets; but that was *not* an old gentleman.' It turned out that the farmer and all his compatriots in bonny Martindale had been taught at the parish school to rob the Patriarch Noah of one clear moiety appertaining in fee simple[75] to that ancient name. But afterwards I found that the farmer was not so entirely absurd as he had seemed. The Septuagint, indeed, is clearly against him; for *there*, as plain as a pikestaff, the farmer might have read Νωϊ.[76] But, on the other hand, Pope, not quite so great a scholar as he was a poet, yet still a fair one, *always* made Noah into a monosyllable;[77] and that seems to argue an old English usage; though I

* The reasons for this anarchy in the naturalisation of Eastern words are to be sought in three causes: 1. In national rivalships: French travellers in India, like Jacquemont,[66] &c., as they will not adopt our English First Meridian, will not, of course, adopt our English spelling. In one of Paul Richter's novels a man assumes the First Meridian to lie generally, not through Greenwich,[67] but through his own skull, and always through his own study. I have myself long suspected the Magnetic Pole to lie under a friend's wine-cellar, from the vibrating movement which I have remarked constantly going on in his cluster of keys towards that particular point. Really, the French, like Sir Anthony Absolute, must 'get an atmosphere of their own,'[68] such is their hatred to holding anything in common with us. 2. They are to be sought in local *Indian* differences of pronunciation. 3. In variety of our own British population – soldiers, missionaries, merchants, who are unlearned or half-learned – scholars, really learned, but often fantastically learned, and lastly (as you may swear) young ladies – anxious, above all things, to mistify us outside barbarians.

really believe Pope's reason for adhering to such an absurdity was with a prospective view to the rhymes *blow*, or *row*, or *stow*, (an important idea to the Ark) which struck him as *likely* words, in case of any call for writing about Noah.

The long and the short of it is – that the whole world lies in heresy or schism on the subject of orthography. All climates alike groan under heterography. It is absolutely of no use to begin with one's own grandmother in such labors of reformation. It is toil thrown away: and as nearly hopeless a task as the proverb insinuates that it is to attempt a reformation in that old lady's mode of eating eggs.[78] She laughs at one. She has a vain conceit that she is able, out of her own proper resources, to do both, viz., the spelling and the eating of the eggs. And all that remains for philosophers, like Mr Landor and myself, is – to turn away in sorrow rather than in anger,[79] dropping a silent tear for the poor old lady's infatuation.

MILTON *VERSUS* SOUTHEY AND LANDOR

First published in *Tait's*, XIV, April 1847, pp. 253–9. The essay was printed as 'BY THOMAS DE QUINCEY.' in a centred line following the title and immediately preceding the text.

Reprinted in *F*, XVIII, *The Note Book of an English Opium-Eater* (1855), pp. 193–216.

Revised text, carrying many accidentals but only one substantive variant from *F*, in *SGG*, *Speculations, Literary and Philosophic, with German Tales* (1859), pp. 176–98.

There are no manuscripts.

Crabb Robinson was unimpressed by the essay:

> A piece of laboured criticism written for bread, a rambling [article] sent to a Scotch magazine…a jumble not easy to find a name for. My correspondence contains a few things equally deserving to be printed, such as Landor's [letters about] Wordsworth (*HCR*, vol. II, p. 818).

John E. Jordan, however, reprinted the essay in its entirety in *De Quincey as Critic* (pp. 465–82), and praised the piece for its 'interesting analysis of versification'.

For the context and occasion of this essay, see headnote, pp. 3–5.

THIS conversation is doubly interesting: interesting by its subject, interesting by its interlocutors; for the subject is Milton, whilst the interlocutors are *Southey*[1] and *Landor*. If a British gentleman, when taking his pleasure in his well-armed yacht, descries, in some foreign waters, a noble vessel, from the Thames or the Clyde,[2] riding peaceably at anchor – and soon after, two smart-looking clippers, with rakish masts, bearing down upon her in company – he slackens sail: his suspicions are slightly raised; they have not shown their teeth as yet, and perhaps all is right; but there can be no harm in looking a little closer; and, assuredly, if he finds any mischief in the wind against his countryman, he will show *his* teeth also; and please the wind, will take up such a position as to rake both of these pirates by turns. The two dialogists are introduced walking out after breakfast, 'each his Milton in his pocket;' and says Southey, 'Let us collect all the graver faults we can lay our hands upon, without a too minute and troublesome research;' – just so; there would be danger in *that* – help might be put off from shore; – 'not,' says he, 'in the spirit of Johnson, but in our own.'[3] Johnson, we may suppose, is some old ruffian well known upon that coast; and '*faults*' may be a flash term for what the Americans call 'notions.'[4] A part of the cargo it clearly is; and one is not surprised to hear Landor, whilst assenting to the general plan of attack, suggesting in a whisper, 'that they should abase their eyes in reverence to so great a man, without absolutely closing them;'[5] which I take to mean – that, without trusting entirely to their boarders, or absolutely closing their ports, they should depress their guns and fire down into the hold, in respect of the vessel attacked standing so high out of the water. After such plain speaking, nobody can wonder much at the junior pirate (Landor) muttering, 'It will be difficult for us always to refrain.'[6] Of course it will: *refraining* was no part of the business, I should fancy, taught by that same buccaneer, Johnson. There is mischief, you see, reader, singing in the air – 'miching malhecho'[7] – and it is our business to watch it.

But, before coming to the main attack, I must suffer myself to be detained for a few moments by what Mr L. premises upon the 'moral' of any great fable,[8] and the relation which it bears, or *should* bear, to the solution of such a fable. Philosophic criticism is so far improved, that, at this day, few people, who have reflected at all upon such subjects, but are agreed as to one point: viz., that in metaphysical language the moral of an epos or a drama should be *immanent*, not *transient;* or, otherwise, that it should be vitally distributed through the whole organization of the tree, not gathered or secreted into a sort of red berry or *racemus*,[9] pendent at the end of its boughs. This view Mr Landor himself takes, as a general view; but, strange to say, by some Landorian perverseness, where there occurs a memorable exception to this rule (as in the 'Paradise Lost'),[10] in that case he insists upon the rule in its rigour – the rule, and nothing *but* the rule. Where, on the contrary, the rule does really and obviously take effect (as in the 'Iliad' and 'Odyssey'),[11] there he insists upon an exceptional case. There *is* a moral, in *his* opinion, hanging like a tassel of gold bullion from the 'Iliad;' – and what is it? Something so fantastic, that I decline to repeat it.[12] As well might he have said, that the moral of 'Othello' was – '*Try Warren's Blacking!*'[13] There is no moral, little or big, foul or fair, to the 'Iliad.' Up to the 17th book, the moral might seem dimly to be this – 'Gentlemen, keep the peace: you see what comes of quarrelling.' But *there* this moral ceases; – there is now a break of guage; the narrow guage takes place after this; whilst up to this point, the broad guage – viz., the wrath of Achilles, growing out of his turn-up with Agamemnon[14] – had carried us smoothly along without need to shift our luggage. There is no more quarrelling after Book 17, how then can there be any more moral from quarrelling? If you can insist on *my* telling *you* what is the moral of the 'Iliad,' I insist upon *your* telling *me* what is the moral of a rattlesnake or the moral of Niagara. I suppose the moral is – that you must get out of their way, if you mean to moralise much longer. The going-up (or anabasis) of the Greeks against Troy, was a *fact;* and a pretty dense fact; and, by accident, the very first in which all Greece had a common interest. It was a joint-stock concern – a representative expedition – whereas, previously there had been none; for even the Argonautic expedition,[15] which is rather of the darkest, implied no confederation except amongst individuals. How could it? For the Argo is supposed to have measured only twenty-seven tons: how she would have been classed at Lloyd's[16] is hard to say, but certainly not as A 1. There was no state-cabin; everybody, demi-gods and all, pigged in the steerage amongst beans and bacon. Greece was naturally proud of having crossed the herring-pond, small as it was, in search of an entrenched enemy; proud also of having licked him 'into Almighty smash;'[17] this was sufficient; or if an impertinent moralist sought for something more, doubtless the moral must have lain in the booty. A peach is the moral of a peach, and moral enough; but if a man *will* have something better – a moral within a moral – why, there is the peach-stone, and its kernel, out of which he may make ratafia, which seems to be the ultimate morality that *can* be extracted from a peach. Mr Archdeacon Williams, indeed, of the Edinburgh Academy,[18] has published an *octavo* opinion upon the case, which asserts that the moral of the Trojan war was (to borrow a phrase from children) *tit for tat*. It was a case of retaliation for crimes against Hellas, committed by Troy in an earlier generation. It may be so; Nemesis[19] knows best. But this moral, if it concerns the total expedition to the Troad, cannot concern the 'Iliad,' which does not take up matters from so early a period, nor go on to the final catastrophe of Ilium.[20]

Now, as to the 'Paradise Lost,' it happens that there is – whether there ought to be or not – a pure golden moral, distinctly announced, separately contemplated, and the very weightiest ever uttered by man or realised by fable. It is a moral rather for the drama of a world than for a human poem. And this moral is made the more prominent and memorable by the grandeur of its annunciation. The jewel is not more splendid in itself than in its setting. Excepting the well-known passage on Athenian oratory in the 'Paradise Regained,'[21] there is none even in Milton where the metrical pomp is made so effectually to aid the pomp of the sentiment. Hearken to the way in which a roll of dactyles is made to settle, like the swell of the advancing tide, into the long thunder of billows breaking for leagues against the shore:

> 'That to the height of this great argument
> I may assert eternal Providence.'[22] ——

Hear what a motion, what a tumult, is given by the dactylic close to each of the introductory lines! And how massily is the whole locked up into the peace of heaven, as the aerial arch of a viaduct is locked up into tranquil stability by its key-stone, through the deep spondaic close.

> 'And justify the ways of God to man.'[23]

That is the moral of the Miltonic epos; and as much grander than any other moral *formally* illustrated by poets, as heaven is higher than earth.

But the most singular moral, which Mr Landor anywhere discovers, is in his own poem of '*Gebir.*'[24] Whether he still adheres to it, does not appear from the present edition. But I remember distinctly, in the original edition, a Preface (now withdrawn) in which he made his acknowledgements to some book read at a Welsh Inn for the outline of the story; and as to the moral, he declared it to be an exposition of that most mysterious offence, *Over-Colonisation*.[25] Much I mused, in my youthful simplicity, upon this criminal novelty. What might it be? Could I, by mistake, have committed it myself? Was it a felony, or a misdemeanour? – liable to transportation, or only to fine and imprisonment? Neither in the Decemviral Tables, nor in the Code of Justinian, nor the maritime Code of Oleron, nor in the Canon Law, nor the Code Napoleon, nor our own Statutes at large, nor in Jeremy Bentham,[26] had I read of such a crime as a possibility. Undoubtedly the vermin, locally called *Squatters*,* both in the wilds of America and Australia, who preoccupy other men's estates, have latterly illustrated the logical possibility of such an offence; but they were quite unknown at the aera of Gebir. Even Dalica,[28] who knew as much wickedness as most people, would have stared at this unheard-of villainy, and have asked, as eagerly as *I* did – 'What is it now? Let's have a shy at it in Egypt.' I, indeed, knew a case, but Dalica did *not*, of shocking over-colonisation. It was the case, which even yet occurs on out-of-the-way roads, where a man, unjustly big, mounts into the inside of a stage-coach already sufficiently crowded. In streets and squares, where men could give him a wide berth, they had tolerated the injustice of his person; but now, in a chamber so confined, the length and breadth of his wickedness shines revealed to every eye. And if the coach should upset, which it would not be the less likely to do for having *him* on board, somebody or other (perhaps myself) must lie beneath this monster, like Enceladus under Mount Etna, calling upon Jove[29] to come quickly with a few thunderbolts and destroy both man and mountain, both *succubus* and *incubus*,[30] if no other relief offered. Meantime, the only case of over-colonisation notorious to all Europe, is that which some German traveller (Riedesel, I think) has reported so eagerly, in ridicule of our supposed English credulity; viz. – the case of the foreign swindler, who advertised that he would get into a quart bottle, filled Drury Lane, pocketed the admission money, and decamped, protesting (in his adieus to the spectators) that 'it lacerated his heart to disappoint so many noble islanders; but that on his next visit he would make full reparation by getting into a vin-

* *Squatters:*[27] – They are a sort of self-elected warming pans. What we in England mean by the political term '*warming-pans*,' are men who occupy, by consent, come official place, or Parliamentary seat, until the proper claimant is old enough in law to assume his rights. When the true man comes to bed, the warming-pan respectfully turns out. But these ultra-marine warming-pans *wouldn't* turn out. They showed fight, and wouldn't hear of the true man, even as a bed-fellow.

egar cruet.'[31] Now, here certainly was a case of over-colonisation, not perpetrated, but meditated. Yet, when one examines this case, the crime consisted by no means in doing it, but in *not* doing it; by no means in getting into the bottle, but in *not* getting into it. The foreign contractor would have been probably a very unhappy man, had he fulfilled his contract by over-colonising the bottle, but he would have been decidedly a more virtuous man. He would have redeemed his pledge; and, if he had even died in the bottle, we should have honoured him as a '*vir bonus, cum malâ fortunâ compositus;*'[32] as a man of honour matched in single duel with calamity, and also as the best of conjurors. Over-colonisation, therefore, except in the one case of the stage-coach, is apparently no crime; and the offence of King Gebir, in my eyes, remains a mystery to this day.

What next solicits notice is in the nature of a digression: it is a kind of parenthesis on Wordsworth.

'*Landor.* – When it was a matter of wonder how Keats, who was ignorant of Greek, could have written his "Hyperion," Shelley, whom envy never touched, gave as a reason – "because he *was* a Greek."[33] Wordsworth, being asked his opinion of the same poem, called it, scoffingly, "a pretty piece of paganism;" yet he himself, in the best verses he ever wrote – and beautiful ones they are – reverts to the powerful influence of the "pagan creed."'[34]

Here are nine lines exactly in the original type. Now, nine tailors are ranked, by great masters of algebra, as = one man; such is the received equation; or, as it is expressed, with more liveliness, in an old English drama, by a man who meets and quarrels with eighteen tailors – 'Come, hang it! I'll fight you *both*.'[35] But, whatever be the algebraic ratio of tailors to men, it is clear that nine Landorian lines are not always equal to the delivery of one accurate truth, or to a successful conflict with three or four signal errors. Firstly – Shelley's reason, if it ever was assigned, is irrelevant as regards any question that must have been intended. It could not have been meant to ask – Why was the 'Hyperion' so Grecian in its spirit? for it is anything but Grecian. We should praise it falsely to call it so; for the feeble, though elegant, mythology of Greece was incapable of breeding anything so deep as the mysterious portents that, in the 'Hyperion,' run before and accompany the passing away of divine immemorial dynasties. Nothing can be more impressive than the picture of Saturn in his palsy of affliction, and of the mighty goddess his grand-daughter, or than the secret signs of coming woe in the palace of Hyperion.[36] These things grew from darker creeds than Greece had ever known since the elder traditions of Prometheus – creeds that sent down their sounding plummets into far deeper wells within the human spirit.[37] What had been meant, by the question proposed to Shelley, was no doubt – How so young a man as Keats, not having had the advantage of a regular classical education, could have been so much at home in the details of the *elder* mythology? Tooke's 'Pantheon'[38] might have been obtained by favour of any English schoolboy, and Dumoustier's '*Lettres à Emilie sur la Mythologie*'[39] by favour of very many young ladies; but these, according to my recollection of them, would hardly have sufficed. Spence's '*Polymetis*,'[40] however, might have been had by favour of any good library; and the '*Bibliotheca*' of Apollodorus,[41] who is the cock of the walk on this subject, might have been read by favour of a Latin translation, supposing Keats really unequal to the easy Greek text. There is no wonder in the case; nor, if there had been, would Shelley's kind remark have solved it. The *treatment* of the facts must, in any case, have been due to Keats's genius, so as to be the same whether he had studied Greek or not: the *facts*, apart from the treatment, must in any case have been had from a book. Secondly – Let Mr Landor rely upon it – that Wordsworth never said the thing ascribed to him here as any formal judgment, or what Scottish law would call *deliverance*, upon the 'Hyperion.'[42] As to what he might have said incidentally and collaterally; the meaning of words is so entirely affected by their position in a conversation – what followed, what went before – that five words dislocated from their context never would be received as evidence in the Queen's Bench. The court which, of all others, least strictly weighs its rules of evidence, is the female tea-table; yet even that tribunal would require the deponent to strengthen his evidence, if he had only five detached words to produce. Wordsworth is a very proud man, as he has good reason to be; and perhaps it was I, myself, who once said in print of him – that it is not the correct way of speaking, to say that Wordsworth is as proud as Lucifer; but, inversely, to say of Lucifer that some people have conceived him to be as proud as Wordsworth.[43] But, if proud, Wordsworth is not haughty, is not ostentatious, is not anxious for display, is not arrogant, and, least of all, is he capable of descending to envy. Who or what is it that *he* should be envious of? Does anybody suppose that Wordsworth would be jealous of Archimedes if he now walked upon earth, or Michael Angelo,[44] or Milton? Nature does not repeat herself. Be assured she will never make a second Wordsworth. Any of us would be jealous of his own duplicate; and, if I had a *doppelganger*, who went about personating me, copying me, and pirating me, philosopher as I am, I might (if the Court of Chancery would not grant an injunction against him) be so far carried away by jealousy as to attempt the crime of murder upon his carcass; and no great matter as regards HIM. But it would be a sad thing for *me* to find myself hanged; and for what, I beseech you? for murdering a sham, that was either nobody at all, or oneself repeated once too often.[45] But if you show to Wordsworth a man as great as himself, still that great man will not be much *like* Wordsworth – the great man will not be Wordsworth's *doppelganger*. If not *impar* (as you say) he will be *dispar*;[46] and why, then, should Wordsworth be jealous of him, unless he is jealous of the sun, and of Abd el Kāder, and of Mr Waghorn[47] – all of whom carry off a great deal of any spare admiration which Europe has to dispose of. But suddenly it strikes me that we are all proud, every man of us; and I daresay with some reason for it, 'be the same more or less.' For I never came to know any man in my whole life intimately, who could not do something or other better than anybody else. The only man amongst us that is thoroughly free from pride, that you may at all seasons rely on as a pattern of humility, is the pickpocket. That man is so admirable in his temper, and so used to pocketing anything whatever Providence sends in his way, that he will even pocket a kicking, or anything in that line of favours which you are pleased to bestow. The smallest donations are by him thankfully received, provided only that you, whilst half-blind with anger in kicking him round a figure of eight, like a dexterous skater, will but allow *him* (which is no more than fair) to have a second 'shy'[48] at your pretty Indian pocket-handkerchief, so as to convince you, on cooler reflection, that he does not *always* miss. Thirdly – Mr Landor leaves it doubtful what verses those are of Wordsworth's which celebrate the power 'of the Pagan creed;' whether that sonnet in which Wordsworth wishes to exchange for glimpses of human life, *then and in those circumstances*, 'forlorn,' the sight

> '—— Of Proteus coming from the sea,
> And hear old Triton wind his wreathed horn;'

whether this, or the passage on the Greek mythology in 'The Excursion.'[49] Whichever he means, I am the last man to deny that it is beautiful, and especially if he means the latter. But it is no presumption to deny firmly Mr Landor's assertion, that these are 'the best verses Wordsworth ever wrote.' Bless the man!

> 'There are a thousand such elsewhere,
> As worthy of your wonder:'[50] –

Elsewhere, I mean, in Wordsworth's poems. In reality it is *impossible* that these should be the best; for even if, in the executive part, they were so, which is not the case, the very nature of the thought, of the feeling, and of the relation, which binds it to the general theme, and the nature of that theme itself, forbid the possibility of merits so high. The whole movement of the feeling is fanciful: it neither appeals to what is deepest in human sensibilities, nor is meant to do so. The result, indeed, serves only to show Mr Landor's slender acquaintance with Wordsworth. And what is worse than being slenderly acquainted, he is erroneously acquainted even with these two short breathings from the Wordsworthian shell. He mistakes the logic. Wordsworth does not celebrate any power at all in Paganism. Old Triton indeed! he's little better, in respect of the terrific, than a mail-coach guard, nor half as good, if you allow the guard his official seat, a coal-black night, lamps blazing back upon his royal scarlet, and his blunderbuss correctly slung. Triton would not stay, I engage, for a second look at the old Portsmouth mail, as once I knew it. But, alas! better things than ever stood on Triton's pins are now as little able to stand up for themselves, or to startle the silent fields in darkness, with the sudden flash of their glory – gone before it had fully come – as Triton is to play the Freyschütz chorus[51] on his humbug of a horn. But the logic of Wordsworth is this – not that the Greek mythology is potent; on the contrary, that it is weaker than cowslip tea, and would not agitate the nerves of a hen-sparrow; but that, weak as it is – nay, by means of that very weakness – it does but the better serve to measure the weakness of something which *he* thinks yet weaker – viz. the death-like torpor of London society in 1808, benumbed by conventional apathy and worldliness –

'Heavy as frost, and deep almost as life.'[52]

This seems a digression from Milton, who is properly the subject of this colloquy. But, luckily, it is not one of *my* sins. Mr Landor is lord within the house of his own book; he pays all accounts whatever; and readers that have either a bill, or bill of exceptions, to tender against the concern, must draw upon *him*. To Milton he returns upon a very dangerous topic indeed – viz. the structure of his blank verse. I know of none that is so trying to a wary man's nerves. You might as well tax Mozart with harshness in the divinest passages of 'Don Giovanni,'[53] as Milton with any such offence against metrical science. Be assured, it is yourself that do not read with understanding, not Milton that by possibility can be found deaf to the demands of perfect harmony. You are tempted, after walking round a line threescore times, to exclaim at last – 'Well, if the Fiend himself should rise up before me at this very moment, in this very study of mine, and say that no screw was loose in that line, then would I reply – "Sir, with submission, you are ——."' 'What!' suppose the Fiend suddenly to demand in thunder; 'what am I?' 'Horribly wrong,' you wish exceedingly to say; but, recollecting that some people are choleric in argument, you confine yourself to the polite answer – 'That, with deference to his better education, you conceive him to lie;' – that's a bad word to drop your voice upon in talking with a fiend, and you hasten to add – 'under a slight, a *very* slight mistake.' Ay, you might venture on that opinion with a fiend. But how if an angel should undertake the case? And angelic was the ear of Milton. Many are *primâ facie*[54] anomalous lines in Milton; many are the suspicious lines, which in many a book I have seen many a critic peering into, with eyes made up for mischief, yet with a misgiving that all was not quite safe, very much like an old raven looking down a marrow-bone. In fact, such is the metrical skill of the man, and such the perfection of his metrical sensibility, that, on any attempt to take liberties with a passage of his, you feel as when coming, in a forest, upon what seems a dead lion; perhaps he may *not* be dead, but only sleeping; nay, perhaps he may *not* be sleeping, but only shamming. And you have a jealousy, as to Milton, even in the most flagrant case of almost palpable error, that, after all, there may be a plot in it. You may be put down with shame by some man reading the line otherwise, reading it with a different emphasis, a different caesura, or perhaps a different suspension of the voice, so as to bring out a new and self-justifying effect. It must be added, that, in reviewing Milton's metre, it is quite necessary to have such books as 'Nares's English Orthoēpy' (*in a late edition*),[55] and others of that class, lying on the table; because the accentuation of Milton's age was, in many words, entirely different from ours. And Mr Landor is not free from some suspicion of inattention as to this point. Over and above this accentual difference, the practice of our elder dramatists in the resolution of the final *tion* (which now is uniformly pronounced *shon*), will be found exceedingly important to the appreciation of a writer's verse. *Contribution*, which now is necessarily pronounced as a word of four syllables, would then, in verse, have five, being read into *con-tri-bu-ce-on*.[56] Many readers will recollect another word, which for years brought John Kemble into hot water with the pit of Drury Lane.[57] It was the plural of the word ache. This is generally made a dissyllable by the Elizabethan dramatists; it occurs in the 'Tempest.' Prospero says –

'I'll fill thy bones with aches.'[58]

What follows, which I do not remember *literatim*,[59] is such metrically as to *require* two syllables for aches. But how, then, was this to be pronounced? Kemble thought *akies* would sound ludicrous; *aitches* therefore he called it: and always the pit howled like a famished *menagerie*, as they did also when he chose (and he constantly chose) to pronounce *beard* like *bird*. Many of these niceties must be known, before a critic can ever allow *himself* to believe that he is right in *obelizing*,[60] or in marking with so much as a ? any verse whatever of Milton's. And there are some of these niceties, I am satisfied, not even yet fully investigated.

It is, however, to be borne in mind, after all allowances and provisional reservations have been made, that Bentley's hypothesis[61] (injudiciously as it was managed by that great scholar) has really a truth of fact to stand upon. Not only must Milton have composed his three greatest poems, the two 'Paradises' and the 'Samson,' in a state of blindness – but subsequently, in the correction of the proofs, he must have suffered still more from this conflict with darkness, and, consequently, from this dependence upon careless readers. This is Bentley's *case*: as lawyers say, 'My lord, that is my case.' It is possible enough to *write* correctly in the dark, as I myself often do, when losing or missing my lucifers[62] – which, like some elder lucifers, are always rebelliously straying into places where they *can* have no business. But it is quite impossible to *correct a proof* in the dark. At least, if there *is* such an art, it must be a section of the black art. Bentley gained from Pope that admirable epithet of *slashing*, ['*the ribbalds – from slashing Bentley down to piddling Theobalds*,' i.e. *Tibbalds* as it was pronounced],[63] altogether from his edition of the 'Paradise Lost.' This the doctor founded on his own hypothesis as to the advantage taken of Milton's blindness; and corresponding was the havoc which he made of the text. In fact, on the really just allegation that Milton must have used the services of an amanuensis; and the plausible one that this amanuensis, being often weary of his task, would be likely to neglect punctilious accuracy; and the most improbable allegation that this weary person would also be very conceited, and add much rubbish of his own; Bentley resigned himself luxuriously, without the whisper of a scruple, to his own sense of what was or was not poetic, which sense happened to be that of the adder for music.[64] The deaf adder heareth not though the musician charm ever so wisely. No scholarship, which so far beyond other men Bentley had,[65] could gain him the imaginative sensibility which, in a degree so far beyond average men, he wanted. Consequently, the world never before beheld such a scene of massacre as his 'Paradise Lost' exhibited. He laid himself down to his work of extermination like the brawniest of reapers going in steadily with his sickle, coat stripped off, and shirt sleeves tucked up, to deal with an acre of barley. One duty, and no other, rested upon *his* conscience; one voice he heard – Slash away, and hew down the rotten growths of this abominable amanuensis. The carnage was like that after a pitched battle. The very finest passages in every book of the poem were marked by italics, as dedicated to fire and slaughter. 'Slashing Dick' went through the whole forest, like a woodman marking with white paint the giant trees that must all come down in a month or so. And one naturally reverts to a passage in the poem itself, where God the Father is supposed to say to his Filial assessor on the heavenly throne, when marking the desolating progress of Sin and Death, –

> 'See with what havoc these fell dogs advance
> To ravage this fair world.'[66]

But still this inhuman extravagance of Bentley, in following out his hypothesis, does not exonerate *us* from bearing in mind so much truth as that hypothesis really must have had, from the pitiable difficulties of the great poet's situation.

My own opinion, therefore, upon the line, for instance, from 'Paradise Regained,' which Mr Landor appears to have indicated for the reader's amazement, viz.: –

> 'As well might recommend
> *Such solitude before choicest society*,'[67]

is – that it escaped revision from some accident calling off the ear of Milton whilst in the act of having the proof read to him. Mr Landor silently prints it in italics, without assigning his objection; but, of course, that objection must be – that the line has one foot too much. It is an Alexandrine, such as Dryden[68] scattered so profusely, without asking himself why; but which Milton never tolerates except in the choruses of the Samson.

> '*Not difficult, if thou hearken to me*'[69] –

is one of the lines which Mr Landor thinks that 'no authority will reconcile'[70] to our ears. I think otherwise. The caesura is meant to fall not with the comma after *difficult*, but after *thou*; and there is a most effective and grand suspension intended. It is Satan who speaks – Satan in the wilderness; and he marks, as he wishes to mark, the tremendous opposition of attitude between the two parties to the temptation.

'Not difficult if *thou* ——'

there let the reader pause, as if pulling up suddenly four horses in harness, and throwing them on their haunches – not difficult if thou (in some mysterious sense the son of God); and then, as with a burst of thunder, again giving the reins to your *quadriga*,[71]

'—— hearken to me:'

that is, to me, that am the Prince of the Air, and able to perform all my promises for those that hearken to my temptations.

Two lines are cited under the same ban of irreconcileability to our ears, but on a very different plea. The first of these lines is –

'Launcelot, or Pellias, or Pellinore;'[72]

The other

'Quintius, Fabricius, Curius, Regulus.'[73]

The reader will readily suppose that both are objected to as 'roll-calls of proper names.'[74] Now, it is very true that nothing is more offensive to the mind than the practice of mechanically packing into metrical successions, as if packing a portmanteau, names without meaning or significance to the feelings. No man ever carried that atrocity so far as Boileau,[75] a fact of which Mr Landor is well aware; and slight is the sanction or excuse that can be drawn from *him*. But it must not be forgotten that Virgil, so scrupulous in finish of composition, committed this fault. I remember a passage ending

'——Noëmonaque Prytaninqué;'[76]

but, having no Virgil within reach, I cannot at this moment quote it accurately. Homer, with more excuse, however, from the rudeness of his age, is a deadly offender in this way.[77] But the cases from Milton are very different. Milton was incapable of the Homeric or Virgilian blemish. The objection to such rolling musquetry of names is, that unless interspersed with epithets, or broken into irregular groups by brief circumstances of parentage, country, or romantic incident, they stand audaciously perking up their heads like lots in a catalogue, arrow-headed palisades, or young larches in a nursery ground, all occupying the same space, all drawn up in line, all mere iterations of each other. But in

'Quintius, Fabricius, Curius, Regulus,'

though certainly not a good line *when insulated*, (better, however, in its connexion with the entire succession of which it forms part) the apology is, that the massy weight of the separate characters enables them to stand like granite pillars or pyramids, proud of their self-supporting independency.

Mr Landor makes one correction by a simple improvement in the punctuation, which has a very fine effect. Rarely has so large a result been distributed through a sentence by so slight a change. It is in the 'Samson.' Samson says, speaking of himself (as elsewhere) with that profound pathos, which to all hearts invests Milton's own situation in the days of his old age, when he was composing that drama –

> 'Ask for this great deliverer now, and find him
> *Eyeless in Gaza at the mill with slaves*.'[78]

Thus it is usually printed; that is, without a comma in the latter line; but, says Landor, 'there ought to be commas after *eyeless*, after *Gaza*, after *mill*.' And why? because thus 'the grief of Samson is aggravated at every member of the sentence.'[79] He (like Milton) was – 1. blind; 2. in a city of triumphant enemies; 3. working for daily bread; 4. herding with slaves; Samson literally, and Milton with those whom politically he regarded as such.

Mr Landor is perfectly wrong, I must take the liberty of saying, when he demurs to the line in 'Paradise Regained:'

> '*From that placid aspéct and meek regard*,'[80]

on the ground that '*meek regard* conveys no new idea to *placid aspéct*.' But *aspéct* is the countenance of Christ when passive to the gaze of others: *regard* is the same countenance in active contemplation of those others whom he loves or pities. The *placid aspéct* expresses, therefore, the divine rest; the *meek regard* expresses the divine benignity: the one is the self-absorption of the total Godhead, the other the eternal emanation of the Filial Godhead.

'By what ingenuity,' says Landor, 'can we erect into a verse –

> "*In the bosom of bliss, and light of light?*"'[81]

Now really it is by my watch exactly three minutes too late for *him* to make that objection. The court cannot receive it now; for the line just this moment cited, the ink being hardly yet dry, is of the same identical structure. The usual iambic flow is disturbed in both lines by the very same ripple, viz., a trochee in the second foot, *placid* in the one line, *bosom* in the other. They are a sort of *snags*, such as lie in the current of the Mississippi. *There* they do nothing but mischief. Here, when the lines are read in their entire *nexus*, the disturbance stretches forwards and backwards with good effect on the music. Besides, if it did *not*, one is willing to take a *snag* from Milton, but one does not altogether like being *snagged* by the Mississippi. One sees no particular reason for bearing it, if one only knew how to be revenged on a river.

But, of these metrical skirmishes, though full of importance to the impassioned text of a great poet (for mysterious is the life that connects all modes of passion with rhythmus), let us suppose the casual reader to have had enough. And now at closing, for the sake of change, let us treat him to a harlequin trick upon another theme. Did the reader ever happen to see a sheriff's officer arresting an honest gentleman, who was doing no manner of harm to gentle or simple, and immediately afterwards a second sheriff's officer arresting the first – by which means that second officer merits for himself a place in history; for at the same moment he liberates a deserving creature (since an arrested officer cannot possibly bag his prisoner), and he also avenges the insult put upon that worthy man? Perhaps the reader did *not* ever see such a sight; and, growing personal, he asks *me* in return, if *I* ever saw it. To say the truth, I never *did;* except once, in a too-flattering dream; and though I applauded so loudly as even to waken myself, and shouted '*encore*,' yet all went for nothing; and I am still waiting for that splendid exemplification of retributive justice. But why? Why should it be a spectacle so uncommon? For surely those official arresters of men must want arresting at times as well as better people. At least, however, *en attendant*,[82] one may luxuriate in the vision of such a thing; and the reader shall now see such a vision rehearsed. He shall see Mr Landor arresting Milton – Milton, of all men! – for a flaw in his Roman erudition; and then he shall see me instantly stepping up, tapping Mr Landor on the shoulder, and saying, 'Officer, you're wanted;' whilst to Milton I say, touching my hat, 'Now, sir, be off; run for your life, whilst I hold this man in custody, lest he should fasten on you again.'

What Milton had said, speaking of the '*watchful* cherubim,' was –

> 'Four faces each
> Had, *like a double Janus;*'[83]

Upon which Southey – but, of course, Landor ventriloquising through Southey – says, 'Better left this to the imagination: double Januses are queer figures.'[84] Not at all. On the contrary, they become so common, that finally there were no other. Rome, in her days of childhood, contented herself with a two-faced Janus; but, about the time of the first or second Caesar, a very ancient statue of Janus was exhumed, which had four faces. Ever afterwards, this sacred resurgent statue became the model for any possible Janus that could show himself in good company. The *quadrifrons Janus* was now the orthodox Janus; and it would have been as much a sacrilege to rob him of any single face, as to rob a king's statute* of its horse. One thing may recall this to Mr Landor's memory. I think it was Nero, but certainly it was one of the first six Caesars, that built, or that finished, a magnificent temple to Janus;[87] and each face was so managed as to point down an avenue leading to a separate market-place. Now, that there were *four* market-places, I will make oath before any Justice of the Peace. One was called the *Forum Julium*, one the *Forum Augustum*, a third the *Forum Transitorium:* what the fourth[88] was called is best known to itself, for really I forget. But if anybody says that perhaps it was called the *Forum Landorium*, I am not the man to object; for few names

* *A king's statue:* – Till very lately, the etiquette of Europe was, that none but royal persons could have equestrian statues. Lord Hopetoun, the reader will object, is allowed to have a horse, in St Andrew's Square, Edinburgh.[85] True, but observe that he is not allowed to mount him. The first person, so far as I remember, that, not being royal, has, in our island, seated himself comfortably in the saddle, is the Duke of Wellington.[86]

have deserved such an honour more, whether from those that then looked forward into futurity with one face, or from our posterity that will look back into the vanishing past with another.

JOAN OF ARC*
[Part I]

First published in *Tait's*, XIV, March 1847, pp. 184–90. The essay was printed as 'BY THOMAS DE QUINCEY.' in a centred line following the title and immediately preceding the text.

Reprinted in *F*, III, *Miscellaneous Essays* (1851), pp. 79–100, 123–4.

Revised text, carrying many accidentals but only two significant variants from *F*, in *SGG*, III, *Miscellanies, Chiefly Narrative* (1854), pp. 209–28.

There are no manuscripts.

Joan of Arc (French, Jeanne d'Arc; 1412–31) was known as La Pucelle, or the Maid of Orléans. She was born of peasant parentage in Domrémy, on the borders of the duchies of Bar and Lorraine. She felt her mission was to expel the English and their Burgundian allies from the Valois kingdom of France, and that she was guided in this task by visions and the celestial voices of St Michael, St Catherine, and St Margaret. In 1428, she led the French army in the momentous victory at Orléans that repulsed an English attempt to conquer France, and decisively turned the Hundred Years' War in France's favour. Joan was captured by the English and their French collaborators in 1430, and burned as a heretic a year later. In 1455–6, the Church retried her case, and she was pronounced innocent. She was canonized by Pope Benedict XV in 1920.

De Quincey wrote his account of Joan 'in reference' to the assessment of the French historian Jules Michelet (1789–1874), who discussed Joan at length in volume five (1841) of his monumental seventeen-volume *Histoire de France* (1833–67). But De Quincey's attitude towards Michelet is decidedly hostile: as

* *Arc:* – Modern France, that should know a great deal better than myself, insists that the name is not d'Arc, *i.e.* of Arc, but *Darc*. Now it happens sometimes, that if a person, whose position guarantees his access to the best information, will content himself with gloomy dogmatism, striking the table with his fist, and saying in a terrific voice – 'It *is* so; and there's an end of it,' – one bows deferentially, and submits. But if, unhappily for himself, won by this docility, he relents too amiably into reasons and arguments, probably one raises an insurrection against him that may never be crushed; for in the fields of logic one can skirmish, perhaps, as well as he. Had he confined himself to dogmatism; he would have entrenched his position in darkness, and have hidden his own vulnerable points. But, coming down to base reasons, he lets in light, and one sees where to plant the blows. Now, the worshipful reason of modern France for disturbing the old received spelling, is – that Jean Hordal, a descendant of *La Pucelle's* brother, spelled the name *Darc*, in 1612.[1] But what of that? Beside the chances that M. Hordal might be a gigantic blockhead, it is notorious that what small matter of spelling Providence had thought fit to disburse amongst man in the seventeenth century, was all monopolised by printers: in France, much more so.

he put it in a letter to his daughter Florence, he 'leveled' the paper 'partly at M. Michelet....He is...an author of prodigious popularity in France, and generally on the Continent....But I gave it him right and left'. As De Quincey makes clear in the second instalment of the essay, however, he did not actually work from Michelet's original French text. Rather, his source is a translation of Michelet by Walter Keating Kelly, whose many works include *Narrative of the French Revolution of 1848* (1848) and *Life of Wellington, for boys* (1853). Kelly published his two-volume version of Michelet's *Histoire* in 1844–6. De Quincey found Kelly's translation 'faithful, spirited, and idiomatically English – liable, in fact, only to the single reproach of occasional provincialisms' (Pforzheimer. Misc. MS 1782; see below, p. 86).

De Quincey had plans for the essay that extended well beyond its original appearance in *Tait's*. 'The *whole* of my paper is printed', he told Florence in February 1847: 'but only 1/3rd will appear in the March No. of the Mag. It will be reprinted immediately – somewhat enlarged. The *closing* page of the art., which will not be published till the April No., I advise you to read. Next after the *Vision of Sudden Death*, it is the most elaborate and solemn *bravura* of rhetoric that I have composed'. Not a third, but a half, of the essay, however, was published in the March number, and the second half did not appear until August. What is more, by that time De Quincey's plans seem to have changed, for he now considered republishing 'Joan of Arc' with 'The Nautico-Military Nun of Spain', and 'a few words of preface telling the public what *I* think of them, and what place *I* expect for them', as he put it in another letter to Florence of September 1847. His enthusiasm for the paper, however, was unchanged. When his daughter Margaret told him that Florence had read his essay on 'Schlosser's Literary History of the Eighteenth Century', De Quincey was again anxious that she read 'Joan of Arc'. 'By what strange fatality is it', he asked, 'that, if I write a hurried paper, by its subject necessarily an inferior one, some friend is sure to show it to you? And no friend thought it worth while to show you the "Spanish Nun's" passage across the Andes, or the "Joan of Arc"' (Pforzheimer. Misc. MS 1782; Japp, p. 266).

De Quincey's essay is one of many remarkable treatments of Joan, extending from Shakespeare's *Henry VI, Part I*, through David Hume's famous account in his *History of England* (1754–62) and Voltaire's *La pucelle d'Orléans* (1755), to Robert Southey's *Joan of Arc* (1796), Friedrich Schiller's *Die Jungfrau von Orleans* (1801), Felicia Hemans's 'Joan of Arc, in Rheims' (1828), Mark Twain's *Personal Recollections of Joan of Arc* (1896), and George Bernard Shaw's *Saint Joan* (1923). De Quincey's essay drew a good deal of contemporary praise. 'I read in De Quincey's beautiful article on *Joan of Arc*, which is excellent in style', wrote Henry Crabb Robinson in 1854. That same year the *Westminster Review* observed, in reference to 'Joan of Arc', that it knew 'of no other author who so thoroughly understands the *melody* of prose: [De Quincey's] finest sentences seem to have a rhythmic flow; and prose writing in his hands rises almost into the dignity of a poem'. The *Eclectic Review* went even further:

> His 'Joan of Arc' is a strain of a loftier mood, and rises to the dignity and power of that highest kind of history which verges on and over the limit of poetry. De Quincey, indeed, we have often pronounced to be, since Tac-

itus, *potentially* the greatest of history writers. He is as eloquent, as epic, as impassioned in his nobler narrative as Carlyle, and he is far more dignified, less melodramatic, and purer in style.

In *Sesame and Lilies* (1865), John Ruskin quoted De Quincey's description of the role played by 'wild and fair nature' in 'the education of Joan of Arc' (*HCR*, vol. II, p. 740; Henry Bright, 'Thomas De Quincey and his Works' in *Westminster Review*, NS 5 (April 1854), p. 533; Anon., '*Selections Grave and Gay*...by Thomas De Quincey' in *Eclectic Review*, NS 8 (October 1854), p. 398; *The Works of John Ruskin*, eds E. T. Cook and Alexander Wedderburn, 39 vols (London: Allen, 1903–12), vol. XVIII, p. 133; see also, Gerard de Contades, 'La *Jeanne D'Arc* de Thomas De Quincey' in *Revue des Deux Mondes*, 115 (15 February 1893), pp. 907–25).

More recently, Angela Leighton explores the implications of De Quincey's claim in 'Joan of Arc' that women 'can do one thing as well as the best of us men – a greater thing than even Mozart is known to have done, or Michael Angelo – you can die grandly, and as goddesses would die were goddesses mortal' (see below, p. 82). Leighton observes: 'The scene of woman's death is the scene of her artistic, emotional and even political success. She is thus generously compensated for her unquestioned intellectual inferiority'. Morrison points out that De Quincey's assertion is strikingly anticipated only a year earlier by Edgar Allan Poe's declaration in 'The Philosophy of Composition' (1846) that 'the death...of a beautiful woman is, unquestionably, the most poetical topic in the world' (Angela Leighton, 'De Quincey and Women' in *Beyond Romanticism: New Approaches to Texts and Contexts*, eds Stephen Copley and John Whale (London: Routledge, 1992), p. 160; Robert Morrison, 'Poe's De Quincey, Poe's Dupin' in *Essays in Criticism*, 51.4 (2001), p. 427).

The annotation for this essay draws on previous editions of 'Joan of Arc' by J. W. Abernethy (New York: Maynard, Merril, 1889), Henry H. Belfield (Boston: Sibley, 1892), J. M. Hart (New York: Holt, 1893), Milton Haight Turk (Boston: Ginn, 1902), Carol M. Newman (New York: Macmillan, 1906), and R. Adelaide Witham (Boston: Houghton, Mifflin, 1906).

In reference to M. Michelet's History of France.

WHAT is to be thought of *her?* What is to be thought of the poor shepherd girl from the hills and forests of Lorraine,[2] that – like the Hebrew shepherd boy from the hills and forests of Judaea – rose suddenly out of the quiet, out of the safety, out of the religious inspiration, rooted in deep pastoral solitudes, to a station in the van of armies, and to the more perilous station at the right hand of kings? The Hebrew boy inaugurated his patriotic mission by an *act*, by a victorious *act*, such as no man could deny.[3] But so did the girl of Lorraine, if we read her story as it was read by those who saw her nearest. Adverse armies[4] bore witness to the boy as no pretender: but so they did to the gentle girl. Judged by the voices of all who saw them *from a station of good will*,[5] both were found true and loyal to any promises involved in their first acts. Enemies it was that made the difference between their subsequent fortunes. The boy rose – to a splendour and a noon-day prosperity, both personal and public, that rang through the records of his people, and became a bye-word amongst his posterity for a thousand years, until the sceptre was departing from Judah.[6] The poor, forsaken girl, on the contrary, drank not herself from that cup of rest which she had secured for France. She never sang together with the songs that rose in her native Domrémy, as echoes to the departing steps of invaders. She mingled not in the festal dances at Vaucouleurs[7] which celebrated in rapture the redemption of France. No! for her voice was then silent: No! for her feet were dust. Pure, innocent, noble-hearted girl! whom, from earliest youth, ever I believed in as full of truth and self-sacrifice, this was amongst the strongest pledges for *thy* side, that never once – no, not for a moment of weakness – didst thou revel in the vision of coronets and honour from man. Coronets for thee! Oh no! Honours, if they come when all is over, are for those that share thy blood.* Daughter of Domrémy, when the gratitude of thy king shall awaken, thou wilt be sleeping the sleep of the dead.[9] Call her, King of France, but she will not hear thee! Cite her by thy apparitors[10] to come and receive a robe of honour, but she will be found *en contumace*.[11] When the thunders of universal France, as even yet may happen,[12] shall proclaim the grandeur of the poor shepherd girl that gave up all for her country – thy ear, young shepherd girl, will have been deaf for five centuries. To suffer and to do, that was thy portion in this life; to *do* – never for thyself, always for others; to *suffer* – never in the persons of generous champions, always in thy own: – that was thy destiny; and not for a moment was it hidden from thyself. Life, thou said'st, is short: and the sleep, which is in the grave,[13] is long! Let me use that life, so transitory, for the glory of those heavenly dreams destined to comfort the sleep which is so long. This pure creature – pure from every suspicion of even a visionary self-interest, even as she was pure in senses more obvious – never once did this holy child, as regarded herself, relax from her belief in the darkness that was travelling to meet her. She might not prefigure the very manner of her death; she saw not in vision perhaps the aërial altitude of the fiery scaffold, the spectators without end on every road pouring into Rouen[14] as to a coronation, the surging smoke, the volleying flames, the hostile faces all around, the pitying eye that lurked but here and there until nature and imperishable truth broke loose from artificial restraints; these might not be apparent through the mists of the hurrying future. But the voice that called her to death, *that* she heard for ever.

Great was the throne of France even in those days, and great was he that sate upon it: but well Joanna knew that not the throne, nor he that sate upon it, was for *her;* but, on the contrary, that she was for *them;* not she by them, but they by her, should rise from the dust. Gorgeous were the lilies of France,

* *Those that share thy blood*: – a collateral relative of Joanna's was subsequently ennobled by the title of *du Lys*.[8]

and for centuries had the privilege to spread their beauty over land and sea, until, in another century, the wrath of God and man combined to wither them;[15] but well Joanna knew, early at Domrémy she had read that bitter truth, that the lilies of France would decorate no garland for *her*. Flower nor bud, bell nor blossom, would ever bloom for *her*.

But stop. What reason is there for taking up this subject of Joanna precisely in this spring of 1847? Might it not have been left till the spring of 1947? or, perhaps, left till called for? Yes, but it *is* called for; and clamorously. You are aware, reader, that amongst the many original thinkers, whom modern France has produced, one of the reputed leaders is M. Michelet. All these writers are of a revolutionary cast; not in a political sense merely, but in all senses: mad, oftentimes, as March hares[16] crazy with the laughing-gas of recovered liberty; drunk with the wine-cup of their mighty Revolution;[17] snorting, whinnying, throwing up their heels, like wild horses in the boundless Pampas,[18] and running races of defiance with snipes, or with the winds, or with their own shadows, if they can find nothing else to challenge. Some time or other, I, that have leisure to read, may introduce *you*, that have not, to two or three dozen of these writers; of whom I can assure you beforehand that they are often profound, and at intervals are even as impassioned as if they were come of our best English blood, and sometimes (because it is not pleasant that people should be too easy to understand) almost as obscure as if they had been suckled by transcendental German nurses.[19] But now, confining our attention to M. Michelet – who is quite sufficient to lead a man into a gallop, requiring two relays, at least, of fresh readers; – we in England – who know him best by his worst book, the book against Priests,[20] &c., which has been most circulated – know him disadvantageously. That book is a rhapsody of incoherence. M. Michelet was light-headed, I believe, when he wrote it: and it is well that his keepers overtook him in time to intercept a second part. But his *History of France* is quite another thing. A man, in whatsoever craft he sails, cannot stretch away out of sight when he is linked to the windings of the shore by towing ropes of history. Facts, and the consequences of facts, draw the writer back to the falconer's lure from the giddiest heights of speculation. Here, therefore – in his *France* – if not always free from flightiness, if now and then off like a rocket for an airy wheel in the clouds, M. Michelet, with natural politeness, never forgets that he has left a large audience waiting for him on earth, and gazing upwards in anxiety for his return: return, therefore, he does. But History, though clear of certain temptations in one direction, has separate dangers of its own. It is impossible so to write a History of France, or of England – works becoming every hour more indispensable to the inevitably-political man of this day – without perilous openings for assault. If I, for instance, on the part of England, should happen to turn my labours into that channel, and (on the model of Lord Percy going to Chevy Chase) –

———————'A vow to God should make
My pleasure in the Michelet woods
Three summer days to take,'[21]

– probably from simple delirium, I might hunt M. Michelet into *delirium tremens*.[22] Two strong angels stand by the side of History, whether French History or English, as heraldic supporters: the angel of Research on the left hand, that must read millions of dusty parchments, and of pages blotted with lies; the angel of Meditation on the right hand, that must cleanse these lying records with fire, even as of old the draperies of *asbestos* were cleansed, and must quicken them into regenerated life. Willingly I acknowledge that no man will ever avoid innumerable errors of detail: with so vast a compass of ground to traverse, this is impossible: but such errors (though I have a bushel on hand, at M. Michelet's service) are not the game I chase: it is the bitter and unfair spirit in which M. Michelet writes against England. Even *that*, after all, is but my secondary object: the real one is Joanna, the Pucelle d'Orleans,[23] for herself.

I am not going to write the History of *La Pucelle*: to do this, or even circumstantially to report the history of her persecution and bitter death, of her struggle with false witnesses and with ensnaring judges, it would be necessary to have before us *all* the documents, and, therefore, the collection only now forthcoming in Paris.[24] But *my* purpose is narrower. There have been great thinkers, disdaining the careless judgments of contemporaries, who have thrown themselves boldly on the judgment of a far posterity, that should have had time to review, to ponder, to compare. There have been great actors on the stage of tragic humanity that might, with the same depth of confidence, have appealed from the levity of compatriot friends – too heartless for the sublime interest of their story, and too impatient for the labour of sifting its perplexities – to the magnanimity and justice of enemies. To this class belongs the Maid of Arc. The Romans were too faithful to the ideal of grandeur in themselves not to relent, after a generation or two, before the grandeur of Hannibal.[25] Mithridates – a more doubtful person – yet, merely for the magic perseverance of his indomitable malice, won from the same Romans the only real honour that ever he received on earth.[26] And we English have ever shown the same homage to stubborn enmity. To work unflinchingly for the ruin of England; to say through life, by word and by deed – *Delenda est Anglia Victrix!*[27] that one purpose of malice, faithfully pursued, has quartered some people upon our national funds of homage as by a perpetual annuity. Better than an inheritance of service rendered to England herself, has sometimes proved the most insane hatred to England. Hyder Ali, even his far inferior son Tippoo, and Napoleon[28] – have all benefitted by this disposition amongst ourselves to exaggerate the merit of diabolic enmity. Not one of these men was ever capable, in a solitary instance, of praising an enemy – [what do you say to *that*, reader?] and yet, in *their* behalf, we consent to forget, not their crimes only, but (which is worse) their hideous bigotry and anti-magnanimous egotism; for nationality it was not.[29] Suffrein,[30] and some half dozen of other French nautical heroes, because rightly they did us all the mischief they could, [which was really great] are names justly reverenced in England. On the same principle, La Pucelle d'Orleans, the victorious enemy of England, has been destined to receive her deepest commemoration from the magnanimous justice of Englishmen.[31]

Joanna, as we in England should call her, but, according to her own statement, Jeanne (or, as M. Michelet asserts, Jean*) d'Arc, was born at Domrémy, a village on the marches of Lorraine and Champagne, and dependent upon the town of Vaucouleurs. I have called her a Lorrainer, not simply because the word is prettier, but because Champagne too odiously reminds us English of what are for *us* imaginary wines, which, undoubtedly, *La Pucelle* tasted as rarely as we English; we English, because the Champagne of London is chiefly grown in Devonshire; *La Pucelle*, because the Champagne of Champagne never, by any chance, flowed into the fountain of Domrémy, from which only she drank. M. Michelet will have her to be a *Champenoise*, and for no better reason than that she 'took after her father,' who happened to be a *Champenois*. I am sure she did *not:* for her father was a filthy old fellow, whom I shall soon teach the judicious reader to hate. But, (says M. Michelet, arguing the case physiologically) 'she had none of the Lorrainian asperity;' no, it seems she had only 'the gentleness of Champagne, its simplicity mingled with sense and acuteness, as you find it in Joinville.'[33] All these things she had; and she was worth a thousand Joinvilles, meaning either the prince so called, or the fine old crusader.[34] But still, though I love Joanna dearly, I cannot shut my eyes entirely to the Lorraine element of 'asperity' in her nature. No; really now, she must have had a shade of *that*, though very slightly developed – a mere soupçon,[35] as French cooks express it in speaking of cayenne pepper, when she caused so many of our English throats to be cut. But could she do less? No: I always say so; but still you never saw a person kill even a trout with a perfectly 'Champagne' face of 'gentleness and simplicity,' though often, no doubt, with considerable 'acuteness.' All your cooks and butchers wear a *Lorraine* cast of expression.

* *'Jean'*: – M. Michelet asserts that there was a mystical meaning at that aera in calling a child *Jean;* it implied a secret commendation of a child, if not a dedication, to St John the Evangelist,[32] the beloved disciple, the apostle of love and mysterious visions. But, really, as the name was so exceedingly common, few people will detect a mystery in calling a *boy* by the name of Jack, though it *does* seem mysterious to call a girl Jack. It may be less so in France, where a beautiful practice has always prevailed of giving to a boy his mother's name – preceded and strengthened by a male name, as *Charles Anne*, *Victor Victoire*. In cases where a mother's memory has been unusually dear to a son, this vocal memento of her, locked into the circle of his own name, gives to it the tenderness of a testamentary relique, or a funeral ring. I presume, therefore, that *la Pucelle* must have borne the baptismal names of Jeanne Jean; the latter with no reference to so sublime a person as St John, but simply to some relative.

These disputes, however, turn on refinements too nice. Domrémy stood upon the frontiers; and, like other frontiers, produced a *mixed* race representing the *cis* and the *trans*.[36] A river (it is true) formed the boundary line at this point – the river Meuse; and *that* in old days might have divided the populations; but in these days it did not – there were bridges, there were ferries, and weddings crossed from the right bank to the left. Here lay two great roads, not so much for travellers, that were few, as for armies that were too many by half. These two roads, one of which was the great high road between France and Germany, *decussated* at this very point; which is a learned way of saying that they formed a St Andrew's cross, or letter of X. I hope the compositor will choose a good large X, in which case the point of intersection, the *locus* of conflux for these four diverging arms, will finish the reader's geographical education, by showing him to a hair's breadth where it was that Domrémy stood. These roads, so grandly situated, as great trunk arteries between two mighty realms,* and haunted for ever by wars or rumours of wars,[38] decussated (for anything I know to the contrary) absolutely under Joanna's bed-room window; one rolling away to the right, past Monsieur D'Arc's old barn, and the other, unaccountably preferring, (but there's no disputing about tastes), to sweep round that odious man's odious pigstye to the left.

Things being situated as is here laid down, viz. in respect of the decussation, and in respect of Joanna's bed-room; it follows that, if she had dropped her glove by accident from her chamber window into the very bull's eye of the target, in the centre of X, not one of several great potentates could (though all animated by the sincerest desires for the peace of Europe) have possibly come to any clear understanding on the question of whom the glove was meant for. Whence the candid reader perceives at once the necessity for at least four bloody wars. Falling indeed a little farther, as, for instance, into the pigstye, the glove could not have furnished to the most peppery prince any shadow of excuse for arming: he would not have had a leg to stand upon in taking such a perverse line of conduct. But, if it fell (as by the hypothesis it did) into the one sole point of ground common to four kings, it is clear that, instead of no leg to stand upon, eight separate legs would have had no ground to stand upon unless by treading on each other's toes. The philosopher, therefore, sees clearly the necessity of a war, and regrets that sometimes nations do not wait for grounds of war so solid.

In the circumstances supposed, though the four kings might be unable to see their way clearly without the help of gunpowder to any decision upon Joanna's intention, she – poor thing! – never could mistake her intentions for a moment. All her love was for France; and, therefore, any glove she might drop into the *quadrivium*[39] must be wickedly missent by the post-office, if it found its way to any king but the king of France.

* And reminding one of that inscription, so justly admired by Paul Richter, which a Russian Czarina placed on a guide post near Moscow – *This is the road that leads to Constantinople*.[37]

On whatever side of the border chance had thrown Joanna, the same love to France would have been nurtured. For it is a strange fact, noticed by M. Michelet and others, that the Dukes of Bar and Lorraine had for generations pursued the policy of eternal warfare with France[40] on their own account, yet also of eternal amity and league with France in case anybody else presumed to attack her. Let peace settle upon France, and before long you might rely upon seeing the little vixen Lorraine flying at the throat of France. Let France be assailed by a formidable enemy, and instantly you saw a Duke of Lorraine or Bar insisting on having his throat cut in support of France; which favour accordingly was cheerfully granted to them in three great successive battles by the English and by the Turkish Sultan, viz., at Crécy, at Nicopolis, and at Agincourt.[41]

This sympathy with France during great eclipses in those that during ordinary seasons were always teasing her with brawls and guerrilla inroads, strengthened the natural piety to France of those that were confessedly the children of her own house. The outposts of France, as one may call the great frontier provinces, were of all localities the most devoted to the Fleurs de Lys.[42] To witness, at any great crisis, the generous devotion to these lilies of the little fiery cousin that in gentler weather was for ever tilting at her breast, could not but fan the zeal of the legitimate daughter: whilst to occupy a post of honour on the frontiers against an old hereditary enemy of France,[43] would naturally have stimulated this zeal by a sentiment of martial pride, had there even been no other stimulant to zeal by a sense of danger always threatening, and of hatred always smouldering. That great four-headed road was a perpetual memento to patriotic ardour. To say, this way lies the road to Paris – and that other way to Aix-la-Chapelle,[44] this to Prague, that to Vienna – nourished the warfare of the heart by daily ministrations of sense. The eye that watched for the gleams of lance or helmet from the hostile frontier, the ear that listened for the groaning of wheels,[45] made the highroad itself, with its relations to centres so remote, into a manual of patriotic enmity.

The situation, therefore, *locally* of Joanna was full of profound suggestions to a heart that listened for the stealthy steps of change and fear that too surely were in motion. But if the place were grand, the times, the burthen of the times, was far more so. The air overhead in its upper chambers was *hurtling* with the obscure sound; was dark with sullen fermenting of storms that had been gathering for a hundred and thirty years. The battle of Agincourt in Joanna's childhood had re-opened the wounds of France. Crécy and Poictiers,[46] those withering overthrows for the chivalry of France, had been tranquillised by more than half a century; but this resurrection of their trumpet wails made the whole series of battles and endless skirmishes take their stations as parts in one drama. The graves that had closed sixty years ago, seemed to fly open in sympathy with a sorrow that echoed their own. The monarchy of France laboured in extremity, rocked and reeled like a ship fighting with the darkness of monsoons. The madness of the poor King (Charles

VI.)[47] falling in at such a crisis, like the case of women labouring in childbirth during the storming of a city, trebled the awfulness of the time. Even the wild story of the incident which had immediately occasioned the explosion of this madness – the case of a man unknown, gloomy, and perhaps maniacal himself, coming out of a forest at noonday, laying his hand upon the bridle of the King's horse, checking him for a moment to say, 'Oh, King, thou art betrayed,' and then vanishing no man knew whither, as he had appeared for no man knew what – fell in with the universal prostration of mind that laid France on her knees as before the slow unweaving of some ancient prophetic doom.[48] The famines, the extraordinary diseases, the insurrections of the peasantry[49] up and down Europe, these were chords struck from the same mysterious harp; but these were transitory chords. There had been others of deeper and more ominous sound. The termination of the crusades, the destruction of the Templars, the Papal interdicts, the tragedies caused or suffered by the House of Anjou, by the Emperor[50] – these were full of a more permanent significance; but since then the colossal figure of feudalism was seen standing as it were on tiptoe at Crécy for flight from earth: that was a revolution unparalleled; yet *that* was a trifle by comparison with the more fearful revolutions that were mining below the Church. By her own internal schisms, by the abominable spectacle of a double Pope[51] – so that no man, except through political bias, could even guess which was Heaven's vicegerent, and which the creature of hell – she was already rehearsing, as in still earlier forms she had rehearsed, the first rent in her foundations (reserved for the coming century) which no man should ever heal.[52]

These were the loftiest peaks of the cloudland in the skies that to the scientific gazer first caught the colours of the *new* morning in advance. But the whole vast range alike of sweeping glooms overhead, dwelt upon all meditative minds, even those that could not distinguish the altitudes nor decipher the forms. It was, therefore, not her own age alone, as affected by its immediate calamities, that lay with such weight upon Joanna's mind; but her own age, as one section in a vast mysterious drama, unweaving through a century back, and drawing nearer continually to crisis after crisis. Cataracts and rapids were heard roaring a-head; and signs were seen far back, by help of old men's memories, which answered secretly to signs now coming forward on the eye, even as locks answer to keys. It was not wonderful that in such a haunted solitude, with such a haunted heart, Joanne should see angelic visions, and hear angelic voices. These voices whispered to her the duty, imposed upon herself, of delivering France. Five years she listened to these monitory voices with internal struggles. At length she could resist no longer. Doubt gave way; and she left her home in order to present herself at the Dauphin's court.

The education of this poor girl was mean according to the present standard; was ineffably grand, according to a purer philosophic standard; and only not good for our age, because for us it would be unattainable. She read nothing, for she could not read; but she had heard others read parts of the Roman martyrology. She wept in sympathy with the sad *Misereres* of the Romish chaunting;[53] she rose to heaven with the glad triumphant *Gloria in Excelcis*:[54] she drew her comfort and her vital strength from the rites of her church. But, next after these spiritual advantages, she owed most to the advantages of her situation. The fountain of Domrémy was on the brink of a boundless forest; and it was haunted to that degree by fairies that the parish priest (*curé*) was obliged to read mass there once a-year, in order to keep them in any decent bounds.[55] Fairies are important, even in a statistical view: certain weeds mark poverty in the soil, fairies mark its solitude. As surely as the wolf retires before cities, does the fairy sequester herself from the haunts of licensed victuallers.[56] A village is too much for her nervous delicacy: at most, she can tolerate a distant view of a hamlet. We may judge, therefore, by the uneasiness and extra trouble which they gave to the parson, in what strength the fairies mustered at Domrémy, and, by a satisfactory consequence, how thinly sown with men and women must have been that region even in its inhabited spots. But the forests of Domrémy – those were the glories of the land: for, in them abode mysterious powers and ancient secrets that towered into tragic strength. 'Abbeys there were, and abbey windows, dim and dimly seen – as Moorish temples of the Hindoos,'[57] that exercised even princely power both in Lorraine and in the German Diets. These had their sweet bells that pierced the forests for many a league at matins or vespers, and each its own dreamy legend. Few enough, and scattered enough, were these abbeys, in no degree to disturb the deep solitude of the region; many enough to spread a net-work or awning of Christian sanctity over what else might have seemed a heathen wilderness. This sort of religious talisman being secured, a man the most afraid of ghosts (like myself, suppose, or the reader), becomes armed into courage to wander for days in their sylvan recesses. The mountains of the Vosges on the eastern frontier of France, have never attracted much notice from Europe, except in 1813–14, for a few brief months, when they fell within Napoleon's line of defence against the Allies.[58] But they are interesting for this, amongst other features – that they do not, like some loftier ranges, repel woods: the forests and they are on sociable terms. *Live and let live*[59] is their motto. For this reason, in part, these tracts in Lorraine were a favourite hunting ground with the Carlovingian princes. About six hundred years before Joanna's childhood, Charlemagne[60] was known to have hunted there. That, of itself, was a grand incident in the traditions of a forest or a chace. In these vast forests, also, were to be found (if the race was not extinct) those mysterious fawns[61] that tempted solitary hunters into visionary and perilous pursuits. Here was seen, at intervals, that ancient stag[62] who was already nine hundred years old, at the least, but possibly a hundred or two more, when met by Charlemagne; and the thing was put beyond doubt by the inscription upon his golden collar. I believe Charlemagne knighted the stag; and, if ever he is met again by a king, he ought to be made an earl – or, being upon the marches of France, a marquess.[63] Observe, I don't absolutely vouch for all these things: my own opinion varies. On a fine breezy forenoon I am audaciously sceptical; but as twilight sets in, my credulity becomes equal to anything that could be desired. And I have heard candid sportsmen declare that, outside of these very forests near the Vosges, they laughed loudly at all the dim tales connected with their haunted solitudes; but, on reaching a spot notoriously eighteen miles deep within them, they agreed with Sir Roger de Coverley that a good deal might be said on both sides.[64]

Such traditions, or any others that (like the stag) connect distant generations with each other, are, for that cause, sublime; and the sense of the shadowy, connected with such appearances that reveal themselves or not according to circumstances, leaves a colouring of sanctity over ancient forests, even in those minds that utterly reject the legend as a fact.

But, apart from all distinct stories of that order, in any solitary frontier between two great empires, as here, for instance, or in the desert between Syria and the Euphrates,[65] there is an inevitable tendency, in minds of any deep sensibility to people the solitudes with phantom images of powers that were of old so vast. Joanna, therefore, in her quiet occupation of a shepherdess, would be led continually to brood over the political condition of her country, by the traditions of the past no less than by the mementoes of the local present.

M. Michelet, indeed, says that La Pucelle was *not* a shepherdess. I beg his pardon: she *was*. What he rests upon, I guess pretty well: it is the evidence of a woman called Haumette,[66] the most confidential friend of Joanna. Now, she is a good witness, and a good girl, and I like her; for she makes a natural and affectionate report of Joanna's ordinary life. But still, however good she may be as a witness, Joanna is better: and she, when speaking to the Dauphin, calls herself in the Latin report *Bergereta*.[67] Even Haumette confesses that Joanna tended sheep in her girlhood. And I believe, that, if Miss Haumette were taking coffee alone with me this very evening (February 12, 1847) – in which there would be no subject for scandal or for maiden blushes, because I am an intense philosopher, and Miss H. would be hard upon 450 years old – she would admit the following comment upon her evidence to be right. A Frenchman, about thirty years ago, M. Simond, in his *Travels*,[68] mentioned incidentally the following hideous scene as one steadily observed and watched by himself in France at a period some trifle before the French Revolution: – A peasant was ploughing; and the team that drew his plough was a donkey and a woman. Both were regularly harnessed: both pulled alike. This is bad enough: but the Frenchman adds – that, in distributing his lashes, the peasant was obviously desirous of being impartial: or, if either of the yoke-fellows had a right to complain, certainly it was not the donkey. Now, in any country, where such degradation of females could be tolerated by the state of manners, a woman of delicacy would shrink from acknowledging, either for herself or her friend, that she had ever been addicted to any mode of labour not strictly domestic; because, if once owning herself a praedial[69] servant, she would be sensible that this confession extended by probability in the hearer's thoughts to having incurred indignities of this horrible kind. Haumette clearly thinks it more dignified for Joanna to have been darning the stockings[70] of her horny-hoofed father, Monsieur D'Arc, than keeping sheep, lest she might then be suspected of having ever done something worse. But, luckily, there was no danger of *that:* Joanna never was in service; and my opinion is that her father should have mended his own stockings, since probably he was the party to make the holes in them, as many a better man than D'Arc does; meaning by *that* not myself, because, though certainly a better man than D'Arc, I protest against doing anything of the kind. If I lived even with Friday in Juan Fernandez,[71] either Friday must do all the darning, or else it must go undone. The better men that I meant were the sailors in the British Navy, every man of whom mends his own stockings. Who else is to do it? Do you suppose, reader, that the junior lords of the Admiralty are under articles to darn for the Navy?

The reason, meantime, for my systematic hatred of D'Arc is this. There was a story current in France before the Revolution, framed to ridicule the pauper aristocracy, who happened to have long pedigrees and short rent rolls, viz., that a head of such a house, dating from the Crusades, was overheard saying to his son, a Chevalier of St Louis,[72] '*Chevalier, as-tu donné au cochon à manger?*' Now, it is clearly made out by the surviving evidence, that D'Arc would much have preferred continuing to say – '*Ma fille, as-tu donné au cochon à manger?*' to saying '*Pucelle d'Orléans, as-tu sauvé les fleurs-de-lys?*'[73] There is an old English copy of verses which argues thus:

'If the man, that turnips cries,
Cry not when his father dies –
Then 'tis plain the man had rather
Have a turnip than his father.'[74]

I cannot say that the logic of these verses was ever *entirely* to my satisfaction. I do not see my way through it as clearly as could be wished. But I see my way most clearly through D'Arc; and the result is – that he would greatly have preferred not merely a turnip to his father, but the saving a pound or so of bacon to saving the Oriflamme[75] of France.

It is probable (as M. Michelet suggests) that the title of Virgin, or *Pucelle*, had in itself, and apart from the miraculous stories about her, a secret power over the rude soldiery and partisan chiefs of that period;[76] for, in such a person, they saw a representative manifestation of the Virgin Mary, who, in a course of centuries, had grown steadily upon the popular heart.

As to Joanna's supernatural detection of the Dauphin (Charles VII.)[77] amongst three hundred lords and knights, I am surprised at the credulity which could ever lend itself to that theatrical juggle. Who admires more than myself the sublime enthusiasm, the rapturous faith in herself, of this pure creature? But I admire not stage artifices, which not *La Pucelle*, but the Court, must have arranged; nor can surrender myself a dupe to a conjuror's *leger-de-*

main,[78] such as may be seen every day for a shilling. Southey's 'Joan of Arc' was published in 1796.[79] Twenty years after, talking with Southey, I was surprised to find him still owning a secret bias in favour of Joan, founded on her detection of the Dauphin. The story, for the benefit of the reader new to the case, was this: – *La Pucelle* was first made known to the Dauphin, and presented to his Court, at Chinon: and here came her first trial. She was to find out the royal personage amongst the whole ark of clean and unclean creatures. Failing in this *coup d'essai*,[80] she would not simply disappoint many a beating heart in the glittering crowd that on different motives yearned for her success, but she would ruin herself – and, as the oracle within had told her, would ruin France. Our own sovereign lady Victoria rehearses annually a trial not so severe in degree, but the same in kind. She 'pricks' for sheriffs.[81] Joanna pricked for a king. But observe the difference: our own lady pricks for two men out of three; Joanna for one man out of three hundred. Happy Lady of the islands and the orient![82] – she *can* go astray in her choice only by one half; to the extent of one half she *must* have the satisfaction of being right. And yet, even with these tight limits to the misery of a boundless discretion, permit me, liege Lady, with all loyalty, to submit – that now and then you prick with your pin the wrong man. But the poor child from Domrémy, shrinking under the gaze of a dazzling court – not because dazzling (for in visions she had seen those that were more so), but because some of them wore a scoffing smile on their features – how should *she* throw her line into so deep a river to angle for a king, where many a gay creature was sporting that masqueraded as kings in dress? Nay, even more than any true king would have done: for, in Southey's version of the story, the Dauphin says, by way of trying the virgin's magnetic sympathy with royalty,

> ———'on the throne,
> I the while mingling with the menial throng,
> Some courtier shall be seated.'[83]

This usurper is even crowned: 'the jewell'd crown shines on a menial's head.'[84] But really, that is '*un peu fort;*'[85] and the mob of spectators might raise a scruple whether our friend the jackdaw upon the throne, and the Dauphin himself, were not grazing the shins of treason. For the Dauphin could not lend more than belonged to him. According to the popular notion, he had no crown for himself, but, at most, a *petit écu*[86] worth thirty pence; consequently none to lend, on any pretence whatever, until the consecrated Maid should take him to Rheims.[87] This was the *popular* notion in France. The same notion as to the indispensableness of a coronation prevails widely in England. But, certainly, it was the Dauphin's interest to support the popular notion, as he meant to use the services of Joanna. For, if he were king already, what was it that she could do for him beyond Orleans? And above all, it he were king without a coronation, and without the oil from the sacred ampulla,[88] what advantage was yet open to him by celerity above his competitor the English boy?[89] Now was to be a race for a coronation: he that should win *that* race, carried the superstition of France along with him. Trouble us not, lawyer, with your quillets. We are illegal blockheads; so thoroughly without law, that we don't know even if we have a right to be blockheads; and our mind is made up – that the first man drawn from the oven of coronation at Rheims,[90] is the man that is baked into a king. All others are counterfeits, made of base Indian meal – damaged by sea-water.

(To be continued.)

JOAN OF ARC
[Part II]

First published in *Tait's*, XIV, August 1847, pp. 535–42. Two centred lines followed the title of the essay and immediately preceded the text. The first stated that the essay was 'BY THOMAS DE QUINCEY.', and the second that it was '*(Concluded from page* 184.*)*' to denote where in *Tait's* Part I of the essay ended.

Reprinted in *F*, III, *Miscellaneous Essays* (1851), pp. 100–21, 124–9.

Revised text, carrying many accidentals but only one significant variant from *F*, in *SGG*, III, *Miscellanies, Chiefly Narrative* (1854), pp. 228–48.

There are no manuscripts.

For the occasion and context of the article, see headnote, pp. 61–3.

In reference to M. Michelet's History of France.

LA PUCELLE,[1] before she could be allowed to practise as a warrior, was put through her manual and platoon exercise, as a juvenile pupil in divinity, before six eminent men in wigs. According to Southey (v. 393, Book III., in the original edition of his 'Joan of Arc') she 'appall'd the doctors.'[2] It's not easy to do *that:* but they had some reason to feel bothered, as that surgeon would assuredly feel bothered, who, upon proceeding to dissect a subject, should find the subject retaliating as a dissector upon himself, especially if Joanna ever made the speech to them which occupies v. 354-391, B. III.[3] It is a double impossibility; 1st, because a piracy from Tindal's *Christianity as Old as the Creation:*[4] now a piracy *à parte post* is common enough; but a piracy *à parte ante*,[5] and by three centuries, would (according to our old English phrase*) drive a coach-and-six through any copyright act that man born of woman could frame.[7] 2dly, It is quite contrary to the evidence on Joanna's trial; for Southey's 'Joan' of A. Dom. 1796 (Cottle, Bristol),[8] tells the doctors, amongst other secrets, that she never in her life attended – 1st, Mass; nor 2d, the Sacramental table; nor 3d, Confession.[9] Here's a precious windfall for the doctors; they, by snaky tortuosities, had hoped, through the aid of a corkscrew (which every D.D. or S.T.P.[10] is said to carry in his pocket), for the happiness

* Yes, old – very old phrase: not, as ignoramuses fancy, a phrase recently minted by a Repealer in Ireland.[6]

of ultimately extracting from Joanna a few grains of heretical powder or small shot, which might have justified their singeing her a little. And just at such a crisis, expressly to justify their burning her to a cinder, up gallops Joanna with a brigade of guns, unlimbers, and serves them out with heretical grape and deistical round-shot enough to lay a kingdom under interdict.[11] Any miracles, to which Joanna might treat the grim D.Ds. after *that*, would go to the wrong side of her little account in the clerical books. Joanna would be created a *Dr* herself, but not of Divinity. For in the Joanna page of the ledger the entry would be – 'Miss Joanna, in acct. with the Church, *Dr* by sundry diabolic miracles, she having publicly preached heresy, shown herself a witch, and even tried hard to corrupt the principles of six church pillars.' In the meantime, all this deistical confession of Joanna's, besides being suicidal for the interest of her cause, is opposed to the depositions upon *both* trials.[12] The very best witness[13] called from first to last deposes that Joanna attended these rites of her Church even too often; was taxed with doing so; and, by blushing, owned the charge as a fact, though certainly not as a fault. Joanna was a girl of natural piety, that saw God in forests, and hills, and fountains; but did not the less seek him in chapels and consecrated oratories.

This peasant girl was self-educated through her own natural meditativeness. If the reader turns to that divine passage in *Paradise Regained*, which Milton has put into the mouth of our Saviour when first entering the wilderness, and musing upon the tendency of those great impulses growing within himself –

'Oh, what a multitude of thoughts arise!' &c.[14]

he will have some notion of the vast reveries which brooded over the heart of Joanna in early girlhood, when the wings were budding that should carry her from Orleans to Rheims,[15] when the golden chariot was dimly revealing itself that should carry her from the kingdom of *France Delivered*[16] to the eternal kingdom.

It is not requisite, for the honour of Joanna, nor is there, in this place, room to pursue her brief career of *action*. That, though wonderful, forms the earthly part of her story: the intellectual part is, the saintly passion of her imprisonment, trial, and execution. It is unfortunate, therefore, for Southey's 'Joan of Arc' (which however should always be regarded as a *juvenile* effort), that, precisely when her real glory begins, the poem ends. But this limitation of the interest grew, no doubt, from the constraint inseparably attached to the law of Epic unity.[17] Joanna's history bisects into two opposite hemispheres, and both could not have been presented to the eye in one poem, unless by sacrificing all unity of theme, or else by involving the earlier half, as a narrative episode, in the latter; – this might have been done – it might have been communicated to a fellow-prisoner, or a confessor, by Joanna herself, in the same way that Virgil has contrived to acquaint the reader, through the hero's mouth, with earlier adventures that, if told by the poet speaking in his own person, would have destroyed the unity of his fable. The romantic interest of the early and *irrelate* incidents (last night of Troy,[18] &c.) is thrown as an affluent into the general river of the personal narrative, whilst yet the capital current of the *epos*, as unfolding the origin and *incunabula*[19] of Rome, is not for a moment suffered to be modified by events so subordinate and so obliquely introduced. It is sufficient, as concerns *this* section of Joanna's life, to say – that she fulfilled, to the height of her promises, the restoration of the prostrate throne. France had become a province of England;[20] and for the ruin of both, if such a yoke could be maintained. Dreadful pecuniary exhaustion caused the English energy to droop; and that critical opening *La Pucelle* used with a corresponding felicity of audacity and suddenness (that were in themselves portentous) for introducing the wedge of French native resources, for rekindling the national pride, and for planting the Dauphin once more upon his feet.[21] When Joanna appeared, he had been on the point of giving up the struggle with the English, distressed as they were, and of flying to the South of France. She taught him to blush for such abject counsels. She liberated Orleans, that great city, so decisive by its fate for the issue of the war, and then beleaguered by the English with an elaborate application of engineering skill unprecedented in Europe.[22] Entering the city after sunset, on the 29th of April, she sang mass on Sunday, May 8, for the entire disappearance of the besieging force. On the 29th of June, she fought and gained over the English the decisive battle of Patay; on the 9th of July, she took Troyes[23] by a coup-de-main from a mixed garrison of English and Burgundians; on the 15th of that month, she carried the Dauphin into Rheims; on Sunday the 17th, she crowned him; and there she rested from her labour of triumph. What remained was – to suffer.

All this forward movement was her own: excepting one man,[24] the whole Council was against her. Her enemies were all that drew power from earth. Her supporters were her own strong enthusiasm, and the headlong contagion by which she carried this sublime frenzy into the hearts of women, of soldiers, and of all who lived by labour. Henceforwards she was thwarted; and the worst error, that she committed, was to lend the sanction of her presence to counsels which she disapproved. But she had accomplished the capital objects which her own visions had dictated. These involved all the rest. Errors were now less important; and doubtless it had now become more difficult for herself to pronounce authentically what *were* errors. The noble girl had achieved, as by a rapture of motion, the capital end of clearing out a free space around her sovereign, giving him the power to move his arms with effect; and, secondly, the inappreciable end of winning for that sovereign what seemed to all France the heavenly ratification of his rights, by crowning him with the ancient solemnities. She had made it impossible for the English now to step before her. They were caught in an irretrievable blunder, owing partly to discord amongst the uncles of Henry VI.,[25] partly to a want of funds, but partly to the very impossibility which they believed to press with tenfold force upon any French attempt to forestal theirs. They laughed at such a thought; and whilst they laughed, she *did* it. Henceforth the single redress for the English of this capital oversight, but which never *could* have redressed it effectually, was – to vitiate and taint the coronation of Charles VII. as the work of a witch. That policy, and not malice (as M. Michelet is so happy to believe),[26] was the moving principle in the subsequent prosecution of Joanna. Unless they unhinged the force of the first coronation in the popular mind, by associating it with power given from hell, they felt that the sceptre of the invader was broken.

But she, the child that, at nineteen, had wrought wonders so great for France, was she not elated? Did she not lose, as men so often *have* lost, all sobriety of mind when standing upon the pinnacle of successes so giddy? Let her enemies declare. During the progress of her movement, and in the centre of ferocious struggles, she had manifested the temper of her feelings by the pity which she had everywhere expressed for the suffering enemy. She forwarded to the English leaders a touching invitation to unite with the French, as brothers, in a common crusade against infidels, thus opening the road for a soldierly retreat. She interposed to protect the captive or the wounded – she mourned over the excesses of her countrymen – she threw herself off her horse to kneel by the dying English soldier,[27] and to comfort him with such ministrations, physical or spiritual, as his situation allowed. 'Nolebat,' says the evidence, 'uti ense suo, aut quemquam interficere.'[28] She sheltered the English, that invoked her aid, in her own quarters. She wept as she beheld, stretched on the field of battle, so many brave enemies that had died without confession. And, as regarded herself, her elation expressed itself thus: – on the day when she had finished her work, she wept; for she knew that, when her task was done, her end must be approaching.[29] Her aspirations pointed only to a place, which seemed to her more than usually full of natural piety, as one in which it would give her pleasure to die. And she uttered, between smiles and tears, as a wish that inexpressibly fascinated her heart, and yet was half fantastic, a broken prayer that God would return her to the solitudes from which he had drawn her, and suffer her to become a shepherdess once more.[30]It was a natural prayer, because Nature has laid a necessity upon every human heart to seek for rest, and to shrink from torment. Yet, again, it was a half-fantastic prayer, because, from childhood upwards, visions that she had no power to mistrust, and the voices which sounded in her ear for ever, had long since persuaded her mind, that for *her* no such prayer could be granted. Too well she felt that her mission must be worked out to the end, and that the end was now at hand. – All went wrong from this time. She herself had created the *funds* out of which the French restoration should grow; but she was not suffered to witness their development, or their prosperous application. More than one military plan was entered upon which she did not approve. But she still continued to expose her person as before. Severe wounds had not taught her caution. And at length, in a sortie from Compiegne, whether through treacherous collusion on the part of her own friends is doubtful to this day, she was made prisoner by the Burgundians, and finally surrendered to the English.[31]

Now came her trial.[32] This trial, moving of course under English influence, was conducted in chief by the Bishop of Beauvais.[33] He was a Frenchman, sold to English interests, and hoping, by favour of the English leaders, to reach the highest preferment. *Bishop that art, Archbishop that shalt be, Cardinal that mayest be*,[34] were the words that sounded continually in his ear; and doubtless, a whisper of visions still higher, of a triple crown,[35] and feet upon the necks of kings, sometimes stole into his heart. M. Michelet is anxious to keep us in mind that this Bishop was but an agent of the English.[36] True. But it does not better the case for his countryman – that, being an accomplice in the crime, making himself the leader in the persecution against the helpless girl, he was willing to be all this in the spirit, and with the conscious vileness of a cats-paw.[37] Never from the foundations of the earth was there such a trial as this, if it were laid open in all its beauty of defence, and all its hellishness of attack. Oh, child of France! shepherdess, peasant girl! trodden under foot by all around thee, how I honour thy flashing intellect, quick as God's lightning, and true as that lightning to its mark, that ran before France and laggard Europe by many a century, confounding the malice of the ensnarer, and making dumb the oracles of falsehood! Is it not scandalous – is it not humiliating to civilisation – that, even at this day, France exhibits the horrid spectacle of judges examining the prisoner against himself; seducing him, by fraud, into treacherous conclusions against his own head; using the terrors of their power for extorting confessions from the frailty of hope; nay (which is worse), using the blandishments of condescension and snaky kindness for thawing into compliances of gratitude those whom they had failed to freeze into terror! Wicked judges! Barbarian jurisprudence! that, sitting in your own conceit on the summits of social wisdom, have yet failed to learn the first principles of criminal justice – sit ye humbly and with docility at the feet of this girl from Domrémy, that tore your webs of cruelty into shreds and dust. 'Would you examine me as a witness against myself?'[38] was the question by which many times she defied their arts. Continually she showed that their interrogations were irrelevant to any business before the court, or that entered into the ridiculous charges against her. General questions were proposed to her on points of casuistical divinity; two-edged questions which not one of themselves could have answered without, on the one side, landing himself in heresy (as then interpreted), or, on the other, in some presumptuous expression of self-esteem. Next came a wretched Dominican that pressed her with an objection, which, if applied to the Bible, would tax every one of its miracles with unsoundness. The monk had the excuse of never having read the Bible. M. Michelet has no such excuse; and it makes one blush for him, as a philosopher, to find him describing such an argument as 'weighty,'[39] whereas it is but a varied expression of rude Mahometan metaphysics. Her answer to this, if there were room to place the whole in a clear light, was as shattering as it was rapid. Another thought to entrap her by asking what language the angelic visiters of her solitude had talked:[40] as though heavenly counsels could want polyglott interpreters for every word, or that God needed language at all in whispering thoughts to a human heart. Then came a worse devil, who asked her whether the archangel Michael had appeared naked. Not comprehending the vile insinuation, Joanna, whose poverty suggested to her simplicity that it might be the *costliness* of suitable robes which caused the demur, asked them if they fancied God, who clothed the flowers of the valleys, unable to find raiment for his servants.[41] The answer of Joanna moves a smile of tenderness, but the disappointment of her judges makes one laugh horribly. Others succeeded by troops, who upbraided her with leaving her father; as if that greater Father,[42] whom she believed herself to have been serving, did not retain the power of dispensing with his own rules, or had not said, that for a less cause than martyrdom, man and woman should leave both father and mother.[43]

On Easter Sunday,[44] when the trial had been long proceeding, the poor girl fell so ill as to cause a belief that she had been poisoned. It was not poison. Nobody had any interest in hastening a death so certain. M. Michelet, whose sympathies with all feelings are so quick that one would gladly see them always as justly directed, reads the case most truly. Joanna had a two-fold malady.[45] She was visited by a paroxysm of the complaint called *home-sickness;* the cruel nature of her imprisonment, and its length, could not but point her solitary thoughts, in darkness, and in chains (for chained she was), to Domrémy. And the season, which was the most heavenly period of the spring, added stings to this yearning. That was one of her maladies – *nostalgia*, as medicine calls it; the other was weariness and exhaustion from daily combats with malice. She saw that everybody hated her, and thirsted for her blood; nay, many kind-hearted creatures that would have pitied her profoundly as regarded all political charges, had their natural feelings warped by the belief that she had dealings with fiendish powers. She knew she was to die; that was *not* the misery; the misery was that this consummation could not be reached without so much intermediate strife, as if she were contending for some chance (where chance was none) of happiness, or were dreaming for a moment of escaping the inevitable. Why, then *did* she contend? Knowing that she would reap nothing from answering her persecutors, why did she not retire by silence from the superfluous contest? It was because her quick and eager loyalty to truth would not suffer her to see it darkened by frauds, which *she* could expose, but others, even of candid listeners, perhaps, could not; it was through that imperishable grandeur of soul, which taught her to submit meekly and without a struggle to her punishment, but taught her *not* to submit – no, not for a moment – to calumny as to facts, or to misconstruction as to motives. Besides, there were secretaries all around the court taking down her words. That was meant for no good to *her*. But the end does not always correspond to the meaning. And Joanna might say to herself – these words, that will be used against me to-morrow and the next day, perhaps in some nobler generation may rise again for my justification. Yes, Joanna, they *are* rising even now in Paris, and for more than justification.

Woman, sister – there are some things which you do not execute as well as your brother, man; no, nor ever will. Pardon me if I doubt whether you will ever produce a great poet from your choirs, or a Mozart, or a Phidias, or a Michael Angelo,[46] or a great philosopher, or a great scholar. By which last is meant – not one who depends simply on an infinite memory, but also on an infinite and electrical power of combination; bringing together from the four winds, like the angel of the resurrection, what else were dust from dead men's bones,[47] into the unity of breathing life. If you *can* create yourselves into any of these great creators, why have you not? Do not ask me to say otherwise; because if you do, you will lead me into temptation.[48] For I swore early in life never to utter a falsehood, and, above all, a sycophantic falsehood; and, in the false homage of the modern press towards women, there is horrible sycophancy. It is as hollow, most of it, and it is as fleeting as is the love that lurks in *uxoriousness*.[49] Yet, if a woman asks me to tell a falsehood, I have long made up my mind – that on moral considerations I *will*, and *ought* to do so, whether it be for any purpose of glory to *her*, or of screening her foibles (for she *does* commit a few), or of humbly, as a vassal, paying a pepper-corn rent[50] to her august privilege of caprice. Barring these cases, I must adhere to my resolution of telling no fibs. And I repeat, therefore, but not to be rude, I repeat in Latin –

> Excudent alii meliùs spirantia signa,
> Credo equidem vivos ducent de marmore vultus:
> Altius ascendent: at tu caput, Eva, memento
> Sandalo ut infringas referenti oracula tanta.*

Yet, sister woman – though I cannot consent to find a Mozart or a Michael Angelo in your sex, until that day when you claim my promise as to falsehood – cheerfully, and with the love that burns in depths of admiration, I acknowledge that you can do one thing as well as the best of us men – a greater thing than even Mozart is known to have done, or Michael Angelo – you can die grandly, and as goddesses would die were goddesses mortal. If any distant

* Our sisters are always rather uneasy when we say anything of them in Latin or Greek. It is like giving sealed orders to a sea captain, which he is not to open for his life till he comes into a certain latitude, which latitude, perhaps, he never *will* come into, and thus may miss the secret till he is going to the bottom. Generally I acknowledge that it is not polite before our female friends to cite a single word of Latin without instantly translating it. But in this particular case, where I am only iterating a disagreeable truth, they will please to recollect that the politeness lies in *not* translating. However, if they insist absolutely on knowing this very night, before going to bed, what it is that those ill-looking lines contain, I refer them to Dryden's Virgil, somewhere in the 6th Book of the Aeneid, except as to the closing line and a-half, which contain a private suggestion of my own to discontented nymphs anxious to see the equilibrium of advantages re-established between the two sexes.[51]

world (which *may* be the case) are so far ahead of us Tellurians[52] in optical resources as to see distinctly through their telescopes all that we do on earth, what is the grandest sight to which we ever treat them? St Peter's at Rome, do you fancy, on Easter Sunday, or Luxor, or perhaps the Himalayas?[53] Pooh! pooh! my friend: suggest something better; these are baubles to *them*; they see in other worlds, in their own, far better toys of the same kind. These, take my word for it, are nothing. Do you give it up? The finest thing, then, we have to show them is a scaffold on the morning of execution. I assure you there is a strong muster in those far telescopic worlds, on any such morning, of those who happen to find themselves occupying the right hemisphere for a peep at *us*. Telescopes look up in the market on that morning, and bear a monstrous premium; for they cheat, probably, in those scientific worlds as well as we do. How, then, if it be announced in some such telescopic world by those who make a livelihood of catching glimpses at our newspapers, whose language they have long since deciphered, that the poor victim in the morning's sacrifice is a woman? How, if it be published on that distant world that the sufferer wears upon her head, in the eyes of many, the garlands of martyrdom? How, if it should be some Marie Antoinette, the widowed queen,[54] coming forward on the scaffold, and presenting to the morning air her head, turned grey prematurely by sorrow, daughter of Caesars kneeling down humbly to kiss the guillotine, as one that worships death? How, if it were the 'martyred wife of Roland,'[55] uttering impassioned truth – truth odious to the rulers of her country – with her expiring breath? How, if it were the noble Charlotte Corday,[56] that in the bloom of youth, that with the loveliest of persons, that with homage waiting upon her smiles wherever she turned her face to scatter them – homage that followed those smiles as surely as the carols of birds, after showers in spring, follow the reappearing sun and the racing of sunbeams over the hills – yet thought all these things cheaper than the dust upon her sandals in comparison of deliverance from hell for her dear suffering France? Ah! these were spectacles indeed for those sympathising people in distant worlds; and some, perhaps, would suffer a sort of martyrdom themselves, because they could not testify their wrath, could not bear witness to the strength of love, and to the fury of hatred, that burned within them at such scenes; could not gather into golden urns some of that glorious dust which rested in the catacombs of earth.

On the Wednesday after Trinity Sunday in 1431, being then about nineteen years of age, the Maid of Arc underwent her martyrdom. She was conducted before mid-day, guarded by eight hundred spearmen, to a platform of prodigious height, constructed of wooden billets supported by occasional walls of lath and plaster, and traversed by hollow spaces in every direction for the creation of air-currents. The pile 'struck terror,' says M. Michelet, 'by its height;'[57] and, as usual, the English purpose in this is viewed as one of pure malignity. But there are two ways of explaining all that. It is probable that the purpose was merciful. – On the circumstances of the execution I shall not linger. Yet, to mark the almost fatal felicity of M. Michelet in finding out whatever may injure the English name, at a moment when every reader will be interested in Joanna's personal appearance, it is really edifying to notice the ingenuity by which he draws into light from a dark corner a very unjust account of it, and neglects, though lying upon the high road, a very pleasing one. Both are from English pens. Grafton, a chronicler but little read, being a stiff-necked John Bull, thought fit to say, that no wonder Joanna should be a virgin, since her 'foule face'[58] was a satisfactory solution of that particular merit. Holinshead, on the other hand, a chronicler somewhat later, every way more important, and universally read, has given a very pleasing testimony to the interesting character of Joanna's person and engaging manners.[59] Neither of these men lived till the following century, so that personally this evidence is none at all. Grafton sullenly and carelessly believed as he wished to believe; Holinshead took pains to inquire, and reports undoubtedly the general impression of France. But I cite the case as illustrating M. Michelet's candour.*

* Amongst the many ebullitions of M. Michelet's fury against us poor English, are four which will be likely to amuse the reader; and they are the more conspicuous in collision with the justice which he sometimes does us, and the very indignant admiration which, under some aspects, he grants to us.

1. Our English literature he admires with some gnashing of teeth. He pronounces it 'fine and sombre,' but, I lament to add, 'sceptical, Judaic, Satanic – in a word, Anti-Christian.' That Lord Byron[60] should figure as a member of this diabolical corporation, will not surprise men. It *will* surprise them to hear that Milton is one of its Satanic leaders. Many are the generous and eloquent Frenchmen, beside Chateaubriand, who have, in the course of the last thirty years, nobly suspended their own burning nationality, in order to render a more rapturous homage at the feet of Milton;[61] and some of them have raised Milton almost to a level with angelic natures. Not one of them has thought of looking for him *below* the earth. As to Shakspere, M. Michelet detects in him a most extraordinary mare's nest. It is this: he does 'not recollect to have seen the name of God'[62] in any part of his works. On reading such words, it is natural to rub one's eyes, and suspect that all one has ever seen in this world may have been a pure ocular delusion. In particular, I begin myself to suspect that the word '*la gloire*' never occurs in any Parisian journal. 'The great English nation,' says M. Michelet, 'has one immense profound vice,' to wit, 'pride.'[63] Why, really, that may be true; but we have a neighbour not absolutely clear of an 'immense profound vice,' as like ours in colour and shape as cherry to cherry. In short, M. Michelet thinks us, by fits and starts, admirable, only that we are detestable; and he would adore some of our authors, were it not that so intensely he could have wished to kick them.

2. M. Michelet thinks to lodge an arrow in our sides by a very odd remark upon Thomas à Kempis; which is, that a man of any conceivable European blood – a Finlander, suppose, or a Zantiote[64] – might have written Tom; only not an Englishman. Whether an Englishman could have forged Tom must remain a matter of doubt, unless the thing had been tried long ago. That problem was intercepted for ever by Tom's perverseness in choosing to manufacture himself. Yet, since nobody is better aware than M. Michelet, that this very point of Kempis *having* manufactured Kempis is furiously and hopelessly litigated, three or four nations claiming to have forged his work for him, the shocking old doubt will raise its snaky head once more – whether this forger, who rests in so much darkness, might not, after all, be of English blood. Tom, it may be feared, is known to modern English literature chiefly by an irreverent mention of his name in a line of Peter Pindar's (Dr Wolcot), fifty years back, where he is described as

The circumstantial incidents of the execution, unless with more space than I can now command, I should be unwilling to relate. I should fear to injure,

---

'Kempis Tom,
Who clearly shows the way to Kingdom Come.'[65]

Few in these days can have read him unless in the Methodist version of John Wesley.[66] Amongst those few, however, happens to be myself; which arose from the accident of having, when a boy of eleven, received a copy of the *De Imitatione Christi*, as a bequest from a relation, who died very young; from which cause, and from the external prettiness of the book, being a Glasgow reprint, by the celebrated Foulis,[67] and gaily bound, I was induced to look into it; and finally read it many times over, partly out of some sympathy which, even in those days, I had with its simplicity and devotional fervor; but much more from the savage delight I found in laughing at Tom's Latinity. *That*, I freely grant to M. Michelet, is inimitable; else, as regards substance, it strikes me that I could forge a better *De Imitatione* myself. But there is no knowing till one tries. Yet, after all, it is not certain whether the original *was* Latin. But, however *that* may have been, if it is possible that M. Michelet* can be accurate in saying that there are no less than *sixty* French versions (not editions, observe, but separate versions) existing of the *De Imitatione*, how prodigious must have been the adaptation of the book to the religious heart of the fifteenth century! Excepting the Bible, but excepting *that* only in Protestant lands, no book known to man has had the same distinction. It is the most marvellous bibliographical fact on record.

3. Our English girls, it seems, are as faulty in one way as we English males in another. None of us lads could have written the *Opera Omnia*[69] of Mr à Kempis; neither could any of our lasses have assumed male attire like *La Pucelle*. But why? Because, says Michelet, English girls and German think so much of an indecorum.[70] Well, that is a good fault, generally speaking. But M. Michelet ought to have remembered a fact in the martyrologies which justifies both parties, the French heroine for doing, and the general choir of English girls for *not* doing. A female Saint, specially renowned in France, had, for a reason as weighty as Joanna's, viz., expressly to shield her modesty amongst men, worn a male military harness. That reason and that example authorised *La Pucelle;* but our English girls, as a body, have seldom any such reason, and certainly no such saintly example, to plead. This excuses *them*. Yet, still, if it is indispensable to the national character that our young women should now and then trespass over the frontier of decorum, it then becomes a patriotic duty in me to assure M. Michelet that we have such ardent females amongst us, and in a long series – some detected in naval hospitals, when too sick to remember their disguise; some on fields of battle; multitudes never detected at all; some only suspected; and others discharged without noise by war offices and other absurd people. In our navy, both royal and commercial, and generally from deep remembrances of slighted love, women have sometimes served in disguise for many years, taking contentedly their daily allowance of burgoo,[71] biscuit, or cannon balls – anything, in short, digestible or indigestible, that it might please Providence to send. One thing, at least, is to their credit: never any of these poor masks, with their deep silent remembrances, have been detected through murmuring, or what is nautically understood by 'skulking.' So, for once, M. Michelet has an *erratum* to enter upon the fly-leaf of his book in presentation copies.

* 'If M. Michelet can be accurate.' However, on consideration, this statement does not depend on Michelet. The bibliographer, Barbier, has absolutely *specified* sixty in a separate dissertation, *soixante traductions*,[68] amongst those even that have not escaped the search. The Italian translations are said to be thirty. As to mere *editions*, not counting the early MSS. for half a century before printing was introduced, those in Latin amount to two thousand, and those in French to one thousand. Meantime, it is very clear to me that this astonishing popularity, so entirely unparalleled in literature, could not have existed except in Roman Catholic times, nor subsequently have lingered in any Protestant land. It was the denial of Scripture fountains to thirsty lands which made this slender rill of Scripture truth so passionately welcome.

by imperfect report, a martyrdom which to myself appears so unspeakably grand. Yet for a purpose pointing, not at Joanna but at M. Michelet – viz., to convince him that an Englishman is capable of thinking more highly of *La Pucelle* than even her admiring countryman, I shall, in parting, allude to one or two traits in Joanna's demeanour on the scaffold, and to one or two in that of the bystanders, which authorise me in questioning an opinion of his upon this martyr's firmness. The reader ought to be reminded that Joanne d'Arc was subjected to an unusually unfair trial of opinion. Any of the elder Christian martyrs had not much to fear of *personal* rancor. The martyr was chiefly regarded as the enemy of Caesar; at times, also, where any knowledge of the Christian faith and morals existed, with the enmity that arises spontaneously in the worldly against the spiritual. But the martyr, though disloyal, was not supposed to be, therefore, anti-national; and still less was *individually* hateful. What was hated (if anything) belonged to his class, not to himself separately. Now Joanna, if hated at all, was hated personally, and in Rouen[76] on national grounds. Hence there would be a certainty of calumny arising against *her*, such as would not affect martyrs in general. That being the case, it would follow of necessity that some people would impute to her a willingness to recant. No innocence could escape *that*. Now, had she really testified this willingness on the scaffold, it would have argued nothing at all but the weakness of a genial nature shrinking from the instant approach of torment. And those will often pity that weakness most, who, in their own persons, would yield to it least. Meantime, there never was a calumny uttered that drew less support from the recorded circumstances. It rests upon no *positive* testimony, and it has a weight of contradicting testimony to stem. And yet, strange to say, M.

---

4. But the last of these ebullitions is the most lively. We English, at Orleans, and after Orleans (which is not quite so extraordinary, if all were told), fled before the Maid of Arc. Yes, says M. Michelet, you *did:* deny it, if you can. Deny it, my dear? I don't mean to deny it. Running away, in many cases, is a thing so excellent, that no philosopher would, at times, condescend to adopt any other step. All of us nations in Europe, without one exception, have shown our philosophy in that way at times. Even people, '*qui ne se rendent pas*,' have deigned both to run and to shout, '*Sauve qui peut!*'[72] at odd times of sunset; though, for my part, I have no pleasure in recalling unpleasant remembrances to brave men; and yet, really, being so philosophic, they ought *not* to be unpleasant. But the amusing feature in M. Michelet's reproach is the way in which he *improves* and varies against us the charge of running, as if he were singing a catch.[73] Listen to him. They '*showed their backs*,' did these English. (Hip, hip, hurrah! three times three!) '*Behind good walls, they let themselves be taken*.' (Hip, hip! nine times nine!) They '*ran as fast as their legs could carry them*.' (Hurrah! twenty-seven times twenty-seven!) They '*ran before a girl;*'[74] they did. (Hurrah! eighty-one times eighty-one!) This reminds one of criminal indictments on the old model in English courts, where (for fear the prisoner should escape) the crown lawyer varied the charge perhaps through forty counts. The law laid its guns so as to rake the accused at every possible angle. Whilst the indictment was reading, he seemed a monster of crime in his own eyes; and yet, after all, the poor fellow had but committed one offence, and not always *that*. N.B. – Not having the French original at hand, I make my quotations from a friend's copy of Mr Walter Kelly's translation, which seems to me faithful, spirited, and idiomatically English – liable, in fact, only to the single reproach of occasional provincialisms.[75]

Michelet, who at times seems to admire the Maid of Arc as much as I do, is the one sole writer amongst her *friends* who lends some countenance to this odious slander. His words are – that, if she did not utter this word *recant* with her lips, she uttered it in her heart. 'Whether she *said* the word is uncertain: but I affirm that she *thought* it.'[77]

Now, I affirm that she did not; not in any sense of the word '*thought*' applicable to the case. Here is France calumniating *La Pucelle:* here is England defending her. M. Michelet can only mean, that, on *à priori* principles, every woman must be presumed liable to such a weakness; that Joanna was a woman; *ergo*,[78] that she was liable to such a weakness. That is, he only supposes her to have uttered the word by an argument which presumes it impossible for anybody to have done otherwise. I, on the contrary, throw the *onus* of the argument not on presumable tendencies of nature, but on the known facts of that morning's execution, as recorded by multitudes. What else, I demand, than mere weight of metal, absolute nobility of deportment, broke the vast line of battle then arrayed against her? What else but her meek, saintly demeanour, won from the enemies, that till now had believed her a witch, tears of rapturous admiration? 'Ten thousand men,' says M. Michelet himself, 'ten thousand men wept;'[79] and of these ten thousand the majority were political enemies knitted together by cords of superstition. What else was it but her constancy, united with her angelic gentleness, that drove the fanatic English soldier – who had sworn to throw a faggot on her scaffold, as *his* tribute of abhorrence, that *did* so, that fulfilled his vow – suddenly to turn away a penitent for life, saying everywhere that he had seen a dove rising upon wings to heaven from the ashes where she had stood? What else drove the executioner to kneel at every shrine for pardon to *his* share in the tragedy? And, if all this were insufficient, then I cite the closing act of her life as valid on her behalf, were all other testimonies against her. The executioner had been directed to apply his torch from below. He did so. The fiery smoke rose upwards in billowing volumes. A Dominican monk was then standing almost at her side. Wrapt up in his sublime office, he saw, not the danger, but still persisted in his prayers. Even then, when the last enemy was racing up the fiery stairs to seize her, even at that moment did this noblest of girls think only for *him*, the one friend that would not forsake her, and not for herself; bidding him with her last breath to care for his own preservation, but to leave *her* to God. That girl, whose latest breath ascended in this sublime expression of self-oblivion, did not utter the word *recant* either with her lips or in her heart. No; she did not, though one should rise from the dead[80] to swear it.

* * * * * * *

Bishop of Beauvais! thy victim died in fire upon a scaffold, thou upon a down bed. But for the departing minutes of life, both are oftentimes alike. At the farewell crisis, when the gates of death are opening, and flesh is resting from its struggles, oftentimes the tortured and the torturer have the same truce from carnal torment; both sink together into sleep; together both, sometimes, kindle into dreams. When the mortal mists were gathering fast upon you two, Bishop and Shepherd-girl – when the pavilions of life were closing up their shadowy curtains about you, let us try, through the gigantic glooms, to decipher the flying features of your separate visions.

The shepherd girl that had delivered France – she, from her dungeon, she, from her baiting at the stake, she, from her duel with fire – as she entered her last dream, saw Domrémy, saw the fountain of Domrémy, saw the pomp of forests in which her childhood had wandered. That Easter festival, which man had denied to her languishing heart – that resurrection of spring-time, which the darkness of dungeons had intercepted from *her*, hungering after the glorious liberty of forests – were by God given back into her hands, as jewels that had been stolen from her by robbers. With those, perhaps (for the minutes of dreams can stretch into ages),[81] was given back to her by God the bliss of childhood. By special privilege, for *her* might be created, in this farewell dream, a second childhood, innocent as the first; but not, like *that*, sad with the gloom of a fearful mission in the rear. This mission had now been fulfilled. The storm was weathered, the skirts even of that mighty storm were drawing off. The blood, that she was to reckon for, had been exacted; the tears, that she was to shed in secret, had been paid to the last. The hatred to herself in all eyes had been faced steadily, had been suffered, had been survived. And in her last fight upon the scaffold, she had triumphed gloriously; victoriously she had tasted the stings of death.[82] For all except this comfort from her farewell dream, she had died – died amidst the tears of ten thousand enemies – died amidst the drums and trumpets of armies – died amidst peals redoubling upon peals, volleys upon volleys, from the saluting clarions of martyrs.

Bishop of Beauvais! because the guilt-burthened man is in dreams haunted and waylaid by the most frightful of his crimes, and because upon that fluctuating mirror – rising (like the mocking mirrors of *mirage* in Arabian deserts) from the fens of death – most of all are reflected the sweet countenances which the man has laid in ruins; therefore I know, Bishop, that you also, entering your final dream, saw Domrémy. That fountain, of which the witnesses spoke so much, showed itself to your eyes in pure morning dews; but neither dews, nor the holy dawn, could cleanse away the bright spots of innocent blood upon its surface. By the fountain, Bishop, you saw a woman seated, that hid her face.[83] But as *you* draw near, the woman raises her wasted features. Would Domrémy know them again for the features of her child? Ah, but *you* know them, Bishop, well! Oh, mercy! what a groan was *that* which the servants, waiting outside the Bishop's dream at his bedside, heard from his labouring heart, as at this moment he turned away from the fountain and the woman, seeking rest in the forests afar off. Yet not *so* to escape the woman, whom once again he must behold before he dies. In the forests, to which he prays for pity, will he find a respite? What a tumult, what a gathering of feet is there! In glades, where only wild deer should run, armies and nations are assembling – towering in the fluctuating crowd are phantoms that belong to departed hours. There is the great English prince, regent of France. There is my lord of Winchester,[84] the princely cardinal, that died and made no sign. There is the Bishop of Beauvais, clinging to the shelter of thickets. What building is that which hands so rapid are raising? Is it a martyr's scaffold? Will they burn the child of Domrémy a second time? No: it is a tribunal that rises to the clouds; and two nations stand around it, waiting for a trial. Shall my lord of Beauvais sit again upon the judgment-seat, and again number the hours for the innocent? Ah! no: he is the prisoner at the bar. Already all is waiting: the mighty audience is gathered, the Court is hurrying to their seats, the witnesses are arrayed, the trumpets are sounding, the judge is going to take his place. Oh! but this is sudden. My lord, have you no counsel? 'Counsel I have none: in heaven above, or on earth beneath, counsellor there is none now that would take a brief from *me:* all are silent.' Is it, indeed, come to this? Alas! the time is short, the tumult is wondrous, the crowd stretches away into infinity, but yet I will search in it for somebody to take your brief: I know of somebody that will be your counsel. Who is this that cometh from Domrémy?[85]Who is she that cometh in bloody coronation robes from Rheims?[86] Who is she that cometh with blackened flesh from walking the furnaces of Rouen? This is she, the shepherd girl, counsellor that had none for herself, whom I choose, Bishop, for yours. She it is, I engage, that shall take my lord's brief. She it is, Bishop, that would plead for you: yes Bishop, SHE – when Heaven and Earth are silent.

THE NAUTICO-MILITARY NUN OF SPAIN
[Part I]

First published in *Tait's*, XIV, May 1847, pp. 324–33. The essay was printed as 'BY THOMAS DE QUINCEY.' in a centred line following the title and immediately preceding the text.

Reprinted in *F*, VII, *Narrative and Miscellaneous Papers* (1852), pp. 109–43, p. 203.

Revised text, carrying many accidentals but only one substantive variant from *F*, in *SGG*, III, *Miscellanies, Chiefly Narrative* (1854), pp. 1–35.

There are five manuscripts, as follows:

MS A: Huntington Library, HM 31019. The manuscript is a set of *SGG* page proofs, with one interleaved sheet, corresponding to the text below running from p. 94.9 'On a night in the year 1592' to p. 101.24 'It was not to the Don, as', with those textual variants from *SGG* running from p. 640, 94.9 '*Section 1. – An Extra Nuisance is introduced into Spain*' to p. 644, 101.24 'protector and official visitor of'. MS A breaks in mid-sentence, but is picked up again at MS B.

MS B: British Library, Department of Printed Books, C. 60. o. 3. The manuscript is a set of galley proofs, corresponding to the text below running from p. 101.24 'harbourer of his daughter, but' to p. 109.35 'was to some degree doubtful.', with those textual variants from *SGG* running from p. 644, 101.25 'as hereditary patron of' to p. 647, 109.26 'none; and she'.

MS C: Huntington Library, HM 31019. The manuscript is a set of *SGG* page proofs that overlaps with MS B by seven lines, and corresponds to the text below running from p. 109.30–1 'down, and unintentionally fell' to p. 110.28 'had a right to expect.', with those textual variants from *SGG* running from p. 647, 109.42 'boat (though a boat…perish),' to p. 647, 110.16 'that, whatever this might be, it'.

MS D: Huntington Library, HM 31019. The manuscript is a set of page proofs from *F*, and corresponds to the footnote below running from p. 105.36 '"*She looked*," &c.' to p. 105.44–5 'now reached (1608)'.

MS E: Buffalo and Erie County Public Library, James Fraser Gluck Collection, Part II. #1 (26). The manuscript is a single sheet of white paper, measuring 115 by 190 mm, with writing in black ink on both sides. There is no watermark. It corresponds to the *SGG* footnote below running from p. 645, 105.4 'Who is Mrs Bobo?' to 'apply for biscuit.'

Taken together, the five manuscripts contain twenty significant variants, and these are listed in the textual notes.

Catalina de Erauso (1592–1650) was born in the coastal town of San Sebastián in the Basque region of northern Spain. She was a middle daughter of Captain Miguel de Erauso and his wife María Pérez de Galarraga. Her four brothers were all military men and adventurers who lived most of their lives in the New World and eventually died there. Like her four sisters, Catalina entered the convent of San Sebastian the Elder, but she escaped at fifteen and did not take final vows. Disguised in men's clothing, she roamed Spain and then set sail for South America, where she led a life of often violent adventure, and fought as a Spanish soldier in campaigns in Chile and Peru, rising to the rank of second lieutenant. Catalina returned to Europe toward the end of 1624, and sometime shortly thereafter she wrote down or dictated to an amanuensis an account of her life. At this time she was also rewarded with a soldier's pension from the Spanish monarch and dispensation from Pope Urban VIII to continue her life in men's clothing. In 1630 she returned to the Americas, this time to Mexico, where she lived the remaining twenty years of her life as Antonio de Erauso, a mule-driver, slave owner, and small merchant. She died at Cuitlaxtla while journeying to Veracruz.

Not all the details of Catalina's life can be affirmed with certainty, and there is contradictory evidence concerning different dates and circumstances, as James Fitzmaurice-Kelly details. Moreover, as Michele Stepto points out, Catalina's account of her life is

> firmly shaped by the Spanish picaresque tradition, which flourished in the century and a half following the Colombian discovery....Catalina's memoir forcefully reminds us that the picaresque is a creature of discovery and conquest, a new mode of storytelling brought to birth in a suddenly vast and changing world.

While De Quincey is quick to emphasize that details surrounding Catalina have been 'trebly authenticated by proofs and attestations direct and collateral', her life story is undoubtedly a combination of historical fact and picaresque fiction (James Fitzmaurice-Kelly, 'Introduction' in *The Nun Ensign*, ed. James Fitzmaurice-Kelly (London: T. Fisher Unwin, 1908), pp. xxxix–xxxiii; Michele Stepto, 'Introduction' in *Lieutenant Nun*, translated by Michele Stepto and Gabriel Stepto (Boston: Deacon Press, 1996), p. xxxiv.

No original copy of Catalina's narrative has been found, though evidence suggests a manuscript was submitted to the publisher Bernardino de Guzmán in 1625. For at least a century following its composition, the manuscript was in the possession of the Urbizu family of Seville. One copy was owned by the Spanish poet Cándido María Trigueros (1737–1801), which in 1784 was transcribed by royal historian Juan Bautista Muñoz (1745–99) and given the title *Vida i sucesos de la Monja Alférez*. Finally, in 1829, the Basque soldier and critic Joaquín María de Ferrer (1777–1861) edited and published the manuscript under the title *Historia de la Monja Alférez, Doña Catalina de Erauso, escrita por ella misma*. English and German translations followed, as did one in French by Alexis de Valon (1818–51), and it is the Valon version of Catalina's story that forms the basis of De Quincey's account.

When he first published the article in *Tait's*, De Quincey suggested that he had done a great deal of research in order to present an accurate assessment of

Catalina's history. 'From the archives of the Royal Marine at Seville', he noted, 'from the autobiography of the heroine, from contemporary chronicles, and from several official sources scattered in and out of Spain, some of them ecclesiastical, the amplest proofs have been drawn, and may yet be greatly extended, of the extraordinary events here recorded' (see below, p. 93). When he revised the article in 1854, however, he was more forthcoming. 'I must not leave the impression upon my readers', he now explained, 'that this complex body of documentary evidence had been searched and appraised by myself. Frankly I acknowledge that, on the sole occasion when any opportunity offered itself for such a labour, I shrank from it as too fatiguing' (see Vol. 20, p. 26). In fact, De Quincey's account is indebted exclusively to Valon's narrative, and Goldman taxed him 'with something very close to plagiarism', for he 'transferred...the entire series of adventures, neither adding nor omitting a single episode'. Masson, however, emphasized that while De Quincey was clearly indebted to Valon, his 'craft in language enabled him to make good his assertion that *his* narrative contained "no one sentence derived from any foreign one."' De Quincey also makes additions that are uniquely his own. The disquisition on Coleridge's 'Ancient Mariner' in Part II, for example, is not in Valon, and suggestively links Catalina's delirium to the 'craziness' that settled upon the 'mariner's brain, driving him, as if he were a Cain, or another Wandering Jew' (Goldman, pp. 127, 129; Masson, vol. XIII, pp. 248, 245; see below, p. 116).

De Quincey rated parts of the essay very highly, especially 'the "Spanish Nun's" passage across the Andes'. The *Eclectic Review* agreed: 'as a writer of narrative, De Quincey shines as an adept; marvellously graphic is his account of the *Spanish Military Nun*'....We should like to embellish our pages by inserting the description of Kate on the summit of the Andes'. The *Continental Monthly* described the essay as 'a narrative of absorbing power'. Crabb Robinson, however, was much less impressed: 'I finished to-day *The Spanish Military Nun*....A real story is told in a very unreal style; an effort about it, as if written for effect. So that it leaves a bad effect' (Japp, p. 266; Anon., '*Selections Grave and Gay*...by Thomas De Quincey' in *Eclectic Review*, NS 8 (October 1854), p. 398; Anon., 'Thomas De Quincey and his Writings' in *Continental Monthly*, 5 (June 1864), p. 657; *HCR*, vol. II, pp. 740-1).

De Quincey clearly thought of 'The Nautico Military Nun of Spain' and his essay on 'Joan of Arc' (see above, pp. 61–89) as two parts of a similar project, for he wrote and published them in *Tait's* almost at the same time, and he planned to issue them together in book form, 'with a few words of preface telling the public what *I* think of them, and what place *I* expect for them'. Plans for book publication did not materialize, but several critics have pointed to the similarities between the stories of Joan and Catalina. 'Two of the *Tait* papers...are among the most vivid of De Quincey's productions', observes Metcalf. 'They are both on women....If the incredible Kate of St Sebastian stirred the lighter fancy of De Quincey, it was the sainted Joan of Arc who fired his heart with lyric transport'. From a very different perspective, Leighton asserts:

> Obscurely, through all his life and writings, De Quincey hints that it is the very closeting protection of men, of fathers, husbands and brothers, which kills women. Those, like Joan of Arc and the Spanish military nun,

> who escape the home, "can die", but on their own terms, and in their own cause. Those others, who stay indoors, are artistically and inevitably murdered.

In her introductory discussion of the narratives that inform Kate's memoir, Garber cites the 'pertinent example' of 'Joan of Arc, the cross-dressed soldier and saint tried for transvestism by the Inquisition' (John Calvin Metcalf, *De Quincey: A Portrait* (Cambridge, Mass.: Harvard University Press, 1940), p. 147; Angela Leighton, 'De Quincey and Women' in *Beyond Romanticism: New Approaches to Texts and Contexts*, eds Stephen Copley and John Whale (London: Routledge, 1992), p. 172; Marjorie Garber, 'Foreword' in *Lieutenant Nun*, translated by Michele Stepto and Gabriel Stepto (Boston: Deacon Press, 1996), p. xii.

The annotation for this essay draws on previous editions of the Catalina de Erauso's narrative by Fitzmaurice-Kelly (cited above), Carol M. Newman (New York: Macmillan, 1906), V. H. Collins (Oxford: Clarendon Press, 1909), Rima de Vallbona (Tempe: Arizona State University Press, 1992) and Pedro Rubio Merino (Seville: Cabildo Metropolitano, 1995).

WHY is it that *Adventures* are so generally repulsive to people of meditative minds? It is for the same reason that any other want of law, that any other anarchy, is repulsive. Floating passively from action to action, as helplessly as a withered leaf surrendered to the breath of winds, the human spirit (out of which comes all grandeur of human motions) is exhibited in mere *Adventures* as either entirely laid asleep, or as acting only by lower organs that regulate the *means*, whilst the *ends* are derived from alien sources, and are imperiously predetermined. It is a case of exception, however, when even amongst such adventures the agent reacts upon his own difficulties and necessities by a temper of extraordinary courage, and a mind of premature decision. Further strength arises to such an exception, if the very moulding accidents of the life, if the very external coercions are themselves unusually romantic. They may thus gain a separate interest of their own. And, lastly, the whole is locked into validity of interest, even for the psychological philosopher, by complete authentication of its truth. In the case now brought before him, the reader must not doubt; for no memoir exists, or personal biography, that is so trebly authenticated by proofs and attestations direct and collateral. From the archives of the Royal Marine at Seville, from the autobiography of the heroine, from contemporary chronicles, and from several official sources scattered in and out of Spain, some of them ecclesiastical, the amplest proofs have been drawn, and may yet be greatly extended, of the extraordinary events here recorded. M. de Ferrer, a Spaniard of much research, and originally incredulous as to the facts, published about seventeen years ago a selection from the leading documents, accompanied by his *palinode* as to their accuracy. His materials have been since used for the basis of more than one narrative, not inaccurate, in French, German, and Spanish journals of high authority. It is seldom the case that French writers err by prolixity. They *have* done so in this case. The present narrative, which contains no sentence derived from any foreign one, has the great advantage of close compression; my own pages, after equating the size, being as 1 to 3 of the shortest continental form.[1] In the mode of narration, I am vain enough to flatter myself that the reader will find little reason to hesitate between us. Mine will, at least, weary nobody; which is more than can be always said for the continental versions.

On a night in the year 1592 (but which night is a secret liable to 365 answers), a Spanish '*son of somebody,*'[*] in the fortified town of St Sebastian, received the disagreeable intelligence from a nurse, that his wife had just presented him with a daughter. No present that the poor misjudging lady could possibly have made him was so entirely useless for any purpose of his. He had three daughters already, which happened to be more by 2+1 than *his* reckoning assumed as a reasonable allowance of daughters. A supernumerary son might have been stowed away; but daughters in excess were the very nuisance of Spain. He did, therefore, what in such cases every proud and lazy Spanish gentleman was apt to do – he wrapped the new[2] little daughter, odious to his paternal eyes, in a pocket handkerchief; and then, wrapping up his own throat with a good deal more care, off he bolted to the neighbouring convent of St Sebastian; not merely of that city, but also (amongst several convents) the one dedicated to that saint. It is well that in this quarrelsome world we quarrel furiously about tastes; since agreeing too closely about the objects to be liked and appropriated would breed much more fighting than is bred by disagreeing. That little human tadpole, which the old toad of a father would not suffer to stay ten minutes in his house, proved as welcome at the nunnery of St Sebastian as she was odious elsewhere. The superior of the convent was aunt, by the mother's side, to the new-born stranger. She, therefore, kissed and blessed the little lady. The poor nuns, who were never to have any babies of their own, and were languishing for some amusement, perfectly doated on this prospect of a wee pet. The superior thanked the hidalgo for his very splendid present. The nuns thanked him each and all; until the old crocodile actually began to cry[3] and whimper sentimentally at what he now perceived to be excess of munificence in himself. Munificence, indeed, he remarked, was his foible next after parental tenderness.

What a luxury it is sometimes to a cynic that there go two words to a bargain.[4] In the convent of St Sebastian all was gratitude; gratitude (as aforesaid) to the hidalgo from all the convent for his present, until, at last, the hidalgo began to express gratitude to *them* for their gratitude to *him*. Then came a rolling fire of thanks to St Sebastian; from the superior, for sending a future saint; from the nuns, for sending such a love of a plaything; and, finally, from papa, for sending such substantial board and well-bolted lodgings, 'from

[*] *i.e.* 'Hidalgo.'

which,' said the malicious old fellow, 'my pussy will never find her way out to a thorny and dangerous world.' Won't she? I suspect, son of somebody, that the next time you see 'pussy,' which may happen to be also the last, will not be in a convent of any kind. At present, whilst this general rendering of thanks was going on, one person only took no part in them. That person was 'pussy,' whose little figure lay quietly stretched out in the arms of a smiling young nun, with eyes nearly shut, yet peering a little at the candles. Pussy said nothing. It's of no great use to say much, when all the world is against you. But, if St Sebastian had enabled her to speak out the whole truth, pussy *would* have said: – 'So, Mr Hidalgo, you have been engaging lodgings for me; lodgings for life. Wait a little. We'll try that question, when my claws are grown a little longer.'

Disappointment, therefore, was gathering ahead. But for the present there was nothing of the kind. That noble old crocodile, papa, was not in the least disappointed as regarded *his* expectation of having no anxiety to waste, and no money to pay, on account of his youngest daughter. He insisted on his right to forget her; and in a week *had* forgotten her, never to think of her again but once. The lady superior, as regarded *her* demands, was equally content, and through a course of several years; for, as often as she asked pussy if she would be a saint, pussy replied that she would, if saints were allowed plenty of sweetmeats. But least of all were the nuns disappointed. Everything that they had fancied possible in a human plaything fell short of what pussy realised in racketing, racing, and eternal plots against the peace of the elder nuns. No fox ever kept a hen-roost in such alarm as pussy kept the dormitory of the senior sisters; whilst the younger ladies were run off their legs by the eternal wiles, and had their chapel gravity discomposed, even in the chapel, by the eternal antics, of this privileged little kitten.

The kitten had long ago received a baptismal name, which was Kitty; this is Catharine, or Kate, or *Hispanice* Catalina. It was a good name, as it recalled her original name of pussy. And, by the way, she had also an ancient and honourable surname, viz., *De Erauso*, which is to this day a name rooted in Biscay.[5] Her father, the *hidalgo*, was a military officer in the Spanish service, and had little care whether his kitten should turn out a wolf or a lamb, having made over the fee simple[6] of his own interest in the little Kate to St Sebastian, 'to have and to hold,'[7] so long as Kate should keep her hold of this present life. Kate had no apparent intention to let slip that hold, for she was blooming as a rose-bush in June,[8] tall and strong as a young cedar. Yet, notwithstanding this robust health and the strength of the convent walls, the time was drawing near when St Sebastian's lease in Kate must, in legal phrase, 'determine;' and any *chateaux en Espagne*,[9] that the Saint might have built on the cloistral fidelity of his pet Catalina, must suddenly give way in one hour, like many other vanities in our own days of Spanish bonds and promises.[10] After reaching her tenth year, Catalina became thoughtful, and not very docile. At times she was even headstrong and turbulent, so that the gentle sisterhood of St

Sebastian, who had no other pet or plaything in the world, began to weep in secret – fearing that they might have been rearing by mistake some future tigress – for as to infancy, *that*, you know, is playful and innocent even in the cubs of a tigress.[11] But *there* the ladies were going too far. Catalina was impetuous and aspiring, but not cruel. She was gentle, if people would let her be so. But woe to those that took liberties with *her!* A female servant of the convent, in some authority, one day, in passing up the aisle to matins, *wilfully* gave Kate a push; and in return, Kate, who never left her debts in arrear, gave the servant for a keep-sake a look which that servant carried with her in fearful remembrance to her grave. It seemed as if Kate had tropic blood in her veins, that continually called her away to the tropics. It was all the fault of that 'blue rejoicing sky,'[12] of those purple Biscayan mountains, of that tumultuous ocean, which she beheld daily from the nunnery gardens. Or, if only half of it was *their* fault, the other half lay in those golden tales, streaming upwards even into the sanctuaries of convents, like morning mists touched by earliest sunlight, of kingdoms overshadowing a new world which had been founded by her kinsmen with the simple aid of a horse and a lance. The reader is to remember that this is no romance, or at least no fiction, that he is reading; and it is proper to remind the reader of real romances in Ariosto or our own Spenser, that such martial ladies as the *Marfisa*, or *Bradamant* of the first, and *Britomart*[13] of the other, were really not the improbabilities that modern society imagines. Many a stout man, as you will soon see, found that Kate, with a sabre in hand, and well mounted, was but too serious a fact.

The day is come – the evening is come – when our poor Kate, that had for fifteen years been so tenderly rocked in the arms of St Sebastian and his daughters, and that henceforth shall hardly find a breathing space between eternal storms, must see her peaceful cell, must see the holy chapel, for the last time.[14] It was at vespers, it was during the chaunting of the vesper service, that she finally read the secret signal for her departure, which long she had been looking for. It happened that her aunt, the Lady Principal, had forgotten her breviary. As this was in a private 'scrutoire, she did not choose to send a servant for it, but gave the key to her niece. The niece, on opening the 'scrutoire, saw, with that rapidity of eye-glance for the one thing needed in any great emergency which ever attended her through life, that *now* was the moment for an attempt which, if neglected, might never return. There lay the total keys, in one massive *trousseau*,[15] of that fortress impregnable even to armies from without. Saint Sebastian! do you see what your pet is going to do? And do it she will, as sure as your name is St Sebastian. Kate went back to her aunt with the breviary and the key; but taking good care to leave that awful door, on whose hinge revolved her whole life, unlocked. Delivering the two articles to the Superior, she complained of a head-ache – [Ah, Kate! what did *you* know of head-aches, except now and then afterwards from a stray bullet, or so?] – upon which her aunt, kissing her forehead, dismissed her to bed. Now, then, through three-fourths of an hour Kate will have free elbow-room for unanchoring her boat, for unshipping her oars, and for pulling ahead right out of St Sebastian's cove into the main ocean of life.

Catalina, the reader is to understand, does not belong to the class of persons in whom chiefly I pretend to an interest. But everywhere one loves energy and indomitable courage. I, for my part, admire not, by preference, anything that points to this world. It is the child of reverie and profounder sensibility who turns *away* from the world as hateful and insufficient, that engages *my* interest: whereas Catalina was the very model of the class fitted for facing this world, and who express their love to it by fighting with it and kicking it from year to year. But, always, what is best in its kind one admires, even though the kind be disagreeable. Kate's advantages for her *rôle* in this life lay in four things, viz., in a well-built person, and a particularly strong wrist; 2d, in a heart that nothing could appal; 3d, in a sagacious head, never drawn aside from the *hoc age*[16] [from the instant question of life] by any weakness of imagination; 4th, in a tolerably thick skin – not literally, for she was fair and blooming, and decidedly handsome, having such a skin as became a young woman of family in northern-most Spain. But her sensibilities were obtuse as regarded *some* modes of delicacy, *some* modes of equity, *some* modes of the world's opinion, and *all* modes whatever of personal hardship. Lay a stress on that word *some* – for, as to delicacy, she never lost sight of the kind which peculiarly concerns her sex. Long afterwards she told the Pope himself, when confessing without disguise her sad and infinite wanderings to the paternal old man (and I feel convinced of her veracity) that in this respect, even then, at middle age, she was as pure as is a child. And, as to equity, it was only that she substituted the equity of camps for the polished (but often more iniquitous) equity of courts and towns. As to the third item – the world's opinion – I don't know that you need lay a stress on *some*; for, generally speaking, *all* that the world did, said, or thought, was alike contemptible in her eyes, in which, perhaps, she was not so *very* far wrong. I must add, though at the cost of interrupting the story by two or three more sentences, that Catalina had also a fifth advantage, which sounds humbly, but is really of use in a world, where even to fold and seal a letter adroitly is not the least of accomplishments. She was a *handy* girl. She could turn her hand to anything, of which I will give you two memorable instances. Was there ever a girl in this world but herself that cheated and snapped her fingers at that awful Inquisition,[17] which brooded over the convents of Spain, that did this without collusion from outside, trusting to nobody, but to herself, and what? to one needle, two hanks of thread, and a very inferior pair of scissors? For, that the scissors were bad, though Kate does not say so in her memoirs, I know by an *à priori*[18] argument viz., because *all* scissors were bad in the year 1607. Now, say all decent logicians, from a universal to a particular *valet consequentia*,[19] *all* scissors were bad: *ergo, some* scissors were bad. The second instance of her handiness will surprise you even more: – She once stood upon a scaffold, under sentence of death – [but, understand, on the evidence of false witnesses]. Jack Ketch was absolutely tying the knot under her ear, and the shameful man of ropes fumbled so deplorably, that Kate (who by much nautical experience had learned from another sort of 'Jack'[20] how a knot *should* be tied in this world,) lost all patience with the contemptible artist, told him she was ashamed of him, took the rope out of his hand, and tied the knot irreproachably herself. The crowd saluted her with a festal roll, long and loud, of *vivas;*[21] and this word *viva* of good augury – but stop: let me not anticipate.

From this sketch of Catalina's character, the reader is prepared to understand the decision of her present proceeding. She had no time to lose: the twilight favoured her; but she must get under hiding before pursuit commenced. Consequently she lost not one of her 45 minutes in picking and choosing. No *shilly-shally*[22] in Kate. She saw with the eyeball of an eagle what was indispensable. Some little money perhaps to pay the first toll-bar of life: so, out of four shillings in Aunty's purse, she took one. You can't say *that* was exorbitant. Which of us wouldn't subscribe a shilling for poor Katy to put into the first trouser pockets that ever she will wear? I remember even yet, as a personal experience, that when first arrayed, at four years old, in nankeen trousers, though still so far retaining hermaphrodite relations of dress as to wear a petticoat above my trousers, all my female friends (because they pitied me, as one that had suffered from years of ague),[23] filled my pockets with half-crowns, of which I can render no account at this day. But what were my poor pretensions by the side of Kate's? Kate was a fine blooming girl of 15, with no touch of ague, and, before the next sun rises, Kate shall draw on her first trousers, and made by her own hand; and, that she may do so, of all the valuables in Aunty's repository she takes nothing beside the shilling, *quantum sufficit*[24] of thread, one stout needle, and (as I told you before, if you would please to remember things), one bad pair of scissors. Now she was ready; ready to cast off St Sebastian's towing rope; ready to cut and run for port anywhere. The finishing touch of her preparations was to pick out the proper keys: even there she showed the same discretion. She did no gratuitous mischief. She did not take the wine-cellar key, which would have irritated the good father confessor; she took those keys only that belonged to *her*, if ever keys did; for they were the keys that locked her out from her natural birthright of liberty. 'Show me,' says the Romish Casuist, 'her right in law to let herself out of that nunnery.' 'Show us,' we reply, '*your* right to lock her in.'[25]

Right or wrong, however, in strict casuistry, Kate was resolved to let herself out; and *did* so; and, for fear any man should creep in whilst vespers lasted, and steal the kitchen grate, she locked her old friends *in*. Then she sought a shelter. The air was not cold. She hurried into a chestnut wood, and upon withered leaves slept till dawn. Spanish diet and youth leaves the digestion undisordered, and the slumbers light. When the lark rose, up rose Catalina. No time to lose, for she was still in the dress of a nun, and liable to be arrested by any man in Spain. With her *armed* finger, [aye, by the way, I forgot the thimble; but Kate did *not*] – she set to work upon her amply embroidered petticoat. She turned it wrong side out; and with the magic that only female hands possess, she had soon sketched and finished a dashing pair of Wellington trousers.[26] All other changes where made according to the materials she possessed, and quite sufficiently to disguise the two main perils – her sex, and her monastic dedication. What was she to do next? Speaking of Wellington trousers would remind *us*, but could hardly remind *her*, of Vittoria,[27] where she dimly had heard of some maternal relative. To Vittoria, therefore, she bent her course; and, like the Duke of Wellington, but arriving more than two centuries earlier, [though *he* too is an early riser], she gained a great victory at that place. She had made a two days' march, baggage far in the rear, and no provisions but wild berries; she depended for anything better, as light-heartedly as the Duke, upon attacking, sword in hand, storming her dear friend's entrenchments, and effecting a lodgment in his breakfast-room, should he happen to have one. This amiable relative,[28] an elderly man, had but one foible, or perhaps one virtue in the world; but *that* he had in perfection, – it was pedantry. On that hint Catalina spoke: she knew by heart, from the services of the convent, a few latin phrases. Latin! – Oh, but *that* was charming; and in one so young! The grave Don owned the soft impeachment;[29] relented at once, and clasped the hopeful young gentleman in the Wellington trousers to his *uncular*[30] and rather angular breast. In this house the yarn of life was of a mingled quality.[31] The table was good, but that was exactly what Kate cared little about. The amusement was of the worst kind. It consisted chiefly in conjugating Latin verbs, especially such as were obstinately irregular. To show him a withered frost-bitten verb, that wanted its preterite, wanted its supines, wanted, in fact, everything in this world, fruits or blossoms, that make a verb desirable, was to earn the Don's gratitude for life. All day long he was marching and countermarching his favourite brigades of verbs – verbs frequentative, verbs inceptive, verbs desiderative – horse, foot, and artillery; changing front, advancing from the rear, throwing out skirmishing parties, until Kate, not given to faint, must have thought of such a resource, as once in her life she had thought so seasonably of a vesper head-ache. This was really worse than St Sebastian's. It reminds one of a French gaiety in Thiebault[32] or some such author, who describes a rustic party, under equal despair, as employing themselves in conjugating the verb *s'ennuyer*, – *Je m'ennuie, tu t'ennuies, il s'ennuit; nous nous ennuyons*, &.; thence to the imperfect – *Je m'ennuyois, tu t'ennuyois*, &.; thence to the imperative – *Qu'il s'ennuye*, &.; and so on through the whole melancholy conjugation. Now, you know, when the time comes that, *nous nous ennuyons*,[33] the best course is, to part. Kate saw *that*; and she walked off from the Don's [of whose amorous passion for defective verbs one would have wished to know the catastrophe], and took from his mantlepiece rather more silver than she had levied on her aunt. But the Don also was a relative; and really he owed her a small cheque on his banker for turning out on his field-days. A man, if he *is* a kinsman, has no right to bore one *gratis*.

From Vittoria Kate was guided by a carrier to Valladolid.[34] Luckily, as it seemed at first, but it made little difference in the end, here, at Valladolid, were the King[35] and his Court. Consequently, there was plenty of regiments and plenty of regimental bands. Attracted by one of these, Catalina was quietly listening to the music, when some street ruffians, in derision of the gay colours and the form of her forest-made costume – [rascals! one would like to have seen what sort of trousers *they* would have made with no better scissors!] – began to pelt her with stones. Ah, my friends, of the genus *blackguard*, you little know who it is that you are selecting for experiments. This is the one creature of fifteen in all Spain, be the other male or female, whom nature, and temper, and provocation have qualified for taking the conceit out of you. This she very soon did, laying open a head or two with a sharp stone, and letting out rather too little than too much of bad Valladolid blood. But mark the constant villany of this world. Certain Alguazils[36] – very like some other Alguazils that I know nearer home – having stood by quietly to see the friendless stranger insulted and assaulted, now felt it their duty to apprehend the poor nun for murderous violence: and had there been such a thing as a treadmill in Valladolid, Kate was booked for a place on it without further inquiry. Luckily, injustice does not *always* prosper. A gallant young cavalier, who had witnessed from his windows the whole affair, had seen the provocation, and admired Catalina's behaviour – equally patient at first and bold at last – hastened into the street, pursued the officers, forced them to release their prisoner, upon stating the circumstances of the case, and instantly offered Catalina a situation amongst his retinue. He was a man of birth and fortune; and the place offered, that of an honorary page, not being at all degrading even to a 'daughter of somebody,' was cheerfully accepted. Here Catalina spent a happy month. She was now splendidly dressed in dark blue velvet, by a tailor that did not work within the gloom of a chestnut forest. She and the young cavalier, Don Francisco de Cardenas,[37] were mutually pleased, and had mutual confidence. All went well – when one evening, but, luckily, not until the sun had been set so long as to make all things indistinct, who should march into the ante-chamber of the cavalier but that sublime of crocodiles, *Papa*, that we lost sight of fifteen years ago, and shall never see again after this night. He had his crocodile tears all ready for use, in working order, like a good industrious fire-engine. It was absolutely to Catalina herself that he advanced; whom, for many reasons, he could not be supposed to recognise – lapse of years, male attire, twilight, were all against him. Still, she might have the family countenance; and Kate thought he looked with a suspicious scrutiny into her face, as he inquired for the young Don. To avert her own face, to announce him to Don Francisco, to wish him on the shores of that ancient river for crocodiles, the Nile, furnished but one moment's work to the active Catalina. She lingered, however, as her place entitled her to do, at the door of the audience chamber. She guessed already, but in a moment she *heard* from papa's lips what was the nature of his errand. His daughter,

Catharine, he informed the Don, had eloped from the convent of St Sebastian, a place rich in delight. Then he laid open the unparalleled ingratitude of such a step. Oh, the unseen treasure that had been spent upon that girl! Oh, the untold sums of money that he had sunk in that unhappy speculation! The nights of sleeplessness suffered during her infancy! The fifteen years of solicitude thrown away in schemes for her improvement! It would have moved the heart of a stone. The *hidalgo* wept copiously at his own pathos. And to such a height of grandeur had he carried his Spanish sense of sublime, that he disdained to mention the pocket-handkerchief which he had left at St Sebastian's fifteen years ago, by way of envelope for 'pussy,' and which, to the best of pussy's knowledge, was the one sole memorandum of papa ever heard of at St Sebastian's. Pussy, however, saw no use in revising and correcting the text of papa's remembrances. She showed her usual prudence, and her usual incomparable decision. It did not appear, as yet, that she would be reclaimed, or was at all suspected for the fugitive by her father. For it is an instance of that singular fatality which pursued Catalina through life, that, to her own astonishment (as she now collected from her father's conference), nobody had traced her to Valladolid, nor had her father's visit any connexion with suspicions travelling in that direction. The case was quite different. Strangely enough, her street row had thrown her into the one sole household in all Spain that had an official connexion with St Sebastian's. That convent had been founded by the young cavalier's family; and, according to the usage of Spain, the young man (as present representative of his house) was the responsible protector of the establishment. It was not to the Don, as harbourer of his daughter, but to the Don, as *ex officio*[38] visitor of the convent, that the hidalgo was appealing. Probably Kate might have staid safely some time longer. Yet, again, this would but have multiplied the clues for tracing her; and, finally, she would too probably have been discovered; after which, with all his youthful generosity, the poor Don could not have protected her. Too terrific was the vengeance that awaited an abettor of any fugitive nun; but above all, if such a crime were perpetrated by an official mandatory[39] of the church. Yet, again, so far it was the more hazardous course to abscond, that it almost revealed her to the young Don as the missing daughter. Still, if it really *had* that effect, nothing at present obliged him to pursue her, as might have been the case a few weeks later. Kate argued (I daresay) rightly, as she always did. Her prudence whispered eternally, that safety there was none for her, until she had laid the Atlantic between herself and St Sebastian's. Life was to be for *her* a Bay of Biscay; and it was odds but she had first embarked upon this billowy life from the literal Bay of Biscay.[40] Chance ordered otherwise. Or, as a Frenchman says with eloquent ingenuity, in connexion with this story, 'chance is but the *pseudonyme* of God for those particular cases which he does not subscribe openly with his own sign manual.'[41] She crept up stairs to her bedroom. Simple are the travelling preparations of those that, possessing nothing, have no imperials[42] to pack. She had Juvenal's qualification for caroling gaily through a forest full of robbers;[43] for she had nothing to lose but a change of linen, that rode easily enough under her left arm, leaving the right free for answering any questions of impertinent customers. As she crept down stairs, she heard the Crocodile still weeping forth his sorrows to the pensive ear of twilight, and to the sympathetic Don Francisco. Now, it would not have been filial or lady-like for Kate to do what I am going to suggest;[44] but what a pity that some gay brother page had not been there to turn aside into the room, armed with a roasted potato, and, taking a sportsman's aim, to have lodged it in the Crocodile's abominable mouth. Yet, what an anachronism! There *were* no roasted potatoes in Spain at that date,[45] and very few in England. But anger drives a man to say anything.

Catalina had seen her last of friends and enemies in Valladolid. Short was her time there; but she had improved it so far as to make a few of both. There was an eye or two in Valladolid that would have glared with malice upon her, had she been seen by *all* eyes in that city, as she tripped through the streets in the dusk; and eyes there were that would have softened into tears, had they seen the desolate condition of the child, or in vision had seen the struggles that were before her. But what's the use of wasting tears upon our Kate? Wait till to-morrow morning at sun-rise, and see if she is particularly in need of pity. What now should a young lady do – I propose it as a subject for a prize essay – that finds herself in Valladolid at nightfall, having no letters of introduction, not aware of any reason great or small for preferring any street in general, except so far as she knows of some reason for avoiding one or two streets in particular? The great problem I have stated, Kate investigated as she went along; and she solved it with the accuracy with which she ever applied to *practical* exigencies. Her conclusion was – that the best door to knock at in such a case was the door where there was no need to knock at all, as being unfastened, and open to all comers. For she argued that within such a door there would be nothing to steal, so that, at least, you could not be mistaken in the dark for a thief. Then, as to stealing from *her*, they might do that if they could.

Upon these principles, which hostile critics will in vain endeavour to undermine, she laid her hand upon what seemed a rude stable door. Such it proved. There was an empty cart inside; certainly there was, but you couldn't take *that* away in your pocket; and there were five loads of straw, but then of those a lady could take no more than her *reticule* would carry, which perhaps was allowed by the courtesy of Spain. So Kate was right as to the difficulty of being challenged for a thief. Closing the door as gently as she had opened it, she dropped her person, dressed as she was, upon the nearest heap of straw. Some ten feet further were lying two muleteers, honest and happy enough, as compared with the lords of the bed-chamber then in Valladolid: but still gross men, carnally deaf from eating garlic and onions, and other horrible substances. Accordingly, they never heard her, nor were aware, until dawn, that such a blooming person existed. But she was aware of *them*, and of their conversation. They were talking of an expedition for America, on the point of sailing under Don Ferdinand de Cordova. It was to sail from some Andalusian port.[46] That was the very thing for *her*. At daylight she woke, and jumped up, needing no more toilet than the birds that already were singing in the gardens, or than the two muleteers, who, good honest fellows, saluted the handsome boy kindly – thinking no ill at his making free with *their* straw, though no leave had been asked.

With these philo-garlic men Kate took her departure. The morning was divine; and leaving Valladolid with the transports that befitted such a golden dawn, feeling also already, in the very obscurity of her exit, the pledge of her escape; she cared no longer for the crocodile, or for St Sebastian, or (in the way of fear) for the protector of St Sebastian, though of *him* she thought with some tenderness; so deep is the remembrance of kindness mixed with justice. Andalusia she reached rather slowly; but many months before she was sixteen years old, and quite in time for the expedition. St Lucar being the port of rendezvous for the Peruvian expedition, thither she went. All comers were welcome on board the fleet; much more a fine young fellow like Kate. She was at once engaged as a mate; and *her* ship, in particular, after doubling Cape Horn without loss, made the coast of Peru. Paita[47] was the port of her destination. Very near to this port they were, when a storm threw them upon a coral reef. There was little hope of the ship from the first, for she was unmanageable, and was not expected to hold together for twenty-four hours. In this condition, with death before their faces, mark what Kate did; and please to remember it for her benefit, when she does any other little thing that angers you. The crew lowered the long-boat. Vainly the Captain protested against this disloyal desertion of a king's ship, which might yet perhaps be run on shore, so as to save the stores. All the crew, to a man, deserted the captain. You may say *that* literally; for the single exception was *not* a man, being our bold-hearted Kate. She was the only sailor that refused to leave her captain, or the king of Spain's ship. The rest pulled away for the shore, and with fair hopes of reaching it. But one half hour told another tale: just about that time came a broad sheet of lightening, which, through the darkness of evening, revealed the boat in the very act of mounting like a horse upon an inner reef, instantly filling, and throwing out the crew, every man of whom disappeared amongst the breakers. The night which succeeded was gloomy for both the representatives of his Catholic Majesty. It cannot be denied by the greatest of philosophers, that the muleteer's stable at Valladolid was worth twenty such ships, though the stable was *not* insured against fire, and the ship *was* insured against the sea and the wind by some fellow that thought very little of his engagements. But what's the use of sitting down to cry? That was never any trick of Catalina's. By day-break, she was at work with an axe in her hand. I knew it, before ever I came to this place, in her memoirs. I felt, as sure as if I had read it, that, when day broke, we should find Kate hard at work. Thimble or axe, trowsers or raft, all one to *her*. The Captain, though true to his duty, seems to have desponded. He gave no help towards the raft. Signs were speaking, however, pretty loudly that he must do something; for notice to quit was now served pretty liberally. Kate's raft was ready; and she encouraged the captain to think that it would give both of them something to hold by in swimming, if not even carry double. At this moment, when all was waiting for a start, and the ship herself was waiting for a final lurch, to say *Good-bye* to the King of Spain, Kate went and did a thing which some misjudging people will object to. She knew of a box laden with gold coins, reputed to be the King of Spain's, and meant for contingencies in the voyage out. This she smashed open with her axe, and took a sum equal to 100 guineas English; which, having well secured in a pillow-case, she then lashed firmly to the raft. Now this, you know, though not '*flotsom*,' because it would not float, was certainly, by maritime law, '*jetsom*.' It would be the idlest of scruples to fancy that the sea or a shark had a better right to it than a philosopher, or a splendid girl who showed herself capable of writing a very fair 8vo,[48] to say nothing of her decapitating in battle several of the king's enemies, and recovering the king's banner. No sane moralist would hesitate to do the same thing under the same circumstances, on board an English vessel, though the First Lord of the Admiralty should be looking on. The raft was now thrown into the sea. Kate jumped after it, and then entreated the captain to follow her. He attempted it; but, wanting her youthful agility, he struck his head against a spar, and sank like lead, giving notice below that his ship was coming. Kate mounted the raft, and was gradually washed ashore, but so exhausted, as to have lost all recollection. She lay for hours until the warmth of the sun revived her. On sitting up, she saw a desolate shore stretching both ways – nothing to eat, nothing to drink, but fortunately the raft and the money had been thrown near her; none of the lashings having given way – only what is the use of a guinea amongst tangle and sea-gulls? The money she distributed amongst her pockets, and soon found strength to rise and march forward. But which *was* forward? and which backward? She knew by the conversation of the sailors that Paita must be in the neighbourhood; and Paita, being a port, could not be in the inside of Peru, but, of course, somewhere on its outside – and the outside of a maritime land must be the shore; so that, if she kept the shore, and went far enough, she could not fail of hitting her foot against Paita at last, in the very darkest night, provided only she could first find out which was *up* and which was *down*; else she might walk her shoes off, and find herself six thousand miles in the wrong. Here was an awkward case, all for want of a guide post. Still, when one thinks of Kate's prosperous horoscope, that after so long a voyage, *she* only, out of the total crew, was thrown on the American shore, with one hundred and five pounds in her purse of clear gain on the voyage, a conviction arises that she *could* not guess wrongly. She might have tossed up, having coins in her pocket, *heads or tails?* but this kind of sortilege was then coming to be thought irreligious in Christendom, as a Jewish and a Heathen mode of questioning the dark future. She simply guessed, therefore;

and very soon a thing happened which, though adding nothing to strengthen her guess as a true one, did much to sweeten it if it should prove a false one. On turning a point of the shore, she came upon a barrel of biscuit washed ashore from the ship. Biscuit is about the best thing I know,[49] but it is the soonest spoiled; and one would like to hear counsel on one puzzling point, why it is that a touch of water utterly ruins it, taking its life, and leaving a *caput mortuum*[50] corpse! Upon this *caput* Kate breakfasted, though *her* case was worse than mine; for any water that ever plagued *me* was always fresh; now *hers* was a present from the Pacific ocean. She, that was always prudent, packed up some of the Catholic king's biscuit, as she had previously packed up far too little of his gold. But in such cases a most delicate question occurs, pressing equally on medicine and algebra. It is this: if you pack up too much, then, by this extra burthen of salt provisions, you may retard for days your arrival at fresh provisions; on the other hand, if you pack up too little, you may never arrive at all. Catalina hit the *juste milieu;*[51] and about twilight on the second day, she found herself entering Paita, without having had to swim any river in her walk.

The first thing, in such a case of distress, which a young lady does, even if she happens to be a young gentleman, is to beautify her dress. Kate always attended to *that*, as we know, having overlooked her in the chestnut wood. The man she sent for was not properly a tailor, but one who employed tailors, he himself furnishing the materials. His name was Urquiza, a fact of very little importance to us in 1847, if it had stood only at the head and foot of Kate's little account. But unhappily for Kate's *début* on this vast American stage, the case was otherwise. Mr Urquiza had the misfortune (equally common in the old world and the new) of being a knave; and also a showy specious knave. Kate, who had prospered under sea allowances of biscuit and hardship, was now expanding in proportions. With very little vanity or consciousness on that head, she now displayed a really fine person; and, when drest anew in the way that became a young officer in the Spanish service, she looked* the representative picture of a Spanish *caballador*.[53] It is strange that such an appearance, and such a rank, should have suggested to Urquiza the presumptuous idea of wishing that Kate might become his clerk. He *did*, however, wish it; for Kate wrote a beautiful hand; and a stranger thing is, that Kate accepted his proposal. This might arise from the difficulty of moving in those

* '*She looked*,' &c. If ever the reader should visit Aix-la-Chapelle, he will probably feel interest enough in the poor, wild impassioned girl, to look out for a picture of her in that city, and the only one known *certainly* to be authentic. It is in the collection of Mr Sempaler.[52] For some time it was supposed that the best (if not the only) portrait of her lurked somewhere in Italy. Since the discovery of the picture at Aix-la-Chapelle, that notion has been abandoned. But there is great reason to believe that, both in Madrid and Rome, many portraits of her must have been painted to meet the intense interest which arose in her history subsequently amongst all the men of rank, military or ecclesiastical, whether in Italy or Spain. The date of these would range between sixteen and twenty-two years from the period which we have now reached (1608).

days to any distance in Peru. The ship had been merely bringing stores to the station of Paita; and no corps of the royal armies was readily to be reached, whilst something must be done at once for a livelihood. Urquiza had two mercantile establishments, one at Trujillo,[54] to which he repaired in person, on Kate's agreeing to undertake the management of the other in Paita. Like the sensible girl, that we have always found her, she demanded specific instruction for her guidance in duties so new. Certainly she was in a fair way for seeing life. Telling her beads at St Sebastian's, manoeuvring irregular verbs at Vittoria, acting as gentleman usher at Valladolid, serving his Spanish majesty round Cape Horn, fighting with storms and sharks off the coast of Peru, and now commencing as book-keeper or *commis*[55] to a draper at Paita, does she not justify the character that I myself gave her, just before dismissing her from St Sebastian's, of being a 'handy' girl? Mr Urquiza's instructions were short, easy to be understood, but rather comic; and yet, which is odd, they led to tragic results. There were two debtors of the shop, (*many*, it is to be hoped, but two meriting his affectionate notice) with respect to whom he left the most opposite directions. The one was a very handsome lady; and the rule as to *her* was, that she was to have credit unlimited, strictly unlimited. That was plain. The other customer, favoured by Mr Urquiza's valedictory thoughts, was a young man, cousin to the handsome lady;[56] and bearing the name of Reyes. This youth occupied in Mr Urquiza's estimate the same hyperbolical rank as the handsome lady, but on the opposite side of the equation. The rule as to *him* was – that he was to have *no* credit; strictly none. In this case, also, Kate saw no difficulty; and when she came to know Mr Reyes a little, she found the path of pleasure coinciding with the path of duty. Mr Urquiza could not be more precise in laying down the rule than Kate was in enforcing it. But in the other case a scruple arose. *Unlimited* might be a word, not of Spanish law, but of Spanish rhetoric; such as '*Live a thousand years*,' which even annuity offices hear, and perhaps utter, without a pang. Kate, therefore, wrote to Trujillo, expressing her honest fears, and desiring to have more definite instructions. These were positive. If the lady chose to send for the entire shop, her account was to be debited instantly with *that*. She had, however, as yet, not sent for the shop, but she began to manifest strong signs of sending for the shop*man*. Upon the blooming young Biscayan had her roving eye settled; and she was in a course of making up her mind to take Kate for a sweetheart. Poor Kate saw this with a heavy heart. And, at the same time that she had a prospect of a tender friend more than she wanted, she had become certain of an extra enemy that she wanted quite as little. What she had done to offend Mr Reyes, Kate could not guess, except as to the matter of the credit: but then, in that, she only executed her instructions. Still Mr Reyes was of opinion that there were two ways of executing orders: but the main offence was unintentional on Kate's part. Reyes, though as yet she did not know it, had himself been a candidate for the situation of clerk; and intended probably to keep the equation precisely as it was with respect to the allowance of credit, only to change places with the handsome lady – keeping *her* on the negative side, himself on the affirmative – an arrangement that you know could have made no sort of pecuniary difference to Urquiza.

Thus stood matters, when a party of strolling players strolled into Paita. Kate, as a Spaniard, being one held of the Paita aristocracy, was expected to attend. She did so; and there also was the malignant Reyes. He came and seated himself purposely so as to shut out Kate from all view of the stage. She, who had nothing of the bully in her nature, and was a gentle creature when her wild Biscayan blood had not been kindled by insult, courteously requested him to move a little: upon which Reyes remarked that it was not in his power to oblige the clerk as to that, but that he *could* oblige him by cutting his throat. The tiger that slept in Catalina wakened at once. She seized him, and would have executed vengeance on the spot, but that a party of young men interposed to part them. The next day, when Kate (always ready to forget and forgive) was thinking no more of the row, Reyes passed; by spitting at the window, and other gestures insulting to Kate, again he roused her Spanish blood. Out she rushed, sword in hand – a duel began in the street, and very soon Kate's sword had passed into the heart of Reyes. Now that the mischief was done, the police were, as usual, all alive for the pleasure of avenging it. Kate found herself suddenly in a strong prison, and with small hopes of leaving it, except for execution. The relations of the dead man were potent in Paita and clamorous for justice, so that the *corrégidor*,[57] in a case where he saw a very poor chance of being corrupted by bribes, felt it his duty to be sublimely incorruptible. The reader knows, however, that, amongst the relatives of the deceased bully, was that handsome lady, who differed as much from her cousin in her sentiments as to Kate, as she did in the extent of her credit with Mr Urquiza. To *her* Kate wrote a note; and using one of the Spanish King's gold coins for bribing the jailor, got it safely delivered. That, perhaps, was unnecessary; for the lady had been already on the alert, and had summoned Urquiza from Trujillo. By some means, not very luminously stated, and by paying proper fees in proper quarters, Kate was smuggled out of the prison at nightfall, and smuggled into a pretty house in the suburbs. Had she known exactly the footing she stood on as to the law, she would have been decided. As it was, she was uneasy, and jealous of mischief abroad; and, before supper, she understood it all. Urquiza briefly informed his clerk, that it would be requisite for him to marry the handsome lady. But why? Because, said Urquiza, after talking for hours with the *corrégidor*, who was infamous for obstinacy, he had found it impossible to make him 'hear reason,'[58] and release the prisoner, until this compromise of marriage was suggested. But how could public justice be pacified for the clerk's unfortunate homicide of Reyes, by a female cousin of the deceased man engaging to love, honour, and obey the clerk for life? Kate could not see her way through this logic. 'Nonsense, my friend,' said Urquiza, 'you don't comprehend. As it stands, the affair is a murder, and hanging the penalty. But, if you marry into the murdered man's house, then it becomes a little family murder, all quiet and comfortable amongst ourselves. What has the *corrégidor* to do with that? or the public either? Now, let me introduce the bride.' Supper entered at that moment, and the bride immediately after. The thoughtfulness of Kate was narrowly observed, and even alluded to, but politely ascribed to the natural anxieties of a prisoner, and the very imperfect state of liberation even yet from prison *surveillance*. Kate had, indeed, never been in so trying a situation before. The anxieties of the farewell night at St Sebastian were nothing to this; because, even if she had failed *then*, a failure might not have been always irreparable. It was but to watch and wait. But now, at this supper table, she was not more alive to the nature of the peril than she was to the fact, that if, before the night closed, she did not by some means escape from it, she never *would* escape with life. The deception as to her sex, though resting on no motive that pointed to these people, or at all concerned them, would be resented as if it had. The lady would resent the case as a mockery; and Urquiza would lose his opportunity of delivering himself from an imperious mistress. According to the usages of the times and country, Kate knew that in twelve hours she would be assassinated.

People of infirmer resolution would have lingered at the supper-table, for the sake of putting off the evil moment of final crisis. Not so Kate.[59] She had revolved the case on all its sides in a few minutes, and had formed her resolution. This done, she was as ready for the trial at one moment as another; and, when the lady suggested that the hardships of a prison must have made repose desirable, Kate assented, and instantly rose. A sort of procession formed, for the purpose of doing honour to the interesting guest, and escorting him in pomp to his bed-room. Kate viewed it much in the same light as the procession to which for some days she had been expecting an invitation from the *corrégidor*. Far ahead ran the servant-woman as a sort of outrider. Then came Urquiza, like a Pasha of two tails,[60] who granted two sorts of credit, viz. unlimited and none at all, bearing two wax-lights, one in each hand, and wanting only cymbals and kettle drums to express emphatically the pathos of his Castillian strut. Next came the bride, a little in advance of the clerk, but still turning obliquely towards him, and smiling graciously into his face. Lastly, bringing up the rear, came the prisoner – our Kate – the nun, the page, the mate, the clerk, the homicide, the convict; and, for this day only, by particular desire, the bridegroom elect.

It was Kate's fixed opinion, that, if for a moment she entered any bedroom having obviously no outlet, her fate would be that of an ox once driven within the shambles. Outside, the bullock might make some defence with his horns; but once in, with no space for turning, he is muffled and gagged. She carried her eye, therefore, like a hawk's, steady, though restless, for vigilant examination of every angle she turned. Before she entered any bed-room, she was resolved to reconnoiter it from the doorway, and, in the case of necessity, show fight at once, before entering – as the best chance, after all, where all chances were bad. Everything ends; and at last the procession reached the bed-room door, the outrider having filed off to the rear. One glance sufficed to satisfy Kate that windows there were none, and, therefore, no outlet for escape. Treachery appeared even in *that;* and Kate, though unfortunately without arms, was now fixed for resistance. Mr Urquiza entered first – 'Sound the trumpets! Beat the drums!'[61] There were, as we know already, no windows; but a slight interruption to Mr Urquiza's pompous tread showed that there were steps downwards into the room. Those, thought Kate, will suit me even better. She had watched the unlocking of the bed-room door – she had lost nothing – she had marked that the key was left in the lock. At this moment, the beautiful lady, as one acquainted with the details of the house, turning with the air of a gracious monitress, held out her fair hand to guide Kate in careful descent of the steps. This had the air of taking out Kate to dance; and Kate, at that same moment, answering to it by the gesture of a modern waltzer, threw her arm behind the lady's waist, hurled her headlong down the steps right against Mr Urquiza, draper and haberdasher; and then, with the speed of lightening, throwing the door *home* within its architrave, doubly locked the creditor and debtor into the rat-trap which they had prepared for herself.

The affrighted out-rider fled with horror; she already knew that the clerk had committed one homicide; a second would cost him still less thought; and thus it happened that egress was left easy. But, when out and free once more in the bright starry night, which way should Kate turn? The whole city would prove but a rat-trap for her, as bad as Mr Urquiza's, if she was not off before morning. At a glance she comprehended that the sea was her only chance. To the port she fled. All was silent. Watchmen there were none. She jumped into a boat. To use the oars was dangerous, for she had no means of muffling them. But she contrived to hoist a sail, pushed off with a boat hook, and was soon stretching across the water for the mouth of the harbour before a breeze light but favourable. Having cleared the difficulties of exit she lay down, and unintentionally fell asleep. When she awoke the sun had been up for three or four hours; all was right otherwise; but had she not served as a sailor, Kate would have trembled upon finding that, during her long sleep of perhaps seven or eight hours, she had lost sight of land; by what distance she could only guess; and in what direction, was to some degree doubtful. All this, however, seemed a great advantage to the bold girl, throwing her thoughts back on the enemies she had left behind. The disadvantage was – having no breakfast, not even damaged biscuit; and some anxiety naturally arose as to ulterior prospects a little beyond the horizon of breakfast. But who's afraid? As sailors whistle for a wind,[62] Catalina really had but to whistle for anything with energy, and it was sure to come. Like Caesar to the pilot of Dyrrhachium, she might have said, for the comfort of her poor timorous boat, (though destined soon to perish,) '*Catalinam vehis, et fortunas ejus.*'[63] Meantime, being very doubtful as to the best course for sailing, and content if her course did but lie off shore, she 'carried on,' as sailors say, under easy sail, going, in fact, just whither and just how the Pacific breezes suggested in the gentlest of whispers. *All right behind*, was Kate's opinion; and, what was better, very soon she might say, *all right ahead*: for some hour or two before sunset, when dinner was for once becoming, even to Kate, the most interesting of subjects for meditation, suddenly a large ship began to swell upon the brilliant atmosphere. In those latitudes, and in those years, any ship was pretty sure to be Spanish: sixty years later the odds were in favour of its being an English buccaneer: which would have given a new direction to Kate's energy. Kate continued to make signals with a handkerchief whiter than the crocodile's of Ann. Dom.[64] 1592, else it would hardly have been noticed. Perhaps, after all, it would not, but that the ship's course carried her very nearly across Kate's. The stranger lay-to for her. It was dark by the time Kate steered herself under the ship's quarter; and *then* was seen an instance of this girl's eternal wakefulness. Something was painted on the stern of her boat, she could not see *what*; but she judged that it would express some connexion with the port that she had just quitted. Now it was her wish to break the chain of traces connecting her with such a scamp as Urquiza; since else, through his commercial correspondence, he might disperse over Peru a portrait of herself by no means flattering. How should she accomplish this? It was dark; and she stood, as you may see an Etonian do at times,[65] rocking her little boat from side to side, until it had taken in water as much as might be agreeable. Too much it proved for the boat's constitution, and the boat perished of dropsy – Kate declining to tap it. She got a ducking herself; but what cared she? Up the ship's side she went, as gaily as ever, in those years when she was called pussy, she had raced after the nuns of St Sebastian; jumped upon deck, and told the first-lieutenant, when he questioned her about her adventures, quite as much truth as any man, under the rank of admiral, had a right to expect.

(*To be concluded in the next Number.*)

THE NAUTICO-MILITARY NUN OF SPAIN
[PART II]

First published in *Tait's*, XIV, June 1847, pp. 369–76. Two centred lines followed the title of the essay and immediately preceded the text. The first stated that the essay was 'BY THOMAS DE QUINCEY.', and the second that it was '*(Continued from page* 333.*)*' to denote where in *Tait's* Part I of the essay ended.

Reprinted in *F*, VII, *Narrative and Miscellaneous Papers* (1852), pp. 143–69, pp. 203–5.

Revised text, carrying many accidentals but only two substantive variants from *F*, in *SGG*, III, *Miscellanies, Chiefly Narrative* (1854), pp. 35–60.

There are three manuscripts, as follows:

MS A: Worcester College, Oxford, MS 128. The manuscript is a single sheet of blue paper, measuring 180 by 225mm, with writing in black ink on the recto only. There is no watermark. It corresponds to the passage below running from p. 120.31 'time and space!' to p. 121.7–8 'thought had struck her all at once,'.

MS B: Huntington Library, HM 31019. The manuscript is a complete set of *SGG* page proofs.

MS C: Huntington Library, HM 31019. The manuscript is three endnotes from *F*, corresponding to the text below running from p. 112.42 '*Alférez*. This rank' to p. 112.43 '*sous-lieutenant* of France.'; from p. 116.43 'The beautiful words' to p. 116.43 '"*Defense of Poesie*."'; and from p. 123.41 'Though not exactly' to p. 124.50 'so fatally frequent.'.

The three manuscripts contain twenty-four significant variants, and these are listed in the textual notes.

For the context and occasion of the article, see headnote, pp. 90–3.

THIS ship was full of recruits for the Spanish army, and bound to Concepcion.[1] Even in that destiny was an iteration, or repeating memorial of the significance that ran through Catalina's most casual adventures. She had enlisted amongst the soldiers; and, on reaching port, the very first person who came off from shore was a dashing young military officer, whom at once by his name and rank, (though she had never consciously seen him,) she identified as her own brother.[2] He was splendidly situated in the service, being the Governor-General's secretary, besides his rank as a cavalry officer; and, his errand on board being to inspect the recruits, naturally, on reading in the roll one of them described as a Biscayan, the ardent young man came up with high-bred courtesy to Catalina, took the young recruit's hand with kindness, feeling that to be a compatriot at so great a distance was to be a sort of relative, and asked with emotion after old boyish remembrances. There was a scriptural pathos in what followed, as if it were some scene of domestic reunion, opening itself from patriarchal ages. The young officer was the eldest son of the house, and had left Spain when Catalina was only three years old. But, singularly enough, Catalina it was, the little wild cat that he yet remembered seeing at St Sebastians, upon whom his earliest inquiries settled. 'Did the recruit know his family, the De Erausos?' Oh yes, every body knew *them*. 'Did the recruit know little Catalina?' Catalina smiled, as she replied that she did; and gave such an animated description of the little fiery wretch, as made the officer's eyes flash with gratified tenderness, and with certainty that the recruit was no counterfeit Biscayan. Indeed, you know, if Kate couldn't give a good description of 'Pussy', who could? The issue of the interview was – that the officer insisted on Kate's making a home of his quarters. He did other services for his unknown sister. He placed her as a trooper in his own regiment, and favoured her in many a way that is open to one having authority. But the person, after all, that did most to serve our Kate, was Kate. War was then raging with Indians, from both Chili and Peru. Kate had always done her duty in action; but at length, in the decisive battle of Puren, there was an opening for doing something more. Havock had been made of her own squadron; most of the officers were killed, and the standard was carried off. Kate gathered around her a small party – galloped after the Indian column that was carrying away the trophy – charged – saw all her own party killed – but (in spite of wounds on her face and shoulder) succeeded in bearing away the recovered standard. She rode up to the general and his staff; she dismounted; she rendered up her prize; and fainted away, much less from the blinding blood, than from the tears of joy which dimmed her eyes, as the general, waving his sword in admiration over her head, pronounced our Kate on the spot an *Alférez*,* or standard-bearer, with a commission from the King of Spain and the Indies. Bonny Kate! Noble Kate! I would there were not two centuries laid between us, so that I might have the pleasure of kissing thy fair hand.

Kate had the good sense to see the danger of revealing her sex, or her relationship, even to her own brother. The grasp of the Church never relaxed, never 'prescribed,'[4] unless freely and by choice. The nun, if discovered, would have been taken out of the horse-barracks, or the dragoon-saddle. She had the firmness, therefore, for many years, to resist the sisterly impulses that sometimes suggested such a confidence. For years, and those years the most important of her life – the years that developed her character – she lived

* *Alférez*. This rank in the Spanish army is, or was, on a level with the modern *sous-lieutenant*[3] of France.

undetected as a brilliant cavalry officer under her brother's patronage. And the bitterest grief in poor Kate's whole life, was the tragical (and, were it not fully attested, one might say the ultra-scenical) event that dissolved their long connexion. Let me spend a word of apology on poor Kate's errors. We all commit many; both you and I, reader. No, stop; that's not civil. You, reader, I know, are a saint; I am *not*, though very near it. I *do* err at long intervals; and then I think with indulgence of the many circumstances that plead for this poor girl. The Spanish armies of that day inherited, from the days of Cortez and Pizarro,[5] shining remembrances of martial prowess, and the very worst of ethics. To think little of bloodshed, to quarrel, to fight, to gamble, to plunder, belonged to the very atmosphere of a camp, to its indolence, to its ancient traditions. In your own defence, you were obliged to do such things. Besides all these grounds of evil, the Spanish army had just there an extra demoralization from a war with savages – faithless and bloody. Do not think, I beseech you, too much, reader, of killing a man. That word '*kill*' is sprinkled over every page of Kate's own autobiography. It ought not to be read by the light of these days. Yet, how if a man that she killed were ——? Hush! It was sad; but is better hurried over in a few words. Years after this period, a young officer one day dining with Kate, entreated her to become his second in a duel. Such things were every-day affairs. However, Kate had reasons for declining the service, and did so. But the officer, as he was sullenly departing, said – that, if he were killed, (as he thought he *should* be) his death would lie at Kate's door. I do not take *his* view of the case, and am not moved by his rhetoric or his logic. Kate *was*, and relented. The duel was fixed for eleven at night, under the walls of a monastery. Unhappily the night proved unusually dark, so that the two principals had to tie white handkerchiefs round their elbows, in order to descry each other. In the confusion they wounded each other mortally. Upon that, according to a usage not peculiar to Spaniards, but extending (as doubtless the reader knows) for a century longer to our own countrymen, the two seconds were obliged in honour to do something towards avenging their principals. Kate had her usual fatal luck. Her sword passed sheer through the body of her opponent: this unknown opponent falling dead, had just breath left to cry out, 'Ah, villain, you have killed me,' in a voice of horrific reproach; and the voice was the voice of her brother!

The monks of the monastery, under whose silent shadows this murderous duel had taken place, roused by the clashing of swords and the angry shouts of combatants, issued out with torches to find one only of the four officers surviving. Every convent and altar had a right of asylum for a short period. According to the custom, the monks carried Kate, insensible with anguish of mind, to the sanctuary of their chapel. There for some days they detained her; but then, having furnished her with a horse and some provisions, they turned her adrift. Which way should the unhappy fugitive turn? In blindness of heart, she turned towards the sea. It was the sea that had brought her to Peru; it was the sea that would perhaps carry her away. It was the sea that had first showed her this land and its golden hopes; it was the sea that ought to hide from her its fearful remembrances. The sea it was that had twice spared her life in extremities; the sea it was that might now, if it chose, take back the bauble that it had spared in vain.

KATE'S PASSAGE OVER THE ANDES.

Three days our poor heroine followed the coast. Her horse was then almost unable to move; and, on *his* account, she turned inland to a thicket for grass and shelter. As she drew near to it, a voice challenged – '*Who goes there?*' Kate answered, '*Spain.*' '*What people?*' '*A friend.*' It was two soldiers, deserters, and almost starving. Kate shared her provisions with these men: and, on hearing their plan, which was to go over the Cordilleras,[6] she agreed to join the party. *Their* object was the wild one of seeking the river *Dorado*, whose waters rolled along golden sands, and whose pebbles were emeralds.[7] *Hers* was to throw herself upon a line the least liable to pursuit, and the readiest for a new chapter of life in which oblivion might be found for the past. After a few days of incessant climbing and fatigue, they found themselves in the regions of perpetual snow. Summer would come as vainly to this kingdom of frost as to the grave of her brother. No fire, but the fire of human blood in youthful veins, could ever be kept burning in these aerial solitudes. Fuel was rarely to be found, and kindling a secret hardly known except to Indians. However, our Kate can do everything, and she's the girl, if ever girl *did* such a thing, or ever girl did *not* such a thing, that I back at any odds for crossing the Cordilleras. I would bet you something now, reader, if I thought you would deposit your stakes by return of post (as they play at chess through the post office), that Kate does the trick, that she gets down to the other side: that the soldiers do *not:* and that the horse, if preserved at all, is preserved in a way that will leave him very little to boast of.

The party had gathered wild berries and esculent roots at the foot of the mountains, and the horse was of very great use in carrying them. But this larder was soon emptied. There was nothing then to carry; so that the horse's value, as a beast of burthen, fell cent. per cent. In fact, very soon he could not carry himself, and it became easy to calculate when he would reach the bottom on the wrong side of the Cordilleras. He took three steps back for one upwards. A council of war being held, the small army resolved to slaughter their horse. He, though a member of the expedition, had no vote, and if he had the votes would have stood three to one – majority, two against him. He was cut into quarters; which surprises me; for unless *one* quarter was considered his own share, it reminds one too much of this amongst the many *facetioe*[8] of English midshipmen, who ask (on any one of their number looking sulky) 'if it is his intention to marry and retire from the service upon a superannuation of £4 4s. $4\frac{1}{2}$d. a year, paid quarterly by way of bothering the purser.' The purser can't do it with the help of farthings. And, as respects aliquot parts, four shares among three persons, are as incommensurable as a guinea is against any attempt at giving change in half-crowns. However, this was all the preservation that the horse found. No saltpetre or sugar could be had: but the frost was antiseptic. And the horse was preserved in as useful a sense as ever apricots were preserved or strawberries.

On a fire, painfully devised out of broom and withered leaves, a horse-steak was dressed; for drink, snow was allowed *a discretion*.[9] This ought to have revived the party, and Kate, perhaps, it *did*. But the poor deserters were thinly clad, and they had not the boiling heart of Catalina. More and more they drooped. Kate did her best to cheer them. But the march was nearly at an end for *them*, and they were going in one half hour to receive their last billet. Yet, before this consummation, they have a strange spectacle to see; such as few places could show, but the upper chambers of the Cordilleras. They had reached a billowy scene of rocky masses, large and small, looking shockingly black on their perpendicular sides as they rose out of the vast snowy expanse. Upon the highest of these, that was accessible, Kate mounted to look around her, and she saw – oh, rapture at such an hour! – a man sitting on a shelf of rock with a gun by his side. She shouted with joy to her comrades, and ran down to communicate the joyful news. Here was a sportsman, watching, perhaps, for an eagle; and now they would have relief. One man's cheek kindled with the hectic of sudden joy, and he rose eagerly to march. The other was fast sinking under the fatal sleep that frost sends before herself as her merciful minister of death; but hearing in his dream the tidings of relief, and assisted by his friends, he also staggeringly arose. It could not be three minutes' walk, Kate thought, to the station of the sportsman. That thought supported them all. Under Kate's guidance, who had taken a sailor's glance at the bearings, they soon unthreaded the labyrinth of rocks so far as to bring the man within view. He had not left his resting-place; their steps on the soundless snow, naturally, he could not hear; and, as their road brought them upon him from the rear, still less could he see them. Kate hailed him; but so keenly was he absorbed in some speculation, or in the object of his watching, that he took no notice of them, not even moving his head. Kate began to think there would be another man to rouse from sleep. Coming close behind him she touched his shoulder, and said, 'My friend, are you sleeping?' Yes, he *was* sleeping; sleeping the sleep from which there is no awaking;[10] and the slight touch of Kate having disturbed the equilibrium of the corpse, down it rolled on the snow; the frozen body rang like a hollow iron cylinder; the face uppermost and blue with mould, mouth open, teeth ghastly and bleaching in the frost, and a frightful grin upon the lips. This dreadful spectacle finished the struggles of the weaker man, who sank and died at once. The other made an effort with so much spirit, that, in Kate's opinion, horror had acted upon him beneficially as a stimulant. But it was not really so. It was a spasm of morbid strength; a collapse succeeded; his blood began to freeze; he sat down in spite of Kate, and *he* also died without further struggle. Gone are the poor suffering deserters; stretched and bleaching upon the snow; and insulted discipline is avenged. Great kings have long arms; and sycophants are ever at hand for the errand of the potent. What had frost and snow to do with the quarrel? Yet *they* made themselves sycophantic servants of the King of Spain; and *they* dogged his deserters up to the summit of the Cordilleras, more surely than any Spanish bloodhound, or any Spanish tirailleur's bullet.[11]

Now is our Kate standing alone on the summits of the Andes, in solitude that is shocking, for she is alone with her own afflicted conscience. Twice before she had stood in solitude as deep upon the wild – wild waters of the Pacific; but her conscience had been then untroubled. Now, is there nobody left that can help; her horse is dead – the soldiers are dead. There is nobody that she can speak to except God; and very soon you will find that she *does* speak to him; for already on these vast aerial deserts He has been whispering to *her*. The condition of Kate is exactly that of Coleridge's '*Ancient Mariner*.'[12] But possibly, reader, you may be amongst the many careless readers that have never fully understood what that condition was. Suffer me to enlighten you, else you ruin the story of the mariner; and by losing all its pathos, lose half the jewels of its beauty.

There are three readers of the 'Ancient Mariner.' The first is gross enough to fancy all the imagery of the mariner's visions delivered by the poet for actual facts of experience; which being impossible, the whole pulverises, for that reader, into a baseless fairy-tale. The second reader is wiser than *that*; he knows that the imagery is *not* baseless; it is the imagery of febrile delirium; really seen, but not seen as an external reality. The mariner had caught the pestilential fever, which carried off all his mates; he only had survived – the delirium had vanished; but the visions that had haunted the delirium remained. 'Yes,' says the third reader, 'they remained; naturally they did, being scorched by fever into his brain; but how did they happen to remain on his belief as gospel truths? The delirium had vanished: why had not the painted scenery of the delirium vanished, except as visionary memorials of a sorrow that was cancelled? Why was it that craziness settled upon this mariner's brain, driving him, as if he were a Cain, or another Wandering Jew, to 'pass like night – from land to land;'[13] and, at uncertain intervals, wrenching him until he made rehearsal of his errors, even at the hard price of 'holding children from their play, and old men from the chimney corner?'* That craziness, as the *third* reader deciphers, rose out of a deeper soil than any bodily affection. It had its root in penitential sorrow. Oh, bitter is the sorrow to a conscientious heart, when, too late, it discovers the depth of a love that has been trampled under foot! This mariner had slain the creature that, on all the earth, loved him best. In the darkness of his cruel superstition he had done it,

* The beautiful words of Sir Philip Sydney, in his '*Defense of Poesie*.'[14]

to save his human brothers from a fancied inconvenience; and yet, by that very act of cruelty, he had himself called destruction upon their heads. The Nemesis[15] that followed punished *him* through *them* – him, that wronged, through those that wrongfully he sought to benefit. That spirit who watches over the sanctities of love is a strong angel – is a jealous angel; and this angel it was

> 'That lov'd the bird, that lov'd the man,
> That shot him with his bow.'[16]

He it was that followed the cruel archer into silent and slumbering seas;

> 'Nine fathom deep he had follow'd him
> Through the realms of mist and snow.'[17]

This jealous angel it was that pursued the man into noon-day darkness, and the vision of dying oceans, into delirium, and finally, (when recovered from disease) into an unsettled mind.

Such, also, had been the offence of Kate; such, also, was the punishment that now is dogging her steps. She, like the mariner, had slain the one sole creature that loved her upon the whole wide earth; she, like the mariner, for this offence, had been hunted into frost and snow – very soon will be hunted into delirium; and from *that* (if she escapes with life) will be hunted into the trouble of a heart that cannot rest. There was the excuse of one darkness for *her;* there was the excuse of another darkness for the mariner. But, with all the excuses that earth, and the darkness of earth, can furnish, bitter it would be for you or me, reader, through every hour of life, waking or dreaming, to look back upon one fatal moment when we had pierced the heart that would have died for *us*. In this only the darkness had been merciful to Kate – that it had hidden for ever from her victim the hand that slew him. But now in such utter solitude, her thoughts ran back to their earliest interview. She remembered with anguish, how, on first touching the shores of America, almost the very first word that had met her ear had been from *him*, the brother whom she had killed, about the 'Pussy' of times long past; how the gallant young man had hung upon her words, as in her native Basque she described her own mischievous little self, of twelve years back; how his colour went and came, whilst his loving memory of the little sister was revived by her own descriptive traits, giving back, as in a mirror, the fawn-like grace, the squirrel-like restlessness, that once had kindled his own delighted laughter; how he would take no denial, but showed on the spot, that, simply to have touched – to have kissed – to have played with the little wild thing, that glorified, by her innocence, the gloom of St Sebastian's cloisters, gave a *right* to his hospitality; how, through *him* only, she had found a welcome in camps; how, through *him*, she had found the avenue to honour and distinction. And yet this brother, so loving and generous, it was that she had dismissed from life. She paused; she turned round, as if looking back for his grave; she saw the dreadful wildernesses of snow which already she had traversed. Silent they were at this season, even as in the panting heats of noon, the Zaarrahs[18] of the torrid zone are oftentimes silent. Dreadful was the silence; it was the nearest thing to the silence of the grave. Graves were at the foot of the Andes, *that* she knew too well; graves were at the summit of the Andes, *that* she saw too well. And, as she gazed, a sudden thought flashed upon her, when her eyes settled upon the corpses of the poor deserters, – could she, like *them*, have been all this while unconsciously executing judgment upon herself? Running from a wrath that was doubtful, into the very jaws of a wrath that was inexorable? Flying in panic – and behold! there was no man that pursued?[19] For the first time in her life, Kate trembled. *Not* for the first time, Kate wept. Far less for the first time was it, that Kate bent her knee – that Kate clapsed her hands – that Kate prayed. But it *was* the first time that she prayed as *they* pray, for whom no more hope is left but in prayer.

Here let me pause a moment for the sake if making somebody angry. A Frenchman, who sadly misjudges Kate, looking at her through a Parisian opera-glass, gives it as *his* opinion – that, because Kate first *records* her prayer on this occasion, therefore, now first of all she prayed.[20] *I* think not so. *I* love this Kate, blood-stained as she is; and I could not love a woman that never bent her knee in thankfulness or in supplication. However, we have all a right to our own little opinion; and it is not *you*, '*mon cher*,'[21] you Frenchman, that I am angry with, but somebody else that stands behind you. You, Frenchman, and your compatriots, I love oftentimes for your festal gaiety of heart; and I quarrel only with your levity and that eternal worldliness that freezes too fiercely – that absolutely blisters with its frost – like the upper air of the Andes. *You* speak of Kate only as too readily you speak of all women; the instinct of a natural scepticism being to scoff at all hidden depths of truth. Else you are civil enough to Kate; and your '*homage*' (such as it may happen to be) is always at the service of a woman on the shortest notice. But behind *you*, I see a worse fellow; a gloomy fanatic; a religious sycophant that seeks to propitiate his circle by bitterness against the offences that are most unlike his own. And against him, I must say one word for Kate to the too hasty reader. This villain, whom I mark for a shot if he does not get out of the way, opens his fire on our Kate under shelter of a lie. For there is a standing lie in the very constitution of civil society, a *necessity* of error, misleading us as to the proportions of crime. Mere necessity obliges man to create many acts into felonies, and to punish them as the heaviest offences, which his better sense teaches him secretly to regard as perhaps among the lightest. Those poor deserters, for instance, were they necessarily without excuse? They might have been oppressively used; but in critical times of war, no matter for the individual palliations, the deserter from his colours *must* be shot: there is no help for it: as in extremities of general famine, we shoot the man [alas! we are *obliged* to shoot him] that is found robbing the common stores in order to feed his own perishing children, though the offence is hardly visible in the sight of God.

Only blockheads adjust their scale of guilt to the scale of human punishments. Now, our wicked friend the fanatic, who calumniates Kate, abuses the advantage which, for such a purpose, he derives from the exaggerated social estimate of all violence. Personal security being so main an object of social union, we are obliged to frown upon all modes of violence as hostile to the central principle of that union. We are *obliged* to rate it, according to the universal results towards which it tends, and scarcely at all, according to the special condition of circumstances, in which it may originate. Hence a horror arises for that class of offences, which is (philosophically speaking) exaggerated; and by daily use, the ethics of a police-office translate themselves, insensibly, into the ethics even of religious people. But I tell that sycophantish fanatic – not this only, viz., that he abuses unfairly, against Kate, the advantage which he has from the *inevitably* distorted bias of society; but also, I tell him this second little thing, viz., that upon turning away the glass from that one obvious aspect of Kate's character, her too fiery disposition to vindicate all rights by violence, and viewing her in relation to *general* religious capacities, she was a thousand times more promisingly endowed than himself. It is impossible to be noble in many things, without having many points of contact with true religion. If you deny *that*, you it is that calumniate religion. Kate *was* noble in many things. Her worst errors never took a shape of self-interest or deceit. She was brave, she was generous, she was forgiving, she bore no malice, she was full of truth – qualities that God loves either in man or woman. She hated sycophants and dissemblers. *I* hate them; and more than ever at this moment on her behalf. I wish she were but here – to give a punch on the head to that fellow who traduces her. And, coming round again to the occasion from which this short digression has started, viz., the question raised by the Frenchman – whether Kate were a person likely to *pray* under other circumstances than those of extreme danger? I offer it as *my* opinion that she was. Violent people are not always such from choice, but perhaps from situation. And, though the circumstances of Kate's position allowed her little means for realising her own wishes, it is certain that those wishes pointed continually to peace and an unworldly happiness, if *that* were possible. The stormy clouds that enveloped her in camps, opened overhead at intervals – showing her a far distant blue serene.[22] She yearned, at many times, for the rest which is not in camps or armies; and it is certain, that she ever combined with any plans or day-dreams of tranquillity, as their most essential ally, some aid derived from that dovelike religion which, at St Sebastian's, as an infant and through girlhood, she had been taught so profoundly to adore.

Now, let us rise from this discussion of Kate against libellers, as Kate herself is rising from prayer, and consider, in conjunction with *her*, the character and promise of that dreadful ground which lies immediately before her. What is to be thought of it? I could wish we had a theodolite here, and a spirit-level, and other instruments, for settling some important questions. Yet no: on consideration, if one *had* a wish allowed by that kind fairy, without whose assistance it would be quite impossible to send, even for the spirit-level, nobody would throw away the wish upon things so paltry; I would not put the fairy upon any such errand: I would order the good creature to bring no spirit-level, but a stiff glass of spirits for Kate – a palanquin, and relays of fifty stout bearers – all drunk, in order that they might not feel the cold. The main interest at this moment, and the main difficulty – indeed, the 'open question' of the case – was, to ascertain whether the ascent were yet accomplished or not; and when would the descent commence? or had it, perhaps, long commenced? The character of the ground, in those immediate successions that could be connected by the eye, decided nothing; for the undulations of the level had been so continual for miles, as to perplex any eye but an engineer's, in attempting to judge whether, upon the whole, the tendency were upwards or downwards. Possibly it was yet neither way; it is, indeed, probable, that Kate had been for some time travelling along a series of terraces, that traversed the whole breadth of the topmost area at that point of crossing the Cordilleras, and which perhaps, but not certainly, compensated any casual tendencies downwards by corresponding reascents. Then came the question – how long would these terraces yet continue? and had the ascending parts *really* balanced the descending? – upon *that* seemed to rest the final chance for Kate. Because, unless she very soon reached a lower level, and a warmer atmosphere, mere weariness would oblige her to lie down, under a fierceness of cold, that would not suffer her to rise after once losing the warmth of motion; or, inversely, if she even continued in motion, mere extremity of cold would of itself, speedily absorb the little surplus energy for moving, which yet remained unexhausted by weariness.

At this stage of her progress, and whilst the agonising question seemed yet as indeterminate as ever, Kate's struggle with despair, which had been greatly soothed by the fervour of her prayer, revolved upon her in deadlier blackness. All turned, she saw, upon a race against time, and the arrears of the road; and she, poor thing! how little qualified could *she* be, in such a condition, for a race of any kind; and against two such obstinate brutes as time and space! This hour of the progress, this noontide of Kate's struggle, must have been the very crisis of the whole. Despair was rapidly tending to ratify itself. Hope, in any degree, would be a cordial for sustaining her efforts. But to flounder along a dreadful chaos of snow-drifts, or snow-chasms, towards a point of rock, which, being turned, should expose only another interminable succession of the same character – might *that* be endured by ebbing spirits, by stiffening limbs, by the ghastly darkness that was now beginning to gather upon the inner eye? And, if once despair became triumphant, all the little arrear of physical strength would collapse at once.

Oh! verdure of human fields, cottages of men and women (that now suddenly seemed all brothers and sisters), cottages with children around them at play, that are so far below – oh! summer and spring, flowers and blossoms, to which, as to *his* symbols, God has given the gorgeous privilege of rehearsing for ever upon earth his most mysterious perfection – Life, and the resurrections of Life – is it indeed true, that poor Kate must never see you more? Mutteringly she put that question to herself. But strange are the caprices of ebb and flow in the deep fountains of human sensibilities. At this very moment, when the utter incapacitation of despair was gathering fast at Kate's heart, a sudden lightening shot far into her spirit, a reflux almost supernatural, from the earliest effects of her prayer. A thought had struck her all at once, and this thought prompted her immediately to turn round. Perhaps it was in some blind yearning after the only memorials of life in this frightful region, that she fixed her eye upon a point of hilly ground by which she identified the spot near which the three corpses were lying. The silence seemed deeper than ever. Neither was there any phantom memorial of life for the eye or for the ear, nor wing of bird, nor echo, nor green leaf, nor creeping thing,[23] that moved or stirred, upon the soundless waste.[24] Oh, what a relief to this burthen of silence would be a human groan! Here seemed a motive for still darker despair. And yet, at that very moment, a pulse of joy began to thaw the ice at her heart. It struck her, as she reviewed the ground, that undoubtedly it had been for some time slowly descending. Her senses were much dulled by suffering; but this thought it was, suggested by a sudden apprehension of a continued descending movement, which had caused her to turn round. Sight had confirmed the suggestion first derived from her own steps. The distance attained was now sufficient to establish the tendency. Oh, yes, yes, to a certainty she had been descending for some time. Frightful was the spasm of joy which whispered that the worst was over. It was as when the shadow of midnight, that murderers had relied on, is passing away from your beleaguered shelter, and dawn will soon be manifest. It was as when a flood, that all day long has raved against the walls of your house, has ceased (you suddenly think) to rise; yes! measured by a golden plummet, it *is* sinking beyond a doubt, and the darlings of your household are saved. Kate faced round in agitation to her proper direction. She saw, what previously, in her stunning confusion, she had *not* seen, that, hardly two stones' throw in advance, lay a mass of rock, split as into a gateway. Through that opening it now became probable that the road was lying. Hurrying forward, she passed within the natural gates. Gates of paradise they were. Ah, what a vista did that gateway expose before her dazzled eye? what a revelation of heavenly promise? Full two miles long, stretched a long narrow glen, everywhere descending, and in many parts rapidly. All was now placed beyond a doubt. She *was* descending – for hours perhaps *had* been descending insensibly, the mighty staircase. Yes, Kate is leaving behind her the kingdom of frost and the victories of death. Two miles farther there may be rest, if there is not shelter. And very soon, as the crest of her new-born happiness, she distinguished at the other end of that rocky vista, a pavilion-shaped mass of dark-green foliage – a belt of trees, such as we see in the lovely parks of England, but islanded by a screen (though not everywhere occupied by the usurpations) of a thick bushy undergrowth. Oh, verdure of dark-olive foliage, offered suddenly to fainting eyes, as if by some winged patriarchal herald of wrath relenting[25] – solitary Arab's tent, rising with saintly signals of peace, in the dreadful desert, must Kate indeed die even yet, whilst she sees but cannot reach you? Outpost on the frontier of man's dominions, standing within life, but looking out upon everlasting death, wilt thou hold up the anguish of thy mocking invitation, only to betray? Never, perhaps, in this world was the line so exquisitely grazed, that parts salvation and ruin. As the dove to her dove-cot from the swooping hawk – as the Christian pinnace to Christian batteries, from the bloody Mahometan corsair, so flew – so tried to fly towards the anchoring thickets, that, alas, could not weigh their anchors and make sail to meet her – the poor exhausted Kate from the vengeance of pursuing frost.

And she reached them; staggering, fainting, reeling, she entered beneath the canopy of umbrageous trees. But, as oftentimes, the Hebrew fugitive to a city of refuge, flying for his life before the avenger of blood, was pressed so hotly that, on entering the archway of what seemed to *him* the heavenly city-gate, as he kneeled in deep thankfulness to kiss its holy merciful shadow, he could not rise again, but sank instantly with infant weakness into sleep – sometimes to wake no more; so sank, so collapsed upon the ground, without power to choose her couch, and with little prospect of ever rising again to her feet, the martial nun. She lay as luck had ordered it, with her head screened by the undergrowth of bushes, from any gales that might arise; she lay exactly as she sank, with her eyes up to heaven; and thus it was that the nun saw, before falling asleep, the two sights that upon earth are fittest for the closing eyes of a nun, whether destined to open again, or to close for ever. She saw the interlacing of boughs overhead forming a dome, that seemed like the dome of a cathedral. She saw through the fret-work of the foliage, another dome, far beyond, the dome of an evening sky, the dome of some heavenly cathedral, not built with hands.[26] She saw upon this upper dome the vesper lights, all alive with pathetic grandeur of colouring from a sunset that had just been rolling down like a chorus. She had not, till now, consciously observed the time of day; whether it were morning, or whether it were afternoon, in her confusion she had not distinctly known. But now she whispered to herself – '*It is evening:*' and what lurked half unconsciously in these words might be – 'The sun, that rejoices, has finished his daily toil; man, that labours, has finished *his;* I, that suffer, have finished mine.' That might be what she thought, but what she *said* was, 'it is evening; and the hour is come when the *Angelus*[27] is sounding through St Sebastians.' What made her think of St Sebastians, so far away in depths of space and time? Her brain was wandering, now that her feet were *not*; and, because her eyes had descended from the heavenly to the earthly dome, *that* made her think of earthly cathedrals, and of catherdral choirs, and of St Sebastian's chapel, with its silvery bells that carried the *Angelus* far into mountain recesses. Perhaps, as her wanderings increased, she thought herself back in childhood; became 'pussy' once again; fancied that all since then was a frightful dream; that she was not upon the dreadful Andes, but still kneeling in the holy chapel at vespers; still innocent as then; loved as then she had been loved; and that all men were liars, who said her hand was ever stained with blood. Little enough is mentioned of the delusions which possessed her; but that little gives a key to the impulse which her palpitating heart obeyed, and which her rambling brain for ever reproduced in multiplying mirrors. Restlessness kept her in waking dreams for a brief half hour. But then fever and delirium would wait no longer; the killing exhaustion would no longer be refused; the fever, the delirium, and the exhaustion, swept in together with power like an army with banners;[28] and the nun ceased through the gathering twilight any more to watch the cathedrals of earth, or the more solemn cathedrals that rose in the heavens above.

All night long she slept in her verdurous St Bernard's hospice[29] without awaking, and whether she would *ever* awake seemed to depend upon an accident. The slumber that towered above her brain was like that fluctuating silvery column which stands in scientific tubes sinking, rising, deepening, lightening, contracting, expanding; or like the mist that sits, through sultry afternoons, upon the river of the American St Peter,[30] sometimes rarefying for minutes into sunny gauze, sometimes condensing for hours into palls of funeral darkness. You fancy that, after twelve hours of *any* sleep, she must have been refreshed; better at least than she was last night. Ah! but sleep is not always sent upon missions of refreshment. Sleep is sometimes the secret chamber in which death arranges his machinery. Sleep is sometimes that deep mysterious atmosphere, in which the human spirit is slowly unsettling its wings for flight from earthly tenements. It is now eight o'clock in the morning; and, to all appearance, if Kate should receive no aid before noon, when next the sun is departing to his rest, Kate will be departing to hers; when next the sun is holding out his golden Christian signal to man, that the hour is come for letting his anger go down,[31] Kate will be sleeping away for ever into the arms of brotherly forgiveness.

What is wanted just now for Kate, supposing Kate herself to be wanted by this world, is, that this world would be kind enough to send her a little brandy before it is too late. The simple truth was, and a truth which I have known to take place in more ladies than Kate, who died or did *not* die, accordingly, as they had or had not an adviser like myself, capable of giving so sound an opinion, that the jewelly star of life had descended too far down the arch towards setting, for any chance of re-ascending by *spontaneous* effort. The fire was still burning in secret, but needed to be rekindled by potent artificial breath. It lingered, and *might* linger, but would never culminate again without some stimulus from earthly vineyards.* Kate was ever lucky, though ever

* Though not exactly in the same circumstances as Kate, or sleeping, *à la belle etoile*,[32] on a declivity of the Andes, I have known (or heard circumstantially reported) the cases of many

unfortunate; and the world, being of my opinion that Kate was worth saving, made up its mind about half-past eight o'clock in the morning to save her. Just at that time, when the night was over, and its sufferings were hidden – in one of those intermitting gleams that for a moment or two lightened the clouds of her slumber, Kate's dull ear caught a sound that for years had spoken a familiar language to *her*. What was it? It was the sound, though muffled and deadened, like the ear that heard it, of horsemen advancing. Interpreted by the tumultuous dreams of Kate, was it the cavalry of Spain, at whose head so often she had charged the bloody Indian scalpers? Was it, according to the

---

ladies besides Kate, who were in precisely the same critical danger of perishing for want of a little brandy.[33] A dessert spoonful or two would have saved them. Avaunt! you wicked 'Temperance' medallist![34] repent as fast as ever you can, or, perhaps the next time we hear of you, *anasarca* and *hydrothorax*,[35] will be running after you to punish your shocking excesses in water. Seriously, the case is one of constant recurrence, and constantly ending fatally from *unseasonable* and pedantic rigor of temperance.[36] The fact is, that the medical profession composes the most generous and liberal body of men amongst us; taken generally, by much the most enlightened; but professionally, the most timid. Want of boldness in the administration of opium, &c., though they can be bold enough with mercury, is their besetting infirmity. And from this infirmity females suffer most. One instance I need hardly mention, the fatal case of an august lady, mourned by nations, with respect to whom it was, and is, the belief of multitudes to this hour, (well able to judge) that she would have been saved by a glass of brandy; and her attendant, who shot himself, came to think so too late – too late for *her*, and too late for himself.[37] Amongst many cases of the same nature, which personally I have been acquainted with, twenty years ago, a man, illustrious for his intellectual accomplishments,[38] mentioned to me that his own wife, during her first or second confinement, was suddenly reported to him, by one of her female attendants, (who slipped away unobserved by the medical people) as undoubtedly sinking fast. He hurried to her chamber, and *saw* that it was so. The presiding medical authority, however, was inexorable. 'Oh, by no means,' shaking his ambrosial wig, 'any stimulant at this crisis would be fatal.' But no authority could overrule the concurrent testimony of all symptoms, and of all unprofessional opinions. By some pious falsehood my friend smuggled the doctor out of the room, and immediately smuggled a glass of brandy into the poor lady's lips. She recovered with magical power. The doctor is now dead, and went to his grave under the delusive persuasion – that not any vile glass of brandy, but the stern refusal of all brandy, was the thing that saved his collapsing patient. The patient herself, who might naturally know something of the matter, was of a different opinion. She sided with the factious body around her bed, (comprehending all beside the doctor) who felt sure that death was rapidly approaching, *barring* that brandy. The same result in the same appalling crisis, I have known repeatedly produced by twenty-five drops of laudanum. An obstinate man will say – 'Oh, never listen to a non-medical man like this writer. Consult in such a case your medical adviser.' You will, will you? Then let me tell you, that you are missing the very logic of all I have been saying for the improvement of blockheads, which is – that you should consult any man *but* a medical man, since no other man has any obstinate prejudice of professional timidity. N.B. – I prescribe for Kate *gratis*, because she, poor thing! has so little to give. But from other ladies, who may have the happiness to benefit by my advice, I expect a fee – not so large a one considering the service – a flowering plant, suppose the *second* best in their collection. I know it would be of no use to ask for the *very* best, (which else I could wish to do) because that would only be leading them into little fibs. I don't insist on a *Yucca gloriosa*, or a *Magnolia speciosissima*,[39] (I hope there *is* such a plant) – a rose or a violet will do. I am sure there is such a plant as that. And if they settle their debts justly, I shall very soon be master of the prettiest little conservatory in England. For, treat it not as a jest, reader; no case of timid practice is so fatally frequent.

legend of ancient days, cavalry that had been sown by her brother's blood, cavalry that rose from the ground on an inquest of retribution, and were racing up the Andes to seize her?[40] Her dreams that had opened sullenly to the sound waited for no answer, but closed again into pompous darkness. Happily, the horsemen had caught the glimpse of some bright ornament, clasp, or aiguillette, on Kate's dress. They were hunters and foresters from below; servants in the household of a beneficent lady; and in some pursuit of flying game had wandered beyond their ordinary limits. Struck by the sudden scintillation from Kate's dress played upon by the morning sun, they rode up to the thicket. Great was their surprise, great their pity, to see a young officer in uniform stretched within the bushes upon the ground, and perhaps dying. Borderers from childhood on this dreadful frontier, sacred to winter and death, they understood the case at once. They dismounted: and with the tenderness of women, raising the poor frozen cornet in their arms, washed her temples with brandy, whilst one, at intervals, suffered a few drops to trickle within her lips. As the restoration of a warm bed was now most likely to be successful, they lifted the helpless stranger upon a horse, walking on each side with supporting arms. Once again our Kate is in the saddle; once again a Spanish Caballador. But Kate's bridle-hand is deadly cold. And her spurs, that she had never unfastened since leaving the monastic asylum, hung as idle as the flapping sail that fills unsteadily with the breeze upon a stranded ship.

This procession had some miles to go, and over difficult ground; but at length it reached the forest-like park and the chateau of the wealthy proprietress. Kate was still half-frozen and speechless, except at intervals. Heavens! can this corpse-like, languishing young woman be the Kate that once, in her radiant girlhood rode with a handful of comrades into a column of two thousand enemies, that saw her comrades die, that persisted when all were dead, that tore from the heart of all resistance the banner of her native Spain? Chance and change have 'written strange defeatures in her face.'[41] Much is changed; but some things are not changed: there is still kindness that overflows with pity; there is still helplessness that asks for this pity without a voice: she is now received by a Senora, not less kind than that maternal aunt, who, on the night of her birth, first welcomed her to a loving home; and she, the heroine of Spain, is herself as helpless now as that little lady who, then at ten minutes of age, was kissed and blessed by all the household of St Sebastian.

Last month, reader, I promised, or some one promised *for* me, that I should drive through to the end of the journey in the next stage. But, oh, dear reader! these Andes, in Jonathan's phrase, are a 'severe' range of hills. It takes 'the kick' out of any horse, or, indeed, out of any cornet of horse, to climb up this cruel side of the range. Rest I really must, whilst Kate is resting. But next month I will carry you down the other side at such a flying gallop, that you shall suspect me (though most unjustly) of a plot against your neck. Now, let me throw down the reins; and then, in our brother Jonathan's sweet sentimental expression, 'let's liquor.'

(To be concluded in our next.)

THE NAUTICO-MILITARY NUN OF SPAIN
[Part III]

First published as the lead article in *Tait's*, XVI, July 1847, pp. 431–40. In *Tait's*, however, there was an error in pagination and the pages were incorrectly numbered '231–40'. Two centred lines followed the title of the essay and immediately preceded the text. The first stated that the essay was 'BY THOMAS DE QUINCEY.', and the second that it was '(*Concluded from page* 376.)' to denote where in *Tait's* Part II of the essay ended.

Reprinted in *F*, VII, *Narrative and Miscellaneous Papers* (1852), pp. 169–201, pp. 205–6.

Revised text, carrying many accidentals but only one substantive variant from *F*, in *SGG*, III, *Miscellanies, Chiefly Narrative* (1854), pp. 60–92.

There are three manuscripts. They are a combination of galley and page proofs for the article as revised for *SGG*, and taken together they form a complete set of proofs for the article. The manuscripts are as follows:

MS A: Huntington Library, HM 31019. The manuscript is a set of *SGG* page proofs, corresponding to the text below running from p. 128.1 'LET us suppose Kate' to p. 139.2 'his traces. What succeeded', with those textual variants from *SGG* running from p. 650, *Title* '20. – *A Second Lull in Kate's Stormy Life*.' to p. 652, 138.28–9 'bushes." But birds…as usual, had'. MS A breaks in mid-sentence, but is picked up again at MS B.

MS B: British Library, Department of Printed Books, C. 60. o. 3. The manuscript is a set of galley proofs, corresponding to the text below running from p. 139.3 'was all one scene of continued, dreadful' to p. 144.40 'a secret for ever and ever!', with those textual variants from *SGG* running from p. 652, 139.6 'In the first moments a' to p. 655, 144.39 'for more than two'.

MS C: Huntington Library, HM 31019. The manuscript is three endnotes from *F*, corresponding to the text below running from p. 128.30 '"*Creole*"*:* – At that time' to p. 128.40 'Casaubon *apud Scriptores. Hist Augustan*.'; from p. 128. 41 'It is well known, that' to p. 129.43 'out upon his forehead.'; and p. 142.42 'Griffith in Shakspere, when' to p. 142.42–3 'Queen Catherine, Cardinal Wolsey.'.

The three manuscripts contain only three significant variants, and these are listed in the textual notes.

For the occasion and context of the article, see headnote, pp. 90–3.

LET us suppose Kate placed in a warm bed. Let us suppose her in a few hours recovering steady consciousness; in a few days recovering some power of self-support; in a fortnight able to seek the gay saloon, where the Senora was sitting alone, and rendering thanks, with that deep sincerity which ever characterised our wild-hearted Kate, for the critical services received from that lady and her establishment.

This lady, a widow, was what the French call a *métisse*, the Spaniards a *mestizza;* that is, the daughter of a genuine Spaniard, and an Indian mother. I shall call her simply a *creole*,* which will indicate her want of pure Spanish blood sufficiently to explain her deference for those who had it. She was a kind, liberal woman; rich rather more than needed where there were no opera boxes to rent – a widow about fifty years old in the wicked world's account, some forty-four in her own; and happy, above all, in the possession of a most lovely daughter, whom even the wicked world did not accuse of more than sixteen years. This daughter, Juana, was – But stop – let her open the door of the saloon in which the Senora and the cornet are conversing, and speak for herself. She did so, after an hour had passed; which length of time, to *her* that never had any business whatever in her innocent life, seemed sufficient to settle the business of the old world and the new. Had Pietro Diaz (as Catalina now called herself) been really a Peter, and not a sham Peter, what a vision of loveliness would have rushed upon his sensibilities as the door opened! Do not expect me to describe her, for which, however, there are materials extant, sleeping in archives, where they have slept for two hundred and twenty years. It is enough that she is reported to have united the stately tread of Andalusian women with the innocent voluptuousness of Peruvian eyes.[2] As to her complexion and figure, be it known that Juana's father was a gentleman from Grenada,[3] having in his veins the grandest blood of all this earth, blood of Goths and Vandals, tainted (for which Heaven be thanked!) twice over with blood of Arabs – once through Moors, once through Jews;† whilst from her

* *'Creole':* – At that time the infusion of negro or African blood was small. Consequently none of the negro hideousness was diffused. After these intercomplexities had arisen between all complications of descent from three original strands, European, American, African, the distinctions of social consideration founded on them bred names so many, that a court calendar was necessary to keep you from blundering. As yet, the varieties were few. Meantime, the word *creole* has always been misapplied in our English colonies to a person (though of strictly European blood) simply because *born* in the West Indies. In this English use, it expresses the same difference as the Romans indicated by *Hispanus* and *Hispanicus*. The first meant a person of Spanish blood, a native of Spain; the second, a Roman born in Spain. So of *Germanus* and *Germanicus*, *Italus* and *Italicus*, *Anglus* and *Anglicus*, &c.; an important distinction, on which see Casaubon *apud Scriptores. Hist Augustan.*[1]

† It is well known, that the very reason why the Spanish of all nations became the most gloomily jealous of a Jewish cross in the pedigree, was because, until the vigilance of the Church rose into ferocity, in no nation was such a cross so common. The hatred of fear is ever the deepest. And men hated the Jewish taint, as once in Jerusalem they hated the leprosy, because even whilst they raved against it, the secret proofs of it might be detected amongst

grandmother Juana drew the deep subtle melancholy and the beautiful contours of limb which belong to the Indian race – a race destined silently and slowly to fade from the earth. No awkwardness was or could be in this antelope, when gliding with forest grace into the room – no town-bred shame – nothing but the unaffected pleasure of one who wishes to speak a fervent welcome, but knows not if she ought – the astonishment of a Miranda, bred in utter solitude, when first beholding a princely Ferdinand[5] – and just so much reserve as to remind you, that if Catalina thought fit to dissemble her sex, she did *not*. And consider, reader, if you look back and are a great arithmetician, that whilst the Senora had only fifty per cent. of Spanish blood, Juana had seventy-five; so that her Indian melancholy after all was swallowed up for the present by her Vandal, by her Arab, by her Spanish fire.

Catalina, seared as she was by the world, has left it evident in her memoirs that she was touched more than she wished to be by this innocent child.[6] Juana formed a brief lull for Catalina in her too stormy existence. And if for *her* in this life the sweet reality of a sister had been possible, here was the sister she would have chosen. On the other hand, what might Juana think of the cornet? To have been thrown upon the kind hospitalities of her native home, to have been rescued by her mother's servants from the fearful death which, lying but a few miles off, had filled her nursery with traditionary tragedies, – *that* was sufficient to create an interest in the stranger.[7] But his bold martial demeanour, his yet youthful style of beauty, his frank manners, his animated conversation that reported a hundred contests with suffering and peril, wakened for the first time her admiration. Men she had never seen before, except menial servants, or a casual priest. But here was a gentleman, young like herself, that rode in the cavalry of Spain – that carried the banner of the only potentate whom Peruvians knew of – the King of the Spains and the Indies[8] – that had doubled Cape Horn, that had crossed the Andes, that had suffered ship-wreck, that had rocked upon fifty storms, and had wrestled for life through fifty battles.

The reader knows all that followed. The sisterly love which Catalina did really feel for this young mountaineer was inevitably misconstrued. Embarrassed, but not able, from sincere affection, or almost in bare propriety, to refuse such expressions of feeling as corresponded to the artless and involuntary kindness of the ingenuous Juana, one day the cornet was surprised by mamma in the act of encircling her daughter's waist with his martial arm, although waltzing was premature by at least two centuries in Peru. She taxed him instantly with dishonourably abusing her confidence. The cornet made but a bad defence. He muttered something about '*fraternal affection*,' about 'esteem,' and a great deal of metaphysical words that are destined to remain untranslated in their original Spanish. The good Senora, though she could

their own kindred, even as in the Temple, whilst once a king rose in mutiny against the priesthood, (Chron. ii. 26) suddenly the leprosy that dethroned him, blazed out upon his forehead.[4]

boast only of forty-four years' experience, was not altogether to be '*had*' in that fashion – she was as learned as if she had been fifty, and she brought matters to a speedy crisis. 'You are a Spaniard,' she said, 'a gentleman, therefore: *remember* that you are a gentleman. This very night, if your intentions are not serious, quit my house. Go to Tucuman;[9] you shall command my horses and servants; but stay no longer to increase the sorrow that already you will have left behind you. My daughter loves you. That is sorrow enough, if you are trifling with us. But, if not, and you also love *her*, and can be happy in our solitary mode of life, stay with us – stay for ever. Marry Juana with my free consent. I ask not for wealth. Mine is sufficient for you both.' The cornet protested that the honour was one never contemplated by *him* – that it was too great – that ——. But, of course, reader, you know that 'gammon' flourishes in Peru, amongst the silver mines, as well as in some more boreal lands that produce little better than copper and tin. 'Tin,'[10] however, has its uses. The delighted Senora overruled all objections, great and small; and she confirmed Juana's notion that the business of two worlds could be transacted in an hour, by settling her daughter's future happiness in exactly twenty minutes. The poor, weak Catalina, not acting now in any spirit of recklessness, grieving sincerely for the gulph that was opening before her, and yet shrinking effeminately from that momentary shock that would be inflicted by a firm adherence to her duty, clinging to the anodyne of a short delay, allowed herself to be installed as the lover of Juana. Considerations of convenience, however, postponed the marriage. It was requisite to make various purchases; and for this, it was requisite to visit Tucuman, where, also, the marriage ceremony could be performed with more circumstantial splendour. To Tucuman, therefore, after some weeks' interval, the whole party repaired. And at Tucuman it was that the tragical events arose, which, whilst interrupting such a mockery for ever, left the poor Juana still happily deceived, and never believing for a moment that hers was a rejected or a deluded heart.

One reporter of Mr De Ferrer's narrative forgets his usual generosity, when he says that the Senora's gift of her daughter to the Alférez was not quite so disinterested as it seemed to be.[11] Certainly it was not so disinterested as European ignorance might fancy it: but it was quite as much so as it ought to have been, in balancing the interests of a child. Very true it is – that, being a genuine Spaniard, who was still a rare creature in so vast a world as Peru, being a Spartan amongst Helots, an Englishman amongst Savages, an Alférez would in those days have been a natural noble. His alliance created honour for his wife and for his descendants. Something, therefore, the cornet would add to the family consideration. But, instead of selfishness, it argued just regard for her daughter's interest to build upon this, as some sort of equipoise to the wealth which her daughter would bring.

Spaniard, however, as he was, our Alférez on reaching Tucuman found no Spaniards to mix with, but instead twelve Portuguese.

Catalina remembered the Spanish proverb – 'Subtract from a Spaniard all his good qualities, and the remainder makes a pretty fair Portuguese;'[12] but, as there was nobody else to gamble with, she entered freely into their society. Very soon she suspected that there was foul play: all modes of doctoring dice had been made familiar to *her* by the experience of camps. She watched; and, by the time she had lost her final coin, she was satisfied that she had been plundered. In her first anger she would have been glad to switch the whole dozen across the eyes; but, as twelve to one were too great odds, she determined on limiting her vengeance to the immediate culprit. Him she followed into the street; and coming near enough to distinguish his profile reflected on a wall, she continued to keep him in view from a short distance. The light-hearted young cavalier whistled, as he went, an old Portuguese ballad of romance; and in a quarter of an hour came up to an house, the front door of which he began to open with a pass-key. This operation was the signal for Catalina that the hour of vengeance had struck; and, stepping hastily up, she tapped the Portuguese on the shoulder, saying – 'Senor, you are a robber!' The Portuguese turned coolly round, and, seeing his gaming antagonist, replied – 'Possibly, Sir; but I have no particular fancy for being told so,' at the same time drawing his sword. Catalina had not designed to take any advantage; and the touching him on the shoulder, with the interchange of speeches, and the known character of Kate, sufficiently imply it. But it is too probable in such cases, that the party whose intention has been regularly settled from the first, will, and must have an advantage unconsciously over a man so abruptly thrown on his defence. However this might be, they had not fought a minute before Catalina passed her sword through her opponent's body; and without a groan or a sigh, the Portuguese cavalier fell dead at his own door. Kate searched the street with her ears, and (as far as the indistinctness of night allowed) with her eyes. All was profoundly silent; and she was satisfied that no human figure was in motion. What should be done with the body? A glance at the door of the house settled *that:* Fernando had himself opened it at the very moment when he received the summons to turn round. She dragged the corpse in, therefore, to the foot of the staircase, put the key by the dead man's side, and then issuing softly into the street, drew the door close with as little noise as possible. Catalina again paused to listen and to watch, went home to the hospitable Senora's house, retired to bed, fell asleep, and early the next morning was awakened by the Corregidor and four alguazils.[13]

The lawlessness of all that followed strikingly exposes the frightful state of criminal justice at that time, wherever Spanish law prevailed. No evidence appeared to connect Catalina in any way with the death of Fernando Acosta. The Portuguese gamblers, besides that perhaps they thought lightly of such an accident, might have reasons of their own for drawing off public attention from their pursuits in Tucuman: not one of these men came forward openly; else the circumstances at the gaming table, and the departure of Catalina so closely on the heels of her opponent, would have suggested reasonable grounds for detaining her until some further light should be obtained. As it was, her imprisonment rested upon no colourable ground whatever, unless the magistrate had received some anonymous information, which, however, he never alleged. One comfort there was, meantime, in Spanish injustice: it did not loiter. Full gallop it went over the ground: one week often sufficed for informations – for trial – for execution; and the only bad consequence was, that a second or third week sometimes exposed the disagreeable fact that everything had been 'premature:' a solemn sacrifice had been made to offended justice, in which all was right except as to the victim: it was the wrong man; and *that* gave extra trouble; for then all was to do over again, another man to be executed, and, possibly, still to be caught.

Justice moved at her usual Spanish rate in the present case. Kate was obliged to rise instantly; not suffered to speak to anybody in the house, though, in going out, a door opened, and she saw the young Juana looking out with saddest Indian expression. In one day the trial was all finished. Catalina said (which was true) that she hardly knew Acosta; and that people of her rank were used to attack their enemies face to face, not by murderous surprises. The magistrates were impressed with Catalina's answers (yet answers to *what?*) Things were beginning to look well, when all was suddenly upset by two witnesses, whom the reader (who is a sort of accomplice after the fact, having been privately let into the truths of the case, and having concealed his knowledge,) will know at once to be false witnesses, but whom the old Spanish buzwigs[14] doated on as models of all that could be looked for in the best. Both were very ill-looking fellows, as it was their duty to be. And the first deposed as follows: – That through *his* quarter of Tucuman, the fact was notorious of Acosta's wife being the object of a criminal pursuit on the part of Alférez (Catalina): that, *doubtless*, the injured husband had surprised the prisoner, which, of course, had led to the murder – to the staircase – to the key – to everything, in short, that could be wished; no – stop! what am I saying? – to everything that ought to be abominated. Finally – for he had now settled the main question – that he had a friend who would take up the case where he himself, from short-sightedness, was obliged to lay it down.' This friend, the Pythias of this short-sighted Damon,[15] started up in a frenzy of virtue at this summons, and, rushing to the front of the alguazils, said, 'that since his friend had proved sufficiently the fact of the Alférez having been lurking in the house, and having murdered a man, all that rested upon *him* to show was, how that murderer got out of the house; which he could do satisfactorily; for there was a balcony running along the windows on the second floor, one of which windows he himself, lurking in a corner of the street, saw the Alférez throw up, and from the said balcony take a flying leap into the said street.' Evidence like this was conclusive; no defence was listened to, nor indeed had the prisoner any to produce. The Alférez could deny neither the staircase nor the balcony; the street is there to this day, like the bricks in Jack Cade's Chimney,[16] testifying all that may be required; and, as to our friend who saw the leap, there he was; nobody could deny *him*. The prisoner might indeed have suggested that she never heard of Acosta's wife, nor had the existence of such a wife been ripened even into a suspicion. But the bench were satisfied; chopping logic[17] was of no use; and sentence was pronounced – that on the eighth day from the day of arrest, the Alférez should be executed in the public square.

It was not amongst the weaknesses of Catalina – who had so often inflicted death, and, by her own journal, thought so lightly of inflicting it (if not under cowardly advantages) – to shrink from facing death in her own person. Many incidents in her career show the coolness and even gaiety with which, in any case where death was apparently inevitable, she would have gone to meet it. But in this case she *had* a temptation for escaping it, which was probably in her power. She had only to reveal the secret of her sex, and the ridiculous witnesses, beyond whose testimony there was nothing at all against her, must at once be covered with derision. Catalina had some liking for fun; and a main inducement to this course was, that it would enable her to say to the judges, 'Now you see what old fools you've made of yourselves; every woman and child in Peru will soon be laughing at you.' I must acknowledge my own weakness; this last temptation I could *not* have withstood; flesh is weak, and fun is strong. But Catalina *did*. On consideration she fancied, that, although the particular motive for murdering Acosta would be dismissed with laughter, still this might not clear her of the murder, which on some *other* motive she might have committed. But supposing that she were cleared altogether, what most of all she feared was, that the publication of her sex would throw a reflex light upon many past transactions in her life – would instantly find its way to Spain – and would probably soon bring her within the tender attentions of the Inquisition. She kept firm to the resolution of not saving her life by this discovery. And so far as her fate lay in her own hands, she would (as the reader will perceive from a little incident at the scaffold) have perished to a certainty. But even at this point, how strange a case! A woman *falsely* accused of an act which she really *did* commit! And falsely accused of a true offence upon a motive that was impossible!

As the sun set upon the seventh day, when the hours were numbered for the prisoner, there filed into her cell four persons in religious habits. They came on the charitable mission of preparing the poor convict for death. Catalina, however, watching all things narrowly, remarked something earnest and significant in the eye of the leader, as of one who had some secret communication to make. She contrived to clasp this man's hands as if in the energy of internal struggles, and *he* contrived to slip into hers the very smallest of billets from poor Juana. It contained, for indeed, it *could* contain, only these three words – 'Do not confess. J.' This one caution, so simple and so brief, was a talisman. It did not refer to any confession of the crime, *that* would have been assuming that Juana was neither entitled nor disposed to assume, but, in the technical sense of the Church, to the act of devotional confession. Catalina found a single moment for a glance at it – understood the whole – resolutely refused to confess, as a person unsettled in her religious opinions, that needed spiritual instructions, and the four monks withdrew to make their report. The principal judge, upon hearing of the prisoner's impenitence, granted another day. At the end of *that*, no change having occurred either in the prisoner's mind, or in the circumstances, he issued his warrant for the execution. Accordingly, as the sun went down, the sad procession formed within the prison. Into the great square of Tucuman it moved, where the scaffold had been built, and the whole city had assembled for the spectacle. Catalina steadily ascended the ladder of the scaffold; even then she resolved not to benefit by revealing her sex; even then it was that she expressed her scorn for the lubberly executioner's mode of tying a knot; did it herself in a 'ship-shape,' orthodox manner; received in return the enthusiastic plaudits of the crowd, and so far ran the risk of precipitating her fate; for the timid magistrates, fearing a rescue from the impetuous mob, angrily ordered the executioner to finish the scene. The clatter of a galloping horse, however, at this instant forced them to pause. The crowd opened a road for the agitated horseman, who was the bearer of an order from the President of La Plata[18] to suspend the execution until two prisoners could be examined. The whole was the work of the Senora and her daughter. The elder lady, having gathered informations against the witnesses, had pursued them to La Plata. There, by her influence with the Governor, they were arrested; recognised as old malefactors; and in their terror had partly confessed their perjury. Catalina was removed to La Plata; solemnly acquitted; and, by the advice of the President, for the present the connexion with the Senora's family was postponed indefinetly.

Now was the last adventure approaching that ever Catalina should see in the new world. Some fine sights she may yet see in Europe, but nothing after this *(which she has recorded)* in America. Europe, if it had ever heard of her name (which very shortly it *shall)*, Kings, Pope, Cardinals, if they were but aware of her existence (which in six months they *shall* be), would thirst for an introduction to our Catalina. You hardly thought now, reader, that she was such a great person, or anybody's pet but yours and mine. Bless you, sir, she would scorn to look at *us*. I tell you, royalties are languishing to see her, or soon *will* be. But how can this come to pass, if she is to continue in her present obscurity? Certainly it cannot without some great *peripetteia*[19] or vertiginous whirl of fortune; which, therefore, you shall now behold taking place in one turn of her next adventure. *That* shall let in a light, *that* shall throw back a Claude Lorraine[20] gleam over all the past, able to make Kings, that would have cared not for her under Peruvian daylight, come to glorify her setting-beams.

The Senora – and, observe, whatever kindness she does to Catalina speaks secretly from two hearts, her own and Juana's – had, by the advice of Mr President Mendonia, given sufficient money for Catalina's travelling expenses. So far well. But Mr M. chose to add a little codicil to this bequest of the

Senora's, never suggested by her or by her daughter. 'Pray,' said this Inquisitive President, who surely might have found business enough in La Plata, 'Pray, Senor Pietro Diaz, did you ever live at Concepcion? And were you ever acquainted there with Senor Miguel de Erauso? That man, sir, was my friend.' What a pity that on this occasion Catalina could not venture to be candid! What a capital speech it would have made to say – '*Friend* were you? I think you could hardly be *that*, with 700 miles between you. But that man was *my* friend also; and, secondly, my brother. True it is I killed him. But if you happen to know that this was by pure mistake in the dark, what an old rogue you must be to throw *that* in my teeth, which is the affliction of my life!' Again, however, as so often in the same circumstances, Catalina thought that it would cause more ruin than it could heal to be candid: and, indeed, if she were really *P. Diaz, Esq.*, how came she to be brother to the late Mr Erauso? On consideration, also, if she could not tell *all*, merely to have professed a fraternal connexion which never was avowed by either whilst living together, would not have brightened the reputation of Catalina, which too surely required a scouring. Still, from my kindness for poor Kate, I feel uncharitably towards the president for advising Senor Pietro 'to travel for his health.' What had *he* to do with people's health? However, Mr Peter, as he had pocketed the Senora's money, thought it right to pocket also the advice that accompanied its payment. That he might be in a condition to do so, he went off to buy a horse. He was in luck to-day. For, beside money and advice, he obtained, at a low rate, a horse both beautiful and serviceable for a journey. To Paz[21] it was, a city of prosperous name, that the cornet first moved. But Paz did not fulfil the promise of its name. For it laid the grounds of a feud that drove our Kate out of America.

Her first adventure was a bagatelle, and fitter for a jest book than a history; yet it proved no jest either, since it led to the tragedy that followed. Riding into Paz, our gallant standard-bearer and her bonny black horse drew all eyes, *comme de raison*,[22] upon their separate charms. This was inevitable amongst the indolent population of a Spanish town; and Kate was used to it. But, having recently had a little too much of the public attention, she felt nervous on remarking two soldiers eyeing the handsome horse and the handsome rider, with an attention that seemed too solemn for mere *aesthetics*. However, Kate was not the kind of person to let anything dwell on her spirits, especially if it took the shape of impudence; and, whistling gaily, she was riding forward – when, who should cross her path, but the Alcalde! Ah! Alcalde, you see a person now that has a mission against you, though quite unknown to herself. He looked so sternly, that Kate asked if his worship had any commands. 'These men,' said the Alcalde, 'these two soldiers, say that this horse is stolen.' To one who had so narrowly and so lately escaped the balcony witness and his friend, it was really no laughing matter to hear of new affidavits in preparation. Kate was nervous; but never disconcerted. In a moment she had twitched off a saddle cloth on which she sat; and throwing it over the horse's head, so as to cover up all between the ears and the mouth, she replied, 'that she had bought and paid for the horse at La Plata. But now, your worship, if this horse has really been stolen from these men, they must know well of which eye it is blind; for it *can* be only in the right eye or the left.' One of the soldiers cried out instantly, that it was the left eye; but the other said, 'No, no, you forget, it's the right.' Kate maliciously called attention to this little schism. But the men said, 'Ah, *that* was nothing; they were hurried; but now, on recollecting themselves, they were agreed that it was the left eye.' Did they stand to that? 'Oh yes, positive they were, left eye, left.'

Upon which our Kate, twitching off the horse-cloth, said gaily to the magistrate – 'Now, sir, please to observe that this horse has nothing the matter with either eye.' And in fact it *was* so. Then his worship ordered his alguazils to apprehend the two witnesses, who posted off to bread and water, with other reversionary advantages, whilst Kate rode in quest of the best dinner that Paz could furnish.

This Alcalde's acquaintance, however, was not destined to drop here. Something had appeared in the young *caballero's*[23] bearing, which made it painful to have addressed him with harshness, or for a moment to have entertained such a charge against such a person. He despatched his cousin, therefore, Don Antonio Calderon,[24] to offer his apologies, and at the same time to request that the stranger, whose rank and quality he regretted not to have known would do him the honour to come and dine with him. This explanation, and the fact that Don Antonio had already proclaimed his own position as cousin to the magistrate and nephew to the Bishop of Cuzco,[25] obliged Catalina to say, after thanking the gentlemen for their obliging attentions, 'I myself hold the rank of Alférez in the service of his Catholic Majesty. I am a native of Biscay, and I am now repairing to Cuzco on private business.' 'To Cuzco!' exclaimed Don Antonio, 'how very fortunate! my cousin is a Basque like you; and, like you, he starts for Cuzco to-morrow morning; so that, if it is agreeable to you, Senor Alférez, we will travel together.' It was settled that they should. To travel – amongst 'balcony' witnesses, and anglers for 'blind horses' – not merely with a just man, but with the very abstract idea and riding allegory of justice, was too delightful to the storm-wearied cornet; and he cheerfully accompanied Don Antonio to the house of the magistrate, called Don Pedro de Chavarria. Distinguished was his reception; the Alcalde personally renewed his regrets for the ridiculous scene of the two scampish oculists, and presented him to his wife, a splendid Andalusian beauty, to whom he had been married about a year.

This lady there is a reason for describing; and the French reporter of Catalina's memoirs dwells upon the theme. She united, he says, the sweetness of the German lady with the energy of the Arabian, a combination hard to judge of. As to her feet, he adds, I say nothing; for she had scarcely any at all. '*Je ne parle point de ses pieds, elle n'en avait presque pas.*'[26] 'Poor lady!' says a compassionate rustic: 'no feet! What a shocking thing that so fine a woman should have been so sadly mutilated!' Oh, my dear rustic, you're quite in the wrong box. The Frenchman means this as the very highest compliment. Beautiful, however, she must have been; and a Cinderella I hope, not a Cinderellula,[27] considering that she had the inimitable walk and step of the Andalusians, which cannot be accomplished without something of a proportionate basis to stand upon.

The reason which there is (as I have said) for describing this lady arises out of her relation to the tragic events which followed. She, by her criminal levity, was the cause of all. And I must here warn the moralising blunderer of two errors that he is too likely to make: 1st, That he is invited to read some extract from a licentious amour, as if for its own interest; 2d, Or on account of Donna Catalina's memoirs, with a view to relieve their too martial character. I have the pleasure to assure him of his being so utterly in the darkness of error, that any possible change he can make in his opinions, right or left, must be for the better: he cannot stir, but he will mend; which is a delightful thought for the moral and blundering mind. As to the first point, what little glimpse he obtains of a licentious amour is, as a court of justice will sometimes show him such a glimpse, simply to make intelligible the subsequent facts which depend upon it. Secondly, As to the conceit, that Catalina wished to embellish her memoirs, understand that no such practice then existed; certainly not in Spanish literature. Her memoirs are electrifying by their facts; else, in the manner of telling these facts, they are systematically dry.[28]

Don Antonio Calderon was a handsome, accomplished cavalier. And in the course of dinner, Catalina was led to judge from the behaviour to each other of this gentleman and the lady, the Alcalde's beautiful wife, that they had an improper understanding. This also she inferred from the furtive language of their eyes. Her wonder was, that the Alcalde should be so blind; though upon that point she saw reason in a day or two to change her opinion. Some people see everything by affecting to see nothing. The whole affair, however, was nothing at all to *her*, and she would have dismissed it from her thoughts altogether, but for what happened on the journey.

From the miserable roads, eight hours a-day of travelling was found quite enough for man and beast; the product of which eight hours was from ten to twelve leagues. On the last day but one of the journey, the travelling party, which was precisely the original dinner party, reached a little town ten leagues short of Cuzco. The Corregidor of this place was a friend of the Alcalde; and through *his* influence the party obtained better accommodations than those which they had usually had in a hovel calling itself a *venta*, or in the sheltered corner of a barn. The Alcalde was to sleep at the Corregidor's house: the two young cavaliers, Calderon and our Kate, had sleeping rooms at the public *locanda;*[29] but for the lady was reserved a little pleasure-house in an enclosed garden. This was a plaything of a house; but the season being summer, and the house surrounded with tropical flowers, the lady preferred it (in spite of its loneliness) to the damp mansion of the official grandee, who, in her humble opinion, was quite as fusty as his mansion, and his mansion not much less so than himself.

After dining gaily together at the *locanda*, and possibly taking a 'rise' out of his worship, the Corregidor, as a repeating echo of Don Quixote,[30] (then growing popular in Spanish America) the young man who was no young officer, and the young officer who was no young man, lounged down together to the little pavilion in the flower-garden, with the purpose of paying their respects to the presiding belle. They were graciously received; and had the honour of meeting there his Mustiness the Alcalde, and his Fustiness the Corregidor; whose conversation was surely improving, but not equally brilliant. How they got on under the weight of two such muffs, has been a mystery for two centuries. But they *did* to a certainty, for the party did not break up till eleven. *Tea and turn out* you could not call it; for there was the *turn out* in rigour but not the *tea*. One thing, however, Catalina by mere accident had an opportunity of observing, and observed with pain. The two official gentlemen had gone down the steps into the garden. Catalina, having forgot her hat, went back into the little vestibule to look for it. There stood the lady and Don Antonio, exchanging a few final words (they *were* final) and a few final signs. Amongst the last Kate observed distinctly this; and distinctly she understood it. First drawing Calderon's attention to the gesture, as one of significant pantomime, by raising her forefinger, the lady snuffed out one of the candles. The young man answered it by a look of intelligence, and all three passed down the steps together. The lady was disposed to take the cool air, and accompanied them to the garden-gate; but in passing down the walk Catalina noticed a second ill-omened sign that was not right. Two glaring eyes she distinguished amongst the shrubs for a moment, and a rustling immediately after. – 'What's that?' said the lady, and Don Antonio answered carelessly – 'a bird flying out of the bushes.'

Catalina, as usual, had read everything. Not a wrinkle or a rustle was lost upon *her*. And, therefore, when she reached the *locanda*, knowing to an iota all that was coming, she did not retire to bed, but paced before the house. She had not long to wait: in fifteen minutes, the door opened softly, and out stepped Calderon. Kate walked forward, and faced him immediately; telling him laughingly that it was not good for his health to go abroad on this night. The young man showed some impatience; upon which, very seriously, Kate acquainted him with her suspicions, and with the certainty that the Alcalde was not so blind as he had seemed. Calderon thanked her for that information; would be upon his guard; but, to prevent further expostulation, he wheeled round instantly into the darkness. Catalina was too well convinced, however, of the mischief on foot, to leave him thus. She followed rapidly, and passed silently into the garden, almost at the same time with Calderon. Both took their stations behind trees; Calderon watching nothing but the burning candles, Catalina watching circumstances to direct her movements. The candles burned brightly in the little pavilion. Presently one was extinguished.

Upon this, Calderon pressed forward to the steps, hastily ascended them, and passed into the vestibule. Catalina followed on his traces. What succeeded was all one scene of continued, dreadful dumb show: different passions of panic, or deadly struggle, or hellish malice absolutely suffocated all articulate words.

In a moment a gurgling sound was heard as of a wild beast attempting vainly to yell over some creature that it was strangling. Next came a tumbling out at the door of one black mass, which heaved and parted at intervals into two figures, which closed, which parted again, which at last fell down the steps together. Then appeared a figure in white. It was the unhappy Andalusian; and she seeing the outline of Catalina's person, ran up to her, unable to utter one syllable. Pitying the agony of her horror, Catalina took her within her own cloak, and carried her out at the garden-gate. Calderon had by this time died; and the maniacal Alcalde had risen up to pursue his wife. But Kate, foreseeing what he would do, had stepped silently within the shadow of the garden wall. Looking down the road to the town, and seeing nobody moving, the maniac, for some purpose, went back to the house. This moment Kate used to recover the *locanda* with the lady still panting in horror. What was to be done? To think of concealment in this little place was out of the question. The Alcalde was a man of local power, and it was certain that he would kill his wife on the spot. Kate's generosity would not allow her to have any collusion with this murderous purpose. At Cuzco, the principal convent was ruled by a near relative of the Andalusian; and there she would find shelter. Kate, therefore, saddled her horse rapidly, placed the lady behind, and rode off in the darkness. About five miles out of the town their road was crossed by a torrent, over which they could not hit the bridge. 'Forward!' cried the lady; and Kate repeating the word to the horse, the docile creature leaped down into the water. They were all sinking at first; but having its head free, the horse swam clear of all obstacles through the midnight darkness, and scrambled out on the opposite bank. The two riders were dripping from the shoulders downward. But, seeing a light twinkling from a cottage window, Kate rode up; obtained a little refreshment, and the benefit of a fire, from a poor labouring man. From this man she also bought a warm mantle for the lady, who, besides her torrent bath, was dressed in a light evening robe, so that but for the horseman's cloak of Kate she would have perished. But there was no time to lose. They had already lost two hours from the consequences of their cold bath. Cuzco was still eighteen miles distant; and the Alcalde's shrewdness would at once divine this to be his wife's mark. They remounted: very soon the silent night echoed the hoofs of a pursing rider; and now commenced the most frantic race, in which each party rode as if the whole game of life were staked upon the issue. The pace was killing: and Kate has delivered it as her opinion, in the memoirs which she wrote, that the Alcalde was the better mounted.[31] This may be doubted. And certainly Kate had ridden too many years in the Spanish cavalry to have any fear of his worship's horsemanship; but it was a prodigious disadvantage that *her* horse had to carry double; while the horse ridden by her opponent was one of those belonging to the murdered Don Antonio, and known to Kate as a powerful animal. At length they had come within three miles of Cuzco. The road after this descended the whole way to the city, and in some places rapidly, so as to require a cool rider. Suddenly a deep trench appeared traversing the whole extent of a broad heath. It was useless to evade it. To have hesitated was to be lost. Kate saw the necessity of clearing it, but doubted much whether her poor exhausted horse, after twenty-one miles of work so severe, had strength for the effort. Kate's maxim, however, which never yet had failed, both figuratively for life, and literally for the saddle, was – to ride at everything that showed a front of resistance. She did so now. Having come upon the trench rather too suddenly, she wheeled round for the advantage of coming down upon it more determinately, rode resolutely at it, and gained the opposite bank. The hind feet of her horse were sinking back from the rottenness of the ground; but the strong supporting bridle-hand of Kate carried him forward; and in ten minutes more they would be in Cuzco. This being seen by the vicious Alcalde, who had built great hopes on the trench, he unslung his carbine, pulled up, and fired after the bonny black horse and its bonny fair riders. But this manoeuvre would have lost his worship any bet that he might have had depending on this admirable steeple chase. Had I been stakeholder, what a pleasure it would have been, in fifteen minutes from this very vicious shot, to pay into Kate's hands every shilling of the deposits. I would have listened to no nonsense about referees or protests. The bullets, says Kate, whistled round the poor clinging lady *en croupe*[32]– luckily none struck her; but one wounded the horse. And that settled the odds. Kate now planted herself well in her stirrups to enter Cuzco, almost dangerously a winner; for the horse was so maddened by the wound, and the road so steep, that he went like blazes; and it really became difficult for Kate to guide him with any precision through narrow episcopal[33] paths. Henceforwards the wounded horse required Kate's continued attention; and yet, in the mere luxury of strife, it was impossible for Kate to avoid turning a little in her saddle to see the Alcalde's performance on this tight rope of the trench. His worship's horsemanship being perhaps rather rusty, and he not perfectly acquainted with his horse, it would have been agreeable to compromise the case by riding round, or dismounting. But all *that* was impossible. The job must be done. And I am happy to report, for the reader's satisfaction, the sequel – so far as Kate could attend the performance. Gathering himself up for mischief, the Alcalde took a sweep, as if ploughing out the line of some vast encampment, or tracing the *pomoerium*[34] for some future Rome; then, like thunder and lightning, with arms flying aloft in the air, down he came upon the trembling trench. But the horse refused the leap; and, as the only compromise that *his* unlearned brain could suggest, he threw his worship right over his ears, lodging him safely in a sand heap that rose with clouds of dust and screams of birds into the morning air. Kate had now no time to send back her compliments in a musical halloo. The Alcalde missed breaking his neck on this occassion very narrowly; but his neck was of no use to him in twenty minutes more, as the reader will soon find. Kate rode right onwards; and, coming in with a lady behind her, horse bloody, and pace such as no hounds could have lived with, she ought to have made a great sensation in Cuzco. But, unhappily, the people were all in bed.

The steeple-chase into Cuzco had been a fine headlong thing, considering the torrent, the trench, the wounded horse, the lovely lady, with her agonising fears, mounted behind Kate, together with the meek dove-like dawn: but the finale crowded together the quickest succession of changes that out of a melodrama can ever have been witnessed. Kate reached the convent in safety; carried into the cloisters, and delivered like a parcel the fair Andalusian. But to rouse the servants caused delay; and on returning to the street through the broad gateway of the convent, whom should she face but the Alcalde! How he escaped the trench, who can tell? He had no time to write memoirs; his horse was too illiterate. But he *had* escaped; temper not at all improved by that adventure, and now raised to a hell of malignity by seeing that he had lost his prey. In the morning light he now saw how to use his sword. He attacked Kate with fury. Both were exhausted; and Kate, besides that she had no personal quarrel with the Alcalde, having now accomplished her sole object in saving the lady, would have been glad of a truce. She could with difficulty wield her sword: and the Alcalde had so far the advantage, that he wounded Kate severely. That roused her ancient blood. She turned on him now with determination. At that moment in rode two servants of the Alcalde, who took part with their master. These odds strengthened Kate's resolution, but weakened her chances. Just then, however, rode in, and ranged himself on Kate's side, the servant of the murdered Don Calderon. In an instant, Kate had pushed her sword through the Alcalde, who died upon the spot. In an instant the servant of Calderon had fled. In an instant the Alguazils had come up. They and the servants of the Alcalde pressed furiously on Kate, who now again was fighting for life. Against such odds, she was rapidly losing ground: when, in an instant, on the opposite side of the street, the great gates of the Episcopal palace rolled open. Thither it was that Calderon's servant had fled. The bishop and his attendants hurried across. 'Senor Caballador,' said the bishop, 'in the name of the Virgin, I enjoin you to surrender your sword.' 'My lord,' said Kate, 'I dare not do it with so many enemies about me.' 'But I,' replied the bishop, 'become answerable to the law for your safe-keeping.' Upon which, with filial reverence, all parties dropped their swords. Kate being severely wounded, the bishop led her into his palace. In an instant came the catastrophe; Kate's discovery could no longer be delayed; the blood flowed too rapidly; the wound was in her bosom. She requested a private interview with the bishop; all was known in a moment; for surgeons and attendants were summoned hastily, and Kate had fainted. The good bishop pitied her, and had her attended in his palace; then removed to a convent;

then to a second at Lima;[35] and, after many months had passed, his report to the Spanish Government at home of all the particulars, drew from the King of Spain and from the Pope an order that the Nun should be transferred to Spain.

Yes, at length the warrior lady, the blooming cornet, this nun that is so martial, this dragoon that is so lovely, must visit again the home of her childhood, which now for seventeen years she has not seen. All Spain, Portugal, Italy, rang with her adventures. Spain, from north to south, was frantic with desire to behold her fiery child, whose girlish romance, whose patriotic heroism electrified the national imagination. The King of Spain must kiss his *faithful* daughter, that would not suffer his banner to see dishonour. The Pope[36] must kiss his *wandering* daughter, that henceforwards will be a lamb travelling back into the Christian fold. Potentates so great as these, when *they* speak words of love, do not speak in vain. All was forgiven; the sacrilege, the bloodshed, the flight and the scorn of St Peter's keys;[37] the pardons were made out, were signed, were sealed, and the chanceries of earth were satisfied.

Ah! what a day of sorrow and of joy was *that* one day, in the first week of November, 1624, when the returning Kate drew near to the shore of Andalusia – when, descending into the ship's barge, she was rowed to the piers of Cadiz[38] by bargemen in the royal liveries – when she saw every ship, street, house, convent, church, crowded, like a day of judgment, with human faces, with men, with women, with children, all bending the lights of their flashing and their loving eyes upon herself. Forty myriads of people had gathered in Cadiz alone. All Andalusia had turned out to receive her. Ah! what joy, if she had not looked back to the Andes, to their dreadful summits, and their more dreadful feet. Ah! what sorrow, if she had not been forced by music, and endless banners, and triumphant clamours, to turn away from the Andes to the joyous shore which she approached!

Upon this shore stood, ready to receive her, in front of all this mighty crowd, the Prime Minister of Spain, the same Condé Olivarez,[39] who but one year before had been so haughty and so defying to our haughty and defying Duke of Buckingham. But a year ago the Prince of Wales[40] was in Spain, and he also was welcomed with triumph and great joy, but not with the hundredth part of that enthusiasm which now met the returning nun. And Olivarez, that had spoken so roughly to the English Duke, to *her* 'was sweet as summer.'* Through endless crowds of festive compatriots he conducted her to the King. The King folded her in his arms, and could never be satisfied with listening to her. He sent for her continually to his presence – he delighted in her conversation, so new, so natural, so spirited – he settled a pension upon her at that time, of unprecedented amount, in the case of a subaltern officer; and by *his* desire, because the year 1625 was a year of jubilee,[42]

* Griffith in Shakspere, when vindicating, in that immortal scene with Queen Catherine, Cardinal Wolsey.[41]

she departed in a few months from Madrid to Rome. She went through Barcelona;[43] there and everywhere welcomed as the lady whom the King delighted to honour.[44] She travelled to Rome, and all doors flew open to receive her. She was presented to his Holiness, with letters from his most Catholic majesty. But letters there needed none. The Pope admired her as much as all before had done. He caused her to recite all her adventures; and what he loved most in her account, was the sincere and sorrowing spirit in which she described herself as neither better nor worse than she had been. Neither proud was Kate, nor sycophantishly and falsely humble. Urban VIII. it was that then filled the chair of St Peter. He did not neglect to raise his daughter's thoughts from earthly things – he pointed her eyes to the clouds that were above the dome of St Peter's cathedral – he told her what the cathedral had told her in the gorgeous clouds of the Andes and the vesper lights, how sweet a thing, how divine a thing it was for Christ's sake to forgive all injuries, and how he trusted that no more she would think of bloodshed. He also said two words to her in Latin, which, if I had time to repeat a Spanish bishop's remark to Kate some time afterwards upon those two mysterious words, with Kate's most natural and ingenuous answer to the Bishop upon what she supposed to be their meaning, would make the reader smile not less than they made myself. You know that Kate *did* understand a little Latin, which, probably, had not been much improved by riding in the Light Dragoons. I must find time, however, whether the press and the compositors are in a fury or not, to mention that the Pope, in his farewell audience to his dear daughter, whom he was to see no more, gave her a general license to wear henceforth in all countries – even *in partibus Infidelium*[45] – a cavalry officer's dress – boots, spurs, sabre, and sabre-tache; in fact, anything that she and the Horse Guards might agree upon. Consequently, reader, remember for your life never to say one word, nor suffer any tailor to say one word, against those Wellington trousers made in the chestnut forest; for, understand that the Papal indulgence, as to this point, runs backwards as well as forwards; it is equally shocking and heretical to murmur against trousers in the forgotten rear or against trousers yet to come.

From Rome Kate returned to Spain. She even went to St Sebastian's – to the city, but – whether it was that her heart failed her or not – never to the convent. She roamed up and down; everywhere she was welcome – everywhere an honoured guest; but everywhere restless. The poor and humble never ceased from their admiration of her; and amongst the rich and aristocratic of Spain, with the King at their head, Kate found especial love from two classes of men. The Cardinals and Bishops all doated upon her – as their daughter that was returning. The military men all doated upon her – as their sister that was retiring.

Some time or other, when I am allowed more elbow-room, I will tell you why it is that I myself love this Kate. Now, at this moment, when it is necessary for me to close, if I allow you one question before laying down my pen –

if I say, 'Come now, be quick, ask anything you *have* to ask, for, in one minute, I am going to write *Finis*, after which (unless the Queen wished it) I could not add a syllable' – twenty to one, I guess what your question will be. You will ask me, What became of Kate? What was her end?

Ah, reader! but, if I answer that question, you will say I have *not* answered it. If I tell you that secret, you will say the secret is still hidden. Yet, because I have promised, and because you will be angry if I do not, let me do my best; and bad is the best. After ten years of restlessness in Spain, with thoughts always turning back to the Andes, Kate heard of an expedition on the point of sailing to Spanish America. All soldiers knew *her*, so that she had information of everything that stirred in camps. Men of the highest military rank were going out with the expedition; but they all loved Kate as a sister, and were delighted to hear that she would join their mess on board ship. This ship, with others, sailed, whither finally bound, I really forget. But, on reaching America, all the expedition touched at *Vera Cruz*.[46] Thither a great crowd of the military went on shore. The leading officers made a separate party for the same purpose. Their intention was, to have a gay happy dinner, after their long confinement to a ship, at the chief hotel; and happy in perfection it could not be, unless Kate would consent to join it. She, that was ever kind to brother soldiers, agreed to do so. She descended into the boat along with them, and in twenty minutes the boat touched the shore. All the bevy of gay laughing officers, junior and senior, like schoolboys escaping from school, jumped on shore, and walked hastily, as their time was limited, up to the hotel. Arriving there, all turned round in eagerness, saying, 'Where is our dear Kate?' Ah, yes, my dear Kate, at that solemn moment, where, indeed, were *you?* She had *certainly* taken her seat in the boat: that was sure. Nobody, in the general confusion, was certain of having seen her on coming ashore. The sea was searched for her – the forests were ransacked.[47] The sea made no answer – the forests gave up no sign. I have a conjecture of my own; but her brother soldiers were lost in sorrow and confusion, and could never arrive even at a conjecture.[48]

That happened two hundred and fourteen years ago! Here is the brief sum of all: – This nun sailed from Spain to Peru, and she found no rest for the sole of her foot.[49] This nun sailed back from Peru to Spain, and she found no rest for the agitations of her heart. This nun sailed again from Spain to America, and she found – the rest which all of us find. But where it was, could never be made known to the father of Spanish camps, that sat in Madrid; nor to Kate's spiritual father, that sat in Rome. Known it is to the great Father that once whispered to Kate on the Andes; but else it has been a secret for two centuries; and to man it remains a secret for ever and ever!

P.S. – The portrait of Kate at Aix-la-Chapelle, mentioned in Part I., is in the gallery of *Herr Sempeller*: Semp*a*ler was a press error.[50] There is reason, however, to think that Velasquez painted a portrait of her in 1624, for his Spanish Majesty. In the year previous, that great artist certainly painted a portrait of Charles I.,[51] then Prince of Wales; and a rumour is abroad that this picture has recently been discovered. Perhaps a little search would bring to light the Nun's. All things were strange that ever connected themselves with Kate; and amongst the latest of these strange things should be mentioned, that, in the Three Days of Paris (July, 1830),[52] nearly all the copies of her memoirs and documents, just then printed by M. de Ferrer, perished by cannon shot.

SECRET SOCIETIES
[Part I]

First published in *Tait's*, XIV, August 1847, pp. 513–22. The essay was printed as 'BY THOMAS DE QUINCEY.' in a centred line following the title and immediately preceding the text.

Reprinted in *F*, XI, *Historical and Critical Essays* (1853), pp. 285–316, 349–52.

Revised text, carrying many accidentals but only one substantive variant from *F*, in *SGG*, VII, *Studies on Secret Records, Personal and Historic* (1858), pp. 234–64, 327–9.

There is one manuscript, as follows:

MS A: British Library, Department of Printed Books, C. 60. o. 3. The manuscript is part of a single endnote from *F*, corresponding to the text below running from p. 163.23 'used his opportunities' to p. 164.12 'the national religion.' The manuscript contains no substantive variants.

As the article demonstrates, De Quincey's interest in secret societies began early and lasted a lifetime. His fascination was often driven by his religious convictions, and his most prominent explorations of the subject include his four-part 'Historico-Critical Inquiry into the Origins of the Rosicrucians and the Free-Masons', published in the *London Magazine* in 1824, and his three-part essay 'On the Essenes', which appeared in *Blackwood's Magazine* in 1840. The publisher James Hogg stated that, 'of all the subjects which exercised a permanent fascination' over De Quincey,

> I would place first in order Thuggism in India and the Cagots of Spain and France. The Thugs gave rise to endless speculation…The far-reaching power of this mysterious brotherhood, the swiftness and certainty of its operations, the strange gradations of official rank, and the curious disguises adopted – all these exercised an influence on his mind which seemed never to wane….In like manner the Cagots – the lepers of France and Spain – excited his deep pity.

In 1858, when De Quincey revised the essay for *SGG*, he added a long 'SUPPLEMENTARY NOTE ON THE ESSENES' (Vol. 4, pp. 1–49; Vol. 11, pp. 442–88; Hogg, p. 174; Vol. 20, pp. 87–98).

AT a very early age commenced my own interest in the mystery that surrounds secret societies; the mystery being often double – 1. *What* they do; and 2. What they do it *for*. Except as to the premature growth of this interest, there was nothing surprising in *that*. For everybody that is by nature meditative must regard, with a feeling higher than any vulgar curiosity, small fraternities of men forming themselves as separate and inner vortices within the great vortex of society, communicating silently in broad daylight by signals not even seen, but if seen, not understood except among themselves, and connected by the link either of purposes not safe to be avowed, or by the grander link of awful truths which, merely to shelter themselves from the hostility of an age unprepared for their reception, must retire, perhaps for generations, behind thick curtains of secrecy. To be hidden amidst crowds is sublime – to come down hidden amongst crowds from distant generations, is doubly sublime.

The first incident in my own childish experience that threw my attention upon the possibility of such dark associations, was the Abbé Baruel's book, soon followed by a similar book of Professor Robison's, in demonstration of a regular conspiracy throughout Europe for exterminating Christianity.[1] This I did not read, but I heard it read and frequently discussed. I had already Latin enough to know that *cancer* meant a crab, and that the disease so appalling to a child's imagination, which in English we call a cancer, as soon as it has passed beyond the state of an indolent schirrous[2] tumour, drew its name from the horrid claws, or spurs, or roots, by which it connected itself with distant points, running underground, as it were, baffling detection, and defying radical extirpation. What I heard read aloud from the Abbé gave that dreadful cancerous character to the plot against Christianity. This plot, by the Abbé's account, stretched its horrid fangs, and threw out its forerunning feelers and *tentacles* into many nations, and more than one century.[3] *That* perplexed me, though also fascinating me by its grandeur. How men, living in distant periods and distant places – men that did not know each other, nay, often had not even heard of each other, nor spoke the same languages – could yet be parties to the same treason against a mighty religion towering to the highest heavens, puzzled my comprehension. Then, also, when wickedness was so easy, *why* did they take all this trouble to be wicked? The *how* and the *why* were alike mysterious to me. Yet the Abbé, everybody said, was a good man; incapable of telling falsehoods, or of countenancing falsehoods; and, indeed, to say *that* was superfluous as regarded myself; for every man that wrote a book was in my eyes an essentially good man, being a revealer of hidden truth. Things in MS. might be doubtful, but things printed were unavoidably and profoundly true. So that if I questioned and demurred as hotly as an infidel would have done, it never was that by the slightest shade I had become tainted with the infirmity of scepticism. On the contrary, I believed everybody as well as every*thing*. And, indeed, the very starting-point of my too importunate questions was exactly that incapacity of scepticism – not any lurking jealousy that even part might be false, but confidence too absolute that the whole must be true; since the more undeniably a thing was certain, the more clamorously I called upon people to make it intelligible. Other people, when they could not comprehend a thing, had often a resource in saying, 'But, after all, perhaps it's a lie.' *I* had no such resource. A lie was impossible in a man that descended upon earth in the awful shape of four volumes octavo. Such a great man as *that* was an oracle for me, far beyond Dodona or Delphi.[4] The same thing occurs in another form to everybody. Often (you know) – alas! *too* often – one's dear friend talks something, which one scruples to call 'rigmarole,' but which, for the life of one (it becomes necessary to whisper), cannot be comprehended. Well, after puzzling over it for two hours, you say, 'Come, that's enough; two hours is as much time as I can spare in one life for one unintelligibility.' And then you proceed, in the most tranquil frame of mind, to take coffee as if nothing had happened. The thing does not haunt your sleep; for you say, 'My dear friend, after all, was perhaps unintentionally talking nonsense.' But how if the thing that puzzles you happens to be a phenomenon in the sky or the clouds – something said by Nature? Nature never talks nonsense. There's no getting rid of the thing in that way. You can't call *that* 'rigmarole.' As to your dear friend, you were sceptical; and the consequence was, that you were able to be tranquil. There was a valve in reserve, by which your perplexity could escape. But as to Nature, you have no scepticism at all; you believe in *her* to a most bigoted extent; you believe every word she says. And that very belief is the cause that you are disturbed daily by something which you cannot understand. Being true, the thing ought to be intelligible. And exactly because it is *not* – exactly because this horrid unintelligibility is denied the comfort of doubt – therefore it is that you are so unhappy. If you could once make up your mind to doubt and to think, 'Oh, as to Nature, I don't believe one word in ten that she says,' then and there you would become as tranquil as when your dearest friend talks nonsense. My purpose, as regarded Baruel, was not tentative, as if presumptuously trying whether I should like to swallow a thing, with an *arrière pensée*[5] that, if not palatable, I might reject it, but simply the preparatory process of a boa-constrictor lubricating the substance offered, whatever it might be, towards its readier deglutition; that result, whether easy or not easy, being one that followed at any rate.

The person, who chiefly introduced me to Baruel, was a lady,[6] a stern lady, and austere, not only in her manners, which made most people dislike her, but also in the character of her understanding and morals – an advantage which made most people afraid of her. Me, however, she treated with unusual indulgence, chiefly, I believe, because I kept her intellectuals in a state of exercise, nearly amounting to persecution. She was just five times my age when our warfare of disputation commenced, I being seven, she thirty-five; and she was not quite four times my age when our warfare terminated by sudden separation, I being then ten and she thirty-eight. – This change, by the way, in the multiple that expressed her chronological relations to myself, used greatly to puzzle me; because, as the interval between us had diminished, within the memory of man, so rapidly, that, from being five times younger, I found myself less than four times younger, the natural inference seemed to be, that, in a few years, I should not be younger at all, but might come to be the older of the two; in which case, I should certainly have 'taken my change' out of the airs she continually gave herself on the score of 'experience.' That decisive word 'experience' was, indeed, always a sure sign to me that I had the better of the argument, and that it had become necessary, therefore, suddenly to pull me up in the career of victory by a violent exertion of authority; as a knight of old, at the very moment when he would else have unhorsed his opponent, was often frozen into unjust inactivity by the king's arbitrary signal for parting the tilters. It was, however, only when very hard pressed that my fair antagonist took this *not* fair advantage in our daily tournaments. Generally, and if I showed any moderation in the assault, she was rather pleased with the sharp rattle of my rolling musketry. Objections she rather liked, and questions, as many as one pleased upon the *pourquoi*, if one did not go on to *le pourquoi du pourquoi*.[7] *That*, she said, was carrying things too far: excess in anything she disapproved. Now, *there* I differed from her: excess was the thing I doated on. The fun seemed to me only beginning, when she asserted that it had already 'over-stepped the limits of propriety.' Ha! those limits, I thought, were soon reached.

But, however much or often I might vault over the limits of propriety, or might seem to challenge both *her* and the Abbé – all this was but anxiety to reconcile my own secret belief in the Abbé, with the arguments for not believing; it was but the form assumed by my earnest desire to see *how* the learned gentleman could be right, whom my intense faith certified beyond all doubt to *be* so, and whom, equally, my perverse logical recusancy whispered to be continually in the wrong. I wished to see my own rebellious arguments, which I really sorrowed over and bemoaned, knocked down like ninepins; shown to be softer than cotton, frailer than glass, and utterly worthless in the eye of reason. All this, indeed, the stern lady assured me that she *had* shown over and over again. Well, it might be so; and to this, at any rate, as a decree of court, I saw a worldly prudence in submitting. But, probably, I must have looked rather grim, and have wished devoutly for one fair turn-up, on Salisbury plain,[8] with herself and the Abbé, in which case my heart told me how earnestly I should pray that they might for ever floor *me*, but how melancholy a conviction oppressed my spirits that my destiny was to floor *them*. Victorious, I should find my belief and my understanding in painful schism: beaten and demolished, I should find my whole nature in harmony with itself.

The mysteriousness to me of men becoming partners (and by no means sleeping partners) in a society of which they had never heard; or, again, of one fellow standing at the beginning of a century, and stretching out his hand as an accomplice towards another fellow standing at the end of it, without either having known of the other's existence – all *that* did but sharpen the interest of wonder that gathered about the general economy of secret societies. Tertullian's profession of believing things, not *in spite* of being impossible, but *because* they were impossible,[9] is not the extravagance that most people suppose it. There is a deep truth in it. Many are the things which, in proportion as they attract the *highest* modes of belief, discover a tendency to repel belief on that part of the scale which is governed by the lower understanding. And here, as so often elsewhere, the axiom, with respect to extremes meeting, manifests its subtle presence. The highest form of the incredible, is sometimes the initial form of the credible. But the point on which our irreconcilability was greatest, respected the *cui bono*[10] of this alleged conspiracy. What were the conspirators to gain by success? and nobody pretended that they could gain anything by failure. The lady replied – that, by obliterating the light of Christianity, they prepared the readiest opening for the unlimited gratification of their odious appetites and passions. But to this the retort was too obvious to escape anybody, and for me it threw itself into the form of that pleasant story, reported from the life of Pyrrhus the Epirot[11] – viz., that one day, upon a friend requesting to know what ulterior purpose the king might mask under his expedition to Sicily, 'why, after *that* is finished,' replied the king, 'I mean to administer a little correction (very much wanted) to certain parts of Italy, and particularly to that nest of rascals in Latium.'[12] 'And then ——' said the friend: 'and then,' said Pyrrhus, 'next we go for Macedon; and, after that job's jobbed, next, of course, for Greece.' 'Which done,' said the friend: 'which done,' interrupted the king, 'as done it shall be, then we're off to tickle the Egyptians.' 'Whom having tickled,' pursued the friend, 'then we' – 'tickle the Persians,' said the king. 'But after that is done,' urged the obstinate friend, 'whither next?' 'Why, really man, it's hard to say; you give one no time to breathe; but we'll consider the case in Persia, and, until we've settled it, we can crown ourselves with roses, and pass the time pleasantly enough over the best wine to be found in Ecbatana.'[13] 'That's a very just idea,' replied the friend; 'but, with submission, it strikes me that we might do *that* just now, and, at the beginning of all these tedious wars, instead of waiting for their end.' 'Bless me!' said Pyrrhus, 'if ever I thought of *that* before. Why, man, you're a conjurer; you've discovered a mine of happiness. So, here boy, bring us roses and plenty of Cretan wine.' Surely, on the same principle, these French Encyclopédistes, and Bavarian Illuminati,[14] did not need to postpone any jubilees of licentiousness which they promised themselves, to so very indefinite a period as their ovation over the ruins of Christianity. True, the *impulse* of hatred, even though irrational, may be a stronger force for action than any *motive* of hatred, however rational, or grounded in self-interest. But the particular motive relied upon by the stern lady, as the central spring of the anti-Christian movement, being obviously insufficient for the weight which it had to sustain, naturally the lady, growing sensible of this herself, became still sterner; very angry with me; and not quite satisfied, in this instance, with the

Abbé. Yet, after all, it was not any embittered remembrance of our eternal feuds, in dusting the jacket of the Abbé Baruel, that lost me, ultimately, the favour of this austere lady. All *that* she forgave; and especially because she came to think the Abbé as bad as myself, for leaving such openings to my inroads. It was on a question of politics that our deadliest difference arose, and that my deadliest sarcasm was launched; not against herself, but against the opinion and party which she adopted. I was right, as usually I am; but, on this occasion, must have been, because I stood up (as a patriot, intolerant, to frenzy, of all insult directed against dear England); and she, though otherwise patriotic enough, in this instance ranged herself in alliance with a false anti-national sentiment. My sarcasm was not too strong for the case. But certainly I ought to have thought it too strong for the presence of a lady; whom, or any of her sex, on a matter of politics in these days, so much am I changed, I would allow to chace me, like a foot-ball, all round the tropics, rather than offer the least show of resistance. But my excuse was childhood; and, though it may be true, as the reader will be sure to remind me, that she was rapidly growing down to my level in that respect, still she had not quite reached it; so that there was more excuse for me, after all, than for *her*. She was no longer five times as old, or even four; but when she would come down to be two times as old, and one time as old, it was hard to say.

Thus I had good reason for remembering my first introduction to the knowledge of Secret Societies, since this knowledge introduced me to the more gloomy knowledge of the strife which gathers in clouds over the fields of human life; and to the knowledge of this strife in two shapes, one of which none of us fail to learn – the personal strife which is awakened so eternally by difference of opinion, or difference of interest; the other, which is felt, perhaps, obscurely by all, but distinctly noticed only by the profoundly reflective, viz., the schism – so mysterious to those even who have examined it most – between the human intellect and many undeniable realities of human experience. As to the first mode of strife, I could not possibly forget it; for the stern lady died before we had an opportunity to exchange forgiveness, and *that* left a sting behind. She, I am sure, was a good forgiving creature at heart; and, especially, she would have forgiven *me*, because it was *my* place (if one only got one's right place on earth) to forgive *her*. Had she even hauled me out of bed with a tackling of ropes in the dead of night, for the mere purpose of reconciliation, I should have said – 'Why, you see, I can't forgive you entirely to-night, because I'm angry when people waken me without notice, but to-morrow morning I certainly will; or, if that won't do, you shall forgive *me*. No great matter *which*, as the conclusion must be the same in either case, viz., to kiss and be friends.'

But the other strife, which perhaps sounds metaphysical in the reader's ears, then first wakened up to my perceptions, and never again went to sleep amongst my perplexities. Oh Cicero! my poor, thoughtless Cicero! in all your shallow metaphysics not once did you give utterance to such a bounce as when you asserted, that never yet did human reason say one thing and Nature say another.[15] On the contrary, every part of Nature – mechanics, dynamics, morals, metaphysics, and even pure mathematics – are continually giving the lie flatly by their facts and conclusions to the very necessities and laws of human understanding. Did the reader ever study the *Antimonics* of Kant?[16] If not, he has read nothing. Now, *there* he will have the pleasure of seeing a set of quadrilles or reels, in which old Mother Reason amuses herself by dancing to the right and left two variations of blank contradiction to old Mother Truth, both variations being irrefragable, each variation contradicting the other, each contradicting the equatorial reality, and each alike (though past all denial) being a lie. But he need not go to Kant for this. Let him look as one having eyes for looking, and everywhere the same perplexing phenomenon occurs. And this first dawned upon myself in the Baruel case. As nature is to the human intellect, so was Baruel to mine. We all believe in nature without limit, yet hardly understand a page amongst her innumerable pages. I believed in Baruel by necessity, and yet everywhere my understanding mutinied against *his*.

But in Baruel I had heard only of Secret Societies that were consciously formed for mischievous ends; or if not always for a distinct purpose of evil, yet always in a spirit of malignant contradiction and hatred. Soon I read of other Societies even more secret, that watched over *truth* dangerous to publish or even to whisper, like the sleepless dragons that Oriental fable associated with the subterraneous guardianship of regal treasures. The secrecy, and the reasons for the secrecy, were alike sublime. The very image, unveiling itself by unsteady glimpses, of men linked by brotherly love and perfect confidence, meeting in secret chambers, at the noontide of night, to shelter, by muffling, with their own persons interposed, and at their own risk, some solitary lamp of truth – sheltering it from the carelessness of the world, and its stormy ignorance – this would soon have blown it out – sheltering it from the hatred of the world, that would soon have found out its nature, and made war upon its life – *that* was superhumanly sublime. The fear of those men was sublime – the courage was sublime – the stealthy thief like means were sublime – the audacious end, viz., to change the kingdoms of earth, was sublime. If they acted and moved like cowards, those men were sublime: if they planned with the audacity of martyrs, those men were sublime – not less, as cowards, not more as martyrs; for the cowardice that appeared above, and the courage that lurked below, were parts of the same machinery.

But another feature of sublimity, which it surprises one to see so many coarse minded men unaware of, lies in the self-perpetuation and phoenix-like defiance to mortality of such Societies. This feature it is that throws a grandeur even on a humbug, of which there have been many examples, and two in particular, which I am soon going to memorialise. Often and often have men of finer minds felt this secret spell of grandeur, and laboured to embody it in external forms. There was a phoenix-club once in Oxford (up and down

Europe there have been several) that by its constitution grasped not only at the sort of immortality aspired after by Phoenix Insurance offices, viz. a legal or notional perpetuation,[17] liable merely to no *practical* interruptions as regarded paying, and *à fortiori*[18] as regarded receiving money, but otherwise fast asleep every night like other dull people – far more faithful, literal, intense, was the realisation in *this* case of an undying life. Such a condition as a '*sede vacante*,'[19] which is a condition expressed in the constitutions of all other societies, was impossible in this, for any office whatever. That great case was realised which has since been described by Chateaubriand as governing the throne of France and its successions.[20] '*His Majesty is dead!*' shouts a voice, and this seems to argue, at least, a moment's interregnum: not at all; not a moment's: the thing is impossible: simultaneous (and not successive) is the breath that ejaculates '*may the King live for ever.*' The birth and the death, the rising and the setting, synchronise by a metaphysical nicety of neck-and-neck, inconceivable to the book keepers of earth. These wretched men imagine that the second rider's foot cannot possibly be in the stirrup until the first rider's foot is out. If the one event occurs in moment M, the other they think must occur in moment N. That may be as regards stirrups, but not as regards metaphysics. I admit that the guard of a mail-coach cannot possibly leave the post-office *before* the coachman, but upon the whole a little after him. Such base rules, however, find themselves compelled to give way in presence of great metaphysicians – in whose science, as I stoop to inform book-keepers, the effect, if anything, goes rather a-head of the cause. Now that Oxford club arose on these sublime principles: no disease like intermitting pulse was known *there*. No fire, but vestal fire, was used for boiling the tea kettle. The rule was – that, if once entered upon the *matricula* of this amaranthine[21] club, thence forwards, come from what zone of the earth you would – come without a minute's notice – send up your card – Mr O. P., from the Anthropophagi – Mr P. O., from the men whose heads do grow beneath their shoulders[22] – instantly you were shown in to the sublime presence. You were not limited to any particular century. Nay, by the rigour of the theory, you had your own choice of millennium. Whatever might be convenient to you, was convenient to the club. The constitution of the club assumed, that, in every successive generation, as a matter of course, a President duly elected, (or his authorised delegate) would be found in the chair; scornfully throwing the *onus* of proof to the contrary upon the presumptuous reptile that doubted it. Public or private calamity signified not. The President reverberated himself through a long sinking fund of Surrogates and Vice-Presidents. There, night and day, summer and winter, seed-time and harvest, sat the august man, looking as grim as the *Princeps Senatûs*[23] amongst the Conscript Fathers of Rome, when the Gauls entered on the errand of cutting their throats.[24] If *you* entered this club on the very same errand, the President was backed to a large amount to keep his seat until his successor had been summoned. Suppose the greatest of revolutions to have passed over the island during your absence abroad; England, let us say, has even been conquered by a polished race of Hottentots.[25] Very good: an accomplished Hottentot will then be found seated in the chair; you will be allowed to kiss Mr President's black paw; and will understand that, although *farewells* might be common enough, as regarded individual members, yet by the eternal laws of this eternal club, the word *adjournment* for the whole concern was a word so treasonable, as not to be uttered without risk of massacre.

The same principle in man's nature, the everlasting instinct for glorifying the everlasting, the impulse for petrifying the fugitive, and arresting the transitory, which shows itself in ten thousand forms, has also, in this field of secret confederations, assumed many grander forms. To strive after a conquest over Time the conqueror, is already great, in whatsoever direction. But it is still greater when it applies itself to objects that are *per se* immortal, and mortal only as respects their alliance with man. Glorification of heaven – litanies, chaunted day and night by adoring hearts – these will doubtless ascend for ever from this planet. That result is placed out of hazard, and needs not the guarantee of princes. Somewhere, from some climate, from some lips, such a worship will not cease to rise. But, let a man's local attachments be what they may, he must sigh to think that no assignable spot of ground on earth, that no nation, that no family, enjoys any absolute privilege in that respect. No land, whether continent or island – nor race, whether free men or slaves, can claim any fixed inheritance, or indefeasible heirlooms of truth. Yet, for that very reason, men of deep piety have but the more earnestly striven to bind down, and chain their own conceptions of truth within the models of some unchanging establishments, even as the Greek Pagans of old chained down their gods* from deserting them; have striven to train the vagrant water-brooks of Wisdom, lest she might desert the region altogether, into the channels of some local homestead; to connect, with a fixed succession of descendants, the conservation of religion; to root, as one would root a forest that is to flourish through ages, a heritage of ancient truth in the territorial heritage of an ancient household. That sounds to some ears like the policy that founded monastic institutions. Whether so or not, it is not necessarily Roman Catholic. The same policy – the same principle – the sighing after peace and the image of perpetuity – have many times moulded the plans of *Protestant* families. Such families, with monastic imaginations linked to Protestant hearts, existed numerously in England through the reigns of the First James and

* *'Chained down their Gods':* – Many of the Greek states, though it has not been sufficiently inquired *which* states and in what age, had a notion that in war-time the tutelary deities of the place, the epichorial[26] gods, were liable to bribery, by secret offers of temples more splendid, altars better served, &c. from the enemy; so that a standing danger existed, lest these gods should desert to the hostile camp; and especially, because, not knowing the rate of the hostile biddings, the indigenous worshippers had no guide to regulate their own counterbiddings. In this embarrassment, the prudent course, as most people believed, was to chain the divine idols by the leg, with golden fetters.[27]

Charles[28] – families amongst the gentry, or what on the Continent would be called the lower nobility, that remembered with love the solemn ritual and services of the Romish Church; but with *this* love combined the love of Protestant doctrines. Amongst these families, and distinguished amongst them, was that of the Farrers.* The name of their patrimonial estate was Little Gidding, and, I think, in the county of Hertford.[32] They were, by native turn of mind, and by varied accomplishments, a most interesting family. In some royal houses of Europe it was once a custom, that every son, if not every daughter, should learn a trade. This custom subsisted down to the days of the unhappy Louis XVI.,[33] who was a locksmith; and I was once assured by a Frenchman, who knew him well, not so bad a one, considering (you know) that one cannot be as rough as might be wished in scolding a locksmith that one is obliged to address as 'your majesty.' A majestic locksmith has a sort of right to be a bad one. The Farrers adopted this custom, and most of them chose the trade of a bookbinder. Why this was a good trade to choose, I will explain in a brief digression. It is a reason which applies only to three other trades, viz. to coining, to printing books, and to making gold or silver plate. And the reason is this – all the four arts stand on an isthmus, connecting them, on one side, with merely mechanic crafts, on the other side, with the Fine Arts. This was the marking distinction between the coinages of ancient classical days and our own. Our European and East Indian[34] coins are the basest of all base products from rude barbaresque handicraft. They are imagined by the man, some horrid Cyclops,[35] who conceived the great idea of a horse-shoe, a poker, and a tenpenny nail. Now, the ancient coins were modelled by the same immortal artists that conceived their exquisite *gems*, the cameos and intaglios, which you may buy, in Tassie's Sulphurs, at a few shillings each, or for much less in the engraved *Glyptothecae*.[36] But, as to coining, our dear lady the Queen (God bless her!)[37] is so avaricious, that she will have it all to herself. She taboos it. She won't let you or me into the smallest share of the business; and she lags us if we poach. That is what *I* call monopoly. And I do wish her Majesty would be persuaded to read a ship-load of political economists that I could point out, on the ruinous consequences of that vice, which, otherwise, it may be feared nobody ever will read. After coining, the next best trade is Printing. This, also, might approach to a Fine Art. When entering the twilight of dotage, reader, I mean to have a printing-press in my own study.[38] I shall print some immaculate editions, as farewell keepsakes, for distribution amongst people that I love; but rich and rare must be the gems on which *I* shall condescend to bestow this manual labour. I mean, also, to print a spelling-book for

* *'The Farrers.'* – There is, but by whom written I really forget, a separate memoir of this family, and published as a separate volume. In the county histories (such as Chauncy's,[29] &c.) will also be found sketches of their history. But the most popular form in which their memorials have been retraced is a biography of Nicholas Farrer,[30] introduced into one of the volumes, I cannot say which, of the Ecclesiastical Biography – an interesting compilation, drawn up by the late Dr Christopher Wordsworth, a brother of the great poet.[31]

the reader's use. As it seems that he reads, he surely ought to spell. I hope he will not be offended. If he *is*, and dreadfully, viewing it as the most awful insult that man could offer to his brother man, in that case he might bequeath it by will to his possible grandson. Two generations might wash out the affront. Or if he accepts, and furnishes me with his name, I will also print on a blank leaf the good old ancestral legend – 'A. B., *his* book, Heaven grant him grace therein to look.' As to Plate-making, it seems to rank with mechanic baseness; you think not of the sculptor, the chaser, and their exquisite tools, but of Sheffield, Birmingham, Glasgow, sledge-hammers, and pincers. It seems to require no art. I think I could make a dessert spoon myself. Yet the openings which it offers are vast, wherever wealth exists, for the lovelier conceptions of higher art. Benvenuto Cellini[39] – what an artist was *he!* There are some few of his most exquisite works in this country, which may be seen by applying in the right quarters. Judge of him by these, and not by his autobiography. There he appears as a vain ostentatious man.* One would suppose, to hear *him* talk, that nobody ever executed a murder but himself. His own are tolerable, that's all you can say; but not one of them is first-rate, or to be named on the same day with the Pope's attempt at murdering Cellini himself, which must command the unqualified approbation of the connoisseur.[41] True, the Papal attempt did not succeed, and most of Cellini's *did.* What of *that?* Who but idiots judge by the event? Much, therefore, as I condemn the man's vanity, and the more so because he claims some murders that too probably were none of *his* (not content with exaggerating his own, he absolutely pirated other men's murders!) yet, when you turn from this walk of art, in which he practised only as an *amateur*, to his *orféverie*[42] – then you feel the interval that divides the *charlatan* from the man of exquisite genius. As a murderer, he was a poor creature; as an artist in gold, he was inimitable. Finally, there remains *book-binding*,[43] of which also one may affirm, that, being usually the vilest of handicrafts, it is susceptible of much higher effects in the enrichments, tooling, architecture, heraldic emblazonries, &c. This art Mr Farrer selected for his trade. He had travelled on foot through Spain; and I should think it not impossible that he had *there* seen some magnificent specimens of book-binding. For I was once told, though I have not seen it mentioned in any book, that a century before the date of Farrer's travels, Cardinal Ximenes, when printing his great Complutensian Bible,[44] gave a special encouragement to a new style of binding – fitted for harmonising with the grandeur of royal furni-

* When a murderer is thoroughly diseased by vanity ones loses all confidence in him. Cellini went upon the plan of claiming all eminent murders, suitable in point of time and place, that nobody else claimed; just as many a short poem in the Greek Anthologies, marked *adespoton* (or, *without an owner*), was sported by one pretender after another as his own. Even simple homicides he would not think it below him to challenge as his own. Two princes, at the very least, a Bourbon and a Nassau,[40] he pretended to have shot; it might be so, but nobody ever came forward to corroborate his statement.

ture, and the carved enrichments of gothic libraries.* This, and the other accomplishments which the Farrers had, they had in perfection. But the most remarkable trait in the family character, was the exaltation of their devotional feelings. Had it not been for their benignity and humility, they might have been thought gloomy and ascetic. Something there was, as in thoughtful minds left to a deep rural solitude there is likely to be, of La Trappism and Madame Guyon Quietism.[45] A nun-like aspiration there was in the females after purity and oblivion of earth: in Mr Farrer, the head of the family, a devotional energy, put forth in continual combat with the earthly energies that tempted him away to the world, and with all that offered itself under the specious name of public usefulness. In this combination of qualities arose the plan which the family organised for a system of perpetual worship. They had a family chapel regularly consecrated, as so many families of their rank still had in England. They had an organ: they had means of forming a choir. Gradually the establishment was mounted: the appointments were completed: the machinery was got into motion. How far the plan was ever effectually perfected, would be hard to say. The increasing ferment of the times, until the meeting of the Long Parliament in Nov. 1640, and in less than two years after *that*, the opening of the great civil war[46] must have made it absolutely impossible to adhere systematically to any scheme of that nature, which required perfect seclusion from worldly cares within the mansion, and public tranquillity outside. Not to mention that the Farrers had an extra source of molestation at that period, when Puritanism was advancing rapidly to a domineering station of power, in the public suspicions which unjustly (but not altogether unplausibly) taxed them with Popish leanings.[47] A hundred years later, Bishop Butler drew upon himself at Durham the very same suspicion,[48] and in some degree by the very same act, viz., by an adoption of some pious symbols, open undeniably to the whole catholic family of Christian Churches, and yet equivocal in their meaning, because popularly appropriated from old associations of habit to the use of Popish communities. Abstracting, however, from the violent disturbances of those stormy times in the way of all religious schemes, we may collect that the scheme of the Farrers was – that the chapel services should be going on, by means of successive 'reliefs' as in camps, or of 'watches' as at sea, through every hour of the day and the night, from year to year, from childhood to old age. Come when you might, come in the dawning, come in the twilight, come at noonday, come through silent roads in the dead of night, always you were to be sure of hearing, through the woods of Little Gidding, the blair of the organ, or the penitential wail of the solitary choristers, or the glad triumphant burst of the full choir in jubilation. There

* This was the earliest attempt at a Polyglot Bible, and had its name from the town of *Complutum*, which is, I think, *Alcala de Henarez*. The Henarez is a little river. Some readers will thank me for mentioning that the accent is on the *first* syllable of Complutum, the *u* in the penultimate being short; not Compultum, but Complutŭm.

was some affinity in Mr Farrer's mind to the Spanish peculiarities, and the Spanish modes of grandeur; awful prostration, like Pascal's,[49] before the divine idea; gloom that sought to strengthen itself by tenfold involution in the night of solitary woods; exaggerated impressions (if such impressions *could* be exaggerated) of human wretchedness, and a brooding sense of some unknown illimitable grandeur[50] – a sense that could sustain itself at its natural level, only by eternal contemplation of objects that had no end.

Mr Farrer's plan for realising a vestal fire, or something beyond it, viz., a *secrecy* of truth, burning brightly in darkness – and, secondly, a *perpetuity* of truth – did not succeed; as many a noble scheme, that men never heard of, has been swept away in its infancy by the ruins of flood, fire, earthquake, which also are forgotten not less completely than what they ruined. Thank Heaven for that! If the noble is often crushed suddenly by the ignoble, one forgetfulness travels after both. The wicked earthquake is forgotten not less than the glorious temples which it ruined. Yet the Farrer plan has repeatedly succeeded and prospered through a course of centuries, and for purposes of the same nature. But the strange thing is (which already I have noticed), that the general principle of such a plan has succeeded most memorably when applied to purposes of humbug. The two best-known of all Secret Societies, that ever *have* been, are the two most extensive monuments of humbug on the one side and credulity on the other. They divide themselves between the ancient world and the modern. The great and illustrious humbug of ancient history was, the ELEUSINIAN MYSTERIES. The great and illustrious humbug of modern history, of the history which boasts a present and a future, as well as a past, is FREEMASONRY.[51] Let me take a few liberties with both.

The Eleusinian humbug was for centuries the opprobrium of scholars. Even in contemporary times it *was* such. The greatest philosopher, or polyhistor, of Athens, or of Rome, could no more tell you the secret – the *to aporeton*[52] (unless he had been initiated, in which case he *durst* not tell it) – than I can. In fact, if you come to *that*, perhaps I myself *can* tell it. The ancient philosopher would retort that we of these days are in the same predicament as to our own humbug – the Freemasons. No, no, my friend, you're wrong *there*. We know all about that humbug, as I mean to show you. But for what we know of Eleusis and its mummeries, which is quite enough for all practical purposes, we are indebted to none of you ancients, but entirely to modern sagacity. Is not *that* shocking, that a hoax should first be unmasqued when it has been defunct for 1,500 years? The interest which attaches to the Eleusinian shows, is not properly an interest in *them*, but an alien interest in accidents indirectly connected with them. Secret there was virtually none; but a mystery at length begins to arise – how it was that this distressing secret, viz., of there being no secret at all, could, through so many generations, pass down in religious conservation of itself from all profane curiosity of outside barbarians. There was an endless file of heroes, philosophers, statesmen, all hoaxed, all of course incensed at being hoaxed, and yet not one of them is known to have blabbed. A great modern poet, musing philosophically on the results amongst the mob 'in Leicester's busy square,' from looking through a showman's telescope at the moon, is surprised at the crowd of spectators going off with an air of disappointment:

> 'One after one they turn aside; nor have I one espied,
> That doth not slackly go away, as if dissatisfied.'[53]

Yes, but I can tell him the reason of that. The fact is, a more pitiful sight for sight-seers, than our own moon, does not exist. The first man that showed *me* the moon through a glass of any power, was a distinguished professor of astronomy.[54] I was so incensed with the hoax (as it seemed) put upon me – such a weak, watery, wicked old harridan, substituted for the pretty creature I had been used to see – that I marched up to him with the angry design of demanding my half-crown back again, until a disgusting remembrance came over me, that, being a learned professor the showman could not possibly have taken my half-crown, which fact also destroyed all ground of action against him as obtaining money under false pretences. I contented myself, therefore, with saying, that until he showed me the man in the moon, with his dog, lanthorn, and bundle of thorns, I must decline corroborating his fancy of being able to exhibit the real old original moon and no mistake. Endymion[55] never could have had such a sweetheart as *that*. Let the reader take my advice, not to seek familiarity with the moon. Familiarity breeds contempt.

It is certain that, like the travellers through 'Leicester's busy square,' all the visiters of Eleusis must have abominated the hoax put upon them –

> — —'nor have I *one* espied,
> That did not slackly walk away, as if dissatisfied.'

See now the different luck of hoaxers in this world. Joseph Ady is smoked pretty nearly by the whole race of man. The Continent is, by this time, wide awake; Belgium has refused to take in his letters; and the cruel Lord Mayor of London[56] has threatened to indict Joe for a fraud, value two-pence, by reason of the said Joe having seduced his lordship into opening an unpaid letter, which was found to contain nothing but an invitation from 'yours respectfully' – not to a dinner party – but to an early remittance of one pound, for reasons subsequently to be disclosed. I should think, but there's no knowing, that there might be a chance still for Joe (whom, really one begins to pity, as a persecuted man – cruising, like the Flying Dutchman, through seas that have all closed their ports), in Astrachan, and, perhaps, in Mecca.[57] Some business might be done, for a few years, in Timbuctoo; and an opening there would undoubtedly be found for a connexion with Abd-el-Kader,[58] if only any opening could be found *to* Abd-el-Kader through the French lines. Now, on the other hand, the goddess, and her establishment of hoaxers at Eleusis did a vast 'stroke of business' for more than six centuries, without any 'unpleasantries'* occurring; no cudgels shaken in the streets, little incidents that custom (by making too familiar,) has made contemptible to the philosophy of Joe: no round robins, signed by the whole maindeck of the academy or the porch; no praetors or lord mayors threatening actions *repetundarum*,[60] and mourning over two-pences that had gone astray. 'Misfortune acquaints a man with strange bed-fellows;'[61] and the common misfortune of having been hoaxed lowers the proudest and the humblest into a strange unanimity, for once, of pocketing their wrongs in silence. Eleusis, with her fine bronzed face, might say proudly and laughingly – 'expose *me*, indeed! – why, I hoaxed this man's great-grandfather, and I trust to hoax his great-grandson; all generations of his house *have* been, or *shall* be hoaxed, and afterwards grateful to me for not exposing that fact of the hoax at their private expense.'

There is a singularity in this case, of the same kind as that stratagem, (but how prodigiously exceeded in its scale,) imperfectly executed on the Greek leaders by the Persian Satrap Tissaphernes,[62] but perfectly, in one or two cases, amongst the savage islands of the South Seas, upon European crews, when one victim, having first been caught, has been used as the means of trepanning all his comrades in succession. Each successive novice has been tamed, by terror, into an instrument for decoying other novices, from A to Z. Next, after this feature of interest about the Eleusinian *Teletai*,[63] is another which modern times have quickened and developed, viz., the gift of enormous nonsense, the inspiration of nonsense, which the enigma of these mysteries has been the fortunate means of blowing into the brains of various able men. It requires such men, in fact, to succeed as speculators in nonsense. None but a man of extraordinary talents can write first-rate nonsense. Perhaps the prince of all men, ever formed by nature and education, for writing superior nonsense was, Warburton.[64] The natural vegetation of his intellect tended to that kind of fungus which is called 'crotchet;' so much so, that, if he had a just and powerful thought (as sometimes he had), or even a wise and beautiful thought, or even a grand one, by the mere perversity of his tortuous brain, it was soon digested into a crotchet. This native tendency of his was cultured and watered, for years, by his practice as an attorney.[65] Making him a bishop was, perhaps, a mistake; it certainly stunted the growth of special pleading, perhaps ruined the science; on the other hand, it saved the twelve judges of that day from being driven mad, as they would have been by this Hermes Trismegistus, this born Titan, in the realms of *La Chicane*.[66] Some fractions of the *virus* descended through the Warburtonian commentaries upon Pope,[67] &c., corroding the flesh to the very bones, wherever it alighted. But the Centaur's shirt[68] of W.'s malignity was destined for the Hebrew lawgiver, and all that

* 'Unpleasantries' – this is a new word, launched a very few years back[59] in some commercial towns. It is generally used – not in any sense that the reader would collect from its antipole, *pleasantry*, but in a sense that he may abstract from the context in the sentence above.

could be made to fall within that field. Did my reader ever read the 'Divine Legation of Moses'?[69] Is he aware of the mighty syllogism, that single block of granite, such as you can see nowhere but at St Petersburg,[70] on which that elaborate work reposes? There is a Welsh bridge, near Llanroost, the birth-place of Inigo Jones,[71] built by that architect with such exquisite skill, that the people astonished me (but the people were two milk-maids), by protesting that invariably a little breeze-footed Camilla, of three years old, in running across, caused the bridge to tremble like a guilty thing.[72] So admirable was the equillibrium, that an infant's foot disturbed it. Unhappily, Camilla had sprained her ancle at that time, so that the experiment could not be tried; and the bridge, to me, seemed not guilty at all (to judge by its trembling), but as innocent as Camilla herself. Now, Warburton must have sought to rival the Welsh *pontifex* in this particular test of architectural skill; for his syllogism is so divinely poised, that if you shake this key-stone of his great arch (as you certainly may), then you will become aware of a vibration – of a nervous tremor – running through the entire dome of his divine legation; you are absolutely afraid of the dome coming down with yourself in the centre; just as the Llanroost bridge used to be near going into hysterics when the light-footed Camilla bounded across it. This syllogism, on account of its connexion with the Eleusinian hoax, I will rehearse: it is the very perfection of a crotchet. Suppose the *major* proposition to be this – That no religion, unless through the advantage of divine inspiration, could dispense with the doctrine of future rewards and punishments. Suppose the *minor* proposition this – That the Mosaic religion *did* dispense with that doctrine. Then the conclusion will be – *ergo* the Mosaic religion was divinely inspired. The monstrous tenor of this argument made it necessary to argue most elaborately that all the false systems of false and cruel religions were affectionately anxious for maintaining the doctrine of a future state; but 2dly, that the only true faith and the only pure worship were systematically careless of that doctrine. Of course it became necessary to show, *inter alia*,[73] that the Grecian States and law-givers maintained officially, as consecrated parts of the public religion, the doctrine of immortality as valid for man's expectations and fears; whilst at Jerusalem, at Hebron, on Mount Sinai,[74] this doctrine was slighted. Generally speaking, a lie is a hard thing to establish. The Bishop of Gloucester was forced to tax his resources as an artist, in building palaces of air, not less than ever Inigo Jones before him in building Whitehall[75] or St Vitus's bridge at Llanroost. Unless he could prove that Paganism fought hard for this true doctrine, then by his own argument Paganism would be found true. Just as, inversely, if he failed to prove that Judaism countenanced the false doctrine, Judaism would itself be found false. Which ever favoured the false, was true; which ever favoured the true, was false. There's a crotchet for you, reader, round and full as any prize turnip ever yet crowned with laurels by great agricultural Societies! I suspect that in Homeric language, twice nine of such degenerate men as the reader and myself could not grow such a crotchet as that!

The Bishop had, therefore, to prove – it was an obligation self-created by his own syllogism – that the Pagan religion of Greece, in some great authorised institution of the land, taught and insisted on the doctrine of a future state as the basis on which all legal ethics rested. This great doctrine he had to suspend as a chandelier in his halls of Pagan mythology. A pretty chandelier for a Christian Bishop to be chaining to the roof and lighting up for the glory of heathenism! Involuntarily one thinks of Aladdin's impious order for a roc's egg, the egg of the very deity whom the slave of the lamp served, to hang up in his principal saloon.[76] The Bishop found his chandelier, or fancied he had found it, in the old lumber garrets of Eleusis. He knew, he could prove, what was taught in the Eleusinian shows. Was the Bishop ever there? No: but what of that? He could read through a milestone. And Virgil, in his 6th Aeneid, had given the world a poetic account of the *Teletai*, which the Bishop kindly translated and expanded into the truth of absolute prose. The doctrine of immortality, he insisted, was the chief secret revealed in the mysteries.[77] And thus he proved decisively that, because it taught a capital truth, Paganism must be a capital falsehood. It is impossible to go within a few pages into the innumerable details. Sufficient it would be for any casual reader to ask, if this were the very hinge of all legislative ethics in Greece, how it happened that it was a matter of pure fancy or accident whether any Greek, or even any Athenian, were initiated or not; 2dly, how the Bishop would escape the following dilemma – if the supposed doctrine were advanced merely as an opinion, one amongst others, then what authority did it draw from Eleusis? If, on the other hand, Eleusis pretended to some special argument for immortality, how came it that many Greek and some Roman philosophers, who had been introduced at Eleusis, or had even ascended to the highest degree of μυησις,[78] did not, in discussing this question, refer to that secret proof which, though not privileged to develop, they might safely have built upon as a postulate amongst initiated brothers? An opinion ungrounded was entitled to no weight even in the mobs of Eleusis – an argument upon good grounds must have been often alluded to in philosophic schools. Neither could a nation of holy cowards, trembling like the bridge at Llanroost, have had it in their power to intercept the propagation of such a truth. The 47th of Euclid I. *might* have been kept a secret by fear of assassination, because no man could communicate *that* in a moment of intoxication;[79] if his wife, for instance, should insist on his betraying the secret of that proposition, he might safely tell her – not a word would she understand or remember; and the worst result would be, that she would box his ears for imposing upon her. I once heard a poor fellow complain, that, being a Freemason, he had been led the life of a dog by his wife, as if *he* were Samson and *she* were Dalilah,[80] with the purpose of forcing him to betray the Masonic secret and sign: and these, he solemnly protested to us all, that he *had* betrayed most regularly and faithfully whenever he happened to be drunk. But what did he get for his goodness? All the return he ever had for the kindness of this invariable treachery was a word, too common, I regret to say, in female lips, viz. *fiddle-de-dee:* and he declared, with tears in his eyes, that peace for *him* was out of the question, until he could find out some plausible falsehood that might prove more satisfactory to his wife's mind than the truth. Now the Eleusinian secret, if it related to the immortality of the soul, could not have the protection of obscurity or complex involution. If it had, then it could not have been intelligible to mobs: if it had *not*, then it could not have been guarded against the fervor of confidential conversation. A very subtle argument could not have been communicated to the multitudes that visited the shows – a very popular argument would have passed a man's lips, in the ardour of argument, before he would himself be aware of it.

But all this is superfluous. Let the reader study the short essay of Lobeck on this subject, forming one section in three of his *Aglaophamus*,[81] and he will treat, with derision, all the irrelevant skirmishing, with the vast roars of artillery pointed at shadows, which amuse the learned, but disgust the philosophic in the 'Divine Legation.' Much remains to be done that Lobeck's rustic seclusion denied him the opportunities for doing;* much that can be done

* It may seem strange to insinuate against the *Aglaophamus* any objection, great or small, as regards its condition – *that* being the main organ of its strength. But precisely here lay the power of Lobeck, and here his weakness; all his strength, and his most obvious defect. Of this he was sensible himself. At the very period of composing *Aglaophamus*, he found reason to complain that his situation denied him access to great libraries: and this, perhaps, is felt by the reader most in the part relating to the Eleusinian mysteries, least in that relating to the Orphic. Previously, however, Lobeck had used his opportunities well. And the true praise of his reading is, not so much that it was unusually extensive, as that it was unusually systematic, and connected itself in all its parts by unity of purpose. At the same time it is a remark of considerable interest, that the student must not look in Lobeck, for luminous logic, or for simplicity of arrangement, which are qualifications for good writing, unknown to the great scholars of modern Germany, to Niebuhr altogether, and in the next degree unknown to Ottfried Mueller,[82] and to Lobeck. Their defects in this respect are so flagrant, as to argue some capital vice in the academic training of Germany. Elsewhere throughout the world no such monstrous result appears of chaotic arrangement from profound research. As regards philosophy, and its direct application to the enigmas of these Grecian mysteries, it is no blame to Lobeck that none must be looked for in *him*, unless he had made some pretence to it, which I am not aware that he did. Yet in one instance he ought to have made such a pretence: mere good sense should have opened his eyes to one elementary blunder of Warburton's. I tax W., I tax all who have ever countenanced W., I tax all who have ever opposed W., I tax Lobeck as bringing up the rear of these opponents, one and all with the inexcusable blindness of torpor in using their natural eyesight. So much of philosophy as resides in the mere natural faculty of reflectiveness would have exposed [pure sloth it was in the exercise of this faculty which concealed] the blunder of W. in confounding a *doctrinal* religion [such as Judaism, Christianity, Islamism] with a Pagan religion, which last has a *cultus* or ceremonial worship, but is essentially insusceptible of any dogma or opinion. Paganism had no creed, no faith, no doctrine, little, or great, shallow, or deep, false or true. Consequently the doctrine of a future state *did* not (because it *could* not) belong to Paganism. Having no doctrines of *any* sort, Grecian idolatry could not have *this*. All other arguments against W. were *a posteriori* from facts of archaeology: this was *a priori*[83] from the essential principle of an idolatrous religion. All other arguments proved the Warburtonian crotchet to be a falsehood: this proves it to be an impossibility. Other arguments contradict it: this leaves it in self-contradiction. And one thing let me warn the reader to beware of. In the Oriental forms of

effectually only in great libraries. *But* I return to my assertion, that the most memorable of all Secret Societies was the meanest. That the Society which made more people hold their tongues than ever the Inquisition did, or the mediaeval Vehm-gericht,[84] was a hoax; nay, except Freemasonry, the hoax of hoaxes.

(To be concluded in next Number.)

Paganism, such as Buddhism, Brahminism, &c., some vestiges of opinion seem at times to intermingle themselves with the facts of the mythology: all which, however, are only an after-growth of sectarian feuds, or philosophic dreams, that having survived opposition, and the memory of their own origin, have finally confounded themselves with the religion itself as parts in its original texture. But in Greece there never *was* any such confusion, even as a natural process of error. The schools of philosophy, always keeping themselves alive, naturally always vindicated their own claims against any incipient encroachments of the national religion.

SECRET SOCIETIES
[Part II]

First published in *Tait's*, XIV, October 1847, pp. 661–70. The essay was printed as 'BY THOMAS DE QUINCEY.' in a centred line following the title and immediately preceding the text.

Reprinted in *F*, XI, *Historical and Critical Essays* (1853), pp. 316–47, 352–4.

Revised text, carrying many accidentals but only one substantive variant from *F*, in *SGG*, VII, *Studies on Secret Records, Personal and Historic* (1858), pp. 265–95, p. 329–33.

There are two manuscript, as follows:

MS A: British Library, Department of Printed Books, C. 60. o. 3. The manuscript is part of a single endnote from *F*, corresponding to the text below running from p. 170.32 '*'Wicked Will Whiston'*' to p. 171.32 'sincerity, and that'.

MS B: Brown University, Department of Rare Books, YQE/D44se. The manuscript is a single sheet of *SGG* page proof, and corresponds to the text below running from p. 182.8 'in behalf of Christ's' to p. 182.17–8 'and its present consolation.', with those textual variants from *SGG* running from p. 669, 182.9 'necessary for' to p. 670, 182.16–17 'and its'.

The two manuscripts contain no substantive variants.

For the occasion and context of this essay, see headnote, p. 146.

PART II.

HAS the modern world no hoax of its own, answering to the Eleusinian mysteries of Grecian days? Oh, yes, it has. I have a very bad opinion of the ancient world; and it would grieve me if such a world could be shown to have beaten us even in the quality of our hoaxes. I have, also, not a very favourable opinion of the *modern* world. But I dare say that in fifty thousand years it will be considerably improved; and, in the meantime, if we are not quite so good or so clever as we ought to be, yet still we are a trifle better than our ancestors; I hope we are up to a hoax any day. A man must be a poor creature that can't invent a hoax. For two centuries we have had a first-rate one; and its name is *Freemasonry*.[1] Do you know the secret, my reader? Or shall I tell you? Send me a consideration, and I will. But stay, the weather being so fine, and philosophers, therefore, so good-tempered, I'll tell it you for nothing; whereas, if you become a mason, you must pay for it. Here is the secret. When the novice is introduced into the conclave of the Freemasons, the grand-master looks very fierce at him, and draws his sword, which makes the novice look very melancholy, as he is not aware of having had time as yet for any profaneness, and fancies, therefore, that somebody must have been slandering him. Then the grand-master, or his deputy, cites him to the bar, saying, 'What's *that* you have in your pocket?' To which the novice replies, 'A guinea.' 'Anything more?' 'Another guinea.' 'Then,' replies the official person in a voice of thunder, 'Fork out.' Of course to a man coming sword in hand few people refuse to do *that*. This forms the first half of the mysteries; the second half, which is by much the more interesting, consists entirely of brandy. In fact, this latter mystery forms the reason, or final cause, for the elder mystery of the *Forking out*. But how did I learn all this so accurately? Isn't a man liable to be assassinated, if he betrays that ineffable mystery or αποῤῥητο of masonry, which no wretch but one since King Solomon's days[2] is reputed ever to have blabbed? And perhaps, reader, the wretch didn't blab the whole; he only got as far as the *Forking out;* and being a churl who grudged his money, he ran away before reaching the *brandy*. So that this fellow, if he seems to you but half as guilty as myself, on the other hand is but half as learned. It's better for you to stick by the guiltier man. And yet, on consideration, I am not so guilty as we have both been thinking. Perhaps it was a mistake. Dreaming on days far back, when I was scheming for an introduction to the honourable society of the masons, and of course to their honourable secret, with the single-minded intention of instantly betraying that secret to a dear female friend (and, you see, in honour it was not possible for me to do otherwise, because she had made me promise that I *would*) – all this time I was soothing my remorse with a belief that woman was answerable for my treachery, she having positively compelled me to undertake it. When suddenly I woke into a bright conviction that all was a dream; that I had never been near the Freemasons; that I had treacherously evaded the treachery which I ought to have committed, by perfidiously forging a secret quite as good, very likely better, than that which I was pledged in honour to betray; and that, if anybody had ground of complaint against myself, it was not the grand-master, sword-in-hand, but my poor ill-used female friend, so confiding, so amiably credulous in my treachery, so cruelly deceived, who had swallowed a mendacious account of Freemasonry forged by myself, the same which, I greatly fear that, on looking back, I shall find myself to have been palming, in this very page, upon the much-respected reader. Seriously, however, the whole bubble of Freemasonry was shattered in a paper which I myself once threw into a London journal about the year 1823 or 4.[3] It was a paper in this sense mine, that from me it had received form and arrangement; but the materials belonged to a learned German, viz., Buhle, the same (Ebelison) that edited the 'Bipont Aristotle,' and wrote a History of philosophy.[4] No German has any conception of style. I therefore did him the favour to wash his dirty face, and make him presentable amongst Christians; but the substance was drawn entirely from this German book. It was there established, that the whole hoax of masonry had been invented in the year 1629 by one Andrea;[5] and the reason that this exposure could have dropped out of remembrance, is probably, that it never reached the public ear; partly because the journal had a limited circulation; but much more because the *title* of the paper was not so constructed as to indicate its object. A title, which seemed to promise only a discussion of masonic doctrines, must have repelled everybody; whereas, it ought to have announced (what in fact it accomplished) the utter demolition of the whole masonic edifice. At this moment I have not space for an abstract of that paper; but it was conclusive; and hereafter, when I have strengthened it by facts since noticed in my own reading, it may be right to place it more effectually before the public eye.

Finally, I will call the reader's attention to the most remarkable by far of all secret societies ever heard of, and for this reason, that it suddenly developed the most critical wisdom in a dreadful emergency; secondly, the grandest purpose; and, lastly, with entire success. The purpose was, to protect a jewel by hiding it from all eyes, whilst it navigated a sea swarming with enemies. The critical wisdom was the most remarkable evidence ever given by the primitive Christians of that serpent's subtlety which they had been warned to combine with the innocence of the dove. The success was, the victory of the Christian church over the armies that waylaid its infancy. Without falsehood, without shadow of falsehood, all the benefits of falsehood – the profoundest – were secured. Without need to abjure anything, all that would have raised a demoniac yell for instant abjuration was suddenly hidden out of sight. In noonday the Christian church was suddenly withdrawn behind impenetrable veils, even as the infant Christ himself was caught up to the secrecies of Egypt and the wilderness from the bloody wrath of Herod.[6] And whilst the enemies of this infant society were roaming around them on every side, seeking for them, walking upon their very traces, absolutely touching them, or divided from their victims only as children in bed have escaped from murderers in thick darkness, sheltered by no screen but a muslin curtain; all the while the inner principle of the church lurked as in the cell at the centre of a labyrinth. Was the hon. reader ever in a real labyrinth, like that described by Herodotus?[7] We have all been in labyrinths of debt, labyrinths of error, labyrinths of metaphysical nonsense. But I speak of literal labyrinths. Now, at Bath, in my labyrinthine childhood, there was such a mystery.[8] This mystery I used to visit; and I can assert that no type ever flashed upon my mind so pathetically shadowing out the fatal irretrievability of early errors in life. Turn but wrong at first entering the thicket, and all was over; you were ruined; no wandering could recover the right path. Or suppose you even took the right turn at first, what of that? You couldn't expect to draw a second prize; five turnings offered very soon after; your chance of escaping error was now reduced to one-fifth of unity; and supposing that again you draw no blank, not very far had you gone before fourteen roads offered. What remained for you to do *now?* Why, if you were a wise man, to lie down and cry. None but a presumptuous fool would count upon drawing for a third time a prize, and such a prize as one amongst fourteen. I mention all of this, I recall this image of the poor Sidney Labyrinth, whose roses, I fear, must long ago have perished, betraying all the secrets of the mysterious house, simply to teach the stranger how secure is the heart of a labyrinth. Gibraltar[9] is nothing to it. You may sit in that deep grave-like recess, you may hear distant steps approaching, but laugh at them. If you are coining, and have all the implements of coining round about you, never trouble yourself to hide them. Nobody will in this life ever reach you. Why, it is demonstrable by the arithmetic of combinations, that if a man spent the flower of his life as a police-officer in trying to reach your coining-shop, he could not do it; you might rest as in a sanctuary, that is, hidden and inaccessible to those who do not know the secret of the concealment. In that recess you might keep a private still for a century without fear of the exciseman. Light, common daylight, will not show you the stars; on the contrary, it hides them; and the brighter this light becomes, the more it hides them. Even so, from the exquisite machinery of the earliest Christian society, whatever suspicions might walk about in the darkness, all efforts of fanatical enemies at forcing an entrance within the air-woven gates of these entrenchments were (as the reader will see) utterly thrown away. Round and round the furious Jews must have circumambulated the camp, like the poor gold fish eternally wheeling round his crystal wall, but, after endless cruisings, never nearer to any opening. That concealment for the Christian nursery was absolutely required, because else martyrdom would have come too soon. Martyrdom was good for watering the church, and quickening its harvests; but, at this early stage of advance, it would utterly have extirpated the church. If a voice had been heard from heaven, saying, 'Let there be martyrs,' soon the great answering return would be heard rolling back from earth, 'And there *were* martyrs.' But for this there must be time; the fire to be sure, will never be extinguished, if once thoroughly kindled; but, in this earliest twilight of the primitive faith, the fire is but a little gathering of scanty fuel fanned by human breath, and barely sufficient to show one golden rallying star in all the mighty wilderness.

There was the motive to the secret society which I am going to describe! *there* was its necessity! 'Masque, or you will be destroyed!' was the private signal among the Christians. 'Fall flat on your faces,' says the Arab to the pilgrims, when he sees the purple haze of the simoom running before the wind. 'Lie down, men,' says the captain to his fusiliers, 'till these hurricanes of the artillery be spent.' To hide from the storm, during its first murderous explosion, was so absolutely requisite, that, simply from its *sine qua non*[10] necessity, and supposing there were no other argument whatever, I should infer that it had been a fact. Because it *must* have been, therefore (I should say), it *was*. However, do as you like; pray use your own pleasure; consider yourself quite at home amongst my arguments, and kick them about with as little apology as if they were *my* children and servants. What makes me so easy in the matter is, that I use the above argument – though, in my opinion, a strong one – *ex abundanti;*[11] it is one string more than I want to my bow; so I can afford to lose it, even if I lose it unjustly. But, by quite another line of argument, and dispensing with this altogether, I mean to *make* you believe, reader, whether you like it or not.

I once threw together a few thoughts upon this obscure question of the *Essenes*, which thoughts were published at the time in a celebrated journal,[12] and my reason for referring to them here is in connexion with a single inappropriate expression since applied to that paper. In a short article on myself in his 'Gallery of Literary Portraits' Mr Gilfillan spoke of that little disquisition in terms beyond its merit, and I thank him for his kind opinion. But as to one word, not affecting myself but the subject, I find it a duty of sincerity to dissent from him. He calls the thesis of that paper '*paradoxical*.'[13] Now paradox is a very charming thing, and, since leaving off opium,[14] I take a great deal too much of it for my health. But, in this case, the paradox lies precisely and outrageously in the opposite direction; that is, when used (as the word *paradox* commonly is) to mean something that startles by its extravagance. Else I have twice or three times explained in print,[15] for the benefit of my female or non-Grecian readers, that *paradox,* being a purely Greek word, ought strictly to be read by a Grecian light, and then it implies nothing, of necessity, that may not be right. Here follows a rigorous definition of *paradox* in a Greek sense. Not *that* only is paradoxical which, being really false, puts on the semblance of truth; but, secondly, *that*, also, which, being really true, puts on the semblance of falsehood. For, literally speaking, everything is paradoxical which contradicts the public *doxa* (δοξα), that is, contradicts the popular opinion, or the public expectation, which may be done by a truth as easily as a falsehood. The very weightiest truths now received amongst men have nearly all of them, in turn, in some one stage of their development, been found strong paradoxes to the popular mind. Hence it is, viz., in the Grecian sense of the word *paradox*, as something extraordinary, but not on that account the less likely to be true, that several great philosophers have published, under the idea and title of *paradoxes*, some first-rate truths on which they desired to fix public attention; meaning, in a short-hand form, to say – 'Here, reader, are some extraordinary truths, looking so very like falsehoods, that you would never take them for anything else if you were not invited to give them a special examination.' Boyle published some elementary principles in hydrostatics as paradoxes.[16] Natural philosophy is overrun with paradoxes. Mathematics, mechanics, dynamics, are all partially infested with them. And in morals the Stoics threw their weightiest doctrines under the rubric of paradoxes – a fact which survives to this day in a little essay of Cicero's.[17] To be paradoxical, therefore, is not necessarily to be unphilosophic; and that being so, it might seem as though Mr Gilfillan had laid me under no obligation to dissent from him; but used popularly, as naturally Mr Gilfillan meant to use it in that situation, the word certainly throws a reproach of extravagance upon any thought, argument, or speculation, to which it is imputed.

Now it is important for the reader to understand that the very first thing which ever fixed my sceptical eye upon the whole fable of the Essenes, as commonly received amongst Christian churches, was the intolerable extravagance of the received story. The outrageousness – the mere Cyclopian enormity of its paradox – this, and nothing else, it was that first extorted from me, on a July day, one long shiver of horror at the credulity, the bottomless credulity, that could have swallowed such a legend of delirium. Why, Pliny,[18] my excellent sir, you were a gentleman mixing with men of the highest circles – you were yourself a man of fine and brilliant intellect – a jealous inquirer – and, in extent of science, beyond your contemporaries – how came you, then to lend an ear, so learned as yours, to two such knaves as your Jewish authorities? For, doubtless, it *was* they, viz., Josephus and Philo-Judaeus, that poisoned the Plinian ear. Others from Alexandria[19] would join the cabal, but these vagabonds were the ringleaders. Now there were three reasons for specially distrusting such men, two known equally well to Pliny and me, one separately to myself. Jews had by that time earned the reputation, in Roman literature, of being credulous by preference amongst the children of earth. That was one reason; a second was, that all men tainted with intense nationality, and especially if not the gay, amiable, nationality of Frenchmen, but a gloomy unsocial nationality, are liable to suspicion as liars. So much was known to Pliny; and a third thing which was not, I could have told him, viz., that Josephus was the greatest knave in that generation. A learned man in Ireland is at this moment bringing out a new translation of Josephus,[20] which has, indeed, long been wanted; for 'wicked Will Whiston'* was a very moderate Grecian – a miserable antiquarian – a coarse writer of English – and, at that time of day, in the

* '*Wicked Will Whiston*.' – In this age, when Swift is so little read, it may be requisite to explain that Swift it was who fastened this epithet of *wicked* to Will Whiston;[21] and the humour of it lay in the very incongruity of the epithet; for Whiston, thus sketched as a profligate, was worn to the bone by the anxieties of scrupulousness: he was, anything but wicked, being pedantic, crazy, and fantastical in virtue after a fashion of his own. He ruined his wife and family, he ruined himself and all that trusted in him, by crotchets that he never could explain to any rational man; and by one thing that he never explained to himself, which a hundred years after I explained very clearly, viz., that all his heresies in religion, all his crazes in ecclesiastical antiquities, in casuistical morals, and even as to the discovery of the longitude, had their rise, not (as his friends thought) in too much conscientiousness and too much learning, but in too little rhubarb and magnesia. In his autobiography he has described his own craziness of stomach in a way to move the gravest reader's laughter, and the sternest reader's pity.[22] Everybody, in fact, that knew his case and history, stared at him, derided him, pitied him, and, in some

absence of the main German and English researches on the many questions (chronological or historical) in Syro-Judaic and Egyptian antiquities, had it not within his physical possibilities to adorn the Sparta[25] which chance had assigned him. From what I hear, the history will benefit by this new labour of editorial culture; the only thing to be feared is, that the historian, the bad Josephus, will not be meritoriously scourged. *I, lictor, colliga manus.*[26] One aspect of Josephus and his character occurs to me as interesting, viz., when placed in collision with the character so different, and the position partially the same, of St Paul.[27] In both, when suddenly detained for inspection at an early stage of their career, we have a bigot of the most intractable quality; and in both the bigotry expressed its ferocity exclusively upon the Christians, as the newborn heretics that troubled the unity of the national church. Thus far the parties agree; and they agree also in being as learned as the limited affinities in their native studies to exotic learning would allow. But from that point, up to which the resemblance in position, in education, in temper, is so close, how entirely opposed! Both erring profoundly; yet the one not only in his errors, but *by* his errors showing himself most single-minded, conscientious, fervent, devout; a holy bigot; as incapable of anything mercenary then, of anything insidious, or of compromise with any mode of self-interest, as after the rectification of his views he was incapable of compromise with profounder shapes of error. The other, a time-serving knave, sold to adulation and servile ministeries; a pimp; a liar; or ready for any worse office, if worse is named on earth. Never on any human stage was so dramatically realised, as by Josephus in Rome, the delineation of the poet:

* * * *

'A fingering meddling slave;
One that would peep and botanise
Upon his mother's grave.'[28]

Yes, this master in Israel, this leader of Sanhedrims,[29] went as to a puppet-show, sat the long day through to see a sight. What sight? Jugglers, was it? buffoons? tumblers? dancing dogs? or a reed shaken by the wind? Oh, no!

---

degree, respected him. For he was a man of eternal self-sacrifice, and that is always venerable; he was a man of primitive unworldly sincerity, and that is always lovely; yet both the one and the other were associated with so many oddities and absurdities, as compelled the most equitable judge at times to join in the general laughter. He and Humphry Ditton, who both held official stations as mathematicians, and were both honoured with the acquaintance of Sir Isaac Newton,[23] had both been candidates for the Parliamentary prize as discoverers of the longitude, and, naturally, both were found wrong: which furnishes the immediate theme for Swift's savage ridicule:

'The longitude mist on
By wicked Will Whiston;
And not better hit on
By good Master Ditton.'[24]

Simply to see his ruined country carried captive in effigy through the city of her conqueror – to see the sword of the Maccabees hung up as a Roman trophy – to see the mysteries of the glorious temple dragged from secrecy before the grooms and gladiators of Rome.[30] Then when this was finished, a woe that would once have caused Hebrew corpses to stir in their graves, he goes home to find his *atrium* made glorious with the monuments of a thousand years that had descended through the princes of Hebrew tribes; and to find his luxury, his palace, and his haram, charged as a perpetual tax upon the groans of his brave unsurrendering countrymen, that had been sold as slaves into marble quarries: *they* worked extra hours, that the only traitor to Jerusalem might revel in honour.[31]

When first I read the account of the *Essenes* in Josephus, I leaned back in my seat, and apostrophised the writer thus: – 'Joe, listen to me; you've been telling us a fairy tale; and, for my part, I've no objection to a fairy tale in any situation; because, if one can make no use of it oneself, one always knows a child that will be thankful for it. But this tale, Mr Joseph, happens also to be a lie; secondly, a fraudulent lie; thirdly, a malicious lie.' It was a fiction of hatred against Christianity. For I shall startle the reader a little when I inform him that, if there were a syllable of truth in the main statement of Josephus, then at one blow goes to wreck the whole edifice of Christianity. Nothing but blindness and insensibility of heart to the *true* internal evidence of Christianity could ever have hidden this from men. Religious sycophants who affect the profoundest admiration, but in their hearts feel none at all, for what they profess to regard as the beauty of the moral revelations made in the New Testament, are easily cheated, and often *have* been cheated, by the grossest plagiarisms from Christianity offered to them as the pure natural growths of paganism. I would engage to write a Greek version somewhat varied and garbled of the Sermon on the Mount, were it hidden in Pompeii,[32] unearthed, and published as a fragment from a posthumous work of a Stoic, with the certain result that very few people indeed should detect in it any signs of forgery. There are several cases of that nature actually unsuspected at this hour, which my deep cynicism and detestation of human hypocrisy yet anticipates a banquet of gratification in one day exposing. Oh, the millions of deaf hearts, deaf to everything really impassioned in music, that pretend to admire Mozart![33] Oh, the worlds of hypocrites who cant about the divinity of Scriptural morality, and yet would never see any lustre at all in the most resplendent of Christian jewels, provided the pagan thief had a little disguised their setting. The thing has been tried long before the case of the *Essenes;* and it takes more than a scholar to detect the imposture. A philosopher, who must also be a scholar, is wanted. The eye that suspects and watches, is needed. Dark seas were those over which the ark of Christianity tilted for the first four centuries; evil men and enemies were cruising, and an Alexandrian Pharos[34] is required to throw back a light broad enough to search and sweep the guilty secrets of those times. The Church of Rome has always thrown a backward telescopic glance of question and uneasy suspicion upon these ridiculous *Essenes*, and has repeatedly come to the right practical conclusion – that they were, and must have been, Christians under some mask or other; but the failure of Rome has been in carrying the Ariadne's thread[35] through the whole labyrinth from centre to circumference. Rome has given the ultimate solution rightly, but has not (in geometrical language) raised the construction of the problem with its conditions and steps of evolution. Shall I tell you, reader, in a brief rememberable form what was the crime of the hound Josephus, through this fable of the *Essenes* in relation to Christ? It was the very same crime as that of the hound Lauder in relation to Milton.[36] Lauder, about the middle of the last century, bearing deadly malice to the memory of Milton, conceived the idea of charging the great poet with plagiarism. He would greatly have preferred denying the value *in toto*[37] of the 'Paradise Lost.' But, as this was hopeless, the next best course was to say – Well, let it be as grand as you please, it is none of Milton's. And, to prepare the way for this, he proceeded to translate into Latin (but with plausible variations in the expression or arrangement) some of the most memorable passages in the poem. By this means he had, as it were, melted down or broken up the golden sacramental plate, and might now apply it to his own felonious purposes. The false swindling travesty of the Miltonic passage he produced as the undoubted original, professing to have found it in some rare or obscure author, not easily within reach, and then saying – Judge (I beseech you) for yourself, whether Milton were indebted to this passage or not. Now, reader, a falsehood *is* a falsehood, though uttered under circumstances of hurry and sudden trepidation; but certainly it becomes, though not more a falsehood, yet more criminally, and hatefully a falsehood, when prepared from afar and elaborately supported by fraud, and dovetailing into fraud, and having no palliation from pressure and haste. A man is a knave who falsely, but in the panic of turning all suspicion from himself, charges you or me with having appropriated another man's jewel. But how much more odiously is he a knave, if with no such motive of screening himself, if out of pure devilish malice to us, he has contrived in preparation for his own lie to conceal the jewel about our persons! This was what the wretch Lauder tried hard to do for Milton. This was what the wretch Josephus tried hard to do for Christ. Josephus grew up to be a mature man about thirty-five years old, during that earliest stage of Christianity, when the divine morality of its founder was producing its first profound impression, through the advantage of a dim religious one, still brooding over the East, from the mysterious death of that founder. I wish that the reader would attend to a thing which I am going to say. In 1839–40 and 41, it was found by our force in Affghanistan[38] that, in a degree much beyond any of the Hindoo races, the Affghan Sirdars and officers of rank were profoundly struck by the beauty of the Evangelists; especially in five or six passages, amongst which were the Lord's Prayer, and the Sermon on the Mount, with one or two Parables. The reason of this was, that the Affghans, though more simple and unpolished than the Hindoos, were also in a far more natural condition of moral feeling; being Mahometans, they were much more advanced in their conceptions of Deity; and they had never been polluted by the fearful distractions of the Hindoo polytheism. Now, I am far from insinuating that the Romans of that first Christian era were no further advanced in culture than the Affghans. Yet still I affirm that, in many features, both moral and intellectual, these two martial races resembled each other. Both were slow and tenacious (that is adhesive) in their feelings. Both had a tendency to dulness, but for that very reason to the sublime. Mercurial races are never sublime. There were two channels through whom the Palestine of Christ's day communicated with the world outside, viz., the Romans of the Roman armies, and the Greek colonists. Syria, under the Syro-Macedonian dynasty; Palestine, under the house of Antipater; and Egypt, under the Ptolemies[39] – were all deluged with Greek emigrants and settlers. Of these two races, the subtle, agile Greek, unprincipled, full of change and levity, was comparitively of little use to Christianity as a centre, waiting and seeking for means of diffusion. Not only were the deeper conscientious instincts of the Romans more suited to a profound religion, as instruments for the radiation of light, but also it is certain that the military condition *per se* supplies some advantages towards a meditative apprehension of vast eternal problems beyond what *can* be supplied by the fractionary life of petty brokerage or commerce. This is also certain, that Rome itself – the idea which predominated in Roman camps – cherished amongst her soldiery, from the very enormities of her state, and from the chaos of her internal life, a tendency to vast fermentations of thought favourable to revolutions in man's internal worlds of feeling and aspirations. Hence it will be found, if once a man's eye is directed into that current, that no classes of people did so much for the propagation of Christianity as the officers of the Roman army, centurions, tribunes, prefects, legates, &c., or as the *aulic*[40] officers, the great ceremonial officers of the imperial court – or as the *aulic* ladies, the great leading ladies that had practically much influence on the ear of Caesar. The utter dying away of the Roman paganism, which had become quite as powerless to all the accomplished men and women of Rome for any purpose of terror or of momentary consolation as to us English at present the mythology of Fairies, left a frightful *vacuum* in the mind of Roman grandees – a horror as of voyagers upon some world floating away without helmsman or governor. In this unhappy agitation of spirit and permanent posture of clamorous demand for light, a *nidus* was already forming for a deep brooding interest in any great spiritual phenomena of breadth and power that might anywhere arise amongst men. Athens was too windy, too conceited, too shallow in feeling, to have been much impressed by the deepest revolutionary movements in religion. But in Rome, besides the far different character of the national mind, there were what may be called *spiritual* horrors arising, which (like dreadful nervous diseases) unfolded terrifically to the experience spiritual capacities and openings beyond what had been suspected. The great domestic convulsions of Rome, the poisonings and assassinations, that gleam so fearfully from the pictures of Juvenal,[41] were beginning about this period. It was not that by any coarse palpable logic, as dull people understood the case, women or men said – 'Accountability there is none; and we will no longer act as if there were.' Accountability there never *had* been any; but the obscure scene of an order with which all things sympathised, men not less than the wheels of society – this had blindly produced an instinct of corresponding self-control. At present, when the Pagan religion had virtually died out, all secret restraints were breaking up; a general delirium carried, and was felt to carry, a license into all ranks; it was not a negative merely, but a positive change. A religion had collapsed – *that* was negative; a mockery had been exposed – that was positive. It was not that restraints were resisted; there were none to resist; they had crumbled away spontaneously. What power still acted upon society? Terror from police, and still, as ever, the Divine restraints of love and pity, honour, and domestic affections. But the conscience spoke no longer through any spiritual organs. Just at this moment it was when the confusions of Roman society, the vast expansion of the empire, the sea-like expansion of the mighty capital, the political tendencies of the whole system, were all moving together towards grandeur and distraction of feeling, that the doctrine of *apotheosis*, applied to a man and often to a monster, towered up to cause still greater distraction.* The pagan pantheon had just sunk away from the support of the Roman mind. It was not only that the Pagan gods were individually too base and polluted to sustain the spiritual feelings of an expanding national intellect, but the whole collective idea of Deity was too feebly conceived by Paganism. Had the individuals of the Pantheon[44] been purer and nobler, their doom was sealed, nevertheless, by their abstract deficiencies as modes of spiritual life for a race so growing as that of man. How unfortunate, therefore, that at this crisis, when ancient religions were crum-

* The Romans themselves saw a monstrosity in this practice which did not really exist in the metaphysical necessity. It was, and it was *not*, monstrous. In reality it was rational, or monstrous, according to theoretic construction. Generally speaking, it was but a variety of that divinity which in Christendom all of us so long ascribed to kings. We English always laughed at the French with their *grand monarque*.[42] The Americans of the United States have always laughed at us English, and the sanctity with which our constitution invests the Sovereign. We English, French, and Americans, have all alike laughed at the Romans upon this matter of *apotheosis*. And when brought before us under the idea of Seneca's *apocolocuntosis*,[43] this practice has seemed too monstrous for human gravity. And yet again, we English, French, Americans, and Romans, should all have united in scorn for the deep Phrygian, Persian, or Asiatic servility to kings. We of European blood have all looked to the constitutional idea, not the individual person of the sovereign. The Asiatics, though *they* also still feebly were groping after the same deep idea, sought it in such a sensual body of externals, that none but a few philosophers could keep their grasp on the original problem. How profound an idea is the sanctity of the English sovereign's constitutional person, which idea first made possible the responsibility of the sovereign's ministers. They could be responsible, only if the sovereign were *not;* let *them* be accountable, and the king might be inviolable. Now really in its secret metaphysics the Roman apotheosis meant little more. Only the accountability lay not in Caesar's ministers, but in the personal and transitory Caesar, as distinguished from the eternal Imperator.

bling into ruins, new gods should be arising from the veriest beasts amongst men – utterly repelled and rejected by the spiritual instinct in man, but suggested by a necessity of political convenience.

But oftentimes the excess of an evil is its cure, or the first impulse in that direction. From the connexion of the great Augustan[45] and Claudian houses with the family of Herod,[46] much knowledge of Jewish peculiarities had been diffused in Rome. Agrippa, the grandson of Herod, Bernice,[47] and others of the reigning house in Judea, had been long resident – had been loved and admired in the imperial family. The tragical events in Herod's own household[48] had drawn the attention of the Roman grandees and senate to Jewish affairs. The migrations to Rome of Jewish settlers, since the era of Pharsalia,[49] had strengthened the interest, by keeping the enigma of the Jewish history and character constantly before the Roman eye. The upper and more intellectual circles in Rome of inquiring men and women kept up this interest through their military friends in the legions quartered upon Syria and Lower Egypt, many of whom must have read the Septuagint version of the Law and the Prophets. Some whispers, though dim and scarcely intelligible, would have made their way to Rome as to the scenes of the Crucifixion, able at least to increase the attraction of mystery. But a much broader and steadier interest would have been diffused by the accounts transmitted of the Temple, so mysterious from the absence of all idol, so magnificent to the eye and the ear from its glorious service. By the time when Vespasian and his son[50] commanded in the East, and when the great insurrection of the Jewish race in Jerusalem was commencing, Josephus must have been well aware of this deep attention to his own people gathering in the highest quarters; and he must have been aware that what was now creeping into the subject of profoundest inquiry amongst the Jews themselves, viz., the true pretensions, the history, doctrines, and new morals, of those Nazarene revolutionists, would, by a natural transfer, soon become the capital object of attention to all Romans interested in Judea. The game was up for the separate glory of Judaism, the honour of the Mosaic legislation was becoming a superannuated thing, if he suffered the grandeur of Christianity, *as* such, and recognised for Christianity to force its way upon the fermenting intellect of Rome. His discernment told him that the new Christian ethics never *would* be put down. That was impossible; but he fancied that it might be possible to disconnect the system of moral truth from the new but still obscure Christian sect, and to transfer its glory upon a pretended race of Hebrew recluses or immemorial eremites. As Lauder meant to say, 'This may be grand, but it is not Milton's;' so did Josephus mean to say, 'This may be very fine and very new, but take notice it is not Christ's.' During his captivity in Roman hands and in Rome, being one of the few cowards who had spiritedly volunteered as a traitor, and being a good scholar for a Jew, as well a good traitor and the best of cowards, he enjoyed the finest opportunities of insinuating his ridiculous legend about the Essenes into the foremost literary heads of the universal metropolis. Imperial favour, and the increasing curiosity of Rome, secured him access to the most intellectual circles. His legend was adopted by the ruling authority in the literature of the earth; and an impossible lie became signed and countersigned for many centuries to come.

But how did this particular form arise for the lie? Were there no such people as the Essenes? Why, no; not as Josephus described them: if there were, or could be, then there were Christians without Christ; there was Christianity invented by man. Under *his* delineation, they existed only as King Arthur existed, or Morgan le Fay, or the sword Excalibur.[51] Considered in their romantic pretensions, connected with the Round Table, these worthy blades of flesh and steel were pure dreams: but, as downright sober realities, known to cutlers and others, they certainly have a hold upon history. So of the Essenes: nobody could be more certain than Josephus that there *were* such people; for he knew the very street of Jerusalem in which they met; and in fact he had been matriculated amongst them himself.[52] Only all that moonshine about remote seclusions, and antique derivations, and philosophic considerations, were fables of the Hesperides, or fit for the future use of Archbishop Turpin.[53] What, then, is my own account of the Essenes?

The earliest great danger to which Christianity was exposed, arose with the Jews. This was the danger that besieged the cradle of the religion. From Rome no danger arose until the time of Trajan;[54] and, as to the nature of this danger, the very wildest mistake is made in books innumerable. No Roman anger ever *did,* or ever *could*, point to any doctrine of Christianity; unless, indeed, in times long subsequent, when the Christian doctrines, though otherwise indifferent to the Roman authorities, would become exponents or convertible signs of the firm disloyalty to Caesar which constitutes the one great offence of Christians. Will you burn incense to Caesar?[55] No. Well, that is your State crime, Christian; *that*, and neither less nor more. With the Jews the case was exactly reversed; they cared nothing about the external ceremonies (or *cultus*) of the Christians, what it was they practised, or what it was they refused to practise. A treasonable distinction would even have been a recommendation in their eyes; and as to any differences between their own ritual and the Christian, for these (had they been more or greater than they were) the ruling Jews would readily have found the same indulgence which they found for other schismatics, or imperfect proselytes, or doubtful brothers, or known Gentiles. All these things were trifles: what *they* cared about was exactly what the Romans did *not* care about, viz., the Christian doctrines in relation to Moses and the Messiah. Was the Messiah come? Were the prophecies accomplished? Was the Mosaic economy of their nation self-dissolved, as having reached its appointed terminus, or natural euthanasy, and lost itself in a new order of things? This concerned their existence as a separate people. If *that* were the Messiah, whom the Christians gave out for such, then all the fabric of their national hopes, their visions of an earthly restoration, were shattered. Into this question shot itself the whole agony of their hereditary interest and pride as the children of Abraham.[56] The Jewish nature was now roused in good earnest. So much we may see sufficiently in the Acts of the Apostles; and we may be assured by more than one reflection, that the Jewish leaders at that time were resolved not again to commit the error of relaxing their efforts until the work of extermination was perfect. They felt, doubtless not without much surprise, but still with some self-reproach, that they had been too negligent in assuming the sect to have been trampled out by the judicial death of its leader. Dispersion had not prevented the members of the sect from recombining; and even the public death as a malefactor of the leader was so far from having dimmed the eyes or dejected the hopes of the body, that, under the new colouring given to it by the Christians, this very death had become the most triumphant of victories. There was, besides, a reason to dread the construction of the Romans upon this heresy, if it continued longer to defy public suppression. And there was yet another uneasiness that must greatly have been increasing – an uneasiness of an affecting nature, and which long afterwards, in ages nearer to our own, constituted the most pathetic feature in Christian martyrdoms. Oftentimes those who resorted to the fiery spectacle in pure hatred of the martyr, or who were purposely brought thither to be warned by salutary fear, were observed by degrees to grow thoughtful; instead of reaping confirmation in their feelings of horror, they seemed dealing with some internal struggle, musing, pausing, reflecting, and at length enamoured as by some new-born love, languishing in some secret fascination. Those that in Pagan days caught in forests a momentary glimpse of the nymphs and sylvan goddesses, were struck with a hopeless passion: they were nympholepts: the affection, as well known as epilepsy, was called nympholepsy.[57] This parallel affection, in those that caught a momentary celestial glimpse from the countenances of dying martyrs, by the side of their fiery couches, might be called martyrolepsy. And many were they that saw the secret glance. In mountainous lands, oftentimes when looking down from eminences far above the level of lakes and valleys, it has happened that I could not see the sun: the sun was hidden behind some gloomy mass of clouds; but far below I beheld, tremulously vibrating on the bosom of some half-hidden lake, a golden pillar of solar splendour which had escaped through rifts and rents in the clouds that to me were as invisible as the sun himself. So in the martyrdom of the proto-martyr St Stephen, Paul of Tarsus, the learned Jew,[58] could see no gates of heaven that opened, could see no solar orb: to him were visible, as the scenery about St Stephen, nothing but darkness of error and clouds. Yet, as I far below in the lake, so he far below in the countenance of St Stephen, saw, with consternation, reflected a golden sunlight, some radiance not earthly, which ought *not* to have been there. That troubled him. Whence came *that?* The countenance of Stephen, when the great chorus was even then arising – '*Stone him to death!*'* shone like the countenance of an angel.[60] That countenance, which brought down to earth some revelation of a brightness in the sky, intercepted to Paul, perplexed him; haunted him sleeping, troubled him when awake. That face of the martyr brought down telegraphically from some altitude inaccessible to himself, a handwriting that *must* be authentic. It carried off to heaven, in the very moment of death, a glory that from heaven it must have borrowed. Upon this we may be sure that Paul brooded intensely; that the effect, noticed as so often occurring at martyrdoms, was already commencing in *him;* and probably that the noonday scene on the road to Damascus[61] did but quicken and ante-date a result which would at any rate have come. That very case of Paul, and no doubt others not recorded, must continually have been causing fresh uneasiness to the Jewish leaders. Their own ministers were falling off to the enemy. And now, therefore, at last they were determined, once for all, that it should be decided who was to be Master in Jerusalem.[62]

The Apostles, on *their* side, and all their flock, though not losing a solemn confidence in the issue, could not fail to be alarmed. A contest of life and death was at hand. By what price of suffering and ruins the victory might need to be achieved, they could not measure. They had now faced, as they saw, without power any more to evade it, a fiery trial. Ordinary counsels would not avail; and, according to the magnitude of the crisis, it became the first of duties to watch warily every step they should take, since the very first *false* one might happen to prove irretrievable. The interests of the youthful church were confided to *their* hands. Less than faithful they could not be; but for the present that was not enough. To be faithful in extremity was all that might remain at last; but for the present, the summons was – to be wise, so as to intercept that extremity, if possible. In this exigency, and with the sudden illumination which very perplexity will sometimes create, which the mere inspiration of distress will sometimes suggest, they devised the scheme of a Secret Society.

Armies of brave men have often not only honourably shut themselves up into impenetrable squares, or withdrawn altogether behind walls and batteries, but have even, by exquisite concert, suddenly dispersed over a thousand hills; have vanished at noon-day on the clapping of hands, as if into thick shadows; and again, by the clapping of hands, in a moment have reässembled in battle array. Such was the magical effect from the new device. The Christians are seen off their guard all around; spearmen wheel suddenly into view, but every Christian has vanished. The Christian is absolutely in the grasp of the serjeant; but, unaccountably, he slips away, and a shadow only remains in the officers' hand. The Christian fugitive is before your face, he rushes round a corner, you see him as he whirls round with a mask upon his face; one bound throws you round the corner upon his traces; and then you see no fugitive at

* There is a chorus of that title, powerfully conceived, in Dr Mendelssohn's Oratorio of St Paul.[59]

all, no mask, but a man walking in tranquillity, who readily joins you in the pursuit.

The reader must consider – 1st, *what* it was that the Christians had to accomplish; and 2dly, how it was that such a thing could be accomplished in such almost impracticable circumstances. If the whole problem had been to bend before the storm, it was easy to do *that* by retiring for a season. But there were two reasons against so timid a course: *first*, the enemy was prepared, and watching for all such momentary expedients, waiting for the sudden forced retirement, waiting for the sudden stealthy attempt at resuming the old station; *secondly*, which was a more solemn reason for demur, this course might secure safety to the individual members of the church, but, in the meantime it left the church, as a spiritual community, in a languishing condition – not only without means of extension, but without means even of repairing its own casual waste. Safety obtained on these terms was not the safety that suited apostolic purposes. It was necessary with the protection (and therefore with the present concealment) of the church to connect some machinery for nursing it – feeding it – expanding it. No theory could be conceived more audacious than the one rendered imperative by circumstances. Echo was not to babble of the whereabouts assigned to the local stations or points of rendezvous for this outcast church; and yet in this naked houseless condition she was to find shelter for her household; and yet, whilst bloodhounds were on her own traces, whilst she durst not look abroad through the mighty storm, this church was to be raising a college and a council, *de propaganda fide*,[63] was to be working all day long in the centre of enemies raging for her blood, and to declare herself in permanent session when she had no foot of ground to stand upon.

This object, seemingly so impracticable, found an opening for all its parts in the *community* of field unavoidably cultivated by the church and the enemy of the church. Did the church seek to demonstrate the realisation of the promised Messiah in the character and history of Christ? This she must do by diligently searching the prophetic types as the inner wards of the lock, and then searching the details of Christ's life and passion as the corresponding wards of the key. Did the enemy of the church seek to refute and confound this attempt to identify the Messiahship with the person of Jesus? This she could attempt only by labours in the opposite direction applied to the very same ground of prophecy and history. The prophecies and the traditions[64] current in Judea that sometimes were held to explain, and sometimes to integrate, the written prophecies about the mysterious Messiah, must be alike important and alike commandingly interesting to both parties. Having, therefore, this fortunate common ground of theological study with her own antagonist, there was no reason at all why the Christian church should not set up a seminary of labourers for her own vineyard under the mask of enemies trained against herself. There was no sort of reason, in moral principle or in prudence, why she should not, under colour of training learned and fervent enemies to the Christian name, silently prepare and arm a succession of servants for doing her own work. In order to stamp from the beginning a patriotic and intensely national character upon her new institution, leading men already by names and sounds into the impression that the great purpose of this institution was, to pour new blood into the life of old Judaic prejudices, and to build up again the dilapidation of Mosaic orthodoxy, whether due to time or to recent assaults, the church selected the name of *Essen* for the designation of the new society, from the name of an important gate in the temple;[65] so that, from the original use, as well as from another application to the religious service of the temple, a college or fraternity of *Essenes* became, by its very name, a brief symbolic profession of religious patriotism and bigotry, or what the real bigots would consider orthodoxy, from the first, therefore, carried clear away from suspicion. But it may occur to the reader that the Christian founders would thus find themselves in the following awkward dilemma. If they carried out the seeming promise of their Judaic name, then there would be a risk of giving from the first an anti-Christian bias to the feelings of the students, which might easily warp their views for life. And on the other hand, if by direct discipline they began at an early stage to correct this bias, there arose a worse risk, viz., that their real purposes might be suspected or unmasked. In reality, however, no such risk would arise in either direction. The elementary studies (that is, suppose in the eight first ascending classes) would be, simply to accumulate a sufficient fund of materials, of the original documents, with the commentaries of every kind, and the verbal illustrations or glosses. In this stage of the studies, at any rate, and whether the first objects had or had not been Christian, all independent judgments upon subjects so difficult and mysterious would be discouraged as presumptuous; so that no opening would arise for suspicion against the teachers, on the one hand, as unfaithful to the supposed bigotry of the institution, nor on the other for encouraging an early pre-occupation of mind against Christian views. After passing No. 8 of the classes, the delicacy of the footing would become more trying. But until the very first or inner-most class was reached, when the last reserves must be laid aside, two circumstances would arise to diminish the risk. The first is this – that the nearer the student advanced to the central and dangerous circles of the art, the more opportunity would the governors have had for observing and appraising his character. Now it is evident that, altogether apart from any considerations of the danger to the society connected with falseness, treachery, or generally with anti-Christian traits of character, even for the final uses and wants of the society, none but pure, gentle, truthful, and benign minds would avail the church for Christian ministrations. The very same causes, therefore, which would point out a student as dangerous to entrust with the capital secrets of the institution, would equally have taken away from the society all motive for carrying him farther in studies that must be thrown away for himself and others. He would be civilly told that his vocation did not seem to such pursuits; would have some sort of degree or literary honour conferred upon him, and would be turned back from the inner chambers, where he was beginning to be regarded as suspicious. Josephus was turned adrift in this way, there is no doubt. He fancied himself to have learned all, whilst in fact there were secret esoteric classes which he had not so much as suspected to exist. Knaves never passed into those rooms. A second reason, which diminished the risk, was, that undoubtedly under the mask of scholastic disputation the student was exercised in hearing all the arguments that were most searchingly profound in behalf of Christ's Messiahship. No danger would attend this: it was necessary for polemic discipline and gymnastics, so that it always admitted of a double explanation, reconcilable alike with the true end and the avowed end. But, though used only as a passage of practice and skill, such a scene furnished means at once to the Christian teachers in disguise for observing the degrees in which different minds melted or froze before the evidence. *There* arose fresh aids to a safe selection. And, finally, whilst the institution of the *Essenes* was thus accomplishing its first mission of training up a succession to the church, and providing for her future growth, it was also providing for the secret meeting of the church and its present consolation.

SCHLOSSER'S LITERARY HISTORY OF THE EIGHTEENTH CENTURY

[Part I]

First published as the lead article in *Tait's*, XIV, September 1847, pp. 575–83. The essay was printed as 'BY THOMAS DE QUINCEY.' in a centred line following the title and immediately preceding the text.

Reprinted in *F*, XVIII, *The Note Book of an English Opium-Eater* (1855), pp. 81–109, 131–2.

Revised text, carrying many accidentals but only three substantive variants from *F*, in *SGG*, VIII, *Essays, Sceptical and Anti-Sceptical, or Problems Neglected or Misconceived* (1858), 35–64.

There are two manuscripts, as follows:

MS A: Buffalo and Erie County Public Library, James Fraser Gluck Collection, Part II. #18 (21). The manuscript is one sheet of *SGG* page proof, and corresponds to the text below running from p. 195.44 'pretends, when he took' to p. 196.20 'Hence, he did not', with those variants from *SGG* running from p. 672, 196.3 'reviews; the editions were still scanty; and' to p. 672, 196.16–17 'published. My'. The manuscript contains no substantive variants.

MS B: Princeton University, Robert H. Taylor Collection. The manuscript is a set of *SGG* page proofs, and corresponds to the text below running from p. 184.1 'IN the person of this Mr Schlosser' to p. 185.20 'scale of proportions from', with those variants from *SGG* running from p. 670, 184.3 'to our provinces,' to p. 670, 185.9–12 'All who dislike...And thus'. At this point the manuscript breaks off and there is a gap of four pages (in *SGG*, pp. 37–40). The manuscript then recommences and corresponds to the text below running from p. 187.23 'There he thrives,' to p. 200.21 'or let *me* get out.', with those variants from *SGG* running from p. 671, 187.30 'themselves. Thus' to p. 673, 200.20 'superficial, a pedant'. The manuscript contains one significant variant, and this is listed in the textual notes.

Friedrich Christoph Schlosser (1776–1861), German historian, studied theology at the University of Göttingen (1794–7). In 1812 he published his *Geschichte des bilderstürmenden Kaiser des oströmischen Reichs (History of the Iconoclastic Emperors of the East)*, which secured him a professorship in history at the University of Frankfurt. In 1817 he began to teach history at the University of Heidelberg, where he remained until his death. Schlosser's principal work was his immense *Weltgeschichte für das deutsche Volk* (*World History for the German People*, 1844–57). In 1823 he published a two-volume *Geschichte des achtzehnten*

Jahrhunderts, which he enlarged and reissued in seven volumes as *Geschichte des achtzehnten Jahrjunderts und des neunzehnten bis zum Sturz des französischen Kaiserreichs* (*History of the Eighteenth Century and of the Nineteenth till the Overthrow of the French Empire*, 1836–49). The work was translated in eight volumes (London: Chapman and Hall, 1843–52) by Rev. David Davison (d. 1858). The present essay is the first of De Quincey's two-part review of Davison's Schlosser, though De Quincey is concerned only with Davison's first two volumes, which explore subjects such as the 'REFORMATION OR REVOLUTION OF PHILOSOPHY AND LITERATURE IN ENGLAND' and the 'PROGRESS AND NATURE OF INTELLECTUAL IMPROVEMENT AND LITERATURE'.

In a September 1847 letter to his daughter Florence, De Quincey contrasted the present essay with 'Joan of Arc' (see above, pp. 61–89) and the 'passage across the Andes' in 'The Nautico-Military Nun of Spain' (see above, pp. 114–26), and described it as 'a hurried paper', and 'by its subject necessarily an inferior one'. In the 1858 *SGG* 'Preface', however, he spoke far more highly of the work. '"Schlosser on Literature"', he declared,

> was not written with the slight or careless purpose to which the reader will probably attach it. The indirect object was to lodge, in such a broad exemplification of German ignorance, a protest against the habit (prevalent through the last fifty years) of yielding an extravagant precedency to German critics (on Shakspere especially), as if better and more philosophic (because more cloudy) than our own.

George Gilfillan thought this review contained 'searching criticisms'. John E. Jordan described it as 'obviously the product of a jocular mood' (Japp, p. 266; Vol. 20, p. 103; George Gilfillan, *Galleries of Literary Portraits*, 2 vols (Edinburgh: Hogg, 1857), vol. II, p. 162; *De Quincey as Critic*, p. 306).

IN the person of this Mr Schlosser is exemplified a common abuse, not confined to literature. An artist from the Italian opera of London and Paris, making a professional excursion to our provinces, is received according to the tariff of the metropolis; no one being bold enough to dispute decisions coming down from the courts above. In that particular case there is seldom any reason to complain – since really out of Germany and Italy there is no city, if you except Paris and London, possessing *materials*, in that field of art, for the composition of an audience large enough to act as a court of revision. It would be presumption in the provincial audience, so slightly trained to good music and dancing, if it should affect to reverse a judgment ratified in the supreme capital. The result, therefore, is practically just, if the original verdict was just; what was right from the first cannot be made wrong by iteration. Yet, even in such a case, there is something not satisfactory to a delicate sense of equity; for the artist returns from the tour as if from some new and independent triumph, whereas, all is but the reverberation of an old one; it seems a new access of sunlight, whereas it is but a reflex illumination from satellites.

In literature the corresponding case is worse. An author, passing by means of translation before a foreign people, ought *de jure* to find himself before a new tribunal; but *de facto*,[1] he does not. Like the opera artist, but not with the same propriety, he comes before a court that never interferes to disturb a judgment, but only to re-affirm it. And he returns to his native country, quartering in his armorial bearings these new trophies, as though won by new trials, when, in fact, they are due to servile ratifications of old ones. When Sue, or Balzac, Hugo, or George Sand,[2] comes before an English audience – the opportunity is invariably lost for estimating them at a new angle of sight. All who dislike them lay them aside – whilst those only apply themselves seriously to their study, who are predisposed to the particular key of feeling, through which originally these authors had prospered. And thus a new set of judges, that might usefully have modified the narrow views of the old ones, fall by mere *inertia* into the humble character of echoes and sounding-boards to swell the uproar of the original mob.

In this way is thrown away the opportunity, not only of applying corrections to false national tastes, but oftentimes even to the unfair accidents of *luck* that befal books. For it is well known to all who watch literature with vigilance, that books and authors have their fortunes, which travel upon a far different scale of proportions from those that measure their merits. Not even the caprice or the folly of the reading public is required to account for this. Very often, indeed, the whole difference between an extensive circulation for one book, and none at all for another of about equal merit, belongs to no particular blindness in men, but to the simple fact, that the one *has*, whilst the other has *not*, been brought effectually under the eyes of the public. By far the greater part of books are lost, not because they are rejected, but because they are never introduced. In any proper sense of the word, very few books are published.[3] Technically they are published; which means, that for six or ten times they are *advertised*, but they are not made known to *attentive* ears, or to ears *prepared* for attention. And amongst the causes which account for this difference in the fortune of books, although there are many, we may reckon, as foremost, *personal* accidents of position in the authors. For instance, with us in England it will do a bad book no *ultimate* service, that it is written by a lord, or a bishop, or a privy counsellor, or a member of Parliament – though, undoubtedly, it will do an *instant* service – it will sell an edition or so. This being the case, it being certain that no rank will reprieve a bad writer from *final* condemnation, the sycophantic glorifier of the public fancies his idol justified; but not so. A bad book, it is true, will not be saved by advantages of position in the author; but a book moderately good will be extravagantly aided by such advantages. Lectures on *Christianity*, that happened to be respectably written and delivered, had prodigious success in my young days, because, also, they happened to be lectures of a prelate; three times the ability would not have procured them any attention had they been the lectures of an obscure curate. Yet, on the other hand, it is but justice to say, that, if written with three times *less* ability, lawn-sleeves would not have given them buoyancy, but, on the contrary, they would have sunk the bishop irrecoverably; whilst the curate favoured by obscurity, would have survived for another chance. So again, and indeed, more than so, as to poetry. Lord Carlisle, of the last generation, wrote tolerable verses. They were better than Lord Roscommon's, which, for 150 years, the judicious public has allowed the booksellers to incorporate, along with other refuse of the seventeenth and eighteenth century, into the costly collections of the 'British Poets.'[4] And really, if you *will* insist on odious comparisons, they were not so very much below the verses of an amiable prime minister known to us all.[5] Yet, because they wanted vital *stamina*, not only they fell, but, in falling, they caused the earl to reel much more than any commoner would have done. Now, on the other hand, a kinsman of Lord Carlisle, viz., Lord Byron,[6] because he brought real genius and power to the effort, found a vast auxiliary advantage in a peerage and a very ancient descent. On these double wings he soared into a region of public interest, far higher than ever he *would* have reached by poetic power alone. Not only all his rubbish – which in quantity is great – passed for jewels, but also what *are* incontestably jewels have been, and will be, valued at a far higher rate than if they had been raised from less aristocratic mines. So fatal for mediocrity, so gracious for real power, is any adventitious distinction from birth, station, or circumstances of brilliant notoriety. In reality, the public, our never-sufficiently-to-be-respected mother, is the most unutterable sycophant that ever the clouds dropped their rheum upon. She is always ready for jacobinical scoffs at a man for being a lord, if he happens to fail; she is always ready for toadying a lord, if he happens to make a hit. Ah, dear sycophantic old lady, I kiss your sycophantic hands, and wish heartily that I were a duke for your sake!

It would be a mistake to fancy that this tendency to confound real merit and its accidents of position is at all peculiar to us or to our age. Dr Sacheverell, by embarking his small capital of talent on the spring-tide of a furious political collision, brought back an ampler return for his little investment than ever did Wickliffe or Luther.[7] Such was his popularity in the heart of love and the heart of hatred, that he would have been assassinated by the Whigs, on his triumphal progresses through England, had he not been canonised by the Tories. He was a dead man if he had not been suddenly gilt and lacquered as an idol. Neither is the case peculiar at all to England. Ronge, the *ci-devant* Romish priest[8] (whose name pronounce as you would the English word *wrong*, supposing that it had for a second syllable the final *a* of 'sopha,' *i. e., Wronguh)*, has been found a wrong-headed man by *all* parties, and in a venial degree is, perhaps, a stupid man; but he moves about with more *eclat* by far than the ablest man in Germany. And, in days of old, the man that burned down a miracle of beauty, viz., the temple of Ephesus,[9] protesting, with tears in his eyes, that he had no other way of getting himself a name, *has* got it in spite of us all. He's booked for a ride down all history, whether you and I like it or not. Every pocket dictionary knows that Erostratus was that scamp. So of Martin, the man that parboiled, or par-roasted York Minster some ten or twelve years back;[10] that fellow will float down to posterity with the annals of the glorious cathedral: he will

'Pursue the triumph and partake the gale,'[11]

whilst the founders and benefactors of the Minster are practically forgotten.

These incendiaries, in short, are as well known as Ephesus or York; but not one of us can tell, without humming and hawing, who it was that rebuilt the Ephesian wonder of the world, or that repaired the time-honoured Minster. Equally in literature, not the weight of service done, or the power exerted, is sometimes considered chiefly – either of these must be very conspicuous before it will be considered at all – but the splendour, or the notoriety, or the absurdity, or even the scandalousness of the circumstances* surrounding the author.

Schlosser must have benefited in some such adventitious way before he ever *could* have risen to his German celebrity. What was it that raised him to his momentary distinction? Was it something very wicked that he did, or something very brilliant that he said? I should rather conjecture that it must have been something inconceivably absurd which he proposed. Any one of the three achievements stands good in Germany for a reputation. But, however it were that Mr Schlosser first gained his reputation, mark what now follows. On the wings of this equivocal reputation he flies abroad to Paris and London. There he thrives, not by any approving experience or knowledge of his works, but through blind faith in his original German public. And back he flies afterwards to Germany, as if carrying with him new and independent testimonies to his merit, and from two nations that are directly concerned in his violent judgments; whereas (which is the simple truth) he carries back a careless reverberation of his first German character, from those who have far too much to read for declining aid from vicarious criticism when it will spare that effort to themselves. Thus it is that German critics become audacious and libellous. Kohl, Von Raumer, Dr Carus, physician to the King of Saxony,[12] by means of introductory letters floating them into circles far above any they had seen in homely Germany, are qualified by our own negligence and indulgence for mounting a European tribunal, from which they pronounce malicious edicts against ourselves. Sentinels present arms to Von Raumer at Windsor, because he rides in a carriage of Queen Adelaide's;[13] and Von Raumer immediately conceives himself the Chancellor of all Christendom, keeper of the conscience

* Even Pope, with all his natural and reasonable interest in aristocratic society, could not shut his eyes to the fact that a jest in *his* mouth became twice a jest in a lord's. But still he failed to perceive what I am here contending for, that if the jest happened to miss fire, through the misfortune of bursting its barrel, the consequences would be far worse for the lord than the commoner. There *is*, you see, a blind sort of compensation.

to universal Europe, upon all questions of art, manners, politics, or any conceivable intellectual relations of England. Schlosser meditates the same career.

But have I any right to quote Schlosser's words from an English translation? I do so only because this happens to be at hand, and the German not. German books are still rare in this country, though more (by 1,000 to 1) than they were thirty years ago. But I have a full right to rely on the English of Mr Davison.[14] 'I hold in my hand,' as gentlemen so often say at public meetings, 'a certificate from Herr Schlosser, that to quote Mr Davison is to quote *him*.' The English translation is one which Mr Schlosser '*durchgelesen hat, und für deren genauigkeit und richtigkeit er bürgt*' [has read through, and for the accuracy and propriety of which he pledges himself].[15] Mr Schlosser was so anxious for the spiritual welfare of us poor islanders, that he not only read it through, but he has even *aufmerksam durchgelesen* it [read it through wide awake] *und geprüft* [and carefully examined it]; nay, he has done all this in company with the translator. 'Oh ye Athenians! how hard do I labour to earn your applause!' And, as the result of such herculean labours, a second time he makes himself surety for its precision; '*er bürgt also dafür, wie für seine eigne arbeit*' [he guarantees it accordingly as he would his own workmanship].[16] Were it not for this unlimited certificate, I should have sent for the book to Germany. As it is, I need not wait; and all complaints on this score I defy, above all from Herr Schlosser.*

In dealing with an author so desultory as Mr Schlosser, the critic has a right to an *extra* allowance of desultoriness for his own share; so excuse me, reader, for rushing at once *in medias res*.[21]

Of Swift, Mr Schlosser selects for notice three works – the 'Drapier's Letters,' 'Gulliver's Travels,' and the 'Tale of a Tub.'[22] With respect to the first, as it is a necessity of Mr S. to be for ever wrong in his substratum of facts, he adopts the old erroneous account of Wood's contract as to the copper coinage, and of the imaginary wrong which it inflicted on Ireland.[23] Of all Swift's vil-

* Mr Schlosser, who speaks English, who has read rather too much English for any good that he has turned it to, and who ought to have a keen eye for the English version of his own book, after so much reading and study of it, has, however, overlooked several manifest errors. I do not mean to tax Mr Davison with general inaccuracy. On the contrary, he seems wary, and in most cases successful as a dealer with the peculiarities of the German. But several cases of error I detect without needing the original: they tell their own story. And one of these I here notice, not only for its own importance, but out of love to Schlosser, and by way of nailing his guarantee to the counter – not altogether as a bad shilling, but as a light one. At p. 5 of Vol. 2, in a foot-note, which is speaking of Kant,[17] we read of his *attempt to introduce the notion of negative greatness into Philosophy. Negative greatness!* What strange bird may *that* be? Is it the *ornithorynchus paradoxus?* Mr Schlosser was not wide awake *there*. The reference is evidently to Kant's essay upon the advantages of introducing into philosophy the algebraic idea of *negative quantities*.[18] It is one of Kant's grandest gleams into hidden truth. Were it only for the merits of this most masterly essay in reconstituting the algebraic meaning of a *negative quantity* [so generally misunderstood as a *negation* of quantity, and which even Sir Isaac Newton misconstrued as regarded its metaphysics], great would have been the service rendered to logic by Kant. But there is a greater. From this little *brochure* I am satisfied was derived originally the German regeneration of the Dynamic philosophy,[19] its expansion through the idea of polarity, indifference, &c. Oh, Mr Schlosser, you had not *geprüft*[20] p. 5 of vol. 2. You skipped the notes.

lainies for the sake of popularity, and still more for the sake of wielding this popularity vindictively, none is so scandalous as this. In any new life of Swift the case must be stated *de novo*.[24] Even Sir Walter Scott is not impartial; and for the same reason as now forces me to blink it, viz., the difficulty of presenting the details in a readable shape.[25] 'Gulliver's Travels' Schlosser strangely considers 'spun out to an intolerable extent.'[26] Many evil things might be said of Gulliver; but not this. The captain is anything but tedious. And, indeed, it becomes a question of mere mensuration, that can be settled in a moment. A year or two since I had in my hands a pocket edition, comprehending all the four parts of the worthy skipper's adventures within a single volume of 420 pages. Some part of the space was also wasted on notes, often very idle. Now the 1st part contains *two* separate voyages (Lilliput and Blefuscu),[27] the 2d, *one*, the 3d, *five*, and the 4th, *one*; so that, in all, this active navigator, who has enriched geography, I hope, with something of a higher quality than your old muffs that thought much of doubling Cape Horn, here gives us *nine* great discoveries, far more surprising than the pretended discoveries of Sinbad (which are known to be fabulous), averaging, *quam proximè*,[28] forty-seven small 16mo pages each. Oh you unconscionable German, built round in your own country with circumvallations of impregnable 4tos, oftentimes dark and dull as Avernus[29] – that you will have the face to describe dear excellent Captain Lemuel Gulliver of Redriff, and subsequently of Newark, that 'darling of children and men,' as tedious. It is exactly because he is *not* tedious, because he does not shoot into German foliosity, that Schlosser finds him '*intolerable*.' I have justly transferred to Gulliver's use the words originally applied by the poet to the robin red-breast,[30] for it is remarkable that *Gulliver* and the *Arabian Nights* are amongst the few books where children and men find themselves meeting and jostling each other. This was the case from its first publication, just one hundred and twenty years since. 'It was received,' says Dr Johnson, 'with such avidity, that the price of the first edition was raised before the second could be made – it was read by the high and the low, the learned and the illiterate. Criticism was lost in wonder.'[31] Now, on the contrary, Schlosser wonders not at all, but simply criticises; which we could bear, if the criticism were even ingenious. Whereas, he utterly misunderstands Swift, and is a malicious calumniator of the captain who, luckily, roaming in Sherwood, and thinking, often with a sigh, of his little nurse,* Glumdalclitch,

* 'Little nurse:' – the word *Glumdalclitch*, in Brobdingnagian,[32] absolutely *means little nurse*, and nothing else. It may seem odd that the captain should call any nurse of Brobdingnag, however kind to him, by such an epithet as *little;* and the reader may fancy that Sherwood forest had put it into his head, where Robin Hood always called his right hand man 'Little John,'[33] not *although*, but expressly *because* John stood seven feet high in his stockings. But the truth is – that Glumdalclitch *was* little; and literally so; she was only nine years old, and (says the captain,) 'little of her age,'[34] being barely forty feet high. She had time to grow certainly, but as she had so much to do before she could overtake other women, it is probable that she would turn out what, in Westmoreland, they call a *little stiffenger* – very little, if at all, higher than a common English church steeple.[35]

would trouble himself slightly about what Heidelberg might say in the next century. There is but one example on our earth of a novel received with such indiscriminate applause as 'Gulliver;' and *that* was 'Don Quixote.'[36] Many have been welcomed joyfully by a class – these two by a people. Now, could that have happened had it been characterised by dulness? Of all faults, it could least have had *that*. As to the 'Tale of a Tub,' Schlosser is in such Cimmerian vapours, that no system of bellows could blow open a shaft or tube through which he might gain a glimpse of the English truth and daylight. It is useless talking to such a man on such a subject. I consign him to the attentions of some patriotic Irishman.

Schlosser, however, is right in a graver reflection which he makes upon the prevailing philosophy of Swift, viz., that 'all his views were directed towards what was *immediately* beneficial, which is the characteristic of savages.'[37] This is undeniable. The meanness of Swift's nature, and his rigid incapacity for dealing with the grandeurs of the human spirit, with religion, with poetry, or even with science, when it rose above the mercenary practical, is absolutely appalling. His own *yahoo*[38] is not a more abominable one-sided degradation of humanity, than is he himself under this aspect. And, perhaps, it places this incapacity of his in its strongest light, when we recur to the fact of his *astonishment* at a religious princess refusing to confer a bishoprick[39] upon one that had treated the Trinity, and all the profoundest mysteries of Christanity, not with mere scepticism, or casual sneer, but with set pompous merriment and farcical buffoonery. This dignitary of the church, Dean of the most conspicuous cathedral in Ireland,[40] had, in full canonicals, made himself into a regular mountebank, for the sake of giving fuller effect, by the force of contrast, to the silliest of jests directed against all that was most inalienable from Christianity. Ridiculing such things, could he, in any just sense, be thought a Christian? But, as Schlosser justly remarks, even ridiculing the peculiarities of Luther and Calvin[41] as he *did* ridicule them, Swift could not be thought other than constitutionally incapable of religion. Even a Pagan philosopher, if made to understand the case, would be incapable of scoffing at any *form*, natural or casual, simple or distorted, which might be assumed by the most solemn of problems – problems that rest with the weight of worlds upon the human spirit –

'Fix'd fate, free-will, fore-knowledge absolute.'[42]

the destiny of man, or the relations of man to God. Anger, therefore, Swift *might* feel, and he felt it* to the end of his most wretched life; but what reasonable ground had a man of sense for *astonishment* – that a princess, who (according to her knowledge) was sincerely pious, should decline to place such a man upon an Episcopal throne? This argues, beyond a doubt, that Swift was in that state of constitutional irreligion, irreligion from a vulgar tempera-

* See his bitter letters to Lady Suffolk.[43]

ment, which imputes to everybody else its own plebeian feelings. People differed, he fancied, not by more and less religion, but by more and less dissimulation. And, therefore, it seemed to him scandalous that a princess, who must, of course, in her heart regard (in common with himself) all mysteries as solemn masques and mummeries, should pretend, in a case of downright serious business, to pump up, out of old dry conventional hoaxes, any solid objection to a man of his shining merit. '*The Trinity*,' for instance, *that* he viewed as the pass-word, which the knowing ones gave in answer to the challenge of the sentinel; but, as soon as it had obtained admission for the party within the gates of the camp, it was rightly dismissed to oblivion or to laughter. No case so much illustrates Swift's essential irreligion; since, if he had shared in ordinary human feelings on such subjects, not only he could not have been surprised at his own exclusion from the bench of bishops, *after* such ribaldries, but originally he would have abstained from them as inevitable bars to clerical promotion, even upon principles of public decorum.

As to the *style* of Swift, Mr Schlosser shows himself without sensibility in his objections, as the often hackneyed English reader shows himself without philosophic knowledge of style in his applause. Schlosser thinks the style of Gulliver 'somewhat dull.'[44] This shows Schlosser's presumption in speaking upon a point where he wanted, 1st, original delicacy of tact; and, 2dly, familiar knowledge of English. Gulliver's style is *purposely* touched slightly with that dulness of circumstantiality which besets the excellent, but 'somewhat dull' race of men – old sea captains.[45] Yet it wears only an aërial tint of dulness; the felicity of this colouring in Swift's management is, that it never goes the length of wearying, but only of giving a comic air of downright Wapping and Rotherhithe verisimilitude.[46] All men grow dull, and ought to be dull, that live under a solemn sense of eternal danger, one inch only of plank (often worm-eaten) between themselves and the grave; and, also, that see for ever one wilderness of waters – sublime, but (like the wilderness on shore) monotonous. All sublime people, being monotonous, have a tendency to be dull, and sublime things also. Milton and Aeschylus,[47] the sublimest of men, are crossed at times by a shade of dulness. It is their weak side. But as to a sea captain, a regular nor'-nor'-wester, and sou'-sou'-easter, he ought to be kicked out of the room if he is *not* dull. It is not 'ship-shape,' or barely tolerable, that he should be otherwise. Yet, after all, considering what I have stated about Captain Gulliver's nine voyages crowding into one pocket volume, he cannot really have much abused his professional licence for being dull. Indeed, one has to look out an excuse for his being so little dull; which excuse is found in the fact that he had studied three years at a learned university. Captain Gulliver, though a sailor, I would have you to know, was a gownsman of Cambridge:[48] so says Swift, who knew more about the Captain than anybody now-a-days. Cantabs are all horsemen, *ergo*, Gulliver was fit for any thing, from the *wooden shoon* of Cambridge up to the Horse Marines.

Now, on the other hand, you, common-place reader, that (as an old tradition) believe Swift's style to be a model of excellence, hereafter I shall say a word to you, drawn from deeper principles. At present I content myself with these three propositions, which overthrow if you can: –

1. That the merit, which justly you ascribe to Swift, is *vernacularity;* he never forgets his mother-tongue in exotic forms, unless we may call Irish exotic; for Hibernicisms he certainly has. This merit, however, is exhibited – not, as *you* fancy, in a graceful artlessness, but in a coarse inartificiality. To be artless, and to be inartificial, are very different things; as different as being natural and being gross; as different as being simple and being homely.

2. That whatever, meantime, be the particular sort of excellence, or the value of the excellence, in the style of Swift, he had it in common with multitudes beside of that age. De Foe[49] wrote a style for all the world the same as to kind and degree of excellence, only pure from Hibernicisms. So did every honest skipper [Dampier[50] was something more] who had occasion to record his voyages in this world of storms. So did many a hundred of religious writers. And what wonder should there be in this, when the main qualification for such a style was plain good sense, natural feeling, unpretendingness, some little scholarly practice in putting together the clockwork of sentences, so as to avoid mechanical awkwardness of construction, but above all the advantage of a *subject*, such in its nature as instinctively to reject ornament, lest it should draw off attention from itself? Such subjects are common; but grand impassioned subjects insist upon a different treatment; and *there* it is that the true difficulties of style commence.

3. [Which partly is suggested by the last remark.] That nearly all the blockheads with whom I have at any time had the pleasure of conversing upon the subject of style (and pardon me for saying that men of the most sense are apt, upon two subjects, viz., poetry and style, to talk *most* like blockheads), have invariably regarded Swift's style not as if *relatively* good [*i. e. given* a proper subject], but as if *absolutely* good – good unconditionally, no matter what the subject. Now, my friend, suppose the case, that the Dean had been required to write a pendant for Sir Walter Raleigh's immortal apostrophe to Death,[51] or to many passages that I will select in Sir Thomas Brown's 'Religio Medici,' and his 'Urn-burial,' or to Jeremy Taylor's inaugural sections of his 'Holy Living and Dying,'[52] do you know what would have happened? Are you aware what sort of ridiculous figure your poor bald Jonathan would have cut? About the same that would be cut by a forlorn scullion or waiter from a greasy eating-house at Rotterdam, if suddenly called away in vision to act as seneschal to the festival of Belshazzar the king, before a thousand of his lords.[53]

Schlosser, after saying any thing right and true (and he really did say the true thing about Swift's *essential* irreligion), usually becomes exhausted, like a boa-constrictor after eating his half-yearly dinner. The boa gathers himself up, it is to be hoped for a long fit of dyspepsy, in which the horns and hoofs that he has swallowed may chance to avenge the poor goat that owned them. Schlosser, on the other hand, retires into a corner, for the purpose of obstinately talking nonsense, until the gong sounds again for a slight refection of sense. Accordingly he likens Swift, before he has done with him, to whom? I might safely allow the reader three years for guessing, if the greatest of wagers were depending between us. He likens him to Kotzebue, in the first place. How faithful the resemblance! How exactly Swift reminds you of Count Benyowski in Siberia, and of Mrs Haller moping her eyes in the 'Stranger!'[54] One really is puzzled to say, according to the negro's logic, whether Mrs Haller is more like the Dean of St Patrick's, or the Dean more like Mrs Haller. Anyhow, the likeness is prodigious, if it is not quite reciprocal. The other *terminus* of the comparison is Wieland.[55] Now there *is* some shadow of a resemblance there. For Wieland had a touch of the comico-cynical in his nature; and it is notorious that he was often called the German Voltaire, which argues some tiger-monkey grin[56] that traversed his features at intervals. Wieland's malice, however, was far more playful and genial than Swift's; something of this is shown in his romance of 'Idris,' and oftentimes in his prose. But what the world knows Wieland by is his 'Oberon.' Now in this gay, musical romance of Sir Huon[57] and his enchanted horn, with its gleams of voluptuousness, is there a possibility that any suggestion of a scowling face like Swift's should cross the festal scenes?

From Swift the scene changes to Addison and Steele.[58] Steele is of less importance; for, though a man of greater intellectual activity* than Addison, he had far less of genius. So I turn him out, as one would turn out upon a heath a ram that had missed his way into one's tulip preserve; requesting him to fight for himself against Schlosser, or others that may molest him. But, so far as concerns Addison, I am happy to support the character of Schlosser for consistency, by assuring the reader that, of all the monstrosities uttered by any man upon Addison, and of all the monstrosities uttered by Schlosser upon any man, a thing which he says about Addison is the worst. But this I reserve for a climax at the end. Schlosser really puts his best leg foremost at starting, and one thinks he's going to mend; for he catches a truth, viz., the following – that all the brilliances of the Queen Anne period (which so many inconsiderate people have called the Augustan age of our literature) 'point to this – that the reading public wished to be entertained, not roused to think; to be

* *'Activity.'* – It is some sign of this, as well as of the more thoroughly English taste in literature which distinguished Steele, that hardly twice throughout the 'Spectator' is Shakspere quoted or alluded to by Addison.[59] 'Even these quotations he had from the theatre, or the breath of popular talk. Generally, if you see a line from Shakspere, it is safe to bet largely that the paper is Steele's; sometimes, indeed, of casual contributors; but, almost to a certainty, *not* a paper of Addison's. Another mark of Steele's superiority in vigour of intellect is, that much oftener in *him* than in other contributors strong thoughts came forward; harsh and disproportioned, perhaps, to the case, and never harmoniously developed with the genial grace of Addison, but original, and pregnant with promise and suggestion.

gently moved, not deeply excited.'[60] Undoubtedly what strikes a man in Addison, or *will* strike him when indicated, is the coyness and timidity, almost the girlish shame, which he betrays in the presence of all the elementary majesties belonging to impassioned or idealised nature. Like one bred in crowded cities, when first left alone in forests or amongst mountains, he is frightened at their silence, their solitude, their magnitude of form, or their frowning glooms. It has been remarked by others that Addison and his companions never rise to the idea of addressing the 'nation' or the 'people:' it is always the 'town.' Even their audience was conceived of by *them* under a limited form. Yet for this they had some excuse in the state of facts. A man would like at this moment to assume that Europe and Asia were listening to him; and as some few copies of his book do really go to Paris and Naples, some to Calcutta, there is a sort of legal fiction that such an assumption is steadily taking root. Yet, unhappily, that ugly barrier of languages interferes. Schamyl, the Circassian chief,[61] though much of a savage, is not so wanting in taste and discernment as to be backward in reading any book of yours or mine. Doubtless he yearns to read it. But then, you see, that infernal *Tchirkass* language steps between our book, the darling, and *him*, the discerning reader. Now, just such a barrier existed for the Spectator in the travelling arrangements of England. The very few old heavies[62] that had begun to creep along three or four main roads, depended so much on wind and weather, their chances of foundering were so uncalculated, their periods of revolution were so cometary and uncertain, that no body of scientific observations had yet been collected to warrant a prudent man in risking a heavy bale of goods; and, on the whole, even for York, Norwich, or Winchester, a consignment of '*Specs*' was not quite a safe spec. Still, I could have told the Spectator who was anxious to make money, where he might have been sure of a distant sale, though returns would have been slow, viz., at Oxford and Cambridge. We know from Milton that old Hobson delivered his parcels pretty regularly eighty years before 1710.[63] And, one generation before *that*, it is plain, by the interesting (though somewhat Jacobinical) letters* of Joseph Mede, the commenter on the Apocalypse, that news and politics of one kind or other (and scandal of *every* kind) found out for themselves a sort of contraband lungs to breathe through between London and Cambridge; not quite so regular in their *systole* and *diastole* as the tides of ebb and flood, but better than nothing. If you consigned a packet into the proper hands on the 1st of May, 'as sure as death' (to speak *Scotticè*) it would be delivered within sixty miles of the capital before midsummer. Still there were delays; and these forced a man into carving his world out of London. That excuses the word *town*. Inexcusable, however, were many other forms of expression in those days, which argued cowardly feelings. One would like to see a searching investigation into the state of society in Anne's days – its extreme artificiality, its sheepish reserve upon all the impassioned grandeurs,

* 'Letters of Joseph Mede,' published more than twenty years ago by Sir Henry Ellis.[64]

its shameless outrages upon all the decencies of human nature. Certain it is, that Addison (because everybody) was in that meanest of conditions which blushes at any expression of sympathy with the lovely, the noble, or the impassioned. The wretches were ashamed of their own nature, and perhaps with reason; for in their own denaturalised hearts they read only a degraded nature. Addison, in particular, shrank from every bold and every profound expression as from an offence against good taste. He durst not for his life have used the word 'passion' except in the vulgar sense of an angry paroxysm. He durst as soon have danced a hornpipe on the top of the 'monument' as have talked of a 'rapturous emotion.' What *would* he have said? Why, 'sentiments that were of a nature to prove agreeable after an unusual rate.' In their odious verses, the creatures of that age talk of love as something that 'burns' them.[65] You suppose at first that they are discoursing of tallow candles, though you cannot imagine by what impertinence they address *you*, that are no tallow-chandler, upon such painful subjects. And, when they apostrophise the woman of their heart (for you are to understand that they pretend to such an organ), they beseech her to 'ease their pain.'[66] Can human meanness descend lower? As if the man, being ill from pleurisy, therefore had a right to take a lady for one of the dressers in an hospital, whose duty it would be to fix a burgundy-pitch plaster between his shoulders. Ah, the monsters! Then to read of their Phillises, and Strephons, and Chloes, and Corydons[67] – names that, by their very non-reality amongst names of flesh and blood, proclaim the fantasticalness of the life with which they are poetically connected – it throws me into such convulsions of rage, that I move to the window, and (without thinking what I am about) throw it up, calling, '*Police! police!*' What's *that* for? What can the police do in the business? Why, certainly nothing. What I meant in my dream was, perhaps [but one forgets *what* one meant upon recovering one's temper], that the police should take Strephon and Corydon into custody, whom I fancied at the other end of the room. And really the justifiable fury, that arises upon recalling such abominable attempts at bucolic sentiment in such abominable language, sometimes transports me into a luxurious vision sinking back through 130 years, in which I see Addison, Phillips, both John and Ambrose, Tickell, Fickell, Budgell, and Cudgell,[68] with many others beside, all cudgelled in a round robin, none claiming precedency of another, none able to shrink from his own dividend, until a voice seems to recall me to milder thoughts by saying, 'But surely, my friend, you never could wish to see Addison cudgelled? Let Stephron and Corydon be cudgelled without end, if the police can show any warrant for doing it. But Addison was a man of great genius.' True, he was so. I recollect it suddenly, and will back out of any angry things that I have been misled into saying by Schlosser, who, by-the-bye, was right, after all, for a wonder. But now I will turn my whole fury in vengeance upon Schlosser. And, looking round for a stone to throw at him, I observe this. Addison could not be so entirely careless of exciting the public to think and feel, as Schlosser pretends, when he took so much pains to inoculate that public with a sense of the Miltonic grandeur. The 'Paradise Lost' had then been published barely forty years,[69] which was nothing in an age without reviews; the editions were still scanty; and though no Addison could eventually promote, for the instant he quickened, the circulation. If I recollect, Tonson's[70] accurate revision of the text followed immediately upon Addison's papers. And it is certain that Addison* must have diffused the knowledge of Milton upon the continent, from signs that soon followed. But does this not prove that I myself have been in the wrong as well as Schlosser? No: that's impossible. Schlosser's always in the wrong; but it's the next thing to an impossibility that I should be detected in an error: philosophically speaking, it is supposed to involve a contradiction. 'But surely I said the very same thing as Schlosser by assenting to what he said.' Maybe I did: but then I have time to make a distinction, because my article is not yet finished; we are only at page 6 or 7; whereas Schlosser can't make any distinction now, because his book's printed; and his list of *errata* (which is shocking, though he does not confess to the thousandth part) is actually published.[72] My distinction is – that, though Addison generally hated the impassioned, and shrank from it as from a fearful thing, yet this was when it combined with forms of life and fleshy realities (as in dramatic works), but not when it combined with elder forms of eternal abstractions. Hence, he did not read, and did not like Shakspere; the music was here too rapid and life-like: but he sympathised profoundly with the solemn cathedral chaunting of Milton. An appeal to his sympathies which exacted quick changes in those sympathies he could not meet, but a more stationary *key* of solemnity he *could*. Indeed, this difference is illustrated daily. A long list can be cited of passages in Shakspere, which have been solemnly denounced by many eminent men (all blockheads) as ridiculous: and if a man *does* find a passage in a tragedy that displeases him, it is sure to seem ludicrous: witness the indecent exposures of themselves made by Voltaire, La Harpe,[73] and many billions beside of bilious people. Whereas, of all the shameful people (equally billions, and not less bilious) that have presumed to quarrel with Milton, not one has thought him ludicrous, but only dull and somnolent. In 'Lear' and in 'Hamlet,' as in a human face agitated by passion, are many things that tremble on the brink of the ludicrous to an observer endowed with small range of sympathy or intellect. But no man ever found the starry heavens ludicrous, though many find them dull, and prefer a near view of a brandy flask. So in the solemn wheelings of the Miltonic movement, Addison could find a sincere delight. But the sublimities of earthly misery and of human frenzy were for him a book sealed. Beside all which, Milton renewed the types of Grecian beauty as to *form*, whilst Shak-

* It is an idea of many people, and erroneously sanctioned by Wordsworth, that Lord Somers gave a powerful lift to the 'Paradise Lost.' He was a subscriber to the sixth edition, the first that had plates; but this was some years before the Revolution of 1688, and when he was simply Mr Somers, a barrister, with no effectual power of patronage.[71]

spere, without designing at all to contradict these types, did so, in effect, by his fidelity to a new nature, radiating from a Gothic centre.

In the midst, however, of much just feeling, which one could only wish a little deeper, in the Addisonian papers on 'Paradise Lost,' there are some gross blunders of criticism, as there are in Dr Johnson,[74] and from the self-same cause – an understanding suddenly palsied from defective passion. A feeble capacity of passion must, upon a question of passion, constitute a feeble range of intellect. But, after all, the worst thing uttered by Addison in these papers is, not *against* Milton, but meant to be complimentary. Towards enhancing the splendour of the great poem, he tells us that it is a Grecian palace as to amplitude, symmetry, and architectural skill; but being in the English language, it is to be regarded as if built in brick; whereas, had it been so happy as to be written in Greek, then it would have been a palace built in Parian marble.[75] Indeed! that's smart – 'that's handsome, I calculate.' Yet, before a man undertakes to sell his mother tongue, as old pewter trucked against gold, he should be quite sure of his own metallurgic skill; because else, the gold may happen to be copper, and the pewter to be silver. Are you quite sure, my Addison, that you have understood the powers of this language which you toss away so lightly, as an old tea-kettle? Is it a ruled case that you have exhausted its resources? Nobody doubts your grace in a certain line of composition, but it is only one line among many, and it is far from being amongst the highest. It is dangerous, without examination, to sell even old kettles; misers conceal old stockings filled with guineas in old tea-kettles; and we all know that Aladdin's servant, by exchanging an old lamp for a new one, caused an Iliad of calamities: his master's palace jumped from Bagdad to some place on the road to Ashantee; Mrs Aladdin and the piccaninies were carried off as inside passengers; and Aladdin himself only escaped being lagged, for a rogue and a conjuror, by a flying jump after his palace.[76] Now, mark the folly of man. Most of the people I am going to mention subscribed, generally, to the supreme excellence of Milton; but each wished for a little change to be made – which, and which only was wanted to perfection. Dr Johnson, though he pretended to be satisfied with the 'Paradise Lost,' even in what he regarded as the undress of blank verse, still secretly wished it in rhyme. That's No. 1. Addison, though quite content with it in English, still could have wished it in Greek. That's No. 2. Bentley, though admiring the blind old poet in the highest degree, still observed, smilingly, that after all he *was* blind; he, therefore, slashing Dick, could have wished that the great man had always been surrounded by honest people; but, as that was not to be, he could have wished that his amanuensis had been hanged; but, as that also had become impossible, he could wish to do execution upon him in effigy, by sinking, burning, and destroying his handywork – upon which basis of posthumous justice, he proceeded to amputate all the finest passages in the poem.[77] Slashing Dick was No. 3. Payne Knight was a severer man even than slashing Dick; he professed to look upon the first book of 'Paradise Lost' as the finest thing that earth had to show; but, for that very reason, he could have wished, by your leave, to see the other eleven books sawed off, and sent overboard; because, though tolerable perhaps in another situation, they really were a national disgrace, when standing behind that unrivalled portico of book 1.[78] There goes No. 4. Then came a fellow, whose name was either not on his title page, or I have forgotten it, that pronounced the poem to be laudable, and full of good materials; but still he could have wished that the materials had been put together in a more workmanlike manner; which kind office he set about himself. He made a general clearance of all lumber: the expression of every thought he entirely re-cast: and he fitted up the metre with beautiful patent rhymes; not, I believe, out of any consideration for Dr Johnson's comfort, but on principles of mere abstract decency: as it was, the poem seemed naked, and yet was not ashamed.[79] There went No. 5. *Him* succeeded a droller fellow than any of the rest. A French bookseller had caused a prose French translation to be made of the 'Paradise Lost,' without particularly noticing its English origin, or at least not in the title page. Our friend, No. 6, getting hold of this as an original French romance, translated it back into English prose, as a satisfactory novel for the season.[80] His little mistake was at length discovered, and communicated to him with shouts of laughter; on which, after considerable kicking and plunging (for a man cannot but turn restive when he finds that he has not only got the wrong sow by the ear, but actually sold the sow to a bookseller), the poor translator was tamed into sulkiness; in which state he observed that he could have wished his own work, being evidently so much superior to the earliest form of the romance, might be admitted by the courtesy of England to take the precedency as the original 'Paradise Lost,' and to supersede the very rude performance of 'Milton, Mr John.'*

Schlosser makes the astounding assertion, that a compliment of Boileau to Addison, and a pure compliment of ceremony upon Addison's early Latin verses, was (*credite posteri!*) the making of Addison in England.[82] Understand, Schlosser, that Addison's Latin verses were never heard of by England, until long after his English prose had fixed the public attention upon him; his Latin reputation was a slight reaction from his English[83] reputation: and, secondly, understand that Boileau had at no time any such authority in England as to *make* anybody's reputation; he had first of all to make his own. A sure proof of this is, that Boileau's name was first published to London, by Prior's burlesque of what the Frenchman had called an ode. This gasconading ode celebrated the passage of the Rhine in 1672, and the capture of that famous fortress called *Skink* ('le fameux fort de'),[84] by Louis XIV., known to London

* *'Milton, Mr John:'* – Dr Johnson expressed his wrath, in an amusing way, at some bookseller's hack who, when employed to make an index, introduced Milton's name among the Ms, under the civil title of – 'Milton, Mr John.'[81]

at the time of Prior's parody by the name of 'Louis Baboon.'* *That* was not likely to recommend Master Boileau to any of the allies against the said Baboon, had it ever been heard of out of France. Nor was it likely to make him popular in England, that his name was first mentioned amongst shouts of laughter and mockery. It is another argument of the slight notoriety possessed by Boileau in England – that no attempt was ever made to translate even his satires, epistles, or 'Lutrin,'[86] except by booksellers' hacks; and that no such version ever took the slightest root amongst ourselves, from Addison's day to this very summer of 1847. Boileau was essentially, and in two senses, viz., both as to mind and as to influence, *un homme borné*.[87]

Addison's 'Blenheim'[88] is poor enough; one might think it a translation from some German original of those times. Gottsched's aunt, or Bodmer's wet-nurse,[89] might have written it; but still no fibs even as to 'Blenheim.' His 'enemies' did not say this thing against 'Blenheim' 'aloud,' nor his friends that thing against it 'softly.'[90] And why? Because at that time (1704–5) he had made no particular enemies, nor any particular friends; unless by friends you mean his Whig patrons, and by enemies his tailor and co.

As to 'Cato,' Schlosser, as usual, wanders in the shadow of ancient night.[91] The English 'people,' it seems, so 'extravagantly applauded' this wretched drama, that you might suppose them to have 'altogether changed their nature,' and to have forgotten Shakspere. That man must have forgotten Shakspere, indeed, and from *ramollissement*[92] of the brain, who could admire 'Cato.' 'But,' says Schlosser, 'it was only a "fashion;" and the English soon repented.'[93] The English could not repent of a crime which they had never committed. Cato was not popular for a moment, nor tolerated for a moment, upon any literary ground, or as a work of art. It was an apple of temptation and strife thrown by the goddess of faction between two infuriated parties. 'Cato,' coming from a man without Parliamentary connexions, would have dropped lifeless to the ground. The Whigs have always affected a special love and favour for popular counsels: they have never ceased to give themselves the best of characters as regards public freedom. The Tories, as contradistinguished to the Jacobites, knowing that without *their* aid, the Revolution could not have been carried, most justly contended that the national liberties had been at least as much indebted to themselves. When, therefore, the Whigs put forth *their* man Cato to mouth speeches about liberty, as exclusively *their* pet, and about patriotism and all that sort of thing, saying insultingly to the Tories, 'How do you like *that?* Does *that* sting?' 'Sting, indeed!' replied the Tories; 'not at all; it's quite refreshing to us, that the Whigs have not utterly disowned such sentiments, which, by their public acts, we really thought they *had*.' And, accordingly, as the popular anecdote tells us, a Tory leader, Lord

* *'Louis Baboon'*: – As people read nothing in these days that is more than forty-eight hours old, I am daily admonished that allusions the most obvious to anything in the rear of our own time, needs explanation. *Louis Baboon* is Swift's jesting name for *Louis Bourbon, i. e.,* Louis XIV own time.[85]

Bolingbroke, sent for Booth[94] who performed Cato, and presented him (*populo spectante*)[95] with fifty guineas 'for defending so well the cause of the people against a perpetual dictator.'[96] In which words, observe, Lord Bolingbroke at once asserted the cause of his own party, and launched a sarcasm against a great individual opponent, viz., Marlborough.[97] Now, Mr Schlosser, I have mended your harness; all right ahead; so drive on once more.

But, oh Castor and Pollux,[98] whither – in what direction is it, that the man is driving us? Positively, Schlosser, you must stop and let *me* get out. I'll go no further with such a drunken coachman. Many another absurd thing I was going to have noticed, such as his utter perversion of what Mandeville said about Addison (viz., by suppressing one word, and misapprehending all the rest).[99] Such, again, as his point-blank misstatement of Addison's infirmity in his official character, which was *not* that 'he could not prepare despatches in a good style,'[100] but diametrically the opposite case – that he insisted too much on style, to the serious retardation of public business. But all these things are as nothing to what Schlosser says elsewhere. He actually describes Addison, on the whole, as a 'dull prosaist,'[101] and the patron of pedantry! Addison, the man of all that ever lived most hostile even to what was good in pedantry, to its tendencies towards the profound in erudition and the non-popular; Addison, the champion of all that is easy, natural, superficial, a pedant and a master of pedantry! Get down, Schlosser, this moment; or let *me* get out.

SCHLOSSER'S LITERARY HISTORY OF THE EIGHTEENTH CENTURY
[Part II]

First published in *Tait's*, XIV, October 1847, pp. 690–6. Contrary to *Tait's* usual practice, the essay was not printed as by De Quincey. A centred line immediately preceding the text stated that it was '*(Continued from page* 583.)' to denote where in *Tait's* Part I of the essay ended.

Reprinted in *F*, XVIII, *The Note Book of an English Opium-Eater* (1855), pp. 109–30, 133–5.

Revised text, carrying many accidentals but only two substantive variants from *F*, in *SGG*, VIII, *Essays, Sceptical and Anti-Sceptical, or Problems Neglected or Misconceived* (1858), pp. 64–87.

There are two manuscripts, as follows:

MS A: Dove Cottage, Grasmere, MS 1989:161.62. The manuscript is a draft fragment from De Quincey's discussion of 'FOX AND BURKE' (see below, pp. 205–8). A full transcript is given below, pp. 500–1.

MS B: Princeton University, Robert H. Taylor Collection. The manuscript is a complete set of *SGG* page proofs. It contains five significant variants, and these are listed in the textual notes.

For the occasion and context of the essay, see headnote, pp. 183–4.

Pope, by far the most important writer, English or Continental, of his own age, is treated with more extensive ignorance by Mr Schlosser than any other, and (excepting Addison)[1] with more ambitious injustice. A false abstract is given, or a false impression, of any one amongst his brilliant works, that is noticed at all; and a false sneer, a sneer irrelevant to the case, at any work dismissed by name as unworthy of notice. The three works, selected as the gems of Pope's collection, are the 'Essay on Criticism,' the 'Rape of the Lock,' and the 'Essay on Man.' On the first, which (with Dr Johnson's leave)[2] is the feeblest and least interesting of Pope's writings, being substantially a mere versification, like a metrical multiplication-table, of common places the most mouldy with which criticism has baited its rat-traps; since nothing is said worth answering, it is sufficient to answer nothing. The 'Rape of the Lock' is treated with the same delicate sensibility that we might have looked for in

Brennus,[3] if consulted on the picturesque, or in Attila the Hun, if adjured to decide aesthetically, between two rival cameos. Attila is said (though no doubt falsely) to have described himself as not properly a man so much as the Divine wrath incarnate.[4] This would be fine in a melodrama, with Bengal lights[5] burning on the stage. But, if ever he said such a naughty thing, he forgot to tell us what it was that had made him angry; by what *title* did *he* come into alliance with the Divine wrath, which was not likely to consult a savage? And why did his wrath hurry, by forced marches, to the Adriatic?[6] Now so much do people differ in opinion, that, to us, who look at him through a telescope from an eminence, fourteen centuries distant, he takes the shape rather of a Mahratta trooper, painfully gathering *chout*,[7] or a cateran levying black-mail, or a decent tax-gatherer with an ink-horn at his button-hole, and supported by a select party of constabulary friends. The very natural instinct which Attila always showed for following the trail of the wealthiest footsteps, seems to argue a most commercial coolness in the dispensation of his wrath. Mr Schlosser burns with the wrath of Attila against all aristocracies, and especially that of England. He governs his fury, also, with an Attila discretion in many cases; but not here. Imagine this Hun coming down, sword in hand, upon Pope and his Rosicrucian light troops, levying *chout* upon Sir Plume, and fluttering the dove-cot of the Sylphs.[8] Pope's 'duty it was,' says this demoniac, to 'scourge the follies of good society,' and also 'to break with the aristocracy.'[9] No, surely? something short of a total rupture would have satisfied the claims of duty? Possibly; but it would not have satisfied Schlosser. And Pope's guilt consists in having made his poem an idyl or succession of pictures representing the gayer aspects of society as it really was, and supported by a comic interest of the mock-heroic derived from a playful machinery, instead of converting it into a bloody satire. Pope, however, did not shrink from such assaults on the aristocracy, if these made any part of his duties. Such assaults he made twice at least[10] too often for his own peace, and perhaps for his credit at this day. It is useless, however, to talk of the poem as a work of art, with one who sees none of its exquisite graces, and can imagine his countryman Zachariä equal to a competition with Pope.[11] But this it may be right to add, that the 'Rape of the Lock' was *not* borrowed from the 'Lutrin' of Boileau.[12] That was impossible. Neither was it suggested by the 'Lutrin.' The story in Herodotus of the wars between cranes and pigmies,[13] or the *Batrachomyomachia* (so absurdly ascribed to Homer)[14] might have suggested the idea more naturally. Both these, there is proof that Pope had read: there is none that he had read the 'Lutrin,' nor did he read French with ease to himself. The 'Lutrin,' meantime, is as much below the 'Rape of the Lock' in brilliancy of treatment, as it is dissimilar in plan or the quality of its pictures.

The 'Essay on Man' is a more thorny subject. When a man finds himself attacked and defended from all quarters, and on all varieties of principle, he is bewildered. Friends are as dangerous as enemies. He must not defy a bristling enemy, if he cares for repose; he must not disown a zealous defender, though making concessions on his own behalf not agreeable to himself; he must not explain away ugly phrases in one direction, or perhaps he is recanting the very words of his 'guide, philosopher, and friend,' who cannot safely be taxed with having first led him into temptation;[15] he must not explain them away in another direction, or he runs full tilt into the wrath of mother Church – who will soon bring him to his senses by penance. Long lents, and no lampreys allowed, would soon cauterise the proud flesh of heretical ethics. Pope did wisely, situated as he was, in a decorous nation, and closely connected, upon principles of fidelity under political suffering, with the Roman Catholics, to say little in his own defence. That defence, and any reversionary cudgelling which it might entail upon the Quixote undertaker, he left – meekly but also slyly, humbly but cunningly – to those whom he professed to regard as greater philosophers than himself. All parties found their account in the affair. Pope slept in peace; several pugnacious gentlemen up and down Europe expectorated much fiery wrath in dusting each other's jackets; and Warburton, the attorney, finally earned his bishoprick in the service of whitewashing a writer, who was aghast at finding himself first trampled on as a deist, and then exalted as a defender of the faith.[16] Meantime, Mr Schlosser mistakes Pope's courtesy, when he supposes his acknowledgments to Lord Bolingbroke sincere in their whole extent.[17]

Of Pope's 'Homer' Schlosser thinks fit to say, amongst other evil things, which it really *does* deserve (though hardly in comparison with the German 'Homer' of the ear-splitting Voss), 'that Pope pocketed the subscription of the "Odyssey," and left the work to be done by his understrappers.'[18] Don't tell fibs, Schlosser. Never do *that* any more. True it is, and disgraceful enough, that Pope (like modern contractors for a railway or a loan) let off to sub-contractors several portions of the undertaking. He was perhaps not illiberal in the terms of his contracts. At least I know of people now-a-days (much better artists) that would execute such contracts, and enter into any penalties for keeping time at thirty per cent. less. But *navies* and bill-brokers, that are in excess now, then were scarce. Still the affair, though not mercenary, was illiberal in a higher sense of art; and no anecdote shows more pointedly Pope's sense of the mechanic fashion, in which his own previous share of the Homeric labour had been executed. It was disgraceful enough, and needs no exaggeration. Let it, therefore, be reported truly: Pope personally translated one-half of the 'Odyssey' – a dozen books he turned out of his own oven; and, if you add the *Batrachomyomachia*, his dozen was a baker's dozen. The journeymen did the other twelve; were regularly paid; regularly turned off when the job was out of hand; and never once had to 'strike for wages.' How much beer was allowed, I cannot say. This is the truth of the matter. So no more fibbing, Schlosser, if you please.

But there remains behind all these labours of Pope, the 'Dunciad,'[19] which is by far his greatest. I shall not, within the narrow bounds assigned to me, enter upon a theme so exacting; for, in this instance, I should have to fight not against Schlosser only, but against Dr Johnson, who has thoroughly misrepresented the nature of the 'Dunciad,' and, consequently, could not measure its merits.[20] Neither he, nor Schlosser, in fact, ever read more than a few passages of this admirable poem. But the villany is too great for a brief exposure. One thing only I will notice of Schlosser's misrepresentations. He asserts (not when directly speaking of Pope, but afterwards, under the head of Voltaire) that the French author's trivial and random *Temple de Gout*[21] 'shows the superiority in this species of poetry to have been greatly on the side of the Frenchman.' Let's hear a reason, though but a Schlosser reason, for this opinion: know, then, all men whom it concerns, that 'the Englishman's satire only hit such people as would never have been known without his mention of them, whilst Voltaire selected those who were still called great, and their respective schools.' Pope's men, it seems, never *had* been famous – Voltaire's might cease to be so, but as yet they had *not* ceased; as yet they commanded interest. Now mark how I will put three bullets into that plank, riddle it so that the leak shall not be stopped by all the old hats in Heidelberg, and Schlosser will have to swim for his life. First, he is forgetting that, by his own previous confession, Voltaire, not less than Pope, had 'immortalised a great many *insignificant* persons;'[22] consequently, had it been any fault to do so, each alike was caught in that fault; and insignificant as the people might be, if they *could* be 'immortalised,' then we have Schlosser himself confessing to the possibility that poetic splendour should create a secondary interest where originally there had been none. Secondly, the question of merit does not rise from the object of the archer, but from the style of his archery. Not the choice of victims, but the execution done is what counts. Even for continued failures it would plead advantageously, much more for continued and brilliant successes, that Pope fired at an object offering no sufficient breadth of mark. Thirdly, it is the grossest of blunders to say that Pope's objects of satire were obscure by comparison with Voltaire's. True, the Frenchman's example of a scholar, viz., the French Salmasius, was most accomplished. But so was the Englishman's scholar, viz., the English Bentley.[23] Each was absolutely without a rival in his own day. But the day of Bentley was the very day of Pope. Pope's man had not even faded; whereas the day of Salmasius, as respected Voltaire, had gone by for more than half a century. As to Dacier, '*which* Dacier, Bezonian?'[24] The husband was a passable scholar – but madame was a poor sneaking fellow, fit only for the usher of a boarding-school. All this, however, argues Schlosser's two-fold ignorance – first, of English authors; second, of the 'Dunciad;' – else he would have known that even Dennis, mad John Dennis, was a much cleverer man than most of those alluded to by Voltaire. Cibber, though slightly a coxcomb, was born a brilliant man. Aaron Hill[25] was so lustrous, that even Pope's venom fell off spontaneously, like rain from the plumage of a pheasant, leaving him to 'mount far upwards with the swans of Thames'[26] – and, finally, let it not be forgotten, that Samuel Clarke, Burnet, of the Charterhouse, and Sir Isaac Newton,[27] did not wholly escape tasting the knout; if *that* rather impeaches the equity, and sometimes the judgment of Pope, at least it contributes to show the groundlessness of Schlosser's objection – that the population of the Dunciad, the characters that filled its stage, were inconsiderable.

FOX AND BURKE.[28]

It is, or it *would* be, if Mr Schlosser were himself more interesting, luxurious to pursue his ignorance as to facts, and the craziness of his judgment as to the valuation of minds, throughout his comparison of Burke with Fox. The force of antithesis brings out into a feeble life of meaning, what, in its own insulation, had been languishing mortally into nonsense. The darkness of his 'Burke' becomes *visible* darkness[29] under the glimmering that steals upon it from the desperate common-places of his 'Fox.' Fox is painted exactly as he *would* have been painted fifty years ago by any pet subaltern of the Whig club, enjoying free pasture in Devonshire House.[30] The practised reader knows well what is coming. Fox is 'formed after the model of the ancients' – Fox is 'simple' – Fox is 'natural' – Fox is 'chaste' – Fox is 'forcible;'[31] Why yes, in a sense, Fox is even 'forcible:' but then, to feel that he was so, you must have *heard* him; whereas, for forty years he has been silent. We of 1847, that can only *read* him, hearing Fox described as *forcible*, are disposed to recollect Shakespere's Mr Feeble amongst Falstaff's recruits, who also is described as *forcible*, viz., as the 'most forcible Feeble.'[32] And, perhaps, a better description could not be devised for Fox himself – so feeble was he in matter, so forcible in manner; so powerful for instant effect, so impotent for posterity.[33] In the Pythian fury of his gestures – in his screaming voice – in his directness of purpose, Fox would now remind you of some demon steam-engine on a railroad, some Fire-king or Salmoneus,[34] that had counterfeited, because he could not steal, Jove's thunderbolts; hissing, bubbling, snorting, fuming; demoniac gas, you think – gas from Acheron[35] must feed that dreadful system of convulsions. But pump out the imaginary gas, and, behold! it is ditch-water. Fox, as Mr Schlosser rightly thinks, was all of a piece – simple in his manners, simple in his style, simple in his thoughts. No waters in *him* turbid with new crystallisations; everywhere the eye can see to the bottom. No music in *him* dark with Cassandra meanings.[36] Fox, indeed, disturb decent gentlemen by 'allusions to all the sciences, from the integral calculus and metaphysics to navigation!'[37] Fox would have seen you hanged first. Burke, on the other hand, did all that, and other wickedness besides, which fills an 8vo page in Schlosser; and Schlosser crowns his enormities by charging him, the said Burke (p. 99), with '*wearisome tediousness*.' Among my own acquaintances are several old women, who think on this point precisely as Schlosser thinks; and they go further, for they even charge Burke with 'tedious wearisomeness.' Oh, sorrowful woe, and also woeful sorrow, when an Edmund Burke arises, like a *cheeta* or hunting leopard coupled in a tiger-chase with a German poodle. To think, in a merciful spirit, of the jungle – barely to contemplate, in a temper of humanity, the incomprehensible cane-thickets, dark and bristly, into which that bloody *cheeta* will drag that unoffending poodle!

But surely the least philosophic of readers, who hates philosophy 'as toad or asp,'[38] must yet be aware, that, where new growths are not germinating, it is no sort of praise to be free from the throes of growth. Where expansion is hopeless, it is little glory to have escaped distortion. Nor is it any blame that the rich fermentation of grapes should disturb the transparency of their golden fluids. Fox had nothing new to tell us, nor did he hold a position amongst men that required or would even have allowed him to tell anything new. He was helmsman to a party; what he had to do, though seeming to *give* orders, was simply to repeat *their* orders – 'Port your helm,' said the party; 'Port it is,' replied the helmsman. But Burke was no steersman; he was the Orpheus that sailed with the Argonauts; he was their *seer*,[39] seeing more in his visions than he always understood himself; he was their watcher through the hours of night; he was their astrological interpreter. Who complains of a prophet for being a little darker of speech than a post-office directory? or of him that reads the stars for being sometimes perplexed?

But, even as to facts, Schlosser is always blundering. Post-office directories would be of no use to *him*; nor link-boys; nor blazing tar-barrels. He wanders in a fog such as sits upon the banks of Cocytus. He fancies that Burke, in his lifetime, was *popular*.[40] Of course, it is so natural to be popular by means of '*wearisome tediousness*,' that Schlosser, above all people, should credit such a tale. Burke has been dead just fifty years, come next autumn. I remember the time from this accident – that my own nearest relative stepped on a day of October 1797, into that same suite of rooms at Bath (North Parade) from which, six hours before, the great man had been carried out to die at Beaconsfield.[41] It is, therefore, you see, fifty years. Now, ever since then, his *collective* works have been growing in bulk by the incorporation of juvenile essays, (such as his 'European Settlements,' his 'Essay on the Sublime,' on 'Lord Bolingbroke,'[42] &c.,) or (as more recently) by the posthumous publication of his MSS.;[*] and yet, ever since then, in spite of growing age and growing bulk, are more in demand. At this time, half a century after his last sigh, Burke *is* pop-

[*] 'Of his MSS.:' – And, if all that I have heard be true, much has somebody to answer for, that so little has been yet published. The two executors of Burke were Dr Lawrence, of Doctors' Commons, a well-known M.P. in forgotten days, and Windham,[43] a man too like Burke in elasticity of mind ever to be spoken of in connexion with forgotten things. Which of them was to blame, I know not. But Mr R. Sharpe,[44] M.P., twenty-five years ago, well known as *River* Sharpe, from the απεραντολογια[45] of his conversation, used to say, that one or both of the executors had offered *him* (the river) a huge travelling trunk, perhaps an Imperial or a Salisbury boot (equal to the wardrobe of a family), filled with Burke's MSS., on the simple condition of editing them with proper annotations. An Oxford man, and also the celebrated Mr Christian Curwen, then member for Cumberland,[46] made, in my hearing, the same report. The Oxford

ular; a thing, let me tell you, Schlosser, which never happened before to a writer steeped to his lips in *personal* politics. What a tilth of intellectual lava must that man have interfused amongst the refuse and scoria of such mouldering party rubbish, to force up a new verdure and laughing harvests, annually increasing for new generations! Popular he *is* now, but popular he was not in his own generation. And how could Schlosser have the face to say that he was? Did he never hear the notorious anecdote, that at one period Burke obtained the *sobriquet* of 'dinner-bell?'[48] And why? Not as one who invited men to a banquet by his gorgeous eloquence, but as one that gave a signal to shoals in the House of Commons, for seeking refuge in a *literal* dinner from the oppression of his philosophy. This was, perhaps, in part a scoff of his opponents. Yet there must have been some foundation for the scoff, since, at an earlier stage of Burke's career, Goldsmith had independently said, that this great orator

——— 'went on refining,
And thought of convincing, whilst *they* thought of dining.'[49]

I blame neither party. It ought not to be expected of any *popular* body that it should be patient of abstractions amongst the intensities of party-strife, and the immediate necessities of voting. No deliberative body would less have tolerated such philosophic exorbitations from public business than the *agora* of Athens, or the Roman senate. So far the error was in Burke, not in the House of Commons. Yet, also, on the other side, it must be remembered, that an intellect of Burke's combining power and enormous compass, could not, from necessity of nature, abstain from such speculations. For a man to reach a remote posterity, it is sometimes necessary that he should throw his voice over to them in a vast arch – it must sweep a parabola – which, therefore, rises high above the heads of those next to him, and is heard by the bye-standers but indistinctly, like bees swarming in the upper air before they settle on the spot fit for hiving.

See, therefore, the immeasurableness of misconception. Of all public men, that stand confessedly in the first rank as to splendour of intellect, Burke was the *least* popular at the time when our blind friend Schlosser assumes him to have run off with the lion's share of popularity. Fox, on the other hand, as the leader of opposition, was at that time a household term of love or reproach, from one end of the island to the other. To the very children playing in the streets, Pitt[50] and Fox, throughout Burke's generation, were pretty nearly as

man, in particular, being questioned as to the probable amount of MS., deposed, that he could not speak upon oath to the cubical contents; but this he could say, that, having stripped up his coat sleeve, he had endeavoured, by such poor machinery as nature had allowed him, to take the soundings of the trunk, but apparently there were none; with his middle finger he could find no bottom; for it was stopped by a dense stratum of MS.; below which, you know, other strata might lie *ad infinitum*.[47] For anything proved to the contrary, the trunk might be bottomless.

broad distinctions, and as much a war-cry, as English and French, Roman and Punic. Now, however, all this is altered. As regards the relations between the two Whigs whom Schlosser so steadfastly delighteth to misrepresent,

'Now is the winter of our discontent
Made glorious summer'[51]

for that intellectual potentate, Edmund Burke, the man whose true mode of power has never yet been truly investigated; whilst Charles Fox is known only as an echo is known, and for any real *effect* of intellect upon this generation, for anything but 'the whistling of a name,'[52] the Fox of 1780-1807 sleeps where the carols of the larks are sleeping, that gladdened the spring-tides of those years – sleeps with the roses that glorified the beauty of their summers.*

JUNIUS.[57]

Schlosser talks of Junius, who is to him, as to many people, more than entirely the enigma of an enigma, Hermes Trismegistus, or the mediaeval Prester John.[58] Not only are most people unable to solve the enigma, but they have no idea of what it is that they are to solve. I have to inform Schlosser that there are three separate questions about Junius, of which he has evidently no distinct knowledge, and cannot, therefore, have many chances to spare for settling them. The three questions are these: – A. Who *was* Junius? B. What was it that armed Junius with a power so unaccountable at this day over the public mind? C. Why, having actually exercised this power, and gained under his masque far more than he ever hoped to gain, did this Junius not come forward *in his own person*, when all the legal danger had long passed away, to claim a distinction that for *him* (among the vainest of men) must have been more precious than his heart's blood? The two questions, B and C, I have

* A man in Fox's situation is sure, whilst living, to draw after him trains of sycophants; and it is the evil necessity of newspapers the most independent, that they *must* swell the mob of sycophants. The public compels them to exaggerate the true proportions of such people as we see every hour in our own day. Those who, for the moment, modify, or *may* modify the national condition, become preposterous idols in the eyes of the gaping public; but with the sad necessity of being too utterly trodden under foot after they are shelved, unless they live in men's memory by something better than speeches in Parliament. Having the usual fate, Fox was complimented, *whilst living*, on his knowledge of Homeric Greek, which was a jest:[53] he knew neither more nor less of Homer, than, fortunately, most English gentlemen of his rank; quite enough that is to read the 'Iliad' with unaffected pleasure, far too little to revise the text of any three lines, without making himself ridiculous. The excessive slenderness of his general literature, English and French, may be seen in the letters published by his Secretary, Trotter.[54] But his fragment of a History, published by Lord Holland,[55] at two guineas, and currently sold for two shillings, (not two *pence*, or else I have been defrauded of 1s. 10d.) most of all proclaims the tenuity of his knowledge. He looks upon Malcolm Laing as a huge oracle; and, having read even less than Hume,[56] a thing not very easy, with great *naiveté*, cannot guess where Hume picked up his facts.

examined in past times,[59] and I will not here repeat my explanations further than to say, with respect to the last, that the reason for the author not claiming his own property was this, because he *dared* not; because it would have been *infamy* for him to avow himself as Junius; because it would have revealed a crime and published a crime in his own earlier life, for which many a man is transported in our days, and for less than which many a man has been in past days hanged, broken on the wheel, burned, gibbeted, or impaled. To say that he watched and listened at his master's key-holes, is nothing. It was not key-holes only that he made free with, but keys; he tampered with his master's seals; he committed larcenies; not, like a brave man, risking his life on the highway, but petty larcenies – larcenies in a dwelling-house – larcenies under the opportunities of a confidential situation – crimes which formerly, in the days of Junius, our bloody code never pardoned in villains of low degree. Junius was in the situation of Lord Byron's Lara, or, because Lara is a plagiarism, of Harriet Lee's Kraitzrer.[60] But this man, because he had money, friends, and talents, instead of going to prison, took himself off for a jaunt to the continent. From the continent, in full security and in possession of the *otium cum dignitate*,[61] he negotiated with the government, whom he had alarmed by publishing the secrets which he had stolen. He succeeded. He sold himself to great advantage. Bought and sold he was; and of course it is understood that, if you buy a knave, and expressly in consideration of his knaveries, you secretly undertake not to hang him. 'Honour bright!' Lord Barrington might certainly have indicted Junius at the Old Bailey, and had a reason for wishing to do so; but George III.,[62] who was a party to the negotiation, and all his ministers, would have said, with fits of laughter – 'Oh, come now, my lord, you must *not* do that. For, since we have bargained for a price to send him out as a member of council to Bengal,[63] you see clearly that we could not possibly hang him *before* we had fulfilled our bargain. Then it is true we might hang him after he comes back. But, since the man (being a clever man) has a fair chance in the interim of rising to be Governor-General, we put it to your candour, Lord Barrington, whether it would be for the public service to hang his excellency?' In fact, he might probably have been Governor-General, had his bad temper not overmastered him. Had he not quarrelled so viciously with Mr Hastings,[64] it is ten to one that he might, by playing his cards well, have succeeded him. As it was, after enjoying an enormous salary, he returned to England – not Governor-General, certainly, but still in no fear of being hanged. Instead of hanging him, on second thoughts, Government gave him a red ribbon. He represented a borough in Parliament.[65] He was an authority upon Indian affairs. He was caressed by the Whig party. He sat at good men's tables. He gave for toasts – *Joseph Surface*[66] sentiments at dinner parties – 'The man that betrays' [something or other] – 'the man that sneaks into' [other men's portfolios, perhaps] – 'is' – aye, *what* is he? Why he is, perhaps, a Knight of the Bath, has a sumptuous mansion in St James's Square,[67] dies full of years and honour, has a pompous funeral, and fears only some such epitaph as this – 'Here lies, in a red ribbon, the man who built a great prosperity on the basis of a great knavery.' I complain heavily of Mr Taylor,[68] the very able unmasquer of Junius, for blinking the whole questions B and C. He it is that has settled the question A, so that it will never be re-opened by a man of sense. A man who doubts, after *really* reading Mr Taylor's work, is not only a blockhead, but an irreclaimable blockhead. It is true that several men, among them Lord Brougham, whom Schlosser (though hating him, and kicking him) cites, still profess scepticism.[69] But the reason is evident: they have not *read* the book, they have only heard of it. They are unacquainted with the strongest arguments, and even with the nature of the evidence.* Lord Brougham, indeed, is generally reputed to have reviewed Mr Taylor's book. *That* may be:[72] it is probable enough: what I am denying is not at all that Lord Brougham *reviewed* Mr Taylor, but that Lord Brougham *read* Mr Taylor. And there is not much wonder in *that*, when we see professed writers on the subject – bulky writers – writers of Answers and Refutations, dispensing with the whole of Mr T.'s book, single paragraphs of which would have forced them to cancel their own. The possibility of scepticism, after really *reading* Mr T.'s book, would be the strongest exemplification upon record of Sancho's proverbial reproach, that a man 'wanted better bread than was made of wheat –'[73] would be the old case renewed from the scholastic grumblers 'that some men do not know when they are answered.' They have got their *quietus*, and they still continue to 'maunder' on with objections long since disposed of. In fact, it is not too strong a thing to say – and Chief Justice Dallas *did* say something like it[74] – that if Mr Taylor is not right, if Sir Philip Francis is *not* Junius, then was no man ever yet hanged on sufficient evidence. Even confession is no absolute proof. Even confessing to a crime, the man may be mad. Well, but at least seeing is believing: if the court sees a man commit an assault, will not *that* suffice? Not at all: ocular delusions on the largest scale are common. What's a court? Lawyers have no better eyes than other people. Their physics are often out of repair, and whole cities have been known to see things that could have no existence. Now, all other evidence is held to be short of this blank seeing or blank confessing. But I am not at all sure of *that*. Circumstan-

* Even in Dr Francis's Translation of Select Speeches from Demosthenes, which Lord Brougham naturally used a little in his own labours on that theme, there may be traced several peculiarities of diction that startle us in Junius. Sir P. had them from his father.[70] And Lord Brougham ought not to have overlooked them. The same thing may be seen in the notes to Dr Francis's translation of Horace.[71] These points, though not *independently* of much importance, become far more so in combination with others. The reply made to me once by a publisher of some eminence upon this question, was the best fitted to lower Mr Taylor's investigation with a *stranger* to the long history of the dispute. 'I feel,' he said, 'the impregnability of the case made out by Mr Taylor. But the misfortune is, that I have seen so many previous impregnable cases made out for other claimants.' Ay, that *would* be unfortunate. But the misfortune for this repartee was, that I, for whose use it was intended, not being in the predicament of a *stranger* to the dispute, having seen every page of the pleadings, knew all (except Mr Taylor's) to be false in their statements; after which their arguments signified nothing.

tial evidence, that multiplies indefinitely its points of *internexus* with known admitted facts, is more impressive than direct testimony. If you detect a fellow with a large sheet of lead that by many (to wit 70) salient angles, that by tedious (to wit 30) reëntrant angles, fits into and owns its sisterly relationship to all that is left of the lead upon your roof – this tight fit will weigh more with a jury than even if my lord chief justice should jump into the witness-box, swearing that, with judicial eyes, he saw the vagabond cutting the lead whilst he himself sat at breakfast; or even than if the vagabond should protest before this honourable court that he *did* cut the lead in order that he (the said vagabond) might have hot rolls and coffee as well as my lord, the witness. If Mr Taylor's body of evidence does *not* hold water, then is there no evidence extant upon any question, judicial or not judicial, that *will*.

But I blame Mr Taylor heavily for throwing away the whole argument applicable to B and C; not as any debt that rested particularly upon *him* to public justice; but as a debt to the integrity of his own book. That book is now a fragment; admirable as regards A; but (by omitting B and C) not sweeping the whole area of the problem. There yet remains, therefore, the dissatisfaction which is always likely to arise – not from the smallest *allegatio falsi*, but from the large *suppressio veri*.[75] B, which, on any other solution than the one I have proposed, is perfectly unintelligible, now becomes plain enough. To imagine a heavy, coarse, hard-working government, seriously affected by such a bauble as *they* would consider performances on the tight rope of style, is mere midsummer madness. 'Hold your absurd tongue,' would any of the ministers have said to a friend descanting on Junius as a powerful artist of style – 'do you dream, dotard, that this baby's rattle is the thing that keeps us from sleeping? Our eyes are fixed on something else: that fellow, whoever he is, knows what he ought *not* to know; he has had his hand in some of our pockets: he's a good locksmith, is that Junius; and before he reaches Tyburn,[76] who knows what amount of mischief he may do to self and partners?' The rumour that ministers were themselves alarmed (which was the naked truth) travelled downwards; but the *why* did not travel; and the innumerable blockheads of lower circles, not understanding the real cause of fear, sought a false one in the supposed thunderbolts of the rhetoric. Opera-house thunderbolts they were: and strange it is, that grave men should fancy newspapers, teeming (as they have always done) with *Publicolas*, with *Catos*, with *Algernon Sydneys*, able by such trivial small shot to gain a moment's attention from the potentates of Downing Street.[77] Those who have despatches to write, councils to attend, and votes of the Commons to manage, think little of Junius Brutus. A Junius Brutus, that dares not sign by his own honest name, is presumably skulking from his creditors. A Timoleon,[78] who hints at assassination in a newspaper, one may take it for granted, is a manufacturer of begging letters. And it is a conceivable case that a £20 note, enclosed to Timoleon's address, through the newspaper office, might go far to soothe that great patriot's feelings, and even to turn aside his avenging dagger. These sort of people were not the sort to frighten a British Ministry. One laughs at the probable conversation between an old hunting squire coming up to comfort the First Lord of the Treasury, on the rumour that he was panic-struck. 'What, surely, my dear old friend, you're not afraid of Timoleon?' First Lord. – 'Yes, I am.' C. Gent. – 'What, afraid of an anonymous fellow in the papers?' F.L. – 'Yes, dreadfully.' C. Gent. – 'Why, I always understood that these people were a sort of shams – living in Grub Street – or where was it that Pope used to tell us they lived?[79] Surely you're not afraid of Timoleon, because some people think he's a patriot?' F.L. – 'No, not at all; but I am afraid because some people think he's a housebreaker!' In that character only could Timoleon become formidable to a Cabinet Minister; and in some such character must our friend, Junius Brutus, have made himself alarming to Government. From the moment that B is properly explained, it throws light upon C. The Government was alarmed – not at such moonshine as patriotism, or at a soap-bubble of rhetoric – but because treachery was lurking amongst their own households; and, if the thing went on, the consequences might be appalling. But this domestic treachery, which accounts for B, accounts at the same time for C. The very same treachery that frightened its objects at the time by the consequences it might breed, would frighten its author afterwards from claiming its literary honours by the remembrances it might awaken. The mysterious disclosure of official secrets, which had once roused so much consternation within a limited circle, and (like the French affair of the diamond necklace)[80] had sunk into neglect only when all clue seemed lost for *perfectly* unravelling it, would revive in all its interest when a discovery came before the public, viz., a claim on the part of Francis to have written the famous letters, which must at the same time point a strong light upon the true origin of the treacherous disclosures. Some astonishment had always existed as to Francis – how he rose so suddenly into rank and station: some astonishment always existed as to Junius, how he should so suddenly have fallen asleep as a writer in the journals. The coincidence of this sudden and unaccountable silence with the sudden and unaccountable Indian appointment of Francis; the extraordinary familiarity of Junius, which had *not altogether escaped notice*, with the secrets of one particular office, viz., the War Office; the sudden recollection, sure to flash upon all who remembered Francis, if again he should become revived into suspicion, that he had held a situation of trust in that particular War Office; all these little recollections would begin to take up their places in a connected story: *this* and *that*, laid together, would become clear as daylight; and to the keen eyes of still surviving enemies – Horne Tooke, 'little Chamier,' Ellis,[81] the Fitzroy, Russell, and Murray houses – the whole progress and catastrophe of the scoundrelism, the perfidy and the profits of the perfidy, would soon become as intelligible as any tale of midnight burglary from without, in concert with a wicked butler within, that was ever sifted by judge and jury at the Old Bailey, or critically reviewed by Mr John Ketch at Tyburn.[82]

Francis was the man. Francis was the wicked butler within, whom Pharaoh ought to have hanged, but whom he clothed in royal apparel, and mounted upon a horse that carried him to a curule chair of honour. So far his burglary prospered. But, as generally happens in such cases, this prosperous crime subsequently avenged itself. By a just retribution, the success of Junius, in two senses so monstrously exaggerated – exaggerated by a romantic over-estimate of its intellectual power through an error of the public, not admitted to the secret – and equally exaggerated as to its political power by the government in the hush-money for its future suppression, became the heaviest curse of the successful criminal. This criminal thirsted for literary distinction above all other distinction, with a childish eagerness, as for the *amreeta*[83] cup of immortality. And, behold! there the brilliant bauble lay, glittering in the sands of a solitude, unclaimed by any man; disputed with him (if he chose to claim it) by nobody; and yet for his life he durst not touch it. He stood – he knew that he stood – in the situation of a murderer who has dropt an inestimable jewel upon the murdered body in the death-struggle with his victim. The jewel is his! Nobody will deny it. He may have it for asking. But to ask is his death-warrant. 'Oh, yes!' would be the answer, 'here's your jewel, wrapt up safely in tissue paper. But here's another lot that goes along with it – no bidder can take them apart – viz. a halter, also wrapt up in tissue paper.' Francis, in relation to Junius, was in that exact predicament. 'You are Junius? You are that famous man who has been missing since 1772? And you can prove it? God bless me! sir; what a long time you've been sleeping: every body's gone to bed. Well, then, you are an exceedingly clever fellow, that have had the luck to be thought ten times more clever than really you were. And also, you are the greatest scoundrel that at this hour rests in Europe unhanged!' – Francis died, and made no sign. Peace of mind he had parted with for a peacock's feather, which feather, living or dying, he durst not mount in the plumage of his cap.

CONVERSATION

First published in *Tait's*, XIV, October 1847, pp. 678–81. Contrary to *Tait's* usual practice, the essay was not printed as by De Quincey.

Reprinted in *F*, *Letters to a Young Man, and Other Papers* (1854), pp. 127–40.

Revised text, carrying many accidentals but only three substantive variants from *F*, in *SGG*, XIV, *Letters to a Young Man Whose Education has been Neglected, and Other Papers* (1860), pp. 150–62. In 1850, De Quincey published another paper called 'Conversation' in *Hogg's Instructor* (see Vol. 17, pp. 3–13). In *SGG*, he simply joined the 1847 and 1850 papers together to form one article called 'Conversation' (see *SGG*, XIV, pp. 150–79).

There are no manuscripts.

De Quincey was regarded as one of the great conversationalists of his age. 'What would one give', Jane Welsh Carlyle once remarked, 'to have him in a box, and take him out to talk!' (cited in Lindop, p. 288). In this essay De Quincey contrasts Samuel Johnson's 'retrogressive, retrospective' intellect with Edmund Burke's 'prodigious elasticity of…thinking'. While Johnson's thought moved 'back on its own steps', the 'very violence of a projective' as thrown out by Burke 'caused it to rebound in fresh forms, fresh angles….Motion propagated motion, and life threw off life' (see below, p. 219). As is so often the case, De Quincey seems to have taken Burke as a model, for his conversation was frequently characterized by the kind of vitality and expansiveness he celebrated in Burke. 'The talk might be of "beeves"', R. P. Gillies remembered,

> and [De Quincey] could grapple with them if expected to do so, but his musical cadences were not in keeping with such work, and in a few minutes (not without some strictly logical sequence) he could escape at will from beeves to butterflies, and thence to the soul's immortality, to Plato, and Kant, and Schelling, and Fichte, to Milton's early years and Shakespeare's sonnets, to Wordsworth and Coleridge, to Homer and Aeschylus, to St Thomas of Aquin, St Basil, and St Chrysostom. (Hogg, pp. 241–2)

Richard Woodhouse was similarly impressed. De Quincey's conversation 'appeared like the elaboration of a mine of results', and one evening ranged from

> Political Economy, into the Greek & Latin Accents, into Antiquities – Roman Roads – Old castles – the origin & analogy of Languages. Upon all these he was informed to considerable minuteness. The same with regard to Shakspeare's Sonnets, Spenser's minor poems & the great writ-

ers & Characters of Elizabeth's age and those of Cromwell's time. (Morrison, pp. 6–7)

Yet De Quincey was different from Samuel Taylor Coleridge, that other great conversationalist of the day, for he was a good listener as well. Like many observers, De Quincey reported that unless Coleridge 'could have all the talk, [he] would have none. But then this was not conversation. It was not *colloquium*, or talking *with* the company, but *alloquium*, or talking *to* the company'. By contrast, John Ritchie Findlay remembered that, while De Quincey had 'a just horror of bores, and carefully avoided them', he 'never monopolised talk, allowed every one to have a fair chance, and listened with respectful patience to the most commonplace remarks from any one present' (Vol. 17, p. 9; Hogg, p. 128).

AMONGST the arts connected with the *elegancies* of social life, in a degree which nobody denies, is the art of Conversation; but in a degree which almost everybody denies, if one may judge by their neglect of its simplest rules, this same art is not less connected with the *uses* of social life. Neither the luxury of conversation, nor the possible benefit of conversation, is to be had under that rude administration of it which generally prevails. Without an art, without some simple system of rules, gathered from experience of such contingencies as are most likely to mislead the practice, when left to its own guidance, no act of man, nor effort, accomplishes its purposes in perfection. The sagacious Greek would not so much as drink a glass of wine amongst a few friends without a systematic art to guide him, and a regular form of polity to control him, which art and which polity (begging Plato's pardon) were better than any of more ambitious aim in his Republic. Every *symposium* had its set of rules, and vigorous they were; had its own *symposiarch* to govern it, and a tyrant he was.[1] Elected democratically, he became, when once installed, an autocrat not less despotic than the King of Persia. Purposes still more slight and fugitive have been organised into arts. Taking soup gracefully, under the difficulties opposed to it by a dinner dress at that time fashionable, was reared into an art about forty-five years ago by a Frenchman, who lectured upon it to ladies in London; and the most brilliant Duchess of that day was amongst his best pupils. Spitting, if the reader will pardon the mention of so gross a fact, was shown to be a very difficult art, and publicly prelected upon about the same time, in the same great capital. The professors in this faculty were the hackney-coachmen; the pupils were gentlemen, who paid a guinea each for three lessons; the chief problem in this system of hydraulics being to throw the salivating column in a parabolic curve from the centre of Parliament Street, when driving four-in-hand, to the foot pavements, right and left, so as to alarm the consciences of guilty peripatetics on either side. The ultimate problem, which closed the *curriculum* of study, was held to lie in spitting round a corner; when *that* was mastered, the pupil was entitled to his doctor's degree. Endless are the purposes of man, merely festal or merely comic, and aiming but at the momentary life of a cloud, which have earned for themselves the distinction and apparatus of a separate art. Yet for conversation, the great paramount purpose of social meetings, no art exists or has been attempted.

That seems strange, but is not really so. A limited process submits readily to the limits of a technical system; but a process, so unlimited as the interchange of thought, seems to reject them. And even, if an art of conversation were less unlimited, the means of carrying such an art into practical effect amongst so vast a variety of minds, seem wanting. Yet again, perhaps, after all, this may rest on a mistake. What we begin by misjudging is the particular phasis of conversation which brings it under the control of art and discipline. It is not in its relation to the intellect that conversation ever has been improved or *will* be improved primarily, but in its relation to manners. Has a man ever mixed with what in technical phrase is called 'good company,' meaning company in the highest degree polished, company which (being or *not* being aristocratic as respects its composition) is aristocratic as respects the standard of its manners and usages? If he really *has*, and does not deceive himself from vanity or from pure inacquaintance with the world, in that case he must have remarked the large effect impressed upon the grace and upon the freedom of conversation by a few simple instincts of real good breeding. Good breeding – what is it? There is no need in this place to answer that question comprehensively; it is sufficient to say, that it is made up chiefly of *negative* elements; that it shows itself far less in what it prescribes, than in what it forbids. Now, even under this limitation of the idea, the truth is – that more will be done for the benefit of conversation by the simple magic of good manners (that is, chiefly by a system of forbearances), applied to the besetting vices of social intercourse, than ever *was* or can be done by all varieties of intellectual power assembled upon the same arena. Intellectual graces of the highest order may perish and confound each other when exercised in a spirit of ill temper, or under the license of bad manners: whereas, very humble powers, when allowed to expand themselves colloquially in that genial freedom which is possible only under the most absolute confidence in the self-restraint of your collocutors, accomplish their purpose to a certainty, if it be the ordinary purpose of liberal amusement, and have a chance of accomplishing it, even when this purpose is the more ambitious one of communicating knowledge or exchanging new views upon truth.

In my own early years, having been formed by nature too exclusively and morbidly for solitary thinking, I observed nothing. Seeming to have eyes, in reality I saw nothing. But it is a matter of no very uncommon experience – that, whilst the mere observers never become meditators, the mere meditators, on the other hand, may finally ripen into close observers. Strength of thinking, through long years, upon innumerable themes, will have the effect of disclosing a vast variety of questions, to which it soon becomes apparent that answers are lurking up and down the whole field of daily experience; and thus an external experience which was slighted in youth, because it was a dark cipher that could be read into no meaning, a key that answered to no lock, gradually becomes interesting as it is found to yield one solution after another to problems that have independently matured in the mind. Thus, for instance, upon the special functions of conversation, upon its powers, its laws, its ordinary diseases, and their appropriate remedies, in youth I never bestowed a thought or a care. I viewed it – not as one amongst the gay ornamental arts of the intellect, but as one amongst the dull necessities of business. Loving solitude too much, I understood too little the capacities of colloquial intercourse. And thus it is, though not for *my* reason, that most people estimate the intellectual relations of conversation. Let these, however, be what they may, one thing seemed undeniable – that this world talked a great deal too much. It would be better for all parties, if nine in every ten of the *winged words*, flying about in this world (Homer's *epea pteroenta*) had their feathers clipped amongst men, or even amongst women, who have a right to a larger allowance of words. Yet, as it was quite out of my power to persuade the world into any such self-denying reformation, it seemed equally out of the line of my duties to nourish any moral anxiety in that direction. *To talk* seemed then in the same category as *to sleep;* not an accomplishment, but a base physical infirmity. As a moralist, I really was culpably careless upon the whole subject. I cared as little what absurdities men practised in their vast tennis-courts of conversation, where the ball is flying backwards and forwards to no purpose for ever, as what tricks Englishmen might play with their monstrous national debt. Yet at length what I disregarded on any principle of moral usefulness, I came to make an object of the profoundest interest on principles of art. *Betting*, in like manner, and *wagering*, which apparently had no moral value, and for that reason had been always slighted as inconsiderable arts (though, by the way, they always had one valuable use, viz., that of evading quarrels, since a bet summarily intercepts an altercation), rose suddenly into a philosophic rank, when successively, Huyghens, the Bernoullis, and De Moivre, were led by the suggestion of these trivial practices amongst men, to throw the light of a high mathematical analysis upon the whole doctrine of Chances.[2] Lord Bacon had been led to remark the capacities of conversation as an organ for sharpening one particular mode of intellectual power. Circumstances, on the other hand, led me into remarking the special capacities of conversation, as an organ for absolutely creating another mode of power. Let a man have read, thought, studied, as much as he may, rarely will he reach his possible advantages as a *ready* man, unless he has exercised his powers much in conversation – that was Lord Bacon's idea.[3] Now, this wise and useful remark points in a direction, not objective, but subjective – that is, it does not promise any absolute extension to truth itself, but only some greater facilities to the man who expounds or diffuses the truth. Nothing will be done for truth objectively that would not at any rate be done, but subjectively it will be done with more fluency, and at less cost of exertion to the doer. On the contrary, my own growing reveries on the latent powers of conversation (which, though a thing that then I hated, yet challenged at times unavoidably my attention) pointed to an absolute birth of new insight into the truth itself, as inseparable from the finer and more scientific exercise of the talking art. It would not be the brilliancy, the ease, or the adroitness of the expounder that would benefit, but the absolute interests of the thing expounded. A feeling dawned on me of a secret magic lurking in the peculiar life, velocities, and contagious ardour of conversation, quite separate from any which belonged to books; arming a man with new forces, and not merely with a new dexterity in wielding the old ones. I felt, and in this I could not be mistaken, as too certainly it was a fact of my own experience, that in the electric kindling of life between two minds, and far less from the kindling natural to conflict (though *that* also is something), than from the kindling through sympathy with the object discussed, in its momentary coruscation of shifting phases, there sometimes arise glimpses, and shy revelations of affinity, suggestion, relation, analogy, that could not have been approached through any avenues of methodical study. Great organists find the same effect of inspiration, the same result of power creative and revealing, in the mere movement and velocity of their own voluntaries, like the heavenly wheels of Milton, throwing off fiery flakes and bickering flames; these *impromptu* torrents of music create rapturous *fioriture*,[4] beyond all capacity in the artist to register, or afterwards to imitate. The reader must be well aware that many philosophic instances exist where a change in the degree makes a change in the kind. Usually this is otherwise; the prevailing rule is, that the principle subsists unaffected by any possible variation in the amount or degree of the force. But a large class of exceptions must have met the reader, though, from want of a pencil, he has improperly omitted to write them down in his pocket-book – cases, viz., where upon passing beyond a certain point in the graduation, an alteration takes place suddenly in the *kind* of effect, a new direction is given to the power. Some illustration of this truth occurs in conversation, where a velocity in the movement of thought is made possible (and often natural), greater than ever can arise in methodical books; and where, 2dly, approximations are more obvious and easily effected between things too remote for a steadier contemplation. One remarkable evidence of a *specific* power lying hid in conversation may be seen in such writings as have moved by impulses most nearly resembling those of conversation; for instance, in those of Edmund Burke. For one moment, reader, pause upon the spectacle of two contrasted intellects, Burke's and Johnson's; one an intellect essentially going forward, governed by the very necessity of growth – by the law of motion in advance; the latter, essentially an intellect retrogressive, retrospective, and throwing itself back on its own steps.[5] This original difference was aided accidentally in Burke by the tendencies of political partisanship, which, both from moving amongst moving things and uncertainties, as compared with the more stationary aspects of moral philosophy, and also from its more fluctuating and fiery passions, must unavoidably reflect in greater life the tumultuary character of conversation. The result from these original differences of intellectual constitution, aided by these secondary differences of pursuit, is, that Dr Johnson never, in any instance, GROWS a truth before your eyes, whilst in the act of delivering it, or moving towards it. All that he offers up to the end of the chapter he had when he began. But to Burke, such was the prodigious elasticity of his thinking, equally in his conversation and in his writings, the mere act of movement became the principle or cause of movement. Motion propagated motion, and life threw off life. The very violence of a projectile, as thrown by *him*, caused it to rebound in fresh forms, fresh angles, splintering, coruscating, which gave out thoughts as new (and that would at the beginning have been as startling) to himself as they are to his reader. In this power, which might be illustrated largely from the writings of Burke, is seen something allied to the powers of a prophetic seer,[6] who is compelled oftentimes into seeing things, as unexpected by himself as by others. Now in conversation, considered as to its *tendencies* and capacities, there sleeps an intermitting spring of such sudden revelation, showing much of the same general character; a power putting on a character *essentially* differing from the character worn by the power of books.

If, then, in the *colloquial* commerce of thought, there lurked a power not shared by other modes of that great commerce, a power separate and *sui generis*,[7] next it was apparent that a great art must exist somewhere, applicable to this power; not in the Pyramids, or in the tombs of Thebes,[8] but in the unwrought quarries of men's minds, so many and so dark. There was an art missing. If an art, then an artist missing. If the art (as we say of foreign mails) were 'due,' then the artist was 'due.' How happened it that this great man never made his appearance? But perhaps he *had*. Many people think Dr Johnson the *exemplar* of conversational power. I think otherwise, for reasons which I shall soon explain, and far sooner I should look for such an *exemplar* in Burke. But neither Johnson nor Burke, however they might rank as *powers*, was the *artist* that I demanded. Burke valued not at all the reputation of a great performer in conversation: he scarcely contemplated the skill as having a real existence; and a man will never be an artist who does not value his art, or even recognise it as an object distinctly defined. Johnson, again, relied sturdily upon his natural powers for carrying him aggressively through all conversational occasions or difficulties that English society, from its known character and composition, could be supposed likely to bring forward, without caring for any art or system of rules that might give further effect to that power. If a man is strong enough to knock down ninety-nine in a hundred of all antagonists, in spite of any advantages as to pugilistic science which they may possess over himself, he is not likely to care for the improbable case of a hundredth man appearing with strength equal to his own, superadded to the utmost excess of that artificial skill which is wanting in himself. Against such a contingency it is not worth while going to the cost of a regular pugilistic training. Half a century might not bring up a case of actual call for its application. Or, if it did, for a single *extra* case of that nature, there would always be a resource in the *extra* (and, strictly speaking, foul) arts of kicking, scratching, pinching, and tearing hair.

The conversational powers of Johnson were narrow in compass, however strong within their own essential limits. As a *conditio sine quâ non*,[9] he did not absolutely demand a *personal* contradictor by way of 'stoker' to supply fuel and keep up his steam, but he demanded at least a *subject* teeming with elements of known contradictory opinion, whether linked to partisanship or not. His views of all things tended to negation, never to the positive and the creative. Hence may be explained a fact, which cannot have escaped any keen observer of those huge Johnsonian *memorabilia* which we possess, viz., that the gyration of his flight upon any one question that ever came before him was so exceedingly brief. There was no process, no evolution, no movements of self-conflict or preparation; – a word, a distinction, a pointed antithesis, and, above all, a new abstraction of the logic involved in some popular fallacy or doubt, or prejudice, or problem, formed the utmost of his efforts.[10] He dissipated some casual perplexity that had gathered in the eddies of conversation, but he contributed nothing to any weightier interest; he unchoked a strangulated sewer in some blind alley, but what river is there that felt his cleansing power. There is no man that can cite any single error which Dr Johnson unmasked, or any important truth which he expanded. Nor is this extraordinary. Dr Johnson had not within himself the fountain of such power, having not a brooding or naturally philosophic intellect. Philosophy in any acquired sense he had none. How else could it have happened that, upon David Hartley, upon David Hume, upon Voltaire, upon Rousseau,[11] the true or the false philosophy of his own day, beyond a personal sneer, founded on some popular slander, he had nothing to say and said nothing? A new world was moulding itself in Dr Johnson's meridian hours, new generations were ascending, and 'other palms were won.'[12] Yet of all this the Doctor suspected nothing. Countrymen and contemporaries of the Doctor's, brilliant men, but (as many think) trifling men, such as Horace Walpole and Lord Chesterfield,[13] already in the middle of that eighteenth century, could read the signs of the great changes advancing, already started in horror from the portents which rose before them in Paris, like the procession of regal phantoms before Macbeth, and have left in their letters records undeniable (such as now read like Cassandra prophecies)[14] that already they had noticed tremors in the ground below their feet, and sounds in the air, running before the great convulsions under which Europe was destined to rock, full thirty years later. Many instances, during the last war, showed us that in the frivolous dandy might often lurk the most fiery and accomplished of *aides-de-camp;* and these cases show that men, in whom the world sees only elegant *roués*,[15] sometimes from carelessness, sometimes from want of opening for display, conceal qualities of penetrating sagacity, and a learned spirit of observation, such as may be looked for vainly in persons of more solemn and academic pretension. But there was a greater defect in Dr Johnson, for purposes of conversation, than merely want of eye for the social phenomena rising around him. He had no eye for such phenomena, because he had a somnolent want of interest in them; and why? because he had little interest in man. Having no sympathy with human nature in its struggles, or faith in the progress of man, he could not be supposed to regard with much interest any forerunning symptoms of changes that to *him* were themselves indifferent. And the reason that he felt thus careless was the desponding taint in his blood. It is good to be of a melancholic temperament, as all the ancient physiologists held,[16] but only if the melancholy is balanced by fiery aspiring qualities, not when it gravitates essentially to the earth. Hence the drooping, desponding character, and the monotony of the estimate which Dr Johnson applied to life. We were all, in *his* view, miserable, scrofulous wretches; the 'strumous diathesis'[17] was developed in our flesh, or soon would be; and but for his piety, which was the best indication of some greatness latent within him, he would have suggested to all mankind a nobler use for garters than any which regarded knees. In fact, I believe, that but for his piety, he would not only have counselled hanging in general, but hanged himself in particular. Now, this gloomy temperament, not as an occasional but as a permanent state, is fatal to the power of brilliant conversation, in so far as that power rests upon raising a continual succession of topics, and not merely of using with lifeless talent the topics offered by others. Man is the central interest about which revolve all the fleeting phenomena of life: these secondary interests demand the first; and with the little knowledge about them which must follow from little care about them, there can be no salient fountain of conversational themes. *Pectus – id est quod disertum facit.*[18] From the heart, from an interest of love or hatred, of hope or care, springs all permanent eloquence; and the elastic spring of conversation is gone, if the talker is a mere showy man of talent, pulling at an oar which he detests.

What an index might be drawn up of subjects interesting to human nature, and suggested by the events of the Johnsonian period, upon which the Doctor ought to have talked, and must have talked, if his interest in man had been catholic, but on which the Doctor is not recorded to have uttered one word! Visiting Paris once in his life, he applied himself diligently to the measuring – of what? Of gilt mouldings and diapered panels![19] Yet books, it will be said, suggest topics as well as life, and the moving sceneries of life. And surely Dr Johnson had *this* fund to draw upon? No: for though he had read much in a desultory way, he had studied nothing;* and, without that sort of systematic reading, it is but a rare chance that books can be brought to bear

* *'Had studied nothing:'* – It may be doubted whether Dr Johnson understood any one thing thoroughly, except Latin; not that he understood even *that* with the elaborate and circumstan-

effectually, and yet indirectly, upon conversation; whilst to make them directly and formally the subjects of discussion, pre-supposes either a learned audience, or, if the audience is not so, much pedantry and much arrogance in the talker.

---

tial accuracy required for the editing critically of a Latin classic. But if he had less than *that*, he had also more: he *possessed* that language in a way that no extent of mere critical knowledge could confer. He wrote it genially, not as one translating into it painfully from English, but as one using it for his original organ of thinking. And in Latin verse he expressed himself at times with the energy and freedom of a Roman. With Greek, his acquaintance was far more slender, and had not been much cultivated after his youthful days.[20]

PROTESTANTISM*

First published in *Tait's*, XIV, November 1847, pp. 758–65. The essay was printed as 'BY THOMAS DE QUINCEY.' in a centred line following the title and immediately preceding the text.

Reprinted in *F*, XVI, *Theological Essays and Other Papers* (1854), pp. 53–77, 115–19.

Revised text, carrying many accidentals but only two substantive variants from *F*, in *SGG*, VIII, *Essays, Sceptical and Anti-Sceptical, or Problems Neglected or Misconceived* (1858), pp. 88–114.

There is one manuscript, as follows:

MS A: Houghton Library, Harvard, MS *EC8. D4436. D858p. The manuscript is a complete set of *SGG* page proofs. It contains two significant variants, and these are listed in the textual notes.

The essay is the first instalment of De Quincey's three-part review of *A Vindication of Protestant Principles* by John William Donaldson (1811–61; *DNB*). Donaldson was of Scottish ancestry, but born in London. He was educated privately, and at fourteen was articled to his uncle, a solicitor. In 1830, he gained first prize in Greek at University College, London, and was sent to Trinity College, Cambridge, where he matriculated the following year. In 1841 he was appointed headmaster of King Edward's School, Bury St Edmunds, a post he held until 1855, when he retired to Cambridge. Donaldson made his name as a philologist and, in addition to contributions to *Fraser's Magazine* and the *Quarterly Review*, his books included a *New Cratylus, or Contributions towards a more accurate knowledge of the Greek Language* (1839), *Jashar; Fragmenta Archetypa Carminum Hebraicorum* (1854), *Classical Scholarship and Classical Learning Considered* (1856), and *Christian Orthodoxy reconciled with the conclusions of Modern Biblical Learning* (1857). Henry Crabb Robinson became acquainted with Donaldson in 1843, and greatly admired him. 'I had a three hours' walk with Donaldson', he wrote in 1846.

> Our talk was on religion. His liberality surprised and delighted me...He declares himself to be a believer in all Church doctrines, but avails himself of the glorious latitude which the Church allows. He maintains that only the Calvinist and the Romanist are excluded from the Church; the Calvinist on account of the doctrine of election and denial of baptismal

* A Vindication of Protestant Principles. By Phileleutheros Anglicanus. London: Parker. 1847.

> regeneration....He declares himself a Trinitarian...He blames Dissenters for needlessly leaving the Church.

When Donaldson died, Robinson described him as 'a man of great learning and excellent colloquial abilities' (*Diary, Reminiscences, and Correspondence of Henry Crabb Robinson*, ed. Thomas Sadler, 3 vols (London: Macmillan, 1869), vol. III, pp. 276–7, 478).

Donaldson published *A Vindication of Protestant Principles* in 1847, under the pseudonym Phileleutherus Anglicanus ('an English lover of liberty'). In the 'Preface' he declared that the work would immediately be recognized as

> an attempt to justify the liberty of the Protestant Philologer, from the point of view originally taken up by the Reformed Anglican Church; and to show...that...liberal and enlightened Protestantism is compatible with an attachment to the Established Church of England (p. v)

Donaldson's *Vindication* is part of a widespread contemporary debate on the history and principles of Protestantism, and takes its place alongside works such as George Hodson's *The Danger of Receding from the Principles of the Protestant Reformation* (1846), James Edward Gordon's *British Protestantism: its Present Position, Responsibilities, and Duties* (1847), and James Taylor's *Popery or Protestantism, which?* (1848). It is also a response to John Henry Newman's recent and highly publicized conversion from the Church of England to Rome, and the publication of his *Essay on the Development of Christian Doctrine* (1845). In the review, De Quincey states that he was still 'too slenderly acquainted with' Newman's *Essay*, but he comments at length on the doctrine of development (see below, pp. 255–63). In 1861 Thomas E. Kebbel wrote that De Quincey 'seems to have thought there was a good deal in Newman's theory of development, not as tending to favour Romanism, but as helping to harmonize Scripture with modern thought'. Newman, however, was unimpressed. 'I wonder', he wrote to John Cowley Fisher,

> if [De Quincey] saw even the outside of my book on doctrinal development. If he ever saw it, he would have known that the object of it, and the matter of it, was solely and entirely to answer the very objection which he makes ‹implies›. I lay down, that no one can religiously speak of development, without giving the *rules* which keep it from extravagating endlessly. And I give seven tests of a true development, founded on the nature of the case. These tests secure the substantial immutability of Christian doctrine.

Quarterly Review 110 (July, 1861) p. 17; *The Letters and Diaries of John Henry Newman*, eds C.S. Dessain, Ian Ker, Thomas Gornall, Edward E. Kelly, Vincent Farrer (London, 1961–continuing), vol. XX, p. 54).

THE work whose substance and theme are thus briefly abstracted is, at this moment, making a noise in the world. It is ascribed by report to two bishops – not jointly, but alternatively – in the sense that, if one did *not* write the book, the other *did*. The Bishops of Oxford and St David's, Wilberforce and Thirlwall, are the two pointed at by the popular finger; and, in some quarters, a third is suggested, viz., Stanley, Bishop of Norwich.[1] The betting, however, is altogether in favour of Oxford. So runs the current of *public* gossip. But the public is a bad guesser, 'stiff in opinion' it is, and almost 'always in the wrong.'[2] Now let *me* guess. When I had read for ten minutes, I offered a bet of seven to one (no takers) that the author's name began with H. Not out of any love for that amphibious letter; on the contrary, being myself what Professor Wilson calls a *hedonist*,[3] or philosophical voluptuary, and murmuring, with good reason, if a rose leaf lies doubled below me, naturally I murmur at a letter that puts one to the expense of an aspiration, forcing into the lungs an extra charge of raw air on frosty mornings. But truth is truth, in spite of frosty air. And yet, upon further reading, doubts gathered upon my mind. The H. that I mean is an Englishman; now it happens that here and there a word, or some peculiarity in using a word, indicates, in this author, a Scotchman; for instance, the expletive 'just,' which so much infests Scotch phraseology, written or spoken, at page 1;[4] elsewhere the word '*shortcomings,*'[5] which, being horridly tabernacular, and such that no gentleman could allow himself to touch it without gloves, it is to be wished that our Scottish brethren would resign, together with '*backslidings,*' to the use of field preachers. But worse, by a great deal, and not even intelligible in England, is the word *thereafter*, used as an adverb of time, *i. e.*, as the correlative of *hereafter. Thereafter,* in pure vernacular English, bears a totally different sense. In 'Paradise Lost,' for instance, having heard the character of a particular angel, you are told that he spoke *thereafter, i.e.*, spoke agreeably to that character.[6] 'How a score of sheep, Master Shallow?' The answer is, '*Thereafter* as they be.'[7] Again, 'Thereafter as a man sows shall he reap.'[8] The objections are overwhelming to the Scottish use of the word; first, because already in Scotland it is a barbarism transplanted from the filthy vocabulary of attorneys, locally called *writers;* secondly, because in England it is not even intelligible, and, what is worse still, sure to be *mis*-intelligible. And yet, after all, these exotic forms may be a mere blind. The writer is, perhaps, purposely leading us astray with his '*thereafters,*' and his horrid '*shortcomings.*' Or, because London newspapers, and Acts of Parliament, are beginning to be more and more polluted with these barbarisms, he may even have caught them unconsciously. And, on looking again at one case of '*thereafter,*' viz., at page 79, it seems impossible to determine whether he uses it in the classical English sense, or in the sense of leguleian[9] barbarism.

This question of authorship, meantime, may seem to the reader of little moment. Far from it! The weightier part of the interest depends upon that very point. If the author really *is* a bishop, or supposing the public rumour so far correct as that he is a man of distinction in the English Church, then, and by that simple fact, this book, or this pamphlet, interesting at any rate for itself, becomes separately interesting through its authorship, so as to be the most remarkable phenomenon of the day; and why? Because the most remarkable expression of a movement, accomplished and proceeding in a quarter that, if any on this earth, might be thought sacred from change. Oh, fearful are the motions of time, when suddenly lighted up to a retrospect of thirty years! Pathetic are the ruins of time in its slowest advance! Solemn are the prospects, so new and so incredible, which time unfolds at every turn of its wheeling flight! Is it come to this? Could any man, one generation back, have anticipated that an English dignitary, and speaking on a very delicate religious question, should deliberately appeal to a writer confessedly infidel, and proud of being an infidel, as a 'triumphant' settler of Christian scruples? But if the infidel is right, a point which I do not here discuss – but if the infidel is a man of genius, a point which I do not deny – was it not open to cite him, even though the citer were a bishop? Why, yes – uneasily one answers, *yes*; but still the case records a strange alteration, and still one could have wished to hear such a doctrine, which ascribes human infirmity (nay, human criminality) to *every* book of the Bible, uttered by anybody rather than by a father of the Church, and guaranteed by anybody rather than by an infidel, in triumph. A boy may fire his pistol unnoticed; but a sentinel, mounting guard in the dark, must remember the trepidation that will follow any shot from *him*, and the certainty that it will cause all the stations within hearing to get under arms immediately. Yet why, if this bold opinion *does* come from a prelate, he being but one man, should it carry so alarming a sound? Is the whole bench of bishops bound and compromised by the audacity of any one amongst its members? Certainly not. But yet such an act, though it should be that of a rash precursor, marks the universal change of position; there is ever some sympathy between the van and the rear of the same body at the same time; and the boldest could not have dared to go ahead so rashly, if the rearmost was not known to be pressing forward to his support, far more closely than thirty years ago he could have done. There have been, it is true, heterodox professors of divinity and free-thinking bishops before now. England can show a considerable list of such people – even Rome has a smaller list. Rome, that weeds all libraries, and is continually burning books, in effigy, by means of her vast *Index Expurgatorius*,* which index, continually, she is enlarging by successive supplements, needs also an *Index Expurgatorius* for the catalogue of her prelates. Weeds there are in the very flower-garden and conservatory of the Church. Fathers of the Church are no more to be relied on, as safe authorities, than we rascally lay authors, that notoriously will say anything. And it is a striking proof of this amongst our English bishops, that the very man who, in

* '*Index Expurgatorius*.' – A question of some interest arises upon the casuistical construction of this Index.[10] We, that are not by name included, may we consider ourselves indirectly licensed? Silence, I should think, gives consent. And if it wasn't that the present Pope, being a horrid Radical, would be sure to blackball *me* as an honest Tory, I would send him a copy of my *Opera Omnia*,[11] requesting his Holiness to say, by return of post, whether I ranked amongst the chaff winnowed by St Peter's flail, or had his gracious permission to hold myself amongst the pure wheat gathered into the Vatican garner.

the last generation, most of all won the public esteem as the champion of the Bible against Tom Paine, was privately known amongst us connoisseurs in heresy (that are always prying into ugly secrets) to be the least orthodox thinker, one or other, amongst the whole brigade of 15,000 contemporary clerks who had subscribed the Thirty-nine Articles.[12] Saving your presence, reader, his lordship was no better than a bigoted Socinian, which, in a petty diocese that he never visited, and amongst South Welshmen, that are all incorrigible Methodists, mattered little, but would have been awkward had he come to be Archbishop of York; and that he did *not*, turned upon the accident of a few weeks too soon, by which the Fates cut short the thread of the Whig ministry in 1807.[13] Certainly, for a Romish or an English bishop to be a Socinian is *un peu fort*.[14] But I contend that it is quite possible to be far less heretical, and yet dangerously bold; yes, upon the free and spacious latitudes, purposely left open by the English Thirty-nine Articles (aye, or by any Protestant Confession), to plant novelties not less startling to religious ears than Socinianism itself. Besides (which adds to the shock), the dignitary now before us, whether bishop or no bishop, does not write in the tone of a conscious heretic; or, like Archdeacon Blackburne[*] of old, in a spirit of hostility to his own fellow-churchmen; but, on the contrary, in the tone of one relying upon support from his clerical brethren, he stands forward as expositor and champion of views now prevailing amongst the *elite* of the English Church. So construed, the book is, indeed, a most extraordinary one, and exposes a history that almost shocks one of the strides made in religious speculation. Opinions change slowly and stealthily. The steps of the changes are generally continuous; but sometimes it happens that the notice of such steps, the publication of such changes, is not continuous, that it comes upon us *per saltum*,[16] and, consequently, with the stunning effect of an apparent treachery. Every thoughtful man raises his hands with an involuntary gesture of awe at the revolutions of so revolutionary an age, when thus summoned to the spectacle of an English prelate serving a piece of artillery against what once were fancied to be main out-works of religion, and at a station sometimes considerably in advance of any occupied by Voltaire.[†]

It is this audacity of speculation, I apprehend, this *étalage*[18] of bold results, rather than any success in their development, which has fixed the public

[*] '*Archdeacon Blackburne*.' – He was the author of *The Confessional*, which at one time made a memorable ferment amongst all those who loved as sons, or who hated as nonconformists, the English Establishment. This was his most popular work, but he wrote many others in the same temper, that fill six or seven octavos.[15]

[†] '*Voltaire*.' – Let not the reader misunderstand me: I do not mean that the clerical writer now before us (bishop or not bishop) is more hostile to religion than Voltaire,[17] or is hostile at all. On the contrary, he is, perhaps, profoundly religious, and he writes with neither levity nor insincerity. But this conscientious spirit, and this piety, do but the more call into relief the audacity of his free-thinking – do but the more forcibly illustrate the prodigious changes wrought by time, and by the contagion from secular revolutions, in the spirit of religious philosophy.

attention. Development, indeed, applied to philosophic problems, or research applied to questions of erudition, was hardly possible within so small a compass as 117 pages, for *that* is the extent of the work, except as regards the notes, which amount to 74 pages more. Such brevity, on such a subject, is unseasonable, and almost culpable. On such a subject as the Philosophy of Protestantism – '*satius erat silere, quam parcius dicere*.' Better were absolute silence, more respectful as regards the theme, less tantalising as regards the reader, than a style of discussion so fragmentary and so rapid.

But, before we go farther, what are we to call this bold man? One must have some name for a man that one is reviewing; and, as he comes abroad *incognito*, it is difficult to see what name *could* have any propriety. Let me consider: there are three bishops in the field, Mr H., and the Scotchman – that makes five. But every one of these, you say, is represented equally by the name in the title – *Phileleutheros Anglicanus*.[19] True, but *that's* as long as a team of horses. If it had but *Esquire* at the end, it would measure against a Latin Hendecasyllable[20] verse. I'm afraid that we must come at last to *Phil.* I've been seeking to avoid it, for it's painful to say 'Jack' or 'Dick' either *to* or *of* an ecclesiastical great gun. But if such big wigs *will* come abroad in disguise, and with names as long as Fielding's Hononchrononthononthologus,[21] they must submit to be hustled by pick-pockets and critics, and to have *their* names docked as well as profane authors.

Phil., then, be it – that's settled. Now, let us inquire what it is that *Phil.* has been saying, to cause such a sensation amongst the gnostics. And, to begin at the beginning, what is *Phil.*'s capital object? *Phil.* shall state it himself – these are his opening words: – 'In the following pages we propose to vindicate the fundamental and inherent *principles* of Protestantism.' Good; but what *are* the fundamental principles of Protestantism? 'They are,' says *Phil.*, 'the sole sufficiency of Scripture,* the right of private judgment in its interpretation, and the authority of individual conscience in matters of religion.'[23] Errors of logic show themselves more often in a man's terminology, and his antitheses, and his subdivisions, than anywhere else. *Phil.* goes on to make this distinction, which brings out his imperfect conception. 'We,' says he (and, by the way, if *Phil.* is *we*, then it must be my duty to call him *they*), 'we do not propose to defend the varieties of *doctrine* held by the different communities of Protestants.' Why, no; that would be a sad task for the most skilful of funam-

* '*Sole sufficiency of Scripture*.' – This is much too elliptical a way of expressing the Protestant meaning. Sufficiency for *what?* 'Sufficiency for salvation' is the phrase of many, and I think elsewhere of *Phil.*[22] But *that* is objectionable on more grounds than one: it is redundant, and it is aberrant from the true point contemplated. *Sufficiency for itself, without alien helps*, is the thing contemplated. The Greek *autarkeia* (αὐτάρκεια), self-sufficiency, or, because that phrase, in English, has received a deflexion towards a bad meaning, the word *self-sufficingness* might answer; sufficiency for the exposition of its own most secret meaning, out of fountains within itself; needing, therefore, neither the supplementary aids of tradition, on the one hand, nor the complementary aids on the other (in the event of unprovided cases, or of dilemmas arising), from the infallibility of a *living* expounder.

bulists or theological tumblers, seeing that many of these varieties stand related to each other as categorical affirmative and categorical negative: it's heavy work to make *yes* and *no* pull together in the same proposition. But this, fortunately for himself, *Phil.* declines. You are to understand that he will not undertake the defence of Protestantism in its *doctrines*, but only in its *principles*. That won't do; that antithesis is as hollow as a drum; and, if the objection were verbal only, I would not make it. But the contradistinction fails to convey the real meaning. It is not that he has falsely expressed his meaning, but that he has falsely developed that meaning to his own consciousness. Not the word only is wrong; but the wrong word is put forward for the sake of hiding the imperfect idea. What he calls *principles* might almost as well be called *doctrines;* and what he calls *doctrines* as well be called *principles*. Out of these terms, apart from the rectifications suggested by the context, no man could collect his drift, which is simply this. Protestantism, we must recollect, is not an absolute and self-dependent idea; it stands in relation to something antecedent, against which it protests, viz., Papal Rome. And under what phasis does it protest against Rome? Not against the Christianity of Rome, because every Protestant Church, though disapproving a great deal of *that*, disapproves also a great deal in its own sister churches of the protesting household; and because every Protestant Church holds a great deal of Christian truth, in common with Rome. But what furnishes the matter of protest is – the *deduction of the title* upon which Rome plants the right to be a church at all. This deduction is so managed by Rome as to make herself, not merely a true church (which many Protestants grant), but the exclusive church. Now, what *Phil.* in effect undertakes to defend is not principles by preference to doctrines (for they are pretty nearly the same thing), but the question of title to teach at all, in preference to the question of what is the thing taught. *There* is the distinction, as I apprehend it. All these terms – 'principle,' 'doctrine,' 'system,' 'theory,' 'hypothesis' – are used nearly always most licentiously, and as arbitrarily as a Newmarket jockey[24] selects the colours for his riding dress. It is true that one shadow of justification offers itself for *Phil.*'s distinction. All principles are doctrines, but all doctrines are not principles; which, then, in particular? Why, those properly are principles which contain the *principia*, the beginnings, or starting-points of evolution, out of which any system of truth is evolved. Now, it may seem that the very starting-point of our Protestant pretensions is first of all to argue our *title* or right to be a church *sui juris;* apparently we must begin by making good our *locus standi*,[25] before we can be heard upon our doctrines. And upon this mode of approach, the pleadings about the *title*, or right to teach at all, taking precedency of the pleadings about the particular things taught, would be the *principia*, or beginning of the whole process, and so far would be entitled by preference to the name of *principles*. But such a mode of approach is merely an accident, and contingent upon our being engaged in a polemical discussion of Protestantism in relation to Popery. *That*, however, is a pure matter of choice; Protestantism may be discussed, as though Rome were not, in relation to its own absolute merits; and this treatment is the logical treatment, applying itself to what is permanent in the *nature* of the object; whereas the other treatment applies itself to what is casual and vanishing in the *history* (or the origin) of Protestantism. For, after all, it would be no great triumph to Protestantism that she should prove her birth-right to revolve as a *primary* planet in the solar system; that she had the same original right as Rome to wheel about the great central orb, undegraded to the rank of satellite or secondary projection – if, in the meantime, telescopes should reveal the fact that she was pretty nearly a sandy desert. *What* a church teaches is true or not true, without reference to her independent right of teaching; and eventually, when the irritations of earthly feuds and political schisms shall be soothed by time, the philosophy of this whole question will take an inverse order. The credentials of a church will not be put in first, and the quality of her doctrine discussed as a secondary question. On the contrary, her credentials will be sought *in* her doctrine. The Protesting Church will say, I have the *right* to stand separate, because I stand; and from my holy teaching I deduce my title to teach. *Jus est ibi summum docendi, ubi est fons purissimus doctrinae.*[26] That inversion of the Protestant plea with Rome is even now valid with many; and, when it becomes universally current, then the *principles*, or great beginnings of the controversy, will be transplanted from the *locus*, or centre, where *Phil.* places them, to the very *locus* which he neglects.

There is another expression of *Phil.'s* (I am afraid *Phil.* is getting angry by this time) to which I object. He describes the doctrines held by all the separate Protestant churches as doctrines *of* Protestantism. I would not delay either *Phil.* or myself for the sake of a trifle; but an impossibility is *not* a trifle. If from orthodox Turkey[27] you pass to heretic Persia, if from the rigour of the *Sonnees* to the laxity of the *Sheeahs*,[28] you could not, in explaining those schisms, go on to say, 'And these are the doctrines *of* Islamism;' for they destroy each other. Both are supported by earthly powers; but one only could be supported by central Islamism. So of Calvinism and Arminianism; you cannot call them doctrines *of* Protestantism, as if growing out of some reconciling Protestant principles; one of the two, though not manifested to human eyes in its falsehood, must secretly be false; and a falsehood cannot be a doctrine of Protestantism. It is more accurate to say that the separate creeds of Turkey and Persia are *within* Mahommedanism: such, viz., as that neither excludes a man from the name of Mussulman; and, again, that Calvinism and Arminianism are doctrines *within* the Protestant Church – as a church of general toleration for all religious doctrines not *demonstrably* hostile to any cardinal truth of Christianity.

Phil., then, we all understand, is not going to traverse the vast field of Protestant opinions as they are distributed through our many sects; *that* would be endless; and he illustrates the mazy character of the wilderness over which these sects are wandering,

— 'ubi passim
Palantes error recto de tramite pellit,'[29]

by the four cases of – 1, the Calvinist; 2, the Newmanite; 3, the Romanist;* 4, the Evangelical enthusiast – as holding systems of doctrine, 'no one of which is capable of recommending itself to the favourable opinion of an impartial judge.'[36] Impartial! but what Christian *can* be impartial? To be free from all

* *'The Romanist'* – What, amongst Protestant sects? Ay, even so. It's *Phil.'s* mistake, not mine. He will endeavour to doctor the case, by pleading that he was speaking universally of Christian error: but the position of the clause forbids this plea. Not only in relation to what immediately precedes, the passage must be supposed to contemplate *Protestant* error; but the immediate inference from it, viz., that 'the world may well be excused for doubting whether there is, after all, so much to be gained by that liberty of private judgment, which is the essential characteristic of Protestantism; whether it be not, after all, merely a liberty to fall into error,'[30] nails *Phil.* to that construction – argues too strongly that it is an oversight of indolence. *Phil.* was sleeping for the moment, which is excusable enough towards the end of a book, but hardly in section I. P.S. – I have since observed (which *not* to have observed is excused, perhaps, by the too complex machinery of hooks and eyes between the text and the notes involving a double reference – 1st, to the section, 2d, to the particular clause of the section) that *Phil.* has not here committed an inadvertency; or, if he *has*, is determined to fight himself through his inadvertency, rather than break up his quaternion of cases. 'In speaking of Romanism as arising from a misapplication of Protestant principles; we refer, not to those who were born, but to those who have become members of the Church of Rome.'[31] What is the name of those people? And where do they live? I have heard of many who think (and there *are* cases in which most of us, that meddle with philosophy, are apt to think) occasional principles of Protestantism available for the defence of certain Roman Catholic mysteries too indiscriminately assaulted by the Protestant zealot; but, with this exception, I am not aware of any parties professing to derive their Popish learnings *from* Protestantism; it is *in spite of* Protestantism, as seeming to *them* not strong enough, or through principles omitted by Protestantism, which therefore seems to *them* not careful enough or not impartial enough, that Protestants have lapsed to Popery. Protestants have certainly been known to become Papists, not through Popish arguments, but simply through their own Protestant books; yet never, that I heard of, through an *affirmative* process, as though any Protestant argument involved the rudiments of Popery, but by a *negative* process, as fancying the Protestant reasons, though lying in the right direction, not going far enough; or, again, though right partially, yet defective as a whole. *Phil.*, therefore, seems to me absolutely caught in a sort of *Furcae Caudinae*,[32] unless he has a dodge in reserve to puzzle us all. In a different point, I, that hold myself a *doctor seraphicus*, and also *inexpugnabilis*[33] upon quillets of logic, justify *Phil.*, whilst also I blame him. He defends himself rightly for distinguishing between the Romanist and Newmanite on the one hand, between the Calvinist and the Evangelical man on the other, though perhaps a young gentleman, commencing his studies on the *Organon*,[34] will fancy that here he has *Phil.* in a trap, for these distinctions, he will say, do not entirely exclude each other as they ought to do. The class calling itself Evangelical, for instance, may also be Calvinistic; the Newmanite is not, *therefore*, anti-Romanish. True, says *Phil.*; I am quite aware of it. But to be aware of an objection is not to answer it. The fact seems to be, that the actual combinations of life, not conforming to the truth of abstractions, compel us to seeming breaches of logic. It would be right practically to distinguish the Radical from the Whig; and yet it might shock *Duns* or *Lombardus*, the *magister sententiarum*,[35] when he came to understand that partially the principles of Radicals and Whigs coincide. But, for all that, the logic which distinguishes them is right; and the apparent error must be sought in the fact, that all cases (political or religious) being cases of life, are *concretes*, which never conform to the exquisite truth of abstractions. Practically, the Radical *is* opposed to the Whig, though casually the two are in conjunction continually; for, as *acting* partizans, they work *from* different centres, and, finally, *for* different results.

bias, and to begin his review of sects in that temper, he must begin by being an infidel. Vainly a man endeavours to reserve in a state of neutrality any preconceptions that he may have formed for himself, or prepossessions that he may have inherited from 'mamma;' he cannot do it any more than he can dismiss his own shadow. And it is strange to contemplate the weakness of strong minds in fancying that they can. Calvin, whilst amiably engaged in hunting Servetus to death,[37] and writing daily letters to his friends, in which he expresses his hope that the executive power would not think of burning the poor man, since really justice would be quite satisfied by cutting his head off, meets with some correspondents who conceive (idiots that they were!) even that little amputation not indispensable. But Calvin soon settles *their* scruples. You don't perceive, he tells them, what this man has been about. When a writer attacks Popery, it's very wrong in the Papists to cut his head off; and why? Because he has only been attacking error. But here lies the difference in this case; Servetus has been attacking the TRUTH. Do you see the distinction, my friends? Consider it, and I am sure you will be sensible that this quite alters the case. It is shocking, it is perfectly ridiculous, that the Bishop of Rome should touch a hair of any man's head for contradicting *him*; and why? Because, do you see? *he* is wrong. On the other hand, it is evidently agreeable to philosophy, that I, John Calvin, should shave off the hair, and, indeed, the head itself (as I heartily hope* will be done in this present case) of any man presumptuous enough to contradict *me*; but then, why? For a reason that makes all the difference in the world, and which, one would think, idiocy itself could not overlook, viz., that I, John Calvin, am right – right, through

* The reader may imagine that, in thus abstracting Calvin's epistolary sentiments, I am a little improving them. Certainly they would bear improvement, but that is not my business. What the reader sees here is but the result of bringing scattered passages into closer juxtaposition; whilst, as to the strongest (viz., the most sanguinary) sentiments here ascribed to him, it will be a sufficient evidence of my fidelity to the literal truth, if I cite three separate sentences. Writing to Farrel,[38] he says, '*Spero* capitale saltem fore judicium.' Sentence of the court, he *hopes*, will, at any rate, reach the life of Servetus. Die he must, and die he shall. But why should he die a cruel death? 'Paenoe vero atrocitatem remitti cupio.' To the same purpose, when writing to Sultzer, he expresses his satisfaction in being able to assure him that a principal civic officer of Geneva was, in this case, entirely upright, and animated by the most virtuous sentiments. Indeed! what an interesting character! and in what way now might this good man show this beautiful tenderness of conscience? Why, by a fixed resolve that Servetus should not in any case escape the catastrophe which I, John Calvin, am longing for, ('ut saltem exitum, *quem optamus*, non fugiat.') Finally, writing to the same Sultzer, he remarks that – when we see the Papists such avenging champions of their own superstitious fables as not to falter in shedding innocent blood, 'pudeat Christianos magistratus [as if the Roman Catholic magistrates were not Christians] in *tuendâ certâ* veritate nihil prorsus habere animi' – 'Christian magistrates ought to be ashamed of themselves for manifesting no energy at all in the vindication of truth undeniable;'[39] yet really since these magistrates had at that time the full design, which design not many days after they executed, of maintaining truth by fire and faggot, one does not see the call upon them for blushes so very deep as Calvin requires. Hands so crimson with blood might compensate the absence of crimson cheeks.

three degrees of comparison – right, righter, or more right, rightest, or most right. Calvin fancied that he could demonstrate his own impartiality.

The self-sufficingness of the Bible, and the right of private judgment – here, then, are the two great charters in which Protestantism commences; these are the bulwarks behind which it entrenches itself against Rome. And it is remarkable that these two great preliminary laws, which soon diverge into fields so different, at the first are virtually one and the same law. The refusal of an oracle alien to the Bible, extrinsic to the Bible, and claiming the sole interpretation of the Bible; the refusal of an oracle that reduced the Bible to a hollow masque, underneath which fraudulently introducing itself any earthly voice could mimic a heavenly voice, was in effect to refuse the coercion of this false oracle over each man's conscientious judgment; to make the Bible independent of the Pope, was to make man independent of all religious controllers. The *self-sufficingness of Scripture*, its independency of any external interpreter, passed in one moment into the other great Protestant doctrine of *Toleration*. It was but the same triumphal monument under a new angle of sight, the golden and silver faces of the same heraldic shield. The very same act which denies the right of interpretation to a mysterious Papal phoenix, renewed from generation to generation, having the antiquity and the incomprehensible omniscience of the Simorg[40] in Southey, transferred this right of mere necessity to the individuals of the whole human race. For where else could it have been lodged? Any attempt in any other direction was but to restore the Papal power in a new impersonation. Every man, therefore, suddenly obtained the right of interpreting the Bible for himself. But the word '*right*' obtained a new sense. Every man has the right, under the Queen's Bench, of publishing an unlimited number of metaphysical systems; and, under favour of the same indulgent Bench, we all enjoy the unlimited right of laughing at him. But not the whole race of man has a right to *coerce*, in the exercise of his intellectual rights, the humblest of individuals. The rights of men are thus unspeakably elevated; for, being now freed from all anxiety, being sacred as merely *legal* rights, they suddenly rise into a new mode of responsibility as *intellectual* rights. As a Protestant, every mature man has the same dignified right over his own opinions and profession of faith that he has over his own hearth. But his hearth can rarely be abused; whereas his religious system, being a vast kingdom, opening by immeasurable gates upon worlds of light and worlds of darkness, now brings him within a new amenability – called upon to answer new impeachments, and to seek for new assistances. Formerly another was answerable for his belief; if that were wrong, it was no fault of his. Now he has new rights, but these have burthened him with new obligations. Now he is crowned with the glory and the palms of an intellectual creature, but he is alarmed by the certainty of corresponding struggles. Protestantism it is that has created him into this child and heir of liberty; Protestantism it is that has invested him with these unbounded privileges of private judgment, giving him in one moment the sublime powers of a Pope within his own conscience; but Protestantism it is that has introduced him to the most dreadful of responsibilities.

I repeat that the twin maxims, the columns of Hercules[41] through which Protestantism entered the great sea of human activities, were originally but two aspects of one law: to deny the Papal control over men's conscience being to affirm man's self-control, was, therefore, to affirm man's universal right to toleration, which again implied a corresponding *duty* of toleration. Under this bi-fronted law, generated by Protestantism, but in its turn regulating Protestantism, *Phil.* undertakes to develope all the principles that belong to a Protestant church. The *seasonableness* of such an investigation – its critical application to an evil now spreading like a fever through Europe – he perceives fully, and in the following terms he expresses this perception: –

> 'That we stand on the brink of a great theological crisis, that the problem must soon be solved, how far orthodox Christianity is possible for those who are not behind their age in scholarship and science; this is a solemn fact, which may be ignored by the partisans of short-sighted bigotry, but which is felt by all, and confessed by most of those who are capable of appreciating its reality and importance. The deep Sibylline vaticinations of Coleridge's philosophical mind, the practical working of Arnold's religious sentimentalism,[42] and the open acknowledgment of many divines who are living examples of the spirit of the age, have all, in different ways, foretold the advent of a Church of the Future.'

This is from the preface, p. ix, where the phrase, *Church of the Future*, points to the Prussian minister's (Bunsen's) *Kirche der Zukunft;*[43] but in the body of the work, and not far from its close, (p. 114,) he recurs to this crisis, and more circumstantially.

Phil. embarrasses himself and his readers in this development of Protestant principles. His own view of the task before him requires that he should separate himself from the consideration of any particular church, and lay aside all partisanship – plausible or not plausible. It is his own overture that warrants us in expecting this. And yet, before we have travelled three measured inches, he is found entangling himself with Church of Englandism. Let me not be misunderstood, as though, borrowing a Bentham word, I were therefore a Jerry Benthamite:[44] I, that may describe myself generally as *Philo-Phil.*, am not less a son of the 'Reformed Anglican Church' than *Phil.*[45] Consequently, it is not likely that, in any vindication of that church, simply *as* such, and separately for itself, I should be the man to find grounds of exception. Loving most of what *Phil.* loves, loving *Phil.* himself, and hating (I grieve to say), with a theological hatred, whatever *Phil.* hates, why should I demur at this particular point to a course of argument that travels in the line of my own partialities? And yet I *do* demur. Having been promised a philosophic defence of the principles concerned in the great European schism of the sixteenth century, suddenly we find ourselves collapsing from that altitude of speculation into a defence of one individual church. Nobody would complain of *Phil.*, if, *after* having deduced philosophically the principles upon which all Protestant separation from Rome should revolve, he had gone forward to show, that in some one of the Protestant churches, more than in others, these principles had been asserted with peculiar strength, or carried through with special consistency, or associated pre-eminently with the other graces of a Christian church, such as a ritual more impressive to the heart of man, or a polity more symmetrical with the structure of English society. Once having unfolded from philosophic grounds the primary conditions of a pure scriptural church, *Phil.* might then, without blame, have turned sharp round upon us, saying, such being the conditions under which the great idea of a true Christian church must be *constructed*, I now go on to show that the Church of England has conformed to those conditions more faithfully than any other. But to entangle the pure outlines of the idealising mind with the practical forms of any militant church, embarrassed (as we know all churches to have been) by pre-occupations of judgment, derived from feuds too local and interests too political, moving too (as we know all churches to have moved) in a spirit of compromise, occasionally from mere necessities of position; this is in the result to injure the object of the writer doubly: 1st, as leaving an impression of partisanship the reader is mistrustful from the first, as against a judge that, in reality, is an advocate; 2d, without reference to the effect upon the reader, directly to *Phil.* it is injurious, by fettering the freedom of his speculations, or, if leaving their freedom undisturbed, by narrowing their compass.

And, if *Phil.*, as to the general movement of his Protestant pleadings, modulates too little in the transcendental key, sometimes he does so too much. For instance, at p. 69, sec. 35, we find him half calling upon Protestantism to account for her belief in God; how then? Is this belief special to Protestants? Are Roman Catholics, are those of the Greek, the Armenian, and other Christian churches, atheistically given? We used to be told that there is no royal road to geometry.[46] I don't know whether there is or not; but I am sure there is no Protestant bye-road, no Reformation short-cut, to the demonstration of Deity. It is true that *Phil.* exonerates his philosophic scholar, when throwing himself in Protestant freedom upon pure intellectual aids, from the vain labour of such an effort. He consigns him, however philosophic, to the evidence of 'inevitable assumptions, upon axiomatic postulates, which the reflecting mind is compelled to accept, and which no more admit of doubt and cavil than of establishment by formal proof.'[47] I am not sure whether I understand *Phil.* in this section. Apparently he is glancing at Kant. Kant was the first person, and perhaps the last, that ever undertook formally to demonstrate the indemonstrability of God.[48] He showed that the three great arguments for the existence of the Deity were virtually one, inasmuch as the two weaker borrowed their value and *vis apodeictica*[49] from the more rigorous metaphysical argument. The physico-theological argument he forced to back, as it were, into the cosmological, and *that* into the ontological. After this reluctant *regressus* of the three into one, shutting up like a spying-glass, which (with the iron hand of Hercules forcing Cerberus up to day-light)[50] the stern man of Koenigsberg[51] resolutely dragged to the front of the arena, nothing remained, now that he had this pet scholastic argument driven up into a corner, than to break its neck – which he did. Kant took the conceit out of all the three arguments; but, if this is what *Phil.* alludes to, he should have added, that these three, after all, were only the arguments of speculating or *theoretic* reason. To this faculty Kant peremptorily denied the power of demonstrating the Deity; but then that same *apodeixis*,[52] which he had thus inexorably torn from reason under one manifestation, Kant himself restored to the reason in another (the *praktische vernunft*.)[53] God he asserts to be a postulate of the human reason, as speaking through the conscience and will, not proved *ostensively*, but indirectly proved as being *wanted* indispensably, and presupposed in other necessities of our human nature. This, probably, is what *Phil.* means by his shorthand expression of 'axiomatic postulates.' But then it should not have been said that the case does not 'admit of formal proof,' since the proof is as 'formal' and rigorous by this new method of Kant as by the old obsolete methods of Sam. Clarke and the schoolmen.*

But it is not the too high or the too low – the too much or the too little – of what one might call by analogy the *transcendental* course, which I charge upon *Phil.* It is, that he is too desultory – too eclectic. And the secret purpose, which seems to me predominant throughout his work, is, not so much the defence of Protestantism, or even of the Anglican Church, as a report of the latest novelties that have found a roosting-place in the English Church, amongst the most temperate of those churchmen who keep pace with modern philosophy; in short, it is a selection from the classical doctrines of religion, exhibited under their newest revision; or, generally, it is an attempt to show, from what is going on amongst the most moving orders in the English Church, how far it is possible that strict orthodoxy should bend, on the one side, to new impulses, derived from an advancing philosophy, and yet, on the other side, should reconcile itself, both verbally and in spirit, with ancient standards. But if *Phil.* is eclectic, then *I* will be eclectic; if *Phil.* has a right to be desultory, then *I* have a right. *Phil.* is my leader. I can't, in reason, be expected to be better than *he* is. If I'm wrong, *Phil.* ought to set me a better example. And here, before this honourable audience of the public, I charge all my errors (whatever they may be, past or coming) upon *Phil.'s* misconduct.

Having thus established my patent of vagrancy, and my license for picking and choosing, I choose out these three articles to toy with: – 1st, Bibliolatry; 2d, Development applied to the Bible and Christianity; 3d, Philology, as the particular resource against false philosophy, relied on by *Phil.*

* The method of Des Cartes[54] was altogether separate and peculiar to himself; it is a mere conjuror's juggle; and yet, what is strange, like some other audacious sophisms, it is capable of being so stated as most of all to baffle the subtle dialectician; and Kant himself, though not cheated, was never so much perplexed in his life as in the effort to make its hollowness apparent.[55]

Bibliolatry. – We Protestants charge upon the Ponteficii, as the more learned of our fathers always called the Roman Catholics, *Mariolatry;* they pay undue honours, say we, to the Virgin. They in return charge upon us, *Bibliolatry*, or a superstitious allegiance – an idolatrous homage – to the words, syllables, and punctuation of the Bible. They, according to *us*, deify a woman; and we, according to *them*, deify an arrangement of printer's types. As to *their* error, we need not mind *that*: let us attend to our own. And to this extent it is evident at a glance that Biblioatrists *must* be wrong, viz., because, as a pun vanishes on being translated into another language, even so would, and must melt away, like ice in a hot-house, a large majority of those conceits which every Christian nation is apt to ground upon the verbal text of the Scriptures in its own separate vernacular version. But once aware that much of their Bibliolatry depends upon ignorance of Hebrew and Greek, and often upon peculiarity of idiom or structures in their mother dialect, cautious people begin to suspect the whole. Here arises a very interesting, startling, and perplexing situation for all who venerate the Bible; one which must always have existed for prying, inquisitive people, but which has been incalculably sharpened for the apprehension of these days by the extraordinary advances made and making in Oriental and Greek philology. It is a situation of public scandal even to the deep reverencers of the Bible; but a situation of much more than scandal, of real grief, to the profound and sincere amongst religious people. On the one hand, viewing the Bible as the word of God, and not merely so in the sense of its containing most salutary counsels, but, in the highest sense, of its containing a revelation of the most awful secrets, they cannot for a moment listen to the pretence that the Bible has benefited by God's inspiration only as other good books may be said to have done. They are confident that, in a much higher sense, and in a sense incommunicable to other books, it is inspired. Yet, on the other hand, as they will not tell lies, or countenance lies, even in what seems the service of religion, they cannot hide from themselves that the materials of this imperishable book are perishable, frail, liable to crumble, and actually *have* crumbled to some extent, in various instances. There is, therefore, lying broadly before us, something like what Kant called an antinomy – a case where two laws equally binding on the mind are, or seem to be, in collision.[56] Such cases occur in morals – cases which are carried out of the general rule, and the jurisdiction of that rule, by peculiar deflexions; and from the word *case* we derive the word *casuistry*, as a general science dealing with such anomalous cases. There is a casuistry, also, for the speculative understanding, as well as for the moral (which is the *practical*) understanding. And this question as to the inspiration of the Bible, with its apparent conflict of forces, repelling it and yet affirming it, is one of its most perplexing and most momentous problems.

My own solution of the problem would reconcile all that is urged against an inspiration with all that the internal necessity of the case would plead in behalf of an inspiration. So would *Phil.'s*. His distinction, like mine, would substantially come down to this – that the grandeur and extent of religious truth is not of a nature to be affected by verbal changes such as *can* be made by time, or accident, or without treacherous design. It is like lightning, which could not be mutilated, or truncated, or polluted. But it may be well to rehearse a little more in detail, both *Phil.'s* view and my own. Let my principal go first; make way, I desire, for my leader: let *Phil.* have precedency, as, in all reason, it is my duty to see that he has.

Whilst rejecting altogether any inspiration as attaching to the separate words and phrases of the Scriptures, *Phil.* insists (Sect. 25, p. 49) upon such an inspiration as attaching to the spiritual truths and doctrines delivered in these Scriptures. And he places this theory in a striking light, equally for what it affirms and for what it denies, by these two arguments – 1st (in affirmation of the real spiritual inspiration), that a series of more than thirty writers, speaking in succession along a vast line of time, and absolutely without means of concert, yet all combine unconsciously to one end – lock like parts of a great machine into one system – conspire to the unity of a very elaborate scheme, without being at all aware of what was to come after. Here, for instance, is one, living nearly 1600 years before the last in the series, who lays a foundation (in reference to man's ruin, to God's promises and plan for human restoration), which is built upon and carried forward by all, without exception, that follow. Here come a multitude that prepare each for his successor – that unconsciously integrate each other – that, finally, when reviewed, make up a total drama, of which each writer's separate share would have been utterly imperfect without corresponding parts that he could not have foreseen. At length all is finished. A profound piece of music, a vast oratorio, perfect and of elaborate unity, has resulted from a long succession of strains, each for itself fragmentary. On such a final creation resulting from such a distraction of parts, it is indispensable to suppose an over-ruling inspiration, in order at all to account for the final result of a most elaborate harmony. Besides, which would argue some inconceivable magic, if we did not assume a providential inspiration watching over the coherencies, tendencies, and intertessellations (to use a learned word)[57] of the whole, – it happens that, in many instances, typical things are recorded – things ceremonial, that could have no meaning to the person recording – prospective words, that were reported and transmitted in a spirit of confiding faith, but that could have little meaning to the reporting parties for many hundreds of years. Briefly, a great mysterious *word* is spelt as it were by the whole sum of the scriptural books – every separate book forming a letter or syllable in that secret and that unfinished word, as it was for so many ages. This co-operation of ages, not able to communicate or concert arrangements with each other, is neither more nor less an argument of an over-ruling inspiration, than if the separation of the contributing parties were by space, and not by time. As if, for example, every island at the same moment were to send its contribution, without previous concert, to a sentence or chapter of a book; in which case the result, if full of meaning, much more if full of awful and profound meaning, could not be explained rationally without the assumption of a supernatural over-ruling of these unconscious co-operators to a common result. So far on behalf of inspiration. Yet, on the other hand, as an argument in denial of any blind mechanic inspiration cleaving to words and syllables, *Phil.* notices this consequence as resulting from such an assumption, viz., that if you adopt any one gospel, St John's suppose, or any one narrative of a particular transaction, as inspired in this minute and pedantic sense, then for every other report, which, adhering to the spiritual *value* of the circumstances, and virtually the same, should differ in the least of the details, there would instantly arise a solemn degradation.[58] All parts of Scripture, in fact, would thus be made active and operative in degrading each other.

PROTESTANTISM
[Part II]

First published in *Tait's*, XIV, December 1847, pp. 843–50. Two centred lines followed the title of the essay and immediately preceded the text. The first stated that the essay was 'BY THOMAS DE QUINCEY.', and the second that it was '*(Continued from page* 765.*)*' to denote where in *Tait's* Part I of the essay ended.

Reprinted in *F*, XVI, *Theological Essays and Other Papers* (1854), pp. 77–99, 119–25.

Revised text, carrying many accidentals but no substantive variants from *F*, in *SGG*, VIII, *Essays, Sceptical and Anti-Sceptical, or Problems Neglected or Misconceived* (1858), pp. 114–39.

There are two manuscripts, as follows:

MS A: Houghton Library, Harvard, MS *EC8. D4436. D858p. The manuscript is a complete set of *SGG* page proofs. It contains fourteen significant variants, and these are listed in the textual notes.

MS B: British Library, Department of Printed Books, C. 60. o. 3. The manuscript is one incomplete, and two complete, endnotes from *F*. The first corresponds to the text below running from p. 253.38 'eye? For the Greek' to p. 253.45 'by the evil eye.' The second corresponds to the text below running from p. 253.46 'I am not referring' to p. 253.47 'or ventriloquists.' The third corresponds to the text below running from p. 254.35 'Does that argument' to p. 254.36 'preceding paragraph? – ED.' There are no substantive variants.

For the context and occasion of the essay, see headnote, pp. 223–4.

SUCH is *Phil.'s* way of explaining θεοπνευστια* *(theopneustia)*, or divine prompting, so as to reconcile the doctrine affirming a *virtual* inspiration, an

* 'θεοπνευστια.' – I must point out to *Phil.* an oversight of his as to this word at p. 45; he there describes the doctrine of *theopneustia* as being that of 'plenary and *verbal* inspiration.' But this he cannot mean, for obviously this word *theopneustia* comprehends equally the verbal inspiration which he is denouncing, and the inspiration of power or spiritual virtue which he is substituting. Neither *Phil.*, nor any one of his school is to be understood as rejecting *theopneustia*, but as rejecting that particular mode of *theopneustia* which appeals to the eye by mouldering symbols, in favour of that other mode which appeals to the heart by incorruptible radiations of inner truth.

inspiration as to the truths revealed, with a peremptory denial of any inspiration at all, as to the mere verbal vehicle of those revelations. He is evidently as sincere in regard to the inspiration which he upholds as in regard to that which he denies. *Phil.* is honest, and *Phil.* is able. Now comes *my* turn. I rise to support my leader, and shall attempt to wrench this notion of a verbal inspiration from the hands of its champions by a *reductio ad absurdum*,[1] viz., by showing the monstrous consequences to which it leads – which form of logic *Phil.* also has employed briefly in the last paragraph of last month's paper; but mine is different and more elaborate. Yet, first of all, let me frankly confess to the reader, that some people allege a point-blank assertion by Scripture itself of its own verbal inspiration; which assertion, if it really *had* any existence, would summarily put down all cavils of human dialectics. *That* makes it necessary to review this assertion. This famous passage of Scripture, this *locus classicus*, or prerogative text, pleaded for the *verbatim et literatim*[2] inspiration of the Bible, is the following; and I will so exhibit its very words as that the reader, even if no Grecian, may understand the point in litigation. The passage is this: πασα γραφη θεοπνευστος και ὠφέλιμος, &c., taken from St Paul (2 Tim. iii. 16.)[3] Let us construe it literally, expressing the Greek by Latin characters: *Pasa graphé*, all written lore (or, every writing) – *theopneustos*, God-breathed, or, God-prompted – *kai*, and (or, also) – *ophelimos*, serviceable – *pros*, towards, *didaskalian*, doctrinal truth. Now this sentence, when thus rendered into English according to the rigour of the Grecian letter, wants something to complete its sense – it wants an *is*. There is a subject, as the logicians say, and there is a predicate (or, something affirmed of that subject), but there is no *copula* to connect them – we miss the *is*. This omission is common in Greek, but cannot be allowed in English. The *is* must be supplied; but *where* must it be supplied? That's the very question, for there is a choice between two places; and, according to the choice, will the word *theopneustos* become part of the subject, or part of the predicate; which will make a world of difference. Let us try it both ways: –

1. All writing inspired by God (*i. e.*, being inspired by God, supposing it inspired, which makes *theopneustos* part of the subject) *is* also profitable for teaching, &c.

2. All writing *is* inspired by God, and profitable, &c. (which makes *theopneustos* part of the predicate.)

Now, in this last way of construing the text, which is the way adopted by our authorised version, one objection strikes everybody at a glance, viz., that St Paul could not possibly mean to say of all writing, indiscriminately, that it was divinely inspired, this being so revoltingly opposed to the truth. It follows, therefore, that, on this way of interpolating the *is*, we must understand the Apostle to use the word *graphé*, writing, in a restricted sense, not for writing generally, but for sacred writing, or (as our English phrase runs) '*Holy Writ;*' upon which will arise three separate demurs – *first*, one already stated by *Phil.*, viz., that, when *graphé* is used in this sense, it is accompanied by the article; the phrase is either ἡ γραφη, 'the writing,' or else (as in St Luke) ἁι γραφαι, 'the writings,'[4] just as in English it is said, 'the Scripture,' or 'the Scriptures.' *Secondly*, that, according to the Greek usage, this would not be the natural place for introducing the *is*. *Thirdly* – which disarms the whole objection from this text, *howsoever* construed – that, after all, it leaves the dispute with the bibliolaters wholly untouched. We also, the anti-bibliolaters, say that all Scripture is inspired, though we may not therefore suppose the Apostle to be here insisting on that doctrine. But no matter whether he is or not, in relation to this dispute. Both parties are contending for the inspiration – so far they are agreed; the question between them arises upon quite another point, viz., as to the *mode* of that inspiration, whether incarnating its golden light in the corruptibilities of perishing syllables, or in the sanctities of indefeasible, word-transcending ideas. Now, upon that question, the apostolic words, torture them how you please, say nothing at all.

There is, then, no such dogma (or, to speak *Germanicè*, no such *machtspruch*)[5] in behalf of verbal inspiration as has been ascribed to St Paul, and I pass to my own argument against it. This argument turns upon the self-confounding tendency of the common form ascribed to θεοπνευστια, or divine inspiration. When translated from its true and lofty sense of an inspiration – brooding, with outstretched wings, over the mighty abyss of *secret* truth – to the vulgar sense of an inspiration, burrowing, like a rabbit or a worm, in grammatical quillets and syllables, mark how it comes down to nothing at all; mark how a stream, pretending to derive itself from a heavenly fountain, is finally lost and confounded in a morass of human perplexities.

First of all, at starting, we have the inspiration (No. 1) to the original composers of the sacred books. *That* I grant, though distinguishing as to its nature.

Next, we want another inspiration (No. 2) for the countless *translators* of the Bible. Of what use is it to a German, to a Swiss, or to a Scotsman, that, three thousand years before the Reformation, the author of the Pentateuch was kept from erring by a divine restraint over his words, if the authors of this Reformation – Luther, suppose, Zwingle, John Knox[6] – either making translations themselves, or *relying* upon translations made by others under no such verbal restraint, have been left free to bias his mind, pretty nearly as much as if the original Hebrew writer had been resigned to his own human discretion?

Thirdly, even if we adopt the inspiration, No. 2, *that* will not avail us; because many *different* translators exist. Does the very earliest translation of the Law and the Prophets, viz., the Greek translation of the Septuagint, always agree verbally with the Hebrew? Or the Samaritan[7] Pentateuch always with the Hebrew? Or do the earliest Latin versions of the entire Bible agree *verbally* with modern Latin versions? Jerome's Latin version,[8] for instance, memorable as being that adopted by the Romish Church, and known under the name of the *Vulgate*, does it agree verbally with the Latin versions of the Bible or parts of the Bible made since the Reformation? In the English, again, if we begin with the translation still sleeping in MS., made five centuries ago, and passing from that to the first *printed* translation (which was, I think, Coverdale's, in 1535),[9] if we thence travel down to our own day, so as to include all that have confined themselves to separate versions of some one book, or even of some one cardinal text, the versions that differ – and to the idolater of words *all* differences are important – may be described as countless. Here, then, on that doctrine of inspiration which ascribes so much to the power of *verbal* accuracy, we shall want a fourth inspiration, No. 4, for the guidance of each separate Christian applying himself to the Scriptures in his mother tongue; he will have to select not one (where is the one that has been uniformly correct?) but a multitude; else the same error will again rush in by torrents through the license of interpretation assumed by these many adverse translators.

Fourthly, as these differences of version arise often under the *same* reading of the original text; but as, in the meantime, there are many *different* readings, here a fifth source of possible error calls for a fifth inspiration overruling us to the proper choice amongst various readings. What may be called a 'textual' inspiration for *selecting* the right reading is requisite for the very same reason, neither more nor less, which supposes any verbal inspiration originally requisite for *constituting* a right reading. It matters not in which stage of the Bible's progress the error commences; first stage and last stage are all alike in the sight of God. There was, reader, as perhaps you know, about six score years ago, another *Phil.*, not the same as this *Phil.* now before us (who would be quite vexed if you fancied him as old as all *that* comes to – oh dear, no! he's not near as old) – well, that earlier *Phil.* was Bentley, who wrote (under the name of *Phileleutheros Lipsiansis)* a pamphlet connected with this very subject, partly against an English infidel of that day.[10] In that pamphlet, *Phil.* the first pauses to consider and value this very objection from textual variation to the validity of Scripture; for the infidel (as is usual with infidels) being no great scholar, had argued as though it were impossible to urge anything whatever for the word of God, since so vast a variety in the readings rendered it impossible to know what *was* the word of God. Bentley, though rather rough, from having too often to deal with shallow coxcombs, was really and unaffectedly a pious man. He was shocked at this argument, and set himself seriously to consider it.[11] Now, as all the various readings were Greek, and as Bentley happened to be the first of Grecians, his deliberate review of this argument is entitled to great attention. There were, at that moment when Bentley spoke, something more (as I recollect) than ten thousand varieties of reading in the text of the New Testament; so many had been collected in the early part of Queen Anne's reign by Wetstein, the Dutchman,[12] who was then at the head of the collators. Mill, the Englishman,[13] was at that very time making further collations. How many he added, I cannot tell without consulting books – a thing which I very seldom do. But since that day, and long after Bentley and Mill were in their graves, Griesbach, the German,[14] has risen to the top of the tree, by towering above them all in the accuracy of his collations. Yet, as the harvest comes before the gleanings, we may be sure that Wetstein's barn housed the very wealth of all this variety. Of this it was, then, that Bentley spoke. And what *was* it that he spoke? Why, he, the great scholar, pronounced, as with the authority of a Chancery decree, that the vast majority of various readings made no difference at all in the sense.[15] In the *sense*, observe; but many things *might* make a difference in the sense which would still leave the doctrine undisturbed. For instance, in the passage about a camel going through the eye of a needle,[16] it will make a difference in the sense, whether you read in the Greek word for *camel* the oriental animal of that name, or a ship's cable; but no difference at all arises in the spiritual doctrine. Or, illustrating the case out of Shakspeare, it makes no difference as to the result, whether you read in Hamlet 'to take arms against a *sea* of troubles,' or (as has been suggested), 'against a *siege* of troubles;' but it makes a difference as to the integrity of the image.[*] What has a sea to do with arms? What has a camel,[†] the quadruped, to do with a needle? A prodigious minority, therefore, there is of such various readings as slightly affect the *sense;* but this minority becomes next to nothing, when we inquire for such as affect any *doctrine*. This was Bentley's opinion upon the possible disturbance offered to the Christian by various readings in the New Testament. You thought that the carelessness, or, at times, even the treachery of men, through so many centuries, must have ended in corrupting the original truth; yet, after all, you see the light burns as brightly and steadily as ever. We, now, that are not bibliolatrists, no more believe that, from the disturbance of a few words here or there, any evangelical truth can have suffered a wound or mutilation, than we believe that the burning of a wood, or even of a forest, which happens in our vast American possessions,[19] sometimes from natural causes (lightning, or spontaneous combustion), sometimes from an Indian's carelessness, can seriously have injured botany. But for *him*, who conceives an inviolable sanctity to have settled upon

[*] 'Integrity of the metaphor.' – One of the best notes ever written by Warburton was in justification of the old reading, *sea*.[17] It was true, that against a *sea* it would be idle to take *arms*. We, that have lived since Warburton's day, have learned by the solemn example of Mrs Partington (which, it is to be hoped, none of us will ever forget), how useless, how vain it is to take up a mop against the Atlantic ocean.[18] Great is the mop, great is Mrs Partington, but greater is the Atlantic. Yet, though all arms must be idle against the sea considered literally, and κατα την φαντασιαν under that image, Warburton contended justly that all images, much employed, *evanesce* into the ideas which they represent. A *sea* of troubles comes to mean only a *multitude* of troubles. No image of the sea is suggested; and arms, incongruous in relation to the literal sea, is not so in relation to a multitude; besides, that the image *arms* itself, evanesces for the same reason into *resistance*. For this one note, which I cite from boyish remembrance, I have always admired the subtlety of Warburton.

[†] Meantime, though using this case as an illustration, I believe that *camel* is, after all, the true translation; first, on account of the undoubted proverb in the east about the *elephant* going through the needle's eye; the relation is that of *contrast* as to magnitude; and the same relation holds as to the camel and the needle's eye; secondly, because the proper word for a cable, it has been alleged, is not 'cam*e*lus,' but 'cam*i*lus.'

each word and particle of the original record, there *should* have been strictly required an inspiration (No. 5) to prevent the possibility of various readings arising. It is too late, however, to pray for *that;* the various readings *have* arisen; here they are; and what's to be done now? The only resource for the bibliolatrist is – to invoke a new inspiration (No. 4) for helping him out of his difficulty, by guiding his choice. We, anti-bibliolaters, are not so foolish as to believe that God having once sent a deep message of truth to man, would suffer it to lie at the mercy of a careless or a wicked copyist. Treasures so vast would not be left at the mercy of accidents so vile. Very little more than two hundred years ago, a London compositor, not wicked at all, but simply drunk, in printing Deuteronomy, left out the most critical of words; the seventh commandment he exhibited thus – 'Thou *shalt* commit adultery;' in which form the sheet was struck off. And though in those days no practical mischief could arise from this singular *erratum*, which English Griesbachs will hardly enter upon the roll of various readings, yet, harmless as it was, it met with punishment. 'Scandalous!' said Laud,[20] 'shocking! to tell men in the seventeenth century, as a biblical rule, that they positively must commit adultery!' The brother compositors of this drunken biblical reviser, being too honourable to betray the individual delinquent, the Star Chamber fined the whole 'chapel.'[21] Now, the copyists of MSS. were as certain to be sometimes drunk as this compositor – famous by his act – utterly forgotten in his person – whose crime is remembered – the record of whose name has perished. We therefore hold, that it never was in the power, or placed within the discretion, of any copyist, whether writer or printer, to injure the sacred oracles. But the bibliolatrist cannot say *that;* because, if he does, then he is formally unsaying the very principle which is meant by bibliolatry. He therefore must require another supplementary inspiration, viz., No. 4, to direct him in his choice of the true reading amongst so many as continually offer themselves.*

* I recollect no variation in the text of Scripture which makes any startling change, even to the amount of an eddy in its own circumjacent waters, except that famous passage about the three witnesses – '*There are three that bear record in heaven*,'[22]&c. This has been denounced with perfect fury as an interpolation; and it is impossible to sum up the quart bottles of ink, black and blue, that have been shed in the dreadful skirmish. Porson even, the all-accomplished Grecian, in his letters to Archdeacon Travis, took a conspicuous part in the controversy;[23] his wish was, that men should think of him as a second Bentley tilting against Phalaris;[24] and he stung like a hornet. To be a Cambridge man in those days was to be a hater of all Establishments in England; things and persons were hated alike. I hope the same thing may not be true at present. It may chance that on this subject Master Porson will get stung through his coffin, before he is many years deader. However, if this particular variation troubles the waters just around itself (for it would desolate a Popish village to withdraw its local saint), yet carrying one's eye from this Epistle to the whole domains of the New Testament – yet, looking away from that defrauded village to universal Christendom, we must exclaim – What does one miss? Surely Christendom is not disturbed because a village suffers wrong; the sea is not roused because an eddy in a corner is boiling; the doctrine of the Trinity is not in danger because Mr Porson is in a passion.

Fifthly, as all words cover ideas, and many a word covers a choice of ideas, and very many ideas split into a variety of modifications, we shall, even after a fourth inspiration has qualified us for selecting the true reading, still be at a loss how, upon this right reading, to fix the right acceptation. So *there*, at that fifth stage, in rushes the total deluge of human theological controversies. One church, or one sect, insists upon one sense; another, and another, 'to the end of time,'[25] insists upon a different sense. Babel is upon us;[26] and, to get rid of Babel, we shall need a fifth inspiration. No. 5 is clamorously called for.*

But we all know, each knows by his own experience, that No. 5 is not forthcoming; and, in the absence of *that*, what avail for *us* the others? 'Man overboard!' is the cry upon deck; but what avails it for the poor drowning creature that a rope being thrown to him is thoroughly secured at one end to the ship, if the other end floats wide of his grasp? We are in prison: we descend from our prison-roof, that seems high as the clouds, by knotting together all the prison bed-clothes, and all the aids from friends outside. But all is too short: after swarming down the line, in middle air, we find ourselves hanging: sixty feet of line are still wanting. To re-ascend – *that* is impossible: to drop boldly – alas! *that* is to die.

Meantime, what need of this eternal machinery, that eternally is breaking like ropes of sand? Or of this earth resting on an elephant, that rests on a tortoise,[28] that, when all is done, must still consent to rest on the common atmosphere of God? These chains of inspiration are needless. The great ideas of the Bible protect themselves. The heavenly truths, by their own imperishableness, defeat the mortality of languages with which for a moment they are associated. Is the lightning enfeebled or dimmed, because for thousands of years it has blended with the tarnish of earth and the steams of earthly graves? Or light, which so long has travelled in the chambers of our sickly air,

* One does not wish to be tedious; or, if one *has* a gift in that way, naturally one does not wish to bestow it *all* upon a perfect stranger, as 'the reader' usually is, but to reserve a part for the fireside, and the use of one's most beloved friends; else I could torment the reader by a longer succession of numbers, and perhaps drive him to despair. But one more of the series, viz., No. 6, as a parting *gage d'amitié*,[27] he must positively permit me to drop into his pocket. Supposing, then, that No. 5 were surmounted, and that, supernaturally, you knew the value to a hair's breadth of every separate word (or, perhaps, composite phrase made up from a constellation of words) – ah, poor traveller in trackless forests, still you are lost again – for, oftentimes, and especially in St Paul, the words may be known, their sense may be known, but their *logical relation* is still doubtful. The word X and the word Y are separately clear; but has Y the dependency of a consequence upon X, or no dependency at all? Is the clause which stands eleventh in the series a direct prolongation of that which stands tenth? or is the tenth wholly independent and insulated? or does it occupy the place of a parenthesis, so as to modify the ninth clause? People that have practised composition as much, and with as vigilant an eye as myself, know also, by thousands of cases, how infinite is the disturbance caused in the logic of a thought by the mere position of a word as despicable as the word *even*. A mote, that is itself invisible, shall darken the august faculty of sight in a human eye – the heavens shall be hidden by a wretched atom that dares not show itself – and the station of a syllable shall cloud the judgment of a council. Nay, even an ambiguous emphasis falling to the right-hand word, or the left hand-word, shall confound a system.

and searched the haunts of impurity – is that less pure than it was in the first chapter of Genesis?[29] Or that more holy light of truth – the truth, suppose, written from his creation upon the tablets of man's heart – which truth never was imprisoned in any Hebrew or Greek, but has ranged for ever through courts and camps, deserts and cities, the original lesson of justice to man and piety to God – has that become tainted by intercourse with flesh? or has it become hard to decipher, because the very heart, that human heart where it is inscribed, is so often blotted with falsehoods? You are aware, perhaps, reader, that in the Mediterranean sea, off the coast of Asia Minor (and, indeed, elsewhere), through the very middle of the salt-sea billows, rise up, in shining columns, fountains of fresh water.* In the desert of the sea are found Arabian fountains of Ishmael and Isaac![31] Are these fountains poisoned for the poor victim of fever, because they have to travel through a contagion of waters not potable? Oh, no! They bound upwards like arrows, cleaving the seas above with as much projectile force as the glittering waterworks of Versailles cleave the air,[32] and rising as sweet to the lip as ever mountain torrent that comforted the hunted deer.

It is impossible to suppose that any truth, launched by God upon the agitations of things so unsettled as languages, *can* perish. The very frailty of languages is the strongest proof of this; because it is impossible to suppose that anything so great can have been committed to the fidelity of anything so treacherous. There is laughter in heaven when it is told of man, that he fancies his earthly jargons, which, to heavenly ears, must sound like the chucklings of poultry, equal to the task of hiding or distorting any light of revelation. Had *words* possessed any authority or restraint over scriptural truth, a much worse danger would have threatened it than any malice in the human will, suborning false copyists, or surreptitiously favouring depraved copies. Even a general conspiracy of the human race for such a purpose would avail against the Bible only as a general conspiracy to commit suicide might avail against the drama of God's providence. Either conspiracy would first become dangerous when first either became possible. But a real danger seems to lie in the insensible corruption going on for ever within all languages, by means of which they are eternally dying away from their own vital powers; and that is a danger which is travelling fast after all the wisdom and the wit, the eloquence and the poetry of this earth, like a mountainous wave, and will finally overtake them – their very vehicles being lost and confounded to human sensibilities. But such a wave will break harmlessly against scriptural truth; and not merely because that truth will for ever evade such a shock by its eternal transfer from language to language – from languages dying out to languages in vernal bloom – but also because, if it could *not* evade the shock, supreme truth would surmount it for a profounder reason. A danger analogous to this once existed

* See Mr Yates's 'Annotations upon Fellowes's Researches in Anatolia,' as *one* authority for this singular phenomenon.[30]

in a different form. The languages into which the New Testament was first translated offered an apparent obstacle to the translation that seemed insurmountable. The Latin, for instance, did not present the spiritual words which such a translation demanded; and how *should* it, when the corresponding ideas had no existence amongst the Romans? Yet, if not spiritual, the language of Rome was intellectual; it was the language of a cultivated and noble race. But what shall be done if the New Testament wishes to drive a tunnel through a rude forest race, having an undeveloped language, and understanding nothing but war? Four centuries after Christ, the Gothic Bishop Ulphilas set about translating the Gospels for his countrymen.[33] He had no words for expressing spiritual relations or spiritual operations. The new nomenclature of moral graces, humility, resignation, the spirit of forgiveness, &c., hitherto unrecognised for such amongst men, having first of all been shown in blossom, and distinguished from weeds, by Christian gardening, had to be reproduced in the Gothic language, with apparently no means whatever of effecting it. In this earliest of what we may call ancestral translations, (for the Goths were of our own blood), and, therefore, by many degrees, this most interesting of translations, may be seen to this day, after fourteen centuries and upwards have passed, *how* the good bishop succeeded, to what extent he succeeded, and by what means. I shall take a separate opportunity for investigating that problem; but at present I will content myself with noticing a remarkable principle which applies to the case, and illustrating it by a remarkable anecdote. The principle is this – that in the grander parts of knowledge, which do not deal much with petty details, nearly all the *building* or constructive ideas (those ideas which build up the system of that particular knowledge) lie involved within each other; so that any one of the series, being awakened in the mind, is sufficient (given a multitude of minds) to lead backwards or forwards, analytically or synthetically, into many of the rest That is the principle;[*] and the story which illustrates it is this: – A great work of Apollo-

[*] '*That* is the principle' – I am afraid, on reviewing this passage, that the reader may still say, '*What* is the principle?' I will add, therefore, the shortest explanation of my meaning. If into any Pagan language you had occasion to translate the word *love*, or *purity*, or *penitence*, &c., you could not do it. The Greek language itself, perhaps the finest (all things weighed and valued) that man has employed, could not do it. The *scale* was not so pitched as to make the transfer possible. It was to execute organ music on a guitar. And, hereafter, I will endeavour to show how scandalous an error has been committed on this subject, not by scholars only, but by religious philosophers. The relation of Christian ethics (which word ethics, however, is itself most insufficient) to natural or universal ethics is a field yet uncultured by a rational thought. The first word of sense has yet to be spoken. There lies the difficulty; and the principle which meets it is this, that what any one idea could never effect for itself (insulated, it must remain an unknown quality for ever), the total system of the ideas developed from its centre would effect for each separately. To know the part, you must first know the whole, or know it, at least, by some outline. The idea of *purity*, for instance, in its Christian altitude, would be utterly incomprehensible, and, besides, could not sustain itself for a moment if by any glimpse it were

nius, the sublime geometer, was supposed in part to have perished: seven of the eight books remained in the original Greek; but the eighth was missing.[36] The Greek, after much search, was not recovered; but at length there was found (in the Bodleian, I think,) an Arabic translation of it. An English mathematician, Halley, knowing not one word of Arabic, determined (without waiting for that Arabic key) to pick the lock of this MS.[37] And he did so. Through strength of preconception, derived equally from his knowledge of the general subject, and from his knowledge of this particular work in its earlier sections, using also to some extent the subtle art of the decipherer,* now become so powerful an instrument of analysis, he translated the whole Arabic MS. He printed it – he published it.[40] He tore – he extorted the truth from the darkness of an unknown language – he would not suffer the Arabic to benefit by its own obscurity to the injury of mathematics. And the book remains a monument to this day, that a system of ideas, having internal coherency and interdependency, is vainly hidden under an unknown tongue; that it may be illuminated and restored chiefly through their own reciprocal involutions. The same principle applies, and *à fortiori*[41] applies, to religious truth, as one which lies far deeper than geometry in the spirit of man, one to which the inner attestation is profounder, and to which the key-notes of Scripture (once awakened on the great organ of the heart) are sure to call up corresponding echoes. It is not in the power of language to arrest or to defeat this mode of truth; because, when once the fundamental base is furnished by revelation, the human heart itself is able to co-operate in developing the great harmonies of the system, without aid from language, and in defiance of language – without aid from human learning, and in defiance of human learning.

Finally, there is another security against the suppression or distortion of any great biblical truth by false readings, which I will state in the briefest terms. The reader is aware of the boyish sport sometimes called 'drake-stone;' a

---

approached. But when a *ruin* was unfolded that had affected the human race, and many things heretofore unobserved, *because uncombined*, were gathered into a unity of evidence to that ruin, spread through innumerable channels, the great altitude would begin dimly to reveal itself by means of the mighty depth in correspondence. One deep calleth to another.[34] One after one the powers lodged in the awful succession of uncoverings would react upon each other; and thus the feeblest language would be as capable of receiving and reflecting the system of truths (because the system is an arch that supports itself) as the richest and noblest; and for the same reason that makes geometry careless of language. The vilest jargon that ever was used by a shivering savage of Terra del Fuego[35] is as capable of dealing with the sublime and eternal affections of space and quantity, with up and down, with more and less, with circle and radius, angle and tangent, as is the golden language of Athens.

* '*Art of the decipherer.*' – An art which, in the preceding century, had been greatly improved by Wallis, Savilian professor of geometry at Oxford, the improver of analytic mathematics, and the great historian of algebra.[38] Algebra it was that suggested to him his exquisite deciphering skill, and the parliamentary war it was that furnished him with a sufficient field of practice. The King's private cabinet of papers, all written in cipher, and captured in the royal coach on the decisive day of Naseby (June, 1645), was (I believe) deciphered by Wallis, *proprio marte*.[39]

flattish stone is thrown by a little dexterity so as to graze the surface of a river, but so, also, as in grazing it to dip below the surface, to rise again from this dip, again to dip, again to ascend, and so on alternately, *à plusieurs reprises*.[42] In the same way, with the same effect of alternate resurrections, all scriptural truths reverberate and diffuse themselves along the pages of the Bible; none is confined to one text, or to one mode of enunciation; all parts of the scheme are eternally chasing each other, like the parts of a fugue; they hide themselves in one chapter, only to restore themselves in another; they diverge, only to recombine; and under such a vast variety of expressions, that, even in that way, supposing language to have powers over religious truth – which it never had, or can have – any abuse of such a power would be thoroughly neutralised. The case resembles the diffusion of vegetable seeds through the air and through the waters; draw a *cordon sanitaire*[43] against dandelion or thistle-down, and see if the armies of earth would suffice to interrupt this process of radiation, which yet is but the distribution of weeds. Suppose, for instance, the text about the *three heavenly witnesses* to have been eliminated finally as an interpolation. The first thought is – *there* goes to wreck a great doctrine! Not at all. That text occupied but a corner of the garden. The truth, and the secret implications of the truth, have escaped at a thousand points in vast arches above our heads, rising high above the garden wall, and have sown the earth with memorials of the mystery which they envelope.

The final inference is this – that Scriptural truth is endowed with a self-conservative and a self-restorative virtue; it needs no long successions of verbal protection by inspiration; it is self-protected; first, internally, by the complex power which belongs to the Christian *system* of involving its own integrations, in the same way as a musical chord involves its own successions of sound, and its own resolutions; secondly, in an external and obvious way, it is protected by its prodigious iteration, and secret *presupposal*[44] in all varieties of form. Consequently, as the peril connected with language is thus effectually barred, the call for any verbal inspiration (which, on separate grounds, is shown to be self-confounding) shows itself now, in a *second* form, to be a gratuitous delusion, since, in effect, it is a call for protection against a danger which cannot have any existence.

There is another variety of bibliolatry arising in a different way – not upon errors of language incident to human infirmity, but upon deliberate errors indispensable to divine purposes. The case is one which has been considered with far too little attention, else it could never have been thought strange that Christ should comply in things indifferent with popular errors. A few words will put the reader in possession of my view. Speaking of the Bible, *Phil.* says, 'We admit that its separate parts are the work of frail and fallible human beings. We do not seek to build upon it systems of cosmogony, chronology, astronomy, and natural history. We know no reason of internal or external probability which should induce us to believe that such matters could ever have been the subjects of direct revelation.'[45] Is *that* all? There is no reason, certainly, for expectations so foolish; but is there no adamantine reason against them? It is no business of the Bible, we are told, to teach science. Certainly not; but that is far too little. It is an obligation resting upon the Bible, if it is to be consistent with itself, that it should *refuse* to teach science; and, if the Bible ever *had* taught any one art, science, or process of life, capital doubts would have clouded our confidence in the authority of the book. By what caprice, it would have been asked, is a divine mission abandoned suddenly for a human mission? By what caprice is this one science taught, and others not? Or these two, suppose, and not all? But an objection, even deadlier, would have followed. It is clear as is the purpose of day-light, that the whole body of the arts and sciences composes one vast machinery for the irritation and development of the human intellect. For this end they exist. To see God, therefore, descending into the arena of science, and contending, as it were, for his own prizes, by teaching science in the Bible, would be to see him intercepting from their self-evident destination (viz., man's intellectual benefit) his own problems by solving them himself. No spectacle could more dishonour the divine idea. *The Bible must not teach anything that man can teach himself.* Does the doctrine require a revelation? – then nobody but God *can* teach it. Does it require none? – then in whatever case God has qualified man to do a thing for himself, he has in that very qualification silently laid an injunction upon man to do it, by giving the power. But it is fancied that a divine teacher, without descending to the unworthy office of teaching science, might yet have kept his own language free from all collusion with human error. Hence, for instance, it was argued at one time, that any language in the Bible implying the earth to be stationary, and central to our system, could not have been a compliance with the popular errors of the time, but must be taken to express the absolute truth. And so grew the anti-Galilean fanatics. Out of similar notions have risen the absurdities of a polemic Bible chronology, &c.* Meantime, if a man sets himself steadily to contemplate the consequences which

* The Bible cosmology stands upon another footing. *That* is not gathered from a casual expression, shaped to meet popular comprehension, but is delivered directly, formally, and elaborately, as a natural preface to the history of man and his habitation. Here, accordingly, there is no instance of accommodation to vulgar ignorance; and the persuasion gains ground continually that the order of succession in the phenomena of creation will be eventually confirmed by scientific geology, so far as this science may ever succeed in unlinking the steps of the process. Nothing, in fact, disturbs the grandeur and solemnity of the Mosaical cosmogony, except (as usual) the ruggedness of the bibliolater. He, finding the English word *day* employed in the measurement of the intervals, takes it for granted that this must mean a *nychthemeron*[46] of twenty-four hours; imports, therefore, into the biblical text this conceit; fights for his own opinion, as for a revelation from heaven; and thus disfigures the great inaugural chapter of human history with this single feature of a fairy-tale, where everything else is told with the most majestic simplicity. But this word, which so ignorantly he presumes to be an ordinary human day, bears that meaning only in common historical transactions between man and man; but never once in the great prophetic writings, where God comes forward as himself the principal agent. It then means always a vast and mysterious duration – undetermined, even to this hour, in Daniel. The *heptameron*[47] is not a week, but a shadowy adumbration of a week.

must inevitably have followed any deviation from the usual erroneous phraseology, he will see the utter impossibility that a teacher (pleading a heavenly mission) could allow himself to deviate by one hair's breadth (and why should he wish to deviate?) from the ordinary language of the times. To have uttered one syllable, for instance, that implied motion in the earth, would have issued into the following ruins: – *First*, it would have tainted the teacher with the suspicion of lunacy; and, *secondly*, would have placed him in this inextricable dilemma. On the one hand, to answer the questions prompted by his own perplexing language, would have opened upon him, as a necessity, one stage after another of scientific cross-examination, until his spiritual mission would have been forcibly swallowed up in the mission of natural philosopher; but, on the other hand, to pause resolutely at any one stage of this public examination, and to refuse all further advance, would be, in the popular opinion, to retreat as a baffled disputant from insane paradoxes which he had not been able to support. One step taken in that direction was fatal, whether the great envoy retreated from his own words to leave behind the impression that he was defeated as a rash speculator, or stood to these words, and thus fatally entangled himself in the inexhaustible succession of explanations and justifications. In either event the spiritual mission was at an end: it would have perished in shouts of derision, from which there could have been no retreat, and no retrieval of character. The greatest of astronomers, rather than seem ostentatious or unseasonably learned, will stoop to the popular phrase of the sun's rising, or the sun's motion in the ecliptic. But God, for a purpose commensurate with man's eternal welfare, is by these critics supposed incapable of the same petty abstinence.

The same line of argument applies to all the compliances of Christ with the Jewish prejudices (partly imported from the Euphrates)[48] as to demonology, witchcraft, &c. By the way, in this last word, 'witchcraft,' and the too memorable histories connected with it, lies a perfect mine of bibliolatrous madness. As it illustrates the folly and the wickedness of the bibliolaters, let us pause upon it.

The word *witch*, these bibliolaters take it for granted, must mean exactly what the original Hebrew means, or the Greek word chosen by the LXX.;[49] so much, and neither more nor less. That is, from total ignorance of the machinery by which language moves, they fancy that every idea and word which exists, or has existed, for any nation, ancient or modern, must have a direct interchangeable equivalent in all other languages; and that, if the dictionaries do not show it, *that* must be because the dictionaries are bad. Will these worthy people have the goodness, then, to translate *coquette*[50] into Hebrew, and *post-office* into Greek? The fact is, that all languages, and in the ratio of their development, offer ideas absolutely separate and exclusive to themselves. In the highly-cultured languages of England, France, and Germany, are words, by thousands, which are strictly untranslateable. They may be approached, but cannot be reflected as from a mirror. To take an image from the language of eclipses, the correspondence between the disk of the original word and its translated representative is, in thousands of instances, not *annular;* the centres do not coincide; the words overlap; and this arises from the varying modes in which different nations *combine* ideas. The French word shall combine the elements, *l, m, n, o* – the nearest English word, perhaps, *m, n, o, p.* For instance, in all words applied to the *nuances* of manners, and generally to *social* differences, how prodigious is the wealth of the French language! How merely untranslateable for all Europe! I suppose, my bibliolater, you have not yet finished your Hebrew or Samaritan translation of *coquette*. Well, you shall be excused from *that*, if you will only translate it into English. You cannot: you are obliged to keep the French word; and yet you take for granted, without inquiry, that in the word 'witchcraft,' and in the word 'witch,' applied to the sorceress of Endor, our authorised English Bible of King James's day must be correct.[51] And your wicked bibliolatrous ancestors proceeded on that idea throughout Christendom to murder harmless, friendless, and oftentimes crazy old women. Meantime the witch of Endor in no respect resembled our modern domestic witch.* There was as much difference as between a Roman Proconsul, surrounded with eagle-bearers, and a commercial Consul's clerk with a pen behind his ear. Apparently she was not so much a Medea as an Erichtho. (See the *Pharsalia*.)[56] She was an *Evocatrix*, or female necromancer, evoking phantoms that stood in some unknown relation to dead men; and then by some artifice (it has been supposed) of ventriloquism,† causing these phantoms to deliver oracular answers upon great political questions. Oh, that one had lived in the times of those New-

* 'The domestic witch.' – It is the common notion that the superstition of the *evil eye*, so widely diffused in the Southern lands, and in some, not a slumbering, but a fiercely operative superstition, is unknown in England and other Northern latitudes. On the contrary, to my thinking, the regular old vulgar witch of England and Scotland was but an impersonatrix of the very same superstition. Virgil expresses this mode of sorcery to the letter, when his shepherd says –

'Nescio quis teneros *oculus* mihi fascinat agnos?'[52]

Precisely in that way it was that the British witch operated. She, *by her eye*, blighted the natural powers of growth and fertility. By the way, I ought to mention, as a case parallel to that of the Bible's recognising witchcraft, and of enlightened nations continuing to punish it, that St Paul himself, in an equal degree, recognises the *evil eye*; that is, he uses the idea, (though certainly not meaning to accredit such an idea,) as one that briefly and energetically conveyed his meaning to those whom he was addressing. 'Oh, foolish Galatians, who hath bewitched you?'[53] That is, literally, who has fascinated your senses by the evil eye? For the Greek is, *tis umas ebaskanen?* Now the word *ebaskanen* is a past tense of the verb *baskaino*, which was the technical term for the action of the evil eye. Without having written a treatise on the Aeolic digamma,[54] probably the reader is aware that F is V, and that, in many languages, B and V are interchangeable letters through thousands of words, as the Italian *tavola*, from the Latin *tabula*. Under that little process it was that the Greek *baskaino* transmigrated into the Latin *fascino;*[55] so that St Paul's word, in speaking to the Galatians, is the very same word as Virgil's, in speaking of the shepherd's flock as charmed by the evil eye.

† I am not referring to German infidels. Very pious commentators have connected her with the *engastrimuthoi* (εγγαστριμυθοι) or ventriloquists.

England wretches that desolated whole districts and terrified vast provinces by their judicial murders of witches, under plea of a bibliolatrous warrant; until at last the fiery furnace, which they had heated for women and children, shot forth flames that, like those of Nebuchadnezzar's furnace,[57] seizing upon his very agents, began to reach some of the murderous judges and denouncers![58]

Yet, after all, are there not express directions in Scripture to exterminate witches from the land?[59] Certainly; but *that* does not argue any scriptural recognition of witchcraft as a possible offence. An imaginary crime may imply a criminal intention that is *not* imaginary; but also, which much more directly concerns the interests of a state, a criminal purpose, that rests upon a pure delusion, may work by means that are felonious for ends that are fatal. At this moment, we English and the Spaniards have laws, and severe ones, against witchcraft, viz., in the West Indies, and indispensable it is that we should. The Obeah man from Africa[60] can do no mischief to one of us. The proud and enlightened white man despises his arts; and for *him*, therefore, these arts have no existence, for they work only through strong preconceptions of their reality, and through trembling faith in their efficacy. But by that very agency they are all-sufficient for the ruin of the poor credulous negro; he is mastered by original faith, and has perished thousands of times under the knowledge that *Obi* had been set for him. Justly, therefore, do our colonial courts punish the Obeah sorcerer, who (though an imposter) is not the less a murderer. Now the Hebrew witchcraft was probably even worse; equally resting on delusions, nevertheless, equally it worked for unlawful ends, and (which chiefly made it an object of divine wrath) it worked *through* idolatrous agencies. It must, therefore, have kept up that connexion with idolatry which it was the unceasing effort of the Hebrew polity to exterminate from the land. Consequently, the Hebrew commonwealth might, as consistently as our own, denounce and punish witchcraft without liability to the inference that it therefore recognised the pretensions of witches as real, in the sense of working their bad ends by the means which they alleged. Their magic was causatively of no virtue at all, but, being believed in, through this belief it became the occasional means of exciting the imagination of its victims; after which the consequences were the same as if the magic had acted physically according to its pretences.*

* Does that argument not cover 'the New England wretches' so unreservedly denounced in a preceding paragraph? – ED.[61]

PROTESTANTISM
[Part III]

First published in *Tait's*, XV, February 1848, pp. 84–8. Two centred lines followed the title of the essay and immediately preceded the text. The first stated that the essay was 'BY THOMAS DE QUINCEY.', and the second that it was '(*Continued from page* 480, *vol.* 14.)' to denote where in *Tait's* Part II of the essay ended. The page number, however, was incorrect: it should read '850', not '480'.

Reprinted in *F*, XVI, *Theological Essays and Other Papers* (1854), pp. 99–114, 125–6.

Revised text, carrying many accidentals but only one substantive variant from *F*, in *SGG*, VIII, *Essays, Sceptical and Anti-Sceptical, or Problems Neglected or Misconceived* (1858), pp. 140–64.

There are two manuscripts, as follows:

MS A: Houghton Library, Harvard, MS *EC8. D4436. D858p. The manuscript is a complete set of *SGG* page proofs. It contains fourteen significant variants, and these are listed in the textual notes.

MS B: British Library, Department of Printed Books, C. 60. o. 3. The manuscript is three endnotes from *F*. The first corresponds to the text below running from p. 260.42 'Filmer's *Patriarcha.*' to p. 260.43 'Locke was answering him.' The second corresponds to the text below running from p. 261.41 'See, for some very' to p. 262.44 'for cheerful Scotland.' The third corresponds to the text below running from p. 263.38 '*From climate to climate.*' to p. 263.43 'a high civilization.' The manuscript contains no substantive variants.

For the context and occasion of the essay, see headnote, pp. 223–4.

II. *Development*, as applicable to Christianity, is a doctrine of the very days that are passing over our heads, and due to Mr Newman, originally the ablest son of Puseyism, but now a powerful architect of religious philosophy on his own account.[1] I should have described him more briefly as a 'master builder,' had my ear been able to endure a sentence ending with two consecutive trochees, and each of those trochees ending with the same syllable *er*. Ah, reader! I would the gods had made thee rhythmical, that thou mightest comprehend the thousandth part of my labours in the evasion of cacophon. *Phil.* has a general dislike to the Puseyites,[2] though he is too learned to be ignorant, (as are often the Low-Church, or Evangelical, party in England,) that, in many of their supposed innovations, the Puseyites were really only restoring what the torpor of the eighteenth century had suffered to go into disuse. They were *reforming* the Church in the sense sometimes belonging to the particle *re*, viz., *retroforming* it, moulding it back into compliance with its original form and model. It is true that this effort for quickening the Church, and for adorning her exterior service, moved under the impulse of too undisguised a sympathy with Papal Rome. But there is no great reason to mind *that* in our age and our country. Protestant zealotry may be safely relied on in this island as a match for Popish bigotry. There will be no love lost between them – be assured of *that* – and justice will be done to both, though neither should do it to her rival; for philosophy, which has so long sought only amusement in either, is in these latter days of growing profundity applying herself steadily to the profound truths which dimly are descried lurking in both. It is these which Mr Newman is likely to illuminate, and not the faded forms of an obsolete ceremonial that cannot now be restored effectually, were it even important that they should. Strange it is, however, that he should open his career by offering to Rome, as a mode of homage, this doctrine of development, which is the direct inversion of her own. Rome founds herself upon the idea, that to *her*, by tradition and exclusive privilege, was communicated, once for all, the whole truth from the beginning. Mr Newman lays his corner stone in the very opposite idea of a gradual development given to Christianity by the motion of time, by experience, by expanding occasions, and by the progress of civilization. Is Newmanism likely to prosper? Let me tell a little anecdote. Twenty years ago, roaming one day (as I had so often the honour to do) with our immortal Wordsworth,[3] I took the liberty of telling him, at a point of our walk, where nobody could possibly overhear me, unless it were old Father Helvellyn,[4] that I feared his theological principles were not quite so sound as his friends would wish. They wanted repairing a little. But, what was worse, I did not see how they *could* be repaired in the particular case which prompted my remark, for in that place, to repair, or in any respect to alter, was to destroy. It was a passage in the 'Excursion,' where the Solitary had described the baptismal rite as washing away the taint of original sin, and, in fact, working the effect which is called technically *regeneration*.[5] In the 'Excursion' this view was advanced, not as the poet's separate opinion, but as the avowed doctrine of the English Church, to which Church Wordsworth and myself yielded gladly a filial reverence. But *was* this the doctrine of the English Church? *That* I doubted – not that I pretended to any sufficient means of valuing the preponderant opinion between two opinions in the Church; a process far more difficult than is imagined by historians, always so ready to tell us fluently what 'the nation' or 'the people' thought upon a particular question, (whilst, in fact, a whole life might be often spent vainly in collecting the popular opinion); but, judging by my own casual experience, I fancied that a considerable majority in the Church gave an interpretation to this Sacrament differing by much from that in the 'Excursion.' Wordsworth was startled and disturbed at hearing it whispered even before Helvellyn, who is old enough to keep a secret, that his divinity might possibly limp a little. I, on *my* part, was not sure that it *did*, but I feared so; and, as there was no chance that I should be murdered for speaking freely, (though the place was lonely, and the evening getting dusky,) I stood to my disagreeable communication with the courage of a martyr. The question between us being one of mere fact, (not what *ought* to be the doctrine, but what *was* the doctrine of our Church at that time,) there was no opening for any discussion; and, on Wordsworth's suggestion, it was agreed to refer the point to his learned brother, Dr Christopher Wordsworth,[6] just then meditating a visit to his native lakes. That visit in a short time 'came off,' and then, without delay, our dispute 'came on' for judgment. I had no bets upon the issue – one can't bet with Wordsworth – and I don't know that I should have ventured to back myself in a case of that nature. However, I felt a slight anxiety on the subject, which was very soon and kindly removed by Dr Wordsworth's deciding, 'sans phrase,'[7] that I, the original mover of the strife, was wrong, wrong as wrong could be. To this decision I bowed at once, on a principle of courtesy. One ought always to presume a man right within his own *profession*, even if privately one should think him wrong. But I could not think *that* of Dr Wordsworth. He was a D.D.; he was head of Trinity College, which has *my* entire permission to hold its head up amongst twenty and more colleges, as the leading one in Cambridge (provided it can obtain St John's permission),[8] 'and which,' says *Phil.*, 'has done more than any other foundation in Europe for the enlightenment of the world, and for the overthrow of literary, philosophical, and religious superstitions.'[9] I quarrel not with this bold assertion, remembering reverentially that Isaac Barrow, that Isaac Newton, that Richard Bentley belonged to Trinity,[10] but I wish to understand it. The total pretensions of the College can be known only to its members; and, therefore, *Phil.* should have explained himself more fully. He *can* do so, for *Phil.* is certainly a Trinity man.[11] If the police are in search of him, they'll certainly hear of him at Trinity. Suddenly it strikes me as a dream, that Lord Bacon belonged to this College.[12] Don't laugh at me, *Phil.*, if I'm wrong, and still less (because then you'll laugh even more ferociously) if I happen to be right. Can one remember everything? Ah! the worlds of distracted facts that one ought to remember. Would to heaven that I remembered nothing at all, and had nothing to remember! This thing, however, I certainly *do* remember, that Milton was *not* of Trinity, nor Jeremy Taylor;[13] so don't think to hoax me there, my parent! Dr Wordsworth was, or had been, an examining chaplain to the Archbishop of Canterbury. If Lambeth could be at fault on such a question, then it's of no use going to Newcastle for coals.[14] Delphi, we all know, and Jupiter Ammon had vanished.[15] What other court of appeal was known to man? So I submitted as cheerfully as if the learned Doctor, instead of kicking me out of court, had been handing me in. Yet, for all that, as I returned musing past Rydal water,[16] I could not help muttering to myself

– Ay, now, what rebellious thought was it that I muttered? You fancy, reader, that perhaps I said, 'But yet, Doctor, in spite of your wig, I am in the right.' No; you're quite wrong: I said nothing of the sort. What I *did* mutter was this – 'The prevailing doctrine of the Church must be what Dr Wordsworth says, viz. that baptism *is* regeneration – he cannot be mistaken as to *that* – and I have been misled by the unfair proportion of Evangelical people, bishops, and others, whom accident has thrown in my way at Barley Wood (Hannah More's).[17] These, doubtless, form a minority in the Church; and yet, from the strength of their opinions, from their being a moving party, as also from their being a growing party, I prophesy this issue, that many years will not pass before this very question, now slumbering, will rouse a feud within the English Church. There is a quarrel brewing. Such feuds, long after they are ripe for explosion, sometimes slumber on, until accident kindles them into flame.' That accident was furnished by the tracts of the Puseyites,[18] and since then, according to the word which I spoke on Rydal water, there has been open war raging upon this very point.

At present, with even more certainty, I prophesy that mere necessity, a necessity arising out of continual collisions with sceptical philosophy, will, in a few years, carry all churches enjoying a learned priesthood into the disputes connected with this doctrine of development. *Phil.*, meantime, is no friend to that Newmanian doctrine; and in sect. 31, p. 66, he thus describes it: – 'According to these writers' (viz., the writers 'who advocate the theory of development'), 'the progressive and gradual development of religious truth, which appears to *us*' (*us*, meaning, I suppose, the *Old*mannians,) 'to have been terminated by the final revelation of the Gospel, has been going on ever since the foundation of the Church, is going on still, and must continue to advance. This theory presumes that the Bible does not contain a full and final exposition of a complete system of religion; that the Church has developed from the Scriptures true doctrines not explicitly contained therein,' &c. &c.

But, without meaning to undertake a defence of Mr Newman (whose book I am as yet too slenderly acquainted with), may I be allowed, at this point, to intercept a fallacious view of that doctrine, as though essentially it proclaimed some imperfection in Christianity. The imperfection is in us, the Christians, not in Christianity. The impression given by *Phil.* to the hasty reader is, that, according to Newmanism, the Scriptures make a good beginning, to which we ourselves are continually adding – a solid foundation, on which we ourselves build the superstructure. Not so. In the course of a day or a year, the sun passes through a vast variety of positions, aspects, and corresponding powers, in relation to ourselves. Daily and annually he is *developed* to us – he runs a cycle of development. Yet, after all, this practical result does not argue any change or imperfection, growth or decay, in the sun. This great orb is stationary as regards his place, and unchanging as regards his power. It is the subjective change in ourselves that projects itself into this endless succession of phantom changes in the object. Not otherwise on the scheme of development; the Christian theory and system are perfect from the beginning. In itself, Christianity changes not, neither waxing nor waning; but the motions of time and the evolutions of experience continually uncover new parts of its stationary disk. The orb *grows*, so far as practically we are speaking of our own benefit; but absolutely, as regards itself, the orb, eternally the same, has simply more or fewer of its digits exposed. Christianity, perfect from the beginning, had a curtain over much of its disk, which Time and Social Progress are continually withdrawing. This I say not as any deliberate judgment on development, but merely as a suspending, or *ad interim*[19] idea, by way of barring too summary an interdict against the doctrine at this premature stage. *Phil.*, however, hardens his face against Newman and all his works. Him and them he defies; and would consign, perhaps secretly, to the care of a well-known (not new, but) old gentleman, if only he had any faith in that old gentleman's existence. On that point, he is a fixed infidel, and quotes with applause the answer of Robinson, the once celebrated Baptist clergyman, who being asked if he believed in the devil, replied, 'Oh, no; *I*, for my part, believe in God – don't *you*?'[20]

Phil., therefore, as we have seen, in effect condemns development. But, at p. 33, when as yet he is not thinking of Mr Newman, he says, 'If knowledge is progressive, the development of Christian doctrine must be progressive likewise.' I do not see the *must;* but I see the Newmanian cloven foot. As to the *must*, knowledge is certainly progressive; but the development of the multiplication table is not therefore progressive, nor of anything else that is finished from the beginning. My reason, however, for quoting the sentence is, because here we suddenly detect *Phil.* in laying down the doctrine which in Mr Newman he had regarded as heterodox. *Phil.* is taken red-hand, as the English law expresses it, crimson with the blood of his offence; assuming, in fact, an original imperfection *quoad* the *scire*, though not *quoad* the *esse;*[21] as to the '*exposition* of the system,' though not as to the '*system*' of Christianity. Mr Newman, after all, asserts (I believe) only one mode of development as applicable to Christianity. *Phil.* having broke the ice, may now be willing to allow of two developments; whilst I, that am always for going to extremes, should be disposed to assert three, viz: –

First, The *Philological* development. And this is a point on which I, *Philo-Phil.* (or, as for brevity you may call me, *Phil-Phil.*), shall, without wishing to do so, vex *Phil.* It's shocking that one should vex the author of one's existence, which *Phil.* certainly is in relation to me, when considered as *Phil-Phil.* Still it is past all denial, that, to a certain extent, the Scriptures must benefit, like any other book, by an increasing accuracy and compass of learning in the *exegesis* applied to them. But if all the world denied this, *Phil.*, my parent, is the man that cannot; since he it is that relies upon Philological knowledge as the one resource of Christian philosophy in all circumstances of difficulty for any of its interests, positive or negative. Philology, according to *Phil.*, is the sheet-anchor of Christianity. Already it is the author of a Christianity more in harmony with philosophy; and, as regards the future, *Phil.* it is that charges Philology with the whole service of divinity. Wherever anything, being right, needs to be defended – wherever anything, being amiss, needs to be improved – oh! what a life he will lead this poor Philology! Philology, with *Phil.*, is the great benefactress for the past, and the sole trustee for the future. Here, therefore, *Phil.* is caught in a fix, *habemus confitentem*.[22] He denounces development when dealing with the Newmanites; he relies on it when vaunting the functions of Philology; and the only evasion for *him* would be to distinguish about the modes of development, were it not that, by insinuation, he has apparently denied all modes.

Secondly, There is the *Philosophic* development, from the reaction upon the Bible of advancing knowledge. This is a mode of development continually going on, and reversing the steps of past human follies. In every age, man has imported his own crazes into the Bible, fancied that he saw them there, and then drawn sanctions to his wickedness or absurdity from what were nothing else than fictions of his own. Thus did the Papists draw a plenary justification of intolerance, or even of atrocious persecution, from the evangelical '*Compel them to come in!*'[23] The right of unlimited coercion was read in these words. People, again, that were democratically given, or had a fancy for treason, heard a trumpet of insurrection in the words, '*To your tents, oh Israel!*'[24] But far beyond these in multitude were those that drew from the Bible the most extravagant claims for kings and rulers. 'Rebellion was as the sin of witchcraft.'[25] This was a jewel of a text; it killed two birds with one stone. Broomsticks were proved out of it most clearly, and also the atrocity of representative government. What a little text to contain so much! Look into Algeron Sydney,[26] or into Locke's controversy with Sir Robert Filmer's* 'Patriarcha,' or into any books of those days on political principles, and it will be found that Scripture was so used as to form an absolute bar against human progress. All public benefits were, in the strictest sense of the word, *precarious*, as depending upon prayers and entreaties to those who had an interest in refusing them. All improvements were eleemosynary; for the initial step in all cases belonged to the Crown. 'The right divine of kings to govern wrong'[28] was in those days what many a man would have died for – what many a man *did* die for; and all in pure simplicity of heart – faithful to the Bible, but to the Bible of misinterpretation. They obeyed (often to their own ruin) an order which they had misread. Their sincerity, the disinterestedness of their folly, is evident; and in that degree is evident the opening for Scripture development. Nobody could better obey Scripture as *they* had understood it. Change in the obedience, there could be none for the better; it demanded only that there should be a change in the interpretation, and that change would be what is meant by a development of Scripture. Two centuries of enormous progress in

* 'Filmer's *Patriarcha*.' – I mention the *book* as the antagonist, and not the man, because (according to my impression) Sir Robert was dead when Locke was answering him.[27]

the relations between subjects and rulers have altered the whole reading. '*How readest thou?*' was the question of Christ himself;[29] that is, in what meaning dost thou read the particular Scripture that applies to this case? All the texts and all the cases remain at this hour just as they were for our ancestors; and our reverence for these texts is as absolute as theirs; but we, applying lights of experience which *they* had not, construe these texts by a different logic. *There* now is development applied to the Bible in one of its many *strata* – that *stratum* which connects itself most with civil polity. Again, what a development have we made of Christian truth! how differently do we now read our Bibles in relation to the poor tenants of dungeons that once were thought, even by Christian nations, to have no rights at all! – in relation to 'all prisoners and captives;'[30] and in relation to slaves! The New Testament had said nothing *directly* upon the question of slavery; nay, by the misreader it was rather supposed *indirectly* to countenance that institution. But mark – it is Mahommedanism, having little faith in its own laws, that dares not confide in its children for developing anything, but must tie them up for every contingency by the *letter* of a rule. Christianity – how differently does *she* proceed! She throws herself broadly upon the pervading spirit which burns within her morals. 'Let them alone,' she says of nations; 'leave them to themselves. I have put a new law into their hearts; and if it is really there, and really cherished, that law will tell them – will develop for them – what it is that they ought to do in every case as it arises, when once its consequences are comprehended.' No need, therefore, for the New Testament *explicitly* to forbid slavery; silently and *implicitly* it is forbidden in many passages of the New Testament, and it is at war with the spirit of all. Besides, the religion which trusts to formal and literal rules breaks down the very moment that a new case arises not described in the rules. Such a case is virtually unprovided for, if it does not answer to a circumstantial textual description; whereas *every* case is provided for, as soon as its tendencies and its moral relations are made known, by a religion that speaks through a spiritual organ to a spiritual apprehension in man. Accordingly, we find that, whenever a new mode of intoxication is introduced, not depending upon grapes, the most devout Mussulmans hold themselves absolved from the restraints of the Koran.[31] And so it would have been with Christians, if the New Testament had laid down *literal* prohibitions of slavery, or of the slave traffic. Thousands of variations would have been developed by time which no *letter* of Scripture could have been comprehensive enough to reach. Were the domestic servants of Greece, the θητες (*thetes*), within the description? Were the *serfs* and the *ascripti glebae*[32] of feudal Europe to be accounted slaves? Or those amongst our own brothers and sisters, that within so short a period were born subterraneously* in Scottish mines,[36] or in the

* See, for some very interesting sketches of this Pariah population, the work (title I forget) of Mr Bald, a Scottish engineer,[33] well known and esteemed in Edinburgh and Glasgow. He

English collieries of Cumberland, and were supposed to be *ascripti metallo*,[37] sold by nature to the mine, and indorsed upon its machinery for the whole term of their lives; in whom, therefore, it was a treason to see the light of upper day – would *they*, would these poor Scotch and English Pariahs, have stood within any Scriptural privilege if the New Testament had legislated by name and letter for this case of *douloi* (slaves)? No attorney would have found them entitled to plead the benefit of the Bible statute. Endless are the variations of the conditions that new combinations of society would bring forward; endless would be the virtual restorations of slavery that would take place under a Mahometan literality; endless would be the defeats that such restorations must sustain under a Christianity relying on no *letter*, but on the *spirit* of God's commandments, and that will understand no equivocations with the secret admonitions of the heart. Meantime, this sort of development, it may be objected, is not a light that Scripture throws out upon human life so much as a light that human life and its development throw back upon Scripture. True; but then how was it possible that life and the human intellect should be carried forward to such developments? Solely through the training which both had received under the discipline of Christian truth. Christianity utters some truth widely applicable to society. This truth is caught up by some influential organ of social life – is expanded prodigiously by human experience, and, when travelling back as an illustrated or improved text to the Bible, is found to be made up, in all its details, of many human developments. Does that argue anything disparaging to Christianity, as though *she* contributed little and man contributed much? On the contrary, man would have contributed nothing at all but for that *nucleus* by which Christianity started and moulded the principle. To give one instance – public charity, when did it commence?[38] – who first thought of it? Who first noticed hunger and cold as awful realities afflicting poor women and innocent children? Who first made a public provision to meet these evils? – Constantine it was, the first Christian that sat upon a throne.[39] Had, then, rich Pagans before his time no charity – no pity? – no money available for hopeless poverty? Not much – very little, I conceive; about so much as Shakspere insinuates that there is of milk in a male tiger.[40] Think, for instance, of that black-hearted reprobate, Cicero, the moralist. This moral knave, who wrote such beautiful Ethics,[41] and *was* so wicked – who

may be relied on. What he tells against Scotland is violently against his own will, for he is intensely national, of which I will give the reader one instance that may make him smile. Much of the rich, unctuous coal, from Northumberland and Durham,[34] gives a deep ruddy light, verging to a blood-red, and certainly is rather sullen, on a winter evening, to the eye. On the other hand, the Scottish coal or most of it, being far poorer as to heat, throws out a very beautiful and animated scarlet blaze; upon which hint, Mr Bald, when patriotically distressed at not being able to deny the double power of the eastern English coal, suddenly revivifies his Scottish heart that had been chilled, perhaps, by the Scottish coals in his fire-grate, upon recurring to this picturesque difference in the two blazes – 'Ah!' he says gratefully, 'that Newcastle blaze is well enough for a "gloomy" Englishman, but it wouldn't do at all for cheerful Scotland.'[35]

spoke so charmingly and acted so horribly – mentions, with a petrifying coolness, that he knew of desolate old women in Rome who passed three days in succession without tasting food.[42] Did not the wretch, when thinking of this, leap up, and tumble down stairs in his anxiety to rush abroad and call a public meeting for considering so dreadful a case? Not he; the man continued to strut about his library, in a huge toga as big as the *Times* newspaper, singing out, '*Oh, fortunatam natam me Consule Romam!*'[43] and he mentioned the fact at all only for the sake of Natural Philosophers or of the curious in old women. Charity, even in that sense, had little existence – nay, as a duty, it had no place or rubric in human conceptions before Christianity. Thence came the first rudiments of all public relief to starving men and women; but the idea, the principle, was all that the Bible furnished, needed to furnish, or could furnish. The practical arrangements, the endless details for carrying out this Christian idea – these were furnished by man; and why not? This case illustrates only one amongst innumerable modes of development applicable to the Bible; and this power of development, in general, proves also one other thing of the last importance to prove, viz. the power of Christianity to work in coöperation with time and social progress; to work variably according to the endless variations of time and place; and *that* is the exact *shibboleth* of a true and spiritual religion – for, on reviewing the history of false religions, and inquiring what it was that ruined them, rarely is it found that any of them perished by external violence.[44] Even the dreadful fury of the early Mahometan Sultans in India, before the house of Timour,[45] failed to crush the monstrous idolatries of the Hindoos. All false religions have perished by their own hollowness, under that searching trial applied by social life and its changes, which awaits every mode of religion. One after another they have sunk away, as by palsy, from new aspects of society and new necessities of man which they were not able to face. Commencing in one condition of society, in one set of feelings, and in one system of ideas, they sank uniformly under any great change in these elements, to which they had no natural power of accommodation. A false religion furnished a key to one subordinate lock; but a religion that is true will prove a master-key for all locks alike. This transcendental principle, by which Christianity transfers herself so readily from climate to climate,* from century to century, from the simplicity of shepherds to the utmost refinement of philosophers, carries with it a necessity, corresponding to such infinite flexibility of endless development.

(To be concluded in our next.)[46]

* '*From climate to climate.*' – Sagacious Mahometans have been often scandalised and troubled by the secret misgiving that, after all, their Prophet must have been an ignorant fellow. It is clear that the case of a cold climate had never occurred to him; and even a hot one had been conceived most narrowly. Many of the Bedouin Arabs complain of ablutions not adapted to their waterless condition. These evidences of oversight would have been fatal to Islamism, had Islamism produced a high civilization.

Article for *Macphail's Edinburgh Ecclesiastical Journal*, 1848

WAR

First published as the lead article in *Macphail's Edinburgh Ecclesiastical Journal and Literary Review*, V, February 1848, pp. 1–20. The essay was printed as 'BY THOMAS DE QUINCEY.' in a centred line following the title and immediately preceding the text.

Reprinted in *F*, VIII, *Narrative and Miscellaneous Papers* (1853), pp. 191–232.

Revised text, carrying many accidentals but only three substantive variants from *F*, in *SGG*, IV, *Miscellanies* (1854), pp. 289–322.

There are six manuscripts, as follows:

MS A: The manuscript is a draft fragment published in Japp, *PW*. The original has not been traced. Japp entitles the fragment 'The True Justifications of War', and describes it as 'evidently intended to appear in the article on *War*' (Japp, *PW*, vol. I, pp. 315–6). A full transcript is given below, pp. 514–5.

MS B: National Library of Scotland, MS 21239. The manuscript is a single white sheet, measuring 190 by 300 mm, and with writing in black ink on the recto only. There is no watermark. The MS corresponds to the passage below running from p. 270.42 'And naturally, to match' to p. 271.22 'stores. Birmingham will'.

MS C: British Library, Department of Printed Books, C. 61. a. 2. The manuscript is an interleaved set of page proofs from *F*. It corresponds to the text below running from p. 269.1 'FEW people need to be told' to p. 276.27 'sovereign, into that far', with those variants from *SGG* running from p. 696, 269.3 'so ubiquitous, so ancient,' to p. 701, 276.27 'in a Council Chamber with'. At this point the manuscript breaks off and there is a gap of four pages (in *F*, pp. 205–8). The manuscript then recommences and corresponds to the passage below running from p. 278.26 '*caused* a war by pulling' to p. 288.25 'reproaches to his humanity.', with those variants from *SGG* running from p. 702, 278.27–8 'and prolonged it, was sure' to p. 706, 288.26–34 'Meantime…who (like myself) deny it.'.

MS D: Berg Collection, New York Public Library. The manuscript is two pages of *SGG* page proof, and corresponds to the text below running from p. 277.22 'an occasion for a cause.' to p. 278.30 'at the utmost have', with those variants from *SGG* running from p. 701, 277.22 'occasion for' to p. 702, 278.30 'they at the utmost might'.

MS E: British Library, Department of Printed Books, C. 60. o. 3. The manuscript is thirteen pages: the first twelve are *SGG* page proofs, and the thirteenth is an interleaved, handwritten *SGG* footnote. The page proof section begins immediately following where MS D ends, and corresponds to the text below running from p. 278.30 'have claimed a distinction' to p. 288.25 'reproaches to his humanity.', with those variants from *SGG* running from p. 702, 278.31 'the captain of a gun' to p. 706, 288.26–34 'What opening...war will no longer'. The final handwritten sheet contains the *SGG* footnote beginning p. 703, 283.21 *'Spartan warfare:'*.

MS F: Berg Collection, New York Public Library. The manuscript is a single page of *SGG* page proof, and begins immediately following where the page proof section of MS E ends. It corresponds to the text below running from p. 706, 288.26–34 'be tolerated by those who pay' to 'something very much worse.'.

MSS B through F contain nearly one hundred and fifty significant variants, and these are listed in the textual notes.

Macphail's Edinburgh Ecclesiastical Journal and Literary Review was founded in 1846 by the Scottish publisher Myles Macphail. It had religious affiliations from the outset, and became known as an unofficial voice of the established Church of Scotland, then embroiled in the debates that had led to the Disruption of 1843, and the formation of the Free Church of Scotland (see Vol. 15, pp. 3–32). The essay is De Quincey's sole contribution to *Macphail's*, which, in 1848, was edited by Peter Landreth, who recalled the circumstances of composition:

> De Quincey said that he was closing – what had been a dull task – an article on that commonplace subject, "War;" and he was writing what, unfortunately, had not been bespoken, – what, perhaps, no journal would buy, and yet he needed the money.

When De Quincey showed the essay to the Scottish chemist and author Samuel Brown (1817–56; *DNB*), however, Brown described it as 'Capital!' He promptly offered 'to dispose of [it] to a magazine' and bring De Quincey the '*honorarium*', an arrangement to which 'De Quincey readily consented'. Brown returned the next day with De Quincey's payment, and the article duly appeared as 'the opening one...of an ecclesiastical journal'. Yet despite the enthusiasm of its supporters, *Macphail's* popular appeal was limited, and it did not play a major role in the controversy over the Free Church of Scotland, or in the more broadly defined theological debates of the day. It attracted even smaller audiences in the 1850s, and folded in 1863 (Josef L. Altholz, *The Religious Press in Britain, 1760–1900* (Westport, Conn.: Greenwood, 1989), pp. 90–1; Emerson, *JMN*, vol. X, p. 223; Peter Landreth, 'Emerson's meeting with De Quincey' in *Blackwood's*, 155 (1894), p. 487).

When De Quincey revised the present essay in 1854 he changed the title to 'On War', and added a long prefatory discussion in which he considered Peace Societies, 'merciful bloodshed', 'Wordsworth's bold doctrine upon war', and the childish state of the French with regard to 'every possible question that connects itself at any point with martial pretensions' (see Vol. 20, pp. 31–3).

FEW people need to be told – that associations exist up and down Christendom having the ambitious object of abolishing war.[1] Some go so far as to believe that this evil of war, so ubiquitous, so ancient, and apparently so inalienable from man's position upon earth, is already doomed; that not the private associations only but the prevailing voice of races the most highly civilised, may be looked on as tending to confederation against it; that sentence of extermination has virtually gone forth, and that all which remains is gradually to execute that sentence. Conscientiously I find myself unable to join in these views. The project seems to me the most romantic of all romances in the course of publication. Consequently, when asked to become a member in any such association, I have always thought it most respectful, because most sincere, to decline. Yet, as it is painful to refuse all marks of sympathy with persons whose motives one honours, I design at my death to bequeath half a crown to the chief association for extinguishing war; the said half-crown to be improved in all time coming for the benefit of the association, under the trusteeship of Europe, Asia, and America, but not of Africa. I really dare not trust Africa with money, she is not able as yet to take care of herself. This half-crown, a fund that will overshadow the earth before it comes to be wanted under the provisions of my will, is to be improved at any interest whatever – no matter what; for the vast period of the accumulations will easily make good any tardiness of advance, long before the time comes for its commencing payment; a point which will be soon understood from the following explanation, by any gentleman that hopes to draw upon it.

There is in Ceylon a granite *cippus*, or monumental pillar, of immemorial antiquity; and to this pillar a remarkable legend is attached.[2] The pillar measures six feet by six, *i.e.* 36 square feet, on the flat tablet of its horizontal surface; and in height several *riyanas*, (which are Ceylonese cubits of 18 inches each,) but of these cubits, there are either 8 or 12; excuse me for having forgotten which. At first, perhaps you will be angry, viz., when you hear that this simple difference of 4 cubits, or six feet, measures a difference for your expectations, whether you count your expectations in kicks or halfpence, that absolutely strikes horror into arithmetic. The singularity of the case is, that the very solemnity of the legend and the wealth of the human race in time, depend upon the cubical contents of the monument, so that a loss of one granite chip is a loss of a frightful infinity; yet, again, for that very reason, the loss of all *but* a chip, leaves behind riches so appallingly too rich, that everybody is careless about the 4 cubits. Enough is as good as a feast. Two bottomless abysses take as much time for the diver as ten; and five eternities are as frightful to look down as four-and-twenty. In the Ceylon legend all turns upon the inexhaustible series of ages which this pillar guarantees. But, as one inexhaustible is quite enough for one race of men, and you are sure of more by ineffable excess than you can use in any private consumption of your own, you become generous; 'and between friends,' you say, in accepting my apologies for the doubtful error as to the 4 cubits, 'what signifies an infinity more or less?'

For the Ceylonese legend is this, that once in every hundred years an angel visits this granite pillar. He is dressed in a robe of white muslin, muslin of that kind which the Romans called *aura textilis*[3] – woven, as might seem, from zephyrs or from pulses of the air, such in its transparency, such in its gossamer lightness. Does the angel touch the pillar with his foot? Oh no! Even *that* would be something, but even *that* is not allowed. In his soundless flight across it, he suffers the hem of his impalpable robe to sweep the surface as softly as a moonbeam. So much and no more of pollution he endures from contact with earthly objects. The lowest extremity of his dress, but with the delicacy of light, grazes the granite surface. And *that* is all the attrition which the sacred granite receives in the course of any one century, and this is all the progress which we, the poor children of earth, in any one century make towards the exhaustion of our earthly imprisonment. But, argues the subtle legend, even *that* attrition, when weighed in metaphysical scales, cannot be denied its value; it has detached from the pillar an atom (no matter that it is an invisible atom) of granite dust, the ratio of which atom to a grain avoirdupois,[4] if expressed as a fraction of unity, would by its denominator stretch from the Accountant-General's office in London to the Milky Way. Now the total mass of the granite represents, on this scheme of payment, the total funded debt of man's race to Father Time and earthly corruption; all this intolerable score, chalked up to our debit, we by ourselves and our representatives have to rub off, before the granite will be rubbed away by the muslin robe of the proud flying angel, (who, if he were a good fellow, might just as well give a sly kick with his heel to the granite,) before time will be at an end, and the burden of flesh accomplished. But you hear it expressed in terms that will astonish Baron Rothschild,[5] what is the progress in liquidation which we make for each particular century. A billion of centuries pays off a quantity equal to a pinch of snuff. Despair seizes a man in contemplating a single *coupon*, no bigger than a visiting card, of such a stock as this; and behold we have to keep on paying away until the total granite is reduced to a level with a grain of mustard seed. But when that is accomplished, thank heaven, our last generation of descendants will be entitled to leave at Master Time's door a visiting card, which the meagre shadow cannot refuse to take, though he will sicken at seeing it; viz., a P. P. C.[6] card, upon seeing which, the old thief is bound to give receipt in full for all debts and pretended arrears.

The reader perhaps knows of debts on both sides the Atlantic that have no great prospect of being paid off sooner than this in Ceylon.

And naturally, to match this order of debts, moving off so slowly, there are funds that accumulate as slowly. My own funded half-crown is an illustration. The half-crown will travel in the inverse order of the granite pillar. The pillar and the half-crown move upon opposite tacks; and there *is* a point of time, (which it is for Algebra to investigate) when they will cross each other in the exact moment of their several bisections – my aspiring half-crown tending gradually towards the fixed stars, so that perhaps it might be right to make the man in the moon trustee for that part of the accumulations which rises above the optics of sublunary bankers; whilst the Ceylon pillar is constantly unweaving its own granite texture, and dwindling earthwards. It is probable that each of the parties will have reached its consummation about the same time. What is to be done with the mustard seed, Ceylon has forgotten to say. But what is to be done with the half crown and its surplus, no body can doubt after reading my last will and testament. After reciting a few inconsiderable legacies to the three continents, and to the man in the moon, for any trouble they may have had in managing the hyperbolical accumulations, I go on to observe, that, when war is reported to have taken itself off for ever, 'and no mistake,' (because I foresee many false alarms of a perpetual peace,)[7] a variety of inconveniences will arise to all branches of the United Service, including the Horse Marines. Clearly there can be no more half-pay; and even more clearly, there is an end to full-pay. Pensions are at an end for 'good service.' Allowances for wounds cannot be thought of, when all wounds shall have ceased except those from female eyes – for which the Horse Guards is too little advanced in civilization to make any allowance at all. Bargains there will be no more amongst auctions of old Government stores. Birmingham will be ruined, or so much of it, as depended on rifles.[8] And the great Scotch works on the river Carron will be hungering for beef, so far as Carron depended for beef upon carronades.[9] Other arrears of evil will stretch after the extinction of war.

Now upon my half-crown fund (which will be equal to any thing by the time it is wanted) I charge once and for ever the general relief of all these arrears – of the poverty, the loss, the bankruptcy, arising by reason of this *quietus* or final extinction applied to war. I charge the fund with a perpetual allowance of half-pay to all the armies of earth; or indeed, whilst my hand is in, I charge it with *full*-pay. And I strictly enjoin upon my trustees and executors, but especially upon the man in the moon, if his unsocial lip has left him one spark of gentlemanly feeling, that he and they shall construe all claims liberally; nay, with that riotous liberality which is safe and becoming, when applied to a fund so inexhaustible. Yes, reader, my fund will be inexhaustible, because the period of its growth will be measured by the concurrent deposition of the Ceylon mustard-seed from the everlasting pillar.

Yet why, or on what principle? It is because I see, or imagine that I see, a twofold necessity for war – a necessity in two different senses – 1st, a physical necessity arising out of man's nature when combined with man's situation; a necessity under which war may be regarded, if you please, as a nuisance, but as a nuisance inalienable from circumstances essential to human frailty. 2dly, a moral necessity connected with benefits of compensation, such as continually lurk in evils acknowledged to be such – a necessity under which it becomes lawful to say, that war *ought* to exist as a balance to opposite tendencies of a still more evil character. War is the mother of wrong and spoliation; war is a scourge of God – granted: but, like other scourges in the divine economy, war purifies and redeems itself in its character of a counterforce to greater evils that could not otherwise be intercepted or redressed. In two different meanings we say that a thing is necessary; either in that case where it is inexorably forced on by some sad overruling principle which it is vain to fight against, though all good men mourn over its existence and view it as an unconditional evil; or secondly, in that case, where an instrument of sorrowful consequences to man is nevertheless invoked and postulated by man's highest moral interests, is nevertheless clamorously indicated as a blessing when looked at in relation to some antagonist cause of evil for which it offers the one only remedy or principle of palliation. The very evil and woe of man's condition upon earth may be oftentimes detected in the necessity of looking to some other woe as the pledge of its purification; so that what separately would have been hateful for itself, passes mysteriously into an object of toleration, of hope, or even of prayer, as a counter-venom to the taint of some more mortal poison. Poverty, for instance, is in both senses necessary for man.[10] It is necessary in the same sense as thirst is necessary (*i.e.* inevitable) in a fever – necessary as one corollary amongst many others, from the eternal hollowness of all human efforts for organizing any perfect model of society – a corollary which, how gladly would all of us unite to cancel, but which our hearts suggest, which Scripture solemnly proclaims, to be ineradicable from the land.[11] In this sense, poverty is a necessity over which we *mourn*, – as one of the dark phases that sadden the vision of human life. But far differently, and with a stern gratitude, we recognise another mode of necessity for this gloomy distinction – a call for poverty, when seen in relation to the manifold agencies by which it developes human energies, in relation to the trials by which it searches the power of patience and religion, in relation to the struggles by which it evokes the nobilities of fortitude; or again, amongst those who are not sharers in these trials and struggles, but sympathizing spectators, in relation to the stimulation by which it quickens wisdom that watches over the causes of this evil, or by which it vivifies the spirit of love that labours for its mitigation. War stands, or seems to stand, upon the same double basis of necessity; a primary necessity that belongs to our human degradations, a secondary one that towers by means of its moral relations into the region of our impassioned exaltations. The two propositions on which I take my stand are these. *First*, that there are no where latent in society any powers by which it can effectually operate on war for its extermination. The machinery is not there. The game is not within the compass of the cards. *Secondly*, that this defect of power is, though sincerely I grieve in avowing such a sentiment, and perhaps, (if an infirm reader had his eye upon me) I might seem, in sympathy with his weakness, to blush – not a curse, no not at all, but on the whole a blessing from century to century, if it is an inconvenience from year to year. The Abolition Committees, it is to be feared, will be very angry at both propositions. Yet, gentlemen, hear me – strike, but hear me. I believe that's a sort of plagiarism from Themistocles.[12] But never mind. I have as good a right to the words, until translated back into Greek, as that most classical of yellow admirals. '*Pereant qui ante nos nostra dixerunt!*'[13]

The first proposition is, that war *cannot* be abolished. The second, and more offensive – that war *ought* not to be abolished. First, therefore, concerning the first. One at a time. Sufficient for the page is the evil thereof! How came it into any man's heart, first of all, to conceive so audacious an idea as that of a conspiracy against war? Whence could he draw any vapour of hope to sustain his preliminary steps? And in framing his plot, which way did he set his face to look out for accomplices? Revolving this question in times past, I came to the conclusion – that, perhaps, this colossal project of a war against war, had been first put in motion under a misconception (natural enough, and countenanced by innumerable books,) as to the true historical origin of wars in many notorious instances. If these had arisen on trivial impulses, a trivial resistance might have intercepted them. If a man has once persuaded himself, that long, costly, and bloody wars had arisen upon a point of ceremony, upon a personal pique, upon a hasty word, upon some explosion of momentary caprice; it is a natural inference, that strength of national will and public combinations for resistance, supposing such forces to have been trained, organized, and from the circumstances of the particular nation, to be permanently disposable for action, might prove redundantly effective, when pointed against a few personal authors of war, so presumably weak, and so flexible to any stern countervolition as those *must* be supposed, whose wars argued so much of vicious levity. The inference is unexceptionable: it is the premises that are unsound. Anecdotes of war as having emanated from a lady's tea-table or toilette would authorize such inference as to the facilities of controling them. But the anecdotes themselves are false, or false substantially. *All* anecdotes, I fear, are false. I am sorry to say so, but my duty to the reader extorts from me the disagreeable confession, as upon a matter specially investigated by myself, that all dealers in anecdotes are tainted with mendacity. Where is the Scotchman, said Dr Johnson, who does not prefer Scotland to truth?[14] but, however this may be, rarer than such a Scotchman, rarer than the phoenix, is that virtuous man, a monster he is, nay, he is an impossible man, who will consent to lose a prosperous anecdote on the consideration that it happens to be a lie. All history, therefore, being built partly, and some of it altogether upon anecdotage, must be a tissue of lies. Such, for the most part, is the history of Suetonius, who may be esteemed the father of anecdotage; and being such he (and not Herodotus) should have been honoured with the title, *Father of lies*.[15] Such is the Augustan history, which is all that remains of the Roman empire: such is the vast series of French memoirs,[16] now stretching through more than three entire centuries. Are these works then to be held cheap, because their truths to their falsehoods are in the ratio of one to five hundred? On the contrary, they are better and more to be esteemed on that account; because *now* they are admirable reading on a winter's night; whereas written on the principle of sticking to the truth, they would have been as dull as ditch water. Generally, therefore, the dealers in anecdotage are to be viewed with admiration as patriotic citizens, willing to sacrifice their own characters, lest their countrymen should find themselves short of amusement. I esteem them as equal to Codrus, Timoleon, William Tell, or to Milton,[17] as regards the liberty of unlicensed printing. And I object to them only in the exceptional case of their being cited as authorities for an inference, or as vouchers for a fact. Universally it may be received as a rule of unlimited application, – that when an anecdote involves a stinging repartee or collision of ideas, fancifully and brilliantly related to each other by resemblance or contrast, then you may challenge it as false to a certainty. One illustration of which is, – that pretty nearly every memorable *propos*, or pointed repartee, or striking *mot*,[18] circulating at this moment in Paris or London, as the undoubted property of Talleyrand (that eminent knave) was ascribed at Vienna, 90 years ago, to the Prince de Ligne, and 30 years previously to Voltaire,[19] and so on, regressively to many other wits (knaves or not;) until, at length, if you persist in backing far enough, you find yourself amongst Pagans, with the very same repartee, &c. doing duty in pretty good Greek;[*] sometimes, for instance, in Hierocles, sometimes in Diogenes Laertius, in Plutarch, or in Athenaeus.[25] Now the thing you know claimed by so many people, could not belong to all of them: *all* of them could not be the inventors. Logic and common sense unite in

[*] This is *literally* true, more frequently than would be supposed. For instance, a jest often ascribed to Voltaire, and of late pointedly reclaimed for him by Lord Brougham,[20] as being one that he (Lord B.) could swear to for *his*, so characteristic seemed the impression of Voltaire's mind upon the *tournure*[21] of the sarcasm, unhappily for this waste of sagacity, may be found recorded by Fabricius[22] in the *Bibliotheca Graeca*, as the jest of a Greek who has been dead for about seventeen centuries. The man certainly *did* utter the jest; and 1750 years ago. But who it was that he stole it from is another question. To all appearance, and according to Lord Brougham's opinion, the party robbed must have been M. de Voltaire. I notice the case, however, of the Greek thefts and frauds committed upon so many of our excellent wits belonging to the 18th and 19th centuries, chiefly with a view to M. de Talleyrand – that rather middling bishop, but very eminent knave. He also has been extensively robbed by the Greeks of the 2d and 3d centuries. How else can you account for so many of his sayings being found amongst *their* pages? A thing you may ascertain in a moment, at any police office, by having the Greeks searched: for surely you would never think of searching a bishop. Most of the Talleyrand jewels will be found concealed amongst the goods of these unprincipled Greeks. But one, and the most famous in the whole jewel-case, sorry am I to confess, was nearly stolen from the Bishop, not by any Greek, but by an English writer, viz. Goldsmith, who must have been dying about the time that his Excellency, the diplomatist, had the goodness to be born.[23] That famous *mot* about language, as a gift made to man for the purpose of *concealing* his thoughts, is lurking in Goldsmith's Essays.[24] Think of *that!* Already, in his innocent childhood, whilst the Bishop was in petticoats, and almost before he had begun to curse and to swear plainly in French, an Irish vagabond had attempted to swindle him out of that famous witticism which has since been as good as a life-annuity to the venerable knave's literary fame.

showing us, that it must have belonged to the moderns, who had clearly been hustled and robbed by the ancients, so much more likely to commit a robbery than Christians, they being all Gentiles – Pagans – Heathen dogs. What do I infer from this? Why, that upon *any* solution of the case, hardly one worthy saying can be mentioned, hardly one jest, pun, or sarcasm, which has not been the occasion and subject of many falsehoods – as having been *au- (and men) - daciously* transferred from generation to generation, sworn to in every age as this man's property, or that man's, by people that must have known they were lying, until you retire from the investigation with a conviction, that under any system of chronology the science of lying is the only one that has never drooped. Date from *Anno Domini*, or from the Julian era, patronize Olympiads,[26] or patronize (as *I* do, from misanthropy, because nobody else *will*) the era of Nabonassar,[27] – no matter, upon every road, thicker than mile-stones, you see records of human mendacity, or – (which is much worse in my opinion) of human sympathy with other people's mendacity.

This digression now on anecdotes[*] is what the learned call an *excursus*, and I am afraid too long by half; not strictly in proportion. But don't mind *that*. I'll make it all right by being too short upon something else at the next opportunity: and then nobody can complain. Meantime, I argue that, as all brilliant or epigrammatic anecdotes are probably false, (a thing that hereafter I shall have much pleasure in making out to the angry reader's satisfaction,) but to a dead certainty those anecdotes in particular which bear marks in their construction that a rhetorical effect of art had been contemplated by the narrator, – we may take for granted, that the current stories ascribing modern wars (French or English) to accidents the most inconsiderable, are false even in a literal sense: but at all events they are so when valued philosophically, and brought out into their circumstantial relations. For instance, we have a French anecdote, from the latter part of the 17th century, which ascribes one bloody war to the accident of a little 'miff,' arising between the king and his minister upon some such trifle as the situation of a palace window. Again, from the early part of the 18th century, we have an English anecdote, ascribing consequences no less bloody to a sudden feud between two ladies, and that feud, (if

[*] The word 'Anecdotes,' first, I believe, came into currency about the middle of the 6th century, from the use made of it by Procopius.[28] *Literally* it indicated nothing that could interest either public malice or public favour: it promised only *unpublished* notices of the Emperor Justinian, his wife Theodora, Narses, Belisarius,[29] &c. But *why* had they been unpublished? Simply because scandalous and defamatory: and hence, from the interest which invested the case of an imperial court so remarkable, this oblique, secondary and purely accidental modification of the word came to influence its *general* acceptation. Simply to have been previously unpublished, no longer raised any statement into an anecdote: it now received a new integration – it must be some fresh publication of *personal* memorabilia; and these having references to *human* creatures, must always be presumed to involve more evil than good – much defamation – true or false – much doubtful insinuation – much suggestion of things worse than could be openly affirmed. So arose the word: but the *thing* arose with Suetonius, that dear, excellent and hard-working 'father of lies.'

I remember) tracing itself up to a pair of gloves; so that in effect the war and the gloves form the two poles of the transaction. Harlequin throws a pair of Limerick gloves into a corn-mill; and the spectator is astonished to see the gloves immediately issuing from the hopper, well-ground into seven armies of 100,000 men each, and with parks of artillery to correspond.[30] In these two anecdotes we recognize at once the able and industrious artist arranging his materials with a pious regard to theatrical effect. This man knows how to group his figures; well he understands where to plant his masses of light and shade; and what impertinence it would be in us spectators, the reader suppose and myself, to go behind the scenes for critical inquiry into day-light realities. All reasonable men see that, the less of such realities our artist had to work with, the more was his merit. I am one of those that detest all insidious attempts to rob men situated as this artist of their fair fame, by going about and whispering that perhaps the thing is true. Far from it! I sympathise with the poor trembling artist, and agree most cordially that the whole story is a lie; and he may rely upon my support at all times to the extent of denying that any vestige of truth probably lay at the foundations of his ingenious apologue. And what I say of the English fable, I am willing to say of the French one. Both, I dare say, were the rankest fictions. But next, what after all if they were *not?* For in the rear of all discussion upon anecdotes, considered simply as true or *not* true, comes finally a *valuation* of those anecdotes in their moral relation, and as to the inferences which they will sustain. The story, for example, of the French minister Louvois, and the adroitness with which he fastened upon great foreign potentates, in the shape of war, that irritability of temper in his royal master[31] which threatened to consume himself; the diplomatic address with which he transmuted suddenly a task so delicate as that of skirmishing daily in a Council Chamber with his own sovereign, into that far jollier mode of disputation where one replies to all objections of the very keenest logician, either with round shot or with grape; here is an anecdote, which (for my own part) I am inclined to view as pure gasconade. But suppose the story true, still it may happen that a better valuation of it may disturb the whole edifice of logical inferences by which it seemed to favour the speculations of the war-abolitionists. Let us see. What *was* the logic through which such a tale as this could lend any countenance to the schemes of these abolitionists? That logic travelled in the following channel. Such a tale, or the English tale of the gloves, being supposed true, it would seem to follow that war and the purposes of war were phenomena of chance growth, not attached to any instinct so ancient, and apparently so grooved into the dark necessities of our nature, as we had all taken for granted. Usually we rank war with hunger, with cold, with sorrow, with death, afflictions of our human state that spring up as inevitably without separate culture and in defiance of all hostile culture, as verdure, as weeds, and as flowers that overspread in spring-time a fertile soil without needing to be sown or watered – awful is the necessity, as it seems, of all such afflictions. Yet, again, if (as these anecdotes imply) war could by possibility depend frequently on accidents of personal temperament, irritability in a sensual king, wounded sensibilities of pride between two sensitive ladies, there in a moment shone forth a light of hope upon the crusade against war.

If *personal* accidents could, to any serious extent, be amongst the causes of war, then it would become a hopeful duty to combine personal influences that should take an opposite direction. If casual causes could be supposed chiefly to have promoted war, how easy for a nation to arrange permanent and determinate causes against it! The logic of these anecdotes seemed to argue that the whole fountains of war were left to the government of chance and the windiest of levities; that war was not in reality roused into activity by the evil that resides in the human will, but on the contrary, by the simple defect of any will energetic enough or steady enough to merit that name. Multitudes of evils exist in our social system, simply because no steadiness of attention, nor action of combined will, has been converged upon them. War, by the silent evidence of these anecdotes, seemed to lie amongst that class of evils. A new era might be expected to commence in new views upon war; and the evil would be half conquered from the moment that it should be traced to a trivial or a personal origin.

All this was plausible, but false. The anecdotes, and all similar anecdotes, might be true, but were delusive. The logical vice in them was – that they substituted an occasion for a cause. The king's ill temper for instance, acting through the levity and impatience of the minister, might be the *causa occasionalis* of the war, but not its true *causa efficiens*. What *was?* Where do the true permanent causes of war, as distinguished from its proximate excitements, find their lodgment and abiding ground? They lie in the system of national competitions; in the common political system to which all individual nations are unavoidably parties; in the system of public forces distributed amongst a number of adjacent nations, with no internal principle for adjusting the equilibrium of these forces, and no supreme *Areopagus*,[32] or court of appeal, for deciding disputes. Here lies the *matrix* of war, because an eternal *matrix* of disputes lies in a system of interests that are continually the same, and therefore the parents of rivalships too close, that are continually different, and so far the parents of alienation too wide. All war is an instinctive *nisus*[33] for redressing the errors of equilibrium in the relative position of nations amongst nations. Every nation's duty, first, midst, and last, is to itself. No nation can be safe from continual (because insensible) losses of ground, but by continual jealousies, watchings, and ambitious strivings to mend its own position. Civilities and high-bred courtesies pass and ought to pass between nations; *that* is the graceful drapery which shrouds their natural, fierce, and tiger-like relations to each other. But the glaring eyes, which express this deep and inalienable ferocity, look out at intervals from below these gorgeous draperies; and sad it is to think that at intervals the acts and the temper suitable to those glaring eyes *must* come forward. Mr Carter[34] was on terms of the most exquisite dissimulation with his lions and tigers; but, as often as he trusted his person amongst them, if, in the midst of infinite politeness exchanged on all sides, he saw a certain portentous expression of mutiny kindling in the eye-ball of any discontented tiger, all was lost, unless he came down instantly upon that tiger's skull with a blow from an iron bar, that suggested something like apoplexy. On such terms do nations meet in diplomacy; high consideration for each other does not conceal the basis of enmity on which they rest; not an enmity that belongs to their feelings, but to the necessities of their position. Every nation in negociating has its right hand upon the hilt of its sword, and at intervals playfully unsheaths a little of its gleaming blade. As things stand at present, war and peace are bound together like the vicissitudes of day and night, of Castor and Pollux.[35] It matters little which bucket of the two is going up at the moment, which going down. Both are steadfastly tied by a system of alternations to a revolving wheel; and a new war as certainly becomes due during the evolutions of a tedious peace, as a new peace may be relied on during the throes of a bloody war, to tranquillize its wounds. Consequently, when the arrogant Louvois carried a war to the credit of his own little account on the national ledger of France, this coxcomb well knew that a war was at any rate due about that time. Really, says he, I must find out some little war to exhaust the *surplus* irritability of this person, or he'll be the death of me. But irritable or not irritable, with a puppy for his minister or not, the French king would naturally have been carried headlong into war by the mere system of Europe, within a very few months. So much had the causes of complaint reciprocally accumulated. The account must be cleansed, the court roll of grievances must be purged. With respect to the two English ladies again, it is still more evident that they could not have *caused* a war by pulling caps with each other, since the grounds of every war, what had caused it, and prolonged it, was sure to be angrily reviewed by Parliament at each annual exposition of the Finance Minister's Budget. These ladies, and the French coxcomb, could at the utmost have claimed a distinction – such as that which belonged to a particular Turkish gunner, the captain of a gun at Navarino,[36] viz., that he, by firing the first shot without orders, did (as a matter of fact) let loose and unmuzzle the whole of that dreadful iron hurricane from four nations which instantly followed, but which (be it known to the gunner) could not have been delayed for fifty minutes longer, whether he had fired the unauthorised gun or not.

But now, let me speak to the second proposition of my two-headed thesis, viz., that war *ought* not to be abolished, if such an abolition were even possible. *Primâ facie,*[37] it seems a dreadful doctrine to claim a place for war as amongst the evils that are salutary to man; but conscientiously I hold it to be such. I hold with Wordsworth, but for reasons which may or may not be the same, since he has not stated *his* –

'That God's most dreaded instrument
In working out a pure intent,
Is man – array'd for mutual slaughter:
Yea, Carnage is his daughter.'[38]

I am obliged to hold, that supposing so romantic a condition realised as the cessation of war, this change, unless other evils were previously abolished, or neutralized in a way still more romantic to suppose, would not be for the welfare of human nature, but would tend to its rapid degradation.

One, in fact, of the earliest aspects under which this moral necessity for war forces itself upon our notice, is its physical necessity. I mean to say that one of the earliest reasons why war *ought* to exist, is because under any mode of suppressing war, virtually it *will* exist. Banish war as now administered, and it will revolve upon us in a worse shape, that is, in a shape of predatory and ruffian war, more and more licentious, as it enjoys no privilege or sufferance, by the supposition, under the national laws. Will the causes of war die away because war is forbidden? Certainly not; and the only result of the prohibition would be to throw back the exercise of war from national into private and mercenary hands; and *that* is precisely the retrograde or inverse course of civilization; for in the natural order of civilization, war passes from the hands of knights, barons, insulated cities, into those of the universal community. If again it is attempted to put down this lawless *guerrilla* state by national forces, then the result will be to have established an interminable warfare of a mixed character, private and public, civil and foreign, infesting the frontiers of all states like a fever, and in substitution for the occasional and intermitting wars of high national police, administered with the dignified responsibility that belongs to supreme rank, with the humanity that belongs to conscious power, and with the diminishing havock that belongs to increasing skill in the arts of destruction. Even as to this last feature in warfare, which in the war of brigands and *condottieri*[39] would for many reasons instantly decay, no reader can fail to be aware of the marvels effected by the forces of inventive science that run along side by side with the advances of civilization; look back even to the grandest period of the humane Roman warfare, listen to the noblest and most merciful of all Roman captains, saying on the day of Pharsalia (and saying of necessity) 'strike at their faces, cavalry,'[40] – yes, absolutely directing his own troopers to plough up with their sabres the blooming faces of the young Roman nobility: and then pass to a modern field of battle, where all is finished by musquetry and artillery amidst clouds of smoke, no soldier recognising his own desolations, or the ghastly ruin of his own right arm, so that war by losing all its brutality is losing half of its demoralization.

War, so far from ending, because war was forbidden and nationally renounced, on the contrary would transmigrate into a more fearful shape. As things are at present, (and, observe, they are always growing better,) what numbers of noble-minded men in the persons of our officers, (yes, and often of non-commissioned officers) do we British, for example, disperse over battle-fields, that could not dishonour their glorious uniform by any countenance to an act of cruelty! They are *eyes* delegated from the charities of our domestic life to overlook and curb the licence of war. I remember in Xenophon some passage where he describes a class of Persian gentlemen who were called the ὀφθαλμοι, or *eyes* of the king:[41] but for a very different purpose. These British officers may be called the *ophthalmoi* or eyes of our Sovereign Lady,[42] that into every corner of the battle carry their scrutiny, lest any cruelty should be committed on the helpless, or any advantage taken of a dying enemy. But mark, such officers would be rare in the irregular troops succeeding to the official armies. And through this channel, amongst others, war, when cried down by act of Parliament, and precisely *because* it was cried down, would become more perilously effective for the degradation of human nature. Being itself dishonoured, war would become the more effective as an instrument for the dishonouring of its agents. However, at length, we will suppose the impossible problem solved – war, we will assume, is at last put down.

At length there is no more war. Though by the way, let me whisper in your ear, (supposing you to be a Christian,) this would be a prelibation drawn prematurely from the cup of millennial happiness: and, strictly speaking, there is no great homage to religion, even thus far – in figuring *that* to be the purchase of man for himself, and through his own efforts, which is viewed by Scripture as a glory removed to the infinite and starry distance of a millennium, and as the τελευταιον ἐπιγεννημα,[43] the last crowning attainment of Christian truth, no longer *militant* on earth. Christianity it is, but Christianity when *triumphant*, and no longer in conflict with adverse, or thwarting, or limiting influences, which only can be equal to a revolution so mighty. But all this, for the sake of pursuing the assumption, let us agree to waive. In reality there are two separate stations taken up by the war-denouncers. One class hold, that an influence derived from political economy is quite equal to the flying leap by which man is to clear this unfathomable gulph of war, and to land his race for ever on the opposite shore of a self-sustaining peace. Simply, the contemplation of national debts,[44] (as a burthen which never would have existed without war,) and a computation of the waste, havock, unproductive labour, &c., attached to any single campaign – these, they imagine, might suffice *per se*, for the extinction of war. But the other class cannot go along with a speculation so infirm. Reasons there are in the opposite scale, tempting man into war – which are far mightier than any motives addressed to his self-interest. Even straining her energies to the utmost, they regard all policy of the *purse* as adequate: any thing short of religion, they are satisfied, must be incommensurate to a result so vast.

I myself certainly agree with this last class; but upon this arises a delusion, which I shall have some trouble in making the reader understand: and of this I am confident – that a majority, perhaps, in every given amount of readers will share in the delusion; will part from me in the persuasion that the error I attempt to expose is no error at all, but that it is myself who am in the wrong. The delusion which I challenge as such, respects the very meaning and value of a sacrifice made to Christianity. What is it, what do we properly mean, by a concession or a sacrifice made to a spiritual power, such as Christianity? If a king and his people, impressed by the unchristian character of war, were to say in some solemn act – 'We, the parties undersigned, for the reasons stated in the body of this document, proclaim to all nations that, from and after Midsummer eve of the year 1850, this being the eve of St John the Baptist, (who was the herald of Christ,)[45] we will no more prosecute any interest of ours, unless the one sole interest of national defence, by means of war – and this sacrifice we make as a concession and act of homage to Christianity' – would *that* vow, I ask, sincerely offered, and steadily observed, really be a sacrifice made to Christianity? Not at all. A sacrifice, that was truly such, to a spiritual religion, must be a sacrifice not verbally (though sincerely) dedicating itself to the religion, but a sacrifice wrought and accomplished by that religion, through and by its own spirit. Midsummer eve of 1850 could clearly make no spiritual change in the king or his people – such they would be on the morning after St John's day, as on the morning before it – *i.e.*, filled with all elements (though possibly undeveloped) of strife, feud, pernicious ambition.

The delusion, therefore, which I charge upon this religious class of war-denouncers is, that whilst they see and recognize this infinite imperfection of any influence which Christianity yet exercises upon the world, they nevertheless rely upon that acknowledged shadow for the accomplishment of what would, in such circumstances, be a real miracle; they rely upon that shadow, as truly and entirely as if it were already that substance which, in a vast revolution of ages, it will finally become. And they rely upon this mockery in *two* senses; first for the *endurance* of the frail human resolution that would thaw in an hour before a great outrage, or provocation suited to the nobler infirmities of man. Secondly, which is the point I mainly aim at, assuming, for a moment, that the resolution *could* endure, amongst all mankind, we are all equally convinced, that an evil so vast is not likely to be checked or controled, except by some very extraordinary power. Well, where *is* it? Show me that power. I know of none but Christianity. *There* undoubtedly is hope. But, in order that the hope may become rational, the power must become practical. And practi-

* *What* section, if you please? I, for my part, do not agree with those that geographically degrade Christianity as occupying but a trifle on the area of our earth. Mark this; all Eastern populations have dwindled upon better acquaintance. Persia that *ought* to have, at least, 250 millions of people, and *would* have them under English government, and once was supposed to have at least 100 millions, how many millions has she? *Eight!* This was ascertained by Napoleon's emissary in 1808, General Gardanne.[46] Afghanistan has very little more, though some falsely count 14 millions. There go two vast chambers of Mahometanism; not twenty millions between them. Hindostan may *really* have 120 millions claimed for her. As to the Burman Empire, I, nor any body else knows the truth. But, as to China, I have never for a moment been

cal it is not in the extent required, until this Christianity from being dimly appreciated by a section* of this world, shall have been the law that overrides the whole. That consummation is not immeasurably distant. Even now, from considerations connected with China, with New Zealand, Borneo, Australia, we may say, that already the fields are white for harvest.[50] But alas! the interval is brief between Christianity small, and Christianity great, as regards space or terraqueous importance, compared with that interval which separates Christianity formally professed, from Christianity thankfully acknowledged by universal man in beauty and power.

Here, therefore, is one spoke in the wheel for so vast a change as war dethroned, viz., that you see no cause, though you should travel round the whole horizon, adequate to so prodigious an effect. What could do it? Why, Christianity could do it. Aye, true; but man disarms Christianity. And no mock Christianity, no lip homage to Christianity, will answer.

But is war then to go on for ever? Are we never to improve! Are nations to conduct their intercourse eternally under the secret understanding that an unchristian solution of all irreconcileable feuds stands in the rear as the ultimate appeal? I answer that war, going on even for ever, may still be for ever amending its modes and its results upon human happiness – secondly, that we not only are under no fatal arrest in our process of improvement, but that, as regards war, history shows how steadily we *have* been improving – and thirdly, that although war may be irreversible as the last resource, this last resource may constantly be retiring further into the rear. Let us speak to this last point. War is the last resource only because other and more intellectual resources for solving disputes are not available. And *why* are they not? Simply because the knowledge, and the logic, which ultimately will govern the case, and the very circumstances of the case itself in its details, as the basis on which this knowledge and logic are to operate, happen not to have been sufficiently developed. A code of law is not a spasmodic effort of gigantic talent in any one man, or any one generation; it is a slow growth of accidents and occasions expanding with civilization; dependant upon time as a multiform element in its development; and presupposing often a concurrent growth of *analogous* cases towards the completion of its system. For instance, the law which regulates the rights of shipping, seafaring men, and maritime commerce – how slow was its development! Before such works as the *Consolato del Mare*[51] had been matured, how wide must have been the experience, and how slow its accumulation! During that long period of infancy for law, how many must have been the openings

---

moved by those ridiculous estimates of the flowery people,[47] which our simple countrymen copy. Instead of 350 millions, a third of the human race upon the most exaggerated estimate, read 80 or 100 millions at most. Africa, as it regards religion, counts for a cipher. Europe, America, and the half of Asia, as to space, are Christian. Consequently, the total *facit*,[48] as regards Christianity, is not what many amiable infidels make it to be. My dears, your wish was father to that thought.[49]

for ignorant and unintentional injustice! How differently again will the several parties to any transaction construe the rights of the case! Discussion, without rules for guiding it, will but embitter the dispute. And in the absence of all guidance from the intellect gradually weaving a *common* standard of international appeal, it is clear that nations *must* fight, and *ought* to fight. Not being convinced, it is base to pretend that you *are* convinced; and failing to be convinced by your neighbour's arguments, you confess yourself a poltroon (and moreover you *invite* injuries from every neighbour) if you pocket your wrongs. The only course in such a case is to thump your neighbour, and to thump him soundly, for the present. This treatment is very serviceable to your neighbour's optics; he sees things in a new light after a sufficient course of so distressing a regimen. But mark, even in this case war has no tendency to propagate war, but tends to the very opposite result. To thump is as costly, and in other ways as painful, as to *be* thumped. The evil to both sides arises in an undeveloped state of law. If rights were defined by a well considered code growing out of long experience, each party sees that this scourge of war would continually tend to limit itself. Consequently the very necessity of war becomes the strongest invitation to that system of judicial logic which forms its sole limitation. But all war whatsoever stands in those circumstances. It follows that all war whatever, unless on the brutal principle of a Spartan warfare[52] that made war its own sufficient object and self-justification, operates as a perpetual bounty offered to men upon the investigation and final adjudication of those disputed cases through which war prospers.

Hence it is, viz., because the true boundaries of reciprocal rights are for ever ascertaining themselves more clearly, that war is growing less frequent. The fields open to injustice (which originally from pure ignorance are so vast) continually (through deeper and more expansive surveys by man's intellect – searching – reflecting – comparing,) are narrowing themselves; narrowing themselves in this sense, that all nations under a common centre of religious civilization, as Christendom suppose, or Islamism, would not fight – no, and would not (by the national sense of wrong and right) be permitted to fight – in a cause *confessedly* condemned by equity as now developed. The causes of war that still remain, are causes on which international law is silent – that large arrear of cases as yet unsettled; or else they are cases in which though law speaks with an authentic voice, it speaks in vain, because the circumstances are doubtful; so that, if the law is fixed as a lamp nailed to a wall, yet the *incidence* of the law on the particular circumstances, becomes as doubtful as the light of the lamp upon objects that are capriciously moving. We see all this illustrated in a class of cases that powerfully illustrate the good and the bad in war, the why and the wherefore, as likewise the why *not*, and therefore I presume the wherefore *not;* and this class of cases belongs to the *lex vicinitatis*. In the Roman law this section makes a great figure. And speaking accurately, it makes a greater in our own. But the reason why this *law of neighbourhood* seems to fill so much smaller a section in ours, is because in English law, being *positively* a longer section, *negatively* to the whole compass of our law, it is less. The Roman law would have paved a road to the moon. And what is *that* expressed in time? Let us see: a railway train, worked at the speed of the Great Western Express,[53] accomplishes easily a thousand miles in 24 hours; consequently in 240 days or 8 months it would run into the moon with its buffers, and break up the quarters of that Robinson Crusoe who (and without any Friday) is the only policeman that parades that little pensive appendage or tender to our fuming engine of an earth.[54] But the English law – oh frightful reader, don't even think of such a question as its relation in space and time to the Roman law. That it would stretch to the fixed stars is plain, but to which of them, – don't now, dear persecuting reader, unsettle our brains by asking. Enough it is that both in Roman and English law the rights of neighbourhood are past measuring. Has a man a right to play the German flute, where the partitions are slender, all day long in the house adjoining to yours? Or, supposing a beneficent jury (beneficent to *him*) finds this to be no legal nuisance, has he a right to play it ill? Or, because juries, when tipsy, will wink at any thing, does the privilege extend to the Jew's harp? to the poker and tongs? to the marrowbones and cleavers? Or, without ranging through the whole of the *Spectator's* culinary music,[55] will the bagpipes be found within benefit of jury law? *War to the knife*[56] I say, before we'll submit to *that*. And if the law won't protect us against it, then we'll turn rebels.

Now this law of neighbourhood, this *lex vicinitatis*, amongst the Romans, righted itself and settled itself, as amongst ourselves it continues to do, by means of actions or legal suits. If a man poisons us with smoke, we compel him by an action to eat his own smoke, or (if he chooses) to make his chimnies eat it. Here you see is a transmuted war; in a barbarous state fire and sword would have avenged this invasion of smoke; but amongst civilised men, paper bullets in the form of *Qui tam* and *Scire facias*,[57] beat off the enemy. And on the same principle, exactly as the law of international rights clears up its dark places, war gradually narrows its grounds, and the *jus gentium*[58] defines itself through national attornies, *i.e.*, diplomatists.

For instance, now I have myself seen a case where a man cultivating a flower-garden, and distressed for some deliverance from his rubbish of dead leaves, litter, straw, stones, took the desperate resolution of projecting the whole upon his neighbour's flower-garden. I, a chance spectator of the outrage, knew too much of this world to lodge any protest against it, on the principle of mere abstract justice; so it would have passed unnoticed, but for the accident that his injured neighbour unexpectedly raised up his head above the dividing wall, and reproached the aggressor with his unprincipled conduct. This aggressor, adding evil to evil, suggested as the natural remedy for his own wrong, that the sufferer should pass the nuisance onwards to the garden next beyond him; from which it might be posted forward on the same principle. The aggrieved man, however, preferred passing it back, without any discount to the original proprietor. Here now, is a ripe case, a *causa teterrima*,[59] for war between the parties, and for a national war had the parties been nations. In fact, the very same injury, in a more aggravated shape, is perpetrated from time to time by Jersey upon ourselves, and would, upon a larger scale, right itself by war. Convicts are costly to maintain; and Jersey, whose national revenue is limited, being too well aware of this, does us the favour to land upon the coasts of Hampshire, Dorset, &c., all the criminals whom she cannot summarily send back to self-support, at each jail-delivery.[60] 'What are *we* do to in England?' is the natural question propounded by the injured scoundrels, when taking leave of their Jersey escort. 'Any thing you please,' is the answer: 'rise, if you can, to be dukes: only never come back hither; since, dukes or *no* dukes, to the rest of Christendom, to *us* of the Channel Islands you will always be transported felons.' There is therefore a good right of action, *i.e.* a good ground of war, against Jersey, on the part of Great Britain, since, besides the atrocious injury inflicted, this unprincipled little island has the audacity to regard our England, (all Europe looking on,) as existing only for the purposes of a sewer or cess-pool to receive *her* impurities. Some time back I remember a Scottish newspaper holding up the case as a newly discovered horror in the social system. But, in a quiet way Jersey has always been engaged in this branch of exportation, and rarely fails to 'run' a cargo of rogues upon our shore, once or so in the season. What amuses one besides, in this Scottish denunciation of the villainy, is, that Scotland* of old, pursued the very same mode of jail-delivery as to knaves that were not thought ripe enough for hanging: she carted them to the English border, unchained them, and hurried them adrift into the wilderness, saying – Now, boys, shift for yourselves, and henceforth plunder none but Englishmen.

What I deduce from all this is, that as the feuds arising between individuals under the relation of neighbours, are so far from tending to a hostile result, that, on the contrary, as coming under a rule of law already ascertained, or furnishing the basis for a new rule, they gradually tighten the cords which exclude all opening for quarrel; not otherwise is the result, and therefore the usefulness, of war amongst nations. All the causes of war, the occasions upon which it is likely to arise, the true and the ostensible motives, are gradually evolved, are examined, searched, valued, by publicists; and by such means, in the further progress of men, a comprehensive law of nations will finally be accumulated, not such as now passes for international law, (a worthless code that *has* no weight in the practice of nations, nor deserves any,) but one which will exhaust the great body of cases under which wars have arisen under the Christian era, and gradually collect a public opinion of Christendom upon the nature of each particular case. The causes that *have* existed for war are

* To banish them 'forth of the kingdom,' was the *euphuismus*;[61] but the reality understood was – to carry the knaves, like foxes in a bag, to the English soil, and there unbag them for English use.

the causes that *will* exist; or, at least, they are the same under modifications that will simply vary the rule, as our law-cases in the courts are every day circumstantiating the particular statute concerned. At this stage of advance, and when a true European opinion has been created, a '*sensus communis*,' or community of feeling on the main classifications of wars, it will become possible to erect a real Areopagus, or central congress for all Christendom, not with any commission to suppress wars, – a policy which would neutralize itself by re-acting as a fresh cause of war, since high-spirited nations would arm for the purpose of resisting such decrees; but with the purpose and the effect of oftentimes healing local or momentary animosities, and also by publishing the opinion of Europe, assembled in council, with the effect of taking away the shadow of dishonour from the act of retiring from war. Not to mention that the mere delay, involved in the waiting for the solemn opinion of congress, would always be friendly to pacific councils. But *would* the belligerents wait? That concession might be secured by general exchange of treaties, in the same way that the co-operation of so many nations has been secured to the suppression of the trade in slaves.[62] And one thing is clear, that when all the causes of war, involving *manifest* injustice, are banished by the force of European opinion, focally converged upon the subject, the range of war will be prodigiously circumscribed. The costliness of war, which, for various reasons has been continually increasing since the Feudal period, will operate as another limitation upon its field, concurring powerfully with the public declaration from a council of collective Christendom.

There is, besides, a distinct and separate cause of war, more fatal to the possibilities of peace in Europe than open injustice; and this cause being certainly in the hands of nations to deal with as they please, there is a tolerable certainty that a congress *sincerely* pacific would cut it up by the roots. It is a cause noticed by Kant in his Essay on Perpetual Peace,[63] and with great sagacity, though otherwise that little work is not free from visionary self-delusions: and this cause lies in the diplomacy of Europe. Treaties of peace are so constructed, as almost always to sow the seeds of future wars. This seems to the inexperienced reader a matter of carelessness or laxity in the choice of expression; and sometimes it may have been so; but more often it has been done under the secret dictation of powerful courts – making peaces only as truces, anxious only for time to nurse their energies, and to keep open some plausible call for war. This is not only amongst the most extensive causes of war, but the very worst: because it gives a colourable air of justice, and almost of necessity to a war, which is, in fact, the most outrageously unjust, as being derived from a pretext silently prepared in former years, with mere subtlety of malice: it is a war growing out of occasions, forged beforehand, lest no occasions should

[*] One great *nidus* of this insidious preparation for war under the very masque of peace, which Kant, from brevity, has failed to particularize, lies in the neglecting to make any provi-

spontaneously arise. Now, this cause of war could and would be healed by a congress, and through an easy reform in European diplomacy.*

It is the strongest confirmation of the power inherent in growing civilization, to amend war, and to narrow the field of war, if we look back for the records of the changes in this direction which have already arisen in generations before our own.

The most careless reviewer of history can hardly fail to read a rude outline of progress made by men in the rights and consequently in the duties of war through the last twenty-five centuries. It is a happy circumstance for man – that oftentimes he is led by pure selfishness into reforms, the very same as high principle would have prompted; and in the next stage of his advance, when once habituated to an improved code of usages, he begins to find a gratification to his sensibilities, (partly luxurious sensibilities, but partly moral) in what originally had been a mere movement of self-interest. Then comes a third stage, in which having thoroughly reconciled himself to a better order of things, and made it even necessary to his own comfort, at length he begins in his reflecting moments to perceive a moral beauty and a fitness in arrangements that had emanated from accidents of convenience, so that finally he generates a sublime pleasure of conscientiousness out of that which originally commenced in the meanest forms of mercenary convenience. A Roman lady of rank, out of mere voluptuous regard to her own comfort, revolted from the harsh clamours of eternal chastisements inflicted on her numerous slaves; she forbade them; the grateful slaves showed their love for her; gradually and unintentionally she trained her feelings, when thus liberated from a continual temptation to the sympathies with cruelty, into a demand for gentler and purer excitement. Her purpose had been one of luxury; but, by the benignity of nature still watching for ennobling opportunities, the actual result was a development given to the higher capacities of her heart. In the same way, when the brutal right (and in many circumstances the brutal duty) of inflicting death upon prisoners taken in battle, had exchanged itself for the profits of ransom or slavery, this relaxation of ferocity (though commencing in selfishness) gradually exalted itself into a habit of mildness, and some dim perception of a sanctity in human life. The very vice of avarice ministered to the purification of barbarism; and the very evil of slavery in its earliest form was applied to the mitigation of another evil – war conducted in the spirit of piratical outrage. The commercial instincts of men having worked one set of changes in war, a second set of changes was prompted by instincts derived from the arts of ornament and pomp. Splendour of arms, of banners, of equi-

sion for cases that are likely enough to arise. A, B, C, D, are all equally possible, but the treaty provides a specific course of action only for A, suppose. Then upon B or C arising, the high contracting parties, though desperately and equally pacific, find themselves committed to war actually by a treaty of lasting peace. Their pacific majesties sigh, and say – Alas! that it should be so, but really fight we must, for what says the treaty?

pages, of ceremonies, and the elaborate forms of intercourse with enemies through conferences, armistices, treatises of peace, &c., having tamed the savagery of war into connexion with modes of intellectual grandeur, and with the endless restraints of superstition or scrupulous religion, – a permanent light of civilisation began to steal over the bloody shambles of buccaneering warfare. Other modes of harmonizing influences arose more directly from the bosom of war itself. Gradually the mere practice of war, and the culture of war though merely viewed as a rude trade of bloodshed, ripened into an intellectual art. Were it merely with a view to more effectual carnage, this art (however simple and gross at first) opened at length into wide scientific arts, into strategies, into tactics, into castrametation, into poliorcetics,[64] and all the processes through which the first rude efforts of martial cunning finally connect themselves with the exquisite resources of science. War, being a game in which each side forces the other into the instant adoption of all improvements through the mere necessities of self-preservation, became continually more intellectual.

It is interesting to observe the steps by which, were it only through impulses of self-conservation, and when searching with a view to more effectual destructiveness, war did and must refine itself from a horrid trade of butchery into a magnificent and enlightened science. Starting from no higher impulse or question than how to cut throats most rapidly, most safely, and on the largest scale, it has issued even at our own stage of advance into a science, magnificent, oftentimes ennobling, and cleansed from all horrors except those which (not being within man's power utterly to divorce from it) no longer stand out as reproaches to his humanity.

Meantime a more circumstantial review of war, in relation to its motives and the causes assigned for its justification, would expose a series of changes greater perhaps than the reader is aware of. Such a review, which would too much lengthen a single paper, may or may not form the subject of a second.[65] And I will content myself with saying, as a closing remark, that this review will detect a principle of steady advance in the purification and elevation of war – such as must offer hope to those who believe in the possibility of its absolute extermination, and must offer consolation to those who (like myself) deny it.[66]

Article for the *Glasgow Athenaeum Album*, 1848

SORTILEGE ON BEHALF OF THE GLASGOW ATHENAEUM

First published in the *Glasgow Athenaeum Album* (Glasgow: James Hedderwick and son, 1848), pp. 9–31. The *Album* is 'respectfully Inscribed' to 'the Ladies of Glasgow, / The generous Patrons / Of every Scheme having the Enlightenment / And Moral Elevation of the Public / For its Aim'. The 'Preface', dated 'Glasgow, 18*th March*, 1848', notes that 'this little volume has been got up as a Contribution to the LADIES' BAZAAR, to be held on the 22d and 23d of this month, in aid of the LIBRARY of the GLASGOW ATHENAEUM' (pp. 3–5). 'Sortilege on Behalf of the Glasgow Athenaeum' was printed as 'BY THOMAS DE QUINCEY.' in a centred line following the title and immediately preceding the text. The essay opened the volume, and was dated 'FEB. 24, 1848'.

Reprinted in *SGG*, IX, *Leaders in Literature, with a Notice of Traditional Errors Affecting Them* (1858), pp. 261–83.

There is one manuscript, as follows:

MS A: Huntington Library, HM 36039. The manuscript is a complete set of *SGG* page proofs. It contains four significant variants, and these are listed in the textual notes.

Judson S. Lyon observes that the present essay shows De Quincey 'in his mood of free, relaxed, self-mocking burlesque. This piece contains the amusing description of his ceremonial random selection of a piece for publication from his chaotic bath-tub file, as well as ridiculous anecdotes and playful satire on astrology' (Judson S. Lyon, *Thomas De Quincey* (New York: Twayne, 1969), p. 149).

SUDDENLY, about the middle of February, I received a request for some contribution of my own proper writing to a meditated ALBUM of the Glasgow Athenaeum. What was to be done? The 13th of the month had already dawned before the request reached me; 'return of post' was the sharp limitation notified within which my communication must revolve; whilst the request itself was dated Feb. 10: so that already three 'returns of post' had finished their brief career on earth. I am not one of those people who, in respect to bread, insist on the discretionary allowance of Paris;[1] but, in respect to time, I *do*. Positively, for all efforts of thought I must have time *à discrétion*.[2] In this case, now, all *discretion* was out of the question; a mounted jockey, in the *melée* of a Newmarket start,[3] might as well demand time for meditation on the philosophy of racing. There was clearly no resource available but one; and it was this: – In my study I have a bath, large enough to swim in, provided the swimmer, not being an ambitious man, is content with going a-head to the extent of six inches at the utmost. This bath, having been superseded (as regards its original purpose) by another mode of bathing, has yielded a secondary service to me as a reservoir for my MSS. Filled to the brim it is by papers of all sorts and sizes. Every paper written *by* me, *to* me, *for* me, *of* or *concerning* me, and, finally, *against* me, is to be found, after an impossible search, in this capacious repertory. Those papers, by the way, that come under the last (or hostile) subdivision, are chiefly composed by shoemakers and tailors – an affectionate class of men, who stick by one to the last like pitch-plasters.[4] One admires this fidelity; but it shows itself too often in waspishness, and all the little nervous irritabilities of attachment too ardent. They are wretched if they do not continually hear what one is 'about,' what one is 'up to,' and which way one is going to travel. Me, because I am a political economist, they plague for my private opinions on the currency, especially on that part of it which consists in bills at two years after date; and they always want an answer by return of post. What the deuce! one can't answer *every*body by return of post. – Now, from this reservoir I resolved to draw some paper for the use of the Athenaeum. It was my fixed determination that this Institution should receive full justice, so far as human precautions could secure it. Four dips into the bath I decreed that the Athenaeum should have; whereas an individual man, however hyperbolically illustrious, could have had but one. On the other hand, the Athenaeum must really content itself with what fortune might send, and not murmur at me as if I had been playing with loaded dice. To cut off all pretence for this allegation, I requested the presence of three young ladies, haters of everything unfair, as female attorneys, to watch the proceedings on behalf of the Athenaeum, to see that the dipping went on correctly, and also to advise the court in case of any difficulties arising. At 6 p.m. all was reported right for starting in my study. The bath had been brilliantly illuminated from above, so that no tricks *could* be played in that quarter; and the young man who was to execute the dips had finished dressing in a new potato sack, with holes cut through the bottom for his legs. Now, as the sack was tied with distressing tightness about his throat, leaving only a loop-hole for his right arm to play freely, it is clear that however sincerely fraudulent in his intentions, and in possible collusion with myself, he could not assist me by secreting any papers about his person, or by any other knavery that we might wish to perpetrate. The young ladies having taken their seats in stations admirably chosen for overlooking the movements of the young man and myself, the proceedings opened. The inaugural step was made in a neat speech from myself, complaining that I was the object of unjust suspicions, and endeavouring to re-establish my character for absolute purity of intentions; but, I regret to say, ineffectually. This angered me, and I declared with some warmth that in the bath, but whereabouts I could not guess, there lay a particular paper which I valued as equal to the half of my kingdom; 'but for all that,' I went on, 'if our hon. friend in the potato sack should chance to haul up this very paper, I am resolved to stand by the event, yes, in that case, to the half of my kingdom I will express my interest in the Institution. Should even *that* prize be drawn, out of this house it shall pack off to Glasgow this very night.' Upon this, the leader of the attorneys, whom, out of honour to Shakspere, I may as well call Portia,[5] chilled my enthusiasm disagreeably by saying – 'There was no occasion for any extra zeal on *my* part in such an event, since, as to packing out of this house to Glasgow, she and her learned sisters would take good care that it *did;*' – in fact, *I* was to have no merit whatever I did. Upon this, by way of driving away the melancholy caused by the obstinate prejudices of the attorneys, I called for a glass of wine, and, turning to the west, I drank the health of the Athenaeum,[6] under the allegoric idea of a young lady about to come of age and enter upon the enjoyment of her estates. 'Here's to your prosperity, my dear lass,' I said; 'you're very young – but that's a fault which, according to the old Greek adage, is mending every day;[7] and I'm sure you'll always continue as amiable as you are now towards strangers in distress for books and journals. Never grow churlish, my dear, as some of your sex are' (saying which, I looked savagely at Portia). And then, I made the signal to the young man for getting to work – Portia's eyes, as I noticed privately, brightening like a hawk's. '*Prepare to dip!*' I called aloud; and soon after – '*Dip!*' At the '*prepare*,' Potato-sack went on his right knee (his face being at right angles to the bath); at the 'Dip!' he plunged his right arm into the billowy ocean of papers. For one minute he worked amongst them as if he had been pulling an oar; and then, at the peremptory order '*Haul up!*' he raised aloft in air, like Brutus refulgent from the stroke of Caesar,[8] his booty. It was handed, of course, to the attorneys, who showed a little female curiosity at first, for it was a letter with the seal as yet unbroken, and might prove to be some old love-letter of my writing,[9] recently sent back to me by the Dead-Letter Office. It still looked fresh and blooming. So, if there was no prize for Glasgow, there might still be an interesting secret for the benefit of the attorneys. What it was, and what each successive haul netted, I will register under the corresponding numbers.

No. 1. – This was a dinner invitation for the 15th of February, which I had neglected to open. It was, as bill-brokers say, 'coming to maturity,' but luckily not *past due* (in which case you have but a poor remedy), for, though twenty days after date, it had still two days to run before it could be presented for payment. A debate arose with the attorneys – Whether this might not do for the *Album*, in default of any better haul? I argued, for the affirmative, – that, although a dinner invitation cannot in reason be looked to for very showy writing, its motto being *Esse quam videri* (which is good Latin for – *To eat rather than make believe to eat*, as at ball suppers or Barmecide banquets),[10] yet, put the case that I should send this invitation to the Athenaeum, accompanied with a power-of-attorney to eat the dinner in my stead – might not *that* solid bonus as an enclosure weigh down the levity of the letter considered as a contribution to the *Album*, and take off the edge of the Athenaeum's displeasure? Portia argued *contra* – that such a thing was impossible; because the Athenaeum had 2,000 mouths, and would therefore require 2,000 dinners; – an argument which I admitted to be showy, but, legally speaking, hardly tenable: because the Athenaeum had power to appoint a plenipotentiary – some man of immense calibre – to eat the dinner, as representative of the collective 2,000. Portia parried this objection by replying, that if the invitation had been to a ball there might be something in what I said; but as to a mere dinner, and full fifty miles to travel for it from Glasgow, the plenipotentiary (whatever might be his calibre) would decline to work so hard for such a trifle. 'Trifle!' I replied – 'But, with submission, a dinner twenty-two days after date of invitation is not likely to prove a trifle. This, however, is always the way in which young ladies, whether attorneys or not, treat the subject of dinner. And as to the fifty miles, the plenipotentiary could go in an hour.' 'How?' said Portia, sternly. 'Per rail,' I replied with equal sternness. What there was to laugh at I don't see; but at this hot skirmish between me and Portia concerning that rather visionary person the plenipotentiary, and what he might choose to do in certain remote contingencies, and especially when the gross reality of '*per rail*' came into collision with his aerial essence, Potato-sack began to laugh so immoderately, that I was obliged to pull him up by giving the word rather imperiously – '*Prepare to dip!*' Before he could obey, I was myself pulled up by Portia, with a triumph in her eye that alarmed me. She and her sister attorneys had been examining the dinner invitation – 'and,' said Portia maliciously to me, 'it's quite correct – as you observe there are two days good to the dinner hour on the 15th; "*Prepare to dine!*" is the signal that *should* be flying at this moment, and in two days more "*Dine!*" – only, by misfortune, the letter is in the wrong year – it is four years old!' Oh! fancy the horror of this; since, besides the mortification from Portia's victory, I had perhaps narrowly escaped an indictment from the plenipotentiary for sending him what might *now* be considered a swindle. I hurried to cover my confusion, by issuing the two orders '*Prepare to dip!*' and '*Dip!*' almost in the same breath. No. 1, after all the waste of legal learning upon it, had suddenly burst like an air-bubble; and the greater stress of expectation, therefore, had now settled on No. 2. With considerable trepidation of voice, I gave the final order – '*Haul up!*'

No. 2. – It is disagreeable to mention that this haul brought up – 'a dun.'[11] Disgust was written upon every countenance; and I fear that suspicion began to thicken upon myself – as having possibly (from my personal experience in these waters) indicated to our young friend where to dredge for duns with most chance of success. But I protest fervently my innocence. It is true that I had myself long remarked that part of the channel to be dangerously infested with duns. In searching for literary or philosophic papers, it would often happen for an hour together that I brought up little else than variegated specimens of the dun. And one vast bank there was, which I called the Goodwin Sands,[12] because nothing within the memory of man was ever known to be hauled up from it except eternal specimens of the dun – some grey with antiquity, some of a neutral tint, some green and lively. With grief it was that I had seen our dipper shoaling his water towards that dangerous neighbourhood. But what could I do? If I had warned him off, Portia would have been sure to fancy that there was some great oyster-bed or pearl-fishery in that region; and all I should have effected by my honesty would have been a general conviction of my treachery. I therefore became as anxious as everybody else for No. 3, which might set all to rights – *might*, but slight were my hopes that it *would*, when I saw in what direction the dipper's arm was working. Exactly below that very spot where he had dipped, lay, as stationary as if he had been anchored, a huge and ferocious dun of great antiquity. Age had not at all softened the atrocious expression of his countenance, but rather aided it by endowing him with a tawny hue. The size of this monster was enormous, nearly two square feet; and I fancied at times that, in spite of his extreme old age, he had not done growing. I knew him but too well; because whenever I happened to search in that region of the bath, let me be seeking what I would, and let me miss what I might, always I was sure to haul up *him* whom I never wanted to see again. Sometimes I even found him basking on the very summit of the papers; and I conceived an idea, which may be a mere fancy, that he came up for air in particular states of the atmosphere. At present he was *not* basking on the surface: better for the Athenaeum if he *had:* for then the young man would have been cautious. Not being above, he was certainly below, and underneath the very centre of the dipper's plunge. Unable to control my feelings, I cried out – 'Bear away to the right!' But Portia protested with energy against this intermeddling of mine, as perfidy too obvious. 'Well,' I said, 'have it your own way: you'll see what will happen.'

No. 3. – This, it is needless to say, turned out the horrid old shark, as I had long christened him: I knew his vast proportions, and his bilious aspect, the moment that the hauling up commenced, which in *his* case occupied some time. Portia was the more angry, because she had thrown away her right to *express* any anger by neutralising my judicious interference. She grew even more angry, because I, though sorry for the Athenaeum, really could not help laughing when I saw the truculent old wretch expanding his huge dimensions – all umbered by time and ill-temper – under the eyes of the wondering young ladies; so mighty was the contrast between this sallow behemoth and a rose-coloured little billet of their own. By the way, No. 2 had been a specimen of the dulcet dun, breathing only zephyrs of request and persuasion; but this No. 3 was a specimen of the polar opposite – the dun horrific and Gorgonian[13] – blowing great guns of menace. As ideal specimens in their several classes, might they not have a value for the *museum* of the Athenaeum, if it *has* one, or even for the *Album?* This was *my* suggestion, but overruled, like everything else that I proposed; and on the ground that Glasgow had too vast a conservatory of duns, native and indigenous, to need any exotic specimens. This settled, we hurried to the next dip, which, being by contract the last, made us all nervous.

No. 4. – This, alas! turned out a lecture addressed to myself by an ultra-moral friend; a lecture on procrastination; and not badly written. I feared that something of the sort was coming; for, at the moment of dipping, I called out to the dipper – 'Starboard your helm! you're going smack upon the Goodwins: in 30 seconds you'll founder!'[14] Upon this, in an agony of fright, the dipper forged off, but evidently quite unaware that vast spurs stretched off from the Goodwins – shoals and sand-banks – where it was mere destruction to sail without a special knowledge of the soundings. He had run upon an ethical sand-bank. 'Yet, after all, since this is to be the last dip,' said Portia, 'if the lecture is well written, might it not be acceptable to the Athenaeum?' 'Possibly,' I replied; 'but it is too personal, besides being founded in error from first to last. I could not allow myself to be advertised in a book as a procrastinator on principle, unless the Athenaeum would add a postscript under its official seal, expressing entire disbelief of the accusation; which I have private reasons for thinking that the Athenaeum may decline to do.'

'Well, then,' said Portia, 'as you wilfully rob the Athenaeum of No. 4, which by contract is the undoubted property of that body, in fee simple and not in fee conditional,'[15] (mark Portia's learning as an attorney,) 'then you are bound to give us a 5th dip; particularly as you've been so treacherous all along.' Tears rushed to my eyes at this most unjust assumption. In agonising tones I cried out, 'Potato-sack! my friend Potato-sack! will you quietly listen to this charge upon me, that am as innocent as the child unborn? If it is a crime in me to know, and in you *not* to know, where the Goodwins lie, why then let you and me sheer off to the other side of the room, and let Portia try if *she* can do better. I allow her motion for a fresh trial. I grant a 5th dip: and the more readily, because it is an old saying – that there is luck in odd numbers: *numero deus impare gaudet;*[16] – only I must request of Portia to be the dipper on this final occasion.' All the three attorneys blushed a rosy red on this unexpected summons. It was one thing to criticise, but quite another thing to undertake the performance; and the fair attorneys trembled for their professional reputation. Secretly, however, I whispered to Potato-sack, 'You'll see now, such is female address, that whatever sort of monster they haul up, they'll swear it's a great prize, and contrive to extract some use from it that may seem to justify this application for a new trial.'

No. 5. – Awful and thrilling were the doubts, fears, expectations of us all, when Portia 'prepared to dip,' and secondly 'dipped.' She shifted her hand, and 'ploitered'[17] amongst the papers for full five minutes. I winked at this in consideration of past misfortunes; but, strictly speaking, she had no right to 'ploiter' for more than one minute. She contended that she knew, by intuition, the sort of paper upon which 'duns' were written; and whatever else might come up, she was resolved it should not be a dun. 'Don't be too sure,' I said; and, at last, when she seemed to have settled her choice, I called out the usual word of command, '*Haul up.*'

'What is it?' we said; 'what's the prize?' we demanded, all rushing up to Portia. Guess, reader; – it was a sheet of blank paper!

I, for my part, was afraid either to laugh or to cry. I really felt for Portia, and, at the same time, for the Athenaeum. Yet I had a monstrous desire to laugh horribly. But, bless you, reader! there was no call for pity to Portia. With the utmost coolness she said, 'Oh! here is *carte blanche*[18] for receiving your latest thoughts. This is the paper on which you are to write an essay for the Athenaeum; and thus we are providentially enabled to assure our client the Athenaeum of something expressly manufactured for the occasion, and not an old wreck from the Goodwins. Fortune loves the Athenaeum; and her four blanks at starting were only meant to tease that Institution, and to enhance the value of her final favour.' 'Ah, indeed!' I said in an under tone, '*meant to tease!* there are other ladies who understand that little science beside Fortune!' However, there is no disobeying the commands of Portia; so I sate down to write a paper on ASTROLOGY. But, before beginning, I looked at Potato-sack, saying only, 'You see: I told you what would happen.'

ASTROLOGY.

As my contribution to their *Album*, I will beg the Athenaeum to accept a single thought on this much-injured subject. Astrology I greatly respect; but it is singular that my respect for the science arose out of my contempt for its professors, – not exactly as a direct logical consequence, but as a casual suggestion from that contempt. I believe in astrology, but not in astrologers; as to *them* I am an incorrigible infidel. First, let me state the occasion upon which my astrological thought arose; and then, secondly, the thought itself.

When about 17 years old, I was wandering as a pedestrian tourist in North Wales. For some little time, the centre of my ramblings (upon which I still revolved from all my excursions, whether elliptical, circular, or zig-zag) was Llangollen in Denbighshire, or else Rhuabon, not more than a few miles distant.[19] One morning I was told by a young married woman, at whose cottage I had received some kind hospitalities, that an astrologer lived in the neighbourhood. 'What might be his name?' Very good English it was that my young hostess had hitherto spoken; and yet, in this instance, she chose to answer me in Welch. *Mochinahante* was her brief reply. I dare say that my spelling of the word will not stand Welch criticism; but what can you expect from a man's first attempt at Welch orthography? I am sure that my *written* word reflects the *vocal* word which I heard – provided you pronounce the *ch* as a Celtic guttural; and I can swear to three letters out of the twelve, viz. the first, the tenth, and the eleventh, as rigorously correct. Pretty well, I think, *that*, for a mere beginner – only seventy-five per cent. by possibility wrong! But what did *Mochinahante* mean? For a man might as well be anonymous, or call himself X Y Z,[20] as offer one his visiting card indorsed with a name so frightful to look at – so shocking to utter – so agonising to spell – as *Mochinahante*. And that it had a translateable meaning – that it was not a proper name but an appellative, in fact some playful *sobriquet*, I felt certain, from observing the young woman to smile whilst she uttered it. My next question drew from her – that this Pagan-looking monster of a name meant *Pig-in-the-dingle*. But really, now, between the original monster and this English interpretation, there was very little to choose; in fact the interpretation, as often happens, strikes one as the harder to understand of the two. 'To be sure it does,' says a lady sitting at my elbow, and tormented by a passion so totally unfeminine as curiosity – 'to be sure – very much harder; for *Mochina – what-do-you-call-it?* might, you know, mean something or other, for anything that you or I could say to the contrary; but as to *Pig-in-the-dingle* – what dreadful nonsense! what an impossible description of an astrologer! A man that – let me see – does something or other about the stars: how can *he* be described as a pig? pig in *any* sense, you know – pig in *any* place? But *Pig-in-a-dingle!* – why, if he's a pig at all, he must be *Pig-on-a-steeple*, or *Pig-on-the-top-of-a-hill*, that he may rise above the mists and vapours. Now I insist, my dear creature, on your explaining all this riddle on the spot. *You* know it – you came to the end of the mystery; but none of *us* that are sitting here can guess at the meaning; we shall all be ill, if you keep us waiting – I've a headach beginning already – so say the thing at once, and put us out of torment!'

What's to be done? I *must* explain the thing to the Athenaeum; and if I stop to premise an oral explanation for the lady's separate use, there will be no time to save the Glasgow post, which waits for no man, and is deaf even to female outcries. By way of compromise, therefore, I request of the lady that she will follow my pen with her radiant eyes, by which means she will obtain the earliest intelligence, and the speediest relief to her headach. I, on my part, will not loiter, but will make my answer as near to a telegraphic answer, in point of speed, as a rigid metallic pen will allow. – I divide this answer into two heads: the first concerning '*in the dingle*,' the second concerning '*pig*.' My philosophic researches, and a visit to the astrologer, ascertained a profound reason for describing him as *in-the-dingle;* viz. because he *was* in a dingle. He was the sole occupant of a little cove amongst the hills – the sole householder; and so absolutely such, that if ever any treason should be hatched in the dingle, clear it was to my mind that *Mochinahante* would be found at the bottom of it; if ever war should be levied in this dingle, *Mochinahante* must be the sole belligerent; and if a forced contribution were ever imposed upon this dingle, *Mochinahante* (poor man!) must pay it all out of his own pocket. The lady interrupts me at this point to say – 'Well, I understand all *that* – that's all very clear. But what I want to know about is – *Pig*. Come to *Pig*. Why *Pig?* How *Pig?* In what sense *Pig?* You can't have any profound reason, you know, for *that*.'

Yes I have: a *very* profound reason; and satisfactory to the most sceptical of philosophers, viz. that he *was* a Pig. I was presented by my fair hostess to the great interpreter of the stars, in person; for I was anxious to make the acquaintance of an astrologer, and especially of one who, whilst owning to so rare a profession, owned also to the soft impeachment of so very significant a name. Having myself enjoyed so favourable an opportunity for investigating the reasonableness of that name, *Mochinahante*, as applied to the Denbighshire astrologer, I venture to pronounce it unimpeachable. About his dress there was a forlornness, and an ancient tarnish or *aerugo*,[21] which went far to justify the name; and upon his face there sate that lugubrious rust (or what medallists technically call *patina*) which bears so costly a value when it is found on the *coined* face of a Syro-Macedonian prince long since compounded with dust, but, alas! bears no value at all if found upon the flesh-and-blood face of a living philosopher. Speaking humanly, one would have insinuated that the star-gazer wanted much washing and scouring; but, astrologically speaking, perhaps he would have been spoiled by earthly waters for his celestial vigils.

Mochinahante was civil enough; a pig is not necessarily rude; and, after seating me in his chair of state, he prepared for his learned labours by cross-examinations as to the day and hour of my birth. The *day* I knew to a certainty; and even about the *hour* I could tell quite as much as ought in reason to be expected from one who certainly had not been studying a chronometer when that event occurred. These points settled, the astrologer withdrew into an adjoining room, for the purpose (as he assured me) of scientifically constructing my horoscope; but unless the drawing of corks is a part of that process, I should myself incline to think that the great man, instead of minding my interests amongst the stars and investigating my horoscope, had been seeking consolation for himself in bottled porter. Within half-an-hour he returned; looking more lugubrious than ever – more grim – more grimy (if *grime* yields any such adjective) – a little more rusty – rather more *patinous*, if numismatists will lend me that word – and a great deal more in want of scouring. He had a paper of diagrams in his hand, which of course contained some short-hand memoranda upon my horoscope; but, from its smokiness, a malicious visitor might have argued a possibility that it had served for more customers than myself. Under his arm he carried a folio book, which (he said) was a manuscript of unspeakable antiquity. This he was jealous of my seeing; and before he would open it, as if I and the book had been two prisoners at the bar suspected of meditating some collusive mischief (such as tying a cracker to the judge's wig), he separated us as widely from each other as the dimensions of the room allowed. These solemnities finished, we were all ready – I, and the folio volume, and Pig-in-the-dingle – for our several parts in the play. *Mochinahante* began: – He opened the pleadings in a deprecatory tone, protesting, almost with tears, that if anything should turn out amiss in the forthcoming revelations, it was much against his will – that *he* was powerless, and could not justly be held responsible for any part of the disagreeable message which it might be his unhappiness to deliver. I hastened to assure him that I was incapable of such injustice; that I should hold the stars responsible for the whole; by nature, that I was very forgiving; that any little malice, which I might harbour for a year or so, should all be reserved for the use of the particular constellations concerned in the plot against myself; and, lastly, that I was now quite ready to stand the worst of their thunders. Pig was pleased with this reasonableness – he saw that he had to deal with a philosopher – and, in a more cheerful tone, he now explained that my 'case' was mystically contained in the diagrams; these smoke-dried documents submitted, as it were, a series of questions to the book; which book it was – a book of unspeakable antiquity – that gave the inflexible answers, like the gloomy oracle that it was. But I was not to be angry with the book, any more than with himself, since —— 'Of course not,' I replied, interrupting him, 'the book did but utter the sounds which were predetermined by the white and black keys struck in the smoky diagrams; and I could no more be angry with the book for speaking what it conscientiously believed to be the truth than with a decanter of port wine, or a bottle of porter, for declining to yield more than one or two wine-glasses of the precious liquor at the moment when I was looking for a dozen, under a transient forgetfulness, incident to the greatest minds, that I myself, ten minutes before, had nearly drunk up the whole.' This comparison, though to a critic wide awake it might have seemed slightly personal, met with the entire approbation of *Pig-in-the-dingle*. A better frame of mind for receiving disastrous news, he evidently conceived, could not exist or be fancied by the mind of man than existed at that moment in myself. *He* was in a state of intense pathos from the bottled porter. *I* was in a state of intense excitement (pathos combined with horror) at the prospect of a dreadful lecture on my future life, now ready to be thundered into my ears from that huge folio of unspeakable antiquity, prompted by those wretched smoke-dried diagrams. I believe we were in magnetical rapport. Think of *that*, reader! – Pig and I in magnetical rapport! Both making passes at each other! What in the world would have become of us if suddenly we should have taken to somnambulising? Pig would have abandoned his dingle to me; and I should have dismissed Pig to that life of wandering which must have betrayed the unscoured and patinous condition of the astrologer to the astonished eyes of Cambria;[22] –

> 'Stout Glo'ster stood aghast [or *might* have stood] in speechless trance.
> *To arms!* cried Mortimer [or at least *might* have cried], and couch'd his
> quivering lance.'[23]

But Pig was a greater man than he seemed. He yielded neither to magnetism nor to bottled porter; but commenced reading from the black book in the most awful tone of voice, and, generally speaking, most correctly. Certainly he made one dreadful mistake; he started from the very middle of a sentence, instead of the beginning; but then *that* had a truly lyrical effect, and also it was excused by the bottled porter. The words of the prophetic denunciation, from which he started, were these – 'also *he* [that was myself, you understand] shall have red hair.' '*There* goes a bounce,' I said in an under tone; 'the stars, it seems, can tell falsehoods as well as other people.' 'Also,' for Pig went on without stopping, 'he shall have seven-and-twenty children.' Too horror-struck I was by this news to utter one word of protest against it. 'Also,' Pig yelled out at the top of his voice, 'he shall desert them.' Anger restored my voice, and I cried out, 'That's not only a lie in the stars, but a libel; and, if an action lay against a constellation, I should recover damages.' Vain it would be to trouble the reader with all the monstrous prophecies that Pig read against me. He read with a steady Pythian[24] fury. Dreadful was his voice: dreadful were the starry charges against myself – things that I *was* to do, things that I *must* do: dreadful was the wrath with which secretly I denounced all participation in the acts which these wicked stars laid to my charge. But this infirmity of good nature besets me, that, if a man shows trust and absolute faith in any agent or agency whatever, heart there is not in me to resist him, or to expose his folly. Pig trusted – oh how profoundly! – in his black book of unspeakable antiquity. It would have killed him on the spot to prove that the black book was a hoax, and that he himself was another. Consequently, I submitted in silence to pass for the monster that Pig, under coercion of the stars, had pronounced me, rather than part in anger from the solitary man, who after all was not to blame, acting only in a ministerial capacity, and reading only what the stars obliged him to read. I rose without saying one word, advanced to the table, and paid my fees; for it is a disagreeable fact to record, that astrologers grant no credit, nor even discount upon prompt payment. I shook hands with *Mochinahante;* we exchanged kind farewells – he smiling benignly upon me, in total forgetfulness that he had just dismissed me to a life of storms and crimes; I, in return, as the very best benediction that I could think of, saying secretly, 'Oh Pig, may the heavens rain their choicest soap-suds upon thee!'

Emerging into the open air, I told my fair hostess of the red hair which the purblind astrologer had obtained for me from the stars, and which, with *their* permission, I would make over to *Mochinahante* for a reversionary wig in his days of approaching baldness. But I said not one word upon that too bountiful allowance of children with which *Moch.* had endowed me. I retreated by nervous anticipation from that inextinguishable laughter which, I was too certain, would follow upon *her* part; and yet, when we reached the outlet of the dingle, and turned round to take a parting look of the astrological dwelling, I myself was overtaken by fits of laughter; for suddenly I figured in vision my own future return to this mountain recess, with the young legion of twenty-seven children. '*I* desert them, the darlings!' I exclaimed, 'far from it! Backed by this filial army, I shall feel myself equal to the task of taking vengeance on the stars for the affronts they have put upon me through Pig their servant. It will be like the return of the Heracleidae to the Peloponnesus.[25] The sacred legion will storm the "dingle," whilst *I* storm Pig; the rising generation will take military possession of "*-inahante*," whilst I deal with "*Moch*" (which I presume to be the part in the long word answering to *Pig*).' My hostess laughed in sympathy with *my* laughter; but I was cautious of letting her have a look into my vision of the sacred legion. We quitted the dingle for ever; and so ended my first visit, being also my last, to an astrologer.

This, reader, was the true general occasion of my one thought upon astrology; and, before I mention it, I may add that the immediate impulse drawing my mind in any such direction was this – on walking to the table where the astrologer sat, in order to pay my fees, naturally I came nearer to the folio book than astrological prudence would generally have allowed. But Pig's attention was diverted for the moment to the silver coins laid before him – these he reviewed with the care reasonable in one so poor, and in a state of the coinage so neglected as it then was. By this moment of avarice in Pig, I profited so far as to look over the astrologer's person, sitting and bending forward full upon the book. It was spread open, and at a glance I saw that it was no MS. but a printed book, printed in black-letter types. The month of August stood as a rubric at the head of the broad margin – and below it stood some days of that month in orderly succession. – 'So then, Pig,' said I in my thoughts, 'it seems that any person whatever, born on my particular day and hour of August, is to have the same exact fate as myself. But a king and a beggar may chance thus far to agree. And be you assured, Pig, that all the infinite variety of cases lying between these two *termini* differ from each other in fortunes and incidents of life as much, though not so notoriously, as king and beggar.'

Hence arose a confirmation of my contempt for astrology. It seemed as if *necessarily* false – false by an *à priori*[26] principle, viz. that the possible differences in human fortunes, which are infinite, cannot be measured by the possible differences in the particular moments of birth, which are too strikingly finite. It strengthened me in this way of thinking, that subsequently I found the very same objection in Macrobius.[27] Macrobius may have stolen the idea; but certainly not from me – *as* certainly I did not steal it from him; so that here is a concurrence of two people independently, *one* of them a great philosopher, in the very same annihilating objection.

Now comes my one thought. Both of us were wrong, Macrobius and myself. Even the great philosopher is obliged to confess it. The objection truly valued is – to astrologers, not to astrology. No two events ever *did* coincide in point of time. Every event has, and must have, a certain duration; this you may call its *breadth;* and the true *locus* of the event in time is the central point of that breadth, which never was or will be the same for any two separate events, though grossly held to be contemporaneous. It is the mere imperfection of our human means for chasing the infinite subdivisibilities of time which causes us to regard two events as even by possibility concurring in their central moments.[28] This imperfection is crushing to the pretensions of astrologers; but astrology laughs at it in the heavens; and astrology, armed with celestial chronometers, is true!

Suffer me to illustrate the case a little: – It is rare that a metaphysical difficulty can be made as clear as a pike-staff. This can. Suppose two events to occur in the same quarter of a minute – that is, in the same 15 seconds; then, if they started precisely together, and ended precisely together, they would not only have the same breadth, but this breadth would accurately coincide in all its parts or fluxions; consequently, the central moment, viz. the 8th, would coincide rigorously with the centre of each event. But, suppose that one of the two events, A for instance, commenced a single second before B the other, then, as we are still supposing them to have the same breadth or extension, A will have ended in the second before B ends; and, consequently, the centres will be different, for the 8th second of A will be the 7th of B. The disks of the two events will overlap – A will overlap B at the beginning; B will overlap A at the end. Now, go on to assume that, in a particular case, this overlapping does not take place, but that the two events eclipse each other, lying as truly surface to surface as two sovereigns in a tight *rouleau*[29] of sovereigns, or one dessert-spoon nestling in the bosom of another; in that case, the 8th or central second will be the centre for both. But even here a question will arise as to the degree of rigour in the coincidence; for divide that 8th second into a thousand parts or sub-moments, and perhaps the centre of A will be found to hit the 450th sub-moment, whilst that of B may hit the 600th. Or suppose, again, even this trial surmounted: the two harmonious creatures, A and B, running neck and neck together, have both hit simultaneously the true centre of the thousand sub-moments which lies half-way between the 500th and the 501st. All is right so far – 'all right behind;'[30] but go on, if you please; subdivide this last centre, which we will call X, into a thousand lesser fractions. Take, in fact, a railway express-train of decimal fractions, and give chase to A and B; my word for it that you will come up with them in some stage or other of the journey, and arrest them in the very act of separating their centres – which is a dreadful crime in the eye of astrology; for, it is utterly impossible that the initial moment, or *sub*-moment, or *sub-sub*-moment of A and B should absolutely coincide. Such a thing as a perfect start was never heard of at Doncaster.[31] – Now, this severe accuracy is not wanted on earth. Archimedes, it is well known, never saw a perfect circle, nor even, with his leave, a decent circle;[32] for, doubtless, the reader knows the following fact, viz. that, if you take the most perfect Vandyking ever cut out of paper or silk, by the most delicate of female fingers, with the most exquisite of Salisbury scissors, upon viewing it through a microscope you will find the edges frightfully ragged; but, if you apply the same microscope to one of God's Vandyking[33] on the corolla or calyx of a flower, you will find it as truly cut and as smooth as a moonbeam. We on earth, I repeat, need no such rigorous truth. For instance, you and I, my reader, want little perhaps with circles, except now and then to bore one with an augre in a ship's bottom, when we wish to sink her and to cheat the underwriters; or, by way of variety, to cut one with a centre-bit through shop-shutters, in order to rob a jeweller; – so *we* don't care much whether the circumference is ragged or not. But that won't do for a constellation! The stars *n'entendent pas la raillerie*[34] on the subject of geometry. The pendulum of the starry heavens oscillates truly; and if the Greenwich time of the *Empyreum*[35] can't be repeated upon earth, without an error, a horoscope is as much a chimera as the perpetual motion,[36] or as an agreeable income-tax. In fact, in casting a nativity, to swerve from the true centre by the trillionth of a centillionth is as fatal as to leave room for a coach and six to turn between your pistol shot and the bull's eye. If you haven't done the trick, no matter how near you've come to it. And to overlook this, is as absurd as was the answer of that Lieutenant M., who, being asked whether he had any connexion with another officer of the same name, replied – 'Oh yes! a very close one.' 'But in what way?' 'Why, you see, I'm in the 50th regiment of foot, and he's in the 49th:' walking, in fact, just behind him! Yet, for all this, horoscopes may be calculated very truly by the stars amongst themselves; and my conviction is – that they are. They are perhaps even printed hieroglyphically, and published as regularly as a nautical almanack; only, they cannot be re-published upon earth by any mode of piracy yet discovered amongst sublunary booksellers. Astrology, in fact, is a very profound, or at least a very lofty science; but astrologers are humbugs.

I have finished, and I am vain of my work; for I have accomplished three considerable things: – I have floored Macrobius; I have cured a lady of her headach; and lastly, which is best of all, I have expressed my sincere interest in the prosperity of the Glasgow Athenaeum.

But the Glasgow post is mounting, and this paper will be lost; a fact which, amongst all the dangers besetting me in this life, the wretched Pig forgot to warn me of.

Articles for the *North British Review*, 1848

THE LIFE AND ADVENTURES OF OLIVER GOLDSMITH

First published in the *North British Review*, IX, May 1848, pp. 187–212. The essay was printed anonymously.

Reprinted in *F*, IX, *Essays on the Poets and Other English Writers* (1853), pp. 99–144.

Revised text, carrying many accidentals but only six substantive variants from *F*, in *SGG*, VI, *Sketches, Critical and Biographic* (1857), pp. 194–233.

There is one manuscript, as follows:

MS A: British Library, Department of Printed Books, C. 60. o. 3. The manuscript is a set of *SGG* page proofs. It corresponds to the text below running from p. 309.3 'THIS book accomplished' to p. 315.9 'invidiously, or with any', with those textual variants from *SGG* running from p. 711, 309.4 'through seventy and odd years.' to p. 712, 315.9 'We do not'. At this point the manuscript breaks off and there is a gap of four pages (in *SGG*, pp. 205–8). The manuscript then recommences and corresponds to the text below running from p. 317.23 'denounces, or by implication' to p. 330.42 'Be thy memorial upon', with those textual variants from *SGG* running from p. 713, 317.24 '*we* believe' to p. 715, 330.38 'precedency. But,'. The manuscript contains no substantive variants.

Oliver Goldsmith (1730–74; *DNB*), essayist, novelist, playwright and poet, was born in County Westmeath, Ireland. At sixteen he went to Trinity College, Dublin, and later spent brief periods at Edinburgh and Leiden Universities. In 1756, he settled in London, where he quickly rose from the obscurity of Grub Street to the fame of membership in the Club, a group that included James Boswell, Samuel Johnson, Edmund Burke, and David Garrick. Goldsmith is best remembered for his novel *The Vicar of Wakefield* (1766), his poem *The Deserted Village* (1770), and his play *She Stoops to Conquer* (1773).

John Forster (1812–76; *DNB*), essayist and biographer, was born in Newcastle, and attended University College, London. He was called to the bar in 1843, but preferred his work as adviser, agent, and proofreader to many of the leading writers of the day, including Thomas Carlyle and Charles Dickens. In 1846 he succeeded Dickens as editor of *The Daily News*, and a year later began editing *The Examiner*. Forster wrote biographies of Goldsmith (1848; enlarged 1854), Walter Savage Landor (1869), and Dickens (1872–4).

De Quincey's review of Forster's *Goldsmith* is the first of three book reviews that he contributed to the *North British Review* in 1848. The *North British* was a quarterly review, and appeared in February, May, August, and November. It was established in Edinburgh in 1844 by the evangelical members of the recently founded Free Church of Scotland and, according to its prospectus, it sought to find the middle ground between the avowedly religious magazines that were too exclusively theological and too rigorously sectarian, and those political, literary, and scientific journals that excluded religion altogether, or gave it only minor notice. The *North British*, the Prospectus continued, was 'not intended to be a Theological Journal. No subject that can occupy the interest of a well-cultivated mind will be excluded. But topics of every kind will be treated of by individuals accustomed to view them in their highest relations'. W. G. Blaikie, the editor of the *North British* from 1860 to 1863, expanded on this theme when he noted that 'neither the *Edinburgh* nor the *Quarterly Review* was quite satisfactory to a considerable number of gentlemen…for the *Edinburgh* was too secular, and the *Quarterly* too conservative. They longed for an organ of a high class that would be both liberal in politics and Christian in tone'. Blaikie, however, observed that while 'the projectors of the *Review* were mostly Free Churchmen…it was never designed to be a Free Church organ'. Indeed, Henry Cockburn went so far as to claim that, while the founders may have declared the opposite, 'the general impression of the work will be against the Church, and in favour of all dissent that is honest and pious'. De Quincey himself described the *North British* as a 'liberal' journal ('The North British Review, 1844–1871' in *The Wellesley Index to Victorian Periodicals*, gen. ed. Walter Houghton, 5 vols (Toronto: University of Toronto Press, 1966–89), vol. I, pp. 663–4; Mark A. Weinstein, 'The North British Review' in *British Literary Magazines: The Victorian and Edwardian Age, 1837–1913* (Westport, Conn.: Greenwood Press, 1984), pp. 275–81; Vol. 19, p. 170).

During De Quincey's one-year tenure with the *North British*, it was edited by William Hanna (1808–82; *DNB*), and its leading contributors included the Scottish physicist and author David Brewster (1781–1868; *DNB*), and the English poet and essayist Coventry Patmore (1823–96; *DNB*). Hanna's time as editor, however, was unsuccessful, at least in terms of sales. In 1846, one year before he took over the position, the total printing of the *North British* was 3,000, but by 1849 that number had declined to 1,650. De Quincey published nothing in the review after 1848. Hanna resigned in 1850. The *North British* recovered in the 1850s, and by 1865 its circulation had again risen to 3,000. In late 1869, however, a group of liberal Catholics took control and circulation again began to drop. When the new editor became seriously ill in early 1871, publication ceased.

When De Quincey revised the present review in 1857 he stated that he owed 'a large apology' to Forster 'for having so inadequately reported the character and qualities of his *Vindiciae Oliverianae*', owing to 'a deep-seated nervous derangement, under which at that time…I had been suffering'. De Quincey added, rather oddly, that he did not write the essay with 'sincere cordiality or with perfect charity' because he had 'always borne a grudge to Goldsmith on behalf of Shakespere, whom so deeply and so deliberately he had presumed to insult'. Yet despite De Quincey's misgivings, the essay drew memorably high praise from the young Wallace Stevens, who in July 1899 was reading De Quincey's *Essays on the Poets* in *F*. 'So far I find the one on Goldsmith to be remarkably well-done', Stevens asserted; 'indeed one of the best things I have ever seen on any poet (or prose-writer either for that)' (Vol. 20, p. 78; *Letters of Wallace Stevens*, ed. Holly Stevens (London: Faber, 1966), pp. 29–30).

In addition to the present review, De Quincey's interest in Forster's biography seems to have prompted his short essay on 'Dr Johnson and Lord Chesterfield' (see below, pp. 516–9).

ART. VI. – *The Life and Adventures of Oliver Goldsmith. A Biography.* In Four Books. By JOHN FORSTER. London, 1848.

THIS book accomplishes a retribution which the world has waited for through seventy and odd years. Welcome at any rate by its purpose, it is trebly welcome by its execution, to all hearts that linger indulgently over the frailties of a national favourite once wickedly exaggerated – to all hearts that brood indignantly over the powers of that favourite once maliciously undervalued.

A man of original genius, shewn to us as revolving through the leisurely stages of a biographical memoir, lays open, to readers prepared for sympathy, two separate theatres of interest: one in his personal career; the other in his works and his intellectual development. Both unfold together; and each borrows a secondary interest from the other: the life from the recollection of the works – the works from the joy and sorrow of the life. There have, indeed, been authors whose great creations, severely preconceived in a region of thought transcendent to all impulses of earth, would have been pretty nearly what they are under any possible changes in the dramatic arrangement of their lives. Happy or not happy – gay or sad – these authors would equally have fulfilled a mission too solemn and too stern in its obligations to suffer any warping from chance, or to bend before the accidents of life, whether dressed in sunshine or in wintry gloom. But generally this is otherwise. Children of Paradise, like the Miltons of our planet, have the privilege of stars – to 'dwell apart.'[1] But the children of flesh, whose pulses beat too sympathetically with the agitations of mother-earth, cannot sequester themselves in that way. They walk in no such altitudes, but at elevations easily reached by ground-winds of humble calamity. And from that cup of sorrow, which upon all lips is pressed in some proportion, they must submit, by the very tenure on which they hold their gifts, to drink, if not more profoundly than others, yet always with more peril to the accomplishment of their earthly mission.

Amongst this household of children too tremulously associated to the fluctuations of earth, stands forward conspicuously Oliver Goldsmith. And there is a belief current – that he was conspicuous, not only in the sense of being constitutionally flexible to the impressions of sorrow and adversity, in case they had happened to occur, but also that he really *had* more than his share of those afflictions. We are disposed to think that this was not so. Our trust is, that Goldsmith lived upon the whole a life which, though troubled, was one of average enjoyment. Unquestionably, when reading at midnight, and in the middle watch of a century which *he* never reached, this record of one so amiable, so guileless, so upright, or seeming to be otherwise for a moment only in the eyes of those who did not know his difficulties, nor could have understood them; when recurring also to his admirable genius, to the sweet natural gaiety of his oftentimes pathetic humour, and to the varied accomplishments from talent or erudition, by which he gave effect to endowments so fascinating – one cannot but sorrow over the strife which he sustained, and over the wrong by which he suffered. A few natural tears one sheds at the rehearsal of so much contumely from fools, which he stood under unresistingly as one bareheaded under a hail-storm;* and worse to bear than the scorn of fools, was the imperfect sympathy and jealous self-distrusting esteem which he received to the last from friends. Doubtless he suffered much wrong; but so, in one way or other, do most men: he suffered also this special wrong, that in his life-time he never was fully appreciated by any one friend – something of a countermovement ever mingled with praise for *him* – he never saw himself enthroned in the heart of any young and fervent admirer, and he was always overshadowed by men less deeply genial, though more showy than himself: – but these things happen, and *have* happened to myriads amongst the benefactors of earth. Their names ascend in songs of thankful commemoration, but not until the ears are deaf that would have thrilled to the music. And these were the heaviest of Goldsmith's afflictions: what are likely to be thought such, viz., the battles which he fought for his daily bread, we do not number amongst them. To struggle is not to suffer. Heaven grants to few of us a life of untroubled prosperity, and grants it least of all to its favourites. Charles I. carried, as it was thought by a keen Italian judge of physiognomy, a predestination to misery written in his features.[3] And it is probable that if any Cornelius Agrippa[4] had then been living, to show him in early life the strife, the bloodshed, the triumphs of enemies, the treacheries of friends, the separation for ever from the familiar faces of his hearth, which darkened the years from 1642 to 1649, he would have said – 'Prophet of wo! if I bear to live through this vista of seven years, it is because at the further end of it thou showest me the consolation of a scaffold.'[5] And yet our persuasion is, that in the midst of its deadly agitations and its torments of suspense, probably enough by the energies of hope, or even of anxiety which exalted it, that period of bitter conflict was found by the king a more ennobling life than he *would* have found in the torpor of a prosperity too profound. To be cloyed perpetually is a worse fate than sometimes to stand within the vestibule of

* We do not allude chiefly to his experience in childhood, when he is reported to have been a general butt of mockery for his ugliness and his supposed stupidity; since, as regarded the latter reproach, he could not have suffered very long, having already at a childish age vindicated his intellectual place by the verses which opened to him an academic destination.[2] We allude to his mature life, and the supercilious condescension with which even his reputed friends doled out their praises to *him*.

starvation; and we need go no farther than the confidential letters of the court ladies in this and other countries to satisfy ourselves how much worse in its effects upon happiness than any condition of alarm and peril, is the lethargic repose of luxury too monotonous, and of security too absolute. If, therefore, Goldsmith's life *had* been one of continual struggle, it would not follow that it had therefore sunk below the standard of ordinary happiness. But the life-struggle of Goldsmith, though severe enough (after all allowances) to challenge a feeling of tender compassion, was not in such a degree severe as has been represented.* He enjoyed two great immunities from suffering that have been much overlooked; and *such* immunities that, in our opinion, four in five of all the people ever connected with Goldsmith's works, as publishers, printers, compositors, (that is, men taken at random,) have very probably suffered more, upon the whole, than he. The immunities were these: – 1*st*, From any *bodily* taint of low spirits. He had a constitutional gaiety of heart; an elastic hilarity; and, as he himself expresses it, 'a knack of hoping'[7] – which knack could not be bought with Ormus and with Ind, nor hired for a day with the peacock-throne of Delhi.[8] How easy was it to bear the brutal affront of being to his face described as '*Doctor minor*,' when one hour or less would dismiss the *Doctor major*, so invidiously contradistinguished from himself, to a struggle with scrofulous melancholy;[9] whilst *he*, if returning to solitude and a garret, was returning also to habitual cheerfulness. *There* lay one immunity, beyond all price, from a mode of strife to which others, by a large majority, are doomed – strife with bodily wretchedness. Another immunity he had of almost equal value, and yet almost equally forgotten by his biographers, viz. from the responsibilities of a family. Wife and children he had not.[10] They it is that, being a man's chief blessings, create also for him the deadliest of his anxieties, that stuff his pillow with thorns, that surround his daily path with snares. Suppose the case of a man who has helpless dependants of this class upon himself summoned to face some sudden failure of his resources: how shattering to the power of exertion, and, above all, of exertion by an organ so delicate as the creative intellect, dealing with subjects so coy as those of imaginative sensibility, to know that instant ruin attends his failure. Success in such paths of literature might at the best be doubtful; but success is impossible with any powers whatever, unless in a genial state of those powers; and this geniality is to be sustained in the case supposed, whilst the eyes are fixed upon the most frightful of abysses yawning beneath his feet. He is to win his inspiration for poetry or romance from the prelusive cries of infants clamouring for daily bread. Now, on the other hand, in the case of an extremity equally sudden alighting on the head of a man in Goldsmith's position, having no burthen to support but the trivial one of his own personal needs, the

* We point this remark not at Mr Forster, who, upon the whole, shares our opinion as to the tolerable comfort of Goldsmith's life; he speaks indeed elsewhere of Goldsmith's depressions;[6] but the question still remains – were they of frequent recurrence, and had they any constitutional settlement? We are inclined to say *no* in both cases.

resources are endless for gaining time enough to look around. Suppose him ejected from his lodgings: let him walk into the country, with a pencil and a sheet of paper; there sitting under a hay-stack for one morning, he may produce what will pay his expenses for a week: a day's labour will carry the sustenance of ten days. Poor may be the trade of authorship, but it is as good as that of a slave in Brazil, whose one hour's work will defray the twenty-four hours' living. As a reader, or corrector of proofs, a good Latin and French scholar (like Goldsmith) would always have enjoyed a preference, we presume, at any eminent printing-office.[11] This again would have given him time for looking round; or, he might perhaps have obtained the same advantage for deliberation from some confidential friend's hospitality. In short, Goldsmith enjoyed the two privileges, one subjective – the other objective – which, when uniting in the same man, would prove more than a match for all difficulties that *could* arise in a literary career to him who was at once a man of genius so popular, of talents so versatile, of reading so various, and of opportunities so large for still more extended reading. The subjective privilege lay in his buoyancy of animal spirits; the objective in his freedom from responsibilities. Goldsmith wanted very little more than Diogenes: now Diogenes *could* only have been robbed of his tub:* which perhaps was about as big as most of poor Goldsmith's sitting-rooms, and far better ventilated. So that the liability of these two men, cynic and non-cynic, to the kicks of fortune, was pretty much on a par; whilst Goldsmith had the advantage of a better temper for bearing them, though certainly Diogenes had the better climate for soothing his temper.

But it may be imagined, that if Goldsmith were thus fortunately equipped for authorship, on the other hand the position of literature, as a money-making resource, was in Goldsmith's days less advantageous than in ours. We are not of that opinion; and the representation by which Mr Forster endeavours to sustain it seems to us a showy but untenable refinement.[16] The outline of his argument is, that the aristocratic patron had, in Goldsmith's day, by the progress of society, disappeared; he belonged to the past – that the mercenary publisher had taken his place – he represented the ugly present – but that the great reading public (that true and equitable patron, as some fancy) had not yet matured its means of effectual action upon literature: this reading public

* Which tub the reader may fancy to have been only an old tar-barrel:[12] if so, he is wrong. Isaac Casaubon, after severe researches into the nature of that tub, ascertained to the general satisfaction of Christendom that it was not of wood, or within the restorative powers of a cooper, but of earthen ware, and once shattered by a horse's kick, quite past repair.[13] In fact, it was a large oil-jar, such as the remnant of the forty thieves lurked in, when waiting for their captain's signal from Ali Baba's house;[14] and in Attica it must have cost fifteen shillings, supposing that the philosopher did not steal it. Consequently a week's loss of house-room and credit to Oliver Goldsmith, at the rate of living then prevalent in Grub Street,[15] was pretty much the same thing in money value as the loss to Diogenes of his crockery house by burglary, or in any nocturnal lark of young Attic wine-bibbers. The underwriters would have done an insurance upon either man at pretty much the same premium.

virtually, perhaps, belonged to the future. All this we steadfastly resist. No doubt the old full-blown patron, *en grand costume*,[17] with his heraldic bearings emblazoned at the head of the Dedication, was dying out, like the golden pippin.[18] But he still lingered in sheltered situations. And part of the machinery by which patronage[19] had ever moved, viz., using influence for obtaining subscriptions, was still in capital working order – a fact which we know from Goldsmith himself (see the *Enquiry;*) for he tells us that a popular mode of publication amongst bad authors, and certainly it needed no publisher's countersign, was by means of subscription papers:[20] upon which, as we believe, a considerable instalment was usually paid down when as yet the book existed only by way of title-page, supposing that the whole sum were not even paid *up*. Then as to the publisher, (a nuisance, we dare say, in all stages of his Natural History,) *he* could not have been a weed first springing up in Goldsmith's time, but must always have been an indispensable broker or middleman between the author and the world. In the days even of Horace and Martial[21] the book-*seller* (bibliopola) clearly acted as book-*publisher*. Amongst other passages proving this, and showing undeniably that Martial at least had sold the copy-right of his work to *his* publisher, is one arguing pretty certainly that the price of a gay drawing-room copy must have been hard upon £1, 11s. 6d. Did ever any man hear the like? A New York newspaper would have been too happy to pirate the whole of Martial had he been three times as big, and would have engaged to drive the bankrupt publisher into a madhouse for twopence. Now, it cannot be supposed that Martial, a gay light-hearted fellow, willing to let the public have his book for a shilling, or perhaps for love, had been the person to put that ridiculous price upon it. We may conclude that it was the publisher. As to the public, *that* respectable character must always have presided over the true and final court of appeal, silently defying alike the *prestige* of patronage and the intriguing mysteries of publishing. Lordly patronage might fill the sails of one edition, and masterly publishing of three. But the books that ran contagiously through the educated circles, or that lingered amongst them for a generation, must have owed their success to the unbiassed feelings of the reader – not over-awed by authority, not mystified by artifice. Varying, however, in whatever proportion as to power, the three possible parties to an act of publication will always be seen intermittingly at work – the voluptuous self-indulging public, and the insidious publisher, of course; but even the brow-beating patron still exists in a new *avatar*. Formerly he made his descent upon earth in the shape of Dedicatee; and it is true that this august being, to whom dedications burned incense upon an altar, withdrew into sunset and twilight during Goldsmith's period;[22] but he still revisits the glimpses of the moon in the shape of author. When the *auctoritas*[23] of a peer could no longer sell a book by standing at the head of a dedication, it lost none of its power when standing on a title-page as the author. Vast catalogues might be composed of books and pamphlets that have owed a transient success to no other cause on earth than the sonorous title, or the distinguished position of those who wrote them. Ceasing to patronise other people's books, the grandee has still power to patronise his own. All *celebrities* have this form of patronage. And, for instance, had the boy Jones* (otherwise called Inigo Jones) possessed enough of book-making skill to forge a plausible curtain-lecture, as overheard by himself when concealed in Her Majesty's bed-room, ten steam-presses working day and night would not have supplied the public demand; and even Her Majesty must herself have sent for a large-paper copy, were it only to keep herself *au courant*[25] of English literature. In short, first, the extrinsic patronage of books; secondly, the self-patronage of books in right of their merits; and thirdly, the artificial machineries for diffusing the knowledge of their existence, are three forces in current literature that ever *have* existed and must exist, in some imperfect degree. Horace recognises them in his

'Non Dî, non homines, non concessere columnae.'[26]

The *Dî* are the paramount public, arbitrating finally on the fates of books, and generally on some just ground of judgment, though it may be fearfully exaggerated on the scale of importance. The *homines* are the publishers; and a sad *homo* the publisher sometimes is, particularly when he commits insolvency. But the *columnae* are those pillars of state, the grandees of our own age, or any other patrons, that support the golden canopy of our transitory pomps, and thus shed an alien glory of coloured light from above upon the books falling within that privileged area.

We are not therefore of Mr Forster's opinion, that Goldsmith fell upon an age less favourable to the expansion of literary powers, or to the attainment of literary distinction, than any other. The patron might be a tradition – but the public was not therefore a prophecy. My lord's trumpets had ceased to sound, but the *vox populi*[27] was not therefore muffled. The means indeed of diffusive advertisement and of rapid circulation, the combinations of readers into reading societies, and of roads into iron net-works, were as yet imperfectly developed. These gave a potent stimulus to periodic literature. And a still more operative difference between ourselves and them is – that a new class of people has since then entered our reading public, viz. – the class of artisans and of all below the gentry, which (taken generally) was in Goldsmith's day a cipher as regarded any real encouragement to literature. In our days, if *The Vicar of Wakefield* had been published as a Christmas tale, it would have produced a fortune to the writer. In Goldsmith's time, few below the gentry were readers on any large scale. So far there really *was* a disadvantage. But it was a

* It may be necessary to explain, for the sake of the many persons who have come amongst the reading public since the period of the incident referred to, that this was a boy called Jones, who was continually entering Buckingham Palace clandestinely, was as regularly ejected by the police, but with respectable pertinacity constantly returned, and on one occasion effected a lodgment in the royal bedchamber. Some happy wit, in just admiration of such perseverance and impudence, christened him *In-I-go Jones*.[24]

disadvantage which applied chiefly to novels. The new influx of readers in our times, the collateral affluents into the main stream from the mechanic and provincial sections of our population, which have centupled the volume of the original current, cannot be held as telling favourably upon literature, or telling at all, except in the departments of popularized science, of religion, of fictitious tales, and of journalism. To be a reader, is no longer as once it was, to be of a meditative turn. To be a *very* popular author is no longer that honorary distinction which once it might have been amongst a more elevated because more select body of readers. We do not say this invidiously, or with any special reference. But it is evident that writers and readers must often act and react for reciprocal degradation. A writer of this day, either in France or England, to be *very* popular, must be a story-teller; which is a function of literature neither very noble in itself, nor, secondly, tending to permanence. All novels whatever, the best equally with the worst, have faded almost with the generation that produced them. This is a curse written as a superscription above the whole class. The modes of combining characters, the particular objects selected for sympathy, the diction, and often the manners,* hold up an imperfect mirror to any generation that is not their own. And the reader of novels belonging to an obsolete era, whilst acknowledging the skill of the groupings, or the beauty of the situations, misses the echo to that particular revelation of human nature which has met him in the social aspects of his own day; or too often he is perplexed by an expression which, having dropped into a lower use, disturbs the unity of the impression, or is revolted by a coarse sentiment, which increasing refinement has made unsuitable to the sex or to the rank of the character. How bestial and degrading at this day seem many of the scenes in Smollett! How coarse are the ideals of Fielding! – his odious Squire Western, his odious Tom Jones. What a gallery of histrionic masqueraders is thrown open in the novels of Richardson,[30] powerful as they were once found by the two leading nations of the earth.[31] A popular writer, therefore, who, *in order* to be popular, must speak through novels, speaks to what is least permanent in human sensibilities. That is already to be self-degraded. *Secondly,* because the novel-reading class is by far the most comprehensive one, and being such, must count as a large majority amongst its members those who

* Often, but not so uniformly (the reader will think) as the diction, because the manners are sometimes not those of the writer's own age, being ingenious adaptations to meet the modern writer's conjectural ideas of ancient manners. These, however, (even in Sir Walter Scott,) are precisely the most mouldering parts in the entire architecture, being always (as, for instance, in Ivanhoe)[28] fantastic, caricatured, and betraying the true modern ground gleaming through the artificial tarnish of antiquity. All novels, in every language, are hurrying to decay;[29] and hurrying by *internal* changes – were those all; but, in the meantime, the everlasting life and fertility of the human mind is for ever accelerating this hurry by *superseding* them, *i. e.*, by an external change. Old forms, fading from the interest, or even from the apprehension, have no chance at all as against new forms embodying the same passions. It is only in the grander passions of poetry, allying themselves with forms more abstract and permanent, that such a conflict of the old with the new is possible.

are poor in capacities of thinking, and are passively resigned to the instinct of immediate pleasure – to these the writer must chiefly humble himself: he must study *their* sympathies, must assume them, must give them back. In our days, he must give them back even their own street slang; so servile is the modern novelist's dependence on his *canaille*[32] of an audience. In France, amongst the Sues, &c., it has been found necessary to give back even the closest portraits of obscene atrocities that shun the light, and burrow only in the charnel-houses of vast manufacturing towns.[33] Finally, the very principle of commanding attention only by the interest of a tale, which means the interest of a momentary curiosity that is to vanish for ever in a sense of satiation, and of a momentary suspense that, having once collapsed, can never be rekindled, is in itself a confession of reliance upon the meaner offices of the mind. The result from all which is – that to be popular in the most extensive walk of popularity, that is, as a novelist, a writer must generally be in a very considerable degree self-degraded by sycophancy to the lowest order of minds, and cannot (except for mercenary purposes) think himself advantageously placed.

To have missed, therefore, this enormous expansion of the reading public, however unfortunate for Goldsmith's purse, was a great escape for his intellectual purity. Every man has two-edged tendencies lurking within himself, pointing in one direction to what will expand the elevating principles of his nature, pointing in another to what will tempt him to its degradation. A mob is a dreadful audience for chafing and irritating the latent vulgarisms of the human heart. Exaggeration and caricature, before such a tribunal, become inevitable, and sometimes almost a duty. The genial but not very delicate humour of Goldsmith would in such circumstances have slipped, by the most natural of transitions, into buffoonery; the unaffected pathos of Goldsmith would, by a monster audience, have been debauched into theatrical sentimentality. All the motions of Goldsmith's nature moved in the direction of the true, the natural, the sweet, the gentle. In the quiet times, politically speaking, through which his course of life travelled, he found a musical echo to the tenor of his own original sensibilities – in the architecture of European history, as it unfolded its proportions along the line of his own particular experience, there was a symmetry with the proportions of his own unpretending mind. Our revolutionary age would have unsettled his brain.[34] The colossal movements of nations, from within and from without; the sorrow of the times, which searches so deeply; the grandeur of the times, which aspires so loftily; these forces, acting for the last fifty years by secret sympathy upon our fountains of thinking and impassioned speculation, have raised them from depths never visited by our fathers, into altitudes too dizzy for *their* contemplating. This generation and the last, with their dreadful records, would have untuned Goldsmith for writing in the key that suited him; and *us* they would have untuned for understanding his music, had we not learned to understand it in childhood, before the muttering hurricanes in the upper air had begun to reach our young ears, and forced them away to the thundering overhead, from the carolling of birds amongst earthly bowers.

Goldsmith, therefore, as regards the political aspects of his own times, was fortunately placed; a thrush or a nightingale is hushed by the thunderings which are awakening to Jove's eagle. But an author stands in relation to other influences than political; and some of these are described by Mr Forster as peculiarly unfavourable to comfort and respectability at the era of Goldsmith's novitiate in literature. Will Mr Forster excuse us for quarrelling with his whole doctrine upon this subject – a subject and a doctrine continually forced upon our attention in these days, by the extending lines of our own literary order, and continually refreshed in warmth of colouring by the contrast as regards *social* consideration, between our literary body and the corresponding order in France. The questions arising have really a general interest, as well as a special one, in connexion with Goldsmith; and therefore we shall stir them a little, not with any view of exhausting the philosophy that is applicable to the case, but simply of amusing some readers, (since Pliny's remark on history is much more true of literature or literary gossip, viz., that '*quoquo* modo scripta delectat;')[35] and with the more ambitious purpose of recalling some other readers from precipitate conclusions upon a subject where nearly all that is most plausible happens to be most untrue.

Mr Forster, in his views upon the *social* rights of literature, is rowing pretty nearly in the same boat as Mr Carlyle[36] in *his* views upon the rights of labour. Each denounces, or by implication denounces, as an oppression and a nuisance, what *we* believe to be a necessity inalienable from the economy and structure of our society. Some years ago Mr Carlyle offended us all (or all of us that were interested in social philosophy) by enlarging on a social affliction, which few indeed needed to see exposed, but most men would have rejoiced to see remedied, if it were but on paper, and by way of tentative suggestion. Precisely at that point, however, where his aid was invoked, Mr Carlyle halted.[37] So does Mr Forster with regard to *his* grievance; he states it, and we partly understand him – as ancient Pistol says – 'we hear him with ears;'[38] and when we wait for him to go on, saying – 'well, here's a sort of evil in life, how would you redress it? you've shewn, or you've made another hole in the tin-kettle of society; how do you propose to tinker it?' – behold! he is suddenly almost silent. But this cannot be allowed. The right to insist upon a well known grievance cannot be granted to that man (Mr Carlyle, for instance, or Mr Forster) who uses it as matter of blame and denunciation, unless at the same time he points out the methods by which it could have been prevented. He that simply bemoans an evil has a right to his moan, though he should make no pretensions to a remedy; but he that criminates – that imputes the evil as a fault – that charges the evil upon selfishness or neglect lurking in some alterable arrangements of society, has no right to do so, unless he can instantly sketch the remedy; for the very first step by which he could have learned that the evil involved a blame, the first step that could have entitled him to denounce it as a wrong, must have been that step which brought him within the knowledge (wanting to everybody else) that it admitted of a cure. A wrong it could not have been even in *his* eyes, so long as it was a necessity, nor a ground of complaint until the cure appeared to him a possibility. And the over-riding motto for these parallel speculations of Messrs. Carlyle and Forster, in relation to the frailties of our social system, ought to have been – '*Sanabilibus aegrotamus malis*.'[39] Unless with this watchword they had no right to commence their crusading march. *Curable* evils justify clamorous complaints; the incurable justify only prayers.

Why it was that Mr Carlyle, in particular, halted so steadily at the point where his work of love was first beginning, it is not difficult to guess. As the 'Statutes at large'[40] have not one word against the liberty of unlicensed hypothesis, it is conceivable the Mr C. might have indulged a little in that agreeable pastime: but this, he was well aware, would have brought him in one moment under the fire of Political Economy, from the whole vast line of its modern batteries.[41] These gentlemen, the economists, would have torn to ribbons, within fifteen minutes, any *positive* speculation for amending the evil. It was better, therefore, to keep within the trenches of the blank negative, pointing to everything as *wrong* – horribly wrong, but never hinting at the mysterious *right:* which, to this day, we grieve to say, remains as mysterious as ever.*

Passing to Mr Forster, who (being capable of a splendour so original) disappoints us most when he reminds us of Mr Carlyle, by the most disagreeable of that gentleman's phraseological forms;[45] and, in this instance, by a speculation twin-sister to the economic one just noticed – we beg to premise, that in anything here said, it is far from our wish to express disaffection to the cause of our literary brothers. We grudge them nothing that they are ever likely to get. We wish even that the House of Commons would see cause for creating *majorats*[46] in behalf of us all; only whispering in the ear of that honourable House to appoint a Benjamin's portion[47] to ourselves – as the parties who

* It ought, by this time, to be known equally amongst governments and philosophers – that for the State to promise with sincerity the absorption of surplus labour, as fast as it accumulates, cannot be postulated as a duty, until it can first be demonstrated as a possibility. This was forgotten, however, by Mr C., whose vehement complaints, that the arable field, without a ploughman, should be in one county, whilst in another county was the stout ploughman without a field;[42] and sometimes (which was worse still,) that the surplus ploughmen should far outnumber the surplus fields, certainly proceeded on the secret assumption that all this was within the remedial powers of the State. The same doctrine was more openly avowed by various sections of our radicals, who (in their occasionally insolent petitions to Parliament) many times asserted that one main use and function of a government was – to find work for everybody. At length, [February and March 1848,] we see this doctrine solemnly adopted by a French body of rulers, self-appointed, indeed, or perhaps appointed by their wives, and so far sure, in a few weeks, to be answerable for nothing;[43] but, on the other hand, adopting it as a practical *undertaking*, in the lawyer's sense, and by no means as a mere gaiety of rhetoric. Meantime, they themselves will be 'broken,' before they will have had time for being reproached with broken promises; though neither fracture is likely to require much above the length of a quarantine.[44]

suggested the idea. But what is the use of benevolently bequeathing larks for dinner to all literary men, in all time coming, if the sky must fall before they can bag our bequest? We shall discuss Mr Forster's views, not perhaps according to any arrangement of his, but according to the order in which they come back to our own remembrance.

Goldsmith's period, Mr F. thinks, was bad – not merely by the transitional misfortune (before noticed) of coming too late for the patron, and too soon for the public, (which is the compound ill-luck of being a day after one fair, and a month too soon for the next) – but also by some coöperation in this evil destiny through misconduct on the part of authors themselves, (p. 70.) Not 'the circumstances' only of authors were damaged, but the 'literary character' itself. We are sorry to hear *that*. But, as long as they did not commit murder, we have a great indulgence for the frailties of authors. If ever the 'benefit of clergy' could be fairly pleaded, it might have been by Grub Street for petty larceny. The 'clergy' they surely could have pleaded; and the call for larceny was so audible in their condition, that in *them* it might be called an instinct of self-preservation, which surely was not implanted in man to be disobeyed. One word allow us to say on these three topics: – 1. The condition of the literary body in its hard-working section at the time when Goldsmith belonged to it. 2. Upon the condition of that body in England as compared with that of the corresponding body in France. 3. Upon the condition of the body in relation to patronage purely *political*.

1. The pauperized (or Grub Street) section of the literary body, at the date of Goldsmith's taking service amongst it, was (in Mr Forster's estimate) at its very lowest point of depression. And one comic presumption in favour of that notion we ourselves remember; viz. that Smart, the prose translator of Horace, and a well-built scholar, actually *let* himself out to a monthly journal on a regular lease of ninety-nine years.* What could move the rapacious publisher to draw the lease for this monstrous term of years, we cannot conjecture. Surely the villain might have been content with threescore years and ten. But think, reader, of poor Smart two years after, upon another publisher's applying to him vainly for contributions, and angrily demanding what possible objection could be made to offers so liberal, being reduced to answer – 'no objection, sir, whatever, except an unexpired term of ninety-seven years yet to run.' The bookseller saw that he must not apply again in *that* century; and, in fact, Smart could no longer let himself, but must be sublet (if let at all) by the original lessee. Query now – was Smart entitled to vote as a freeholder, and Smart's children (if any were born during the currency of the lease) would they be serfs, and *ascripti prelo?*[49] Goldsmith's own terms of self-conveyance to Griffiths[50] – the terms we mean on which he 'conveyed' his person and free-agency to the uses of the said Griffiths (or his assigns?) – do not appear to

* When writing this passage, we were not aware (as we now are) that Mr Forster had himself noticed the case.[48]

have been much more dignified than Smart's in the quality of the *conditions*, though considerably so in the duration of the *term;* Goldsmith's lease being only for one year, and not for ninety-nine, so that he had (as the reader perceives) a clear ninety-eight years at his own disposal. We suspect that poor Oliver, in his guileless heart, never congratulated himself on having made a more felicitous bargain. Indeed, it was not so bad, if everything be considered; Goldsmith's situation at the time was bad; and for that very reason the lease (otherwise monstrous) was *not* bad. He was to have lodging, board, and 'a small salary,'[51] *very* small, we suspect; and in return for all these blessings, he had nothing to do, but to sit still at a table, to work hard from an early hour in the morning until 2 P.M., (at which elegant hour we presume that the parenthesis of dinner occurred,) but also – which, not being an article in the lease, might have been set aside, on a motion before the King's Bench – to endure without mutiny the correction and revisal of all his MSS. by *Mrs* Griffiths,[52] wife to Dr G. the lessee. This affliction of Mrs *Dr* G. surmounting his shoulders, and controlling his pen, seems to us not at all less dreadful than that of Sinbad when indorsed with the old man of the sea;[53] and we, in Goldsmith's place, should certainly have tried how far Sinbad's method of abating the nuisance had lost its efficacy by time, viz. the tempting our oppressor to get drunk once or twice a-day, and then suddenly throwing Mrs Dr G. off her perch. From that 'bad eminence,'[54] which she had audaciously usurped, what harm could there be in thus dismounting this 'old *woman* of the sea?' And as to an occasional thump or so on the head, which Mrs Dr G. might have caught in tumbling, that was *her* look-out; and might besides have improved her style. For really now, if the candid reader will believe us, we know a case, odd certainly but very true, where a young man, an author by trade,* who wrote pretty well, happening to tumble out of a first-floor in London, was afterwards observed to grow very perplexed and almost unintelligible in his style; until some years later, having the good fortune (like Wallenstein at Vienna) to tumble out of a two-pair of stairs window,[56] he slightly fractured his skull, but on the other hand, recovered the brilliancy of his long fractured style. Some people there are of our acquaintance who would need to tumble out of the attic story before they could seriously improve their style.

Certainly these conditions – the hard work, the being chained by the leg to the writing-table, and above all the having one's pen chained to that of Mrs Dr Griffiths, *do* seem to countenance Mr F.'s idea, that Goldsmith's period was the purgatory of authors. And we freely confess – that excepting Smart's ninety-nine years' lease, or the contract between the Devil and Dr Faustus,[57] we never heard of a harder bargain driven with any literary man. Smart, Faustus, and Goldsmith, were clearly overreached. Yet, after all, was this treatment in any important point (excepting as regards Dr Faustus) worse

* His name began with A, and ended with N;[55] there are but three more letters in the name, and if doubt arises upon our story, in the public mind, we shall publish them.

than that given to the whole college of Grub Street, in the days of Pope? The first edition of the Dunciad dates from 1727; Goldsmith's matriculation in Grub Street dates from 1757[58] – just thirty years later; which is one generation. And it is important to remember that Goldsmith, at this time in his twenty-ninth year, was simply an usher at an obscure boarding-school; had never practised writing for the press; and had not even himself any faith at all in his own capacity for writing. It is a singular fact, which we have on Goldsmith's own authority, that until his thirtieth year (that is, the year spent with Dr and Mrs Griffiths) it never entered into his head that literature was his natural vocation.[59] That vanity, which has been so uncandidly and sometimes so falsely attributed to Goldsmith, was compatible, we see, if at all it existed, with the humblest estimate of himself. Still, however much this deepens our regard for a man of so much genius united with so much simplicity and unassumingness – humility would not be likely to raise his salary; and we must not forget that his own want of self-esteem would reasonably operate on the terms offered by Griffiths. A man, who regarded himself as little more than an amanuensis, could not expect much better wages than an under-gardener, which perhaps he had. And, weighing all this, we see little to have altered in the lease – that was fair enough; only as regarded the execution of the lease, we really must have protested, under any circumstances, against Mrs Doctor Griffiths. That woman would have broken the back of a camel, which must be supposed tougher than the heart of an usher. There we should have made a ferocious stand; and should have struck for much higher wages, before we could have brought our mind to think of a capitulation. It is remarkable, however, that this year of humble servitude was not only (or, as if by accident) the epoch of Goldsmith's intellectual development, but also the occasion of it. Nay, if all were known, perhaps it may have been to Mrs Doctor Griffiths in particular, that we owe that revolution in his self-estimation which made Goldsmith an author by deliberate choice. Hag-ridden every day, he must have plunged and kicked violently to break loose from this harness; but, not impossibly, the very effort of contending with the hag, when brought into collision with his natural desire to soothe the hag, and the inevitable counter-impulse in any continued practice of composition, towards the satisfaction at the same time of his own reason and taste, must have furnished a most salutary *paloestra*[60] for the education of his literary powers. When one lives at Rome, one must do as they do at Rome:[61] when one lives with a hag, one must accommodate oneself to haggish caprices; besides, that once in a month the hag might be right; or, if not, and supposing her *always* in the wrong, which perhaps is too much to assume even of Mrs Dr G., *that* would but multiply the difficulties of reconciling *her* demands with the demands of the general reader and of Goldsmith's own judgment. And in the pressure of these difficulties would lie the very value of this rough Spartan education. Rope-dancing cannot be very agreeable in its elementary lessons; but it must be a capital process for calling out the agilities that slumber in a man's legs.

Still, though these hardships turned out so beneficially to Goldsmith's intellectual interests, and consequently so much to the advantage of all who have since delighted in his works, not the less on that account they *were* hardships, and hardships that imposed heavy degradation. So far, therefore, they would seem to justify Mr Forster's characterisation of Goldsmith's period by comparison with Addison's period* on the one side, and our own on the other.[62] But, on better examination, it will be found that this theory is sustained only by an unfair selection of the antithetic objects in the comparison. Compare Addison's age *generally* with Goldsmith's – authors, prosperous or unprosperous, in each age taken indiscriminately – and the two ages will be found to offer 'much of a muchness.'[63] But, if you take the paupers of one generation to contrast with the grandees of another, how is there any justice in the result? Goldsmith at starting was a penniless man. Except by random accidents he had not money enough to buy a rope, in case he had fancied himself in want of such a thing. Addison, on the contrary, was the son of a tolerably rich man; lived gaily at a most aristocratic college (Magdalen), in a most aristocratic university;[64] formed early and brilliant connexions with the political party that were magnificently preponderant until the last four years of Queen Anne;[65] travelled on the Continent, not as a pedestrian mendicant, housing with owls, and thankful for the bounties of a village fair, but with the appointments and introductions of a young nobleman; and became a secretary of state not by means of his 'delicate humour,' as Mr Forster chooses to suppose, but through splendid patronage,[66] and (speaking *Hibernicè*) through a 'strong back.' His bad verses, his Blenheim, his Cato,[67] in later days, and other rubbish, had been the only part of his works that aided his rise; and even these would have availed him little, had he not originally possessed a *locus standi*,[68] from which he could serve his artilleries of personal flattery with commanding effect, and could *profit* by his successes. As to the really exquisite part of his writings, *that* did him no yeoman's service at all, nor *could* have done; for he was a made man, and had almost received notice to quit this world of prosperous whiggery before he had finished those exquisite prose miscellanies. Pope, Swift, Gay, Prior, &c., all owed their social positions to early accidents of good connexions and sometimes of luck,[69] which would not indeed have supplied the place of personal merit, but which gave lustre and effect to merit where it existed in strength. There were authors, quite as poor as Goldsmith in the Addisonian age; there were authors quite as rich as Pope, Steele,[70] &c., in Goldmith's age, and having the same social standing. Goldsmith struggled with so much distress, not because his period was more inauspicious, but because his connexions and starting advantages were incom-

* If Addison died (as we think he did) in 1717, then, because Goldsmith commenced authorship in 1757, there would be forty years between the two periods. But, as it would be fairer to measure from the centre of Addison's literary career, *i.e.*, from 1707, the difference would be just half a century.

parably less important. His profits were so trivial because his capital was next to none.

So far, as regards the comparison between Goldsmith's age and the one immediately before it. But now, as regards the comparison with our own, removed by two generations – can it be said truly that the literary profession has risen in estimation, or is rising? There is a difficulty in making such an appraisement; and from different minds there would proceed very different appraisements; and even from the same mind, surveying the case at different stations. For, on the one hand, if a greater breadth of social respectability catches the eye on looking carelessly over the body of our modern literati, which may be owing chiefly to the large increase of gentlemen that in our day have entered the field of literature, on the other hand, the hacks and *handicraftsmen* whom the shallow education of newspaper journalism has introduced to the press, and whom poverty compels to labours not meriting the name of literature, are correspondingly expanding their files. There is, however, one reason from analogy, which may incline us to suppose that a higher consideration is now generally conceded to the purposes of literature, and consequently, a juster estimate made of the persons who minister to those purposes. Literature – provided we use that word not for the mere literature of knowledge, but for the literature of power[71] – using it for literature as it speaks to what is genial in man, viz. – to the human *spirit*, and *not* for literature, (falsely so called,) as it speaks to the meagre understanding – is a fine art; and not only so, it is the supreme of the fine arts; nobler, for instance, potentially, than painting, or sculpture, or architecture. Now, *all* the fine arts, *that popularly are called such*, have risen in esteem within the last generation. The most aristocratic of men will now ask into his own society an artist, whom fifty years ago he would have transferred to the house-steward's table. And why? Not simply because more attention having been directed to the arts, more notoriety has gathered about the artist; for that sort of *eclat* would not work any durable change; but it is because the interest in the arts having gradually become much more of an enlightened interest, the public has been slowly trained to fix its attention upon the *intellect* which is pre-supposed in the arts, rather than upon the offices of *pleasure* to which they minister. The fine arts have now come to be regarded rather as powers that are to mould, than as luxuries that are to embellish. And it has followed that artists are valued more by the elaborate agencies which they guide, than by the fugitive sensations of wonder or sympathy which they evoke.

Now this is a change honourable to both sides. The public has altered its estimate of certain men; and yet has not been able to do so, without previously enlarging its idea of the means through which those men operate. It could not elevate the men, without previously elevating itself. But, if so, then, in correcting their appreciation of the fine arts, the public must simultaneously have corrected their appreciation of literature; because, whether men have or have not been in the habit of regarding literature as a fine art, this they must have felt, viz., that literature in its more genial functions, works by the very same organs as the liberal arts, speaks to the same heart, operates through the same compound nature, and educates the same deep sympathies with mysterious ideals of beauty. *There* lies the province of the arts usually acknowledged as fine or liberal: *there* lies the province of fine or liberal literature. And with justifiable pride a *littérateur* may say – that *his* fine art wields a sceptre more potent than any other; literature is more potent than other fine arts, because *deeper* in its impressions according to the usual tenor of human sensibilities; because more *extensive*, in the degree that books are more diffused than pictures or statues; because more *durable*, in the degree that language is durable beyond marble or canvass, and in the degree that vicarious powers are opened to books for renewing their phoenix immortality through unlimited translations: powers denied to painting except through copies that are feeble, and denied to sculpture except through casts that are costly.

We infer that, as the fine arts have been rising, literature (on the secret feeling that essentially it moves by the same powers) must also have been rising; that, as the arts will continue to rise literature will continue to rise; and that in both cases the men, the ministers, must ascend in social consideration as the things, the ministrations ascend. But there is another form in which the same result offers itself to our notice; and this should naturally be the last paragraph in this section 1, but, as we have little room to spare, it may do equally well as the first paragraph in section 2, viz., on the condition of our own literary body by comparison with the same body in France.

2. Who were the people amongst ourselves that throughout the eighteenth century chiefly came forward as undervaluers of literature? They belonged to two very different classes – the aristocracy and the commercial body, who agreed in the thing, but on very different impulses. To the mercantile man the author was an object of ridicule, from natural poverty; *natural*, because there was no regular connexion between literature and any mode of money-making. By accident the author might *not* be poor, but professionally or according to any obvious opening for an income he *was*. Poverty was the badge of all his tribe. Amongst the aristocracy the instinct of contempt or at least of slight regard towards literature was supported by the irrelation of literature to the *state*. Aristocracy itself was the flower and fruitage of the state; a nobility was possible only in the ratio of the grandeur and magnificence developed for *social* results; so that a poor and unpopulous nation cannot create a great aristocracy: the flower and foliation must be in relation to the stem and the radix out of which they germinate. Inevitably, therefore, a nobility so great as the English – that not in pride but in the mere logic of its political relations, felt its order to be a sort of heraldic shield, charged with the trophies and ancestral glories of the nation – could not but in its *public* scale of appreciation estimate every profession and rank of men by the mode of their natural connexion with the state. Law and arms, for instance, were honoured, not because any capricious precedent had been established of a title to public honour in

favour of those professions, but because through their essential functions they opened for themselves a permanent necessity of introsusception[72] into the organism of the state. A great law-officer, a great military leader, a popular admiral, *is* already, by virtue of his functions, a noble in men's account, whether you gave or refused him a title; and in such cases it has always been the policy of an aristocratic state to confer, or even impose, the title, lest the disjunction of the virtual nobility from the titular should gradually disturb the estimate of the latter. But literature, by its very grandeur, is degraded socially; for its relations are essentially cosmopolitan, or, speaking more strictly, not cosmopolitan, which might mean to all other peoples considered as national states, whereas literature has no relation to any sections or social schisms amongst men – its relations are to the race. In proportion as any literary work rises in its pretensions; for instance, if it works by the highest forms of passion, its *nisus* – its natural effort – is to address the race, and not any individual nation. That it found a bar to this *nisus*, in a limited language, was but an accident: the essential relations of every great intellectual work are to those capacities in man by which he tends to brotherhood, and not to those by which he tends to alienation. Man is ever coming nearer to agreement, ever narrowing his differences, notwithstanding that the interspace may cost an eternity to traverse. Where the agreement is, not where the difference is, in the centre of man's affinities, not of his repulsions, *there* lies the magnetic centre towards which all poetry that is potent, and all philosophy that is faithful, are eternally travelling by natural tendency. Consequently, if indirectly literature may hold a patriotic value as a gay plumage in the cap of a nation, directly, and by a far deeper tendency, literature is essentially alien. A poet, a book, a system of religion, belongs to the nation best qualified for appreciating their powers, and not to the nation that, perhaps by accident, gave them birth. How, then, is it wonderful that an intense organ of the social principle in a nation, viz., a nobility, should fail, in their professional character, to rate highly, or even to recognise as having any proper existence, a fine art which is by tendency anti-social; (anti-social in this sense, that what it seeks, it seeks by transcending all social barriers and separations?) Yet it is remarkable that in England, where the aristocracy for three centuries (16th, 17th, 18th) paid so little honour, in their public or corporate capacity, to literature, privately they honoured it with a rare courtesy. That same grandee, who would have looked upon Camden, Ben Jonson, Selden, or Hobbes,[73] as an audacious intruder, if occupying any prominent station at a State festival, would have received him with a kind of filial reverence in his own mansion; for in this place, as having no national reference, as sacred to hospitality, which regards the human tie, and not the civic tie, he would be at liberty to regard the man of letters in his cosmopolitan character. And on the same instinct, a prince in the very meanest State would, in a State-pageant commemorating the national honours, assign a distinguished place to the national high-admiral, though he were the most stupid of men, and would utterly neglect the stranger Columbus.[74] But in his own palace, and at his own table, he would perhaps invert this order of precedency, and would place Columbus at his own right hand.

Some such principle, as is here explained, did certainly prevail in the practice (whether consciously perceived or not in the philosophy) of that England which extended through the sixteenth and seventeenth centuries. First in the eighteenth century all honour to literature under *any* relation began to give way. And why? Because expanding politics, expanding partisanship, and expanding journalism, then first called into the field of literature an inferior class of labourers. Then first it was that – from the noblest of professions, literature became a trade. Literature it was that gave the first wound to literature; the hack scribbler it was that first degraded the lofty literary artist.[75] For a century and a half we have lived under the shade of this fatal Revolution. But, however painful such a state of things may be to the keen sensibilities of men pursuing the finest of vocations – carrying forward as inheritors from past generations the eternal chase after truth, and power, and beauty – still we must hold that the dishonour to literature has issued from internal sources proper to herself, and not from without. The nobility of England have for three and a half centuries personally practised literature as an elevated accomplishment: our royal and noble authors are numerous; and they would have continued the same cordial attentions to the literary body, had that body maintained the same honourable composition. But a *littérateur*, simply *as* such, it is no longer safe to distinguish with favour; once, but not now, he was liable to no misjudgment. Once he was pretty sure to be a man of some genius, or, at the least, of unusual scholarship. Now, on the contrary, a mob of traitors have mingled with the true men; and the loyal perish with the disloyal, because it is impossible in a mob, so vast and fluctuating, for the artillery of avenging scorn to select its victims.

All this, bitter in itself, has become *more* bitter from the contrast furnished by France. We know that literature has long been misappreciated amongst ourselves. In France it has long been otherwise appreciated – more advantageously appreciated. And we infer that therefore it is in France more wisely appreciated. But this does not follow. We have ever been of opinion that the valuation of literature in France, or at least of current literature, and as it shews itself in the treatment of literary men, is unsound, extravagant, and that it rests upon a basis originally false.[76] Simply to have been the translator from the English of some prose book, a history or a memoir, neither requiring nor admitting any display of mastery over the resources of language, conferred, throughout the eighteenth century, so advantageous a position in society upon one whom we English should view as a literary scrub or mechanic drudge, that we really had a right to expect the laws of France and the court ceremonies to reflect this feature of public manners. Naturally, for instance, any man honoured so preposterously ought in law to have enjoyed, in right of his book, the *jus trium liberorum*,[77] and perpetual immunity from taxes. Or again, as regards ceremonial honours, on any fair scale of proportions, it was reasonable to expect that to any man who had gone into a fourth edition, the royal sentinels should present arms; that to the author of a successful tragedy, the guard should everywhere turn out; and that an epic poet, if ever such a difficult birth should make its epiphany in Paris, must look to have his approach towards a *soirée*[78] announced by a salvo of a hundred and one guns.

Our space will not allow us to go into the illustrative details of this monstrous anomaly in French society. We confine ourselves to its cause – as sufficiently explaining why it is that no imitation of such absurdities can or ought to prosper in England. The same state of things, under a different modification, takes place in Germany; and from the very same cause. Is it not monstrous, or *was* it not until within recent days, to find every German city drawing the pedantic materials, and the pedantic interest of its staple conversation from the systems and the conflicts of a few rival academic professors? Generally these paramount lords of German conversation, that swayed its movements this way or that, as a lively breeze sways a corn-field, were metaphysicians; Fichte, for instance, and Hegel.[79] These were the arid sands that bibulously absorbed all the perennial gushings of German enthusiasm. France of the last century and the modern Germany were as to this point on the same level of foolishness. But France had greatly the advantage in point of liberality. For general literature furnishes topics a thousand times more graceful and fitted to blend with social pleasure than the sapless problems of ontological systems meant only for scholastic use.

But what then was the cause of this social deformity? Why was literature allowed eventually to disfigure itself by disturbing the natural currents of conversation, to make itself odious by usurpation, and thus virtually to operate as a mode of pedantry? It was because in neither land had the people any power of free discussion. It was because every question growing out of religion, or connecting itself with laws, or with government, or with governors, with political interests or political machineries, or with judicial courts, was an interdicted theme. The mind sought in despair for some free area wide enough to allow of boundless openings for individualities of sentiment – human enough to sustain the interests of festive discussion. That open area was found in books. In Paris to talk of politics was to talk of the king; *l'état c'est moi;*[80] to talk of the king in any spirit of discussion, to talk of that *Jupiter optimus maximus*,[81] from whom all fountains flowed of good and evil things, before whom stood the two golden urns, one filled with *lettres de cachet*[82] – the other with crosses, pensions, offices, what was it but to dance on the margin of a volcano, or to swim cotillions in the suction of a maelstrom? Hence it was that literature became the only safe colloquial subject of a general nature in old France; hence it was that literature furnished the only 'open questions;' and hence it *is* that the mode and the expression of honour to literature in France has continued to this hour tainted with false and histrionic feeling, because originally it grew up from spurious roots, prospered unnaturally upon deep abuses in the system, and at this day (so far as it still lingers) memorialises the political bondage of the nation. Cleanse therefore – is our prayer – cleanse, oh, unknown Hercules, this Augéan stable[83] of our English current literature, rich in dunghills, rich therefore in precipitate mushroom and fraudulent fungus, yet rich also (if we may utter our real thoughts) – rich preëminently at this hour in seed-plots of immortal growths, and in secret vegetations of volcanic strength; – cleanse it (oh coming man!) but not by turning through it any river of Lethe,[84] such as for two centuries swept over the literature of France. Purifying waters were these in one sense; they banished the accumulated depositions of barbarism; they banished Gothic tastes; yes, but they did this by laying asleep the nobler activities of a great people, and reconciling them to forgetfulness of all which commanded them as duties, or whispered to them as rights.

If, therefore, the false homage of France towards literature still survives, it is no object for imitation amongst *us;* since it arose upon a vicious element in the social composition of that people. Partially it *does* survive, as we all know by the experience of the last twenty years, during which authors, and *as* authors, (not like Mirabeau or Talleyrand in spite of authorship,) have been transferred from libraries to senates and privy councils.[85] This has done no service to literature, but, on the contrary, has degraded it by seducing the children of literature from their proper ambition. It is the glory of literature to rise as if on wings into an atmosphere nobler than that of political intrigue. And the whole result to French literature has been – that some ten or twelve of the leading literati have been tempted away by bribes from their appropriate duties, whilst some 5000 have been made envious and discontented.

At this point, when warned suddenly that the hourglass is running out, which measures our residuum of flying minutes, we first perceive on looking round, that we have actually been skirmishing with Mr Forster, from the beginning of our paper to this very line; and thus we have left ourselves but a corner for the main purpose (to which our other purpose of 'argle-bargling'[86] was altogether subordinate) of expressing emphatically our thanks to him for this successful labour of love in restoring a half-subverted statue to its upright position. We are satisfied that many thousands of readers will utter the same thanks to him, with equal fervour and with the same sincerity. Admiration for the versatile ability with which he has pursued his object is swallowed up for the moment in gratitude for his perfect success. It might have been imagined, that exquisite truth of household pathos, and of humour, with happy graces of style plastic as the air or the surface of a lake to the pure impulses of nature sweeping them by the motions of her eternal breath, were qualities authorized to justify themselves before the hearts of men, in defiance of all that sickly scorn or the condescension of masquerading envy could avail for their disturbance. And so they are: and left to plead for themselves at such a bar as unbiassed human hearts, they could not have their natural influences intercepted. But in the case of Goldsmith, literary traditions have *not* left these qualities to their natural influences. It is a fact that up to this hour the contemporary falsehoods at Goldsmith's expense, and (worse perhaps than those falsehoods,) the malicious constructions of incidents partly true, having wings lent to them by the levity and amusing gossip of Boswell,[87] continue to obstruct the full ratification of Goldsmith's pretensions. To this hour the scorn from many of his own age, runs side by side with the misgiving sense of his real native power. A feeling still survives, originally derived from his own age, that the 'inspired idiot,'[88] wherever he succeeded, ought *not* to have succeeded – having owed his success to accident, or even to some inexplicable perverseness in running counter to his own nature. It was by shooting awry that he had hit the mark; and, when most he came near to the bull's eye, most of all 'by rights' he ought to have missed it. He had blundered into the Traveller, into Mr Croaker, into Tony Lumkin;[89] and not satisfied with such dreadful blunders as these, he had consummated his guilt by blundering into the Vicar of Wakefield, and the Deserted Village;[90] atrocities over which in effect we are requested to drop the veil of human charity; since the more gem-like we may choose to think these works, the more unnatural, audacious, and indeed treasonable, it was in an idiot to produce them.

In this condition of Goldsmith's traditionary character, so injuriously disturbing to the natural effect of his inimitable works, (for in its own class each of his best works *is* inimitable,) Mr Forster steps forward with a three-fold exposure of the falsehood inherent in the anecdotes upon which this traditional character has arisen. Some of these anecdotes he challenges as *literally* false; others as virtually so; they are true perhaps, but under such a version of their circumstances as would altogether take out the sting of their offensive interpretation. For others again, and this is a profounder service, he furnishes a most just and philosophic explanation, that brings them at once within the reader's toleration, nay, sometimes within a deep reaction of pity. As a case, for instance, of downright falsehood, we may cite the well-known story told by Boswell – that, when Goldsmith travelled in France with some beautiful young English women, (meaning the Miss Hornecks,) he was seriously uneasy at the attentions which they received from the gallantry of Frenchmen, as intruding upon his own claims.[91] Now this story, in logical phrase, proves too much. For the man who *could* have expressed such feelings in such a situation, must have been ripe for Bedlam.[92] Coleridge mentions a man who entertained so exalted an opinion of himself, and of his own right to apotheosis, that he never uttered that great pronoun '*I*,' without solemnly taking off his hat. Even to the oblique case '*me*,' which no compositor ever honours with a capital *M*, and to the possessive pronoun *my* and *mine*, he held it a duty to kiss his hand.[93] Yet this bedlamite would not have been a competitor with a lady for the attentions paid to her in right of her sex. In Goldsmith's case, the whole allegation was dissipated in the most decisive way. Some years after Goldsmith's death, one of the sisters personally concerned in the case, was unaffectedly shocked at the printed story when coming to her knowledge, as a gross calumny; her sorrow made it evident that the whole had been a malicious distortion of some light-hearted gaiety uttered by Goldsmith. There is little doubt that the story of the bloom-coloured coat, and of the puppet-show,[94] rose on a similar basis – the calumnious perversion of a jest.

But in other cases, where there really *may* have been some fretful expression of self-esteem, Mr Forster's explanation transfers the foible to a truer and a more pathetic station. Goldsmith's own precipitancy, his overmastering defect in proper reserve, in self-control, and in presence of mind, falling in with the habitual undervaluation of many amongst his associates, placed him at a great disadvantage in animated conversation. His very truthfulness, his simplicity, his frankness, his hurry of feeling, all told against him. They betrayed him into inconsiderate expressions that lent a colour of plausibility to the malicious ridicule of those who disliked him the more, from being compelled, after all, to respect him. His own understanding oftentimes sided with his disparagers. He *saw* that he had been in the wrong; whilst secretly he *felt* that his meaning – if properly explained – had been right. Defrauded in this way, and by his own co-operation, of distinctions that naturally belonged to him, he was driven unconsciously to attempt some restoration of the balance, by claiming for a moment distinctions to which he had no real pretensions. The whole was a trick of sorrow, and of sorrowing perplexity: he felt that no justice had been done to him, and that he had himself made an opening for the wrong: the result he saw, but the process he could not disentangle; and, in the confusion of his distress, natural irritation threw him upon blind efforts to recover his ground by unfounded claims, when claims so well founded had been maliciously disallowed.

But a day of accounting comes at last – a day of rehearing for the cause, and of revision for the judgment. The longer this review has been delayed, the more impressive it becomes in the changes which it works. Welcome is the spectacle when, after three-fourths of a century have passed away, a writer – qualified for such a task, by ample knowledge of things and persons, by great powers for a comprehensive estimate of the case, and for a splendid exposition of its results, with deep sensibility to the merits of the man chiefly concerned in the issue, enthusiastic, but without partisanship – comes forward to unsettle false verdicts, to recombine misarranged circumstances, and to explain anew misinterpreted facts. Such a man wields the authority of heraldic marshals. Like the Otho of the Roman theatre, he has power to raise or to degrade – to give or to take away precedency. But, like this Otho, he has so much power, because he exercises it on known principles, and without caprice.[95] To the man of true genius, like Goldsmith, when seating himself in humility on the lowest bench, he says – 'Go thou up to a higher place. Seat thyself above those proud men, that once trampled thee in the dust. Be thy memorial upon earth – not (as of some who scorned thee) "the whistling of a name."[96] Be thou remembered amongst men by tears of tenderness, by happy laughter, untainted with malice, and by the benedictions of those that, reverencing man's nature, see gladly its frailties brought within the gracious smile of human charity, and its nobilities levelled to the apprehension of simplicity and innocence.'

Over every grave, even though tenanted by guilt and shame, the human heart, when circumstantially made acquainted with its silent records of suffering or temptation, yearns in love or in forgiveness to breathe a solemn *Requiescat!*[97] how much more, then, over the grave of a benefactor to the human race! But it is a natural feeling, with respect to such a prayer, that, however fervent and sincere, it has no perfect faith in its own validity so long as any unsettled feud from ancient calumny hangs over the buried person. The unredressed wrong seems to haunt the sepulchre in the shape of a perpetual disturbance to its rest. First of all, when this wrong has been adjudicated and expiated, is the *Requiescat* uttered with a perfect faith in itself. By a natural confusion we then transfer our own feelings to the occupant of the grave. The tranquillization to our own wounded sense of justice seems like an atonement to *his:* the peace for *us* transforms itself under a fiction of tenderness into a peace for *him:* the reconciliation between the world that did the wrong and the grave that seemed to suffer it, is accomplished; the reconciler in such a case, whoever he may be, seems a double benefactor – to *him* that endured the injury – to *us* that resented it; and in the particular case now before the public, we shall all be ready to agree that this reconciling friend, who might have entitled his work *Vindicioe Oliverianae,*[98] has, by the piety of his service to a man of exquisite genius, so long and so foully misrepresented, earned a right to interweave for ever his own cipher and cognizance in filial union with those of OLIVER GOLDSMITH.

THE WORKS OF ALEXANDER POPE, Esquire

First published as the lead article in the *North British Review*, IX, August 1848, pp. 299–333. The essay was printed anonymously.

Reprinted in *F*, IX, *Essays on the Poets and Other English Writers* (1853), pp. 145–204.

Revised text, carrying many accidentals and nineteen substantive variants from *F*, in *SGG*, IX, *Leaders in Literature, With a Notice of Traditional Errors Affecting Them*, (1858), pp. 1–53.

There is one manuscript, as follows:

MS A: Huntington Library, HM 36039. The manuscript is a complete set of *SGG* page proofs. It contains six significant variants, and these are listed in the textual notes.

De Quincey's interest in Alexander Pope (1688–1744; *DNB*) was persistent and wide-ranging, though his opinion of the poet was often antagonistic. The present review, his second of three for the *North British*, took for its occasion an edition of Pope by William Roscoe (1753–1831; *DNB*), attorney and MP for Liverpool, and author of the highly successful *Life of Lorenzo dé Medici* (1795), and the *Life and Pontificate of Leo the Tenth* (1805). Roscoe's edition of *The Works of Alexander Pope* first appeared in ten volumes in 1824 (London: C. and J. Rivington), and De Quincey used the biography of Pope in volume one as the basis for his 1838–9 *Encyclopaedia Britannica* article on Pope (Vol. 13, pp. 238–72). Roscoe's edition was reissued in eight volumes in 1847, with additional manuscript material by Charles Wentworth Dilke (1789–1864; *DNB*), critic and editor, best remembered now for his friendship with John Keats. The present review is of the 1847 reissue.

De Quincey's attitude toward Pope in the review is frequently dismissive. Pope is 'a man of genius', but De Quincey debunks notions of his 'correctness', mocks the manufactured nature of his satiric wrath, and ridicules his 'gallery of female portraits' (see below, p. 348). De Quincey is more positive about Roscoe's edition. It is 'certainly the most agreeable of all that we possess', and while his notes want 'compactness', they are 'written with a peculiar good sense, temperance, and kind feeling' (see below, p. 363). De Quincey expanded these comments in his 1851 *Tait's* essay on 'Lord Carlisle on Pope', where he characterized Roscoe as 'by far the most agreeable' of 'all editors of Pope' (Vol. 17, p. 221). His personal recollections of Roscoe, however, were less generous: he possessed, said De Quincey, 'the feebleness of a mere *belles-lettrist*...in the style of his sentiments on most subjects' (Vol. 10, p. 190). For De Quincey, Roscoe, and the literary society of Liverpool, see Daniel Roberts, *Revisionary*

Gleam: De Quincey, Coleridge, and the High Romantic Argument (Liverpool: University of Liverpool Press, 2000), pp. 76–82.

The most famous section of the review, however, concerns neither Pope nor Roscoe, but De Quincey's extended and final examination of his well-known distinction between the 'literature of knowledge' and the 'literature of power'. He first examined the concept in his 1823 *London Magazine* 'Letters to a Young Man Whose Education has been Neglected', where he acknowledged that he owed the idea to 'many years' conversation with Mr Wordsworth' (Vol. 3, p. 70). Wordsworth touches on the formulation occasionally in his published work. In a footnote to the 1800 'Preface', he remarks that 'much confusion has been introduced into criticism by this contradistinction of Poetry and Prose, instead of the more philosophical one of Poetry and Science' (Wordsworth, *Prose*, vol. I, p. 134). In Book VIII of the 1805 *Prelude*, he recollects his feelings on his first visit London in 1788: 'teeming as it did / Of past and present', he writes,

> such a place must needs
> Have pleased me, in those times; I sought not then
> Knowledge; but craved for power, and power I found
> In all things. (ll. 752–6)

In the 1815 'Essay, Supplementary to the Preface', Wordsworth insists that the aims of literature cannot be achieved 'by the mere communication of *knowledge*', and that the poet must 'call forth and...communicate *power*' (Wordsworth, *Prose*, vol. III, pp. 81–2; Wordsworth's italics). De Quincey would, of course, have known these written sources. Yet as he stressed in the 1823 essay, and as seems so often to have been the case, the idea originated in 'conversation with Mr Wordsworth'.

Critics have discussed De Quincey's conception of 'knowledge' and 'power' at length. René Wellek was unimpressed: 'The...distinction seems to amount to little more than the distinction between imaginative and applied literature', he argues; and 'the vagueness and multiplicity of meaning which it is possible to assign to the term "power" and the fact that also "knowledge is power" have discredited De Quincey's terminology'. But for John E. Jordan, the distinction provides 'the best single example of what De Quincey expected of literature and of the persistent dualism in his thought'. D. D. Devlin writes that the idea enabled De Quincey to build 'a substantial theory of criticism'. For Robert Lance Snyder, the concept is meaningful to De Quincey 'principally because it enables him to surmount a metaphysics of absence', but also because it provides him 'with a paradigmatic but equivocal myth of the agency of power'. Several commentators have written revealingly on the differences between the 1823 and the 1848 formulations of the distinction, and how 'the later essay...shifts the ground of the discussion...from the affective to the ethical', as Jonathan Bate puts it (René Wellek, 'De Quincey's Status in the History of Ideas' in *Philological Quarterly*, 23 (July 1944), pp. 268–9; John E. Jordan, *Thomas De Quincey, Literary Critic* (Berkeley: University of California Press, 1952), p. 38; D. D. Devlin, *De Quincey, Wordsworth and the Art of Prose* (London: Macmillan, 1983), p. 78; Robert Lance Snyder, 'De Quincey's Literature of Power: A Mythic Paradigm' in *Studies in English Literature*, 26 (1986), p. 692; Jonathan Bate, 'The

Literature of Power: Coleridge and De Quincey' in *Coleridge's Visionary Languages*, eds Tim Fulford and Morton D. Paley (Cambridge: D. S. Brewer, 1993), p. 149).

ART. I. – *The Works of Alexander Pope, Esquire*. By W. Roscoe, Esq. A New Edition. In eight vols. London, 1847.

EVERY great classic in our native language should from time to time be reviewed anew; and especially if he belongs in any considerable extent to that section of the literature which connects itself with manners; and if his reputation originally, or his style of composition, is likely to have been much influenced by the transient fashions of his own age. The withdrawal, for instance, from a dramatic poet, or a satirist, of any false lustre which he has owed to his momentary connexion with what we may call the *personalities* of a fleeting generation, or of any undue shelter to his errors which may have gathered round them from political bias, or from intellectual infirmities amongst his partizans, will sometimes seriously modify, after a century or so, the fairest *original* appreciation of a fine writer. A window, composed of Claude Lorraine glasses,[1] spreads over the landscape outside a disturbing effect, which not the most practised eye can evade. The *idola theatri*[2] affect us all. No man escapes the contagion from his contemporary bystanders. And the reader may see further on, that, had Pope been merely a satiric poet, he must in these times have laid down much of the splendour which surrounds him in our traditional estimate of his merit. Such a renunciation would be a forfeit – not always to errors in himself – but sometimes to errors in that stage of English society, which forced the ablest writer into a collusion with its own meretricious tastes. The antithetical prose 'characters,' as they were technically termed, which circulated amongst the aristocracy in the early part of the last century, the style of the dialogue in such comedy as was then popular, and much of the occasional poetry in that age, expose an immoderate craving for glittering effects from contrasts too harsh to be natural, too sudden to be durable, and too fantastic to be harmonious. To meet this vicious taste, from which (as from any diffusive taste) it is vain to look for *perfect* immunity in any writer lying immediately under its beams, Pope sacrificed in *one* mode of composition, the simplicities of nature and sincerity; and had he practised no other mode, we repeat that *now* he must have descended from his pedestal. To some extent he is degraded even as it is; for the reader cannot avoid whispering to himself – what quality of thinking must *that* be which allies itself so naturally (as will be shewn) with distortions of fact or of philosophic truth? But, had his whole writings been of that same cast, he must have been degraded altogether, and a star would have fallen from our English galaxy of poets.

We mention this particular case as a reason generally for renewing by intervals the examination of great writers, and liberating the verdict of their contemporaries from the casual disturbances to which every age is liable in its judgments and in its tastes. As books multiply to an unmanageable excess, selection becomes more and more a necessity for readers, and the power of selection more and more a desperate problem for the busy part of readers. The possibility of selecting wisely is becoming continually more hopeless, as the necessity for selection is becoming continually more crying. Exactly as the growing weight of books overlays and stifles the power of comparison, *pari passu*[3] is the call for comparison the more clamorous; and thus arises a duty, correspondingly more urgent, of searching and revising until everything spurious has been weeded out from amongst the Flora of our highest literature; and until the waste of time for those who have so little at their command, is reduced to a *minimum*. For, where the good cannot be read in its twentieth part, the more requisite it is that no part of the bad should steal an hour of the available time; and it is not to be endured that people without a minute to spare should be obliged first of all to read a book before they can ascertain whether it was at all *worth* reading. The public cannot read by proxy as regards the good which it is to appropriate, but it *can* as regards the poison which it is to escape. And thus, as literature expands, becoming continually more of a household necessity, the duty resting upon critics (who are the vicarious readers for the public) becomes continually more urgent – of reviewing all works that may be supposed to have benefited too much or too indiscriminately by the superstition of a name. The *praegustatores*[4] should have tasted of every cup, and reported its quality, before the public call for it; and, above all, they should have done this in all cases of the higher literature – that is, of literature properly so called.

What is it that we mean by *literature*? Popularly, and amongst the thoughtless, it is held to include everything that is printed in a book. Little logic is required to disturb *that* definition; the most thoughtless person is easily made aware that in the idea of *literature* one essential element is – some relation to a general and common interest of man, so that what applies only to a local – or professional – or merely personal interest, even though presenting itself in the shape of a book, will not belong to literature. So far the definition is easily narrowed; and it is as easily expanded. For not only is much that takes a station in books not literature; but inversely, much that really *is* literature never reaches a station in books. The weekly sermons of Christendom, that vast pulpit literature which acts so extensively upon the popular mind – to warn, to uphold, to renew, to comfort, to alarm, does not attain the sanctuary of libraries in the ten thousandth part of its extent. The drama again, as, for instance, the finest of Shakspere's plays in England, and all leading Athenian plays in the noontide of the Attic stage, operated as a literature on the public mind, and were (according to the strictest letter of that term) *published* through the audiences that witnessed[*] their representation some time before they were published as things to be read; and they were published in this scenical mode of publication with much more effect than they could have had as books, during ages of costly copying or of costly printing.

Books, therefore, do not suggest an idea co-extensive and interchangeable with the idea of literature; since much literature, scenic, forensic, or didactic, (as from lecturers and public orators,) may never come into books; and much that *does* come into books, may connect itself with no literary interest.[6] But a far more important correction, applicable to the common vague idea of literature, is to be sought – not so much in a better definition of literature, as in a sharper distinction of the two functions which it fulfils. In that great social organ, which collectively we call literature, there may be distinguished two separate offices that may blend and often *do* so, but capable severally of a severe insulation, and naturally fitted for reciprocal repulsion. There is first the literature of *knowledge*, and secondly, the literature of *power*. The function of the first is – to *teach;* the function of the second is – to *move:* the first is a rudder, the second an oar or a sail. The first speaks to the *mere* discursive understanding; the second speaks ultimately it may happen to the higher understanding or reason, but always *through* affections of pleasure and sympathy. Remotely, it may travel towards an object seated in what Lord Bacon calls *dry* light;[7] but proximately it does and must operate, else it ceases to be a literature of *power*, on and through that *humid* light which clothes itself in the mists and glittering *iris* of human passions, desires, and genial emotions. Men have so little reflected on the higher functions of literature, as to find it a paradox if one should describe it as a mean or subordinate purpose of books to give information. But this is a paradox only in the sense which makes it honourable to be paradoxical. Whenever we talk in ordinary language of seeking information or gaining knowledge, we understand the words as connected with something of absolute novelty. But it is the grandeur of all truth which *can* occupy a very high place in human interests, that it is never absolutely novel to the meanest of minds: it exists eternally by way of germ or latent principle in the lowest as in the highest, needing to be developed but never to be planted. To be capable of transplantation is the immediate criterion of a truth that ranges on a lower scale. Besides which, there is a rarer thing than truth, namely, *power* or deep sympathy with truth. What is the effect, for instance, upon society – of children? By the pity, by the tenderness, and by the peculiar modes of admiration, which connect themselves with the helplessness, with the innocence, and with the simplicity of children, not only are the primal affections strengthened and continually renewed, but the qualities which are dearest in the sight of heaven – the frailty for instance, which

[*] Charles I., for example, when Prince of Wales, and many others in his father's court, gained their known familiarity with Shakspere – not through the original quartos, so slenderly diffused, nor through the first folio of 1623, but through the court representations of his chief dramas at Whitehall.[5]

appeals to forbearance, the innocence which symbolizes the heavenly, and the simplicity which is most alien from the worldly, are kept up in perpetual remembrance, and their ideals are continually refreshed. A purpose of the same nature is answered by the higher literature, viz. the literature of power. What do you learn from Paradise Lost? Nothing at all. What do you learn from a cookery-book? Something new, something that you did not know before, in every paragraph. But would you therefore put the wretched cookery-book on a higher level of estimation than the divine poem? What you owe to Milton is not any knowledge, of which a million separate items are still but a million of advancing steps on the same earthly level; what you owe – is *power*, that is, exercise and expansion to your own latent capacity of sympathy with the infinite, where every pulse and each separate influx is a step upwards – a step ascending as upon a Jacob's ladder[8] from earth to mysterious altitudes above the earth. *All* the steps of knowledge, from first to last, carry you farther on the same plane, but could never raise you one foot above your ancient level of earth: whereas, the very *first* step in power is a flight – is an ascending into another element where earth is forgotten.

Were it not that human sensibilities are ventilated and continually called out into exercise by the great phenomena of infancy, or of real life as it moves through chance and change, or of literature as it recombines these elements in the mimicries of poetry, romance, &c., it is certain that, like any animal power or muscular energy falling into disuse, all such sensibilities would gradually droop and dwindle. It is in relation to these great *moral* capacities of man that the literature of power, as contradistinguished from that of knowledge, lives and has its field of action. It is concerned with what is highest in man: for the Scriptures themselves never condescend to deal by suggestion or co-operation, with the mere discursive understanding: when speaking of man in his intellectual capacity, the Scriptures speak not of the understanding, but of '*the understanding heart*,'[9] – making the heart, *i.e.*, the great *intuitive* (or non-discursive) organ,[10] to be the interchangeable formula for man in his highest state of capacity for the infinite. Tragedy, romance, fairy-tale, or epopee,[11] all alike restore to man's mind the ideals of justice, of hope, of truth, of mercy, of retribution, which else, (left to the support of daily life in its realities,) would languish for want of sufficient illustration. What is meant for instance by *poetic justice*? – It does not mean a justice that differs by its object from the ordinary justice of human jurisprudence; for then it must be confessedly a very bad kind of justice; but it means a justice that differs from common forensic justice by the degree in which it *attains* its object, a justice that is more omnipotent over its own ends, as dealing – not with the refractory elements of earthly life – but with the elements of its own creation, and with materials flexible to its own purest preconceptions. It is certain that, were it not for the literature of power, these ideals would often remain amongst us as mere arid notional forms; whereas, by the creative forces of man put forth in literature, they gain a vernal life of restoration, and germinate into vital activities. The commonest novel, by moving in alliance with human fears and hopes, with human instincts of wrong and right, sustains and quickens those affections. Calling them into action, it rescues them from torpor. And hence the pre-eminency over all authors that merely *teach*, of the meanest that *moves;* or that teaches, if at all, indirectly *by* moving. The very highest work that has ever existed in the literature of knowledge, is but a *provisional* work: a book upon trial and sufferance, and *quamdiu bene se gesserit*.[12] Let its teaching be even partially revised, let it be but expanded, nay, even let its teaching be but placed in a better order, and instantly it is superseded. Whereas the feeblest works in the literature of power, surviving at all, survive as finished and unalterable amongst men. For instance, the *Principia* of Sir Isaac Newton[13] was a book *militant* on earth from the first. In all stages of its progress it would have to fight for its existence: 1*st*, as regards absolute truth; 2*dly*, when that combat is over, as regards its form or mode of presenting the truth. And as soon as a La Place,[14] or anybody else, builds higher upon the foundations laid by this book, effectually he throws it out of the sunshine into decay and darkness; by weapons won from this book he superannuates and destroys this book, so that soon the name of Newton remains, as a mere *nominis umbra*,[15] but his book, as a living power, has transmigrated into other forms. Now, on the contrary, the Iliad, the Prometheus of Aeschylus,[16] – the Othello or King Lear, – the Hamlet or Macbeth,[17] – and the Paradise Lost, are not militant but triumphant for ever as long as the languages exist in which they speak or can be taught to speak. They never *can* transmigrate into new incarnations. To reproduce *these* in new forms, or variations, even if in some things they should be improved, would be to plagiarize. A good steam-engine is properly superseded by a better. But one lovely pastoral valley is not superseded by another, nor a statue of Praxiteles by a statue of Michael Angelo.[18] These things are not separated by imparity, but by disparity. They are not thought of as unequal under the same standard, but as differing in *kind*, and as equal under a different standard. Human works of immortal beauty and works of nature in one respect stand on the same footing: they never absolutely repeat each other: never approach so near as not to differ; and they differ not as better and worse, or simply by more and less: they differ by undecipherable and incommunicable differences, that cannot be caught by mimicries, nor be reflected in the mirror of copies, nor become ponderable in the scales of vulgar comparison.

Applying these principles to Pope, as a representative of fine literature in general, we would wish to remark the claim which he has, or which any equal writer has, to the attention and jealous winnowing of those critics in particular who watch over public morals. Clergymen, and all the organs of public criticism put in motion by clergymen, are more especially concerned in the just appreciation of such writers, if the two canons are remembered, which we have endeavoured to illustrate, viz., that all works in this class, as opposed to those in the literature of knowledge, 1*st*, work by far deeper agencies; and, 2*dly*, are more permanent; in the strictest sense they are κτηματα ἐς ἀει:[19]

and what evil they do, or what good they do, is commensurate with the national language, sometimes long after the nation has departed. At this hour, 500 years since their creation, the tales of Chaucer,* never equalled on this earth for tenderness, and for life of picturesqueness, are read familiarly by many in the charming language of their natal day, and by others in the modernizations of Dryden, of Pope, and Wordsworth.[20] At this hour, 1800 years since their creation, the Pagan tales of Ovid,[21] never equalled on this earth for the gaiety of their movement and the capricious graces of their narrative, are read by all Christendom. This man's people and their monuments are dust; but *he* is alive: he has survived them, as he told us that he had it in his commission to do, by a thousand years; 'and *shall* a thousand more.'[22]

All the literature of knowledge builds only ground-nests, that are swept away by floods, or confounded by the plough; but the literature of power builds nests in aerial altitudes of temples sacred from violation, or of forests inaccessible to fraud. *This* is a great prerogative of the *power* literature: and it is a greater which lies in the mode of its influence. The *knowledge* literature, like the fashion of this world, passeth away.[23] An Encyclopaedia is its abstract; and, in this respect, it may be taken for its speaking symbol – that, before one generation has passed, an Encyclopaedia is superannuated; for it speaks through the dead memory and unimpassioned understanding, which have not the *rest* of higher faculties, but are continually enlarging and varying their phylacteries.[24] But all literature, properly so called – literature Κατ' ἐξοχην,[25] for the very same reason that it is so much more durable than the literature of knowledge, is (and by the very same proportion it is) more intense and electrically searching in its impressions. The directions in which the tragedy of this planet has trained our human feelings to play, and the combinations into which the poetry of this planet has thrown our human passions of love and hatred, of admiration and contempt, exercises a power bad or good over human life, that cannot be contemplated when seen stretching through many generations, without a sentiment allied to awe.† And of this let every one be assured – that he owes to the impassioned books which he has read, many a thousand more of emotions than he can consciously trace back

* The Canterbury Tales were not made public until 1380 or thereabouts: but the composition must have cost 30 or more years; not to mention that the work had probably been finished for some years before it was divulged.

† The reason why the broad distinctions between the two literatures of power and knowledge so little fix the attention, lies in the fact, that a vast proportion of books – history, biography, travels, miscellaneous essays, &c., lying in a middle zone, confound these distinctions by interblending them. All that we call 'amusement' or 'entertainment,' is a diluted form of the power belonging to passion, and also a mixed form; and where threads of direct *instruction* intermingle in the texture with these threads of *power*, this absorption of the duality into one representative *nuance* neutralises the separate perception of either. Fused into a *tertium quid*,[26] or neutral state, they disappear to the popular eye as the repelling forces, which in fact they are.

to them. Dim by their origination, these emotions yet arise in him, and mould him through life like the forgotten incidents of childhood.

In making a revaluation of Pope as regards some of his principal works, we should have been glad to examine more closely than we shall be able to do, some popular errors affecting his whole intellectual position; and especially these two, *first*, That he belonged to what is idly called the *French* School of our literature;[27] *secondly*, That he was specially distinguished from preceding poets by *correctness*. The first error has infected the whole criticism of Europe. The Schlegels,[28] with all their false airs of subtlety, fall into this error in discussing every literature of Christendom. But, if by a mere accident of life any poet *had* first turned his thoughts into a particular channel on the suggestion of some French book, *that* would not justify our classing what belongs to universal nature, and what *inevitably* arises at a certain stage of social progress, under the category of a French creation. Somebody must have been first in point of time upon every field: but this casual precedency establishes no title whatever to authority, or plea of original dominion over fields that lie within the inevitable line of march upon which nations are moving. Had it happened that the first European writer on the higher geometry was a Graeco-Sicilian, *that* would not have made it rational to call geometry the Graeco-Sicilian Science. In *every* nation first comes the higher form of passion, next the lower. This is the mere order of nature in governing the movements of human intellect, as connected with social evolution; this is therefore the universal order, that in the earlier stages of literature, men deal with the great elementary grandeurs of passion, of conscience, of the will in self-conflict; they deal with the capital struggles of the human race in raising empires, or in overthrowing them – in vindicating their religion, (as by crusades,) or with the more mysterious struggles amongst spiritual races allied to our own, that have been dimly revealed to us. We have an Iliad, a Jerusalem Delivered,[29] a Paradise Lost. These great subjects exhausted, or exhausted in their more inviting manifestations, inevitably, by the mere endless motion of society, there succeeds a lower key of passion. Expanding social intercourse in towns, multiplied and crowded more and more, banishes those gloomier and grander phases of human history from literature. The understanding is quickened: the lower faculties of the mind – fancy and the habit of minute distinction, are applied to the contemplation of society and manners. Passion begins to wheel in lower flights, and to combine itself with interests that in part are addressed to the insulated understanding – observing, refining, reflecting. This may be called the *minor* key of literature in opposition to the *major*, as cultivated by Shakspere, Spenser, Milton. But this key arises spontaneously in *every* people, and by a necessity as sure as any that moulds the progress of civilization. Milton and Spenser were *not* of any Italian school. Their Italian studies were the result and not the cause of the determination given to their minds by nature working in conjunction with their social period. It is equally childish to say of Dryden and Pope – that they belonged to any French school. That thing which they did, they *would* have done though France had been at the back of China. The school to which they belonged, was a school developed at a certain stage of progress in all nations alike by the human heart as modified by the human understanding: it is a school depending on the peculiar direction given to the sensibilities by the reflecting faculty, and by the new phases of society. Even as a fact, (though a change as to the fact could not make any change at all in the philosophy of the case,) it is not true that either Dryden or Pope was influenced by French literature. Both of them had a very imperfect acquaintance with the French language. Dryden ridiculed French literature;[30] and Pope, except for some purposes connected with his Homeric translations, read as little of it as convenience would allow. But, had this been otherwise, the philosophy of the case stands good; that, after the primary formations of the fermenting intellect, come everywhere – in Thebes[31] or Athens, in France or England, the secondary: that, after the creating passion comes the reflecting and recombining passion: that after the solemnities and cloistral grandeurs of life – solitary and self-conflicting, comes the recoil of a self-observing and self-dissecting stage, derived from life social and gregarious. After the Iliad, but doubtless many generations after, comes a Batrachomyomachia:[32] after the gorgeous masque of our forefathers came always the anti-masque, that threw off echoes as from some devil's laughter in mockery of the hollow and transitory pomps that went before.

It is an error equally gross, and an error in which Pope himself participated, that his plume of distinction from preceding poets consisted in *correctness*. Correctness in what? Think of the admirable qualifications for settling the scale of such critical distinctions which that man must have had who turned out upon this vast world the single oracular word 'correctness' to shift for itself, and explain its own meaning to all generations. Did he mean logical correctness in maturing and connecting thoughts? But of all poets that have practised reasoning in verse, Pope is the one most inconsequential in the deduction of his thoughts, and the most severely distressed in any effort to effect or to explain the dependency of their parts. There are not ten consecutive lines in Pope unaffected by this infirmity. All his thinking proceeded by insulated and discontinuous jets:[33] and the only resource for *him*, or chance of even seeming correctness, lay in the liberty of stringing his aphoristic thoughts like pearls – having no relation to each other but that of contiguity. To *set* them like diamonds was for Pope to risk distraction: to systematize was ruin. – On the other hand, if this elliptical word *correctness* is to be understood with such a complementary qualification as would restrict it to Pope's use of *language*, that construction is even more untenable than the other – more conspicuously untenable – for many are they who have erred by illogical thinking, or by distracted evolution of thoughts: but rare is the man amongst classical writers in any language who has disfigured his meaning more remarkably than Pope by imperfect expression. We do not speak of plebeian phrases, of exotic phrases, of slang, from which Pope was not free, though *more* free than many of his contemporaries. From vulgarism indeed he was shielded, though imperfectly, by the aristocratic society which he kept: *they* being right, *he* was right: and he erred only in the cases where they misled him; for even the refinement of that age was oftentimes coarse and vulgar. His grammar, indeed, is often vicious: preterites and participles he constantly confounds, and registers this class of blunders for ever by the cast-iron index of rhymes that never *can* mend. But worse than this mode of viciousness is his syntax, which is so bad as to darken his meaning at times, and at other times to defeat it. But these were errors cleaving to his times; and it would be unfair to exact from Pope a better quality of diction than belonged to his contemporaries. Still it is indisputable that a better model of diction and of grammar prevailed a century before Pope. In Spenser, in Shakspere, in the Bible of King James' reign,[34] and in Milton, there are very few grammatical errors.* But Pope's defect in language was almost peculiar to himself. It lay in an inability, nursed doubtless by indolence, to carry out and perfect the expression of the thought which he wishes to communicate. The language does not realize the idea: it simply suggests or hints it. Thus to give a single illustration, –

> 'Know, God and Nature only are the same:
> In man the judgment shoots at flying game.'[40]

* And this purity of diction shews itself in many points arguing great vigilance of attention, and also great anxiety for using the language powerfully as the most venerable of traditions, when treating the most venerable of subjects. For instance, the Bible never condescends to the mean colloquial preterites of *chid* for *did chide*, or *writ* for *did write*, but always uses the full dress word *chode*, and *wrote*. Pope might have been happier had he read his Bible more: but assuredly he would have improved his English. A question naturally arises – How it was that the elder writers – Shakspere in particular, (who had seen so little of higher society when he wrote his youthful poems of Lucrece and Adonis,)[35] should have maintained so much purer a grammar? Dr Johnson indeed, but most falsely, says that Shakspere's grammar is licentious. 'The style of Shakspere' (these are the exact words of the Doctor in his preface) 'was in itself ungrammatical, perplexed, and obscure.'[36] An audacious misrepresentation! In the doctor himself, a legislator for the language, we undertake to shew more numerically of trespasses against grammar, but (which is worse still) more unscholarlike trespasses. Shakspere is singularly correct in grammar. One reason, we believe, was this: from the restoration of Charles II.[37] decayed the *ceremonious* exteriors of society. Stiffness and reserve melted away before the familiarity and impudence of French manners. Social meetings grew far more numerous as towns expanded; social pleasure far more began now to depend upon conversation; and conversation, growing less formal, quickened its pace. Hence came the call for rapid abbreviations: the *'tis* and *'twas*, the *can't* and *don't* of the two post-Miltonic generations arose under this impulse; and the general impression has ever since subsisted amongst English writers – that language, instead of being an exquisitely beautiful vehicle for the thoughts – a robe that never can be adorned with too much care or piety, is in fact a dirty high-road which all people detest whilst all are forced to use it, and to the keeping of which in repair no rational man ever contributes a trifle that is not forced from him by some severity of Quarter Sessions.[38] The great corrupter of English was the conversational instinct for rapidity.[39] A more honourable source of corruption lay in the growth of new ideas, and the continual influx of foreign words to meet them. Spanish words arose, like *reformado*, *privado*, *desperado*, and French ones past counting. But as these retained their foreign forms of structure, they reacted to vitiate the language still more by introducing a piebald aspect of books which it seemed a matter of necessity to tolerate for the interests of wider thinking. The perfection of this horror was never attained except amongst the Germans.

The first line one would naturally construe into this: that God and Nature were in harmony, whilst all other objects were scattered into incoherency by difference and disunion. Not at all; it means nothing of the kind; but that God and Nature only are exempted from the infirmities of change. *They* only continue uniform and self-consistent. This might mislead many readers; but the second line *must* do so: for who would not understand the syntax to be – that the judgment, as it exists in man, shoots at flying game? But, in fact, the meaning is – that the judgment, in aiming its calculations at man, aims at an object that is still on the wing, and never for a moment stationary. We give this as a specimen of a fault in diction – the very worst amongst all that are possible; to write bad grammar or colloquial slang does not necessarily obscure the sense; but a fault like this is a treachery, and hides the true meaning under the cloud of a conundrum: nay worse; for even a conundrum has fixed conditions for determining its solution, but this sort of mutilated expression is left to the solutions of conjecture.

There are endless varieties of this fault in Pope, by which he sought relief for himself from half-an-hour's labour, at the price of utter darkness to his reader.

One editor distinguishes amongst the epistles that which Pope addressed to Lord Oxford some years after his fall, as about the most '*correct*, musical, dignified, and affecting'[41] that the poet has left. Now, even as a specimen of vernacular English, it is conspicuously bad: the shocking gallicism, for instance, of '*attend*' for 'wait his leisure,' in the line 'For *him*, *i.e.* on his behalf, thou oft hast bid the world attend,'[42] would alone degrade the verses. To bid the world attend – is to bid the world listen attentively; whereas what Pope means is, that Lord Oxford bade the world wait in his ante-chamber, until he had leisure from his important conferences with a poet, to throw a glance upon affairs so trivial as those of the human race. This use of the word *attend* is a shocking violation of the English idiom; and even the slightest would be an unpardonable blemish in a poem of only forty lines, which ought to be polished as exquisitely as a cameo. It is a still worse disfiguration of the very same class, viz. a silent confession of defeat, in a regular wrestling-match with the difficulties of a metrical expression, that the poem terminates thus –

'Nor fears to tell that *Mortimer* is he;'[43]

why *should* he fear? Really there is no very desperate courage required for telling the most horrible of secrets about Mortimer. Had Mortimer even been so wicked as to set the Thames on fire, safely it might have been published by Mortimer's bosom-friend to all magistrates, sheriffs, and constables; for not a man of them would have guessed in what hiding-place to look for Mortimer, or who Mortimer might be. True it is, that a secondary earldom, conferred by Queen Anne upon Robert Harley, was that of Mortimer; but it lurked unknown to the public ear; it was a coronet that lay hid under the beams of *Oxford* – a title so long familiar to English ears, when descending through six and twenty generations of de Veres.[44] Quite as reasonable it would be, in a birth-day ode to the Prince of Wales, if he were addressed as my Lord of Chester, or Baron of Renfrew, or your Grace of Cornwall. To express a thing in cipher may do for a conspirator; but a poet's *correctness* is shown in his intelligibility.

Amongst the early poems of Pope, the 'ELOISA TO ABELARD'[45] has a special interest of a double order: first, it has a *personal* interest as the poem of Pope, because indicating the original destination of Pope's intellect, and the strength of his native vocation to a class of poetry in deeper keys of passion than any which he systematically cultivated. For itself also, and abstracting from its connexion with Pope's natural destination, this poem has a *second* interest, an intrinsic interest, that will always make it dear to impassioned minds. The self-conflict – the flux and reflux of the poor agitated heart – the spectacle of Eloisa now bending penitentially before the shadowy austerities of a monastic future, now raving upon the remembrances of the guilty past – one moment reconciled by the very anguish of her soul to the grandeurs of religion and of prostrate adoration, the next moment revolting to perilous retrospects of her treacherous happiness – the recognition by shining gleams through the very storm and darkness evoked by her earthly sensibilities, of a sensibility deeper far in its ground, and that trembled towards holier objects – the lyrical tumult of the changes, the hope, the tears, the rapture, the penitence, the despair – place the reader in tumultuous sympathy with the poor distracted nun. Exquisitely imagined, among the passages towards the end, is the introduction of a voice speaking to Eloisa from the grave of some sister nun, that, in long-forgotten years, once had struggled and suffered like herself,

> 'Once (like herself) that trembled, wept, and pray'd,
> Love's victim then, though now a sainted maid.'[46]

Exquisite is the passage in which she prefigures a visit yet to come from Abelard to herself – no more in the character of a lover, but as a priest, ministering by spiritual consolations to her dying hours, pointing her thoughts to heaven, presenting the Cross to her through the mists of death, and fighting for her as a spiritual ally against the torments of flesh. That anticipation was not gratified. Abelard died long before her; and the hour never arrived for *him* of which with such tenderness she says, –

> 'It will be *then* no crime to gaze on me.'[47]

But another anticipation *has* been fulfilled in a degree that she could hardly have contemplated; the anticipation, namely –

> 'That ages hence, when all her woes were o'er,
> And that rebellious heart should beat no more,'

wandering feet should be attracted from afar

'To Paraclete's white walls and silver springs,'[48]

as the common resting-place and everlasting marriage-bed of Abelard and Eloisa; that the eyes of many that had been touched by their story, by the memory of their extraordinary accomplishments in an age of darkness, and by the calamitous issue of their attachment, should seek, first and last, for the grave in which the lovers trusted to meet again in peace; and should seek it with interest so absorbing, that even amidst the ascent of hosannahs from the choir, amidst the grandeurs of high mass, the raising of the host, and 'the pomp of dreadful sacrifice,'[49] sometimes these wandering eyes should steal aside to the solemn abiding-place of Abelard and his Eloisa, offering so pathetic a contrast, by its peaceful silence, to the agitations of their lives; and that there, amidst thoughts which by right were all due and dedicated

'to heaven,
One *human* tear should drop and be forgiven.'[50]

We may properly close this subject of Abelard and Eloisa, by citing, in English, the solemn Latin inscription placed in the last century – six hundred years after their departure from earth, over their common remains. They were buried in the same grave, Abelard dying first by a few weeks more than twenty-one years; his tomb was opened again to admit the coffin of Eloisa; and the tradition at Quincey, the parish near Nogent-sur-Seine, in which the monastery of the Paraclete[51] is situated, was – that at the moment of interment Abelard opened his arms to receive the impassioned creature that once had loved *him* so frantically, and whom *he* had loved with a remorse so memorable. The epitaph is singularly solemn in its brief simplicity, considering that it came from Paris, and from Academic wits: 'Here, under the same marble slab, lie the founder of this monastery, Peter Abelard, and its earliest Abbess, Heloisa – once united in studies, in love, in their unhappy nuptial engagements, and in penitential sorrow; but now, our hope is, reunited for ever in bliss.'[52]

The SATIRES of Pope, and what under another name *are* satires, viz. his MORAL EPISTLES,[53] offer a second variety of evidence to his voluptuous indolence. They offend against philosophic truth more heavily than the Essay on Man;[54] but not in the same way. The Essay on Man sins chiefly by want of central principle, and by want therefore of all coherency amongst the separate thoughts. But taken *as* separate thoughts, viewed in the light of fragments and brilliant aphorisms, the majority of the passages have a mode of truth; not of truth central and coherent, but of truth angular and splintered.[55] The Satires on the other hand were of false origin. They arose in a sense of talent for caustic effects, unsupported by any satiric heart. Pope had neither the malice (except in the most fugitive form) which thirsts for leaving wounds, nor on the other hand the deep moral indignation which burns in men whom Providence has from time to time armed with scourges for cleansing the sanctuaries of truth or justice. He was contented enough with society as he found it: bad it might be, but it was good enough for *him*: and it was the merest self-delusion if at any moment the instinct of glorying in his satiric mission (the *magnificabo apostolatum meum*)[56] persuaded him that in *his* case it might be said – *Facit indignatio versum*. The indignation of Juvenal[57] was not always very noble in its origin, or pure in its purpose: it was sometimes mean in its quality, false in its direction, extravagant in its expression: but it was tremendous in the roll of its thunders, and as withering as the scowl of a Mephistopheles.[58] Pope having no such internal principle of wrath boiling in his breast, being really (if one must speak the truth) in the most pacific and charitable frame of mind towards all scoundrels whatever, except such as might take it into their heads to injure a particular Twickenham grotto,[59] was unavoidably a hypocrite of the first magnitude when he affected (or sometimes really conceited himself) to be in a dreadful passion with offenders as a body. It provokes fits of laughter, in a man who knows Pope's real nature, to watch him in the process of brewing the storm that spontaneously will not come; whistling, like a mariner, for a wind to fill his satiric sails; and pumping up into his face hideous grimaces in order to appear convulsed with histrionic rage. Pope should have been counselled never to write satire, except on those evenings when he was suffering horribly from indigestion. By this means the indignation would have been ready-made. The rancour against all mankind would have been sincere; and there would have needed to be no extra expense in getting up the steam. As it is, the short puffs of anger, the uneasy snorts of fury in Pope's satires, give one painfully the feeling of a steam-engine with unsound lungs. Passion of any kind may become in some degree ludicrous, when disproportioned to its exciting occasions. But it is never entirely ludicrous, until it is self-betrayed as counterfeit. Sudden collapses of the manufactured wrath, sudden oblivion of the criminal, announce Pope's as *always* counterfeit.

Meantime insincerity is contagious. One falsehood draws on another. And having begun by taking a station of moral censorship, which was in the uttermost degree a self-delusion, Pope went on to other self-delusions in reading history the most familiar, or in reporting facts the most notorious. Warburton had more to do with Pope's satires, as an original suggestor,* and not merely as a commentator, than with any other section of his works. Pope and he hunted in couples over this field: and those who know the absolute craziness of Warburton's mind, the perfect frenzy and *lymphaticus*[61] *error* which possessed him for leaving all high-roads of truth and simplicity in order to trespass over hedge and ditch after coveys of shy paradoxes, cannot be surprised that Pope's good sense should often have quitted him under such guidance. – There is, amongst the earliest poems of Wordsworth, one which has interested many readers by its mixed strain of humour and tenderness. It

* It was *after* his connexion with Warburton that Pope introduced several of his *living* portraits into the Satires.[60]

describes two thieves who act in concert with each other. One is a very aged man, and the other is his great-grandson of three years old:

> 'There are ninety good years of fair and foul weather
> Between them, and both go a stealing together.'

What reconciles the reader to this social iniquity – is the imperfect accountability of the parties; the one being far advanced in dotage, and the other an infant. And thus

> 'Into what sin soever the couple may fall,
> *This* child but half-knows it, and *that* not at all.'

Nobody besides suffers from their propensities: since the child's mother makes good in excess all their depredations: and nobody is duped for an instant by their gross attempts at fraud: for

> 'Wherever they carry their plots and their wiles,
> Every face in the village is dimpled with smiles.'[62]

There was not the same disparity of years between Pope and Warburton as between old Daniel and his descendant in the third generation: Warburton was but ten years younger. And there was also this difference, that in the case of the two thieves neither was official ringleader: on the contrary, they took it turn about; great grand-papa was ringleader to-day, and the little great grandson to-morrow:

> 'Each in his turn was both leader and led:'[63]

whereas, in the connexion of the two literary accomplices, the Doctor was latterly always the instigator to any outrage on good sense; and Pope, from mere habit of deference to the Doctor's theology and theological wig, as well as from gratitude for the Doctor's pugnacity in his defence (since Warburton really was as good as a bull-dog in protecting Pope's advance or retreat,) followed with docility the leading of his reverend friend into any excess of folly. It is true, that oftentimes in earlier days Pope had run into scrapes from his own heedlessness: and the Doctor had not the merit of suggesting the *escapade*, but only of defending it; which he always does, (as sailors express it) 'with a will:'[64] for he never shows his teeth so much, or growls so ferociously, as when he suspects the case to be desperate. But in the satires, although the original absurdity comes forward in the text of Pope, and the Warburtonian note in defence is apparently no more than an after-thought of the good Doctor in his usual style of threatening to cudgel anybody who disputes his friend's assertion, yet sometimes the thought expressed and adorned by the poet had been prompted by the divine. This only can account for the savage crotchets, paradoxes, and conceits, which disfigure Pope's later edition of his satires.[65]

Truth, even of the most appreciable order, truth of history, goes to wreck continually under the perversities of Pope's satire applied to celebrated men;

and as to the higher truth of philosophy, it was still less likely to survive amongst the struggles for striking effects and startling contrasts. But worse are Pope's satiric sketches of women, as carrying the same outrages on good sense to a far greater excess; and as these expose the false principles on which he worked more brightly, and have really been the chief ground of tainting Pope's memory with the reputation of a woman-hater, (which he was *not*), they are worthy of separate notice.

It is painful to follow a man of genius through a succession of inanities descending into absolute nonsense, and of vulgarities sometimes terminating in brutalities. These are harsh words: but not harsh enough by half as applied to Pope's gallery of female portraits. What is the key to his failure? It is simply that, throughout this whole satiric section, not one word is spoken in sincerity of heart, or with any vestige of self-belief. The case was one of those so often witnessed, where either the indiscretion of friends, or some impulse of erring vanity in the writer, had put him upon undertaking a task in which he had too little natural interest to have either thought upon it with originality, or observed upon it with fidelity. Sometimes the mere coercion of system drives a man into such a folly. He treats a subject which branches into A, B, and C. Having discussed A and B, upon which he really *had* something to offer, he thinks it necessary to integrate his work by going forward to C, on which he knows nothing at all, and, what is even worse, for which in his heart he cares nothing at all. Fatal is all falsehood. Nothing is so sure to betray a man into the abject degradation of self-exposure as pretending to a knowledge which he has not, or to an enthusiasm which is counterfeit. By whatever mistake Pope found himself pledged to write upon the characters of women, it was singularly unfortunate that he had begun by denying to woman any characters at all.

> 'Matter too soft a lasting mark to bear,
> And best distinguished by black, brown, or fair.'[66]

Well for *him* if he had stuck to that liberal doctrine: 'Least said soonest mended.'[67] And *much* he could not easily have said upon a subject that he had pronounced all but a nonentity. In Van Troil's work, or in Horrebow's, upon Iceland, there is a well-known chapter regularly booked in the index – *Concerning the Snakes of Iceland*. This is the title, the running rubric; and the body of the chapter consists of these words – 'There *are* no snakes in Iceland.'[68] That chapter is soon studied, and furnishes very little opening for footnotes or supplements. Some people have thought that Mr Van T. might with advantage have amputated this unsnaky chapter on snakes; but at least nobody can accuse him of forgetting his own extermination of snakes from Iceland, and proceeding immediately to describe such horrible snakes as eye had never beheld amongst the afflictions of the island. Snakes there are none, he had protested; and, true to his word, the faithful man never wanders into any description of Icelandic snakes. Not so our satiric poet. He, with Mahometan liberality had denied characters, *i.e.*, souls, to women. 'Most women,' he says, 'have* no character at all;'[71] yet, for all that, finding himself pledged to treat this very subject of female characters, he introduces us to a museum of monsters in that department such as few fancies could create, and no logic can rationally explain. What was he to do? He had entered upon a theme concerning which, as the result has shewn, he had not one solitary thought – good, bad, or indifferent. Total bankruptcy was impending. Yet he was aware of a deep interest connected with this section of his satires; and to meet this interest he invented what was pungent, when he found nothing to record which was true.

It is a consequence of this desperate resource – this plunge into absolute fiction – that the true objection to Pope's satiric sketches of the other sex ought not to arise amongst women, as the people that suffered by his malice, but amongst readers generally, as the people that suffered by his fraud. He has promised one thing, and done another. He has promised a chapter in the zoology of nature, and he gives us a chapter in the fabulous zoology of the herald's college. A tigress is not much within ordinary experience, still there *is* such a creature; and in default of a better choice, that is, of a choice settling on a more familiar object, we are content to accept a good description of a tigress. We are reconciled; but we are *not* reconciled to a description, however spirited, of a basilisk. A viper might do; but not, if you please, a dragoness or a harpy. The describer knows, as well as any of us the spectators know, that he is romancing; the *incredulus odi*[72] overmasters us all; and we cannot submit to be detained by a picture which, according to the shifting humour of the poet – angry or laughing, is a lie where it is not a jest, is an affront to the truth of nature, where it is not confessedly an extravagance of drollery. In a playful fiction, we can submit with pleasure to the most enormous exaggerations; but then they must be offered as such. These of Pope's are not *so* offered, but as serious portraits – and in that character they affect us as odious and malignant libels. The malignity was not real – as indeed nothing was real, but a condiment for hiding insipidity. Let us examine two or three of them, equally with a view to the possibility of the object described, and to the delicacy of the description.

* By what might seem a strange oversight, but which in fact is a very natural oversight to one who was not uttering one word in which he seriously believed, Pope, in a prose note on verse 207, roundly asserts 'that the particular characters of women are *more various* than those of men.'[69] It is no evasion of this insufferable contradiction, that he couples with the greater variety of *characters* in women a greater uniformity in what he presumes to be their *ruling passion*. Even as to this ruling passion he cannot agree with himself for ten minutes; generally he says, that it is the love of pleasure; but sometimes (as at verse 208) forgetting this monotony, he ascribes to women a dualism of passions – love of pleasure and love of power – which dualism of itself must be a source of self-conflict, and therefore of inexhaustible variety in character:

> 'Those only fix'd, they first or last obey —
> The love of pleasure and the love of sway.'[70]

'How soft is Silia! fearful to offend;
The frail one's advocate, the weak one's friend.
To *her* Calista proved her conduct nice;
And good Simplicius asks of *her* advice.'[73]

Here we have the general outline of Silia's character; not particularly striking, but intelligible. She has a suavity of disposition that accommodates itself to all infirmities. And the worst thing one apprehends in her is – falseness: people with such honeyed breath for *present* frailties, are apt to exhale their rancour upon them when a little out of hearing. But really now this is no foible of Silia's. One likes her very well, and would be glad of her company to tea. For the dramatic reader knows who Calista is[74] – and if Silia has indulgence for *her*, she must be a thoroughly tolerant creature. Where is her fault then? You shall hear –

'Sudden she storms! she raves! – You tip the wink:
But spare your censure; Silia does *not* drink.
All eyes may see from what the change arose:
All eyes may see – (see what?) – a pimple on her nose.'[75]

Silia, the dulcet, is suddenly transformed into Silia the fury. But why? The guest replies to that question by *winking* at his fellow-guest; which most atrocious of vulgarities is expressed by the most odiously vulgar of phrases – he *tips* the wink – meaning to tip an insinuation that Silia is intoxicated. Not so, says the poet – drinking is no fault of hers – everybody may see [why not the winker then?] that what upsets her temper is a pimple on the nose. Let us understand you, Mr Pope. A pimple! – what, do you mean to say that pimples jump up on ladies' faces at the unfurling of a fan? If they really *did* so in the 12th of George II.,[76] and a lady, not having a pimple on leaving her dressing-room, might grow one whilst taking tea, then we think that a saint might be excused for storming a little. But how is it that the wretch who winks, does *not* see the pimple, the *causa teterrima*[77] of the sudden wrath; and Silia, who has no looking-glass at her girdle, *does*? And then who is it that Silia 'storms' at – the company, or the pimple? If at the company, we cannot defend her; but if at the pimple – oh, by all means – storm and welcome – she can't say anything worse than it deserves. Wrong or right, however, what moral does Silia illustrate more profound than this – that a particular lady, otherwise very amiable, falls into a passion upon suddenly finding her face disfigured? But then one remembers the song – '*My face is my fortune, sir, she said, sir, she said*'[78] – it is a part of *every* woman's fortune, so long as she is young. Now to find one's fortune dilapidating by changes so rapid as this – pimples rising as suddenly as April clouds, is far too trying a calamity, that a little fretfulness should merit either reproach or sneer. Dr Johnson's opinion was that the man, who cared little for dinner, could not be reasonably supposed to care much for anything.[79] More truly it may be said that the woman who is reckless about her face must be an unsafe person to trust with a secret. But seriously, what moral, what philosophic thought can be exemplified by a case so insipid, and so imperfectly explained as this? But we must move on.

Next, then, let us come to the case of Narcissa:[80] –

> 'Odious! in *woollen*?* 'Twould a saint provoke;'
> Were the last words that poor Narcissa spoke.
> 'No, let a charming chintz and Brussels lace
> Wrap my cold limbs, and shade my lifeless face;
> One would not sure be frightful when one's dead:
> And, Betty, give this cheek a little red.'[82]

Well, what's the matter now? What's amiss with Narcissa, that a satirist must be called in to hold an inquest upon her corpse, and take Betty's evidence against her mistress? Upon hearing any such question, Pope would have started up in the character (very unusual with *him*) of religious censor, and demanded whether one approved of a woman's fixing her last dying thought upon the attractions of a person so soon to dwell with darkness and worms? Was *that* right – to provide for coquetting in her coffin? Why no, not strictly right, its impropriety cannot be denied; but what strikes one even more is – the suspicion that it may be a lie. Be this as it may, there are two insurmountable objections to the case of Narcissa, even supposing it not fictitious – viz. first, that so far as it offends at all, it offends the religious sense, and not any sense of which satire takes charge; secondly, that without reference to the special functions of satire, *any* form of poetry whatever, or *any* mode of moral censure, concerns itself not at all with anomalies. If the anecdote of Narcissa were other than a fiction, then it was a case too peculiar and idiosyncratic to furnish a poetic illustration; neither moral philosophy nor poetry condescends to the monstrous or the abnormal; both one and the other deal with the catholic and the representative.

There is another *Narcissa* amongst Pope's tulip-beds of ladies,[83] who is even more open to criticism – because offering not so much an anomaly in one single trait of her character as an utter anarchy in all. *Flavia* and *Philomedé*[84] again present the same multitude of features with the same absence of all central principle for locking them into unity. They must have been distracting to themselves; and they are distracting to us a century later. *Philomedé*, by the way, stands for the second Duchess of Marlborough,† daughter of the great Duke. And these names lead us naturally to Sarah, the original, and (one may call her) the *historical* Duchess, who is libelled under the name of *Atossa*.[87] This character amongst all Pope's satiric sketches has been celebrated the

* This refers to the Act of Parliament for burying corpses in woollen, which greatly disturbed the fashionable costume in coffins *comme il faut*.[81]

† The sons of the Duke having died, the title and estates were so settled as to descend through this daughter, who married the Earl of Sunderland. In consequence of this arrangement, *Spencer* (until lately) displaced the great name of *Churchill*;[85] and the Earl became that second Duke of Marlborough, about whom Smollett tells in his History of England (Reign of George II.) so remarkable and to this hour so mysterious a story.[86]

most, with the single exception of his *Atticus*.[88] But the *Atticus* rested upon a different basis – it was true; and it was noble. Addison really *had* the infirmities of envious jealousy, of simulated friendship, and of treacherous collusion with his friend's enemies – which Pope imputed to him under the happy parisyllabic name of Atticus; and the mode of imputation, the tone of expostulation – indignant as regarded Pope's own injuries, but yet full of respect for Addison, and even of sorrowful tenderness – all this in combination with the interest attaching to a feud between two men so eminent, has sustained the *Atticus* as a classic remembrance in satiric literature. But the *Atossa* is a mere chaos of incompatibilities, thrown together as into some witch's cauldron. The witch, however, had sometimes an unaffected malignity, a sincerity of venom in her wrath, which acted chemically as a solvent for combining the heterogeneous ingredients in her kettle; whereas the want of truth and earnestness in Pope leave the incongruities in his kettle of description to their natural incoherent operation on the reader. We have a great love for the great Duchess of Marlborough, though too young by a hundred years* or so to have been that true and faithful friend which, as contemporaries, we *might* have been.

What we love Sarah for, is partly that she has been ill-used by all subsequent authors, one copying from another a fury against her which even in the first of these authors was not real. And a second thing which we love is her very violence, qualified as it was. Sulphureous vapours of wrath rose up in columns from the crater of her tempestuous nature against him that *deeply* offended her, but she neglected petty wrongs. Wait, however – let the volcanic lava have time to cool, and all returned to absolute repose. It has been said that she did not write her own book.[90] We are of a different opinion. The mutilations of the book were from other and inferior hands: but the main texture of the narrative and of the comments were, and must have been, from herself, since there could have been no adequate motive for altering them, and nobody else could have had the same motive for uttering them. It is singular that, in the case of the Duchess, as well as that of the Lady M. W. Montagu,[91] the same two men, without concert, were the original aggressors amongst the *gens de plume*,[92] viz., Pope, and subsequently Horace Walpole.[93] Pope suffered more from his own libellous assault upon *Atossa*, through a calumny against himself rebounding from it, than *Atossa* could have done from the point-blank shot of fifty such batteries. The calumny circulated was, that he had been bribed by the Duchess with a thousand pounds to suppress the character – which of itself was bad enough; but as the consummation of baseness it was added, that after all, in spite of the bribe, he caused it to be published. This calumny we believe to have been utterly without foundation. It is repelled by

* The Duchess died in the same year as Pope, viz., just in time by a few months to miss the Rebellion of 1745, and the second Pretender; spectacles which for little reasons (vindictive or otherwise) both of them would have enjoyed until the spring of 1746.[89]

Pope's character, incapable of any act so vile, and by his position, needing no bribes. But what we wish to add is, that the calumny is equally repelled by Sarah's character, incapable of any propitiation so abject. Pope wanted no thousand pounds; but neither did Sarah want his clemency. *He* would have rejected the £1000 cheque with scorn; but *she* would have scorned to offer it. Pope cared little for Sarah; but Sarah cared less for Pope.

What *is* offensive, and truly so, to every generous reader, may be expressed in two items: first, not pretending to have been himself injured by the Duchess, Pope was in this instance meanly adopting some third person's malice, which sort of intrusion into other people's quarrels is a sycophantic act, even where it may not have rested upon a sycophantic motive; secondly, that even as a second-hand malice it is not sincere. More shocking than the malice is the self-imposture of the malice: in the very act of puffing out his cheeks like Aeolus,[94] with ebullient fury, and conceiting himself to be in a passion perfectly diabolic, Pope is really unmoved, or angry only by favour of dyspepsy; and at a word of kind flattery from Sarah, (whom he was quite the man to love,) though not at the clink of her thousand guineas, he would have fallen at her feet, and kissed her beautiful hand with rapture. To enter a house of hatred as a junior partner, and to take the stock of malice at a valuation – (we copy from advertisements) – *that* is an ignoble act. But then how much worse in the midst of all this unprovoked wrath, real as regards the persecution which it meditates, but false as the flatteries of a slave in relation to its pretended grounds, for the spectator to find its malice counterfeit, and the fury only a plagiarism from some personated fury in an Opera.

There is no truth in Pope's satiric sketches of women – not even colourable truth; but if there were, how frivolous – how hollow, to erect into solemn monumental protestations against the whole female sex what, if examined, turn out to be pure casual eccentricities, or else personal idiosyncracies, or else foibles shockingly caricatured, but, above all, to be such foibles as could not have connected themselves with *sincere* feelings of indignation in any rational mind.

The length and breadth [almost we might say – the *depth*] of the shallowness, which characterizes Pope's Philosophy, cannot be better reflected than from the four well-known lines –

> 'For modes of faith let graceless zealots fight,
> *His* can't be wrong, whose life is in the right:
> For forms of government let fools contest,
> Whate'er is best administer'd is best.'[95]

In the first couplet, what Pope says is, that a life, which is irreproachable on a *human* scale of appreciation, neutralises and practically cancels all possible errors of creed, opinion, or theory. But this schism between the moral life of man and his moral faith, which takes for granted that either may possibly be true whilst the other is entirely false, can wear a moment's plausibility only by understanding *life* in so limited a sense as the sum of a man's external actions, appreciable by man. He whose life is in the right, cannot, says Pope, in any sense calling for blame, have a wrong faith; that is, if his life *were* right, his creed might be disregarded. But the answer is – that his life, according to any adequate idea of life in a moral creature, *cannot* be in the right unless in so far as it bends to the influences of a true faith. How feeble a conception must that man have of the infinity which lurks in a human spirit, who can persuade himself that its total capacities of life are exhaustible by the few gross *acts* incident to social relations or open to human valuation. An act, which may be necessarily limited and without opening for variety, may involve a large variety of motives – motives again, meaning grounds of action that are distinctly recognised for such, may (numerically speaking) amount to nothing at all when compared with the absolutely infinite influxes of feeling or combinations of feeling that vary the thoughts of man; and the true internal *acts* of moral man are his thoughts – his yearnings – his aspirations – his sympathies – his repulsions of heart. This is the life of man as it is appreciable by heavenly eyes. The scale of an alphabet – how narrow is that! Four or six and twenty letters, and all is finished. Syllables range through a wider compass. Words are yet more than syllables. But what are words to thoughts? Every word has a thought corresponding to it, so that not by so much as one solitary counter can the words outrun the thoughts. But every thought has *not* a word corresponding to it: so that the thoughts may outrun the words by many a thousand counters. In a developed nature they *do* so. But what are the thoughts when set against the modifications of thoughts by feelings, hidden even from him that feels them – or against the intercombinations of such modifications with others – complex with complex, decomplex with decomplex – these can be unravelled by no human eye. This is the infinite music that God only can read upon the vast harp of the human heart. Some have fancied that musical combinations might be exhausted. A new Mozart[96] might be impossible. All that he could do, might already have been done. Music laughs at *that*, as the sea laughs at palsy for its billows, as the morning laughs at old age and wrinkles for itself. But a harp, though a world in itself, is but a narrow world by comparison with the world of a human heart.

Now these thoughts, tinctured subtly with the perfume and colouring of human affections, make up the sum of what merits Κατ' ἐξοχην[97] the name of *life*: and these in a vast proportion depend for their possibilities of truth upon the degree of approach which the thinker makes to the appropriation of a pure faith. A man is thinking all day long, and putting thoughts into words: he is acting comparatively seldom. But are any man's thoughts brought into conformity with the openings to truth that a faith like the Christian's faith suggests? Far from it. Probably there never was one thought, from the foundation of the earth, that has passed through the mind of man, which did not offer some blemish, some sorrowful shadow of pollution, when it came up for review before a heavenly tribunal: that is, supposing it a thought entangled at all with human interests or human passions. But it is the *key* in which the thoughts move, that determines the stage of moral advancement. So long as we are human, many among the numerous and evanescent elements that enter (half-observed or not observed at all) into our thoughts, cannot *but* be tainted. But the governing – the predominant element it is which gives the character and the tendency to the thought: and this must become such, must become a governing element, through the quality of the ideals deposited in the heart by the quality of the religious faith. One pointed illustration of this suggests itself from another poem of Pope's, in which he reiterates his shallow doctrine. In his Universal Prayer he informs us, that it can matter little whether we pray to Jehovah or to Jove, so long as in either case we pray to the First Cause.[98] To contemplate God under that purely ontological relation to the world would have little more operative value for what is most important in man than if he prayed to gravitation. And it would have been more honest in Pope to say, as virtually he has said in the couplet under examination, that it can matter little whether man prays at all to any being. It deepens the scandal of this sentiment, coming from a poet professing Christianity, that a clergyman, (holding preferment in the English Church,) viz., Dr Joseph Warton, justifies Pope for this Pagan opinion, upon the ground that an ancient philosopher had uttered the same opinion long before.[99] What sort of philosopher? A Christian? No: but a Pagan. What then is the value of the justification? To a Pagan it could be no blame that he should avow a reasonable Pagan doctrine. In Irish phrase, it was 'true for *him*.' Amongst gods that were all utterly alienated from any scheme of moral government, all equally remote from the executive powers for sustaining such a government, so long as there was a practical anarchy and rivalship amongst themselves, there could be no sufficient reason for addressing vows to one rather than to another. The whole pantheon collectively could do nothing for moral influences, *a fortiori*,[100] no separate individual amongst them. Pope indirectly confesses this elsewhere by his own impassioned expression of Christian feelings, though implicitly denying it here by his mere understanding. For he reverberates elsewhere, by deep echoes, that power in Christianity which even in a legendary tale he durst not on mere principles of good sense and taste have ascribed to Paganism. For instance, how could a God, having no rebellion to complain of in man, pretend to any occasion of large forgiveness to man, or of framing means for reconciling this forgiveness with his own attribute of perfect holiness? What room, therefore, for ideals of mercy, tenderness, long-suffering, under any Pagan religion – under any worship of Jove! How again from Gods, disfigured by fleshly voluptuousness in every mode, could any countenance be derived to an awful ideal of purity? Accordingly we find, that even among the Romans, (the most advanced, as regards moral principle, of all heathen nations,) neither the deep fountain of benignity, nor that of purity, was unsealed in man's heart. So much of either was sanctioned as could fall within the purposes of the magistrate, but beyond that level neither fountain could have been permitted to throw up its column of waters, nor could in fact have had any impulse to sustain it in ascending; and not merely because it would have been repressed by ridicule as a deliration[101] of the human mind, but also because it would have been frowned upon gravely by the very principle of the Roman polity, as wandering away from *civic* objects. Even for so much of these great restorative ventilations as Rome enjoyed, she was indebted not to her religion but to elder forces that acted *in spite of* her religion, viz., the original law written upon the human heart. Now, on the other hand, Christianity has left a separate system of ideals amongst men, which (as regards their development) are continually growing in authority. Waters, after whatever course of wandering, rise to the level of their original springs. Christianity lying so far above all other fountains of religious influence, no wonder that its irrigations rise to altitudes otherwise unknown, and from which the distribution to every level of society becomes comparatively easy. Those men are reached oftentimes – choosing or not choosing – by the healing streams, who have not sought them, nor even recognised them. Infidels of the most determined class talk in Christian lands the morals of Christianity, and exact that morality with their hearts, constantly mistaking it for a morality co-extensive with man; and why? Simply from having been moulded unawares by its universal pressure through infancy, childhood, manhood, in the nursery, in the school, in the market-place. Pope himself, not by system or by affectation an infidel, not in any coherent sense a doubter but a careless and indolent assenter to such doctrines of Christianity as his own Church prominently put forward,[102] or as social respectability seemed to enjoin, – Pope therefore, so far a very lukewarm Christian, was yet unconsciously to himself searched profoundly by the Christian types of purity. This we may read in his

'Hark, the herald angels say,
— Sister spirit, come away!'[103]

Or again, as some people read the great lessons of spiritual ethics more pathetically in those that have transgressed them than in those that have been faithful to the end – read them in the Magdalen that fades away in penitential tears rather than in the virgin martyr triumphant on the scaffold – we may see in his own Eloisa, and in her fighting with the dread powers let loose upon her tempestuous soul, how profoundly Pope also had drunk from the streams of Christian sentiment through which a new fountain of truth had ripened a new vegetation upon earth. What was it that Eloisa fought with? What power afflicted her trembling nature, that any Pagan religions *could* have evoked? The human love, 'the nympholepsy of the fond despair,'[104] might have existed in a Vestal Virgin[105] of ancient Rome: but in the Vestal what counter-influence could have come into conflict with the passion of love through any operation whatever of religion? None of any ennobling character that could reach the Vestal's own heart. The way in which religion connected itself with the case was through a traditional superstition – not built upon any fine spiritual sense of female chastity as dear to heaven – but upon a gross fear of alienating a tutelary goddess by offering an imperfect sacrifice. This sacrifice, the sacrifice of the natural household* charities[106] in a few injured women on the altar of the goddess, was selfish in all its stages – selfish in the dark deity that could be pleased by the sufferings of a human being simply *as* sufferings, and not at all under any fiction that they were voluntary ebullitions of religious devotion – selfish in the senate and people who demanded these sufferings as a ransom paid through sighs and tears for *their* ambition – selfish in the Vestal herself, as sustained altogether by fear of a punishment too terrific to face, sustained therefore by the meanest principle in her nature. But in Eloisa how grand is the collision between deep religious aspirations and the persecuting phantoms of her undying human passion! The Vestal feared to be walled up alive, abandoned to the pangs of hunger – to the trepidations of darkness – to the echoes of her own lingering groans – to the torments perhaps of frenzy rekindling at intervals the decaying agonies of flesh. Was *that* what Eloisa feared? Punishment she had none to apprehend: the crime was past, and remembered only by the criminals: there was none to accuse but herself: there was none to judge but God. Wherefore should Eloisa fear? Wherefore and with what should she fight? She fought by turns against herself and against God, against her human nature and against her spiritual yearnings. How grand were the mysteries of her faith, how gracious and forgiving its condescensions! – How deep had been her human love, how imperishable its remembrance on earth! – 'What is it,' the Roman Vestal would have said, 'that this Christian lady is afraid of? What is the phantom that she seems to see?' Vestal! it is not fear, but grief. She sees an immeasurable heaven that seems to touch her eyes: so near is she to its love. Suddenly, an Abelard – the glory of his race – appears, that seems to touch her lips. The heavens recede, and diminish to a starry point twinkling in an unfathomable abyss; they are all but lost for *her*. Fire, it is in Eloisa that searches fire: the holy that fights with the earthly: fire that cleanses with fire that consumes; like cavalry the two fires wheel and counterwheel, advancing and retreating, charging and countercharging through and through each other. Eloisa trembles, but she trembles as a guilty creature[107] before a tribunal unveiled within the secrecy of her own nature: there was no such trembling in the heathen worlds, for there was no such secret tribunal. Eloisa fights with a shadowy enemy: there was no such fighting for Roman Vestals; because all the temples of our earth, (which is the crowned Vesta,) no, nor all the glory of her altars, nor all the pomp of her cruelties, could cite from the depths of a human spirit any such fearful shadow as Christian faith evokes from an afflicted conscience.

* The Vestals not only renounced marriage, at least for those years in which marriage could be a natural blessing, but also left their fathers' houses at an age the most trying to the human heart as regards the pangs of separation.

Pope therefore, wheresoever his heart speaks loudly, shows how deep had been his early impressions from Christianity. That is shown in his intimacy with Crashaw, in his Eloisa, in his Messiah, in his adaptation to Christian purposes of the Dying Adrian,[108] &c. It is remarkable also, that Pope betrays, in all places where he has occasion to *argue* about Christianity, how much grander and more faithful to that great theme were the subconscious perceptions of his heart than the explicit commentaries of his understanding. He, like so many others, was unable to read or interpret the testimonies of his own heart, which is a deep over which diviner agencies brood than are legible to the intellect. The cipher written on his heaven-visited heart was deeper than his understanding could interpret.

If the question were asked, What ought to have been the best among Pope's poems? most people would answer, the *Essay on Man*. If the question were asked, What *is* the worst? all people of judgment would say, the *Essay on Man*. Whilst yet in its rudiments this poem claimed the first place by the promise of its subject: when finished, by the utter failure of its execution, it fell into the last. The case possesses a triple interest – first, as illustrating the character of Pope modified by his situation; secondly, as illustrating the true nature of that 'didactic' poetry to which this particular poem is usually referred; thirdly, as illustrating the anomalous condition to which a poem so grand in its ambition has been reduced by the double disturbance of its proper movement; one disturbance through the position of Pope, another through his total misconception of didactic poetry. First, as regards Pope's situation, it may seem odd – but it is not so – that a man's social position should overrule his intellect. The scriptural denunciation of riches, as a snare to any man that is striving to rise above worldly views,[109] applies not at all less to the intellect, and to any man seeking to ascend by some aerial arch of flight above ordinary intellectual efforts. Riches are fatal to those continuities of energy without which there is no success of that magnitude. Pope had £800 a-year. *That* seems not so much. No, certainly not, with a wife and six children; but by accident Pope had no wife and no children. He was luxuriously at his ease: and this accident of his position in life fell in with a constitutional infirmity that predisposed him to indolence. Even his religious faith, by shutting him out from those public employments which else his great friends would have been too happy to obtain for him,[110] aided his idleness, or sometimes invested it with a false character of conscientious self-denial. He cherished his religion confessedly as a plea for idleness. The result of all this was, that in his habits of thinking and of study, (if *study* we can call a style of reading so desultory as *his*,) Pope became a pure *dilettante;* in his intellectual eclecticism he was a mere epicure, toying with the delicacies and varieties of literature; revelling in the first bloom of moral speculations, but sated immediately; fastidiously retreating from all that threatened labour, or that exacted continuous attention; fathoming, throughout all his vagrancies amongst books, no foundation; filling up no chasms; and with all his fertility of thought expanding no germs of new life.

This career of luxurious indolence was the result of early luck which made it possible, and of bodily constitution which made it tempting. And when we remember his youthful introduction to the highest circles in the metropolis,[111] where he never lost his footing, we cannot wonder that, without any sufficient motive for resistance, he should have sunk passively under his constitutional propensities, and should have fluttered amongst the flower-beds of literature or philosophy far more in the character of a libertine butterfly for casual enjoyment, than of a hard-working bee pursuing a premeditated purpose.

Such a character, strengthened by such a situation, would at any rate have disqualified Pope for composing a work severely philosophic, or where philosophy did more than throw a coloured light of pensiveness upon some sentimental subject. If it were necessary that the philosophy should enter substantially into the very texture of the poem, furnishing its interest and prescribing its movement, in that case Pope's combining and theorizing faculty would have shrunk as from the labour of building a pyramid. And wo to him where it did *not*, as really happened in the case of the Essay on Man. For his faculty of execution was under an absolute necessity of shrinking in horror from the enormous details of such an enterprise to which so rashly he had pledged himself. He was sure to find himself, as find himself he did, landed in the most dreadful embarrassment upon reviewing his own work. A work which, when finished, was not even begun; whose arches wanted their keystones; whose parts had no coherency; and whose pillars, in the very moment of being thrown open to public view, were already crumbling into ruins. This utter prostration of Pope in a work so ambitious as an Essay on Man – a prostration predetermined from the first by the personal circumstances which we have noticed, was rendered still more irresistible in the *second* place by the general misconception in which Pope shared as to the very meaning of 'didactic' poetry. Upon which point we pause to make an exposition of our own views.

What *is* didactic poetry? What does 'didactic' mean when applied as a distinguishing epithet to such an idea as a poem? The predicate destroys the subject: it is a case of what logicians call *contradictio in adjecto* – the unsaying by means of an attribute the very thing which in the subject of that attribute you have just affirmed. No poetry can have the function of teaching. It is impossible that a variety or species should contradict the very purpose which contradistinguishes its *genus*. The several species differ partially; but not by the whole idea which differentiates their class. Poetry, or any one of the fine arts, (all of which alike speak through the genial nature of man and his excited sensibilities,) can teach only as nature teaches, as forests teach, as the sea teaches, as infancy teaches, viz., by deep impulse, by hieroglyphic suggestion. Their teaching is not direct or explicit, but lurking, implicit, masked in deep incarnations. To teach formally and professedly is to abandon the very differential character and principle of poetry. If poetry could condescend to teach anything, it would be truths moral or religious. But even these it can utter only through symbols and actions. The great moral, for instance, the last result of the Paradise Lost, is once formally announced: but it teaches itself only by diffusing its lesson through the entire poem in the total succession of events and purposes: and even this succession teaches it only when the whole is gathered into unity by a reflex act of meditation; just as the pulsation of the physical heart can exist only when all the parts in an animal system are locked into one organization.

To address the *insulated* understanding is to lay aside the Prospero's robe of poetry.[112] The objection, therefore, to didactic poetry, as vulgarly understood, would be fatal even if there were none but this logical objection derived from its definition. To be in self-contradiction is, for any idea whatever, sufficiently to destroy itself. But it betrays a more obvious and practical contradiction when a little searched. If the true purpose of a man's writing a didactic poem were to teach, by what suggestion of idiocy should he choose to begin by putting on fetters? wherefore should the simple man volunteer to handcuff and manacle himself, were it only by the encumbrances of metre, and perhaps of rhyme? But these he will find the very least of his encumbrances. A far greater exists in the sheer necessity of omitting in any poem a vast variety of details, and even capital sections of the subject, unless they will bend to purposes of ornament. Now this collision between two purposes, the purpose of use in mere teaching and the purpose of poetic delight, shows, by the uniformity of its solution, which is the true purpose, and which the merely ostensible purpose. Had the true purpose been instruction, the moment that this was found incompatible with a poetic treatment, as soon as it was seen that the sound education of the reader-pupil could not make way without loitering to gather poetic flowers, the stern cry of 'duty' would oblige the poet to remember that he had dedicated himself to a didactic mission, and that he differed from other poets, as a monk from other men, by his vows of self-surrender to harsh ascetic functions. But, on the contrary, in the very teeth of this rule, wherever such a collision does really take place, and one or other of the supposed objects must give way, it is always the vulgar object of *teaching* (the pedagogue's object) which goes to the rear, whilst the higher object of poetic emotion moves on triumphantly. In reality not one didactic poet has ever yet attempted to use any parts or processes of the particular art which he made his theme, unless in so far as they seemed susceptible of poetic treatment, and only *because* they seemed so. Look at the poem of *Cyder*, by Philips, of the *Fleece* of Dyer, or (which is a still weightier example) at the *Georgics* of Virgil,[113] – does any of these poets show the least anxiety for the correctness of your principles, or the delicacy of your manipulations in the worshipful arts they affect to teach? No; but they pursue these arts through every stage that offers any attractions of beauty. And in the very teeth of all anxiety for teaching, if there existed traditionally any very absurd way of doing a thing which happened to be eminently picturesque, and, if opposed to this, there were some improved mode that had recommended itself to poetic hatred by being dirty and ugly, the poet (if a good one) would pretend never to have heard of this disagreeable improvement. Or if obliged, by some rival poet, not absolutely to ignore it, he would allow that such a thing could be done, but hint that it was hateful to the Muses or Graces, and very likely to breed a pestilence.

This subordination of the properly didactic function to the poetic, which, leaving the old essential distinction of poetry [viz., its sympathy with the genial motions of man's heart] to override all accidents of special variation, and showing that the essence of poetry never *can* be set aside by its casual modifications, – will be compromised by some loose thinkers, under the idea that in didactic poetry the element of instruction is in fact one element, though subordinate and secondary. Not at all. What we are denying is – that the element of instruction enters *at all* into didactic poetry. The subject of the Georgics, for instance, is Rural Economy as practised by Italian farmers: but Virgil not only *omits* altogether innumerable points of instruction insisted on as articles of religious necessity by Varro, Cato, Columella,[114] &c.; but, even as to those instructions which he *does* communicate, he is careless whether they are made technically intelligible or not. He takes very little pains to keep you from capital mistakes in *practising* his instructions; but he takes good care that you shall not miss any strong impression for the eye or the heart to which the rural process, or rural scene, may naturally lead. He pretends to give you a lecture on farming, in order to have an excuse for carrying you all round the beautiful farm. He pretends to show you a good plan for a farm-house, as the readiest means of veiling his impertinence in shewing you the farmer's wife and her rosy children. It is an excellent plea for getting a peep at the bonny milkmaids to propose an inspection of a model dairy. You pass through the poultry-yard, under whatever pretence, in reality to see the peacock and his harem. And so on to the very end, the pretended instruction is but in secret the connecting tie which holds together the laughing flowers going off from it to the right and to the left; whilst if ever at intervals this prosy thread of pure didactics is brought forward more obtrusively, it is so by way of foil, to make more effective upon the eye the prodigality of the floral magnificence.

We affirm therefore that the didactic poet is so far from seeking even a secondary or remote object in the particular points of information which he may happen to communicate, that much rather he would prefer the having communicated none at all. We will explain ourselves by means of a little illustration from Pope, which will at the same time furnish us with a miniature type of what we ourselves mean by a didactic poem, both in reference to what it *is* and to what it is *not*. In the Rape of the Lock there is a game at cards played, and played with a brilliancy of effect and felicity of selection, applied to the circumstances, which make it a sort of gem within a gem.[115] This game was not in the first edition of the poem,[116] but was an after-thought of Pope's, laboured therefore with more than usual care. We regret that *ombre*, the game described, is no longer played, so that the entire skill with which the mimic battle is fought cannot be so fully appreciated as in Pope's days. The strategics have partly perished, which really Pope ought not to complain of, since he suffers only as Hannibal, Marius, Sertorius,[117] suffered before him. Enough however survives of what will tell its own story. For what is it, let us ask, that a poet has to do in such a case, supposing that he were disposed to weave a didactic poem out of a pack of cards, as Vida has out of the chess-board?[118] In describing any particular game he does not seek to *teach* you that game – he postulates it as *already* known to you – but he relies upon separate resources. 1*st*, he will revive in the reader's eye, for picturesque effect, the well-known personal distinctions of the several kings, knaves, &c., their appearances and their powers. *2dly*, he will choose some game in which he may display a happy selection applied to the chances and turns of fortune, to the manoeuvres, to the situations of doubt, of brightening expectation, of sudden danger, of critical deliverance, or of final defeat. The interest of a war will be rehearsed – *lis est de paupere regno*[119] – that is true; but the depth of the agitation on such occasions, whether at chess, at draughts, or at cards, is not measured of necessity by the grandeur of the stake; he selects, in short, whatever fascinates the eye or agitates the heart by mimicry of life; but so far from *teaching*, he presupposes the reader already *taught*, in order that he may go along with the movement of the descriptions.

Now, in treating a subject so vast, indeed so inexhaustible, as man, this eclecticism ceases to be possible. Every part depends upon every other part: in such a *nexus* of truths to insulate is to annihilate. Severed from each other the parts lose their support, their coherence, their very meaning; you have no liberty to reject or to choose. Besides, in treating the ordinary themes proper for what is called didactic poetry – say, for instance, that it were the art of rearing silk-worms or bees – or suppose it to be horticulture, landscape-gardening, hunting, or hawking, rarely does there occur anything polemic; or, if a slight controversy *does* arise, it is easily hushed asleep – it is stated in a line, it is answered in a couplet. But in the themes of Lucretius[120] and Pope, *every* thing is polemic – you move only through dispute, you prosper only by argument and never-ending controversy. There is not positively one capital proposition or doctrine about man, about his origin, his nature, his relations to God, or his prospects, but must be fought for with energy, watched at every turn with vigilance, and followed into endless mazes, not under the choice of the writer, but under the inexorable dictation of the argument.

Such a poem, so unwieldy, whilst at the same time so austere in its philosophy, together with the innumerable polemic parts essential to its good faith and even to its evolution, would be absolutely unmanageable from excess and from disproportion, since often a secondary demur would occupy far more space than a principal section. Here lay the impracticable dilemma for Pope's

Essay on Man. To satisfy the demands of the subject, was to defeat the objects of poetry. To evade the demands in the way that Pope has done, is to offer us a ruin for a palace. The very same dilemma existed for Lucretius, and with the very same result. The *De Rerum Naturâ*, (which might, agreeably to its theme, have been entitled *De omnibus rebus*), and the Essay on Man, (which might equally have borne the Lucretian title *De Rerum Naturâ*,)[121] are both, and from the same cause, fragments that could not have been completed. Both are accumulations of diamond-dust without principles of coherency. In a succession of pictures, such as usually form the materials of didactic poems, the slightest thread of interdependency is sufficient. But, in works essentially and everywhere argumentative and polemic, to omit the connecting links, as often as they are insusceptible of poetic effect, is to break up the unity of the parts, and to undermine the foundations, in what expressly offers itself as a systematic and architectural whole. Pope's poem has suffered even more than that of Lucretius from this want of cohesion. It is indeed the realization of anarchy; and one amusing test of this may be found in the fact, that different commentators have deduced from it the very opposite doctrines. In some instances this apparent antinomy is doubtful, and dependent on the ambiguities or obscurities of the expression. But in others it is fairly deducible: and the cause lies in the elliptical structure of the work: the ellipsis, or (as sometimes it may be called) the chasm may be filled up in two different modes essentially hostile: and he that supplies the *hiatus*, in effect determines the bias of the poem this way or that – to a religious or to a sceptical result. In this edition the commentary of Warburton has been retained, which ought certainly to have been dismissed. The Essay is, in effect, a Hebrew word with the vowel-points omitted: and Warburton supplies one set of vowels, whilst Crousaz[122] with equal right supplies a contradictory set.

As a whole, the edition before us is certainly the most agreeable of all that we possess. The fidelity of Mr Roscoe to the interests of Pope's reputation, contrasts pleasingly with the harshness at times of Bowles, and the reckless neutrality of Warton.[123] In the editor of a great classic, we view it as a virtue, wearing the grace of loyalty, that he should refuse to expose frailties or defects in a spirit of exultation. Mr Roscoe's own notes are written with peculiar good sense, temperance, and kind feeling. The only objection to them, which applies however still more to the notes of former editors, is the want of compactness. They are not written under that austere instinct of compression and verbal parsimony, as the ideal merit in an annotator, which ought to govern all such ministerial labours in our days. Books are becoming too much the oppression of the intellect, and cannot endure any longer the accumulation of undigested commentaries, or that species of diffusion in editors which roots itself in laziness: the efforts of condensation and selection are painful; and they are luxuriously evaded by reprinting indiscriminately whole masses of notes – though often in substance reiterating each other. But the interests of readers clamorously call for the amendment of this system. The principle of selection must now be applied even to the *text* of great authors. It is no longer advisable to reprint the whole of either Dryden or Pope. Not that we would wish to see their works mutilated. Let such as are selected, be printed in the fullest integrity of the text. But some have lost their interest;* others, by the elevation of public morals since the days of those great wits, are felt to be now utterly unfit for general reading. Equally for the reader's sake and the poet's, the time has arrived when they may be advantageously retrenched: for they are painfully at war with those feelings of entire and honourable esteem with which all lovers of exquisite intellectual brilliancy must wish to surround the name and memory of POPE.

* We do not include the DUNCIAD[124] in this list. On the contrary, the arguments by which it has been generally undervalued, as though antiquated by lapse of time and by the fading of names, are all unsound. We ourselves hold it to be the greatest of Pope's efforts. But for that very reason we retire from the examination of it, which we had designed, as being wholly disproportioned to the narrow limits remaining to us.

FINAL MEMORIALS OF CHARLES LAMB

First published in the *North British Review*, X, November 1848, pp. 179–214. The essay was printed anonymously.

Reprinted in *F*, II, *Biographical Essays* (1851), 167–228.

Revised text, carrying many accidentals and eighteen substantive variants from *F*, in *SGG*, IX, *Leaders in Literature, With a Notice of Traditional Errors Affecting Them*, (1858), pp. 108–60.

There are five manuscripts. The first four constitute a consecutive set of manuscript pages for the closing section of the essay, with the exception of two words dropped between MS C and MS D.

MS A: Cornell University, Wordsworth Collection, 2809. The manuscript is a single sheet of buff paper, measuring 230 by 185 mm, with writing in dark brown ink on the recto only. There is an incomplete crown watermark. MS A corresponds to the passage below running from p. 394.5 'On the table lay a copy' to p. 394.34 'But these, you tell me,'.

MS B: Berg Collection, New York Public Library. The manuscript is a single sheet of wove paper, measuring 150 by 185 mm, with writing in black ink on the recto only. There is no watermark. It begins immediately following where MS A ends, and corresponds to the passage below running from p. 394.34–5 'allow of no such thing;' to p. 395.6 'the evening terminated.'

MS C: Cornell University, Wordsworth Collection, 2809. The manuscript is a single sheet of buff paper, measuring 230 by 185 mm, with writing in dark brown ink on the recto only. There is an incomplete crown watermark. It begins immediately following where MS B ends, and corresponds to the passage below running from p. 395.7 'We have left ourselves' to p. 396.12 'amongst his friends,'.

MS D: Boston University, Special Collections. The manuscript is a single sheet of white paper, measuring 185 by 230 mm, with writing in black ink on both recto and verso. There is no watermark. It begins where MS C ends, except that the words 'which made' have been dropped between the two manuscripts. MS D corresponds to the passage below running from p. 396.12 'him reserved in the expression' to p. 397.34 'his memory is hallowed for ever!'.

MS E: Huntington Library, HM 36039. The manuscript is a complete set of *SGG* page proofs.

The five manuscripts contain nearly one hundred significant variants, and these are listed in the textual notes.

Charles Lamb (1775–1834; *DNB*), essayist and critic, was born in London and educated at Christ's Hospital. His early works included *A Tale of Rosamund*

Gray (1798), *John Woodvil* (1802), and *Specimens of English Dramatic Poets* (1808). In 1820 he began to write his *Elia Essays*, and over the next three years he published in the *London Magazine* alongside contributors such as De Quincey, William Hazlitt, John Clare, Walter Savage Landor, and Thomas Carlyle. *The Essays of Elia* were collected in book form in 1823, and a second collection, *The Last Essays of Elia*, was published in 1833. Lamb died at Edmonton.

De Quincey's writings are filled with references to Lamb, from the 1803 *Diary* to the revised 1856 version of *Confessions of an English Opium-Eater*. De Quincey was still a teenager when the two met in late 1804 or early 1805, and though the friendship had an unpropitious start, De Quincey soon came to appreciate Lamb's strength, keen wit, and large capacity for friendship. 'As a *moral* being', De Quincey observed in 1838, 'I am disposed...to pronounce him the best man...that I have known or read of' (Vol. 1, p. 44; Vol. 2, p. 136; Vol. 10, pp. 243–4).

The present essay is a book review of the *Final Memorials of Charles Lamb* by Thomas Noon Talfourd (1785–1854; *DNB*), judge, playwright, and critic. Talfourd knew most of the leading literary figures of the early nineteenth century, and gained contemporary recognition for his influential magazine essays on the poetry of Wordsworth, and for his blank-verse tragedy *Ion* (1836). Charles Dickens dedicated *Pickwick Papers* (1837) to him. De Quincey uses Talfourd's text as a prompt to consider topics ranging from the *Elia Essays*, Lamb's prose style, his humour, and his religious convictions, to the key features of his biography, including the tragic killing of his mother by his sister Mary. De Quincey also discusses friends of Lamb such as Coleridge, Hazlitt, Robert Southey and, most strikingly, Thomas Griffiths Wainewright, art critic and murderer, and a key contributor to the *London* under the pseudonym Janus Weathercock. Oscar Wilde was much impressed by De Quincey's portrait of Wainewright, and drew on it in his famous 1889 essay, 'Pen, Pencil and Poison' (Norbert Kohl, *Oscar Wilde: The works of a conformist rebel*, trans. by David Henry Wilson (Cambridge: Cambridge University Press, 1989), pp. 116–8).

This is De Quincey's third and final essay for the *North British Review.*

ART. VI. – *Final Memorials of Charles Lamb.* By THOMAS NOON TALFOURD. 2 vols. London: 1848.

IT sounds paradoxical, but is not so in a bad sense, to say – that in every literature of large compass some authors will be found to rest much of the interest which surrounds them on their essential *non*-popularity. They are good for the very reason that they are not in conformity to the current taste. They interest because to the world they are *not* interesting. They attract by means of their repulsion. Not as though it could separately furnish a reason for loving a book – that the majority of men had found it repulsive. *Prima facie*,[1] it must suggest some presumption *against* a book – that it has failed to engage public attention. To have roused hostility indeed, to have kindled a feud against its own principles or its temper, may happen to be a good sign.

That argues power. Hatred may be promising. The deepest revolutions of mind sometimes begin in hatred. But simply to have left a reader unimpressed – is in itself a neutral result, from which the inference is doubtful. Yet even *that*, even simple failure to impress, may happen at times to be a result from positive powers in a writer, from special originalities, such as rarely reflect themselves in the mirror of the ordinary understanding. It seems little to be perceived – how much the great scriptural* idea of the *worldly* and the *unworldly* is found to emerge in literature as well as in life. In reality the very same combinations of moral qualities, infinitely varied, which compose the harsh physiognomy of what we call worldliness in the living groups of life, must unavoidably present themselves in books. A library divides into sections of worldly and unworldly, even as a crowd of men divides into that same majority and minority. The world has an instinct for recognising its own; and recoils from certain qualities when exemplified in books, with the same disgust or defective sympathy as would have governed it in real life. From qualities for instance of childlike simplicity, of shy profundity, or of inspired self-communion, the world does and must turn away its face towards grosser, bolder, more determined, or more intelligible expressions of character and intellect; – and not otherwise in literature, nor at all less in literature, than it does in the realities of life.

Charles Lamb, if any ever *was*, is amongst the class here contemplated; he, if any ever *has*, ranks amongst writers whose works are destined to be for ever unpopular, and yet for ever interesting; interesting, moreover, by means of those very qualities which guarantee their non-popularity. The same qualities which will be found forbidding to the worldly and the thoughtless, which will be found insipid to many even amongst robust and powerful minds, are exactly those which will continue to command a select audience in every generation. The prose essays, under the signature of *Elia*, form the most delightful section amongst Lamb's works. They traverse a peculiar field of observation, sequestered from general interest; and they are composed in a spirit too delicate and unobtrusive to catch the ear of the noisy crowd, clamouring for strong sensations. But this retiring delicacy itself, the pensiveness chequered by gleams of the fanciful, and the humour that is touched with cross-lights of pathos, together with the picturesque quaintness of the objects casually described, whether men, or things, or usages, and, in the rear of all this, the constant recurrence to ancient recollections and to decaying forms of household life, as things retiring before the tumult of new and revolutionary generations; – these traits in combination communicate to the papers a grace and strength of originality which nothing in any literature approaches,[2]

* '*Scriptural*' we call it, because this element of thought, so indispensable to a profound philosophy of morals, is not simply *more* used in Scripture than elsewhere, but is so exclusively significant or intelligible amidst the correlative ideas of Scripture, as to be absolutely insusceptible of translation into classical Greek or classical Latin. It is disgraceful that more reflection has not been directed to the vast causes and consequences of so pregnant a truth.

whether for degree or kind of excellence, except the most felicitous papers of Addison, such as those on Sir Roger de Coverly,[3] and some others in the same vein of composition. They resemble Addison's papers also in the diction, which is natural and idiomatic, even to carelessness. They are equally faithful to the truth of nature; and in this only they differ remarkably – that the sketches of Elia reflect the stamp and impress of the writer's own character, whereas in all those of Addison the personal peculiarities of the delineator (though known to the reader from the beginning through the account of the Club)[5] are nearly quiescent. Now and then they are recalled into a momentary notice, but they do not act, or at all modify his pictures of Sir Roger or Will Wimble. *They* are slightly and amiably eccentric; but the Spectator himself, in describing them, takes the station of an ordinary observer.[4]

Everywhere, indeed, in the writings of Lamb, and not merely in his *Elia*, the character of the writer co-operates in an under current to the effect of the thing written. To understand in the fullest sense either the gaiety or the tenderness of a particular passage, you must have some insight into the peculiar bias of the writer's mind – whether native and original, or impressed gradually by the accidents of situation; whether simply developed out of predispositions by the action of life, or violently scorched into the constitution by some fierce fever of calamity. There is in modern literature a whole class of writers, though not a large one, standing within the same category; some marked originality of character in the writer becomes a coefficient with what he says to a common result; you must sympathize with this *personality* in the author before you can appreciate the most significant parts of his views. In most books the writer figures as a mere abstraction, without sex or age or local station, whom the reader banishes from his thoughts. What is written seems to proceed from a blank intellect, not from a man clothed with fleshly peculiarities and differences. These peculiarities and differences neither do, nor (generally speaking) *could* intermingle with the texture of the thoughts so as to modify their force or their direction. In such books, and they form the vast majority, there is nothing to be found or to be looked for beyond the direct objective. (*Sit venia verbo!*)[5] But, in a small section of books, the objective in the thought becomes confluent with the subjective in the thinker – the two forces unite for a joint product; and fully to enjoy that product, or fully to apprehend either element, both must be known. It is singular, and worth inquiring into, for the reason, that the Greek and Roman literature had no such books. Timon of Athens, or Diogenes,[6] one may conceive qualified for this mode of authorship, had Journalism existed to rouse them in those days; their 'articles' would no doubt have been fearfully caustic. But, as *they* failed to produce anything, and Lucian[7] in an after age is scarcely characteristic enough for the purpose, perhaps we may pronounce Rabelais and Montaigne[8] the earliest of writers in the class described. In the century following *theirs*, came Sir Thomas Brown, and immediately after *him* La Fontaine. Then came Swift, Sterne,[9] with others less distinguished: in Germany Hippel, the friend of Kant, Hamann the obscure, and the greatest of the whole body – John Paul Fr. Richter.[10] In *him*, from the strength and determinateness of his nature, as well as from the great extent of his writings, the philosophy of this interaction between the author as a human agency and his theme as an intellectual reagency, might best be studied. From *him* might be derived the largest number of cases illustrating boldly this absorption of the universal into the concrete – of the pure intellect into the human nature of the author. But nowhere could illustrations be found more interesting, – shy, delicate, evanescent – shy as lightning, delicate and evanescent as the coloured pencillings on a frosty night from the Northern Lights, than in the better parts of Lamb.

To appreciate Lamb, therefore, it is requisite that his character and temperament should be understood in their coyest and most wayward features. A capital defect it would be if these could not be gathered silently from Lamb's works themselves. It would be a fatal mode of dependency upon an alien and separable accident if they needed an external commentary. But they do *not*. The syllables lurk up and down the writings of Lamb which decipher his eccentric nature. His character lies there dispersed in anagram; and to any attentive reader the regathering and restoration of the total word from its scattered parts is inevitable without an effort. Still it is always a satisfaction in knowing a result, to know also its *why* and *how;* and in so far as every character is likely to be modified by the particular experience, sad or joyous, through which the life has travelled, it is a good contribution towards the knowledge of that resulting character as a whole to have a sketch of that particular experience. What trials did it impose? What energies did it task? What temptations did it unfold? These calls upon the moral powers, which in music so stormy, many a life is doomed to hear, how were they faced? The character in a capital degree moulds oftentimes the life, but the life *always* in a subordinate degree moulds the character. And the character being in this case of Lamb so much of a key to the writings, it becomes important that the life should be traced, however briefly, as a key to the character.

That is *one* reason for detaining the reader with some slight record of Lamb's career. Such a record by preference and of right belongs to a case where the intellectual display, which is the sole ground of any public interest at all in the man, has been intensely modified by the *humanities* and moral *personalities* distinguishing the subject. We read a Physiology, and need no information as to the life and conversation of its author: a meditative poem becomes far better understood by the light of such information; but a work of genial and at the same time eccentric sentiment, wandering upon untrodden paths, is barely intelligible without it. There is a good reason for arresting judgment on the writer, that the court may receive evidence on the life of the man. But there is another reason, and, in any other place, a better; which reason lies in the extraordinary value of the life considered separately for itself. Logically, it is not allowable to say that *here;* and, considering the principal purpose of this paper, any possible *independent* value of the life must rank as a better reason for reporting it. Since, in a case where the original object is professedly to estimate the writings of a man, whatever promises to further that object must, merely by that tendency, have, in relation to that place, a momentary advantage which it would lose if valued upon a more abstract scale. Liberated from this casual office of throwing light upon a book – raised to its grander station of a solemn deposition to the moral capacities of man in conflict with calamity – viewed as a return made into the chanceries of heaven – upon an issue directed from that court to try the amount of power lodged in a poor desolate pair of human creatures for facing the very anarchy of storms – this obscure life of the two Lambs, brother and sister, (for the two lives were one life,) rises into a grandeur that is not paralleled once in a generation.

Rich, indeed, in moral instruction was the life of Charles Lamb; and perhaps in one chief result it offers to the thoughtful observer a lesson of consolation that is awful, and of hope that ought to be immortal, viz., in the record which it furnishes, that by meekness of submission, and by earnest conflict with evil, in the spirit of cheerfulness, it is possible ultimately to disarm or to blunt the very heaviest of curses – even the curse of lunacy. Had it been whispered, in hours of infancy, to Lamb, by the angel who stood by his cradle – 'Thou, and the sister that walks by ten years before thee, shall be through life, each to each, the solitary fountain of comfort; and except it be from this fountain of mutual love, except it be as brother and sister, ye shall not taste the cup of peace on earth!' – here, if there was sorrow in reversion, there was also consolation.

But what funeral swamps would have instantly engulfed this consolation had some meddling fiend prolonged the revelation, and, holding up the curtain from the sad future a little longer, had said scornfully – 'Peace on earth! Peace for you two, Charles and Mary Lamb! What peace is possible under the curse which even now is gathering against your heads? Is there peace on earth for the lunatic – peace for the parenticide – peace for the girl that, without warning, and without time granted for a penitential cry to heaven, sends her mother to the last audit?' And then, without treachery, speaking bare truth, this prophet of woe might have added – 'Thou also, thyself, Charles Lamb, thou in thy proper person, shalt enter the skirts of this dreadful hail-storm: even thou shalt taste the secrets of lunacy,[11] and enter as a captive its house of bondage; whilst over thy sister the accursed scorpion shall hang suspended through life, like Death hanging over the beds of hospitals, striking at times, but more often threatening to strike; or withdrawing its instant menaces only to lay bare her mind more bitterly to the persecutions of a haunted memory!' Considering the nature of the calamity, in the first place; considering, in the second place, its life-long duration; and, in the last place, considering the quality of the resistance by which it was met, and under what circumstances of humble resources in money or friends – we have come to the deliberate judgment, that the whole range of history scarcely presents a more affecting spectacle of perpetual sorrow, humiliation, or conflict, and that was supported to the end, (that is, through forty years,) with more resignation, or with more absolute victory.

Charles Lamb was born in February of the year 1775. His immediate descent was humble; for his father, though on one particular occasion civilly described as a 'scrivener,' was in reality a domestic servant to Mr Salt – a bencher (and therefore a barrister of some standing) in the Inner Temple.[12] John Lamb the father belonged by birth to Lincoln; from which city, being transferred to London whilst yet a boy, he entered the service of Mr Salt without delay; and apparently from this period throughout his life continued in this good man's household to support the honourable relation of a Roman client to his *patronus*[13] – much more than that of a mercenary servant to a transient and capricious master. The terms on which he seems to have lived with the family of the Lambs, argue a kindness and a liberality of nature on both sides. John Lamb recommended himself as an attendant by the versatility of his accomplishments; and Mr Salt, being a widower without children, which means in effect an old bachelor, naturally valued that encyclopaedic range of dexterity which made his house independent of external aid for every mode of service. To kill one's own mutton is but an operose way of arriving at a dinner, and often a more costly way; whereas to combine one's own carpenter, locksmith, hair-dresser, groom, &c., all in one man's person, – to have a Robinson Crusoe,[14] up to all emergencies of life, always in waiting, is a luxury of the highest class for one who values his ease.

A consultation is held more freely with a man familiar to one's eye, and more profitably with a man aware of one's peculiar habits. And another advantage from such an arrangement is – that one gets any little alteration or repair executed on the spot. To hear is to obey, and by an inversion of Pope's rule, –

One always *is*, and never *to be*, blest.[15]

People of one sole accomplishment, like the *homo unius libri*,[16] are usually within that narrow circle disagreeably perfect, and therefore apt to be arrogant. People who can do all things, usually do every one of them ill; and living in a constant effort to deny this too palpable fact, they become irritably vain. But Mr Lamb the elder seems to have been bent on perfection. He did all things; he did them all well; and yet was neither gloomily arrogant, nor testily vain. And being conscious apparently that all mechanic excellencies tend to illiberal results, unless counteracted by perpetual sacrifices to the muses – he went so far as to cultivate poetry: he even printed his poems,[17] and were we possessed of a copy, (which we are *not*, nor probably is the Vatican,) it would give us pleasure at this point to digress for a moment, and to cut them up, purely on considerations of respect to the author's memory. It is hardly to be supposed that they did not really merit castigation; and we should best shew the sincerity of our respect for Mr Lamb, senior, in all those cases where we *could* conscientiously profess respect by an unlimited application of the knout in the cases where we could *not*.

The whole family of the Lambs seem to have won from Mr Salt the consideration which is granted to humble friends; and from acquaintances nearer to their own standing, to have won a tenderness of esteem such as is granted to decayed gentry. Yet, naturally, the social rank of the parents, as people still living, must have operated disadvantageously for the children. It is hard, even for the practised philosopher, to distinguish aristocratic graces of manner, and capacities of delicate feeling, in people whose very hearth and dress bear witness to the servile humility of their station. Yet such distinctions, as wild gifts of nature, timidly and half-unconsciously asserted themselves in the unpretending Lambs. Already in *their* favour there existed a silent privilege analogous to the famous one of Lord Kinsale. He, by special grant from the Crown, is allowed, when standing before the King, to forget that he is not himself a king: the bearer of that Peerage, through all generations, has the privilege of wearing his hat in the Royal Presence.[18] By a general though tacit concession of the same nature, the rising generation of the Lambs, John[19] and Charles, the two sons, and Mary Lamb, the only daughter, were permitted to forget that their grandmother had been a housekeeper for sixty years, and that their father had worn a livery. Charles Lamb, individually, was so entirely humble, and so careless of social distinctions, that he has taken pleasure in recurring to these very facts in the family-records amongst the most genial of his Elia recollections.[20] He only continued to remember, without shame, and with a peculiar tenderness, these badges of plebeian rank, when everybody else, amongst the few survivors that could have known of their existence, had long dismissed them from their thoughts.

Probably through Mr Salt's interest, Charles Lamb, in the autumn of 1782, when he wanted something more than four months of completing his eighth year, received a presentation to the magnificent school of Christ's Hospital.[21] The late Dr Arnold,[22] when contrasting the school of his own boyish experience, Winchester, with Rugby, the school confided to his management, found nothing so much to regret in the circumstances of the latter as its forlorn condition with respect to historical traditions. Wherever these were wanting, and supposing the school of sufficient magnitude, it occurred to Dr Arnold that something of a compensatory effect for impressing the imagination might be obtained by connecting the school with the nation through the link of annual prizes issuing from the Exchequer. An official basis of national patronage might prove a substitute for an antiquarian or ancestral basis. Happily for the great educational foundations of London, none of them is in the naked condition of Rugby. Westminster, St. Paul's, Merchant Tailors', the Charter-House,[23] &c., are all crowned with historical recollections: and Christ's Hospital, besides the original honours of its foundation, so fitted to a consecrated place in a youthful imagination – an asylum for boy-students, provided by a boy-king[24] – innocent, religious, prematurely wise, and prematurely called away from earth – has also a mode of perpetual connexion with the State. It enjoys, therefore, *both* of Dr Arnold's advantages. Indeed, all the great foundation-schools of London, bearing in their very codes of organisation the impress of a double function – viz., the conservation of sound learning and of pure religion – wear something of a monastic or cloisteral character in their aspect and usages which is peculiarly impressive, and even pathetic, amidst the uproars of a capital the most colossal and tumultuous upon earth.

Here Lamb remained until his fifteenth year, which year threw him on the world, and brought him alongside the golden dawn of the French Revolution.[25] Here he learned a little elementary Greek, and of Latin more than a little; for the Latin notes to Mr Cary (of Dante celebrity)[26] though brief, are sufficient to reveal a true sense of what is graceful and idiomatic in Latinity. *We* say this, who have studied that subject more than most men. It is not that Lamb would have found it an easy task to compose a long paper in Latin – nobody *can* find it easy to do what he has no motive for habitually practising; but a single sentence of Latin, wearing the secret countersign of the 'sweet Roman hand,'[27] ascertain sufficiently that, in reading Latin classics, a man feels and comprehends their peculiar force or beauty. That is enough. It is requisite to a man's expansion of mind that he should make acquaintance with a literature so radically differing from all modern literatures as is the Latin. It is *not* requisite that he should practise Latin composition. Here, therefore, Lamb obtained in sufficient perfection one priceless accomplishment, which even singly throws a graceful air of liberality over all the rest of a man's attainments: having rarely any pecuniary value, it challenges the more attention to its intellectual value. Here also Lamb commenced the friendships of his life: and, of all which he formed, he lost none. Here it was, as the consummation and crown of his advantages from the time-honoured Hospital, that he came to know 'Poor S. T. C.'* Τον θαυμασιωτατον.[29]

Until 1796, it is probable that he lost sight of Coleridge, who was then occupied with Cambridge – having been transferred thither as a 'Grecian' from the house of Christchurch.[30] That year, 1796, was a year of change and fearful calamity for Charles Lamb. On that year revolved the wheels of his after-life. During the three years succeeding to his school-days, he had held a clerkship in the South Sea House. In 1795, he was transferred to the India House.[31] As a junior clerk he could not receive more than a slender salary: but even this was important to the support of his parents and sister. They lived together in lodgings near Holborn; and in the spring of 1796, Miss Lamb, (having previously shown signs of lunacy at intervals,) in a sudden paroxysm of her disease, seized a knife from the dinner table, and stabbed her mother, who died upon the spot.[32] A coroner's inquest easily ascertained the nature of

* The affecting expression by which Coleridge indicates himself in the few lines written during his last illness for an inscription upon his grave;[28] lines ill constructed in point of diction and compression, but otherwise speaking from the depths of his heart.

a case which was transparent in all its circumstances, and never for a moment indecisive as regarded the medical symptoms. The poor young lady was transferred to the establishment for lunatics at Hoxton:[33] she soon recovered, we believe; but her relapses were as sudden as her recoveries, and she continued through life to revisit, for periods of uncertain seclusion, this house of wo. This calamity of his fireside, followed soon after by the death of his father,[34] who had for some time been in a state of imbecility, determined the future destiny of Lamb. Apprehending, with the perfect grief of perfect love, that his sister's fate was sealed for life – viewing her as his own greatest benefactress, which she really *had* been through her advantage by ten years in age – yielding with impassioned readiness to the depth of his fraternal affection, what at any rate he would have yielded to the sanctities of duty as interpreted by his own conscience – he resolved for ever to resign all thoughts of marriage with a young lady whom he loved,[35] for ever to abandon all ambitious prospects that might have tempted him into uncertainties, humbly to content himself with the *certainties* of his Indian clerkship, to dedicate himself for the future to the care of his desolate and prostrate sister, and to leave the rest to God. These sacrifices he made in no hurry or tumult, but deliberately, and in religious tranquility. These sacrifices were accepted in heaven – and even on this earth they *had* their reward. She for whom he gave up all, in turn gave up all for *him*. She devoted herself to his comfort. Many times she returned to the lunatic establishment, but many times she was restored to illuminate the household hearth for *him;* and of the happiness which for forty years more he had, no hour seemed true that was not derived from *her*. Henceforwards, therefore, until he was emancipated by the noble generosity of the East India Directors, Lamb's time, for nine and twenty years, was given to the India House.[36]

'*O fortunati nimium, sua si bona nôrint*,' is applicable to more people than '*agricolae*.'[37] Clerks of the India House are as blind to their own advantages as the blindest of ploughmen. Lamb was summoned, it is true, through the larger and more genial section of his life, to the drudgery of a copying clerk – making confidential entries into mighty folios, on the subject of calicoes and muslins. By this means, whether he would or not, he became gradually the author of a great 'serial' work, in a frightful number of volumes, on as dry a department of literature as the children of the great desert could have suggested. Nobody, he must have felt, was ever likely to study this great work of his, not even Dr Dryasdust.[38] He had written in vain, which is not pleasant to know. There would be no second edition called for by a discerning public in Leadenhall Street: not a chance of *that*. And consequently the *opera omnia*[39] of Lamb, drawn up in a hideous battalion, at the cost of labour so enormous, would be known only to certain families of spiders in one generation, and of rats in the next. Such a labour of Sisyphus[40]– the rolling up a ponderous stone to the summit of a hill only that it might roll back again by the gravitation of its own dulness, seems a bad employment for a man of genius in his meridian energies. And yet, perhaps not. Perhaps the collective wisdom of Europe could not have devised for Lamb a more favourable condition of toil than this very India House clerkship. His works (his Leadenhall Street works) were certainly not read; popular they *could* not be, for they were not read by anybody; but then, to balance *that*, they were not reviewed. His folios were of that order, which (in Cowper's words) 'not even critics criticise.'[41] *Is that* nothing? Is it no happiness to escape the hands of scoundrel reviewers? Many of us escape being *read;* the worshipful reviewer does not find time to read a line of us; but we do not for that reason escape being criticised, 'shewn up,' and martyred. The list of *errata* again, committed by Lamb, was probably of a magnitude to alarm any possible compositor; and yet these *errata* will never be known to mankind. They are dead and buried. They have been cut off prematurely; and for any effect upon their generation, might as well never have existed. Then the returns, in a pecuniary sense, from these folios – how important were *they!* It is not common, certainly, to write folios; but neither is it common to draw a steady income of from £300 to £400 per annum from volumes of any size. This will be admitted; but would it not have been better to draw the income without the toil? Doubtless it would always be more agreeable to have the rose without the thorn. But in the case before us, taken with all its circumstances, we deny that the toil is truly typified as a thorn; – so far from being a thorn in Lamb's daily life, on the contrary, it was a second rose engrafted upon the original rose of the income, that he had to earn it by a moderate but continued exertion. Let us consider what this exertion really amounted to. Holidays, in a national establishment so great as the India House, and in our too fervid period, naturally could not be frequent; yet all great English corporations are gracious masters, and indulgences of this nature could be obtained on a special application. Not to count upon these accidents of favour, we find that the regular toil of those in Lamb's situation began at ten in the morning and ended as the clock struck four in the afternoon. Six hours composed the daily contribution of labour, that is precisely one-fourth part of the total day. Only that, as Sunday was exempted, the rigorous expression of the quota was one-fourth of six-sevenths, which makes six twenty-eighths and not six twenty-fourths of the total time. Less toil than this would hardly have availed to deepen the sense of value in that large part of the time still remaining disposable. Had there been any resumption whatever of labour in the evening, though but for half an hour, that one encroachment upon the broad continuous area of the eighteen free hours would have killed the tranquility of the whole day, by *sowing* it (so to speak) with intermitting anxieties – anxieties that, like tides, would still be rising and falling. Whereas now, at the early hour of four, when day-light is yet lingering in the air, even at the dead of winter, in the latitude of London, and when the *enjoying* section of the day is barely commencing – every thing is left which a man would care to retain. A mere *dilettante* or amateur student, having no mercenary interest concerned, would, upon a refinement of luxury – would, upon choice, give up so much time to study, were it only to sharpen the value of what remained for pleasure. And thus the only difference between the scheme of the India House distributing his time for Lamb, and the scheme of a wise voluptuary distributing his time for himself, lay, not in the *amount* of time deducted from enjoyment, but in the particular mode of appropriating that deduction. An *intellectual* appropriation of the time, though casually fatiguing, must have pleasures of its own; pleasures denied to a task so mechanic and so monotonous as that of reiterating endless records of sales or consignments not *essentially* varying from each other. True: it is pleasanter to pursue an intellectual study than to make entries in a ledger. But even an intellectual toil is toil: few people can support it for more than six hours in a day. And the only question, therefore, after all, is, at what period of the day a man would prefer taking this pleasure of study. Now, upon that point, as regards the case of Lamb, there is no opening for doubt. He, amongst his *Popular Fallacies*, admirably illustrates the necessity of evening and artificial lights to the prosperity of studies.[42] After exposing, with the perfection of fun, the savage unsociality of those elder ancestors who lived (if life it was) before lamp-light was invented, showing that 'jokes came in with candles,' since 'what repartees *could* have passed' when people were 'grumbling at one another in the dark,' and 'when you must have felt about for a smile, and handled a neighbour's cheek to be sure that he understood it?' He goes on to say, 'this accounts for the seriousness of the elder poetry,' viz., because they had no candle-light. Even eating he objects to as a very imperfect thing in the dark: you are not convinced that a dish tastes as it should do by the promise of its name, if you dine in the twilight without candles. Seeing is believing. 'The senses absolutely give and take reciprocally.' The sight guarantees the taste. For instance, 'Can you tell pork from veal in the dark, or distinguish Sherries from pure Malaga?'[43] To all enjoyments whatsoever candles are indispensable as an adjunct: but, as to *reading*, 'there is,' says Lamb, 'absolutely no such thing but by a candle. We have tried the affectation of a book at noon-day in gardens, but it was labour thrown away. It is a mockery, all that is reported of the influential Phoebus.[44] No true poem ever owed its birth to the sun's light. The mild internal light, that reveals the fine shapings of poetry, like fires on the domestic hearth, goes out in the sunshine. Milton's morning hymn in Paradise, we would hold a good wager, was penned at midnight; and Taylor's rich description of a sunrise smells decidedly of the taper.'[45] This view of evening and candle-light as involved in literature may seem no more than a pleasant extravanganza; and no doubt it is in the nature of such gaieties to travel a little into exaggeration, but substantially it is certain that Lamb's feelings pointed habitually in the direction here indicated. His literary studies, whether taking the colour of tasks or diversions, courted the aid of evening, which, by means of physical weariness, produces a more luxurious state of repose than belongs to the labour-hours of day, and courted the aid of lamp-light, which, as Lord Bacon remarked, gives a gorgeousness to human pomps and pleasures, such as would be vainly sought from the homeliness of day-light.[46] The hours, therefore, which were withdrawn from his own control by the India House, happened to be exactly that part of the day which Lamb least valued and could least have turned to account.

The account given of Lamb's friends, of those whom he endeavoured to love, because he admired them, or to esteem intellectually because he loved them personally, is too much coloured for general acquiescence by Sergeant Talfourd's own early prepossessions. It is natural that an intellectual man like the Sergeant, personally made known in youth to people whom from childhood he had regarded as powers in the ideal world, and in some instances as representing the eternities of human speculation, since their names had perhaps dawned upon his mind in concurrence with the very earliest suggestion of topics which they had treated, should overrate their intrinsic grandeur. Hazlitt accordingly is styled 'the great thinker.'[47] But had he been such potentially, there was an absolute bar to his achievement of that station in act and consummation. No man *can* be a great thinker in our days upon large and elaborate questions without being also a great student. To think profoundly, it is indispensable that a man should have read down to his own starting point, and have read as a collating student to the particular stage at which he himself takes up the subject. At this moment, for instance, how could geology be treated otherwise than childishly by one who should rely upon the encyclopaedias of 1800? or comparative Physiology by the most ingenious of men unacquainted with Marshall Hall, and with the apocalyptic glimpses of secrets unfolding under the hands of Professor Owen?[48] In such a condition of undisciplined thinking, the ablest man thinks to no purpose. He lingers upon parts of the inquiry that have lost the importance which once they had, under imperfect charts of the subject; he wastes his strength upon problems that have become obsolete; he loses his way in paths that are not in the line of direction upon which the improved speculation is moving; or he gives narrow conjectural solutions of difficulties that have long since received sure and comprehensive ones. It is as if a man should in these days attempt to colonize, and yet through inertia or through ignorance, should leave behind him all modern resources of chemistry, of chemical agriculture, or of steam-power. Hazlitt had read nothing.[49] Unacquainted with Grecian philosophy, with Scholastic philosophy, and with the recomposition of these philosophies in the looms of Germany, during the last sixty and odd years, trusting merely to the untrained instincts of keen mother-wit, – whence should Hazlitt have had the materials for great thinking? It is through the collation of many abortive voyages to Polar regions that a man gains his first chance of entering the Polar basin, or of running ahead on the true line of approach to it. The very reason for Hazlitt's defect in eloquence as a lecturer,[50] is sufficient also as a reason why he could not have been a comprehensive thinker. 'He was not eloquent,' says the Sergeant, 'in the true sense of the term.' But why? Because it seems 'his thoughts were too weighty to be moved along by the shallow stream of feeling which an evening's excitement can rouse;'[51] – an explanation which leaves us in doubt whether Hazlitt forfeited his chance of eloquence by accommodating himself to this evening's excitement, or by gloomily resisting it. Our own explanation is different. Hazlitt was not eloquent, because he was discontinuous. No man can be eloquent whose thoughts are abrupt, insulated, capricious, and (to borrow an impressive word from Coleridge) non-sequacious.[52] Eloquence resides not in separate or fractional ideas, but in the relations of manifold ideas, and in the mode of their evolution from each other. It is not indeed enough that the ideas should be many, and their relations coherent: the main condition lies in the *key* of the evolution, in the *law* of the succession. The elements are nothing without the atmosphere that moulds, and the dynamic forces that combine. Now Hazlitt's brilliancy is seen chiefly in separate splinterings of phrase or image, which throw upon the eye a vitreous scintillation for a moment, but spread no deep suffusions of colour, and distribute no masses of mighty shadow. A flash, a solitary flash, and all is gone. Rhetoric, according to its quality, stands in many degrees of relation to the permanencies of truth; and all rhetoric, like all flesh, is partly unreal, and the glory of both is fleeting. Even the mighty rhetoric of Sir Thomas Brown, or Jeremy Taylor,[53] to whom only it has been granted to open the trumpet-stop on that great organ of passion, oftentimes leaves behind it the sense of sadness which belongs to beautiful apparitions starting out of darkness upon the morbid eye only to be reclaimed by darkness in the instant of their birth, or which belongs to pageantries in the clouds. But if all rhetoric is a mode of pyrotechny, and all pyrotechnics are by necessity fugacious, yet even in these frail pomps there are many degrees of frailty. Some fire-works require an hour's duration for the expansion of their glory; others, as if formed from fulminating powder, expire in the very act of birth. Precisely on that scale of duration and of power stand the glitterings of rhetoric that are not worked into the texture, but washed on from the outside. Hazlitt's thoughts were of the same fractured and discontinuous order as his illustrative images – seldom or never self-diffusive; and *that* is a sufficient argument that he had never cultivated philosophic thinking.

Not however to conceal any part of the truth, we are bound to acknowledge that Lamb thought otherwise on this point, manifesting what seemed to us an extravagant admiration of Hazlitt, and perhaps even in part for that very glitter which we are denouncing – at least he did so in a conversation with ourselves. But, on the other hand, as this conversation travelled a little into the tone of a disputation, and *our* frost on this point might seem to justify some undue fervour by way of balance, it is very possible that Lamb did not speak his absolute and most dispassionate judgment. And yet again, if he *did*, may we, with all reverence for Lamb's exquisite genius, have permission to say – that his own constitution of intellect sinned by this very habit of discontinuity. It was a habit of mind not unlikely to be cherished by his habits of life. Amongst these habits was the excess of his social kindness. He scorned so much to deny his company, and his redundant hospitality to any man who manifested a wish for either by calling upon him, that he almost seemed to think it a criminality in himself if, by accident, he really *was* from home on your visit, rather than by possibility a negligence in you, that had not forewarned him of your intention. All his life, from this and other causes, he must have read in the spirit of one liable to sudden interruption; like a dragoon, in fact, reading with one foot in the stirrup, when expecting momentarily a summons to mount for action. In such situations, reading by snatches, and by intervals of precarious leisure, people form the habit of seeking and unduly valuing condensations of the meaning, where in reality the truth suffers by this short-hand exhibition, or else they demand too vivid illustrations of the meaning. Lord Chesterfield himself, so brilliant a man by nature, already therefore making a morbid estimate of brilliancy, and so hurried throughout his life as a public man, read under this double coercion for craving instantaneous effects. At one period, his only time for reading was in the morning, whilst under the hands of his hair-dresser: compelled to take the hastiest of flying shots at his author, naturally he demanded a very conspicuous mark to fire at. But the author could not, in so brief a space, be always sure to crowd any very prominent objects on the eye, unless by being audaciously oracular and peremptory as regarded the sentiment, or flashy in excess as regarded its expression. 'Come now, my friend,' was Lord Chesterfield's morning adjuration to his author; 'come now, cut it short – don't prose – don't hum and haw.'[54] The author had doubtless no ambition to enter his name on the honourable and ancient roll of gentlemen prosers: probably he conceived himself not at all tainted with the asthmatic infirmity of humming and hawing; but, as to 'cutting it short,' how could he be sure of meeting his Lordship's expectations in that point, unless by dismissing the limitations that might be requisite to fit the idea for use, or the adjuncts that might be requisite to integrate its truth, or the final consequences that might involve some deep *arrière pensée*,[55] which, coming last in the succession, might oftentimes be calculated to lie deepest on the mind. To be lawfully and usefully brilliant after this rapid fashion, a man must come forward as a refresher of old truths, where *his* suppressions are supplied by the reader's memory; not as an expounder of new truths, where oftentimes a dislocated fraction of the true is more dangerous than the false itself.

To read therefore habitually, by hurried instalments, has this bad tendency – that it is likely to found a taste for modes of composition too artificially irritating, and to disturb the equilibrium of the judgment in relation to the colourings of style. Lamb, however, whose constitution of mind was even ideally sound in reference to the natural, the simple, the genuine, might seem of all men least liable to a taint in this direction. And undoubtedly he *was* so as regarded those modes of beauty which nature had specially qualified him for apprehending. Else, and in relation to other modes of beauty, where his sense of the true, and of its distinction from the spurious, had been an acquired sense, it is impossible for us to hide from ourselves – that not through habits only, not through stress of injurious accidents only, but by original structure and temperament of mind, Lamb had a bias towards those very defects on which rested the startling characteristics of style which we have been noticing. He himself, we fear, not bribed by indulgent feelings to another, not moved by friendship, but by native tendency, shrank from the continuous, from the sustained, from the elaborate.

The elaborate, indeed, without which much truth and beauty must perish in germ, was by name the object of his invectives. The instances are many in his own beautiful essays where he literally collapses, literally sinks away from openings suddenly offering themselves to flights of pathos or solemnity in direct prosecution of his own theme. On any such summons, where an ascending impulse, and an untired pinion were required, he *refuses* himself (to use military language)[56] invariably. The least observing reader of *Elia* cannot have failed to notice that the most felicitous passages always accomplish their circuit in a few sentences. The gyration within which his sentiment wheels, no matter of what kind it may be, is always the shortest possible. It does not prolong itself, and it does not repeat itself. But in fact, other features in Lamb's mind would have argued this feature by analogy, had we by accident been left unaware of it directly. It is not by chance, or without a deep ground in his nature *common* to all his qualities, both affirmative and negative, that Lamb had an insensibility to music more absolute than can have been often shared by any human creature, or perhaps than was ever before acknowledged so candidly.[57] The sense of music, as a pleasurable sense, or as any sense at all other than of certain unmeaning and impertinent differences in respect to high and low – sharp or flat – was utterly obliterated as with a sponge by nature herself from Lamb's organization. It was a corollary from the same large *substratum* in his nature, that Lamb had no sense of the rhythmical in prose composition. Rhythmus, or pomp of cadence, or sonorous ascent of clauses, in the structure of sentences, were effects of art as much thrown away upon *him* as the voice of the charmer upon the deaf adder. We ourselves, occupying the very station of polar opposition to that of Lamb, being as morbidly, perhaps, in the one excess as he in the other, naturally detected this omission in Lamb's nature at an early stage of our acquaintance. Not the fabled Regulus, with his eyelids torn away, and his uncurtained eye-balls exposed to the noon-tide glare of a Carthaginian sun,[58] could have shrieked with more anguish of recoil from torture than we from certain sentences and periods in which Lamb perceived no fault at all. *Pomp*, in our apprehension, was an idea of two categories; the *pompous* might be spurious, but it might also be genuine. It is well to love the simple: *we* love it;[59] nor is there any opposition at all between *that* and the very glory of pomp. But, as we once put the case to Lamb, if as a musician, as the leader of a mighty orchestra, you had this theme offered to you – 'Belshazzar the king gave a great feast to a thousand of his lords'[60] – or this, 'And on a certain day, Marcus Cicero stood up, and in a set speech rendered solemn thanks to Caius Caesar for Quintus Ligarius pardoned, and for Marcus Marcellus restored,'[61]—Surely no man would deny that, in such a case, simplicity, though in a passive sense not lawfully absent, must stand aside as totally insufficient for the *positive* part. Simplicity might guide, even here, but could not furnish the power; a rudder it might be, but not an oar or a sail. This, Lamb was ready to allow; as an intellectual *quiddity*, he recognised pomp in the character of a privileged thing; he was obliged to do so; for take away from great ceremonial festivals, such as the solemn rendering of thanks, the celebration of national anniversaries, the commemoration of public benefactors, &c., the element of pomp, and you take away their very meaning and life; but, whilst allowing a place for it in the rubric of the logician, it is certain that, *sensuously*, Lamb would not have sympathized with it, nor have *felt* its justification in any concrete instance. We find a difficulty in pursuing this subject, without greatly exceeding our limits. We pause, therefore, and add only this one suggestion as partly explanatory of the case. Lamb had the dramatic intellect and taste, perhaps in perfection; of the Epic, he had none at all. Here, as happens sometimes to men of genius preternaturally endowed in one direction, he might be considered as almost starved. A favourite of nature, so eminent in some directions, by what right could he complain that her bounties were not indiscriminate? From this defect in his nature it arose, that except by culture and by reflexion, Lamb had no genial appreciation of Milton.[62] The solemn planetary wheelings of the Paradise Lost were not to his taste. What he *did* comprehend, were the motions like those of lightning, the fierce angular coruscations of that wild agency which comes forward so vividly in the sudden περιπέτεια,[63] in the revolutionary catastrophe, and in the tumultuous conflicts, through persons or through situations, of the tragic drama.

There is another vice in Mr Hazlitt's mode of composition, viz., the habit of trite quotation, too common to have challenged much notice, were it not for these reasons: – 1st, that Sergeant Talfourd speaks of it in equivocal terms, as a fault perhaps, but as a 'felicitous' fault, 'trailing after it a line of golden associations;'[64] 2dly, because the practice involves a dishonesty. On occasion of No. 1, we must profess our belief that a more ample explanation from the Sergeant would have left him in substantial harmony with ourselves. We cannot conceive the author of Ion, and the friend of Wordsworth, seriously to countenance that paralytic 'mouth-diarrhoea,' (to borrow a phrase of Coleridge's)[65] – that *fluxe de bouche* (to borrow an earlier phrase of Archbishop Huet's)[66] which places the reader at the mercy of a man's tritest remembrances from his most schoolboy reading. To have the verbal memory infested with tags of verse and 'cues' of rhyme is in itself an infirmity as vulgar and as morbid as the stable-boy's habit of whistling slang airs upon the mere mechanical excitement of a bar or two whistled by some other blockhead in some other stable. The very stage has grown weary of ridiculing a folly, that having been long since expelled from decent society has taken refuge amongst the most imbecile of authors. Was Mr Hazlitt then of that class? No: he was a man of great talents, and of capacity for greater things than he ever attempted, though without any pretensions of the philosophic kind ascribed to him by the Sergeant. Meantime the reason for resisting the example and practice of Hazlitt lies in this – that essentially it is at war with sincerity, the foundation of all good writing, to express one's own thoughts by another man's words. This dilemma arises. The thought is, or it is not, worthy of that emphasis which belongs to a metrical expression of it. If it is *not*, then we shall be guilty of a mere folly in pushing into strong relief that which confessedly cannot support it. If it *is*, then how incredible that a thought strongly conceived, and bearing about it the impress of one's own individuality, should naturally, and without dissimulation or falsehood, bend to another man's expression of it! Simply to back one's own view by a similar view derived from another may be useful; a quotation that repeats one's own sentiment, but in a varied form, has the grace which belongs to the *idem in alio*,[67] the same radical idea expressed with a difference; similarity in dissimilarity; but to throw one's own thoughts, matter, and form, through alien organs so absolutely as to make another man one's interpreter for evil and good, is either to confess a singular laxity of thinking that can so flexibly adapt itself to any casual form of words, or else to confess that sort of carelessness about the expression which draws its real origin from a sense of indifference about the things to be expressed. Utterly at war this distressing practice is with all simplicity and earnestness of writing; it argues a state of indolent ease inconsistent with the pressure and coercion of strong fermenting thoughts, before we can be at leisure for idle or chance quotations. But lastly, in reference to No. 2, we must add that the practice is signally dishonest. It 'trails after it a line of golden associations.' Yes, and the burglar, who leaves an army-tailor's after a midnight visit, trails after him perhaps a long roll of gold bullion epaulettes which may look pretty by lamp-light.

But *that*, in the present condition of moral philosophy amongst the police, is accounted robbery. And to benefit too much by quotations is little less. At this moment we have in our eye a work, at one time not without celebrity, which is one continued *cento* of splendid passages from other people.[68] The natural effect from so much fine writing is – that the reader rises with the impression of having been engaged upon a most eloquent work. Meantime the whole is a series of mosaics; a tessellation made up from borrowed fragments: and first, when the reader's attention is expressly directed upon the fact, he becomes aware that the nominal author has contributed nothing more to the book than a few passages of transition or brief clauses of connexion.

In the year 1796 the main incident occurring of any importance for English literature was the publication by Southey of an epic poem. This poem, the *Joan of Arc*,[69] was the earliest work of much pretension amongst all that Southey wrote; and by many degrees it was the worst. In the four great narrative poems of his later years, there is a combination of two striking qualities, viz., a peculiar command over the *visually* splendid, connected with a deep-toned grandeur of moral pathos. Especially we find this union in the *Thalaba* and the *Roderick*;[70] but in the *Joan of Arc* we miss it. What splendour there is for the fancy and the eye belongs chiefly to the Vision, contributed by Coleridge, and this was subsequently withdrawn.[71] The fault lay in Southey's political relations at that era; his sympathy with the French Revolution in its earlier stages had been boundless: in all respects it was a noble sympathy, fading only as the gorgeous colouring faded from the emblazonries of that awful event, drooping only when the promises of that golden dawn sickened under stationary eclipse. In 1796 Southey was yet under the tyranny of his own earliest fascination: in *his* eyes the Revolution had suffered a momentary blight from refluxes of panic; but blight of some kind is incident to every harvest on which human hopes are suspended. Bad auguries were also ascending from the unchaining of martial instincts. But that the Revolution having ploughed its way through unparalleled storms, was preparing to face other storms, did but quicken the apprehensiveness of his love – did but quicken the duty of giving utterance to this love. Hence came the rapid composition of the poem, which cost less time in writing than in printing. Hence also came the choice of his heroine. What he needed in his central character was – a heart with a capacity for the wrath of Hebrew prophets applied to ancient abuses, and for evangelic pity applied to the sufferings of nations. This heart, with this double capacity – where should he seek it? A French heart it must be, or how should it follow with its sympathies a French movement? *There* lay Southey's reason for adopting the Maid of Orleans[72] as the depositary of hopes and aspirations of behalf of France as fervid as his own. In choosing this heroine, so inadequately known at that time, Southey testified at least his own nobility of feeling;* but in executing his choice, he and his friends overlooked two faults

* It is right to remind the reader of this, for a reason applying forcibly to the present moment. Michelet has taxed Englishmen with yielding to national animosities in the case of Joan, having no plea whatever for that insinuation but the single one drawn from Shakspeare's Henry VI.[73] To this the answer is – first, that Shakspeare's share in that trilogy is not nicely ascertained.[74] Secondly, that M. Michelet forgot (or, which is far worse, *not* forgetting it, he dissembled) the fact, that in undertaking a series of dramas upon the basis avowedly of national chronicles, and for the very purpose of profiting by old traditionary recollections connected with ancestral glories, it was mere lunacy to recast the circumstances at the bidding of antiquarian research, so as entirely to disturb these glories. Besides that to Shakspeare's age no such spirit of research had blossomed. Writing for the stage a man would have risked lapidation by uttering a whisper in that direction. And, even if not, what sense could there have been in openly running counter to the very motive that had originally prompted that particular class of chronicle plays? Thirdly, if one Englishman had, in a memorable situation, adopted the popular view of Joan's conduct, (*popular* as much in France as in England); on the other hand, fifty years before M. Michelet was writing this flagrant injustice, another Englishman (viz. Southey) had, in an epic poem, reversed this misjudgment, and invested the shepherd girl with a glory nowhere else accorded to her, unless indeed by Schiller.[75] Fourthly, we are not entitled to view as an *attack* upon Joanna, what, in the worst construction, is but an unexamining adoption of

fatal to his purpose. One was this: sympathy with the French Revolution meant sympathy with the opening prospects of man – meant sympathy with the Pariah of every clime – with all that suffered social wrong, or saddened in hopeless bondage.

That was the movement at work in the French Revolution. But the movement of Joanne d'Arc took a different direction. In *her* day also, it is true, the human heart had yearned after the same vast enfranchisement for the children of labour as afterwards worked in the great vision of the French Revolution. In *her* days also, and shortly before them, the human hand had sought by bloody acts to realize this dream of the heart. And in her childhood, Joanna had not been insensible to these premature motions upon a path too bloody and too dark to be safe. But this view of human misery had been utterly absorbed to *her* by the special misery then desolating France. The lilies of France had been trampled under foot by the conquering stranger. Within fifty years, in three pitched battles that resounded to the ends of the earth, the chivalry of France had been exterminated. Her oriflamme had been dragged through the dust.[77] The eldest son of Baptism had been prostrated. The daughter of France had been surrendered on coercion as a bride to her English conqueror. The child of that marriage, so ignominious to the land, was king of France by the consent of Christendom: that child's uncle domineered as regent of France:[78] and that child's armies were in military possession of the land. But were they undisputed masters? No; and *there* precisely lay the sorrow of the time. Under a perfect conquest there would have been repose; whereas the presence of the English armies did but furnish a plea, masking itself in patriotism, for gatherings everywhere of lawless marauders; of soldiers that had deserted their banners; and of robbers by profession. This was the wo of France more even than the military dishonour. That dishonour had been palliated from the first by the genealogical pretensions of the English royal family to the French throne, and these pretensions were strengthened in the person of the present claimant. But the military desolation of France, this it was that woke the faith of Joanna in her own heavenly mission of deliverance. It was the attitude of her prostrate country, crying night and day for purification from blood, and not from feudal oppression, that swallowed up the thoughts of the impassioned girl. But *that* was not the cry that uttered itself afterwards in the French revolution. In Joanna's days, the first step towards rest for France was by expulsion of the foreigner. Independence of a foreign yoke, liberation as

---

the contemporary historical accounts. A poet or a dramatist is not responsible for the accuracy of chronicles. But what *is* an attack upon Joan, being briefly the foulest and obscenest attempt ever made to stifle the grandeur of a great human struggle, viz., the French burlesque poem of *La Pucelle*,[76] – What memorable man was it that wrote *that?* Was he a Frenchman, or was he not? That M. Michelet should *pretend* to have forgotten this vilest of pasquinades, is more shocking to the general sense of justice than any special untruth as to Shakspeare *can* be to the particular nationality of an Englishman.

between people and people, was the one ransom to be paid for French honour and peace. *That* debt settled there might come a time for thinking of civil liberties. But this time was not within the prospects of the poor shepherdess. The field – the area of her sympathies never coincided with that of the revolutionary period. It followed, therefore, that Southey *could* not have raised Joanna (with her condition of feeling) by any management, into the interpreter of his own. *That* was the first error in his poem, and it was irremediable. The second was, and strangely enough this also escaped notice, that the heroine of Southey is made to close her career precisely at the point when its grandeur commences. She believed herself to have a mission for the deliverance of France; and the great instrument which she was authorized to use towards this end, was the king, Charles VII. Him she was to crown. With this coronation her triumph, in the plain historical sense, ended. – And *there* ends Southey's poem.[79] But exactly at this point, the grander stage of her mission commences, viz., the ransom which she, a solitary girl, paid in her own person for the national deliverance. The grander half of the story was thus sacrificed, as being irrelevant to Southey's political object; and yet, after all, the half which he retained did not at all symbolize that object. It is singular, indeed, to find a long poem, on an ancient subject, adapting itself hieroglyphically to a modern purpose; 2dly, to find it failing of this purpose; and 3dly, if it had *not* failed, so planned that it could have succeeded only by a sacrifice of all that was grandest in the theme.

To these capital oversights Southey, Coleridge, and Lamb, were all joint parties; the two first as concerned in the composition, the last as a frank though friendly reviewer of it in his private correspondence with Coleridge.[80] It is, however, some palliation of these oversights, and a very singular fact in itself, that neither from English authorities nor from French, though the two nations were equally brought into close connexion with the career of that extraordinary girl, could any adequate view be obtained of her character and acts. The *official* records of her trial, apart from which nothing can be depended upon, were first in the course of publication from the Paris press during the currency of last year. First in 1847,[81] about four hundred and sixteen years after her ashes had been dispersed to the winds, could it be seen distinctly, through the clouds of fierce partisanships and national prejudices, what had been the frenzy of the persecution against her, and the utter desolation of her position, – what had been the grandeur of her conscientious resistance.

Anxious that our readers should see Lamb from as many angles as possible, we have obtained from an old friend of his a memorial – slight, but such as the circumstances allowed – of an evening spent with Charles and Mary Lamb, in the winter of 1821–2. The record is of the most unambitious character; it pretends to nothing, as the reader will see – not so much as to a pun, which it really required some singularity of luck to have missed from Charles Lamb, who often continued to fire puns, as minute guns, all through the evening. But the more unpretending this record is, the more appropriate it becomes by that very fact to the memory of *him* who, amongst all authors, was the humblest and the least pretending. We have often thought that the famous epitaph written for his own grave by Piron, the cynical author of *La Métromanie*,[82] might have come from Lamb, were it not for one objection: Lamb's benign heart would have recoiled from a sarcasm, however effective, inscribed upon a grave-stone; or from a jest, however playful, that tended to a vindictive sneer amongst his own farewell words. We once translated this Piron epitaph into a kind of rambling Drayton couplet;[83] and the only point needing explanation is, – that, from the accident of scientific men, Fellows of the Royal Society, being usually very solemn men, with an extra chance, therefore, for being dull men in conversation, naturally it arose that some wit amongst our great-grandfathers translated F. R. S. into a short-hand expression for a Fellow Remarkably Stupid; to which version of the three letters our English epitaph alludes. The French original of Piron is this: –

> 'Ci git Piron; qui ne fut rien;
> Pas même académicien.'

The bitter arrow of the second line was feathered to hit the French Académie,[84] who had declined to elect him a member. Our translation is this: –

> Here lies Piron; who was – nothing; or, if *that* could be, was less:
> How! – nothing? Yes, nothing: not so much as F. R. S.

But now to our friend's memorandum![85]

October 6, 1848.

'MY DEAR X., – You ask me for some memorial, however trivial, of any dinner party, supper party, water party – no matter what – that I can circumstantially recall to recollection, by any features whatever, puns or repartees, wisdom or wit, connecting it with Charles Lamb. I grieve to say that my meetings of *any* sort with Lamb were few, though spread through a score of years. That sounds odd for one that loved Lamb so entirely, and so much venerated his character. But the reason was, that I so seldom visited London, and Lamb so seldom quitted it. Somewhere about 1810 and 1812 I must have met Lamb repeatedly at the *Courier Office* in the Strand; that is, at Coleridge's, to whom, as an intimate friend, Mr Stuart (a proprietor of the paper) gave up for a time the use of some rooms in the office.[86] Thither, in the London season, (May especially and June,) resorted Lamb, Godwin, Sir H. Davy, and, once or twice, Wordsworth, who visited Sir George Beaumont's Leicestershire residence of Coleorton early in the spring, and then travelled up to Grosvenor Square[87] with Sir George and Lady Beaumont: "spectatum veniens, veniens spectetur ut ipse."'[88]

But in these miscellaneous gatherings, Lamb said little, except when an opening arose for a pun.[89] And how effectual that sort of small shot was from *him*, I need not say to anybody who remembers his infirmity of stammering, and his dexterous management of it for purposes of light and shade. He was often able to train the roll of stammers into settling upon the words immediately preceding the effective one; by which means the key-note of the jest or sarcasm, benefiting by the sudden liberation of his embargoed voice, was delivered with the force of a pistol-shot. That stammer was worth an annuity to him as an ally of his wit. Firing under cover of that advantage he did triple execution; for, in the first place, the distressing sympathy of the hearers with *his* distress of utterance won for him unavoidably the silence of deep attention; and then, whilst he had us all hoaxed into this attitude of mute suspense by an appearance of distress that he perhaps did not really feel, down came a plunging shot into the very thick of us with ten times the effect it would else have had. If his stammering however often did him true 'yeoman's service,'[90] sometimes it led him into scrapes. Coleridge told me of a ludicrous embarrassment which it caused him at Hastings.[91] Lamb had been medically advised to a course of sea-bathing; and accordingly at the door of his bathing machine, whilst he stood shivering with cold, two stout fellows laid hold of him, one at each shoulder, like heraldic supporters: they waited for the word of command from their principal, who began the following oration to them: 'Hear me, men! Take notice of this – I am to be dipped.' What more he would have said is unknown to land or sea or bathing machines; for having reached the word dipped, he commenced such a rolling fire of Di-di-di-di, that when at length he descended *à plomb*[92] upon the full word *dipped*, the two men, rather tired of the long suspense, became satisfied that they had reached what lawyers call the 'operative' clause of the sentence; and both exclaiming at once, 'Oh yes, Sir, we're quite aware of *that*' – down they plunged him into the sea. On emerging, Lamb sobbed so much from the cold, that he found no voice suitable to his indignation; from necessity he seemed tranquil; and again addressing the men, who stood respectfully listening, he began thus: – 'Men! is it possible to obtain your attention?' – 'Oh surely, sir, by all means.' – 'Then listen: once more I tell you, I am to be di-di-di- ' – and then, with a burst of indignation, 'dipped, I tell you' – 'Oh decidedly, sir,' rejoined the men, 'decidedly' – and down the stammerer went for the second time. Petrified with cold and wrath, once more Lamb made a feeble attempt at explanation – 'Grant me pa-pa-patience; is it mum-um-murder you me-me-mean? Again and a-ga-ga-gain, I tell you, I'm to be di-di-di-dipped,' now speaking furiously, with the voice of an injured man. 'Oh yes, sir,' the men replied, 'we know that – we fully understood it' – and for the third time down went Lamb into the sea. 'Oh limbs of Satan!' he said, on coming up for the third time, 'it's now too late; I tell you that I am – no, that I *was* – to be di-di-di-dipped only *once*.'

Since the rencontres with Lamb at Coleridge's I had met him once or twice at literary dinner parties. One of these occurred at the house of Messrs. Taylor and Hessey, the publishers.[93] I myself was suffering too much from illness at the time to take any pleasure in what passed, or to notice it with any vigilance of attention. Lamb, I remember, as usual, was full of gaiety;[94] and as usual he rose too rapidly to the zenith of his gaiety: he shot upwards like a rocket, and, as usual, people said he was 'tipsy.'[95] To me Lamb never seemed intoxicated, but at most aerially elevated. He never talked nonsense, which is a great point gained; nor polemically, which is a greater; for it is a dreadful thing to find a drunken man bent upon converting oneself: nor sentimentally, which is greatest of all. You can stand a man's fraternizing with you; or if he swears an eternal friendship[96] – only once in an hour, you do not think of calling the police: but once in every three minutes is too much. Lamb did none of these things: he was always rational, quiet, and gentlemanly in his habits. Nothing memorable, I am sure, passed upon this occasion, which was in November of 1821; and yet the dinner was memorable by means of one fact not discovered until many years later. Amongst the company, all literary men, sate a murderer, and a murderer of a freezing class; cool, calculating, wholesale in his operations, and moving all along under the advantages of unsuspecting domestic confidence and domestic opportunities. This was Mr Wainwright, who was subsequently brought to trial, but not for any of his murders, and transported for life.[97] The story has been told both by Sergeant Talfourd, in the second volume of these 'Final Memoirs,' and previously by Sir Edward B. Lytton.[98] Both have been much blamed for the use made of this extraordinary case; but we know not why. In itself it is a most remarkable case for more reasons than one. It is remarkable for the appalling revelation which it makes of power spread through the hands of people not liable to suspicion, for purposes the most dreadful. It is remarkable also by the contrast which existed in this case between the murderer's appearance and the terrific purposes with which he was always dallying. He was a contributor to a journal in which I also had written several papers. This formed a shadowy link between us; and, ill as I was, I looked more attentively at *him* than at anybody else. Yet there were several men of wit and genius present, amongst whom Lamb (as I have said) and Thomas Hood, Hamilton Reynolds, and Allan Cunningham.[99] But *them* I already knew, whereas Mr W. I now saw for the first time and the last. What interested me about *him* was this – the papers which had been pointed out to me as his (signed *Janus Weathercock*, *Vinkbooms*, &c.)[100] were written in a spirit of coxcombry that did not so much disgust as amuse. The writer could not conceal the ostentatious pleasure which he took in the luxurious fittings-up of his rooms, in the fancied splendour of his *bijouterie*, &c. Yet it was easy for a man of any experience to read two facts in all this idle *étalage* – one being, that his finery was but of a second-rate order; the other, that he was a *parvenu*,[101] not at home even amongst his second-rate splendour. So far there was nothing to distinguish Mr W——'s papers from the papers of other triflers. But in this point there *was*, viz., that in his judgments upon the great Italian masters of painting, Da Vinci, Titian, &c., there seemed a tone of sincerity and of native sensibility, as in one who spoke from himself, and was not merely a copier from books. This it was that interested me; as also his reviews of the chief Italian engravers – Morghen, Volpato,[102] &c.; not for the manner, which overflowed with levities and impertinence, but for the substance of his judgments in those cases where I happened to have had an opportunity of judging for myself. Here arose also a claim upon Lamb's attention: for Lamb and his sister had a deep feeling for what was excellent in painting. Accordingly Lamb paid him a great deal of attention, and continued to speak of him for years with an interest that seemed disproportioned to his pretensions. This might be owing in part to an indirect compliment paid to Miss Lamb in one of W——'s papers:[103] else his appearance would rather have repelled Lamb; it was commonplace, and better suited to express the dandyism which overspread the surface of his manner than the unaffected sensibility which apparently lay in his nature. Dandy or not, however, this man on account of the schism in his papers, so much amiable puppyism on one side, so much deep feeling on the other, (feeling, applied to some of the grandest objects that earth has to shew,) did really move a trifle of interest in me, on a day when I hated the face of man and woman. Yet again, if I had known this man for the murderer that even then he was, what sudden loss of interest – what sudden growth of another interest, would have changed the face of that party! Trivial creature, that didst carry thy dreadful eye kindling with perpetual treasons! Dreadful creature, that didst carry thy trivial eye, mantling with eternal levity, over the sleeping surfaces of confiding household life – oh, what a revolution for man wouldst thou have accomplished had thy deep wickedness prospered! What *was* that wickedness? In a few words I will say.

At this time (October 1848)[104] the whole British island is appalled by a new chapter in the history of poisoning. Locusta in ancient Rome, Madame Brinvilliers in Paris,[105] were people of original genius; not in any new artifice of toxicology, not in the mere management of poisons, was the audacity of their genius displayed. No; but in profiting by domestic openings for murder, unsuspected through their very atrocity. Such an opening was made some years ago by those who saw the possibility of founding purses for parents upon the murder of their children. This was done upon a larger scale than had been suspected, and upon a plausible pretence. To bury a corpse is costly; but of a hundred children only a few, in the ordinary course of mortality, will die within a given time. Five shillings a-piece will produce £25 annually, and *that* will bury a considerable number. On this principle arose Infant Burial-societies.[106] For a few shillings annually, a parent could secure a funeral for every child. If the child died, a few guineas fell due to the parent, and the funeral was accomplished without cost of *his*. But on this arose the suggestion – Why not execute an insurance of this nature twenty times over? One single insurance pays for the funeral – the other nineteen are so much clear gain, a *lucro ponatur*,[107] for the parents. Yes; but on the supposition that the child died! twenty are no better than one, unless they are gathered into the garner. Now, if the child died naturally, all was right; but how, if the child did *not* die? Why, clearly this: – the child that *can* die, and won't die, may be made to die. There are many ways of doing that; and it is shocking to know, that, according to recent discoveries, poison is comparatively a very merciful mode of murder. Six years ago a dreadful communication was made to the public by a medical man, viz., that three thousand children were annually burned to death under circumstances shewing too clearly that they had been left by their mothers with the means and the temptations to set themselves on fire in her absence. But more shocking, because more lingering, are the deaths by artificial appliances of wet, cold, hunger, bad diet, and disturbed sleep, to the frail constitutions of children. By that machinery it is, and not by poison, that the majority qualify themselves for claiming the funeral allowances. Here, however, there occur to any man on reflection, two eventual restraints on the extension of this domestic curse: – 1st, as there is no pretext for wanting more than one funeral on account of one child, any insurances beyond one are in themselves a ground of suspicion. Now, if any plan were devised for securing the *publication* of such insurances, the suspicions would travel as fast as the grounds for them. 2dly, it occurs, that eventually the evil checks itself, since a society established on the ordinary rates of mortality would be ruined when a murderous stimulation was applied to that rate too extensively. Still it is certain that, for a season, this atrocity *has* prospered in manufacturing districts for some years, and more recently, as judicial investigations have shown, in one agricultural district of Essex. Now, Mr W——'s scheme of murder was, in its outline, the very same, but not applied to the narrow purpose of obtaining burials from a public fund. He persuaded, for instance, two beautiful young ladies, visitors in his family, to insure their lives for a short period of two years. This insurance was repeated in several different offices, until a sum of £18,000 had been secured in the event of their deaths within the two years. Mr W—— took care that they *should* die, and very suddenly, within that period;[108] and then, having previously secured from his victims an assignment to himself of this claim, he endeavoured to make this assignment available. But the offices, which had vainly endeavoured to extract from the young ladies any satisfactory account of the reasons for this limited insurance, had their suspicions at last strongly roused. One office had recently experienced a case of the same nature, in which also the young lady had been poisoned by the man in whose behalf she had effected the insurance: all the offices declined to pay; actions at law arose; in the course of the investigation which followed, Mr W——'s character was fully exposed. Finally, in the midst of the embarrassments which ensued, he committed forgery, and was transported.

From this Mr W——, some few days afterwards, I received an invitation to a dinner party, expressed in terms that were obligingly earnest. He mentioned the names of his principal guests, and amongst them rested most upon those of Lamb and Sir David Wilkie.[109] From an accident I was unable to attend, and I greatly regretted it. Sir David one might rarely happen to see except at a crowded party. But as regarded Lamb, I was sure to see him or to hear of him again in some way or other within a short time. This opportunity in fact offered itself within a month through the kindness of the Lambs themselves. They had heard of my being in solitary lodgings, and insisted on my coming to dine with them, which more than once I did in the winter of 1821–2.[110]

The mere reception by the Lambs was so full of goodness and hospitable feeling, that it kindled animation in the most cheerless or torpid of invalids. I cannot imagine that any *memorabilia* occurred during the visit; but I will use the time that would else be lost upon the settling of that point, in putting down any triviality that occurs to my recollection. Both Lamb and myself had a furious love for nonsense; headlong nonsense. Excepting Professor Wilson,[111] I have known nobody who had the same passion to the same extent. And things of that nature better illustrate the *realities* of Lamb's social life than the gravities which weighing so sadly on his solitary hours he sought to banish from his moments of relaxation.

There were no strangers; Charles Lamb, his sister, and myself made up the party. Even this was done in kindness. They knew that I should have been oppressed by an effort such as must be made in the society of strangers; and they placed me by their own fireside, where I could say as little or as much as I pleased.

We dined about five o'clock, and it was one of the hospitalities inevitable to the Lambs, that any game which they might receive from rural friends in the course of the week, was reserved for the day of a friend's dining with them.

In regard to wine, Lamb and myself had the same habit – perhaps it rose to the dignity of a principle – viz., to take a great deal *during* dinner – none *after* it. Consequently, as Miss Lamb (who drank only water) retired almost with the dinner itself, nothing remained for men of our principles, the rigour of which we had illustrated by taking rather too much of old port before the cloth was drawn, except talking; amoebaean colloquy, or, in Dr Johnson's phrase, a dialogue of 'brisk reciprocation.'[112] But this was impossible: over Lamb, at this period of his life, there passed regularly, after taking wine, a brief eclipse of sleep.[113] It descended upon him as softly as a shadow. In a gross person, laden with superfluous flesh, and sleeping heavily, this would have been disagreeable; but in Lamb, thin even to meagerness, spare and wiry as an Arab of the desert, or as Thomas Aquinas,[114] wasted by scholastic vigils, the affection of sleep seemed rather a network of aerial gossamer than of earthly cobweb – more like a golden haze falling upon him gently from the heavens than a cloud exhaling upwards from the flesh. Motionless in his chair as a bust, breathing so gently as scarcely to seem certainly alive, he presented the image of repose midway between life and death, like the repose of sculpture; and to one who knew his history a repose affectingly contrasting with the calamities and internal storms of his life. I have heard more persons than I can now distinctly recall, observe of Lamb when sleeping – that his countenance in that state assumed an expression almost seraphic, from its intellectual beauty of outline, its childlike simplicity, and its benignity. It could not be called a transfiguration that sleep had worked in his face; for the features wore essentially the same expression when waking; but sleep spiritualized that expression, exalted it, and also harmonized it. Much of the change lay in that last process. The eyes it was that disturbed the unity of effect in Lamb's waking face. They gave a restlessness to the character of his intellect, shifting, like Northern Lights, through every mode of combination with fantastic playfulness, and sometimes by fiery gleams obliterating for the moment that pure light of benignity which was the predominant reading on his features. Some people have supposed that Lamb had Jewish blood in his veins,[115] which seemed to account for his gleaming eyes. It might be so; but this notion found little countenance in Lamb's own way of treating the gloomy mediaeval traditions propagated throughout Europe about the Jews, and their secret enmity to Christian races. Lamb, indeed, might not be more serious than Shakspeare is supposed to have been in his Shylock;[116] yet he spoke at times as from a station of wilful bigotry, and seemed (whether laughingly or not) to sympathize with the barbarous Christian superstitions upon the pretended bloody practices of the Jews, and of the early Jewish physicians. Being himself a Lincoln man, he treated Sir Hugh[*] of Lincoln, the young child that suffered death by secret assassination in the Jewish quarter rather than suppress his daily anthems to the Virgin, as a true historical personage on the rolls of martyrdom; careless that this fable, like that of the apprentice murdered out of jealousy by his master, the architect,[118] had destroyed its own authority by ubiquitous diffusion. All over Europe the same legend of the murdered apprentice and the martyred child reappears under different names – so that in effect the verification of the tale is none at all, because it is unanimous; is too narrow, because it is too impossibly broad. Lamb, however, though it was often hard to say whether he were not secretly laughing, swore to the truth of all these old fables, and treated the liberalities of the present generation on such points as mere fantastic and effeminate affectations, which no doubt, they often are as regards the sincerity of those who profess them. The bigotry, which it pleased his fancy to assume, he used like a sword against the Jew, as the official weapon of the Christian, upon the same principle that a Capulet would have drawn upon a Montague,[119] without conceiving it any duty of *his* to rip up the grounds of so ancient a quarrel; it was a feud handed down to him by his ancestors, and it was *their* business to see that originally it had been an honest feud. I cannot yet believe that Lamb, if seriously aware of any family interconnexion with Jewish blood, would, even in jest, have held that one-sided language. More probable it is, that the fiery eye recorded not any alliance with Jewish blood, but that disastrous alliance with insanity which tainted his own life, and laid desolate his sister's.

[*] The story which furnishes a basis to the fine ballad in Percy's Reliques, and to the Canterbury Tale of Chaucer's Lady Abbess.[117]

On awaking from his brief slumber, Lamb sat for some time in profound silence, and then, with the most startling rapidity, sang out – 'Diddle, diddle, dumpkins;'[120] not looking at me, but as if soliloquizing. For five minutes he relapsed into the same deep silence; from which again he started up into the same abrupt utterance of – 'Diddle, diddle, dumpkins.' I could not help laughing aloud at the extreme energy of this sudden communication, contrasted with the deep silence that went before and followed. Lamb smilingly begged to know what I was laughing at, and with a look of as much surprise as if it were I that had done something unaccountable, and not himself. I told him (as was the truth) that there had suddenly occurred to me the possibility of my being in some future period or other called on to give an account of this very evening before some literary committee. The committee might say to me – (supposing the case that I outlived him) – 'You dined with Mr Lamb in January 1822; now, can you remember any remark or memorable observation which that celebrated man made before or after dinner?'

I as *Respondent.* 'Oh yes, I can.'

Com. 'What was it?'

Resp. 'Diddle, diddle, dumpkins.'

Com. 'And was this his only observation? Did Mr Lamb not strengthen this remark by some other of the same nature?'

Resp. 'Yes, he did.'

Com. 'And what was it?'

Resp. 'Diddle, diddle, dumpkins.'

Com. 'What is your secret opinion of Dumpkins? Do you conceive Dumpkins to have been a thing or a person?'

Resp. 'I conceive Dumpkins to have been a person, having the rights of a person.'

Com. 'Capable, for instance, of suing and being sued?'

Resp. 'Yes, capable of both; though I have reason to think there would have been very little use in suing Dumpkins?'

Com. 'How so? Are the Committee to understand that you, the Respondent, in your own case have found it a vain speculation, countenanced only by visionary lawyers, to sue Dumpkins?'

Resp. 'No; I never lost a shilling by Dumpkins, the reason for which may be that Dumpkins never owed me a shilling; but from his *praenomen*[121] of "diddle" I apprehend that he was too well acquainted with joint-stock companies?'

Com. 'And your opinion is, that he may have diddled Mr Lamb?'

Resp. 'I conceive it to be not unlikely.'

Com. 'And, perhaps, from Mr Lamb's pathetic reiteration of his name, "Diddle, diddle," you would be disposed to infer that Dumpkins had practised his diddling talents upon Mr L. more than once?'

Resp. 'I think it probable.'

Lamb laughed, and brightened up; tea was announced; Miss Lamb returned. The cloud had passed away from Lamb's spirits, and again he realized the pleasure of evening, which, in *his* apprehension, was so essential to the pleasure of literature.

On the table lay a copy of Wordsworth, in two volumes; it was the edition of Longman, printed about the time of Waterloo.[122] Wordsworth was held in little consideration, I believe, amongst the house of Longman; at any rate, *their* editions of his works were got up in the most slovenly manner. In particular, the table of contents was drawn up like a short-hand bill of parcels. By accident the book lay open at a part of this table, where the sonnet beginning –

'Alas! what boots the long laborious quest' –

had been entered with mercantile speed, as –

'Alas! what boots, ——'[123]

'Yes,' said Lamb, reading this entry in a dolorous tone of voice, 'he may well say *that*. I paid Hoby[124] three guineas for a pair that tore like blotting paper, when I was leaping a ditch to escape a farmer that pursued me with a pitch-fork for trespassing. But why should W. wear boots in Westmoreland? Pray, advise him to patronize shoes.'

The mercurialities of Lamb were infinite; and always uttered in a spirit of absolute recklessness for the quality or the prosperity of the sally. It seemed to liberate his spirits from some burthen of blackest melancholy which oppressed it, when he had thrown off a jest; he would not stop one instant to improve it; nor did he care the value of a straw whether it were good enough to be remembered, or so mediocre as to extort high moral indignation from a collector who refused to receive into his collection of jests and puns any that were not felicitously good or revoltingly bad.

After tea, Lamb read to me a number of beautiful compositions which he had himself taken the trouble to copy out into a blank paper folio from unsuccessful authors. Neglected people in every class won the sympathy of Lamb. One of the poems, I remember, was a very beautiful sonnet from a volume recently published by Lord Thurlow[125] – which, and Lamb's just remarks upon it, I could almost repeat *verbatim* at this moment, nearly twenty-seven years later, if your limits would allow me. But these, you tell me, allow of no such thing; at the utmost they allow only twelve lines more. Now all the world knows that the sonnet itself would require fourteen lines; but take fourteen from twelve, and there remains very little, I fear; besides which, I am afraid two of my twelve are already exhausted. This forces me to interrupt my account of Lamb's reading by reporting the very accident that *did* interrupt it in fact; since *that* no less characteristically expressed Lamb's peculiar spirit of kindness, (always quickening itself towards the ill-used or the down-trodden,) than it had previously expressed itself in his choice of obscure readings. Two ladies came in, one of whom at least had sunk in the scale of worldly consideration. They were ladies who would not have found much recreation in literary discussions; elderly, and habitually depressed. On *their* account, Lamb proposed whist[126] – and in that kind effort to amuse *them*, which naturally drew forth some momentary gaieties from himself, but not of a kind to impress themselves on the recollection, the evening terminated.

We have left ourselves no room for a special examination of Lamb's writings, some of which were failures, and some were so memorably beautiful as to be uniques in their class. The character of Lamb it is, and the life-struggle of Lamb, that must fix the attention of many, even amongst those wanting in sensibility to his intellectual merits. This character and this struggle, as we have already observed, impress many traces of themselves upon Lamb's writings. Even in that view, therefore, they have a ministerial value; but separately, for themselves, they have an independent value of the highest order. Upon this point we gladly adopt the eloquent words of Sergeant Talfourd: –

> 'The sweetness of Lamb's character, breathed through his writings, was felt even by strangers; but its heroic aspect was unguessed even by many of his friends. Let them now consider it, and ask if the annals of self-sacrifice can shew anything in human action and endurance more lovely than its self-devotion exhibits? It was not merely that he saw, through the ensanguined cloud of misfortune which had fallen upon his family, the unstained excellence of his sister, whose madness had caused it; that he was ready to take her to his own home with reverential affection, and cherish her through life; that he gave up, for *her* sake, all meaner and more selfish love, and all the hopes which youth blends with the passion which disturbs and ennobles it; not even that he did all this cheerfully, and without pluming himself upon his brotherly nobleness as a virtue, or seeking to repay himself (as some uneasy martyrs do) by small instalments of long repining; – but that he carried the spirit of the hour in which he first knew and took his course to his last. So far from thinking that his sacrifice of youth and love to his sister gave him a license to follow his own caprice at the expense of her feelings, even in the lightest matters, he always wrote and spoke of her as his wiser self, his generous benefactress, of whose protecting care he was scarcely worthy.'[127]

It must be remembered also, which the Sergeant does not overlook, that Lamb's efforts for the becoming support of his sister lasted through a period of forty years. Twelve years before his death, the munificence of the India House, by granting him a liberal retiring allowance,[128] had placed his own support under shelter from accidents of any kind. But this died with himself: and he could not venture to suppose that, in the event of his own death, the India House would grant to his sister the same allowance as by custom is granted to a wife. This they did; but not venturing to calculate upon such nobility of patronage, Lamb had applied himself through life to the saving of a provision for his sister under any accident to himself. And this he did with a persevering prudence, so little known in the literary class, amongst a continued tenor of generosities, often so princely as to be scarcely known in any class.

Was this man, so memorably good by life-long sacrifice of himself, in any profound sense a Christian? The impression is – that he was *not*. We, from private communications with him, can undertake to say that, according to his knowledge and opportunities for the study of Christianity, he *was*.[129] What has injured Lamb in this point is, – that his early opinions (which, however, from the first were united with the deepest piety) are read by the inattentive, as if they had been the opinions of his mature days; secondly, that he had few religious persons amongst his friends, which made him reserved in the expression of his own views; thirdly, that in any case where he altered opinions for the better, the credit of the improvement is assigned to Coleridge. Lamb, for example, beginning life as a Unitarian, in not many years became a Trinitarian. Coleridge passed through the same changes in the same order: and, here at least, Lamb is supposed simply to have obeyed the influence, confessedly great, of Coleridge. This, on our own knowledge of Lamb's views, we pronounce to be an error. And the following extracts from Lamb's letters will show – not only that he was religiously disposed on impulses self-derived, but that, so far from obeying the bias of Coleridge, he ventured, on this one subject, firmly as regarded the matter, though humbly as regarded the manner, affectionately to reprove Coleridge.

In a letter to Coleridge, written in 1797, the year after his first great affliction, he says –

> 'Coleridge, I have not one truly elevated character among my acquaintance; not one Christian; not one but undervalues Christianity. Singly, what am I to do? Wesley – [have you read his life?] – was not he an elevated character? Wesley has said religion is not a solitary thing. Alas! it is necessarily so with me, or next to solitary.' 'Tis true you write to me; but correspondence by letter and personal intimacy are widely different. Do, do write to me; and do some good to my mind – already how much "warped and relaxed" by the world!'[130]

In a letter written about three months previously, he had not scrupled to blame Coleridge at some length for audacities of religious speculation, which seemed to him at war with the simplicities of pure religion. He says –

> 'Do continue to write to me. I read your letters with my sister, and they give us both abundance of delight. Especially they please us two when you talk in a religious strain. Not but we are offended occasionally with a certain freedom of expression, a certain air of mysticism, more consonant to the conceits of pagan philosophy than consistent with the humility of genuine piety.'[131]

Then, after some instances of what he blames, he says –

> 'Be not angry with me, Coleridge. I wish not to cavil: I know I cannot instruct you; I only wish to remind you of that humility which best becometh the Chris-

tian character. God in the New Testament, our best guide, is represented to us in the kind, condescending, amiable, familiar light of a parent; and, in my poor mind, 'tis best for us so to consider him as our Heavenly Father, and our best friend, without indulging too bold conceptions of His character.'[132]

About a month later, he says —

'Few but laugh at me for reading my Testament. They talk a language I understand not: I conceal sentiments that would be a puzzle to *them*.'[133]

We see by this last quotation *where* it was that Lamb originally sought for consolation. We personally can vouch that at a maturer period, when he was approaching his fiftieth year, no change had affected his opinions upon that point; and, on the other hand, that no changes had occurred in his needs for consolation, we see, alas! in the records of his life. Whither, indeed, could he fly for comfort,[134] if not to his Bible? And to whom was the Bible an indispensable resource, if not to Lamb? We do not undertake to say, that in his knowledge of Christianity he was everywhere profound or consistent, but he was always earnest in his aspirations after its spiritualities, and had an apprehensive sense of its power.

Charles Lamb is gone: his life was a continued struggle in the service of love the purest, and within a sphere visited by little of contemporary applause. Even his intellectual displays won but a narrow sympathy at any time, and in his earlier period were saluted with positive derision and contumely on the few occasions when they were not oppressed by entire neglect. But slowly all things right themselves. All merit, which is founded in truth and is strong enough, reaches by sweet exhalations in the end a higher sensory – reaches higher organs of discernment, lodged in a selecter audience. But the original obtuseness or vulgarity of feeling that thwarted Lamb's just estimation in life, will continue to thwart its popular diffusion. There are even some that continue to regard him with the old hostility. And we, therefore, standing by the side of Lamb's grave, seemed to hear, on one side (but in abated tones,) strains of the ancient malice – 'this man, that thought himself to be somebody, is dead – is buried – is forgotten!' and, on the other side, seemed to hear ascending, as with the solemnity of an anthem – 'This man, that thought himself to be nobody, is dead – is buried; his life has been searched; and his memory is hallowed for ever!'

Articles for *Blackwood's Edinburgh Magazine*, 1849

THE ENGLISH MAIL-COACH, OR THE GLORY OF MOTION

First published in *Blackwood's*, LXVI, October 1849, pp. 485–500. The essay was printed anonymously.

Reprinted in *F*, III, *Miscellaneous Essays* (1851), pp. 131–70.

Revised text, carrying many accidentals and eleven substantive variants from *F*, in *SGG*, IV, *Miscellanies* (1854), pp. 289–322.

In *SGG*, De Quincey grouped the present essay and its companion piece on 'The Vision of Sudden Death' (see below, pp. 429–49) under the common title 'The English Mail-Coach'. This headnote introduces both 'The Glory of Motion' and 'The Vision of Sudden Death', and surveys the manuscript material related to both essays. For clarity, the two manuscripts related to the present essay on 'The Glory of Motion' carry the abbreviation 'GM':

MS GM A: University of Chicago Library, MS 611-V. The manuscript is an interleaved copy of *F*, with extensive revisions in De Quincey's hand. It corresponds to the passage below running from *Title* 'THE ENGLISH MAIL-COACH' to 427.35 'He was a trooper in the 23d Dra'. The manuscript contains over one hundred significant variants, and these are listed in the textual notes.

MS GM B: University of Chicago Library, MS 611–V. The manuscript is a complete set of *SGG* page proofs, with extensive revisions in De Quincey's hand. The manuscript contains over fifty significant variants, and these are listed in the textual notes.

There are six manuscripts related to 'The Vision of Sudden Death'. For clarity, they carry the abbreviation 'VSD'. For details of these six manuscripts, see below, p. 429.

'The English Mail-Coach' is one of De Quincey's most admired and influential works. The text follows the narrative pattern first established by De Quincey in *Confessions of an English Opium-Eater* (1821), where autobiographical episodes and engaging conversational banter gradually give way to nightmare worlds of personal tragedy and apocalypse played out with horrifying repetitiveness in the tortured mind of the dreamer. De Quincey originally conceived the text as part of *Suspiria de Profundis* (1845), but it soon took on its own identity as a separate and unique narrative. Manuscript evidence reveals the meticulous attention De Quincey paid to details of sound, rhythm, and meaning as he repeatedly revised and rewrote the 'Mail-Coach' for *Blackwood's* in 1849, and then again for its appearance in *SGG* in 1854. The text draws heavily on a wide-ranging series of literary, political and personal sources. At its core is the near-fatal accident between a mail-coach and a small gig, and De Quincey's exploitation and transformation of that event. Contemporary responses to the 'Mail-Coach' were divided, but in the twentieth century the text became a centrepiece of De Quinceyean criticism. It has also held remarkable appeal for several important literary figures, from George Eliot and Stéphane Mallarmé to James Joyce and Sylvia Plath.

I. Composition

The 'Mail-Coach' was written over a number of years, and went through a series of elaborate revisions. De Quincey's initial intention was that it would form part of *Suspiria*, and he sometimes referred to the two texts as mutually interdependent. In a 15 January 1849 *Suspiria* manuscript fragment, he wrote that in order 'to account for the elements of the dream, the reader must remember the leading facts in my travelling experience', a clear reference to the adventures and anxieties of the 'Mail-Coach' (Vol. 15, p. 583). More usually, though, De Quincey described the 'Mail-Coach' as a separate text, and in 1854 declared that he 'did not scruple...to publish it apart, as sufficiently intelligible even when dislocated from its place in a larger whole' (Vol. 20, p. 34). The impression that the 'Mail-Coach' is part of *Suspiria* was later encouraged by Japp, who gave it as item three in a list of titles for *Suspiria* (Japp, *PW*, vol. I, pp. 4–5). Inspection of the original manuscript, however, reveals that the 'Mail-Coach' is Japp's own unwarranted insertion, and not part of De Quincey's plan, at least at the time of the manuscript (see Vol. 15, p. 567). De Quincey conceived and wrote the 'Mail-Coach' during the same period as *Suspiria*, but he seems most often to have thought of it as a separate text.

Publication of *Suspiria* began in *Blackwood's* in March 1845, but was complicated and fractious, and broke off abruptly in July 1845 after the appearance of only four instalments. Five months later, however, De Quincey wrote to Blackwood to say that he would 'send the remainder of the *Suspiria* (now nearly finished) – making in all from 72 to 80pp of the Magazine', and Eaton speculates that 'the long paper "nearly finished" in 1845' was the 'Mail-Coach'. No part of the work was forthcoming at this point, but by February 1847 large portions of the text existed, for De Quincey told his daughter Florence that he considered 'the *Vision of Sudden Death*...the most elaborate and solemn *bravura* of rhetoric that I have composed'. De Quincey was perhaps referring to MS VSD E, which is almost a complete version of 'Sudden Death', and which carries four sheets watermarked '1847'. This dating in turn suggests that MSS VSD A through D were composed prior to 1847, and possibly as early as 1844. MS VSD A contains a set of early draft notes for the 'Dream Fugue':

> 3. The ship running upon the rocks of a port har[b]. a narrow channel. Lights torches all the town stretching y[r] arms to save: your children are on deck: almost you touch the arms y[t] are stretched out
> 4. All have perished: but you – hatefully to yourself – why you know not – *how* you ask not – are again walking in smouldering cities

MSS VSD B, C, and D are most probably discarded fragments from 'Sudden Death' as it evolved into MS VSD E, which served as printer's copy for the essay as it appeared in *Blackwood's* (Eaton, p. 427; Pforzheimer, Misc. MS 1782).

De Quincey published the 'Mail-Coach' in *Blackwood's* for October and December, 1849. On 20 November 1849 John Blackwood sent him proofs for 'Sudden Death', which Blackwood felt was 'quite able to stand by itself separated from the Mail Coach'. De Quincey, however, was not so certain, and inserted a note at the beginning of the second instalment instructing 'the reader...to understand this present paper, in its two sections of *The Vision*, &c., and *The Dream-Fugue*, as connected with a previous paper on *The English Mail-Coach*'. Blackwood also suggested giving the second instalment two separate titles: '1st the Vision of Sudden Death 2nd Dream Figures'. De Quincey apparently agreed, for the essay was printed with the two different headings, though De Quincey of course amended 'Dream Figures' to 'Dream-Fugue' (National Library of Scotland, MS 30315). The two parts of the 'Mail-Coach' are De Quincey's last published works in *Blackwood's*, and bring to a close a relationship that had lasted over thirty years.

De Quincey republished the 'Mail-Coach' in volume four of *SGG*, but with extensive revisions, as the page proofs from both instalments of the original essay ('The English Mail-Coach', MSS GM A and B, and 'The Vision of Sudden Death', MS VSD F) reveal. 'To examine these proof-sheets is to receive a lesson from a master of style', wrote Edward Dowden. The variants from these page proofs are given in the textual notes (see below, pp. 723-51). Among scores of changes, De Quincey grouped the two separate essays together under the common title 'The English Mail-Coach', and made a major cut to the nightmare that closes the opening section of the first instalment, removing from p. 421.17 'upwards to heaven,' to p. 423.11 'transfigured coachman of the Bath mail.' The 'Mail-Coach' evolved over a period of several years, and is perhaps the most thoroughly revised of all De Quincey's essays. The extant manuscript material provides remarkable evidence of how meticulously he laboured at the process of revision, and how many striking variations he considered on his central themes (Edward Dowden, 'How De Quincey Worked' in *Saturday Review*, 79 (1895), p. 246).

II. Sources

The 'Mail-Coach' draws on an extensive series of sources. De Quincey cites classical authors such as Cicero, Virgil, Suetonius, and most prominently Homer, whose *Iliad* features the shout of Achilles that De Quincey invokes in 'Sudden Death'. There are Biblical allusions, quotations from Spenser's *Faerie Queene*, Shakespeare's *Richard III*, and Milton's *Paradise Lost*, as well as references to lesser-known writers like the Welsh historian Giraldus Cambrensis and the Italian antiquary Stefano Morcelli. De Quincey's opening discussion is indebted to William Cowper's account of the arrival of the post in Book IV of *The Task*, and to Robert Southey's description of mail-coach travel in his *Letters from England*. The dreams of Fanny that close 'The Glory of Motion' section draw on the poetry of Alexander Pope and William Wordsworth, while in the 'Dream-Fugue', the 'Dying Trumpeter' sounding 'his stony trumpet' of resurrection seems to recollect William Blake's title-page engraving for Robert Blair's *The Grave*, a book which De Quincey is known to have seen, and which depicts a trumpeter sounding notes that bring a skeleton to life (G. E. Bentley, *The Stranger from Paradise: A Biography of William Blake* (New Haven, Conn.: Yale University Press, 2001), p. 485; for De Quincey and Blake, see Vol. 11, p. 205).

The 'Mail-Coach' is also informed by the political and social events of the day. De Quincey highlights Britain's military victories in battles such as Trafalgar, Salamanca, Vittoria, and especially Talavera, all of which prepared the way for the final defeat of Napoleon at Waterloo, an event that resonates through the final two sections of the 'Dream Fugue'. De Quincey records his complex response to the consequences of mechanization and the industrial revolution, as he moves from the heyday of the mail-coach service in the early nineteenth century to nearly fifty years later, by which time the mail-coaches have been replaced by a national system of railways. De Quincey's account of the near-fatal accident between the mail-coach and the gig is dilated into mythic proportions, but accidents of the road were commonplace, and often described in the newspapers of the day. 'MAIL COACH ACCIDENT' on the road 'from Edinburgh to Carlisle', reported *The True Weekly Sun*:

> There were three passengers outside and four inside, none of whom...received any serious injury, although two of the former were pitched into a field by the roadside. Had the coach been thrown over on the opposite side of the road, the consequences might have been dreadful. (5 January 1834, p. 147)

Even the dreaded crocodile, so intimately associated with De Quincey's dreamscapes and his loathing of Eastern imagery, was sometimes to be found alive in an English countryside that De Quincey might have expected to be free from such freak horrors. 'A few days ago', reported the *Staffordshire Advertizer* in July 1830,

> an animal answering in every particular the description of a crocodile, was caught...in this county, in a culvert. It was first discovered by a woman, who heard it *cry out* from her own door...It is nearly four feet in length, and is still living. It is said that, last year, a man and woman were travelling the country with some young animals of this species....one of them escaped, and is believed to be the one caught. (cited in *The Chat of the Week*, IX, 31 July 1830, p. 25)

In the 'Mail-Coach', political fantasy and apocalyptic vision are informed by the pressing demands and bewildering anxieties of contemporary life.

The 'Mail-Coach' also features key circumstances from De Quincey's own experience. As in other autobiographical works such as *Confessions of an English Opium-Eater* and *Suspiria*, the revelatory power of the dreaming mind is given a central role, as is the inexorable agency of opium. De Quincey returns again to the seminal events of his years as a student at Oxford, for in both *Confessions* and the 'Mail-Coach', the teenager is father of the man, and it is his preoccupations that shape the dream terrors of the older De Quincey. The most crucial circumstance, however, is the near-fatal collision between the mail-coach and the small gig, for it is from this scene that, as De Quincey put it, 'the whole of this paper radiates as a natural expansion' (Vol. 20, p. 34). In 1854, De Quincey recorded that the accident happened 'in the dead of night' when he was a 'solitary spectator...seated on the box of the Manchester and Glasgow mail, in the second or third summer after Waterloo' (see below, p. 741, 433.18–19). De Quincey describes the scene in considerable minuteness, and includes in his account such information as the month of the accident, the time, the location, the speed of the mail-coach, the distances separating the two vehicles, the positions of the passengers, and the results of the collision. The incident clearly made a profound impression on him, and the horror of the scene was still with him thirty years later.

Yet it seems very unlikely that the accident happened as De Quincey describes. De Quincey stressed that the collision occurred in 'the second or third summer after Waterloo', and yet as the coach thunders down on the small carriage, he is unable to make his way to the guard's seat because of the 'extra accumulation of foreign mails this night, owing to irregularities caused by war' (see below, p. 435). For all the specificity of his account, then, De Quincey has apparently misremembered whether or not the accident happened before or after Waterloo, though this may be intentional, as it allows him to incorporate both the chaotic mood of wartime and the superficially serene but actually ominous atmosphere of the post-war period between Waterloo and Peterloo. Similarly, the young, vulnerable female victims who haunt De Quincey's texts – as Ann of Oxford Street and Catherine Wordsworth in *Confessions*; as Agnes in the tale of terror 'The Household Wreck'; as Elizabeth in *Suspiria* – reappear in De Quincey's representation of the accident scene in the 'Mail-Coach', as the terrified young woman awaits the impact of the runaway coach, and the female infant in the 'Dream-Fugue' sits helplessly in the path of the on-coming vehicle.

De Quincey's presentation of the collision was also undoubtedly shaped by a number of similar accident scenes. In a fragment discarded from his 1839 *Tait's* article on Wordsworth, he recollects how he once witnessed the 'ludicrous spectacle in a long and narrow Devonshire lane' of a clergyman 'meeting a chaise-and-four tearing along at a mail coach pace', and 'finding it vain to force his horse up into facing the terrific equipage'. De Quincey also seems to have in mind the opening chapter of Walter Scott's *Heart of Mid-Lothian* (1818), where a collision is described in which a mail-coach has 'over-turned so completely, that it was literally resting upon the ground, with the roof undermost, and the four wheels in the air'. Most strikingly, De Quincey draws on a passage that he had previously translated from Ernst Moritz Arndt, in which Arndt is aboard a small coach and sees

> a heavy travelling carriage half a mile ahead escorted by cavalry, and nearing us with prodigious speed. I stood up bare-headed as he passed, and I remarked that, from the brute obstinacy of my own Polish postillion, my slight equipage was within one finger's breath of being actually run down by his majesty's heavy one. As it was, the royal carriage grazed mine, and injured the wheels: but for the flying velocity with which it moved, undoubtedly, I should have been swept into the ditch.

De Quincey seems certain to have been involved in some kind of mail-coach accident, but he undoubtedly altered and embellished the event in light of his central preoccupations and his knowledge of similar accident scenes. In the 'Mail-Coach', he weaves literary, political, and personal incident into a mythic vision of death, the apocalypse, Waterloo, industrialization, and lost innocence (Vol. 11, p. 580; Scott, *Mid-Lothian*, pp. 6–10; Vol. 12, p. 328).

III. Reception

Contemporary reaction to the 'Mail-Coach' was mixed. 'I read to-day in the new volume of De Quincey his powerful papers on the *English Mail-Coach*', wrote Henry Crabb Robinson. 'Written with diseased strength, but still evidently stretched out unduly for the sake of pay'. *The British Quarterly Review* complained, 'How elaborately he delays the catastrophe...and hunts, Diogenes fashion, for every item of excitement and fear. What a master-of-ceremonies formality in introducing you to everybody you don't want, and in hindering from what you do want'. Leslie Stephen criticized the 'Mail-Coach' for its 'exaggerated patriotism', which leads De Quincey into 'a rather vulgar bit of claptrap'. Yet other contemporary critics responded sympathetically, and particularly to the 'Dream-Fugue', which in the view of the *Continental Monthly* should be read by anyone who 'desires to see what can be done with the English language'. *The Gentleman's Magazine* concurred:

> So full of the sweetest and the choicest inspiration of imagination, so rich in trembling tenderness, with interserted symphonies of grandeur, as to require only the accident of metre, if indeed it requires even that, to deserve a place amongst the choicest and most charming specimens of genuine poetry.

(*HCR*, vol. II, pp. 747–8; *The British Quarterly Review*, 38 (July 1863), p. 20; Leslie Stephen, *Hours in a Library* (London: Smith, Elder, 1874), p. 362; *Continental Monthly*, 5 (June 1864), p. 660; *The Gentleman's Magazine*, 203 (August 1857), p. 111).

For the past one hundred years, the 'Mail-Coach' has been examined from several critical perspectives, and has been a cornerstone of De Quinceyean criticism. George Saintsbury scanned long sections of the text in his *History of English Prose Rhythm*, and described De Quincey as 'a great and a very early master of our later rhythmed prose'. Sackville-West read the 'Dream-Fugue' in Freudian terms: 'The prevalence throughout of anxiety, the suspicion of persecution, the feeling of dread, of irrevocability, above all of guilt – in short all the preoccupations, expressed in easily recognizable symbols, which harassed his waking mind in moments of unhappiness'. John E. Jordan characterized the 'Mail-Coach' as written in a style 'that is not so much "impassioned" as "theatrical" and "rhetorical"....The feeling which it contains is artfully controlled and sometimes perhaps even artfully contrived' (George Saintsbury, *A History of English Prose Rhythm* (London: Macmillan, 1912), p. 306; Edward Sackville-West, *A Flame in Sunlight: The Life and Work of Thomas De Quincey*, (London: Cassell, 1936), p. 172; John E. Jordan, 'Introduction' in *Thomas De Quincey: The English Mail-Coach and Other Essays*, ed. John E. Jordan (London: Dent, 1961), p. x).

More recently, Robert Maniquis writes of the 'Dream-Fugue', 'No more mind-boggling fantasy of patriotism was ever written in the nineteenth century. The self, the nation, the world, Christendom are gathered into one historical light cast against the darkness'. V. A. De Luca notes that 'there is something decidedly chilling in De Quincey's absorption of pain and death as contrapuntal notes in an artfully composed fugue, in his preference, finally, for order in any form at the expense of what is certainly a genuinely felt outrage at the brutalities of experience'. For Robert Hopkins the 'Mail-Coach' is 'a meaningful, coherent imaginative prose work', but for Arden Reed, the 'vibrations and slippages' of the text demonstrate that 'the mail-coach could hardly be less steady'. John Barrell observes that the 'Mail-Coach' 'either records or invents a fascinating moment in the history of class division, the moment when – according to De Quincey – it became fashionable...for young gentlemen to travel on the outside of the coach...rather than on the inside'. Frederick Burwick examines the 'Mail-Coach' as 'a case study in ekphrastic paralysis', and Grevel Lindop concentrates on the 'complex...ramifications' of the crocodile, which in the 'Mail-Coach' comes to symbolise 'the moral problem from which De Quincey's finest writing and most original insights come'. In Angela Leighton's view,

> De Quincey...emphasizes, through "The English Mail-Coach", something that has been present in all his work....As the documentary and historical realism of the first part insidiously slides into surrealistic nightmare, De Quincey seems to expose the hollowness of Victorian patriotism and patriarchy, from the point of view of the female outsider.

But for Thomas McFarland, the 'Mail-Coach'

> emphasizes the endless resurrections of De Quincey's own love for his sister even as it celebrates the endless resurrection of divine love. One of the final guarantees of the Book of Revelation is that in the New Jerusalem "there shall be no night". As the English mail-coach wheels into the courtyard of apocalypse, its journey to the end of night breaks and ceases in the abrogation of night.

(Robert Maniquis, 'Lonely Empires: Personal and Public Visions of Thomas De Quincey' in *Literary Monographs*, vol. 8, eds Eric Rothstein and Joseph Anthony Wittreich (Madison: University of Wisconsin Press, 1976), p. 75; V. A. De Luca, *Thomas De Quincey: The Prose of Vision* (Toronto: University of Toronto Press, 1980), p. 116; Robert Hopkins, 'De Quincey on War and the Pastoral Design of "The English Mail-Coach"' in *Studies in Romanticism*, 6.3 (Spring 1967), p. 129; Arden Reed, '"Booked for Utter Perplexity" on De Quincey's "English Mail-Coach"' in *Thomas De Quincey: Bicentenary Studies*, ed. Robert Lance Snyder (Norman: University of Oklahoma Press, 1985), p. 303; John Barrell, *The Infection of Thomas De Quincey* (New Haven, Conn.: Yale University Press, 1991), p. 8; Frederick Burwick: *Thomas De Quincey: Knowledge and Power* (London: Palgrave, 2001), p. 127; Grevel Lindop, 'De Quincey and the Cursed Crocodile' in *Essays in Criticism*, 45.2 (1994), pp. 124, 139; Angela Leighton, 'De Quincey and Women' in *Beyond Romanticism: New Approaches to Texts and Contexts*, eds Stephen Copley and John Whale (London: Routledge, 1992), p. 176; Thomas McFarland, *Romantic Cruxes: The English Essayists and the Spirit of the Age* (Oxford: Clarendon Press, 1987), p. 121).

Yet the 'Mail-Coach' has not only been a source of fascination to critics. From its original publication in 1849, it has had a remarkable literary influence, and on a number of major figures. Frederick Rockwell explores Herman Melville's 'indebtedness to the "Mail-Coach" for essentials of the last three chapters of *Moby Dick*', and as a contributing factor in 'the transmuting of *The*

Whale into *Moby Dick*'. Walter Pater cites the 'Mail-Coach' in his essay on 'Aesthetic Poetry'. Kathleen McCormack describes how the incidents and images of De Quincey's text are a 'presence hovering over' George Eliot's *Felix Holt*. Francis Thompson borrowed from the 'Mail-Coach' in 'The Hound of Heaven', and Stéphane Mallarmé is almost certainly indebted to the same source in *Un Coup de dés*. In her essay entitled 'The English Mail-Coach', Virginia Woolf observes that De Quincey's 'writing at its best has the effect of rings of sound which break into each other and widen out and out till the brain can hardly expand far enough to realise the last remote vibrations which spend themselves on the verge of everything where speech melts into silence'. James Joyce could recite from the 'Mail-Coach' 'by the page', and draws on it in 'The Oxen of the Sun' chapter in *Ulysses*, while in *Finnegans Wake* quotations from the 'Mail-Coach' help make up 'De Quinceys salade'. Sylvia Plath marked many passages from the 'Mail-Coach' in her copy of De Quincey's works, and her 'celebrations of equine movement in poems like "Years" and "Ariel"' share both the 'terms and attitudes' of De Quincey's text (Frederick Rockwell, 'De Quincey and the Ending of *Moby Dick*' in *Nineteenth-Century Fiction*, 9 (1954), p. 168; Walter Pater, 'Aesthetic Poetry' in *Appreciations, with an Essay on Style* (London: Macmillan, 1889), p. 222; Kathleen McCormack, *George Eliot and Intoxication: Dangerous Drugs and the Condition of England* (New York: Palgrave, 2000), p. 147; John Walsh, *Strange Harp, Strange Symphony: The Life of Francis Thompson* (New York: Hawthorn, 1967), pp. 94, 100; Calvin Brown, 'De Quincey and the participles in Mallarmé's *Coup de dés*' in *Comparative Literature*, 16 (1964), pp. 65–9; Virginia Woolf, 'The English Mail-Coach' in *The Essays of Virginia Woolf*, ed. Andrew McNeillie, 4 vols (London: Hogarth Press, 1986-continuing), vol. I, p. 367; J. S. Atherton, 'The Oxen of the Sun' in James Joyce's *Ulysses: Critical Essays* (Berkeley: University of California Press, 1974), p. 329–30; J. S. Atherton, *The Books at the Wake* (Appel: Mamaroneck, 1974), p. 246; Al Strangeways, *Sylvia Plath: The Shaping of Shadows* (London: Associated University Presses, 1998), p. 74).

The annotation for this essay draws on previous editions of 'The English Mail-Coach' by Henry H. Belfield (Boston: Sibley, 1892), Cecil M. Barrow and Mark Hunter (London: Bell, 1896), Milton Haight Turk (Boston: Ginn, 1902), Carol M. Newman (New York: Macmillan, 1906), R. Adelaide Witham (Boston: Houghton, Mifflin, 1906), and Grevel Lindop (Oxford: Oxford University Press, 1996).

THE ENGLISH MAIL-COACH, OR THE GLORY OF MOTION.

SOME twenty or more years before I matriculated at Oxford, Mr Palmer, M.P. for Bath,[1] had accomplished two things, very hard to do on our little planet, the Earth, however cheap they may happen to be held by the eccentric people in comets: he had invented mail-coaches, and he had married the daughter* of a duke. He was, therefore, just twice as great a man as Galileo, who certainly invented (or *discovered*)[3] the satellites of Jupiter,[4] those very next things extant to mail-coaches in the two capital points of speed and keeping time, but who did *not* marry the daughter of a duke.

These mail-coaches, as organised by Mr Palmer, are entitled to a circumstantial notice from myself – having had so large a share in developing the anarchies of my subsequent dreams, an agency which they accomplished, first, through velocity, at that time unprecedented; they first revealed the glory of motion: suggesting, at the same time, an under-sense, not unpleasurable, of possible though indefinite danger; secondly, through grand effects for the eye between lamp-light and the darkness upon solitary roads; thirdly, through animal beauty and power so often displayed in the class of horses selected for this mail service; fourthly, through the conscious presence of a central intellect, that, in the midst of vast distances,† of storms, of darkness, of night, overruled all obstacles into one steady co-operation in a national result. To my own feeling, this Post-office service recalled some mighty orchestra, where a thousand instruments, all disregarding each other, and so far in danger of discord, yet all obedient as slaves to the supreme *baton* of some great leader, terminate in a perfection of harmony like that of heart, veins, and arteries, in a healthy animal organisation. But, finally, that particular element in this whole combination which most impressed myself, and through which it is that to this hour Mr Palmer's mail-coach system tyrannises by terror and terrific beauty over my dreams, lay in the awful political mission which at that time it fulfilled. The mail-coaches it was that distributed over the face of the land, like the opening of apocalyptic vials,[6] the heart-shaking news[7] of Trafalgar, of Salamanca, of Vittoria, of Waterloo.[8] These were the harvests that, in the grandeur of their reaping, redeemed the tears and blood in which they had been sown.[9] Neither was the meanest peasant so much below the grandeur and the sorrow of the times as to confound these battles, which were gradually moulding the destinies of Christendom, with the vulgar conflicts of ordinary warfare, which are oftentimes but gladiatorial trials of national prowess. The victories of England in this stupendous contest rose of themselves as natural *Te Deums*[10] to heaven; and it was felt by the thoughtful that such victories, at such a crisis of general prostration,[11] were not more beneficial to ourselves than finally to France, and to the nations of western and central Europe, through whose pusillanimity it was that the French domination had prospered.

The mail-coach, as the national organ for publishing these mighty events, became itself a spiritualised and glorified object to an impassioned heart; and

* Lady Madeline Gordon.[2]

† '*Vast distances*.' – One case was familiar to mail-coach travellers, where two mails in opposite directions, north and south, starting at the same minute from points six hundred miles apart, met almost constantly at a particular bridge which exactly bisected the total distance.[5]

naturally, in the Oxford of that day, all hearts were awakened. There were, perhaps, of us gownsmen, two thousand *resident** in Oxford, and dispersed through five-and-twenty colleges. In some of these the custom permitted the student to keep what are called 'short terms;' that is, the four terms of Michaelmas, Lent, Easter, and Act,[12] were kept severally by a residence, in the aggregate, of ninety-one days, or thirteen weeks. Under this interrupted residence, accordingly, it was possible that a student might have a reason for going down[13] to his home four times in the year. This made eight journeys to and fro. And as these homes lay dispersed through all the shires of the island, and most of us disdained all coaches except his majesty's mail, no city out of London could pretend to so extensive a connexion with Mr Palmer's establishment as Oxford.[14] Naturally, therefore, it became a point of some interest with us, whose journeys revolved every six weeks on an average, to look a little into the executive details of the system. With some of these Mr Palmer had no concern; they rested upon bye-laws not unreasonable, enacted by posting-houses for their own benefit, and upon others equally stern, enacted by the inside passengers for the illustration of their own exclusiveness. These last were of a nature to rouse our scorn, from which the transition was not *very long* to mutiny. Up to this time, it had been the fixed assumption of the four inside people, (as an old tradition of all public carriages from the reign of Charles II.,)[15] that they, the illustrious quaternion, constituted a porcelain variety of the human race, whose dignity would have been compromised by exchanging one word of civility with the three miserable delf ware[16] outsides. Even to have kicked an outsider might have been held to attaint[17] the foot concerned in that operation; so that, perhaps, it would have required an act of parliament to restore its purity of blood. What words, then, could express the horror, and the sense of treason, in that case, which *had* happened, where all three outsides, the trinity of Pariahs, made a vain attempt to sit down at the same breakfast-table or dinner-table with the consecrated four? I myself witnessed such an attempt; and on that occasion a benevolent old gentleman endeavoured to soothe his three holy associates, by suggesting that, if the outsides were indicted for this criminal attempt at the next assizes, the court would regard it as a case of lunacy (or *delirium tremens*)[18] rather than of treason. England owes much of her grandeur to the depth of the aristocratic element in her social composition. I am not the man to laugh at it. But sometimes it expressed itself in extravagant shapes. The course taken with the infatuated outsiders, in the particular attempt which I have noticed, was, that the waiter, beckoning them away from the privileged *salle-à-manger*,[19] sang out, 'This way, my good men;' and then enticed them away off to the kitchen. But that plan had not always answered. Sometimes, though very rarely, cases occurred

* '*Resident*.' – The number on the books was far greater, many of whom kept up an intermitting communication with Oxford. But I speak of those only who were steadily pursuing their academic studies, and of those who resided constantly as *fellows*.

where the intruders, being stronger than usual, or more vicious than usual, resolutely refused to move, and so far carried their point, as to have a separate table arranged for themselves in a corner of the room. Yet, if an Indian screen could be found ample enough to plant them out from the very eyes of the high table, or *dais*, it then became possible to assume as a fiction of law – that the three delf fellows, after all, were not present. They could be ignored by the porcelain men, under the maxim, that objects not appearing, and not existing, are governed by the same logical construction.[20]

Such now being, at that time, the usages of mail-coaches, what was to be done by us of young Oxford? We, the most aristocratic of people, who were addicted to the practice of looking down superciliously even upon the insides themselves as often very suspicious characters, were we voluntarily to court indignities? If our dress and bearing sheltered us, generally, from the suspicion of being 'raff,'[21] (the name at that period for 'snobs,'[*]) we really *were* such constructively, by the place we assumed. If we did not submit to the deep shadow of eclipse, we entered at least the skirts of its penumbra. And the analogy of theatres was urged against us, where no man can complain of the annoyances incident to the pit or gallery, having his instant remedy in paying the higher price of the boxes. But the soundness of this analogy we disputed. In the case of the theatre, it cannot be pretended that the inferior situations have any separate attractions, unless the pit suits the purpose of the dramatic reporter. But the reporter or critic is a rarity. For most people, the sole benefit is in the price. Whereas, on the contrary, the outside of the mail had its own incommunicable advantages. These we could not forego. The higher price we should willingly have paid, but *that* was connected with the condition of riding inside, which was insufferable. The air, the freedom of prospect, the proximity to the horses, the elevation of seat – these were what we desired; but, above all, the certain anticipation of purchasing occasional opportunities of driving.

Under coercion of this great practical difficulty, we instituted a searching inquiry into the true quality and valuation of the different apartments about the mail. We conducted this inquiry on metaphysical principles; and it was ascertained satisfactorily, that the roof of the coach, which some had affected to call the attics, and some the garrets, was really the drawing-room, and the box was the chief ottoman or sofa in that drawing-room; whilst it appeared that the inside, which had been traditionally regarded as the only room tenantable by gentlemen, was, in fact, the coal-cellar in disguise.

Great wits jump.[23] The very same idea had not long before struck the celestial intellect of China.[24] Amongst the presents carried out by our first embassy[25] to that country was a state-coach. It had been specially selected as a

[*] 'Snobs,' and its antithesis, 'nobs,' arose among the internal factions of shoemakers perhaps ten years later.[22] Possibly enough, the terms may have existed much earlier; but they were then first made known, picturesquely and effectively, by a trial at some assizes which happened to fix the public attention.

personal gift by George III.; but the exact mode of using it was a mystery to Pekin. The ambassador, indeed, (Lord Macartney,)[26] had made some dim and imperfect explanations upon the point; but as his excellency communicated these in a diplomatic whisper, at the very moment of his departure, the celestial mind was very feebly illuminated; and it became necessary to call a cabinet council on the grand state question – 'Where was the emperor[27] to sit?' The hammer-cloth[28] happened to be unusually gorgeous; and partly on that consideration, but partly also because the box offered the most elevated seat, and undeniably went foremost, it was resolved by acclamation that the box was the imperial place, and, *for the scoundrel who drove, he might sit where he could find a perch*. The horses, therefore, being harnessed, under a flourish of music and a salute of guns, solemnly his imperial majesty ascended his new English throne, having the first lord of the treasury[29] on his right hand, and the chief jester on his left. Pekin gloried in the spectacle; and in the whole flowery people,[30] constructively present by representation, there was but one discontented person, which was the coachman. This mutinous individual, looking as blackhearted as he really was, audaciously shouted – 'Where am *I* to sit?' But the privy council, incensed by his disloyalty, unanimously opened the door, and kicked him into the inside. He had all the inside places to himself; but such is the rapacity of ambition, that he was still dissatisfied. 'I say,' he cried out in an extempore petition, addressed to the emperor through a window, 'how am I to catch hold of the reins?' – 'Any how,' was the answer; 'don't trouble *me*, man, in my glory; through the windows, through the key-holes – how you please.' Finally, this contumacious coachman lengthened the check-strings into a sort of jury-reins,[31] communicating with the horses; with these he drove as steadily as may be supposed. The emperor returned after the briefest of circuits: he descended in great pomp from his throne, with the severest resolution never to remount it. A public thanksgiving was ordered for his majesty's prosperous escape from the disease of a broken neck; and the state-coach was dedicated for ever as a votive offering to the god Fo, Fo – whom the learned more accurately call Fi, Fi.[32]

A revolution of this same Chinese character did young Oxford of that era effect in the constitution of mail-coach society. It was a perfect French revolution; and we had good reason to say, *Ca ira*.[33] In fact, it soon became *too* popular. The 'public,' a well-known character, particularly disagreeable, though slightly respectable, and notorious for affecting the chief seats in synagogues,[34] had at first loudly opposed this revolution; but when all opposition showed itself to be ineffectual, our disagreeable friend went into it with headlong zeal. At first it was a sort of race between us; and, as the public is usually above 30, (say generally from 30 to 50 years old,) naturally we of young Oxford, that averaged about 20, had the advantage. Then the public took to bribing, giving fees to horse-keepers, &c., who hired out their persons as warming-pans on the box-seat. *That*, you know, was shocking to our moral sensibilities. Come to bribery, we observed, and there is an end to all morality,

Aristotle's, Cicero's,[35] or anybody's. And, besides, of what use was it? For *we* bribed also. And as our bribes to those of the public being demonstrated out of Euclid[36] to be as five shillings to sixpence, here again young Oxford had the advantage. But the contest was ruinous to the principles of the stable-establishment about the mails. The whole corporation was constantly bribed, rebribed, and often sur-rebribed; so that a horse-keeper, ostler, or helper, was held by the philosophical at that time to be the most corrupt character in the nation.

There was an impression upon the public mind, natural enough from the continually augmenting velocity of the mail, but quite erroneous, that an outside seat on this class of carriages was a post of danger. On the contrary, I maintained that, if a man had become nervous from some gipsy prediction in his childhood, allocating to a particular moon now approaching some unknown danger, and he should inquire earnestly, – 'Whither can I go for shelter? Is a prison the safest retreat? Or a lunatic hospital? Or the British Museum?' I should have replied – 'Oh, no; I'll tell you what to do. Take lodgings for the next forty days on the box of his majesty's mail. Nobody can touch you there. If it is by bills at ninety days after date that you are made unhappy – if noters and protesters[37] are the sort of wretches whose astrological shadows darken the house of life – then note you what I vehemently protest, viz., that no matter though the sheriff in every county should be running after you with his *posse*,[38] touch a hair of your head he cannot whilst you keep house, and have your legal domicile, on the box of the mail. It's felony to stop the mail; even the sheriff cannot do that. And an *extra* (no great matter if it grazes the sheriff) touch of the whip to the leaders at any time guarantees your safety.' In fact, a bed-room in a quiet house seems a safe enough retreat; yet it is liable to its own notorious nuisances, to robbers by night, to rats, to fire. But the mail laughs at these terrors. To robbers, the answer is packed up and ready for delivery in the barrel of the guard's blunderbuss.[39] Rats again! there *are* none about mail-coaches, any more than snakes in Von Troil's Iceland;[40] except, indeed, now and then a parliamentary rat,[41] who always hides his shame in the 'coal-cellar.' And, as to fire, I never knew but one in a mail-coach, which was in the Exeter mail, and caused by an obstinate sailor bound to Devonport. Jack, making light of the law and the lawgiver that had set their faces against his offence, insisted on taking up a forbidden seat[42] in the rear of the roof, from which he could exchange his own yarns with those of the guard. No greater offence was then known to mail-coaches; it was treason, it was *laesa majestas*,[43] it was by tendency arson; and the ashes of Jack's pipe, falling amongst the straw of the hinder boot, containing the mail-bags, raised a flame which (aided by the wind of our motion) threatened a revolution in the republic of letters. But even this left the sanctity of the box unviolated. In dignified repose, the coachman and myself sat on, resting with benign composure upon our knowledge – that the fire would have to burn its way through four inside passengers before it could reach ourselves. With a quotation rather too trite, I remarked to the coachman, –

——'Jam proximus ardet
Ucalegon.'[44]

But, recollecting that the Virgilian part of his education might have been neglected, I interpreted so far as to say, that perhaps at that moment the flames were catching hold of our worthy brother and next-door neighbour Ucalegon. The coachman said nothing, but by his faint sceptical smile he seemed to be thinking that he knew better; for that in fact, Ucalegon, as it happened, was not in the way-bill.[45]

No dignity is perfect which does not at some point ally itself with the indeterminate and mysterious. The connexion of the mail with the state and the executive government – a connexion obvious, but yet not strictly defined – gave to the whole mail establishment a grandeur and an official authority which did us service on the roads, and invested us with seasonable terrors. But perhaps these terrors were not the less impressive, because their exact legal limits were imperfectly ascertained. Look at those turnpike gates; with what deferential hurry, with what an obedient start, they fly open at our approach! Look at that long line of carts and carters ahead, audaciously usurping the very crest of the road: ah! traitors, they do not hear us as yet, but as soon as the dreadful blast of our horn[46] reaches them with the proclamation of our approach, see with what frenzy of trepidation they fly to their horses' heads, and deprecate our wrath by the precipitation of their crane-neck quarterings.[47] Treason they feel to be their crime; each individual carter feels himself under the ban of confiscation and attainder: his blood is attainted through six generations,[48] and nothing is wanting but the headsman and his axe, the block and the sawdust to close up the vista of his horrors. What! shall it be within benefit of clergy,[49] to delay the king's message on the highroad? – to interrupt the great respirations, ebb or flood, of the national intercourse – to endanger the safety of tidings running day and night between all nations and languages? Or can it be fancied, amongst the weakest of men, that the bodies of the criminals will be given up to their widows for Christian burial? Now, the doubts which were raised as to our powers did more to wrap them in terror, by wrapping them in uncertainty, than could have been effected by the sharpest definitions of the law from the Quarter Sessions.[50] We, on our parts, (we, the collective mail, I mean,) did our utmost to exalt the idea of our privileges by the insolence with which we wielded them. Whether this insolence rested upon law that gave it a sanction, or upon conscious power, haughtily dispensing with that sanction, equally it spoke from a potential station; and the agent in each particular insolence of the moment, was viewed reverentially, as one having authority.[51]

Sometimes after breakfast his majesty's mail would become frisky; and in its difficult wheelings amongst the intricacies of early markets, it would upset an apple-cart, a cart loaded with eggs, &c. Huge was the affliction and dismay, awful was the smash, though, after all, I believe the damage might be levied upon the hundred.[52] I, as far as was possible, endeavoured in such a case to represent the conscience and moral sensibilities of the mail; and, when wildernesses of eggs were lying poached[53] under our horses' hoofs, then would I stretch forth my hands in sorrow, saying (in words too celebrated in those days from the false* echoes of Marengo) – 'Ah! wherefore have we not time to weep over you?' which was quite impossible, for in fact we had not even time to laugh over them. Tied to post-office time, with an allowance in some cases of fifty minutes for eleven miles, could the royal mail pretend to undertake the offices of sympathy and condolence? Could it be expected to provide tears for the accidents of the road? If even it seemed to trample on humanity, it did so, I contended, in discharge of its own more peremptory duties.

Upholding the morality of the mail, *à fortiori*[56] I upheld its rights, I stretched to the uttermost its privilege of imperial precedency, and astonished weak minds by the feudal powers which I hinted to be lurking constructively in the charters of this proud establishment. Once I remember being on the box of the Holyhead mail, between Shrewsbury and Oswestry,[57] when a tawdry thing from Birmingham, some *Tallyho* or *Highflier*,[58] all flaunting with green and gold, came up alongside of us. What a contrast to our royal simplicity of form and colour is this plebeian wretch! The single ornament on our dark ground of chocolate colour was the mighty shield of the imperial arms, but emblazoned in proportions as modest as a signet-ring bears to a seal of office. Even this was displayed only on a single panel, whispering, rather than proclaiming, our relations to the state; whilst the beast from Birmingham had as much writing and painting on its sprawling flanks as would have puzzled a decipherer from the tombs of Luxor.[59] For some time this Birmingham machine ran along by our side, – a piece of familiarity that seemed to us sufficiently jacobinical. But all at once a movement of the horses announced a desperate intention of leaving us behind. 'Do you see *that?*' I said to the coachman. 'I see,' was his short answer. He was awake, yet he waited longer than seemed prudent; for the horses of our audacious opponent had a disagreeable air of freshness and power. But his motive was loyal; his wish was that the Birmingham conceit should be full-blown before he froze it. When *that* seemed ripe, he unloosed, or, to speak by a stronger image, he sprang his known resources, he slipped our royal horses like cheetas, or hunting leopards after the affrighted game. How they could retain such a reserve of fiery power after the work they had accomplished, seemed hard to explain. But on our side, besides the physical superiority, was a tower of strength, namely, the king's name, 'which they upon the adverse faction wanted.'[60] Passing them

* 'False echoes' – yes, false! for the words ascribed to Napoleon, as breathed to the memory of Desaix, never were uttered at all.[54] They stand in the same category of theatrical inventions as the cry of the foundering *Vengeur*, as the vaunt of General Cambronne at Waterloo, '*La Garde meurt, mais ne se rend pas*,' as the repartees of Talleyrand.[55]

without an effort, as it seemed, we threw them into the rear with so lengthening an interval between us, as proved in itself the bitterest mockery of their presumption; whilst our guard blew back a shattering blast of triumph, that was really too painfully full of derision.

I mention this little incident for its connexion with what followed. A Welshman, sitting behind me, asked if I had not felt my heart burn within me[61] during the continuance of the race? I said – No; because we were not racing with a mail, so that no glory could be gained. In fact, it was sufficiently mortifying that such a Birmingham thing should dare to challenge us. The Welshman replied, that he didn't see *that;* for that a cat might look at a king,[62] and a Brummagem[63] coach might lawfully race the Holyhead mail. '*Race* us perhaps,' I replied, 'though even *that* has an air of sedition, but not *beat* us. This would have been treason; and for its own sake I am glad that the Tallyho was disappointed.' So dissatisfied did the Welshman seem with this opinion, that at last I was obliged to tell him a very fine story from one of our elder dramatists,[64] viz. – that once, in some Oriental region, when the prince of all the land, with his splendid court, were flying their falcons, a hawk suddenly flew at a majestic eagle; and in defiance of the eagle's prodigious advantages, in sight also of all the astonished field sportsmen, spectators, and followers, killed him on the spot. The prince was struck with amazement at the unequal contest, and with burning admiration for its unparalleled result. He commanded that the hawk should be brought before him; caressed the bird with enthusiasm, and ordered that, for the commemoration of his matchless courage, a crown of gold should be solemnly placed on the hawk's head; but then that, immediately after this coronation, the bird should be led off to execution, as the most valiant indeed of traitors, but not the less a traitor that had dared to rise in rebellion against his liege lord the eagle. 'Now,' said I to the Welshman, 'how painful it would have been to you and me as men of refined feelings, that this poor brute, the Tallyho, in the impossible case of a victory over us, should have been crowned with jewellery, gold, with Birmingham ware, or paste diamonds, and then led off to instant execution.' The Welshman doubted if that could be warranted by law. And when I hinted at the 10th of Edward III. chap. 15,[65] for regulating the precedency of coaches, as being probably the statute relied on for the capital punishment of such offences, he replied drily – That if the attempt to pass a mail was really treasonable, it was a pity that the Tallyho appeared to have so imperfect an acquaintance with law.

These were among the gaieties of my earliest and boyish acquaintance with mails. But alike the gayest and the most terrific of my experiences rose again after years of slumber, armed with preternatural power to shake my dreaming sensibilities; sometimes, as in the slight case of Miss Fanny on the Bath road, (which I will immediately mention,) through some casual or capricious association with images originally gay, yet opening at some stage of evolution into sudden capacities of horror; sometimes through the more natural and fixed alliances with the sense of power so various lodged in the mail system.

The modern modes of travelling cannot compare with the mail-coach system in grandeur and power. They boast of more velocity, but not however as a consciousness, but as a fact of our lifeless knowledge, resting upon *alien* evidence; as, for instance, because somebody *says* that we have gone fifty miles in the hour, or upon the evidence of a result, as that actually we find ourselves in York four hours after leaving London.[66] Apart from such an assertion, or such a result, I am little aware of the pace. But, seated on the old mail-coach, we needed no evidence out of ourselves to indicate the velocity. On this system the word was – *Non magna loquimur*, as upon railways, but *magna vivimus*.[67] The vital experience of the glad animal sensibilities made doubts impossible on the question of our speed; we heard our speed, we saw it, we felt it as a thrilling; and this speed was not the product of blind insensate agencies, that had no sympathy to give, but was incarnated in the fiery eyeballs of an animal, in his dilated nostril, spasmodic muscles, and echoing hoofs. This speed was incarnated in the *visible* contagion amongst brutes of some impulse, that, radiating into their natures, had yet its centre and beginning in man. The sensibility of the horse uttering itself in the maniac light of his eye, might be the last vibration of such a movement; the glory of Salamanca might be the first – but the intervening link that connected them, that spread the earthquake of the battle into the eyeball of the horse, was the heart of man – kindling in the rapture of the fiery strife, and then propagating its own tumults by motions and gestures to the sympathies, more or less dim, in his servant the horse.

But now, on the new system of travelling, iron tubes and boilers have disconnected man's heart from the ministers of his locomotion. Nile nor Trafalgar[68] has power any more to raise an extra bubble in a steam-kettle. The galvanic cycle is broken up for ever; man's imperial nature no longer sends itself forward through the electric sensibility of the horse; the inter-agencies are gone in the mode of communication between the horse and his master, out of which grew so many aspects of sublimity under accidents of mists that hid, or sudden blazes that revealed, of mobs that agitated, or midnight solitudes that awed. Tidings, fitted to convulse all nations,[69] must henceforwards travel by culinary process; and the trumpet that once announced from afar the laurelled mail, heart-shaking, when heard screaming on the wind, and advancing through the darkness to every village or solitary house on its route, has now given way for ever to the pot-wallopings of the boiler.

Thus have perished multiform openings for sublime effects, for interesting personal communications, for revelations of impressive faces that could not have offered themselves amongst the hurried and fluctuating groups of a railway station. The gatherings of gazers about a mail-coach had one centre, and acknowledged only one interest. But the crowds attending at a railway station have as little unity as running water, and own as many centres as there are separate carriages in the train.

How else, for example, than as a constant watcher for the dawn, and for the London mail that in summer months entered about dawn into the lawny thickets of Marlborough Forest,[70] couldst thou, sweet Fanny of the Bath road, have become known to myself? Yet Fanny, as the loveliest young woman for face and person that perhaps in my whole life I have beheld, merited the station which even *her* I could not willingly have spared; yet (thirty-five years later) she holds in my dreams; and though, by an accident of fanciful caprice, she brought along with her into those dreams a troop of dreadful creatures, fabulous and not fabulous, that were more abominable to a human heart than Fanny and the dawn were delightful.

Miss Fanny of the Bath road, strictly speaking, lived at a mile's distance from that road, but came so continually to meet the mail, that I on my frequent transits rarely missed her, and naturally connected her name with the great thoroughfare where I saw her; I do not exactly know, but I believe with some burthen of commissions to be executed in Bath, her own residence being probably the centre to which these commissions gathered. The mail coachman, who wore the royal livery, being one amongst the privileged few,* happened to be Fanny's grandfather. A good man he was, that loved his beautiful granddaughter; and, loving her wisely, was vigilant over her deportment in any case where young Oxford might happen to be concerned. Was I then vain enough to imagine that I myself individually could fall within the line of his terrors? Certainly not, as regarded any physical pretensions that I could plead; for Fanny (as a chance passenger from her own neighbourhood once told me) counted in her train a hundred and ninety-nine professed admirers, if not open aspirants to her favour; and probably not one of the whole brigade but excelled myself in personal advantages. Ulysses even, with the unfair advantage of his accursed bow, could hardly have undertaken that amount of suitors.[72] So the danger might have seemed slight – only that woman is universally aristocratic: it is amongst her nobilities of heart that she *is* so. Now, the aristocratic distinctions in my favour might easily with Miss Fanny have compensated my physical deficiencies. Did I then make love to Fanny? Why, yes; *mais oui donc;*[73] as much love as one *can* make whilst the mail is changing horses, a process which ten years later did not occupy above eighty seconds; but *then,* viz. about Waterloo, it occupied five times eighty. Now, four hundred seconds offer a field quite ample enough for whispering into a young woman's ear a great deal of truth; and (by way of parenthesis) some trifle of falsehood. Grandpapa did right, therefore, to watch me. And yet, as happens

* 'Privileged few.' The general impression was that this splendid costume belonged of right to the mail coachmen as their professional dress. But that was an error. To the guard it *did* belong as a matter of course, and was essential as an official warrant, and a means of instant identification for his person, in the discharge of his important public duties. But the coachman, and especially if his place in the series did not connect him immediately with London and the General Post Office, obtained the scarlet coat only as an honorary distinction after long or special service.[71]

too often to the grandpapas of earth, in a contest with the admirers of granddaughters, how vainly would he have watched me had I meditated any evil whispers to Fanny! She, it is my belief, would have protected herself against any man's evil suggestions. But he, as the result showed, could not have intercepted the opportunities for such suggestions. Yet he was still active; he was still blooming. Blooming he was as Fanny herself.

> 'Say, all our praises why should lords — '[74]

No, that's not the line:

> 'Say, all our roses why should girls engross?'

The coachman showed rosy blossoms on his face deeper even than his granddaughter's, – *his* being drawn from the ale-cask, Fanny's from youth and innocence, and from the fountains of the dawn. But, in spite of his blooming face, some infirmities he had; and one particularly (I am very sure, no *more* than one,) in which he too much resembled a crocodile. This lay in a monstrous inaptitude for turning round. The crocodile, I presume, owes that inaptitude to the absurd *length* of his back; but in our grandpapa it arose rather from the absurd *breadth* of his back, combined, probably, with some growing stiffness in his legs. Now upon this crocodile infirmity of his I planted an easy opportunity for tendering my homage to Miss Fanny. In defiance of all his honourable vigilance, no sooner had he presented to us his mighty Jovian back (what a field for displaying to mankind his royal scarlet!) whilst inspecting professionally the buckles, the straps, and the silver turrets[75] of his harness, than I raised Miss Fanny's hand to my lips, and, by the mixed tenderness and respectfulness of my manner, caused her easily to understand how happy it would have made me to rank upon her list as No. 10 or 12, in which case a few casualties amongst her lovers (and observe – they *hanged* liberally in those days) might have promoted me speedily to the top of the tree; as, on the other hand, with how much loyalty of submission I acquiesced in her allotment, supposing that she had seen reason to plant me in the very rearward of her favour, as No. 199+1. It must not be supposed that I allowed any trace of jest, or even of playfulness, to mingle with these expressions of my admiration; that would have been insulting to her, and would have been false as regarded my own feelings. In fact, the utter shadowyness of our relations to each other, even after our meetings through seven or eight years had been very numerous, but of necessity had been very brief, being entirely on mail-coach allowance – timed, in reality, by the General Post-Office – and watched by a crocodile belonging to the antepenultimate generation, left it easy for me to do a thing which few people ever *can* have done – viz., to make love for seven years, at the same time to be as sincere as ever creature was, and yet never to compromise myself by overtures that might have been foolish as regarded my own interests, or misleading as regarded hers. Most truly I loved this beautiful and ingenuous girl; and had it not been for the Bath and Bristol mail, heaven only knows what might have come of it. People talk of being over head and ears in love – now, the mail was the cause that I sank only over ears in love, which, you know, still left a trifle of brain to overlook the whole conduct of the affair.[76] I have mentioned the case at all for the sake of a dreadful result from it in after years of dreaming. But it seems, *ex abundanti*,[77] to yield this moral – viz. that as, in England, the idiot and the half-wit are held to be under the guardianship of Chancery,[78] so the man making love, who is often but a variety of the same imbecile class, ought to be made a ward of the General Post-Office, whose severe course of *timing* and periodical interruption might intercept many a foolish declaration, such as lays a solid foundation for fifty years' repentance.

Ah, reader! when I look back upon those days, it seems to me that all things change or perish. Even thunder and lightning, it pains me to say, are not the thunder and lightning which I seem to remember about the time of Waterloo. Roses, I fear, are degenerating, and, without a Red revolution, must come to the dust.[79] The Fannies of our island – though this I say with reluctance – are not improving; and the Bath road is notoriously superannuated. Mr Waterton[80] tells me that the crocodile does *not* change – that a cayman, in fact, or an alligator, is just as good for riding upon as he was in the time of the Pharaohs. *That* may be; but the reason is, that the crocodile does not live fast – he is a slow coach. I believe it is generally understood amongst naturalists, that the crocodile is a blockhead. It is my own impression that the Pharaohs were also blockheads. Now, as the Pharaohs and the crocodile domineered over Egyptian society, this accounts for a singular mistake that prevailed on the Nile. The crocodile made the ridiculous blunder of supposing man to be meant chiefly for his own eating. Man, taking a different view of the subject, naturally met that mistake by another; he viewed the crocodile as a thing sometimes to worship, but always to run away from.[81] And this continued until Mr Waterton[82] changed the relations between the animals. The mode of escaping from the reptile he showed to be, not by running away, but by leaping on its back, booted and spurred. The two animals had misunderstood each other. The use of the crocodile has now been cleared up – it is to be ridden; and the use of man is, that he may improve the health of the crocodile by riding him a fox-hunting before breakfast.[83] And it is pretty certain that any crocodile, who has been regularly hunted through the season, and is master of the weight he carries, will take a six-barred gate now as well as ever he would have done in the infancy of the Pyramids.

Perhaps, therefore, the crocodile does *not* change, but all things else *do:* even the shadow of the Pyramids grows less. And often the restoration in vision of Fanny and the Bath road, makes me too pathetically sensible of that truth. Out of the darkness, if I happen to call up the image of Fanny from thirty-five years back, arises suddenly a rose in June;[84] or, if I think for an instant of the rose in June, up rises the heavenly face of Fanny. One after the other, like the antiphonies in a choral service, rises Fanny and the rose in June, then back again the rose in June and Fanny. Then come both together, as in a chorus; roses and Fannies, Fannies and roses, without end – thick as blossoms in paradise.[85] Then comes a venerable crocodile, in a royal livery of scarlet and gold, or in a coat with sixteen capes; and the crocodile is driving four-in-hand from the box of the Bath mail. And suddenly we upon the mail are pulled up by a mighty dial, sculptured with the hours, and with the dreadful legend of TOO LATE. Then all at once we are arrived in Marlborough forest, amongst the lovely households* of the roe-deer: these retire into the dewy thickets; the thickets are rich with roses; the roses call up (as ever) the sweet countenance of Fanny, who, being the granddaughter of a crocodile, awakens a dreadful host of wild semi-legendary animals – griffins, dragons, basilisks, sphinxes – till at length the whole vision of fighting images crowds into one towering armorial shield, a vast emblazonry of human charities and human loveliness that have perished, but quartered heraldically with unutterable horrors of monstrous and demoniac natures; whilst over all rises, as a surmounting crest, one fair female hand, with the fore-finger pointing, in sweet, sorrowful admonition, upwards to heaven, and having power (which, without experience, I never could have believed) to awaken the pathos that kills in the very bosom of the horrors that madden the grief that gnaws at the heart, together with the monstrous creations of darkness that shock the belief, and make dizzy the reason of man.[87] This is the peculiarity that I wish the reader to notice, as having first been made known to me for a possibility by this early vision of Fanny on the Bath road. The peculiarity consisted in the confluence of two different keys, though apparently repelling each other, into the music and governing principles of the same dream; horror, such as possesses the maniac, and yet, by momentary transitions, grief, such as may be supposed to possess the dying mother when leaving her infant children to the mercies of the cruel. Usually, and perhaps always, in an unshaken nervous system, these two modes of misery exclude each other – here first they met in horrid reconciliation. There was also a separate peculiarity in the quality of the horror. This was afterwards developed into far more revolting complexities of misery and incomprehensible darkness; and perhaps I am wrong in ascribing any value as a *causative* agency to this particular case on the Bath road – possibly it furnished merely an *occasion* that accidentally introduced a mode of horrors certain, at any rate, to have grown up, with or without the Bath road, from more advanced stages of the nervous derangement. Yet, as the cubs of tigers or leopards, when domesticated, have been observed to suffer a sudden development of their latent ferocity under too eager an appeal to their playfulness – the gaieties of sport in *them* being too closely connected with the fiery brightness of their

* '*Households*.' – Roe-deer do not congregate in herds like the fallow or the red deer, but by separate families, parents, and children; which feature of approximation to the sanctity of human hearths, added to their comparatively miniature and graceful proportions, conciliate to them an interest of a peculiarly tender character, if less dignified by the grandeurs of savage and forest life.[86]

murderous instincts – so I have remarked that the caprices, the gay arabesques, and the lovely floral luxuriations of dreams, betray a shocking tendency to pass into finer maniacal splendours. That gaiety, for instance, (for such at first it was,) in the dreaming faculty, by which one principal point of resemblance to a crocodile in the mail-coachman was soon made to clothe him with the form of a crocodile, and yet was blended with accessory circumstances derived from his *human* functions, passed rapidly into a further development, no longer gay or playful, but terrific, the most terrific that besieges dreams, viz. – the horrid inoculation upon each other of incompatible natures. This horror has always been secretly felt by man; it was felt even under pagan forms of religion, which offered a very feeble, and also a very limited gamut for giving expression to the human capacities of sublimity or of horror. We read it in the fearful composition of the sphinx. The dragon, again, is the snake inoculated upon the scorpion. The basilisk unites the mysterious malice of the evil eye, unintentional on the part of the unhappy agent, with the intentional venom of some other malignant natures. But these horrid complexities of evil agency are but *objectively* horrid; they inflict the horror suitable to their compound nature; but there is no insinuation that they *feel* that horror. Heraldry is so full of these fantastic creatures, that, in some zoologies, we find a separate chapter or a supplement dedicated to what is denominated heraldic zoology. And why not? For these hideous creatures, however visionary,* have a real traditionary ground in medieval belief – sincere and partly reasonable, though adulterating with mendacity, blundering, credulity, and intense superstition. But the dream-horror which I speak of is far more frightful. The dreamer finds housed within himself – occupying, as it were, some separate chamber in his brain – holding, perhaps, from that station a secret and detestable commerce with his own heart – some horrid alien nature. What if it were his own nature repeated, – still, if the duality were

* *However visionary.*' – But *are* they always visionary? The unicorn, the kraken,[88] the sea-serpent, are all, perhaps, zoological facts. The unicorn, for instance, so far from being a lie, is rather *too* true; for, simply as a *monokeras*,[89] he is found in the Himalaya, in Africa, and elsewhere, rather too often for the peace of what in Scotland would be called the *intending* traveller. That which really *is* a lie in the account of the unicorn – viz., his legendary rivalship with the lion – which lie may God preserve, in preserving the mighty imperial shield that embalms it[90] – cannot be more destructive to the zoological pretensions of the unicorn, than are to the same pretensions in the lion our many popular crazes about his goodness and magnanimity, or the old fancy (adopted by Spenser, and noticed by so many among our elder poets)[91] of his graciousness to maiden innocence. The wretch is the basest and most cowardly among the forest tribes; nor has the sublime courage of the English bull-dog ever been so memorably exhibited as in his hopeless fight at Warwick with the cowardly and cruel lion called Wallace.[92] Another of the traditional creatures, still doubtful, is the mermaid, upon which Southey[93] once remarked to me, that, if it had been differently named (as, suppose, a mer-ape,) nobody would have questioned its existence any more than that of sea-cows, sea-lions, &c. The mermaid has been discredited by her human name and her legendary human habits. If she would not coquette so much with melancholy sailors, and brush her hair so assiduously upon solitary rocks, she would be carried on our books for as honest a reality, as decent a female, as many that are assessed to the poor-rates.[94]

distinctly perceptible, even *that* – even this mere numerical double[95] of his own consciousness – might be a curse too mighty to be sustained. But how, if the alien nature contradicts his own, fights with it, perplexes, and confounds it? How, again, if not one alien nature, but two, but three, but four, but five, are introduced within what once he thought the inviolable sanctuary of himself? These, however, are horrors from the kingdoms of anarchy and darkness, which, by their very intensity, challenge the sanctity of concealment, and gloomily retire from exposition. Yet it was necessary to mention them, because the first introduction to such appearances (whether causal, or merely casual) lay in the heraldic monsters, which monsters were themselves introduced (though playfully) by the transfigured coachman of the Bath mail.

GOING DOWN WITH VICTORY.

But the grandest chapter of our experience, within the whole mail-coach service, was on those occasions when we went down from London with the news of victory. A period of about ten years stretched from Trafalgar to Waterloo: the second and third years of which period (1806 and 1807) were comparatively sterile; but the rest, from 1805 to 1815 inclusively, furnished a long succession of victories; the least of which, in a contest of that portentous nature, had an inappreciable value of position – partly for its absolute interference with the plans of our enemy, but still more from its keeping alive in central Europe the sense of a deep-seated vulnerability in France. Even to tease the coasts of our enemy, to mortify them by continual blockades, to insult them by capturing if it were but a baubling schooner[96] under the eyes of their arrogant armies, repeated from time to time a sullen proclamation of power lodged in a quarter to which the hopes of Christendom turned in secret. How much more loudly must this proclamation have spoken in the audacity* of having bearded the *élite* of their troops, and having beaten them in pitched battles! Five years of life it was worth paying down for the privilege of an outside place on a mail-coach, when carrying down the first tidings of any such event. And it is to be noted that, from our insular situation, and the multitude of our frigates disposable for the rapid transmission of intelligence, rarely did any unauthorised rumour steal away a prelibation from the aroma

* *'Audacity!'* Such the French accounted it; and it has struck me that Soult would not have been so popular in London, at the period of her present Majesty's coronation,[97] or in Manchester, on occasion of his visit to that town, if they had been aware of the insolence with which he spoke of us in notes written at intervals from the field of Waterloo. As though it had been mere felony in our army to look a French one in the face, he said more than once – 'Here are the English – we have them: they are caught *en flagrant delit*.'[98] Yet no man should have known us better; no man had drunk deeper from the cup of humiliation than Soult had in the north of Portugal, during his flight from an English army, and subsequently at Albuera, in the bloodiest of recorded battles.[99]

of the regular despatches. The government official news was generally the first news.

From eight P.M. to fifteen or twenty minutes later, imagine the mails assembled on parade in Lombard Street, where, at that time, was seated the General Post-Office.[100] In what exact strength we mustered I do not remember; but, from the length of each separate *attelage*,[101] we filled the street, though a long one, and though we were drawn up in double file. On *any* night the spectacle was beautiful. The absolute perfection of all the appointments about the carriages and the harness, and the magnificence of the horses, were what might first have fixed the attention. Every carriage, on every morning in the year, was taken down to an inspector for examination – wheels, axles, linchpins, pole, glasses, &c., were all critically probed and tested. Every part of every carriage had been cleaned, every horse had been groomed, with as much rigour as if they belonged to a private gentleman; and that part of the spectacle offered itself always. But the night before us is a night of victory; and behold! to the ordinary display, what a heart-shaking addition! – horses, men, carriages – all are dressed in laurels and flowers, oak leaves and ribbons. The guards, who are his Majesty's servants, and the coachmen, who are within the privilege of the Post-Office, wear the royal liveries of course; and as it is summer (for all the *land* victories were won in summer,) they wear, on this fine evening, these liveries exposed to view, without any covering of upper coats. Such a costume, and the elaborate arrangement of the laurels in their hats, dilated their hearts, by giving to them openly an *official* connection with the great news, in which already they have the general interest of patriotism. That great national sentiment surmounts and quells all sense of ordinary distinctions. Those passengers who happen to be gentlemen are now hardly to be distinguished as such except by dress. The usual reserve of their manner in speaking to the attendants has on this night melted away. One heart, one pride, one glory, connects every man by the transcendant bond of his English blood.[102] The spectators, who are numerous beyond precedent, express their sympathy with these fervent feelings by continual hurrahs. Every moment are shouted aloud by the Post-Office servants the great ancestral names of cities known to history through a thousand years, – Lincoln, Winchester, Portsmouth, Gloucester, Oxford, Bristol, Manchester, York, Newcastle, Edinburgh, Perth, Glasgow – expressing the grandeur of the empire by the antiquity of its towns, and the grandeur of the mail establishment by the diffusive radiation of its separate missions. Every moment you hear the thunder of lids locked down upon the mail-bags. That sound to each individual mail is the signal for drawing off, which process is the finest part of the entire spectacle. Then come the horses into play; – horses! can these be horses that (unless powerfully reined in) would bound off with the action and gestures of leopards? What stir! – what sea-like ferment! – what a thundering of wheels, what a trampling of horses! – what farewell cheers – what redoubling peals of brotherly congratulation, connecting the name of the particular mail – 'Liverpool for ever!' – with the name of the particular victory – 'Badajoz for ever!' or 'Salamanca[103] for ever!' The half-slumbering consciousness that, all night long and all the next day – perhaps for even a longer period – many of these mails, like fire racing along a train of gunpowder, will be kindling at every instant new successions of burning joy, has an obscure effect of multiplying the victory itself, by multiplying to the imagination into infinity the stages of its progressive diffusion. A fiery arrow seems to be let loose, which from that moment is destined to travel, almost without intermission, westwards for three hundred* miles – northwards for six hundred; and the sympathy of our Lombard Street friends at parting is exalted a hundredfold by a sort of visionary sympathy with the approaching sympathies, yet unborn, which we were going to evoke.

Liberated from the embarrassments of the city, and issuing into the broad uncrowded avenues of the northern suburbs, we begin to enter upon our natural pace of ten miles an hour. In the broad light of the summer evening, the sun perhaps only just at the point of setting, we are seen from every storey of every house. Heads of every age crowd to the windows – young and old understand the language of our victorious symbols – and rolling volleys of sympathising cheers run along behind and before our course. The beggar, rearing himself against the wall, forgets his lameness – real or assumed – thinks not of his whining trade, but stands erect, with bold exulting smiles, as we pass him. The victory has healed him, and says – Be thou whole![105] Women and children, from garrets alike and cellars, look down or look up with loving eyes upon our gay ribbons and our martial laurels – sometimes kiss their

* *'Three hundred.'* Of necessity this scale of measurement, to an American, if he happens to be a thoughtless man, must sound ludicrous. Accordingly, I remember a case in which an American writer[104] indulges himself in the luxury of a little lying, by ascribing to an Englishman a pompous account of the Thames, constructed entirely upon American ideas of grandeur, and concluding in something like these terms: – 'And, sir, arriving at London, this mighty father of rivers attains a breadth of at least two furlongs, having, in its winding course, traversed the astonishing distance of 170 miles.' And this the candid American thinks it fair to contrast with the scale of the Mississippi. Now, it is hardly worth while to answer a pure falsehood gravely, else one might say that no Englishman out of Bedlam ever thought of looking in an island for the rivers of a continent; nor, consequently, could have thought of looking for the peculiar grandeur of the Thames in the length of its course, or in the extent of soil which it drains: yet, if he *had* been so absurd, the American might have recollected that a river, not to be compared with the Thames even as to volume of water – viz. the Tiber – has contrived to make itself heard of in this world for twenty-five centuries to an extent not reached, nor likely to be reached very soon, by any river, however corpulent, of his own land. The glory of the Thames is measured by the density of the population to which it ministers, by the commerce which it supports, by the grandeur of the empire in which, though far from the largest, it is the most influential stream. Upon some such scale, and not by a transfer of Columbian standards, is the course of our English mails to be valued. The American may fancy the effect of his own valuations to our English ears, by supposing the case of a Siberian glorifying his country in these terms: – 'Those rascals, sir, in France and England, cannot march half a mile in any direction without finding a house where food can be had and lodging: whereas, such is the noble desolation of our magnificent country, that in many a direction for a thousand miles, I will engage a dog shall not find shelter from a snow-storm, nor a wren find an apology for breakfast.'

hands, sometimes hang out, as signals of affection, pocket handkerchiefs, aprons, dusters, anything that lies ready to their hands. On the London side of Barnet,[106] to which we draw near within a few minutes after nine, observe that private carriage which is approaching us. The weather being so warm, the glasses are all down; and one may read, as on the stage of a theatre, everything that goes on within the carriage. It contains three ladies, one likely to be 'mama,' and two of seventeen or eighteen, who are probably her daughters. What lovely animation, what beautiful unpremeditated pantomime, explaining to us every syllable that passes, in these ingenuous girls! By the sudden start and raising of the hands, on first discovering our laurelled equipage – by the sudden movement and appeal to the elder lady from both of them – and by the heightened colour on their animated countenances, we can almost hear them saying – 'See, see! Look at their laurels. Oh, mama! there has been a great battle in Spain; and it has been a great victory.' In a moment we are on the point of passing them. We passengers – I on the box, and the two on the roof behind me – raise our hats, the coachman makes his professional salute with the whip; the guard even, though punctilious on the matter of his dignity as an officer under the crown, touches his hat. The ladies move to us, in return, with a winning graciousness of gesture: all smile on each side in a way that nobody could misunderstand, and that nothing short of a grand national sympathy could so instantaneously prompt. Will these ladies say that we are nothing to *them?* Oh, no; they will not say *that*. They cannot deny – they do not deny – that for this night they are our sisters: gentle or simple, scholar or illiterate servant, for twelve hours to come – we on the outside have the honour to be their brothers. Those poor women again, who stop to gaze upon us with delight at the entrance of Barnet, and seem by their air of weariness to be returning from labour – do you mean to say that they are washerwomen and charwomen? Oh, my poor friend, you are quite mistaken; they are nothing of the kind. I assure you, they stand in a higher rank: for this one night they feel themselves by birthright to be daughters of England, and answer to no humbler title.

Every joy, however, even rapturous joy – such is the sad law of earth – may carry with it grief, or fear of grief, to some.[107] Three miles beyond Barnet, we see approaching us another private carriage, nearly repeating the circumstances of the former case. Here also the glasses are all down – here also is an elderly lady seated; but the two amiable daughters are missing; for the single young person, sitting by the lady's side, seems to be an attendant – so I judge from her dress, and her air of respectful reserve. The lady is in mourning; and her countenance expresses sorrow. At first she does not look up; so that I believe she is not aware of our approach, until she hears the measured beating of our horses' hoofs. Then she raises her eyes to settle them painfully on our triumphal equipage. Our decorations explain the case to her at once; but she beholds them with apparent anxiety, or even with terror. Some time before this, I, finding it difficult to hit a flying mark, when embarrassed by the coachman's person and reins intervening, had given to the guard a *Courier* evening paper, containing the gazette,[108] for the next carriage that might pass. Accordingly he tossed it in so folded that the huge capitals expressing some such legend as – GLORIOUS VICTORY, might catch the eye at once. To see the paper, however, at all, interpreted as it was by our ensigns of triumph, explained everything; and, if the guard were right in thinking the lady to have received it with a gesture of horror, it could not be doubtful that she had suffered some deep personal affliction in connexion with this Spanish war.

Here now was the case of one who, having formerly suffered, might, erroneously perhaps, be distressing herself with anticipations of another similar suffering. That same night, and hardly three hours later, occurred the reverse case. A poor woman, who too probably would find herself, in a day or two, to have suffered the heaviest of afflictions by the battle, blindly allowed herself to express an exultation so unmeasured in the news, and its details, as gave to her the appearance which amongst Celtic Highlanders is called *fey*.[109] This was at some little town, I forget what, where we happened to change horses near midnight. Some fair or wake had kept the people up out of their beds. We saw many lights moving about as we drew near; and perhaps the most impressive scene on our route was our reception at this place. The flashing of torches and the beautiful radiance of blue lights (technically Bengal lights)[110] upon the heads of our horses; the fine effect of such a showery and ghostly illumination falling upon flowers and glittering laurels,[111] whilst all around the massy darkness seemed to invest us with walls of impenetrable blackness, together with the prodigious enthusiasm of the people, composed a picture at once scenical and affecting. As we staid for three or four minutes, I alighted. And immediately from a dismantled stall in the street, where perhaps she had been presiding at some part of the evening, advanced eagerly a middle-aged woman. The sight of my newspaper it was that had drawn her attention upon myself. The victory which we were carrying down to the provinces on *this* occasion was the imperfect one of Talavera.[112] I told her the main outline of the battle. But her agitation, though not the agitation of fear, but of exultation rather, and enthusiasm, had been so conspicuous when listening, and when first applying for information, that I could not but ask her if she had not some relation in the Peninsular army. Oh! yes: her only son was there. In what regiment? He was a trooper in the 23d Dragoons. My heart sank within me as she made that answer. This sublime regiment, which an Englishman should never mention without raising his hat to their memory, had made the most memorable and effective charge recorded in military annals. They leaped their horses – *over* a trench, where they could *into* it, and with the result of death or mutilation when they could *not*. What proportion cleared the trench is nowhere stated. Those who *did*, closed up and went down upon the enemy with such divinity of fervour – (I use the word *divinity* by design: the inspiration of God must have prompted this movement to those whom even then he was calling to his presence) – that two results followed. As regarded the enemy, this 23d Dragoons, not, I believe, originally 350 strong, paralysed a French column, 6000 strong, then ascending the hill, and fixed the gaze of the whole French army. As regarded themselves, the 23d were supposed at first to have been all but annihilated; but eventually, I believe, not so many as one in four survived.[113] And this, then, was the regiment – a regiment already for some hours known to myself and all London as stretched, by a large majority, upon one bloody aceldama[114] – in which the young trooper served whose mother was now talking with myself in a spirit of such hopeful enthusiasm. Did I tell her the truth? Had I the heart to break up her dream? No. I said to myself, To-morrow, or the next day, she will hear the worst. For this night, wherefore should she not sleep in peace? After to-morrow, the chances are too many that peace will forsake her pillow. This brief respite, let her owe this to *my* gift and *my* forbearance. But, if I told her not of the bloody price that had been paid, there was no reason for suppressing the contributions from her son's regiment to the service and glory of the day. For the very few words that I had time for speaking, I governed myself accordingly. I showed her not the funeral banners under which the noble regiment was sleeping. I lifted not the overshadowing laurels from the bloody trench in which horse and rider lay mangled together. But I told her how these dear children of England, privates and officers, had leaped their horses over all obstacles as gaily as hunters to the morning's chase. I told her how they rode their horses into the mists of death, (saying to myself, but not saying to *her*,) and laid down their young lives for thee, O mother England! as willingly – poured out their noble blood as cheerfully – as ever, after a long day's sport, when infants, they had rested their wearied heads upon their mothers' knees, or had sunk to sleep in her arms. It is singular that she seemed to have no fears, even after this knowledge that the 23d Dragoons had been conspicuously engaged, for her son's safety: but so much was she enraptured by the knowledge that *his* regiment, and therefore *he*, had rendered eminent service in the trying conflict – a service which had actually made them the foremost topic of conversation in London – that in the mere simplicity of her fervent nature, she threw her arms round my neck, and, poor woman, kissed me.

THE VISION OF SUDDEN DEATH

First published in *Blackwood's*, LXVI, December 1849, pp. 741–55. The essay was printed anonymously.

Reprinted in *F*, III, *Miscellaneous Essays* (1851), pp. 171–208.

Revised text, carrying many accidentals but only three substantive variants from *F*, in *SGG*, IV, *Miscellanies* (1854), pp. 323–55.

There are six manuscripts, as follows:

MS VSD A: Bodleian MS Eng. Lett. c. 461, f. 103 and f. 116. The manuscript is two fragments of a set of notes apparently relating to 'The English Mail-Coach'. A full transcript is given below, pp. 453–5.

MS VSD B: Dove Cottage MS 1989: 161.44. The manuscript is a short passage that De Quincey apparently discarded from 'The Vision of Sudden Death' or its revisions. The most likely point for inclusion is following the line '...the mail was not even yet ready to start' (below, p. 433). A full transcript is given below, pp. 456–7.

MS VSD C: National Library of Scotland, MS 21239, ff. 62–3. The manuscript contains six short drafts of different sections from 'The Vision of Sudden Death'. A full transcript is given below, pp. 458–9.

MS VSD D: Berg Collection, New York Public Library. The manuscript contains a draft of the fourth section of the 'Dream-Fugue'. A full transcript is given below, pp. 460–2.

MS VSD E: National Library of Scotland, MS 4789, ff.1–32. The manuscript is 'The Vision of Sudden Death' and most of the 'Dream-Fugue'. It served as printer's copy for the essay as it appeared in *Blackwood's*. A full transcript is given below, pp. 463–89.

MS VSD F: University of Chicago Library, MS 611–V. The manuscript is a set of interleaved *SGG* and *F* page proofs of 'The Vision of Sudden Death'. The *SGG* page proofs correspond to the text below running from *Title* 'THE VISION OF SUDDEN DEATH' to p. 438.4 'woods and fields, but with a', with those variants from *SGG* running from p. 738, *Title* 'THE VISION OF SUDDEN DEATH' to p. 746, 438.1–2 'were by this time blending;'. The *SGG* page proofs then break off, but the text recommences at roughly the same point in page proofs from *F*, which correspond to the passage below running from p. 437.3–4 'it must have been thought.,' to p. 440.7 'Strange it is, and to a mere'. The manuscript contains nearly one hundred significant variants, and these are listed in the textual notes.

For the occasion and context of the essay, see headnote, pp. 401–8.

[The reader is to understand this present paper, in its two sections of *The Vision*, &c., and *The Dream-Fugue*, as connected with a previous paper on *The English Mail-Coach*, published in the Magazine for October. The ultimate object was the Dream-Fugue,[1] as an attempt to wrestle with the utmost efforts of music in dealing with a colossal form of impassioned horror. The Vision of Sudden Death contains the mail-coach incident, which did really occur, and did really suggest the variations of the Dream, here taken up by the Fugue, as well as other variations not now recorded. Confluent with these impressions, from the terrific experience on the Manchester and Glasgow mail, were other and more general impressions, derived from long familiarity with the English mail, as developed in the former paper; impressions, for instance, of animal beauty and power, of rapid motion, at that time unprecedented, of connexion with the government and public business of a great nation, but, above all, of connexion with the national victories at an unexampled crisis, – the mail being the privileged organ for publishing and dispersing all news of that kind. From this function of the mail, arises naturally the introduction of Waterloo into the fourth variation of the Fugue; for the mail itself having been carried into the dreams by the incident in the Vision, naturally all the accessory circumstances of pomp and grandeur investing this national carriage followed in the train of the principal image.]

WHAT is to be thought of sudden death? It is remarkable that, in different conditions of society, it has been variously regarded, as the consummation of an earthly career most fervently to be desired,[2] and, on the other hand, as that consummation which is most of all to be deprecated. Caesar the Dictator, at his last dinner party, (*caena*,)[3] and the very evening before his assassination, being questioned as to the mode of death which, in *his* opinion, might seem the most eligible, replied – 'That which should be most sudden.[4] On the other hand, the divine Litany of our English Church, when breathing forth supplications, as if in some representative character for the whole human race prostrate before God, places such a death in the very van of horrors. 'From lightning and tempest; from plague, pestilence, and famine; from battle and murder, and from sudden death, – *Good Lord, deliver us*.'[5] Sudden death is here made to crown the climax in a grand ascent of calamities; it is the last of curses; and yet, by the noblest of Romans, it was treated as the first of blessings. In that difference, most readers will see little more than the difference between Christianity and Paganism. But there I hesitate. The Christian church may be right in its estimate of sudden death; and it is a natural feeling, though after all it may also be an infirm one, to wish for a quiet dismissal from life – as that which *seems* most reconcilable with meditation, with penitential retrospects, and with the humilities of farewell prayer. There does not, however, occur to me any direct scriptural warrant for this earnest petition of the English Litany. It seems rather a petition indulged to human infirmity, than exacted from human piety. And, however *that* may be, two remarks suggest themselves as prudent restraints upon a doctrine, which else *may* wander, and *has* wandered, into an uncharitable superstition. The first is this: that many people are likely to exaggerate the horror of a sudden death, (I mean the *objective* horror to him who contemplates such a death, not the *subjective* horror to him who suffers it) from the false disposition to lay a stress upon words or acts, simply because by an accident they have become words or acts.[6] If a man dies, for instance, by some sudden death when he happens to be intoxicated, such a death is falsely regarded with peculiar horror; as though the intoxication were suddenly exalted into a blasphemy. But *that* is unphilosophic. The man was, or he was not, *habitually* a drunkard. If not, if his intoxication were a solitary accident, there can be no reason at all for allowing special emphasis to this act, simply because through misfortune it became his final act. Nor, on the other hand, if it were no accident, but one of his *habitual* transgressions, will it be the more habitual or the more a transgression, because some sudden calamity, surprising him, has caused this habitual transgression to be also a final one? Could the man have had any reason even dimly to foresee his own sudden death, there would have been a new feature in his act of intemperance – a feature of presumption and irreverence, as in one that by possibility felt himself drawing near to the presence of God. But this is no part of the case supposed. And the only new element in the man's act is not any element of extra immorality, but simply of extra misfortune.[7]

The other remark has reference to the meaning of the word *sudden*. And it is a strong illustration of the duty which for ever calls us to the stern valuation of words – that very possibly Caesar and the Christian church do not differ in the way supposed; that is, do not differ by any difference of doctrine as between Pagan and Christian views of the moral temper appropriate to death, but that they are contemplating different cases. Both contemplate a violent death; a Βιαθανατος – death that is Βιαιος:[8] but the difference is – that the Roman by the word 'sudden' means an *unlingering* death: whereas the Christian litany by 'sudden' means a death *without warning*, consequently without any available summons to religious preparation. The poor mutineer, who kneels down to gather into his heart the bullets from twelve firelocks of his pitying comrades, dies by a most sudden death in Caesar's sense: one shock, one mighty spasm, one (possibly *not* one) groan, and all is over. But, in the sense of the Litany, his death is far from sudden; his offence originally, his imprisonment, his trial, the interval between his sentence and its execution, having all furnished him with separate warnings of his fate – having all summoned him to meet it with solemn preparation.

Meantime, whatever may be thought of a sudden death as a mere[9] variety in the modes of dying, where death in some shape is inevitable – a question which, equally in the Roman and the Christian sense, will be variously answered according to each man's variety of temperament – certainly, upon one aspect of sudden death there can be no opening for doubt, that of all agonies incident to man it is the most frightful, that of all martyrdoms it is the most freezing to human sensibilities – namely, where it surprises a man under circumstances which offer (or which seem to offer) some hurried and inappreciable chance of evading it. Any effort, by which such an evasion can be accomplished, must be as sudden as the danger which it affronts. Even *that*, even the sickening necessity for hurrying in extremity where all hurry seems destined to be vain, self-baffled, and where the dreadful knell of *too* late is already sounding in the ears by anticipation – even that anguish is liable to a hideous exasperation in one particular case, namely, where the agonising appeal is made not exclusively to the instinct of self-preservation, but to the conscience, on behalf of another life besides your own, accidentally cast upon *your* protection. To fail, to collapse in a service merely your own, might seem comparatively venial; though, in fact, it is far from venial. But to fail in a case where Providence has suddenly thrown into your hands the final interests of another – of a fellow-creature shuddering between the gates of life and death; this, to a man of apprehensive conscience, would mingle the misery of an atrocious criminality with the misery of a bloody calamity. The man is called upon, too probably, to die; but to die at the very moment when, by any momentary collapse, he is self-denounced as a murderer. He had but the twinkling of an eye[10] for his effort, and that effort might, at the best, have been unavailing; but from this shadow of a chance, small or great, how if he has recoiled by a treasonable *lâcheté?*[11] The effort *might* have been without hope; but to have risen to the level of that effort – would have rescued him, though not from dying, yet from dying as a traitor to his duties.

The situation here contemplated exposes a dreadful ulcer, lurking far down in the depths of human nature. It is not that men generally are summoned to face such awful trials. But potentially, and in shadowy outline, such a trial is moving subterraneously in perhaps all men's natures – muttering under ground in one world, to be realised perhaps in some other. Upon the secret mirror of our dreams such a trial is darkly projected at intervals, perhaps, to every one of us. That dream, so familiar[12] to childhood, of meeting a lion, and, from languishing prostration in hope and vital energy, that constant sequel of lying down before him, publishes the secret frailty of human nature – reveals its deep-seated Pariah falsehood to itself – records its abysmal treachery. Perhaps not one of us escapes that dream; perhaps, as by some sorrowful doom of man, that dream repeats for every one of us, through every generation, the original temptation in Eden. Every one of us, in this dream, has a bait offered to the infirm places of his own individual will; once again a snare is made ready for leading him into captivity to a luxury of ruin; again, as in aboriginal Paradise, the man falls from innocence; once again, by infinite iteration, the ancient Earth groans to God, through her secret caves, over the weakness of her child; 'Nature from her seat, sighing through all her works,' again 'gives signs of woe that all is lost;'[13] and again the counter sigh is repeated to the sorrowing heavens of the endless rebellion against God. Many people think that one man, the patriarch of our race, could not in his single person execute this rebellion for all his race. Perhaps they are wrong. But, even if not, perhaps in the world of dreams every one of us ratifies for himself the original act. Our English rite of 'Confirmation,' by which, in years of awakened reason, we take upon us the engagements contracted for us in our slumbering infancy, – how sublime a rite is that![14] The little postern gate, through which the baby in its cradle had been silently placed for a time within the glory of God's countenance, suddenly rises to the clouds as a triumphal arch, through which, with banners displayed and martial pomps, we make our second entry as crusading soldiers militant for God, by personal choice and by sacramental oath. Each man says in effect – 'Lo! I rebaptise myself; and that which once was sworn on my behalf, now I swear for myself.' Even so in dreams, perhaps, under some secret conflict of the midnight sleeper, lighted up to the consciousness at the time, but darkened to the memory as soon as all is finished, each several child of our mysterious race completes for himself the aboriginal fall.

As I drew near to the Manchester post-office, I found that it was considerably past midnight;[15] but to my great relief, as it was important for me to be in Westmorland[16] by the morning, I saw by the huge saucer eyes of the mail, blazing through the gloom of overhanging houses, that my chance was not yet lost. Past the time it was; but by some luck, very unusual in my experience, the mail was not even yet ready to start.[17] I ascended to my seat on the box, where my cloak was still lying as it had lain at the Bridgewater Arms. I had left it there in imitation of a nautical discoverer, who leaves a bit of bunting on the shore of his discovery, by way of warning off the ground the whole human race, and signalising to the Christian and the heathen worlds, with his best compliments, that he has planted his throne for ever upon that virgin soil; henceforward claiming the *jus dominii* to the top of the atmosphere above it, and also the right of driving shafts to the centre of the earth below it; so that all people found after this warning, either aloft in the atmosphere, or in the shafts, or squatting on the soil, will be treated as trespassers – that is, decapitated by their very faithful and obedient servant, the owner of the said bunting. Possibly my cloak might not have been respected, and the *jus gentium*[18] might have been cruelly violated in my person – for, in the dark, people commit deeds of darkness, gas being a great ally of morality[19] – but it so happened that, on this night, there was no other outside passenger; and the crime, which else was but too probable, missed fire for want of a criminal.[20] By the way, I may as well mention at this point, since a circumstantial accuracy is essential to the effect of my narrative, that there was no other person of any description whatever about the mail – the guard, the coachman, and myself being allowed for – except only one – a horrid creature of the class known to the world as insiders, but whom young Oxford called sometimes 'Trojans,' in opposition to our Grecian selves, and sometimes 'vermin.' A Turkish

Effendi,[21] who piques himself on good-breeding, will never mention by name a pig. Yet it is but too often that he has reason to mention this animal; since constantly, in the streets of Stamboul, he has his trousers deranged or polluted by this vile creature running between his legs. But under any excess of hurry he is always careful, out of respect to the company he is dining with, to suppress the odious name, and to call the wretch 'that other creature,' as though all animal life beside formed one group, and this odious beast (to whom, as Chrysippus observed, salt serves as an apology for a soul)[22] formed another and alien group on the outside of creation. Now I, who am an English Effendi, that think myself to understand good-breeding as well as any son of Othman,[23] beg my reader's pardon for having mentioned an insider by his gross natural name. I shall do so no more: and, if I should have occasion to glance at so painful a subject, I shall always call him 'that other creature.' Let us hope, however, that no such distressing occasion will arise. But, by the way, an occasion arises at this moment; for the reader will be sure to ask, when we come to the story, 'Was this other creature present?' He was *not*; or more correctly, perhaps, *it* was not. We dropped the creature – or the creature, by natural imbecility, dropped itself – within the first ten miles from Manchester. In the latter case, I wish to make a philosophic remark of a moral tendency. When I die, or when the reader dies, and by repute suppose of fever, it will never be known whether we died in reality of the fever or of the doctor. But this other creature, in the case of dropping out of the coach, will enjoy a coroner's inquest; consequently he will enjoy an epitaph. For I insist upon it, that the verdict of a coroner's jury makes the best of epitaphs. It is brief, so that the public all find time to read it; it is pithy, so that the surviving friends (if any *can* survive such a loss) remember it without fatigue; it is upon oath, so that rascals and Dr Johnsons cannot pick holes in it.[24] 'Died through the visitation of intense stupidity, by impinging on a moonlight night against the off hind wheel of the Glasgow mail! Deodand[25] upon the said wheel – twopence.' What a simple lapidary inscription! Nobody much in the wrong but an off-wheel; and with few acquaintances; and if it were but rendered into choice Latin, though there would be a little bother in finding a Ciceronian word for 'off-wheel,' Morcellus[26] himself, that great master of sepulchral eloquence, could not show a better. Why I call this little remark *moral*, is, from the compensation it points out. Here, by the supposition, is that other creature on the one side, the beast of the world; and he (or it) gets an epitaph. You and I, on the contrary, the pride of our friends, get none.

But why linger on the subject of vermin? Having mounted the box, I took a small quantity of laudanum, having already travelled two hundred and fifty miles – viz., from a point seventy miles beyond London, upon a simple breakfast. In the taking of laudanum there was nothing extraordinary. But by accident it drew upon me the special attention of my assessor on the box, the coachman. And in *that* there was nothing extraordinary. But by accident, and with great delight, it drew my attention to the fact that this coachman was a monster in point of size, and that he had but one eye. In fact he had been foretold by Virgil as –

> 'Monstrum horrendum, informe, ingens, cui lumen ademptum.'[27]

He answered in every point – a monster he was – dreadful, shapeless, huge, who had lost an eye. But why should *that* delight me? Had he been one of the Calendars in the Arabian Nights, and had paid down his eye as the price of his criminal curiosity,[28] what right had *I* to exult in his misfortune? I did *not* exult: I delighted in no man's punishment, though it were even merited. But these personal distinctions identified in an instant an old friend of mine, whom I had known in the south for some years as the most masterly of mail-coachmen. He was the man in all Europe that could best have undertaken to drive six-in-hand full gallop over *Al Sirat* – that famous bridge of Mahomet[29] across the bottomless gulf, backing himself against the Prophet and twenty such fellows. I used to call him *Cyclops mastigophorus*, Cyclops the whip-bearer, until I observed that his skill made whips useless, except to fetch off an impertinent fly from a leader's head; upon which I changed his Grecian name to Cyclops *diphrélates* (Cyclops the charioter.) I, and others known to me, studied under him the diphrelatic[30] art. Excuse, reader, a word too elegant to be pedantic. And also take this remark from me, as a *gage d'amitié*[31] – that no word ever was or *can* be pedantic which, by supporting a distinction, supports the accuracy of logic; or which fills up a chasm for the understanding. As a pupil, though I paid extra fees, I cannot say that I stood high in his esteem. It showed his dogged honesty, (though, observe, not his discernment,) that he could not see my merits. Perhaps we ought to excuse his absurdity in this particular by remembering his want of an eye. *That* made him blind to my merits. Irritating as this blindness was, (surely it could not be envy?) he always courted my conversation, in which art I certainly had the whip-hand of him. On this occasion, great joy was at our meeting. But what was Cyclops doing here? Had the medical men recommended northern air, or how? I collected, from such explanations as he volunteered, that he had an interest at stake in a suit-at-law pending at Lancaster; so that probably he had got himself transferred to this station, for the purpose of connecting with his professional pursuits an instant readiness for the calls of his law-suit.

Meantime, what are we stopping for? Surely we've been waiting long enough. Oh, this procrastinating mail, and oh this procrastinating post-office! Can't they take a lesson upon that subject from *me?* Some people have called *me* procrastinating.[32] Now you are witness, reader, that I was in time for *them*. But can *they* lay their hands on their hearts, and say that they were in time for me? I, during my life, have often had to wait for the post-office: the post-office never waited a minute for me. What are they about? The guard tells me that there is a large extra accumulation of foreign mails this night, owing to irregularities caused by war and by the packet-service,[33] when as yet nothing is done by steam. For an *extra* hour, it seems, the post-office has been engaged in threshing out the pure wheaten correspondence of Glasgow, and winnowing it from the chaff of all baser intermediate towns. We can hear the flails going at this moment. But at last all is finished. Sound your horn, guard. Manchester, good bye; we've lost an hour by your criminal conduct at the post-office: which, however, though I do not mean to part with a serviceable ground of complaint, and one which really *is* such for the horses, to me secretly is an advantage, since it compels us to recover this last hour amongst the next eight or nine. Off we are at last, and at eleven miles an hour:[34] and at first I detect no changes in the energy or in the skill of Cyclops.

From Manchester to Kendal, which virtually (though not in law) is the capital of Westmoreland,[35] were at this time seven stages of eleven miles each. The first five of these, dated from Manchester, terminated in Lancaster, which was therefore fifty-five miles north of Manchester, and the same distance exactly from Liverpool. The first three terminated in Preston (called, by way of distinction from other towns of that name, *proud* Preston,) at which place it was that the separate roads from Liverpool and from Manchester to the north became confluent.[36] Within these first three stages lay the foundation, the progress, and termination of our night's adventure. During the first stage, I found out that Cyclops was mortal: he was liable to the shocking affection of sleep[37] – a thing which I had never previously suspected. If a man is addicted to the vicious habit of sleeping, all the skill in aurigation[38] of Apollo himself, with the horses of Aurora[39] to execute the motions of his will, avail him nothing. 'Oh, Cyclops!' I exclaimed more than once, 'Cyclops, my friend; thou art mortal. Thou snorest.' Through this first eleven miles, however, he betrayed his infirmity – which I grieve to say he shared with the whole Pagan Pantheon – only by short stretches. On waking up, he made an apology for himself, which, instead of mending the matter, laid an ominous foundation for coming disasters. The summer assizes were now proceeding at Lancaster: in consequence of which, for three nights and three days, he had not lain down in a bed. During the day, he was waiting for his uncertain summons as a witness on the trial in which he was interested; or he was drinking with the other witnesses, under the vigilant surveillance of the attorneys. During the night, or that part of it when the least temptations existed to conviviality, he was driving. Throughout the second stage he grew more and more drowsy. In the second mile of the third stage, he surrendered himself finally and without a struggle to his perilous temptation. All his past resistance had but deepened the weight of this final oppression. Seven atmospheres of sleep seemed resting upon him; and, to consummate the case, our worthy guard, after singing 'Love amongst the Roses,' for the fiftieth or sixtieth time, without any invitation from Cyclops or myself, and without applause for his poor labours, had moodily resigned himself to slumber – not so deep doubtless as the coachman's, but deep enough for mischief; and having, probably, no similar excuse. And thus at last, about ten miles from Preston, I found myself left in charge of his Majesty's London and Glasgow mail then running about eleven miles an hour.

What made this negligence less criminal than else it must have been thought, was the condition of the roads at night during the assizes. At that time all the law business of populous Liverpool, and of populous Manchester, with its vast cincture of populous rural districts, was called up by ancient usage to the tribunal of Lilliputian Lancaster.[40] To break up this old traditional usage required a conflict with powerful established interests, a large system of new arrangements, and a new parliamentary statute.[41] As things were at present, twice in the year[42] so vast a body of business rolled northwards, from the southern quarter of the county, that a fortnight at least occupied the severe exertions of two judges for its despatch. The consequence of this was – that every horse available for such a service, along the whole line of road, was exhausted in carrying down the multitudes of people who were parties to the different suits. By sunset, therefore, it usually happened that, through utter exhaustion amongst men and horses, the roads were all silent. Except exhaustion in the vast adjacent county of York from a contested election,[43] nothing like it was ordinarily witnessed in England.

On this occasion, the usual silence and solitude prevailed along the road. Not a hoof nor a wheel was to be heard. And to strengthen this false luxurious confidence in the noiseless roads, it happened also that the night was one of peculiar solemnity and peace. I myself, though slightly alive to the possibilities of peril, had so far yielded to the influence of the mighty calm as to sink into a profound reverie. The month was August, in which lay my own birthday; a festival to every thoughtful man suggesting solemn and often sigh-born thoughts.* The county was my own native county[45] – upon which, in its southern section, more than upon any equal area known to man past or present, had descended the original curse of labour in its heaviest form, not mastering the bodies of men only as of slaves, or criminals in mines, but working through the fiery will. Upon no equal space of earth, was, or ever had been, the same energy of human power put forth daily. At this particular season also of the assizes, that dreadful hurricane of flight and pursuit, as it might have seemed to a stranger, that swept to and from Lancaster all day long, hunting the county up and down, and regularly subsiding about sunset, united with the permanent distinction of Lancashire as the very metropolis and citadel of labour, to point the thoughts pathetically upon that counter vision of rest, of saintly repose from strife and sorrow, towards which, as to their secret haven, the profounder aspirations of man's heart are continually travelling. Obliquely we were nearing the sea upon our left,[46] which also must, under the present circumstances, be repeating the general state of halcyon repose. The sea, the atmosphere, the light, bore an orchestral part in this

* 'Sigh-born:' I owe the suggestion of this word to an obscure remembrance of a beautiful phrase in Giraldus Cambrensis, viz., *suspiriosae cogitationes*.[44]

universal lull. Moonlight, and the first timid tremblings of the dawn, were now blending; and the blendings were brought into a still more exquisite state of unity, by a slight silvery mist, motionless and dreamy, that covered the woods and fields, but with a veil of equable transparency. Except the feet of our own horses, which, running on a sandy margin of the road, made little disturbance, there was no sound abroad. In the clouds, and on the earth, prevailed the same majestic peace; and in spite of all that the villain of a schoolmaster has done for the ruin of our sublimer thoughts, which are the thoughts of our infancy,[47] we still believe in no such nonsense as a limited atmosphere. Whatever we may swear with our false feigning lips, in our faithful hearts we still believe, and must for ever believe, in fields of air traversing the total gulf between earth and the central heavens. Still, in the confidence of children that tread without fear *every* chamber in their father's house,[48] and to whom no door is closed,[49] we, in that Sabbatic vision which sometimes is revealed for an hour upon nights like this, ascend with easy steps from the sorrow-stricken fields of earth, upwards to the sandals of God.

Suddenly from thoughts like these, I was awakened to a sullen sound, as of some motion on the distant road. It stole upon the air for a moment; I listened in awe; but then it died away. Once roused, however, I could not but observe with alarm the quickened motion of our horses. Ten years' experience had made my eye learned in the valuing of motion; and I saw that we were now running thirteen miles an hour. I pretend to no presence of mind.[50] On the contrary, my fear is, that I am miserably and shamefully deficient in that quality as regards action. The palsy of doubt and distraction hangs like some guilty weight of dark unfathomed remembrances upon my energies,[51] when the signal is flying for *action*. But, on the other hand, this accursed gift I have, as regards *thought*, that in the first step towards the possibility of a misfortune, I see its total evolution: in the radix,[52] I see too certainly and too instantly its entire expansion; in the first syllable of the dreadful sentence, I read already the last. It was not that I feared for ourselves. What could injure *us?* Our bulk and impetus charmed us against peril in any collision. And I had rode through too many hundreds of perils that were frightful to approach, that were matter of laughter as we looked back upon them, for any anxiety to rest upon *our* interests. The mail was not built, I felt assured, nor bespoke, that could betray *me* who trusted to its protection. But any carriage that we could meet would be frail and light in comparison of ourselves. And I remarked this ominous accident of our situation. We were on the wrong side of the road. But then the other party, if other there was, might also be on the wrong side; and two wrongs might make a right. *That* was not likely. The same motive which had drawn *us* to the right-hand side of the road, viz., the soft beaten sand, as contrasted with the paved centre, would prove attractive to others.[53] Our lamps, still lighted, would give the impression of vigilance on our part. And every creature that met us, would rely upon *us* for quartering.* All this, and if the separate links of the anticipation had been a thousand times more, I saw – not discursively or by effort – but as by one flash of horrid intuition.

Under this steady though rapid anticipation of the evil which *might* be gathering ahead, ah, reader! what a sullen mystery of fear, what a sigh of woe, seemed to steal upon the air, as again the far-off sound of a wheel was heard! A whisper it was – a whisper from, perhaps, four miles off – secretly announcing a ruin that, being foreseen, was not the less inevitable. What could be done – who was it that could do it – to check the storm-flight of these maniacal horses? What! could I not seize the reins from the grasp of the slumbering coachman? You, reader, think that it would have been in *your* power to do so. And I quarrel not with your estimate of yourself. But, from the way in which the coachman's hand was viced between his upper and lower thigh, this was impossible. The guard subsequently found it impossible, after this danger had passed. Not the grasp only, but also the position of this Polyphemus, made the attempt impossible. You still think otherwise. See, then, that bronze equestrian statue. The cruel rider has kept the bit in his horse's mouth for two centuries. Unbridle him, for a minute, if you please, and wash his mouth with water. Or stay, reader, unhorse me that marble emperor: knock me those marble feet from those marble stirrups of Charlemagne.[55]

The sounds ahead strengthened, and were now too clearly the sounds of wheels. Who and what could it be? Was it industry in a taxed cart?[56] – was it youthful gaiety in a gig? Whoever it was, something must be attempted to warn them. Upon the other party rests the active responsibility, but upon *us* – and, woe is me! that *us* was my single self – rests the responsibility of warning. Yet, how should this be accomplished? Might I not seize the guard's horn? Already, on the first thought, I was making my way over the roof to the guard's seat. But this, from the foreign mails being piled upon the roof, was a difficult, and even dangerous attempt, to one cramped by nearly three hundred miles of outside travelling. And, fortunately, before I had lost much time in the attempt, our frantic horses swept round an angle of the road, which opened upon us the stage where the collision must be accomplished, the parties that seemed summoned to the trial, and the impossibility of saving them by any communication with the guard.

Before us lay an avenue, straight as an arrow, six hundred yards, perhaps, in length; and the umbrageous trees, which rose in a regular line from either side, meeting high overhead, gave to it the character of a cathedral aisle.[57] These trees lent a deeper solemnity to the early light; but there was still light enough to perceive, at the further end of this gothic aisle, a light, reedy gig, in which were seated a young man, and, by his side, a young lady. Ah, young sir! what are you about? If it is necessary that you should whisper your communi-

* '*Quartering*' – this is the technical word; and, I presume, derived from the French *cartayer*, to evade a rut or any obstacle.[54]

cations to this young lady – though really I see nobody at this hour, and on this solitary road, likely to overhear your conversation – is it, therefore, necessary that you should carry your lips forward to hers? The little carriage is creeping on at one mile an hour; and the parties within it, being thus tenderly engaged, are naturally bending down their heads. Between them and eternity, to all human calculation, there is but a minute and a half. What is it that I shall do? Strange it is, and to a mere auditor of the tale, might seem laughable, that I should need a suggestion from the *Iliad* to prompt the sole recourse that remained. But so it was. Suddenly I remembered the shout of Achilles, and its effect. But could I pretend to shout like the son of Peleus, aided by Pallas?[58] No, certainly: but then I needed not the shout that should alarm all Asia militant; a shout would suffice, such as should carry terror into the hearts of two thoughtless young people, and one gig horse. I shouted – and the young man heard me not. A second time I shouted – and now he heard me, for now he raised his head.

Here, then, all had been done that, by me, *could* be done: more on *my* part was not possible. Mine had been the first step: the second was for the young man: the third was for God. If, said I, the stranger is a brave man, and if, indeed, he loves the young girl at his side – or, loving her not, if he feels the obligation pressing upon every man worthy to be called a man, of doing his utmost for a woman confided to his protection – he will at least make some effort to save her. If *that* fails, he will not perish the more, or by a death more cruel, for having made it; and he will die, as a brave man should, with his face to the danger, and with his arm about the woman that he sought in vain to save. But if he makes no effort, shrinking, without a struggle, from his duty, he himself will not the less certainly perish for this baseness of poltroonery. He will die no less: and why not? Wherefore should we grieve that there is one craven less in the world? No; *let* him perish, without a pitying thought of ours wasted upon him; and, in that case, all our grief will be reserved for the fate of the helpless girl, who, now, upon the least shadow of failure in *him*, must, by the fiercest of translations – must, without time for a prayer – must, within seventy seconds, stand before the judgment-seat of God.

But craven he was not: sudden had been the call upon him, and sudden was his answer to the call. He saw, he heard, he comprehended, the ruin that was coming down: already its gloomy shadow darkened above him; and already he was measuring his strength to deal with it. Ah! what a vulgar thing does courage seem, when we see nations buying it and selling it for a shilling a-day: ah! what a sublime thing does courage seem, when some fearful crisis on the great deeps of life carries a man, as if running before a hurricane, up to the giddy crest of some mountainous wave, from which accordingly as he chooses his course, he descries two courses, and a voice says to him audibly – 'This way lies hope; take the other way and mourn for ever!' Yet, even then, amidst the raving of the seas and the frenzy of the danger, the man is able to confront his situation – is able to retire for a moment into solitude with God, and to seek all his counsel from *him!* For seven seconds, it might be, of his seventy, the stranger settled his countenance steadfastly upon us, as if to search and value every element in the conflict before him. For five seconds more he sate immovably, like one that mused on some great purpose. For five he sate with eyes upraised, like one that prayed in sorrow, under some extremity of doubt, for wisdom to guide him towards the better choice. Then suddenly he rose; stood upright; and, by a sudden strain upon the reins, raising his horse's forefeet from the ground, he slewed him round on the pivot of his hind legs, so as to plant the little equipage in a position nearly at right-angles to ours. Thus far his condition was not improved; except as a first step had been taken towards the possibility of a second. If no more were done, nothing was done;[59] for the little carriage still occupied the very centre of our path, though in an altered direction. Yet even now it may not be too late: fifteen of the twenty seconds may still be unexhausted; and one almighty bound forward may avail to clear the ground. Hurry then, hurry! for the flying moments – *they* hurry! Oh hurry, hurry, my brave young man! for the cruel hoofs of our horses – *they* also hurry! Fast are the flying moments, faster are the hoofs of our horses. Fear not for *him*, if human energy can suffice: faithful was he that drove, to his terrific duty; faithful was the horse to *his* command. One blow, one impulse given with voice and hand by the stranger, one rush from the horse, one bound as if in the act of rising to a fence, landed the docile creature's fore-feet upon the crown or arching centre of the road. The larger half of the little equipage had then cleared our over-towering shadow: *that* was evident even to my own agitated sight. But it mattered little that one wreck should float off in safety, if upon the wreck that perished were embarked the human freightage. The rear part of the carriage – was *that* certainly beyond the line of absolute ruin? What power could answer the question? Glance of eye, thought of man, wing of angel, which of these had speed enough to sweep between the question and the answer, and divide the one from the other? Light does not tread upon the steps of light more indivisibly, than did our all-conquering arrival upon the escaping efforts of the gig. *That* must the young man have felt too plainly. His back was now turned to us; not by sight could he any longer communicate with the peril; but by the dreadful rattle of our harness, too truly had his ear been instructed – that all was finished as regarded any further effort of *his*. Already in resignation he had rested from his struggle; and perhaps, in his heart he was whispering – 'Father, which art above, do thou finish in heaven what I on earth have attempted.' We ran past them faster than ever mill-race[60] in our inexorable flight. Oh, raving of hurricanes that must have sounded in their young ears at the moment of our transit! Either with the swingle-bar,[61] or with the haunch of our near leader, we had struck the off-wheel of the little gig, which stood rather obliquely and not quite so far advanced as to be accurately parallel with the near wheel. The blow, from the fury of our passage, resounded terrifically. I rose in horror, to look upon the ruins we might have caused. From my elevated station I looked down, and looked back upon the scene, which in a moment told its tale, and wrote all its records on my heart for ever.

The horse was planted immovably, with his fore-feet upon the paved crest of the central road. He of the whole party was alone untouched by the passion of death. The little cany carriage – partly perhaps from the dreadful torsion of the wheels in its recent movement, partly from the thundering blow we had given to it – as if it sympathised with human horror, was all alive with tremblings and shiverings. The young man sat like a rock. He stirred not at all. But *his* was the steadiness of agitation frozen into rest by horror. As yet he dared not to look round; for he knew that, if anything remained to do, by him it could no longer be done. And as yet he knew not for certain if their safety were accomplished. But the lady ———

But the lady ———! Oh heavens! will that spectacle ever depart from my dreams, as she rose and sank upon her seat, sank and rose, threw up her arms wildly to heaven, clutched at some visionary object in the air, fainting, praying, raving, despairing! Figure to yourself, reader, the elements of the case; suffer me to recal before your mind the circumstances of the unparalleled situation. From the silence and deep peace of this saintly summer night, – from the pathetic blending of this sweet moonlight, dawnlight, dreamlight, – from the manly tenderness of this flattering, whispering, murmuring love, – suddenly as from the woods and fields, – suddenly as from the chambers of the air opening in revelation, – suddenly as from the ground yawning at her feet, leaped upon her, with the flashing of cataracts, Death the crownèd[62] phantom, with all the equipage of his terrors, and the tiger roar of his voice.

The moments were numbered. In the twinkling of an eye our flying horses had carried us to the termination of the umbrageous aisle; at right-angles we wheeled into our former direction; the turn of the road carried the scene out of my eyes in an instant, and swept it into my dreams for ever.[63]

DREAM-FUGUE.

ON THE ABOVE THEME OF SUDDEN DEATH.

'Whence the sound
Of instruments, that made melodious chime,
Was heard, of harp and organ; and who mov'd
Their stops and chords, was seen; his volant touch
Instinct through all proportions, low and high,
Fled and pursued transverse the resonant fugue.'
Par. Lost, B. xi.[64]

Tumultuosissimamente.[65]

Passion of Sudden Death! that once in youth I read and interpreted by the shadows of thy averted* signs; – Rapture of panic taking the shape, which amongst tombs in churches I have seen, of woman bursting her sepulchral bonds – of woman's Ionic[66] form bending forward from the ruins of her grave, with arching foot, with eyes upraised, with clasped adoring hands – waiting, watching, trembling, praying, for the trumpet's call to rise from dust for ever; – Ah, vision too fearful of shuddering humanity on the brink of abysses! vision that didst start back – that didst reel away – like a shrivelling scroll from before the wrath of fire racing on the wings of the wind! Epilepsy so brief of horror – wherefore is it that thou canst not die? Passing so suddenly into darkness, wherefore is it that still thou sheddest thy sad funeral blights upon the gorgeous mosaics of dreams? Fragment of music too stern, heard once and heard no more, what aileth thee[67] that thy deep rolling chords come up at intervals through all the worlds of sleep, and after thirty years have lost no element of horror?

1.

Lo, it is summer, almighty summer![68] The everlasting gates of life and summer are thrown open wide; and on the ocean, tranquil and verdant as a savannah, the unknown lady from the dreadful vision and I myself are floating: she upon a fairy pinnace, and I upon an English three-decker. But both of us are wooing gales of festal happiness within the domain of our common country – within that ancient watery park – within that pathless chase where England takes her pleasure as a huntress through winter and summer, and which stretches from the rising to the setting sun. Ah! what a wilderness of floral beauty was hidden, or was suddenly revealed, upon the tropic islands through which the pinnace moved. And upon her deck what a bevy of human flowers – young women how lovely, young men how noble, that were dancing together, and slowly drifting towards *us* amidst music and incense, amidst blossoms from forests and gorgeous corymbi[69] from vintages, amidst natural caroling and the echoes of sweet girlish laughter. Slowly the pinnace nears us, gaily she hails us, and slowly she disappears beneath the shadow of our mighty bows. But then, as at some signal from heaven, the music and the carols, and the sweet echoing of girlish laughter – all are hushed. What evil has smitten the pinnace, meeting or overtaking her? Did ruin to our friends couch within our own dreadful shadow? Was our shadow the shadow of death?[70] I looked over the bow for an answer; and, behold! the pinnace was dismantled;

* '*Averted* signs.' – I read the course and changes of the lady's agony in the succession of her involuntary gestures; but let it be remembered that I read all this from the rear, never once catching the lady's full face, and even her profile imperfectly.

the revel and the revellers were found no more; the glory of the vintage was dust; and the forest was left without a witness to its beauty upon the seas. 'But where,' and I turned to our own crew – 'where are the lovely women that danced beneath the awning of flowers and clustering corymbi? Whither have fled the noble young men that danced with *them?*' Answer there was none. But suddenly the man at the masthead, whose countenance darkened with alarm, cried aloud – 'Sail on the weather-beam! Down she comes upon us; in seventy seconds she will founder!'

2.

I looked to the weather-side, and the summer had departed. The sea was rocking, and shaken with gathering wrath. Upon its surface sate mighty mists, which grouped themselves into arches and long cathedral aisles. Down one of these, with the fiery pace of a quarrel from a cross-bow, ran a frigate right athwart our course. 'Are they mad?' some voice exclaimed from our deck. 'Are they blind? Do they woo their ruin?' But in a moment, as she was close upon us, some impulse of a heady current[71] or sudden vortex gave a wheeling bias to her course, and off she forged without a shock. As she ran past us, high aloft amongst the shrouds stood the lady of the pinnace. The deeps opened ahead in malice to receive her, towering surges of foam ran after her, the billows were fierce to catch her. But far away she was borne into desert spaces of the sea: whilst still by sight I followed her, as she ran before the howling gale, chased by angry sea-birds and by maddening billows; still I saw her, as at the moment when she ran past us, amongst the shrouds, with her white draperies streaming before the wind. There she stood with hair dishevelled, one hand clutched amongst the tackling – rising, sinking, fluttering, trembling, praying – there for leagues I saw her as she stood, raising at intervals one hand to heaven, amidst the fiery crests of the pursuing waves and the raving of the storm; until at last, upon a sound from afar of malicious laughter and mockery, all was hidden for ever in driving showers; and afterwards, but when I know not, and how I know not,

3.

Sweet funeral bells from some incalculable distance, wailing over the dead that die before the dawn, awakened me as I slept in a boat moored to some familiar shore. The morning twilight even then was breaking; and, by the dusky revelations which it spread, I saw a girl adorned with a garland of white roses about her head for some great festival, running along the solitary strand with extremity of haste. Her running was the running of panic; and often she looked back as to some dreadful enemy in the rear. But when I leaped ashore, and followed on her steps to warn her of a peril in front, alas! from me she fled as from another peril; and vainly I shouted to her of quicksands that lay ahead. Faster and faster she ran; round a promontory of rock she wheeled out of sight; in an instant I also wheeled round it, but only to see the treacherous sands gathering above her head. Already her person was buried; only the fair young head and the diadem of white roses around it were still visible to the pitying heavens; and, last of all, was visible one marble arm. I saw by the early twilight this fair young head, as it was sinking down to darkness – saw this marble arm, as it rose above her head and her treacherous grave, tossing, faultering, rising, clutching as at some false deceiving hand stretched out from the clouds – saw this marble arm uttering her dying hope, and then her dying despair. The head, the diadem, the arm, – these all had sunk; at last over these also the cruel quicksand had closed; and no memorial of the fair young girl remained on earth, except my own solitary tears, and the funeral bells from the desert seas, that, rising again more softly, sang a requiem over the grave of the buried child, and over her blighted dawn.

I sate, and wept in secret the tears that men have ever given to the memory of those that died before the dawn, and by the treachery of earth, our mother. But the tears and funeral bells were hushed suddenly by a shout as of many nations, and by a roar as from some great king's artillery advancing rapidly along the valleys, and heard afar by its echoes among the mountains. 'Hush!' I said, as I bent my ear earthwards to listen – 'hush! – this either is the very anarchy of strife, or else' – and then I listened more profoundly, and said as I raised my head – 'or else, oh heavens! it is *victory* that swallows up all strife.'[72]

4.

Immediately, in trance, I was carried over land and sea to some distant kingdom, and placed upon a triumphal car, amongst companions crowned with laurel. The darkness of gathering midnight, brooding over all the land, hid from us the mighty crowds that were weaving restlessly about our carriage as a centre – we heard them, but we saw them not. Tidings had arrived, within an hour, of a grandeur that measured itself against centuries; too full of pathos they were, too full of joy that acknowledged no fountain but God, to utter themselves by other language than by tears, by restless anthems, by reverberations rising from every choir, of the *Gloria in excelsis*.[73] These tidings we that sate upon the laurelled car had it for our privilege to publish amongst all nations. And already, by signs audible through the darkness, by snortings and tramplings, our angry horses, that knew no fear of fleshly weariness, upbraided us with delay. Wherefore *was* it that we delayed? We waited for a secret word, that should bear witness to the hope of nations, as now accomplished for ever. At midnight the secret word arrived; which word was – Waterloo and Recovered Christendom! The dreadful word shone by its own light; before us it went; high above our leaders' heads it rode, and spread a golden light over the paths which we traversed. Every city, at the presence of the secret word, threw open its gates to receive us. The rivers were silent as we crossed. All the infinite forests, as we ran along their margins, shivered in homage to the secret word. And the darkness comprehended it.[74]

Two hours after midnight we reached a mighty minster. Its gates, which rose to the clouds, were closed. But when the dreadful word, that rode before us, reached them with its golden light, silently they moved back upon their hinges; and at a flying gallop our equipage entered the grand aisle of the cathedral. Headlong was our pace; and at every altar, in the little chapels and oratories to the right hand and left of our course, the lamps, dying or sickening, kindled anew in sympathy with the secret word that was flying past. Forty leagues we might have run in the cathedral, and as yet no strength of morning light had reached us, when we saw before us the aërial galleries of the organ and the choir. Every pinnacle of the fret-work, every station of advantage amongst the traceries, was crested by white-robed choristers, that sang deliverance; that wept no more tears, as once their fathers had wept; but at intervals that sang together to the generations, saying –

'Chaunt the deliverer's praise in every tongue,'

and receiving answers from afar,

– 'such as once in heaven and earth were sung.'[75]

And of their chaunting was no end; of our headlong pace was neither pause nor remission.

Thus, as we ran like torrents – thus, as we swept with bridal rapture over the Campo Santo* of the cathedral graves – suddenly we became aware of a vast necropolis rising upon the far-off horizon – a city of sepulchres, built within the saintly cathedral for the warrior dead that rested from their feuds on earth. Of purple granite was the necropolis; yet, in the first minute, it lay like a purple stain upon the horizon – so mighty was the distance. In the second minute it trembled through many changes, growing into terraces and towers of wondrous altitude, so mighty was the pace. In the third minute

* *Campo Santo*. – It is probable that most of my readers will be acquainted with the history of the Campo Santo at Pisa – composed of earth brought from Jerusalem[76] for a bed of sanctity, as the highest prize which the noble piety of crusaders could ask or imagine. There is another Campo Santo at Naples, formed, however, (I presume,) on the example given by Pisa. Possibly the idea may have been more extensively copied. To readers who are unacquainted with England, or who (being English) are yet unacquainted with the cathedral cities of England, it may be right to mention that the graves within-side the cathedrals often form a flat pavement over which carriages and horses might roll; and perhaps a boyish remembrance of one particular cathedral, across which I had seen passengers walk and burdens carried, may have assisted my dream.

already, with our dreadful gallop, we were entering its suburbs. Vast sarcophagi rose on every side, having towers and turrets that, upon the limits of the central aisle, strode forward with haughty intrusion, that ran back with mighty shadows into answering recesses. Every sarcophagus showed many bas-reliefs – bas-reliefs of battles – bas-reliefs of battle-fields; of battles from forgotten ages – of battles from yesterday – of battle-fields that, long since, nature had healed and reconciled to herself with the sweet oblivion of flowers – of battle-fields that were yet angry and crimson with carnage. Where the terraces ran, there did *we* run; where the towers curved, there did *we* curve. With the flight of swallows our horses swept round every angle. Like rivers in flood, wheeling round headlands; like hurricanes that ride into the secrets of forests; faster than ever light unwove the mazes of darkness, our flying equipage carried earthly passions – kindled warrior instincts – amongst the dust that lay around us; dust oftentimes of our noble fathers that had slept in God from Créci to Trafalgar.[77] And now had we reached the last sarcophagus, now were we abreast of the last bas-relief, already had we recovered the arrow-like flight of the illimitable central aisle, when coming up this aisle to meet us we beheld a female infant that rode in a carriage as frail as flowers. The mists, which went before her, hid the fawns that drew her, but could not hide the shells and tropic flowers with which she played – but could not hide the lovely smiles by which she uttered her trust in the mighty cathedral, and in the cherubim that looked down upon her from the topmost shafts of its pillars. Face to face she was meeting us; face to face she rode, as if danger there were none. 'Oh baby!' I exclaimed, 'shalt thou be the ransom for Waterloo? Must we, that carry tidings of great joy to every people,[78] be messengers of ruin to thee?' In horror I rose at the thought; but then also, in horror at the thought, rose one that was sculptured on the bas-relief – a Dying Trumpeter.[79] Solemnly from the field of battle he rose to his feet; and, unslinging his stony trumpet, carried it, in his dying anguish, to his stony lips – sounding once, and yet once again; proclamation that, in *thy* ears, oh baby! must have spoken from the battlements of death. Immediately deep shadows fell between us, and aboriginal silence. The choir had ceased to sing. The hoofs of our horses, the rattling of our harness, alarmed the graves no more. By horror the bas-relief had been unlocked into life. By horror we, that were so full of life, we men and our horses, with their fiery fore-legs rising in mid air to their everlasting gallop, were frozen to a bas-relief. Then a third time the trumpet sounded;[80] the seals were taken off all pulses; life, and the frenzy of life, tore into their channels again; again the choir burst forth in sunny grandeur, as from the muffling of storms and darkness; again the thunderings of our horses carried temptation into the graves. One cry burst from our lips as the clouds, drawing off from the aisle, showed it empty before us – 'Whither has the infant fled? – is the young child caught up to God?' Lo! afar off, in a vast recess, rose three mighty windows to the clouds; and on a level with their summits, at height insuperable to man, rose an altar of purest alabaster. On its eastern face was trembling a crimson glory. Whence came *that?* Was it from the reddening dawn that now streamed *through* the windows? Was it from the crimson robes of the martyrs that were painted *on* the windows? Was it from the bloody bas-reliefs of earth? Whencesoever it were – there, within that crimson radiance, suddenly appeared a female head, and then a female figure. It was the child – now grown up to woman's height. Clinging to the horns of the altar,[81] there she stood – sinking, rising, trembling, fainting – raving, despairing; and behind the volume of incense that, night and day, streamed upwards from the altar, was seen the fiery font, and dimly was descried the outline of the dreadful being that should baptise her with the baptism of death. But by her side was kneeling her better angel, that hid his face with wings; that wept and pleaded for *her;* that prayed when *she* could *not;* that fought with heaven by tears for *her* deliverance; which also, as he raised his immortal countenance from his wings, I saw, by the glory in his eye, that he had won at last.

5.

Then rose the agitation, spreading through the infinite cathedral, to its agony; then was completed the passion of the mighty fugue. The golden tubes of the organ, which as yet had but sobbed and muttered at intervals – gleaming amongst clouds and surges of incense – threw up, as from fountains unfathomable, columns of heart-shattering music. Choir and anti-choir were filling fast with unknown voices. Thou also, Dying Trumpeter! – with thy love that was victorious, and thy anguish that was finishing, didst enter the tumult: trumpet and echo – farewell love, and farewell anguish – rang through the dreadful *sanctus*.[82] We, that spread flight before us, heard the tumult, as of flight, mustering behind us. In fear we looked round for the unknown steps that, in flight or in pursuit, were gathering upon our own. Who were these that followed? The faces, which no man could count – whence were *they?* 'Oh, darkness of the grave!' I exclaimed, 'that from the crimson altar and from the fiery font wert visited with secret light – that wert searched by the effulgence in the angel's eye – were these indeed thy children? Pomps of life, that, from the burials of centuries, rose again to the voice of perfect joy, could it be *ye* that had wrapped me in the reflux of panic?' What ailed me, that I should fear when the triumphs of earth were advancing? Ah! Pariah heart within me, that couldst never hear the sound of joy without sullen whispers of treachery in ambush; that, from six years old, didst never hear the promise of perfect love,[83] without seeing aloft amongst the stars fingers as of a man's hand writing the secret legend – '*ashes to ashes, dust to dust!*' – wherefore shouldst *thou* not fear though all men should rejoice? Lo! as I looked back for seventy leagues through the mighty cathedral, and saw the quick and the dead[84] that sang together to God, together that sang to the generations of man – ah! raving, as of torrents that opened on every side: trepidation, as of female and infant steps that fled – ah! rushing, as of wings that chased! But I heard a voice from heaven, which said – 'Let there be no reflux of panic – let there be no more fear, and no more sudden death! Cover them with joy as the tides cover the shore!' *That* heard the children of the choir, *that* heard the children of the grave. All the hosts of jubilation made ready to move. Like armies that ride in pursuit, they moved with one step. Us, that, with laurelled heads, were passing from the cathedral through its eastern gates, they overtook, and, as with a garment, they wrapped us round with thunders that overpowered our own. As brothers we moved together; to the skies we rose – to the dawn that advanced – to the stars that fled: rendering thanks to God in the highest[85] – that, having hid his face through one generation behind thick clouds of War, once again was ascending – was ascending from Waterloo – in the visions of Peace: – rendering thanks for thee, young girl! whom having overshadowed with his ineffable passion of Death – suddenly did God relent; suffered thy angel to turn aside his arm; and even in thee, sister unknown! shown to me for a moment only to be hidden for ever, found an occasion to glorify his goodness. A thousand times, amongst the phantoms of sleep, has he shown thee to me, standing before the golden dawn, and ready to enter its gates – with the dreadful Word going before thee – with the armies of the grave behind thee; shown thee to me, sinking, rising, fluttering, fainting, but then suddenly reconciled, adoring: a thousand times has he followed thee in the worlds of sleep – through storms; through desert seas; through the darkness of quicksands; through fugues and the persecution of fugues; through dreams, and the dreadful resurrections that are in dreams – only that at the last, with one motion of his victorious arm, he might record and emblazon the endless resurrections of his love![86]

Manuscript Transcripts

[THE VISION OF SUDDEN DEATH]
MS VSD A

The manuscript is held at the Bodleian Library, University of Oxford, as Eng. Lett. c. 461, f. 103 and f. 116. It consists of two fragments of white paper, written on both sides in blue ink: 103 measures 92 by 160 mm, and 116 measures 135 by 134 mm. There are no watermarks. The two fragments originally formed a single piece, cut in turn from a larger written sheet. Thus the text on 103 r. continues on 116 r., but both carry only incomplete lines from the original larger sheet. 116 r. is written in two columns, but only a few words of the right hand column remain. The line 'An opus operatim...' is written vertically up the left margin. After cutting, each of the resulting two fragments was written on the verso. 103 v. carries a set of notes related to 'The Vision of Sudden Death'.

For details of the 'Conventions for Manuscript Transcription', see above, p. xvii. For the occasion and context of 'The Vision of Sudden Death', see headnote, pp. 401–8.

[103 r.]

Let us inquire 1. What were the duties{*cut*}
2. What ‹the› ‹are› is the m{*cut*}
3. What is the ‹aspect of› {↑ crisis in}{*cut*}
4. What is the specific d{*cut*}

Disposing of these objections below
1. ‹W› If 9000 ‹x› why not 7000 more?
Answer – for the most manifest of reasons{*cut*}

[116 r.]

An opus operatim does not mean actum agere.[1]

1. Bec. the quant.{*cut*}

2. Because the ‹7000 added to› 9000 given with no prospect of giving more – that is ‹given› given in {↑ mere} commiser^{-}. to the receivers, as then utterly without secrecy stands upon a{*cut*}

If some humble cooperator in a partic. serv. of warfare had looked cravingly toward a p^{t} of the Spoils, you m^{t}. in generosity allow him the share which he did not claim. But if ‹embolden› after he had assuming a bolder attitude he now held out his hand ‹as› with the air of one claiming a debt{*cut*}

Thirdly. There mt. be reason enough for giving the 9000 be it stood on a{*cut*}

according to the law of{*cut*}
can be collected only{*cut*}
2. Pop{*cut*}
3. In an{*cut*}
who op. this qu{*cut*}
to Popery ac{*cut*}
In limiting it{*cut*}
again an{*cut*}
nexing bet{*cut*}
defect bot{*cut*}
differ on{*cut*}
polit. rel^{-}.{*cut*}
agree upon{*cut*}
in earnest{*cut*}
peril of the{*cut*}

[103 v.]
1. The preaching of Noah – shooting like rockets out of sleep
2. The sea running with pursuing billows
3. The ship running upon the rocks of a port har^{b}. a narrow channel. Lights torches all the town stretching y^{r} arms to save: your children are on deck: almost you touch the arms y^{t} are stretched out
4. All have perished: but you – hatefully to yourself – why you know not – *how* you ask not – are again walking in smouldering cities – burnt out decaying relics of ravage and havock:
Or stretching away thro' dark roads upon what hurrying impulse – you see – but understand you do not.
5. The Mail Coach break^{g} down: – all news rep. but ruin.
6. The faces of the Marble mantle-piece.

[116 v.]

I have a natur. love of intel. power; and moreover I have a nat. hatred of the injustice which thro' life I have witnessed to all such power resting {↑ in simplicity} ‹on› upon its own simple power. If a man courts pop. favor by means of a *narrative* interest, by an int. of curiosity vulgar and in which all can sympathise in a vulg. degree, – or if he is the pet of a coterie combined by ‹hatred› jealousy and envy (as a body of dissenters) then his name travels by powers of which tho' he may be a man of {↑ real} genius not one part in a hund. is his own. ‹But› Strip him of this novelish int^{t}. which is like bladders to a swimmer, strip him of this dissenting support, and he w^{d} sink often to nothing at all. Wanting therefore such adv. aids, coming forward anonymously, and resting upon profound specul^{s}. a man is sure of neglect for a time long enough to mark the utter treachery to their duties of those who in newspapers undertake every month to review

[THE VISION OF SUDDEN DEATH]
MS VSD B

The manuscript is held at Dove Cottage, Grasmere as MS 1989: 161.44. It is a single sheet of white paper, measuring 183 by 225 mm, with writing in black ink on the recto only. There is part of a crown watermark, but no date is discernible. References to 'mounting the box' and the repeated use of the phrase 'too late' suggest that this is a discarded passage from 'The Vision of Sudden Death'. The most likely point for insertion is following the line '…the mail was not even yet ready to start' (see above, p. 433).

For details of the 'Conventions for Manuscript Transcription', see above, p. xvii. For the occasion and context of 'The Vision of Sudden Death', see headnote, pp. 401–8.

But how came I to run any risk?

At my birth, among the fairies that honored that event by their presence, was one – an excellent creature – who said, "The gift, which I bring for the young child, is this: among the dark lines in the woof of his life I ‹mark› {↑ observe} one which indicates a trifle of procrastination as lying amongst his frailties:[1] and {↑ from ‹out of› that frailty} I am resolved to take {↑ out} the sting ‹out of this›. My gift therefore is – that, if he must always {↑ seem} ‹be› in danger of being too late, he shall very seldom {↑ really} ‹indeed› be ‹really› so {↑ ‹x›in fact}." ‹All his errors in that respect shall not through his whole life cost him 10 guineas. Now then I ‹hope› trust to have taken the sting out of that infirmity."› Upon which up jumped a wicked old fairy, ‹ugly and cankered›, vexed ‹also› at not having received a special invitation to the {↑ ‹birth›} ‹ceremony› {↑ natal festivity}, who said – "*You*'ll take the sting out, will you? But now, Madam, please to see me put it back again. *My* gift is – that, if seldom actually in danger of being too late, he shall always be in fear of it. ‹x› Not often com‹mitting›{↑ pleting} the offence, he shall for ever be suffering {↑ its} ‹the penalty of it› penalties." Yes, reader, so she said; and so it happened. The curse, which she imposed, I could not evade. My only resource was – to take out my revenge in affronting her. On this occasion I whispered to her, whilst mounting the box, – "Well, old girl, here I am; and, *as usual*, quite in time." That word – '*as usual*' – must I knew be wormwood to her {↑ heart}: so I repeated it, saying – "Your malice, old cankered lady, is defeated; ‹you› {↑ defeated, you} see, *as usual*." "Certainly my son" – was her horrid reply – "You are in time; and generally you are so. ‹But I grieve to know, I never said that you would *not*. be so.› But it grieves me know that for the last half hour you have been suffering horrid torments of mind.

[THE VISION OF SUDDEN DEATH]
MS VSD C

The manuscript is held at the National Library of Scotland as MS 21239, ff. 62–3. It is two sheets of faded blue paper, measuring 187 by 226 mm, with writing in black ink on the recto only. There are no watermarks. The manuscript contains six discarded passages from different sections of 'The Vision of Sudden Death'.

For details of the 'Conventions for Manuscript Transcription', see above, p. xvii. For the occasion and context of 'The Vision of Sudden Death', see headnote, pp. 401–8.

[62 r.]

Suff. me, reader, to recal ‹into› bef. your memory Suffer me to converge the elements of the case. {↑ They were these.} {↑ [or these they were.]} from the ‹deaf› breathless, ‹hush and peace› {↑ hush, from the} of this saintly sum. night, – from the pathetic blending of this sweet moonlight dawn-light, dreamlight, – [notice to the r. the imposs. of fixing an absol. point in things so varying as a succession of time.] – from the tenderness of this manly flattering – whispering – murmuring, love ——— suddenly, as f^{r}. the f^{ds} and w^{ds} sud.^{ly} as from the chambers of the air – sud. as f^{r}. the g^{d}. opening at her feet – leaped upon her, with the flashing of cataracts – Death the crowned phantom, with all the eq. of his ter., and with the ‹xxx› tiger roar of his voice

the young man sat like a rock: All which *could* be done ‹he› *had* {↑ been} done: if it were too little, {↑ what remained but that} to God ‹it remained that› he should {↑ speak his parting} utter his farewell ‹and› prayer? Even now, even at this instant his fate was not {↑ sealed} ‹decided› but *being* {↑ sealed} ‹decided›. {↑ *That*} He knew: {↑ *That*} *he felt* and [*that* prevented] *him* from turning round. ‹it› and ‹human› nature {↑ in *him*} shrank from looking round at the yet {↑ unfinished} ‹imperfect› case. We {↑ the Mail} ‹ran› and its

with our inexorable pace ran past the little gig ‹with the fury of› {↑ like} a mill-race*:[1] – ‹the› these were the living creatures y^{t} c^{d} support so stood, so sate, the horse, {↑ the shock} the young man: {↑ ‹on the other hand› they seemed ‹in› lifeless and of granite: on the other {↑ hand}} the little reedy carriage, whether it were by the torsion of the wheel, or by the resounding blow {↑ with} which we had struck ‹the› upon it, ‹was› shivered all over ‹like› as ‹**xx**› some

we ran past as fluently as swallows flie – as liquidly (which some people feel a cause of sickness) as ever sudden plunge into the trough of the sea carried a royal ship

[63 r.]

When ‹we› reached the inn at Preston,[2] what was it that I ‹did› proceeded to do? Never trouble yourself reader to be angry, ‹but› when I tell you that I ‹do› had the baseness to think (or at least to speak) chiefly on the subject of cold beef and port wine. There is not much to be said in defence of such conduct, but there is {↑ always} something to be said in defence of any possible conduct. I had travelled 250 miles, by Paterson‹s›. (the g^{t}. authority of those days)[3] – fasting from everything but ‹a› tea, a trifle of opium, and (as Falstaff observes of himself) from sin.[4] But this is ‹a› secondary matter: the first is – that in the recent event which at the time, and soon {↑ not long} afterwards struck me with hor. – so prof^{d}. There {↑ lurked} was in fact ‹buried› a funeral and a ‹mo› festival of joy: being on the very brink of the 1st, we issued into the second.

The young man settled his count. Steadfastly upon us [for a second]; and it ‹might be› for ‹x› {↑ 5} seconds {↑ (it maybe)} he sate like one y^{t} mused on some great purpose; for 5 he sate like one that prayed {↑ to God} in some ‹dre› vast {↑ perplexity} ‹extremity›, between 2 {↑ infinite dangers} ‹possible attempts› {↑ for wisdom} to make the better choice

[THE VISION OF SUDDEN DEATH]
MS VSD D

The manuscript is held in the Berg Collection, New York Public Library, and is catalogued as 'The English mail coach: Dream-fugue'. It is one page, measuring 285 by 185 mm, with writing in black ink on both recto and verso. The recto, however, is actually two separate pieces of paper: a shorter sheet has been aligned at the top and sides, and then pasted down over a longer sheet. The paste down is the opening passage of the manuscript, running from 'Thus as we ran like torrents' to '‹in a moment›'. It has not been possible to read or retrieve the writing underneath the paste down. The bottom sheet becomes visible at 'of {↑ massiest} purple granite'. The paste down is gray wove; the bottom sheet is a yellowing laid paper with part of a watermark visible.

Japp is more than likely responsible for the pasting together of the two manuscript sheets. This would be in line with his habitually unwarranted editorial interventions. He reprints an inaccurately edited version of the manuscript as 'The Ransom for Waterloo' (Japp, *PW*, vol.I pp. 323–5). For details of the 'Conventions for Manuscript Transcription', see above, p. xvii. For the occasion and context of 'The Vision of Sudden Death', see headnote, pp. 401–8.

[1 r.]

Thus as we ran like torrents, thus as with bridal rapture our flying equipage swept over the *Campo santo* of the graves, – thus as our burning wheels carried warrior instincts, kindled earthly passions, amongst the trembling dust below us – ‹dust of our noble fathers that had slept in God since Créci,› suddenly we became aware of a vast Necropolis from afar {↑ to which we were hurrying}. In a moment ‹from afar we were ‹a› bending› our maddening wheels were nearing it ‹in a moment we were running through its gates › ‹in a moment›

of {↑ massiest} purple granite {↑ in massiest piles} was this city of the dead, and yet {↑ ‹at again›} ‹for the› {↑ ‹in the› for one} ‹first› moment it lay like a {↑ visionary} purple stain on the horizon, so mighty was the distance. ‹Through› {↑ In} the second moment {↑ this purple city} ‹it› trembled through many changes, {↑ and grew ‹by› by fiery ‹coruscations› puli‹as›ations, so mighty was the pace. In the third moment {↑ already} with our dreadful gallop ‹already› we were entering, ‹The› {↑ its} suburbs ‹of this ancient›. ‹V Towers and› Systems of sarcophagi, ‹becrested with› {↑ having rose with ‹pl› crests,} aerial ‹turrets rising high into› {↑ of terraces and turrets ‹rose› ‹to› into the upper glooms, –} strode forward with haughty encroachment upon the central ‹ais› aisle, – ran back with mighty shadows into answering recesses. ‹Where the towers of› ‹As› {↑ Like} rivers in {↑ ‹the pomp of› horned} floods ‹that› wheeling {↑ in ‹soundless› pomps} round headlands {↑ of unfathom‹edless›{↑ ed} ‹of› waters} ‹as› {↑ like} hurricanes that ride into the secrets of forests, faster than ever light ‹unravelled the images› {↑ ‹linked›} {↑ travels through the wilderness} of darkness, ‹and our horses sweep shoot every angle and angle› we shot the angles – we ‹curved› {↑ fled} round the ‹fluent› curves of the ‹labyrinths before us.› {↑ labyrinthine ‹sarcophagi› infinite city.} ‹Where the ‹so› streets wheeled, there did our horses wheel. Up or down, by secret or by open wards, where the streets curved› – {↑ with the storms of our horses' feet,} ‹there did our horses curve – there did› {↑ and ‹with the chasm› of our} our burning wheels {↑ did we} carry earthly passions, kindle warrior instincts, amongst the {↑ silent} dust ‹below› {↑ around} us ‹and around› us – dust of our noble fathers that had slept in God since Créci. Every sarcophagus shewed many basreliefs; basreliefs of battles, basreliefs of battle-fields; ‹of› battles from forgotten ages, ‹of› battles from yesterday; ‹of› battle-fields that long since nature had healed and reconciled to herself with the sweet oblivion of flowers; ‹of› battle-fields, that were yet angry and crimson with carnage in all ‹And now had we reached the last sarcophagus,› And now had we reached the last sarcophagus already we were abreast

[1 v.]

of the last basrelief, already we were recovering the arrow-like flight of the ‹endless› central aisle, when coming up it in counterview to ourselves we beheld the frailest of cars – built as it might seem from floral wreaths, and ‹xx› and {↑ from} the shells of Indian Seas. ‹Silvery mists that went before it› half concealed {↑ hidden were} the fawns that drew it – by the {↑ floating] mists that {↑ floated} went before it in pomp. But the mists hid not the lovely countenance of the ‹in› infant girl that sate {↑ with a} upon the car, and hid not the birds of tropic plumage with which she played – Face to face she ‹came moved› rode {↑ forward} to meet us, And baby laughter ‹was› in her {↑ ‹confiding›} eyes {↑ at the ruin that approached} saluted {↑ under misgiving} ‹our laureled equipage, as for a moment we contemplated the ruin that was at hand.› {↑ the gorgeous cathedral} Oh baby, I ‹exclaimed› said in anguish, must we, that carry tidings of great joy to every people, be {↑ God's} messengers of ruin to thee. In horror I rose at the thought. But then also, in horror at the thought, rose one that was sculptured in the basrelief, – a dying trumpeter. Solemnly ‹to› from the field of Waterloo he rose to his feet; and, unslinging his stony trumpet, carried it in his dying anguish to his stony lips —— sounding once, and yet once again: proclamation, that to *thy* ears, oh baby, must have spoken from the battlements of death. Immediately deep shadows fell between us, and ‹mighty› {↑ mightiest} shuddering silence. The choir had ceased to sing: the uproar of our laureled equipage alarmed the graves no more. By horror the basrelief had been unlocked into life – By horror we that were so full of life – we men, and our horses with their fiery forelegs rising in mid air to their everlasting gallop were petrified to a basrelief. Oh glacial pagentry of death, that through {↑ from end to end} of the gorgeous cathedral {↑ for a moment} froze every eye ‹to› by contagion of ‹fr› panic! Then for the third time the trumpet sounded. Back with the shattering burst came the infinite rushing of life ‹once more›. The seals of frost were raised from our stiffening hearts ‹the roar of our thunders of›

THE VISION OF SUDDEN DEATH
MS VSD E

The manuscript is held at the National Library of Scotland as MS 4789, ff. 1–32. It consists of sixteen single sheets and eight geminate leaves. The entire manuscript is written in black ink now faded to brown. Ff. 1–26 and 31–2 are on white paper; ff. 27–30 are on blue paper. Most sheets measure 180 by 230 mm, but others vary in size from 110 by 185 mm to 190 by 320 mm. Ff. 8, 10, 13 and 15 are watermarked 1847; f. 26 appears to be watermarked 'J Dewdrey 1848', but this is difficult to read and cannot be confirmed. No other sheets carry watermarks. All sheets are written on the recto only, except f. 21, which contains writing on the recto and verso, and f. 27, which contains writing on the recto and a fragment in De Quincey's hand taped to the verso. The manuscript contains hundreds of substantive variants, including three discarded footnotes, one of which concerns an Oxford student's '*act* of gambling' and '*habit* of gambling' (see below, p. 465), and another of which incorporates lines from Dante's *Divine Comedy* (see below, p. 480). John Wilson, a close friend and astute critic of De Quincey, once observed that, in De Quincey, 'the best word always comes up'. The manuscript is perhaps the finest example of how hard De Quincey worked to ensure that happened (George Gilfillan, 'De Quincey' in *Sketches Literary and Theological*, ed. Frank Henderson (Edinburgh: Douglas, 1881), p. 33). For the most detailed discussion of the manuscript, see Richard H. Byrns, 'De Quincey's Revisions in the "Dream-Fugue"' in *Publications of the Modern Language Association*, 77 (1962), pp. 97–101; see also Byrns, 'A Note on De Quincey's "The Vision of Sudden Death"' in *Notes and Queries*, 9 (1962), pp. 184–5.

For details of the 'Conventions for Manuscript Transcription', see above, p. xvii. For the occasion and context of 'The Vision of Sudden Death', see headnote, pp. 401–8.

[1 r.]
B1

II. The Vision of Sudden Death

What is to be thought of Sudden Death? It is remarkable that {↑ in different conditions of society} it has been {↑ variously regarded} ‹specially noticed, in different conditions of society› as the ‹thing› consummation of an earthly career most fervently to be desired, and ‹again› on the other hand as that consummation which is most {↑ of all} ‹devoutly› to be deprecated. Caesar the Dictator, at his last dinner party [*caena*], and the very evening before his assassination, being questioned as to the mode of death which {↑ ‹he regarded as› in *his* opinion might seem the} ‹in his opinion seemed the› most eligible, replied – 'That which should be ‹the› most sudden'. On the other hand, the divine Litany of our English Church, when breathing forth supplications {↑ as if} ‹as if› {↑ in some representative character} for the whole human race prostrate before God, places such a death in the very van of horrors. "From lightning and tempest; from plague, pestilence, and famine; from battle and murder, and from sudden death, – *Good Lord, deliver us*." {↑ ‹Strange schism›} Sudden death is here made to crown the {↑ very} climax in a grand ascent of calamities: {↑ it is the last of curses;} ‹Possibly the reader may wonder that I notice› ‹It is treated as a capital curse› and yet by {↑ the noblest of} ‹a stern› Romans it is treated as the {↑ first} ‹greatest› of blessings. In that difference, most readers will see {↑ little more than} ‹only› the ‹the› difference between Christianity and Paganism. But there I hesitate. The ‹English› Christian church may be right in its estimate of Sudden Death; and it is {↑ a} natural feeling, though after all it may {↑ also} be {↑ an infirm one}, ‹a mere expression of human weakness›, to wish for a quiet dismissal from life – as that which {↑ *seems*} ‹is› most reconcilable with meditation, with penitential retrospects, and with the humilities of farewell prayer. There does not however occur to me any direct scriptural warrant for this ‹petition› earnest petition of the English litany. ‹And, however *that* may be, ‹**x**› two remarks I desire to offer as tending to correct or to modify a doctrine, which else has sometimes passed into a superstition. The first›

[2 r.][1]

It seems rather a petition ‹allowable› {↑ indulged} to human infirmity ‹as an indulgence›, than ex‹pected› {↑ acted} from human piety ‹as a debt to God›. And, however *that* may be, two remarks suggest themselves as prudent ‹modifi› restraints upon a doctrine, which else {↑ *may* wander and ‹**x**› sometimes} *has* ‹often› wandered into ‹a superstition› an uncharitable superstition. The first is this: that many people {↑ are likely to} exaggerate the horror of a sudden death [I mean the *objective* horror to him who contemplates such a death, not the *subjective* horror to him who suffers it] {↑ ‹since›} ‹for *that* can admit of no conceivable mis valuation›] from the false disposition to lay a stress upon words or acts {↑ simply because by an} ‹simply as› accident‹ally being› {↑ ‹they were›} ‹the final words or acts of the dying person›. {↑ not foreseen they have become final words or acts.} If a man dies for instance by some sudden death when he ‹is in› happens to be intoxicated, such a death is regarded with peculiar horror; {↑ as though the intoxication were suddenly exalted into a blasphemy.} But ‹this› *that* is unphilosophic. The man was, or he was not, *habitually* a drunkard. If not, if his intoxication were a ‹rare or› solitary accident, there can be no reason ‹x› at all for allowing a‹ny› special emphasis to this ‹trespass sim› act simply because {↑ through misfortune it became} ‹it was casually it was› his final act. Nor on the other hand, if {↑ it were} no accident but one of his *habitual* transgressions, will it be {↑ the} more habitual or the more a transgression, because ‹during its a› {↑ some} sudden calamity surprising him has caused this habitual ‹transgressive act› {↑ transgression} to be also a final {↑ one.} ‹act transgression›. ‹Had› {↑ Could} the man {↑ have had any reason} even dimly ‹foreseen› to foresee his {↑ own} sudden death, there would have been a new feature in his act of intemperance {↑ intemperance} – a feature of presumption and irreverence ‹But this is not part of the case supposed› {↑ as} in one that by possibility felt himself {↑ drawing near to} ‹approaching› the presence of God. But this is no part of the case supposed. And the only new element in ‹his› {↑ the man's} act is not any element of extra immortality, but {↑ simply} of extra misfortune.*

The other remark has reference to the meaning of the word *sudden*.

[3 r.]

* If a father, visiting without {↑ warning} ‹notice› his son ‹a student› an Oxford student, should find him at a gaming table, he would naturally be entitled to ‹view› {↑ argue from} this ‹vice a sin as› *act* of gambling as {↑ from} a *habit* of gambling: {↑ since there} ‹for he› could {↑ be} ‹have› no reasonable licence for presuming ‹that that the› {↑ any} act, in which by chance he should detect his son, ‹was› {↑ to be} one contradicting the whole tenor of that son's ordinary life. The laws of probability would not allow of such ‹an an indulgent› {↑ construction} ‹judgement›. ‹Yet› And yet by possibility the case might really be of that exceptional {↑ and improbable} character. It is the limited vision of man, and the necessity of his adhering to the laws of probability, which would coerce an earthly father into error in such circumstances. But a heavenly father‹,›, not limited in vision, not tied to laws of ‹pro› likelihood, is under no such coercion. And it is therefore deliberately to load God with the infirmities of man, when we allow ourselves to think that a man's intoxication has any separate horror in it from the accident of his dying under that intoxication. This ‹x› in effect to suppose that God would anthropomorphitically judge an act – not by its intrinsic qualities or tendencies – but by its scenical position, as a dramatic incident calculated for stage effects.

[4 r.]
B 3
‹It› {↑ And it} is a ‹xxx› strong illustration of the {↑ duty} ‹call› which ‹alwa› forever {↑ calls us} ‹summons us› to the stern valuation of words – that very possibly Caesar ‹on the one hand› and the Christian Church ‹on the other,› do not differ in the way supposed; that is {↑ do not differ} ‹not› by any difference of doctrine as between Pagan and Christian views of {↑ the} moral temper {↑ appropriate to death}; but that they are contemplating different cases. Both contemplate a violent death; a {↑ Βιαθανατος} death that is Βιαιος: but the difference is – that the Roman by the word ‹*sudden*› "sudden" means an *unlingering* death: whereas the Christian litany ‹means› by ‹*sudden*› "sudden" {↑ means} a death *without warning*, consequently without any {↑ available} summons to {↑ religious} preparation. The poor mutineer, who kneels down to gather into his heart the bullets from twelve firelocks of his pitying comrades, dies by a most sudden death in Caesar's sense: one ‹mighty› shock, one mighty spasm, ‹and all is over› one (‹and perhaps› {↑ ‹but›} {↑ possibly} *not* one) groan, and all is over. But in the sense of the Litany his death is ‹*not*› {↑ far from} sudden: {↑ his offence originally,} his imprisonment, his trial, the interval between his sentence and its execution, having all furnished him with separate warnings of his fate; having all summoned him to meet it with solemn preparation.

Meantime, whatever may be thought of a sudden death as a {↑ mere} ‹mode of anguish that is inevitable› variety in the modes of {↑ dying} ‹death›, when death is {↑ in some shape} ‹at any rate› inevitable, – [a question which ‹either on› equally in the Roman and the Christian sense will be ‹di› variously answered according to {↑ each man's variety of} ‹every man's› temperament,] – ‹the capital anxiety it is certain that› {↑ certainly} upon one aspect of sudden death there can be no {↑ ‹rational›} {↑ opening for} doubt ‹or variety of opinions, viz.›{↑ ‹rational›} that ‹if› of all agonies incident to man it is the most frightful, ‹this› {↑ that of all martyrdoms it is *the* most} ‹most of a› freezing ‹martyrdom› to human sensibilities {↑ viz.} where it surprises a man under circumstances which offer (or which seem to offer) some {↑ hurried and} inappreciable chance of ‹facing it and› evading it. Any effort, by which such an

[5 r.]
B 4
evasion can be accomplished, must be as sudden as the danger which it affronts. Even *that*, even the sickening necessity for hurrying in extremity where all hurry {↑ seems destined to} ‹may› be vain, {↑ or ‹if not vain it seems sure to be›} ‹where may be› self-baffled, and where the dreadful knell of *Too late* is already {↑ sounding in the ears by anticipation} ‹killing the fluttering energies›, even that anguish is ‹surer› liable to a hideous exasperation in

one particular case, viz. where the agonizing appeal ‹of the moment› is made not {↑ exclusively} ‹merely› exclusively to the instinct of self-preservation, but to the conscience on behalf of another life besides your ‹own thrown upon your› {↑ own} accidentally {↑ cast} upon *your* ‹protection› protection. To fail, to collapse, in a service {↑ merely} ‹exclusively› your own – ‹may› {↑ might} seem comparatively venial; {↑ though in fact it is far from venial.} But to fail in a case, where providence has suddenly thrown into your hands the final interests of another – of a fellow creature shuddering between the gates of life and ‹instant› death, this to a ‹consci› man of apprehensive conscience would mingle the misery of an atrocious criminality with the misery of a bloody calamity. ‹You are He› {↑ The man} is called upon ‹pr› {↑ too probably} to die; but to die at the very moment when by ‹a› {↑ any} momentary collapse he is self-{↑ denounced} ‹convicted› as a murderer. He had but the twinkling of an eye for his effort; and that effort might at the best have been unavailing: but from this ‹c› shadow of a chance, ‹however valued› {↑ small or great} on the scale of heaven, he has recoiled by a treasonable *lacheté*. The effort *might* have been ‹utterly› without hope: but to have risen to the ‹alti› level of that effort – would have rescued him, though not from dying, yet from dying as a conscious traitor.

The situation here contemplated exposes a dreadful ulcer ‹in› lurking far down in the depths of human nature. It is not that men generally are summoned to face such awful trials. But potentially ‹and darkly the {↑ ‹dark›} shadows are›

[6 r.]
B 5

{↑ and in shadowy} outline ‹of› such a trial is moving ‹under ground› subterraneously in perhaps all men's natures, {↑ muttering under ground in one world to be realised perhaps in some other.} Upon the secret mirror of our dreams such a trial is {↑ darkly} exhibited at intervals perhaps to every one of us. That dream ‹of› so familiar to childhood of meeting a lion, and from ‹sick› languishing ‹surrender of hope› prostration in hope and vital energy ‹of› that {↑ constant} sequel of lying down before him, publishes the secret vice of human nature – {↑ reveals} its deep-seated {↑ Pariah} falsehood to itself – {↑ records} its abysmal treachery. Perhaps not one of us escapes that dream: perhaps, as by some sorrowful doom of man, that dream repeats for every one of us {↑ through every generation} the original temptation in Eden. Every one of us in this dream has a bait offered to the infirm places of his {↑ own individual} will: once again a snare is made ready for leading {↑ him} ‹us› into captivity to the ‹vol› {↑ ‹a›} luxury of ruin: ‹once› again {↑ as in aboriginal Paradise} the man falls {↑ from innocence}: ‹and› {↑ once} again ‹the› by infinite iteration ‹the› the ancient ‹mother› Earth ‹sighs› {↑ groans} to God ‹for the› through ‹all› her {↑ secret} caves over the weakness of her child; ‹and forth this once again does› "Nature from her seat sighing through all her works" {↑ again "gives} ‹Give› sighs of woe that all is lost": and again the counter sigh is repeated {↑ to the sorrowing ‹heavens› heavens} of the endless rebellion against God. Many people think that one man, the patriarch of ‹his› {↑ our} race, could not in his single person execute {↑ this rebellion} ‹the rebellion of› {↑ for} all his race. Perhaps they are wrong. But, {↑ even} if {↑ not} ‹they are right›, perhaps in {↑ the world ‹of›} ‹some shadowy trials› of dreams everyone of us ratifies {↑ for himself} the original act. {↑ ‹through›} ‹by which imperfectly he was {↑ ‹already›} affected from his birth.› Our English rite of 'Confirmation,' by which in years of awakened reason we take upon us the ‹unconscious› engagements contracted for us in our slumbering infancy, how sublime a‹n act of satisfaction› {↑ rite} is that! The little postern gate through which the baby ‹had been› in its cradle had been silently placed for a time within the glory of God's countenance, suddenly rises to the clouds as a triumphal arch through

[7 r.]
B 6
which, with banners displayed {↑ and martial pomps}, we make our second ‹en› entry as crusading soldiers militant {↑ for God} by {↑ personal} choice and {↑ by} sa‹**x**›{↑ cra}mental oath ‹for God›. Each man says in effect – "Lo! I rebaptise myself, and that, which once was {↑ sworn} ‹promised› on my behalf, now I ‹promise› {↑ swear} for myself." Even so in dreams ‹there is involved› ‹**x**› perhaps {↑ under} ‹in› some ‹shadowy› {↑ secret} conflict of the {↑ midnight} sleeper, ‹as is couched a ratification of woe corresponding to this baptismal ratification of joyous hope rest and hope a God Perhaps, though in darkness as regards his› lighted up to the consciousness at the time, but darkened to the memory as soon as all ‹a› is finished, – each several child of our mysterious race completes ‹**x**› for himself the

[8 r.]
B 7
As I drew near to the Manchester P. Office, I found that it was considerably past midnight, but to my great relief, as it was important for me to be in Westmorland by the morning, I saw by the huge saucer eyes of the mail, blazing through the gloom of ‹a d› overhanging ‹houss›, {↑ houses} that ‹I wa the› my chance was not yet lost. Past the time it was; but ‹for some› by some luck‹ily**x**› very unusual {↑ in *my* experience,} ‹for *me* to meet with› the mail was not even yet ready to start. I ascended to my ‹seat› seat on the box, where my cloak was still lying as {↑ it had lain} ‹I had left it› at the Bridgewater arms. {↑ I had left it there ‹in› in imitation of ‹that›} ‹a› a nautical discoverer, who leaves a bit of bunting {↑ on ‹his› the shore of his discovery} ‹to› by way

of warning ‹all mankind› off the ground {↑ the whole human race,} and signalising to ‹Chr› the Christian and the Heathen worlds, with his best Compliments, that he has planted his throne for ever upon that virgin soil; ‹has› henceforward ‹has› {↑ claiming} the *jus dominii* to the top of the atmosphere above it, and {↑ also} the right of driving shafts to the centre of the earth below it; ‹and› {↑ so} that all people found ‹in there› after this warning {↑ either aloft in the atmosphere, or ‹**xx**› in the shafts, or squatting on the soil} will be treated as trespassers, {↑ that is, decapitated,} by their very faithful and obedient servant, the owner of the said bunting. Possibly my cloak might ‹have› not have been respected, and the *jus gentium* might have been cruelly violated in my person, – for, ‹if the› in the dark, people commit deeds of darkness, gas being a great ally of morality, – but it so happened that on this night there was no other outside passenger; and the crime, {↑ which else was but too probable,} missed fire for want of a criminal. By the way, I may as well mention (‹since› at this point, since ‹it› {↑ a ‹severe› circumstantial accuracy ‹is›} is essential ‹that› to the effect of my narration, ‹that *all* its circum› that there was no other person of any ‹class or› description {↑ whatsoever} about the mail, ‹except a› the guard, the coachman, and myself being allowed for, except only one – a horrid creature of the class {↑ known to the world as} ‹called› insiders, but whom young Oxford called sometimes 'Trojans' in opposition to our Grecian selves, and sometimes 'vermin'. A Turkish effendi, who piques himself on ‹politeness› good breeding, will never mention by name a pig. ‹Too› {↑ Yet it} ‹It› is but too often that he has occasion to mention this animal;

[9 r.]
B 8

since constantly in the streets of Stamboul he ‹is› has his trousers deranged {↑ or polluted} by this vile creature running between his legs. But ‹un› under any excess of hurry he {↑ is} always {↑ careful} ‹thinks it› {↑ out of} respect‹ful› to the company he is dining with, to ‹call the wretch› suppress the odious name, and to call the wretch "that other creature"; as though all ‹organised› animal life beside formed one groupe, and this odious beast (to whom, as Chrysippus observed, salt serves as an apology for a soul) formed another and alien groupe on the outside of creation. Now I who am an English effendi, that think myself ‹as well-bred› to understand good-breeding as well as any son of Othman, beg my reader's pardon for {↑ having} mention‹ing›{↑ ed} an insider by his gross natural name. I shall do so no more: and, if I should have occasion to ‹speak of so› glance at so painful a subject, I shall always call him "that other creature." Let us hope however that no such distressing {↑ occasion} ‹necessity› will arise. But by the way {↑ an occasion} ‹a necessity› arises {↑ at} this moment. For the reader will be sure to ask, when we come to the story, "Was this other creature present?" He was *not*: or more correctly perhaps ‹I should have said› – *It* was not. We dropped the creature, or the creature by natural imbecility dropped itself, within the first 11 miles from Manchester. In the latter case, I wish to make a ‹high› philosophic remark of a moral tendency. When I die, or when the reader dies, and by repute suppose of fever, – it will never be known whether he died ‹by› {↑ in reality of} the fever or ‹by› {↑ of} the doctor. But ‹such are the compensations observed in› this other creature in the case of dropping out of the coach will enjoy a coroner's inquest: consequently he will enjoy an epitaph. For I insist upon it – that the verdict of a coroner's jury makes the best of epitaphs. It is brief, so that the public all find time to read it; it is ‹pithy› pithy, so that the ‹fr› surviving friends (if any *can* survive such a loss) remember it without fatigue; it is upon oath, so that rascals and Dr Johnsons cannot ‹pick it to pieces.› {↑ pick holes in it.} "Died ‹by› {↑ through} the visitation of intense stupidity ‹by› {↑ by ‹through›} impinging on a moonlight night against the off hind wheel of the Glasgow Mail!‹"› – Deodand upon the said wheel – 2 pence." What a simple lapidary inscription! ‹How clearly the› All the {cut across manuscript removes half the final line} {↑ nobody much in the wrong but an off wheel with few acquaintances;} railways shares; ‹all accounts settled on the spot,›

[10 r.]
B 9

and if it were but rendered into ‹classical› {↑ choice} Latin, though there would be a {↑ little bother} ‹difficulty› in finding a Ciceronian ‹phrase› {↑ word} for 'off-wheel', ‹Morcellus h› Morcellus himself that great master of Sepulchral eloquence could not shew a better. Why I call this little remark *moral*, is – ‹that› from the compensations it points out. Here {↑ by the supposition} is ‹a› that other creature on the one side, the beast of the world; and he (or it) gets an epitaph. You and I on the contrary ‹get none› the pride of our friends, get none,

But why linger on the subject of vermin? – Having mounted the box, I took a small quant‹t›ity of laudanum, having already travelled 250 miles, viz. {↑ from a point} 70 miles beyond London, upon a simple breakfast. In ‹this› {↑ thus taking the laudanum} there was nothing extraordinary. But by accident it drew upon me the {↑ special} attention of my assessor on the box, the coachman. And in *that* there was nothing extraordinary. But by accident, and with great delight, {↑ it drew my attention to the fact} ‹I saw› that ‹x› {↑ the} coachman was a monster in point of size, and that he had but one eye. In fact he had been foretold by Virgil as

> Monstrum horrendum, ‹in› informe, ingens, cui lumen ademptum.

He ‹was l› answered in every point: a monster he was – dreadful, shapeless, huge, who had lost an eye. But why should *that* delight me? Had he been one of the calendars in the Arabian Nights, and had paid down his eye as the price of his criminal curiosity, what right had *I* to exult in his misfortune? I did *not* exult: I delighted in no man's punishment, though it were {↑ even} merited. But these personal distinctions identified in an instant an old friend of mine, whom I had known in the ‹Sou› South for some years as the most masterly of mail coachmen. He was the man {↑ in all Europe} that could ‹have› {↑ best have} undertaken to drive six-in-hand full gallop over *Al Sirat*, that famous bridge of Mahomet over the bottomless gulph, ‹on which as where the error of a› backing himself against the Prophet and 20 such fellows. I used to call him *Cyclops mastigophorous* Cyclops the whip-bearer, until I observed that his skill made whips useless, except to fetch off an impertinent fly from ‹his› a leader's head: upon which I changed his Grecian name to Cyclops *diphrélates* (Cyclops the Charioteer). I and others known to me studied under him the diphre‹a›latic art. Excuse reader a word too elegant to be pedantic. And also take this remark from me, as a

[11 r.]
B 10
gage d'amitié – that no word ever was or *can* be pedantic which ‹is› {↑ by} support‹s›{↑ ing} a distinction {↑ supports} ‹useful to› the accuracy of logic, or {↑ which} fills up a chasm for the understanding. As a pupil, though I paid extra fees, I cannot say that I stood high in his esteem. It shewed his dogged honesty, (though observe not his discernment) that he could not see my merits. ‹And he vexed me by not even *hoping* well of me: which was intolerable: charity hopeth all things.›[2] Perhaps we ought to excuse his absurdity in this particular by remembering his want of an eye. *That* made him blind to my merits. ‹However we always met and parted excellent friends. In my heart I honored his honest refusal to flatter me on my ‹driving› accomplishments, since he really could not see them, absurd and› Irritating as {↑ this} ‹that› blindness was, {↑ (‹it› surely it could not be envy?) he always courted} ‹He on his part liked› my conversation; in which ‹great› art I certainly had the whip hand of him. On this occasion great joy was at our meeting. ‹All our little pointings and miffs were went unremembered. My inflated stupidity was forgotten by utterly forgotten by me the insulted party, by him the insulter his dense brutal insensibility› But what was ‹he› Cyclops doing here? ‹Was he the› Had the medical men recommended northern air, or how? – I collected from such ‹**xxx** {↑ ‹partial›} explanations ‹which› {↑ as} he volunteered – that he had some interest at stake in a ‹trial› suit-at-law depending at Lancaster; so that probably he had got himself transferred to this station for the purpose of connecting ‹his diphre‹**x**›latic with his legaling› {↑ with his} professional pursuits {↑ an instant readiness for the} ‹with his the momentary› calls of his law-suit.

Meantime, what are we stopping for? Surely we've been waiting long enough. Oh this procrastinating ‹Post Office› Mail, and {↑ oh} this procrastinating Post-Office! – Can't they take a lesson {↑ upon that subject} from *me?* ‹You› {↑ Some people have called *me* procrastinating. Now you} are witness, reader, that I was in time for *them*. But can *they* lay their hands on their hearts, and say that they were in time for me? ‹They've kept me waiting {↑ ‹for›} a full 20 minutes, which it is ‹not› not every man than that can bear philosophically›. {↑ I during my life have often had to wait for the Post-office: the Post-Office never waited a minute for me.} – What are they about? The guard tells me – that there ‹are› is ‹**xx** an unusually› large extra {↑ accumulation} ‹amount.› of foreign mails this night, owing to the irregularities caused by war and by ‹the› the packet-service, where ‹all› as yet ‹is› {↑ nothing is} done by ‹sailing vessels› steam. For an *extra* hour, it seems, the P. Office has been {tear} thrashing out the pure wheaten correspondence of Glasgow, and winnowing it from the {cut across manuscript removes final line}

[12 r.]
B 11
chaff of all baser intermediate towns. We can hear their flails {↑ going} at this moment. But at last all is finished. ‹S› Sound your horn, guard. Manchester, good bye; ‹and Salford,[3] good bye **x**› we've lost an hour by your criminal conduct at the Post Office: which, ‹though› however, though I do not mean to part with a‹s ostensible› {↑ servicable} ground of complaint, and one which ‹is› really {↑ is} such for the horses, to me ‹is› secretly {↑ is} an advantage, since it compels us to recover ‹our› this {↑ lost} hour amongst the next 8 or 9. Off we are {↑ at last} and at ‹12› {↑ 11} miles an hour: and ‹as yet› {↑ at first} I detect no change in the energy, or {↑ in} the skill ‹without an effort,› of ‹my› Cyclops. ‹my worthy but undiscerning friend.›

From Manchester to Kendal, which ‹virt› virtually (though not ‹for› in law) is the capital of Westmorland, were at this time ‹11› 7 stages of eleven miles each. The first 5 of these {↑ ‹where if› dated from Manchester} terminated ‹at› in Lancaster, which was therefore 55 miles north of Manchester, and the same distance exactly from Liverpool. The first 3 terminated in Preston (called, by way of distinction from other {↑ towns of that name} ‹Prestons›, *proud* Preston); at which {↑ place} ‹town› it was, {↑ that the separate roads from} ‹the› Liverpool and {↑ from} Manchester ‹roads› to the North became confluent. Within these first 3 stages lay ‹our› the {↑ foundation, the progress ‹in steps,›} ‹growth› and termination of our night's adventure. During the first stage I found out that Cyclops was mortal: he was liable to the ‹dread› shocking affection of sleep: a thing which I had ‹not› {↑ never} previously ‹supposed as possible› suspected. If a man is addicted to {↑ the vicious habit of} sleeping, all the skill in aurigation of Apollo himself ‹will not› with the horses of ‹Apollo's car› Aurora to execute ‹his w› the motions of his will, avail him nothing. "Oh Cyclops!" I exclaimed more than once, "Cyclops, my friend, thou art mortal. Thou snorest." Through this first eleven miles however ‹Cyclops› he betrayed his infirmity, which I grieve to say he shared with the whole Pagan Pantheon, only by short snatches. ‹He› On waking up, he made an apology for himself which instead of mending the matter laid an ominous foundation for coming disasters ‹he had in fact been kept out of his bed for 3 nights and days› The summer Assizes were now proceeding at Lancaster: in consequence of which for 3 nights and 3 days he had not lain down in a bed. During the day he was waiting for the uncertain summons ‹to› as a witness on the trial in which he was interested; or he was drinking with the other witnesses under the vigilant

[13 r.]
B 12

‹inspection suf› surveillance of the attorneys. During the night, ‹he was› or that part of it when the least temptations existed to ‹drink› conviviality, he was driving. Throughout the second stage he grew more and more drowsy. In the second mile of the third {↑ stage} he ‹fell yielded› surrendered himself finally and without a struggle to this perilous temptation. ‹Seven atmospheres of sleep seemed› All his past resistance had but deepened the weight of ‹his› this final oppression. Seven atmospheres of sleep seemed resting upon him. And, to consummate the case, our worthy guard, ‹soon after had› after singing 'Love amongst the roses' for the $50^{th.}$ or $60^{th.}$ time without any invitation from ‹the co› Cyclops or myself, and without applause for his past labors, had moodily resigned himself to {↑ slumbers} ‹a sleep› – not so deep {↑ doubtless} ‹probably› as the coachman's, but deep enough for mischief; and having probably no similar excuse. And thus at last about ten miles from Preston I found myself left in charge of H. M's London and Glasgow mail – then running about eleven miles an hour.

What makes this negligence less criminal, than else it must have been thought, was the general condition of the roads during the assizes. At that time all the law business of populous Liverpool, and of populous Manchester with its ‹populous› vast cincture of populous rural districts, was ‹xx› called up by ‹law› ancient usage to the ‹Lilliputian› tribunal of Lilliputian Lancaster. To break up this old traditional usage required a conflict with powerful established interests, ‹and with› a ‹new› large ‹preparation› {↑ system} of new arrangements, and a new Parliamentary statute. ‹At present› As things were at present, twice in the year so vast a body of business rolled northwards from the southern quarter of the country, that a fortnight at least ‹was› occupied {↑ the severe exertions of two judges for its} ‹by› its despatch. ‹two judges sitting constantly All day long the› The consequence of this was – that every horse available for such a service along the whole line of road and working ‹to exhaustion› in carrying down the multitudes of people who were parties to the different suits. ‹A› By sunset therefore it usually happened that, through utter exhaustion amongst men and horses, the roads were all silent. Except the exhaustion in the {↑ vast} adjacent county of York from a contested election, nothing like it was ordinarily witnessed

[14 r.]
B 13
in England.

On this occasion‹ally› the usual silence and solitude prevailed along the road. Not a hoof nor a wheel {↑ was to} ‹could› be heard. And ‹it happened also›, to strengthen this {↑ false luxurious} confidence in the noiseless roads, {↑ it happened also} that the night was one of peculiar solemnity and peace. ‹The› I myself, though slightly alien to the possibilities of peril, had so far yielded to the influence of the ‹mighty› {↑ mighty} calm as to sink into a profound reverie. The month was August, in which ‹(as it happened)› lay my own birth-day; a‹n› ‹solemn anniversary moving profound› {↑ festival to every thoughtful man suggesting solemn} and often {↑ sigh-born[*]} ‹half-sorrowful› thoughts. ‹to every meditative man's› The county was my own native county, – upon which in its southern section, more than upon any equal area known to man, {↑ past or present,} had descended the {↑ original} curse of labor in its heaviest form {↑ not mastering the bodies of men only as of slaves {↑ or criminals} in mines, but working through the fiery wills} Upon no equal space of earth, was or ever had been ‹were equal› {↑ the same} energy of human powers ‹been› put forth daily. ‹The drea› At this particular ‹period› {↑ season} also of {↑ the Assizes} that dreadful hurricane of {↑ flight and pursuit, ‹as› it ‹seemed› might have seemed to a stranger,} ‹a flying motions› that swept ‹the length of the county› to and from Lancaster all day long, hunting the county up and down, and regularly subsiding ‹at› about sunset, united with the permanent ‹character› distinction‹s› of ‹the cou› Lancashire as ‹a› the very metropolis and citadel of labor, to point the thoughts pathetically upon that ‹rest› {↑ counter} vision of rest, ‹and› of saintly repose from {↑ strife ‹strife› and} sorrow, ‹to› {↑ towards} which as to their secret haven ‹all› the profoundest {↑ aspirations} ‹feelings› of ‹man's› man's heart are continually ‹tending› {↑ travelling}. Obliquely we were ‹n› nearing the {↑ sea} ‹sea› upon our left, which also must under the present circumstances be {↑ repeating the general} ‹profoundly at rest› state of halcyon repose. ‹And And› The ‹air› atmosphere and the light ‹were› bore {↑ an orchestral} part ‹like› in this {↑ universal} ‹exquisite› lull. Moonlight

[*] "sigh-born": I owe {↑ the suggestion of this word} ‹this expression› to ‹the› {↑ an obscure} remembrance of a beautiful {↑ phrase} ‹expression› in Giraldus Cambrensis viz. *suspiriosae cogitationes*.

and the first ‹timid› ‹brief› trembling of the dawn were now blending; and ‹both were› the blendings were brought into a still more exquisite state of unity by a slight silvery mist ‹that› motionless and dreamy that covered the woods and fields, but with a ‹transparent covering› veil of equable transparency. Except the feet of our own horses, which, ‹made little sound› ‹made little disturbance› running on a sandy margin of the road, made little disturbance, there was no sound abroad. In ‹spite of all which the villain of a schoolmaster›

[15 r.]
B 14
the clouds and on the earth, prevailed the same majestic peace: and in spite of all that the villain of a schoolmaster has done for the ruin of our sublimer thoughts, which are the thoughts of our infancy, we still ‹like an› believe in no such nonsense as a limited atmosphere. Whatever we may swear with our {↑ ‹lying›} ‹lips, we still believe with our› {↑ false feigning lips, in our faithful} hearts {↑ we still} believe {↑ and must forever believe} in ‹aerial› fields of air traversing the total gulph between earth and the central heavens. Still in the confidence of children that tread without fear *every* chamber in their father's house, and to ‹whom› whom no ‹portals are› {↑ door is} closed, we ‹ascend› in that sabbatic vision which sometimes is revealed {↑ for an hour} upon nights ‹holy as› {↑ like} this {↑ ascend with easy steps} from the sorrow-stricken fields of earth ‹to the› upwards to the sandals of God.

Suddenly from thoughts like these I was awakened to a ‹far off› {↑ sullen} sound as of some motion on the distant roads. ‹The murmur› {↑ It} stole upon the ‹x› air for a moment; I listened in ‹fear› awe; but then it died away. Once ‹awakened› {↑ roused} however I could not but observe with alarm the ‹in› quickened motion of our horses. ‹M from long ex› Ten years' experience had made my eye learned in ‹the› the valuing of motion; and I saw that we were {↑ now} running thirteen ‹motions› miles an hour. I pretend to no presence of mind. On the contrary my fear is – that I am {↑ miserably and shamefully} ‹unusually› deficient in that quality as regards action. The palsy of doubt and {↑ distraction} ‹hesitation› hangs like ‹a› {↑ some} guilty weight of dark unfathomed remembrances upon my energies, when the signal is flying for *action*. But on the other hand this accursed gift I have, as regards *thought*, that in the first step {↑ towards} ‹of any calamity› the possibility of a misfortune I see its total evolution: in the radix {↑ already} I ‹read› see too certainly and too instantly its ‹wh› entire expansion – in the first ‹elu› syllable of the dreadful sentence I read already the last. ‹On the present occasion› {↑ ‹At› }It was not that I feared for ourselves. What could injure *us*? Our bulk and impetus charmed us ‹from› {↑ against} peril in any collision. And I had {↑ survived} rode through {↑ too} ‹so› many {↑ hundreds of} perils, that were frightful to approach, that were matter of laughter as we ‹flew› looked back upon them‹.› for any anxiety to rest upon *our* interests. ‹On the box of the mail I had› The mail was not built, ‹nor› I felt assured, nor

[16 r.]
B 15
bespoke, that could betray *us* who trusted to its protection. But any carriage that we could meet would be frail‹er› and light‹er› in comparison of ourselves. And I remarked this ominous ‹circums› accident of our situation. We were on the wrong side of the road. ‹the› {↑ But then the} other party, if other there was, ‹seeing our lamps which were still lighted, would ex trust to us for quartering. But perhaps they› {↑ might} also ‹might› be on the wrong side; and two wrongs might make a right. *That* was not likely. The same motion which had drawn ‹*our* horses› *us* to the right{↑ -hand} side of the road, viz. the soft beaten sand as contrasted with the paved centre, would ‹have drawn› {↑ prove attractive to} others. Our lamps, still lighted, would give the impression of vigilance on our part. And every creature, that met us, would rely upon *us* for quartering.* All this, and if the separate links of the anticipation had been a thousand times more, I saw – not discursively {↑ or by effort} – but {↑ as} by one flash of ‹intuition› horrid intuition.

Under this steady, though rapid anticipation of the evil which *might* be gathering ahead, ah {↑ readers!} what a sullen mystery of fear, what a sigh of {↑ woe} ‹sorrow›, seemed to steal upon the air – as again the far off sound of a wheel was heard! – A whisper it was, a whisper from perhaps 4 miles off, ‹that› secretly announc{↑ ing}‹ed› a ruin that, being foreseen, was not the less inevitable. What could be done, who was it that could ‹attempt anything› {↑ do it,}, to ‹stop› check the storm flight of these maniacal horses. But could I not seize the ‹reig› reins from the grasp of the ‹slu› slumbering coachman? You, reader, think that it would have been in *your* power to do so. And I quarrel not with your estimate of yourself. But from the way in which the coachman's hand was {↑ viced} ‹locked› between his upper and lower ‹le› thigh, this was impossible. The guard sub-

[17 r.]
B 16
sequently found it impossible, after this danger had passed. Not the grasp only but also the position of ‹Cyclops› this Polyphemus made ‹it› the attempt impossible. You {↑ still think otherwise. See then} ‹see› that bronze equestrian statue. The cruel rider has kept the bit in his horse's ‹mouth› mouth for two centuries. ‹Take› Unbridle him for a minute, if you please, and wash his

* "*quartering*": – this is the technical word; and, I presume, derived from the French *cartayer*, to evade a rut or any obstacle.

mouth with water. Or stay, reader, unhorse me that marble emperor: knock me those marble feet from those marble stirrups of Charlemagne.

The sounds ahead strengthened, and were now clearly the sounds of wheels. Who ‹could› and what could it be? Was it industry in a taxed cart? Was it youthful gaiety in a gig? – Whoever it was, something must be attempted to warn them. ‹In› {↑ Upon} the other party rests the active {↑ responsibility}: but upon *us,* and, woe is me, that *us* was my‹self› single self, rests the responsibility of warning. Yet how should this be accomplished? Might I not seize the guard's horn? – Already on the first thought I was making my way over the roof to the guard's seat. But this, from the foreign mails being piled upon the roof, was a difficult and even dangerous attempt to one cramped by nearly 300 miles of outside travelling. And ‹as lu› fortunately, before I had lost much {↑ time in the} attempt, our frantic horses swept round an angle of the road, which opened upon us the stage where the collision ‹would› {↑ must} be accomplished, the parties that seemed summoned to the trial, and the impossibility of ‹acting› {↑ saving them} by any communication with the guard.

Before us lay ‹a str› an avenue strait as an arrow, 600 yards perhaps in length. And ‹from› the umbrageous trees, ‹that› which rose in a regular line from either side, meet‹ing› high overhead, gave to it the character of a ca

[18 r.]
B 17
-thedral {↑ ‹the›} aisle. These trees {↑ gave a deeper solemnity to} ‹made› the early light ‹more›: but there was still light enough to perceive at the further end of this gothic aisle a light reedy gig, in which were seated a young man and {↑ by his side ‹a›} a young lady. Ah young Sir! what are you about? ‹x› ‹x› If it is necessary that you should whisper your communications to this young lady, though really I see nobody ‹likely› at this hour and on this solitary road {↑ likely} to overhear your conversation, – is it ‹as› therefore necessary that you should carry your lips forward to hers? – The little carriage is {↑ creeping} ‹coming› on at one mile an hour; and the parties within it, being thus tenderly engaged, are naturally bending down their heads. ‹How shall I rous› Between ‹them› {↑ them} and eternity {↑ to all human calculation} there is but a minute and a half. What is it that I shall do? – Strange it is, ‹that› and ‹might› to a mere auditor of the tale {↑ might} seem laughable, that I should ‹need› {↑ need} a suggestion from the Iliad to prompt the sole recourse that remained. {↑ But so it was.} Suddenly I remembered the shout of Achilles and its effect. But could I pretend to shout like the son of Peleus, aided by Pallas ‹Athena›? No certainly: but then I ‹had not› needed not the shout that should alarm all Asia militant: a shout would suffice, ‹that› such as should carry terror into {↑ the hearts of} two thoughtless young people, and

one gig horse. I shouted: and the young man heard me not. A second time I shouted: and now he heard me: for now he raised his head.

[19 r.]
B 18

Now then ‹I had› {↑ all had been} done ‹all› that {↑ by me} *could* be done: more on *my* part was not possible. Mine {↑ ‹I said›} ‹was› {↑ had been} the first step: the second {↑ ‹I said is to myself, is›} was ‹was› for the young man: the third ‹was› {↑ I said silently is} for God. If the ‹young› stranger is a brave man, and if indeed he ‹loves› loves the young girl ‹at by› {↑ at} his side, – or, loving her not, if he feels the obligation, ‹which› {↑ pressing upon} every man worthy to be called a man, ‹of› ‹acknowledges,› of doing his utmost for a woman confided to his protection {↑ – } he will at least make ‹an› {↑ some} effort to save her. If *that* fails, he will not perish the more {↑ or by a death more cruel} for having made it; and he will die, as a ‹m› brave man should, with his face to the danger, and {↑ with} his arm about the woman that he sought in vain to save. ‹If *that*› But, if he makes no effort, ‹if he shrinks from his duty,› {↑ shrinking without a struggle from his duty, his} he himself will not the less certainly perish for ‹having shrunk by› {↑ this} baseness {↑ of poltroonery} ‹from his duty›. {↑ He will die no less} And why not? Wherefore should we grieve that there is one craven less in the ‹world?› world? No: *let* him ‹p› perish, {↑ without a pitying thought of ours} ‹and in that case all› wasted upon him; and {↑ in that case} ‹in that case› all our grief will be reserved for the {↑ fate of the} poor helpless girl, ‹that› {↑ who now, upon the least shadow of failure in *him*, ‹will› must} by the fiercest of translations, {↑ must without time for ‹know›} ‹and within› {↑ ‹seventy›} ‹seventy to ninety› {↑ a prayer, must within seventy} seconds ‹will› stand before the judgement-seat of God.

But craven he was not: sudden had been the call upon him; and sudden was his answer to the call. He saw, he heard, he comprehended, the ruin that was coming down: already ‹its› its {↑ gloomy} shadow darkened above him; and already he was measuring his strength to ‹fight› {↑ deal with} it. Ah what a vulgar thing does courage seem, when we see nations buying it and selling it for a shilling a day: ah

[20 r.]
B 19

ah what a sublime thing does courage seem, when ‹in› some fearful ‹and unfore sudden› crisis {↑ on the great deeps of} ‹of› life ‹a man driven by as b› carries a man ‹with the› as if running ‹on the sea› before ‹some mighty› {↑ a} hurricane up to the giddy ‹edge› {↑ crest} of some mountainous wave, from which {↑ accordingly as he chooses his course} he decries two courses, and a voice says, to him audibly – 'This way lies hope, ‹that way› take the other way and mourn for ever!' – yet even then, amidst the raving of the seas and the frenzy of the danger, the man is able to confront his situation, is able to retire for a moment into solitude with God, and to ‹as› seek all his counsel from *him*! For {↑ ‹five› seven seconds} ‹5› ‹fiv of his› it might be of his seventy ‹seconds› the stranger settled his countenance steadfastly upon us, as if to {↑ search and} value every element in the conflict before him. For five seconds {↑ more} he sate {↑ immoveably} like one that mused ‹upon› {↑ on} some great purpose. For five he sate {↑ with eyes upraised ‹to heaven›} like one that prayed in sorrow under some ‹dire perplexity agony› {↑ extremity} of doubt {↑ ‹between two courses›} for wisdom ‹to a› ‹from above› to guide him {↑ towards} ‹in making› the better choice. Then, {↑ suddenly} he rose; {↑ stood upright;} ‹to his feet;› and, by a sudden strain upon the reins, raising his horse's forefeet, {↑ from the ground} he slewed him round on the pivot of his hind legs, so as to {↑ plant} ‹place› the little equipage in a position nearly at right angles to ours. Thus far his condition was not improved; ‹If as› except as a first step had been taken towards the possibility of a second. ‹Yet› If no more {↑ were} ‹were› done, nothing was done; for the little carriage still occupied the very centre of our path, though in an altered ‹position› {↑ direction}. Yet {↑ is it} ‹perhaps› {↑ even now it may not be too late} ‹there is still time› : ‹twenty seconds or› fifteen of the seventy seconds may still {↑ be unexhausted} ‹remain›: and ‹a› one almighty ‹leap› bound forward {↑ may} ‹might still› {↑ ‹ava› avail to} clear the ground. ‹But› {↑ Hurry} then, hurry, {↑ ‹hurry,› }‹hurry,› ‹my› for the flying moments – *they* hurry: oh hurry, hurry, my brave young man, for the cruel hoofs of our horses – *they* also ‹are› hurry‹ing› {↑ Fast are the flying moments, faster ‹fast› are the hoofs of our horses.} {↑ Fear not for *him*, if human energy can suffice:} ‹But› faithful was he, that drove, to his

[21 r.]
B 20
terrific duty: faithful was the horse to *his* command. {↑ One blow} One impulse given with voice and hand by the stranger, one such from the {↑ ‹docile›} horse, one bound as if in the act of rising to ‹l› a ‹leap› fence, landed the docile creature's fore-feet upon the crown or arching centre of the road. ‹The better {↑ ‹forward›} half› The larger half of the little equipage had then ‹evidently› cleared ‹the› our ‹overhanging› overt‹**x**›owering shadow: *that* was evident even to my own agitated sight. But it mattered little that ‹a› one wreck should ‹have› float‹ed› off in safety, if, upon the wreck that {↑ ‹should›} perish‹ed›{↑ ed} were embarked the human freightage. The rear ‹section› {↑ part} of the carriage, ‹was all that concerned the› {↑ ‹lent›} ‹horror of {↑ ‹to›} the case: and› was *that* ‹beyond as yet› ‹altogether› {↑ certainly} beyond the line of **xx**› {↑ absolute} ruin? What power could

answer ‹that› {↑ the} question? ‹What glance of› {↑ Glance of} eye, {↑ ‹what›} thought of man, {↑ ‹what›} ‹or› wing of angel {↑ – which of these} ‹was› had speed enough to sweep between the question and the answer, ‹?› and divide {↑ find a division between} the one from the other? ‹Rules of light› Light does not ‹travel after {↑ ‹pursue›} light in the same sunbeam› {↑ tread upon the steps of light} more indivisibly, than {↑ apparently} did our all-conquering arrival {↑ upon} the escaping efforts of the gig. *That* ‹knew› {↑ must} the young man {↑ have felt} too ‹certainly› plainly. His back was {↑ now} turned to us: ‹But his ear had been already instructed by the dreadful rattle of our harness› ‹he could no longer see› not by sight could he any longer communicate with the peril: but ‹his ear had› by the dreadful rattle of our harness too truly had his ear been instructed – that all was finished as regarded any further effort of *his*. Already in ‹a posture› ‹spirit› ‹no doubt of› resignation he had rested from his struggle; and perhaps in his heart he was whispering – "Father, which art in Heaven, ‹what I on earth have attempted›, ‹I› do thou ratify ‹above› ‹"› and finish ‹above› ‹"› what I on earth have attempted." We ran past them ‹like› {↑ faster than ever} mill-race* in our inexorable flight. Oh

[22 r.]
B 21
raving of hurricanes that must have sounded in their young ears at the moment of our transit. Either with the swingle-bar, or with the haunch of our ‹left› near leader, we had struck the off wheel of the little gig, which stood a little obliquely and not quite {↑ so} ‹as› far advanced as to be accurately parallel with the near wheel. The blow, from the fury of our passage, resounded terrifically. I rose in horror to ‹look down and› look ‹back› upon the ruins we might have caused. From my elevated station I looked down and I looked back upon the scene, which in a moment told its tale, and wrote all its records on my heart for ever.

* "a mill-race": – There needs no authority for such ‹a› an image. But ‹lest the reader should fancy ‹the› it not grand enough for the occasion, let me cite remind him of three lines in the Com. Div. of Dante's Inf. Dante's Inferno, ‹x›Canto III. v. 46–7–8 it› {↑ it} may be thought to want {↑ the} dignity. {↑ ‹suitable›} As some argument that it does *not*, let ‹me remind the reader remember› me remind the

[21 v.]
remind the reader of Dante [Inferno Canto XXIII. v. 46–7–8.]

> Non corse mai sì tosto acqua per doccia
> A volger ruota di mulin terragno,
> Quand' ella più verso le pale approccia."[4]

The horse was planted immoveably with his forefeet upon the paved crest of the central road. He of the whole party was alone untouched by {↑ the} passion of ‹sudden› death. The little cany carriage, ‹from the› partly perhaps from the dreadful torsion of the wheels in its recent movement, partly from the ‹dreadful› thundering blow we had given to it, – ‹and› as if it sympathised with human horror, was all ‹a-shiver with trembling› alive with tremblings and shiverings. The young man sate like a rock. He stirred not at all. But *his* was the steadiness of ‹frozen› agitation frozen into rest by horror. As yet he dared not to look round. For he knew that, ‹more› if anything remained to do, by him it could no‹t› {↑ longer} be done. And as yet he knew not for certain if ‹his› {↑ their} safety ‹was› {↑ were} accomplished. But the lady

---

But the lady ————! Oh heavens will that spectacle ever depart from my dreams, as she rose and ‹ros› sank {↑ sank and rose} upon her seat, ‹tos›sed {↑ threw up} her arms wildly to heaven, clutched at some visionary object {tear} air, fainting, praying, raving despairing! – Figure to yourself, reader, the ‹unpa› elements of the case: suffer me to ‹real› recal before your mind the circumstances of the unparalleled situation. From the {↑ silence and} ‹pea› deep peace of this saintly summer night, from the pathetic blending of this sweet

[23 r.]
B 22
moonlight, dawnlight, dreamlight, – from the manly tenderness of this flattering, whispering, murmuring love, – suddenly as from the woods and fields, – suddenly as from the chambers of the air opening in revelations, – suddenly as from the ground yawning at her feet, leaped upon her, with the flashing of cataracts, Death the crownéd* phantom, with all the equipage of terrors, and the tiger roar of his voice.

The moments were numbered. In the twinkling of an eye our flying horses had carried us to the termination of the umbrageous aisle; at right angles we wheeled into our former direction: the turn of the road carried the scene out of my eyes in an instant, and swept it into my dreams for ever.

[24 r.]
‹D 7› DF ‹I›1

* It is important to the rhythmus that this {↑ word *crowned*} should be read, and therefore should be printed, as a dissyllable – crownéd.

Dream-Fugue

on the above theme of Sudden Death.

Tumultuosissimamente.

Passion of Sudden Death! that once in youth I read and interpreted by the ‹light› {↑ shadows} of thy averted* signs ‹x›, ‹xxxx› Rapture of panic taking the shape, which {↑ ‹on›} {↑ ‹on›} ‹in church monuments› {↑ amongst tombs in churches} I have seen, of woman bursting her sepulchral bonds – of woman's Ionic form ‹in act to soar› {↑ bending forward ‹in act to soar›} from the ruins of her grave, with arching foot, with eyes upraised, with clasped adoring hands, {↑ –} waiting, {↑ watching} ‹watching› ‹listening›, trembling, praying, for the trumpet's call to rise from dust for ever; ‹Vision› {↑ ‹an›} {↑ – ah Vision} too fearful, {↑ ‹crowned with marble grandeur›} of shuddering humanity {↑ on the brink} ‹that didst start aside, that record› {↑ of abysses ‹that›, Vision that didst start back,} that didst reel away like a shriveling scroll from before the wrath of fire racing on the wings of the wind, – ‹oh› wherefore {↑ epilepsy so brief of horror, ‹that› wherefore should it be that} {↑ ‹is it, should it be,›} ‹epilepsy so brief of horror,› {↑ ‹so transient›} {↑ that thou} *canst* ‹thou› not die? ‹Wherefore› {↑ Passing ‹away› so suddenly into darkness wherefore} is it that ‹now for thirty years thy› {↑ still} thou sheddest {↑ thy sad ‹blights› funeral} ‹perennial› blights {↑ upon} ‹amongst› the gorgeous mosaics of dreams? {↑ ‹Yes, yes I ask – ›} Fragment of music too stern, heard once and heard no more, {↑ what aileth thee} ‹wherefore is it› that ‹now for thirty years› thy deep rolling chords come up {↑ at intervals} through all the worlds of sleep, {↑ ‹yes! what aileth thee – that after›} ‹and› after thirty ‹years have lost no element of horror? thirty and five› years they have lost no element of horror?

[25 r.]
Dr. F. 2

1.

Lo! it is summer, almighty summer. The everlasting gates of life and summer are thrown open wide; and on the ocean, tranquil and verdant as a savanna, the unknown lady from the dreadful vision and {↑ I} myself are floating: she upon a fairy pinnace; ‹and› {↑ and} I upon ‹an› an ‹vast› English three-decker. But both of us are wooing gales of ‹pleasure› {↑ festal happiness} within the domain of our common country, within that {↑ ancient}

* "*averted* signs": – I read the course and {↑ changes} ‹process› of the lady's agony in ‹the› the succession of her ‹attitudes as› involuntary gestures; {↑ but let it be remembered that} ‹but› {↑ ‹let to be remembered›} I read ‹it› all {↑ this} from the rear, never once catching the lady's full face, ‹an› and even her profile ‹most› imperfectly.

watery park {↑ within that ‹wild billowy chase› pathless chase} ‹of ocean›, where England takes her pleasure {↑ as a huntress} through winter and summer, and which stretches from the rising to the setting sun. Ah! what a wilderness of floral beauty ‹is› {↑ was} hidden, ‹from› or ‹is› {↑ was} ‹kind timidly› {↑ suddenly} revealed, upon the {↑ tropic} ‹sky› islands ‹amongst› {↑ through} which the pinnace, {↑ ‹is moving!›} ‹moves!› moved. And upon her deck what a bevy of human flowers ‹x› – young woman {↑ how} ‹the› lovely ‹est›, young men {↑ how noble} ‹the noblest›, that ‹are› {↑ were} dancing together, and slowly drifting towards *us*, amidst music and incense, ‹bells and› {↑ amidst} blossoms ‹and bells, the› {↑ from forests and gorgeous corymbi ‹of› from vintages amidst ‹wild› natural} caroling and the echoes of sweet girlish laughter. Slowly the pinnace ‹disappears under the shadow of this bows› near‹ed› us, ‹and› gaily she hail‹ed›{↑ s} us, and slowly she disappear‹ed›{↑ s} within the shadow of our mighty bows. But then, ‹suddenly› {↑ as ‹by› at some signal from heaven,} the music and the carols and the ‹echoing› sweet echo‹s›ing ‹from› of girlish laughter – all, {↑ ‹were› are} ‹are› hushed. What evil ‹had› {↑ has} smitten the pinnace, ‹?› ‹M›{↑ m}eeting or overtaking her? Did ruin to ‹her› our friends couch within our {↑ own dreadful} ‹mighty› shadow? {↑ Was our shadow the shadow of death?} I looked over the {↑ bow} ‹taffarel› for an answer; and behold! the pinnace was dismantled, the revel‹lers› and the revellers {↑ were found ‹vanished› ‹fled› no more,} ‹had departed›, the glory of the vintages was dust, and the forest was left without a witness to its‹elf on› {↑ ‹upon›} ‹the seas› beauty upon the seas. "But where," and I turned to our own crew, "where are the ‹lovely› lovely ‹women› {↑ women} that danced beneath the awning of flowers ‹and blossoms› and clustering corymbi? Whither have fled the noble

[26 r.]
DF. 3
{↑ young men} that danced with *them*?" Answer there was none: {↑ vainly I sought for any} ‹and at that I asked {↑ ‹sought›} in vain for› answer. But suddenly {↑ the} ‹the› {↑ a} man at the mast-head, whose countenance darkened ‹as he spok› with alarm, cried ‹**xx**› aloud – "‹Sail› {↑ ‹Ship› Sail} on the weather beam!‹"› Down she comes ‹with› upon us: ‹with all sail set!" She will founder in› in seventy seconds she will founder!"

2.

I looked {↑ to the weather side,} and ‹beheld› the summer {↑ had departed} ‹was gone›. The Sea was {↑ rocking, and shaken with ‹with› gathering wrath.} ‹convulsed with motion.› ‹Mighty mists sate› Upon its surface ‹which› sate mighty mists, which ‹form formed› {↑ grouped} themselves into arches and long cathedral aisles. Down one of these, with the ‹velocity of› fiery pace of {↑ a quarrel from a cross-bow} ‹an arrow,› ran a ‹light› frigate

{↑ right} ‹right› ‹upon our› athwart our course. "‹Is she› {↑ Are they} mad?" ‹I heard the helmsman say,› {↑ some ‹a› voice exclaimed from our deck,} ‹in seventy seconds she will founder› "‹Ar› Are they blind? {↑ Do they woo their ruin?"} ‹In seventy seconds they {↑ ‹she›} will founder›." But, ‹a› in a moment, as she was close upon us, some ‹strong current to› impulse of {↑ heady} current or {↑ sudden} vortex gave a {↑ wheeling} bias to her course; {↑ and off} ‹And as› she {↑ forged ‹off›} ‹ran past us,› ‹without a shock:› ‹and for a moment alongside of us› without a shock. ‹And› As she {↑ ran past us} ‹ran› high aloft amongst the shrouds‹,› stood the lady {↑ of the pinnace} ‹whom I had seen in the carriage›. The deeps opened {↑ ahead in malice} ‹from afar in malice› to receive her, {↑ towering ‹crests of› surges of foam ran after her,} ‹the waves crests of angry foam pursued her›, the billows {↑ ‹with their fiery crests›} were fierce to catch her. ‹Far› But far away she was borne into desert spaces of the sea: ‹but› {↑ whilst} still {↑ by sight} I followed her ‹and with my eye› {↑ ‹by sight›} as she ran before the howling gale, ‹**x**› chased by angry sea-birds and ‹fiery crests of› by maddening billows: still I saw her, {↑ as at the moment when she ‹passe› ran past us ran past us,} ‹as she rose› amongst the shrouds, with her white draperies streaming before the wind {↑ ‹and the spray›} ‹catching at the›. There {↑ ‹for leagues I saw horrors›} she stood ‹ – › with hair dishevelled, {↑ one} hand‹**x**› clutched amongst the tackling, – rising, sinking,

[27 r.]
DF 4
fluttering, trembling, praying; – {↑ there for leagues I saw her as she stood raising at intervals {↑ one} ‹a› hand to heaven} amidst ‹the spray and› the fiery crests of the pursuing waves {↑ and the raving of the storm}; until at last, ‹with a dis sound› {↑ upon a ‹signal› sound} from the distant waters ‹as of {↑ from} malicious› of ‹loud› {↑ malicious} laughter {↑ and mockery}, all was hidden {↑ for ever} in driving showers; and ‹immediately› afterwards, but when I know not, and how I know not,

3.

Sweet funeral bells {↑ from some incalculable distance} ‹coming from some secret recess often with their› wailing {↑ over the dead that die before the dawn,} awakened me {↑ as} ‹as I lay asleep› {↑ ‹the and as› I ‹found› slept} in a boat ‹that was› moored to {↑ ‹a familiar›} ‹some unknown› {↑ some familiar} shore. The ‹grey dawn was› {↑ ‹earliest›} morning ‹has› twilight even ‹**xxx**› {↑ then} was breaking; and, by the dusky ‹l› revelations which it {↑ spread} ‹made› ‹of the solitary shore strand›, I saw a girl, ‹with› {↑ ‹having›} ‹her ha head› adorned {↑ with a garland of white roses about her head,} ‹as› for some great festival, running along {↑ the solitary ‹sho› strand} ‹it› with extremity of haste. {↑ Her running was the running of panic;} ‹In panic she fled›, and often she looked back {↑ as} to some dreadful {↑ enemy} ‹danger› {↑ ‹peril object›} in the rear. But, ‹I leaped ashore as› {↑ when} ‹she passed my station,› I leaped ashore {↑ and followed ‹her› on her steps} to warn her of a ‹danger› {↑ peril} ‹that perhaps was gloomiest› in front, {↑ alas!} ‹Alas›! from me she fled as from ‹another› {↑ an ‹second› other} peril; and vainly I {↑ shouted to ‹would have warned›} ‹shouted to› her of quicksands that lay ahead. Faster and faster she ran; round a ‹rock› promontory of rock she wheeled out of sight; ‹and {↑ ten seconds more} I myself› {↑ in an instant I also} wheeled round it, {↑ but} only ‹in time› to see the {↑ treacherous sands} ‹cruel quicksand› {↑ gathering} ‹closing› a{↑ bove}‹bove› her ‹fair young› head‹;›. ‹The white roses in her hair› Already her ‹person› {↑ person} was buried; ‹alive;› only the {↑ fair young} head and the ‹white› diadem of white roses around it were {↑ still} ‹yet› visible {↑ to the ‹heavens above›}, ‹and **xx**› {↑ pitying ‹**xx**› heavens; and ‹one› last of all {↑ was visible} one} ‹her› marble arm‹,›. ‹with which {↑ arm} she clutched {↑ as if} at some {↑ false delusive hand misleading hand} visionary hand stretched out to save, amongst the clouds, {↑ with which {↑ arm} she uttered her lingering {↑ trembling} hope and her final despair}› The head, the diadem, the ‹poor› arm, – these also {↑ had sunk at last} ‹di sank›: over ‹all› these {↑ also} ‹also› the cruel quicksand {↑ had} closed; and no memorial of the ‹you› fair young girl remained on earth, except my own {↑ solitary} tears, and the {↑ funeral bells from the desart seas that {↑ rising} ‹rose› again more softly, ‹and›} ‹sighing of the early breeze along the solitary shore› sang a requiem over the grave of the buried child and {↑ over} her blighted dawn.

I sate, and wept in secret {↑ the tears that ‹ever› were {↑ ever given} ‹held due› to} ‹over› the memory of ‹the› those ‹her› that died be-

[27 v.]
[DF 4]

I saw by the early ‹ho› twilight ‹her the› this fair young head as it was sinking down to darkness, saw this marble arm as it rose above her head and her treacherous grave – tossing, faultering, rising, clutching as at some false deceiving hand stretched out from the clouds; saw this marble arm uttering her ‹last› {↑ dying} hope, and then her ‹last› {↑ dying} despair.

[28 r.]
DF 5

-fore the dawn, and by the treachery of earth our mother. ‹And as I sate, suddenly I heard› {↑ ‹caught from afar›} a roar as of some great king's artillery advancing rapidly along› {↑ (But ‹the› tears ‹wer› and funeral bells were hushed suddenly by a} ‹the› shout as of {↑ many} nations, and a roar as

{↑ from} ‹of› some great king's artillery advancing rapidly along the ‹distant› vallies, ‹and› but heard ‹chiefly› {↑ afar} by ‹the echoes› its echoes among the mountains. "Hush!" I said, as I {↑ bent my ear earthwards to} ‹stood in the attitude of› listen‹ing›, "hush! – this either is the very anarchy of strife, ‹amongst men›, or else" – and then I listened more profoundly – ‹"or else" it is Victory which swallows up all strife." and I raised my head in {↑ secret} thanksgiving›, "or else {↑ oh heavens!} it is Victory that swallows up all strife."

4.

Immediately in trance I was carried over land and sea to some distant ‹land› {↑ kingdom}, and placed upon a triumphal car amongst companions crowned with laurel. The darkness of gathering midnight brood‹ed›{↑ ing} over {↑ all} the {↑ land} ‹country›. ‹and was saw but dimly heard but did not see Egyptian darkness› hid from ‹us› {↑ us} the mighty crowds that were weaving restlessly about our carriage as a centre: we heard them, but we saw them not. Tidings ‹of› had arrived ‹two› within an hour ‹too full of› of a grandeur {↑ that measured itself against} ‹commensurate with› centuries; too full of pathos they were, ‹too› too full of ‹almighty› joy {↑ that acknowledged no fountain but God,} to utter themselves by other languages than {↑ by} tears, ‹this› by restless ‹murmurs of thanksgiving, by› anthems, by ‹*Te deums*:[5] by the echoes from every church endless› reverberations, {↑ rising ‹continually›} ‹of the *Gloria in excelsis*› {↑ ‹that rose to heavenwards›} from every choir, ‹in every church› of the *Gloria in Excelsis*. These tidings {↑ – we that sate upon the laurelled ‹char› car had it for} ‹it it was a our great office to carry› our ‹publish the› privilege ‹of us› {↑ ‹that we sate upon the laurelled car›} ‹on the triumphal car› to publish amongst all nations. And already ‹the› by {↑ angry} ‹their› {↑ signs audible through the darkness, by} ‹impatient angry tramplings, our immortal {↑ demoniac} horses›, snortings and tramplings, our demoniac horses

[29 r.]
DF 6

that knew no fear of fleshy weariness, ‹ropes› upbraided us with ‹our› delay. {↑ Wherefore *was* it that we delayed?} ‹But we waited. Wherefore *did* we delay?› We waited for a secret ‹word› word, that should bear witness to the hope of nations as now ‹indeed› {↑ ‹at last›} accomplished {↑ for ever}. At midnight the secret word arrived; which word was – Waterloo and Recov{↑ e}red Christendom? The {↑ dreadful} word shone by ‹internal›{↑ its own} light: before us it ‹rode›; {↑ ‹w›went;} ‹and› high above our leaders' heads it rode, and spread a golden light over ‹every road› the paths which we traversed. Every city, at the ‹summons› {↑ ‹sight›} {↑ presence} of the secret word, threw open its gates to receive us. The rivers

{↑ felt its approach, ‹its›} ‹under lig golden light› {↑ and} were silent as we ‹passed› {↑ crossed}. {↑ ‹Sorry›} ‹The forest›, {↑ All the mighty forests,} as we ran along ‹their› {↑ ‹its›} {↑ their} margins‹,› {↑ shivered in} ‹bowed› {↑ ‹its.›} ‹in› homage {↑ to the secret word. And the}. ‹The› darkness comprehended it.

‹Two hours {↑ one hour} before after midnight› Two hours {↑ 2 hours} after midnight we reached a ‹vast cathedral› {↑ mighty minster}. The gates, which rose to the clouds, were closed. But when the dreadful word, that rode before us, reached them with its {↑ golden} ‹l› light, silently they moved back upon their hinges; and at a flying gallop our equipage entered the ‹cathedral› grand aisle of the cathedral. Headlong was our pace; and at every altar, in the little chapels and oratories to the right hand and the left of our course, the {↑ lamps} dying {↑ or sickening,} ‹lamps› kindled {↑ anew} in sympathy with the ‹dreadful› {↑ secret} word that was flying past. ‹Forty leagues it might be that we had› ‹leagues past counting we had measured› {↑ Forty leagues we might have run} in the cathedral, ‹when› and as yet no {↑ strength of} morning light had reached us, when we saw before us the {↑ aerial} galleries ‹and fret work› of the organ and the choir. Every pinnacle ‹of fret› {↑ of the fretwork, every station of advantage amongst the traceries, ‹were› was crested} ‹fret-work, and flyer carved tracery of flying buttress was occupied› by white-robed choristers, that sang deliverance; that wept no more ‹as› tears, as once

[30 r.]
DF 7
‹the› their fathers had wept; but at intervals {↑ 7} that ‹sung› {↑ sang} together to the generations ‹to the generations that lay beneath them in the graves, to the generations that were coming yet to come›, saying ——

"Chaunt the deliverer's praise in every tongue,"

and receiving answers from afar

——"such as once in heaven and earth were sung."

{↑ And of} ‹Of› their chaunting was no end; of our headlong ‹gallop› {↑ pace} was ‹no› {↑ neither pause nor} remission. Thus as we ran like torrents, etc.

[31 r.]
DF 8 DF 8

Thus as we ran like torrents, – thus as {↑ we swept} ‹our flying equipage› with bridal rapture ‹swept› over the Campo Santo of the cathedral graves, – suddenly we became aware of a vast Necropolis rising ‹like a clouds out of the sea from› {↑ upon} the far-off horizon – a {↑ city of} Necropolis {↑ sepulchres built within the saintly cathedrals} for the warrior dead that rested from their feuds {↑ on earth} Of purple granite was the Necropolis; yet {↑ in the first minute} it lay like a purple stain upon the sky; so mighty was the distance. In the second minute it trembled ‹as› through many changes, {↑ growing} ‹and grew› into {↑ terraces, ‹or› and towers of} wonderous attitude, so mighty was the pace. In the third minute already ‹we were› with our dreadful gallop ‹at› we were entering ‹the› {↑ its} suburbs. Vast ‹sar› sarcophagi rose on every side, ‹belted with› having towers and turrets that ‹strode forward with haughty intrusion upon› {↑ ‹over› upon} the limits of the central aisle {↑ strode forward with haughty intrusion,} that {↑ ‹into answering recesses›} ran back with ‹answ› mighty shadows into ‹into answering recesses›. {↑ answering recesses}. ‹Where the towers ran, there did our horses run› Every sarcophagus showed many bas-reliefs; ‹basreliefs› {↑ bas-reliefs} of battles, ‹bas-reliefs of› {↑ bas-reliefs of ‹and›} battle-fields; of battles from forgotten ages, {↑ of} battles from yesterday; {↑ of} battlefields that long since nature had healed and reconciled to herself with the sweet oblivion of flowers; ‹battlefields› of battlefields that were yet angry and crimson with carnage. Where the {↑ terraces› ‹towers› ran,

---

Campo Santo: – (but ‹no› to come in at the end, not as a foot-note). ‹I presume› It is probable that most, {↑ of *my*} readers will be acquainted with the history of the Campo Santo at Pisa – composed of earth brought from ‹the Holy Land› {↑ Jerusalem for ‹the› a bed of sanctity} as the highest prize which the noble piety of crusad‹ing›{↑ ers} ‹success› could ask or imagine. There is ‹a› {↑ another} Campo Santo ‹also› at Naples, formed however (I {↑ presume} ‹believe› on the ‹fine› example {↑ given by} ‹of› Pisa. Possibly the idea may have been more extensively copied. – To readers who are unacquainted with England ‹and› or {↑ who (being English) are ‹yet› unacq.} with the Cathedral cities of England, it may be right to mention that the graves within side ‹the› cathedrals‹,› ‹lie f› form a flat pavement over which carriages and horses might roll: and perhaps a boyish remembrance of one particular cathedral across which I had seen passengers ‹and ever burth› walk and burthens carried may have favored ‹the› in this respect.

[32 r.]
DF 9
there ‹our horses› did *we* run; where the towers curved, there did *we* curve. ‹Like› {↑ With the flight of} swallows our horses swept round every angle. Like rivers in flood wheeling round ‹headla obstructing› headlands like hurricanes that ride into the secrets of forests, faster than ever light unwove the mazes of darkness, our flying equipage carried earthly passions – kindled warrior instincts {↑ – } ‹in› {↑ amongst} the dust that lay around us; ‹ – › dust {↑ oftentimes} of our noble fathers that had slept in God ‹since› {↑ from}

Créci {↑ to Trafalgar.} And now had we reached the last sarcophagus, {↑ now} ‹already we› were {↑ we} ‹coming› abreast of the last bas-relief, already {↑ had} we ‹had› recovered the arrow-like flight of the ‹central ail› {↑ ‹great endless›} {↑ illimitable central} aisle, – when coming up it {↑ to meet us} ‹we beheld› {↑ ‹rode› we beheld} a female infant ‹sitting› {↑ that rode} in a carriage as ‹x› frail as flowers. The ‹silvery› mists, which ‹ran› {↑ went} before her, hid the fawns ‹which› that drew her; but could not hide the shells and tropic flowers with which she played, ‹no› but could not hide the lovely smiles by which she uttered her trust in the mighty cathedral, and in the cherubim that looked down upon her from {↑ the topmost shafts of} its pillars. Face to face she was meeting us, {↑ face to face she rode,} as if danger there were none. "‹Ah,› {↑ Oh} baby," I exclaimed, "shalt thou be the ransom for Waterloo?‹"› Must we, that carry tidings of great joy to every people, be messengers of ruin to thee?" In horror I rose at the thought‹,›. ‹but then› But then also, in horror at the thought, rose one that was sculptured on the bas-relief – a dying trumpeter. Solemnly from the field of battle he rose to his feet; and, unslinging his stony trumpet, carried it in his dying anguish to his stony lips – sounding once, and yet once again: proclamation, that in *thy* ears, oh baby! must have spoken from the battlements of death. Immediately deep shadows fell between us, and {↑ aboriginal} ‹mighty {↑ ies}› silence. The choir had ceased to sing. The

[ON MIRACLES]
MS A

The manuscript is held in the collection of Frederick Burwick. It is two sheets of light blue paper, written in blue-black ink, and measuring 230 by 190 mm. There are no watermarks. De Quincey dates the manuscript 'Monday morn^{g}, June 7, 1847'.

De Quincey was keenly interested in the great controversy over David Hume's account 'Of Miracles' in *An Enquiry Concerning Human Understanding* (1758). He wrote 'On Hume's Argument Against Miracles' in *Blackwood's* for 1839, and returned to related theological issues in *Tait's* essays such as 'On Christianity, as an Organ of Political Movement' and 'Protestantism'. The present manuscript, and the two that follow, extend his deliberations on miracles (Vol. 13, pp. 333–46; Vol. 15, pp. 343–69; see above, pp. 223–63; see also, 'Fragments on Christianity', Vol. 20, pp. 410–44).

De Quincey shared his interest in miracles with Samuel Taylor Coleridge, who explored the subject throughout his career. Burwick writes:

> Both Coleridge and De Quincey, of course, were outspoken opponents of the materialist and mechanist assumptions of Enlightenment philosophy. Reinterpreting the argument in Romantic terms, they sought to clear the faith in supernatural mystery from all taint of weak-minded credulity. Hume approaches the miracle as if it had to be documented as an historical event. Coleridge answers Hume by arguing that a miracle works subjectively rather than objectively. Endorsing a doctrine of immanence similar to Coleridge's definition of symbol, De Quincey insists upon the semiotic mediation of all humanly intelligible manifestations of the divine.

See Frederick Burwick, 'Coleridge and De Quincey on Miracles' in *Christianity and Literature*, 39 (1990), pp. 387–421.

Japp published a version of the present manuscript but, characteristically, altered it in a number of ways. In this instance, he goes so far as to splice 'On Miracles' MS B (see below, p. 494–5) onto the end of the present manuscript, silently turning two different manuscripts into one seamless whole (Japp, *PW*, vol. I, pp. 173–6).

For details of the 'Conventions for Manuscript Transcription', see above, p. xvii.

[1 r.]
Christ's going about and doing good. By showing what commands one sense or other, there is Mystery. A mystery in that case – but even by presenting Christ alive forever.
Truth. Martyrs. Convers^{s}. Prone and Supine – To the spirit and to Christ – to With wind in the starboard, larb, weather lee, then withershins &c.

What else is it than the case of "a wicked and adulterous gener^{ation} asking a Sign"[1] – laying {↑ such} a stress on miracles?

But what are then miracles *for*? To prove a legislation from God. But lst this could not be proved even if miracle-working *were* the test of divine mission by doing miracles until we knew whether the power were genuine, i.e., not like the magicians of Pharaoh or the Witch of Endor,[2] from below. 2ndly, you are a poor pitiful creature, that think *power* to do miracles of any kind that can exhibit itself in an act, the note of a godlike commission. Better is one ray of truth (not seen previously by man), of moral truth – e.g. forgiveness of enemies – than all the power which could create the world, which after all

Oh yes {↑ says objector} but Xst was holy as a man – this we know lst. Then we judge by his power y^{t} he must be f^{m} God. But, if it were doubtful whether his p were f^{m} God – then until this doubt is *otherwise*, is *independently* removed {↑ by a test of holiness irrelevant as power to knock men down}, you cannot decide y^{t} he *was* holy. With other holiness – apparent holiness – ‹of› a simul$^{a\text{-}tion}$ m^{t} be combined.

In passage of Truslar and Ld Sinclair's Speech June 1, 47.[3]

‹Thus he› Let him come down from the cross,[4] and we – &c. Yes, they fancied so. But see what w^{d} really have followed. They would have been stunned and confounded for the moment, not at all con

[1 v.]
verted in heart. Their hatred {↑ to X^{t}} was not built on their unbelief, but their unbelief {↑ in X^{t} was built} on their hatred: ‹H› and this hatred w^{d} not have been mitigated by another (however astounding) miracle. This I said (Monday morn^{g}, June 7, 1847) – in ref. to my saying on the gen^{l} q of miracles – Why these *dubious* miracles? Such as curing blindness[5] that may have been cured by a *process*? Since the *unity* given to the act of healing is {↑ probably (more probably y^{n} otherwise)} but the figurative unity of the tendency to mythus;[6] or else it is this unity misapprehended and mistranslated by the reporters. ‹Or› Such again as the miracle of the loaves[7] – so liable to be utterly gossip, so incapable of being watched or examined amongst a crowd of 7000

people. Besides, were these people mad? The very fact, which is said to have drawn X^{t}'s pity – viz. their situ^{ation} in the desert, surely could not have escaped their own attention on going thither. Think of 7000 people rushing to a sort of destruction; for if less than that, the mere inconven. were not worthy of divine attention. Now, ‹said› said I, why not give us (if Mir *are* required) one that nobody could doubt – removing a mountain, e.g.? Yes: but here the other party begin to *see* the evil of miracles. Oh, this w^{d} have *coerced* people into believing. Rest you safe as to that. It would have been no believing in any proper sense; it w^{d}, at the utmost, and supposing no vital {↑ demur} ‹doubt› to every pop miracle‹,› have led ‹people› into that belief which X^{t} himself describes (and rejects) as calling him Lord! lord? The pretended belief w^{d} have just been put where they were as to any real belief in X^{t}. Previously however, or over and above all this, there would be the ‹as› demur (let the mir have been what it might) of – by what power, by whose agency or help? For if X^{t} does a mir prob he may do it by alliance with some Z standing behind, out of sight. Or if by his own skill, how or whence derived, or of what nature. This obstinately recurrent question remains.

[2 r.]
There is not the meanest court in Cendom or Islam y^{t} w^{d} not say – if called on to adjudicate the rights of an estate on such evid as the mere *facts* of the Gospel – Oh good God, how we can do this? Which of us knows who this Matthew[8] was – whether ever he lived – or if so wrote a line of all this – or, if he did, how situated as to motives, as to means of inform^{ation}, as to judgment and discernment? ‹In› Who knows anything of the combin^{ations} as to circ^{ces}, persons, interests in which the whole narrative originated, or when? All is dark and dusty. Nothing in such a case *can* be proved but what shines by its own light.

[written vertically in right hand margin]
The old man = the original man, as in Timon of Athens.[9]

[written inverse to the rest of the text on the page]
Ah reader you little dream of our mission. You shall see both of us – getting ‹at the› within the next 5 years getting at the heart and rending the heart of some old nuisances – it was unavoidable and granted as they draw themselves {↑ seem to others}, and ‹a› as safe as they seems to y^{m}selves.

[text continued, right side up, from top of page]
I was thinking how impossible it is to avoid a certain shade of dissimul^{ation} – E.g. a lady asked in the amenity of convers^{ation} as to ‹how she› if she does not think such an overture beaut &c., could not without intol pedantry deny unless she had a strong neg opinion. Up to a certain depth therefore within

this field of dissimul^{ation} you must go. ‹How far?› Now this is very remarkable – y^{t} in this necessity is = to the issue of *demonstr*^{ation} in religion. No demonstr-^{ation} as to God: no *absolute* boundary as to moral compliance. You must compromise, and shew your religion by temperating and ‹*managing*› *management* of every poss miracle. Nay, God himself could not attest a miracle – *but* (listen to this) – *but* (hear this my friend) – *but* by the internal revelation or visiting of the spirit – to evade which, to dispense with which, a miracle is ever resorted to.

XYZ.[10] – You never *can* tell that a man is holy: and for the plain reason that God only can read the heart.

[ON MIRACLES]
MS B

The manuscript is held in the collection of Frederick Burwick. It is one sheet, measuring 180 by 115 mm, folded geminate to form four pages, first and fourth recto, second and third verso. It is written in black ink. There are no watermarks.

For details of the 'Conventions for Manuscript Transcription', see above, p. xvii. For the context of the manuscript, as well as its presentation by Japp, see headnote, p. 490.

[1 r., right column]
Besides {↑ ye obj to} miracles y^{t} they are not capable of attestation, Hume's objection[1] is not y^{t} they are false but incommunicable. Two diff. duties arise for the man who witnesses a miracle, and for him who receives it traditionally. The duty of the 1st is to confide in his own xperience which may besides have been repeated; of the 2nd to confide in his und which says – Less marvel y^{t} the reporter sh^{d} have erred y^{n} that nat sh^{d} have been violated.

By the way – it is said: No miracle can be greater y^{n} another. But even objecting

[1 v., left column]
this is only as to Spirit. All force is equal subjectively, even X^{t} {ink stain}. Tells you y^{t} i.e. as regards to powers required for doing y^{m} – y^{se} differ greatly.

How clearly do the villains betray y^{r} own hypocr ab^{t} the divinity of X^{ty}, and at the same time the meanness of their own natures, who think the Messiah or God's Messenger must 1st prove his own com by an act

[1v., right column]
of power. Whereas 1. a new revel^{ation} of moral forces c^{d} not be invented by all gener^{ations}. 2. an act of power much more probably argues an alliance with the devil. – I should gloomily suspect a man who comes forward as a magician.

Sup the gospels written 30 y^{rs} after the events – and by ignorant superst men who have adopted the fables y^{t} old women have surrounded X^{t} with. How does this supposition vitiate their report of X^{ts}

[1 r., left column]
Parables? –But, on ye other hand they c^{d} no more have invented the Parables y^{n} a man alleging a diamond mine c^{d} invent a diamond as attest^{ation}. The Parables prove y^{m} selves.

[ON MIRACLES]
MS C

The manuscript is held in the collection of Frederick Burwick. It is two pieces of paper, written in black ink, and trimmed to measure 90 by 125 mm. The two pieces are glued to a backing sheet, which has rendered the verso illegible.

For details of the 'Conventions for Manuscript Transcription', see above, p. xvii. For the context of the manuscript, see headnote, p. 490.

Miracles: – Every such case is separated f^{m} the hearer by a resistance which may be represented as a moat or canal. It requires a power to waft it across to the hearer. Testimony is too weak. – The fact is a *weight* which testimony cannot raise to the level of the hearer. – Here the resistance to be overcome is considerable: whatever it is, call it X. If you say – But what does X mean. Why this it means – that it is a *quantum:* a certain amount. And tho' it is very true y^{t} you do not know what it is, and for that reason m^{t} think it useless at first sight. Yet upon consider^{ation} – you will see y^{t} ‹it› tho' ignorant of X, you yet know that the ½ of X – or X divided amgst 2 (written thus x/2) is doubtless x/4. This single Fact makes this apparently useless sum useful.

[paste on slip:]

useful! useful for comparisons with a million of *things* henceforward to be placed in comparison to this miracle as to its strength of credibility. Each of the million ms no have ‹a› {↑ it's} separate valu^{ation} ‹which you brought›.

[LET HIM COME DOWN FROM THE CROSS]

The manuscript is held at Dove Cottage, Grasmere, as MS 1989: 130. It is a single sheet folded once, and then opened out flat before writing, the resulting fold-mark being used as a column divider. The order of writing is recto (left column), recto (right column); verso (left column), verso (right column). The paper is lined and written in black ink. There is no watermark.

The present manuscript is related in theme and tone to De Quincey's theological writings of the mid-1840s, and is clearly linked to MS A of 'On Miracles', for both feature the phrase 'Let him come down from the cross' from Matthew 27: 42 (see above, p. 491).

Japp published a version of this manuscript but, characteristically, altered it in a number of ways (cf. Japp, *PW*, vol. I, pp. 177–9).

For details of the 'Conventions for MS Transcription', see above, p. xvii.

[1 r., left column]

Let him come down f^{m}. the Cross. &c. Now this is exceedingly worth consider^{n}. I know not at all whether what I am going to say has been said already: ‹f› life w^{d}. not suffice in every field or section of a field to search every nook and section of a nook for the poss^{ties}. of chance utterance given to any stray opinion. But this I know without any doubt at all – that it cannot have been said effectually, cannot have been so said as to publish and disperse itself: else it is impossible that the crazy logic current upon these topics sh^{d}. have lived, or that many separate arg^{ts}. sh^{d}. ever for very shame have been uttered. – Said or not said, let us presume it unsaid: and let me state the true ans^{r}. as if de novo[1] even if by acc^{t}. somewhere the darkness shelters this same ans^{r}. as uttered long ago. – Now therefore I will sup. y^{t}. he *had* come down from the Cross. No case can so powerfully illustrate the filthy falsehood and pollution of that idea which men generally entertain, which ‹*creditable*› the sole creditable books universally build upon. What w^{d}. have follow-

[1 r., right column]
2)
ed? This w^{d}. have followed: that, inverting the order of every true eman^{-}. f^{m}. God, instead of growing and expanding forever like a

[diagram]

it would have attained its *maximum* at the first. ‹In› The effect for the half hour w^{d}. have been prodigious: and from that moment when it began to flag, it w^{d}. degrade rapidly until in 3 days a far fiercer hatred ‹and› ag^{t}. X^{t}. would have been moulded. For observe: into what state of mind w^{d}. this marvel have been received? Into any good will towards X^{t}., which previously had been defeated by the belief y^{t} he was an impostor in the sense y^{t} he pretended to a ‹m› power of miracles which in fact he had not? By no means. The sense in which X^{t}. ‹w› had been an impostor for them, was – in assuming a commission, a spiritual embassy with appropriate functions, promises, prospects, to which he had no title. How had that notion – not viz. of miraculous impostorship but of spiritual impostorship – been able to maintain itself? Why, what should have reasonably destroyed the notion? This viz. the sublimity of his moral system. But does the reader imagine – that this sublimity is of a nature to be seen intellectually: that is, insulated and *in vacuo*[2] for the intellect

[1 v., left column]
3)
No more y^{n} by geometry or by a sorites[3] any man constitutionally imperfect could come to understand the nature of the sexual appetite: or a man born deaf could make representable to himself the living truth of ‹col› music, a man born blind could make rep^{ble}. the living truth of colors. All men are not equally deaf in heart: far f^{m}. it: the differences are infinite: and some men never ^{c}d. comprehend the beauty of sp. truth. But no man ^{c}d. comp. it without prepar^{-} That prepar^{-} was found in his training of Judaism: which to those whose hearts were hearts of flesh not stony and charmed ag^{t}. hearing, had already anticipated the first outlines of X^{tian}. ideas. Sin, purity, holiness unimaginable, these had already been inoculated into the Jewish mind. And amongst the rare inoculated Xt. found enough for a central nucleus to his future church. But the nat^{l}. tendency under the fever mist of strife and passion evoked by the present ‹sh› posit^{n}. in the world operating upon robust full blooded life unshaken by grief or tenderness of nature or constit^{l}. ‹m› sadness is to fail altogether of seeing the features which so powerfully mark X^{ty}. Those features instead of coming out into strong relief resemble what we see in mountainous regions

[1 v., right column]
4)
We have heard of men saying – give me such titles of honor, so many myriads of pounds, and then I will consider of your proposal y^{t} I sh^{d}. turn X$^{tian.}$ ‹What› Now survey – pause for one mom^{t}. to survey – the immeasurable effrontery of this speech. First it ‹is› replies to a proposal hav^{g}. what object – our happiness or his? Why of course his: how are we interested, except on a sublime principle of benevolence, in his faith being right. Secondly, it is a ‹pr› reply presum^{g}. money the most fleshly of objects to modify or any way control a religion i.e. a spiritual concern. This in itself is already monstrous: and pretty much the same as it w^{d}. be to order a charge of bayonets ag^{t}. gravit^{-} or ag^{t}. an avalanche, or against an earthquake, or ag^{t}. a deluge. But, suppose it were *not* so, what incomprehensible reasoning justifies the notion – y^{t} not we are to be paid but that he is to be paid for a change not concerning or affecting our ‹own› happiness but his?

[DRAFT PAGES ON BURKE FOR REVIEW OF SCHLOSSER'S *LITERARY HISTORY OF THE EIGHTEENTH CENTURY*]

The manuscript is held at Dove Cottage, Grasmere, as MS 1989: 161.62. It consists of two sheets of white paper, written in black ink on the recto only. Page one is 182 by 226 mm; page two is 182 by 102 mm. There are no watermarks.

The manuscript was intended by De Quincey to form part of his discussion of 'FOX AND BURKE' in his review of Schlosser's *Literary History of the Eighteenth Century* (see above, pp. 205–8). The fragment features De Quincey's castigation of Germany as 'a nation of babies', and his most explicit denunciation of Schlosser for his hostile attitude toward Burke. 'Schlosser', declares De Quincey, 'is a jacobin', and 'therefore he hates' Burke, 'the great leader of Anti-jacobins'.

For details of the 'Conventions for Manuscript Transcription', see above, p. xvii.

[1 r.]
{↑ a} smouldering fire. But because Burke has never been adequately translated, not in German, not in French, ‹he still› {↑ locally he} moves forward with disadvantage: amongst foreigners he appeals only to those, an increasing body however, that speak English: and on this account the more to be resented would be any disparaging notice of Burke; how much more then the ‹outrageous› scandalous outrages of Schlosser! – Everything in fact reminds us in Germany, both ‹in› its history from year to year, and its literature, ‹that› {↑ even ‹their› the possibility of such a treatment for Burke, that} whatever may be the German merits in other directions, upon all questions of politics, of social philosophy, of legislation, or of political economy, the Germans are a nation of babies. Having all lived, grown up, and been trained, under despotisms, ‹and but› {↑ yet} called {↑ too hastily} ‹suddenly› ‹and from› by the contagion of opinions in {↑ the} 3 leaders of ‹civil› civilization – England, France, and America, to participate practically in political reforms for which they are utterly unprepared by habits ‹and history›, they ‹would› {↑ would find it their destiny} at any rate {↑ to} make many mistakes. But unhappily,

‹they are› if infants ‹in› politically, they are almost grey-headed in ‹philos› speculative philosophy. All the delirium of metaphysics, that ever *could* be brought to bear on human life, **x** stands ready {↑ therefore} at the very vestibule of their political existence to combine with their rude essays in national police, ‹and› and to {↑ invest} ‹give› them {↑ with} the character of projects in Laputa.[1] ‹If› {↑ Such then being their circumstances, if ‹that› in Europe} there were a man that could ‹rescue them› reveal to them ‹their› this besetting danger, if there were a man that by the grandeur of his natural authority as a potent intellect could balance ‹th› for Germany the excessive bias of that people to the metaphysical, to the *à priori*,[2] to the non-practical, that man ‹is› {↑ seemed to be} Burke. ‹And› Yet him, ‹this good ‹{↑ better}› angel for the cradle of the {↑ a} newborn people›, this lamp for the feet of ‹pol› a race under triple chances of going astray, ‹does Schlosser strive to intercept. Schloss–›

[2 r.]

this better angel for the cradle of a newborn nation, ‹who› an angel that rose too late for the French revolution, ‹coming when already› first raising his trumpet when the hurricane was let loose, and the great deeps were breaking up, but now whilst ‹yet› {↑ Germany is moving ‹surely›} it is not too late might speak with effect to so intellectual a race as the Germans, ‹who are moving quietly for› *him* would Schlosser intercept. Schlosser is a jacobin. Naturally therefore he hates the great leader of Anti-jacobins: and in this instance probably he does not act without ‹a› secret promptings from secret German Societies moving in darkness. – Well: right enough: be a jacobin, Schlosser, *meinetwegen:*[3] only don't speak the language of barbarians upon the merits of great human leaders. Else perhaps it will be time for us Anti-jacobins to be ‹subscribing to a fund for› {↑ turning our thoughts towards} the assassination of Herr Schlosser: and that would be distressing to our feelings.

ON THE RELIGIOUS OBJECTIONS TO THE USE OF CHLOROFORM IN OBSTETRIC MEDICINE

The manuscript is a letter by De Quincey that forms part of the graduation thesis of his son Francis John De Quincey (1823–61), and is held in the University of Edinburgh Library, Special Collections (MD 1849). Francis's thesis is entitled *On the Religious Objections to the use of Chloroform in Obstetric Medicine*, and is eighty-five pages in total. It is written on blue-lined white paper with red horizontal marginal lines. The pages measure 212 by 272 mm, and are bound in black leather, now badly scuffed. The thesis itself covers from page one to page sixty-six. De Quincey's letter begins at the bottom of page sixty-six and concludes on page eighty-five. The entire work, including De Quincey's letter, is written in Francis's hand. De Quincey's letter is dated 'December, 1847'. Francis completed the thesis, and copied out his father's letter, sometime in the following fifteen months, for pages three, thirteen, fifteen, forty-seven, seventy-nine and eighty-five are watermarked '1848', and on the title page the thesis is dated '31st March, 1849'.

Francis John was De Quincey's third son. He was born in the Lake District, but grew up in Edinburgh. In 1840 he went to work in Manchester for a family friend, but was back in Scotland by 1845, living with his father and sisters at Lasswade, and studying at the University of Edinburgh. He graduated with his medical degree in 1849, and two years later travelled to Brazil. In 1853 his sister Florence described him as

> like a May morning, he is of such a bright nature. He seems sometimes beset by a demon of fun that sweeps him along he doesn't know where....We have no fears now, however, as he has gone through the dry hard studies necessary for his profession with great credit, and under very disadvantageous circumstances, and now he has been gone from home for nearly three years to pursue his profession in a place where the people seem so childish that tho. he finds them good natured, and can extract the most exquisite amusement from them, in all other respects it is extremely distasteful (Eaton, p. 440).

Francis died in Rio de Janeiro of Yellow Fever in 1861.

De Quincey's letter to Francis on the religious objections to chloroform was highly topical. Chloroform was discovered, described, and named in the early 1830s. In January 1847, James Simpson (1811–70; *DNB*), Professor of Obstetrics at the University of Edinburgh, became the first to use ether in obstetric practice. But he sought a more effective and manageable agent, and later that year he substituted chloroform for ether, with great success. In November 1847, in Edinburgh, he made a report to the Edinburgh Medical and Chirurgical Society: *Account of a New Anaesthetic Agent, as a substitute for sulphuric ether in surgery and midwifery.* His use of chloroform as an anaesthetic, however, was immediately objected to on several grounds, including religious, based on a literal understanding of Genesis 3: 16, in which God curses Eve: 'in sorrow thou shalt bring forth children'. Simpson replied a month later, in December 1847, with an *Answer to the Religious Objections Advanced Against the Employment of Anaesthetic Agents in Midwifery and Surgery.* De Quincey must have read Simpson's pamphlet as soon as it was published, and written his letter immediately thereafter, for it also carries the date of 'December, 1847'. In his thesis (p. 66), Francis recorded that

> Soon after the discovery of chloroform I wrote to my father upon the subject of the religious objections, and in reply received from him the following letter. Coming from one of consummate learning, of great powers of mind and a constant student of the Bible I regard {↑ it} as of great importance. Indeed...{↑ this} letter ought to settle the matter. Especially when opposed only by men, who, alike by mental qualifications, by education and by pursuits, are unfitted for expressing an opinion upon such a subject.

The views of Simpson and De Quincey soon came to be accepted, and as early as the middle of 1848 Simpson could write that 'here, in Edinburgh, I never now meet with any objections on this point, for the religious, like the other forms of opposition to chloroform, have ceased amongst us'. Widespread acceptance of chloroform came in 1853 when it was administered to Queen Victoria during the birth of her eighth child, Prince Leopold (A. D. Farr, 'Early opposition to obstetric anaesthesia' in *Anaesthesia*, 35 (1980), p. 905).

De Quincey's letter was first published in Masson (vol. XIV, pp. 286–93), who used an ellipsis to remove the passage on diarrhoea that runs from [505.28] 'For in a diarrhoea' to [506.3–4] 'Strange almost as those of nature.' De Quincey's letter is published here in its entirety for the first time.

For details of the 'Conventions for Manuscript Transcription', see above, p. xvii.

[66]
December, 1847.

My Dear Francis,

Say this fact to your heart (whether a great fact, a middle sized fact, or a little fact I know not, but a fact it is) that between sending a letter to Astrachan, or to the Imaum of

[67]

Muscat, and sending a letter to your shoemaker in George Street Edinburgh,[1] the difference, as to trouble of body, as to anxiety of mind and indeed as to postage is next door to nothing. The Shoemaker, it is true, receives your letter, if once it is lodged in the post office, without farther trouble on your part. But so does His Highness of Muscat. The true point of difficulty is – (and in that stage of the transaction the shoemaker costs you quite as much trouble as the Imaum) first of all to reach the post office. Hic labor; hoc opus est.[2] And for us especially it is so. The interval remember between us and this particular post office at Lasswade[3] – (meaning by interval the total diaulos[4] of *to* and *fro*, outward and homeward ‹xxxxxxx› voyage) is a good three miles. Hence my delay, and also from this other cause; that having mislaid your jotting of doubts and queries, I had lost the only guide to my own replies and suggestions.

I. As to Dr Simpson's citation from the

[68]

dramatic poet Middleton, I feel satisfied (from the internal evidence) that it is genuine. The only demur connects itself with the date – 1657 – (If you are right in reporting *that* as the date it puzzles me.)[5] What motive or encouragement could a publisher have for bringing out any Book connected with the stage between 1640 and 1660? Cromwell died in 1658[6] and certainly the period of his Protectorate was not the gloomiest of that puritanical *Vicennium*,[7] but it was gloomy enough. There was no motive of gain at that time, and there might be some dangers in publishing what were viewed as wicked books by the dominant party.

II. But why should there be any difficulty as to Middleton's having noticed a fact, which Dr Simpson, I think, shews, (but here I am speaking from memory) to have been known amongst the Greek Physicians?

[69]

Medicine was much attended to by the literary men of the 17th century: for instance the use of *friction*, the application of the *metallic tractors*, as practised 40 or 50 years ago by the American Empiric – all this was elaborately anticipated by Greatorex in Charles II d's reign.[8] He again had certainly been anticipated by Greeks and Romans. Somewhere in Plautus, I remember a jesting allusion to the medical treatment by traction, in which allusion the adverb *tractim* occurs as part of the expression.[9] And subsequently I remember to have met with cryptical allusions to most of the *medical raving*, which we regard as most peculiarly of modern growth, in Greek writers before the 9th Century of our aera. I must also have pointed out to you the still more singular fact that Hahnemann's doctrine (not as to

[70]

infinitesimal doses but) as to Homoiopathy and Alloiopathy[10] is most distinctly stated and ably exemplified by Milton about 1671 – viz: in the preface to his Samson Agonistes.[11] It is clear that Milton had reflected deeply on Physiology, and other branches of your splendid and infinite profession.

Any reader of this assertion will naturally be startled even more by the *situation* of such a strange hypothesis, than by it's Authorship – by it's local connexion with a Hebrew Tragedy, than by it's personal connexion with Milton. Strange enough in all conscience, that a great poet of the 17th Century should anticipate the German medical innovator of the 19th Century; but stranger still, that for a medical or physiological hypothesis, this great poet should have devised no more suitable situation than in a critical disputation on the principles

[71]

of art, concerned in the Greek tragic drama. So it is however; and really the Miltonic Hahnemannism is more satisfactory than the Miltonic criticism on Grecian Art. Those difficult questions that arise upon the Greek ideas of tragedy, are but grazed or ruffled upon the surface. True – there was not room for doing much more – But then the room was even less that was ‹disposable› disposable for Hahnemann = and yet in the very few words uttered, a most comprehensive outline of the doctrine is sketched, which scarcely allows of improvement. Neither is the introduction of this medical digression, after all, so violent an intrusion as he imagines before hand. It arises naturally enough upon the well known but obscure passage in Aristotle, ascribing to Tragedy the office of purifying the passions by ministrations of pity and terror.[12] The first demur of any note upon this passage is –

[72]

"How? – purify a passion by a *passion*?" "Why yes – even so." is virtually Milton's reply. It seems a strange rationale of medical practice; but in effect it is the very logic nature prompts us to, in the treatment of our own bodily morbid affections. For in a diarrhoea we do not proceed by introducing a counter agency, but a *similar* agency. We do not curb the diarrhoea: on the contrary we ‹curb **xxx** late **xxx**› mimic the natural diarrhoea by an artificial diarrhoea through medicine. Again if a man suffers from a morbid discharge of blood, is it the policy of medicine violently to restrain that discharge? Far from it. The first step is to bleed the patient. The morbid hoemorrhage is attacked by an artificial hoemorrhage, which often succeeds in re-establishing the disordered system. That is to say *pathé* or morbid affections are *redressed* by *homoiopathé*, similar affections

[73]
and not by *alloiopathé*, affections of an alien nature.

What strange vagaries does literature present! Strange almost as those of nature.

Now, as regards the monstrous objections, calling themselves religious, to Dr Simpson's immortal discovery (which discovery I should think will be found to have done more for human comfort, and for the mitigation of animal suffering, than any other discovery whatever). The Doctor's own arguments seem quite sufficient. In the same spirit as these arguments might be suggested such as the following.

I. *Three-score years and ten.*

This is the limit assigned to human life in the Psalms[13] – Consequently in the logic‹al› of these "religious" cavillers, it must be impious to prescribe for a man of 80. And the whole science of *Macrobiotics* must rank with witchcraft and necromancy

[74]
in point of wickedness. Lord Bacon thought otherwise.[14]

II. "*Poverty shall never cease from the land*".[15]

Ergo, it must be profane to attempt the limitation of poverty; and absolutely blasphemous to effect it's extirpation, as was once done in the New England states and elsewhere.

III. "*In Sorrow shall thou bring forth.*"[16]

Dr Simpson's improved interpretation of the Hebrew word, making it to indicate the muscular uterine exertion which attends parturition, (and attends it so pre-eminently in the *human* female) rather than to indicate the pain generally connected with this exertion, seems quite sufficient for the occasion.[17] Another argument suggests itself: viz: that if all pain when carried to the stage which we call agony (or intense struggle amongst vital functions) brings with it some danger to life (as I presume must be the case) then it will follow – that knowingly to

[75]
reject a means of mitigating, or wholly cancelling the danger, now that such a means has been discovered and tested, travels on the road towards suicide. If I am right in supposing a danger to life, lying in this direction, then clearly the act of rejecting the remedy, being wilful, lies in a suicidal direction. It is even worse than an ordinary movement in that direction; because it makes God an accomplice, through the scriptures, in this suicidal movement; nay the primal instigator to it by means of a supposed curse interdicting the use of any means whatever (though revealed by Himself) for annulling that curse. This turns the tables on the *religiosity* people; landing them in the guilt of abetting what

will be henceforward be regarded as a step towards suicide – viz: by abetting the rejection of a known anodyne, potent enough to reduce

[76]

the chances of a fatal issue.

IV. On the argument which would forbid the use of this almost magical anodyne, all the prophylactic means hitherto used for lessening the violence of symptoms in parturition, must have been lawful only in the inverse ratio of their efficacy. To be altogether clear of guilt, the means used must be confessedly and altogether ineffective. I do not pretend to any knowledge upon this subject – but I have a general ‹xxxxx› impression that bleeding and other means are employed in long stages antecedent to childbirth, for the purpose of disarming the symptoms beforehand of their violence, and preparing an easier course of gestation, as well as an easier delivery. Now, if so, what wretches these practitioners must suddenly discover themselves to have been! Do they fancy that it is any different offence to disarm

[77]

a sting partially and before hand, from that newly discovered offence of plucking out the sting completely at the moment of it's hostile action? Is their only excuse for this long series of crime, that after all, their work was done imperfectly? That they failed to give relief – is that their plea? My advice to these {↑ villains} ‹villains› is – to remember the old argument – *"In for a penny, in for a pound."*:[18] they are already up to the lips in guilt: let them therefore, like sensible reprobates, *go the whole hog*[19] by patronising chloroform.

V. There is a case parallel to this in the popish Codes of Casui‹x›stry. Is it not a scriptural doctrine that we should *mortify the flesh*?[20] Certainly it is. No protestant denies it. And upon that argument many a young woman in Convents, with the sanction of her directors and confessors, has founded a reputation for Saintliness upon the practice

[78]

of swallowing the most revolting selections of filth. Southey illustrated a shocking case of that nature in the Quarterly Review.[21] But in the Dublin newspapers, and I think about the same time, occurred a case of the same kind, that terminated in consequences, over which no veils of cloister secrecy could be drawn. A young girl, under some popish superstition, ate large quantities of the earth around the grave of some Priest who had died in the odor of sanctity. This odor, meantime, had not availed to banish the larvae of some hideous beetles. These established themselves in the poor girls intestines. A dreadful illness ensued, with what final result I do not remember.

Now this mode of mortifying the flesh by positive acts; viz: by eating vermin, resembles the present anti-chloroform mode of mortifying the flesh by

[79]

negative acts – viz:, by abstaining from chloroform, in the final consequences: both modes augment the chance of death, and therefore load with the guilt of suicide, those who knowingly become parties to either. The two practices are akin also in this – that both have drawn a furious support from superstition – both plead scriptural words for practices that are essentially unscriptural.

VI. Dr Simpson's notice of the exemption from the worst sufferings of childbirth enjoyed by some races of women is much strengthened by various Polynesian experiences. I fancy that Ellis notices these cases in his Polynesian Researches.[22] In a separate work (not by Ellis) on the particular Island of Tonga (i.e. Tonga ta boo, or Tonga the sacred) I remember a case of total immunity from pain or even momentary lassitude in a native woman during parturition.[23]

[80]

VII. Now, addressing myself no longer to every body, but to you in particular, I am of opinion that your own exegesis or suggestion for a proper exegesis of the original curse – is plausible, and will be thought so by Dr Simpson. No VI argues that the curse is not unconditional, but is perhaps dependant on conditions of diet, of habits engrafted on civilization &c Once removed, the curse loses it's sanctity. Dr Simpson again by his new ‹xxxxxxx› version of the Hebrew word, so transmutes the whole bearings of the passage, as to ‹connect› disconnect it from all liability to these religious scruples against chloroform in childbirth: nothing is disturbed by the chloroform that ever was fixed by the primal decree. Next, comes your own suggestion,[24] which while retaining the curse, evades it by a new interpretation. If it were said, "In sorrow shalt thou eat thy bread" –

[81]

we should not understand the sorrow as settling upon the act of taking food, which on the contrary is one of the commonest enjoyments of life; but we should understand that life itself as a general function of the body, was described by one of it's most general necessities. So also in this case you understand the curse addressed to woman; being simply that she, not less than her partner man, should sorrow through life. But life in *her* is described by a variation of phrase suited to her sexual differences. In man it had been expressed by his peculiar and separate form of activity; viz: by labor applied to the creation of food. In woman the characteristic and differential form of activity being applied – not to the gaining of a livlihood – but to the necessities, cares, innumerable duties connected with the bringing into the world and

[82]
the rearing of children, the expression of the curse has varied itself ‹xxx› correspondingly. The two modes of expression vary with the sex: but the thing expressed is exactly the same; viz: the whole tenor of life; denoted in each by the function which lies upon the surface and strikes the understanding as most distinguishing. It might have been said, with the same exact meaning – to man, "*Thou shalt plough the ground in sorrow*" – to woman, "*Thou shalt spin the garments of thy household in sorrow*": but the scriptural expression has settled upon still wider forms for indicating most comprehensively the process of life. The Curse therefore, is by you so read as to extend itself to life generally; and not as limiting itself to the sources of sorrow involved in the production of children. But lastly if the curse were so limited; I say, if the curse were understood as limited to the

[83]
evils arising through maternity, why should those evils be contemplated as lying chiefly in the very ‹transitory› transient and physical act of parturition? Agonizing as the sufferings from childbirth have occasionally proved (as many great obstetric surgeons have assured us), expressing their fury sometimes by sudden lunacy the most frantic, sometimes by infanticide unconscious or semi conscious – consequences that henceforth are doomed to subside as the billows of the tormented Red Sea before the uplifted rod of Amram's son,[25] – still these sufferings are transitory as compared with the lifelong fears, cares, and trepidations connected with the rearing, training, and disposal of children. *There* lies the sorrow; *there* the opening for a real curse; viz: in the moral and not in the mere physical woe; in the moral woe that lasts through a lifetime; and

[84]
not in the physical woe that after a few days' fearful heaving and convulsion is hushed into a deep rest from the storm – either that rest which lies in restoration to health, or in the deeper rest which lies in the sabbath of Death.

VIII. If it were possible that, in this age of the world, religious scruples such as those now passed in review could maintain their ground, it is certain that a conflict absolutely without precedent, and shocking to contemplate, would arise between the scrupulous practitioner and his patients. A general knowledge of the new anodyne, and of it's instantaneous efficacy will be diffused with a rapidity corresponding to the extensive field of it's application. The whole female sex have within a few weeks come into possession of a great inheritance, of a talisman, suddenly, as it were, *revealed* to them; and the powers of

[85]
this talisman apply themselves to the very class of cases {↑ that} naturally besiege‹ing› the terrified imaginations of females beyond all others. A new anchor has been made known, fitted for the special order of storms that are the most widely appalling to females, as being the catholic inheritance of their sex. This they will now demand when suffering in extremity. To refuse would be – to create scenes the most dreadful of feud between the medical attendant and his patients. The issue of such feuds could not be long doubtful. But in the meantime they would create a scandal shocking to a profession of gentlemen.

IX. And finally, is there any real religious scruple at the bottom of these objections? Is it not a jealousy of Professor Simpson's great discovery that *really* speaks through this jesuitical masquerade of conscientious scruples? Thomas de Quincey.

[RALPH WALDO EMERSON'S *ESSAYS: FIRST SERIES*]

The manuscript is a set of notes written by De Quincey on the rear endpapers of his copy of Ralph Waldo Emerson's *Essays: First Series, New Edition* (Boston: James Munroe, 1847). The volume was presented to De Quincey by Emerson in February 1848, when Emerson was lecturing and visiting in Edinburgh. Emerson wrote an inscription on the front free endpaper: 'Thomas De Quincey, Esq / With the respects of / R. W. Emerson'. The volume is now in private hands. De Quincey's notes are published here for the first time.

De Quincey and Emerson met in Edinburgh in February 1848. Accounts of the visit are mixed. On the one hand, according to the editor and essayist Peter Landreth, De Quincey had not been 'deeply impressed by his few glances at Emerson's first essays', and had been heard 'depreciating' him as 'the *palimpsest* of a small Thomas Carlyle'. Landreth attended a dinner designed to bring the two writers together, but over the course of the evening they spoke very little, and later De Quincey fell asleep at Emerson's lecture. Yet on the other hand, letters by both De Quincey and Emerson indicate that they spent a good deal of time together, and seem genuinely to have enjoyed one another's company. 'De Quincey is a small old man', Emerson wrote shortly after his arrival,

> with a very handsome face, and a face too expressing the highest refinement, a very gentle old man, speaking with the greatest deliberation & softness....He talked of many matters, all easily & well, but chiefly social & literary, & did not venture into any voluminous music....He invited me to dine with him on the following Saturday at Lass Wade...& I accepted.

During Emerson's dinner at Lasswade there was 'a good deal of talk'. The party then traveled into Edinburgh and, to Emerson's delight, De Quincey was 'at [the] lecture!' he gave. The next day the two dined together for a third time. At some point Emerson presented De Quincey with an inscribed copy of the new edition of his *Essays*, and told him that 'the Op. Eater is ruler of the *Night*' (see below, p. 512). When Emerson left Edinburgh the following day to journey north to Dundee, De Quincey was at the station to see him off. At the same time, Emerson asked De Quincey for 'a few lines' of introduction to Derwent Coleridge, and De Quincey happily obliged. 'Emerson...will speak for himself', De Quincey told Derwent,

> and I dare say he *has* spoken to you already through his books; which have this amongst their other fascinations – that, whatever good one may

> have raised out of their mines, always a suspicion remains of deeper treasures left behind....It can be little...to add – that he has been greatly admired in this place by most of those who concern themselves with literature or with philosophy, and by none more than by your old friend (of 41 years' standing).

The present notes indicate that De Quincey continued to engage with Emerson after he had left Edinburgh (Peter Landreth, 'Emerson's meeting with De Quincey' in *Blackwood's*, 155 (1894), pp. 481, 491; *The Letters of Ralph Waldo Emerson*, ed. Ralph L. Rusk (New York: Columbia University Press, 1939), vol. IV, pp. 19–20, 22, 25; Houghton Library, Harvard bMS Am 1280. 226 (3340)).

For details of the 'Conventions for Manuscript Transcription', see above, p. xvii.

[1 v.]
"I have no xpect."[1] No: it is the vain folly, which so often I have secretly laughed at of fancying that the village 4 miles off and therefore idealized by a purple haze – has not its own dunghills – puddles – dust-heaps just as this before us. How childish to fancy that our village, ‹with› the vills which ‹**xx**› we overlook f^r. our bedroom window as lying all around us, will not have its own purple haze if you go 4 miles away.

p. 123 – I read this pass. ab^t. simplicity[2] just as I was think^g. of that wretched cant applying ‹the› {↑ some supposed} scriptural "idea of *simplicity* to the incremen^-. of Greek church. See Blackwood[3]

[2 r.]
p. 132 – "are wiser men than others."[4] No: nor that the peasantry of Alps have any Alpine elevation of sentiment.

314 From 10th. l. to the end. sh^d. be Emerson's motto[5]

p. – What he says somewhere of "that yellow Iachimo"[6] – the Turkish Op. Eater is in effect Virgils case of Jove and Caesar. *Dio. imp. cum J. Caesar habet.*[7] By Emerson's own confession the Op. Eater is ruler of the *Night*.[8]

244 of *six* thousand years – oh shameful![9]

247 A wise old proverb – to end of par. Quote in Op. Conf.[10] – Say. so also acts Fear. the walls give way. Muslin curtains only are stretched around an infinite Bivouac on ‹a› an endless plain heath ‹on› over which are stealing

[2 v.]
upon us in darkness infinite Titan[11] nurseries

burst

67 out of *the* window – not out of window so I here no doubt burst out a laughing[12]

[War]

The manuscript is a draft fragment published in Japp, *PW.* The original has not been traced. Japp entitles the fragment 'The True Justifications of War', and describes it as 'evidently intended to appear in the article on *War*' (Japp, *PW,* vol. I, pp. 315–6).

For the occasion and context of De Quincey's essay on 'War', see headnote, pp. 267–8.

Most of what has been written on this subject (the cruelty of war), in connection with the apparently fierce ethics of the Old Testament, is (with submission to sentimentalists) false and profoundly unphilosophic. It is of the same feeble character as the flashy modern moralizations upon War. The true justifications of war lie far below the depths of any soundings taken upon the charts of effeminate earth-born ethics. And ethics of God, the Scriptural ethics, search into depths that are older and less measurable, contemplate interests that are more mysterious and entangled with perils more awful than merely human philosophy has resources for appreciating. It is not at all impossible that a crisis has sometimes arisen for the human race, in which its capital interest may be said to have ridden at single anchor. Upon the issue of a single struggle between the powers of light and darkness – upon a motion, a bias, an impulse given this way or that – all may have been staked. Out of Judaism came Christianity, and the mere possibility of Christianity. From elder stages of the Hebrew race, hidden in thick darkness to us, descended the only pure glimpse allowed to man of God's nature. Traditionally, but through many generations, and fighting at every stage with storms or with perils more than ever were revealed to *us*, this idea of God, this holy seed of truth, like some secret jewel passing onwards through armies of robbers, made its way downward to an age in which it became the matrix of Christianity. The solitary acorn had reached in safety the particular soil in which it was first capable of expanding into a forest. The narrow, but at the same time austere, truth of Judiasm, furnished the basis which by magic, as it were, burst suddenly and expanded into a vast superstructure, no longer fitted for the apprehension of one single unamiable race, but offering shelter and repose to the whole family of man. These things are most remarkable about this memorable transmigration of one faith into another, of an imperfect into a perfect religion, viz., that the early stage had but a slight resemblance to the latter, nor could have prefigured it to a human sagacity more than a larva could prefigure a chrysalis; and, secondly, that whereas the product, viz., Christianity, never has been nor will be in any danger of ruin, the germ, viz., the Judaic idea of God, the great radiation through which the Deity kept open His communication with man, apparently must more than once have approached an awful struggle for life. This solitary taper of truth, struggling across a howling wilderness of darkness, had it been ever totally extinguished, could probably never have been reillumined. It may seem an easy thing for a mere human philosophy to recover, and steadily to maintain a pure Hebrew conception of God; but so far is this from being true, that we believe it possible to expose in the closest Pagan approximation to this Hebrew type some adulterous elements such as would have ensured its relapse into idolatrous impurity.

[DR JOHNSON AND LORD CHESTERFIELD]

The location of the original manuscript of this essay is not known. It was first published by A. H. Japp in 'Some Unconscious Confessions of De Quincey' in *The Gentleman's Magazine*, 261 (1886), pp. 128–30. It was then republished, in facsimile and with a transcription, by Ben Abramson of New York, as *Thomas De Quincey: Dr Johnson and Lord Chesterfield* (1945). Abramson, however, was unaware that the manuscript had been previously published by Japp, for his title page stated that it was 'printed now for the first time'. Abramson's 'Forward' records that 'the original manuscript was in the possession of the late Mr Frank Hogan, and is now in the collection of Mr Harry Glickman' (p. 9). Based on Abramson's facsimile reproduction, the manuscript is two sheets, measuring approximately 210 by 255 mm, with writing on the recto only. Neither Japp's nor Abramson's transcription records De Quincey's deletions or the placement of his insertions. This information appears here for the first time.

The subject of the essay is the famous quarrel between Samuel Johnson (1709–84; *DNB*) and Philip Dormer Stanhope, fourth Earl of Chesterfield (1694–1773; *DNB*). Johnson had been persuaded to address his *Plan* (1747) for his *Dictionary of the English Language* (1755) to Chesterfield, but his appeal had been met with years of neglect. Just before the *Dictionary* appeared, however, Chesterfield praised it in two essays in a weekly newspaper, *The World*. Johnson did not appreciate Chesterfield's belated endorsement and proprietary tone, and in a stinging rebuke condemned him as self-satisfied and uncharitable:

> Is not a Patron, My Lord, one who looks with unconcern on a Man struggling for Life in the water and when he has reached ground encumbers him with help. The notice which you have been pleased to take of my Labours, had it been early, had been kind; but it has been delayed till I am indifferent and cannot enjoy it, till I am solitary and cannot impart it, till I am known and do not want it. (Johnson, *Letters*, vol. I, p. 96)

De Quincey's essay dates almost certainly from 1848. In May of that year, he published his review of John Forster's *Life and Adventures of Oliver Goldsmith* (see above, pp. 307–31). Forster quotes Johnson's letter to Chesterfield at length, and discusses how it was 'the mission of Johnson' to place the 'writer's craft...on a dignified and honourable basis' (Forster, pp. 188–9, 72). De Quincey cites this passage in the first sentence of the present essay when he asserts that Johnson's 'mission' was to elevate 'the social rank of literary men in England'. De Quincey also observes that Thomas Carlyle had 'held the same language' as Forster, a reference to Carlyle's discussion of Johnson in *On Heroes,*

Hero-Worship, and the Heroic in History (1841). Forster knew Carlyle's work intimately, and in his *Goldsmith* he repeatedly drew on Carlyle's portrait of Johnson in *On Heroes*. De Quincey had also grouped the two writers together in his review of *Goldsmith*, when he noted that 'Mr Forster, in his views upon the *social* rights of literature, is rowing pretty nearly in the same boat as Mr Carlyle in *his* views upon the rights of labour' (see above, p. 317).

For details of the 'Conventions for Manuscript Transcription', see above, p. xvii.

[1 r.]

‹M^{r}. Forster› According to Mr Forster, {↑ (and Mr Carlyle has held the same {↑ language} ‹doctrine›)} Dr Johnson elevated the social rank of literary men in England; nay, he had even "a mission" for doing so. He came as a Hercules[1] to cleanse the earth for the openings of civilisation. We venture to put in our *caveat* against too deep an {↑ acquiescence in} ‹acceptation of› this ‹notice› belief. Dr J. elevated literature amongst us only as every man does so who strikes, by books written in various degrees of power, some chord of human sentiment or opinion not previously struck with the same effect of instant vibration or of lingering echo. But by his *acts* he did not elevate literature. We utterly deny the ordinary construction of the case between Dr J. and lord Chesterfield. So far from being the dignified course to take, so far from the famous letter being the dignified letter to write, that both have been represented, we insist ‹it› upon it – that Dr Johnson's behaviour was that of a sturdy beggar {tear} refuses to ask for money, but expects to have it ‹x› delivered to him *instanter*[2] on looking through the window with {tear} -rific face like that of Frankenstein's monster.[3] And {↑ as to} Dr Johnson's letter, {↑ *that* (we say)} was petulant and boyish at the best: but at the worst it bore a {↑ more sinister} construction ‹that virtually and morally would bring it within the penalties of law›. ‹This we proceed to› {↑ All this let us} show: and, if any reader can overthrow us, let him do it and welcome. What was it that Dr J. was angry with lord Ch. about? It was – that lord Ch. had not sent him money. No very dignified ground therefore of expostulation, even in the case of his having had a right to expect the {↑ money} ‹it›. Certainly it is not the first time by many that we have heard of bullies in threatening letters ordering a man to put a certain bank-note under a certain stone by a certain day: but it *is* the first time that we ever heard a letter, breathing the same essential spirit of malignant extortion, held up as a model of dignity, and ‹the proper› {↑ as} a lesson on the art of – How to treat a lord, if you {↑ happen to be} ‹are› angry with him. Well; ‹to go on›. The Doctor was angry at not finding a cheque on lord Ch's banker lying under a certain stone: and it is natural to be angry at such a neglect, in case one has a right to look for that cheque under that stone. But ‹what right› how had the doctor such a right?

Had he ever condescended to ask for such a cheque? Beggars mustn't be choosers,[4] but at least they should beg; or, if too proud to beg, they should insinuate their wishes: all of which Dr J. had omitted. Perhaps then my lord had {↑ created the right by} volunteered a cheque? Not at all: ‹he› {↑ it} no more occurred to him that any reason existed for his sending a cheque to Dr J. beyond all men in England than for sending him a challenge to fight a duel. Here then we have reached the middle of the tragedy. The cheque

[2 r.]

had not been sent, and punishment must follow. Now let us see in what way *that* was administered. He reproaches lord Ch. *inter alia*[5] with having kept him waiting in his anti-chamber. We have no means of knowing how lord C. would have told that story: all depends on the duration of the waiting, and the number of its recurrences: for public men, peers of Parliament, with splendid stations, splendid estates, splendid talents, cannot ‹be at the› sit in their closets as tenants-at-will[6] to the first o‹b›streperous claimant on their time. ‹Giving› Giving interviews to a long succession of applicants, they must unavoidably cause many to wait. If the doctor waited, others ‹of› waited. But now try it both ways: Did the doctor wait often? Then behold a man dangling ‹in› after rich men in hope of patronage.[7] So far from elevating literature, here we have him as the last recorded man, that clung as a suitor to the degradation of patronage. And he rejects patronage only after patronage has {↑ rejected} ‹failed to court› *him*. Now take it the other way: the doctor was too dignified to wait. ‹oh no! *he* wait indeed to have a bone tossed to him!› – Well then, what's his charge against lord Chesterfield? Such is the dilemma: *having* any charge, {↑ ‹then› in that case} he confesses to ‹a› continued acts of self-degradation; confessing to *no* such acts, ‹then› {↑ in that case} he has no charge. Here then we have disposed of lord Chesterfield's *omissa*, as moralists say: next come his *commissa*.[8] He did *not* grant the interviews at the moment of {tear} doctor's summons; but he *did* grant two separate papers[9] to ‹a› {↑ fashionable} ‹journal› periodic ‹p› miscellany in co {tear} -tion of the doctor's dictionary. Was *that* an insult? If they were ineffectual to aid, at least they were kindly meant. But lord Ch wrote too gracefully to ‹fail› be utterly ineffectual with *any* class of readers: and it happens that the {↑ particular} class which his commendations reached, was exactly that which by influence and wealth and education was best qualified for giving effect to those commendations. And our private belief is – that the sale of the dictionary must have benefited materially (because instantly) by ‹xx› a sort of advertisement so commanding as anything in the shape of praise from the pen of Stanhope. Waive all this however, and suppose the 2 papers to have done no good; at least they ‹have done› {↑ did} no harm. And yet, except the danglings in ante-rooms which ‹we› have been discussed, nothing else is there, small or great, in the doctor's bill of exception against lord C. He says in effect that the praises had come too late, and that he could now do without them. Pause on *that*. How ‹a› was lord C. to praise a book before it was finished? That was impossible for *him*. And to Dr J. it would have been useless: for the value of the praise ‹was› as regarded *his* interest was – to sell the book: which was impossible, until it had been published. But it was a great misrepresentation ‹of› to ‹say› talk of the papers as useless because the book had now ‹been p› been published. A book is not really published, that is ‹made public› dispersed amongst the public, simply because it has announced its own existence. Books that *in posse* are published, in the sense that at the publishers' they may be had on applying for them, very often *in esse*[10] are never published at all. And it is notorious that in {↑ the case of} heavy books like large dictionaries moving off slowly for years until they have ‹become› been talked into currency, no greater service can be done than to proclaim their merits at an early stage and through an effectual organ.

[TESTIMONIAL LETTER FOR WILLIAM NICHOL]

The manuscript is held in the National Library of Scotland as MS 21239, ff. 9–10. It is two sheets of cream laid paper, each sheet measuring 181 by 104 mm, with writing in dark grey ink. There are no watermarks.

William Nichol, lithographic draftsman and printer, younger brother of John Pringle Nichol (1804–59; *DNB*), Professor of Astronomy at the University of Glasgow. William had evidently been active in Edinburgh literary circles for at least a decade, for in 1838 he invited Thomas Carlyle to the city to repeat his recent London lecture series *On the History of Literature*. Carlyle 'gracefully declined'. In 1846, William became secretary of the newly founded Edinburgh Philosophical Institution, but the appointment seems to have lasted only one year. In the present letter, De Quincey cites his 'long personal acquaintance' with Nichol, and endorses him for 'the Secretaryship of a popular institution for literary purposes', but it is not known which institution, or if Nichol received the position (Carlyle, *Letters*, vol. X, p. 120; W. Addis Miller, *The "Philosophical": a short history of the Edinburgh Philosophical Institution* (Edinburgh: C. J. Cousland and Sons, 1949), p. 8).

Although it was common to publish testimonial letters, no record of a volume of letters for Nichol has been traced. Cf. De Quincey's 1852 testimonial letter for J. F. Ferrier (Vol. 17, pp. 250–4).

For details of the 'Conventions for Manuscript Transcription', see above, p. xvii.

[9 r.]

I do not pretend to any circumstantial acquaintance with the duties incident to the Secretaryship of a popular institution for literary purposes. But generally I presume that those duties rest upon a double basis – first, upon the accomplishments of an *energetic* man, practised in business – and, secondly, upon the accomplishments of a *literary* man, who has dedicated much time to study. Travelling in such opposite directions, these separate accomplishments are not likely oftentimes to meet in the same individual. In Mr William Nichol, after a long personal acquaintance with him, I feel satisfied that they

[9 v.]
do. Generally speaking, to have been too ardently a man of business – unsettles the habits of study: to have been too sedentary a student – must be unfavorable to habits of promptness and decision. Yet sometimes a happy equilibrium may be found with regard to *these*, as with regard to *other*, natural gifts of difficult reconciliation. And in sincerity I, for my own part, have never seen this equilibrium so well exemplified as in the person of Mr Nichol. One advantage ‹which› on his part, towards this result, may have lain in his opportunities for *oral* communication with his distinguished elder brother the Astronomical Professor, and other eminent men within his circle of intimacy: he must naturally have found his intellectual attainments facilitated and shortened by such counsels, so as to

[10 r.]
leave a larger portion ‹than› of his time, than might else have been possible, available for the business of active life. But, however this may have been, the result has impressed me strongly – that for this particular occasion, imposing mixed functions active and intellectual, Mr Nichol possesses a combination of qualities which is not common: – whilst for any occasion whatever, requiring address and the management of public bodies, his peculiar kindness of manner and self-possession must be conspicuous qualifications.

Thomas de Quincey

Edinburgh
September 19, 1848.

EXPLANATORY NOTES

The abbreviation *DNB* in a note indicates that an article on the person last named will be found in the *Dictionary of National Biography.*

Notes on Walter Savage Landor {Part I}

1 The Spectator.] *The Spectator* (1711–2) was a daily newspaper founded and jointly conducted by Richard Steele (1672–1729; *DNB*) and Joseph Addison (1672–1719; *DNB*).

2 *asserted there...green man,*] Addison opened the first number of *The Spectator* by observing 'that a Reader seldom peruses a Book with Pleasure 'till he knows whether the Writer of it be a black or a fair Man, of a mild or cholerick Disposition, Married or a Batchelor, with other Particulars of the like nature, that conduce very much to the right Understanding of an Author' (*Spectator*, vol. I, p. 1).

3 *Southey...the year 1810.*] Robert Southey (1774–1843; *DNB*), historian, biographer, essayist and poet laureate, *Letters from England: By Don Manuel Alvarez Espriella* (1807).

4 *Birmingham...metallic fumes;*] In his description of Birmingham, Southey writes that 'every man whom I meet stinks of train-oil and emery. Some I have seen with red eyes and green hair; the eyes affected by the fires to which they are exposed, and the hair turned green by the brass works' (Southey, *Letters*, p. 197).

5 *Trosachs,'*] 'The Trossachs', an area in the Scottish highlands extending west of Callander to Loch Katrine, became a favourite destination for tourists after Walter Scott's descriptions in *The Lady of the Lake* (1810) and *Rob Roy* (1817).

6 *medical advisers of insurance offices;*] cf. De Quincey's discussion of 'surgical examination' and 'insurance offices' in his 1856 *Confessions* (Vol. 2, pp. 249–52).

7 *satyriasis*...Reckoner...Tithe,] 'Satyriasis' means 'excessively great venereal desire in the male' (*OED*, which cites this example from De Quincey). A 'Ready Reckoner' is 'a table...showing at a glance the results of such arithmetical calculations as are most frequently required' (*OED*). The 'Agistment Tithe' is 'the tithe of cattle or other produce of grass lands...paid to the vicar' (*OED*).

8 *Claude...dying dolphin,*] Claude Lorrain (1600–82), French artist best known for ideal-landscape painting. For the 'dying dolphin', see Pliny the Younger, *Letters*, IX. 33.

9 that *is all nonsense.*] cf. Landor's comment when he was eighty and discussing a lost love: 'My future property was equal to hers, my expectancies greater. But, having nothing, I would not ask the hand of one to whom something would be given by her uncle' (Super, p. 29).

10 *Stanhope...Syrian mountains,*] Lady Hester Lucy Stanhope (1776–1839; *DNB*) left England in 1810, and travelled from Egypt to Jerusalem. She reached Palmyra in April 1813, but had to leave suddenly to escape hostile desert tribes. She eventually settled in Syria. De Quincey was fascinated by her story (cf. Vol. 9, p. 626).

11 *novels upon him,*] De Quincey seems here prophetically to anticipate Dickens's portrait of Landor as Boythorn in *Bleak House* (1852–3).

12 *old joke...French...Dutch.*] untraced.

13 *Phrygian...Demosthenes...Plato,*] To the classical Greeks, 'Phrygian' was equivalent to 'slave'. Demosthenes (384–22 BC), Athenian statesman and orator. Plato (*c.* 427–347 BC), Greek philosopher.

14 *'filthy dowlas'...Falstaff,*] 'Dowlas' is 'a course kind of linen' (*OED*). De Quincey is quoting Falstaff in *1 Henry IV*, III.iii.69–70: 'Dowlas, filthy dowlas. I have given them away to baker's wives, they have made bolters of them'.

15 *M. Sue;*] Eugène Sue (1804–57), French author of sensational novels depicting the seamy side of urban life.

16 *Mr Hegel,*] Georg Wilhelm Friedrich Hegel (1770–1831), German philosopher.

17 Gebir...*Southey...Oxford*] Landor's exotic poem *Gebir* (1798) was enthusiastically praised by Southey in the *Critical Review*, and later described by him as containing 'miraculous beauties'. De Quincey matriculated at Worcester College, Oxford, in the latter half of December 1803 (Super, p. 45; Lindop, p. 110).

18 *Landors...preceding my own,*] Landor's father took his BA at Worcester College, Oxford in 1754, half a century before De Quincey entered the same College (Super, p. 2).

19 'Single-Speech Hamilton;'] William Gerard Hamilton (1729–96; *DNB*), politician, became Chancellor of the Exchequer in Ireland in 1763. His popular nickname 'Single Speech' is misleading, as he spoke with success on other occasions, both in the House of Commons and in the Irish parliament.

20 *'a brother near the throne,'*] Alexander Pope (1688–1744; *DNB*), 'Epistle to Dr Arbuthnot', ll. 197–8: 'Should such a man, too fond to rule alone, / Bear, like the Turk, no brother near the throne'.

21 *Gibraltar...very Gebir;*] Tariq ibn Ziyad (d. *c.* AD 720), general, who in May 711 led the Muslim conquest of Gibraltar, which thereafter became known as Jabal Tariq (Mount Tarik), from which the Anglicized form of the name is adapted.

22 *Pitt's 'indemnity...past...future.'*] William Pitt the Elder, first Earl of Chatham (1708–78; *DNB*), British statesman and twice virtual Prime Minister (1756–61 and 1766–8). In a 29 September 1770 letter to the Earl of Shelburne, Pitt insisted upon 'reparation for our rights at home, and security against the like future violations'.

23 *'Incenst...land of Nile.'*] Landor, *Works*, vol. II, p. 488.

24 *'stiff...in the wrong.'*] Not Alexander Pope (see above, n. 20), but John Dryden (1631–1700; *DNB*), *Absalom and Achitophel*, ll. 547–8: 'Stiff in opinions, always in the wrong; / Was every thing by starts, and nothing long'.

25 *'Deep...woe, Masar.'*] Landor, *Works*, vol. II, p. 496: 'Bereft of beauty, bare of ornament, / Stood in the wilderness of woe, Masar'.

26 *Nessus.*] In Greek mythology, Deianeira gave her husband Hercules a shirt soaked in the blood of Nessus, a centaur that Hercules had shot with a poison arrow. The shirt killed Hercules.

27 *'viscous poison'...cerastes,*] Landor, *Works*, vol. II, p. 498: 'But Myrthyr seiz'd with bare bold-sinew'd arm / The grey cerastes, writhing from her grasp, / And twisted off his horn, nor fear'd to squeeze / The viscous poison from his glowing gums'.

28 mise en scene] (Fr.), the arrangement of actors and scenery on a stage for a theatrical production.

29 *'Living...called him Aroar.'*] Landor, *Works*, vol. II, p. 492: 'Living men called him Aroar'.

30 *Aeneas...of the future.*] In Virgil, *Aeneid*, Book VI, Aeneas visits the underworld and meets his father Anchises, who points out the souls of men who are destined to be illustrious in Roman history.

31 *George III...Windsor to Kew,*] George III (1738–1820), King of Great Britain and Ireland, 1760–1820. De Quincey envisages George III moving from the castle at Windsor to the royal estate at Kew, where the famous gardens afforded him much greater privacy.

32 *'Aroar...from north-east.'*] Landor, *Works*, vol. II, p. 493.

33 *Hanover.*] Hanover is a former state of northwestern Germany. The House of Hanover is the British royal house of German origin, descended from George Louis, who succeeded to the British throne as George I (1660–1727).

34 *'He was a warrior...sling, &c. &c.'*] Landor, *Works*, vol. II, p. 493.

35 Tom-Painish,] Thomas Paine (1737–1809; *DNB*), radical writer and revolutionary activist best known for his *Rights of Man* (Part I 1791; Part II 1792) and *Age of Reason* (Part I 1794; Part II 1795).

36 *Socrates...Alcibiades*] Socrates (469–399 BC), Greek philosopher, and Alcibiades (*c.* 450–404 BC), Athenian politician and military commander. The two men were friends, and served together at the siege of Potidaea (432–30 BC) and the Battle of Delium (424 BC).

37 *'wisest of men'*] Milton, *Paradise Regained*, IV. 274–6: 'Of Socrates, see there his tenement, / Whom well inspired the oracle pronounced / Wisest of men'.

38 *Xantippe*] Xanthippe, the reputedly shrewish wife of Socrates.

39 *disciple to write books,*] Socrates himself wrote no books, so information about his personality and doctrines is derived chiefly from the writings of Aristophones, Xenophon and especially Plato.

40 scandalum magnatum] (Lt.), 'offence to the authorities'.

41 *Buckland*] William Buckland (1784–1856; *DNB*), geologist, best known for *Geology and Mineralogy Considered with Reference to Natural Theology* (1836).

42 *Valerius Flaccus.*] Gaius Valerius Flaccus (*fl.* first century AD), epic poet, author of an *Argonautica*.

43 *'But Gebir...nought severe.'*] Landor, *Works*, vol. II, p. 488.

44 *'And the long...*up-rear'd.'] Landor, *Works*, vol. II, p. 490.

45 *'The king...*setting sun.'] Landor, *Works*, vol. II, p. 496.

46 Marshal Bugeaud...Arab Chieftain.] The dialogue was first published in 1846 (Landor, *CW*, vol. VIII, pp. 12–5). Thomas-Robert Bugeaud, marquis de la Piconnerie (1784–1849), marshal of France, played an important part in the French conquest of Algeria.

47 *freshness in the public mind,*] In 1858, De Quincey appended a footnote to this passage in which he made clear that Landor's dialogue concerned 'the atrocity at *Dahra*' (see below, p. 633, 12.10). In June 1845, the French under Aimable-Jean-Jacques Pélissier (1794–1864), suffocated a whole Arab tribe in the Dahra caves near Mustaganem in northern Algeria. The French troops filled the mouths of the caves with logs, and then set them on fire.

48 *'Of seven hundred...motion.'*] Landor, *Works*, vol. II, p. 242.

49 ex hypothesi,] (Lt.), 'hypothetically'.

50 *'Thief...are from thee.'*] Landor, *Works*, vol. II, p. 243.

51 *old Scottish story*] De Quincey's source has not been traced.

52 *'jaloused'*] 'Jalouse' means 'to suspect; to be suspicious about' (*OED*).

53 *'Enter...But* is *it ended?'*] Landor, *Works*, vol. II, p. 243.

54 *martyr...'Brother...for ever'*] De Quincey refers to Hugh Latimer (*c.* 1485–1555; *DNB*), one of the celebrated 'Oxford martyrs', who immortalized himself at the stake by exhorting his fellow victim Nicholas Ridley (*c.* 1500–55; *DNB*) with the words, 'we shall this day light such a candle, by God's grace, in England as I trust shall never be put out'.

55 *'Their moans...bloody Piedmontose.'*] John Milton (1608–74; *DNB*), 'On the late Massacre in Piedmont', ll. 7–10. Milton's sonnet deplores the 1655 massacre of the Vaudois by Charles Emmanuel II (1634–75), Duke of Savoy.

56 *Sidney's...ambitious aim;*] Sir Philip Sidney (1554–86; *DNB*), courtier and poet, *The Countess of Pembroke's Arcadia* (The New Arcadia), ed. Victor Skretkowicz (Oxford: Clarendon Press, 1987), p. 158: 'Who shoots at the midday sun, though he be sure he shall never hit the mark, yet as sure he is he shall shoot higher than who aims but at a bush'.

57 *purification of war...abolition;*] cf. De Quincey in his 1848 essay on 'War': 'And I will content myself with saying, as a closing remark, that this review will detect a principle of steady advance in the purification and elevation of war – such as must offer hope to those who believe in the possibility of its absolute extermination, and must offer consolation to those who (like myself) deny it' (see above, p. 288).

58 *sublime name of* Christendom] cf. De Quincey in 'The English Mail-Coach': 'At midnight the secret word arrived; which word was – Waterloo and Recovered Christendom! The dreadful word shone by its own light' (see above, p. 446).

59 *Bonaparte...has recorded.*] Napoleon Bonaparte (1769–1821), Emperor of the French, who in March 1799 took the port city of Jaffa and then ordered the massacre of about 3000 Turks, rather than weaken his own forces by providing the prisoners with food and an escort.

60 *'insurgent rustics,'*] untraced.

61 *question in casuistry,*] De Quincey examined the case of the Jaffa Massacre in his 1832 *Blackwood's* essay on Charlemagne, and 1839–40 *Blackwood's* essay on casuistry (Vol. 8, pp. 202–3; Vol. 11, pp. 351–2).

62 *Wilson,*] Sir Robert Wilson (1777–1849; *DNB*), general and governor of Gibraltar, who in his *History of the British Expedition to Egypt* (1802) damned the actions of the French at Jaffa and celebrated what he described as 'an uninterrupted series of successes on the part of the English' (second edition (1803), p. xvii).

63 *Magdeburg,*] Magdeburg is in east-central Germany. In 1631, Imperial troops massacred 20,000 of the city's 30,000 inhabitants.

64 *Sweden...Tilly...showed none.*] Gustavus Adolphus (1594–1632), King of Sweden, 1611–32. He tried unsuccessfully to save Magdeburg from capture and sack at the hands of Johann Tserclaes, Graf von Tilly (1559–1632), outstanding military commander, and known as the 'butcher of Magdeburg'.

65 *'Signor Drew' {see Henry V.},*] In Shakespeare, *Henry V*, IV.iv, Pistol's unfortunate French prisoner exclaims '*Seigneur Dieu!*', and Pistol assumes that he is giving his own name, 'Signieur Dew', which De Quincey misremembers as 'Drew'.

66 *Hart...Lutheran clergyman.*] Walter Harte (1709–74; *DNB*), miscellaneous writer, *A History of the Life of Gustavus Adolphus, King of Sweden* (London Hawkins,1759), pp. 313–8. The Lutheran clergyman was M. Theodanus, minister of the church of St Catherine. It is not clear how De Quincey formed the impression that 'no real departures were made from the customary routine'. Harte writes that there was 'a massacre

not to be parrelled in modern ages...disgraceful to common humanity' (pp. 307, 309). Theodanus evidently survived because of his clerical status, and good fortune in encountering soldiers who were relatively humane. Philip Dormer Stanhope, fourth Earl of Chesterfield (1694–1773; *DNB*), statesman, diplomat and wit.

67 *proverb...very little wool.*] cf. Dickens, *Barnaby Rudge*, p. 256. '"The party make noise, enough, but don't call for much. There's great cry there, Mr Willet, but very little wool"'.

68 *Syrian hospital...d'Enguien's execution*] In May 1799 Napoleon gave orders that about fifty plague patients at Jaffa be poisoned. Cf. Hazlitt: 'With the name of Jaffa are connected two of the ugliest charges ever brought against Buonaparte, those of massacring the Turkish prisoners and poisoning his own troops in the hospital there' (Hazlitt, *Works*, vol. XIV, p. 37). Louis Antoine Henri de Bourbon, Duc d'Enghien (1772–1804), was shot after being tried on trumped-up charges of conspiracy.

69 *Timur,*] 'Timur', or 'Tamerlane' (1336–1405), Turkic conqueror of Islamic faith, chiefly remembered for the barbarity of his conquests.

Notes on Walter Savage Landor {Part II}

1 *MELANCHTHON AND CALVIN.*] Philipp Melanchthon (1497–1560), German humanist, reformer and theologian. Jean Calvin (1509–64), leading French Protestant reformer.

2 'Jewish;'] Landor, *Works*, vol. II, p. 224: '*Melancthon.* The Jewish law; the Jewish idolatry. You fear the approach of this, and do not suspect the presence of a worse'.

3 *argued...evil of idolatry.*] Landor, *Works*, vol. II, p. 224: '*Melancthon*....The wickedness of idolatry does not consist in any inadequate representation of the Deity, for whether our hands or our hearts represent him, the representation is almost alike inadequate. Every man does what he hopes and believes will be most pleasing to his God; and God, in his wisdom and mercy, will not punish gratitude in its error'.

4 *golden bow...snake;*] Apollo is associated with a lyre and golden bow, and Aesculapius (the god of medicine and healing) with a snake.

5 *Juvenal's...kitchen-gardens.*] Juvenal (AD*c.* 55–*c.* 127), Roman poet, *Satires*, XIV. 9–10.

6 *vol. I.:*] in fact, 'vol. II'.

7 *Cadis,*] judges.

8 Schwarzerd *(black earth)*;] Whilst still a boy, Philipp had his name changed from Schwartzerd to its Greek equivalent, Melanchthon.

9 *fish, flesh...red herring.*] cf. Scott, *Old Morality*, p. 238: 'Langcale...cannot be suitably, or preceesely, termed either fish, or flesh, or gude red herring'.

10 *Persian symbol of God*] De Quincey is probably thinking of the cult of Mithras, the Persian sun god. The cult became popular in the later Roman Empire.

11 *PORSON AND SOUTHEY.*] The dialogue was first published in the *London Magazine* for July 1823 (Landor, *CW*, vol. V, p. 213). Richard Porson (1759–1808; *DNB*), foremost classical scholar of his day, became a Fellow of Trinity College, Cambridge, in 1782 and Regius Professor of Greek in the University in 1792. For Southey, see above, p. 523, n. 3.

12 *Wordsworth*;] William Wordsworth (1770–1850; *DNB*) was regarded by De Quincey as the greatest poet of the age.

13 *'Avoid...his own name.'*] Landor, *Works*, vol. I, p. 1.

14 *Wordsworth...tipsy...Porson...otherwise*] Wordsworth attended St John's College, Cambridge, 1787–91. De Quincey draws here on his knowledge of Wordsworth's unpublished *Prelude*, III. 299–313, where Wordsworth describes his undergraduate days, and drinking too much wine in rooms that formerly belonged to Milton. Porson drank heavily.

15 *Rolliad,*] *The Rolliad* was a collection of Whig political satires directed against William Pitt the Younger (1759–1806; *DNB*) and his followers after their success in the election of 1784. A complete collection appeared in 1791.

16 *Obereea...Joseph Banks,*] Sir Joseph Banks (1743–1820; *DNB*), explorer and naturalist, met Queen Oberea of Tahiti during his travels around the world with Captain James Cook (1728–79; *DNB*). Banks reputedly fell asleep in Oberea's canoe, and they became lovers. John Scott (1747–1819; *DNB*) published *An Epistle from Oberea, Queen of Otaheite, to Joseph Banks* (1774) in which he alleged amorous incidents between the two.

17 *Pope...Abelard*] Peter Abelard (1079–1142), French theologian and philosopher, and the husband of Héloïse (*c.* 1098–1164). Alexander Pope (see above, p. 524, n. 20) published a bleak study of their love, *Eloisa to Abelard*, in 1717.

18 *Waller*] Edmund Waller (1606–87; *DNB*), poet.

19 *Mathias...*Pursuits of Literature,] Thomas James Mathias (*c.* 1754–1835; *DNB*), satirist and Italian scholar, produced the immensely popular *Pursuits of Literature: a Satirical Poem in Four Dialogues* (1794–7). Many editions and revisions followed. Cf. Landor, *Works,* vol. I, p. 11.

20 *Southey...mentioned slightingly,*] In the *Pursuits*, Mathias wrote that Southey 'gave the public a long quarto volume of epick verses, JOAN OF ARC, written as he says, in the preface, in *six weeks*. Had he meant to write well, he should have kept it at least six years....I wish also that he would review *some of his principles*'. Southey growled: 'They tell me I am civilly wiped in that stupid poem *The Pursuits of Literature*' (Southey, *New Letters*, vol. I, pp. 139–40).

21 *Mathias...died,*] Mathias lived in London for many years, but eventually settled in Naples, where he died.

22 gens de plume...Chronicle *Office,*] 'Gens de plume' (Fr.), 'writers'. Porson wrote for *The Morning Chronicle*. 'I hope this very learned and gifted man will now begin some work of importance', Mathias wrote of Porson: 'but it is, and it ever was, beneath his great abilities to write in the little *democratick closet* fitted up for the wits at the Morning Chronicle office' (*The Pursuits of Literature* (London: Becket and Porter, 1812), p. 341).

23 *he drew it from an Index.*] '*Porson*. I have demonstrated that...[Mathias] could not construe a Greek sentence or scan a verse; and I have fallen on the very *Index* from which he drew out his forlorn hope on the parade' (Landor, *Works*, vol. I, p. 11).

24 *Hetman Platoff.*] Matvei Ivanovich Platoff (1757–1818), last Hetmann of the Cossacks of the Don. Cf. Hazlitt in 1828: 'We are not therefore surprised that the Parisians find fault with the only actor of much genius we possess: he must puzzle them almost as much as the Hetman Platoff' (Hazlitt, *Works*, vol. XVIII, p. 416).

25 *'Brantome...Parish Clerk.'*] Pierre de Brantôme (*c.* 1540–1614), soldier and chronicler, whose works are chiefly accounts of battles and tales of chivalry. Jonathan Swift (1667–1745; *DNB*), Irish satirist and poet. 'The Memoirs of P. P., Clerk of this Parish' were included in Scott, *Swift*, vol. XIII, pp. 166–81. But they were written by Pope (*The Prose Works of Alexander Pope*, ed. Rosemary Cowler (Hamden, Conn. Archon Books, 1986), pp. 99–128).

26 *'Why do you repeat...the white.'"*] a slightly truncated version of Landor, *Works*, vol. I, p. 17.

27 *Deucalion's flood,*] In Greek mythology, Deucalion is the son of Prometheus. When Zeus resolved to destroy all humanity by a flood, Deucalion constructed an ark in which he and his wife floated until the waters subsided.

28 *Mrs Cl——nt...Pestalozzi...Yverdun,*] 'Mrs Clermont' (see below, p. 635, 23.17) has not been identified. Johann Heinrich Pestalozzi (1746–1827), Swiss educational reformer, who from 1805 to 1825 ran a boarding school at Yverdon, in western Switzerland. Porson took notoriously little care of his health or appearance.

29 aerugo...sine qua non] (Lt.), respectively, 'copper rust' and 'absolute requirement'.

30 susurrus] In 1858, De Quincey appended a footnote to this word (see below, p. 635, 23.39).

31 *Mambrino's helmet...Medea's kettle*;] In Ariosto's *Orlando Furioso*, Mambrino is a pagan king who possesses a helmet of pure gold that makes the wearer invisible. De Quincey has in mind Miguel de Cervantes (1547–1616) in his comic novel *Don Quixote* (1605, 1615), where the hero mistakes a barber's brass bowl, worn as a makeshift hat in the rain, for the magical helmet. In Greek mythology, Medea restores Aeson to youth by boiling him in a cauldron with magic herbs.

32 rete mucosum,] 'the under portion of the epidermis, in which the pigment cells are situated' (*OED*).

33 Plica Polonica...*1807–8...snakes;*] 'Plica Polonica', 'a matted filthy condition of the hair due to disease' (*OED*). In Greek mythology, Medusa was a winged female creature with a head of hair consisting of snakes.

34 *Orson...Caliban's...Nebuchadnezzar's?*] 'Orson', from the Old Norman French, means 'bear-cub'. Caliban, a deformed, sullen creature in Shakespeare's *The Tempest*, II.ii.168: 'And I with my long nails will dig the pig-nuts'. Nebuchadrezzar II (*c.* 630 –*c.* 561 BC), second king of the Chaldean dynasty of Babylonia, Daniel 4: 33: 'Nebuchadnezzar...was driven from men...till his hairs were grown like eagles' feathers, and his nails like birds' claws'.

35 *bosom is called her* neck.] *'Porson...*I then understood for the first time that *neck* signifies *bosom* when we speak of women, though not so when we speak of men or other creatures' (Landor, *Works*, vol. I, p. 18).

36 *when people had* thighs.] 'This conversation led me to reflect that I was born in the time when people had *thighs*; before your memory, I imagine' (Landor, *Works*, vol. I, p. 18).

37 *slang from the street*] cf. De Quincey on *Blackwood's* and its 'occasional use of street slang' (Vol. 7, p. 80).

38 venter?] 'belly'.

39 *'every little helps.'*] *Proverbs*, p. 228.

40 doigt-de-pied] (Fr.), literally, 'digit of the foot'.

41 *toe...never to be named?*] *'Porson...*I know not what offence the Great Toe can have committed, that he never should be mentioned by the graver and more stately members of the family' (Landor, *Works*, vol. I, p. 18).

42 Menenius...*foremost.'*] Menenius Agrippa is the patrician adviser and friend of Coriolanus in Shakespeare's *Coriolanus*. De Quincey's quotation is *Coriolanus*, I.i.157–8 (inexact; cf. Vol. 8, p. 39).

43 parrhesia...*wider than of old),*] In his 1857 revision of his essay on Samuel Parr, De Quincey translated 'parresia' as 'the Greek word for *freedom of speech*' (Vol. 8, p. 464).

44 Imperium Germanicum] De Quincey draws from Landor's footnote on 'an *emperor of Germany*' in the conversation between 'Richard I and the Abbot of Boxley' (Landor, *Works*, vol. I, pp. 3–4). The dialogue was first published in 1824 (Landor, *CW*, vol. IV, pp. 7–14). 'Imperium Germanicum' (Lt.), 'German Empire'.

45 Imperator...Rex.] cf. De Quincey in his third essay on 'The Caesars': 'The very title of *Imperator*, from which we have derived our modern one of *Emperor*, proclaims the nature of the government, and the tenure of that office. It was purely a government by the sword, or permanent *stratocracy* having a movable head' (Vol. 9, p. 61). 'Rex' is 'King'.

46 *elder Scaliger on Manilius},*] Julius Caesar Scaliger (1484–1558), classical scholar who worked in botany, zoology, grammar and literary criticism. De Quincey, however, intends his son, Joseph Justus Scaliger (1540–1609), philologist and historian. Marcus Manilius (*fl.* first century AD), whose didactic poem *Astronomicon* deals with astronomy and astrology. De Quincey's reference is to a note on book four, line eighteen of Manilius, *Astronomicon*, ed. Scaliger (Paris, 1579), p. 223.

47 *Caesar...Cicero...Cato,*] Julius Caesar (100–44 BC), Rome's greatest general, dictator and statesman. Marcus Tullius Cicero (106–43 BC), eminent Roman statesman, scholar and writer. Marcus Porcius Cato (95–46 BC), republican supporter who joined with Pompey (106–48 BC) in an unsuccessful attempt to thwart Caesar's dictatorial ambitions.

48 Barbara *and* Celarent,] two kinds of syllogisms.

49 *S. P. Q. R.*] 'SPQR', in Roman documents and inscriptions, is an abbreviation for 'senatus populusque Romanus', 'the senate and people of Rome'.

50 *ourselves and China.*] De Quincey refers to the recent 'Opium wars' (1839–42) between China and Britain, which had been as much about clashes of imperial interest as the specific issue of the opium trade. For De Quincey's extended commentary, see Vol. 11, pp. 532–72.

51 *Herod...Antipater...Persia;*] Antipater (d. 43 BC) and his son Herod the Great (73–4 BC), Roman-appointed King of Judaea, 37–4 BC.

52 ipse dixit] Cicero, *De Natura Deorum,* I.v.10: 'He himself said so'.

53 *Seymour,*] Sir Edward Seymour (1633–1708; *DNB*), Tory politician and Speaker of the Commons, 1673–8, 1678–9.

54 *Newgate*] the main prison in London from the thirteenth until the nineteenth century.

55 *'thill'*] 'the pole or shaft by which a wagon...is attached to the animal drawing it' (*OED*). In 1858, De Quincey appended a footnote to this word and referenced Shakespeare's *Love's Labour's Lost* (see below, p. 635, 29.1).

56 auctoritas...*Cilician...laughter},*] 'Auctoritas' (Lt.), 'authority'; in Roman law, from 'auctor', 'the person who warrants the right of possession' (*OED*). De Quincey must have in mind Plutarch, *Parallel Lives*, Cicero, XXXVI. 1: 'When Caelius the orator asked Cicero to send him panthers from Cilicia for a certain spectacle at Rome, Cicero, pluming himself upon his exploits, wrote to him that there were no panthers in Cilicia'.

57 paludamentum,] In 1858, De Quincey translated 'paludamentum' as 'supreme martial robe' (see below, p. 635, 29.32).

58 '*Rex Regum.*'] 'King of Kings'.

59 *Lupercalia.*] an ancient Roman festival of obscure origin. De Quincey refers to the Lupercalia in February, 44 BC, when Antony offered Caesar a diadem, which Caesar refused (see Shakespeare, *Julius Cesar*, III.ii.95–7).

60 Pompey...*his thighs:*] untraced.

61 *Dogberry*] the self-important constable in Shakespeare's *Much Ado About Nothing*.

62 *incivism;*] 'In reference to the French Revolution: want of loyalty to the principles of the Revolution' (*OED*). Cf. De Quincey in his December 1830 *Blackwood's* essay on 'The Late Cabinet', where he discusses '"civism" (to revive that Jacobin word)' (Vol. 7, p. 258).

63 Basileus...*Artaxerxes*...regulus,] 'Basileus' (Lt.), 'king'; 'regulus' (Lt.), 'minor king'. 'Artaxerxes' is the name of several Persian kings.

64 *Dioclesian...aulic*] Diocletian (AD 245–316), Roman emperor, 284–305. He laid the foundation for the Byzantine Empire in the East. 'Aulic' means 'of or pertaining to a court' (*OED*).

65 *Trajan's time...Commodus,*] Trajan (AD 53–117), Roman emperor, 98–117. Commodus (AD 161–92), Roman emperor, 177–92.

66 *'and from his pockets...sceptres.'*] Shakespeare, *Antony and Cleopatra*, V.ii.90–2: 'In his livery / Walk'd crowns and crownets; realms and islands were / As plates dropp'd from his pocket'.

67 *reaped in glory...sown in dishonour.*] 1 Corinthians 15: 43: 'It is sown in dishonour, it is raised in glory'.

68 *tilting...Semper Augustus?*] Francis II (1768–1835), Emperor of Austria, 1804–35. He was the last Holy Roman emperor, abdicating the title in 1806. 'The late emperor of Austria formally laid down a title which never belonged to him; he and all his ministers were ignorant of this' (Landor, *Works*, vol. I, p. 4).

69 dorypheroi...somatophulakes] 'Dorypheroi' (Gk.), 'spear-bearers'. In 1858, De Quincey translated 'somatophulakes' as 'body-guards' (see below, p. 635, 30.10).

70 *Byzantium,*] The Byzantine Empire (the eastern half of the former Roman Empire) fell to the Ottoman Turks in 1453.

71 *fisherman...Mount Palatine,*] De Quincey's reference is to the Pope, the successor of St Peter (d. *c.* AD 64), a fisherman and disciple of Jesus Christ, and the first Bishop of Rome. Mount Palatine was the seat of the palace of the Roman emperors.

72 *Mamelukes... janizaries...the Porte*] The 'mamelukes' were members of a politically powerful Egyptian military class. The 'janissaries' were the elite corps in the standing army of the Ottoman Empire. The 'Porte' was the government of the Ottoman Empire.

73 *Caliphs,*] a caliph is a successor of Muhammad as temporal and spiritual head of Islam.

74 *Professor Wilson*] De Quincey's close friend John Wilson (1785–1854; *DNB*), a leading writer with *Blackwood's*, and Professor of Moral Philosophy at the University of Edinburgh, 1820–51.

75 *licking...from Napoleon.*] Napoleon's military victories forced the German states to implement wide-ranging reforms. The map of Germany was redrawn at the Congress of Vienna (1814–5).

76 Surena...*Persian expedition*] 'surena', 'Persian grand vizier'. Julian (AD *c.* 331–63), Roman emperor, AD 361–3. Julian invaded Persia and was killed during a disastrous retreat.

77 Count Julian,] For the historical background of Landor's tragedy *Count Julian* (1811), see Landor, *CW*, vol. XIII, p. 390.

78 *Roderick...Thermopylae*] In Landor's play, 'Roderigo' is King of Spain. Thermopylae is a narrow pass on the east coast of central Greece, about 85 miles northwest of Athens. It has been the site of many battles, including in 480 BC when the Persians outflanked and annihilated the Greek defenders.

79 *Marathon,*] At the decisive Battle of Marathon (September 490 BC), the Athenians repulsed the first Persian invasion of Greece.

80 *Metius Fuffetius,*] Metiuis Fufetiuis was King of the Albans, and waged war against the Romans. He was put to death by Tullus Hostilius, traditionally the third King of Rome, who tied him to colts and tore him apart (see Livy, I. 27–8).

81 *'To this pass...reduced him;'*] Plutarch, *Parallel Lives*, Caesar, XLVI. 1: 'They brought me to such a pass that if I, Caius Caesar, after waging successfully the greatest wars, had dismissed my forces, I should have been condemned in their courts'.

82 *dogs of the Crescent,*] The Crescent was the emblem of the Byzantine and Turkish empires.

83 *Oedipus...Escurial,*] In Greek mythology, Oedipus is the King of Thebes, who unwittingly killed his father and married his mother. El Escorial is in central Spain, 26 miles northwest of Madrid. El Escorial library houses a rare collection of more than 4,700 manuscripts and 40,000 printed books.

84 *Satan...Teneriffe...Atlas,*] Tenerife is the largest of the Canary Islands, and lies in the Atlantic Ocean opposite the northwest coast of Africa. The Atlas Mountains are a series of mountain ranges in northwestern Africa, running generally northeast to southwest. De Quincey has in mind Milton, *Paradise Lost*, IV. 985–7: 'On the other side Satan alarmed / Collecting all his might dilated stood, / Like Teneriff or Atlas unremoved'.

85 *'delicious calm...dews of morn.'*] Landor, *Works*, vol. II, p. 519.

86 *rhythmus...entire passage;*] cf. De Quincey on 'the rhythmus' of the closing paragraph of 'The Vision of Sudden Death' (see above, p. 481).

87 *'For his own sake...once!'*] Landor, *Works*, vol. II, p. 519.

88 *that work on* Style,] De Quincey had published a four-part essay on 'Style' in *Blackwood's* in 1840–1 (Vol. 12, pp. 3–84).

89 *''Tis not...who* wish'd *to die.'*] Landor, *Works*, vol. II, p. 519.

90 *Mount Athos...demigod,*] Mount Athos is in northern Greece. Dinocrates (*fl.* fourth century BC), Greek architect who tried to captivate the attention of Alexander the Great with a design for carving Mount Athos into a gigantic seated statue. The plan was not carried out.

91 *phylactories...Ionia...Rubens.*] A 'phylactery' is 'a small leathern box containing four texts of Scripture...worn by Jews during morning prayer' (*OED*). Ionia is an ancient region comprising the central sector of the western coast of Anatolia (in present day Turkey). Peter Paul Rubens (1577–1640), Flemish painter.

92 *'Sed fugit...amore.'*] Virgil, *Georgics*, III. 284–5: 'But time meanwhile is flying, flying beyond recall, while we, charmed with love of our theme, linger around each detail!'.

93 *horrid railway whistle;*] cf. De Quincey in 'The English Mail-Coach': 'the laurelled mail, heart-shaking, when heard screaming on the wind, and advancing through the darkness to every village or solitary house on its route, has now given way for ever to the pot-wallopings of the boiler' (see above, p. 417).

94 *Shelley...Prometheus,*] Percy Bysshe Shelley (1792–1822; *DNB*), poet. In Greek religion, Prometheus is one of the Titans and a god of fire. Shelley published his drama *Prometheus Unbound* in 1820.

95 *Aeschylus...Milton in his Satan),*] Aeschylus (525–456 BC), Greek tragic poet, who wrote approximately ninety plays, including *Prometheus Bound*. De Quincey refers to the portrayal of Satan in Milton's *Paradise Lost*.

96 'non imitable fulgur,'] Virgil, *Aeneid*, VI. 590: 'non imitable fulmen' ('inimitable thunder').

97 *Memnon's statue,*] The statue was in fact one of a pair representing the Egyptian king Amenhotep III (*fl.* 14th century BC), outside his funerary temple on the west bank at Thebes. It was long thought that the statue held a lyre which, when struck by the sun, sounded forth. Cf. John Keats, *Hyperion*, II. 373–6: 'like the bulk / Of Memnon's image at the set of sun / To one who travels from the dusking east: / Sighs, too, as mournful as that Memnon's harp'.

98 *'deep-grooved'*] Wordsworth, 'In the Pleasure-Grounds on the Banks of the Bran, Near Dunkeld', ll. 97–100: 'Solicit a Memnonian strain; / Yet, in some fit of anger sharp, / The wind might force the deep-grooved harp / To utter melancholy moans'.

99 *'burn'd after him...bottomless pit,'*] Milton, *Paradise Lost*, VI. 865–6: 'Down from the verge of heaven, eternal wrath / Burnt after them to the bottomless pit'.

Orthographic Mutineers

1 'Roberte the Deville...to chaste.'] Robert the Devil is a legendary son of a duke of Normandy, born in answer to prayers addressed to the devil. *Robert le Diable* is a late twelfth-century romance; other versions of the legend are told in two fourteenth-century poems. De Quincey cites Anonymous, *The Lyfe of Roberte the Devyll* (*c.* 1510), ll. 201–2: 'Naye, sayde hys master, ye be to bolde; / And toke a rodde for to chaste him soone'. Landor attended Rugby for eight years, but was removed at the age of sixteen for rebelliousness (Super, p. 9).

2 *'justice rul'd the ball,'*] Pope, 'Elegy to the Memory of an Unfortunate Lady', ll. 35–6: 'Thus, if eternal justice rules the ball, / Thus shall your wives, and thus your children fall'.

3 *schoolmaster...always a villain)*] cf. De Quincey in 'The English Mail-Coach': 'In the clouds, and on the earth, prevailed the same majestic peace; and in spite of all that the villain of a schoolmaster has done for the ruin of our sublimer thoughts...we still believe in no such nonsense as a limited atmosphere' (see above, p. 438).

4 *Entick's Dictionary*] John Entick (*c.* 1703–1773; *DNB*), schoolmaster and author of a *Spelling Dictionary of the English Language* (1764).

5 abalienate *and* ablaqueation] 'Abalienate' means 'to make that another's which was our own before'; 'ablaqueation' means 'the breaking up or removal of the soil around the roots of trees' (*OED*).

6 *'occasional conformist;'*] 'Occasional conformity' is 'a phrase applied after 1700 to the practice of persons who, in order to qualify themselves for office...received the Sacrament according to the rites of the Church of England, and afterwards during their office were present at any dissenting meeting for worship' (*OED*).

7 *Old Bailey,*] the central Criminal Court in London

8 *Cowper...Olney...*émeute] William Cowper (1731–1800; *DNB*), poet, who in 1767 took up residence at Olney, in Buckinghamshire. 'Émeute' (Fr.), 'riot'.

9 Greecian *throughout his Homer.*] Cowper's translation of Homer was published in 1791.

10 *Mitford...Redesdale...'wrath...partialilty,'*] William Mitford (1744–1827; *DNB*), historian, *History of Greece* (1784–1810). His younger brother was John Freeman-Mitford, Baron Redesdale (1748–1830; *DNB*), lord chancellor of Ireland. George Gordon, Lord Byron (1788–1824; *DNB*), the most famous poet of his age. In a note in *Don Juan*, Canto XII, Byron writes that Mitford's 'great pleasure' in his *History of Greece* 'consists in praising tyrants, abusing Plutarch, spelling oddly, and writing

quaintly....Having named his sins, it is but fair to state his virtues – learning, labour, research, wrath, and partiality' (Byron, *PW*, vol. V. p. 753).

11 *Mueller...Grecian history.*] Karl Otfried Müller (1797–1840), *Geschichten hellenischer Stämme und Städte* (*History of Greek Peoples and Cities*; 1820).

12 *Gillies,*] John Gillies (1747–1836; *DNB*), historian and classical scholar, *The History of Ancient Greece, its colonies and conquests* (1786).

13 *'the Harmony of Language,'*] Mitford, *An Essay on the Harmony of Language* (1774).

14 *Milton has been able to show.*] De Quincey of course intends Wordsworth. For Milton, see above, p. 526, n. 55.

15 *Samson...Harapha.*] Samson is the Israelite hero in an epic narrative in the Old Testament (see Judges: 13–16). In Milton's *Samson Agonistes*, Harapha is the giant of Gath who comes to mock the blind Samson in prison.

16 *Bishop of St David's...stead.*] Connop Thirlwall (1797–1875; *DNB*), Bishop of St David's, *The History of Greece* (1835–44).

17 Heracleidae *and* Pelopidae,] Heracleidae are the children of Heracles, son of Zeus and Alcmena, and the most famous Greco-Roman legendary hero. Pelopidae are children of Pelops, the grandson of Zeus, and the father of Atreus.

18 fuit Ilium.] (Lt.) 'Ilium is finished'; see Virgil, *Aeneid*, II. 325, where the Trojan priest Panthus acknowledges that Tory is doomed. Cf. De Quincey in his 1831 *Blackwood's* essay 'On the Approaching Revolution in Great Britain' (Vol. 8, p. 99).

19 *Elphinstone...Webster...Yankee*] James Elphinston (1721–1809; *DNB*), educationalist, *Inglish Orthoggraphy epittomized, and Propriety's Pocket Diccionary* (1790). Noah Webster (1758–1843), lexicographer, *American Spelling Book* (1783) and *American Dictionary of the English Language* (1828).

20 *Ritson.*] Joseph Ritson (1752–1803; *DNB*), antiquarian and irascible eccentric.

21 *Shem, Ham...Japhet,*] Shem, Ham and Japheth were the children of the biblical Noah.

22 Pall-Mall...Pel-Mel,] cf. Thomas Blount (1618–79; *DNB*), *Glossographia*: 'Pale-Maille' is 'a game wherein a round bowle is with a Mallet struck through a high arch of iron (standing at either end of an Ally) which he that can do at the fewest blows, or at the number agreed on, wins. This Game was heretofore used at the long alley near St James's, and vulgarly called *Pell-Mell*' (Blount, *Glossographia: or a Dictionary Interpreting the Hard Words of Whatsoever Language, now used in our refined English Tongue* (London: Newcomb, 1670), p. 464).

23 *Pitt of old,*] William Pitt the Elder, see above, p. 524, n. 22. His second son was William Pitt the Younger (see above, p. 528, n. 15).

24 *Chelsea pensioners*] The 'Chelsea Pensioners' are army veterans who live in the Chelsea Royal Hospital, built by Sir Christopher Wren (1632–1723; *DNB*) to house invalid soldiers.

25 *black-letter scholar,*] 'Black-letter' was a style of alphabet used for handwriting throughout Latin Christendom from the early ninth century until the Renaissance.

26 *'Rimes, by Mr Pinkerton,'*] John Pinkerton (1758–1826; *DNB*), Scottish antiquary and historian, *Rimes by Mr Pinkterton* (1782).

27 struttare struttissimamente.] (It.),'taught to strut most struttingly'.

28 *'As I sat on the top of a rock,'*] The passage in question is from Addison's '*Visions of Mirzah*' (1 September 1711), and begins, 'He then led me to the highest Pinnacle of the Rock, and placing me on the Top of it, Cast thy Eyes Eastward, said he' (*Spectator*, vol. II, p. 123).

29 'Letters of Literature...*Heron.*'] Pinkerton, *Letters of Literature, By Robert Heron, esq.* (1785). Pickerton actually wrote as follows: 'Az I waz heré airing my self on thea

topa of thea mountaina, I fell into a profound contemplation on the vanité of human lifé' (*Letters of Literature* (London: Robinson, 1785), p. 255). Cf. De Quincey's comments on Pinkerton in his 1824 *London Magazine* article on 'Goethe' (Vol. 4, p. 198).

30 *Landor…elder reformers.*] cf. Landor in his imaginary conversation between himself and Southey: '*Southey.* I should have adopted all your suggestions in orthography, if I were not certain that my bookseller would protest against it as ruinous' (Landor, *Works*, vol. II, p. 164).

31 *Tooke.*] John Horne Tooke (1736–1812; *DNB*), radical politician, whose *Epea Pteroenta: or, the Diversions of Purley* (1786–1805) launched the science of comparative philology.

32 *Spencer,*] Edmund Spenser (*c.* 1552–1599; *DNB*), poet of *The Faerie Queene* (1590–6).

33 *'The eagle…him fe-al-ty.'*] Wordsworth, 'Song, at the Feast of Brougham Castle', ll. 120–1.

34 feal-ty…*bisects it.*] De Quincey's reference is unclear. In his poetry Landor used the word 'fealty' only twice, and on both occasions he trisected it. The first occasion is *Giovanna of Naples*, V.i.26: 'His duty and his fealty enforce'. The second occasion is *Fra Rupert*, III.iv.1: 'Fealty sworn, should I retract so soon?' (Landor, *CW*, vol. XIV, pp. 41, 71).

35 *authority of Milton…before the* s,] The 'sdeign' of Milton is an Italianism, compromised with Anglo-French spelling, from 'sdegno' or 'sdegnare', meaning 'to disdain'. In Italian, the prefix 'dis' can become plain 's', with no apostrophe to represent the 'missing' letters. In Landor's imaginary conversation between 'Andrew Marvel and Bishop Parker', Marvell states that Milton 'is the only writer whom it is safe to follow in spelling: others are inconsistent; some for want of learning, some for want of reasoning, some for want of memory, some for want of care' (Landor, *Works*, vol. II, p. 100).

36 *Bible, published in Milton's infancy,*] The King James version of the Bible was published in 1611. Milton was born in 1608.

37 Trinity Jones.] De Quincey presumably refers to William Jones of Nayland (1726–1800; *DNB*), whose *Catholic Doctrine of the Trinity* (1756) went through several editions.

38 Nous autres *say 'Aristotle,'*] 'Nous autres' is 'the rest of us'. Aristotle (384–22 BC), philosopher and scientist of ancient Greece. De Quincey refers to Landor's imaginary conversation between 'Aristoteles and Callisthenes' (Landor, *Works*, vol. I, pp. 225–32).

39 *Empedocles,*] Empedocles (*c.* 490–430 BC), Greek philosopher, poet and statesman.

40 *Terence…Horace*] Terence (*c.* 195–*c.* 159 BC), Roman comic dramatist. Horace (65–8 BC), Latin lyric poet and satirist.

41 *Lucretius…Propertius*] Lucretius (*fl.* first century BC), Roman poet and philosopher, whose only known work is *De rerum natura* (*On the Nature of Things*). Sextus Propertius (*c.* 50–after 16 BC), Roman elegiac poet.

42 *Virgil…Valerius…Tullius,*] Virgil (70–19 BC), Roman poet. Valerius Maximus (*fl. c.* AD 20), Roman historian and moralist. For Gaius Valerius Flaccus, see above, p. 525, n. 42. For Marcus Tullius Cicero, see above, p. 530, n. 47.

43 *Ovid*] Ovid (43 BC – AD 17), Roman poet, best known for *Ars Amatoria* and *Metamorphoses* (see Landor, *Works*, vol. I, p. 103; vol. II, p. 219).

44 *Didius Julianus…public auction.*] Marcus Didius Julianus (*c.* AD 135–193), Roman emperor for two months, AD 193. Cf. De Quincey in his 1832–4 *Blackwood's* essays on 'The Caesars': 'The throne was again empty after a reign of about eighty days;

and now came the memorable scandal of putting up the Empire to auction' (Vol. 9, p. 104).

45 *Livy...Livius Andronicus*] Livy (59 BC–AD 17), Roman historian. Lucius Livius Andronicus (*c.* 284 – *c.* 204 BC), founder of Roman epic poetry and drama.

46 *Mark Antony...Marcus Brutus*] Mark Antony (*c.* 82–30 BC), Roman general under Julius Caesar. He is one of the triumvirs in Shakespeare's *Julius Caesar*, and the hero of *Antony and Cleopatra*. Marcus Junius Brutus (85–42 BC) played a leading role in the assassination of Julius Caesar.

47 *Pliny,*] Pliny the Elder (AD 23–79), Roman savant and author of the celebrated *Natural History*; and Pliny the Younger (*c.* AD 61–*c.* 113), Roman author and administrator.

48 *Marius*] Gaius Marius (*c.* 157–86 BC), Roman politician and general.

49 *first Caesar...Caius Julius,*] see above, p. 530, n. 47.

50 *Homer...Hesiod...Pindar,*] Homer (probably eighth century BC), Greek epic poet. Hesiod (*fl. c.* 700 BC), Greek poet. Pindar (518–after 446 BC), the greatest lyric poet of ancient Greece.

51 *Theocritus. Anacreon*] Theocritus (*c.* 300–260 BC) and Anacreon (*c.* 582–*c.* 485 BC), Greek poets.

52 *Aeschylus;*] see above, p. 532, n. 95.

53 *Sallust*] Sallust (*c.* 86–*c.* 35 BC), Roman historian.

54 *President des Brosses,*] Charles de Brosses (1709–77), French magistrate and scholar, and first president of the parliament of Burgundy. He was occupied during the greater part of his life with a translation of Sallust, which he eventually published as *Histoire de la république romaine, dans le cours du VIIe. Siecle* (1777).

55 *Lerminier...(*'Etudes Historiques'*);*] Jean Louis Eugène Lerminier (1803–57), *Études d'histoire et de philosophie* (1836).

56 *Milton,*] John Milton (see above, p. 526, n. 55) preferred 'Sallust to any other Latin historian' (Milton, *Works*, vol. XII, p. 93).

57 *Tacitus,*] Tacitus (*c.* AD 56– *c.* 120), Roman orator and historian.

58 *Lucretius...Statius...Valerius Flaccus,*] For Lucretius, see above, n. 41. Statius (*c.* AD 45–96), Roman epic and lyric poet. For Valerius Flaccus, see above, n. 42.

59 *Catullus...the Atys:*] Gaius Valerius Catullus (*c.* 84–*c.* 54 BC), Roman poet. 'The Atys' is Catullus's poem 'Attis' (number sixty-three).

60 *Plautus:*] Plautus (*c.* 254–184 BC), Roman comic dramatist.

61 *Lucan, Martial, Claudian,*] Lucan (AD 39–65), Martial (*c.* AD 40–*c.* 103) and Claudian (*c.* AD 370 – *c.* 404), Roman poets.

62 *Ovid...favourite of Milton;*] Milton praised Ovid as the 'most elegant of poets' (Milton, *Works*, vol. XII, p. 145).

63 *Council of Trent...Inquisition*] The Roman Catholic Council of Trent (1545–63) introduced sweeping decrees on self-reform. In 1231, Pope Gregory IX instituted the Inquisition for the apprehension and trial of heretics.

64 trivial] '*Nat. Hist.*...popular, vernacular, vulgar' (*OED*).

65 *sixes and sevens;*] 'the creation or existence of, or neglect to remove, confusion, disorder, or disagreement' (*OED*).

66 *Jacquemont,*] Victor Jacquemont (1801–32), French botanist and geologist, *Correspondance de V. J. avec sa famille et plusieurs de ses amis pendant son voyage, dans l'Inde (1828–1832)* (1841–4).

67 *First Meridian...Richter's...Greenwich,*] Johann Paul Friedrich Richter (1763–1825), known as 'Jean Paul', German novelist and prose-poet, *Hesperus* 38: he 'brought over

the whole first circle of his existence out of the India Eden into this narrow housing before the two latest objects of his affection'.

68 *'get an atmosphere of their own,'*] In *The Rivals* (1775) by Richard Brinsley Sheridan (1751–1816; *DNB*), Sir Anthony Absolute is the warm-hearted but demanding old gentleman. De Quincey's reference is *The Rivals*, II.i: 'Don't enter the same hemisphere with me! don't dare to breathe the same air, or use the same light with me; but get an atmosphere and a sun of your own!'.

69 Sepoy...Tiffin?] 'Sepoys' were Indian troops in the service of the British East India Company. A 'tiffin' 'in India and neighbouring eastern countries' was 'a light midday meal' (*OED*).

70 disjune...*Tillietudlem.*] De Quincey has in mind Sir Walter Scott (1771–1832; *DNB*) and his novel *The Tale of Old Mortality* (1816), in which Lady Margaret Bellenden, the Royalist owner of Tillietudlem Castle, remembers 'his sacred Majesty King Charles, when he took his disjune at Tillietudlem' (Scott, *Old Mortality*, p. 24). 'Disjune' means 'breakfast' (*OED*).

71 *Luther. Solomon...Euclid.*] Martin Luther (1483–1546), German Protestant theologian. Solomon (*fl.* mid-tenth century BC), King of Israel. For Samson, see above, n. 15. Euclid (*c.* 330–*c.* 260 BC), Greek mathematician. Robert Simson (1687–1768; *DNB*), mathematician, *Elements of Euclid* (1756).

72 *Lancashire man;*] De Quincey was born in Manchester, Lancashire.

73 *fresh from Oxford,*] De Quincey bolted from Oxford in 1808, and settled in the Lakes in October 1809 (see Lindop, pp. 159–60, 184).

74 *Jupiter,'*] Jupiter, or Jove, was the supreme god of the Romans.

75 *Martindale...Noah...fee simple*] Martindale is a valley near Ullswater in the English Lake District. Noah is the hero of the biblical Flood story in the Old Testament book of Genesis. 'Fee simple' means 'absolute possession' (see below, p. 593, n. 15).

76 *Νωϊ.*], (Gk.),'Noï'; more commonly, 'Noë', which De Quincey wrote in revision (see below, p. 636, 45.30.

77 *Pope...monosyllable;*] see, for example, Pope, 'The Fourth Satire of Dr John Donne', ll. 26–7: '*Noah* had refus'd it lodging in his Ark, / Where all the Race of *Reptiles* might embark'.

78 *proverb...eating eggs.*] *Proverbs,* p. 806: 'Teach your grandmother to suck eggs'.

79 *sorrow rather than in anger,*] Shakespeare, *Hamlet*, I.ii.231–2: 'A countenance more / In sorrow than in anger'.

Milton Versus Southey and Landor

1 *Milton...*Southey] For Milton, see above, p. 526, n. 55. For Southey, see above, p. 523, n. 3. The imaginary conversation between 'Southey and Landor' was first published in 1846 (Landor, *CW,* vol. V, pp. 230–80). A 'second conversation' was similarly published in 1846 (Landor, *CW,* vol. V, pp. 281–334).

2 *Thames...Clyde,*] the major rivers of, respectively, England and Scotland.

3 *'each his Milton...in our own.'*] Landor, *Works*, vol. II, p. 58. Samuel Johnson (1709–84; *DNB*), critic, lexicographer, poet, and man of letters. His 1779 *Life of Milton* was notoriously uneven, and particularly scathing about 'Lycidas'.

4 *Americans call 'notions.'*] '*U.S.*...articles or wares of various kinds forming a miscellaneous cargo' (*OED*).

5 *'that they should...closing them;'*] inexact: '*Landor.* That is, abasing our eyes in reverence to so great a man, but without closing them' (Landor, *Works*, vol. II, p. 58).

6 *'It will be difficult...to refrain.'*] *'Landor*....It will be difficult for us always to refrain. Johnson, I think, has been charged unjustly with expressing too freely and inconsiderately the blemishes of Milton. There are many more than he has noticed' (Landor, *Works*, vol. II, p. 58).

7 *'miching malhecho'*] Shakespeare, *Hamlet*, III.ii.137–8: 'Marry, this [miching] mallecho; it means mischief'.

8 *premises...any great fable,*] *'Southey*....Surely it is a silly and stupid business to talk mainly about the moral of a poem, unless it professedly be a fable' (Landor, *Works*, vol. II, p. 59).

9 racemus,] 'cluster of grapes / berries'.

10 *exception...'Paradise Lost'),*] Milton's *Paradise Lost* 'lays down a principle which concerns every man's welfare...that great and irremediable misery may arise from apparently small offences' (Landor, *Works*, vol. II, p. 60).

11 *'Iliad...Odyssey'*),] epic poems by Homer (see above, p. 536, n. 50). *The Iliad* tells the story of the Trojan war; *The Odyssey* describes the return of Odysseus from Troy.

12 *I decline to repeat it.*] In *The Iliad*, Homer demonstrated 'the evil effects of arbitrary power, in alienating an elevated soul from the cause of his country' (Landor, *Works*, vol. II, p. 59).

13 *'Othello'*...'Try Warren's Blacking!'] De Quincey refers to Shakespeare's tragedy *Othello* and the paste blacking (boot polish) made by Robert Warren and Jonathan Warren, who ran rival, separate businesses. Robert was more famous from his extensive use of advertising jingles. It was in Jonathan's factory that the twelve-year-old Charles Dickens toiled so unhappily.

14 *Achilles...Agamemnon*] In Greek mythology, Achilles is the bravest, handsomest and greatest warrior of the army of Agamemnon, King of Mycenae, or Argos. The subject of *The Iliad* is the 'wrath of Achilles', arising from an affront to his honour given by Agamemnon. Cf. De Quincey in his 1841–2 *Blackwood's* series on 'Homer and the Homeridae': 'WHAT is the *Iliad* about? What is the true and proper subject of the *Iliad?*' (Vol. 13, p. 27).

15 *Argonautic expedition,*] in Greek legend, the band of fifty heroes who went with Jason to recover the Golden Fleece.

16 *Lloyd's*] Lloyd's of London is a corporation of underwriters and insurance brokers specializing in marine insurance.

17 *'into Almighty smash;'*] untraced.

18 *Williams...Academy,*] John Williams (1792–1858; *DNB*), first rector of Edinburgh Academy, which was founded in 1824. De Quincey refers to Williams, *Homerus* (London: Murray, 1842) p. 151: Williams argues that Troy enjoyed 'ten years of prosperous crime and false security' while the Greeks organised their forces, 'nor did the lapse of time soften the hearts of their princes, and incline them to make reparation for their wanton aggressions'.

19 *Hellas...Nemesis*] 'Hellas' is the Greek name for Greece. In Greek myth, 'Nemesis' is the personification of retribution or vengeance.

20 *Troad...Ilium.*] 'The Troad' is 'the land of Troy'; 'Ilium' is the Latin name for 'Troy'.

21 *Athenian...'Paradise Regained,'*] Milton, *Paradise Regained*, IV. 236–364.

22 *'That to the...Providence.'*] Milton, *Paradise Lost*, I. 24–5.

23 *'And justify...to man.'*] Milton, *Paradise Lost*, I. 26. Milton of course wrote 'men'.

24 'Gebir.'] see above, p. 524, n. 17.

25 *original edition*...Over-Colonisation.] 'In the moral are exhibited the folly, the injustice, and the punishment of Invasion, with the calamities which must ever attend the superfluous colonization of a peopled country'. This sentence was not part of the

original 1798 'Preface'. Landor added it for the 1803 edition (Landor, *CW*, vol. XIII, p. 344).

26 *Decemviral...Oleron...Napoleon...Bentham,*] In 451 BC, the 'decemviri' ('ten men') drew up the 'Twelve Tables', the earliest Roman code of laws. Justinian I (482–565), Byzantine emperor who codified Roman law in the Justinian Code. The twelfth-century Rolls of Oléron codified the customary laws of the Atlantic ports and formed the basis of the maritime law in England. Canon law is the body of laws made within certain Christian churches. The Code Napoléon is the systematic collection of the civil law of France. Jeremy Bentham (1748–1832; *DNB*), utilitarian and philosophical radical, whose central preoccupations included the codification of law.

27 Squatters:] In 1859, De Quincey expanded this passage (see below, p. 636, 50.n.6). Cf. De Quincey in 'On Reform as Affecting the Habits of Private Life', where he borrows the term '"squatter"...from America to express the corresponding nuisance' (Vol. 8, p. 355).

28 *Dalica,*] In *Gebir*, Dalica is the nurse whose treachery results in Gebir's death.

29 *Enceladus...Etna...Jove*] Eruptions of Mount Etna were attributed to the mythical monster Enceladus. De Quincey has in mind Virgil, *Aeneid*, III. 578–81.

30 succubus...incubus,] a 'succubus' is a demon assuming female form to have sexual intercourse with men in their sleep; an 'incubus' is an evil spirit that lies on persons in their sleep, and especially one that has sexual intercourse with women in their sleep.

31 *Riedesel...'it lacerated...vinegar cruet.'*] De Quincey has in mind Fredrike Charlotte Luise, Freifrau von Riedesel (1746–1808) or her husband Friedrich Adolf, Freiherr von Riedesel (1738–1800). But the reference has not been traced in their writings.

32 'vir bonus...compositus;'] Seneca, *de Providentia*, II. 9: 'a brave man matched against ill-fortune'.

33 *Keats...Shelley..."because...a Greek."*] De Quincey has switched from the first to the second 'imaginary conversation' between 'Southey and Landor' (see above, n. 1; Landor, *Works*, vol. II, p. 156). John Keats (1795–1821; *DNB*) published 'Hyperion' in *Lamia, Isabella, The Eve of St Agnes, and Other Poems* (1820). Cf. Richard Hengist Horne (1803–84; *DNB*) in his 1844 essay on Alfred Tennyson: 'When somebody expressed his surprise to Shelley, that Keats, who was not very conversant with the Greek language, could write so finely and classically of their gods and goddesses, Shelley replied "He *was* a Greek"' (*Keats: The Critical Heritage*, ed. G. M. Matthews (New York: Barnes and Noble, 1971), p. 298).

34 *Wordsworth... "pagan creed."*'] In an 1845 letter, Benjamin Robert Haydon (1786–1846; *DNB*) recollected how Wordsworth described Keats's 'exquisite ode to Pan' from *Endymion* as '"a Very pretty piece of Paganism" – This was unfeeling, & unworthy of his high Genius to a young Worshipper like Keats – & Keats felt it *deeply*' (*The Keats Circle*, ed. Hyder Edward Rollins, 2 vols (Cambridge, Mass.: Harvard University Press, 1965), vol. II, p. 144).

35 *'Come...fight you* both.'] For 'Nine tailors make a man', see *Proverbs*, p. 567. De Quincey's reference to an 'old English drama' has not been traced. But cf. Thomas Carlyle in *Sartor Resartus*: 'Does it not stand on record that the English Queen Elizabeth, receiving a deputation of Eighteen Tailors, addressed them with a: Good morning, gentlemen both!' (Thomas Carlyle, *Sartor Resartus*, ed. Rodger L. Tarr (Berkeley: University of California Press, 2000), p. 212).

36 *Nothing can be more...Hyperion.*] In Greek mythology, Saturn is leader of the Titans, and Hyperion's brother. De Quincey is thinking in particular of the opening of Keats's poem.

37 *Prometheus...plummets...human spirit.*] For Prometheus, see above, p. 532, n. 94. De Quincey echoes Shakespeare, *The Tempest*, III.iii.101: 'I'll seek him deeper than e'er plummet sounded'.

38 *Tooke's 'Pantheon'*] Andrew Tooke (1673–1732; *DNB*), *The Pantheon, representing the Fabulous Histories of the heathen gods and most Illustrious Heroes* (1698).

39 *Dumoustier's* 'Lettres...Mythologie'] Charles Albert Demoustier (1760–1801), *Lettres à Émilie sur la mythologie* (1786–90).

40 *Spence's* 'Polymetis,'] Joseph Spence (1699–1768; *DNB*), clergyman, anecdotist and scholar, *Polymetis; or An Enquiry concerning the Agreement between the Works of the Roman Poets and the Remains of the Antient Artists* (1747).

41 *'Bibliotheca' of Apollodorus*,] Apollodorus (*fl. c.* 140 BC), Athenian grammarian and author of *Bibliotheca*, a study of Greek heroic mythology.

42 *upon the 'Hyperion.'*] According to Haydon (see above, n. 34), Wordsworth made his disparaging comments after hearing Keats recite, not 'Hyperion', but part of *Endymion*.

43 *Lucifer...Wordsworth.*] De Quincey originally made this comparison in his October 1840 *Tait's* article on 'Walking Stewart' (see Vol. 11, p. 256).

44 *Archimedes...Michael Angelo,*] Archimedes (*c.* 287–212 BC), Greek mathematician and inventor. Michelangelo (1475–1564), Italian painter, sculptor, architect and poet.

45 doppelganger...*once too often.*] cf. De Quincey in his 1826 *Blackwood's* essay on 'Gillies's German Stories': 'We have an example in the *Doppelgänger*, or cases of double identity – where a man runs in a curricle, as it were, with a repetition or duplicate of himself: all the world is duped by the swindling fac-simile' (Vol. 6, p. 17).

46 impar...dispar;] 'impar' is unequal, inferior'; 'dispar' is indifferent'.

47 *Abd el Kâder...Waghorn*] Abdelkader (1808–83), military and religious leader, who led the Algerians in their struggle against French domination (1840–6). Thomas Waghorn (1800–50; *DNB*), promoter of an overland route to India, whose many pamphlets include *Overland Mails to India and China* (1843).

48 *'shy'*] 'a trial, an experiment' (*OED*).

49 *'Of Proteus...wreathed horn;'...'The Excursion.'*] De Quincey slightly misquotes Wordsworth, 'The World is too much with us', ll. 13–14. In Greek mythology, Proteus is the prophetic old man of the sea and Triton is a demigod of the sea. De Quincey's second reference is to Wordsworth, *The Excursion* (1814), IV. 847–87.

50 *'There are...your wonder:'*] Wordsworth, 'Yallow Unvisited', ll. 27–8.

51 *Freyschütz chorus*] Carl Maria von Weber (1786–1826), German composer best known for his opera *Der Freischütz* (*The Freeshooter*, 1821). Cf. Leigh Hunt in 1826: 'I then made tour of the book-stalls at Covent-garden...went to the theatre, and saw Der Freyschutz' (Hunt, p. 46).

52 *'Heavy as frost, and deep almost as life.'*] Wordsworth, 'Intimations of Immortality', l. 131.

53 *Mozart...'Don Giovanni,'*] Wolfgang Amadeus Mozart (1756–91), Austrian composer, whose operas include *The Marriage of Figaro* (1786) and *Don Giovanni* (1787).

54 primâ facie] (Lt.), 'at first sight'.

55 *'Nares's English Orthoëpy'* (in a late edition),] Robert Nares (1753–1829; *DNB*), philologist, *Elements of Orthoepy: containing a distinct view of the whole analogy of the English language; so far as it relates to pronunciation, accent, and quantity* (1784).

56 con-tri-bu-ce-on.] In 1859, De Quincey appended a footnote to this word (see below, p. 637, 55.7).

57 *Kemble...Drury Lane.*] John Philip Kemble (1757–1823; *DNB*), actor and manager of the Covent Garden and Drury Lane theatres in London.

58 *'I'll fill thy bones with aches.'*] Shakespeare, *The Tempest*, I.ii.369–71: 'I'll rack thee with old cramps, / Fill all thy bones with aches, make thee roar / That beasts shall tremble at thy din'.

59 literatim,] (Lt.), 'literally'.

60 obelizing,] To 'obelize' is 'to condemn as spurious or corrupt' (*OED*).

61 *Bentley's hypothesis*] Richard Bentley (1662–1742; *DNB*), Cambridge classicist and antiquarian, who produced a highly idiosyncratic edition of Milton's *Paradise Lost* (1732). Cf. De Quincey in his 1830 *Blackwood's* essay on Bentley: 'His edition of Milton had the same merits as his other editions; peculiar defects it had, indeed, from which his editions of Latin classics were generally free....The romantic, or Christian, poetry, was alien to Bentley's taste' (Vol. 7, p. 131).

62 *lucifers*] matches.

63 Tibbalds *as it was pronounced},*] Pope, 'Epistle to Dr Arbuthnot', ll. 163–4: 'Yet ne'er one sprig of Laurel grac'd these ribalds, / From slashing Bentley down to pidling Tibbalds'. De Quincey also has in mind Pope, 'The First Epistle of the Second Book of Horace Imitated', l. 104: 'Like slashing Bentley with his desp'rate hook'. Cf. De Quincey in 1830: 'Not that [Bentley] had a peculiarly fine sense for the rhythmus of verse, – else the divine structure of the Miltonic blank verse would have preserved numerous fine passages from his "slashing" proscription' (Vol. 7, pp. 156–7).

64 *adder for music.*] Psalms 58: 4–5.

65 *beyond other men Bentley had,*] cf. De Quincey in 1830: 'Bentley expired on the 14th of July, 1742; and in his person England lost the greatest scholar by far that she ever has produced; greater than she *will* produce, according to all likelihood, under the tendencies of modern education' (Vol. 7, p. 117).

66 *'See with what...fair world.'*] Milton, *Paradise Lost*, X. 616–17: 'See with what heat these dogs of hell advance / To waste and havoc yonder world'.

67 *'As well...*choicest society,'] Milton, *Paradise Regained*, I. 301–2. Cf. Landor, *Works*, vol. II, p. 156. In 1859, De Quincey appended a footnote to this quotation (see below, p. 637, 56.28).

68 *Dryden*] For John Dryden, see above, p. 524, n. 24.

69 'Not difficult...hearken to me'] Milton, *Paradise Regained*, II. 428.

70 *'no authority will reconcile'*] Landor, *Works*, vol. II, p. 157.

71 quadriga,] 'chariot'.

72 'Launcelot, or Pellias, or Pellinore;'] Milton, *Paradise Regained*, II. 361.

73 'Quintius, Fabricius, Curius, Regulus.'] Milton, *Paradise Regained*, II. 446.

74 *'roll-calls of proper names.'*] Landor, *Works*, vol. II, p. 157.

75 *Boileau,*] Nicolas Boileau-Despréaux (1636–1711), poet, satirist and literary critic, best known for *Art poétique* (1674). Cf. Landor in the imaginary conversation between himself and the Abbé Delille: 'These names are tacked together for no other purpose than the rhyme...whenever a Frenchman finds a difficulty in spelling a word, he throws in a handful of consonants to help him over: these are the fascines of M. Boileau's approaches' (Landor, *Works*, vol. I, p. 99).

76 *'——Noëmonaque Prytaninqué;'*] Virgil (see above, p. 535, n. 42), *Aeneid*, IX. 767: 'Alcandrumque Haliumque Noëmonaque Prytanimque' ('then, as, all unwitting, on the walls they rouse the fray, Alcander and Halius, Noemon and Prytanis').

77 *Homer...in this way.*] cf. De Quincey's discussion of '*Homer's metre*' in his 1841–2 *Blackwood's* series on 'Homer and the Homeridae' (Vol. 13, pp. 51–3).

78 *'Ask for this great...*with slaves.'] Milton, *Samson Agonistes*, ll. 40–1.

79 *'the grief...of the sentence.'*] Landor, *Works*, vol. II, p. 160.
80 'From that placid...regard,'] Milton, *Paradise Regained*, III. 217; see Landor, *Works*, vol. II, p. 158.
81 "In the bosom...of light?"'] Milton, *Paradise Regained*, IV. 597; see Landor, *Works*, vol. II, p. 159.
82 en attendant,] (Fr.), literally, 'while we wait'.
83 *'Four faces...*double Janus;'] Milton, *Paradise Lost*, XI. 128–9: 'Of watchful cherubim; four faces each / Had, like a double Janus, all their shape'.
84 *'Better left ...are queer figures.'*] Landor, *Works*, vol. II, p. 72.
85 *Hopetoun...Edinburgh.*] John Hope, fourth Earl of Hopetoun (1765–1823; *DNB*), general, whose bronze equestrian statue stands in St Andrew's Square, Edinburgh.
86 *Duke of Wellington.*] Arthur Wellesley, first Duke of Wellington (1769–1852; *DNB*), hero of Waterloo and British Prime Minister, 1828–30.
87 *Nero... temple to Janus;*] Nero (AD 37–68), Roman emperor, AD 54–68. Janus was the Roman god of gates, doorways and bridges. De Quincey is probably referring to the Janus Geminus, a shrine of Janus at the north side of the Forum. It likely dates back to Vespasian (AD 9–79), Roman emperor, AD 69–79.
88 Julium...Augustum...Transitorium...*fourth*] De Quincey seems here to refer to Martial, *Epigrams*, X.xxviii: 'Now your threshold is encircled by Caesar's gifts, and you number as many forums, Janus, as you have faces'. The passage has been taken to mean that the god looked upon the Fora Romanum, Augustum, Transitorium, and Pacis, though the topography makes this improbable.

Joan of Arc {Part I}

1 *Hordal...*Darc, *in 1612.*] The original source is Jean Hordal (1552–1618), *Heroinae nobilissimae Ioannae Darc* (1612), but De Quincey is drawing from Michelet, vol. II, p. 517.
2 *Lorraine,*] At the time of Joan's birth, Upper Lorraine was an independent duchy lying between France and Germany. It now lies in northeastern France.
3 *Hebrew boy...no man could deny.*] David, whose inaugural act was his victory over Goliath (1 Samuel 17).
4 *Adverse armies*] cf. 2 Samuel 5: 3: 'So all the elders of Israel came to the king at Hebron...and they anointed David king over Israel'.
5 from a station of good will,] De Quincey italicizes these words as a way of emphasizing his objection to Michelet's animosity toward Joan.
6 *the sceptre was departing from Judah.*] Genesis 49: 10: 'The sceptre shall not depart from Judah, nor the ruler's staff from between his feet'.
7 *Domrémy...Vaucouleurs*] Domrémy is a village in northeastern France. Vaucouleurs is nearby.
8 *title of* du Lys.] Michelet, vol. II, p. 518: The 'surname of Du Lis' was 'conferred on one of her brothers'.
9 *sleeping the sleep of the dead.*] cf. Psalm 13: 3: 'Consider and hear me, O Lord my God! / Give light to my eyes, lest I sleep the sleep of death'.
10 *apparitors*] legal officers; the summoners of the ecclesiastical courts.
11 en contumace.] (Fr.), a legal term applied to an accused person who fails to appear in court when summoned.
12 *even yet may happen,*] De Quincey's prophecy has been fully realized. Joan was canonized in 1920, and is accepted by France as a national heroine.

13 *sleep, which is in the grave,*] cf. De Quincey in *Confessions*: 'Here were the hopes which blossom in the paths of life, reconciled with the peace which is in the grave' (Vol. 2, pp. 51, 228).

14 *Rouen*] situated on the Seine, some ninety miles northwest of Paris. Joan was burned alive in the city square.

15 *lilies of France...wither them;*] The *fleur-de-lys* (lily flower) was the royal emblem of France from the time of King Clovis (465–511) until the Revolution of 1789.

16 *March hares;*] proverbial; hares are wildest in March.

17 *their mighty Revolution;*] The second French Revolution of 1830 had expelled the restored Bourbon King Charles X, and crowned Louis Philippe, Duke of Orleans, as 'king of the French'. De Quincey discussed these events at great length as a key political writer for *Blackwood's* in the early 1830s (Vol. 7, pp. 160–286). De Quincey may also be prophesying the approach of the third French Revolution of 1848.

18 *Pampas,*] the vast, treeless plain extending westward across central Argentina from the Atlantic coast to the Andean foothills.

19 *transcendental German nurses.*] that is, like De Quincey, schooled in the German transcendentalism of Immanuel Kant and his disciples.

20 *book against Priests,*] Michelet's *Du Pr{e}tre, de la Femme et de la Famille* (1844) was translated by Charles Cocks as *Priests, Women, and Families* (1845).

21 *Percy...'A vow...take,'*] Thomas Percy (1729–1811; *DNB*), antiquarian, whose *Reliques of Ancient English Poetry* (1765) contained 'The Modern Ballad of Chevy Chace'. De Quincey parodies the opening lines: 'The stout Erle of Northumberland / A vow to God did make, / His pleasure in the Scottish woods / Three summers days to take'.

22 delirium tremens.] 'a species of delirium induced by excessive indulgence in alcoholic liquors' (*OED*).

23 *Pucelle d'Orleans,*] (Fr.), 'Maid of Orleans'. Joan was given the title because in 1429 she helped to expel the English from Orleans, the first important act in her career and the military turning point in the One Hundred Years' War.

24 *collection...forthcoming in Paris.*] In 1854 De Quincey appended a footnote to this passage (see below, p. 637, 66.20). The collection in question is Jules Quicherat, *Procès de Condemnation et de Réhabilitation de Jeanne d'Arc, dite La Pucelle*, 5 vols (Paris: Société de l'Histoire de France, 1841–9).

25 *Hannibal.*] Hannibal (247–183 BC) at an early age swore an oath of eternal enmity to Rome, which he kept by ravaging Italy for fifteen years.

26 *Mithridates...received on earth.*] Mithradates the Great, King of Pontus (d. 63 BC) was the most formidable enemy of Rome in Asia Minor. He was finally defeated by Pompey (106–48 BC), and received the 'real honour' of being buried in the royal sepulchre at Sinope.

27 Delenda est Anglia Victrix!] 'Victorious England must be destroyed'. De Quincey imitates the words of Cato the Elder (234–149 BC), who concluded each of his speeches before the Roman Senate with the declaration, *Delenda est Carthago*, 'Carthage must be destroyed'. De Quincey himself uses the phrase '*Delenda est Carthago*' in his 1829 essay on 'The Duke of Wellington and Mr Peel' (Vol. 7, p. 37).

28 *Ali...Tippoo...Napoleon*] Hyder Ali (1722–82), Muslim ruler of Mysore and England's most formidable enemy in India. His son Tippu Sultan (*c.* 1749–1799) continued the war against the English. Napoleon Bonaparte (see above, p. 526, n. 59) was reviled by De Quincey, who in his 1832 *Blackwood's* essay on 'Charlemagne' described him as 'the sole barbarian of his time; presenting, in his deficiencies, the

picture of a low mechanic – and, in his positive qualities, the violence and brutality of a savage' (Vol. 8, p. 195).

29 *nationality it was not.*] cf. De Quincey in 'Revolt of the Tartars', where he speaks of the Kalmucks as a tribe whose 'native ferocity was exasperated by…a nationality as well as an inflated conceit' (Vol. 9, p. 173).

30 *Suffrein,*] Pierre André de Suffren Saint-Tropez (1726–88), distinguished French naval officer, who fought the British in Indian waters during the American Revolutionary War. He concerted with Hyder Ali (see above, n. 28).

31 *magnanimous justice of Englishmen.*] De Quincey has in mind Southey's 'Joan of Arc', not Shakespeare's treatment of her in *Henry VI, Part I.*

32 Jean…*St John the Evangelist,*] Jean is the 'baptismal name…of a great number of celebrated men of the middle ages', including Saint John the Baptist (*fl.* early first century AD), Jewish prophet. The name 'seems to bespeak a sort of mystical tendency in those families that bestowed it on their children' (Michelet, vol. II, p. 518).

33 *'took after…Joinville.'*] Michelet, vol. II, p. 517.

34 *prince…old crusader.*] François de Lorraine, second duc de Guise, duc d'Aumale, Prince de Joinville (1519–63), soldier and political intriguer; and Jean, Sire de Joinville (*c.* 1224–1317), author of the famous *Histoire de saint-Louis*, a chronicle of the Seventh Crusade (1248–54).

35 *soupçon,*] (Fr.), a little bit; a trace.

36 cis…trans.] The territories on this side (*cis*) and on the other side (*trans*) of the boundary line.

37 *Richter*…This…leads to Constantinople.] De Quincey is thinking of Johann Paul Friedrich Richter (see above, p. 536, n. 67), *Hesperus*: 'on the western gate of Cherson stood the sublime description: Here leads the way to Byzantium' (Jean Paul, *Hesperus*, vol. I, p. xxiii).

38 *wars or rumours of wars,*] Matthew 24: 6: 'And ye shall hear of wars and rumours of wars'.

39 quadrivium] (Lt.), 'crossroads'.

40 *Bar and Lorraine…warfare with France*] Bar was a small duchy, later united to Lorraine. 'Though constantly at war with France, these princes of Lorraine and Bar never missed as opportunity of dying for her' (Michelet, vol. II, p. 505).

41 *Crécy…Nicopolis…Agincourt.*] The English defeated the French at the battle of Crécy (1346), and among those killed were Rudolf of Lorraine and the Count of Bar. At Nicopolis (1396), the allied armies of France, Poland and Hungary were defeated by the Turkish Sultan Bayezid I (*c.* 1360–1403), and a third Duke of Lorraine was among those slain. King Henry V of England (1387–1422) won the battle of Agincourt (1415), and those killed included Frederick of Lorraine, the Duke of Bar, and the latter's two brothers.

42 *Fleurs de Lys.*] the lilies of France.

43 *an old hereditary enemy of France,*] the German Empire.

44 *Aix-la-Chapelle,*] now Aachen in northwestern Germany.

45 *ear that listened…groaning of wheels,*] The moment recalls several in De Quincey: cf. his 1839 recollection of Wordsworth when he 'stretched himself at length on the high road, applying his ear to the ground so as to catch any sound of wheels that might be groaning along at a distance' (Vol. 11, p. 74); and 'The English Mail-Coach', when 'a sigh of woe, seemed to steal upon the air, as again the far-off sound of a wheel was heard! A whisper it was' (see above, p. 439).

46 *Poictiers,*] more commonly, 'Poitiers'. Like Crécy and Agincourt (see above, n. 41), the Battle of Poitiers (1356) was part of the Hundred Years' War (conventionally

dated 1337–1453), and a key moment in the English attempt to establish King Edward III (1312–77) on the French throne.

47 *King (Charles VI.)*] Charles VI (1368–1422), King of France who came to power in 1380, but suffered from madness after 1392. He declared Henry V of England his successor.

48 *wild story...prophetic doom.*] The story is related in Michelet, vol. II, pp. 304–5.

49 *famines...diseases...peasantry*] Famine hit France and England particularly hard in 1315, 1336, and 1353. De Quincey has in mind insurrections such as the 1381 Peasants' Revolt, led by Wat Tyler (d. 1381; *DNB*).

50 *crusades...Templars...Interdicts... Emperor*] The Crusades took place from 1095 to 1270. Knight Templars were members of a religious military order established at the time of the Crusades, and eventually suppressed by the Pope in 1312. An interdict is a decree, usually by a Pope, forbidding administration of the sacraments, celebration of public worship and use of the burial service. England was put under interdict by Alexander III in 1170 and by Innocent III in 1209; France, by Innocent III in 1200. The 'tragedies' De Quincey refers to include the beheading of Conradin (1252–68) by Charles of Anjou (1226–85) in 1268, and Charles's subsequent cruelties in Sicily, which caused the bloody popular uprising known as the Sicilian Vespers (1282).

51 *spectacle of a double Pope*] i.e. during the 'Great Schism' (1378–1417), when there were two, and later three, rival popes. It was sparked by the election of Urban VI (*c.* 1318–89).

52 *rent...which no man could ever heal.*] The Reformation, which saw the final separation of the Protestant from the Romish church, as effected by Martin Luther (1483–1546).

53 *sad* misereres *of the Romish chaunting;*] 'Miserere' is the first word of the fifty-first Psalm in the Latin version. It means 'have mercy', and is usually sung for penitential acts.

54 Gloria in Excelcis:] 'We praise thee, O God'. The first words of a Latin hymn.

55 *The fountain...bounds.*] De Quincey draws here from Michelet: Joan's 'village was close on the verge of the great forests of the Vosges...The fairies haunted that wood...the curé used to go once every year and read a mass at the fountain in order to drive them away' (vol. II, p. 519).

56 *licensed victuallers.*] tavern-keepers. Cf. Charles Dickens, *Barnaby Rudge*, p. 115: 'believing, moreover, that the publicans coupled with sinners in Holy Writ were veritable licensed victuallers'.

57 *'Abbeys...Moorish temples...Hindoos,'*] De Quincey is adapting Wordsworth, *Peter Bell*, ll. 728–30: 'Temples like those among the Hindoos, / And mosques, and spires, and abbey windows, / And castles all with ivy green!'.

58 *Vosges...Napoleon's line...Allies.*] The Vosges separate Lorraine from Alsace in north-eastern France. In 1813–4, Napoleon fought against great odds to protect France from invasion by the Allies (Austria, Russia, Prussia and Great Britain). His failure resulted in the fall of Paris and his own abdication on 6 April 1814.

59 Live and let live] proverbial. Cf. 'Dum vivimus vivamus' (Lt.), 'Let us live while we live'; and Hunt, p. 101.

60 *Carlovingians princes...Charlemagne*] the line of kings founded by Charlemagne (AD 742–814), King of the Franks from 768, and by 800 the undisputed ruler of Western Europe. De Quincey draws here from Michelet: 'This elevated part of France...was covered with forests so vast, that the Carlovingians esteemed them the most suitable for their imperials hunts' (Michelet, vol. II, p. 516). For De Quincey's 1832 *Blackwood's* essay on 'Charlemagne', see Vol. 8, pp. 183–205.

61 *mysterious fawns*] In the romances of the Middle Ages, a knight while hunting was sometimes led by a white doe or hart into the 'Happy Other-World'.

62 *ancient stag*] Charles Hardwick, *Traditions, Superstitions, and Folk Lore* (London: Simpkin, Marshall and Co., 1872), pp. 154–5: 'Alexander the Great is said by Pliny to have caught a white stag, placed a collar of gold about its neck, and afterwards set it free....Julius Caesar took the place of Alexander, and Charlemagne caught a white hart at both Magdebourg, and in the Holstein woods'.

63 *marches...marquess.*] De Quincey knows his etymology. 'Marches' are 'borderlands'. 'Marquess' derives from 'marches' and refers to the title originally given to the governor of a march or frontier.

64 *Coverley...said on both sides.*] Sir Roger de Coverley is the landed Tory squire in the fictional sketches that appeared in *The Spectator* (1711–12), a daily newspaper founded and jointly conducted by Richard Steele and Joseph Addison (see above, p. 523, n. 1). De Quincey's reference is to Addison's *Spectator* essay for 20 July 1711: 'Sir ROGER...told them, with the Air of a Man who would not give his Judgment rashly, that *much might be said on both Sides*' (*Spectator*, vol. I, p. 499).

65 *desert between Syria...Euphrates,*] the Syrian desert.

66 not *a shepherdess...Haumette,*] Michelet, vol. II, p. 518: Haumette was Joan's 'bosom friend and companion from childhood, three or four years her junior'. Joan 'did not go to the fields to tend the sheep or other beasts'.

67 Bergereta.] Latin form of the French 'bergerette', a shepherd girl.

68 *Simond, in his* Travels,] Louis Simond (1767–1831), *Switzerland; or, a Journal of a Tour and Residence in that Country, in the years 1817, 1818 and 1819*, second edition (London: John Murray, 1823), vol. I, pp. 14–5. Simond describes a scene observed in 1817 at Dijon in France: 'They plough with all sorts of cattle...we are told that a woman has been yoked with a hog of the species just described, patiently ploughing together'. De Quincey is wrong in that the scene is post-Revolutionary, and no whip is used. He told this same anecdote in his 1838–9 *Encyclopedia Britannica* essay on 'Shakspeare' (Vol. 13, p. 309).

69 *praedial*] performing duties connected with a farm.

70 *darning the stockings*] Michelet, vol. II, p. 518: according to Haumette, Joan 'used to spin and attend to the business of the house like other girls'.

71 *Friday in Juan Fernandez,*] Robinson Crusoe's 'man Friday' in Daniel Defoe's famous novel (1719), which is supposedly based on the experiences of Alexander Selkirk (1676–1721; *DNB*), who for four years lived in solitude on the island of Juan Fernandez.

72 *Chevalier of St Louis,*] a knight of the order of St Louis, founded by Louis XIV (1638–1715) in 1693 for military service, and taking its name from Louis IX (1214–70), who was canonized in 1297.

73 'Chevalier...fleurs-de-lys?'] 'Chevalier, have you fed the hog?', 'My daughter, have you fed the hog?', 'Maid of Orleans, have you saved the fleurs-de-lys?'.

74 *'If the man...his father.'*] De Quincey probably read this stanza in *Anecdotes of the late Samuel Johnson* (1786) by Hester Lynch Piozzi (1740–1821; *DNB*). Johnson is criticizing some verses by the Spanish dramatist Lope de Vega (1562–1635), and remarks, 'you might as well say, that "If the man who turnips cries, / Cry not when his father dies, / 'Tis a proof that he had rather / Have a turnip than his father' (Heather Lynch Piozzi, *Anecdotes of the late Samuel Johnson*, ed. S. C. Roberts (Westport, Conn.: Greenwood Press, 1971), p. 46).

75 *Oriflamme*] the ancient royal standard of France: a red flag, deeply split into flame-shaped streamers, and borne on a gilded lance.

76 *Michelet...*Pucelle...*of that period;*] Michelet, vol. II, p. 545: 'What had she to fear among loyal knights, she a prisoner of war, a girl, so young, and, above all, a virgin?....the worship of the Virgin constantly advancing in the middle ages, having now become the predominant religion, virginity ought apparently to have been an inviolable safeguard'.

77 *detection of the Dauphin (Charles VII.)*] Charles VII (1403–61), King of France, became Dauphin in 1417 and was King, 1422–61. In 1429 Joan travelled to Chinon, a town near Tours in western France, and a castle occupied by Charles. He hid himself among courtiers, but Joan identified him at a glance, 'and though he insisted, at first, he was not the king, she embraced his knees' (Michelet, vol. II, p. 525).

78 leger-de-main,] 'legerdemain': 'sleight of hand...jugglery' (*OED*).

79 *Southey's...published in 1796.*] Robert Southey (see above, p. 523, n. 3) expressed keen sympathy for the French Revolution in his long and hastily written poem on *Joan of Arc* (1796), which De Quincey discusses at greater length in his 1848 *North British Review* essay on Charles Lamb (see above, pp. 382–5). 'Twenty years after', in 1816, Southey and De Quincey were neighbours in the Lake District.

80 coup d'essai,] (Fr.), 'first attempt'.

81 *Victoria...'pricks' for sheriffs.*] Victoria (1819–1901), Queen of Great Britain and Ireland, 1837–1901. De Quincey refers to an ancient ceremony, in which the Sovereign chooses a sheriff by the prick of a pin. Cf. Shakespeare, *Julius Caesar*, IV.i.1: 'These many then shall die, their names are prick'd'.

82 *Lady of the islands and the orient!*] De Quincey prophetically anticipates the title assumed by Victoria in 1876: 'Queen of Great Britain and Ireland, and Empress of India'.

83 *on the throne...be seated.'*] Southey, *Joan of Arc*, III. 175–7.

84 *'the jewell'd crown...menial's head.'*] Southey, *Joan of Arc*, III. 188–9.

85 'un peu fort;'] (Fr.), 'a little too strong'.

86 petit écu] (Fr.), 'petit écu' or 'écu blanc', in contrast with 'écu d'or', was a silver coin, first struck in 1641.

87 *take him to Rheims.*] The English declared Charles VII (see above, n. 77) illegitimate, and in 1422 crowned the infant Henry VI (1421–71) King of France and England. The English controlled the greater part of Northern France, including Rheims, the historic place for the coronation of the French Kings, and as long as Charles remained unconsecrated, the rightfulness of his claim to be King of France was open to challenge. With Joan's help, he was eventually crowned in Rheims in 1429.

88 *ampulla,*] the vase in which the holy oil for coronation was kept.

89 *the English boy?*] Henry VI (see above, n. 87).

90 *oven of coronation at Rheims,*] Rheims (see above, n. 87) was famous for its biscuits and gingerbread.

Joan of Arc {Part II}

1 *LA PUCELLE,*] see above, p. 543, n. 23.

2 *Southey...'appall'd the doctors.'*] For Robert Southey, see above, p. 523, n. 3.

3 *occupies v. 354–391, B. III.*] For example, Southey, *Joan of Arc*, III. 356–9: 'the chaunted mass, / The silver altar and religious robe, / The mystic wafer and the hallowed cup, / Gods priest-created, are to me unknown'.

4 *Tindal's* Christianity...Creation:] Matthew Tindal (1657–1733; *DNB*), English jurist and learned Deist best known for *Christianity as old as the Creation, or the Gospel*

of Republication of the Religion of Nature (1730). In Tindal, as in Joan's speech in Southey's poem, Nature is set above the Church as a religious teacher.

5 à parte post...à parte ante,] (Fr.), respectively, 'from the later period' and 'from the earlier period'. Joan's speech was made three hundred years before Tindal's book was written.

6 *Repealers in Ireland.*] a reference to the Corn Laws, which had finally been repealed in 1846, just a year before the present essay was written.

7 *coach-and-six...woman could frame.*] Sir Stephen Rice (1637–1715; *DNB*), 'I will drive a coach and six horses through the Act of Settlement'.

8 *(Cottle, Bristol),*] Joseph Cottle (1770–1853; *DNB*), a bookseller at Bristol who published works by Southey (including *Joan of Arc*), Samuel Taylor Coleridge and William Wordsworth, and is best known for his lively and inaccurate *Early Recollections; chiefly relating to the late Samuel Taylor Coleridge* (1837). 'I called upon him, whenever I passed through Bristol, simply as a man of letters', De Quincey wrote of Cottle in 1833; 'and I thought him a very agreeable companion' (Vol. 9, p. 347).

9 *Mass...Sacramental table...Confession.*] For example, Southey, *Joan of Arc*, III. 382–5: 'For sins confest / To holy Priest and absolution given / I knew them not; for ignorant of sin / Why should I seek forgiveness?'.

10 *D.D. or S.T.P.*] 'Doctor of Divinity' or 'Sanctae Theologiae Professor' ('Professor of Sacred Theology').

11 *kingdom under interdict.*] see above, p. 545, n. 50.

12 *depositions upon* both *trials.*] De Quincey refers to the trial of condemnation in 1431, and the trial of rehabilitation in 1455–6.

13 *The very best witness*] De Quincey here intends Haumette (see above, p. 546, n. 66), who testified that Joan 'used to blush when they told her she was too devout and went too much to church' (Michelet, vol. II, p. 518).

14 *'Oh, what...thoughts arise!' &c.*] Milton, *Paradise Regained*, I. 196. In 1854 De Quincey quoted Milton at greater length (see below, p. 639, 77.24).

15 *Orleans to Rheims,*] In 1429, Joan expelled the English from Orleans, and then travelled with Charles VII to Rheims, where his coronation finally took place (see above, p. 547, n. 87).

16 France Delivered] De Quincey invokes *Jerusalem Delivered* (1581), the title of the great epic of the crusades by the Italian poet Torquato Tasso (1544–95).

17 *law of Epic unity.*] Aristotle, *Poetics*, XXIV: the epic poem 'should have for its subject a single action, whole and complete, with a beginning, a middle, and an end'.

18 *Virgil...fable...Troy,*] In *The Aeneid*, Virgil (see above, p. 535, n. 42) tells the story of Rome's legendary founder, and proclaims the Roman mission to civilize the world. Book II contains the best-known account of the sacking of the ancient city of Troy.

19 epos...incunabula] respectively, 'epic poem' and 'the earliest stages or first traces in the development of anything' (both *OED*).

20 *France...province of England;*] After the death of Charles VI in 1422 (see above, p. 545, n. 47), the country in France north of the Loire was under the control of England, while southern France, excluding English Aquitaine, was loyal to the Dauphin as Charles VII.

21 *Dauphin once more upon his feet.*] see above, p. 547, n. 77.

22 *engineering skill...in Europe.*] The English began their assault on Orleans in October 1428, and undertook impressive siegeworks, including forts.

23 *Patay...Troyes*] The English were routed by the French at Patay, a small village about fifteen miles northwest of Orleans. Troyes is the historic capital of Champagne.

24 *excepting one man,*] De Quincey refers to Robert Le Maçon (*c.* 1365–1443), chancellor of France, and a leading adviser of Charles VII (see Michelet, vol. II, pp. 536–7).

25 *uncles of Henry VI.,*] De Quincey refers to John Plantagenet, Duke of Bedford (1389–1435; *DNB*), and Humphrey Plantagenet, Duke of Gloucester (1391–1447; *DNB*). Both were uncles to the infant King Henry VI (see above, p. 547, n. 87). Bedford was the official Regent and led the troops in France. Gloucester was the acting Regent in England. The two engaged in a bitter struggle for supremacy.

26 *Michelet...happy to believe),*] Michelet, vol. II, p. 549: 'If the Maid herself was not condemned and burned as a witch, if her victories were not ascribed to the fiend, they would remain miracles and works of God...in that case God was the foe of the English'.

27 *by the dying English soldier,*] Michelet, vol. II, p. 536: when Joan saw a badly wounded English soldier, 'she sprang from her horse, supported the poor fellow's head, had a priest brought to him, comforted him, and helped him to die'.

28 *'Nolebat...quemquam interficere.'*] (Lt.), 'She was unwilling to use her sword or to kill any one'.

29 *she wept...he approaching.*] Michelet, vol. II, p. 538: 'At the instant the king was crowned, the Maid threw herself on her knees, clasped his legs, and wept vehemently'.

30 *shepherdess once more.*] Michelet, vol. II, p. 538: Joan is reported to have said that she wished it were God's pleasure 'that I might go and tend the sheep with my sister and my brothers'.

31 *Compiegne...English.*] Compiègne is a town in northern France. Joan was captured there by the Burgundians in May 1430, and then passed on to the English. Michelet, vol. II, p. 544: 'it was probable that the Maid was bought and sold....The English would have given any money for such a prize'.

32 *Now came her trial.*] The trial began on 13 January 1431. Joan was burned as a heretic on 30 May 1431.

33 *Bishop of Beauvais.*] Pierre Cauchon (1371–1442) was educated at the University of Paris, and became Bishop of Beauvais in 1420. Michelet, vol. II, p. 551: 'Cauchon...was a man not without merit'.

34 Bishop that art...mayest be,] De Quincey echoes Shakespeare, *Macbeth*, I.v.15–6, where Lady Macbeth comments on the witches' prediction concerning her husband: 'Glamis thou art, and Cawdor, and shalt be / What thou art promis'd'.

35 *a triple crown,*] The Pope's crown consists of a long cap, or tiara, of golden cloth, encircled by three coronets, and surmounted by a ball and cross of gold.

36 *agent of the English.*] Michelet, vol. II, p. 552: 'Cauchon, in his exceeding zeal' made himself 'the agent and courier of the English'.

37 *cats-paw.*] 'a person used as a tool by another to accomplish a purpose' (*OED*).

38 *'Would you examine me...against myself?'*] Michelet, vol. II, p. 560.

39 *Dominican...Michelet...'weighty,'*] The Dominicans were an order of mendicant friars established by Domino de Guzmán in 1215. De Quincey's memory is at fault here, for he intends a reference, not to Joan's trial, but to her examination before the doctors at Poictiers: 'A Dominican met her with a single objection, but it was one of weight' (Michelet, vol. II, p. 526). The Dominican at Joan's trial was Jean Lemaître, the vice-inquisitor of France.

40 *what language...had talked:*] De Quincey's memory is again at fault (see above, n. 39; Michelet, vol. II, p. 526).

41 *archangel Michael...raiment for his servants.*] Michelet, vol. II, p. 558: 'Among other hostile and unbecoming questions, she was asked whether St Michael was naked when he appeared to her'.

42 *her father...that greater Father,*] Michelet, vol. II, p. 560: 'Do you think you did well in leaving home without permission from your father and mother?'. Cf. De Quincey in 'The Daughter of Lebanon' (1856): '"Wilt thou, therefore, being now wiser in thy thoughts, suffer God thy new Father to give by seeming to refuse...?"' (Vol. 2, p. 269).

43 *martyrdom...father and mother.*] cf. Genesis: 2: 24: 'Therefore a man leaves his father and his mother and clings to his wife, and they become one flesh'.

44 *Easter Sunday,*] cf. De Quincey in the *Confessions*: 'I thought that it was a Sunday morning in May, that it was Easter Sunday, and as yet very early in the morning' (Vol. 2, p. 72).

45 *two-fold malady.*] Michelet, vol. II, pp. 568–9.

46 *Mozart...Phidias...Michael Angelo,*] For Mozart, see above, p. 540, n. 53. Phidias (*fl.* 490–30 BC), Athenian sculptor responsible for the construction of the Parthenon. For Michelangelo, see above, p. 540, n. 44.

47 *four winds...dead men's bones,*] cf. Ezekiel 37: 1–10.

48 *lead me into temptation.*] cf. Matthew 6: 13 and Luke 11: 4.

49 uxoriousness.] 'doting or submissive fondness of one's wife' (*OED*).

50 *pepper-corn rent*] 'nominal rent'; 'very small, insignificant, trivial' (*OED*).

51 *Excudent...tanta...Dryden's Virgil...sexes.*] The Latin quotation reads as follows: 'Others will hammer out breathing signs – so indeed do I believe – [and] will draw living countenances from marble. They will climb higher. But you, Eve, remember to smite with [your] slipper the head of him who delivers such great oracles'. Cf. Virgil, *Aeneid*, VI. 847–53. De Quincey deliberately distorts the Latin for comic effect. In his famous 1697 translation, John Dryden (see above, p. 524, n. 24) renders the passage as Virgil, VI. 1168–72: 'Let others better mold the running Mass / Of Mettals, and inform the breathing Brass; / And soften into Flesh a Marble Face: / Plead better at the Bar; describe the Skies, / And when the Stars descend, and when they rise'. In 1854, De Quincey omitted this passage and footnote (see below, p. 640, 82.12–27).

52 *Tellurians*] a Tellurian is 'an inhabitant of the earth' (*OED*, which cites this example from De Quincey).

53 *St Peter's...Luxor...Himalayas?*] St Peter's basilica is the church of the popes. Luxor is one of the four quarters of the ancient Egyptian city of Thebes. The Himalayas are the great mountain system of Asia.

54 *Antoinette, the widowed queen,*] Marie Antoinette (1755–93), Queen of France as the wife of King Louis XVI (1754–93). Her father was the Holy Roman emperor Francis I (1708–65), making her a 'daughter of Caesars'. She was guillotined on 16 October 1793.

55 *'martyred wife of Roland,'*] Jean-Marie Roland (1734–93), civil servant and a leader of the moderate Girondin faction. He committed suicide after hearing of the execution of his wife Jeanne-Marie Roland (1754–93), who is best known for her *Appeal to Impartial Posterity* (1795). Cf. De Quincey's reference to 'Roland and his illustrious wife' in his 1830 *Blackwood's* essay on 'The French Revolution' (Vol. 7, p. 175).

56 *Charlotte Corday,*] Charlotte Corday (1768–93) assassinated the French revolutionary Jean-Paul Marat (1743–93) while he was in his bath. Four days later she was guillotined.

57 *'struck terror...by its height;'*] Michelet, vol. II, p. 580.

58 *Grafton…'foule face'*] Richard Grafton (d. *c.* 1572; *DNB*), chronicler and printer. Grafton 'says…that it was easy enough for her to remain a maid, "because of her foul face"' (Michelet, vol. II, p. 524).

59 *Holinshead…engaging manners.*] Raphael Holinshed (d. *c.* 1580; *DNB*), chronicler, who describes Joan as 'a young wench of an eighteene yeeres old', whose father was 'a sorie sheepheard' (*Holinshed's Chronicles of England, Scotland, and Ireland*, 6 vols (London: Johnson, 1807–8), vol. III, p. 163).

60 *'sceptical, Judaic, Satanic'…Byron*] Michelet, vol. II, p. 575. For George Gordon, Lord Byron, see above, p. 533, n. 10. In the 'Preface' to *A Vision of Judgement*, Robert Southey (see above, p. 523, n. 3) attacked the 'Satanic school of poetry', which included Byron, Percy Shelley (see above, p. 532, n. 94) and Leigh Hunt (1784–1859; *DNB*).

61 *Chateaubriand…Milton;*] Michelet, vol. II, p. 574: 'Milton's real hero is Satan'. François-Auguste-René, vicomte de Chateaubriand (1768–1848), author and diplomat, *Le Paradis Perdu de Milton* (1836).

62 *'not recollect…name of God'*] Michelet, vol. II, p. 574.

63 'la gloire'…*'The great English…pride.'*] 'La gloire' means 'glory', but can also denote the 'honour' or 'reputation' of an individual, a family, or a nation (Michelet, vol. II, p. 574).

64 *Kempis…Zantiote*] Thomas à Kempis (*c.* 1379–1471), Christian theologian and the author of *De Imitatione Christi* (*Imitation of Christ*), a devotional manual first published in 1418 and immensely popular throughout medieval Europe. Its authorship was long a matter of dispute. A 'Zantiote' is an inhabitant of Zante, one of the Seven Islands in the Ionian Sea.

65 *Pindar's…Kingdom Come.'*] 'Peter Pindar' was the pseudonym of John Wolcot (1738–1819; *DNB*), who produced a running commentary in satirical verse on society, politics and personalities, 1778–1817. De Quincey quotes Wolcot, 'Dinah; or, my Lady's Housekeeper', ll. 87–8: 'John Bunyan read she too, and Kempis Tom / Who plainly show'd the way to kingdom-come'.

66 *Methodist version…Wesley.*] John Wesley (1703–91; *DNB*), evangelist and co-founder (with his brother Charles) of the Methodist movement in the Church of England, *The Christian's Pattern; or, a treatise on the Imitation of Christ…Compared with the Original and corrected throughout by John Wesley* (1735).

67 De Imitatione Christi…*Foulis,*] Robert Foulis (1707–76; *DNB*), Scottish printer, *De Imitatione Christi* (In aedibus Academicis excudebant R. et A. Coulis: Glasguae, 1751. 12o). It is not clear which relation bequeathed the eleven-year-old De Quincey a copy of the book. He was six when his sister Elizabeth died, and seven when his father died (see Eaton, pp. 14–7).

68 *Barbier…*soixante traductions,] Antoine-Alexandre Barbier (1765–1825), French librarian and bibliographer, *Dissertation sur soixante traductions françaises de l'Imitation de Jésus Christ* (1812).

69 Opera Omnia] *Complete Works.*

70 *English girls…German…indecorum.*] Michelet, vol. II, p. 576: 'The Englishwomen above all…were sure to regard such a disguise as monstrous and intolerably indecent'.

71 *burgoo,*] a thick oatmeal gruel or porridge used by seamen.

72 'qui ne se…qui peut!'] (Fr.), respectively, 'who do not surrender' and 'headlong flight'.

73 *singing a catch.*] 'a short composition for three or more voices…a ROUND' (*OED*).

74 showed their...before a girl;'] These are De Quincey's embellishments. Michelet observes that 'the pursuit was murderous' or 'Falstoff [sic] fled like the rest' (Michelet, vol. II, p. 536).

75 *Kelly's translation...provincialisms.*] Walter Keating Kelly, whose many works include *Narrative of the French Revolution of 1848* (1848) and *Life of Wellington, for boys* (1853).

76 *Rouen*] see above, p. 543, n. 14.

77 *'Whether she* said...*she* thought *it.'*] Michelet, vol. II, p. 581 (De Quincey's italics).

78 à priori...ergo,] (Lt.), respectively, 'from what is already known' and 'thus'.

79 *'Ten thousand men...wept;'*] Michelet, vol. II, p. 583. The rest of De Quincey's passage draws on the same paragraph in Michelet.

80 *though one should rise from the dead*] Luke 16: 31: 'And he said unto him, "If they hear not Moses and the prophets, neither will they be convinced, even if someone rises from the dead"'.

81 *(for the minutes...into ages),*] cf. De Quincey in *Confessions* on his opium dreams: 'the sense of time' was 'powerfully affected...I sometimes seemed to have lived for 70 or 100 years in one night; nay, sometimes had feelings representative of a millennium passed in that time, or, however, of a duration far beyond the limits of any human experience' (Vol. 2, pp. 66–7).

82 *stings of death.*] cf. 1 Corinthians 15: 55: '"Where, O death, is your victory? / Where, O death, is your sting?"'.

83 *hid her face.*] cf. De Quincey in *Confessions*: 'Electra...wept sometimes, and hid her face' (Vol. 2, p. 41).

84 *English prince...lord of Winchester,*] For the Regent of France, see above, n. 25. Henry Beaufort (c. 1374–1447; *DNB*), cardinal and bishop of Winchester. De Quincey has in mind Shakespeare *2 Henry VI*, III.iii.27–9: 'Lord Card'nal, if thou think'st on heaven's bliss, / Hold up thy hand, make signal of thy hope. / He dies, and makes no sign. O God, forgive him!'.

85 *Who is this that cometh from Domrémy?*] cf. Isaiah 63: 1: '"Who is this that cometh from Edom...?"'.

86 *bloody coronation robes from Rheims?*] Joan reportedly appeared at Charles's coronation in her armor, which might reasonably be imagined as 'bloody'. De Quincey may also be emphasizing the fact that she shed her blood to bring about the crowning of Charles.

The Nautico-Military Nun of Spain {Part I}

1 *foreign one...continental form.*] De Quincey may at this point have been intent on 'close compression', but in the event his narrative grew to more than 28,000 words. By comparison, Valon's is approximately 26,000 words, so that De Quincey is roughly 1 to 1 with his continental model, rather than his boasted '1 to 3'. In revision, De Quincey removed this prefatory paragraph (see below, p. 640, 93.1–94.8).

2 *gentleman...wrapped the new*] In 1854, De Quincey expanded this passage (see below, p. 640, 94.18).

3 *old crocodile actually began to cry*] cf. De Quincey in 'The English Mail-Coach', where Fanny's grandfather has 'some infirmities...and one particularly...in which he too much resembled a crocodile' (p. 419). 'Crocodile tears' denote hypocritical sorrow (*Proverbs*, p. 155).

4 *two words to a bargain.*] 'Polite Conversations' in Swift, *Prose*, vol. IV, p. 198: 'There's two Words to that bargain'.

5 *Biscay.*] a province in the Basque Country of northern Spain.
6 *fee simple*] see above, p. 537, n. 75.
7 *'to have and to hold,'*] from the Marriage Ceremony of the Church of England.
8 *blooming as a rose-bush in June,*] cf. De Quincey in 'The English Mail-Coach': 'if I think for an instant of the rose in June, up rises the heavenly face of Fanny' (see above, p. 420).
9 chateaux en Espagne,] (Fr.), 'Castles in Spain' denote any baseless hopes of the future (*Proverbs*, p. 107).
10 *Spanish bonds and promises.*] De Quincey alludes to the savage civil strife in Spain, which produced the first Carlist war (1833–9) and another unsuccessful uprising in the late 1840s. The government was forced to sell large quantities of church lands to finance the war. The Carlist strength lay in the north, especially in the Basque provinces.
11 *playful...cubs of a tigress.*] cf. De Quincey in 'The English Mail-Coach': 'the cubs of tigers or leopards, when domesticated, have been observed to suffer a sudden development of their latent ferocity under too eager an appeal to their playfulness' (see above, p. 421).
12 *'blue rejoicing sky,'*] Coleridge, 'France: An Ode', l. 17: 'Thou rising sun! Thou blue rejoicing sky!'.
13 Marfisa...Bradamant...Britomart] Ludovico Ariosto (1474–1533), Italian poet celebrated for his epic *Orlando furioso*, which features a warlike Indian queen named Marfisa and a Christian amazon named Bradamant. In *The Faerie Queene* of Edmund Spenser (see above, p. 535, n. 32) Britomart is the female knight of chastity.
14 *last time.*] cf. De Quincey in *Confessions*: 'On the evening before I left ——— for ever, I grieved when the ancient and lofty school-room resounded with the evening service, performed for the last time in my hearing' (Vol. 2, p. 15).
15 trousseau,] (Fr.), 'bunch'.
16 hoc age] (Lt.), literally, 'do this'.
17 *that awful Inquisition,*] In 1478 Pope Sixtus IV authorized the Spanish Inquisition.
18 à priori] see above, p. 552, n. 78.
19 valet consequentia,] (Lt.), In 1854, De Quincey translated this phase as 'the right of inference is good' (see below, p. 642, 97.41).
20 *Jack Ketch...'Jack'*] John Ketch (*d.* 1686; *DNB*), English executioner notorious for his barbarous inefficiency. 'Jack Tar' is a familiar name for a sailor.
21 vivas;] literally, 'may you live'.
22 shilly-shally] 'vacillation, irresolution' (*OED*, which cites this example from De Quincey).
23 *years of ague),*] From his second to his fourth year De Quincey 'was continuously ill with some ailment called, in the vague terminology of the day, "an ague"' (Lindop, p. 4).
24 quantum sufficit] (Lt.), 'as much as is sufficient'.
25 *liberty...lock her in.'*] In 1854, De Quincey expanded this passage (see below, p. 643, 98.34–5).
26 *Wellington trousers.*] knee trousers that could be worn with Wellington boots, which were named after the Duke of Wellington (see above, p. 542, n. 86).
27 *Vittoria,*] Vitoria is the capital of Álava province in northeastern Spain. At the Battle of Vitoria (21 June 1813), the British under the Duke of Wellington won a decisive victory over the French.
28 *amiable relative,*] In Valon, the man's name is given as Don Francisco de Cerralta, a distant relative of Catalina's mother (Valon, p. 591).

29 *owned the soft impeachment;*] De Quincey draws on Sheridan, *The Rivals*, V. iii: 'I own the soft impeachment'.

30 uncular] 'belonging to an uncle' (*OED*, which cites this example from De Quincey).

31 *yarn of life...mingled quality.*] cf. Shakespeare, *All's Well that End's Well*, IV.iii.71–2: 'The web of our life is of a mingled yarn, good and ill together'.

32 *Thiebault*] Dieudonné Thiebault (1733–1807), *Mes Souvenirs de Vingt Ans de Séjour a Berlin* (Paris, 1804), vol. II, p. 319.

33 s'ennuyer...nous nous ennuyons,] (Fr.), 'to be bored'; 'I am bored'; 'you are bored'; 'he is bored'; 'we are bored'; 'I was bored'; 'you were bored'; 'let him be bored'; 'we are bored'.

34 *Valladolid.*] Valladolid is the capital of Valladolid province in northwestern Spain.

35 *King*] Philip III (1578–1621), King of Spain, 1598–1621.

36 *Alguazils*] (Sp.), police.

37 *Franciso de Cardenas,*] In Valon, the cavalier's name is given as 'don Carlos de Arellano'. Perhaps De Quincey thought 'Franciso de Cardenas' more euphonious.

38 ex officio] (Lt.), 'by virtue of his office'.

39 *mandatory*] more usually 'mandatary' 'one who is appointed to a benefice by a papal mandate' (*OED*).

40 *Bay of Biscay.*] a wide inlet indenting the coast of western Europe, bounded on the east by the west coast of France and on the south by the north coast of Spain. It is noted for its rough seas.

41 *'chace is but...sign manual.'*] Valon, p. 602: 'Le hazard, a dit quelqu'un, c'est peut-être le pseudonyme de Dieu, quand il ne veut pas signer'.

42 *imperials*] An imperial is 'a case or trunk for luggage' (*OED*).

43 *Juvenal's qualification...robbers;*] Juvenal (see above, p. 527, n.5), *Satire*, X. 22: 'cantabit vacuus coram latrone viator' ('the empty-handed traveller will whistle in the robber's face').

44 *I am going to suggest;*] In 1854, De Quincey expanded this passage with an anecdote about a 'mob orator' (see below, p. 644, 102.5–7).

45 *potatoes in Spain at that date,*] Potatoes were first brought to Spain from South America around the middle of the sixteenth century, and so would have been available to Kate.

46 *Andalusian port.*] Andalusia is a historic region of Spain, and encompasses the southernmost Spanish provinces. Departure from Andalusia means that Kate must travel from the extreme north of Spain to the extreme south, a distance of more than four hundred and fifty miles.

47 *St Lucar...Cape Horn...Paita*] St Lucar, or Sanlúcar de Barrameda, is a port city in southwestern Spain. Cape Horn is located off the southern tip of mainland South America. Paita is a coastal town in northern Peru.

48 *8vo,*] Ferrer's 1829 edition of Catalina's memoirs was published in octavo.

49 *best thing I know,*] In 1854, De Quincey appended a footnote to this passage (see below, p. 645, 105.4).

50 caput mortuum] literally, (Lt.), 'dead head'.

51 juste milieu;] (Fr.), 'happy medium'.

52 *Aix-la-Chapelle...Sempaler.*] Aix-la-Chapelle is now Aachen, in northwestern Germany. De Quincey has mistaken the name of 'Mr Sempaler'. He means Andreas Daniel Berthold von Schepeler, who translated Catalina's narrative as *Die Nonne-Fähnrich, oder Geschichte der Doña Catalina de Erauso, von ihr selbst geschrieben* (Aachen and Leipzig, 1830). Schepeler owned the so-called 'Pacheco portrait' of Catalina,

which was painted by Francisco Pacheco (1564–1654). In 1829, Ferrer was in Aix-la-Chapelle, and became acquainted with 'M. Shepeler' (Valon, p. 634).

53 caballador.] (Sp.), cavalier.

54 *Trujillo,*] Trujillo lies on the Peruvian coast, roughly two hundred and fifty miles south of Paita (see above, n. 47).

55 commis] (Fr.), clerk.

56 *very handsome lady;*] In Valon, the lady's name is given as 'señora Beatrix de Cardenas' (Valon, p. 596).

57 corrégidor,] (Sp.), the chief magistrate.

58 *'hear reason,'*] The phrase is common, but De Quincey probably has in mind Shakespeare, *King Lear*, V.iii.82–3: 'Stay yet, hear reason. Edmund I arrest thee / On capital treason'.

59 *evil crisis...Not so Kate.*] As De Quincey makes clear in 'The English Mail-Coach', he is thinking of 'people' like himself: 'I pretend to no presence of mind....The palsy of doubt and distraction hangs like some guilty weight of dark unfathomed remembrances upon my energies, when the signal is flying for *action*' (see above, p. 438).

60 *Pasha of two tails,*] 'Pasha' is a Turkish title of rank, given to high civil and military authorities. His rank is shown by the number of horse tails on his standard.

61 *'Sound the Trumpets! Beat the drums!'*] Dryden, 'Alexander's Feast', l. 50.

62 *sailors whistle for a wind,*] *Proverbs*, p. 884.

63 'Catalinam vehis, et fortunas ejus.'] (Lt.), 'You carry Catalina, and her fortunes'. The phrase was used by Caesar to encourage a boat captain who was anxious to turn back to port on account of a storm (Plutarch, *Parallel Lives,* Caesar, XXXVIII).

64 *Ann. Dom.*] (Lt.), 'Anno Domini' ('in the year of the Lord').

65 *Etonians do at times,*] Eton College was founded by Henry VI in 1440–1, and is located across the River Thames from Windsor.

The Nautico-Military Nun of Spain {Part II}

1 *Concepcion.*] Concepción lies near the mouth of the Bío-Bío River in south-central Chile. It is more than 2000 miles south of Paita.

2 *her own brother.*] In Valon, Catalina's brother's name is given as 'Miguel de Erauso' (Valon, p. 602).

3 sous-lieutenant] (Fr.), 'second lieutenant'. De Quincey draws directly from Valon: 'Le grade d'*alferez*, dans l'armée espagnole, correspond aujourd'hui à celui de sous-lieutenant en France' (Valon, p. 603).

4 *'prescribed,'*] In Scottish law, to prescribe is 'to become invalid or void by passage of time' (*OED*, which cites this example from De Quincey).

5 *Cortez...Pizarro,*] Hernán Cortés (1485–1547), Spanish conquistador who overthrew the Aztec empire. Francisco Pizarro (*c.* 1475–1541), Spanish conqueror of the Inca empire.

6 *Cordilleras,*] the Andes.

7 Dorado...*emeralds.*] El Dorado was a district of fabulous wealth long believed to exist in the northern part of South America.

8 facetioe] (Lt.), witticisms.

9 a discretion.] 'without limit'.

10 *sleeping the sleep...no awaking;*] cf. Scott, *Lady of the Lake*, I. xxxi: 'Sleep the sleep that knows not breaking, / Morn of toil, nor night of waking'.

11 *tirailleur's bullet.*] soldier or rifleman's bullet.

12 *Coleridge's* 'Ancient Mariner.'] Samuel Taylor Coleridge (1772–1834; *DNB*), poet, critic and philosopher. His 'Rime of the Ancyent Marinere' was published as the lead poem in the 1798 version of *Lyrical Ballads*. De Quincey read the volume in 1799, and described it as 'the greatest event in the unfolding of my own mind' (Vol. 10, p. 287).

13 *Cain... Wandering Jew... 'pass... land;'*] In Genesis 4: 1–16, Cain murders his brother Abel, and is banished by the Lord. According to medieval legend, the Wandering Jew was doomed to wander the earth until Judgment Day because he taunted Jesus on the way to the Crucifixion. De Quincey quotes Coleridge, 'The Rime of the Ancyent Marinere', l. 619.

14 *Sydney...* 'Defense of Poesie.'] Sir Philip Sidney (see above, p. 526, n. 56), 'A Defence of Poetry' in *Miscellaneous Prose of Sir Philip Sidney*, eds Katherine Duncan-Jones and Jan Van Dorsten (Oxford: Clarendon Press, 1973), p. 92 (inexact).

15 *Nemesis*] see above, p. 538, n. 19.

16 *'That lov'd...his bow.'*] Coleridge, 'The Rime of the Ancyent Marinere', ll. 109–10: 'He loved the bird that loved the man / Who shot him with his bow'.

17 *'Nine fathom...mist and snow.'*] Coleridge, 'The Rime of the Ancyent Marinere', ll. 382–3: 'Under the keel nine fathom deep, / From the land of mist and snow'.

18 *Zaarrahs*] variant of Sahara (*OED*).

19 *Flying...no man that pursued?*] cf. Proverbs: 28: 1: 'The wicked flee when no man pursueth'.

20 *Frenchman...all she prayed.*] Valon, p. 609; see also Masson, vol. XIII, pp. 245–50.

21 'mon cher,'] (Fr.), 'my dear'.

22 *far distant blue serene.*] cf. Shelley, *The Revolt of Islam*, I.iv.5: 'Beneath that opening spot of blue serene'.

23 *creeping thing,*] Genesis 1: 24: 'every creeping thing that creepeth upon the earth'; cf. Milton, *Paradise Lost*, VII. 523.

24 *soundless waste.*] De Quincey has in mind Wordsworth, 'The French Army in Russia, 1812–13', l. 38: 'A soundless waste, a trackless vacancy!'.

25 *winged patriarchal herald...relenting*] De Quincey alludes to the dove sent out from the ark that returned with an olive leaf to show that the waters had subsided (Genesis 8: 10–11).

26 *not built with hands.*] 2 Corinthians 5: 1: 'We have a building from God, a house not made with hands, eternal in the heavens'.

27 Angelus] a devotion of the Western church that commemorates the Incarnation and is said at dawn, noon and sunset, at the sound of a bell.

28 *army with banners;*] Song of Solomon 6: 4: 'Terrible as an army with banners'.

29 *St Bernard's hospice*] St Bernard of Menthon (923–1008) established hospices on two Alpine passes.

30 *American St Peter,*] De Quincey apparently has in mind the Minnesota River, which was once known as the St Peter River, and which joins the Mississippi River just south of St Paul.

31 *sun...anger go down,*] Ephesians 4: 26: 'Do not let the sun go down upon your anger'.

32 à la belle etoile,] (Fr.), 'out in the open'.

33 *perishing...a little brandy.*] De Quincey is also thinking of his teenage collapse on a London street, and the actions of Ann as described in *Confessions*: 'Without some powerful and reviving stimulus, I should either have died on the spot – or should at least have sunk to a point of exhaustion from which all reäscent...would soon have become hopeless....She ran off into Oxford Street, and...returned to me with a glass

of port wine and spices, that acted upon my empty stomach...with an instantaneous power of restoration' (Vol. 2, p. 26).

34 *'Temperance' medallist!*] The Temperance movement promoted abstinence or moderation in the consumption of alcohol. In Britain, the movement began in the late 1820s, and grew into a powerful social and political force in Victorian Britain.

35 anasarca...hydrothorax,] 'Anasarca', or dropsy, is a severe, generalized form of edema. 'Hydrothorax' is an accumulation of watery fluid in the pleural cavity.

36 *rigor of temperance.*] In 1854, De Quincey expanded this passage with a reference to 'Dr Darwin' (see below, p. 649, 124.n. 6).

37 *august lady...himself.*] The 'august lady' was Princess Charlotte (1796–1817), who died giving birth to a stillborn child. Her 'attendant', as De Quincey makes clear in his 1854 revisions (see below, p. 650, 124.n.12–13), was Sir Richard Croft (1762–1818; *DNB*), who shot himself three months after Charlotte's death.

38 *his intellectual accomplishments,*] In 1854, De Quincey identified the person in question as 'Robert Southey' (see below, p. 650, 124.n.15).

39 Yucca gloriosa...Magnolia speciosissima,] (Lt.), respectively, 'glorious Yucca' and 'most beautiful magnolia'.

40 *legend...Andes to seize her?*] De Quincey seems to have in mind the Greek legend of Cadmus, who killed a dragon and sowed its teeth in the ground. From these sprang up a race of fierce, armed men.

41 *'written strange...her face.'*] Shakespeare, *The Comedy of Errors*, V.i.299–300: 'And careful hours with time's deformed hand / Have written strange defeatures in my face'.

The Nautico-Military Nun of Spain {Part III}

1 *Casaubon*...Hist. Augustan.] Isaac Casaubon (1559–1614), French classical scholar and author of *Historiae Augustae scriptores* (Paris, 1603), part 2, p. 5. The distinction noted by Casaubon is actually between Hispanus and Hispaniensis.

2 *Andalusian...Peruvian eyes.*] In this description of 'Juana', De Quincey follows Valon. But cf. Stepto, where Catalina does not give the daughter a name, and where she describes her as 'black and ugly as the devil himself' (Valon, p. 611; Stepto, p. 28).

3 *Grenada,*] The historic province of Grenada is in southern Spain. Roman power in the region collapsed during the fifth century when a number of Germanic peoples, including the Vandals and Visigoths, invaded. In the eighth century the Moors conquered Spain and established Muslim states that were to last until 1492.

4 *king...upon his forehead.*] 2 Chronicles 26: 16–20, as De Quincey made clear in 1854 (see below, p. 651, 129.n.1–2).

5 *Miranda...Ferdinand*] Shakespeare, *The Tempest*, I.ii.418–20: 'I might call him / A thing divine, for nothing natural / I ever saw so noble'.

6 *her memoirs...innocent child.*] Valon, p. 611; but cf. Stepto, p. 28.

7 *interest in the stranger.*] In 1854, De Quincey inserted into this passage a reference to Shakespeare's *Othello* (see below, p. 651, 129.21).

8 *King of the Spains and the Indies*] see above, p. 554, n. 35.

9 *Tucuman;*] province in northwestern Argentina.

10 *'gammon'...*'Tin,'] 'Gammon' is to hoax or deceive. 'Tin' is slang for money.

11 *Ferrer's narrative...seemed to be.*] Valon, pp. 613–4.

12 *'Subtract from...fair Portuguese;'*] Robert Christy, *Proverbs, Maxims and Phrases* (London: T. Fisher Unwin, 1888), vol. II, p. 296: 'Strip a Spaniard of every virtue and you have a Portuguese'.

13 *Corregidor...alguazils.*] see above, p. 555, n. 57, and p. 554, n. 36.

14 *buzwigs*] 'bigwigs' (*OED*, which cites this example from De Quincey).

15 *Pythias...Damon,*] Pythias and Damon were two Syracusian youths whose friendship has become proverbial.

16 *Jack Cade's Chimney,*] Jack Cade (d. 1450; *DNB*), English rebel who led a Kentish revolt against Henry VI. He appears as a character in Shakespeare's *2 Henry VI*, and De Quincey's reference is to IV.ii.148–50: 'Sir, he made a chimney in my father's house, and the bricks are alive at this day to testify it; therefore deny it not'.

17 *chopping logic*] 'bandying of arguments' (*OED*).

18 *President of La Plata*] In Valon, the president's name is given as 'Martin de Mendiola' (Valon, p. 618). La Plata, now Sucre, is in southern Bolivia.

19 peripetteia] more commonly, 'peripeteia', the sudden turn of reversal in fortune which Aristotle in his *Poetics* described as part of the tragic action.

20 *Claude Lorraine*] see above, p. 523, n. 8.

21 *Paz*] La Paz is the capital of Bolivia.

22 comme de raison,] (Fr.), 'as a matter of course'.

23 caballero's] see above, p. 555, n. 53.

24 *Antonio Calderon,*] Valon, p. 621.

25 *Cuzco,*] city in south-central Peru.

26 'Je ne parle...presque pas.'] Valon, p. 622.

27 *Cinderella...Cinderellula,*] respectively, 'a small cinder-girl' and 'a very small cinder-girl'.

28 *memoirs...systematically dry.*] De Quincey follows Valon, p. 635: 'C'est moins un récit que la matière d'un récit; c'est un sec et court sommaire sans animation et sans vie'.

29 locanda;] (Sp.), 'inn'.

30 *Don Quixote,*] see above, p. 529, n. 31.

31 *her opinion...better mounted.*] Valon, pp. 626–8.

32 en croupe] (Fr.), 'riding behind'.

33 *episcopal*] In 1854, De Quincey appended a footnote to this word (see below, p. 653, 140.30).

34 pomoerium] the open space round a Roman camp.

35 *Lima;*] the capital of Peru, located on the south bank of the Río Rímac, about eight miles inland from the Pacific Ocean port of Callao.

36 *King of Spain...Pope*] Philip IV (1605–65), King of Spain, 1621–65. Urban VIII, (1568–1644), Pope, 1623–44.

37 *St Peter's keys;*] Matthew 16: 19.

38 Cadiz] port in southwestern Spain.

39 *Olivarez,*] Gaspar de Guzmán y Pimental Olivares (1587–1645), Prime Minister (1623–43) and court favourite of King Philip IV.

40 *Buckingham...Wales*] George Villiers, first Duke of Buckingham (1592–1628; *DNB*), statesman and royal favourite of Charles I (1600–49), King of Great Britain and Ireland, 1625–49. In 1623, Buckingham and Charles, then Prince of Wales, visited Madrid to arrange a marriage between Charles and the daughter of Philip IV. Buckingham's arrogance contributed to the collapse of the negotiations.

41 *Catherine...Wolsey.*] 'Queen Catherine' is Catherine of Aragon (1485–1536), first wife of King Henry VIII (1491–1547), King of England, 1509–47. Thomas Wolsey (1475–1530; *DNB*), Cardinal and statesman who dominated the government of Henry VIII from 1515 to 1529. De Quincey cites Shakespeare, *Henry VIII*, IV.ii.53–4: 'Lofty and sour to them that lov'd him not, / But to those men that sought him, sweet as summer'.

42 *year of jubilee,*] a year recurring at stated intervals, during which those who made a pilgrimage to Rome could obtain a remission of punishment for their sins.

43 *Barcelona;*] port in northeastern Spain.

44 *King delighted to honour.*] cf. Esther 6: 6: 'What shall be done unto the man whom the king delighteth to honour?'.

45 in partibus Infidelium] (Lt.), 'in heathen countries'.

46 Vera Cruz.] port on the Gulf of Mexico.

47 *forests were ransacked.*] In 1854, De Quincey expanded this passage, and added a reference to Revelation (see below, p. 654, 144.28–30).

48 *even at a conjecture.*] De Quincey follows Valon, who writes that Catalina probably fell overboard and drowned before being eaten by a shark (Valon, pp. 632–3).

49 *sole of her foot.*] Cf. Genesis 8: 9: 'the dove found no rest for the sole of her foot'.

50 *Aix-la-Chapelle*...Sempeller...*error.*] see above, p. 554, n. 52.

51 *Velasquez*...*Charles I.*] Diego Velázquez (1599–1660), one of the greatest Spanish painter, was court painter at Madrid in 1623, when the future Charles I of England (see above, n. 40) visited. Velázquez painted a portrait of Phillip IV of Spain (see above, n. 36) in that year, but is not thought to have painted Charles.

52 *Three Days of Paris (July, 1830),*] For the second French Revolution of 27–9 July 1830, see above, p. 543, n. 17.

Secret Societies {Part I}

1 *Baruel's*...*Robison's*...*Christianity.*] Augustin de Barruel (1741–1820), Jesuit polemicist, *Memoirs, Illustrating the History of Jacobinism* (1797–8). John Robison (1739–1805; *DNB*), science writer and Professor of Natural Philosophy at Edinburgh, *Proofs of a Conspiracy against all the Religions and Governments of Europe, carried on in the Secret Meetings of Freemasons, Illuminati, and Reading Societies* (1797).

2 *schirrous*] A 'scirrhus' is 'a hard, firm, and almost painless swelling or tumor' (*OED*).

3 *Abbé's account*...*one century.*] In his *Memoirs*, Barruel claimed that the French Revolution was the carefully orchestrated fulfilment of an ancient conspiracy that had its roots in the medieval Order of Templars, and that sought the overthrow of the Papacy and all monarchies.

4 *Dodona or Delphi.*] The oracles at Dodona originated with Zeus. The oracle at Delphi belonged to Gaea, the Earth goddess; later, Apollo founded his own oracle there.

5 arriére pensée] (Fr.), 'ulterior motive'.

6 *a lady,*] The 'stern lady' has not been identified.

7 pourquoi du pourquoi.] (Fr.), 'the why of the why'.

8 *Salisbury plain,*] a plateau-like area covering about 300 square miles in Wiltshire, southern England.

9 *Tertullian's profession*...*impossible,*] Tertullian (*c.* AD 155–220), Christian theologian and moralist, *De Carne Christi*, 5: 'Certum est quia impossibile est' ('It is certain because it is impossible'). De Quincey's interest in the quotation may have been prompted by his reading of John William Donaldson's *A Vindication of Protestant Principles*, which De Quincey began to review in *Tait's* three months after the present essay appeared. Cf. 'Tertullian's maxim: *prorsus credible est, quia ineptum est; certum est, quia impossibile est (de Carne Christi,* 5), strikes at the root of all Protestantism, and must in these days be rejected with scorn' (Donaldson, p. 191).

10 cui bono] Cicero, *Pro Milone,* XII. 32: '"Who stood to gain?"'.

11 *Pyrrhus the Epirot*] Pyrrhus (*c.* 318–272 BC), King of Epirus, *c.* 307–272 BC. De Quincey is drawing from Plutarch, *Parallel Lives*, Pyrrhus, XIV. 2–7.

12 *Latium.'*] ancient area in west-central Italy.

13 *Ecbatana.'*] ancient city on the site of which stands the modern city of Hamadan, in west-central Iran.

14 *Encyclopédistes*...*Illuminati,*] The Encyclopédistes were the French intellectuals who contributed to Diderot's *Encyclopédie* (1751–72), and whose appeal to reason rather than faith threatened the authority of church and state. The Bavarian Illuminati were a secret, rationalist, anticlerical sect founded in 1776 by Adam Weishaupt (1748–1830), professor of canon law at Ingolstadt, and an ex-Jesuit.

15 *Cicero*...*bounce*...*another.*] Cicero (see above, p. 530, n. 47), *De Re Publica*, III. 22: 'True law is right reason in agreement with nature'.

16 Antimonics *of Kant?*] Immanuel Kant (1724–1804), German philosopher. De Quincey refers to 'The Antinomy of Pure Reason' in Kant, *CPR*, pp. 459–550.

17 *phoenix-club*...*notional perpetuation,*] The phoenix was a legendary bird which lived for five hundred years, burned itself on a pyre, and rose alive from the ashes to live another period.

18 à fortiori] (Lt.), with greater reason or more convincing force.

19 'sede vacante,'] (Lt.), 'empty seat'.

20 *Chateaubriand*...*France and its successions.*] De Quincey refers to Chateaubriand (see above, p. 551, n. 61) and his pamphlet *Le Roi est mort: vive le Roi!'*, which he wrote shortly after the death of Louis XVIII (12 September 1824), at the behest of his successor, Charles X. The new King paid him handsomely for it.

21 matricula...*amaranthine*] 'Matricula' (Lt.), 'register'. In 1858, De Quincey appended a footnote to the word 'amaranthine' (see below, p. 656, 153.26).

22 *Anthropophagi*...shoulders] The 'Anthropophagi' were cannibals. De Quincey alludes to Shakespeare, *Othello*, I.iii.144–5: 'The Anthropophagi, and men whose heads / Do grow beneath their shoulders'.

23 Princeps Senatûs] (Lt.), first man of the senate.

24 *Gauls*...*cutting their throats.*] The Gauls plundered Rome in 390 BC.

25 *Hottentots.*] a member of any of a group of Khoisan-speaking pastoral peoples of southern Africa.

26 *epichorial*] 'proper or peculiar to a particular country or district' (*OED*).

27 *divine idols*...*golden fetters.*] De Quincey seems to refer to the Roman (not Grecian) practice of evocatio, whereby a general would pray to the god of a city that he was besieging with an offer of a better temple at Rome. The classic case is Livy, V.xxi.1–7.

28 *First James and Charles*] James (1566–1625), King of Scotland (as James VI), 1567–1625; and King of England (as James I), 1603–25. For Charles I, see above, p. 558, n. 40.

29 *Chauncy's,*] Sir Henry Chauncy (1632–1719; *DNB*), *The Historical Antiquities of Hertfordshire* (1700).

30 *Farrer,*] Nicholas Ferrar (1592–1637; *DNB*), Anglican clergyman and mystic, and founder of a celebrated Christian community devoted to spiritual discipline. The community mastered assorted crafts, including bookbinding.

31 *Wordsworth*...*poet.*] Christopher Wordsworth (1774–1846; *DNB*), clergyman, educator and the youngest brother of William Wordsworth. His *Ecclesiastical Biography* (1810) includes a detailed consideration of Farrer (see above, n. 30).

32 *Little Gidding*...*Hertford.*] Little Gidding is in Huntingdonshire (now Cambridgeshire), not Hertfordshire.

33 *Louis XVI.*] see above, p. 550, n. 54.
34 *Indian*] In 1858, De Quincey appended a footnote to this word (see below, p. 656, 155.21).
35 *Cyclops,*] one-eyed giants.
36 *Tassie's Sulphurs*...Glyptothecae.] James Tassie (1735–99; *DNB*), Scottish gem engraver and modeller known for reproductions of engraved gems made from a hard, fine-textured substance. 'Glyptothecae' (Lt.), 'carved box'.
37 *Queen (God bless her!)*] for Queen Victoria, see above, p. 547, n. 81.
38 *printing-press in my own study.*] De Quincey had had such plans for a long time. In 1809, he planned to establish a printing press at Grasmere. 'It is his determination', wrote Coleridge, 'to have printed under his own Eye immaculate Editions of such of the eminently great Classics, English and Greek as most need it' (*The Letters of Samuel Taylor Coleridge*, ed. Earl Leslie Griggs, 6 vols (Oxford: Clarendon Press, 1956–71), vol. III, p. 177).
39 *Benvenuto Cellini*] Benvenuto Cellini (1500–71), Italian goldsmith and sculptor.
40 *Bourbon...Nassau,*] The royal houses of, respectively, France and Germany. Cellini does not mention Nassau, but he does claim that he 'killed the Constable of Bourbon' (*The Life of Benvenuto Cellini Written by Himself*, ed. John A. Symonds, 2 vols. (New York: Brentano's, 1906), vol. I, p. 167).
41 *Pope's attempt...connoisseur.*] In his autobiography, Cellini describes several attempts on his life, but none directly concerned the pope.
42 orféverie] (Fr.), 'fine work in gold art as a goldsmith'.
43 book-binding,] In 1858, De Quincey appended a footnote to this passage (see below, p. 657, 156.28).
44 *Cardinal Ximenes...Complutensian Bible,*] Cardinal Francisco Jiménez de Cisneros (1436–1517), religious reformer and twice regent of Spain. His famous Complutensian Polyglot Bible (1514–17) provided for the first time a printed text of the scriptures in their original languages. It was prepared at the University of Alcalá de Henares, in central Spain. De Quincey is right: under the Romans, the city was known as Complutum.
45 *La Trappism...Guyon Quietism.*] 'Trappists' were members of a branch of the Cistercian order of monks founded in 1664 at La Trappe in Normandy and noted for an extreme austerity of diet, penitential exercises, and absolute silence. Jean-Marie Guyon (1648–1717), French mystic and writer known for her advocacy of the passive mysticism known as quietism.
46 *Long Parliament...civil war*] The Long Parliament was summoned by Charles I in November 1640, and quickly introduced sweeping changes to the legal and constitutional structures of Britain. The Civil War broke out in the autumn of 1642.
47 *Puritanism...Popish leanings.*] Christopher Wordsworth, 'Nicholas Ferrar' in *Ecclesiastical Biography*, 4 vols (London: Rivington, 1853), vol. IV, p. 207: 'They were at the time, notwithstanding all the real good they did, severally slandered and vilified: by some they were abused as papists; by others as puritans'.
48 *Butler...Durham...suspicion,*] Joseph Butler (1692–1752; *DNB*), Bishop of Durham. His most famous work, *The Analogy of Religion, Natural and Revealed, to the Constitution and Course of Nature* (1736), is a defence of Christianity against the 'natural' religion of Deism. In 1858, De Quincey appended a footnote to this passage (see below, p. 657, 157.29–30).
49 *Pascal's,*] Blaise Pascal (1623–62), French mathematician, physicist and moralist.
50 *illimitable grandeur*] In 1858, De Quincey inserted a quotation from Wordsworth's 'Tintern Abbey' into this passage (see below, p. 658, 158.2).

51 *ELEUSINIAN MYSTERIES...FREEMASONRY.*] The Eleusinian Mysteries are the most famous of the secret religious rites of ancient Greece. Freemasonry evolved from the guilds of stonemasons and cathedral builders of the Middle Ages. In 1717 the first Grand Lodge was established in England.

52 to aporeton] (Lt.), 'forbidden secret'.

53 *'in Leicester's busy square...dissatisfied.'*] Wordsworth, 'Star-gazers', ll. 5, 31–2 (inexact).

54 *professor of astronomy.*] John Pringle Nichol (1804–59; *DNB*), Professor of Astronomy at the University of Glasgow. De Quincey's 1846 *Tait's* essay on 'The System of the Heavens as Revealed by Lord Rosse's Telescope' is ostensibly a review of Nichol's *Thoughts on some Important Points relating to the System of the World* (Vol. 15, pp. 393–420).

55 *Endymion*] In Greek mythology, Endymion was a beautiful youth put into an everlasting sleep by Selene, goddess of the moon, so that she could enjoy his beauty forever.

56 *Ady...Lord Mayor of London*] Joseph Ady (1770–1852; *DNB*), a notorious impostor, bilked the English public by circulating letters promising, on the receipt of a suitable fee, to inform those whom he addressed of 'something to their advantage'. In 1858, De Quincey appended a long footnote on '*Adyism* and *Ady*' (see below, p. 658, 159.27).

57 *Flying Dutchman...Astrachan...Mecca.*] In European maritime legend, the Flying Dutchman is a spectre ship doomed to sail forever. Astrakhan is a province in Russia, along the lower Volgar River. Mecca is a city in the Sirat Mountains inland from the Red Sea coast of Saudi Arabia.

58 *Timbuctooo...Abd-el-Kader,*] Timbuktu is a region in northern Mali, and borders Algeria on the northeast. Abdelkader (see above, p. 540, n. 47) founded the Algerian state.

59 *new word...few years back*] The *OED* cites this example of 'unpleasantries' from De Quincey, and gives the first usage of the word as 1830.

60 *porch...*repetundarum,] Zeno of Citium (*c.* 335 – *c.* 263 BC), Stoic philosopher who lectured in the Stoa or collonnade at Athens. 'Repetundarum' is a legal term meaning 'for the recovery of goods'.

61 *'Misfortune...bed-fellows;'*] Shakespeare, *The Tempest*, II.ii.37: 'Misery acquaints a man with strange bedfellows'.

62 *Persian Satrap Tissaphernes,*] Tissaphernes (d. 395 BC), Persian satrap (governor) of coastal Asia Minor. He played a leading part in Persia's struggle to reconquer the Ionian Greek cities of Asia Minor.

63 Teletai,] (Gk.), literally, 'celebration of mysteries'.

64 *Warburton.*] William Warburton (1698–1779; *DNB*), Bishop of Gloucester, literary critic and controversialist.

65 *practice as an attorney.*] Warburton articled for five years (1714–9) to an attorney in Nottinghamshire, and may briefly have practiced himself.

66 *Hermes Trismegistus...*La Chicane.] Hermes Trismegistus ('thrice-greatest') was regarded by Neoplatonists as the author of certain works on astrology and alchemy. In Greek mythology, the Titans were the twelve children of Uranus and Gaea. 'La Chicane' (Fr.) is 'chicanery'.

67 *Warburtonian commentaries upon Pope,*] Warburton wrote a series of essays (1738–9) defending Pope's *Essay on Man*, and thereafter became Pope's editor and literary executor.

68 *Centaur's shirt*] see above, p. 524, n. 26.

69 *'Divine Legation of Moses'?*] In *The Divine Legation of Moses Demonstrated* (1737–41), Warburton sought to establish, on deist principles, the divine authority of the Mosaic writings, which deists denied. The book caused immense controversy.

70 *granite...St Petersburg,*] In 1858, De Quincey appended a long footnote to this passage (see below, p. 659, 161.3).

71 *Llanroost...Inigo Jones,*] Inigo Jones (1573–1652; *DNB*), architect and stage designer. The son of a London clockmaker, Jones was not born in Llanrwst in North Wales, though in 1636 he did reputedly design the famous stone bridge leading into the village.

72 *tremble like a guilty thing.*] Wordsworth, 'Intimations of Immortality", l. 150: 'did tremble like a guilty Thing surpriz'd'. The source is of course Shakespeare, *Hamlet*, I.i.148.

73 inter alia,] (Lt.), 'among other things'.

74 *Jerusalem...Hebron...Sinai,*] Jerusalem and Hebron are two of the four holy cities of Judaism. Mount Sinai is the principal site of divine revelation in Jewish history, where God is reported to have given Moses the Ten Commandments.

75 *Whitehall*] Inigo Jones's greatest achievement is the Banqueting House, Whitehall (1619–22).

76 *Aladdin's...principal saloon.*] De Quincey draws from 'Aladdin; or, the wonderful lamp' in *The Arabian Nights' Entertainment* (see below, p. 572, n. 76).

77 *Virgil...mysteries.*] In *Aeneid*, VI, Virgil (see above, p. 535, n. 42) describes Aeneas's visit to the Underworld. De Quincey refers to the general argument of Warburton's *Divine Legation of Moses Demonstrated*, and in particular to the exposition of *Aeneid*, VI, in Book 2, section 4. Warburton sees this as a disguised account of initiation in to the Eleusinian mysteries.

78 μυησις] 'initiation'.

79 *47th of Euclid...intoxication;*] Euclid (see above, p. 537, n. 71) is best known for his treatise on geometry, the *Elements*. The forty-seventh proposition of Euclid is the most famous, and known as the 'Pythagorean Theorem'. It features prominently in the literature of the freemasons.

80 *Samson...Dalilah,*] Samson (see above, p. 534, n. 15) was deprived of his great strength when Delilah, his Philistine lover, had his long hair cut.

81 *Lobeck...*Aglaophamus,] Christian August Lobeck (1781–1860), grammarian, *Aglaophamus; sive, De theologiae mysticae Graecorum causis libri tres* (1829). Lobeck refuted the theory that the mythology of Homer and Hesiod contained symbolic elements of an ancient Oriental revelation.

82 *Niebuhr...Mueller,*] Barthold Georg Niebuhr (1776–1831), German historian. Karl Otfried Müller (1797–1840), German classicist.

83 a posteriori...a priori] (Lt.), respectively, 'from effect to cause' and 'from what is already known'.

84 *Inquisition...Vehm-gericht,*] For the Inquisition, see above, p. 536, n. 63. The 'Vehmgericht' was 'a form of secret tribunal which exercised great power in Westphalia from the end of the 12th to the middle of the 16th century' (*OED*).

Secret Societies {Part II}

1 *Eleusinian mysteries...*Freemasonry.] see above, p. 562, n. 51.

2 αποῤῥητο*...Solomon's days*] (Gk.), 'forbidden secret'. In 1858, De Quincey gave the correct inflectional ending (see below, p. 661, 166.17). Solomon (*fl.* tenth century BC), traditionally regarded as Israel's greatest king.

3 *1823 or 4.*] De Quincey published his 'Historico-Critical Inquiry into the Origin of the Rosicrucians and the Free-Masons' in the *London Magazine* for January 1824 (Vol. 4, pp. 1–49).

4 *Buhle...History of philosophy.*] Johann Gottlieb Buhle (1763–1821), Professor at the University of Göttingen. De Quincey states that he has 'abstracted, rearranged, and in some respects...improved' Buhle's *Ueber den Ursprung und die vornehmsten Schicksale der Orden der Rosenkreuzer und Freymaurer: eine historisch-kritische Untersuchung* (1804; Vol. 4, p. 1). De Quincey also refers to Buhle's edition of Aristotle (1791–1800), and his *Geschichte der neuern Philosophie seit der Epoche der Wiederherstellung der Wissenschaften* (1800–5).

5 *1629 by one Andrea;*] The Rosicrucian Brotherhood was announced in two anonymous manifestos published at Kassel, Germany, in 1614–5. Johann Valentin Andreä (1586–1654), Lutheran pastor and mystic, was at one time thought to have written both pamphlets, but is now considered to have been only closely associated with whoever wrote them.

6 *Christ...wrath of Herod.*] Herod (see above, p. 530, n. 51) ordered the massacre of the innocents. Jesus is thought to have been born during his reign.

7 *described by Herodotus?*] Herodotus (*c.* 485–425 BC), Greek historian, *Histories*, II. 148.

8 *Bath...such a mystery.*] When De Quincey was eleven and living with his mother in Bath, he used to go 'play in Sydney Gardens, whose attractions included a fascinating maze' (Lindop, p. 23; see below, p. 661, 167.40).

9 *Gibraltar*] a heavily fortified British military base on Spain's southern Mediterranean coast.

10 sine qua non] see above, p. 529, n. 29.

11 ex abundanti;] (Lt.), 'abundantly'.

12 Essenes*...celebrated journal,*] The Essenes were a religious sect or brotherhood which flourished in Palestine between the second century BC and the second century AD, and believed in communistic society, extreme piety and the practice of celibacy. De Quincey published a three-part series on 'The Essenes' in *Blackwood's* for January, April and May 1840 (Vol. 11, pp. 442–88).

13 *Gilfillan...*'paradoxical.'] George Gilfillan (1813–78; *DNB*), miscellaneous writer, *A Gallery of Literary Portraits* (Edinburgh: Tait, 1845), p. 162: 'We were particularly interested by his paper on the "Essenes"....He begins...by the statement of what seems a hopeless paradox; but, ere he be done, he has surrounded it with such plausible analogies...that you lay down the paper, believing, or, at least, wishing to believe, that the Essenes and the Christians were identical'.

14 *since leaving off opium,*] De Quincey made this claim many times, and most famously at the close of both the 1821 and 1856 *Confessions* (Vol. 2, pp. 75, 265). De Quincey never left off opium.

15 *explained in print,*] see, for example, De Quincey in *Tait's* in 1834: 'universally, it must be borne in mind – that not *that* is paradox which, seeming to be true, is upon examination false, but that which, seeming to be false, may upon examination be found true' (Vol. 10, p. 42).

16 *Boyle...paradoxes.*] Robert Boyle (1627–91; *DNB*), chemist, *Hydrostatical Paradoxes Made Out by New Experiments* (1666).

17 *little essay of Cicero's.*] The Stoics were a philosophical school founded by Zeno of Citium (see above, p. 562, n. 60), who stressed abstemious living and control of the passions. De Quincey has in mind Cicero (see above, p. 530, n. 47), *Paradoxa Stoicorum*.

18 *Pliny,*] Pliny the Elder (see above, p. 536, n. 47), *Natural History*, V.xv.73: 'On the west side of the Dead Sea...is the solitary tribe of the Essenes'.

19 *Josephus...Philo-Judaeus...Alexandria*] Flavius Josephus (AD 37–100), Jewish historian, who discusses the Essenes in *History of the Jewish War* (Book II), and *Jewish Antiquities* (Books XIII, XV, XVII and XVIII). Philo Judaeus, also known as Philo of Alexandria (*c.* 15 BC-AD c. 45), Greek-speaking Jewish philosopher, *Every Good Man is Free*, 75, 91; and *On the Contemplative Life*, 1–2.

20 *Ireland...translation of Josephus,*] Brunetti of Dublin, *Description of the model of ancient Jerusalem: illustrative of the sacred scriptures and the writings of Josephus* (Dublin: John F. Fowler, 1846).

21 *Swift...Will Whiston;*] For Jonathan Swift, see above, p. 528, n. 25. William Whiston (1667–1752; *DNB*), mathematician and Anglican priest, became Professor of Mathematics at Cambridge in 1703, but his advocacy of the heretical views of Arianism caused him to be expelled in 1710. He achieved great contemporary notoriety with his attempts to devise a means of discovering the longitude. In 1858, De Quincey expanded this passage (see below, p. 662, 170.30).

22 *autobiography...reader's pity.*] Whiston writes that he has been 'a Valetudinarian, and greatly subject to the *Flatus Hypochondriaci* in various Shapes all my Life long'. Cf. De Quincey in his 1830 *Blackwood's* essay on 'Richard Bentley': 'The secret of all Whiston's lunacies may be found in that sentence of his Autobiography, where he betrays the fact of his liability, from youth upwards, to flatulency. What he mistook for conscience was flatulence, which others (it is well known) have mistaken for inspiration' (*Memoirs of the Life and Writings of Mr William Whiston*, 2 vols (London, 1749), vol. I, p. 18; Vol. 7, p. 99).

23 *Ditton...Newton,*] Humphrey Ditton (1675–1715; *DNB*), mathematician and clergyman. In 1706, through the influence of Isaac Newton (1642–1727; *DNB*), Ditton was appointed master of a new mathematical school at Christ's Hospital.

24 *Swift's...'The longitude...Ditton.'*] The lines 'The Longitude mist on / By wicked *Will. Whiston*' appear in the scatological *Ode, for Musick, on the Longitude*, first published in *The Last Volume* of the Pope-Swift *Miscellanies* (1727), and variously attributed to Pope, Swift and John Gay.

25 *to adorn the Sparta*] In 1858, De Quincey appended a footnote to this phrase (see below, p. 662, 171.3).

26 I, lictor, colliga manus.] Livy (see above, p. 536, n. 45), *History of Rome*, I. 26: 'go, lictor, bind his hands'.

27 *St Paul.*] St Paul (AD*c.* 3–*c.* 64), Christian apostle.

28 *'A fingering...mother's grave.'*] Wordsworth, 'A Poet's Epitaph', ll. 18–20: 'Philosopher! A fingering slave, / One that would peep and botanize / Upon his mother's grave'.

29 *Sanhedrims,*] The Sanhedrin was the highest Jewish council in Ancient Jerusalem.

30 *Maccabees...Rome.*] The Maccabees were a Jewish dynasty founded in Jerusalem by Judas Maccabee (d. 161 BC), who expelled the Syrians and restored the Temple of Jerusalem (164 BC). In the First Jewish Revolt (AD 66–70), Josephus led the Jewish forces against the Romans, but was quickly overwhelmed. Jerusalem fell in AD 70. The Temple was burned, and the Jewish state collapsed. Josephus's first work, *History of the Jewish War*, chronicles the events of the war.

31 *traitor...might revel in honour.*] After the Fall of Jerusalem, Josephus took up residence in Rome, where he was granted citizenship and a pension, and where he became a favourite at court.

32 *Mount...Pompeii,*] For the Sermon on the Mount, see Matthew 5–7. Pompeii, Italian ancient city fourteen miles southeast of Naples, was destroyed by the violent eruption of Mount Vesuvius in AD 79.

33 *Mozart!*] For Wolfgang Amadeus Mozart, see above, p. 540, n. 53.

34 *Alexandrian Pharos*] The Pharos of Alexandria was one of the Seven Wonders of the World, and the most famous lighthouse in antiquity. It was built about 280 BC on the island of Pharos in the harbour of Alexandria.

35 *Ariadne's thread*] In Greek mythology, Ariadne gave Theseus a ball of thread in order to enable him to find his way out of the labyrinth of Minos.

36 *Lauder...Milton.*] William Lauder (d. 1771; *DNB*), literary forger, whose *Essay on Milton's Use and Imitation of the Moderns in his Paradise Lost* (1750) was a fraudulent attempt to prove Milton a plagiarist.

37 in toto] (Lt.), 'in its entirety'.

38 *1839–40 and 41...Affghanistan*] Britain tried to extend its control over Afghanistan in three Anglo-Afghan wars, the first of which was fought 1839–42.

39 *Antipater...Ptolemies*] Antipater (d. 43 BC) was the founder of the Herodian dynasty in Palestine. The Ptolemies were a Macedonian dynasty that ruled Egypt, 323–30 BC.

40 aulic] see above, p. 531, n. 64.

41 *Juvenal,*] see above, p. 527, n. 5.

42 grand monarque.] (Fr.), 'great king'.

43 *Seneca's* apocolocuntosis,] Seneca (*c.* 4 BC–AD 65), tragedian, philosopher and statesman. His *Apocolocyntosis divi Claudii* (*The Pumpkinification of the Divine Claudius*) is a satirical burlesque that concerns the deification – or 'pumpkinification' – of Claudius (10 BC–AD 54), Roman emperor, AD 41–54.

44 *Pantheon*] The Roman Pantheon, a temple dedicated to the worship of many gods, was begun in 27 BC and completed about AD 118.

45 *great Augustan*] In 1858, De Quincey appended a footnote to this passage (see below, p. 664, 176.5).

46 *Augustan...Claudian...Herod,*] The Roman emperors Augustus (63 BC-AD 14) and Claudius (see above, n. 43) had a long and close association with the family of Herod (see above, p. 530 n. 51).

47 *Agrippa...Bernice,*] Herod Agrippa I (*c.* 10 BC-AD 44), King of Judaea, AD 41–4. He demonstrated great skill in conciliating the Romans and Jews. His eldest daughter was Berenice (b. AD 28), Judean princess.

48 *Herod's own household*] In 1858, De Quincey appended a footnote to this passage (see below, p. 664, 176.10).

49 *Pharsalia,*] The *Pharsalia* is the only surviving work of Lucan (see above, p. 536, n. 61), and recounts the civil war between Julius Caesar and Pompey.

50 *Vespasian and his son*] Vespasian (AD 9–79), Roman emperor, AD 69–79. His son was Titus (AD 39–81), Roman emperor, AD 79–81. Titus conquered Jerusalem in AD 70.

51 *Arthur...le Fay...Excalibur.*] In Arthurian legend, Arthur is King of Britain, Morgan le Fay is his sister and Excalibur his magic sword.

52 *matriculated amongst them himself.*] Josephus, *The Life*, 9–11.

53 *Hesperides...Turpin.*] In Greek mythology, the Hesperides were a group of nymphs who guarded the golden apples. Archbishop Turpin of Rheims (d. *c.* 800) was for

many years regarded as the author of the legendary *Historia de vita Caroli Magni et Rolandi*.

54 *Trajan;*] Trajan (AD 53–117), Roman emperor, AD 98–117.

55 *Will you burn incense to Caesar?*] Every year Roman citizens were expected to burn incense to Caesar. Many Christians refused, and were put to death.

56 *Abraham.*] Abraham (*fl.* early second century BC), first of the Hebrew patriarchs.

57 *nympholepsy.*] In 1858, De Quincey appended a footnote to this passage in which he quoted an 'exquisite line' from Lord Byron (see below, p. 665, 178.26–7). De Quincey quoted this same line from Byron in his 1848 essay on Alexander Pope (see above, p. 356).

58 *St Stephen, Paul of Tarsus, the learned Jew,*] St Stephen (d. *c.* AD 36), the first Christian martyr. For St Paul, born Saul or Tarsus, see above, n. 27.

59 *Mendelssohn's Oratorio of St Paul.*] Felix Mendelssohn (1809–47), German composer and conductor, completed his oratorio *St Paul* in 1835. The reference here is to Acts 7: 58: 'And cast him out of the city, and stoned him: and the witnesses laid down their cloths at a young man's feet, whose name was Saul'.

60 *shone like...an angel.*] Acts 6: 15: 'And all that sate in the Council, looking steadfastly on him, saw his face as it had been the face of an Angel'.

61 *road to Damascus*] Paul was converted to Christianity by a vision of Christ while on the road to Damascus (Acts 9).

62 *Master in Jerusalem.*] In 1858, De Quincey expanded the conclusion of this paragraph, and appended a long footnote (see below, p. 665, 179.12–14).

63 de propaganda fide,] (Lt.), 'for the spreading of the faith'.

64 *traditions*] In 1858, De Quincey appended a footnote to this word (see below, p. 668, 180.36).

65 Essen...*gate in the temple;*] In 1858, De Quincey expanded this passage (see below, p. 669, 181.8–10). For the derivation of 'the name of Essen', see Christian D. Ginsburg, *The Essenes: Their History and Doctrines* (London: Longmans, Green and Co., 1864), p. 27.

Schlosser's Literary History of the Eighteenth Century. {Part I}

1 de jure...de facto,] (Lt.), respectively, 'by law' and 'in reality'.

2 *Sue...Balzac, Hugo...Sand,*] For Eugene Sue, see above, p. 524, n. 15. Honoré de Balzac (1799–1850), French writer who produced a vast series of novels and short stories called *La Comédie humaine* (*The Human Comedy*). Victor Hugo (1802–85, Paris), French poet, novelist and dramatist best known for *Notre-Dame de Paris* (1831) and *Les Misérables* (1862). George Sand (1804–76), pseudonym of Amandine Aurore Lucie Dupin, French writer celebrated for her studies of rustic life in novels such as *La Mare au diable* (1846). In revision, De Quincey added a reference to Alexandre Dumas to this passage (see below, p. 670, 185.8).

3 *few books are published.*] cf. De Quincey in 'Dr Johnson and Lord Chesterfield': 'A book is not really published, that is <made public> dispersed amongst the public, simply because it has announced its own existence' (see above, p. 519).

4 *Carlisle...Roscommon's...'British Poets.'*] Frederick Howard, fifth Earl of Carlisle (1748–1825; *DNB*), is best known for his tragedy, *The Father's Revenge* (1783). Wentworth Dillon, fourth Earl of Roscommon (1633–85; *DNB*), author of a blank-verse translation of Horace's *Ars Poetica* (1680). De Quincey has in mind collections

such as the *Pocket Edition of Select British Poets* (published by John Cooke) and the *Specimens of the British Poets* (published by William Suttaby).

5 *prime minister known to us all.*] John Russell, first Earl Russell (1792–1878; *DNB*), Prime Minister of Great Britain, 1846–52, 1865–6. He wrote a large number of plays, novels, essays and histories, including *Don Carlos; or, Persecution* (1822).

6 *Lord Byron,*] Lord Carlisle was the guardian of Lord Byron (see above, p. 533, n. 10) during his minority. Carlisle was the first cousin of Byron's father.

7 *Sacheverell... Wickliffe... Luther.*] Henry Sacheverell (*c.* 1674–1724; *DNB*), preacher and fanatical High Church Anglican. John Wycliffe (*c.* 1330–1384; *DNB*), theologian, philosopher, church reformer. Martin Luther (1483–1546), priest and theologian, whose work precipitated the Reformation which gave birth to Protestantism.

8 *Ronge, the* ci-devant *Romish priest*] Johannes Ronge (1813–87) was an excommunicated Roman Catholic priest who in 1844 helped to found the German Catholic church on Protestant principles. 'Ci-devant' (Fr.), 'former'. In revision, De Quincey appended a footnote to this passage (see below, p. 671, 186.40).

9 *temple of Ephesus,*] In 356 BC, the Temple of Artemis at Ephesus was burned by a maniac named Herostratus.

10 *Martin... twelve years back;*] In 1829, York Minster was set on fire and partly destroyed by a madman named Jonathan Martin.

11 *'Pursue the triumph and partake the gale,'*] Pope, *An Essay on Man*, IV. 386.

12 *Kohl, Von Raumer... Carus... King of Saxony,*] Johann Georg Kohl (1808–78), German historian and geographer, *England, Wales and Scotland* (1844). Friedrich von Raumer (1781–1873), German historian, *England in 1835; being a series of letters written to friends in Germany, during a residence in London* (1836). Carl Gastuv Carus (1789–1869), naturalist, amateur painter, psychologist, and court physician to Frederick Augustus II (1797–1854), King of Saxony. De Quincey is thinking in particular of Carus's *The King of Saxony's journey through England and Scotland in the year 1844* (1846).

13 *Adelaide's;*] Adelaide (1792–1849), Queen of William IV (1765–1837), King of Great Britain and Ireland, 1830–7. Raumer describes how the queen 'most graciously lent us her box', and how he found 'Windsor far exceeded my expectations'. But he makes no mention of sentinels presenting arms (Friedrich von Raumer, *England in 1835*, trans. Sarah Austin, 3 vols (London: Murray, 1836), vol II, pp. 92–8).

14 *Davison.*] see headnote above, p. 184.

15 *Schlosser... pledges himself}.*] Schlosser, vol. I, p. xvii.

16 *second time... workmanship}.*] Schlosser, vol. I, p. xvii.

17 *Kant,*] see above, p. 560, n. 16.

18 *Kant's*... negative quantities.] Kant's *Attempt to Introduce the Concept of Negative Magnitudes into Philosophy* (1763). In his 1830 *Blackwood's* essay on 'Kant in his Miscellaneous Essays', De Quincey observes that Kant's 'subtlety in paths more peculiarly his own would be best sustained by a little essay *On the Introduction into Philosophy of the idea of Negative Quantities*' (Vol. 7, p. 78).

19 *Newton... Dynamic philosophy,*] According to the algebraic meaning, opposites simply cancel out, and this is the meaning of negative quantity that De Quincey argues a scientist like Isaac Newton (see above, p. 565, n. 23) presupposes. The 'dynamic philosophy', however, refers to the dialectic method of Johann Gottlieb Fichte (1762–1814), Friedrich Wilhelm Joseph von Schelling (1775–1854), and Georg Wilhelm Friedrich Hegel (see above, p., 524, n. 16), which develops a superior and more inclusive insight ('synthesis') out of a clash of opposing insights ('thesis' and 'antithe-

sis'). For the scientist, negative quantity produces mutual cancellation. For the philosopher, it produces mutual production.

20 geprüft] (Ger.), 'examined'.

21 in medias res.] (Lt.), 'into the middle of things'.

22 *Drapier's...Gulliver's...Tub.'*] Jonathan Swift (see above, p. 528, n. 25), *Drapier's Letters* (1724), *Gulliver's Travels* (1726) and *Tale of a Tub* (1704).

23 *Wood's...inflicted on Ireland.*] 'Wood's halfpence' was a copper coinage minted in Ireland from 1723 to 1725 by the English mine owner and ironmaster William Wood (1671–1730; *DNB*). The Irish parliament was not consulted, and vigorously protested, forcing the withdrawal of the coins (see Schlosser, vol. I, pp. 92–3).

24 de novo.] (Lt.), 'anew'.

25 *Scott...readable shape.*] Scott, *Swift*, vol. VI, p. 348: 'The following historical account of the rise, progress, and termination of Wood's project, will enable the reader to understand completely the celebrated Drapier's Letters'. Eleven pages of summary then follow.

26 *'spun...intolerable extent.'*] Schlosser, vol. I, p. 94.

27 *(Lilliput and Blefuscu),*] In Book I of *Gulliver's Travels*, Gulliver is shipwrecked on the Island of Lilliput, where the inhabitants are only six inches tall. He gains their favour when he wades into the sea and captures an invasion fleet from neighbouring Blefescu.

28 *Cape Horn...Sinbad...*quam proximè,] For Cape Horn, see above, p. 554, n. 47. Sinbad the sailor, the hero of one of the tales in *The Arabian Nights' Entertainment*, relates the fantastic adventures he meets with in his voyages. The Latin phrase is 'as closely as possible'.

29 *Avernus*] The Lake of Averno, in southern Italy, was represented as the entrance to Hades by Virgil, *Aeneid,* VI. 237–40: 'A deep cave there was, yawning wide and vast, shingly, and sheltered by dark lake and woodland gloom'.

30 *poet to the robin red-breast,*] Wordsworth, 'The Redbreast chasing the Butterfly', l. 11.

31 *'It was...lost in wonder.'*] 'Swift' in Johnson, *Lives*, vol. III, p. 38 (inexact).

32 *Brobdingnagian,*] In Book II of *Gulliver's Travels*, Gulliver is stranded in Brobdingnag, a kingdom where the gigantic inhabitants are twelve times taller than himself.

33 *Sherwood...Robin Hood...'Little John,'*] Sherwood Forest is in Nottinghamshire, and well known for its association with Robin Hood, the outlaw hero of medieval legend. His friends included Friar Tuck and Little John.

34 *'little of her age,'*] 'MY Mistress had a daughter of nine Years old....She was...not above forty Foot high, being little for her Age' (Swift, *Prose*, vol. XI, p. 79).

35 *Westmoreland...church steeple.*] For De Quincey's enduring interest in the dialect spoken in Westmorland and Cumberland, see Vol. 1, pp. 292–310.

36 *Hiedelberg...'Don Quixote.'*] Schlosser began to teach at the University of Hiedelberg in 1817. For *Don Quixote*, see above, p. 529, n. 31.

37 *'all his views...of savages.'*] Schlosser, vol. I, p. 93.

38 yahoo] In Book IV of *Gulliver's Travels*, Gulliver describes the country of the Houyhnhnms, rational and virtuous horses who share their island with the vicious and filthy Yahoos.

39 *religious princess...bishoprick*] Caroline of Brandenburg-Ansbach (1683–1737) married George Augustus (later King George II) in 1705, and exercised an often decisive influence over him.

40 *conspicuous cathedral in Ireland,*] In 1713, Swift became Dean of St Patrick's Cathedral in Dublin.

41 *Luther and Calvin*] Schlosser discusses Swift's attitude toward Luther (see above, n. 7) and Calvin (see above, p. 527, n. 1), and how in *Tale of a Tub* he 'wished to ridicule and hold up to contempt the prevailing doctrines of the church' (Schlosser, vol. I, p. 95).

42 *'Fix'd fate...absolute.'*] Milton, *Paradise Lost*, II. 560.

43 *letters to Lady Suffolk.*] Henrietta Howard, Countess of Suffolk (1681–1767), mistress to George II (see above, n. 39).

44 *'somewhat dull.'*] Schlosser, vol. I, p. 93.

45 *old sea captains.*] De Quincey recalls Wordsworth's discussion of retired sea captains in the 1800 'Note to *The Thorn*': 'Such men having little to do become credulous and talkative from indolence'.

46 *Wapping...Rotherhithe verisimilitude.*] Wapping and Rotherhithe are on the Thames in the London dock area.

47 Milton...*Aeschylus,*] De Quincey often groups Milton and Aeschylus together as examples of literary sublimity and power (see above, p. 34).

48 *gownsman of Cambridge:*] 'MY Father...sent me to *Emanuel-College* in *Cambridge*, at Fourteen Years old, where I resided three Years' (Swift, *Prose*, vol. XI, p. 3).

49 *De Foe*] Daniel Defoe (1660–1731; *DNB*), English novelist, pamphleteer and journalist.

50 *Dampier*] William Dampier (1651–1715; *DNB*), buccaneer and writer celebrated for his *New Voyage round the world* (1697).

51 *Raleigh's...apostrophe to Death,*] Sir Walter Raleigh (*c.* 1554–1618; *DNB*), adventurer and writer, *The History of the World* (1614): '0 eloquent, just and mightie Death!'. De Quincey echoes this line in his famous apostrophe from *Confessions*: 'Oh! just, subtle, and mighty opium!' (Sir Walter Raleigh, *The History of the World*, ed. C. A. Patrides (London: Macmillan, 1971), p. 396; Vol. 2, p. 51).

52 *'Urn-Burial...Dying,'*] Sir Thomas Browne (1605–82; *DNB*), physician and author, *Religio Medici* (1642) and *Hydriotaphia, Urne-Buriall, or, A Discourse of the Sepulchrall Urnes lately found in Norfolk* (1658). Jeremy Taylor (1613–67; *DNB*), Anglican clergyman and writer, *The Rules and Exercises of Holy Living* (1650) and *The Rules and Exercises of Holy Dying* (1651). Cf. De Quincey's discussion of 'the mighty rhetoric of Sir Thomas Brown, or Jeremy Taylor' in his essay on Charles Lamb (see above, p. 378).

53 *Rotterdam...Belshazzar...lords.*] Rotterdam is a major European port, and the second largest city in the Netherlands. Belshazzar (d. *c.* 539 BC), coregent of Babylon. De Quincey refers to Daniel 5: 1: 'King Belshazzar made a great festival for a thousand of his lords'.

54 *Kotzebue...Benyowski...'Stranger!'*] August Friedrich Ferdinand von Kotzebue (1761–1819), German playwright, *Count von Benyovszky, or the Conspiracy at Kamtshatka* (1792) and *The Stranger* (1789–90).

55 *Wieland.*] Christoph Martin Wieland (1733–1813), German poet. 'Swift worked upon the English mind after his fashion, in the same way as Kotzebue, Wieland and others among us Germans, in theirs; he hit the point in which the common people and the fashionable vulgar meet' (Schlosser, vol. I, p. 94).

56 *Voltaire...tiger-monkey grin*] François-Marie Arouet de Voltaire (1694–1778), French poet, novelist and philosopher celebrated for his courageous crusades against tyranny, bigotry and cruelty. He frequently referred to the French as 'tigers and monkeys'. In a 13 June 1768 letter to Joseph Michel Antoine Servan, he observed, '...notre nation, aussi atroce quelquefois que frivole, est composé de singes et de Tigres' (*Voltaire's Correspondence*, ed. Theodore Besterman (Genève: Institut et Mesée

Voltaire, 1961), vol. LXVIII, letter 13,748). Cf. De Quincey in his 1830 *Blackwood's* essay on 'France and England': 'it...is the old union of the tiger and the monkey, for which, as representing the elements of *their* character, we have the warrant of the most celebrated amongst their countrymen' (Vol. 7, p. 192).

57 *'Idris...Oberon.'...Huon*] Wieland's *Idris und Zenide* (1767); and *Oberson* (1780), based on the medieval French romance *Huon de Bordeaux*.

58 *Addison and Steele.*] For Addison and Steele, see above, p. 523, n. 1.

59 *Shakspere...by Addison.*] cf. De Quincey in his 1830 *Blackwood's* essay on 'Richard Bentley': 'It is a fact that Addison has never cited Shakspeare but once...and Addison had certainly never read Shakspeare' (Vol. 7, p. 158).

60 *Anne...'point...deeply excited.'*] Anne (1665–1714), Queen of Great Britain, 1702–14. De Quincey cites Schlosser, vol. I, p. 98.

61 *Schamyl, the Circassian chief,*] more commonly, 'Shamil' (*c.* 1797–1871), leader of Muslim Dagestan and Chechen mountaineers, whose fierce resistance delayed Russia's conquest of the Caucasus for twenty-five years.

62 *heavies*] 'a stage wagon for the conveyance of goods' (*OED*, which cites this example from De Quincey).

63 *Hobson...before 1710.*] De Quincey refers to Thomas Hobson (*c.* 1544–1631; *DNB*), the subject of Milton's 'On the University Carrier' (1631).

64 *Mede...Ellis.*] more commonly, Joseph 'Mead' (1586–1638; *DNB*), biblical scholar best known for *Clavis apocalyptica* (1627). Mead maintained an extensive correspondence and had a keen interest in foreign affairs. Sir Henry Ellis (1777–1869; *DNB*), principal librarian of the British Museum, published a selection of Mede's letters in his *Original letters, illustrative of English History*, 3 vols (1824), vol. III.

65 *'burns' them.*] De Quincey has in mind examples such as George Lillo (1693–1739; *DNB*), *Elmerick: or, Justice Triumphant*, II.ii.1–2: 'Her charms are still the same, and at her sight / Love burns with double fury'.

66 *'ease their pain.'*] De Quincey is perhaps aiming at Dryden, 'The Hind and the Panther', III. 84: 'Complaints of Lovers help to ease their pain'.

67 *Phillises...Corydons*] These names were associated with the hackneyed 'pastoral' tradition of idealized rustics and their amours. Cf. Charles Dickens, *Little Dorrit*, ed. Harvey Peter Sucksmith (Oxford: Oxford University Press, 1999), pp. 305–6: 'The poor little old man knew some pale and vapid little songs, long out of date, about Chloe, and Phyllis, and Strephon being wounded by the son of Venus'.

68 *Phillips...Budgell...Cudgell,*] John Philips (1676–1709; *DNB*), Ambrose Philips (*c.* 1675–1749 *DNB*), poets. De Quincey is punning on the names of the poet Thomas Tickell (1686–1740; *DNB*) and the miscellaneous writer Eustace Budgell (1686–1737; *DNB*).

69 *'Paradise Lost'...forty years,*] *Paradise Lost* was published in 1667. Addison's *Spectator* essay on the poem was published forty-five years later, in 1712.

70 *Tonson's*] Jacob Tonson (1655–1736; *DNB*), publisher and bookseller.

71 *Revolution of 1688...patronage.*] De Quincey has only some of his facts straight. The edition of *Paradise Lost* in question is the fourth, not 'the sixth', and it was published in 1688, not 'some years' earlier. De Quincey, however, is right when he states that it was the first to include plates, and that it was patronized by John Somers (1651–1716; *DNB*), lawyer and statesman, who was not raised to the peerage as Baron Somers of Evesham until 1697. In the 1815 'Essay, Supplementary to the Preface', Wordsworth appends a footnote in which Somers is praised for 'encouraging a beautiful edition of Paradise Lost that first brought that incomparable Poem to be generally known and esteemed' (Wordsworth, *Prose*, vol. III, p. 71).

72 *list of* errata...*published.*] Schlosser, vol. I, p. xviii, vol. II, pp. iv, xxi. There are thirty-two errors listed in total.

73 *La Harpe,*] Both Voltaire and the French playwright Jean-François de La Harpe (1739–1803) published hostile criticism of Shakespeare.

74 *blunders of criticism...Johnson,*] for example, in *The Spectator* for 9 February 1712, Addison wrote that the English language 'sank under' Milton (*Spectator*, vol. III, p. 62). For Johnson's *Life of Milton*, see above, p. 537, n. 3.

75 *brick...Parian marble.*] In *The Spectator* for 28 June 1712, Addison wrote that if '*Paradise Lost* falls short of the *Aeneid* or *Iliad*...it proceeds rather from the Fault of the Language in which it is written, than from any Defect of Genius in the Author. So Divine a Poem in *English*, is like a stately Palace built of Brick, where one may see Architecture in as great a Perfection as in one of Marble, tho' the Materials are of a coarser Nature' (*Spectator*, vol. III, p. 566).

76 *Aladdin's servant...palace.*] De Quincey is drawing details from 'Aladdin; or, the wonderful lamp', one of the most popular tales from *The Arabian Nights' Entertainment.*

77 *slashing Dick...the poem.*] For Richard Bentley's edition of *Paradise Lost*, and Alexander Pope's reference to 'slashing Bentley', see above, p. 541, notes 61 and 63. In revision, De Quincey appended a footnote to this passage (see below, p. 672, 197.37).

78 *Knight...portico of book 1.*] Richard Payne Knight (1750–1824; *DNB*), collector and connoisseur. 'In the Paradise Lost, we are perpetually tugging at the oar; and though we discover, at every turn, what fills us with astonishment and delight, the discovery is, nevertheless, a work of toil and exertion: consequently we can only enjoy it, when the powers of attention are fresh and vigorous' (Richard Payne Knight, *An Analytical Inquiry into the Principles of Taste* (London: Hansard, 1805) p. 121).

79 *naked...not ashamed.*] Genesis: 2: 25: 'And they were both naked, the man and his wife, and were not ashamed'.

80 *French translation...novel for the season.*] De Quincey seems most likely to have in mind Nicolas-François, Dupré de Saint-Maur (1695–1774), whose well-known French prose translation of *Paradise Lost* first appeared in 1729. De Quincey's assertion that the French prose was then translated back into English seems apocryphal.

81 *'Milton, Mr John.'*] Boswell, vol. IV, p. 325: '"That is the fellow who made the Index to my Ramblers, and set down the name of Milton thus: Milton, *Mr* John"'.

82 *Boileau...*credite posteri!...*England.*] Nicolas Boileau-Despréaux (see above, p. 541, n. 75) paid Addison a 'polite compliment' on his Latin verses. It was 'duly circulated', and 'Addison's character was made' (Schlosser, vol. I, p. 99). The Latin phrase is 'believe it, oh later generations'.

83 *reaction from his English*] In revision, De Quincey appended a footnote to this passage (see below, p. 673, 198.34).

84 *Prior's...('le...fort de'),*] De Quincey's reference is somewhat confused. In 1672, Louis XIV led 100,000 troops across the Rhine in an easy conquest of southern Holland. Boileau commemorated the event in *Epistre IV*, ll. 73–4: 'En ce moment, il part, et couvert d'une nuë, / Du fameux fort de Skinq prend la route connuë'. It was, however, Boileau's 'Ode Sur la Prise de Namur, Par les Armes du Roy, L'Année 1692', which was satirized by Matthew Prior (1664–1721; *DNB*), poet and diplomat, in 'An English Ballad, On the Taking of Namur by the King of Great Britain, 1695'.

85 Louis Baboon...*Swift's...Louis XIV.*] see, for example, John Arbuthnot, *The History of John Bull*, eds Alan W. Bower and Robert A. Erickson (Oxford: Clarendon Press, 1976), p. 6: '*How* Bull *and* Frog *grew jealous that the Lord* Strutt *intended to give all his Custom to his Grandfather* Lewis Baboon'.

86 *'Lutrin,'*] Boileau's *Le Lutrin* (1674–83) begins with a quarrel between two ecclesiastical dignitaries about where to place a lectern in a chapel. It ends with a battle in a bookstore.
87 un homme borné.] (Fr.), 'a limited man'.
88 *'Blenheim'*] Addison's *The Campaign* (1704) is a poem in heroic couplets commemorating the English victory at Blenheim.
89 *Gottsched's…Bodmer's wet-nurse,*] Johann Jakob Bodmer (1698–1783), Swiss historian, professor and critical writer. Johann Christoph Gottsched (1700–66), German literary theorist, critic and dramatist.
90 *'enemies…aloud…softly.'*] Schlosser, vol. I, p. 99.
91 *'Cato…shadow of ancient night.*] Addison's blank-verse tragedy *Cato* (1713) was staged to great success in Drury Lane. Cf. Milton, *Paradise Lost*, II. 969–70: 'this nethermost abyss, / Chaos and ancient Night'.
92 ramollissement] (Fr.),'softening'.
93 *'But…soon repented.'*] Schlosser, vol. I, p. 99.
94 *Bolingbroke…Booth*] Henry St John, first Viscount Bolingbroke (1678–1751; *DNB*), prominent Tory politician. Barton Booth (1681–1733; *DNB*), actor.
95 (populo spectante)] (Lt.), 'with the people watching'.
96 *'for defending…perpetual dictator.'*] 'Addison' in Johnson, *Lives*, vol. II, p. 101.
97 *Marlborough.*] John Churchill, first Duke of Marlborough (1650–1722; *DNB*), diplomat and one of England's greatest generals.
98 *Castor and Pollux,*] In Greek and Roman mythology, Castor and Pollux were twin deities who succoured shipwrecked sailors and received sacrifices for favourable winds.
99 *Mandeville…all the rest).*] Bernard de Mandeville (1670–1733), Dutch prose writer and philosopher celebrated for *The Fable of the Bees*. De Quincey's objection to Schlosser's 'utter perversion of what Mandeville said about Addison' is unclear. In Johnson, *Lives*, vol. II, p. 123, Mandeville describes Addison as 'a parson in a tye-wig'. These are Schlosser's exact words (vol. I, p. 98).
100 *'he could not…good style,'*] Schlosser, vol. I, p. 98.
101 *'dull prosaist,'*] see Schlosser, vol. I, p. 98.

Schlosser's Literary History of the Eighteenth Century {Part II}

1 *Pope…Addison)*] For Alexander Pope, see above, p. 524, n. 20. For Joseph Addison, see above, p. 523, n. 1.
2 *'Essay…Lock…Man.'…Johnson's leave)*] Pope's *An Essay on Criticism* (1711), *The Rape of the Lock* (1712–4) and *An Essay on Man* (1733–34). According to Samuel Johnson (see above, p. 537, n. 3), *An Essay on Criticism* 'displays such extent of comprehension, such nicety of distinction, such acquaintance with mankind, and such knowledge both of ancient and modern learning as are not often attained by the maturest age and longest experience' (Johnson, *Lives*, vol. III, p. 94).
3 *Brennus,*] De Quincey refers to either Brennus (*fl.* early fourth century BC), leader of the band of Gauls who captured Rome about 390 BC; or a second Brennus (d. 279 BC), Gallic chieftain who led an unsuccessful invasion of Greece in 279 BC.
4 *Attila…wrath incarnate.*] Attila (d. AD 453), King of the Huns, AD 434–53. His Latin byname was 'Flagellum Dei' ('Scourge of God').
5 *Bengal lights*] A sort of fireworks producing a blue-coloured light of great steadiness and intensity, largely used for signals.

6 *forced marches...Adriatic?*] The Adriatic Sea lies between the Italian and Balkan peninsulas. Attila assailed the Roman Empire from the southern Balkan provinces and Greece to Gaul and Italy.

7 chout,] 'the black-mail of one-fourth of the revenue exacted by the Mahrattas in India from provinces within reach of their arms' (*OED*).

8 *Rosicrucian...Plume...Sylphs.*] In the dedication to *The Rape of the Lock*, Pope writes of raising the 'Machinery' of his poem 'on a very new and odd foundation, the Rosicrucian doctrine of Spirits'. 'Sir Plume' is a character in the poem.

9 *'duty...with the aristocracy.'*] Schlosser, vol. I, p. 86.

10 *twice at least*] In 1858, De Quincey appended a footnote to this phrase (see below, p. 673, 202.29).

11 *Zachariä...with Pope.*] Friedrick William Zachariä (1726–77), German poet.

12 *'Lutrin' of Boileau.*] Boileau's *Le Lutrin* (see above, p. 573, n. 86) is 'the pattern which Pope had in his eye in writing "The Rape of the Lock"' (Schlosser, vol. I, p. 85).

13 *Herodotus...cranes and pigmies,*] The battle of the cranes and the pygmies is not in Herodotus but Homer, *Iliad*, III. 3–7, to which Herodotus refers in *Histories*, II. 22, but without mentioning the pygmies. Herodotus does mention the pygmies in *Histories*, II. 32 and IV. 43.

14 Batrachomyomachia...*Homer)*] *The Battle of the Frogs and Mice* is a short Greek mock-epic poem in the style of the Homeric epic sometimes attributed to Homer in antiquity, and dating perhaps from the fifth century BC.

15 *'guide...friend,'...temptation;*] Pope, *Essay on Man*, IV. 390: 'Thou wert my guide, philosopher, and friend?' Cf. Matthew 6: 13: 'and lead us not into temptation'.

16 *Warburton...defender of the faith.*] see above, p. 562, n. 64.

17 *Bolingbroke sincere...extent.*] Schlosser, vol. I, p. 88.

18 *Voss...'that Pope...understrappers.'*] Johann Heinrich Voss (1751–1826), German poet best known for his translations of Homer. De Quincey cites Schlosser, vol. I, p. 82.

19 *'Dunciad,'*] Pope's satire *The Dunciad* was published in three books in 1728, and a fourth book, *The New Dunciad*, was added in 1742.

20 *Johnson...measure its merits.*] Schlosser condemns the 'rudeness and vulgarity' of *The Dunciad*, and the ways in which Pope 'heaps abuse upon his enemies and opponents of another class' (Schlosser, vol. I, p. 86). Johnson believed that Pope wrote *The Dunciad* 'for fame. That was his primary motive. Had it not been for that, the dunces might have railed against him till they were weary, without his troubling himself about them' (Boswell, vol. II, p. 334).

21 Temple de Gout] Voltaire (see above, p. 570, n. 56) published his satiric *Temple of Taste* in 1733.

22 *'shows* ... insignificant *persons;'*] Schlosser, vol. I, p. 120.

23 *Salmasius...Bentley.*] Claudius Salmasius (1588–1653), French classical scholar. For Richard Bentley, see above, p. 541. n. 61.

24 'which *Dacier, Bezonian?'*] André Dacier (1651–1722) and his wife Anne Dacier (1654–1720) were classical scholars and translators. 'Bezonian' means 'base fellow' or 'knave' (*OED*). In 1858, De Quincey appended a footnote on André Dacier's edition of Horace to this passage (see below, p. 674, 204.34–5).

25 *Dennis...Cibber...Hill*] John Dennis (1657–1734; *DNB*), dramatist and critic. Colley Cibber (1671–1757; *DNB*), actor, theatre manager, playwright and poet laureate. Aaron Hill (1685–1750; *DNB*), dramatist, poet and essayist.

26 *'mount far...swans of Thames'*] Pope, *The Dunciad*, II. 298: 'And mounts far off among the Swans of Thames'.

27 *Clarke, Burnet...Newton,*] Samuel Clarke (1675–1729; *DNB*), theologian and philosopher. Thomas Burnet *(c.* 1635–1715; *DNB*), theologian, who in 1685 was appointed Master of Charterhouse. For Isaac Newton, see above, p. 565, n. 23. In 1858, De Quincey appended a footnote on 'Gilbert Burnet' to this passage (see below, p. 674, 204. 43–4).

28 *FOX AND BURKE.*] Charles James Fox (1749–1806; *DNB*), Whig politician, Britain's first foreign secretary and a famous champion of liberty. Edmund Burke (1729–97; *DNB*), Whig politician and political philosopher. For the manuscript fragment related to this section, see above pp. 500–1.

29 visible *darkness*] cf. Milton, *Paradise Lost*, I. 63: 'No light, but rather darkness visible'.

30 *Devonshire House.*] The Devonshires were a highly political Whig family, and Devonshire House their principal London residence.

31 Fox...*'formed...simple...forcible;'*] Schlosser, vol. II, p. 99.

32 *'most forcible Feeble.'*] Shakespeare, *2 Henry IV,* III.ii.167–8: 'Let that suffice, most forcible Feeble'.

33 *impotent for posterity.*] cf. De Quincey on Fox in his 1831 *Blackwood's* essay on Samuel Parr (Vol. 8, p. 53).

34 *Salmoneus,*] In Greek mythology, Salmoneus claimed arrogantly to be the equal of Zeus. He drove about in a chariot of bronze to imitate thunder, and threw firebrands to imitate lightning.

35 *Jove's thunderbolt...Acheron*] For Jove, see above, p. 537, n. 74. In Greek mythology, Acheron is one of the rivers of the underworld.

36 *Cassandra meanings.*] In Greek mythology, Cassandra has the power of prophecy.

37 *'allusions...to navigation!'*] Schlosser, vol. II, p. 99.

38 *'as toad or asp,'*] Milton, 'Sonnet, XI', l. 13: 'Hated not learning worse than toad or asp'.

39 *Burke...Orpheus...*seer,] cf. Samuel O'Sullivan, 'A Conversation on the Reform Bill' in *Blackwood's*, 30 (August 1831), p. 313: 'Where is the seer-like sagacity of Burke...?' In Greek mythology, Orpheus joined the expedition of the Argonauts, and saved them from the music of the Sirens by playing his own, more powerful music.

40 *link-boys...Cocytus...*popular.] A 'link-boy' was 'a boy employed to carry a link to light passengers along the streets' (*OED*). In Greek mythology, Cocytus is one of the rivers of the Underworld. Of Burke's 'popularity', De Quincey is objecting to observations such as 'Burke first made himself renowned as a zealous defender of freedom' (Schlosser, vol. II, p. 93).

41 *Bath...Beaconsfield.*] De Quincey is out by a year. In the throes of his final illness, Burke left his lodgings in North Parade, Bath, in September 1796, and died on 9 July 1797 at Beaconsfield, his house in Buckinghamshire. The next occupant of Burke's Bath rooms was De Quincey's mother (see Lindop, pp. 23–4).

42 *'European...Bolingbroke,'*] Burke's *An Account of the European settlements in America* (1757), *A Philosophical Enquiry into the Origin of Our Ideas of the Sublime and Beautiful* (1757) and *A Vindication of Natural Society in a Letter to Lord* ——— (1756).

43 *Lawrence...Windham,*] French Laurence (1757–1809; *DNB*), Regius Professor of Civil Law at Oxford, and M.P. for Peterborough. He was Burke's literary executor. William Windham (1750–1810; *DNB*), politician and an intimate of Burke's.

44 *Mr R. Sharpe,*] Richard Sharp (1759–1835; *DNB*), M.P. for Castle Rising, Portarlington and Ilchester.

45 απεραντολογια] (Gk.), in 1858, De Quincey translated this word as 'world-without-ending-ness' in a greatly expanded version of this footnote (see below, p. 675, 206.n 5–6).

46 *Curwen...for Cumberland,*] John Christian Curwen (1756–1828), M.P. and wealthy owner of mines and farmland. Cumberland is a former county in extreme northwestern England.

47 ad infinitum.] (Lt.), 'without limit'.

48 sobriquet *of 'dinner-bell?'*] cf. Hazlitt, *Works*, vol. XII, pp. 266–8: Burke 'was emphatically called the *Dinner-Bell*. They went out by shoals when he began to speak'.

49 *'went on refining...dining.'*] Goldsmith, 'Retaliation', ll. 35–6.

50 *Pitt*] For William Pitt the Younger, see above, p. 528, n. 15.

51 *'Now is the winter...summer'*] Shakespeare, *Richard III*, I.i.1–2.

52 *'the whistling of a name,'*] Pope, *Essay on Man*, IV. 283: 'Or ravish'd with the whistling of a Name'.

53 *Homeric Greek, which was a jest:*] cf. De Quincey in his 1830 *Blackwood's* essay on 'France and England': Fox's 'reading had been very limited, (and, in particular, by way of shewing how little truth there often is in old inveterate popular notions, he neither had read more than a few pages of Demosthenes, nor did he particularly profess to admire that orator' (Vol. 7, pp. 187–8).

54 *Secretary, Trotter.*] John Bernard Trotter (1775–1818; *DNB*), private secretary to Charles James Fox and author of *Memoirs of the Latter Years of C. J. Fox* (1811).

55 *Holland,*] Henry Richard Vassall Fox, third Baron Holland (1773–1840; *DNB*), a nephew and disciple of Charles James Fox. He wrote the preface and helped to ensure the posthumous publication of Fox's *History of the Early Part of the Reign of James the Second* (London: Miller, 1808).

56 *Laing...Hume,*] Malcolm Laing (1762–1818; *DNB*), Scottish historian best known for his *History of Scotland from the Union of the Crowns* (1800); he was intimately acquainted with Fox. David Hume (1711–76; *DNB*), Scottish historian and philosopher whose most popular work was *The History of Great Britain* (1754–62).

57 *JUNIUS.*] Junius is the pseudonym adopted by the author of a series of shrewd and unsparing letters (1769–72) that attacked the policies of George III. Junius's identity has never been discovered, though Sir Philip Francis (1740–1818; *DNB*), civil servant and politician, remains the leading candidate.

58 *Trismegistus...Prester John.*] two figures from legend: Hermes Trismegistus (see above, p. 562, n. 66) and Prester John, a Christian ruler of the East, popularized in medieval chronicles.

59 *in past times,*] By the time of the present essay, De Quincey had already considered the Junius question at length: see Vol. 1, pp. 24, 34; Vol. 5, pp. 205–26; Vol. 11, pp. 265–72.

60 *Byron's Lara...Lee's Kraitzrer.*] Lord Byron (see above, p. 533, n. 10) published *Lara* in 1814. Harriet Lee (1757–1851; *DNB*), dramatist and novelist, wrote 'Kruitzner, or the German's Tale' as part of her contribution to *Canterbury Tales* (1797), a five-volume edition she produced in collaboration with her sister Sophia Lee (1750–1824; *DNB*). Seven years earlier De Quincey made the same accusation against Byron of 'a gross plagiarism from Miss H. Lee' (Vol. 11, p. 257). The Byron text in question, however, is not *Lara*, but his 1823 domestic tragedy *Werner*, which he states is 'taken entirely from the "*German's Tale, Kruitzner,*" published many years ago in "*Lee's Canterbury Tales*"' (Byron, *PW*, vol. VI, p. 384). In 1858, De Quincey

expanded this passage (see below, p. 677, 209.15). De Quincey's 1832 Gothic novel *Klosterheim* draws on Lee's 'Kruitzner' (Vol. 8, pp. 225, 434).

61 otium cum dignitate,] (Lt.), 'leisure with honour'; cf. Cicero, *Pro Sestio*, 98.

62 *'Honour bright!'...Barrington...George III.,]* 'Honour bright' is colloquial and 'used as a protestation of...one's honour or sincerity' (*OED*). Junius fiercely attacked William Wildman Barrington, second Viscount Barrington (1717–93; *DNB*), secretary at war. For the Old Bailey, see above, p. 533, n. 7. For George III, see above, p. 525, n. 31.

63 *council to Bengal,]* Francis became councilor to the Governor General of India in 1773.

64 *Hastings,]* Warren Hastings (1732–1818; *DNB*), first British Governor General of India. He and Francis fought a duel in 1780.

65 *represented...in Parliament.]* Francis entered Parliament in 1784, and held a seat for the next twenty years.

66 Joseph Surface] Joseph Surface is the sanctimonious hypocrite in Richard Brinsley Sheridan's comedy *The School for Scandal* (1777).

67 *Knight of the Bath...St James's Square,]* The Knights of the Bath is a British order of knighthood traditionally founded by Henry IV in 1399. St James was a fashionable area for London high society.

68 *Taylor,]* John Taylor (1781–1864; *DNB*), co-owner and editor of the *London Magazine*, *The Identity of Junius with a Distinguished Living Character Established* (1816) and *A Supplement to Junius Identified* (1817).

69 *Brougham...still profess scepticism.]* Henry Brougham (1778–1868; *DNB*), co-founder of the *Edinburgh Review* (1802), lawyer, reformer, and Whig Lord Chancellor. Schlosser damns 'the muddy-flowing Scottish stream of speech' with which Brougham condemns Junius (vol. II, p. 90).

70 *Francis's...Demonsthenes...father.]* Francis's father was Dr Philip Francis (*c.* 1708–1773; *DNB*), classical scholar, whose *Orations of Demosthenes* appeared in 1757. Brougham produced his *Oration of Demosthenes upon the Crown* in 1840.

71 *translation of Horace.]* Dr Philip Francis, *Ode, Epodes, and Carmen Seculare of Horace* (1743–6).

72 *reviewed...*That *may be:]* Brougham reviewed Taylor's *The Identity of Junius* and the *Supplement* (see above, n. 68) in the *Edinburgh Review*, 29 (1818), pp. 94–114 (*The Wellesley Index to Victorian Periodicals*, gen. ed. Walter E. Houghton, 5 vols (Toronto: University of Toronto Press, 1966–89), vol. I, p. 457).

73 *'wanted better bread...wheat –']* Miguel de Cervantes's *Don Quixote* (see above, p. 529, n. 31), where the proverb is used at least twice, and not only by Sancho Panza, the hero's reluctant squire. In Part I Chapter 7, Quixote's niece urges him to stay at home rather than 'roaming the world in search of better bread than was ever made of wheat'. In Part II, Chapter 67, Sancho Panza announces that he has no intention of hunting for 'better bread than is made of wheat'.

74 *Dallas...like it]* Sir Robert Dallas (1756–1824; *DNB*), judge.

75 allegatio falsi...suppressio veri.] (Lt.), respectively, 'allegations of falsehood' and 'suppression of truth'.

76 *Tyburn,]* the location of the infamous Middlesex Gallows.

77 Publicolas...*Downing Street.]* 'Publicola' was supposed to be typical of the pseudonyms used by late eighteenth- and early nineteenth-century political pamphleteers and journalists. Cf. De Quincey in *Walladmor*: 'set Junius upon them – set Publicola upon them in the newspaper' (Vol. 4, p. 318). The Cato Street conspiracy (1820) was a revolutionary plot involving some twenty radical extremists, who planned to assas-

sinate members of the cabinet and seize power. Algernon Sidney (1622–83; *DNB*) was executed for his alleged part in the Rye House Plot (1683). Downing Street has been the official residence of the British Prime Minister since 1732.

78 *Timoleon,*] Timoleon of Corinth (d. *c*. 337 BC), Greek statesman and general, and a lifelong enemy of tyranny.

79 *Pope...tell us they lived?*] 'Grub Street' was an actual street in Moorfields in London, that was renamed Milton Street in 1830, and no longer exists. It was associated with literary hacks who wrote for hire. De Quincey seems to have in mind Pope's footnote to *The Dunciad*, I. 126, where he condemns George Wither as 'a great pretender', and observes that 'the *Marshalsea* and *Newgate* were no strangers to him'.

80 *French...diamond necklace)*] The Affair of the Diamond Necklace was a scandal at the court of Louis XVI in 1785–6. It was widely but mistakenly believed that Queen Marie Antoinette (1755–93) had sold herself to Cardinal de Rohan (1734–1801) for a piece of jewellery.

81 *Tooke...Chamier...Ellis,*] For John Horne Took, see above, p. 535, n. 31. Anthony Chamier (1725–80; *DNB*), whose appointment as deputy secretary of war provoked a series of private and public attacks by Francis. George Ellis (1753–1815; *DNB*), political satirist.

82 *Ketch at Tyburn.*] For Jack Ketch, see above, p. 553, n. 20.

83 amreeta] more commonly, 'amrita', meaning 'immortal' or 'ambrosial'. Cf. Southey, *The Curse of Kehama*, XVIII. 107–8: 'The Amreeta-drink divine / Of immortality'.

Conversation

1 *Plato's...Republic...tyrant he was.*] The philosophical dialogues of Plato (see above, p. 524, n. 13) include *The Republic* and *The Symposium*.

2 *Huyghens...Bernoullis...De Moivre...Chances.*] De Quincey refers to Christian Huyghens (1629–95), Dutch mathematician and author of *On Ratiocination in Dice Games* (1657); Jakob Bernoulli (1655–1705), member of a distinguished Swiss family of mathematicians, whose works include *The Conjectural Arts* (1713); Abraham de Moivre (1667–1754), French mathematician celebrated for his *Doctrine of Chances* (1718).

3 *Lord Bacon's idea.*] Francis Bacon (1561–1626; *DNB*), lawyer, statesman and philosopher, observes in his essay 'Of Studies' that 'Reading maketh a Full Man; Conference a Ready Man; And Writing an Exact man'. But De Quincey may also have in mind Bacon's comments in his essay 'Of Friendship': 'certaine it is that, whosoever hath his Minde fraught, with many Thoughts, his Wits and Understanding doe clarifie and breake up, in the Communicating and discoursing with Another: He tosseth his Thoughts, more easily; He marshalleth them more orderly; He seeth how they looke when they are turned into Words; Finally, He waxeth wiser then Himselfe; And that more by an Houres discourse, then by a Dayes Meditation' (Bacon, *Essayes*, pp. 153, 84).

4 *Milton...bickering flames...*fioriture,] Milton, *Paradise Lost*, VI. 750–1, 765–6: 'The Chariot of Paternal deity, / Flashing thick flames, wheel within wheel undrawn, ...And from about him fierce effusion rolled / Of smoke and bickering flame'. A 'fioritura' is 'a florid ornament or embellishment in music' (*OED*, which cites this example from De Quincey).

5 *Burke's and Johnson's...own steps.*] Edmund Burke (see above, p. 575, n. 28) and Samuel Johnson (see above, p. 537, n. 3) are similarly contrasted by De Quincey in his

1831 *Blackwood's* essay on Samuel Parr: 'Those who carry a spirit of distinguishing refinement into their classifications of the various qualities of conversation, may remark one peculiar feature in Edmund Burke's style of talking, which contra-distinguished it from Dr Johnson's: it grew....Burke's motion...was all a going forward. Johnson's, on the other hand, was purely regressive and analytic'. Cf. John Forster: Burke 'penetrated deeper into the principles of things, below common life and what is called good sense, than Johnson could' (Vol. 8, p. 15; Forster, p. 279).

6 *Burke...prophetic seer,*] see above, p. 575, n. 39.

7 sui generis,] (Lt.), 'one of a kind'.

8 *Thebes,*] the capital of the ancient Egyptian empire.

9 conditio sine quâ non,] see above, p. 529, n. 29.

10 *exceedingly brief...his efforts.*] cf. De Quincey on Hazlitt in his 1848 essay on Charles Lamb: 'Hazlitt was not eloquent, because he was discontinuous. No man can be eloquent whose thoughts are abrupt, insulated, capricious' (see above, p. 378).

11 *Hartley...Hume...Voltaire...Rousseau,*] David Hartley (1705–57; *DNB*), English physician and philosopher. For David Hume, see above, p. 576, n. 56. For Voltaire, see above, p. 570, n. 56. Jean-Jacques Rousseau (1712–78), French philosopher and educational theorist.

12 *'other palms were won.'*] Wordsworth, 'Intimations of Immortality', l. 202.

13 *Walpole...Chesterfield,*] Horace Walpole, fourth Earl of Orford (1717–97; *DNB*), letter-writer, connoisseur and author of the Gothic novel *The Castle of Otranto* (1764). Philip Dormer Stanhope, fourth Earl of Chesterfield (see above, p. 526, n. 66), is chiefly remembered for his *Letters to His Son* (1774) and *The Art of Pleasing* (1774).

14 *Paris...Macbeth...Cassandra prophecies)*] Paris was the seat of the French Revolution of 1789. De Quincey refers to *MacBeth*, IV. i. For 'Cassandra prophecies', see above, p. 575, n. 36.

15 aides-de-camp...roués,] (Fr.), respectively, 'military aids' and 'libertines'.

16 *melancholic...ancient physiologists held,*] For the most famous survey, see Robert Burton (1577–1640; *DNB*), *Anatomy of Melancholy* (1621), 'Of the Species or Kindes of Melancholy'.

17 *scrofulous wretches...'strumous diathesis'*] 'scrofulous' and 'strumous' are terms formerly interchangeable with 'tuberculosis'; 'diathesis' is 'a constitutional tendency or disposition'. Scrofula was the 'King's evil', and was supposedly cured by the royal touch. In 1712, Queen Anne touched the infant Samuel Johnson without effecting a cure.

18 Pectus – id est quod disertum facit.] Quintilian, *Institutio oratoria*, X.vii.15. De Quincey's own translation is '*The heart* (and not the brain) *is that which makes a man eloquent*' (see below, p. 679, 221.27). Cf. Landor: 'The heart is the creator of the poetical world; only the atmosphere is from the brain' (Landor, *Works*, vol. II, p. 164).

19 *Paris...diapered panels!*] Johnson toured France for two months in 1775. De Quincey is maligning what he regards as Johnson's trivial preoccupation with interior decor. One house was 'almost wainscotted with looking-glasses, and covered with gold', while another featured 'a table of porphyry, about five feet long, and between two and three broad' (Boswell, vol. II, pp. 390, 395).

20 studied nothing...*youthful days.*] cf. De Quincey in his 1830 *Blackwood's* essay on Immanuel Kant: 'One fact, which struck me by accident, and not until after a long familiarity with Kant's writings, is this, that in all probability Kant never read a book in his life' (Vol. 7, p. 52); also cf. his comments in his 1831 *Blackwood's* essay on Samuel Parr: 'Certainly, we are satisfied that Dr Johnson was no very brilliant Grecian', but as a Latin scholar he was 'excellent' (Vol. 7, p. 52; Vol. 8, p. 45).

Protestantism {Part I}

1 *Oxford...St David's...Norwich.*] Samuel Wilberforce (1805–73; *DNB*), Bishop of Oxford. For Connop Thirlwall, see above, p. 534, n. 16. Edward Stanley (1779–1849; *DNB*), Bishop of Norwich.

2 *'stiff...in the wrong.'*] see above, p. 524, n. 24.

3 *Wilson...*hedonist,] cf. De Quincey in the 1856 *Confessions*, where he notes that John Wilson (see above, p. 531, n. 74) 'coined the English word *Hedonist*, which he sometimes applied in playful reproach to myself and others' (Vol. 2, p. 251). The *OED* lists the first recorded usage of the word as in *Confessions*, but the reference in the present essay is nine years earlier.

4 *'just'...at page 1;*] 'We are well aware that it is just these varieties of doctrine...which have thrown discredit on the principles which we desire to maintain' (Donaldson, p. 1).

5 'shortcomings,'] Donaldson, p. 73: 'The impression of fear on account of their own impurity, imperfection, and short-comings'.

6 *'Paradise Lost,'...character.*] Milton, *Paradise Lost*, II. 49–50: 'of God, or hell, or worse / He recked not, and these words thereafter spake'.

7 *'How a score...as they be.'*] Shakespeare, *2 Henry IV*, III.ii.49–50 (inexact).

8 *'Thereafter as a man sows shall he reap.'*] De Quincey has in mind Galatians 6: 7: 'Whatsoever a man soweth, that shall he also reap'.

9 *page 79...leguleian*] 'For all those who should thereafter *be* good and *do* good, in the faith which exhibits its energy in self-denying love of God and man, for all those there would be two Paracletes' (Donaldson, p. 79). 'Leguleian' means 'of or pertaining to petty questions of law...pettifogging' (*OED*, which cites this example from De Quincey).

10 'Index Expurgatorius.'...*Index.*] 'Index Expurgatorius', or 'list of banned books', is 'an authoritative specification of the passages to be expunged or altered in works otherwise permitted' (*OED*). De Quincey addresses Pius IX (1792–1878), whose pontificate (1846–78) was marked by a transition from liberalism to conservatism.

11 Opera Omnia,] see above, p. 551, n. 69.

12 *Paine...Thirty-nine Articles.*] Thomas Paine (1737–1809; *DNB*), radical writer and revolutionary activist celebrated for his *Rights of Man* (Part I 1791; Part II 1792). The bishop in question is Richard Watson (1737–1816; *DNB*), Bishop of Llandaff, who is best known for his *Apology for the Bible...Letters...to Thomas Paine* (1796). The Thirty-Nine Articles are a set of doctrinal statements intended to define the position of the reformed Church of England in crucial matters of faith.

13 *Socinian...Whig ministry in 1807.*] The Socinians were a rationalist Christian group that rejected the doctrine of the Trinity. The Whigs shared power in the coalition government of 1806–7, the so-called 'Ministry of all the Talents'.

14 un peu fort.] see above, p. 547, n. 85.

15 Confessional...*six or seven octavos.*] Francis Blackburne (1705–87; *DNB*), Archdeacon of Cleveland, *The Confessional: or, a Full and Free Inquiry into the Right, Utility, Edification, and Success of Establishing Systematical Confessions of Faith and Doctrine in the Protestant Churches* (1766). His *Works, Theological and Miscellaneous* were published in seven volumes (1804).

16 per saltum,] (Lt.), 'by leaps and bounds'.

17 *Voltaire,*] see above, p. 570, n. 56.

18 étalage] (Fr.), 'display'.

19 Phileleutheros Anglicanus.] (Lt.), 'the English lover of freedom'.

20 *Hendecasyllable*] a line of poetry consisting of eleven syllables.

21 *Fielding's Hononchrononthononthologus,*] De Quincey has misremembered the reference. He has in mind Henry Carey (*d.* 1743; *DNB*), poet and musician, *Chrononhotonthologos; the most tragical tragedy that ever was tragedized by any company of tragedians* (1734). But he cites Henry Fielding (1707–54; *DNB*), novelist and playwright, whose *Tom Thumb* (1730) served Carey as a model.

22 *'Sufficiency for salvation'*...Phil.] Donaldson, pp. 3–4: 'William of Ockham did proclaim, in so many words, the Protestant doctrine of "the sufficiency of the Holy Scriptures for salvation"'.

23 *'They are...matters of religion.'*] Donaldson, p. 1.

24 *Newmarket jockey*] Newmarket lies seventy miles north of London, and has been celebrated for its horse races since the early seventeenth-century.

25 sui juris...locus standi,] (Lt.), respectively, 'independently; not subject to authority' and 'place to stand'.

26 Jus est ibi...purissimus doctrinae.] (Lt.), 'The right to teach exists where there is the purest fount of doctrine'.

27 *orthodox Turkey*] In 1858, De Quincey appended a footnote to this phrase (see below, p. 680, 230.26).

28 Sonnees...Sheeahs,] variants of, respectively, 'Sunni' and 'Shia'.

29 *'ubi passim...tramite pellit,'*] Horace, *Satires*, II.iii.48–9: 'Just as in a forest, where some error drives men to wander to and fro from the proper path, and this one goes off to the left and that one to the right'.

30 *'the world may...fall into error,'*] Donaldson, p. 2

31 *'In speaking...Church of Rome.'*] Donaldson, p. 121.

32 Furcae Caudinae,] (Lt.), literally, 'Caudine Forks', a narrow mountain pass in southern Italy where, in 321 BC, the Samnites defeated a Roman army. The Romans acknowledged the defeat by passing under a 'yoke' of Samnite spears, a further disgrace.

33 doctor seraphicus...inexpugnabilis] 'Doctor Seraphicus' is the name given to St Bonaventure (1221–74), leading medieval theologian. 'Doctor Inexpugnabilis' is the name given to Alexander of Hales (*c.* 1170–1245), theologian and philosopher, and an important influence on Bonaventure.

34 *young gentleman...studies...*Organon,] The logical treatises of Aristotle (see above, p. 535, n. 38) are collectively known as the *Organon* (Lt.), literally, 'tool' or 'instrument'. As a student at Oxford, De Quincey 'studied Aristotle's *Organon* throughout, and he meant to have given up that book in logic' (Morrison, p. 32).

35 Duns...Lombardus...magister sententiarum,] Joannes Duns Scotus (*c.* 1266–1308; *DNB*), Franciscan realist philosopher and scholastic theologian. Peter Lombard (*c.* 00–1160), Bishop of Paris whose *Four Books of Sentences* was the standard theological text of the Middle Ages. 'Magister sententiarum' (Lt.), 'master of opinions'.

36 *'no one...impartial judge.'*] Donaldson, p. 2.

37 *Calvin...Servetus to death,*] John Calvin (1509–64), French Protestant reformer and the founder of Calvinism. Michael Servetus (*c.* 1511–53), Spanish physician and theologian whose attack on the doctrine of the Trinity led to his condemnation as a heretic by both Protestants and Roman Catholics. He was burnt at the stake by Calvinists.

38 *Farrel,*] Calvin, *Letters*, vol. II, pp. 417–8: De Quincey cites Calvin's 26 October 1553 letter to Guillaume Farel (1489–1565). The Latin sentence is, 'I hope that it will be at least a capital sentence'.

39 *Sultzer...'Christian magistrates...undeniable;'*] Calvin, *Letters*, vol. II, pp. 409–12: De Quincey cites Calvin's 8 September 1553 letter to Simon Sulzer (1508–85).

40 *Simorg*] In 1858, De Quincey appended a footnote to this word, in which he explained the reference to Robert Southey's epic *Thalaba the Destroyer* (see below, p. 681, 233.20), VIII. 254–6: 'In Kaf the Simorg hath his dwelling-place, / The all-knowning Bird of Ages, who hath seen / The World, with all its children, thrice destroyed'.

41 *columns of Hercules*] more commonly, the 'Pillars of Hercules', two mountains at the Straits of Gibraltar, one in Europe and one in Africa. They have been variously identified.

42 *Coleridge's…Arnold's…sentimentalism,*] For Samuel Taylor Coleridge, see above, p. 556, n. 12. Thomas Arnold (1795–1842; *DNB*), educator, historian and scholar who published five volumes of sermons.

43 *p. ix…(Bunsen's)* Kirche der Zukunft;] The full reference is Donaldson, pp. ix-x. Christian Karl Josias, Freiherr von Bunsen (1791–1860), liberal Prussian diplomat and theologian, *Kirche der Zukunft* (*The Church of the Future*; 1845), which is quoted by Donaldson on a number of occasions (pp. 127, 160, 163, 188).

44 *Englandism…Jerry Benthamite:*] Jeremy Bentham (see above, p. 539, n. 26), *Church of Englandism and its Catechism examined* (1818).

45 *not less a son…than* Phil.] cf. *Suspiria de Profundis*, where De Quincey describes himself as a 'dutiful' child of 'a pure, holy, and magnificent church' (Vol. 15, p. 137).

46 *no royal road to geometry.*] the words of Euclid (see above, p. 537, n. 71) to Ptolemy I (Proclus, *Commentary on the First Book of Euclid's Elementa,* Prologue, Part Two).

47 *'inevitable assumptions…formal proof.'*] Donaldson, p. 70.

48 *Kant…indemonstrability of God.*] De Quincey refers to 'The Ideal of Pure Reason' in Kant, *CPR*, pp. 551–623.

49 vis apodeictica] (Lt.), 'demonstrative power'.

50 *Hercules forcing Cerberus up to day-light)*] In Greek mythology, Cerberus is the three-headed dog who guarded the entrance to the underwold. Heracles's final task was to overpower this monster.

51 *Koenigsberg*] Kant was born, spent his entire life and died in Königsberg, in East Prussia.

52 apodeixis,] (Lt.), 'demonstration'.

53 *(the* praktische vernunft.*)*] Kant, *Kritik der praktischen Vernunft* (*Critique of Practical Reason*, 1788).

54 *Clarke…schoolmen…Des Cartes*] Samuel Clarke (1675–1729; *DNB*), philosopher and theologian, best known for *A Demonstration of the Being and Attributes of God* (1705). The 'schoolmen' are the major philosophers of the thirteenth and fourteenth centuries, namely, St Thomas Aquinas (1224/5–74), Joannes Duns Scotus (*c.* 1266–*c.* 1308; *DNB*), and William Ockham (1285–1347; *DNB*). René Descartes (1596–1650), French mathematician, scientist and philosopher. Cf. De Quincey in his 1830 *Blackwood's* essay on 'Kant in his Miscellaneous Essays': 'God – does he exist by laws capable of a regular demonstration, as Des Cartes (borrowing from the Schoolmen), and, upon different grounds, Samuel Clarke, imagine?' (Vol. 7, p. 47).

55 *Kant…hollowness apparent.*] De Quincey refers to Descartes's version of the ontological argument in Book V of the *Meditations*, as opposed to the medieval version. Kant dismissed Descartes's argument in Kant, *CPR*, p. 569: 'Thus the famous ontological (Cartesian) proof of the existence of a highest being from concepts is only so much trouble and labor lost'.

56 *Kant called…in collision.*] see above, p. 560, n. 16.

57 *intertessellations (to use a learned word)*] 'Tessellate' means 'to make into a mosaic'. Under 'intertessellation' the *OED* cites only the present example from De Quincey.

58 Phil... *solemn degradation.*] 'The doctrine of plenary inspiration would make the most inspired book the work of a number of writing machines, and the legislator and prophet, the evangelist and apostle, would be degraded from their rational position to the rank of mesmeric dreamers and wooden automatons' (Donaldson, p. 50).

Protestantism {Part II}

1 reductio ad absurdum,] (Lt.), 'reduction to absurdity'.

2 locus classicus...verbatim et literatim] (Lt.), respectively, 'a classical source' and 'by word and letter'.

3 *St Paul (2 Tim., iii. 16.)*] In the King James version of the Bible, the passage is rendered thus: 'All scripture *is* given by inspiration of God, & *is* profitable for doctrine, for reproof, for correction, for instruction in righteousness'.

4 *St Luke...'the writings,'*] see Luke 24.

5 macht-spruch)] (Ger.), a legal decision made through the statement of someone in power, outside the general codified law.

6 *Luther...Zwingle...Knox*] For Martin Luther, see above, p. 537, n. 71. Huldrych Zwingli (1484–1351), Swiss Protestant reformer. John Knox (*c.* 1514–1572; *DNB*), foremost leader of the Scottish Reformation.

7 *Samaritan*] a member of a community of Jews that claims to be related by blood to those Jews of ancient Samaria.

8 *Jerome's Latin version,*] St Jerome (*c.* AD 347–*c.* 419), biblical translator and monastic leader.

9 *Coverdale's, in 1535),*] Miles Coverdale (*c.* 1488–1569; *DNB*), Bishop of Exeter, who translated the first printed English Bible in 1535

10 *Bentley...infidel of that day.*] Richard Bentley (see above, p. 541, n. 61) produced his *Remarks Upon a late Discourse of Free-Thinking...by Phileleutherus Lipsiensis* (1713) as a rebuttal to *A Discourse of Free-thinking* (1713) by Anthony Collins (1676–1729; *DNB*), prolific and provocative English Deist. Cf. Donaldson: 'The name, which I have placed, instead of my own, on the title-page, was suggested by that which was adopted under similar circumstances by Dr Bentley' (p. x). 'Phileleutherus Lipsiensis' (Lt.), 'freedom-loving follower of Lipsius'. Justus Lipsius (1547–1606), Flemish humanist and classical scholar.

11 *variety in the readings...seriously to consider it.*] De Quincey is thinking in particular of Bentley's comments from Section XXXII of his *Remarks*: 'If there had been but one manuscript of the Greek Testament at the restoration of learning about two centuries ago, then we had had no *various readings* at all....'Tis a good providence and a great blessing, that so many manuscripts of the New Testament are still amongst us' (Bentley, *Works*, vol. III, pp. 349–50).

12 *Anne's reign...Wetstein, the Dutchman,*] For Queen Anne, see above, p. 571, n. 60. De Quincey has confused Johann Rudolf Wettstein (1647–1711), a German Swiss classicist, with his son Johann Jakob Wettstein (1693–1754), a Biblical scholar celebrated for his edition of the New Testament, *Novum Testamentum Graecum: editionis receptae cum lectionibus variantibus codicum mss* (1751–2).

13 *Mill, the Englishman,*] John Mill (1645–1707; *DNB*), Principal of St Edmund Hall, Oxford. His 1707 edition of the Greek text of the *New Testament* was a great advance on any of its predecessors, as it included a critical apparatus that contained the readings of nearly 100 manuscripts.

14 *Griesbach, the German,*] Johann Jakob Griesbach, (1745–1812) Protestant German theologian, and the earliest biblical critic to subject the Gospels to systematic literary analysis.

15 *various readings...no difference...in the sense.*] 'So it is with the sacred text; make your 30,000 as many more...even put them into the hands of a knave or a fool, and yet...he shall not extinguish the light of any one chapter, nor so disguise Christianity but that every feature of it will still be the same' (Bentley, *Works*, vol. III, p. 360).

16 *camel...eye of a needle,*] Matthew 19: 24; cf. Shakespeare, *Richard II*, V.v.16–7.

17 *Warburton...old reading,* sea.] Shakespeare, *Hamlet*, III.i.58: 'Or to take arms against a sea of troubles'. De Quincey has in mind *The Works of Shakespear...with a comment and notes, critical and explanatory by Mr Pope and Mr Warburton* (1747). But the footnote in question appears in *The Works of Shakespear*, ed. Alexander Pope, 8 vols (London: Tonson, 1723–5), vol. VI, p. 400: 'Perhaps *siege*, which continues the metaphor of *slings, arrows, taking arms;* and represents the being encompass'd on all sides with troubles'.

18 *Partington...Atlantic ocean.*] De Quincey refers to a 12 October 1831 speech at Taunton by Sydney Smith (1771–1845; *DNB*), co-founder of the *Edinburgh Review* and a champion of Parliamentary reform: 'I do not mean to be disrespectful, but the attempt of the Lords to stop the progress of reform, reminds me very forcibly of the great storm at Sidmouth....Dame Partington, who lived upon the beach, was seen at the door of her house with mop and pattens, trundling her mop, squeezing out the sea-water, and vigorously pushing away the Atlantic Ocean. The Atlantic was roused. Mrs Partington's spirit was up; but I need not tell you that the contest was unequal. The Atlantic Ocean beat Mrs Partington' (*The Works of the Rev. Sydney Smith* (London: Longmans, Green, Reader, and Dyer, 1869), p. 664).

19 *forest...vast American possessions,*] cf. De Quincey in his 1832 *Blackwood's* review of John MacGregor's *British America*, where he discusses 'those tremendous fires which sometimes arise in the American forests, and spread havoc by circles of longitude and latitude' (Vol. 8, p. 174).

20 *Laud,*] William Laud (1573–1645; *DNB*), Archbishop of Canterbury and religious adviser to Charles I. De Quincey refers to the 'Wicked Bible' (1631), so called because the word 'not' was omitted from the Seventh Commandment. The mistake cost the King's printer, Robert Barker (d. 1645; *DNB*), a £200 fine.

21 *Star Chamber...'chapel.'*] The Star Chamber is an English court of law that evolved out of the medieval king's council. 'Chapel' means 'a printers' workshop' (*OED*).

22 'There are three...record in heaven,'] 1 John 5: 7.

23 *Travis...controversy;*] George Travis (1741–97; *DNB*), Archdeacon of Chester, whose *Letters to Edward Gibbon* (1784) defended the genuineness of 1 John 5: 7. In *Letters to Archdeacon Travis* (1790), Richard Porson (see above, p. 527, n. 11) conclusively proved the spuriousness of the disputed passage.

24 *Bentley tilting against Phalaris;*] Sir William Temple's *Essay upon the Ancient and Modern Learning* (1690) compared modern writers unfavourably and condescendingly with their classical counterparts, and praised in particular the epistles of Phalaris, a tyrant of Acragas in Sicily in the mid-sixth century BC. Bentley replied in *Epistles of Phalaris* (1699), in which he showed the letters to be forgeries written in Attic, not Sicilian Doric Greek, and mentioning several towns that were not in fact founded until long after the time of Phalaris. De Quincey discusses the Phalaris controversy at length in his 1830 *Blackwood's* essay on Bentley (Vol. 7, pp. 133–55).

25 *'to the end of time,'*] cf. Wordsworth, 'The Old Cumberland Beggar', ll. 107–9: 'authors of delight / And happiness, which to the end of time / Will live'.

26 *Babel is upon us;*] Genesis 11: 1–9.

27 gage d'amitié,] (Fr.), 'pledge of friendship'.

28 *elephant, that rests on a tortoise,*] In Hindu mythology, the tortoise Chukwa supports the elephant Maha-pudma, which upholds the world.

29 *first chapter of Genesis?*] Genesis 1: 3: 'And God said, Let there be light: and there was light'.

30 *'Annotations...Anatolia,'...phenomenon.*] De Quincey refers to James Yates (1789–1871; *DNB*) and his notes to Sir Charles Fellows (1799–1860; *DNB*), *A Journal written during an excursion in Asia Minor* (London: Murray, 1839), pp. 336–7. In 1858, De Quincey expanded this footnote with a reference to 'Generals Outram and Havelock' (see below, p. 682, 247.n. 2).

31 *Ishmael and Isaac!*] In the Old Testament, Ishmael and Isaac are the sons of Abraham (see above, p. 567, n. 56). Muslims believe the Arabs to be descendants of Ishmael. Isaac's son Jacob had twelve sons, traditionally the ancestors of the twelve tribes of Israel.

32 *Versailles cleave the air,*] The palace of Versailles was the principal residence of the kings of France for much of the eighteenth-century.

33 *Ulphilas...for his countrymen.*] more commonly, 'Ulfilas' (*c*. AD 311–*c*. 382), Christian bishop who evangelized the Goths, and wrote the earliest translation of the Bible into a Germanic language.

34 *One deep calleth to another.*] Psalms 42: 7: 'Deep calleth unto deep'.

35 *Terra del Fuego*] an archipelago, at the southern extremity of South America.

36 *Apollonius...eighth was missing.*] Apollonius of Perga (*c*. 262–*c*. 190 BC), mathematician, known as 'The Great Geometer'. The first four books of his *Conics* survive in the original Greek and the next three in Arabic translation. Book eight is lost.

37 *Bodleian...Halley...MS.*] The Bodleian is the library of the University of Oxford. Edmond Halley (1656–1742; *DNB*), astronomer and mathematician, who conjecturally restored the eighth book of Apollonius's *Conics*.

38 *Wallis, Savilian professor...algebra.*] John Wallis (1616–1703; *DNB*), mathematician, who in 1649 was appointed Savilian Professor of Geometry at the University of Oxford. In the English civil war (see above, p. 561, n. 46), he demonstrated his skill in mathematics by deciphering cryptic messages from Royalist partisans that had fallen into the hands of the Parliamentarians.

39 *Naseby*...proprio marte.] At the Battle of Naseby (14 June 1645), the Parliamentary New Model Army routed the royalists, and largely decided the first phase of the civil war. 'Proprio marte' (Lt.), means 'by his own struggle'.

40 *he published it.*] John Wallis, *Apollonii Pergaei Conicorum libri octo* (1710).

41 à fortiori] see above, p. 560, n. 18.

42 à plusieurs reprises.] (Fr.), 'several times'.

43 cordon sanitaire] 'a guarded line between infected and uninfected districts, to prevent intercommunication and spread of a disease' (*OED*).

44 presupposal] 'a "supposal" or supposition formed beforehand' (*OED*, which cites this example from De Quincey).

45 *'We admit...direct revelation.'*] Donaldson, pp. 50–1.

46 nychthemeron] (Gk.), 'night and day'.

47 *Daniel*...heptameron] For example, Daniel 5: 11: 'In the days of thy father light and understanding and wisdom like the wisdom of the gods, was found in him'. In 1858, De Quincey defined 'heptameron' as 'seven days' work of Creation and Rest', and expanded the footnote with a reference to 'Dr Arnold of Rugby' (see below, p. 684, 251.n.17).

48 *Euphrates)*] the largest river of western Asia.
49 *LXX.;*] an abbreviation for the Septuagint, the earliest extant Greek translation of the Old Testament from the original Hebrew.
50 coquette] In 1858, De Quincey appended a footnote to this word in which he referenced Virgil (see below, p. 684, n. 253.10).
51 *sorceress of Endor...must be correct.*] In the Old Testament (1 Samuel 28: 3–25), the Witch of Endor is a sorceress who prophesises the defeat and death of Saul, the first King of Israel.
52 *'Nescio quis teneros* oculus *mihi fascinat agnos?'*] Virgil, *Eclogues*, III. 103: 'Some evil eye bewitches my tender lambs'.
53 *'Oh, foolish Galatians, who hath bewitched you?'*] Galatians 3: 1.
54 *Aeolic digamma,*] The digamma was the sixth letter of the original Greek alphabet, and obsolete by the classical Greek period.
55 tabula...fascino;] respectively, 'tablet' and 'I bewitch'. In 1858, De Quincey expanded this footnote (see below, p. 684, 253.n.21).
56 *Medea...Erichtho...*Pharsalia.*)*] In Greek mythology, Medea is an enchantress who helped Jason to obtain the Golden Fleece. Erichtho is a Thessalian sorceress mentioned in Lucan, *Pharsalia*, VI. 507–826.
57 *Nebuchadnezzar's furnace,*] Daniel 3; for Nebuchadnezzar, see above (p. 529, n. 34).
58 *murderous judges and denouncers!*] De Quincey refers to the Salem witch trials (May-October 1692), in which nineteen convicted 'witches' were hanged and many other suspects imprisoned in the town of Salem in the Massachusetts Bay Colony. Public opinion first stopped, and then condemned, the trials.
59 *exterminate witches from the land?*] 1 Samuel 28: 3: 'and Saul had put away those that had familiar spirits, and the wizards out of the land'.
60 *Obeah man from Africa*] 'Obeah' is 'a kind of pretended sorcery or witchcraft practiced...in Africa' (*OED*); for details, see Alan Richardson, 'Romantic Voodoo: Obeah and British Culture, 1797–1807' in *Studies in Romanticism*, 32 (1993), pp. 3–28).
61 *preceding paragraph? – Ed.*] The editor of *Tait's* at this time was George Troup (1811–79). In 1858, De Quincey expanded this footnote with references to Maria Edgeworth, Samuel Taylor Coleridge and William Wordsworth (see below, p. 685, 254.n. 2).

Protestantism. {Part III}

1 *Newman...Puseyism...account.*] John Henry Newman (1801–90; *DNB*), theologian, *Essay on the Development of Christian Doctrine* (1845). Edward Bouverie Pusey (1800–82; *DNB*), theologian. Both Newman and Pusey were leading members of the Oxford Movement (1833–45), a group of theologians centred at the University of Oxford who sought a renewal of 'catholic' thought and practice within the Church of England. In 1845 Newman became a Roman Catholic; Pusey remained an Anglican.
2 Phil...*general dislike...Puseyites,*] for example, Donaldson, p. 32: 'Add to this the foppish and coxcombical imitation of medieval practices which has directly emanated from the aesthetical adjuncts of Oxford Theology...and it will not, we think, be maintained...that the effects of this movement have been unmixed good to the religious mind of this country'.
3 *Wordsworth,*] If De Quincey has remembered the date correctly, he was walking with William Wordsworth (see above, p. 527, n. 12) in 1828, at a time when their closest intimacy had long since passed.

4 *Helvellyn,*] one of the principal summits in the Lake District in north-west England. It lies behind the lakes of Thirlmere and Ullswater.

5 *'Excursion,'...*regeneration.] Wordsworth, *The Excursion* (1814), V. 279–85:

And when the pure
And consecrating element hath cleansed
The original stain, the child is there received
Into the second ark, Christ's church, with trust
That he, from wrath redeemed, therein shall float
Over the billows of this troublesome world
To the fair land of everlasting life.

6 *Christopher Wordsworth*] see above, p. 560, n. 31.

7 *'sans phrase,'*] (Fr.),'without mincing one's words'.

8 *Trinity...St John's permission),*] Trinity and St John's are colleges of the University of Cambridge. Christopher Wordsworth was Master of Trinity, 1820–41.

9 *'and which...superstitions.'*] Donaldson, p. 36.

10 *Barrow...Newton...Bentley...Trinity,*] Isaac Barrow (1630–77; *DNB*), divine and author of *Exposition of the Creed, Decalogue and Sacraments* (1669). For Isaac Newton, see above, p. 565, n. 23. For Richard Bentley, see above, p. 541, n. 61. All three were members of Trinity College.

11 Phil. *is certainly a Trinity man.*] De Quincey is right. Donaldson matriculated at Trinity College in 1831, and was fellow and tutor until 1840.

12 *Bacon belonged to this College.*] Francis Bacon (see above, p. 578, n. 3) was a member of Trinity College.

13 *Milton...Trinity, nor Jeremy Taylor;*] John Milton (see above, p. 526, n. 55) was a member of Christ's College, Cambridge. Jeremy Taylor (see above, p. 570, n. 52) was a member of Gonville and Caius College, Cambridge.

14 *Lambeth...Newcastle for coals.*] In 1805, Christopher Wordsworth (see above, p. 560, n. 31) was appointed domestic chaplain to Charles Manners-Sutton (1755–1828; *DNB*), Archbishop of Canterbury. Lambeth Palace is the London residence of the Archbishop of Canterbury. Cf. Walter Scott in his 1822 letter to Joanna Baillie: 'I am seriously tempted, though it would be sending coals to Newcastle with a vengeance, not to mention salt to Dysart, and all other superfluous importations' (J. G. Lockhart, *The Life of Sir Walter Scott*, 10 vols (Edinburgh: Constable, 1902–3), vol. VII, p. 6).

15 *Delphi...Ammon had vanished.*] The oracle of Jupiter Ammon was in the Libyan desert, and its fame at one time rivaled that of Delphi (see above, p. 559, n. 4).

16 *Rydal water,*] Rydal Water is situated between Ambleside and Grasmere in the English Lake District. Wordsworth lived at Rydal Mount. De Quincey lived in The Nab, an old farmhouse at the edge of Rydal Water (Lindop, p. 206).

17 *Barley Wood (Hannah More's).*] De Quincey knew Hannah More (1745–1833; *DNB*), and was first brought into her circle when he was a young boy of about eight and his mother moved to Bath. More was the leading representative of Evangelicalism in the area, and the two women soon became close friends. In 1801, More moved to Barley Wood, a house near Wrington, in Somerset. For De Quincey's 1833 *Tait's* essay on Hannah More, see Vol. 9, pp. 323–57; see also, Grevel Lindop, 'Pursuing the Throne of God: De Quincey and the Evangelical Revival' in *The Charles Lamb Bulletin*, 52 (1985), pp. 97–111.

18 *tracts of the Puseyites,*] The ideas of the Oxford Movement were published in ninety *Tracts for the Times* (1833–41). When Newman left for Rome, Pusey fought to prevent others from following. His supporters became known as 'Puseyites'.

19 ad interim] (Lt.),'in the meantime'.

20 *'Oh, no...don't* you?'] Donaldson, p. 168. Robert Robinson (1735–90; *DNB*), Baptist minister and hymn-writer.

21 quoad *the* scire...quoad *the* esse;] respectively, (Lt.), 'insofar as the knowing' and 'insofar as the being'.

22 habemus confitentem.] (Lt.), 'we have him confessing'.

23 'Compel them to come in!'] Luke 14: 23.

24 'To your tents, oh Israel!'] see 1 Kings 12: 16 and 2 Chronicles 10: 16.

25 *'Rebellion...sin of witchcraft.'*] 1 Samuel 15: 23.

26 *Algernon Sydney,*] Algernon Sidney (see above, p. 577, n. 77), *Discourses Concerning Government* (1698).

27 *'Filmer's* Patriarcha.'...*answering him.*] Sir Robert Filmer (*c.* 1588–1653; *DNB*), political theorist, who in *Patriarcha* (1680) championed the divine right of kings. John Locke (1632–1704; *DNB*), philosopher, refuted Filmer in the first of his *Two Treatises of Government* (1690).

28 *'The right...to govern wrong'*] Pope, *The Dunciad*, IV. 188.

29 'How readest thou?'...*Christ himself;*] Luke 10: 26: 'What is written in the law? how readest thou?'.

30 *'all prisoners and captives;'*] from 'The Litany' in *The Book of Common Prayer* (see below, p. 687. 261.12).

31 *restraints of the Koran.*] In 1858, De Quincey expanded this passage and appended a footnote on the 'Bee-like limitation of prophetic vision' (see below, p. 688, 261.33).

32 ascripti glebae] (Lt.), 'bound to the land'. In 1858, De Quincey expanded this passage, and appended a long footnote detailing 'hideous abuses' (see below, p. 688, 261.31–3).

33 *Bald, a Scottish engineer,*] Robert Bald (1776–1861), author and engineer.

34 *Northumberland and Durham,*] counties in northeastern England.

35 *'Ah!...cheerful Scotland.'*] Robert Bald, *A general view of the coal trade of Scotland* (Edinburgh: Oliphant and Brown, 1808; 2nd edn, 1812). De Quincey, however, has misremembered the reference, for there is no such anecdote in either edition. In MS B, De Quincey indicated his own uncertainty regarding the reference when he told the compositor he gave 'the sense of Mr B., not his words which I do not recollect'.

36 *in Scottish mines,*] cf. the Scottish judge and writer Henry Cockburn (1779–1854; *DNB*) in his posthumously published *Memorials of his Time* (1856): 'There are few people who now know that so recently as 1799 there were slaves in this country. Twenty-five years before, that is, in 1775, there must have been thousands of them; for this was then the condition of all our colliers and salters. They were literally slaves' (*Memorials of his Time*, ed. Karl F. C. Miller (Chicago: University of Chicago Press, 1974), p. 70).

37 *Cumberland...*ascripti metallo,] For Cumberland, see above, p. 576, n. 46. 'Ascripti metallo' (Lt.), 'bound to the mine'.

38 *public charity, when did it commence?*] In 1858, De Quincey greatly expanded this passage, and appended four new footnotes (see below, p. 691, 262.25–263.23).

39 *Constantine...Christian...throne.*] Constantine the Great (*c.* 285–337), sole Roman emperor, AD 324–37. He was the first Roman emperor to profess Christianity.

40 *Shakspere...male tiger.*] Shakespeare, *Coriolanus*, V.iv.27–8: 'There is no more mercy in him than there is milk in a male tiger'.

41 *Cicero...such beautiful Ethics,*] Cicero (see above, p. 530, n. 47) was the author of several ethical treatises, of which the most noted is the *De Officiis*.

42 *old women...without tasting food.*] Cicero, *Tusculan Disputations*, II. 40. 'Old women often endure going without food for two or three days: take away an athlete's food for a single day...he will cry out that he cannot endure it'.

43 'Oh, fortunatam natam me Consule Romam!'] De Quincey quotes Cicero, *De suo Consulatu*. The wretched quality of the line has been much ridiculed, and most famously by Juvenal, *Satire*, X. 123: '"O happy Fate for the Roman State / Was the date of my great Consulate!"'.

44 *This case illustrates...external violence.*] In 1858, De Quincey expanded this passage (see below, p. 691, 262.25–263.23).

45 *Timour,*] more commonly, 'Timur' or 'Tamerlane' (1336–1405), Turkic conqueror of Islamic faith, chiefly remembered for the barbarity of his conquests from Russia and India to the Mediterranean Sea.

46 (To be concluded in our next.)] There were no further instalments.

War

1 *associations...abolishing war.*] With the conclusion of the Napoleonic Wars, peace societies were established throughout America and Europe. The New York Peace Society was founded in 1815, and The Society for the Promotion of Universal and Permanent Peace, often known as the London Peace Society, was founded in 1816.

2 *Ceylon...legend is attached.*] De Quincey's source for this legend has not been traced.

3 aura textilis] (Lt.), 'woven breeze'.

4 *avoirdupois,*] system of weights based on a pound of 16 ounces.

5 *Rothschild,*] The Rothschild banking dynasty was founded by Mayer Amschel Rothschild (1744–1812). All five of his sons were made barons of the Austrian Empire.

6 *P. P. C.*] 'pour prendre congé' (Fr.), 'to take leave'.

7 *perpetual peace,*)] De Quincey alludes to Immanuel Kant (see above, p. 560, n. 16) and his essay *Toward Perpetual Peace: A Philosophical Project* (1795), perhaps the most widely read of his informal works. The treatise is thought to have been inspired by the conclusion of the Treaty of Basle on 5 April 1795.

8 *Birmingham...depended on rifles.*] Conrad Gill, *History of Birmingham*, 2 vols (London: Oxford University Press, 1952), vol. I, p. 98: the gun trade flourished in early nineteenth-century Birmingham, 'but it was an unhealthy boon, caused by the Napoleonic war....When peace returned there was a serious reaction and much unemployment'.

9 *Carron...carronades.*] A carronade is a short, large-calibre cannon. The name derives from Cannon, near Falkirk in Scotland, where this kind of cannon was first made.

10 *Poverty...necessary for man.*] cf. below, p. 596, n. 37. In revision, De Quincey expanded this passage (see below, p. 699, 271.19–34).

11 *Scripture...ineradicable...land.*] Deuteronomy 15: 11: 'For the poor shall never cease out of the land'.

12 *Themistocles.*] Themistocles (*c.* 524–*c.* 460 BC), Athenian politician and naval strategist.

13 'Pereant qui ante nos nostra dixerunt!'] (Lt.), 'Confound those who have said our remarks before us'. The phrase is attributed to Aelius Donatus (*fl.* mid-fourth century AD), grammarian and rhetorician, by St Jerome (*c.* 342–420) in his *Commentary*

on Ecclesiastes (*Patrologiae cursus completes*, 221 vols (Paris: Migne, 1844–64), vol. XXIII, col. 1019).

14 *Scotland to truth?*] Samuel Johnson (see above, p. 537, n. 3) claimed that 'a Scotsman must be a sturdy moralist, who does not prefer Scotland to truth' (Boswell, vol. V, p. 110).

15 *Suetonius*...Father of lies.] Suetonius (*c.* AD 69–122), Roman antiquarian and biographer best known for his *De vita Caesarum* (*Lives of the Caesars*). Herodotus (see above, p. 564, n. 7) is called the 'father of history' in Cicero, *De Legibus*, I.i.5; cf. De Quincey in his 1842 *Blackwood's* essay on the 'Philosophy of Herodotus' (Vol. 13, p. 83).

16 *Augustan history...French memoirs,*] The *Augustan History* (or *Historia Augusta*) is the name given to a collection of biographies of Roman emperors from Hadrian (AD 76–138) to Numerianus (d. AD 284). Numerous works in French include the term 'Mémoires', but De Quincey may be thinking specifically of Louis de Rouvroy, duc de Saint-Simon (1675–1755). His *Mémoires* cover the later years of Louis XIV and then the Regency, and are a vivid blend of fact and petty intrigue. Cf. De Quincey's discussion of 'the quality of historical narratives' in his 1832 *Blackwood's* essay on 'James's History of Charlemagne' (Vol. 8, p. 186).

17 *Codrus, Timoleon...Tell...Milton,*] Codrus, traditionally the last King of Athens. For Timoleon, see above, p. 578, n. 78. William Tell, legendary Swiss hero. For John Milton, see above, p. 526, n. 55.

18 propos...mot,] (Fr.), respectively, 'remark' and 'word'.

19 *Talleyrand...de Ligne...Voltaire,*] For Talleyrand, see below, p. 599, n. 85. Charles-Joseph, prince de Ligne (1735–1814), Belgian military officer and man of letters. For Voltaire, see above, p. 570, n. 56.

20 *Brougham,*] For Henry Brougham, see above, p. 577, n. 69.

21 tournure] (Fr.), 'turn of phrase'.

22 *Fabricius*] Johann Albert Fabricius (1668–1736), German classical scholar, *Bibliotheca Graeca* (1705–28).

23 *Goldsmith...goodness to be born.*] De Quincey's calculation is out by two decades. Oliver Goldsmith (see above, pp. 307–31) died in 1774. Talleyrand was born twenty years earlier in 1754.

24 *Goldsmith's Essays.*] In his periodical *The Bee* for 20 October 1759, Goldsmith observed that 'the true use of speech is not so much to express our wants as to conceal them' (Goldsmith, *CW*, vol. I, p. 394).

25 *Hierocles...Laertius...Plutarch...Athenaeus.*] De Quincey has in mind a little-known grammarian named Hierocles, who co-authored a collection of some two hundred and sixty witticisms (see *Philogelos Hieroclis et Philagrii facetiae*, ed. Alfred Eberhard (Ebeling, 1869)). Diogenes Laërtius (*fl.* third century), Greek author celebrated for his *Lives, Teachings, and Sayings of Famous Philosophers*. Plutarch (*c.* AD 46–*c.* 120), biographer and author whose works include the *Parallel Lives*. Athenaeus (*fl. c.* AD 200), Greek grammarian and author *The Gastronomers*.

26 Anno Domini...*Julian...Olympiads,*] For 'Anno Domini', see above, p. 555, n. 64. The Julian calendar was introduced in 46 BC, and fixed the ordinary year at three hundred and sixty five days. An Olympiad is one of the four-year intervals by which time was calculated in ancient Greece.

27 *Nabonassar,*] Nabonassar was the founder of the Babylonian and Chaldean kingdom. The so-called 'era of Nabonassar' commenced 26 February 747 BC, the day of

Nabonassar's accession. The date was used by Ptolemy in his astronomical calculations.

28 *'Anecdotes,'...Procopius.*] Procopius (*c.* AD 500–*c.* 562), Byzantine historian, *Anecdota* (*Secret History*).

29 *Justinian...Theodora, Narses, Belisarius,*] Justinian I (AD 483–565), Byzantine emperor, 527–65. Theodora (*c.* AD 497–548), Byzantine empress and wife of Justianian I. Narses (*c.* AD 480–574) and Belisarius (*c.* AD 505–565), Byzantine generals.

30 *French anecdote...window...English anecdote... correspond.*] The source of these anecdotes has not been traced.

31 *Louvois...royal master*] François-Michel Le Tellier, Marquis de Louvois (1639–91), Secretary of State for War under Louis XIV (see above, p. 546, n. 72).

32 Areopagus,] the name of the highest court in ancient Athens.

33 nisus] (Lt.) striving / effort.

34 *Carter*] For an account of 'Carter, the American "lion King"', see Richard D. Altick, *The Shows of London* (Cambridge, Mass.: Harvard University Press, 1978), p. 226.

35 *Castor and Pollux.*] see above, p. 573, n. 98.

36 *Navarino,*] The Battle of Navarino (20 October 1827) was a decisive naval engagement in the War of Greek Independence against Turkey. The battle took place in the Bay of Navarin in the southwestern Peloponnese.

37 Primâ facie,] see above, p. 540, n. 54.

38 *'That God's...his daughter.'*] Wordsworth (see above, p. 527, n. 12), 'Ode 1815', ll. 106–9 (inexact).

39 condottieri] 'A professional military leader or captain, who raised a troop, and sold his service to states or princes at war' (*OED*).

40 *'strike at their faces, cavalry,'*] Pharsalia was the decisive battle of the Roman civil war (48 BC) in which Julius Caesar (see above, p. 530, n. 47) defeated Pompey (see above, p. 543, n. 26). De Quincey's reference is to Appian (*fl.* second century AD), Greek historian, *Roman History*, The Civil Wars, II. 78: Caesar's cohorts 'advanced to meet the cavalry, and with spears elevated aimed at the faces of the riders, who could not endure the enemy's savagery'.

41 *Xenophon...king:*] Xenophon (431–*c.* 350 BC), Greek historian, *Cyropaedia*, VIII.vi.16.

42 *Sovereign Lady,*] For Queen Victoria, see above, p. 547, n. 81.

43 τελευταιον ἐπιγεννημα,] 'final growth / creation'.

44 *contemplation of nation debts,*] Financial constraints did not prevent De Quincey from urging England to consider war. Cf. his 1830 *Blackwood's* essay on 'France and England': 'War, indeed, is now possible upon other grounds...and some of them are such as may almost compel England, however crippled by her financial condition...to move in that direction' (Vol. 7, p. 208).

45 *St John...herald of Christ,)*] St John the Baptist (*fl.* early first century AD), Jewish prophet revered in the Christian Church as the forerunner of Jesus Christ. Midsummer Day is 24 June, celebrated as the feast of the nativity of St John the Baptist.

46 *General Gardanne.*] It is unclear who De Quincey intends, but General Gaspard Amédée Gardanne (1758–1807) died while on a mission to Silesia.

47 *flowery people,*] One of the Chinese names for China is 'Zhong hua guo' ('Middle Flowery Kingdom').

48 facit,] (Lt.), 'achievement'.

49 *wish was father to that thought.*] Shakespeare, *2 Henry IV,* IV.v.91: 'Thy wish was father, Harry, to that thought'.

50 *fields are white for harvest.*] cf. John 4: 35: 'Look on the fields: for they are white already to harvest'.

51 Consolato del Mare] The 'Consulship of the sea' was the name of a written code of international laws of the thirteenth century for regulating the commerce of the Mediterranean. It consisted of a tribunal of leading merchants authorized to determine disputes.

52 *Spartan warfare*] In revision, De Quincey appended a footnote to this phrase (see below p. 703, 283.21).

53 *Great Western Express,*] The Great Western Railway ran between Bristol and London. The line opened in 1841.

54 *Robinson Crusoe...Friday...earth.*] see above, p. 546, n. 71.

55 Spectator's *culinary music,*] De Quincey's reference is to *The Spectator* for 21 July 1714: 'upon which he called for a Cas-Knife, and applying the Edge of it to his Mouth, converted it into a musical Instrument, and entertained me with an *Italian* Solo' (*Spectator*, vol. IV, p. 545).

56 War to the knife] 'deadly strife'; cf. Byron, *Childe Harold's Pilgrimage*, I.lxxxvi.890: 'War, war is still the cry, "War even to the knife!"'.

57 Qui tam *and* Scire facias,] 'Qui tam' is an abbreviated form of 'qui tam pro domino rege quam pro sic ipso in hoc parte sequitur' (Lt.), 'who as well for the king as for himself sues in this matter'. Qui tam actions were a way for private citizens to gain access to royal courts. 'Scire facias' (Lt.), 'you should let [a party] know', an obsolete writ for processes based on the record.

58 jus gentium] see below, p. 621, n. 18.

59 causa teterrima,] see below, p. 603, n. 77.

60 *Jersey...Hampshire, Dorset...jail-delivery.*] Jersey is the largest and southernmost of the Channel Islands, located twelve miles west of the Cotentin peninsula of France. Hampshire and Dorset are English counties bordered to the south by the English Channel.

61 euphuismus;] In revision, De Quincey defined this word as 'the sweet, caressing mode of expressing the case' (see below, p. 705, 285.n.1).

62 *trade in slaves.*] Britain abolished the slave trade in 1807. It was declared illegal in Venezuela and Mexico in 1810. In 1817 Spain agreed to abolish the slave trade. Chile freed its black slaves in 1823.

63 *Essay on Perpetual Peace,*] 'Toward Perpetual Peace: A Philosophical Project' in Kant, *Practical Philosophy*, ed. Mary J. Gregor (Cambridge: Cambridge University Press, 1996), pp. 317–8: 'No treaty of peace shall be held to be such if it is made with a secret reservation of material for a future war'.

64 *castrametation...poliorcetics,*] respectively, 'the art or science of laying out a camp' (*OED*), and 'the art of conducting and resisting sieges' (*OED*, which cites this example from De Quincey).

65 *subject of a second.*] De Quincey did not write a second instalment.

66 *who (like myself) deny it.*] In revision, De Quincey greatly altered and expanded the conclusion of the essay (see below, p. 706, 288.26–34).

Sortilege on Behalf of the Glasgow Athenaeum.

1 *bread...allowance of Paris;*] In 1846 a crop failure quickly developed into a full-scale economic crisis throughout France. Food became scarce, and had to be rationed. Remarkably, De Quincey is writing at precisely the moment of the third French Rev-

olution, for he dates his essay 24 February 1848, the day Louis-Philippe (1773–1850) abdicated.

2 à discrétion.] see above, p. 555, n. 9.

3 *Newmarket start*,] For Newmarket, see above, p. 581, n. 24.

4 *pitch-plasters.*] Plasters 'made of pitch, formerly used to remove hair' (*OED*).

5 *Portia,*] In Shakespeare's *The Merchant of Venice*, IV. i, Portia (as Balthazar) is arbiter in the case between Antonio and Shylock.

6 *west...Athenaeum,*] De Quincey is in Mavis Bush Cottage, Lasswade, outside Edinburgh, and he looks west toward Glasgow.

7 *Greek adage...mending every day*;] De Quincey is perhaps drawing on Plutarch, *Parallel Lives*, Solon, II. 2: 'he would say that he "grew old ever learning many things"'.

8 *Brutus...stroke of Caesar,*] Suetonius, *De vita Caesarum*, I. 82: Caesar 'was stabbed with three and twenty wounds...when Marcus Brutus rushed at him, he said in Greek, "You too, my child?"'.

9 *old love-letter of my writing,*] cf. De Quincey in *Confessions*: 'Sometimes I wrote letters of business for cottagers...more often I wrote love-letters to their sweethearts for young women' (Vol. 2, p. 20).

10 Esse quam videri...*Barmecide banquets),*] The Latin phrase is literally 'to be rather than to seem'; see Cicero, *de Amnicitia*, 26. In *The Arabian Nights' Entertainment*, Barmecide is a wealthy man who gives a beggar a feast consisting of ornate but empty dishes; hence, a giver of illusory benefits. In 1858, De Quincey appended a footnote to this passage (see below, p. 709, 293.42).

11 *'a dun.'*] 'a demand for payment' (*OED*).

12 *Goodwin Sands,*] Goodwin Sands are dangerous sandbanks located approximately five miles off the east coast of Kent in southern England.

13 *Gorgonian*] In Greek mythology, the Gorgon was a monster figure.

14 *in 30 seconds you'll founder!'*] cf. De Quincey in 'The English Mai-Coach': 'Sail on the weather-beam! Down she comes upon us; in seventy seconds she will founder!' (see above, p. 444).

15 *fee simple...fee conditional,'*] in 'absolute' and 'conditional' possession.

16 numero deus impare gaudet;] Virgil, *Eclogues*, VIII. 75: 'In an uneven number heaven delights'.

17 *'ploitered'*] 'To work in an ineffective way' (*OED*, which cites this example from De Quincey).

18 carte blanche] (Fr.), literally, 'blank slate'.

19 *17...Llangollen...distant.*] In *Confessions*, De Quincey describes how at seventeen he bent his 'steps toward North Wales...wandering about for some time in Denbighshire, Merionethshire, and Caernarvonshire' (Vol. 2, p. 18). Llangollen is a market town in Clwyd county, North Wales.

20 *X Y Z,*] De Quincey's signature for many of his *London Magazine* articles, including 'Letters to a Young Man whose Education has been Neglected' and 'On the Knocking at the Gate in *Macbeth*' (see Vol. 3).

21 aerugo,] see above, p. 529, n. 29.

22 *Cambria;*] Wales.

23 *'Stout Glo'ster ...quivering lance.'*] Thomas Gray, 'The Bard', ll. 13–4.

24 *Pythian*] 'Of or relating to Delphi, or to the oracle and priestess Apollo there' (*OED*).

25 *Heracleidae to the Peloponnesus.*] The return of the mythical Heracleidae (see above, p. 534, n. 17) is often associated with the Dorian invasion of Greece in the twelfth century BC.

26 à priori] see above, p. 522, n. 78.

27 *Macrobius.*] Ambrosius Theodosius Macrobius, (*fl.* AD 400), Latin grammarian and philosopher best known for his *Saturnalia*. But De Quincey seems to have taken the idea from St Augustine's refutation of astrology in his *City of God*, V. 2: 'But arbitrarily to drag in the position of the sky and the stars at the time of conception or birth...this is a strange piece of arrogance'.

28 *subdivisibilities...central moments.*] cf. De Quincey in 'Savannah-la-Mar': 'You see, therefore, how narrow, how incalculably narrow, is the true and actual present....For again subdivide that solitary drop' (Vol. 15, p. 186).

29 rouleau] 'a number of gold coins made up into a cylindrical packet' (*OED*).

30 *'all right behind;'*] cf. Charles Dickens, *Nicholas Nickleby*, ed. Paul Schlicke (Oxford: Oxford University Press, 1998), p. 50: '"All right behind there, Dick?" cried the coachman'.

31 *perfect start...Doncaster.*] Doncaster is in South Yorkshire, and one of the oldest centres of horse racing in England.

32 *Archimedes...decent circle;*] For Archimedes, see above, p. 540, n. 44.

33 *Vandyking*] Sir Anthony Van Dyck (1599–1641), the most eminent Flemish painter of the seventeenth century. 'Vandyking' means 'the drawing or sketching of portraits' (*OED*); De Quincey extends the meaning here to include figures cut out with scissors.

34 n'entendent pas la raillerie] (Fr.), 'are very touchy (on that point)'.

35 *Greenwich time...*Empyreum] The Greenwich meridian serves as the basis for the world's standard time zone system. The 'Empyreum' is 'the fiery heaven or sphere of fire' (*OED*).

36 *perpetual motion,*] Perpetual-motion machines cannot work because they violate the laws of thermodynamics.

Forster's Life of Oliver Goldsmith

1 *'dwell apart.'*] The phrase is common, but De Quincey has in mind Wordsworth, 'Milton! Thou should'st be living at this hour', l. 9: 'Thy soul was like a Star and dwelt apart'.

2 *verses...academic destination.*] Goldsmith had originally been intended for 'a common trade', but was sent to the University of Dublin based on 'some verses he had written at Elphin School, and other evidence of some liveliness of talent, being suddenly brought to light' (Forster, p. 11).

3 *Charles I...his features.*] For Charles I, see above, p. 558, n. 40. The 'keen Italian judge of physiognomy' has not been identified.

4 *Cornelius Agrippa*] Heinrich Cornelius Agrippa von Nettesheim (1486–1535), physician, philosopher and occultist best known for *De occulta philosophia* (1529).

5 *'Prophet...seven years...scaffold.'*] The English Civil War began in 1642. Charles I was beheaded on 30 January 1649. Cf. De Quincey in *Confessions*: 'I had also, though no great reader of history, made myself minutely and critically familiar with one period of English history, viz. the period of the Parliamentary War' (Vol. 2, pp. 67–8).

6 *Goldsmith's depressions;*] De Quincey has in mind Forster's observation that, near the end of Goldsmith's life, 'his spirits were...unusually depressed and uncertain, and...his health had become visibly impaired' (Forster, p. 663).

7 *'a knack of hoping'*] De Quincey quotes the 'philosophic vagabond' in *The Vicar of Wakefield*: 'No person ever had a better knack of hoping than I' (Goldsmith, *CW*, vol. IV, p. 107).

8 *Ormus...Ind...Delhi.*] 'Ormus' is an island in the Persian Gulf, now known as Hormuz, and famous for pearls. 'Ind' means 'India', the capital of which is Delhi. De Quincey invokes Milton, *Paradise Lost*, II. 1–2: 'High on a throne of royal state, which far / Outshone the wealth of Ormus and of Ind'.

9 'Doctor minor,'...major...*melancholy*;] De Quincey refers to a Boswellian anecdote concerning a drunken assistant from Eton College who referred to Johnson as 'Dr *Major*' and Goldsmith as 'Dr *Minor*'. 'Goldsmith was excessively hurt by this. He afterwards spoke of it himself' (Boswell, vol. V, p. 97).

10 *bodily wretchedness...Wife...he had not.*] De Quincey is of course speaking of himself here, for his own bodily sufferings and large family contrast tellingly with Goldsmith's 'habitual cheerfulness' and 'solitude'.

11 *reader...eminent printing-office.*] cf. De Quincey in *Confessions*: 'As a corrector of Greek proofs (if in no other way), I might doubtless have gained enough for my slender wants' (Vol. 2, p. 28).

12 *tub...old tar-barrel:*] Diogenes (*c.* 400–325 BC), archetype of the Greek philosophical sect known as the Cynics, and the subject of numerous apocryphal stories, including one in which he lived in a tub of earthenware (see Diogenes Laertius, *Lives of Eminent Philosophers*, Diogenes, VI. 23).

13 *Casaubon...tub...quite past repair.*] The reference here is somewhat confused, but De Quincey seems most likely to have in mind Gilles Ménage (1613–92), French scholar and man of letters, who in 1692 produced a popular variorum edition of Diogenes Laertius's *Lives of the Eminent Philosophers*, which featured a discussion of the materials of Diogenes the Cynic's tub. Ménage thinks it must have been made of wood: 'Testaceum non fuisse Diogenis dolium, sed legneum'. He also quotes Juvenal, *Satire*, XIV. 308–10: 'The nude Cynic fears no fire for his tub; if broken, he will make himself a new house to-morrow, or keep it repaired with clamps of lead'. Ménage's edition features notes by Isaac Casaubon (see above, p. 557, n. 1), which has led De Quincey to associate the reference with him, though Casaubon is not cited in this part of the discussion.

14 *Ali Baba's house;*] De Quincey refers to *The Arabian Nights' Entertainment*, and the tale of 'Ali Baba and the Forty Thieves'.

15 *Grub Street,*] For Grub Street, see above, p. 578, n. 79. 'Samuel Johnson...was but a Grub Street man...when Goldsmith entered Grub Street' (Forster, p. 73).

16 *Forster... untenable refinement.*] 'The patron was gone; and the public had not come. The seller of books had as yet exclusive command over the destiny of those who wrote them; and he was difficult of access; without certain prospect of the trade wind, hard to move' (Forster, pp. 69–70).

17 en grand costume,] (Fr.), 'in full dress'; 'on the grand scale'.

18 *golden pippin.*] The 'golden pippin' is a variety of apple.

19 *patronage*] cf. De Quincey's 1821 comments to Richard Woodhouse: '"Now," said the Opium-Eater, "the word Patron is a favorite word with me, from its association with those high & noble instances of patronage, about the age of Elizabeth"' (Morrison, p. 12).

20 Enquiry...*subscription papers:*] In his *Enquiry into the Present State of Polite Learning in Europe* (1759), Goldsmith argues that 'Every encouragement given to stupidity, when known to be such, is a negative insult to genius. This appears in nothing more evident than the undistinguished success of those who solicit subscriptions' (Forster, p. 174).

21 *Horace...Martial*] For Horace, see above p. 535, n. 40. Martial (*c.* AD 40–*c.* 103), Roman poet and epigrammatist.

22 *dedications...Goldsmith's period;*] cf. De Quincey to Woodhouse: 'The Dedicators of the next age, rather insinuated than expressly assigned to those they addressed all the virtues & perfections incident to humanity....Even Addison has too much of this – see the prefaces to his *Spectators*. But I was about to observe that, whether for this, or some other reason, the word Patron has fallen into unrepute' (Morrison, p. 13).

23 auctoritas] see above, p. 530, n. 56.

24 In-I-go Jones.] Edward Jones broke into Buckingham Palace at least three times between December 1838 and March 1841. Charles Dickens visited him in prison. For details, see Edna Healey, *The Queen's House: A Social History of Buckingham Palace* (London: Michael Joseph, 1997), pp. 149–50. The nickname plays on the famous Inigo Jones (see above, p. 563, n. 71), painter, architect and designer.

25 au courant] 'conversant'; 'fully informed'.

26 *'Non Dî...columnae.'*] Horace, *Ars Poetica*, l. 373: 'that poets be of middling rank, neither men nor gods nor booksellers ever brooked'.

27 vox populi] (Lt.), 'voice of the people'.

28 *(Sir Walter Scott...Ivanhoe)*] Sir Walter Scott (see above, p. 537, n. 70), *Ivanhoe* (1819).

29 *All novels...hurrying to decay;*] cf. De Quincey's 1830 observation that the novelist strives 'to realize an ideal; and to reproduce the actual world under more harmonious arrangements'. De Quincey's daughter later observed that 'he simply lived in the romances of his youth. He cared nothing for delineations of character, and I do not think he cared much for pictures of modern life, or even for fun or humour – at all events of the later type, in novels' (Vol. 7, p. 290; Japp, p. 439).

30 *Smollett...Fielding...Richardson,*] Tobias Smollett (1721–71; *DNB*), novelist best known for *The Expedition of Humphry Clinker* (1771). Henry Fielding (see above, p. 581, n. 21), whose *Tom Jones* (1749) features a vast gallery of characters, including the cantankerous Squire Western. Samuel Richardson (1689–1761; *DNB*), novelist celebrated for *Clarissa* (1747–8).

31 *two leading nations...earth.*] 'Our own and the French', as De Quincey makes plain in his 1857 revisions (see below, p. 712, 315.29).

32 canaille] (Fr.), 'rabble, riffraff'.

33 *Sues...manufacturing towns.*] see above, p. 524, n. 15.

34 *revolutionary age...unsettled his brain.*] De Quincey has in mind most prominently the third French Revolution, which took place in February 1848, just three months before he published this review.

35 'quoquo *modo scripta delectat;')*] Pliny the Younger, *Letters*, V.viii.4: 'Oratory and poetry win small favour unless they reach the highest standard of eloquence, but history cannot fail to give pleasure however it is presented'.

36 *Forster...Carlyle*] Forster asserts, for example, that 'no man throve that was connected with letters unless connected with their trade and merchandise as well' (Forster, p. 69). Thomas Carlyle (1795–1881; *DNB*), historian, philosopher, essayist and critic, whose best known works include *Sartor Resartus* (1833–4), *The French Revolution* (1837), *Chartism* (1839) and *Past and Present* (1843).

37 *social affliction...Carlyle halted.*] In 1840, De Quincey complained that in *Chartism* Carlyle was long on problems and short on solutions: 'He and others are assuming that something must be dreadfully amiss in our social conditions; and, when you look into the nature of the grievance, it turns out to be nothing at all special to us and our age, – but only the eternal facts of poverty &c. Accordingly he has no cure even by way of hint. And even those, who adopt his views as a handle of change, admit that he is very obscure when he comes to the remedies' (cited in Robert Morri-

son, '"The Bog School": Carlyle and De Quincey' in *Carlyle Studies Annual* (Special Issue, 1995), p. 17).

38 *'we hear him with ears;'*] Shakespeare *The Merry Wives of Windsor*, I.i.148: 'He hears with ears'.

39 'Sanabilibus aegrotamus malis.'] Seneca, 'On Anger', II.xiii.1. In 1857, De Quincey translated this phrase as 'We are sick – but by maladies that are curable' (see below, p. 713, 318.7) .

40 *'Statutes at large'*] The Statutes at Large are a chronological arrangement of the laws exactly as they have been enacted.

41 *Political Economy...modern batteries.*] De Quincey preened himself on his knowledge of political economy, and was quick to point to his superiority in this area: Wordsworth, Coleridge, and Southey 'were ignorant of every principle belonging to every question alike in political economy, and they were obstinately bent upon learning nothing' (Vol. 11, p. 136).

42 *Mr C... ploughman without a field;*] The reference seems to be a generalized recollection of the argument of Carlyle's *Past and Present*. Carlyle writes of 'an Earth all lying around, crying, Come and till me, come and reap me; – yet we here sit enchanted!' He describes how 'soil, with or without ploughing, is the gift of God', and condemns the 'Organization of Labour' as 'not sufficiently advanced'. De Quincey may also have seen Carlyle's 13 May 1848 article on 'Irish Regiments': 'never can the world cease writhing and meaning...till the disorganic perishing spademan begin to get fairly in contact with his spade-work' (Carlyle, *Works,* vol. X pp. 2, 175, 267; *The Spectator*, 21 (no. 1037), p. 465).

43 *French...answerable for nothing;*] After the abdication of Louis-Philippe (see above, p. 592, n. 1) on 24 February 1848, the Chamber of Deputies proclaimed the Second Republic. The government issued a right-to-work declaration, obligating the state to provide jobs for all citizens.

44 *length of a quarantine.*] forty days.

45 *Carlyle...phraseological forms;*] cf. De Quincey's comments on Carlyle's translation of Goethe's *Wilhelm Meister's Apprenticeship*, which he found 'overrun' by 'provincialisms, vulgarisms' and 'barbarisms' (Vol. 4, p. 174).

46 majorats] 'Majorat' means 'the right of primogeniture' (*OED*).

47 *Benjamin's portion*] Genesis: 43: 34: 'Portions were taken to them from Joseph's table, but Benjamin's portion was five times as much as any of theirs'.

48 *Smart...Forster...noticed the case.*] Christopher Smart (1722–71; *DNB*), religious poet and classical scholar, who translated Horace (see above, p. 535, n. 40) into prose (1756) and verse (1767). 'The agreement was for ninety-nine years; and the terms were that Smart was to write nothing else, and be rewarded with one-sixth of the profits!' (Forster, p. 330).

49 ascripti prelo?] (Lt.), 'bound to the olive oil / wine press'.

50 *Griffiths*] Ralph Griffiths (1720–1803; *DNB*), bookseller and founder of *The Monthly Review*, 1749–1845.

51 *'a small salary,'*] Goldsmith was 'to board and lodge with the bookseller, to have a small regular salary, and to devote himself to the *Monthly Review*' (Forster, p. 67).

52 Mrs *Griffiths,*] Goldsmith stated 'that all he wrote was tampered with by Griffiths or his wife' (Forster, p. 79).

53 *Sinbad...old man of the sea;*] In *The Arabian Nights' Entertainment*, the Old Man of the Sea clings to Sinbad's shoulders and refuses to dismount. Sinbad released himself from the burden by getting the Old Man drunk.

54 *'bad eminence,'*] Milton, *Paradise Lost*, II. 5–6: 'by merit raised / To that bad eminence'.

55 *began with A, and ended with N;*] the writer has not been identified.

56 *Wallenstein...stairs window,*] Albrecht Wenzel Eusebius von Wallenstein (1583–1634), Bohemian soldier and commander of the armies of the Holy Roman Empire under Ferdinand II (1578–1637). De Quincey refers here to Act III, Scene ii in Friedrich von Schiller's *Wallenstein* (1800), which De Quincey knew best in Samuel Taylor Coleridge's translation: 'But was it where he fell two story high / From a window-ledge, on which he had fallen asleep; / And rose up free from injury?' (Coleridge, *PW*, vol. III, p. 775).

57 *Devil and Dr Faustus,*] According to German legend, Dr Faustus was an astrologer or necromancer who sold his soul to the devil in exchange for power and knowledge.

58 *Dunciad...1727...Goldsmith's...1757*] Alexander Pope (see above, p. 524, n. 20), whose *Dunciad* was first published in three books in 1728. Forster writes that Goldsmith became an 'Author by Profession' in 1757 (Forster, p. 77).

59 *never entered...natural vocation.*] Goldsmith's 'assertion of later years, that he was past thirty before he was really attached to literature and sensible that he had found his vocation, is no doubt true' (Forster, p. 78).

60 paloestra] literally, (Lt.), 'wrestling place'.

61 *Rome...do at Rome:*] *Proverbs*, p. 683.

62 *one side...the other.*] Joseph Addison (see above, p. 523, n. 1), essayist, poet and playwright. He was a leading contributor to *The Tatler* (1709–11) and co-founder of *The Spectator* (1711–2).

63 *'much of a muchness.'*] *Proverbs*, p. 549.

64 *lived gaily...university;*] Addison was the eldest son of the Reverend Lancelot Addison (1632–1703; *DNB*), Archdeacon of Coventry and Dean of Lichfield. Addison attended Magdalen College, Oxford, where he took an M.A. in 1693, and was a fellow from 1697 to 1711.

65 *brilliant connexions... Anne;*] Addison was closely associated with the Whigs, who were expelled by Queen Anne (see above, p. 571, n. 60) in 1710.

66 *'delicate humour'...patronage,*] Forster, p. 70; Addison's two chief patrons were John Somers (see above, p. 571, n. 71) and Charles Montagu, first Earl of Halifax (1661–1715; *DNB*).

67 *Blenheim...Cato,*] For Addison's *The Campaign* and *Cato*, see above, p. 573, notes 88 and 91.

68 locus standi,] see above, p. 581, n. 25.

69 *Pope, Swift, Gay, Prior...luck,*] For Alexander Pope, see above, p. 524, n. 20. For Jonathan Swift, see above, p. 528, n. 25. John Gay (1685–1732; *DNB*), poet and dramatist. For Matthew Prior, see above, p. 572, n. 84.

70 *Steele,*] For Sir Richard Steele, see above, p. 523, n. 1.

71 *literature of knowledge...power*] De Quincey's principal pronouncements of this famous distinction are in his 1823 series of 'Letters to a Young Man whose Education has been Neglected' (Vol. 3, pp. 69–74) and, three months following the publication of the present essay, in his August 1848 review of the works of Alexander Pope (see above, pp. 336–40).

72 *introsusception*] 'The action of taking up or receiving within' (*OED*, which cites this example from De Quincey).

73 *Camden...Jonson, Selden...Hobbes,*] William Camden (1551–1623; *DNB*), antiquary. Ben Jonson (1572–1637; *DNB*), dramatist, poet and critic. John Selden (1584–1654; *DNB*), antiquarian and Orientalist. Thomas Hobbes (1588–1679; *DNB*), philosopher.

74 *Columbus.*] Christopher Columbus (1451–1506), mariner and navigator.

75 *hack scribbler...literary artist.*] cf. De Quincey in an 1825 letter to John Wilson: 'To fence with these ailments with the one hand, and with the other to maintain the war with the wretched business of hack-author, with all its horrible degradations, is more than I am able to bear' (Lindop, p. 277).

76 *literature in France...false.*] cf. De Quincey to Woodhouse: 'the Opium-Eater found throughout the whole of french literature an universal weakness, & poverty of thought; & that, when the french writers wished to be more than usually grand, they loaded their thoughts with glittering & tinsel expressions – but their conceptions are poor, low & imbecile' (Morrison, p. 29).

77 jus trium liberorum,] (Lt.), 'right of the three children' (see Pliny, *Epistle* II. 13).

78 soirée] (Fr.), 'evening party'.

79 *Fichte...Hegel.*] For Johann Gottlieb Fichte, see above, p. 568, n. 19. For Georg Wilhelm Friedrich Hegel, see above, p. 524, n. 16.

80 l'état c'est moi;] (Fr.), 'I am the state'. The words are attributed to Louis XIV at a session of the Parlement de Paris, 13 April 1655.

81 Jupiter optimus maximus,] (Lt.), 'Jupiter the Best and the Greatest'.

82 lettres de cachet] (Fr.), 'a written order permitting imprisonment without trial'.

83 *Hercules, this Augéan stable*] The Augean stables were the filthiest in Greece. Hercules's fifth labour was to clean them in a single day.

84 *river of Lethe,*] in Greco-Roman mythology, the river of forgetfulness.

85 *Mirabeau...Talleyrand...councils.*] Honoré–Gabriel Riqueti, comte de Mirabeau (1749–91), politician and orator, author of *The Prussian Monarchy Under Frederick the Great* (1788) and *Secret History of the Court of Berlin* (1789). Charles-Maurice, Prince de Talleyrand-Périgord (1754–1838), politician, diplomat and wit, who published a series of essays, letters and addresses, including *Des Loteries* (1789) and *Éloge de M. le comte Reinhard* (1838). More recently, De Quincey has in mind French writers like Alphonse de Lamartine (1790–1869) and Victor Hugo (see above, p. 567, n. 2), both of whom had prominent political careers.

86 *'argle-bargling'*] 'to argue obstinately' (*OED*).

87 *Boswell,*] James Boswell (1740–95; *DNB*), diarist and biographer celebrated for his *Life of Samuel Johnson* (1791), where he comments at length on Goldsmith.

88 *'inspired idiot,'*] Famously, Horace Walpole (see above, p. 579, n. 13) described Goldsmith as 'an inspired ideot' [*sic*] (Boswell, vol. I, p. 413).

89 *Traveller...Croaker...Lumkin;*] Goldsmith's poem *The Traveller; or, A Prospect of Society* (1764); Croaker is the doleful guardian in Goldsmith's first comedy, *The Good-Natured Man* (1768); Lumpkin is the dissolute oaf in Goldsmith's brilliant second comedy, *She Stoops to Conquer* (1773).

90 *Wakefield...Deserted Village;*] Goldsmith's novel *The Vicar of Wakefield* (1766) and his most important poem, *The Deserted Village* (1770).

91 *Hornecks...his own claims.*] According to Boswell, Goldsmith 'was seriously angry' that more attention was paid to the Hornecks than to him. But Forster records that 'when Hazlitt met the younger sister...some twenty years ago...she was talking of her favourite Doctor Goldsmith, with recollection and affection unabated by time' (Boswell, vol. I, p. 414; Forster, p. 501).

92 *Bedlam.*] the first asylum for the insane in England.

93 *Coleridge...kiss his hand.*] The anecdote has not been traced in the published writings of Samuel Taylor Coleridge (see above, p. 556, n. 12). De Quincey may of course be recollecting a conversation with Coleridge.

94 *bloom-coloured coat...puppet-show,*] For the 'bloom-coloured coat', see Boswell, vol. II, p. 83 and Forster, p. 514. For the puppet-show, see Boswell, vol. I, p. 141 and Forster, p. 609.
95 *Otho...without caprice.*] Otho Roscius was author of the law that the *equites* (knights) should occupy the first fourteen rows in the theatre (see Cicero, *Pro Murena*, 19).
96 *"the whistling of a name."*] See above, p. 576, n. 52.
97 Requiescat!] (Lt.), 'May he / she rest in peace'.
98 Vindiciae Oliverianae,] (Lt.), 'Vindication of Oliver'.

The Works of Alexander Pope, Esquire

1 *Claude Lorraine glasses,*] The Claude Lorrain glass was black convex glass used by artists to reflect the landscape in miniature. The effect was to merge details and reduce the strength of colour.
2 idola theatri] In *Novum Organum* (1620), Francis Bacon (see above, p. 578, n. 3) advocated the repudiation of four intellectual idols, one of which was dogmatic philosophical systems (the 'Idols of the Theatre').
3 pari passu] (Lt.), 'at an equal pace'.
4 praegustatores] (Lt.), 'foretasters'.
5 *Charles I...Whitehall.*] For Charles I, see above, p. 558, n. 40. Whitehall Palace, former royal residence in Westminster, London, was destroyed by fire in 1698.
6 *Books...literary interest.*] In 1858, De Quincey appended a footnote on '*The Blue Books*' to this passage (see below, p. 715, 336.8).
7 *Bacon calls* dry *light;*] 'Of Friendship' in Bacon, *Essayes*, p. 84: '*Heraclitus* saith well, in one of his aenigmaes; *Dry Light is ever the best*. And certaine it is, that the Light, that a Man receiveth, by Counsell from Another, is Drier, and purer, then that which commeth from his owne Understanding, and Judgement; which is ever infused and drenched in his Affections and Customes'.
8 *Jacob's ladder*] Genesis, 28. 12: Jacob 'dreamed, and behold, a ladder set up on earth, and the top of it reached to heaven'.
9 'the understanding heart,'] In 1 Kings 3: 9–12, King Solomon asks God for 'an understanding heart' with which to rule his people.
10 intuitive *(or non-discursive) organ,*] cf. Wordsworth, *The Prelude,* XIII. 112–3: 'And endless occupation for the soul / Whether discursive or intuitive'. Wordsworth is echoing Raphael's lesson to Adam in Milton, *Paradise Lost*, V. 486–8: 'Fancy and understanding, whence the soul / Reason receives, and reason is her being, / Discursive, or intuitive'.
11 *epopee,*] epic poem.
12 quamdiu bene se gesserit.] (Lt.), 'as long as it shall conduct itself well'.
13 Principia...*Newton*] Isaac Newton (see above, p. 565, n. 23), physicist and mathematician, whose *Philosophiae Naturalis Principia Mathematica* (1687; *Mathematical Principles of Natural Philosophy*) sets forth the laws of motion and the theory of gravitation.
14 *La Place,*] Pierre-Simon, marquis de Laplace (1749–1827), French mathematician and physicist who successfully applied the Newtonian theory of gravitation to the solar system.
15 nominis umbra,] (Lt.), 'shadow of a name'.
16 *Iliad...Aeschylus,*] In *The Iliad*, Homer (see above, p. 536, n. 50) tells the story of the Trojan War. For Aeschylus, see above, p. 532, n. 95.

17 *Othello...King Lear...Hamlet...Macbeth,*] Shakespeare's four major tragedies.
18 *Praxiteles...Michael Angelo.*] Praxiteles (*fl.* 370–330 BC), Greek sculptor. For Michelangelo, see above, p. 540, n. 45.
19 κτηματα ἐς ἀει:] (Gk.) 'everlasting possessions'. De Quincey draws from Thucydides, *The Peloponnesian War*, I.xxii.4.
20 *Dryden...Pope...Wordsworth.*] Geoffrey Chaucer (*c.* 1340–1400; *DNB*), poet, whose work was translated and modernized by John Dryden (see above, p. 524, n. 24), Alexander Pope and William Wordsworth (see above, p. 527, n. 12).
21 *Ovid,*] Ovid (BC 43–AD 17), Roman poet, best known for *Ars Amatoria* and *Metamorphoses*.
22 '*and* shall *a thousand more.*'] Ovid, *Metamorphoses*, XV. 871–9; and Wordsworth, 'The Force of Prayer; or, The Founding of Bolton Priory', ll. 23–4: 'A thousand years hath it borne that name, / And shall a thousand more'.
23 *world, passeth away.*] 1 Corinthians 7: 31: 'for the fashion of this world passeth away'.
24 *phylacteries.*] see above, p. 532, n. 91.
25 ἐξοχην,] (Gk.), 'in the highest degree'.
26 tertium quid,] (Lt.), 'third factor'.
27 French *School...literature*;] cf. Leigh Hunt in 1818: 'The downfall of the French school of poetry has of late been increasing in rapidity; its cold and artificial compositions have given way...and imagination breathes again in a more green and genial time' (*Leigh Hunt's Literary Criticism*, eds L. H. Houtchens and C. W. Houtchens (New York: Columbia University Press, 1956), p. 129).
28 *Schlegels,*] August Wilhelm von Schlegel (1767–1845) and his younger brother Friedrich von Schlegel (1772–1829), German scholars and critics.
29 *Jerusalem Delivered,*] see above, p. 548, n. 16.
30 *Dryden...French literature;*] see 'Dedication to the Aeneis' in *The Works of John Dryden*, gen. ed. Alan Roper (Berkeley: University of California Press, 1956 – continuing) vol. v, p. 287.
31 *Thebes*] see above, p. 579, n. 8.
32 *Batrachomyomachia:*] see above, p. 574, n. 14.
33 *discontinuous jets:*] cf. De Quincey three months later on Hazlitt: 'Hazlitt was not eloquent, because he was discontinuous. No man can be eloquent whose thoughts are abrupt, insulated, capricious' (see above, p. 378).
34 *King James' reign,*] see above, p. 560, n. 28.
35 *Lucrece and Adonis,)*] Shakespeare's *Venus and Adonis* (1593) and *The Rape of Lucrece* (1594).
36 *'The style...perplexed, and obscure.'*] Johnson's comments appear in the 'Preface' to his 1765 edition of Shakespeare (see Boswell, vol. IV, p. 19).
37 *Charles II.*] Charles II (1630–85), King of England, 1660–85.
38 *Quarter Sessions.*] A general court held quarterly by the justices of the peace of each county, and having jurisdiction over all but the highest crimes..
39 *conversational...rapidity.*] cf. De Quincey's thoughts in his 1850 essay on 'Conversation' (Vol. 17, pp. 3–13).
40 *'Know, God and Nature...flying game.'*] Pope, 'Epistle to Cobham', ll. 154–5.
41 *Lord Oxford...*'correct...*affecting*'] Roscoe, vol. II, p. 51: the editor in question is William Lisle Bowles (1762–1850; *DNB*), poet, critic and clergyman; the poem in question is 'Epistle to Robert, Earl of Oxford and Earl Mortimer'. Robert Harley, first Earl of Oxford and Earl Mortimer (1661–1724; *DNB*), Prime Minister.
42 *'For* him*...world attend,'*] Pope, 'Epistle to Robert, Earl of Oxford and Earl Mortimer', l. 7.
43 *'Nor fears to tell that* Mortimer *is he;'*] Pope, 'Epistle to Robert, Earl of Oxford and Earl Mortimer', l. 40.

44 Oxford...*de Veres.*] The Vere family held the hereditary office of Lord Great Chamberlain from 1133 to 1779, and the Earldom of Oxford from 1142 to 1703. The Mortimer family attained political eminence in the thirteenth century, and possessed a claim to the English throne in the fifteenth.

45 *'ELOISA TO ABELARD'*] see above, p. 528, n. 17.

46 *'Once...a sainted maid.'*] Pope, 'Eloisa to Abelard', ll. 311–2 (inexact).

47 *'It will...gaze on me.'*] Pope, 'Eloisa to Abelard', l. 330.

48 *'That ages hence...silver springs,'*] Pope, 'Eloisa to Abelard', ll. 345–6, 348 (inexact).

49 *'the pomp of dreadful sacrifice,'*] Pope, 'Eloisa to Abelard', l. 354.

50 *'to heaven...be forgiven.'*] Pope, 'Eloisa to Abelard', ll. 357–8 (inexact).

51 *Nogent-sur-Seine...Paraclete*] Nogent-sur-Seine is a town in north-central France, thirty-five miles northwest of Troyes. Abelard established a monastery, the Paraclete, which he gave to Héloïse, who became an abbess of a convent there.

52 *'Here, under...for ever in bliss.'*] Roscoe, vol. III, pp. 21–2: De Quincey has used his own translation from the Latin text rather than Roscoe's.

53 *SATIRES...MORAL EPISTLES,*] Pope, *Imitations of Horace* (1733–8) and *Moral Essays* (1731–5)

54 *Essay on Man;*] Pope, *Essay on Man* (1733–4).

55 *truth angular and splintered.*] cf. De Quincey three months later on Hazlitt: 'Now Hazlitt's brilliancy is seen chiefly in separate splinterings of phrase or image' (see above, p. 378).

56 *(the* magnificabo apostolatum meum*)*] Romans 11: 13: 'I will magnify my office'.

57 Facit indignatio versum...*Juvenal*] Juvenal (*c.* AD 55– *c.* 127), Roman poet, *Satires*, I. 79: 'Indignation produces the verse'.

58 *Mephistopheles.*] Mephistopheles is a familiar spirit of the Devil in late settings of the legend of Faust.

59 *Twickenham grotto,*] In 1719, Pope moved to Twickenham, where he built a shell-lined grotto.

60 *Warburton...Satires.*] see above, p. 562, n. 64.

61 lymphaticus] (Lt.), 'mad' or 'frenzied'. Warburton was an enduring figure of interest to De Quincey (see Vol. 2, pp. 274–5; Vol. 7, p. 85; Vol. 8, pp. 81–2).

62 *'There are ninety...with smiles.'*] slightly misquoted from Wordsworth, 'The Two Thieves', ll. 15–6, 35–6, 39–40.

63 *'Each in his turn...led:'*] Wordsworth, 'The Two Thieves', l. 38.

64 *'with a will:'*] cf. Dickens, *Dombey and Son*, p. 208: '"Come on then," said the Captain. "With a will, my lad!"'

65 *disfigure Pope's...satires.*] Warburton encouraged Pope to write *The New Dunciad* (1742), and added many notes to his various editions of Pope's *Works*, the first of which appeared in 1751.

66 *'Matter too soft...or fair.'*] Pope, 'Epistle to a Lady', ll. 3–4.

67 *'Least said soonest mended.'*] *Proverbs*, p. 472.

68 *'There* are *no snakes in Iceland.'*] One of De Quincey favourite anecdotes: cf. 'The English Mail-Coach', where he observes that there are no rats 'about mail-coaches, any more than snakes in Von Troil's Iceland' (see above, p. 413). The laconic chapter on snakes appeared, not in Uno Von Troil (1746–1803), Archbishop of Uppsala, *The Letters on Iceland* (1780), but in Niels Horrebow (1712–60), *The Natural History of Iceland* (1758), Chapter 72: '*Concerning snakes.* No snakes of any kind are to be met with throughout the whole island'. De Quincey undoubtedly knew the anecdote from Boswell, vol. III, p. 279.

69 *'that the particular...men.'*] Roscoe, vol. IV, p. 221.

70 *'Those only fix'd...love of sway.'*] Pope, 'Epistle to a Lady', ll. 209–10.

71 *no character at all;'*] Pope, 'Epistle to a Lady', l. 2.

72 incredulus odi] Horace, *Ars Poetica*, l. 188: 'I discredit and abhor'.

73 *'How soft is...*her *advice.'*] Pope, 'Epistle to a Lady', ll. 29–32.

74 *who Calista is*] Calista is the heroine in *The Fair Penitent* (1703), a tragedy by Nicholas Rowe (1674–1718; *DNB*).

75 *'Sudden...pimple on her nose.'*] Pope, 'Epistle to a Lady', ll. 33–6.

76 *George II.,*] George II (1683–1760), King of Great Britain, 1727–60.

77 causa teterrima] (Lt.), 'most shocking cause'. De Quincey is adapting Horace, *Satires*, I.iii.107–8: 'nam fuit ante Helenam cunnus taeterrima belli / causa' ('for before Helen's day a wench was the most dreadful cause of war').

78 'My face...she said'] 'Where are you going to, my Pretty Maid?', ll. 18–9.

79 *Johnson's opinion...for anything.*] Boswell, vol. I, p. 467: '"I mind my belly very studiously, and very carefully; for I look upon it, that he who does not mind his belly will hardly mind any thing else"'.

80 *Narcissa:*] Narcissa is a character in *Love's Last Shift* (1696), a comedy by Colly Cibber (1671–1757; *DNB*).

81 comme il faut.] (Fr.), 'proper.' The Act for Burying in Woollen was passed in 1660 and reinforced in 1678. It was designed to support the woollen trade by making it an offence to wrap corpses in any material other than wool.

82 *give this cheek a little red.'*] Pope, 'Epistle to Cobham', ll. 242–7.

83 Narcissa...*tulip-beds of ladies*,] Pope, 'Epistle to a Lady', ll. 53–68.

84 Flavia *and* Philomedé] Pope, 'Epistle to a Lady', ll. 83–100.

85 *Duke...Sunderland...*Churchill;] De Quincey has his facts slightly confused. John Churchill, first Duke of Marlborough (1650–1722; *DNB*), diplomat and one of England's greatest generals. His eldest daughter Henrietta Churchill became second Duchess of Marlborough (1681–1733; *DNB*) upon the death of her father. It was Marlborough's second daughter Anne Churchill (1684–1716), however, who married Charles Spencer, third Earl of Sunderland (1674–1722; *DNB*). George Spencer, fifth Duke of Marlborough (1766–1840; *DNB*), took the additional name of Churchill by royal license in 1817.

86 *Smollett...story.*] *The History of England...by David Hume...continued to the Death of George the Second by T Smollett* (London: Bohn, 1853), p. 1263: in a long footnote, Smollett details 'the secret practices' of an 'incendiary correspondent', who had given the Duke of Marlborough 'to understand, that this vengeance, though slow, would not be the less certain'.

87 *Sarah...*Atossa.] Pope, 'Epistle to a Lady', ll. 115–6: But what are these to great Atossa's mind? / Scare once herself, by turns all Womankind!' The character of Atossa was once thought to be Sarah Jennings, Duchess of Marlborough (1660–1744; *DNB*), wife of John Churchill (see above, n. 85), and a close friend of Queen Anne. It is now thought more likely that Pope's satire was directed soley against Katherine Darnley, Duchess of Buckingham (*c.* 1682–1743). For details, see 'Who was Atossa?' in Alexander Pope, *Epistles to Several Persons*, ed. F. W. Bateson (New Haven: Yale University Press, 1951), pp. 159–70.

88 Atticus.] see Pope, 'Atticus' and 'Epistle to Dr Arbuthnot', ll, 193–214.

89 *Duchess...1745...1746.*] In the rising of 1745, Charles Edward Stuart (1720–88; *DNB*), the 'Younger Pretender' and the Jacobite Prince of Wales, conquered Scotland and led his troops as far as Derby in England. Lack of support from the English and French forced him to retreat to the Highlands, where he was routed at the Battle of Culloden (16 April 1746).

90 *write her own book.*] The book in question seems to be Nathaniel Hooke (d. 1763; *DNB*), *An Account of the Conduct of the Dowager Duchess of Marlborough from her first coming to Court to the year 1710* (privately printed, 1742).

91 *Montagu,*] Lady Mary Wortley Montagu (1689–1762; *DNB*), poet and letter-writer, was a friend of Pope's, but he later turned against her.

92 gens de plume,] see above, p. 528, n. 22.

93 *Horace Walpole.*] see above, p. 579, n. 13.

94 *Aeolus,*] In the works of Homer, Aeolus is the controller of the winds.

95 *'For modes of faith...is best.'*] Pope, *An Essay on Man*, III. 303–6. De Quincey has inverted the two couplets.

96 *Mozart*] see above, p. 540, n. 53.

97 Κατ' ἐξοχην] see above, n. 25.

98 *Universal Prayer...First Cause.*] Pope, 'The Universal Prayer', ll. 3–5: 'By Saint, by Savage, and by Sage, / Jehovah, Jove, or Lord! / Thou Great First Cause, least understood'.

99 *Warton...same opinion long before.*] Joseph Warton (1722–1800; *DNB*), critic, best remembered for his two essays on *The Writings and Genius of Pope* (1756, 1782). De Quincey refers to a note in which Warton cites Seneca's *De Beneficiis* (Roscoe, vol. IV, p. 163).

100 a fortiori,] see above, p. 560, n. 18.

101 *deliration*] 'delirium...frenzy, madness' (*OED*).

102 *own Church...put forward,*] Pope was Catholic.

103 *'Hark...come away!'*] Pope, 'The Dying Christian to his Soul', ll. 7–8: 'Hark! they whisper; Angels say, / Sister Spirit, come away'.

104 *'the nympholepsy...despair,'*] Byron, *Childe Harold's Pilgrimage*, IV.cxv.1031: 'The nympholepsy of some fond despair'. In Greek mythology, 'nympholepsy' is a state of self-destructive rapture suffered by a mortal man who has seen a nymph.

105 *Vestal Virgin*] in Roman religion, any of the six priestesses, representing the daughters of the royal house, who tended the state cult of Vesta, the goddess of the hearth. They were chosen between the ages of six and ten.

106 *charities*] Southey, *Carmen Nuptiale*, l. 668: 'The Virtues and the Household Charities'.

107 *trembles as a guilty creature*] see above, p. 563, n. 72.

108 *Crashaw...Messiah...Dying Adrian,*] Richard Crashaw (*c.* 1613–49; *DNB*) religious poet and Anglo-Catholic. De Quincey refers to Pope's *Messiah: A Sacred Eclogue* and 'The Dying Christian to his Soul', which Warburton asserted was an imitation of Hadrian's verses to his soul, and reportedly uttered as he lay dying

109 *scriptural denunciation...worldly views,*] there are several such denunciations: see Psalm 73: 12; Proverbs 13: 7; Matthew 13: 22.

110 *religious faith...obtain for him,*] As a Catholic, Pope could not hold civil or military office, or a seat in Parliament.

111 *youthful introduction...metropolis,*] Pope was twenty-four when he published the first version of *The Rape of the Lock* (1712), which established his reputation in London society.

112 *Prospero's robe of poetry.*] In Shakespeare, *The Tempest*, Prospero is the master magician who uses his extensive powers to transform the island and its inhabitants.

113 *Philips...Dyer...Virgil,*] John Philips (see above, p. 571, n. 68), *Cider: A Poem in Two Books* (1709). John Dyer (1699–1757; *DNB*), *The Fleece* (1757). Virgil (see above, p. 535, n. 42) composed his *Georgics* between 37 and 30 BC.

114 *Varro, Cato, Columella,*] Marcus Terentius Varro (116–27 BC), scholar and satirist, whose only complete work to survive is *Res rustica* (*Farm Topics*). Marcus Porcius Cato, 'Cato the Elder' (234–149 BC), statesman and orator, whose only surviving work is *De agri cultura* (*On Farming*). Lucius Junius Moderatus Columella (b. first century AD), Roman soldier and farmer, best known for *De re rustica*.

115 *gem within a gem.*] Pope, *The Rape of the Lock*, III. 19–100.

116 *first edition of the poem,*] Pope published a two-canto version of *The Rape of the Lock* in 1712, and an expanded five-canto version in 1714.

117 *Hannibal, Marius, Sertorius,*] Hannibal (247–*c.* 182 BC), Carthaginian general. Gaius Marius (*c.* 157–86 BC), Roman general and politician. Quintus Sertorius (*c.* 123–72 BC), Roman statesman and military commander.

118 *Vida...chess-board?*] Marco Girolamo Vida (*c.* 1490–1566), Italian humanist and author of a Latin poem on *The Game of Chess*.

119 lis est de paupere regno] (Lt.), 'the quarrel is concerning a poor realm'.

120 *Lucretius*] see above, p. 535, n. 41.

121 De omnibus rebus....De Rerum Naturâ,)] (Lt.), respectively, 'Concerning all Things' and 'Concerning the Nature of Things'.

122 *Crousaz*] Jean-Pierre de Crousaz (1663–1740), Swiss theologian, philosopher and controversialist, *Examen de l'essai de M. Pope sur l'homme* (1737). De Quincey draws here on Roscoe, vol. IV, p. 3–18: Roscoe argues in favour of Warburton's reading of the poem, and rejects that of Warton, who supports Crousaz.

123 *Bowles...Warton.*] William Lisle Bowles (1762–1850; *DNB*), poet and critic, whose 1806 edition of the works of Pope gave rise to the so-called 'Pope-Bowles' controversy. For Joseph Warton, see above, n. 99.

124 *DUNCIAD*] Pope published a three-book version of *The Dunciad* in 1728, and added a fourth book in 1742 (see above, n. 65).

Final Memorials of Charles Lamb

1 Prima facie,] (Lt.), see above, p. 540, n. 54.

2 *pensiveness...literature approaches,*] cf. Leigh Hunt on Lamb in 1834: 'His essays, especially those collected under the signature of ELIA, will take their place among the daintiest productions of English *wit-melancholy*, – an amiable melancholy being the ground-work of them, and serving to throw out their delicate flowers of wit and character with the greater nicety' (Hunt, p. 298).

3 *Addison...Roger de Coverly,*] see above, p. 546, n. 64.

4 *Club...Wimble...observer.*] *The Spectator* adopted a fictional method of presentation through a 'Spectator Club', whose imaginary members included Roger de Coverley, Will Wimble and the detached observer Mr Spectator.

5 *(*Sit venia verbo!*)*] (Lt.), 'if you will pardon the expression'.

6 *Timon of Athens...Diogenes,*] Timon is a semi-legendary Athenian who, owing to the ingratitude of his friends, became a misanthrope. Diogenes of Sinope (see above, p. 595, n. 12) may have written a number of works, but nothing has survived.

7 *Lucian*] Lucian (b. 120 AD), Greek rhetorician, pamphleteer and satirist.

8 *Rabelais...Montaigne*] François Rabelais (*c.* 1494–1553) and Michel de Montaigne, French writers.

9 *Brown...La Fontaine...Swift...Sterne,*] For Sir Thomas Browne, see above, p. 570, n. 52. Jean de La Fontaine (1621–95), poet. For Jonathan Swift, see above, p. 528, n. 25. Laurence Sterne (1713–68; *DNB*), novelist.

10 *Hippel...Kant...Hamann...Richter.*] Theodor Gottlieb von Hippel (1741–96) and Johann Georg Hamann (1730–88) were both German writers and disciples of the philosopher Immanuel Kant (see above, p. 560, n. 16) For Jean Paul Richter, see above, p. 536, n. 67.

11 *parenticide...secrets of lunacy,*] In 1796 Charles's older sister Mary Ann (1764–1847; *DNB*) murdered their mother in a fit of insanity. For the rest of her life Mary was subject to recurrent bouts of mental illness. Lamb himself suffered a period of insanity in 1795–6.

12 *Salt...Inner Temple.*] Lamb's father John (*c.* 1722–99) is described as a scrivener on Lamb's Christ's Hospital application form. He was the right-hand man of Samuel Salt (d. 1792), who became a Bencher in 1782, and who was M.P. for Liskeard.

13 patronus] (Lt.), 'patron'.

14 *Robinson Crusoe,*] The eponymous hero of Daniel Defoe's novel *The Life and Strange Surprising Adventures of Robinson Crusoe* (1719). Crusoe is shipwrecked and shows great resourcefulness in dealing with his island isolation.

15 *One always* is...*blest.*] Pope, *An Essay on Man*, I. 96: 'Man never Is, but always To be blest'.

16 homo unius libri,] (Lt.), 'a man of one book'. Cf. Southey: 'The *homo unius libri* is indeed proverbially formidable to all conversational figurantes' (Robert Southey, *The Doctor* (London: Longmans, Green, and Co., 1865), p. 164).

17 *printed his poems,*] John Lamb, *Poetical Pieces on Several Occasions* (London: P. Shatwell, 1770).

18 *Kinsale...Royal Presence.*] De Quincey's reference is not to a particular Lord Kinsale, but to whoever happens to be the holder of the title at a given time. The representative of the family enjoys the privilege of wearing his hat in the royal presence, as granted to John de Courcy (d. *c.* 1219; *DNB*) by John (1167–1216), King of England, 1199–1216. In 1858, De Quincey appended a footnote to this passage (see below, p. 718, 372.13).

19 *John*] Charles's older brother John (1763–1821).

20 *genial...Elia recollections.*] see, for example, 'The Old Benchers of the Inner Temple' (Lamb, *Works*, vol. II, pp. 82–91).

21 *Christ's Hospital.*] a London school founded in 1552 for the sons of needy clergy. The main building was on the site of a Franciscan friary. Lamb and Samuel Taylor Coleridge both entered the school in 1782. For Lamb's recollections, see 'Christ's Hospital Five and Thirty Years Ago' in Lamb, *Works*, vol. II, pp. 12–22.

22 *Arnold,*] Thomas Arnold (1795–1842; *DNB*), educated at Winchester and Oxford, was headmaster of Rugby School.

23 *Westminster...Charter-House,*] all old and well-known British schools. Saint Paul's School was founded in 1509, and Merchant Taylors' in 1560–1

24 *boy-king*] Christ's Hospital was founded by Edward VI (1537–53), King of England and Ireland, 1547–53.

25 *dawn...French Revolution.*] Lamb left Christ's Hospital in 1789, and found employment in the counting-house of a merchant, Joseph Paice (d. 1810).

26 *Cary (of Dante celebrity)*] Henry Francis Cary (1772–1844; *DNB*), biographer and translator, best known for his blank verse translation of *The Divine Comedy* by Dante Alighieri (1265–1321), Italy's greatest poet.

27 *'sweet Roman hand,'*] Shakespeare, *Twelfth Night*, III.iv.28: 'I think we do know the sweet Roman hand'.

28 *inscription upon his grave;*] Samuel Taylor Coleridge, 'Epitaph', 3–4: 'A poet lies, or that which once seem'd he, – / O, lift one thought in prayer for S. T. C.'.

29 Τον θαυμασιωτατον.] 'the most amazing'.

30 *Coleridge...Christchurch.*] Coleridge was Senior Grecian in his year, and in January 1791 was awarded a School Exhibition worth £40 to take him to Cambridge. Lamb himself made it to the rank of Deputy Grecian.

31 *India House.*] De Quincey's dates are wrong here. Lamb was employed as a clerk in the South-Sea House in 1791, and joined the Accountant's Office of East India House a year later. For Lamb's own record of his days at 'The South-Sea House', see Lamb, *Works*, vol. II, pp. 1–7.

32 *Holborn...died upon the spot.*] The Lambs lived at 7 Little Queen Street, Holborn. Mary stabbed her mother to death on 22 September 1796.

33 *lunatics at Hoxton:*] Mary Lamb was confined to an asylum, not at Hoxton, but at Islington (1796–7). Charles had previously spent six weeks in the Hoxton asylum.

34 *death of his father,*] see above, n. 12.

35 *young lady whom he loved,*] The 'young lady' is almost certainly Ann Simmons, 'the fair-hair'd maid' in Lamb's youthful poetry. Cf. Talfourd: 'we know how nobly that love, and all hope of the earthly blessings attendant on such an affection, were resigned on the catastrophe which darkened the following year' (Lamb, *Works*, vol. V, pp. 3, 21; Talfourd, vol. I, p. 2)

36 *given to the India House.*] Lamb retired from the East India House in 1825 after thirty-three years' service.

37 'O fortunati...agricolae.'] Virgil, *Georgics*, II. 458: 'O happy husbandmen! Too happy, should they come to know their blessings!'.

38 *Dr Dryasdust.*] the name of a fictitious person to whom Walter Scott (see above, p. 537, n. 70) pretended to dedicate some of his novels; hence, a writer of antiquities or statistics who is occupied by the driest and most uninteresting details.

39 *Leadenhall*...opera omnia] Lamb's East India House offices were located at Numbers 12–21 Leadenhall Street. For 'opera omnia', see above, p. 551, n. 69.

40 *Sisyphus*] in Greek mythology, the cunning king who was punished by having repeatedly to roll a huge stone up a hill only to have it roll down again.

41 *'not even critics criticise.'*] Cowper, *The Task*, IV. 50–1; cf. Vol. 7, p. 193.

42 *artificial lights...studies.*] In 1826, Lamb contributed a series of 'Popular Fallacies' to *The New Monthly Magazine*.

43 *Malaga?'*] Lamb, *Works*, vol. II, p. 271. Málaga is a sweet, usually red, wine.

44 *Phoebus.*] in Greek mythology, the byname of Apollo, the god of light.

45 *Milton's...Taylor's...taper.'*] Lamb, *Works*, vol. II, p. 272. Lamb refers to the morning hymn in Milton, *Paradise Lost*, V. 153–208, and to the description of a sun-rise by Jeremy Taylor (see above, p. 570, n. 52) in Chapter I, section iii of *The Rule and Exercises of Holy Dying* (1651).

46 *Bacon...day-light.*] 'Of Truth' in Bacon (see above, p. 578, n. 3), *Essayes*, p. 7: 'This same *Truth*, is a Naked, and Open day light, that doth not shew, the Masques, and Mummeries, and Triumphs of the world, halfe so Stately, and daintily, as Candelights'.

47 *'the great thinker.'*] Talfourd, vol. II, p. 177.

48 *Hall...Owen?*] Marshall Hall (1790–1857; *DNB*), physiologist. Sir Richard Owen (1804–92; *DNB*), anatomist and palaeontologist.

49 *Hazlitt had read nothing.*] cf. De Quincey on Hazlitt in *Confessions*: 'he has obviously not had the advantage of a regular scholastic education: he has not read Plato in his youth (which most likely was only his misfortune); but neither has he read Kant in his manhood (which is his fault)' (Vol. 2, p. 13).

50 *Hazlitt's...as a lecturer,*] De Quincey has in mind particularly Hazlitt's 1812 series of public lectures on English philosophy.

51 *'He...excitement can rouse;'*] Talfourd, vol. II, p. 176.

52 *Coleridge) non-sequacious.*] cf. Coleridge, 'The Eolian Harp', l. 18: 'Boldier swept, the long sequacious notes'.

53 *Brown...Taylor,*] For Sir Thomas Browne and Jeremy Taylor, see above, p. 570.n.52. Cf. De Quincey's daughter Florence on his high regard for Taylor: 'I should think any one would guess from his works what a great admiration he had for Shakspear and Milton but I do not think that people would gather the same opinion as regards Jeremy Taylor and yet I think he would have placed him beside those two great towers of strength' (Bonner, p. 47).

54 *Chesterfield...hum and haw.'*] Philip Dormer Stanhope, fourth Earl of Chesterfield (1694–1773; *DNB*), statesman, diplomat and wit, chiefly remembered for his *Letters to His Son*. He frequently mentions reserving the morning for reading. The anecdote to which De Quincey refers does not appear in Chesterfield's letters or works, but was presumably one of the many sayings commonly attributed to him. According to Horace Walpole, 'For a series of years nothing was more talked of than Lord Chesterfield's bon mots, and many of them were excellent; but many, too, of others were ascribed to him' (*Horace Walpole's Marginal Notes, written in Dr Maty's Miscellaneous Works of Memoirs of the Earl of Chesterfield* (1866), p. 7).

55 arrière pensée,] (Fr.), 'ulterior motive'.

56 refuses...*military language)*] '*Mil.* To decline to oppose (troops) to the enemy' (*OED*).

57 *insensibility to music...candidly.*] see Lamb in his 'Chapter on Ears': 'I have no ear....You will understand me to mean – *for music*' (Lamb, *Works*, vol. II, p. 38).

58 *Regulus...Carthaginian sun,*] Marcus Atilius Regulus (*fl.* third century BC), Roman general and statesman. According to tradition, he remained in captivity at Carthage until he was sent to Rome on parole to arrange a peace. He urged the Roman Senate to refuse the proposals, returned to Carthage according to his oath, and was brutally tortured to death.

59 *simple:* we *love it;*] cf. De Quincey to Richard Woodhouse: 'The Opium-Eater always disliked in modern Composition what is termed Ciceronian Latin – that style, in which twenty or thirty words are used to express what might be as well or better given in five or ten. The declamation he gave at Oxford was framed more after the style of Caesar in his Commentaries than after that of Cicero. It was studiously clear, simple, & short' (Morrison, p. 33).

60 *'Belshazzar...his lords'*] see above, p. 570, n. 55.

61 *'And...Cicero ...Marcellus restored.'*] see Cicero, *Pro Ligario* and *Pro Marcello*.

62 *genial appreciation of Milton.*] De Quincey may have in mind Lamb's observation that 'the names of some of our poets sound sweeter...to the ear – to mine, at least – than that of Milton or of Shakspeare....The sweetest names...are, Kit Marlowe, Drayton, Drummond of Hawthornden, and Cowley' (Lamb, *Works*, vol. II, p. 174).

63 περιπέτεια,] 'peripeteia'; see above, p. 558, n. 19.

64 *'trailing...associations;'*] Talfourd, vol. II, p. 161.

65 *Ion...Wordsworth...Coleridge's),*] Talfourd's blank-verse tragedy *Ion* appeared in 1836. Lamb introduced Talfourd to William Wordsworth (see above, p. 527, n. 12).

66 fluxe de bouche...*Huet's)*] Pierre-Daniel Huet (1630–1721), bishop, antiquary, and scientist. His miscellaneous opinions on literature were posthumously collected in *Huetiana* (1722). 'Fluxe de bouche' (Fr.), 'flow from the mouth', by analogy with

'fluxe de ventre' ('diarrhoea'); cf. De Quincey in the first instalment of his 1840–1 *Blackwood's* essay on 'Style' (Vol. 12, p. 19).

67 idem in alio,] (Lt.), 'the same in another'.

68 cento…*other people.*] cf. De Quincey in his 1831 *Blackwood's* essay on Samuel Parr: Thomas James Mathias's *Pursuits of Literature 'is* a cento…in any fair sense' (Vol. 8, p. 65).

69 Joan of Arc,] For De Quincey's full-length consideration of Joan of Arc, see above, pp. 61–89. For Southey's poem, see above p. 528, n. 20.

70 *four…*Thalaba…Roderick;] Southey's *Thalaba the Destoyer* (1801), *Madoc* (1805), *The Curse of Kehama* (1810) and *Roderick the Last of the Goths* (1814).

71 *Coleridge…subsequently withdrawn.*] see Coleridge, *PW,* vol. I, pp. 205–25.

72 *Maid of Orleans*] see above, p. 61.

73 *Michelet…Henry VI.*] For Jules Michelet, see above, p. 61–2. De Quincey had earlier complained of 'the bitter and unfair spirit in which M. Michelet writes against England' (see above, p. 66). For Shakespeare's coarse depiction of Joan of Arc, see *1 Henry VI, Part I.*

74 *Shakespeare's share…ascertained.*] Though still a matter of dispute, the *Henry VI* trilogy is now thought to be mainly if not entirely Shakespeare's work.

75 *glory…indeed by Schiller.*] Friedrich Schiller (1759–1805), dramatist and poet, *Die Jungfrau von Orleans* (1801).

76 *burlesque…*La Pucelle,] François-Marie Arouet de Voltaire (see above, p. 570, n. 56), *La pucelle d'Orléans* (1755).

77 *battles… dust.*] De Quincey refers to the Hundred Years' War, and battles such as Crécy, Poictiers, and Agincourt (see above, p. 544, notes 41 and 46).

78 *Baptism…regent of France:*] In 1420, Henry V married the French princess Catherine of Valois (1401–37). Their son was Henry VI, who in 1422 became the King of England and the disputed King of France. His Regent in France was John Plantagenet, Duke of Bedford (see above, p. 549, note 25).

79 *Charles VII…Southey's poem.*] For Charles VII, see above p. 547, n. 77. Cf. De Quincey in 'Joan of Arc': 'It is unfortunate, therefore, for Southey's "Joan of Arc"…that, precisely when her real glory begins, the poem ends' (see above, p. 77).

80 *friendly reviewer…Coleridge.*] Lamb tells Coleridge that 'on the whole, considering the celerity wherewith ['Joan of Arc'] was finished, I was astonished at the unfrequency of weak lines. I had expected to find it verbose. Joan, I think, does too little in battle' (Talfourd, vol. I, p. 22).

81 official *records…1847,*] see above, p. 543, n. 24.

82 *Piron…*La Métromanie,] Alexis Piron (1689–1773), French dramatist and wit who became famous for his epigrams and for his comedy *La Métromanie* (1738; *The Poetry Craze*).

83 *Drayton couplet;*] Michael Drayton (1563–1631; *DNB*), poet.

84 *French Académie,*] Piron was elected to the Académie Française in 1753. His licentious compositions, however, were shown to the King, who forbade him to take his seat.

85 *our friend's memorandum!*] De Quincey himself is clearly responsible for this 'memorandum' from a 'friend'.

86 *Strand…Coleridge's…office.*] Daniel Stuart (1766–1846; *DNB*), owner of *The Morning Post* and then an evening newspaper, *The Courier.* Lamb discusses him in 'Newspapers Thirty-Five Years Ago'. In 1808 Stuart gave Coleridge a set of rooms above *The Courier* offices at Number 348, the Strand (Lamb, *Works*, vol. II, pp. 220–25).

87 *Godwin…Davy…Coleorton…Square*] William Godwin (1756–1836; *DNB*), philosopher and novelist. Humphrey Davy (1778–1829; *DNB*), chemist, lecturer and

inventor. Sir George Howland Beaumont (1753–1827; *DNB*), connoisseur and patron, owned Coleorton Hall in Leicestershire, but also had a house in Grosvenor Square, London.

88 *"spectatum veniens…ipse."'*] (Lt.), 'coming to look, coming to be looked at himself'. De Quincey inserted a close single quotation mark at this point, but he clearly intended the friend's memorandum to extend to 'the evening terminated' (see p. 395.6).

89 *opening arose for a pun.*] Cf. Lamb's thoughts in 'That the worst puns are the best' (Lamb, *Works*, vol. II, pp. 257–9).

90 *'yeoman's service,'*] Shakespeare, *Hamlet*, V.ii.36.

91 *Hastings.*] Hastings is a famous port and resort in East Sussex, but Lamb did not enjoy the place. 'There is no sense of home at Hastings', he wrote. 'It is a place of fugitive resort, an heterogeneous assemblage of sea-mews and stock brokers' (Lamb, *Works*, vol. II, p. 182).

92 à plomb] (Fr.), 'straight down'.

93 *Taylor and Hessey, the publishers.*] As publishers, James Augustus Hessey (1785–1870) and John Taylor (see above, p. 577, n. 68) produced books by De Quincey, William Hazlitt, John Keats, Charles Lamb, Walter Savage Landor, John Clare, and Thomas Carlyle. In April 1821, they bought the *London Magazine* and, with Taylor as editor, owned and operated it until June 1825. Richard Woodhouse was one of several guests at the dinner party in question, which was held by Taylor and Hessey on 6 December 1821 (Morrison, pp. 20–3).

94 *Lamb…full of gaiety;*] cf. Richard Woodhouse: 'Lamb, observing the Opium Eater to be very still, began a sort of playful attack upon him by way of rousing him, & desired he would (as he knew of old he could) be entertaining & facetious: he also added something in a jeering but good humoured way about Oxford Street' (Morrison, p. 22).

95 *people said he was 'tipsy.'*] cf. Haydon in December 1817: 'Lamb soon gets tipsey, and tipsey he got very shortly, to our infinite amusement' (Haydon, vol. II, p. 173).

96 *swears an eternal friendship*] cf. De Quincey's discussion in *Confessions of an English Opium-Eater* on the effects of wine: 'Men shake hands, swear eternal friendship, and shed tears – no mortal knows why' (Vol. 2, p. 44–5).

97 *Wainwright… for life.*] Thomas Griffiths Wainewright (1794–1847; *DNB*), painter, forger and murderer, wrote over two dozen articles for the *London Magazine* under pseudonyms such as 'Janus Weathercock' and 'Cornelius Van Vinkbooms'. Though he almost certainly committed at least two murders, Wainewright was transported on charges of forgery, and spent the last ten years of his life as a convict in Van Dieman's Land.

98 *Talfourd…Lytton.*] 'Among the contributors…was a gentleman whose subsequent career has invested the recollection of his appearances in the familiarity of social life with fearful interest – Mr Thomas Griffiths Wainwright' (Talfourd, vol. II, p. 7–27). Edward George Earle Bulwer-Lytton, first Baron Lytton (1803–73; *DNB*), novelist, poet and politician, whose *Lucretia, or the Children of the Night* (1846) is based on Wainewright's career.

99 *Hood…Reynolds…Cunningham.*] Thomas Hood (1799–1845; *DNB*), poet, was sub-editor of the *London Magazine,* and wrote over seventy articles for it. John Hamilton Reynolds (1796–1852; *DNB*), barrister and poet, published over eighty articles in the *London*, often over the signature 'Edward Herbert'. Allan Cunningham (1784–1842; *DNB*), chiefly remembered for his *Lives of the Most Eminent British Painters, Sculptors, and Architects* (1829–33), contributed over five dozen articles to the *London*.

100 *(signed...*Weathercock, Vinkbooms, *&c.)*] cf. Lamb to Hessey in 1822: 'Above all what is become of Janus Weathercock – or by his worse name of Vink....He is much wanted. He was the genius of the Lond. Mag. The rest of us are single Essayists' (Tim Chilcott, *A Publisher and his Circle* (London: Routledge & Kegan Paul, 1972), p. 149).

101 bijouterie...étalage...parvenu,] (Fr.), respectively, 'jewellery', 'display', 'upstart'.

102 *Da Vinci, Titian... Morghen, Volpato,*] Leonardo Da Vinci (1452–1519), Titian (*c.* 1488–1576), Raffaello Morghen (1768–1833) and Giovanni Volpato (1733–1803). Wainewright's finest art criticism appeared in two *London Magazine* series: 'Sentimentalities on the Fine Arts' (February – April 1820) and 'Notices of the Fine Arts' (February – June 1820).

103 *Miss Lamb...papers:*] Wainewright's 'indirect compliment' has not been traced.

104 *(October 1848)*] In 1858, De Quincey appended a footnote to this passage (see below, p. 720, 389.26).

105 *Locusta...Brinvilliers in Paris,*] Locusta was one of the most notorious Roman poisoners (Suetonius, *De vita Caesarum*, VI. 33). Marie-Madeleine-Marguérite d'Aubray, marquise de Brinvilliers (*c.* 1630–76), French poisoner.

106 *Infant Burial-societies.*] cf. Thomas Carlyle in the first chapter of *Past and Present*: 'At Stockport Assizes...a Mother and a Father are arraigned and found guilty of poisoning three of their children, to defraud a "burial-society" of some 3*l.* 8*s.* due on the death of each child' (Carlyle, *Works*, vol. X, p. 4). For details of these burial societies, see Judith Knelman, *Twisting in the Wind: The Murderess and the English Press* (Toronto: University of Toronto Press, 1998), pp. 49–52.

107 lucro ponatur,] (Lt.), 'something we reckon a gain'.

108 *die...within that period;*] For details, see Andrew Motion, *Wainewright the Poisoner* (New York: Alfred A. Knopf, 2000). In 1858, De Quincey expanded this passage (see below, p. 720, 390.30).

109 *Wilkie.*] David Wilkie (1785–1841; *DNB*), Scottish-born painter whose best known works include *The Blind Fiddler* (1806), *The Village Festival* (1811) and *The Waterloo Gazette* (1821).

110 *winter of 1821–2.*] De Quincey has misremembered these dates, for Woodhouse's *Cause Book* makes it clear that he left London for his home in Westmorland on 29 December 1821. De Quincey did not return to London until 12 December 1822 (Morrison, p. 33; Lindop, p. 259).

111 *Wilson,*] John Wilson (see above, p. 531, n. 74) was one of the mainstays of *Blackwood's Edinburgh Magazine* for over three decades. He was one of De Quincey's closest friends, and the subject of essays in 1829 (Vol. 7, pp. 3–27) and 1850 (Vol. 17, pp. 33–42),

112 *Johnson's...'brisk reciprocation.'*] 'amoebaean' means 'alternatively answering, responsive' (*OED*). For Samuel Johnson, see above, p. 537, n. 3. The phrase 'brisk reciprocation' has not been traced in Johnson's works. De Quincey may be conflating at least two different references. Boswell records Johnson's observation that 'Tom Birch is as brisk as a bee in conversation'. In *The Lives of the Poets*, Johnson writes that 'Pope and Philips lived in a perpetual reciprocation of malevolence' (Boswell, vol. I, p. 159; Johnson, *Lives*, vol. III, p. 319).

113 *brief eclipse of sleep.*] Cf. Haydon in December 1817: 'Lamb, who had been dosing as usual, suddenly opened his mouth and said, "What did you say, Sir?"' (Haydon, vol. II, p. 174).

114 *Aquinas,*] Saint Thomas Aquinas (1224/25–74), the greatest of the medieval philosopher-theologians.

115 *Lamb had Jewish blood in his veins,*] cf. William Maginn (1793–1842; *DNB*), who argued that Lamb's real name was Lomb, and that he was of Jewish extraction (Lamb, *Works*, vol. II, p. 338).

116 *Shylock;*] Shylock is the Jewish moneylender in Shakespeare's comedy *The Merchant of Venice*.

117 *Percy's...Lady Abbess.*] Hugh of Lincoln (1245–55; *DNB*), legendary English child martyr who was supposedly murdered by members of the local Jewish community. For Thomas Percy, see above, p. 543, n. 21. The legend of Hugh may have influenced Geoffrey Chaucer (see above, p. 601, n. 20) in his composition of 'The Prioress's Tale' from *Canterbury Tales*. In 'Imperfect Sympathies', Lamb writes that he has, 'in the abstract, no disrespect for Jews....but I should not care to be in habits of familiar intercourse with any of that nation. ...Old prejudices cling about me. I cannot shake off the story of Hugh of Lincoln' (Lamb, *Works*, vol. II, p. 61).

118 *murdered...architect,*] Rosslyn chapel, just south of Edinburgh, contains the Apprentice Pillar, which is said to have been carved by an apprentice to the master mason. The master went to Rome to seek inspiration and, in his absense, the apprentice decided to try to carve the pillar himself. When the master returned and discovered the apprentice had created a masterpiece, he struck him dead on the spot in a fit of jealous rage.

119 *Capulet...Montague,*] the two feuding Veronese families in Shakespeare's *Romeo and Juliet*.

120 *'Diddle, diddle, dumpkins;'*] cf. Haydon in December 1817: 'Lamb roared out, "Diddle iddle don / My son John / Went to bed with his breeches on"' (Haydon, vol. II, p. 175).

121 praenomen] the first of the usual three names of a Roman male.

122 *Wordsworth...time of Waterloo.*] Wordsworth's two-volume collected *Poems* of 1815, the year of Napoleon's defeat at Waterloo. The edition was published by Longman, a publishing house founded in 1724 by Thomas Longman (1699–1755; *DNB*).

123 *'Alas! What boots,—'*] Wordsworth, 'Alas! what boots the long laborious quest'. De Quincey quotes the sonnet in his 1830 *Blackwood's* essays on 'Kant in his Miscellaneous Essays' and the 'French Revolution' (Vol. 7, pp. 69, 175, 309, 348).

124 *Hoby*] Hoby, boot maker to George III, was based in St James's Street, Piccadilly. His sympathy for Queen Caroline in her dispute with George IV came to the attention of Byron, who penned an epigram on the subject ('Mr Hoby the Bootmaker's soft heart is sore') in August 1820 (Byron, *PW*, vol. IV, pp. 289, 519).

125 *poems...Thurlow*] Edward Hovell-Thurlow, second Baron Thurlow (1781–1829; *DNB*), whose *Select Poems* appeared in 1821. The sonnet in question is 'To a Bird that Haunted the Waters of Lacken in the Winter', which 'for quiet sweetness, and unaffected morality, has scarcely a parallel in our language', as Lamb put it in the *London Magazine*. In 1827, De Quincey himself described the sonnet as 'fine' (Lamb, *Works*, vol. II, pp. 438–9; Vol. 5, p. 94).

126 *Lamb proposed whist*] cf. Lamb on 'Mrs Battle's Opinions on Whist' (Lamb, *Works*, vol. II, pp. 32–7).

127 *'The sweetness...scarcely worthy.'*] a slightly truncated version of Talfourd, vol. II, pp. 208–9.

128 *liberal retiring allowance,*] Lamb retired from East India House in March 1825, with a pension of £441, less a small annual deduction as a provision for his sister. Lamb 'had amassed, by annual savings, a sufficient sum...to secure comfort to Miss Lamb' (Talfourd, vol. II, p. 215).

129 *he was* not....*he* was.] De Quincey's thoughts in this regard may have been prompted by Lamb's letter to Walter Wilson (1781–1847; *DNB*): 'Do not, I pray you, conclude that I am an inveterate enemy to all religion. I have had a time of seriousness, and I have known the importance and reality of a religious belief' (Talfourd, vol. I, p. 133).

130 *'Coleridge...by the world!'*] Lamb, *Letters*, vol. I, p. 86.

131 *'Do continue...genuine piety.'*] Lamb, *Letters*, vol. I, p. 48

132 *'Be not angry...His character.'*] Lamb, *Letters*, vol. I, p. 49.

133 *'Few but laugh...to* them.'] Lamb, *Letters*, vol. I, p. 74.

134 *could he fly for comfort,*] Psalms 55: 6: 'O that I had wings like a dove; *for then* would I fly away and be at rest'; cf. De Quincey in *Confessions*, Vol. 2, p. 41.

The English Mail-Coach, or The Glory of Motion

1 *Oxford, Mr Palmer, M.P. for Bath,*] De Quincey matriculated at Worcester College, Oxford, in 1803. He left four years later without taking a degree. In 1784, John Palmer (1742–1818; *DNB*), a theatre manager in Bath and Bristol, and William Pitt (see above, p. 528, n. 15), then Chancellor of the Exchequer, arranged the first trial mail coach run. Palmer organized the many changes of horses from drivers and innkeepers. The trial took place on the Bath to London road, and was highly successful. Other mail coach routes were quickly established. Palmer became Comptroller General of the Post Office in 1786. He became M.P. for Bath in 1801. Cf. Southey in 1807: 'Before this plan of Mr Palmer's was established, the ordinary pace of traveling in England differed little from what it still is in other countries: an able-bodied man might walk the usual day's journey' (Southey, *Letters*, p. 202).

2 *Lady Madeline Gordon.*] De Quincey has his facts confused. Lady Madelina [*sic*] Gordon was the second daughter of Alexander, fourth Duke of Gordon (*c.* 1745–1827), and in 1805 she married (not John Palmer) but Charles Palmer of Lockley Park, Berkshire.

3 *invented (or* discovered*)*] In revision, De Quincey added a footnote to this passage (see below, p. 723, 409.3).

4 *Galileo...satellites of Jupiter,*] Galileo (1564–1642), Italian mathematician, astronomer and physicist. He discovered four of Jupiter's satellites in 1610.

5 'Vast distances...*total distance.*] cf. Southey on mail coaches: 'no unnecessary delays are permitted, and the traveler who goes in them can calculate his time accurately' (Southey, *Letters*, p. 201).

6 *apocalyptic vials,*] cf. Revelation 16: 1: 'pour out the vials of the wrath of God upon the earth'.

7 *heart-shaking news*] cf. Cowper's description of the arrival of the mail-coach in *The Task*, IV. 23–7: 'Usher'd in / With such heart-shaking music, who can say / What are its tidings? have our troops awaked? / Or do they still, as if with opium drugg'd, / Snore to the murmurs of th' Atlantic wave?'.

8 *Trafalgar...Salamanca...Vittoria...Waterloo.*] decisive British victories in the Napoleonic wars. Horatio Nelson (1758–1805; *DNB*) destroyed the French fleet in the Battle of Trafalgar (1805). Wellington (see above, p. 542, n. 86) won dramatic battles at Salamanca (1812) and Vitoria (1813). Napoleon's final defeat came at Waterloo (1815).

9 *reaping...tears...sown.*] Psalm 126: 5: 'They that sow in tears shall reap in joy'.

10 Te Deums] a Christian Latin hymn sung on occasions of public thanksgiving. The opening words are 'Te Deum laudamus' ('We praise thee, O Lord').

11 *general prostration,*] At the height of the Napoleonic Wars, Napoleon proclaimed the so-called 'Continental system', a blockade designed to paralyze Britain through the destruction of British commerce: neutrals and French allies were not to trade with the British. Cf. De Quincey in his 1829 essay on John Wilson: 'The fierce *acharnement* of Bonaparte' was 'pointedly directed to every thing English, and the prostration of the Continent' (Vol. 7, p. 25).

12 *Act,*] an old name for Trinity (summer) term at Oxford, and derived from the 'act' or thesis submitted for a degree.

13 *going down*] It is 'up' to Oxford, and 'down' to all other towns and cities. Thus, in 'Going down with victory', De Quincey travels from London into the country.

14 *Palmer's establishment as Oxford.*] In revision, De Quincey expanded this passage (see below, p. 724, 410.12).

15 *four inside...Charles II.,)*] cf. Southey: the mail coaches 'carry four inside passengers, two outside' (Southey, *Letters*, p. 201). De Quincey's point is that during the reign of Charles II (see above, p. 601, n. 37), passengers did not sit on the outside of the coach.

16 *delf ware*] cheap glazed earthenware, originally from Delft in Holland. It is much coarser than porcelain.

17 *attaint*] 'to infect with corruption, poison, etc.' (*OED*, which cites this example from De Quincey).

18 delirium tremens)] see above, p. 543, n. 22.

19 salle-à-manger,] (Fr.), 'dining room'.

20 *maxim...same logical construction.*] De Quincey's free translation of the Roman legal phrase 'De non apparentibus et non existentibus eadem est lex' (see below, p. 725, 411.8).

21 *'raff,'*] persons of the lowest class. Cf. Dickens, *Dombey and Son*, p. 119: 'Mrs Mac Stinger immediately demanded whether an Englishwoman's house was her castle or not: and whether she was to be broke in upon by "raff"'.

22 *'Snobs,'...'nobs,'...ten years later.*] A 'snob' was 'a shoemaker or cobbler'; as a piece of university slang, a 'snob' also meant 'any one not a gownsman; a townsman' (*OED*). A 'nob' was 'a person of some wealth or social distinction' (*OED*).

23 *Great wits jump.*] a proverbial phrase meaning 'men of great minds arrive independently at the same conclusions'. Cf. Shakespeare, *The Taming of the Shrew*, I.i.190: 'Both our inventions meet and jump in one'; cf. also Sterne, *Tristram Shandy*: 'GREAT wits jump: for the moment Dr *Slop* cast his eyes upon his bag...the very same thought occurred' (Laurence Sterne, *The Life and Opinions of Tristram Shandy*, ed. Ian Campbell Ross (Oxford: Oxford University Press, 1998), p. 132).

24 *celestial intellect of China.*] De Quincey is punning. One of the names for China is 'Tian Chan' ('Celestial Empire').

25 *our first embassy*] in MS GM A, De Quincey appended a footnote to this passage (see below, p. 725, p. 411.39–40).

26 *George III...Lord Macartney,)*] In 1792, George III (see above, p. 525, n. 31) appointed George Macartney, Earl Macartney (1737–1806; *DNB*) as first British emissary to Peking. De Quincey's anecdote, however, is fictional, and elaborated from the description in Sir George Staunton (1737–1801; *DNB*), *An Authentic Account of an Embassy from the King of Great Britain to the Emperor of China*, 3 vols (London: Nicol, 1797), vol. II, p. 343: 'It was a new spectacle to the Chinese, accustomed only to the low, clumsy, two-wheeled carriages....When a splendid chariot intended

as a present for the Emperor was unpacked and put together, nothing could be more admired; but it was necessary to give directions for taking off the box; for when the mandarines found out that so elevated a seat was destined for the coachman...they expressed the utmost astonishment that it should be proposed to place any man in a situation *above* the Emperor'.

27 *the emperor*] Qianlong (1711–99), fourth Emperor of the Qing dynasty, 1735–96.

28 *hammer-cloth*] 'a cloth covering the driver's seat or "box" in a state or family coach' (*OED*).

29 *first lord of the treasury*] in England, the Prime Minister.

30 *flowery people,*] see above, p. 591, n. 47.

31 *checkstrings...jury-reins,*] A 'checkstring' is 'a string by which an occupant of a carriage may signal to the driver to stop' (*OED*). A 'jury-rein' is a 'temporary rein'.

32 *god Fo, Fo...call Fi, Fi.*] There is no Chinese god 'Fo, Fo', but De Quincey may be playing on 'Fu Xi', the name of the first of China's mythical emperors.

33 Ca ira.] (Fr.), 'that will succeed'. The expression, many times repeated, comprised about half the words of a revolutionary song that later became the official song of the French Revolution. It is said to have originated on 5 October 1789 when the French mob marched to Versailles to bring the King and royal family to Paris.

34 *chief seats in synagogues,*] Matthew 23: 6: 'And love the uppermost rooms at feasts, and the chief seats in the Synagogues'.

35 *Aristotle's, Cicero's,*] Aristotle (see above, p. 535, n. 38) was the author of the *Nicomachean Ethics*, and founded the Peripatitic school of Philosophy. For Cicero and ethics, see above, p. 589, n. 41.

36 *Euclid*] For Euclid, see above, p. 537, n. 71.

37 *ninety days...notes and protesters*] Bills of exchange committed someone to pay a certain sum of money on a specified date. A bill was negotiable and could be passed from hand to hand unless someone 'protested' it (formally refused to accept it on the grounds that the person named in it would not or could not pay), in which case it would be 'noted' (recorded as worthless). Legal action for debt might follow. De Quincey had suffered the whole process numerous times.

38 posse,] 'Posse comitatus' (literally, 'the power of the county') is a legal term for the band of assistants which may be summoned by a sheriff.

39 *guard's blunderbuss.*] cf. Southey: 'Every coach has its guard, armed with a blunderbuss, who has charge of the mails' (Southey, *Letters*, p. 201).

40 *snakes in Von Troil's Iceland;*] De Quincey used this same anecdote in his 1848 essay on Alexander Pope (see above, p. 602, n. 68). In revision, he also appended a footnote to this passage (see below, p. 726, 413.31).

41 *parliamentary rat,*] a Member of Parliament who goes over from his own party to the opposition, in order to gain some personal advantage.

42 *forbidden seat*] during the process of revision, De Quincey appended a footnote to this passage (see below, p. 726, 413.35).

43 laesa majestas,] (Lt.), 'violated majesty'; a crime committed against the sovereign power in a state.

44 *'Jam proximus ardet Ucalegon.'*] Virgil, *Aeneid*, II. 311–12. The lines are taken from the description, given by Aeneas to Dido, of the destruction of Troy: 'Even now the spacious house of Deiphobus has fallen, as the fire-god towers above; even now his neighbour Ucalegon blazes'.

45 *way-bill.*] a list of passengers booked on the coach.

46 *dreadful blast of our horn*] cf. Southey: the guard 'has a seat affixed behind the coach, from whence he overlooks it, and gives notice with a horn to clear the road when any thing is in the way' (Southey, *Letters*, p. 201).

47 *crane-neck quarterings.*] manoeuvres to remove vehicles urgently from the path of oncoming traffic. The crane-neck was a curved iron rod diagonally connecting the back and front axles of a cart, both of which pivoted to allow turning in the smallest possible space. 'Quartering' was moving a vehicle from the centre of the road to allow another to pass (see below, p. 623, n. 54).

48 *attainder...six generations,*] 'Attainder' was the deprivation of the rights of a person convicted of a felony and sentenced to death or outlawry. The blood of the attainted person was regarded as being corrupted (see above, n. 17), and the person could neither inherit land nor pass it on to an heir. Cf. Shakespeare, *Love's Labor's Lost*, I.i. 155–7: 'The laws at large I write my name, / And he that breaks them... / Stands in attainder of eternal shame'.

49 *benefit of clergy,*] Formerly under the English law, all persons in holy orders, and ultimately all persons who could read, might, by pleading 'benefit of clergy', be exempted from criminal punishment at the hands of a secular judge. The right survived for some offences until 1827.

50 *Quarter Sessions.*] see above, p. 601, n. 38.

51 *having authority.*] Matthew 7: 29: 'For he taught them as one having authority, and not as their scribes'.

52 *levied upon the hundred.*] charged to the hundred, an administrative subdivision of a county, already almost obsolete in 1800.

53 *lying poached*] De Quincey is punning on 'poach', which means 'to thrust or stamp down with the feet', and 'of an egg; cooked in boiling water, without the shell' (*OED*).

54 *Napoleon...Desaix, never were uttered at all.*] Louis-Charles-Antoine Desaix de Veygoux, (1768–1800), French military hero who led forces in the German, Egyptian and Italian campaigns. He was killed at the Battle of Marengo, in northern Italy. When Napoleon heard of his death, he is reported to have said, 'Alas! it is not permitted to me to weep' (J. G. Lockhart, *The History of Napoleon Buonaparte*, ed. J. Holland Rose (London: Oxford University Press, 1916), p. 154); cf. Hazlitt, *Works*, vol. XIV, p. 151.

55 Vengeur...*Cambronne*...'La Garde...pas,'...*Talleyrand.*] In the 'Glorious First of June' victory (1794), Richard Howe, Earl Howe (1726–99; *DNB*) commanded the British fleet, capturing six French ships and sinking a seventh, the *Vengeur*, which was reported to have gone down with her streamers flying and her crew all shouting, '*Vive la République*'. Pierre Cambronne (1770–1842), French general, commanded Napoleon's Old Guard, which was decimated at the Battle of Waterloo. His 'vaunt' was 'The Guards die, but do not surrender'. He later denied using the phrase. For Charles-Maurice, Prince de Talleyrand-Périgord, see above, p. 599, n. 85.

56 à fortiori] see above, p. 560, n. 18.

57 *Holyhead...Shrewsbury and Oswestry,*] Holyhead is a port on Holy Island, in Anglesey, north Wales. Shrewsbury and Oswestry are in Shropshire.

58 Tallyho *or* Highflier,] 'Tally-ho' is 'originally, the proper name given to a fast day-coach between London and Birmingham, started in 1823; subsequently appropriated by other fast coaches on this and other roads' (*OED*). A 'Highflier' is 'a fast stage-coach'; cf. Scott, 'mail-coach races against mail-coach, and high-flyer against high-flyer, through the most remote districts of Britain' (*OED*; Scott, *Mid-Lothian*, p. 7).

59 *tombs of Luxor.*] Luxor is on the East bank of the Nile. It includes part of the ruins of ancient Thebes, and is rich in tombs with hieroglyphic inscriptions.

60 *'which they upon the adverse faction wanted.'*] Shakespeare, *Richard III*, V.iii.12–13: 'Besides, the King's name is a tower of strength, / Which they upon the adverse faction want'.

61 *burn within me*] cf. Luke 24: 32: 'Did not our heart burn within us'.

62 *cat might look at a king,*] *Proverbs*, p. 109.

63 *Brummagem*] 'Brummagem' is a contemptuous name for Birmingham. Cf. De Quincey in his 1830 *Blackwood's* essay on Richard Bentley, where he writes of 'the gold and silver words, and...the base Brummagem copper coinage' (Vol. 7, p. 158).

64 *very fine story...elder dramatists,*] Thomas Heywood (1573–1641; *DNB*), actor and playwright, *The Royal King and the Loyal Subject*, V. v. It is most probable, however, that De Quincey knew the story from its inclusion by Charles Lamb (see above, pp. 365–97) in his *Specimens of the English Dramatic Poets* (1808), where it appears under the title 'Noble Traitor' (Lamb, *Works*, vol. IV, pp. 88–9).

65 *10th of Edward III. chap. 15,*] Edward III (1312–77), King of England, 1327–77. No such statute exists. In revision, De Quincey deleted this reference and inserted 'the 6th of Edward Longshanks, chap. 18' (see below, 729. 416.32–3).

66 *York four hours after leaving London.*] This would have been impossible even by the fastest train in 1849.

67 Non magna loquimur...magna vivimus.] In revision, De Quincey translated this phrase as 'we do not make verbal ostentation of our grandeurs, we realise our grandeurs in act, and in the very experience of life' (see below, p. 729, 417.11).

68 *Nile nor Trafalgar*] At the Battle of the Nile (1798), the English fleet under Nelson (see above, n. 8) routed the French under Napoleon (see above, p. 526, n. 59). For Trafalgar, see above, n. 8.

69 *Tidings, fitted to convulse all nations,*] cf. Cowper, *The Task*, IV. 5–7: 'He comes, the herald of a noisy world, / With spatter'd boots, strapp'd waist, and frozen locks, / News from all nations lumb'ring at his back'.

70 *Marlborough Forest,*] Marlborough is in Wiltshire, and on the highroad between London and Bath.

71 *honorary distinction...special service.*] Southey makes this 'error', for he observed that 'guard and coachmen all wear the royal livery' (Southey, *Letters*, p. 201).

72 *Ulysses...accursed bow...suitors.*] In Homer, *Odyssey*, XXI-XXII, Ulysses slays the suitors of his wife, Penelope, using his magic bow.

73 mais oui donc;] (Fr.), 'but of course'.

74 *'Say, all our praises why should lords –'*] Pope, 'Epistle to Allen Lord Bathurst', l. 249: 'But all our praises why should lords engross?'.

75 *silver turrets*] In revision, De Quincey appended a footnote to this passage in which he cited Chaucer (see below, p. 732, 419.22).

76 *conduct of the affair.*] In revision, De Quincey deleted the rest of this paragraph (see below, p. 732, 420.4–11).

77 ex abundanti,] (Lt.), 'out of an abundance'.

78 *guardianship of Chancery,*] The Court of Chancery was the court of equity under the lord high chancellor. It was abolished in 1873.

79 *change or perish...to the dust.*] In revision, De Quincey added a quotation from Wordsworth's *Excursion* to this passage (see below, p. 732, 420.13–16).

80 *Mr Waterton*] Charles Waterton (1782–1865; *DNB*), naturalist, best known for *Wanderings in South America* (1825).

81 *always to run away from.*] cf. De Quincey in *Confessions*: 'The cursed crocodile became to me the object of more horror than almost all the rest....his leering eyes, looked out at me, multiplied into a thousand repetitions: and I stood loathing and fascinated' (Vol. 2, p. 71).

82 *continued until Mr Waterton*] In revision, De Quincey appended a footnote to this passage (see below, p. 733, 420.29.

83 *crocodile...fox-hunting before breakfast*] De Quincey refers to Waterton's account of crocodile riding in *Wanderings in South America*: 'By the time the Cayman was within two yards of me, I saw he was in a state of fear and perturbation; I instantly dropped the mast, sprung up, and jumped on his back, turning half round as I vaulted, so that I gained my seat with my face in the right position. I immediately seized his legs, and, by main force, twisted them on his back; thus they served me for a bridle....Should it be asked, how I managed to keep my seat, I would answer, – I hunted some years with Lord Darlington's fox hounds' (cited in Grevel Lindop, 'De Quincey and the Cursed Crocodile' in *Essays in Criticism*, 45 (1995), p. 130). Cf. Shelley, 'The Mask of Anarchy', ll. 24–5: 'Like Sidmouth next Hypocrisy / On a crocodile rode by'.

84 *rose in June;*] cf. Wordsworth, 'Strange Fits of Passion I have Known', ll. 1–2: 'When she I loved was strong and gay, / And like a rose in June'.

85 *thick as blossoms in paradise.*] cf. Milton, *Paradise Lost*, I. 302–3: 'Thick as autumnal leaves that strew the brooks / In Vallombrosa'.

86 *of a peculiarly...forest life.*] In MS GM B, De Quincey expanded this passage (see below, p. 733, 421.n.4–5).

87 *reason of man.*] In revision, De Quincey deleted the rest of this paragraph, a deep cut of over one thousand words (see below, p. 734, 421.21–423.11).

88 *kraken,*] a vast mythical sea-monster.

89 monokeras,] the Greek form of 'monoceros', unicorn. It is not clear which one-horned animal De Quincey has in mind, but he may be thinking of the rhinoceros.

90 *shield that embalms it*] The lion and the unicorn are heraldic symbols of Britain.

91 *Spenser...our elder poets)*] Edmund Spenser (see above, p. 535, n. 32), *The Faerie Queene*, I.iii.5–7.

92 *fight at Warwick...lion called Wallace.*] A menagerie-keeper named Wombwell organized the public baiting of two lions by bulldogs at Warwick on 30 July 1825. The first lion, Nero, refused to fight, but Wallace rose to the occasion and killed two dogs (Thomas Kemp, *A History of Warwick and its People* (Warwick: Cooke, 1905), p. 83).

93 *Southey*] For Robert Southey, see above, p. 523, n. 3.

94 *poor-rates.*] 'A rate or assessment, for the relief or support of the poor' (*OED*).

95 *mere numerical double*] For De Quincey on 'oneself repeated once too often', see above, p. 540, n. 45.

96 *baubling schooner*] cf. Shakespeare, *Twelfth Night*, V.i.54–5: 'A baubling vessel was he captain of, / For shallow draught and bulk unprizable'.

97 *Soult...Majesty's coronation,*] Nicolas-Jean de Dieu Soult, Duc de Dalmatia (1769–1851), military leader and political figure, commanded Napoleon's armies in the Peninsula from 1803. After Napoleon's fall he became a royalist, and he represented the French government at Victoria's coronation (see Peter Hayman, *Soult: Napoleon's Maligned Marshall* (London: Arms and Armour Press, 1990), pp. 254–8).

98 en flagrant delit.] from the Latin 'flagrante delicto', 'in flagrant transgression'.

99 *Albuera...battles.*] In May 1811, Soult was defeated with heavy losses at Albuera, in southwestern Spain. It was one of the bloodiest battles of the Napoleonic Wars.

100 *at that time...General Post-Office.*] Lombard Street is in the City of London, and the centre of the money market. In 1829, the Lombard Street post office was replaced by a new post office in St Martin's le Grand, just north of St Paul's Cathedral (see below, p. 735, 424.4).

101 attelage,] equipage, team of horses.

102 *One heart...English blood.*] cf. De Quincey in his 1831 *Blackwood's* essay on Samuel Parr: 'If ever, in this world, a nation had one heart and one soul, it was the British nation in the spring of 1803' (Vol. 8, p. 92).

103 *Badajoz...Salamanca*] Badajoz in southwestern Spain was stormed by Wellington (see above, p. 542, n. 86) in 1812. For Salamanca, see above, n. 8.

104 *American writer*] untraced.

105 *Be thou whole!*] Cf. Mark 5: 34: 'And he said unto her, Daughter, thy faith hath made thee whole'.

106 *Barnet*,] Barnet was a village in Hertfordshire, but is now an outer borough of Greater London.

107 *Every joy...grief, to some.*] cf. Cowper's description of the mailman in *The Task*, IV. 13–15: 'messenger of grief / Perhaps to thousands, and of joy to some'.

108 Courier...*gazette*,] *The Courier* was a London evening paper established in 1792. 'The gazette' is 'one of the three official journals entitled *The London Gazette*, *The Edinburgh Gazette*, and *The Dublin Gazette*, issued by authority twice a week, and containing lists of government appointments and promotions...and other public notices' (*OED*).

109 *Celtic Highlanders...*fey.] 'Fey' means 'fated to die, doomed to death' (*OED*). 'Not a Celtic word, but an Anglo-Saxon word preserved in Lowland Scotch. "You are surely *fey*" would be said in Scotland to a person observed to be in extravagantly high spirits, or in any mood surprisingly beyond the bounds of his ordinary temperament, – the notion being that the excitement is supernatural, and a presage of his approaching death or of some other calamity about to befall him' (Masson, vol. XIII, p. 298).

110 *Bengal lights)*] see above, p. 573, n. 5.

111 *glittering laurels,*] In revision, De Quincey appended a footnote to this phrase (see below, p. 736, n. 427.22).

112 *Talavera.*] On 27–28 July 1809 Wellesley routed the French at Talavera in central Spain, but suffered heavy casualties and was forced to retreat soon afterwards. In revision, De Quincey expanded this passage with a reference to the 'virtual treachery of the Spanish general, Cuesta' (see below, p. 737, 427.30).

113 *23d Dragoons...four survived.*] De Quincey may be drawing in part on Sir William Francis Patrick Napier's famous account of the charge in his *History of the War in the Peninsula* (1828–40): 'Sir Arthur ordered Anson's brigade of cavalry, composed of the 23rd light dragoons and the first German hussars, to charge the head of these columns. They went off at a canter, increasing their speed as they advanced and riding headlong against the enemy; but in a few moments, a hollow cleft which was not perceptible at a distance intervened, and at the same moment the French, throwing themselves into squares, opened their fire....The twenty-third found the chasm more practicable, the English blood is hot, and the regiment plunged down without a check, men and horses rolling over each other in dreadful confusion; yet the survivors, untamed, mounted the opposite bank by twos and threes' (Napier, *History of the War in the Peninsula*, 6 vols (London: Warne, 1892), vol. II, pp. 175–6).

114 *aceldama*] Acts 1: 19: 'field of blood'.

The Vision of Sudden Death

1 *ultimate object...Dream-Fugue,*] cf. De Quincey in his 1838 *Tait's* essay on Charles Lamb, where he states that the dream finale in *Confessions of an English Opium-Eater* was 'the real object of the whole work' (Vol. 10, p. 265). In revision, De Quincey omitted this parenthetical prefatory note (see below, 738, 430.1–20).

2 *consummation...most fervently to be desired,*] cf. Shakespeare, *Hamlet*, III.i.63–4: ''tis a consummation / Devoutly to be wish'd'. De Quincey almost certainly has in mind the Greek legend of Biton and Cleobis. Their mother prayed that they would receive the highest gift the gods had to bestow. The next morning she found them both dead.

3 *Caesar...(*caena,*)*] cf. De Quincey in his 1839 *Blackwood's* essay on 'Dinner: Real and Reputed': 'Great misconceptions have always prevailed about the Roman *dinner.* Dinner [*caena*] was the only meal which the Romans as a nation took' (Vol. 11, p. 409).

4 *'That which should be most sudden.'*] Suetonius, *De vita Caesarum*, I. 87: 'The day before his murder, in a conversation which arose...as to what manner of death was most to be desired, he had given his preference to one which was sudden and unexpected'. The story is also told by Plutarch, *Parallel Lives*, Caesar, LXIII. 7–8; and Appian, *Roman History*, The Civil Wars, II. 115. Cf. Shakespeare, *Julius Caesar*, II.ii.34–7: 'Of all the wonders that I yet have heard, / It seems to me most strange that men should fear, / Seeing that death, a necessary end, / Will come when it will come'.

5 *'From Lightning...sudden death...*deliver us.'] from 'The Litany' in *The Book of Common Prayer.*

6 *words or acts.*] As De Quincey makes clear in revision, he intends '*final* words or acts' (see below, p. 739, 431.8).

7 *simply of extra misfortune.*] In MS VSD E, De Quincey drafted a footnote for this passage, in which he distinguished between the '*act*' and '*habit* of gambling' (see above, p. 465).

8 *βιαθανατος...Βιαιος:*] respectively, 'violent death' and 'violent'. De Quincey draws on John Donne (1572–1631; *DNB*) and his casuistic defence of suicide, *βιαθανατος*, A *Declaration of that Paradoxe or Thesis, That Self-homicide is not so naturally Sin, that it may never be otherwise* (1644). Cf. De Quincey in his 1823 *London Magazine* essay 'On Suicide': 'IT is a remarkable proof of the inaccuracy with which most men read – that Donne's Biathanatos has been supposed to countenance Suicide' (Vol. 3, p. 164). In revision, De Quincey expanded his discussion of these terms (see below, p. 739, 431.30).

9 *Meantime...sudden death as a mere*] In revision, De Quincey expanded this passage (see below, p. 739, 431.41).

10 *twinkling of an eye*] De Quincey invokes 1 Corinthians 15: 51–2: 'We will not all die, but we will all be changed, in a moment, in the twinkling of an eye, at the last trumpet. For the trumpet will sound, and the dead will be raised imperishable, and we will be changed'. Fittingly, De Quincey uses this same phrase again in the closing paragraph of 'The Vision of Sudden Death' (see above, p. 442).

11 lâcheté?] (Fr.), cowardliness.

12 *That dream, so familiar*] cf. the 1856 *Confessions*, where De Quincey discusses the 'languishing impotence...most of us have felt in the dreams of our childhood when lying down without a struggle before some all-conquering lion' (Vol. 2, p. 170).

13 *'Nature...all is lost;'*] Milton, *Paradise Lost*, IX. 782–4: 'Earth felt the wound, and nature from her seat / Sighing through all her works gave signs of woe, / That all was lost'.

14 *'Confirmation...rite is that!*] De Quincey seems to have in mind Wordsworth, 'Confirmation', ll. 4–6: 'For they are taking the baptismal Vow / Upon their conscious selves; their own lips speak / The solemn promise'.

15 *As I drew near...past midnight;*] In revision, De Quincey greatly altered the opening of this paragraph (see below, p. 741, 433.18–19).

16 *Westmorland*] Westmorland is a former county of northwestern England. It became part of the new county of Cumbria in 1974. De Quincey moved to Dove Cottage, Grasmere in Westmorland in 1809. It was his primary place of residence for the next twenty years.

17 *mail was not even yet ready to start.*] MS VSD B is a discarded fragment that De Quincey seems to have considered for insertion at this point (see above, p. 456–7).

18 jus dominii...jus gentium] legal terms meaning, respectively, 'the law of ownership' and 'the law of nations'.

19 *deeds of darkness...ally of morality*] cf. John 3: 19: 'men loved darkness rather than light, because their deeds were evil'. The first street-lighting using coal-gas was installed in Westminster, London, in 1814.

20 *want of a criminal.*] In revision, De Quincey omitted the rest of this paragraph, and the first sentence of the following paragraph (see below, p. 742, 433.38–40).

21 *Effendi,*] 'a Turkish title of respect' (*OED*).

22 *Chrysippus...salt...for a soul)*] Chrysippus (*c.* 280–*c.* 206 BC), Greek philosopher who regarded animals as created solely for the use of man. De Quincey draws from Cicero, *De Natura deorum*, II.lxiv.160: 'As for the pig, it can only furnish food; indeed Chrysippus actually says that its soul was given it to serve as salt and keep it from putrefaction'. De Quincey attributes the converse of this view to Chrysippus.

23 *son of Othman,*] a Turk; the Ottoman dynasty had ruled Turkey since 1300.

24 *Dr Johnsons cannot pick holes in it.*] Samuel Johnson (see above, p. 537, n. 3) published two well-known examinations of epitaphs in 'Essay on Epitaphs' (1740) and 'A Dissertation on Epitaphs Written by Pope' (1756).

25 *Deodand*] a fine charged against the owner of an object that has caused injury or death. In MS VSD F, De Quincey appended a footnote on Morcellus (see below, p. 743, 434.33).

26 *Morcellus*] Stefano Antonio Morelli (1737–1822), Italian antiquary and expert on Latin inscriptions, *De stilo Inscriptionum Latinarum* (1780). Cf. De Quincey on Samuel Parr and epitaphs: 'Dr Parr prescribed to himself, for this department of composition, very peculiar and very refined maxims. The guide whom he chiefly followed, was one not easily obtained for love or money – *Morcellus de Stylo Inscriptionum*' (Vol. 8, p. 75).

27 *Virgil...'Monstrum...lumen ademptum.'*] Virgil, *Aeneid*, III. 658: 'a monster awful, shapeless, huge, bereft of light'. The reference is to the Cyclops Polyphemus. The Cyclopes had only one eye in the centre of the forehead, and even this eye Polyphemus had lost in his battle with Odysseus (Homer, *Odyssey*, IX).

28 *Calendars...Arabian Nights...curiosity,*] Calendars belonged to a religious order of Dervishes. The three Calendars in *The Arabian Nights' Entertainment* were princes in disguise. Each tells the story of how he lost his right eye. Only the third 'paid down his eye as the price of his criminal curiosity'.

29 Al Sirat...*Mahomet*] 'Al Sirat' is the bridge swinging over Hell, leading from Earth to Paradise, according to Mahometan teaching. It was narrower than a hair and sharper than a sword. The righteous will pass safely; the wicked will fall into the abyss.

30 *diphrelatic*] 'relating to the driving of a chariot' (*OED*, which cites this example from De Quincey).

31 gage d'amitié] see above, p. 585, n. 27.

32 *called* me *procrastinating.*] cf. De Quincey in 'Sortilege on behalf of the Glasgow Athenaeum', where he speaks of 'a lecture addressed to myself by an ultra-moral friend; a lecture on procrastination' (see above, p. 296). In MS VSD B, De Quincey cites 'a trifle of procrastination as lying amongst his frailties' (see above, p. 456).

33 *packet-service,*] the boats that ran at regular intervals between two ports for the conveyance of mail.

34 *eleven miles an hour:*] cf. De Quincey in his 1833 *Tait's* essay on Hannah More: 'In the year 1809...even the Bristol mail, the swiftest in the kingdom, did not then perform much above seven miles an hour' (Vol. 9, pp. 333–4).

35 *Kendal...Westmoreland,*] In 1849 Appleby was still the County Town, though Kendal had long been the real commercial and administrative centre of Westmorland (see above, n. 16).

36 proud *Preston...confluent.*] cf. De Quincey in the 1856 *Confessions*: 'Proud Preston' is the 'point of confluence for the Liverpool and Manchester roads northwards' (Vol. 2, p. 173). In revision, De Quincey appended a footnote to this passage (see below, p. 744, 436.17).

37 *first stage...shocking affection of sleep*] cf. De Quincey in *Confessions*: 'The fine fluent motion...of this Mail soon laid me asleep: it is somewhat remarkable, that the first easy or refreshing sleep which I had enjoyed for some months, was on the outside of a Mail-coach' (Vol. 2, p. 31).

38 *aurigation*] 'The action or art of driving a chariot or coach' (*OED*, which cites this example from De Quincey).

39 *horses of Aurora*] the horses of the dawn, which pulled the chariot of the Greek sun-god Apollo (see above, p. 607, n. 44).

40 *Lilliputian Lancaster.*] Lancaster was the county town, but it was much smaller than Manchester or Liverpool. In Jonathan Swift's *Gulliver's Travels* (1726), the Lilliputians are only six inches tall.

41 *new parliamentary statute.*] In 1798, the Lancashire Sessions Act empowered the Lancashire justices to hold a Court of Annual General Session. In 1838, however, four Lancashire boroughs, including Manchester and Liverpool, secured separate courts of quarter sessions.

42 *twice in the year*] In revision, De Quincey appended a footnote to this passage (see below, p. 746, 437.10).

43 *York from a contested election,*] Prior to the 1832 Reform Bill, the number of constituencies in Yorkshire was small, and for each constituency there was only one voting centre. As there were few borough members, the vast majority of the electors were obliged to flock together from different parts of the county to record their vote.

44 *Giraldus Cambrensis*...suspiriosae cogitationes.] Giraldus Cambrensis (*c.* 1146–*c.* 1223; *DNB*), historian, whose works include *Itinerarium Cambriae* (1191; *Itinerary of Wales*) and *De rebus a se gestis* (*c.* 1204–5; *Concerning the Facts of My History*). The phrase has not been traced in his works.

45 *my own birth-day...my own native county*] De Quincey was born 15 August 1785 in Manchester.

46 *sea upon our left,*] De Quincey is nearing Preston, which is located at the lowest bridging point of the Irish Sea estuary, on the north bank of the River Ribble.

47 *schoolmaster...thoughts...infancy,*] cf. De Quincey in his 1847 *Tait's* essay on 'Orthographic Mutineers', where he describes 'the schoolmaster' as 'always a villain' (see above, p. 36). De Quincey also invokes Wordsworth, 'Intimations of Immortality,' l. 66: 'Heaven lies about us in our infancy!'.

48 *chamber in their father's house,*] cf. John 14: 2: 'In my Father's house are many mansions'.

49 *no door is closed,*] cf. De Quincey in *Suspiria de Profundis* when describing the death of his sister Elizabeth: 'I crept again to the room, but the door was now locked – the key was taken away – and I was shut out for ever' (Vol. 15, p. 146).

50 *presence of mind.*] cf. De Quincey in his 1850 *Instructor* essay 'Presence of Mind: A Fragment': 'To face a sudden danger by a corresponding weight of sudden counsel or sudden evasion – *that* was a privilege essentially lodged in the Roman mind. But in every nation some minds much more than others are representative of the national type' (Vol. 17, p. 50).

51 *guilty weight...dark unfathomed...energies,*] cf. De Quincey in *Confessions*: 'I had the power, if I could raise myself, to will it; and yet again had not the power, for the weight of twenty Atlantics was upon me, or the oppression of inexpiable guilt'.

52 *radix*,] root.

53 *attractive to others.*] In revision, De Quincey expanded this passage and appended a footnote (see below, p. 746, 438.41).

54 *'Quartering'...rut or any obstacle.*] 'Quartering' is to move out of the way of an oncoming vehicle. De Quincey's etymology is wrong; the 'quarters' were the four parts into which the width of the road was divided by the two wheel ruts and the central track of the horses. 'Quartering' involved moving the vehicle out of the ruts to drive on the 'quarters'.

55 *Charlemagne.*] Charlemagne (AD 742–814), King of the Franks, 768–814.

56 *a taxed cart?*] an open two-wheeled cart used for trade purposes, on which reduced road-tax was paid.

57 *umbrageous trees...cathedral aisle.*] cf. De Quincey in his 1832 Gothic novel *Klosterheim*: 'Every where they saw alleys, arched high overhead, and resembling the aisles of a cathedral, as much in form as in the perfect darkness which reigned in both at this solemn hour of midnight' (Vol. 8, p. 242).

58 Iliad...*Achilles...Pallas?*] For Achilles, see above, p. 538, n. 14. Pallas, or Pallas Athena, is the Greek goddess of war. De Quincey refers to Homer, *Iliad*, XVIII. 217–9: 'There stood [Achilles] and shouted, and from afar Pallas Athene uttered her voice; but amid the Trojans he roused confusion unspeakable'.

59 *If no more were done, nothing was done;*] cf. Lucan, *Pharsalia,* II. 657: '[Caesar] thought nothing done while anything remained to do'. De Quincey cites this 'famous line' in the first instalment of his 1832–4 *Blackwood's* series on 'The Caesars' (Vol. 9, p. 16).

60 *mill-race*] In MS VSD E, De Quincey appended a footnote to this term, and cited Dante (see above, p. 480).

61 *swingle-bar,*] a pivoted crossbar to which the horses' traces were fastened.

62 *crownèd*] In MS VSD E, De Quincey appended a footnote to this word, in which he observed that it was 'important to the rhythmus' that it 'should be read, and therefore should be printed, as a dissyllable – crownéd' (see above, p. 481). De Quincey has in mind Milton's description of Death in *Paradise Lost*, II. 672–3: 'What seemed his head / The likeness of a kingly crown had on'.

63 *dreams for ever.*] MS VSD C contains a discarded fragment apparently intended for insertion at this point in which De Quincey describes what he did following the accident (see above, p. 459).

64 Par. Lost, *B. xi*] Milton, *Paradise Lost*, XI. 558–63.

65 Tumultuosissimamente.] (It.), 'most tumultuously'.

66 *Ionic*] Vitruvius (*fl.* first century BC), Roman architect and engineer, in writing of the origin of the different orders of architecture, observed that the Greeks shaped the Ionic column in 'a new style' of 'feminine slenderness' (*De architectura*, IV.i.7).

67 *what aileth thee*] cf. Psalms 114: 5: 'What aileth thee, O thou sea'.

68 *Lo, it is summer, almighty summer!*] cf. De Quincey in *Confessions*: 'I find it impossible to banish the thought of death when I am walking alone in the endless days of summer; and any particular death, if not more affecting, at least haunts my mind more obstinately and besiegingly in that season' (Vol. 2, p. 72).

69 *corymbi*] 'a cluster of ivy-berries or grapes' (*OED*, which cites this example from De Quincey).

70 *the shadow of death?*] a familiar Biblical phrase: see, for example, Job 38: 17: 'Have the gates of death been opened unto thee? or hast thou seen the doors of the shadow of death?'.

71 *heady current*] De Quincey recalls Shakespeare, *Henry V*, I.i.33–4: 'Never came reformation in a flood / With such a heady currance'.

72 victory *that swallows up all strife.'*] cf. Isaiah 25: 7–8: 'And he will destroy on this mountain...the veil that is spread over all nations; he will swallow up death for ever'.

73 Gloria in excelsis.] Luke 19: 38: 'glory in the highest'.

74 *darkness comprehended it.*] cf. John 1: 5: 'And the light shineth in darkness, and the darkness comprehended it not'.

75 *'Chaunt the deliverer's...earth were sung.'*] Wordsworth, 'Siege of Vienna raised by John Sobieski', ll. 11–4: 'Chant the Deliverer's praise in every tongue! / The Cross shall spread, the Crescent hath waxed dim; / He conquering, as in joyful Heaven is sung, / HE CONQUERING THROUGH GOD, AND GOD BY HIM'.

76 *Campo Santo at Pisa...Jerusalem*] 'Campo Santo' (It.), literally, 'holy field'. The Campo Santo at Pisa was completed in 1278 and, according to legend, on the site where the Crusaders placed soil they had brought from the Holy Land.

77 *Créci to Trafalgar.*] For the battle of Crécy, see above, p. 544, n. 41. For the battle of Trafalgar, see above, p. 613, n. 8.

78 *tidings of great joy to every people,*] cf. Luke 2: 10: 'And the Angel said unto them, "fear not: for behold, I bring you good tidings of great joy, which shall be to all people"'.

79 *Dying Trumpeter.*] In his 1854 *SGG* 'Preface', De Quincey writes that 'the incident of the Dying Trumpeter, who rises from a marble bas-relief, and carries a marble trumpet to his marble lips for the purpose of warning the female infant, was doubtless secretly suggested by my own imperfect effort to seize the guard's horn, and to blow a warning blast' (Vol. 20, p. 35).

80 *third time the trumpet sounded;*] cf. Revelation 8: 10: 'The third angel blew his trumpet, and a great star fell from heaven, blazing like a torch'.

81 *horns of the altar,*] In the Old Testament, sacrifices were placed upon the horns of the altar (for example, Exodus 29: 12); they were also clasped by those seeking sanctuary (for example, 1 Kings 1: 50).

82 sanctus.] (Lt.), literally, 'holy'. De Quincey has in mind Revelation 4: 8: 'Holy, holy, holy, Lord God Almighty, which was, and is, and is to come'.

83 *six years old...promise of perfect love,*] De Quincey is thinking in particular of the death of his sister Elizabeth. 'About the close of my sixth year, suddenly the first chapter of my life came to a violent termination', he writes in 'The Affliction of Childhood'; 'that chapter which, even within the gates of recovered Paradise, might merit a remembrance. "*Life is Finished!*" was the secret misgiving of my heart' (Vol. 19, p. 3).

84 *the quick and the dead*] a familiar Biblical phrase: see, for example, Acts 10: 42: 'It is he which was ordained of God to be the Judge of the quick and the dead'.

85 *thanks to God in the highest*] see above, n. 73.

86 *victorious arm...his love!*] cf. Milton, *Paradise Lost*, X. 633–7: 'At one sling / Of thy victorious arm, well-pleasing Son, / Both Sin, and Death, and yawning grave at last / Through chaos hurled, obstruct the mouth of hell / For ever, and seal up his ravenous jaws'.

{*The Vision of Sudden Death*}

MS VSD A

1 *opus operatim...actum agere.*] (Lt.), respectively, 'deed as done' and 'carrying out the deed'.

{*The Vision of Sudden Death*}

MS VSD B

1 *procrastination...amongst his frailties:*] cf. De Quincey in his 1846 review of 'The Antigone of Sophocles': 'It had been generally reported as characteristic of myself, that in respect to all coaches, steamboats, railroads, wedding-parties, baptisms, and so forth, there was a fatal necessity of my being a trifle too late. Some malicious fairy, not invited to my own baptism, was supposed to have endowed me with this infirmity. It occurred to me that for once in my life I would show the scandalousness of such a belief by being a trifle too soon, say, three minutes' (Vol. 15, p. 326).

{*The Vision of Sudden Death*}

MS VSD C

1 *mill-race**:] Though marked with an asterisk, the manuscript does not contain the footnote De Quincey intended to append to this term. As MS VSD E makes clear, however, the missing footnote concerned the 'authority' of Dante (see above, p. 480).

2 *Preston,*] Remarkably, this appears to be an account of what De Quincey did after the accident.

3 *Paterson<s>...authority of those days)*] Daniel Paterson (1738–1825; *DNB*), *A new and accurate description of all the direct and principal cross roads in Great Britain* (1771). The eighteenth and final edition appeared in 1829.

4 *(as Falstaff observes of himself) from sin.*] De Quincey has in mind Shakespeare, *1 Henry IV*, V.iv.162–5: 'I'll follow, as they say, for reward. He that rewards me, God reward him! If I do grow great, I'll grow less, for I'll purge and leave sack, and live cleanly as a nobleman should do'.

The Vision of Sudden Death

MS VSD E

1 *{2 r.}*] The pages of De Quincey's manuscript have been numbered from '1' to '32' in the top right-hand corner, and by a hand other than De Quincey's. The page containing the draft footnote on an Oxford student's 'act of gambling' is numbered '2', and the present page is numbered '3'. Such an ordering, however, disrupts the continuity of De Quincey's text, and places the footnote a page before the word that cues it. The present transcription reverses the order of these two pages. The present page is a continuation of the text on '1. r.', and appears here as '2 r.'. The footnote on the Oxford student is clearly meant to be appended to the word 'misfortune.*' at the bottom of '2 r'., and appears here as '3 r.'.

2 *charity hopeth all things.>*] 1 Corinthians 13: 7.

3 *Salford,*] Salford lies immediately west of Manchester.

4 *Non corse...le pale approccia."*] Dante (see above, p. 606, n. 26), *The Inferno*, XXIII. 46–8: 'Water has never coursed more swiftly down a sluice to turn the wheels of a land mill, as it approaches the paddles'.

5 Te deums:] see above, p. 614, n. 10.

{On Miracles}

MS A

1 *"a wicked and adulterous gener*^{ation} *asking a Sign"*] Matthew 16: 4.

2 *Witch of Endor,*] see above, p. 586, n. 51.

3 *Truslar...Sinclair's Speech June 1, 47.*] untraced.

4 *Let him come down from the cross,*] Matthew 27: 42.

5 *curing blindness*] for example, Matthew 12: 22.

6 *tendency to mythus*;] cf. De Quincey's fragments on the 'Mythus' (Vol. 15 pp. 608–18).

7 *miracle of the loaves*] Mathew 15: 35–8.

8 *Matthew*] Matthew is one of the Twelve Apostles.

9 *Timon of Athens.*] In Shakespeare's tragedy, Timon of Athens spends his fortune and is rejected when he asks his friends for help. While they are still enjoying his generosity, one of them observes, 'This is the old man still' (III.vi.61).

10 XYZ.] De Quincey's most popular signature during his first ten years with the magazines, and one he used in both the *London* and *Blackwood's*.

{On Miracles}

MS B

1 *Hume's objection*] In the chapter 'On Miracles' in *An Enquiry Concerning Human Understanding*, the Scottish empiricist and skeptic David Hume (1711–76; *DNB*) did not deny miracles because they were inconsistent with the law of nature. Rather, he emphasized the importance of examining historical evidence, and argued that miracles were highly unlikely.

{Let Him Come Down from the Cross}

1 *de novo*] see above p. 569, n. 24.
2 in vacuo] (Lt.), literally, 'in a vacuum'; 'isolated'.
3 *sorites*] 'a series of propositions, in which the predicate of each is the subject of the next, the conclusion being formed of the first subject and the last predicate' (*OED*).

{Draft Pages on Burke for Review of Schlosser's Literary History of the Eighteenth Century}

1 *Laputa.*] In Book Three of Jonathan Swift's *Gulliver's Travels* (1726), Gulliver travels to the flying island of Laputa, where the nobles quite literally have their heads in the clouds.
2 à priori,] see above, p. 552, n. 78.
3 meinetwegen:] (Ger.) 'for all I care'.

On the Religious Objections to the use of Chloroform in Obstetric Medicine

1 *Astrachan...Muscat...Edinburgh,*] Astrakhan city is situated in southwestern Russia, on the delta of the Volga River. An 'Imaum' (or 'Imam') is the head of the Muslim community. Muscat is the capital of Oman. George Street is one of the main thoroughfares in Edinburgh.
2 *Hic labor; hoc opus est.*] cf. Virgil, *Aenied*, VI. 129: 'hoc opus, hic labor est' ('this is work, this is labour').
3 *Lasswade*] Lasswade is a village seven miles outside Edinburgh. De Quincey and his family lived in Mavis Bush Cottage, just outside the village (Lindop, p. 337).
4 *diaulos*] 'a double course, in which the racers turned round a goal and returned to the starting point' (*OED*).
5 *Middleton...puzzles me.)*] Thomas Middleton (1580–1627; *DNB*), dramatist. Simpson's citation of Middleton has not been traced, but the lines in question are almost certainly from *Women Beware Women*, IV.i.172–4: 'I'll imitate the pities of old surgeons / To this lost limb, – who, ere they show their art, / Cast one asleep, then cut the diseased part'. De Quincey's confusion arises from the fact that the play was written *c.* 1621, but not published until 1657.
6 *Cromwell died in 1658*] Oliver Cromwell (1599–1658; *DNB*), general and Lord Protector.
7 Vicennium,] 'a period of twenty years' (*OED*).
8 *American Empiric...Greatorex...reign.*] The 'American Empiric' is the Yale-trained surgeon Elisha Perkins (1741–99), who announced that his studies of muscle contractions had led him to the discovery of subtle electrical fields in the human body. He used 'metallic tractors' – one brass and one iron – to draw pain out of a sick person. His techniques were associated with mesmerism and animal magnetism, and he was discredited in the 1790s. Ralph Greatorex (d. *c.* 1712; *DNB*), inventor and maker of mathematical instruments. For Charles II, see above, p. 601, n. 37.
9 *Plautus...*tractim*...expression.*] Plautus (*c.* 254–184 BC), Roman comic dramatist, *Amphitruo*, l. 313: 'Quid si ego illum tractim tangam, ut dormiat?' ('What if I should stroke him softly into somnolence?').

10 *Hahnemann's doctrine...Alloiopathy*] Samuel Hahnemann (1755–1843), German physician and founder of homeopathy. De Quincey intends 'allopathy', 'a term applied by homoeopathists to the ordinary or traditional medical practice' (*OED*).

11 *Milton...Samson Agonistes.*] 'TRAGEDY, as it was anciently composed, hath been ever held the gravest, moralist, and most profitable of all other poems: therefore said by Aristotle to be of power by raising pity and fear, or terror, to purge the mind of those and such-like passions, that is to temper and reduce them to just measure with a kind of delight, stirred up by reading or seeing those passions well imitated. Nor is nature wanting in her own effects to make good his assertion: for so in physic things of melancholic hue and quality are used against melancholy, sour against sour, salt to remove salt humours' (Milton, 'Of that sort of Dramatic Poem which is called Tragedy' in *Samson Agnosites,* ll. 1–9).

12 *Aristotle...pity and terror.*] Aristotle, *Poetics*, XIII.

13 Threescore years and ten...*Psalms*] Psalms 90: 10: 'The days of our years are threescore and ten'.

14 Macrobiotics...*Bacon thought otherwise.*] 'Macrobiotics' is 'the science of prolonging life' (*OED*). De Quincey has in mind Francis Bacon (see above, p. 578, n. 3), *The History of Life and Death* (London: Okes, 1638), pp. 199–200: 'To effect this Operation, powder of Gold, or Leaf-Gold, or powder of Pearl, precious Stones and Corrals, are good; being therefore much esteemed by the *Arabians*, *Grecians*, and also Moderns. Therefore...insinuation being made into the substance of the Blood, the spirits and heat having no power to work thereon, putrefaction and dying would be thereby prevented, and Life *prolonged*'.

15 "Poverty shall never cease from the land".] Deuteronomy 15: 11: 'For the poor shall never cease out of the land'.

16 "In Sorrow shall thou bring forth."] Genesis 3: 16.

17 *Hebrew word...occasion.*] Simpson contended that the Hebrew word *'etzebh*, translated 'sorrow' in the phrase 'In sorrow thou shalt bring forth', actually meant 'great effort of any kind', like the English word 'labour, the severe muscular *efforts* and *struggles* of which parturition – and more particularly human parturition – essentially consists' (James Young Simpson, *Answer to the Religious Objections Advanced Against the Employment of Anaesthetic Agents in Midwifery and Surgery* (Edinburgh: Sutherland and Knox, 1847), pp. 13–4).

18 In...for a pound.":] *Proverbs*, p. 402.

19 go the whole hog] *Proverbs*, p. 307.

20 mortify the flesh?] Romans 8: 13: 'if you through the spirit do mortify the deeds of the body, you shall live'.

21 *Southey...Quarterly Review.*] Robert Southey, 'The Roman Catholic Question – Ireland' in the *Quarterly Review*, 38 (October 1828), p. 594: 'A more frightful superstition is that which induces the ignorant Romans (as they style themselves) of that poor be-darkened land, to swallow earth from the grave of a holy priest'. De Quincey's next example is clearly drawn from Southey's footnote to the passage: 'A most extraordinary case, arising from this hideous practice, may be seen in the transactions of the College of Physicians of Dublin, vol. IV. p. 189. A woman...discharged at intervals, by vomiting, &c., a great quantity of church-yard beetles...in all stages of their existence'.

22 *Ellis...Polynesian Researches.*] William Ellis (1794–1872; *DNB*), *Polynesian Researches* (1829).

23 *Island of Tonga...during parturition.*] The Kingdom of Tonga, or the Friendly Islands, are located in the southwestern Pacific Ocean. De Quincey's source has not been

traced. But cf. the account by William Mariner (1791–1853; *DNB*): 'respecting the circumstances of parturition, and the separation of the child, these things are kept a profound secret from the men' (John Martin, *An Account of the Natives of the Tonga Islands...compiled and arranged from the extensive communication of Mr William Mariner* (London: Murray, 1817), vol. II, p. 273).

24 *comes your own suggestion,*] Francis De Quincey's 'own opinion is that in the form of expression – "in sorrow thou shalt bring forth children" – there is no command, but a simple prophetic intimation that woman would never be perfectly happy. She would give birth in sorrow of mind, knowing that sorrow is the lot of the human race' (Francis De Quincey, *On the Religious Objections to the use of Chloroform in Obstetric Medicine*, (unpublished MD, University of Edinburgh, 1849), pp. 27–8).

25 *Red Sea...Amram's son,*] Amram's son Moses in Exodus 14: 21–9; De Quincey also invokes *Paradise Lost*, I. 338–40: 'As when the potent Rod / Of Amram's son in Egypt's evil day / Waved round the coast'.

{Ralph Waldo Emerson's Essays: First Series}

1 *"I have no xpect."*] 'I have no expectations that any man will read history aright, who thinks that what was done in a remote age, by men whose names have resounded far, has any deeper sense than what he is doing today' (Emerson, *Essays*, p. 7).

2 *p. 123...simplicity*] 'The simplicity of the universe is very different from the simplicity of a machine. He who sees moral nature out and out, and thoroughly knows how knowledge is acquired and character formed, is a pedant. The simplicity of nature is not that which may easily be read, but is inexhaustible' (Emerson, *Essays*, p. 123).

3 *"idea of* simplicity...*Blackwood*] untraced.

4 *p. 132 – "are wiser men than others."*] The page would certainly have arrested De Quincey's attention. Emerson observes that 'people are not the better for the sun and moon, the horizon and the trees; as it is not observed that the keepers of Roman galleries, or the valets of painters, have any elevation of thought, or that librarians are wiser men than others'. He discusses the dreaming mind: 'Our dreams are the sequel of our waking knowledge. The visions of the night bear some proportion to the visions of the day. Hideous dreams are exaggerations of the sins of the day'. De Quincey's 'Apparition of the Brocken' from *Suspiria de Profundis* explores the same phenomenon Emerson discusses: 'On the Alps, the traveller sometimes beholds his own shadow magnified to a giant, so that every gesture of his hand is terrific' (Emerson, *Essays*, pp. 132–3; Vol. 15, pp. 182–5).

5 *314...Emerson's motto*] In his eleventh essay on 'Intellect', Emerson praises 'prophets' such as 'Hermes, Heraclitus, Empedocles, Plato', and the 'truth and grandeur of their thought'. Emerson, however, concludes the chapter as follows, and this is the passage De Quincey intends, beginning from the tenth line on page 314: 'But what marks its elevation, and has even a comic book look to us, is the innocent serenity with which these babe-like Jupiters sit in their clouds, and from age to age prattle to each other, and to no contemporary. Well assured that their speech is intelligible, and the most natural thing in the world, they add thesis to thesis, without a moment's heed of the universal astonishment of the human race below, who do not comprehend their plainest argument; nor do they ever relent so much as to insert a popular or explaining sentence; nor testify the least displeasure or petulance at the dulness of their amazed auditory. The angels are so enamoured of the language that is spoken in heaven, that they will not distort their lips with the hissing and unmusi-

cal dialects of men, but speak their own, whether there be any who understand it or not' (Emerson, *Essays*, p. 314).

6 *"that yellow Iachimo"*] De Quincey's quotation is, not Emerson, but Shakespeare, *Cymbeline*, II.v.13–4: 'O, all the devils! / This yellow Jachimo'. But De Quincey clearly has in mind the following passage from Emerson: 'The scholar shames us by his bifold life. Whilst something higher than prudence is active, he is admirable; when common sense is wanted, he is an encumbrance. Yesterday, Caesar was not so great; to-day, the felon at the gallows' foot is not more miserable. Yesterday, radiant with the light of an ideal world, in which he lives, the first of men; and now oppressed by wants and by sickness, for which he must thank himself. He resembles the pitiful drivellers, whom travellers describe as frequenting the bazaars of Constantinople, who skulk about all day, yellow, emaciated, ragged, sneaking; and at evening, when the bazaars are open, slink to the opium-shop, swallow their morsel, and become tranquil and glorified seers' (Emerson, *Essays*, p. 212).

7 Dio. imp. cum J. Caesar habet.] De Quincey seems to have intended 'Dios imperium cum Julius Caesar habet' ('when Julius has dominion from Jove'). But the line is not in Virgil (see above, p. 535, n. 42).

8 *Op. Eater is ruler of the* Night.] cf. Jorges Luis Borges in 1940: 'De Quincey plunged deep into labyrinths on his nights of meticulously detailed horror' (Jorges Luis Borges, *Selected Non-Fictions*, ed. Eliot Weinberger, trans. Ester Allen, Suzanne Jill Levine, and Eliot Weinberger (New York: Viking, 1999), p. 244).

9 *244 of* six *thousand years – oh shameful!*] 'The philosophy of six thousand years has not searched the chambers and magazines of the soul. …Man is a stream whose source is hidden' (Emerson, *Essays*, p. 244).

10 *247…proverb…Op. Conf.*] 'A wise old proverb says, "God comes to see us without bell"; that is, as there is no screen or ceiling between our heads and the infinite heavens, so there is no bar or wall in the soul where man, the effect, ceases, and God, the cause, begins'. De Quincey does not use this quotation in the *Confessions*, though this note indicates that he may have intended to consider it for his 1856 revisions of that text. Cf. the passage in the 1821 text beginning, 'the visible heavens in summer appear far higher, more distant, and…more infinite' (Emerson, *Essays*, p. 247; Vol. 2, p. 72).

11 *Titan*] see above, p. 562, n. 66.

12 *out of* the *window…laughing*] 'that a man is the word made flesh, born to shed healing to the nations, that he should be ashamed of our compassion, and that the moment he acts from himself, tossing the laws, the books, idolatries, and customs out of the window, we pity him no more, but thank and revere him, – and that teacher shall restore the life of man to splendor, and make his name dear to all history' (Emerson, *Essays*, p. 67).

{Dr Johnson and Lord Chesterfield}

1 *Hercules*] see above, p. 524, n. 26.

2 instanter] (Lt.), 'immediately'.

3 *Frankenstein's monster.*] Mary Shelley (1797–1851; *DNB*), novelist and editor. De Quincey has in mind the moment in her best known novel *Frankenstein* (1818) when Victor's wife Elizabeth has just been murdered, and he sees 'at the open window a figure the most hideous and abhorred. A grin was on the face of the monster; he

seemed to jeer' (*Frankenstein, or The Modern Prometheus*, ed. Marilyn Butler (Oxford: Oxford University Press, 1994), p. 166).

4 *Beggars mustn't be choosers,*] *Proverbs*, p. 42.

5 inter alia] see above, p. 563, n. 73.

6 *tenants-at-will*] 'a tenant who holds at the will or pleasure of the lessor' (*OED*).

7 *patronage.*] see above, p. 595, n. 19.

8 omissa…commissa.] (Lt.), respectively, 'omitted' and 'committed'.

9 *two separate papers*] Chesterfield's essays appeared in numbers 100 (28 November 1754) and 101 (5 December 1754) of a weekly newspaper called *The World*.

10 in posse…in esse] (Lt.), 'potential' and 'existence'.

TEXTUAL NOTES

Notes are keyed to the main text by page, line number and (in bold type) word or phrase with any immediately following punctuation. Line numbering excludes the main title of the item, running titles and any headnote material. Textual notes relating to footnotes are given at the points at which footnotes occur, keyed to page number followed by 'n.' and the number of the line counting continuously through all footnote material on that page. Changes between single and double quotation marks are not recorded. All substantive variants, and all accidental variants deemed to be of interest, are recorded. Where a variant introduces new material which requires an explanatory note, the explanatory note follows the textual note in square brackets, keyed to superscript letters within the variant.

Notes on Walter Savage Landor {Part I}

5.2 **No. 1. In** *F, SGG* No. 1; in

5.18–19 **are before … offices; fellows** *SGG* are from the medical advisers of insurance offices before having over our lives insured; fellows

6.4 **should in** *SGG* should not, in

7.5 **'traduced' in** *SGG* traduced (*traduit*) in

7.5 **'overset' in** *SGG* overset (*oversat*) in

7.23 **luxurious:** *SGG* voluptuous;

7.42 ***his*****,** *SGG* his,

8.7–8 **and (nominally) published; whereas, in fact, all** *SGG* and *published*, *i.e.*, nominally made *public;* whereas all

8.12 **the Landors** *SGG* the two Landors

9.12–13 **Dalica, considered as a woman, is** *SGG* But, considered as a woman, Dalica is

9.14 **worse, in fact. She** *SGG* worse. In fact, she

9.16 **known best** *SGG* best known

9.22 **it is close** *SGG* it happens to be close

9.29–30 ***osis*****, necessarily** *MS A osis* <*chlorosis* of course therefore> necessarily

9.34 **incantations. From** *MS A* incantations. <Strichnine no doubt> For

9.36 **their princes** *SGG* their two princes

10.8 **he had** *SGG* Gebir had

11.9 **with those** *F, SGG* with these

11.12 **reason that** *SGG* reason why

11.27 **eye seemed to rest everywhere** *SGG* eye of the reader rested everywhere

11.28 **pannels** *F* panels *SGG* storied panels

12.10 **mind,** *MS A, SGG append footnote and conform, with the exception of six significant deletions in MS A given here in angle brackets* Ten or a dozen years ago, when this was written, the atrocity of *Dahra*[a] was familiar to the readers of newspapers: it is now forgotten;

and therefore I retrace it briefly. The French in Algiers, upon occasion of some <expedition> *razzia*[b] against a party of Arabs, hunted them into the cave or caves of Dahra; and, upon the refusal of the Arabs to surrender, filled up the mouth <the cavern> of their retreat with combustibles, <so that> and eventually roasted alive the whole party – men, women, and children. The Maréchel St Arnaud,[c] who subsequently died in <the> supreme command of the French army before Sebastopol,[d] was *said* to have been concerned as a principal in this atrocity. Meantime the Arabs are not rightfully or specially any objects of legitimate sympathy in such a case; for they are quite capable of similar cruelties <in> under any movement of <their> religious fanaticism.

[a See above, p. 525, n. 47.

b 'War, battle, military expedition' (*OED*).

c Armand-Jacques Leroy de Saint-Arnaud (1798–1854), army officer, went to Algiers in 1837, where he rose rapidly in rank. In 1854 he accepted command of the French forces in the Crimea.

d Sevastopol is a city and seaport in the southwestern Crimean Peninsula. The Siege of Sevastopol (1854–5) was the major operation of the Crimean War.]

12.13 **caverns, thirty'** *SGG* caverns of Dahra, thirty,'

13.n.4 **lawful** *SGG omits*

13.n.7 **fell into** *SGG* fell together into

13.n.7 **were fished** *SGG* were together fished

13.n.10 **the memorable reply** *SGG* this most conclusive reply

13.21–2 **civilization. A quarrel** *F* civilization; – quarrel *SGG* civilisation; quarrel

13.25 **cannot** *F* can not *SGG* will not

13.26–7 **civilization and barbarism, provoked** *SGG* civilisation on the one side, and barbarism on the other, provoked

13.27–8 **passage rising up from the Atlantic deep, suddenly** *SGG* passage amongst the children of Africa, rising again from the Atlantic, suddenly

13.33 **Dahra.** *MS A appends deleted footnote material, of which the first thirteen words are in type, and the remainder in De Quincey's hand:* <* St Arnaud, who died in supreme command of the French army before Sebastopol. was, I believe, y[e] man mainly responsible as regarded the *personal*>

14.20 **soon** *SGG* permanently

14.34 **more significant,** *F, SGG* more and more significant,

16.6–7 **Napoleon, excepting Sir Robert Wilson, no writer in Europe, no section** *SGG* Napoleon, no European writer, with the solitary exception of Sir Robert Wilson,[a] no section

[[a] See above, p. 526, n. 62]

16.n.1 **war. In** *SGG* war by the battle of Prague in the year 1618.[a] In

[[a] In the Battle or Defenestration of Prague (May 1618), the governors of Bohemia were thrown from the windows of the council room in Prague Castle. The incident hastened the outbreak of the Thirty Years' War.]

16.n.16 **that. Magdeburg,** *SGG* that. Mind that distinction, reader. Tilly might forego a parchment that was his own; but how if it belonged to, his hungry army? Magdeburg,[a]

[[a] See above, p. 526, n. 63.]

16.n.24 **hogs,** *SGG* boars,

16.12 **d'Enguien's** *F, SGG* d'Enghien's

16.15 **not less** *SGG* not at all less

16.16–17 **worst which have been ascribed to the Mahometan Timur, or even to any Hindoo Rajah, which hardly** *SGG* worst of Asiatic murders: and yet this Christian atrocity hardly

16.20 **Fifty years** *SGG* Fifty and odd years

Notes on Walter Savage Landor {Part II}

Title **NOTES ON WALTER SAVAGE LANDOR.** *SGG omits*
19.n.6 **not that** *SGG* not (we find) that
19.n.7 **fighting.** *Editorial; 1847* fighting.'
20.n.5 **Melancthon would** *SGG* Melancthon for Melan*chthon* would
20.6 **and centrally** *F, SGG omit*
20.9–10 **by a revelation** *F, SGG* by revelation
21.33 **sing** *SGG sing*
22.n.12 **Mr L.** *F, SGG* Mr Landor
22.n.13 **probably of** *SGG* probably very much of
22.n.14 **compass.** *SGG* compass; and even his metrical efforts in that language were admired by Italians.
22.14 **dining out;** *SGG dining out;*
23.15 **by any means** *F, SGG omit*
23.17 **Cl—nt,** *SGG* Clermont,
23.23 ***qua*** *SGG quo*
23.24 **Cl.** *SGG* Clermont
23.35 **cleansed** *F, SGG* cleaned
23.39 **up** *F, SGG omit*
23.39 ***susurrus*** *MS A, SGG append footnote and conform, with the exception of one significant deletions in MS A given here in angle brackets Susurrus:* – The reader, who has had any experience of stable usages, will know that <they> grooms always keep up a *hissing* accompaniment whilst currycombing a horse, as paviours do a groaning.
24.11 **look** *F, SGG* looks
24.19 **signify nails,** *SGG* signify Porson's nails,
25.18 **Gothic** *SGG* cathedral
25.22 **needlessly offend** *F* needlessly affect *SGG* needlessly revolt
25.25 **revolt** *SGG* recoil
25.30 **walk…dance,** *SGG* walk, or could be supposed to dance,
26.32 **regarded** *F, SGG* regards
26.38 **powers** *SGG* power
28.n.3 **made not** *SGG* not made
28.25 **nothing. Of** *F, SGG insert paragraph break*
29.1 **'thill'** *SGG appends footnote: i.e.,* Shaft-horse. – See Shakspere's *Love's Labour's Lost.*[a]
[[a] Shakespeare, *Love's Labour's Lost*, III.i.]
29.19 **for Cilician** *SGG* on account of Cilician
29.19 **he reports** *SGG* he himself reports
29.20 **sense. Even** *SGG* sense, even
29.27 **out** *SGG* outside
29.32 ***paludamentum*, he** *SGG paludamentum*, of this supreme martial robe, he
30.n.6 **now *white,*** *SGG* for *white,*
30.n.11 **are** *SGG* art
30.9 **advance – before** *SGG* advance, επομπεθσ – before
30.10 ***somatophulakes*** **were** *SGG somatophulakes* or body-guards, were
32.11 **with one** *SGG* with equal
32.39 **see** *SGG see*

34.n.3 **since 1740 they** *SGG* since an early part of the last century they
34.n.7 **nations...He** *SGG* nations. He
34.n.8 **So do I at times.** *SGG omits*
34.23 **avenging** *F, SGG* Avenging
34.24 **fiery visitations** *F, SGG* Fiery Visitations
35.n.3 **circumstances.** *SGG* circumstances. – See some travels, I forget whose, in the neighbourhood of Mount Sinai and its circumjacencies.
35.7 **same...anguish.** *SGG* same eternity of abysmal sorrow.

Orthographic Mutineers

37.1 **we may account** *F, SGG* we account
40.n.7 **This most extravagant** *F, SGG* The most extravagant
40.35 ***adoptado*** *SGG adaptado*
41.10–12 **analogy with itself, that he would distort or retrotort the language; sometimes on the principle of external analogy with** *SGG* analogy with
41.n.9–42.n.1 **to the 27th verse, chap. xiii. of 1st Kings, 'And he'** *SGG* to 1 Kings xiii.27, 'And he,'
42.n.6 ***I* examine** *SGG* I examine
43.14 **him, we – that** *F, SGG* him – that
45.8 **Luther. Solomon** *SGG* Luther; Solomon
45.30 **Νωι** *F, SGG* Νωε
46.8 **nearly hopeless a task** *SGG* nearly a hopeless task

Milton Versus Southey and Landor

48.42–3 **of Niagara.** *F, SGG* of a Niagara.
50.14 **Bentham, had** *SGG* nor in Jeremy Diddler,[a] had
[[a] Jeremy Diddler is a character in *Raising the Wind*, a farce by James Kenney (1780–1849; *DNB*). The name was used generally for anyone adept at raising money on false pretences.]
50.n.6 **bed-fellow.** *SGG* bed-fellow. It is a remarkable illustration of the rapidity with which words submit to new and contradictory modifications that a *squatter*, who is a violent intruder upon other men's rights, consequently a scoundrel, in America, ranks in Australia as a virtuous citizen, and a pioneer of colonisation.
50.25 **tolerated the injustice** *SGG* tolerated the iniquity
50.30 **a few thunderbolts** *SGG* a thunderbolt
50.35–6 **Lane, pocketed** *SGG* Lane Theatre by his fraudulent promise, pocketed
51.4 **but in *not* getting into it. The** *SGG* but in *not* doing it. The
51.11 **Gebir, in** *SGG* Gebir therefore, in
51.35–6 **grand-daughter, or than** *SGG* grand-daughter, who touches the shoulder of the collapsing god – nothing more awful than
52.23–4 **Wordsworth is not haughty, is not ostentatious, is not anxious for display, is not arrogant, and, least** *SGG* Wordsworth is not ostentatious, is not anxious for display, and least
53.23 **Elsewhere,** *SGG inserts paragraph break*
53.37 **Portsmouth mail,** *SGG* Portsmouth or Bristol mail,

54.26 **slight, a *very*** *SGG* slight, *very*

54.26 **opinion with** *SGG* opinion even with

55.7 ***con-tri-bu-ce-on.*** *SGG appends footnote* This is a most important *caveat:* many thousands of exquisite lines in the days of Elizabeth, James, Charles, down even to 1658 (last of Cromwell),[a] are ruined by readers untrained to the elder dissyllabic (not monosyllabic) treatment of the *tion*.

[[a] See above, p. 627, n. 6.]

55.31 **business. But** *SGG* business; but

55.41–2 **conceited, and add** *SGG* conceited, and a scoundrel, and would add

56.28 ***society,*'** *SGG appends footnote* Mr Craik,[a] who is a great authority on such subjects, favoured me some ten or twelve years ago with a letter on this line. He viewed it as a variety more or less irregular, but regular as regarded its model, of the dramatic or scenical verse – privileged to the extent of an extra syllable, but sometimes stretching its privilege a little further.

[[a] George Lillie Craik (1798–1866; *DNB*), Scottish miscellaneous writer.]

58.3 **hearts invests** *SGG* hearts recalls

58.16–7 ***aspéct.*' But *aspéct* is** *SGG* aspéct. But the difference is – as between Christ regarding, and Christ *being* regarded: *aspéct* is

58.20 **the divine** *SGG* the radiation of the divine

59.2 **at the same** *SGG* at one and the same

59.2–3 **since an arrested** *SGG* since the arrested

Joan of Arc {Part I}

61.n.12–13 **that? Beside the chances that M. Hordal might be a gigantic blockhead, it** *SGG* that? It

61.n.15 **printers: in France, much more so.** *SGG* printers; now, M. Hordal was *not* a printer.

64.12 **side, that** *SGG* truth, that

64.22–4 **life; to *do* – never for thyself, always for others; to *suffer* – never in the persons of generous champions, always in thy own: – that** *SGG* life; that

64.40 ***her*;** *SGG inserts six asterisks at paragraph break.*

65.6 **But stop.** *SGG* But stay.

65.7 **this spring** *F, SGG* the spring

65.20–2 **blood, and sometimes…German nurses. But** *SGG* blood. But

65.23–4 **Michelet – who is quite sufficient to lead a man into a gallop, requiring two relays, at least, of fresh readers; – we** *SGG* Michelet, we

65.25–6 **&c., which has been most circulated – know** *SGG* &c. – know

65.27–8 **incoherence. M. Michelet…intercept a second part. But** *SGG* incoherence. But

65.40 **assault.** *SGG* error.

66.4 **probably** *Editorial; 1847* propably

66.20 **only** *SGG appends footnote* 'Only *now* forthcoming:' – In 1847 *began* the publication (from official records) of Joanna's trial. It was interrupted, I fear, by the convulsions of 1848; and whether even yet finished, I do not know.

66.29 **The Romans** *SGG* The ancient Romans

66.39–40 **his far inferior son Tippoo, and** *SGG* his son Tippoo, though so far inferior, and

67.n.11 **reference to** *SGG* reference, perhaps, to

67.19–33 **I am sure...*Lorraine* cast of expression** *SGG omits*
68.10 **letter of X.** *F, SGG* letter X.
68.12 **conflux for** *SGG* conflux and intersection for
68.14 **These roads** *SGG* Those roads
68.18–19 **preferring, (but there's no disputing about tastes), to** *SGG* preferring to
68.19 **man's odious pigstye** *SGG* man's pig-sty
68.20–41 **Things being situated...king of France.** *SGG omits*
69.1 **whatever side** *SGG* whichever wide
69.8–9 **Lorraine or Bar insisting** *SGG* Lorraine insisting
69.10 **granted to them** *SGG* granted to him
69.10–12 **battles by the English and by the Turkish Sultan, viz., at Crécy, at Nicopolis, and at Agincourt.** *SGG* battles – twice by the English, viz., at Crécy and Agincourt, once by the Sultan at Nicopolis.
69.19 **at her breast,** *SGG* at the breast of France,
69.20 **of the legitimate daughter: whilst** *SGG* of France's legitimate daughters: whilst
69.22 **naturally have stimulated** *SGG* naturally stimulate
69.22–3 **pride, had there even been no other stimulant to zeal by** *SGG* pride, by
69.30 **enmity.** *SGG* duty.
69.33–4 **times, the burthen of the times,** *SGG* time, the burden of the time,
69.35–6 **had been** *SGG* had, before Agincourt occurred, been
70.15 **Anjou, by the** *SGG* Anjou, and by the
70.16 **significance; but** *SGG* significance. But,
70.22 **hell – she was** *SGG* hell – the church was
70.22 **was already rehearsing** *SGG* was rehearsing
70.23 **had rehearsed** *SGG* had already rehearsed
70.23 **rehearsed, the first rent in** *SGG* rehearsed, those vast rents in
70.23–4 **foundations (reserved for the coming century) which** *SGG* foundations which
70.28 **even those** *SGG* even upon those
70.28 **altitudes** *SGG* tendencies
70.32 **to crisis after crisis.** *SGG* to some dreadful crisis.
70.37–8 **her the duty, imposed on herself, of** *SGG* her for ever the duty, self-imposed, of
70.40 **home in** *SGG* home for ever in
71.1–2 **Romish chaunting;** *SGG* Romish church;
71.2 **triumphant *Gloria in Excelcis*: she** *SGG* triumphant *Te Deums* of Rome: she
71.3 **of her church.** *SGG* of the same church.
71.10 **of licensed victuallers.** *SGG* of the licensed victualler.
71.18–19 **windows, dim and dimly seen – as Moorish temples of the Hindoos,' that** *SGG* windows,' – 'Like Moorish temples of the Hindoos,' that
71.22 **abbeys, in no** *SGG* abbeys, so as in no
71.23 **region; many** *SGG* region; yet many
71.32 **and they are** *SGG* and the hills are
71.37 **found (if the race was not extinct) those** *SGG* found (if anywhere to be found) those
71.38–9 **seen, at intervals, that** *SGG* seen (if anywhere seen) that
71.39–40 **old, at the least, but** *SGG* old, but
72.2 **credulity becomes** *SGG* credulity grows steadily, till it becomes
72.4 **forests near the Vosges, they** *SGG* forests, they
72.33 **thirty years** *SGG* forty years

72.35 **in France at a period some trifle before** *SGG* in chivalrous France, not very long before
73.2 **to having** *SGG* to the having
73.9 **certainly** *SGG* probably
73.42 **admire not stage** *SGG* am far from admiring stage
73.43 **myself a dupe to a conjuror's** *SGG* myself to the conjuror's
74.6 **trial. She was** *SGG* trial. By way of testing her supernatural pretensions, she was
74.10 **her, would ruin** *SGG* her, would, by ruining herself, ruin
74.20 **because dazzling** *SGG because* dazzling
74.35 **himself, but, at most, a** ***petit écu*** **worth thirty pence; consequently** *SGG* himself; consequently
74.37–8 **France. The same notion as to the indispensableness of a coronation prevails widely in England. But,** *SGG* France. But
74.41 **Orleans? And** *SGG* Orleans? That is to say, what more than a merely *military* service could she render him? And,
75.2–6 **him. Trouble us not....man that is baked** *SGG* with him: he that should first be drawn from the ovens of Rheims, was under that superstition baked
75.6–7 **All others are counterfeits, made of base Indian meal – damaged by seawater.** *SGG omits*

Joan of Arc {Part II}

76.3 **a juvenile pupil** *SGG* a pupil
76.3–4 **divinity, before six** *SGG* divinity, at the bar of six
76.11–14 ***Creation:*** **now...woman could frame. 2dly,** *SGG* Creation' – a piracy *á parte* ante, and by three centuries. 2dly,
76.15 **trial; for Southey's 'Joan' of A. Dom. 1796** *SGG* trial. Southey's 'Joan,' of A.D. 1796
76.17–77.11 **Here's a precious....six church pillars.'** *SGG omits*
77.24 **Oh...arise!' &c.** *SGG*

> Oh, what a multitude of thoughts at once
> Awaken'd in me swarm, while I consider
> What from within I feel myself, and hear
> What from without comes often to my ears,
> Ill sorting with my present state compared!
> When I was yet a child, no childish play
> To me was pleasing; all my mind was set
> Serious to learn and know, and thence to do
> What might be public good; myself I thought
> Born to that end[a] –

[[a] Milton, *Paradise Regained*, I. 196–205.]

77.32 **intellectual** *SGG* spiritual
77.40 **latter; – this might have been done – it** *SGG* latter; which, however, might have been done, for it
77.41–78.5 **herself, in the same way.... introduced. It** *SGG* herself. It
78.25–6 **triumph. What remained was – to suffer.** *SGG* triumph. All that was to be *done*, she had now accomplished: what remained was – to *suffer.*
78.33 **disapproved.** *SGG* had ceased to approve.
78.33 **had accomplished** *SGG* had now accomplished

79.12 **successes** *F, SGG* success
79.26–7 **her task** *SGG* her *triumphal* task
80.19 **as that lightning** *SGG* as God's lightning
81.11 **horribly.** *SGG* exultingly.
82.12–27 **Do not ask me...oracula tanta.*** *SGG omits text and footnote*
82.29–30 **sex, until that day when you claim my promise as to falsehood – cheerfully,** *SGG* sex, cheerfully
82.32 **Mozart** *SGG* Milton
83.1 **world** *SGG* worlds
83.4–5 **Himalayas? Pooh! pooh! My** *SGG* Himalayas? Oh, no! my
83.11–13 ***us.* Telescopes look...worlds as well as we do. How,** *SGG us.* How
83.19–20 **grey prematurely by** *SGG* grey by
83.21–3 **death? How, if it were...with her expiring breath? How,** *SGG* death? How,
84.10 **and universally** *SGG* and at one time universally
85.n.10–12 **inimitable; else, as regards....till one tries. Yet,** *SGG* inimitable. Yet,
85.n.20 **lads** *SGG* men
85.n.20 **lasses** *SGG* girls
86.n.3 **my dear?** *SGG mon cher?*
89.8 **child of Domrémy** *Editorial; 1847* child o Domrémy
89.13–14 **is going to take** *SGG* is taking
89.20 **she that cometh in bloody** *SGG* she in bloody

The Nautico-Military Nun of Spain {Part I}

Title **THE NAUTICO-MILITARY NUN OF SPAIN.** *F* THE SPANISH NUN. *SGG* THE SPANISH MILITARY NUN.
93.1–94.8 **WHY is it that *Adventures*....continental versions.** *SGG omits*
94.9 *F inserts line space. SGG inserts heading: Section* 1. *– An Extra Nuisance is introduced into Spain. MS A includes deletion: Nuisance is* <*Born.*> *Introduced*
94.10 ***somebody,'**** *SGG moves footnote into text: 'son of somebody'* (*i.e.*, hidalgo),
94.13 **useless for** *SGG* useless towards
94.14–15 **2+1 than *his* reckoning assumed as a reasonable** *SGG* 2+1, according to *his* reckoning, than any reasonable
94.16 **but daughters in excess were** *SGG* but supernumerary daughters were
94.18 **gentleman was apt to do – he wrapped the new** *MS A, SGG conform, with the exception of several significant deletions in MS A given here in angle brackets* gentleman endeavoured to do. And surely I need not interrupt myself by any parenthesis to inform the base British reader, who makes it his glory to work hard, that the peculiar point of honour for the Spanish gentleman lay precisely in these two qualities of pride and laziness: for, if he were not proud, or had anything to do, what could you look for but ruin to the old Spanish aristocracy? some of whom boasted that no members of their house (unless illegitimate, and a mere *terrae filius*[a]) had done a day's work since the flood. In the ark, they admitted that Noah kept them tightly to work; because, in fact, there was work to do, that must be done by somebody. But once <after the Ark> anchored upon Ararat,[b] they insisted upon it most indignantly that no ancestor of the Spanish *noblesse* had ever worked, except through his slaves. And with a view to new leases of idleness, through new generations of slaves, it was (as many people think), that Spain went so <cheerfully> heartily into the enterprises of Cortez and Pizarro.[c] A sedentary body of Dons, without needing to uncross their thrice noble legs, would thus

levy eternal tributes of gold and silver upon <inexhaustible> eternal mines, through eternal successions of <slaves> nations that had been, and were to be, enslaved. Meantime, until these golden visions should be realised, aristocratic *daughters*, who constituted the hereditary <nuisance> torment of the true Castilian Don, were to be disposed of in the good old way; viz., by quartering them for life upon nunneries: a plan which entailed no sacrifice whatever upon any of the parties concerned, except, indeed, the <absolute and total> little insignificant sacrifice of happiness and natural birthrights to the daughters <too probably a set of silly romantic girls>. But this little inevitable wreck, when placed in the counter-scale to the magnificent purchase of eternal idleness for an aristocracy so ancient, was surely entitled to little attention amongst philosophers. Daughters must perish by generations, and ought to be proud of perishing, in order that their papas, being hidalgos, might luxuriate in laziness. Accordingly, on this system, our hidalgo of St Sebastian[d] wrapped the new

[[a] A son of the earth; a person of low birth or obscure origin.

[b] Mount Ararat is in extreme eastern Turkey, and is traditionally known as the mountain on which Noah's Ark came to rest at the end of the Flood.

[c] See above, p. 555, n. 5.

[d] Saint Sebastian (d. *c.* AD 288), one of the most celebrated martyrs of the early Christian church.]

94.21 **St Sebastian; not merely of** *SGG* St Sebastian; meaning by that term not merely a convent of

94.24 **liked and appropriated would** *SGG* liked, we should agree too closely about the objects to be appropriated; which would

94.27 **odious elsewhere. The superior** *SGG* odious at home. The lady superior

94.33 **to cry and whimper** *SGG* to whimper

94.35–6 **tenderness. / What** *SGG inserts title:* 2. – *Wait a little, Hidalgo!*

95.12–13 **longer. / Disappointment,** *SGG inserts title:* 3. – *Symptoms of Mutiny.*

95.26 **their chapel gravity** *SGG* their gravity

95.28–9 **was Kitty; this is Catharine, or Kate, or *Hispanice* Catalina. It** *SGG* was Kitty, or Kate; and *that* in Spanish is Catalina. It

95.38 **health and the strength** *SGG* health, which forbade one to think of separation from St Sebastian by death, and notwithstanding the strength

95.38 **walls, the** *SGG* walls, which forbade one to think of any other separation, the

95.42 **Spanish bonds and promises.** *MS A, SGG conform, with the exception of one significant deletion in MS A given here in angle brackets* Spanish growth; such as Spanish constitutions and charters, Spanish financial reforms, Spanish bonds, and other little varieties of Spanish of Spanish <fungus and rottenness> ostentatious mendacity. *followed by paragraph break and heading:* 4. – *The Symptoms Thicken.*

96.5 **aspiring, but not cruel. She** *SGG* aspiring, violent sometimes, headstrong and haughty towards those who presumed upon her youth, absolutely rebellious against all open harshness, but still generous and most forgiving, disdainful of petty arts, and emphatically a noble girl. She

96.9 **keep-sake a look which that** *SGG* keepsake such a look, as that

96.12 **that tumultuous** *SGG* that glad tumultuous

96.23 **was but too** *SGG* was no romance at all, but far too

96.23 **fact. / The** *SGG inserts heading:* 5. – *Good Night, St Sebastian!*

96.31 **'scrutoire, she did** *SGG* the prudent lady did

96.33–4 **in any great emergency which** *SGG* in great emergencies which

96.35 **moment for an attempt which,** *SGG* moment, *now* had the clock struck, for an opportunity which,

96.36 **that fortress impregnable** *SGG* that monastic fortress, impregnable
96.40 **whole life,** *SGG* whole future life,
96.41 **of a head-ache** *SGG* of headache
96.42–3 **head-aches, except now and then afterwards from a stray bullet, or so?] – upon** *SGG* head-aches?) – upon
97.4 **I pretend to an** *SGG* I profess an
97.5–10 **I, for my part…from year to year.** *SGG omits*
97.10 **But, always,** *SGG* And always
97.10–11 **even though the kind be disagreeable. Kate's** *SGG* even where the kind may happen to be not especially attractive. Kate's
97.16 **decidedly** *SGG* eminently
97.16 **skin as** *SGG* skin, in fact, as
97.17 **Spain. But** *SGG* Spain; but
97.20 **the kind** *SGG* that kind
97.22–3 **disguise her sad and infinite wanderings to the paternal old man (and** *SGG* disguise to the paternal old man her sad and infinite wanderings (and
97.23 **respect, even** *SGG* respect – viz., all which concerned her sexual honour – even
97.23–4 **then, at middle age, she** *SGG* then she
97.24 **as is a child** *SGG* as a child
97.24 **equity** *SGG* the rude natural equity
97.25–6 **for the polished (but often more iniquitous) equity** *SGG* for the specious and conventional equity
97.26–9 **As to the third item… not so *very* far wrong.** *SGG omits*
97.32 **least** *SGG* lowest
97.37 **what? to** *SGG* what beside? to
97.37 **hanks** *SGG* skeins
97.38 **a very inferior pair** *SGG* a bad pair
97.41 ***consequentia*, *all* scissors** *SGG consequentia*, the right of inference is good. All *scissors*
97.44 **Ketch was** *SGG* Ketch, or, as the present generation calls him, *'Mr Calcraft,'* or '----- *Calcraft, Esq.,*'[a] was
[[a] William Calcraft (1800–79; *DNB*) was Britain's principal executioner from 1829 to 1874. He was noted for his 'short drops', which caused most of his victims to die a slow and agonizing death.]
98.6 ***viva* of** *SGG viva* being a word of
98.10 **twilight favoured** *SGG* twilight, it is true, favoured
98.10 **but she** *SGG* but in any season twilight is as short-lived as a farthing rushlight; and she
98.13 **perhaps to** *SGG* perhaps, in the first place, to
98.14 **purse, she** *SGG* purse, or what amounted to that English sum in various Spanish coins, she
98.15 **Katy** *SGG* Kate,
98.24 **trousers, and made** *SGG* trousers, made
98.25–6 **beside the shilling, *quantum sufficit* of thread, one stout needle,** *SGG* beside, *first* (for I detest your ridiculous and most pedantic neologism of *firstly*) – *first*, the shilling for which I have already given a receipt; *secondly*, two skeins of suitable thread; thirdly, one stout needle,
98.28–9 **anywhere. The** *SGG* anywhere, which port (according to a smart American adage) is to be looked 'at the back of beyond.' The

98.32 **confessor; she took** *SGG* confessor; she did not take the key of the closet which held the peppermint water and other cordials, for *that* would have distressed the elderly nuns. *She* took

98.34–5 **liberty....'your right to lock her in.'** liberty. Very different views are taken by different parties of this particular act now meditated by Kate. The Court of Rome treats it as the immediate suggestion of Hell, and open to no forgiveness. Another Court, far loftier, ampler, and of larger authority, viz., the Court which holds its dreadful tribunal in the human heart and conscience, pronounces this act an inalienable privilege of man, and the mere reassertion of a birthright that can neither be bought nor sold. *followed by heading:* 6. – *Kate's First Bivouac and First March.*

98.36 **strict casuistry,** *SGG* Romish casuistry,

98.37 ***did* so; and,** *SGG did;* and

98.39 **was not cold. She** *SGG* was moderately warm. She

98.40 **leaves slept till dawn.** *SGG* leaves, which furnished to Kate her very first bivouac in a long succession of such experiences, she slept till earliest dawn.

98.40 **youth leaves** *SGG* youth leave

98.42–3 **nun, and liable to be arrested by any man in Spain.** *SGG* nun; and therefore, by a law too flagrantly notorious, liable to the peremptory challenge and arrest of any man – the very meanest or poorest – in all Spain.

99.6 **trousers would** *SGG* trousers anywhere in the north of Spain would

99.9 **earlier, [though *he* too is an early riser], she** *SGG* earlier, she

99.10 **march, baggage far in the rear, and** *SGG* march, with

99.14 **have one.** *SGG* possess one.

99.14 **relative, an** *SGG* relative proved to be an

99.15 **perhaps one virtue in the world; but *that* he had in perfection, – it was** *SGG* perhaps it was a virtue, which had by continual development overshadowed his whole nature – it was

99.17 **a few latin phrases.** *SGG* a good number of Latin phrases.

99.21–2 **cared little about. The amusement was** *SGG* cared least about. On the other hand, the amusement was

99.24 **preterite, wanted** *SGG* preterite, wanted its gerunds, wanted

99.26–7 **was marching** *SGG* was, as you may say, marching

99.33 **Thiebault or some such author, who** *SGG* Thiebault, who

99.37 **melancholy conjugation.** *SGG* dolorous conjugation.

99.40 **catastrophe], and took from** *SGG* catastrophe), taking from

99.41 **But the** *SGG* But then, observe, the

99.43–4 **no right to bore one *gratis*.** *SGG* no unlimited privilege of boring one: an uncle has a qualified right to bore his nephews, even when they happen to be nieces; but he has no right to bore either nephew or niece *gratis*. *followed by heading:* 7. – *Kate at Court, where she Prescribes Phlebotomy and is Promoted.*

100.2 **but it** *SGG* but, in fact, it

100.3 **were the** *SGG* were assembled the

100.6 **the form** *SGG* the particular form

100.6–7 **[rascals! one would like to have...better scissors!]** *SGG* (rascals! What sort of trousers would *they* have made with no better scissors?)

100.10 **fifteen in** *SGG* fifteen years old in

100.12 **open a head or two with a sharp stone, and letting** *SGG* open with sharp stones more heads than either one or two, and letting

100.15 **know nearer** *SGG* know of nearer

100.17 **for murderous violence: and** *SGG* for her most natural retaliation: and

100.24 **offered Catalina** *SGG* offered to Catalina
100.26 **accepted. Here** *SGG inserts paragraph break and heading:* 8. – *Too Good to Last!*
100.27 **happy month. She** *SGG* happy quarter of a year! She
100.30 **well – when one** *SGG* well – until one
100.31 **until** *SGG* before
100.33 ***Papa*, that we** *SGG papa*, whom we
100.35 **fire-engine. It** *SGG* fire-engine. Whom will he speak to first in this lordly mansion? It
100.38 **Kate thought he** *SGG* Kate fancied (but it must have been a fancy) that he
100.40 **wish him on** *SGG* wish papa on
100.41 **river for crocodiles, the** *SGG* river, the
101.2 **delight. Then** *SGG* delight, radiant with festal pleasure, overflowing with luxury. Then
101.4 **money that** *SGG* money, the unknown amounts of cash, that
101.9 **mention the pocket-handkerchief** *SGG* mention – yes! positively not even in parenthesis would he condescend to notice – that pocket-handkerchief
101.15 **father. For** *SGG* father, or by Don Cardenas. For
101.17–18 **with suspicions travelling in** *SGG* with any suspicious traveller in
101.20 **her into** *SGG* her, by the purest of accidents, into
101.24 **protector of** *SGG* protector and official visitor of
101.25 **as *ex officio* visitor of** *SGG* as hereditary patron of
101.26 **appealing. Probably Kate** *SGG* appealing. This being so, Kate
101.27 **again, this** *SGG* again, that
101.41–2 **not subscribe** *SGG* not choose to subscribe
102.3 **answering any** *SGG* answering the
102.5–7 **Francisco. Now, it would not have been filial or lady-like for Kate to do what I am going to suggest; but what a pity that** *SGG* Francisco. Ah, what a beautiful idea occurs to me at this point! Once on the hustings at Liverpool I saw a mob orator, whose brawling mouth, open to its widest expansion, suddenly some larking sailor, by the most dexterous of shots, plugged up with a paving-stone. Here, now, at Valladolid, was another mouth that equally required plugging. What a pity, then, that
102.7 **page had** *SGG* page of Kate's had
102.10 **date, and very** *SGG* date (1608), which can be apodeictically proved, because in Spain there were no potatoes at all; and very
102.11–12 **anything. / Catalina** *SGG inserts* 9. – *How to Choose Lodgings.*
102.21–2 **introduction, not** *SGG* introduction, and not
102.22 **preferring any street** *SGG* preferring this or that street
102.23–4 **one or two streets in** *SGG* one street in
102.25 **accuracy with which** *SGG* accuracy which
102.28 **being unfastened, and open** *SGG* being deliberately left open
102.33–4 **proved. There was an empty cart inside; certainly there was, but** *SGG* proved; and the stable was not absolutely empty: for there was a cart inside – a four-wheeled cart. True, there was so; but
102.35 **were five** *SGG* were also five
102.39 **person, dressed** *SGG* person, handsomely dressed
102.44–103.1 **conversation. They were talking of an** *SGG* conversation. In the intervals of their sleep, they talked much of an
103.1 **expedition for** *SGG* expedition to
103.3 **the very thing** *SGG* the thing
103.4 **needing no more** *SGG* needing little more

103.10–11 **her escape;** *SGG* her final escape;
103.11 **crocodile, or** *SGG* crocodile, nor
103.11 **Sebastian, or** *SGG* Sebastian, nor
103.14 **slowly; but many** *SGG* slowly; many weeks the journey cost her; but, after all, what are weeks? She reached Seville many
103.15 **expedition. St. Lucar** *SGG* expedition. *followed on new line by heading:* 10. – *An Ugly Dilemma, where Right and Wrong is reduced to a Question of Right or Left.* / Ugly indeed is that dilemma where shipwreck and the sea are on one side of you, and famine on the other; or, if a chance of escape is offered, apparently it depends upon taking the right road where there is no guide-post. / St Lucar
103.36–7 **the greatest of philosophers, that** *SGG* the underwriters at Lloyd's, that
103.43 **Kate hard at** *SGG* Kate at
103.44 ***her.* The** *F, SGG insert paragraph break*
103.44–104.1 **duty, seems to have desponded. He** *SGG* duty, faithful to his king, and on his king's account even hopeful, seems from the first to have desponded on his own. He
104.6 **waiting for a final** *SGG* waiting only for a final
104.7–8 **some misjudging people will object to. She** *SGG* some erring people will misconstrue. She
104.9 **contingencies in** *SGG* contingencies on
104.10 **sum equal** *SGG* sum in ducats and pistoles equal
104.16 **battle several of** *SGG* battle, as you will find, more than one of
104.18 **circumstances, on** *SGG* circumstances, even on
104.18 **vessel, though** *SGG* vessel, and though
104.18–19 **Admiralty should** *SGG* Admiralty, and the Secretary, that pokes his nose into everything nautical, should
104.22–3 **coming. Kate mounted the raft and was** *MS B* coming after him as fast as she could make ready. Kate's <trick> luck was better: she mounted the raft, and by the rising tide was *SGG* coming after him as fast as she could make ready. Kate's luck was better: she mounted the raft and by the rising tide was
104.27–8 **a guinea amongst** *SGG* a golden ducat, though worth nine shillings in silver, or even of a hundred, amongst
104.35 **darkest night, provided** *SGG* darkest of nights, provided
104.36–7 **herself six thousand** *SGG* herself, after all, a thousand
104.37 **case, all** *SGG* case, and all
105.4 **is about the best thing I know, but it but** *SGG* is one of the best things I know, even if not made by Mrs Bobo;* but *MS E, SGG append footnote and conform, with the exception of six significant deletions in MS E given here in angle bracketes* Who is Mrs Bobo? The reader will say, 'I know not Bobo.' Possibly; but for all *that*, Bobo is known to senates. From the American Senate [Friday, March 10, 1854] Bobo received the amplest testimonials of merits, that have not yet been <received> matched. In the debate on <Mr> William Nevins's <pretensions to> claim for the extension of his patent for a machine that rolls and cuts crackers and biscuits, thus spoke Mr Adams, [a] a most distinguished senator <for the>, against Mr Badger:[b] – 'It is said this is a discovery of the patentee for making the best biscuits. Now, if it be so, he must have got his invention from Mrs Bobo of Alabama; for she certainly makes better biscuit than anybody in the world. I can prove by my friend <Mr> from Alabama (Mr Clay),[c] who sits beside me, and by any man who ever stayed at <Alabama> Mrs Bobo's house, that she makes better biscuit than anybody else in the world; and if this man has the best plan for making biscuit, he must have got it from *her*.' Henceforward I hope we know where

to apply for biscuit.

[[a] Stephen Adams (1807–57), United States senator from Mississippi.

[b] George Edmund Badger (1795–1866), United States senator from North Carolina.

[c] Clement Claiborne Clay (1816–82), United States senator from Alabama.]

105.7 ***mortuum* corpse! Upon** *SGG mortuum.* Upon

105.7–9 ***caput* Kate breakfasted...Pacific Ocean. She, that** *SGG caput*, in default of anything better, Kate breakfasted. And breakfast being over, she rang for the waiter to take away, and to – Stop! what nonsense! There could be no bell, besides which, there could be no waiter. Well, then, without asking the waiter's aid, she that

105.12 **medicine** *SGG* dietetics

105.15 **may never** *SGG* may famish and never

105.16 **second day,** *SGG* third day,

105.17 **any river** *SGG* any *very* broad river

105.17–18 **walk. / The** *SGG inserts heading:* 11. – *From the Malice of the Sea, to the Malice of Man and Woman.*

105.20–1 ***that*, as we know, having overlooked her in the chestnut wood. The** *SGG that.* The

105.23 **1847,** *SGG* 1854,

105.29 **fine person;** *SGG* magnificent person;

106.1 **ship had** *SGG* ship which threw Kate ashore had

106.18–19 **That was plain.** *SGG* That seemed plain.

106.29 **offices hear, and perhaps utter, without** *SGG* offices utter without

106.35 **in a course** *SGG* in the course

106.40 **only executed** *SGG* only followed

107.2 **arrangement that you know could** *SGG* arrangement, you know, that in the final result could

107.4 **of strolling players strolled** *SGG* of vagrant comedians strolled

107.5 **Kate, as a Spaniard, being one held of the Paita aristocracy, was** *SGG* Kate, being a native Spaniard, ranked as one of the Paita aristocracy, and was

107.10 **Reyes remarked that** *SGG* Reyes replied, that

107.14 **interposed to** *SGG* interposed, for the present, to

107.21 **execution. The relations of** *MS B* execution. *Followed by paragraph break and heading:* 12. – *From the <Dungeon with> Steps leading up to the Scaffold, to the <Dungeon with> Steps leading down to Assassination.* / The relati<ons>ves of *SGG* execution. *followed by paragraph break and heading:* 12. – *From the Steps leading up to the Scaffold, to the Steps leading down to Assassination.* / The relatives of

107.24 **relatives** *SGG* connections

107.36 **him to** *SGG* him (the clerk) to

108.6 **of liberation** *SGG* of his liberation

108.15 **resent the case** *SGG* regard the case

108.17 **in twelve** *SGG* within twelve

108.26–7 **as the procession** *SGG* as that procession

108.28–9 **outrider. Then** *SGG* outrider; then

108.32 **Castillian strut. Next** *SGG* Castilian strut; next

108.34 **prisoner – our Kate – the** *SGG* prisoner – our poor ensnared Kate – the

108.35 **this day only** *SGG* this night only

108.44 **chance, after all, where** *SGG* chance in a crisis where

109.5 **first – 'Sound** *SGG* first, with a strut more than usually grandiose, and inexpressibly sublime – 'Sound

109.18 **and debtor** *SGG* and unlimited debtor

109.20–1 **she already knew that the clerk had committed** *SGG* she knew that the clerk had already committed

109.22 **easy. But,** *MS B inserts paragraph break, followed by heading:* 13. – *From <the Persecution of> Human Malice back again to the <Persecution> of Winds and Waves.*/ But, *SGG inserts paragraph break, followed by heading:* 13. – *From Human Malice, back again to the Malice of Winds and Waves*. But,

109.22 **when out and** *SGG* when abroad, and

109.24 **but a rat-trap** *SGG* but one vast rat-trap

109.26 **none. She** *SGG* none; and she

109.42 **boat, (though destined** *SGG* boat (though a boat that in fact was destined

110.16 **that it** *SGG* that, whatever this might be, it

The Nautico-Military Nun of Spain {Part II}

Title **THE NAUTICO-MILITARY NUN OF SPAIN.** *SGG omits*

Title SGG inserts heading: 14. – *Bright Gleams of Sunshine.*

112.34–5 **hand. / Kate** *SGG inserts heading:* 15. – *The Sunshine is Overcast.*

113.13 **just there an** *SGG* just then an

113.14–15 **think, I beseech you, too much, of killing a man. That** *SGG* think too much, reader, of killing a man – do not, I beseech you! That

113.38 **had a right** *SGG* had the right

114.5 **KATE'S PASSAGE OVER THE ANDES.** *SGG* 16. – *Kate's Ascent of the Andes.*

114.17 **Summer would come as vainly** *SGG* Summer came even hither; but came as vainly

114.20 **kindling a secret hardly known except to Indians. However,** *MS B* kindling a fire by <friction of two> interfriction[a] of dry sticks was a secret almost exclusively Indian. However, *SGG* kindling a fire by interfriction of dry sticks was a secret almost exclusively Indian. However,

[[a] 'Rubbing together' (*OED*, which cites this example from De Quincey.)]

114.21–2 **thing, or ever girl did *not* such a thing, that** *SGG* thing, that

114.37–115.5 **quarters; which surprises me....found. No** *SGG* quarters; a difficult fraction to distribute amongst a triad of claimants. No

115.7 **strawberries. / On** *SGG* strawberries; and *that* was the kind of preservation which one page ago I promised the horse. / On

115.20 **side. She shouted with joy to** *SGG* side. Joyously she shouted to

115.21 **joyful news.** *SGG* good news.

115.34–5 **head. Kate began to think there would be another man to rouse from sleep. Coming** *SGG* head. Coming

115.35 **him she touched** *SGG* him, Kate touched

115.44–116.1 **was a spasm of morbid strength; a collapse** *SGG* was simply a spasm of morbid strength. A collapse

116.2 **struggle. Gone are** *SGG* struggle. Yes, gone are

116.3 **stretched and** *SGG* stretched out and

116.6 **servants of** *SGG* servants to

116.6–7 ***they* dogged** *SGG they* it was that dogged

116.8–9 **bullet. / Now** *SGG inserts heading:* 17. – *Kate stands alone on the Summit of the Andes.*

116.10 **shocking,** *SGG* frightful,

116.16 **Kate is exactly that** *SGG* Kate in some respects resembled that

116.19–20 **half the jewels of its** *SGG* half its

116.25 **is *not* baseless; it is the** *SGG* is the

116.36 **the hard price of** *SGG* the difficult cost of

117.14–15 **mind. / Such, also, had** *SGG* mind. / Not altogether unlike, though free from the criminal intention of the mariner, had

117.15 **Kate; such, also,** *SGG* Kate; not unlike, also,

117.20 **one darkness for** *SGG* one darkness, physical darkness, for

117.21 **another darkness for** *SGG* another darkness, the darkness of superstition, for

117.23 **for you or me, reader** *SGG* for any of us, reader

117.28 **on first touching** *SGG* on touching

117.28–9 **the very first** *SGG* the first

117.41 **generous, it was that she had** *SGG* generous, who, without knowing, had cherished and protected her, and all from pure holy love for herself as the innocent plaything of St Sebastian's, *him* in a moment she had

118.2 **Zaarrahs** *SGG* Saharas

118.33 **villain, whom I mark for a shot if he does not get out of the way, opens** *SGG* villain opens

118.38 **poor deserters,** *SGG* poor mutineers or deserters,

118.41 **the deserter from his colours *must*** *SGG* the mutineer *must*

119.14 **thing, viz., that** *SGG* thing, that,

119.37–8 **as an infant and through girlhood, she** *SGG* from her infant days she

119.38–9 **adore. / Now,** *SGG inserts heading:* 18. – *Kate begins to Descend the Mighty Staircase.*

120.2 **paltry; I** *F, SGG* paltry. I

120.3 **upon any such errand** *SGG* upon such an errand

120.4 **Kate – a** *SGG* Kate; also, next after which I would request a

120.11 **eye but an** *SGG* eye, even an

120.16 **Cordilleras, and which perhaps, but not certainly, compensated any** *SGG* Cordilleras; and this area, perhaps, but not certainly, might compensate any

120.23 **motion, mere extremity** *SGG* motion, continued extremity

120.25 **weariness.** *SGG* weariness; that is, in short, the excessive weariness would give a murderous advantage to the cold, or the excessive cold would give a corresponding advantage to the weariness.

120.31–2 **space! This hour** *MS A* space! <Like the that, like the tides, are deaf to human rhetoric.> This <half> hour

120.37 **character – might** *MS A* character <similar impediments,> – might

120.38 **ghastly darkness** *MS A* ghastly <visions of> darkness

120.38–9 **that was now beginning to gather upon the inner eye?** *MS A* that {↑ was} now {↑ beginning to} <towered> {↑ gather} upon the <speculat> inner eye?

120.41–2 **suddenly seemed** *SGG* suddenly, in the eyes of Kate, seemed

120.41–3 **suddenly seemed all brothers and sisters), cottages with children around them at play,** *MS A* {↑ suddenly seemed all} <became all of them> brothers and sisters), cottages with children {↑ <around them all,> around them} at play,

120.43 **oh! summer and spring, flowers and blossoms, to** *SGG* oh! spring and summer, blossoms and flowers, to

121.1 **Life, and** *MS A* Life {↑ <in its fountains, Life>} and

121.2 **Kate must** *MS A* Kate <(as she {↑ now} muttered to herself)> must

121.3–4 **strange are the caprices of ebb and flow in** *MS A* strange <Strange> are the caprices of <human> ebb<s> and flow<s> in

121.6 **heart, a** *MS A* heart, <she turned round scarcely knowing> a

121.6 **lightening shot** *SGG* lightening, as it were, or flashing inspiration of hope, shot

121.6–7 **spirit, a reflux almost supernatural, from the earliest effects** *MS A* spirit, <what seemed to her> a {↑ reflux almost} supernatural <reflux> from the <first> {↑ earliest} effects

121.7–11 **prayer. A thought....identified the spot** *MS A* prayer. <stole back upon her <bes> hopes. She had turned round, blindly and suddenly a thought {↑ had} struck her, that which> *SGG* prayer. Dimmed and confused had been the accuracy of her sensations for hours; but all at once a strong conviction came over her – that more and more was the sense of descent becoming steady and continuous. Turning round to measure backwards with her eye the ground traversed through the last half hour, she identified, by a remarkable point of rock, the spot

121.17 **ground, that** *SGG* ground, from that point where the corpses lay, that

121.23 **she had been** *SGG* she was *descending* – she *had* been

121.27 **house, has ceased (you** *SGG* houses, ceases (you

121.33 **became probable** *SGG* became certain

121.34 **the natural** *SGG* these natural

121.35 **dazzled eye?** *SGG* dazzled eye!

121.36 **promise?** *SGG* promise!

121.44–122.1 **screen (though not everywhere occupied by the usurpations) of a thick bushy** *SGG* screen of thick bushy

122.9 **to Christian** *SGG* to the shelter of Christian

122.32–3 **in her confusion she** *SGG* in the confusion of her misery, she

122.38 **Sebastians.'** *Editorial; 1847* Sebastian,'

122.42–3 **the *Angelus*** *SGG* the echoing *Angelus*

122.44 **back in** *SGG* back into

123.4 **Little enough is** *SGG* Little is

123.12–13 **above. / All** *SGG inserts heading:* 19. – *Kate's Bedroom is Invaded by Horsemen.*

123.23 **machinery. Sleep** *SGG* machinery, and stations his artillery. Sleep

123.27 **rest, Kate** *SGG* rest, then, alas! Kate

123.35–6 **giving so sound an opinion, that the jewelly** *SGG* giving an opinion equal to Captain Bunsby's,[a] on this point, viz., whether the jewelly
[[a] Jack Bunsby, old sailor, friend, and adviser of Captain Cuttle in Charles Dickens's *Dombey and Son* (1846–8). 'If so be...as he's dead, my opinion is he won't come back no more. If so be as he's alive, my opinion is he will. Do I say he will? No! Why not? Because the bearings of this obserwation lays in the application on it' (Dickens, *Dombey and Son*, p. 530).]

123.38 **needed to** *SGG* needed, perhaps, to

123.39 **but would** *SGG* but apparently would

124.n.2 **little** *Editorial; 1847* littly

124.n.6 **temperance. The** *MS C, SGG conform, with the exception of two significant deletions in MS C given here in angle brackets* temperance. Dr Darwin, the famous author of 'Zoonomia,' 'The Botanic Garden,'[a] &c., sacrificed his life to the very pedantry and superstition of temperance, by refusing a glass of brandy in obedience to a system, at a moment when (according to the opinion of all around him) one single glass <of brandy might> would have saved his <him> life. The
[[a] Erasmus Darwin (1731–1802; *DNB*), physician, biologist, and poet, whose works include *The Botanic Garden* (1789–91) and *Zoonomia; or, the Laws of Organic Life* (1794–6). Darwin was a strong advocate of temperance. He died in April 1802, probably of a lung infection. Cf. another account of Darwin's deathbed as related by his famous grandson Charles Darwin: 'I have heard from a connection of the family that an old

and faithful maid-servant, who was present when my grandfather died, afterwards told his step-daughter that on hearing him faintly saying something, she bent down her head to listen, but the only word she caught was "Jesus"....But it is incredible that my grandfather should have wholly changed his judgment on so important a subject' (*Charles Darwin's The Life of Erasmus Darwin*, ed. Desmond King-Hele (New York: Cambridge University Press, 2002), p. 63).]

124.n.12–13 **her attendant, who** *SGG* her chief medical attendant, Sir R.C.,[a] who [[a] See above, p. 557, n. 37.]

124.n.14–15 **twenty years** *SGG* thirty years

124.n.15 **accomplishments,** *MS C, SGG append footnote and conform, with the exception of one significant deletion in MS C given here in angle brackets* On second thoughts, I see no reason <why I should impl> for scrupling to mention that this man was Robert Southey.[a] [[a] See above, p. 523, n. 3.]

124.n.18 **so. The** *SGG* so. On this, he suggested earnestly some stimulant – laudanum or alcohol. The

124.n.19 **inexorable.** *Editorial; 1847* inexorable,

124.n.23 **recovered with magical power. The** *SGG* recovered as if under the immediate afflatus of magic; so sudden was her recovery, and so complete. The

124.n.29 **laudanum. An obstinate man will say – 'Oh,** *SGG* laudanum. Many will say, 'Oh,

124.n.33–41 **N.B. – I prescribe for Kate....practice is so fatally frequent.** *SGG omits*

125.7–8 **in some pursuit of flying game had wandered beyond** *SGG* in pursuit of some flying game had wandered far beyond

125.11 **perhaps dying.** *SGG* apparently dying.

125.16–17 **be successful, they** *SGG* be the one thing needed, they

125.22 **some miles** *SGG* many miles

125.30 **changed: there** *SGG* changed, either in herself or in those about her: there

125.37–126.2 **Last month, reader, I promised....expression, 'let's liquor.'** *F, SGG omit*

The Nautico-Military Nun of Spain {Part III}

Title **THE NAUTICO-MILITARY NUN OF SPAIN.** *SGG omits*

Title SGG inserts heading: 20. –. *A Second Lull in Kate's Stormy Life.*

128.4 **and rendering thanks,** *SGG* and able to render thanks,

128.9 **shall call** *SGG* will call

128.n.2 **After these** *SGG* After those

128.n.3 **complications of** *SGG* complications and interweavings of

128.n.5 **yet, the** *SGG* yet (*i.e.*, in Kate's time), the

128.n.7 **because *born*** *SGG* if born

128.n.7 **use, it expresses the** *SGG* use, the word *Creole* expresses exactly the

128.n.10–11 **see Casaubon** *SGG* see Isaac Casaubon

128.13 **forty-four** *SGG* forty-two

128.23 **twenty years** *SGG* twenty-eight years

128.n.12 **Spanish of** *SGG* Spanish beyond

128.n.12–13 **became the most gloomily** *SGG* became so gloomily

129.n.1 **a king** *SGG* a Hebrew king

129.n.1–2 **priesthood, (Chron. ii. 26) suddenly** *SGG* priesthood (2 Chron. xxvi,16-20), suddenly

129.2 **destined silently** *SGG* destined [ah, wherefore?] silently
129.12 **her Vandal,** *SGG* her Visigothic, by her Vandal,
129.21 **stranger. But** *SGG* stranger. Such things it had been that wooed the heavenly Desdemona.[a] But
[[a] Shakespeare, *Othello*, I.iii.128–70.]
129.25–6 **herself, that** *SGG* herself, a splendid cavalier, that
129.31 **reader knows all** *SGG* reader already guesses all
130.1 **of forty-four years' experience, was** *MS A* of forty-two years' experience, <or supposing> was *SGG* of forty-two years' experience, or say forty-four, was
130.36–7 **Helots, an Englishman amongst Savages, an Alférez would in those days have** *MS A* Helots – a Spanish Alférez would in those days, and in that <reign> region, have *SGG* Helots – a Spanish Alférez would in those days, and in that region, have
130.38 **Something, therefore** *MS A* <A good deal>, therefore *SGG* Something, therefore
130.42 **as he was** *SGG* as she was
130.43–131.1 **Portuguese. / Catalina** *SGG inserts heading:* 21. – *Kate once more in Storms.*
131.1 **proverb – 'Subtract from a Spaniard** *SGG* proverb, 'Pump out of Spaniard
131.3–4 **society. Very soon she** *SGG* society. Soon she
131.4 **play: all** *SGG* play: for all
131.13 **an house** *SGG* a house
131.15 **stepping hastily up, she** *SGG* stepping up hastily, she
132.7 **or third** *F, SGG* or a third
132.15 **with saddest** *SGG* with her saddest
132.15 **was all finished.** *SGG* was finished.
132.19 **to *what*?) Things** *SGG* to *what*, or to *whom*, in a case where there was no distinct charge, and no avowed accuser?) Things
132.24 **were very ill-looking** *SGG* were ill-looking
132.37 **the house; which** *SGG* that house; which
133.3 **been ripened** *SGG* been proved, or even ripened
133.4 **logic was of no use; and** *SGG* logic in defence was henceforward impertinence; and
133.8 **it (if not under** *SGG* it (unless under
133.11 **gone to** *SGG* gone forward to
133.12 **was probably** *SGG* was certainly
133.23 **might have committed. But supposing that** *SGG* might be supposed to have committed. But, allowing that
133.27 **firm to** *SGG* firm, therefore, to
133.28–30 **would (as the reader will perceive from a little incident at the scaffold) have perished to a certainty. But** *SGG* would to a certainty have perished – which to me seems a most fantastic caprice; it was to court a certain death and a present death, in order to evade a remote contingency of death. But
133.30 **accused of** *SGG* accused (because accused by lying witnesses) of
133.33 **sun set upon** *SGG* sun was setting upon
133.38 **contrived to** *SGG* contrived, therefore, to
133.41 **brief, was** *SGG* brief, proved
133.43 **assume, but, in** *SGG* assume; but it referred, in
134.15 **the impetuous** *SGG* the fiery clamours of the impetuous
134.25 **was postponed indefinitely.** *SGG* was indefinitely postponed. *followed on new line by heading:* 22. – *Kate's Penultimate Adventure.*

134.26 **last adventure approaching that** *SGG* last-but-one adventure at hand that
134.29 **(which very...*shall*),** *SGG* (as very shortly it *shall* hear),
134.33 **you, royalties are** *SGG* you, that Eminencies, Excellencies, Highnesses – nay, even Royalties and Holinesses, are
135.2–3 **enough in La Plata, 'Pray,'** *SGG* enough within his own neighbourhood – 'pray,
135.16–17 **Catalina, which too surely required a scouring. Still, from my kindness** *SGG* Catalina. Still a kindness
135.22 **horse. He was in luck to-day. For,** *SGG* horse. On that errand, in all lands, for some reason only half explained, you must be in luck if you do not fall in, and eventually fall out, with a knave. But on this particular day Kate *was* in luck. For,
135.27 **jest book than a history;** *SGG* jest-book than for a serious history;
135.34 **too solemn** *SGG* too earnest
135.37 **Alcalde! Ah! Alcalde, you** *SGG* Alcalde of Paz! Ah! alcalde, you
135.38–9 **you, though quite unknown to herself. He looked** *SGG* you and all that you inherit; though known to herself as little as to you. Good were it for you, had you never crossed the path of this Biscayan Alférez. The alcalde looked
135.39 **commands. 'These** *SGG* 'commands. 'Yes. These
136.12 **so. Then his** *SGG* so. Upon *that*, his
136.15–16 **furnish. / This** *SGG inserts heading:* 23. – *Preparation for Kate's Final Adventure in Peru.*
136.28 **exclaimed Don Antonio, 'how very fortunate! my** *SGG* exclaimed Don Antonio; 'and you from dear lovely Biscay! How very fortunate! My
136.37 **presented him to his wife, a splendid** *SGG* presented Kate to his wife – a most splendid
137.3 **hope, not** *SGG* hope, but still not
137.4–5 **of the Andalusians, which** *SGG* of Andalusian women, which
137.22–3 **dry. / Don** *SGG* dry. / But let us resume. Don
137.30 **it from** *SGG* it altogether from
137.31–2 **for what happened on the journey. / From the miserable** *SGG* for the dreadful events on the journey. / *SGG* This went on but slowly, however steadily. Owing to the miserable
137.34 **leagues. On** *SGG* leagues, taking the league at 2¼ miles. On
137.38 **usually had** *SGG* usually commanded
137.38 **in the sheltered** *SGG* in a sheltered
137.42 **a plaything of** *SGG* a mere toy of
138.5 **man who** *SGG* man Don Antonio, who
138.6 **officer who** *SGG* officer Catalina, who
138.10 **conversation was surely improving, but not equally brilliant.** *SGG* conversation ought surely to have been edifying, since it was anything but brilliant.
138.20–1 **First drawing Calderon's attention to the gesture, as one of significant pantomime, by raising her forefinger, the lady snuffed** *SGG* First of all, by raising her forefinger, the lady drew Calderon's attention to the act which followed as one of significant pantomime; which done, she snuffed out one of the candles.
138.28–9 **bushes.' / Catalina, as usual, had** *SGG* bushes.' But birds do not amuse themselves by staying up to midnight; and birds do not wear rapiers. / Catalina had
139.6 **In a moment** *SGG* In the first moments
139.25 **darkness. About five miles** *SGG inserts paragraph break and heading:* 24. – *A Steeple Chase.*
139.27 **lady; and** *SGG* lady; 'Oh, heavens! forward!' and
139.32 **up; obtained** *SGG* up; obtaining

140.10 **effort. Kate's maxim, however, which** *SGG* effort. However, the race was nearly finished: a score of dreadful miles had been accomplished; and Kate's maxim, which

140.14 **it more determinately, rode resolutely at it, and** *SGG* it with more impetus, rode resolutely at it, cleared it, and

140.17–18 **the vicious Alcalde, who** *SGG* the vengeful alcalde, who

140.19 **its bonny fair riders.** *SGG* its two bonny riders.

140.20 **this manoeuvre** *SGG* this vicious manoeuvre

140.21–4 **steeple chase. Had I been stakeholder....The bullets, says Kate, whistled** *SGG* steeple-chase. For the bullets, says Kate, in her memoirs, whistled

140.30 **episcopal** *SGG appends footnote 'Episcopal:'* – The roads around Cuzco were made, and maintained, under the patronage and control of the bishop.

140.31 **required Kate's continued attention;** *SGG* required unintermitting attention;

140.35 **agreeable to** *SGG* agreeable for *him* to

140.42 **leap; and, as the only** *SGG* leap; to take the leap was impossible; absolutely to refuse it, the horse felt, was immoral; and therefore, as the only

141.3–4 **will soon find.** *SGG* will find.

141.6 **people were all in bed.** *SGG* people of Cuzco, the spectators that *should* have been, were fast asleep in bed.

141.8 **lovely lady,** *SGG* lovely Andalusian lady,

141.13 **servants caused delay;** *SGG* servants, and obtain admission to the convent, caused a long delay;

141.18 **prey. In the morning light he now saw how to use his sword. He attacked** *SGG* prey. The morning light showed him how to use his sword, and who he had before him, and he attacked

141.23–4 **ancient blood. She turned on him now with determination.** *SGG* ancient Biscayan blood; and she turned on him now with deadly determination.

141.30–1 **who now again was fighting for life. Against** *SGG* who was again fighting for life with persons not even known to her by sight. Against

141.39 **In an instant** *SGG* In another instant

141.41 **rapidly; the** *SGG* rapidly; and the

141.42 **moment; for surgeons** *SGG* moment; surgeons

142.1 **second at** *SGG* second convent at

142.1–3 **report to the Spanish Government at home of all the particulars, drew from the King of Spain and from the Pope an order** *SGG* report of the whole extraordinary case in all details to the supreme government at Madrid, drew from the king, Philip IV.,[a] and the papal legate, an order
[[a] See above, p. 558, n. 36.]

142.4–5 **Spain. / Yes** *SGG inserts heading: 25. – St Sebastian is finally Checkmated.*

142.15 **of St Peter's keys;** *SGG* of St Sebastian's (consequently of St Peter's) keys;

142.21 **crowded, like a day** *SGG* crowded, as if on some mighty day

142.22–3 **flashing and their loving eyes upon herself. Forty** *SGG* flashing eyes upon herself! Forty

142.24 **joy, if** *SGG* joy for *her*, if

142.27–8 **and triumphant clamours, to turn away from the Andes to the joyous shore which she approached!** *SGG* and the triumphant jubilations of her countrymen, to turn away from the Andes, and to fix her thoughts for the moment upon the glad tumultuous shore which she approached.

142.30 **Spain, the same** *SGG* Spain, that same

142.32 **Wales was in Spain, and** *SGG* Wales had been in Spain, seeking a Spanish bride, and

142.36 **festive compatriots** *SGG* welcoming compatriots

142.40–1 **her at that time, of unprecedented amount, in the case of a subaltern officer; and** *SGG* her (at that time, of unprecedented amount); and

143.11 **were above** *SGG* were floating in mighty volumes above

143.12–13 **her in the** *SGG* her amongst the

143.13 **the vesper** *SGG* the solemn vesper

143.15–23 **bloodshed. He also said two words....fury or not, to mention that** *SGG* bloodshed; but that, if again she should suffer wrongs, she would resign all vindictive retaliation for them into the hands of God, the final Avenger.[a] I must also find time to mention, although the press and the compositors are in a fury at my delays, that
[[a] Romans 12: 19: 'Vengeance is mine, I will repay, said the Lord'.]

143.25–6 **sabre, and sabre-tache; in** *SGG* sabre; in

143.27–8 **reader, remember for your life never to say one word, nor suffer any tailor to say one word, against** *SGG* reader, say not one word, or the ninth part of a word, against

143.30–1 **forwards; it is equally shocking and heretical to murmur against trousers in the forgotten rear or against trousers** *SGG* forwards; it sanctions equally those trousers in the forgotten rear, and all possible trousers

143.41–3 **retiring. / Some time or other, when I am allowed more elbow-room, I will tell you why it is that I myself love this Kate. Now** *SGG inserts heading:* 26. – *Farewell to the Daughter of St Sebastian!* Now

143.43 **moment, when it is necessary for me to close, if I allow you one** *SGG* moment, it has become necessary for me to close, but I allow to the reader one

143.44–144.3 **pen – if I say, 'Come now, be quick, ask anything...twenty to one,** *SGG* pen. Come now, reader, be quick; 'look sharp;' and ask what you *have* to ask; for in one minute and a half I am going to write in capitals the word FINIS; after which, you know, I am not at liberty to add a syllable. It would be shameful to do so; since that word *Finis* enters into a secret covenant with the reader that he shall be molested no more with words small or great. Twenty to one,

144.3–4 **You will ask** *SGG* You desire to ask

144.7–8 **best; and bad is the best. After.** *SGG* best. After

144.9 **the Andes,** *SGG* the dreadful Andes,

144.11 **everything that** *SGG* everything which

144.12–13 **but they all loved Kate as a sister, and were delighted to hear** *SGG* but Kate was a sister everywhere privileged; she was as much cherished and as sacred, in the eyes of every brigade or *tertia*, as their own regimental colours; and every member of the staff, from the highest to the lowest, rejoiced to hear

144.18 **perfection it could** *SGG* perfection the dinner could

144.22 **like schoolboys escaping from** *SGG* like so many schoolboys let loose from

144.26 **had *certainly* taken** *SGG* had, beyond all doubt, taken

144.26–7 **was sure. Nobody in** *SGG* was certain, though nobody, in

144.27 **her on coming ashore.** *SGG* her actually step ashore.

144.28–30 **ransacked. The sea....lost in sorrow and confusion, and could** *SGG* ransacked. But the sea did not give up its dead,[a] if *there* indeed she lay; and the forests made no answer to the sorrowing hearts which sought her amongst *them*. Have I never formed a conjecture of my own upon the mysterious fate which thus suddenly enveloped her, and hid her in darkness for ever? Yes I have. But it is a conjecture too dim and unsteady to be worth repeating. Her brother soldiers, that should naturally have had more materials for guessing than myself, were all lost in sorrowing perplexity, and

could
[a Revelation 20: 13: 'And the sea gave up the dead which were in it'.]
144.31 **conjecture.** *SGG* plausible conjecture.
144.32 **fourteen years** *SGG* twenty-one years
144.32 **ago! Here** *SGG* ago! And here
144.32 **brief sum** *SGG* brief upshot
144.38 **great Father that** *SGG* great Father of all, that
144.39 **for two** *SGG* for more than two
145.1–10 **P.S. – The Portrait of Kate…perished by cannon shot.** *F omits; SGG omits, but incorporates the material into an extensive Postscript, for which* see Vol. 20, p. 24-8.

Secret Societies {Part I}

147.3–5 **Except as to the premature growth of this interest, there was nothing surprising in *that*. For everybody that is by nature meditative must regard,** *SGG* Except for the prematurity of this interest, in itself it was not surprising. Generally speaking, a child may *not* – but every adult *will*, and must, if at all by nature meditative – regard,
147.5 **than any vulgar** *SGG* than vulgar
147.8 **seen, but if** *SGG* seen; or, *if*
147.11 **reception, must retire, perhaps for** *SGG* reception, are forced to retire, possibly for
147.33 **comprehension.** *SGG* understanding.
147.34 **they take** *SGG* people take
147.35 **mysterious** *SGG* incomprehensible
148.27 **to think,** *SGG* to say,
148.28 **she says,'** *SGG* she utters,'
148.34 **deglutition; that** *SGG* deglutition, under the absolute certainty that, come what would, I *must* swallow it; that
148.34 **that followed** *SGG* that finally followed
148.37 **most people** *SGG* some people
149.7 **of 'experience.'** *SGG* of closer logic, but especially of longer 'experience.'
149.13 **fair antagonist** *SGG* fair (or rather, brown) antagonist
149.18 **anything she** *SGG* everything she
149.25 **the arguments** *SGG* the strong arguments
149.39 **schism: beaten** *SGG* schism: since my arguments, which I so much wished to see refuted, would on that assumption be triumphant; on the other hand, beaten
150.4 **but *because*** *SGG* but simply *because*
150.11 ***bono* of** *SGG bono* (the ultimate purpose) of
150.28 **case in Persia, and** *SGG* case as soon as we come to Persia; and
152.6 **not, he has read nothing. Now, *there* he** *SGG* not, he *shall;* and I am the man that will introduce him to that study. *There* he
152.17 ***his.*** *SGG his.* Superstitiously I believed the aggregate of what he said: rebelliously I contradicted each separate sentence.
152.28–9 **ignorance – this world soon** *SGG* ignorance; *that* would soon
152.30 **have found out its nature, and made** *SGG* have made
152.31 **life – *that* was** *SGG* life – all this was
152.38 **surprises one** *SGG* surprises me
152.39 **coarse minded** *SGG* irreflective

153.6 ***this* case** *SGG* this Oxford case
153.11 **interregnum: not at all; not** *SGG* interregnum. Not at all – not
153.12 **impossible: simultaneous** *SGG* impossible. Simultaneous
153.18–19 **metaphysics. I** *SGG* metaphysical successions. I
153.23 **Now that Oxford** *SGG* Now this Oxford
153.26 **amaranthine** *SGG appends footnote 'Amaranthine:'* – This word, familiar even to non-Grecian readers through the flower *amaranth*, and its use amongst poets, is derived from α, not (equivalent to our *un*), and *maraino*, to wither or decay.
153.34 **a President** *SGG* some president
153.38 **of Surrogates and Vice-Presidents.** *SGG* of vice-presidents.
153.41 **the errand** *SGG* the well-known little errand
153.42 **entered this club on** *SGG* entered on
154.12 **conqueror, is** *SGG* conqueror, to confound the grim confounder, is
154.n.2–3 **the place, the epichorial** *SGG* the *place*, the local or epochorial
154.n.8 **leg, with golden fetters.** *SGG* leg with golden fetters – or perhaps silver-gilt would suffice.
155.2 **solemn ritual** *SGG* gorgeous ritual
155.3 **with *this* combined the** *SGG* having *this* combined with the
155.4 **amongst them,** *SGG* amongst these families,
155.n.2–3 **histories (such as Chauncy's, &c.) will** *SGG* histories will
155.n.4 **the volumes,** *SGG* the six volumes,
155.n.6 **poet.** *SGG* poet, and for many years examining chaplain to the Archbishop of Canterbury, Manners Sutton.[a]
[[a] See above, p. 587, n. 14.]
155.6 **the county of Hertford. They** *SGG* the County of Huntingdon. They
155.11 **well, not** *SGG* well, and knew his workmanship, not
155.19 **with merely** *SGG* with the vast continent of merely
155.19 **the Fine** *SGG* the far smaller continent of Fine
155.21 **Indian** *SGG appends footnote* For proof, look only at two coins of our British Empire – first, at our current *rupee* throughout Hindostan. When a child, I was presented by Bengal relatives[a] with a rouleau of rupees by way of playthings: anything so rude in workmanship, so truly Hunnish, and worthy of Attila,[b] I have not seen on this earth of ours. And yet, secondly, our own English *florin*, though less brutally inartificial, is even more offensive to good taste, because less unpretending as a work of display. Oh, that dreadful woman, with that dreadful bust![c] – the big woman, and the big bust! – whom and which to encircle in 'a chaste salute' would require a man with arms fourteen feet long!
[[a] De Quincey' s uncle Colonel Thomas Penson (d. 1835), an army officer in the service of the East India Company. In the 1856 *Confessions of an English Opium-Eater*, De Quincey described him as 'my bronzed Bengal uncle!' (Vol. 2, p. 168).
[b] See above, p. 573, n. 4.
[c] The 'gothic' florin of 1852 featured a large bust of Queen Victoria (see above, p. 547, n. 81), crowned, and with a long hair braid.]
155.22 **handicraft. They are imagined by the man,** *SGG* handicraft. Originally they must have been conceived by that man,
155.23 **who conceived** *SGG* who revealed
155.23 **horse-shoe, a poker, and a** *SGG* horseshoe, of a poker, and of a
155.25 **and intaglios,** *SGG* and the intaglios,
155.28–9 **herself. She taboos it. She** *SGG* herself. She
155.31 **economists that** *SGG* economists (generally in octavo) that

155.37–8 ***I* shall condescend to bestow this manual labour** *SGG I* shall bestow this labour

156.1 **reads, he** *SGG* reads (else how can he be the reader?), he

156.3–4 **bequeath it by** *SGG* bequeath the spelling-book by

156.4–7 **might wash out the affront. Or if he accepts...therein to look.' As** *SGG* might dilute the affront, while it left the spelling-book undamaged. As

156.7–8 **with mechanic baseness; you** *SGG* with the most mechanic of handiworks; you

156.11–12 **lovelier conceptions** *SGG* loveliest conceptions

156.16–17 **own are** *SGG* own, I grant, are

156.28 ***book-binding,*** *SGG appends footnote* In youth I saw frequently *chefs d'oeuvre* of book-binding from the studios of some London artists (Hering, Lewis,[a] &c.), and of several Germans – especially Kaltoeber, Staggemeier,[b] and others (names forgotten by reason of prickliness and thorniness). But read the account of Mr Farrer's Bible,[c] and you see how far *he*, in 1635, must have outshone them.

[[a] Charles Hering (Senior), Charles Hering (Junior), and Charles Lewis (1786–1836; *DNB*), bookbinders.

[b] Christian Samuel Kalthoeber and Lebrecht Staggemeier, German bookbinders, both of whom lived in London in the late eighteenth century.

[c] see above, p. 560, n. 30.]

156.28 **being usually** *SGG* being often

156.30 **architecture, heraldic** *SGG* architecture (for an architecture there is), heraldic

156.31 **trade. He** *SGG* trade, by which I mean his daily mechanic occupation; but he pursued it with the enthusiasm and the inventive skill which belongs to a fine art. He

156.34 **travels, Cardinal Ximenes, when** *SGG* travels – which travels, I should say conjecturally, must be dated about ten to fifteen years after Shakspere's death – Cardinal Ximenes, about 1520, when

157.n.2 **think, *Alcala*** *SGG* think, the Latin name of *Alcala*

157.n.4 **Complutm.** *SGG* Complutum, the adjective from which is *Complutensis*.

157.6 **deep rural** *SGG* deep sylvan

157.6–7 **and Madame** *SGG* and of Madame

157.16–17 **How far the plan was ever effectually perfected, would** *SGG* How long the plan was effectually carried on, would

157.18–19 **after *that*, the** *SGG* after that meeting, the

157.21–2 **tranquillity outside.** *SGG* tranquility *without*.

157.27 **degree by** *SGG* degree justified by

157.27 **same act, viz.,** *SGG* same thoughtless act – viz.,

157.27 **of some pious** *SGG* of pious

157.29–30 **because popularity appropriated from old associations of habit to the use of Popish communities. Abstracting,** *SGG* because specially in the popular mind appropriated to the use of popish churches.* Abstracting, *SGG appends footnote* Was it not Bishop Halifax who apologised for Butler[a] in this instance? If Butler were in deep sincerity a Protestant, no apology was sufficient.

[[a] Samuel Hallifax (1733–90; *DNB*), Bishop of Gloucester, wrote a 'Preface...to a Charge delivered by Bishop Butler' (1786), which from 1788 was added to numerous separate editions of Joseph Butler's *Analogy of Religion, Natural and Revealed, to the Constitution and Course of Nature* (see above, p. 561, n. 48).]

157.37 **you were to be sure of hearing,** *SGG* you could rely on hearing,

157.38 **organ, or the** *SGG* organ, the

158.6 **grandeur – a sense** *SGG* grandeur, 'Whose dwelling is the light of setting suns'[a] – a sense
[[a] Wordsworth, 'Tintern Abbey', l. 97 (cf. Vol. 7, p. 397).]
158.11 **infancy by the** *SGG* infancy, amongst the
158.14 **earthquake is** *SGG* earthquake which ruins is
158.17 **nature. But** *SGG inserts paragraph break*
158.20 **of humbug** *SGG* of elaborate humbug
158.27 **philosopher, or polyhistor, of** *SGG* philosopher and polyhistor of
158.28 ***aporeton*** *SGG aporreton*
158.37 **for 1,500 years? The** *SGG* fifteen hundred years, and after it has done business as a swindle through thirty generations? Dreadful – an't it? The
159.1 **have blabbed. A** *SGG* have revenged himself by blabbing. A
159.6 **one they turn aside;** *SGG* one, they move apart;
159.16 **taken my half-crown,** *F, SGG* taken any half-crown,
159.18–19 **lanthorn,** *SGG* lantern,
159.20 **the real old** *SGG* the old
159.22 **contempt.** *SGG* contempt; and in this more eminently than in any other instance that I know.
159.27 **See, now** *SGG inserts paragraph break*
159.27 **Ady** *SGG appends footnote* Joseph Ady[a] was a useful public servant, although in some degree a disreputable servant; and through half a generation (say sixteen or seventeen years, in these days) a purveyor of fun and hilarity to the great nation of newspaper-readers. His line of business was this: – Naturally, in the case of a funded debt so vast as ours in Great Britain, it must happen that very numerous lodgments of sums not large enough to attract attention, are dropping into the list of dividends with no apparent claimant every fortnight. Death is always at work in removing the barriers between ourselves – whoever this *ourselves* may happen to be – and claims upon the national debt that have lost (perhaps long ago) their original owners. The reader, for instance, or myself, at this very moment, may unconsciously have succeeded to some lapsed claim, between which and us five years ago there may have stood thirty or forty claimants with a nearer title. In a nation so adventurous and given to travelling as ours, deaths abroad by fire and water, by contagious disease, and by the dagger or the secret poison of the assassin) to which of all nations our is most exposed, from inveterate habits of generous unsuspecting confidence), annually clear off a large body of obscure claimants, whose claims (as being not conspicuous from their small amount) are silently as snow-flakes gathering into a vast fund (if I recollect, forty millions sterling) of similar noiseless accumulations. When you read the periodical list published by authority of the countless articles (often valuable) left by the owners in public carriages, out of pure forgetfulness, to the mercy of chance, or of needy public servants, it is not possible that you should be surprised if some enterprising countryman, ten thousand miles from home, should forget in his last moments some deposit of one, two, or three hundred pounds in the British Funds. In such a case, it would be a desirable thing for the reader and myself that some person practised in such researches should take charge of our interests, watch the future fortunes of the unadvertised claim, and note the steps by which sometimes it comes nearer and nearer to our own door. Now, such a vicarious watchman was Joseph Ady. In discharge of his self-assumed duties, he addressed letters to all the world. He communicated the outline of the case; but naturally stipulated for a retaining fee (not much, usually twenty shillings), as the *honorarium* for services past and coming. Out of five thousand addressees, if nine-tenths declined to take any notice of his letters, the remaining tenth secured to him £500 annually. Gradually he

extended his correspondence to the Continent. And general merriment attended his continual skirmishes with police-offices. But this lucrative trade was at last ungenerously stifled by a new section in the Post-Office Bill, which made the *writer* of letters that were refused liable for the postage. That legislative blow extinguished simultaneously *Adyism* and *Ady.*

[[a] See above, p. 562, n. 56.]

159.28 **man. The** *SGG* man; though, by the way, not until after a prosperity of some twenty years. The

159.33 **dinner party – but** *SGG* dinner, good or bad, but

159.38 **opening there would** *SGG* opening would

160.n.1 **new word,** *SGG* new and ludicrous word,

160.3 **making too familiar,)** *SGG* making familiar)

160.4 **the academy or the porch; no** *SGG* the Platonic Academy or the Stoic Porch; no

160.11 **great-grandson; all** *SGG* great-grandson. All

160.12 **hoaxed, and afterwards** *SGG* hoaxed; and having been hoaxed inevitably, they must afterwards

160.21 **interest about the Eleusinian** ***Teletai*****, is** *SGG* interest in the Eleusinian mysteries, is

160.23 **the enigma of** *SGG* the standing riddle of

160.30 **sometimes he** *SGG* sometimes in germ he

160.30 **or even a** *SGG* or a

160.30–1 **thought, or even a grand one, by** *SGG* thought, yet, by

160.33 **his practice as** *SGG* his original profession as

160.36–7 **Trismegistus, this born Titan, in** *SGG* Trismegistus in

160.40 **W.'s** *SGG* Warburton's

161.3 **St. Petersburg, on** *SGG* St Peterburg* – on *SGG appends footnote* 'THAT SINGLE BLOCK OF GRANITE' – ST PETERSBURG. This block is, I believe, a *monolith*. Even to obtain in an accessible situation, and still more to remove into its present site, such a granite mass insusceptible of partition, was a triumph of mechanic art; and consequently superadds to the attraction of the statue (an equestrian statue of Peter the Great[a] – founder at once of the city and the possibility of the city in that situation) – a scenical record of engineering power. So far, and considered as a conquest over difficulties, the entire mass must be very striking. But two objections must interfere with the spectator's pleasure. If, as I have been told, the monolith is itself the *basis* of the statue, in that case what is ordinarily viewed as a *hors-d'oeuvre*, no more belonging to the statue than the terrace, street, square, or public hall in which it may happen to be placed, suddenly enters into the artist's work as an essential and irremovable member, or integrant feature of his workmanship. Secondly, this granite monolith, being chiselled into the mimic semblance of an ascending precipice, or section of a precipice, unavoidably throws the horse into an unnatural action; not perhaps into an unnatural or false attitude; for the attitude may be true to the purpose: but that purpose is itself both false and ungraceful, unless for an ibex or an Alpine chamois. A horse is easily trained to ascent a flight of stairs; and with no training at all, at the request of Mr Pitt, a little horse of the Shetland breed was trotted up-stairs into the front drawing-room at the London mansion of the penultimate Duke of Gordon.[b] That was more than fifty years ago: for Pitt has been dead *now* [viz., November, 1857] for nearly fifty-two years. But within the recent knowledge of us all, a full-sized horse carried his rider in a flying leap over a splendid dinner table – glass, china, tureens, decanters, and blazing wax-lights – ambling gently down-stairs on taking his leave, and winning a heavy wager. Such feats are accounted noble and brilliant amongst the princes and sirdars round the throne of

Persia. But with us of the western world they are reputed more becoming to a Franconi or an Astley[c] than to a Czar of all the Russias, who speaks as God's vicegerent to three hundred nations and languages. But even a flying leap is better than a *scrambling*: and up-hill over the asperities of a granite rock neither horse nor man is able to do more than scramble: and this is undignified for the Czar; is perilous and more unnatural than running up-stairs for the horse; and to the poor spectator (unless paid for spectating) is sympathetically painful.

{[a] Peter I the Great (1672–1725), tsar of Russia from 1682, and emperor from 1721. He founded St Petersburg in 1703.

[b] For William Pitt the Younger, see above, p. 528, n. 15. Alexander Gordon, fourth Duke of Gordon (1743–1827; *DNB*); his wife Jane, Duchess of Gordon (1749–1812; *DNB*) was a confidant of Pitt's.

[c] Antonio Franconi (1737–1836) and Philip Astley (1742–1814; *DNB*), co-founders of the modern circus.}

161.5 **exquisite skill** *SGG* perfect skill

161.6 **(but the people were** *SGG* (but then 'the people' were

161.8 **thing. So admirable was** *SGG* thing: so exquisite was

161.11 **the bridge, to me,** *SGG* the guilty bridge to me

161.20–1 **Suppose the** *SGG* Suppose, secondly, the

161.25 **inspired. The** *SGG* inspired; else confessedly it could *not* have dispensed with it. The

161.30–1 **Grecian States and law-givers maintained officially, as consecrated** *SGG* Grecian lawgivers, being Pagans, offered officially, for consecrated

161.44 **myself could** *SGG* myself, though manuring with unlimited doses of guanao, could

161.44 **that!** *SGG* that.

162.10 **could prove, what** *SGG* could circumstantially reveal, what

162.17 **impossible to go within a few pages into** *SGG* impossible, within a few pages, to go into

162.20 **pure fancy** *SGG* pure caprice

162.20–1 **any Greek, or even any Athenian, were** *SGG* any Greeks were

162.26 **μνησις** *Editorial; 1847* μνητις

162.28 **to develop, they might safely have built upon as a** *SGG* to publish it *as* the Eleusinian secret, they were quite at liberty to use as a

162.38 **fellow complain, that,** *SGG* fellow, who complained that,

162.40 **Dalilah, with the purpose of** *SGG* Delilah, on the motive of

162.41 **protested to us all, that** *SGG* protested that

163.1 ***fiddle-de-dee:* and** *SGG fiddle-de-dee*. And

163.5 **involution. If** *SGG* involution; and upon the following dilemma: – If

163.16 **doing;*** *SGG omits footnote*

164.1 **libraries.** *Editorial; 1847* libraries,

164.4–5 **the hoax of hoaxes.** *SGG* the transcendent and supreme of hoaxes.

164.6 **(*To be concluded in next Number.*)** *SGG omits*

Secret Societies {Part II}

Title **SECRET SOCIETIES.** BY THOMAS DE QUINCEY. PART **II.** *F, SGG* PART II.

165.5–6 **have, also, not a very favourable opinion** *SGG* have also a very bad opinion

165.8–9 **ancestors; I** *SGG* ancestors; and I

165.10 **can't invent a** *SGG* can't lend a hand to a
166.7 **novice look very melancholy,** *SGG* novice melancholy,
166.17**ακοῤῥητο** *SGG* ακοῤῥητον
166.20–1 **money, he ran** *SGG* money, ran
166.30 **that woman was** *SGG* that Woman, as usual, was
166.34–5 **better than that which I was pledged in honour** *SGG* better, than the true one, but still not that particular secret which I had pledged my honour
166.38 **treachery, so** *SGG* treachery, but so
166.39 **the same** *SGG* the very same
166.39 **I greatly fear** *SGG* I fear
166.41 **reader. Seriously, however, the** *SGG* reader. As regards my own criminality, however, long ago it was consummated: for the
166.42 **myself once threw** *SGG* myself threw
166.43 **1823 or 4.** *SGG* 1823 or 1824.
167.1 **German, viz., Buhle, the same (Ebelison) that** *SGG* German – viz., Buhle, the same that
167.7 **that this exposure could have** *SGG* that my exposure *could* have
167.10 **object. A title, which** *SGG* object; or to throw out any promises of gratification to malice. But it *was* malicious: though I was foolish enough to dissemble in its title that part of its pretensions. A title which
167.19–20 **secondly, the grandest purpose; and, lastly with** *SGG* secondly, revealed to us that now are, but hid profoundly from its murderous contemporaries, the grandest of purposes; and, lastly, did all this with
167.25–6 **without shadow** *SGG* without any shadow
167.26 **falsehood – the profoundest – were** *SGG* falsehead were
167.32 **roaming around** *SGG* roaming round
167.40 **mystery. This** *SGG* mystery – viz., in what were then called the Sydney Gardens, opening upon Great Pulteney Street. This
167.42 **of early errors in life.** *SGG* of errors early in life.
167.42 **but wrong** *SGG* but once wrong
167.43 **the thicket, and** *SGG* the inextricable jungle, and
168.1 **prize; five** *SGG* prize: yet five
168.4 **fourteen roads** *SGG* sixteen roads
168.5 **to lie down and cry. None** *SGG* to cry like a girl. None
168.9 **mysterious house,** *SGG* mysterious and pathless house,
168.9–10 **secure is the heart of** *SGG* secure, how impregnable is the central cell or *heart* of
168.11 **hear distant steps approaching,** *SGG* hear steps of the Avenger approaching,
168.14–15 **man spent the** *SGG* man should spend the
168.15 **his life** *SGG* his age
168.16 **sanctuary, that is, hidden** *SGG* sanctuary, hidden
168.17–18 **that recess** *SGG* that central recess
168.18–19 **exciseman.** *SGG* exciseman – that ancient traditional horror; or of Forbes Mackenzie[a] – the new-born revelation of wo.
[[a] The Forbes Mackenzie Act (1853) closed ordinary licensed premises on a Sunday, and pubs at 11 p.m. during the rest of the week.]
168.19 **Light,** *SGG inserts paragraph break*
168.25 **the camp,** *SGG* the Christian camp,
168.26 **endless cruisings,** *SGG* endless circumgyrations,
168.33 **fire to be sure, will** *SGG* fire, beyond all doubt, will

168.35 **primitive faith,** *SGG* primitive church,

168.35 **fire is but** *SGG* fire was but

168.39–40 **necessity! 'Masque, or you will be destroyed!' was the private signal among the Christians. 'Fall** *SGG* necessity! 'Fall

168.43–169.10 **spent.' To hide from the storm....like it or not.** *SGG* spent.' 'Mask all! – man and woman, in the service of God, mask, till this fiery wrath have passed away,' was the order of the Christian leaders. Mask they did: not a Christian at this perilous era but hid himself from pursuing wrath: God said, Let my people reserve themselves for happier days. And all with one heart became Essenes.

169.12–170.6 **journal, and my reason for referring....to which it is imputed** *SGG omits*

170.9–11 **was the intolerable extravagance of the received story. The outrageousness – the mere Cyclopian enormity of its paradox – this,** *SGG* was its intolerable extravagance. This,

170.30 **Whiston'* was a very moderate Grecian – a** *SGG* Whiston,'* whose English version is the one current at this day, was a blockhead at starting, by special favour of nature; was a prig of formidable dimensions; and (according to his own confession) a ruined dyspeptic, knocked up (and sometimes knocked down) by a long course of constitutional flatulency.[a] He was also a miserable Grecian, a miserable

[[a] See above, p. 565, n. 22.]

170.n.4 **of scrupulousness: he** *SGG* of a conscience too scrupulous: he

170.n.5 **own. He** *SGG* own, that *must* have been sincere, as it neither brought nor promised anything but ruin. He

171.n.12 **Ditton.'** *SGG* Ditton; / Sing Whiston, sing Ditton.' After which Swift grows too atrociously Swiftian for quotation.

171.3 **Sparta** *SGG appends footnote 'To adorn the Sparta:'* – This is an old proverbial form of expression amongst the ancients: when any man had assigned to him for culture or for embellishment a barren, a repulsive, or an ungenial field of labour, his friends would often cheer him up by saying, 'Spartam, quam nactus es, exorna;'[a] *i.e.,* 'That Sparta (or homely province) which you have obtained as your allotment, improve and make the best of.'

[[a] The phrase is adapted from Cicero, *Letters to Atticus*, IV.vi.2, which itself quotes Euripides, *Fragments*, 723: 'Sparta is your homeland: adorn that!'. Cf. De Quincey in the first instalment of 'On Murder Considered as One of the Fine Arts' (Vol. 6, p. 115).]

171.6 **scourged.** ***I, lictor, colliga manus.*** **One** *SGG* scourged. One

171.8–9 **position partially the same, of** *SGG* position so similar, of

171.9 **both, when** *SGG* both these men, when

171.13–14 **the limited affinities in their native studies to exotic learning would** *SGG* the limitations of their native literature would

171.19 **with any mode of** *SGG* with modes of

171.21–2 **servile ministeries;** *SGG* servile ministrations;

171.24 **of the poet:** *SGG* of our English poet:

171.28–9 **to a puppet-show,** *SGG* to something that he thought a puppet-show,

172.3 **temple dragged** *SGG* temple – to see the Holy of Holies (which even the High Priest could enter only once in the year) by its representative memorials – dragged

172.6–8 **find his** ***atrium*** **made glorious with the monuments of a thousand years that had descended through the princes of Hebrew tribes; and to find his luxury,** *SGG* find his luxury,

172.13 **my seat,** *SGG* my chair,

172.13 **thus: – 'Joe,** *SGG* thus: – 'Wicked Joseph,

172.15 **oneself, one always knows** *SGG* one's-self, always one knows

172.17 **fiction of** *SGG* fiction – not at all of ignorance or error, but of

172.34 **Mozart!** *SGG* Mozart?

173.1 **question and** *SGG* question, of doubt, and

173.34–9 **Christ. Josephus grew up to be....I am going to say. In** *SGG* Christ. In

174.5 **Affghans. Yet** *F* Affghans, yet *SGG* Affghans; yet

174.21 **itself – the idea** *SGG* itself – that great idea

174.27 **officers** *SGG appends footnote 'Officers:'* – I take advantage of this accidental notice directed to the class which amongst ourselves bears the designation of *officers*, for the purpose of calling attention to this most singular and inexplicable fact – that the Romans, by whom more than by any other people was developed the whole economy of war, consequently the whole corresponding nomenclature, had no term expressing the distinction of officers. If you were a *captain*, they called you a *centurion*; if a colonel, *tribunus*; and if a *private – i.e.*, a common soldier, or soldier in the ranks, which logically stands in contra-position to the term *officer* – they called you *miles gregarius*. But if, in speaking of you or me, they wished to say that either of us was a bad officer, though of what rank they could not say, by Mercury they had no word for conveying their meaning. The *thing* officer was as well known at Rome as coals at Newcastle:[a] but not the *word*, or the *idea* as abstracted from all varieties of rank. Does not this go far to prove that there were blockheads in those days? As again the continuity of succession in that great race (viz., blockheads) seems implied in the possibility that to my unworthy self should be left the very first indication of this unaccountable *lacuna* in the Roman vocabulary.

[[a] See above, p. 587, n. 14.]

174.27–8 **army, centurions, tribunes, prefects, legates, &c., or as** *SGG* army, tribunes (or even officers no higher than centurions), prefects, legates, &c.; or (secondly), as

174.29 **court – or as** *SGG* court; or (thirdly), as

174.29–30 **leading ladies that had practically much influence on the ear of Caesar. The** *SGG* leading official women that stood on the steps of Caesar's throne. The

174.33 **present the** *SGG* present is the

174.34–5 **voyagers upon some world floating away without helmsman or governor. In** *SGG* voyagers embarked upon some fragment of a wreck into unknown darkness, without a taper for guidance, or helmsman, or anchorage. In

174.38 **of breadth** *SGG* of sufficient breadth

174.43 **terrifically to the experience spiritual** *SGG* terrifically spiritual

175.11 **been exposed – that was** *SGG* been drawn into high relief – *that* was

175.17 **sea-like expansion** *SGG* sea-like infinity

175.21 **greater distraction.*** *SGG* greater Babylonian distraction.*

175.n.2 **metaphysical necessity.** *SGG* metaphysical theory.

175.n.5 ***monarque.* The** *SGG monarque*, although we ourselves, until after Charles I.,[a] never presented anything to the sovereign without going down upon our knees. The

[[a] See above, p. 558, n. 40.]

175.n.12 **also still feebly** *SGG* also feebly

175.n.17 **might be** *SGG* might then safely be

176.2–3 **man, but suggested** *SGG* man, yet suggested

176.5 **Augustan** *SGG appends footnote 'Great Augustan:'* – The house of Augustus individually, it will be objected, was *not* great: the Octavian house was petty; but it was elevated by its matrimonial alliance with the Julian house,[a] and otherwise.

[[a] Octavius's mother was the daughter of Julia, the sister of Julius Caesar. Octavius was launched in Roman public life by Caesar, who adopted him as his son and made him his chief personal heir.]

176.7 **Bernice,** *SGG* Berenice,

176.10 **household** *SGG appends footnote 'Herod's own Household:'* – Viz., the murder of his wife Mariamne, to whom (as representing the Asmonéan house)[a] he was indebted for his regal rank; next, the murder of her youthful brother, who stood nearest to the crown upon *her* death; lastly, the murder of the two most distinguished amongst his own sons. All which domestic carnage naturally provoked the cutting remark ascribed to Augustus Caesar (himself bloody enough, as controller of his female household), that it was far better to be numbered amongst Herod's swine, than amongst his kinsfolk;[b] seeing that his swine were protected by the Mosaic law against the butcher's knife; whereas his kinsfolk enjoyed no such immunity.

[[a] Mariamne (*c.* 57–29 BC), Jewish princes, whose marriage to Herod the Great (see above, p. 530, n. 51) united his family with the deposed Hasmonean royal family. Herod had her put to death for adultery. He also executed her two sons.

[b] Macrobius, *Saturnalia*, II.iv.11: 'It is better to be Herod's hog than his son'.]

176.21 **mysterious from** *SGG* mysterious to all nations from

176.21 **of all idol,** *SGG* of idol,

176.36 **but still obscure** *SGG* but as yet obscure

176.38 **'This may** *SGG* 'This system of morals may

176.41 **traitor, and** *SGG* traitor to Jerusalem, and

176.44 **literary heads** *SGG* literary circles

177.7–8 **Christ; there was Christianity** *SGG* Christ; then there was a Christianity

177.12 **cutlers and others, they** *SGG* cutlers as regards one of these classes, and to creditors as regards the other, they

177.16–17 **philosophic considerations,** *SGG* philosophic monasticism,

177.19 **arose with** *SGG* arose, not with that mighty power, which subsequently molested or threatened them – *i.e.*, Rome and Caesar – but with

177.20 **the cradle** *SGG* the very cradle

177.26 **constitutes** *SGG* constituted

177.33 **been more or greater than they were) the** *SGG* been far more or far greater) the

177.35 **known Gentiles.** *SGG* undoubted Gentiles.

177.40–1 **and lost itself in a new order of things? This** *SGG* and having lost itself in a new order of things – viz., Christianity? This

178.1 **question shot** *SGG* question, into this final issue, shot

178.2 **roused in** *SGG* roused and stung in

178.9 **Dispersion had** *SGG* Dispersion, they now became aware, had

178.10 **leader was** *SGG* leader in that sect was

178.11–12 **the body, that, under the new colouring given to it by the Christians, this** *SGG* the main body, that, in fact, this

178.12–13 **the most triumphant of victories. There** *SGG* the triumphant glory and corner-stone of the rising Christian temple. There

178.15 **And there** *SGG* And lastly, there

178.19 **thither to** *SGG* thither by public authority as suspected criminals needing to

178.25 **were struck** *SGG* were sometimes struck

178.26–7 **nympholepsy.** *SGG appends footnote 'Nympholepsy:'* – The English reader will here be reminded of Lord Byron's exquisite line – 'The nympholepsy of some fond despair.'[a]

[[a] See above, p. 604, n. 104.]

178.27 **This parallel** *SGG* The parallel

178.28 **martyrs, by** *SGG* martyrs, when standing by

178.37–8 **him were visible,** *SGG* him *was* visible,

178.39 **Yet, as** *SGG* Yet, even as

178.41 **earthly, which ought** *SGG* earthly, coming through avenues not revealed to himself, some radiance from far-off fountains, such as, upon any theory yet opened to *him*, ought

178.42 **of Stephen,** *SGG* of St Stephen,

179.n.1–2 **title, powerfully conceived, in Dr Mendelssohn's Oratorio of St Paul.** *SGG* title, 'Stone him to death,' as grand and tumultuous as a pitched battle, in Mendelssohn's Oratorio of 'St Paul.'[a]

[[a] See above, p. 567, n. 59.]

179.1 **countenance, which brought down** *SGG* countenance, bringing down

179.2 **sky, intercepted** *SGG* sky, the fountains of which were intercepted

179.4–5 **authentic. It carried** *SGG* authentic, a secret reading that would not be refused. That face carried

179.10 **have come. That** *SGG* have followed in the end. That

179.10 **no doubt others** *SGG* doubtless others

179.12–14 **last they were determined, once for all, that it should be decided who was to be Master in Jerusalem.** *SGG* last, the chief priests, the Sanhedrims, and the representatives of the great national Temple, that mighty Temple which everywhere, by Arabian tribes over the infinite and pathless deserts, had been known as *El Koda** (*the Saintly*), all at once as one man, with one heart, rose under one overmastering impulse, and with one voice swore fiercely by the Law and the Prophets, that now at length, once and for ever, it should be settled who was master in Jerusalem. *SGG appends footnote* The reader is referred to a note upon this Arabic name *El Koda* (which involves a very momentous revelation on behalf of the Biblical records) in the Appendix. *SGG Appendix*

THE JERUSALEM OF HERODOTUS.[a] With the reader's permission, I will premise a brief remark on the letter A, which enjoys this advantage over the rest of the alphabet, that to many young friends of mine, not even two years old, it is tolerably familiar; though very often their erudition does not extend further. The remark which I wish to offer on this distinguished letter is, that it enjoys in our language five separate sounds: –

1. A very broad sound, *aw*, as in *water*, and very commonly before the letter *l*, as in *all, wall, call, tall, talk, walk*, &c.; but not always, as in *calm*; or, again, in *rally, tally, dally.*

2. An ascending sound, *ah*, as in *father, rather, bath*.

3. A very flat sound, as in *man, can, shall, hand, rank, dandy, pandy.*

4. A very long sound, as in *mane, Jane, brave, lake, James.*

5. A borrowed sound, properly the short or flat sound of the vowel *o*, particularly after the letter *w*, as in *what, want, was*; for which reason it has this sound of *o* after *qu*, since that is in effect *kw*, as in *quantity, quality*; though, in reading Latin, the English restore the common flat sound of the *a* (No. 3) to *qualitas, quantitas, quantus*, &c.

And these several sounds are readily transformed into each other, according to their greater or less affinity.

This preliminary explanation made, in order that it may not interrupt me further on, let me come to Herodotus. He was the first man (and of course a Grecian, being a native of a Greek Asiatic colony), not that travelled, for *that* cannot be known, but certainly that wrote an account of his travels, and published this account (or part of it), by reading it at a Panhellenic assembly. And this work survives to our own times, as the most valuable monument by far which we still possess of Greek prose. The loss of Thucydides[b] would injure us comparatively not at all; of Xenophon[c] a little; but that of

Herodotus would break down the earlier arches of that long bridge which connects Christian Europe with Pagan Greece, with Asia, with Egypt, with the Euphrates, and the Nile, with Babylon and Hekatompylos.[d] Herodotus was equally a *traveller*, the most inquiring and exploring; an *archaeologist* that described minutely the antiquities of all the civilised races on every radius protended from the center of Greece; the earliest of *geographers*; and a delightful *historian*; towards the improvement of which last function he enjoyed the unparalleled advantage of coming with his sickle into the whole harvest of human records, whilst yet untouched, except in its Biblical sections. This great man, of whom I have elsewhere said, that his picturesque vivacity, and his shifting scenery, entitle him to the name of the Grecian Froissart,[e] amongst other regions visited Lower Egypt, saw with bodily eyes the Nile and the Pyramids, and the mighty city of Memphis, of which last, in our day, *etiam periere ruinae* (even the ruins are ruined).[f] The main Egyptian monuments he saw, and reported upon them circumstantially as a privileged visiter, enjoying probably the hospitality and friendly explanations of the priestly order. Consequently, being then so near to Judea, naturally this question arises, did he visit Jerusalem? The impression was, for a long time, that he did not. But that was a trifle; the difficulties of access, or dangers from robbers on the land route, or innumerable accidents of disappointment to a stranger having no commercial objects to determine his route, might easily account for this apparent neglect. But another apparent neglect is less to be accounted for: to a hasty reader he does not seem to mention Jerusalem, or any part of Judea. How is that?

Let us pause and consider for a moment at what period it was that Herodotus must have visited Egypt; perhaps *that* may help us to a solution of the difficulty. His own central year, or year in which you might say that he flourished, was probably about 444 before Christ. Now, if Herodotus had happened to travel some 100 years earlier, Judea would have been lying half-desolate, the Temple of Solomon a heap of ruins,[g] and Jerusalem dismantled of her towers and battlements; little, in fact, to be seen of life but the gentle restorations of nature,

'Softening and concealing,
And busy with a hand of healing;'[h]

but, for the monuments of human art and labour, all would be crumbling dilapidations, scoria, and bleaching bones, with endless heaps of dust and ashes. For at that time the remnant of the Hebrew race, the two tribes that had survived the captivity of the ten, were themselves captive on the Euphrates and elsewhere. But at present a happier generation had arisen. The *élite* of the Jews had been suffered to return and re-occupy their solitary homesteads. A second Temple had risen.[i] And the glorious service of daily adorations, however shorn of its pomps, was again in the morning and in the evening throwing up clouds of incense, with peals of far-resounding music, to the astonishment of Edom[j] and of the Arabian wilderness beyond. This was the age of Pericles. Cyrus was gone; Darius was gone; Xerxes was gone;[k] and Jerusalem was now lustrous again with a resurrection of national glories. Considerations of time therefore do but quicken and exasperate the problem either against Herodotus or against Jerusalem – why it was that this man did not glorify that city? Plainly it would seem, either that the man was grossly in fault, and betraying the confidence placed in the comprehensiveness of his travelling reports; or else the city was in fault; possibly he found nothing in the rumours about Jerusalem, not even amidst the Delta of Egypt, that tempted his curiosity, or excited his interest, or justified a circumstantial report.

Meantime, what is it that anti-Biblical writers have inferred from this neglect of Herodotus, supposing it fully established? Would they infer that Jerusalem had no local existence, but was a visionary creation of Jewish romancers? In that case, the romancers might also be visionary. No, they do not go so far as that; but they infer an obscurity in Jerusalem and her Temple which allowed neighbouring peoples to be indifferent and careless about them, in a degree which would argue all the Hebrew records to be fantastic exaggerations.

At this point, therefore, let us again pause, and ask whether it is so entirely certain that Herodotus has *not* mentioned Jerusalem. The name Jerusalem (Iero Solyma, or Holy Solyma) was a Greek name, and doubtless not current in Greece, or heard by any Grecian ear, for at least three centuries later than Herodotus. By what name would *he* know it? Most undoubtedly by the name which must continually have resounded in his ears – the Arabic name El Koda (*the Saintly*). But it will be seen that, about the locality where Jerusalem should be looked for, Herodotus places a great city, which he calls *Cadytis* or *Kadeitis*. Now make the requisite corrections: cut away the *ytis* or *eitis*, as a mere terminal form (such as we see in *Gaulonitis*, *Trachonitis*, &c.), which simply indicated the territory or immediate area investing the city: there remains a word which Herodotus would pronounced *Kauda* (for *el* he would have learned to be simply his own article ο, η, τό). Now the *a*, when pronounced *aw,* passes in all languages into *o*. Thus the Roman noble *Claudius* was indifferently called *Clodius*; *plaustrum* was the same as *plostrum*; the Latin *aurum* (gold) has become the French *or*. At this moment, amongst the English lakes, within a very small cincture of ground, the natives pronounce the word *cause* generally as *cose*. This suggestion, as a key to the apparent neglect of Jerusalem by Herodotus, was indicated some eighty years ago by Larcher[l] and by others. I really do not know who was first. Strangely enough, however, since Larcher's time, several writers have thrown doubts on this solution, which to myself seems unimpeachable. But, on the whole, I impute this skepticism in part to embarrassment from the *ytis*, in not treating it as a mere terminal form, and in part to the error of denoting the *a* of *Ca* by an English long sound (No. 4), that would fail to indicate the *o* of *Koda*, which *o* is virtually represented by the *a* (when pronounced *aw*) of *Kadytis*. Call it *Kaw*ditis, which in all languages would pass into (or out of) *Ko*dytis, and at once you trace the steps of Herodotus. 1. *El Koda*, dropping the article, is *Koda*; 2. *Koda*, by the commonest of all vowel permutations, becomes *Kauda*; 3. *Kauda*, by terminal Hellenisation (*i.e.*, adjustment to the Greek model), becomes *Kaudytis*; and that word, to the eye of Herodotus, would be spelt K*a*dytis. On this account it was that I introduced my notice by a table of the different sounds given to the English A.

[[a] For Herodotus, see above, p. 564, n. 7.

[b] Thucydides (*c*. 460–*c*. 404 BC), Greek historian.

[c] For Xenophon, see above, p. 591, n. 41.

[d] Hecatompylos is an ancient Parthian city whose precise site has not been established.

[e]Jean Froissart (1337–1410) French chronicler, poet and courtier, whose *Chronicles* of the fourteenth century provide a detailed account of feudal times. De Quincey refers to his 1842 *Blackwood's* essay on the 'Philosophy of Herodotus': 'Once, in a public station, we ourselves denominated Herodotus the Froissart of antiquity' (Vol. 13, p. 89).

[f] Lucan, *Pharsalia*, IX. 969.

[g] Nebuchadrezzar (see above, p. 529, n. 34) destroyed the Temple of Solomon in 587–6 BC.

[h] Wordsworth, 'The White Doe or Rylstone', ll. 118–9.

[i]Building on the Second Temple was completed in 515 BC.

j Edom is an ancient land bordering Israel, in what is now southwestern Jordan.

[k] Pericles (*c*. 495–429 BC), Athenian statesman. Cyrus the Great (*c*. 590–*c*. 529 BC), conqueror. Darius the Great (550–486 BC), King of Persia, 522-486. Xerxes the Great

(*c*. 519–465), son and successor of Darius.

[1] Pierre-Henri Larcher (1726–1812), French classical scholar and archaeologist, whose edition of Herodotus was published in 1786.]

179.18 **They had now faced, as** *SGG* They now at last stood face to face, as

179.19 **it, a fiery** *SGG* it, right over against a fiery

179.25 **be wise, so** *SGG* be prudent, cautious, vigilant, forecasting, so

179.28 **of distress** *SGG* of a deep distress

179.33 **hills; have vanished** *SGG* hills; vanished

179.33–4 **into thick shadows; and** *SGG* into some mighty world of shadows; and

179.34 **reässembled** *SGG* reconverged

179.35–6 **device. The Christians** *SGG* device. Image to yourself, reader, the issue of their stratagem, under the following aspect: – Suddenly the Christians

179.37 **vanished. The Christian** *SGG* vanishes. Again the Christian

179.38 **serjeant;** *SGG* officer;

179.39 **face, he** *SGG* eyes; he

180.6 **season. But** *SGG* season: retiring *locally*, as from this particular neighbourhood, where they might be watched and suspected, to some other, where they would be unmolested and unregarded; or *virtually* retiring, as from all modes of activity that could be open to suspicion. But

180.10 **demur, this course might secure** *SGG* demur, such a course might possibly secure

180.14 **repairing its** *SGG* repairing her

180.14 **waste. Safety** *SGG* waste, as bound up with the natural agencies of time and death. Safety

180.15 **purposes. It** *SGG* purposes. The several members of the church might in this way be secured; but the great spiritual interest, for which only they ran risks or evaded them, was chained to inertia, and therefore in effect hurrying to decay. It

180. 20–1 **in this naked houseless condition she was** *SGG* in that houseless condition this church was

180.21–2 **her household; and yet, whilst blood-hounds** *SGG* her total household; bloodhounds

180.22 **traces, whilst she** *F* traces, while she *SGG* traces, she

180.23 **storm, this** *SGG* storm; and yet this

180.23 **college and a** *SGG* college; a

180.25 **blood, and to** *SGG* blood; and yet then first she was to

180.30–1 **by diligently searching the** *SGG* by searching, as keenly as any hostile Jew, the

180.33–4 **to refute and confound this attempt to identify the Messiahship** *SGG* to fight against this identification of Messiahship

180.35 **opposite direction** *SGG* counter direction

180.36 **history. The** *SGG* history. The fanatical miso-Christian Jew, and the Christian himself, could work only by the same means, in the same mines of Hebrew literature, and trimming their lamps by the same golden light of old prophetic inspiration. The

180.36 **and the traditions** *SGG* and traditions *SGG appends footnote 'Traditions:'* – By this term, as distinguished from *prophecies*, I mean to indicate those special characteristics of the expected Messiah, current everywhere amongst the populace of Judea, which had been sent down through possibly sixty generations from Abraham, but were not expressly noticed in the Prophets. There were apparently many of these; and it is certain that some of them were regarded with reverence by Christ, and deliberately fulfilled by him.

180.39–40 **parties. Having, therefore, this** *SGG* parties. There lay the starting-point of the new Christian tactics. A study, that must equally belong to the Christian and to the demoniac persecutor of Christians, could not of itself, and unconditionally, furnish grounds of suspicion. Having this

181.1 **silently prepare and arm a** *SGG* silently arm and discipline a

181.3 **character upon** *SGG* character of Judaism – bigoted or even fanatical – upon

181.5 **this institution was, to** *SGG* this new-born institution (vitally so uniquely Christian, speciously and ostensibly so antichristian) was to

181.6 **dilapidation** *SGG* dilapidations

181.7 **church selected** *SGG* Christians selected

181.8 **society, from the** *SGG* society, *that* being the

181.8 **important** *SGG* venerated

181.8–10 **the temple; so that, from the original use, as well as from another application to the religious service of the temple, a college** *SGG* the fortified cincture of the TEMPLE. Pause upon that great word: for it is here intensely significant. Against the Temple and the vast machineries of its pompous ritual and elaborate sacrificial system, multitudes believed that the hostility of the young Christian establishment was mainly directed. Any institution, therefore, which began by deriving its very name and baptismal sanction, its omen and inauguration, from a part of the Temple, by opening to admit with welcome – by closing to exclude with wrath – did by this one symbolic agency of the Temple gate seem to pledge and implicate the whole mighty overshadowing edifice – *i.e.*, the whole Judaic nationality in the brotherhood of the Essenes, and in the doctrines which they taught. A college

181.24–5 **first objects** *SGG* final objects

181.30 **No. 8 of** *SGG* No. 9 or 10 of

181.31 **very first** *SGG* very last

181.31–2 **when the last reserves** *SGG* when all reserves

181.34 **of the art,** *SGG* of the school,

181.36–8 **from any considerations...final uses and wants of the society, none** *SGG* from considerations of treason applying itself specially to the one perilous secret of the society, even for general secular uses, and the wants of *any* religious community, none

181.39 **for Christian ministrations.** *SGG* for its future ministrations.

181.44 **not seem to such** *SGG* not lie towards such

182.2–3 **Josephus was turned adrift in this way, there is no doubt.** *SGG* Josephus, there can be no doubt, was turned adrift in this way.

182.4–5 **which he had not so much as suspected** *SGG* which, so far from entering and learning experimentally to appreciate, Mr Joe had not suspected

182.9 **necessary for** *SGG* necessary, were it only for

182.11 **end and the avowed end. But,** *SGG* end that was dissembled, and with the false end that was simulated. But,

182.14 **evidence. *There* arose** *SGG* evidence for Christ as the true Messiah. *There* again arose

182.15 **first mission** *SGG* primary mission

182.16–17 **to the church, and providing for her future growth, it was also providing for the secret meeting of the church and its** *SGG* to a church which durst not show its face to the world, or avow its own existence; and thus was providing concurrently for the future growth of that church; it was also in a secondary way providing for the secret meeting of the church, and for its

Schlosser's Literary History of the Eighteenth Century {Part I}

Title **BY THOMAS DE QUINCEY.** *SGG omits*
184.3 **to our provinces, is received according** *SGG* to the French and English provinces, is received deferential and almost passively according
184.4 **no one being** *SGG* no rural judge being
184.7 **possessing *materials*, in that field of art, for** *SGG* possessing musical resources for
184.10 **to reverse** *SGG* to disturb
184.11 **therefore, is practically** *SGG* therefore, will be practically
184.16 **from satellites.** *SGG* from lunar satellites.
185.1–2 **passing by means of translation before** *SGG* passing (by means of translation) before
185.3 ***facto*, he** *SGG facto* too often he
185.4 **to disturb** *SGG* to unsettle
185.8 **Hugo,** *SGG* Dumas[a]
[[a] Alexandre Dumas (1802–70), French novelist best known for *The Count of Monte Cristo* (1844–5) and *The Three Musketeers* (1845).]
185.9 **estimating them at** *SGG* estimating the men at
185.9–12 **sight. All who dislike...authors had prospered. And** *SGG* sight. What is thought of Dumas in Paris? asks the London reviewer; and shapes his notice to catch the *aroma* of the Parisian verdicts just then current. But exactly this is what he should prudently have shunned. He will never learn his own natural and unbiassed opinion of the book when he thus deliberately intercepts all that would have been spontaneous in his impressions, by adulterating with alien views – possibly not even sincere. And
185.28 **Technically they are published;** *SGG* Technically, no doubt, they *are* published;
185.28–9 **for six or ten times** *SGG* for ten or twenty times
185.34 **or a bishop, or a privy counsellor, or a member of Parliament – though,** *SGG* or by a bishop, or by a privy counsellor, or by a member of Parliament; though
186.4–5 **Carlisle, of the last generation, wrote** *SGG* Carlisle (not of this generation, but the earl of fifty years back) wrote
186.7 **other refuse** *SGG* other rubbish
186.9 **not so very much** *SGG* not much
186.10 **minister known** *SGG* minister (John Woburn)[a] known
[[a] Woburn Abbey was the ancestral home of John Russell, first Earl Russell (see above, p. 568, n. 5).]
186.13 **real genius** *SGG* dazzling genius
186.14 **in a peerage** *SGG* in his peerage
186.18 **jewels have** *SGG* jewels more gorgeous that the Koh-i-noor,[a] have
[[a] The Koh-i-noor diamond has the longest history of an extant stone. It was recut in 1852 at Garrards of London.]
186.21 **birth, station, or circumstances of** *SGG* birth, from station, or from accidents of
186.26 **lady, I** *SGG* lady! I
186.31 **collision, brought** *SGG* collision between the Whigs and the Tories, brought
186.40 **moves** *SGG appends footnote* Not at all. He *did* move when this was written; but that was in 1847. He is now as sedentary, or as stationary, as a milestone.
186.44 **down all** *SGG* down through all
187.3 **some ten or twelve years** *SGG* some twenty years
187.17–18 **something very brilliant that** *SGG* something too clever that
187.19 **he proposed.** *SGG* he suggested.

187.30 **themselves. Thus** *MS B* themselves. Schlosser has simply had his old passport *vise'd* up and down Europe; <which cannot promote any man's glory> fresh passports he has none to show. Thus *SGG* themselves. Schlosser has simply had his old passport *vise'd* up and down Europe; fresh passports he has none to show. Thus
187.36 **rides** *SGG* rode
187.37 **conceives** *SGG* conceived
188.5 **more (by 1,000 to 1) than** *F* more (by one thousand to one) than *SGG* more numerous (by one thousand to one) than
188.6 **full right** *SGG* special right
188.18–19 **unlimited certificate,** *SGG* unlimited guarantee,
188.23 **once *in medias res*.** *SGG* once into angry business.
189.15–16 **great discoveries, far** *SGG* great voyages of discovery, far
189.17 **forty-seven small 16mo** *SGG* forty-seven 16mo
189.24 **words originally** *SGG* words, 'darlings of children and men,'[a] originally
[[a] See above, p. 569, n. 30.]
189.25 **poet** *SGG appends footnote 'By the poet:'* – viz., Wordsworth.
189.28 **twenty** *SGG* thirty
189.35 **Sherwood, and** *SGG* Sherwood Forest, and
190.n.1 **would** *Editorial; 1847* wou
190.8 **daylight. It** *SGG* daylight, or we gain a glimpse of Schlosser sitting over his German black-beer. It
190.35 **absolute.'** *SGG* absolute' –
190.41–191.1 **irreligion, irreligion from a vulgar temperament, which** *SGG* irreligion – irreligion not from intellectual scepticism, but from a vulgar temperament – which
191.17 **the often hackneyed** *SGG* the hackneyed
191.19 **'somewhat dull'** *SGG* somewhat dull
191.25 **of wearying,** *SGG* of actual wearying,
191.28 **and the grave; and,** *SGG* and eternity; and
191.32 **dulness. It is** *SGG* dulness. So is Bilidulgerid,[a] so is the Sahara, so is the sea. Dulness is
[[a] More commonly, 'Biledulgerid', the area in north Africa that lies between the Sahara and the Barbary coast.]
191.36 **crowding** *SGG* crowded
191.42–3 **Cantabs are all…up to the Horse Marines.** *SGG omits*
192.5 ***vernacularity*; he** *SGG* venacularity; and nothing better or finer; he
192.7 **for Hibernicisms** *SGG* for some Hibernicisms
192.13 **De Foe** *SGG* Defoe
192.24 **commence.** *SGG* commence; and there it is that your worshipful Master Jonathan would have broke down irrecoverably.
192.33 **will select** *SGG* could select
192.37 **scullion or waiter from** *SGG* scullion from
193.8 **moping** *SGG* mopping
193.9 **logic, whether** *SGG* distinction, whether
193.24 **far less** *SGG* immeasurably less
193.24–6 **So I turn him out…others that may molest him.** *SGG* genius. But
193.28–9 **by any man** *SGG* by man
193.29–30 **upon any man** *SGG* upon man
193.31 **climax at the end. Schlosser** *SGG* climax ahead. Schlosser
194.4 **idealised nature.** *SGG* idealised human nature.
194.9 **limited form** *SGG* miniature form

194.10 **facts. A man would** *SGG* facts. An author would
194.23–4 **a prudent man in risking a** *SGG* a man in risking by *them* a
194.30–1 **letters*** *SGG moves footnote to* Mede,*
194.n.1 **Mede,** *SGG moves footnote* from letters
194.n.1 **twenty** *SGG* thirty
194.34 **regular in their *systole* and *diastole* as** *SGG* regular as
194.39 ***town*. Inexcusable,** *F, SGG insert paragraph break*
195.19 **in an hospital** *SGG* in a hospital
195.20 **shoulders. Ah, the monsters! Then** *SGG* shoulders. Then
195.21–2 **that, by their very non-reality amongst names of flesh and blood, proclaim** *SGG omit* names that
195.23 **connected** *SGG* associated
195.31 **sentiment** *F, SGG* sentiments
195.41 **wonder. But now I** *F inserts paragraph break* wonder. But now I *SGG inserts paragraph break* wonder. Now then I
195.43 **this. Addison** *SGG* this: Addison
196.3 **reviews; the editions were still scanty; and** *SGG* reviews or any other organs of literary advertisement; and
196.n.4 **of patronage.** *SGG* of *literary* patronage.
196.8 **does this not prove** *SGG* does not this prove
196.9 **Schlosser's** *SGG* Schlosser is
196.14 **at page 6 or 7; whereas** *SGG* at the beginning: whereas
196.15 **book's** *SGG* book is
196.16–17 **published. My** *SGG* published and finished. My
196.22 **cathedral chaunting** *SGG* cathedral-chanting
196.24 **Indeed,** *Editorial; 1847* Indeed;
196.27 **that displeases** *SGG* which displeased
196.28 **ludicrous: witness** *SGG* ludicrous. Witness
196.36 **prefer a near view of a brandy flask. So** *SGG* prefer, for a near view, a decanter of brandy. So,
197.14 **Indeed!** *SGG* Indeed?
197.14 **calculate.'** *SGG* calculate!'
197.16 **gold may** *SGG* gold that he buys may
197.17 **pewter to** *SGG* pewter that he sells to
197.35 **blind; he,** *SGG* blind. He,
197.37 **Dick,** *SGG appends footnote Slashing* was the characteristic epithet by which Pope described Bentley,[a] in allusion, generally, to Bentley's bold style of practice in critical correction, but specially to his furious ravages up and down the 'Paradise Lost,' on the plea that Milton's amanuensis, whosoever he might be, had taken a base advantage of the great poet's blindness.
[[a] See above, p. 541, n. 61.]
197.39 **hanged; but,** *SGG* hanged; yet,
197.43 **Knight was** *SGG* Knight, who in his own person had rendered services to literature, was
197.43 **slashing Dick; he** *SGG* Slashing Dick. He
198.n.2–3 **the Ms, under the civil title of – 'Milton, Mr** *SGG* the M's, and by way of being particularly civil, as 'Milton, Mr
198.34 **reputation was** *SGG* reputation, so far from being the fountain upon which he built, was

198.34 **English** *SGG appends footnote* In Oxford, where naturally an academic reputation forestalls for any scholarlike student his more national reputation, some of Addison's Latin verses were probably the ground of his first premature notoriety. But in London, I believe that Addison was first made known by his 'Blenheim' in 1704; most assuredly not by any academic exercise whatever.

198.37 **published to London, by** *SGG* published in London by

198.39–40 **of that famous fortress called *Skink* ('le fameux fort de'), by** *SGG* of a famous fortress (*'le fameux for de Skink'*) by

199.n.1–2 **than forty-eight hours old,** *SGG* than a month old,

199.n.3 **Swift's jesting name** *SGG* Swift's allegorico-jocular name

199.4 **amongst shouts** *SGG* amidst shouts

199.8 **ourselves, from** *SGG* ourselves, in spite of Skink, from

199.8–9 **day to this very summer of 1847. Boileau** *SGG* day to our own. Boileau

199.17 **enemies his tailor and co. As** *SGG* enemies his creditors.

199.31–2 **contradistinguished to the** *SGG* contradistinguished from the

200.14–15 **insisted too much on style, to the serious retardation of public** *SGG* insisted – so microscopically insisted on scruples of diction, that a serious retardation was threatened to the course of public

200.19 **erudition and** *SGG* erudition, to its minute precision and

200.20 **superficial, a** *SGG* superficial – Addison a

200.20–1 **a master of** *SGG* a patron of

200.21 **Get down, Schlosser, this moment; or let *me* get out.** *SGG omits*

Schlosser's Literary History of the Eighteenth Century {Part II}

202.6 **angry; by** *SGG* angry. By

202.9 **us, who** *SGG* me, who

202.11 **a cateran** *MS B* a Scotch cateran *SGG* a Scottish cateran

202.29 **he made twice** *SGG* he did actually make four times over, and twice

202.29 **least** *SGG appends footnote 'Twice as least:'* – Viz., upon Aaron Hill, and upon the Duke of Chandos.[a] In both cases the aggrieved parties sharpened the edge of the unprovoked assault by the dignity of their own behaviour, by their command of temper, and by their manly disdain of all attempts to retaliate, by undervaluing their splendid assailant. Evil is the day for a conscientious man, when his sole resource for self-defence lies in a falsehood. And such, unhappily, was Pope's situation. His assaults upon Lady M. W. Montagu, and upon the two Duchesses of Marlborough,[b] stand upon another basis.

{[a] For Aaron Hill, see above, p. 574, n. 25. James Brydges Chandos, first Duke of Chandos (1673–1744; *DNB*), nobleman, and patron of composer George Frideric Handel.

[b] For Lady Mary Wortley Montagu, see above, p. 604, n. 91. For Sarah Jennings, first Duchess of Marlborough, see above, p. 603, n. 87. For Henrietta Churchill, second Duchess of Marlborough, see above, p. 603, n. 85.}

202.36 **Homer) might have suggested the idea more naturally. Both** *SGG* Homer), was *more* likely, though very unlikely, to have suggested the idea. Both

202.40 **treatment, as** *SGG* treatment, and in the festive gaiety of its incidents, as

202.40 **plan or the** *SGG* plan and in the

202.41 **man finds** *SGG* writer finds

202.44–203.1 **though making** *SGG* though defending him perhaps on a principle potentially ruinous, and making

203.1 **behalf not agreeable to** *SGG* behalf abominable to

203.3–4 **friend,' who cannot safely be taxed with having first led him into temptation; he** *SGG* friend;' he

203.6 **penance. Long** *SGG* penance and discipline. Long

203.8–9 **upon principles of fidelity** *SGG* upon motives of honourable fidelity

203.12 **but cunningly** *SGG* but yet cunningly

203.18 **then exalted** *SGG* then enthroned

203.18–19 **mistakes Pope's** *SGG* misinterprets Pope's

203.22–3 **German 'Homer'** *SGG* German hexamertrical 'Homer'

203.25–6 **enough, that** *SGG* enough in itself without lying, that

203.43–4 **within the narrow bounds assigned to me, enter** *SGG* within narrow bounds, enter

204.8 **Let's** *SGG* Let us

204.9 **opinion: know,** *SGG* opinion. Know,

204.12 **still called** *SGG still* (meaning even in Voltaire's day) called

204.13 **might cease** *SGG* might possibly cease

204.21–2 **poetic splendour should create** *SGG* poetic emblazonries might create

204.22–3 **none. Secondly,** *SGG* none: a concession which is abundantly sufficient for the justification of Pope. Secondly,

204.23 **not rise from the** *SGG* not graduate itself by the

204.23–4 **but from the** *SGG* but by the

204.28–9 **Voltaire's. True, the** *SGG* Voltaire's. Grant that the

204.29–30 **was most accomplished. But** *SGG* was commandingly impressive. But

204.31 **day. But** *SGG* day. Meantime,

204.32 **even faded; whereas** *SGG* even *begun* to fade; whereas

204.34 **Dacier, '*which* Dacier, Bezonian?'** *MS B* Dacier, *which* Dacier? 'which king Bezonian?' *SGG* Dacier, whom Schlosser cites, *which* Dacier? 'which king Bezonian?'

204.34–5 **a passable scholar – but** *SGG* a good* scholar; but *SGG appends footnote* See his edition of 'Horace' in nine volumes,[a] from which any man may learn, and be thankful. [[a] André Dacier (see above, p. 574, n. 24) published his edition of Horace in Paris, 1681-9.]

204.37 **second,** *SGG* secondly,

204.40–1 **venom fell off spontaneously, like rain from the plumage of a pheasant, leaving** *SGG* venom (and by Pope's own confession) fell off spontaneously from *him*, like rain from oily plumage, leaving

204.42 **Thames** *Editorial; 1847* Thanes

204.43 **Clarke,** *Editorial; 1847* Clarke

204.43–4 **Samuel Clarke, Burnet, of the Charterhouse, and Sir Isaac Newton, did** *SGG* Samuel Clark, for one; Burnet, of the Charterhouse, for a second, and Sir Isaac Newton, for a third, did *SGG appends footnote 'Burnet of the Charterhouse:'* – Let not the reader confound this Burnet with Gilbert Burnet, the Bishop of Salisbury.[a] The latter was a gossiper, a slanderer, and, by the Duchess of Portsmouth's report, so notorious a falsifier of facts, that to repeat a story on *his* authority was – to insure its scoffing rejection by the whole court. Such was his character in that section of Europe (viz., the Court of Whitehall in the days of Charles II.) where he was most familiarly and experimentally known. That one of his sermons was burned by the hangman under orders from the House of Commons, is the sole consolatory fact in his most worldly career. Would there have been much harm in tying his lordship to the sermon? But the other

Burnet, though too early for a sound Cosmogony (anarchon ara kai ateleutaion to Pan),[c] was amongst the elect of earth by his eloquence.

[[a] Gilbert Burnet (1643–1715; *DNB*), divine and author of *The History of my Own Time* (1724–34).

[b] Louise-Renée de Kéroualle, Duchess of Portsmouth (1649–1734), French mistress of Charles II (see above, p. 601, n. 37).

[c] In a marginal note in MS B, De Quincey asks, 'Oh Mr Comp[ositor], did you never read the Vicar of Wakefield? Well, these Greek words are those by which '*the Cosmogony man*' imposes on the Vicar as a man of learning. It is a passage notorious to all Europe and the U.S.' In *The Vicar of Wakefield* (1766), Oliver Goldsmith (see above, pp. 307–31) writes that 'Ocellus Lucanus...has these words *Anarchon ara kai atelutaion to pan*, which imply that all things have neither beginning nor end' (Goldsmith, *CW*, vol. IV, p. 74).]

204.44 **escape tasting the knout; if** *SGG* escape Pope's knout. Now, if

205.5 **luxurious** *SGG* a luxury

205.10 **his** 'Burke' *SGG* Schlosser's 'Burke'

205.10 **steals upon** *SGG* steals over

205.15 **forcible;' Why** *SGG* forcible.' Why,

205.17 **forty years** *SGG* fifty-and-one years

205.17 **1847,** *SGG* 1858,

205.23 **voice – in** *SGG* voice (for Fox's voice was shrill as a women's) – in

205.25–6 **counterfeited, because he could not steal, Jove's** *SGG* counterfeited Jove's

205.31 **eye can** *SGG* eye could

205.33 **metaphysics to** *SGG* metaphysics down to

206.2 **in a merciful spirit,** *SGG* in any Christian spirit,

206.3 **of humanity,** *SGG* of merciful humanity,

206.5 **philosophy 'as toad** *SGG* philosophy 'worse than toad

206.13 **orders – 'Port** *SGG* orders. 'Port

206.16 **than he always understood himself;** *SGG* than was always intelligible even to himself;

206.16–17 **the hours of night; he** *SGG* the starry hours; he

206.20 **But, even** *SGG* Yet, even

206.22 **Cocytus. He fancies that** *SGG* Cocytus, fancying that

206.23 ***popular*. Of** *SGG popular*, perhaps too popular. Of

206.24 **should credit** *SGG* ought to credit

206.25 **fifty** *SGG* sixty-one

206.26–7 **a day of October 1797,** *SGG* a golden day of 1797,

206.28 **six hours** *SGG* three hours

206.29 **see, fifty years. Now,** *SGG* see, threescore years and one. Now,

206.n.3–4 **in elasticity** *SGG* in compass and elasticity

206.n.5–6 **M.P., twenty-five years ago, well known as *River* Sharpe, from the απεραντολογια of his conversation, used to say, that** *MS B, SGG conform, with the exception of two significant deletions in MS B given here in angle brackets* M.P. for I know not what borough, told the following story. Let me pause at this name. R., as the reader will rightly suppose, represented the Christian name which his godfathers and his godmothers had indorsed upon him at the baptismal font. Originally this R. had represented *Richard*: but when Richard had swelled into portly proportions, had become an adult, and taken his seat in the House of Commons, the Pagan public of London raised him to the rank of *River*; and thenceforwards R.S. stood for '*River* Sharpe' – this honorary augmentation of old hereditary name being understood to indicate the απεραντολογια (or world-without-ending-ness of his eternal talk); in prophetic anticipation of which the poet Horace is supposed to have composed his two famous lines* –

> 'Rusticus expectat dum defluat amnis at ille
> Labitur et labetur in omne volubilis aevum.'[a]

This Mr R Sharpe, by the way, was a man of multitudinous dodges. He could (and he did, if you look into the parliamentary mirrors of those days) make a very neat speech upon occasion, and when time was plentiful, else he was generally hurried by business; for he was a London merchant (in the English sense, observe – not the Scottish), exporting, therefore, to every latitude in countless longitudes; so that his own mercantile letters exhausted his whole power of franking. This made him wear a selfish expression of countenance to that army of letter-writing ladies in whose eyes the final cause of an M.P. was, that he might give franks to his female acquaintances – a matter of some importance when a double letter usually cost you a pretty half-crown, which, and not five shillings, is what the French always mean by an *écu*.[b] Mr Sharpe was chivalrous, nevertheless, and conceived himself a master in the most insinuating modes of deferential gallantry. But his seat in Parliament cost him exactly a thousand pounds sterling per annum. This sum he had to <filch> fetch back by franking, which lucrative privilege he applied naturally to all the heaviest despatches of his own firm. And under such circumstances, where each civility to his fair friends could be put into scales and weighed in his counting-house, reasonably he neither stood nor understood any 'nonsense.' *Usque ad aras*[c] – *i.e.*, so far as the ledger permitted – he wished to conduct himself towards women *en grand seigneur*, or even *en prince*.[d] But to waste a frank upon their 'nonsense' – a frank that paid all expenses from the Cornish Scillys northwards to John Groat, Esq.,[e] in Caithness – was the high road to bankruptcy. Consequently, Mr Sharpe was less popular than else he might have been, with so abundant a treasure of anecdotes, of gossip, and (amongst select friends) of high-flavoured scandal. Him, the said Sharpe, I heard more than once at Wordsworth's say, that *SGG appends footnote 'Famous lines:'* – Of which the following translation was executed, the first line by the late Mr William Cobbett[f] (who hated Sharpe), and the last by Dryden:[g] –

> 'Chaw-bacon[h] loiters till the stream be gone;
> Which flows – and as it flows, for ever shall flow on.'

But naturalists object (to Horace more properly than to Mr Cobbett) that of all men Chaw-bacon, <as a peasant, or paysan, familiar with the pays>as a rusticus familiar with all features of the *rus*, is least likely to make such a mistake as that of waiting for a river to run down. A *cit*, a townsman bred and born, is what Horace must have meant.

[[a] Horace, *Epistles*, I.ii.42–3: 'He who puts off the hour of right living is like the bumpkin waiting for the river to run out: yet on it glides, and on it will glide, rolling its flood forever'.

[b] See above, p. 547, n. 86.

[c] Literally, 'even to the altars'.

[d] '*En grand seigneur*' (Fr.), is 'like a lord', and '*en prince*' is 'like royalty'.

[e] From one end of Britain to the other: the Isles of Scilly are a group of about fifty small islands lying southwest of Cornwall, 25–36 miles off Land's End; John o'Groats is the northernmost point in the district of Caithness, Highland region, Scotland.

[f] William Cobbett (1763–1835; *DNB*), popular journalist and champion of traditional rural England.

[g] For John Dryden, see above, p. 524, n. 24.

[h] 'Chaw-bacon' is 'a bumpkin' (*OED*).]

206.n.7 **offered *him*** *SGG* offered to *him*
206.n.9 **with proper annotations** *SGG* with annotation
207.n.1 **MS., deposed, that** *SGG* MS., lamented that the gods had not made him an exciseman, with the gift of gauging barrels and other repositories; that
206.33–4 **are more** *SGG* are becoming more
207.1 **before to** *SGG* before, in island or in continent, amongst Christians or Pagans, to
207.12 **opponents.** *SGG appends footnote* I do not believe that at any time he was so designated, unless playfully and in special coteries. That the young, who were wearied, that the intensely practical, who distrusted him as a spectator, that the man of business, *natus rebus agendis*,[a] who viewed him as a trespasser on the disposable time of the House, should combine intermittingly in giving expression to their feelings is conceivable, or even probable. The rest is exaggeration.
[[a] Horace, *Ars poetica*, 82: 'natum rebus agendis' ('by nature fit for action').]
207.27 **those next** *SGG* those that stand next
208.6 **for that** *SGG* as respects that
208.9 **but 'the whistling** *F, SGG* but the 'whistling
208.n.3–4 **see every** *SGG* see or hear every
208.n.9 **Homer, than, fortunately, most** *SGG* Homer and his Ionic Greek than most
208.n.11 **three lines** *SGG* ten lines
208.14 **enigma, Hermes Trismegistus, or the** *SGG* enigma, a vapoury likeness of Hermes Trismegistus, or a dark shadow of the
208.16 **are to solve. I** *SGG* are required to solve. Schlosser is in that predicament. I
208.17–18 **evidently no distinct knowledge, and** *SGG* evidently never heard, and
208.20–1 **power so unaccountable at this day over the public mind? C.** *SGG* power over the public mind so unaccountable at this day. C.
208.21 **this power** *SGG* such a power
209.1 **explanations further** *SGG* conclusions further
209.3–4 **because it would have been *infamy* for him to** *SGG* because, for that man who *was* Junius, it would have been mere *infamy* to
209.5 **crime and published** *SGG* crime, and would have published
209.6–7 **been in past days hanged,** *SGG* been, in neighbouring lands, hanged,
209.14–15 **a plagiarism, of** *SGG* a foul plagairism – of
209.15 **Kraitzrer. But** *SGG* Kruitzner. All the world over, *or nearly*, Lara moved in freedom as a nobleman, haughtily and irreproachably. But one spot there was on earth in which he durst not for his life show himself – one spot in which instantly he would be challenged as a criminal – nay, whisper it not, ye forests and rivers! challenged as a vile midnight thief. But
209.22 **undertake not** *SGG* undertake, even without a special contract, not
209.29 **back. But,** *SGG* back; but
209.32 **fact, he might probably** *SGG* fact, Sir Philip might very probably
209.33 **bad temper** *SGG* vile temper
209.38 **Parliament. He** *SGG* Parliament; he
209.39 **affairs. He** *SGG* affairs; he
209.39 **party. He** *SGG* party; he
210.2 **of a great knavery.'** *SGG* of an unparalleled knavery.'
210.8 **profess scepticism.** *SGG* profess, or are *said to profess*, scepticism.
210.n.2 **Brougham naturally used a little in** *SGG* Brougham would be likely to consult in
210.n.3 **Sir P.** *SGG* Sir Philip
210.n.3 **father. And** *SGG* father, Dr Francis. And

210.n.4 **seen in** *SGG* seen, as was pointed out by Mr Taylor, in
210.n.5 **much importance** *SGG* conclusive importance
210.n.7–8 **question, was the best fitted to lower Mr Taylor's investigation with a *stranger* to the long history of the dispute. 'I** *SGG* question is remarkable, and worth repeating. 'I
210.n.8–9 **made out by** *SGG* made out for Sir Philip Francis by
210.n.13 **statements; after which their arguments signified** *SGG* statements of fact, after which, that their arguments should be ingenious or subtle, signified
210.12 **enough: what** *SGG* enough. What
210.16 **Mr T.'s** *F, SGG* Mr Taylor's
210.17 **cancel their** *SGG* cancel the sum total of their
210.17 **Mr T.'s** *F, SGG* Mr Taylor's
210.19 **that a man 'wanted better** *SGG* that some men 'want better
210.26 **mad. Well, but at** *SGG* mad, or a knavish simulator. Well, at
211.1 ***internexus* with** *SGG internexus*, its nodes of intersection, with
211.2 **than direct** *SGG* than any direct possible direct
211.3 **(to wit 70) salient angles, that** *F* (to wit seventy) salient angles, that *SGG* (to wit, seventy) salient angles – that
211.4 **(to wit 30) reëntrant angles, fits** *F* (to wit thirty) reëntrant angles, fits *SGG* (to wit, sixty-nine) re-entrant angles – fits
211.8 **if the vagabond** *SGG* if that very vagabond
211.13–14 **argument applicable to B** *SGG* argument deducible from B
212.21 **disclosure** *F, SGG* disclosures
212.24 **its interest** *SGG* its mystical interest
212.27 **disclosures. Some** *SGG* disclosures made in those letters. Some
212.30–1 **with the sudden** *SGG* with that sudden
212.37 **together, would** *SGG* together, *that* and *this*, spelled into most significant words, would
212.39 **Ellis, the Fitzroy, Russell, and Murray houses – the** *SGG* Ellis, to the English houses of Fitzroy and Russell, to the Scottish houses of Murray and Wedderburne – the
213.4–5 **subsequently avenged itself. By** *SGG* subsequently became the killing curse of long years to Francis. By
213.9 **the heaviest curse of the** *SGG* the self-avenger to the
213.10–11 **criminal thirsted for literary distinction above all other distinction, with a childish eagerness, as** *SGG* criminal was one who, with a childish eagerness, thirsted for literary distinction above all other distinction, as
213.14–15 **He stood** *SGG* Sir Philip stood
213.17–18 **is his death warrant. 'Oh** *SGG* is – to die; to die the death of a felon. 'Oh
213.21 **'You are** *SGG* 'You, then, are
213.24–6 **bed. Well, then, you an exceedingly clever....greatest scoundrel** *MS B, SGG conform, with the exception of one significant deletion in MS B given here in angle brackets* bed from that generation. But let us have a look at you, before you move off to prison. I like to look at clever men; particularly men that are *too* clever; and you, my dear sir, are too clever by half. I <consider> regard you as the brightest specimen of the swell-mob,[a] and in fact as the very ablest scoundrel
[[a] 'A class of pickpockets who assume the dress and manners of respectable people in order to escape detection' (*OED*).]

Conversation

215.5 **to be had under that** *F* to be under that *SGG* to be found under that
215.14 **vigorous** *SGG* rigorous
215.20 **Duchess of that day was amongst** *SGG* duchess of that day, viz., the Duchess of Devonshire,[a] was amongst
[[a] Georgina Cavendish, Duchess of Devonshire (1757–1806; *DNB*), poet and letter writer.]
216.11 **seem wanting.** *SGG* seems wanting.
216.42 **become** *SGG* became
217.11–12 **understood too little the capacities of colloquial intercourse. And** *SGG* understood the capacities of colloquial intercourse too little. And
217.21 **seemed then in** *SGG* seemed to me at that time in
217.32 **Huyghens** *SGG* Huygens
217.41 **that was** *SGG* that, I think, was
219.13 **(and that would at the beginning have been as startling)** *SGG* (and as startling)
220.21 **cleansing power.** *F, SGG* cleansing power?
220.35 **already started** *SGG* already they started
221.27 ***Pectus – id*** *SGG* '*Pectus*,' says Quintilian,[a] '*id*
[[a] Quintilian (AD *c.*35–after 96), teacher and writer celebrated for his *Institutio oratoria*.]
221.27 ***facit*. From** *SGG facit*:' – *The heart* (and not the brain) *is that which makes a man eloquent*. From
221.35 **his life,** *SGG* his whole life,
221.37 **life. And** *SGG* life; and
222.n.1–2 ***that*, he had also more: he** *F that,* he also had more: he *SGG that,* he also had more: He
222.n.5–6 **slender, and had not been much cultivated after his youthful days** *F, SGG* slender.

Protestantism {Part I}

223.n.1 **A Vindication of Protestant Principles. By Phileleutheros Anglicanus. London: Parker. 1847.** *SGG* This little paper, founded on a 'Vindication of Protestant Principles' – by Phileleutheros Anglicanus – might perhaps sufficiently justify itself by the importance of the principles discussed, if it replied to a mere imaginary antagonist. But this was not so. 'The Vindication' was a real book, and, as a startling phenomenon, made a sudden and deep impression.
224.2 **moment, making** *SGG* moment (1847) making
225.5 **opinion' it is, and** *SGG* opinion,' and
225.9 **voluptuary, and murmuring** *SGG* voluptuary, murmuring
225.16 **Scotch** *SGG* Scottish
225.27 **reap.' The** *SGG* reap' – *i. e.*, conformably or answerably to what he sows. The
226.n.3 **think,** *SGG* hope,
227.4 **15,000** *SGG* eighteen thousand
227.n.4 **octavos.** *SGG* octavos. I fear that it may be a duty to read him; and if it is, then I think of his seven octavos with holy horrors.
227.22 **history** *SGG* record

227.32 **any occupied** *SGG* any station ever occupied

227.n.9–11 **changes wrought by time, and by the contagion from secular revolutions, in the spirit of religious philosophy.** *SGG* changes in the spirit of religious philosophy wrought by time, and by the contagion from secular revolutions.

228.11 **to see what** *SGG* to say what

228. 16 **Hendecasyllable** *SGG* Hexameter

229.6 **won't** *Editorial; 1847* wont

229.12 ***principles.* Out of** *SGG principles.* But of

229.33 **principles; which,** *SGG* principles. Which,

229.35 **evolved.** *SGG* developed.

229.40 **beginning of** *SGG* beginnings of

230.6 **the solar system;** *SGG* the Christian system;

230.12 **soothed** *SGG* tranquillised

230.16 **I stand;** *SGG* I *do* stand;

230.20 **the *locus*, or centre,** *SGG* the centre,

230.21 **to the very** *SGG* to that very

230.21 **neglects.** *MS A, SGG conform, with the exception of one significant deletion in MS A given here in angle brackets* neglects. One church may say – My doctrine must be holy, because it is admitted that I have the authentic commission from Heaven to teach. But equally another church may say – My commission to teach must be conceded, because my teaching is holy. The first deduces the <irreproachable> purity of her doctrine from her divine commission to teach. But the second, with logic as forcible, deduces her divine commission to teach from the purity of her doctrine.

230.22–3 ***Phil.'s* (I am afraid *Phil.* is getting angry by this time) to** *SGG Phil.'s* to

230.26 **Turkey** *MS A, SGG append footnote and conform, with the exception of one significant deletion in MS A given here in angle brackets 'Orthodox Turkey:'* – At Mecca, or more <properly> probably throughout the Mussulman world, the Ottoman Sultan is regarded as the true filial champion *ed deen* [*i.e.*, of the faith]. He is the *right*-hand pillar; whereas the Shah of Persia is a heterodox believer, and therefore an unsound pillar. But it illustrates powerfully the non-spirituality of this religion (though pirated chiefly from the Bible), that this great schism in Islamism does not turn upon any point of doctrine, but simply upon a most trivial question of historic fact – viz., who were *de jure*[a] the immediate successors of Mahomet.

[[a] See above, p. 567, n. 1.]

230.27 ***Sonnees* to** *SGG Sonnees* (orthodox Mussulmans) to

230.27 ***Sheeahs*, you** *SGG Sheeahs* (Mahometan heretics), you

230.30 **by central Islamism. So** *SGG* by a central organ of Islamism, if such there were. So

231.4 **Evangelical** *F, SGG* Evangelican

231.n.30 ***inexpugnabilis*** *Editorial; 1847 inexpugnabi is*

231.n.45 **are in conjunction continually; for,** *SGG* are continually in conjunction; for,

232.5 **shadow. And** *SGG* shadow. Every man that lives, has (or has had) a *mamma*, who has made it impossible for him to be neutral in religious beliefs. And

232.11 **not indispensable.** *SGG* not absolutely indispensable.

232.15 **Servetus has** *F, SGG* Servetus had

232.19 **see? *he*** *SGG* see, *he*

233.2 **right. Calvin fancied that he could demonstrate his own impartiality.** *SGG* right.

233.4 **charters** *SGG* characters

233.8 **of an oracle alien** *SGG* of a Delphic oracle at Rome alien

233.20 **Simorg in Southey,** *SGG* Simorg,* that ancient bird in Southey, *SGG appends footnote 'The Simorg:'* – If the reader has not made the acquaintance of this mysterious bird, eldest of created things, it is time he should. The Simorg would help him out of all his troubles, if the reader could find him at home. Let him consult Southey's 'Thalaba.'[a] [[a] See above, p. 582, n. 40.]
233.25 **right, under the** *SGG* right, protected by the
233.28 **man has** *SGG* man, the very humblest and poorest, has
234.1 **within his own conscience;** *SGG* within one solitary conscience;
235.6 **man, or** *SGG* man – where lies the defence for the sublime Anglican Liturgy; or
235.7 **society. Once** *SGG* society – where lies the defence of Episcopacy. Once
235.16 **moving too (as** *SGG* moving, also (as
235.26 **God; how** *SGG* God. How
235.44 **spying-glass,** *SGG* spy-glass,
236.33 **than** *Editorial; 1847* then
237.4–5 **words, syllables, and punctuation** *SGG* words, to the syllables, and to the very punctuation
237.13 **often upon** *SGG* often depends upon
237.14 **in their mother dialect, cautious** *SGG* in modern tongues, cautious
237.19 **and making in** *SGG* and being made in
237.34 **seem** *SGG* seemed
237.38 **(which is** *SGG* (which in Kant's terminology is
238.6 **let *Phil.* have** *SGG* let this honourable man *Phil.*, whom I, *Philo-Phil.*, now take by the right hand, and solemnly present to the public – let this Daniel who has come to judgment have
238.9 **insists (Sect. 25, p. 49) upon** *SGG* insists upon
238.10 **inspiration,** *Editorial; 1847* inspiratiou,

Protestantism {Part II}

241.8 **employed briefly in the last paragraph of last month's paper; but** *SGG* employed; but
242.30 **years before** *SGG* years (plus two hundred) before
243.1 **ago, and** *SGG* ago – in fact, about Chaucer's time – and
243.5 **text, the** *SGG* text, countless are the
243.7–8 **important – may be described as countless. Here,** *SGG* important. Here,
243.8 **a fourth inspiration, No. 4, for** *SGG* a third inspiration (No. 3) for
243.10–13 **tongue; he will have to select....many adverse translators.** *SGG* tongue. The man who seeks to benefit by inspiration in his choice of a translator will have to select from a multitude, since nobody contends that the truth is uniformly exhibited throughout any one version, but grants that it is dispersed in fractions through a multitude.
243.16 **fifth** *SGG* fourth
243.16 **fifth** *SGG* fourth
243.44 **German, has risen to** *SGG* German, rose to
244.9 **sense, whether** *SGG* sense, and a very noticeable difference, whether
244.11 **cable; but** *SGG* cable, sometimes so called; but
244.n.1 **metaphor.' – One** *SGG image:'* – One

244.n.5 **ocean. Great** *SGG* Ocean. Can it be said that Mrs Partington[a] lived in vain, if she demonstrated this relation between mops and the Atlantic? Great
[[a] See above, p. 584, n. 18.]

244.n.15 **needle's** *Editorial; 1847* neddle's

244.n.17 **'cam*i*lus.'** *SGG* 'cam*i*lus.' What has an elephant to do with a needle? Why, he has this to do: the needle's eye, under its narrow function, takes charge of physical magnitude in one extreme – the elephant of the same idea in another extreme.

244.24 **here or there** *SGG* here and there

244.28 **carelessness, can** *SGG* carelessness in lighting his culinary fires, sometimes from an Englishman's carelessness, when throwing away into a drift of dry leaves the fuming reliques of his cigar, can

245.4 **are; and** *SGG* are, thirty thousand in amount; and

245.5 **inspiration (No. 4) for** *SGG* inspiration for

245.19–20 **'chapel.' Now,** *SGG* 'chapel.' A black Monday *that* must have been for the self-accusing compositors. Now,

245.27 **No. 4, to** *SGG* No. 5, if I count right, to

245.n.6 **controversy; his** *SGG* controversy. His

245.n.9–10 **alike. I hope the same thing may not be true at present. It** *SGG* alike. It

246.3 **fourth inspiration** *SGG* fifth inspiration

246.4 **how, upon this** *SGG* how, with regard to this

246.4 **to fix** *SGG* to select

246.6 **sense; another, and another, 'to** *SGG* sense; second church or second sect, 'to

246.7 **upon a different sense. Babel** *SGG* upon another. Babel

246.8 **a fifth inspiration. No. 5 is** *SGG* a sixth inspiration. No. 6 is

246.n.2 **a perfect stranger,** *SGG* a stranger,

246.n.2 **reserve a part** *SGG* reserve part

246.n.4 **longer succession** *SGG* long succession

246.n.4 **numbers, and perhaps drive him to despair. But** *SGG* numbers. But

246.n.5 **viz., No. 6, as** *SGG* viz., No. 7, as

246.n.6 **that No. 5 were** *SGG* that No. 6 were

246.n.8 **words) – ah, poor traveller in trackless forests, still** *SGG* words), still

246.n.11 **all? Is** *SGG* all? Does Y modify X, or not? Is

246.n.14–15 **composition as much, and with as vigilant an eye as myself, know** *SGG* composition with a vigilant eye, know

246.9 **that No. 5 is** *SGG* that No. 6 is

246.25 **lightning enfeebled or dimmed, because** *SGG* lightning dimmed or emasculated, because

247.5–6 **man and piety** *SGG* man – of piety

247.10–11 **billows, rise up, in shining columns, fountains of fresh water.*** *SGG* billows, rises up, in silvery brightness, an aspiring column of *fresh* water.*

247.n.2 **phenomenon.** *MS A, SGG conform, with the exception of three significant deletions in MS A given here in angle brackets* phenomenon, which has since been noticed <by our shipping> in the Persian Gulf. This most interesting phenomenon was <again> witnessed by the Generals Outram and Havelock,[a] in company with most of their army, on the expedition against Persia, within the last twelve months [February, 1858]. In fact, if a fountain bursts out with the sudden impetus of a fiery projectile, forced upwards by earthquake, which may happen on the barren floor of <a sea> the ocean as probably as in many other situations, then, supposing the column of water above not too dense, the fountain of fresh water will naturally cleave the marine water like an arrow.

[[a] Sir James Outram (1803-63; *DNB*) successfully commanded an English expedition against Iran in 1857. He was accompanied by Sir Henry Havelock (1795-1857; *DNB*).]

247.11–12 **found Arabian fountains of Ishmael and Isaac! Are** *SGG* found fountains – sister fountains to those of Ishmael and Isaac in the Arabian sands! Are

247.17 **hunted deer.** *SGG* hunted fawn.

247.30–1 **when first either** *SGG* when either

248.7 **Testament wishes** *SGG* Testament seeks

248.9 **Christ, the** *SGG* Christ, such a case did actually occur: the

248.13 **such amongst** *SGG* virtues amongst

248.13 **shown in blossom, and** *SGG* shown as blossoms and flowers, and

248.18 **translations, may** *SGG* translations for *us*, may

248.18–19 **day, after fourteen centuries and upwards have** *SGG* day, when nearly fifteen centuries have

248.28 **synthetically** *Editorial; 1847* symthetically

249.n.11–12 **preceding century** *SGG* seventeenth century

249.n.17 ***marte.*** *SGG marte;* that is to say, without assistance.

249.12 **He tore – he extorted the truth from the darkness of an unknown** *SGG* He tore the hidden truth – he extorted it from the darkness of a perfectly unknown

249.13 **to benefit by its own obscurity to the injury of mathematics. And** *SGG* to hide a treasure from man. And

249.15 **under an unknown tongue; that** *SGG* under a mask of words; that

249.16–17 **through their own reciprocal involutions. The** *SGG* through the reciprocal involutions of the hidden ideas themselves. The

249.20 **the heart)** *SGG* the human heart)

249.25 **learning.** *SGG* learning, by a machinery of spiritual counterpoint.

250.2 **dip below** *SGG* dip slightly below

250.3 **to ascend,** *SGG* to rise,

250.3 **alternately, *à*** *SGG* alternately dipping and rising *à*

250.27 **own resolutions; secondly,** *SGG* own technical *resolutions;* secondly,

250.29–30 **effectually barred,** *SGG* effectually neutralised

250.30–1 **grounds, is shown to** *SGG* grounds, appears to

250.31–2 **gratuitous delusion,** *SGG* gratuitous and superfluous delusion,

251.1 **so foolish;** *SGG* so unreflecting;

251.17 **idea. *The*** *SGG* idea – could more injure man under the mask of aiding him. *The*

251.17–8 **Does the doctrine** *SGG* Does a doctrine

251.21 **it, by giving the power. But** *SGG* it. But

251.24 **it was argued at one time, that** *SGG* it has been argued that

251.25–6 **not have been a compliance** *MS A* not <be received for a> express a mere compliance *SGG* not express a mere compliance

251.26 **to express** *SGG* to indicate

251.n.3–4 **there is no instance of accommodation** *SGG* there should be no call for accommodation

251.n.4–7 **ignorance; and the persuasion....Nothing, in fact, disturbs** *MS A* ignorance, because the ignorant populace starts with no <distinct> creed or preconceptions, <either> false or true. In fact, what most disturbs *SGG* ignorance, because the ignorant populace starts with no creed or preconceptions, false or true. In fact, what most disturbs

251.n.7–8 **cosmogony, except (as usual) the ruggedness of** *SGG* cosmogony is the perverseness of

251.n.10–11 **for his own opinion, as** *SGG* for this conceit as

251.n.12–13 **this single feature** *SGG* this feature

251.n.13 **fairy-tale, where everything else is told with the most majestic simplicity. But** *SGG* fairy tale. But

251.n.14 **meaning only** *SGG* meaning biblically only

251.n.14–15 **man; but never** *SGG* man – never

251.n.17 **hour, in Daniel. The *heptameron* is** *SGG* hour. The *heptameron*, or seven days' work of Creation and Rest, is

251.n.17 **week.** *SGG* week, compromising perhaps millions of years. Let me ask this question – In Daniel, whether considered (as in past ages he was) a prophet, or (as in this generation he is, even by pious men like Dr Arnold of Rugby)[a] simply a writer of history, and posterior to the events contemplated – has any man been foolish enough to regard his 1260 *days* as literally such – viz., as no more than 180 weeks?

[[a] In 1840, Thomas Arnold (see above, p. 582, n. 42) wrote that 'the greater part of the book of Daniel is most certainly a very late work…and the pretended prophecy about the Kings of Grecia and Persia…is mere history, like the poetical prophecies in Virgil and elsewhere' (A. P. Stanley, *The Life and Correspondence of Thomas Arnold* (London: Fellowes, 1844), vol. II, p. 188.]

252.1–2 **the usual erroneous phraseology, he** *SGG* the customary erroneous phraseology of the people, he

252.6–7 **the suspicion of lunacy; and, secondly, would** *SGG* the reputation of lunacy. Secondly, it would

252.14–15 **which he had not been able to** *SGG* which it had not been found possible to

252.15–16 **great envoy** *SGG* great heavenly envoy

252.26 **The same line** *SGG* A similar line

253.6 ***p.* For** *SGG p* – by one element richer, by one element poorer. For

253.8 **Europe! I** *SGG* Europe! In the language of high passion, how bare and beggarly is the French! how incapable of rendering Shakspere! I

253.9 **Samaritan translation** *SGG* Arabic translation

253.10 ***coquette.*** *SGG appends footnote 'Coquette:'* – Virgil comes near to one phasis of this idea – Malo me Galatea petit lasciva puella, et fugit ad salices, *et se cupit ante videri. Lasciva* is merely *frolicsome:* in the last line appears the coquette.

[[a] Virgil, *Eclogues*, III. 64-5: 'Galatea, saucy girl, pelts me with an apple, then runs off to the willows – and hopes to be seen first'.]

253.n.2 **in the Southern lands,** *SGG* in southern lands,

253.n.2 **some, not** *SGG* some, as Portugal, for example, not

253.n.7 **agnos?'** *SGG* agnos.'

253.n.8 ***eye,* blighted the** *SGG eye*, was supposed to blight the

253.n.18 ***tabula.* Under** *MS A tabula*, dia*v*olo, from the <Latin dia*b*olus> Greek *diabolos*, &c. Under *SGG tabula*, dia*v*olo, from the Greek *diabolos*, &c. Under

253.n.21 **eye.** *SGG* eye. For first of all, St Paul's word *Baskaino* was undoubtedly pronounced *Vaskaino;* just as *Sebastopol* is orientally pronounced Se*v*astopol, and as *Sebastos*, which is the Greek equivalent for the Roman *Augustus*, was always pronounced Se*v*astos. By this process, the Grecian word *Baskaino* became *V*askaino, and then, with hardly any change, the Latin *Fascino* pronounced 'Fas*k*ino.' For the Roman '*c*' had in *all* situations the force of '*k*.' Thus Caesar was always Keysar (therefore in Greek Καισαρ); and our wicked friend Cicero was always *Kikero* (in Greek therefore Κιχερων). Except for the accent on the first syllable of Fascino, the Greek and the Roman word were therefore identical to the ear, though slightly different to the eye.

253.n.23 **(εγγαστριμνθοι** *Editorial; 1847* εγγαστριμνθοι

254.4–6 **upon his very agents, began to reach some of the murderous judges and denouncers!** *MA A, SGG conform, with the exception of two significant deletions in MS A given here in angle brackets* upon the very agents of his cruelty, began to reach the murderous judges themselves and the denouncers! Oh, glory of re<taliation>tribution to see the wicked judge of New England roasted in the fire which himself had kindled – to see the cruel bibliolater, in <Shakspeare's> Hamlet's words, 'hoist by his own petard.'[a]

[[a] Shakespeare, *Hamlet*, III.iv.207: 'Hoist with his own petar'.]

254.20 **perished thousands** *SGG* perished by a languishing decay thousands

254.23–4 **delusions, nevertheless, equally it** *SGG* delusion, equally nevertheless it

254.25–6 **agencies. It must, therefore, have** *SGG* agencies. All the spells, the rites, the invocations were doubtless Pagan. The witchcraft of Judea therefore must have

254.28 **own, denounce** *SGG* own in Trinidad and Jamaica, denounce

254.32 **in, through this belief it became the occasional** *SGG* in like the equally false but equally operative belief of the African negro in *Obi*, it became, through and by that potent belief, the occasional

254.n.2 **paragraph? – ED.** *MS A, SGG conform, with the exception of five significant deletions in MS A given here in angle brackets* paragraph? – American[a] ED. *Answer from this side of the Atlantic.* – No, surely the difference is vast between the two cases. The persons denounced and arrested in New England were entirely passive; or were so generally; they did nothing at all – they were not seeking to injure others. But the Obeah man never moved except for evil purposes; either as an agent in the service of some other man's malice, or in the service of his own rapacity – as an extortioner relying upon the <uncontrollable agonizing> mystic terrors of his negro victims. Let the reader consult Bryan Edwards in his 'West Indies'[b] – a well-known book of 60 years back. Or, as I now dimly remember, in Miss Edgeworth's earliest novel of 'Belinda,'[c] he will find a lively sketch embodying most of the features characterising <this> the African form of magic; <but for> that is, the special magic of Obi (which, by the way, was popularised in London and Liverpool some 50 years back by the picturesque drama of 'Obi, or Three-fingered Jack').[d] But for a larger view of African magic, not limited to the Koromantyn form of *Obi*, I would refer <him> the reader to some interesting disclosures (founded on personal experience) in the 'African Memoranda' of captain Beavor.[e] The book belongs to the last generation, and must be more than 40 years old. The author was a Post-captain in our navy: and I may mention incidentally that he was greatly <respected> admired by Coleridge and Wordsworth[f] for the meditative and philosophic style of mind exhibited in his book.

[[a] In MS B, De Quincey inserted the word 'American' into the *Tait's* footnote as it appeared in *F*, and thus 'ED.' appeared as 'American ED.' in *SGG*. De Quincey, however, has forgotten that the footnote was originally inserted by the British editor of *Tait's*, and was simply reproduced by the American typesetters for *F*.

[b] Bryan Edwards (1743-1800; *DNB*), *The History, Civil and Commercial, of the British Colonies of the West Indies*, 2 vols (London: Stockdale, 1793).

[c] Maria Edgeworth (1767-1849; *DNB*), Anglo-Irish writer, *Belinda* (1801).

[d] For the most detailed account, see Charles J. Rzepka, 'Thomas De Quincey's "Three-Fingered Jack": The West Indian Origins of the "Dark Interpreter"' in *European Romantic Review*, 8.2 (1997), pp. 117-38.

[e] Philip Beaver (1766-1813; *DNB*), *African Memoranda: Relative to an attempt to establish a British Settlement on the Island of Bulama, on the Western Coast of Africa, in the year 1792* (London: Baldwin, 1805).

[f] In 1809, Wordsworth described 'Commodore Beaver' as 'one of the most enlightened

men any Country ever produced' (*The Letters of William and Dorothy Wordsworth*: *The Middle Years, Part I*, ed. Mary Moorman (Oxford: Clarendon Press, 1969), p. 297).]

Protestantism {Part III}

255.8 **cacophon.** *SGG* cacophony.
256.25 **day (as I had so often the honour to do) with** *SGG* day (as I so often did) with
256.29 **wanted repairing** *SGG* wanted tinkering
256.30 **be repaired** *SGG* be tinkered
256.31 **to repair,** *SGG* to tinker,
256.38–43 **doubted – not that I pretended...the popular opinion); but, judging** *SGG*
doubted; and judging
257.3 **his divinity** *SGG* his theology
257.6 **dusky,) I** *SGG* dusky, and W.W. had a natural resemblance to Mrs Ratcliffe's Schedoni[a] and other assassins roaming through prose and verse), I
[[a] De Quincey compares William Wordsworth to Schedoni, the villain in *The Italian* (1797), one of a series of highly successful Gothic novels by Ann Radcliffe (1764-1823; *DNB*).]
257.8 **our Church** *SGG* our English Church
257.9 **any discussion;** *SGG* much discussion;
257.17 **be. To** *SGG* be; without an opening in fact to any possibility of being *more* wrong. To
257.21–2 **twenty and more colleges,** *SGG* twenty colleges.
257.22 **can obtain** *SGG* can also obtain
257.26 **bold assertion,** *SGG* bold appreciation,
257.31 **him, they'll certainly hear** *SGG* him, beyond a doubt they'll hear
257.32 **Bacon belonged** *SGG* Bacon also belonged
257.32–8 **College. Don't laugh at me....Dr Wordsworth was, or** *SGG* College. As to Dr Wordsworth, he was, or
257.39–41 **Canterbury. If Lambeth...and Jupiter Ammon had vanished. What** *MS A* Now to suppose Lambeth <at> in fault on such a question, <it's of no use going to Newcastle for coals, Delphia, we all know, and Jupiter Ammon, have long vanished.> *SGG* Now to suppose Lambeth in fault on such a question, is equivalent to the old Roman formula of *Solem dicere falsum*.[a] What
[[a] Cf. Virgil, *Georgics*, I. 463: 'solem quis dicere falsum audeat?' ('Who dare say the Sun is false?').]
258.24 **(*us*, meaning, I suppose, the *Old*mannians,) 'to** *SGG* (*us*, in the mouth of an *anti-Newmanite*, meaning the *Old*-mannians) 'to
258.36 **adding – a solid foundation,** *SGG* adding – furnish a foundation,
258.44 **phantom changes** *SGG* *apparent* changes
258.44–259.1 **of development;** *SGG* of religious development;
259.4 **stationary disk.** *SGG* *unchanging* disk.
259.5 **benefit; but absolutely as regards itself, the** *MS A* benefit <of> or our own perception; but absolutely, as regards itself in its essence, the *SGG* benefit or our own perceptions; but absolutely, as regards itself in its essence, the
259.7 **had a curtain** *SGG* had in its earlier stages a curtain
259.17 ***you?'*** *MS A* *you*?' as if <the one> belief <negatived> the other. SGG *you*?' as if each belief alternately involved a negation of the other.

259.25 ***Phil.* in laying down the doctrine** *SGG Phil.* laying down in his own person that doctrine

259.29 **'*system*' of** *SGG* '*system*' itself of

259.32 **extremes, should** *SGG* extremes, finding moderation to be the worst thing in this present world, should

259.35 ***Phil-Phil.* Still** *SGG Phil-Phil*; for I, in my incarnation of *Phil-Phil.*, certainly could not have existed, had not *Phil.* pre-existed. Still

260.3–4 **improved – oh! what** *SGG* improved – on Philology it is that the burden rests. Oh, what

260.5 **future. Here,** *MS A, SGG conform, with the exception of two significant deletions in MS A given here in angle brackets* future. Philology is the Mrs Partington[a] that not only engages in single duel with the Atlantic Ocean, armed <only> simply with her mop, but also undertakes to mop out the Atlantic from all <inroads and attempts at> trespass or intrusion through all time coming. Here,

[[a] See above, p. 584, n. 18.]

260.11–12 **from the reaction upon the Bible of advancing** *SGG* from that constant reaction upon the Bible which is maintained by advancing

260.16 **than fictions of his own. Thus** *SGG* than reflexes projected from his own monstrous errors, or, at best, puerile conceits of adventurous ignorance. Thus

260.18 **these words.** *F, SGG* those words.

260.23–4 **stone. Broomsticks were** *MS A, SGG conform, with the exception of one significant deletion in MS A given here in angle brackets* stone – viz., simultaneously condemning all constitutional resistance, the most wise and indispensable, to the most profligate of kings, and also <countenancing> consecrating the filthiest of man's follies as to witchcraft. Broomsticks, as aerial horses, were

260.26 **Filmer's*** *SGG moves footnote to* 'Patriarchia,'*

260.26–7 **'Patriarchia,'** *SGG moves footnote from* Filmer's

260.29 **were, in the strictest sense of the word, *precarious*,** *SGG* were, in the most *verbal* sense, made to be *precarious*,

260.30 **prayers and entreaties to** *SGG* prayers (*preces* – whence *precor*, and our own *precarious*) to

260.32 **Crown. 'The** *SGG* crown; and except as bounty or lordly alms from the crown, no reform was possible. 'The

260.35 **obeyed (often** *SGG* obeyed (and most sincerely, because often

261.3 **case? All** *SGG* case, so as to escape a superstitious obedience to its mere *letter*, which so often 'killeth?' All

261.7–8 **that *stratum*** *SGG* that particular *stratum*

261.9 **truth! how** *F* truth; how *SGG* truth, how

261.12 **captives;'** *SGG appends footnote* Words from one of the beautiful petitions in the Litany of the Anglican Church.

261.12 **relation to** *SGG* relation, above all, to

261.15 **Mahommedanism,** *SGG* Mahometanism,

261.15 **own laws, that** *SGG* own *spiritual* power of rectification, that

261.20 **hearts; and if** *SGG* hearts, and a new heart (a heart of flesh, where before was a stony heart)[a] into all my children; and if

[[a] Ezekiel 11: 19: 'And I will give them one heart, and I will put a new spirit within you: and I will take the stony heart out of their flesh, and will give them an heart of flesh'.]

261.21 **law will** *SGG* law, read by that heart, will

261.22 **arises, when** *SGG* arises, though never noticed in words, when

261.27–8 **for, if it does not answer to a circumstantial textual description; whereas** *SGG* for, unless it answer circumstantially to a type laid down by anticipation in some great premonitory model of legislation; whereas

261.28–9 **case is provided for, as soon as its tendencies and its moral relations are made known, by** *SGG* case, together with its moral relations, is expounded by

261.30 **to a spiritual apprehension in** *SGG* to an apprehension spiritually trained in

261.31 **whenever** *SGG* when

261.31–3 **introduced, not depending upon grapes, the most devout Mussulmans hold themselves absolved from the restraints of the Koran.** *SGG* introduced, or a mode which, *not* being new, was unknown to Mahomet (or at least was overlooked by him), devout Mussulmans hold themselves absolved from the interdict of the Koran as to strong drink, on the ground that this interdict applied itself to the fermentations of grapes, and scandalously unaware, in its bee-like limitation of prophetic vision,* that such blessings would arise in the Christian world, as brown stout and Bass's medicinal ale, which the Prophet himself might have found useful as a *viaticum*,[a] on his *flight* to (or *from*, was it?) Medina.[b] *SGG appends footnote 'Bee-like limitation of prophetic vision:'* – Grosser ignorance than my own in most sections of natural history is not easily imagined. I retreat in panic from a cross-examination upon such themes by a child of five years. But, nevertheless, I am possessed of various odd fragments in this field of learning, mostly achieved by my own casual observation up and down innumerable solitary roamings. I am also possessed of one solitary zoological fact, borrowed, and not self-originated (which I fear may turn out to be a falsehood), as to the optics of the bee. I picked it up about fifty years ago in a most unlikely quarter – viz., the little work of a sentimentalist and a discounting poet – namely, Samuel Rogers – which is my chief reason for viewing it sceptically. He, in his 'Pleasures of Memory,' asserts that the bee, too busy for star-gazing, sees only to the extent of half-an-inch beyond his own eye.[c] I know people with a range of vision considerably less.[d] Will the reader permit me to present him with this little contribution to his stores of zoological science, before it has time to explode (in the event of being unsound)? I expect no premium or *bonus*, by way of *commission* on fifty years' porterage.

[[a] an allowance for traveling expenses.

[b] Medina is one of the two most holy cities of Islam. In 622 the Prophet Muhammad arrived at Medina from Mecca.

[c] Samuel Rogers (1763-1855; *DNB*), banker and poet, *The Pleasures of Memory* (1792), I, 344-5: 'Hark! the bee winds her small but mellow horn, / Blithe to salute the sunny smile of morn'. Rogers appends a footnote to these lines in which he observes that 'this little animal, from the extreme convexity of her eye, cannot see many inches before her'.

[d] De Quincey himself was very short-sighted (Lindop, p. 194).]

261.33 **And so it would** *SGG inserts paragraph break*

261.34 **had laid down *literal*** *SGG* had contented itself with *literal*

261.35 **the slave traffic.** *SGG* the commerce in slaves.

261.35 **of variations** *SGG* of verbal variations

261.35–6 **been developed by time which** *SGG* been introduced, which

261.36 **of Scripture could** *SGG* of the Scriptures could

261.34–262.4 **to reach. Were the domestic servants of Greece....the light of upper day** – would *SGG* to intercept. For instance, did servants, praedial and household, such as the Greeks termed θητες [*Thetes*], fall within the description of Δουλοι (*i.e.*, slaves)? *SGG* Were serfs, again, to be accounted slaves, or the bondsmen and *ascripti glebae*[a] of feudal Europe? At what point was the line to be drawn? or what was the essential and logical distinction by which Greek and Roman slavery determined its own more or less of assimilation to the modern negro slavery in the West Indies for the three-and-a-half last centuries, and (in the Spanish South American colonies) of the Indian slavery? Or again, speaking more frankly and nationally, of those amongst our own brothers and sisters, both in England and Scotland, that until very lately were born and bred subterraneously, and passed their whole lives subterraneously in mines or collieries, Scotch or English alike, and were by lawyers regarded as *ascripti metallo*[b] borne upon the establishment as regular working tools, indorsed upon the machinery as so many spokes in a mighty wheel, shafts and tubes in the 'plant' of the concern, and liable to be pursued as fugitive slaves, in the case of their coming up to daylight, and walking off to some other district.* Would *SGG appends footnote* These hideous abuses, which worked for generations through the silent aid of dense ignorance in some quarters, and of old traditional maxims in others, under the darkness of general credulity, and riveted locally by brazen impudence in lawyers, gave way (I believe), not to any express interference of the legislature [for in these monstrous inroads upon human rights the old proverbial saying was exemplified – *Out of sight, out of mind;*[c] and no bastille[d] can be so much out of sight as a mine or a colliery], but simply to the instincts of truth and knowledge slowly diffusing their contagious light. Latterly, indeed, the House of Commons interfered powerfully to protect *women* from working in mines, and the poor creatures most fervently returned thanks to the House – but, as I saw and said at the time, under the unfortunate misconception that the gracious and paternal senate would send a supplementary stream of gold and silver, in lieu of that particular stream which the honourable House had seen cause suddenly to freeze up for ever. Not that I would insinuate the reasonableness, or even the possibility, of Parliament's paying permanent wages to these poor mining women; but I *do* contend, that in the act of correcting a ruinous social evil, that never could have reached its climax unless under the criminal negligence of Parliament, naturally and justly the duty fell upon that purblind Parliament of awarding to these poor mining families such an indemnification, once for all, as might lighten and facilitate the harsh transition from double pay to single pay which the new law had suddenly exacted. As a sum to be paid by a might nation, it was nothing at all: as a sum to be received by a few hundreds of working households, at a moment of unavoidable hardship and unforeseen change, it would have been a serious and seasonable relief, acknowledged with gratitude. Meantime, I am not able to say whether *all* the evils of female participation in mining labour, as contemplated by the wisdom of Parliament, so fearfully disturbing the system of their natural household functions, and lowering so painfully the dignity of their sexual position, have even yet been purified. Mr Bald,[e] a Scottish engineer, chiefly applying his science to collieries, describes a state of degradations as pressing upon the female co-operators in the system of some collieries, which is likely enough to prevail at this hour [February, 1858], inasmuch as the substitution of male labour would often prove too costly, besides that the special difficulty of the case would thus be aggravated: I speak of cases where the avenues of descent into the mine are too low to admit of horses; and the women, whom it is found necessary to substitute, being obliged to assume a cowering attitude, gradually subside into this unnatural posture (as a fixed memorial of their brutal degradation). The spine in these poor women, slaving on behalf of their children, becomes permanently horizontal, and at right angles to their legs. In process of time they lose the power of bending back into the perpendicular attitude conferred by nature as a symbolic privilege of grandeur upon the human race; at least if we believe the Roman poet, who tells us that *She* (meaning Nature)

'Os homini sublime dedit, coelumque tueri
Jussit, et erectos ad sidera tollere vultus:'[f]

i.e., to the race of man she gave an aspiring countenance, and laid her commands upon that race to fix his gaze upon the heavens overhead, and to lift up all faces erect and bold to the imperishable stars. But these faithful mothers, loyal to their duties in scorn of their own personal interests, oftentimes exulted in tossing away from them, as a worthless derelict, their womanly graces of figure and motion – dedicating and using up these graces as a fund for ransoming their daughters from all similar degradation in time to come.

[[a] See above, p. 588, n. 32.

[b] See above, p. 588, n. 37.

[c] *Proverbs*, p. 602.

[d] The Bastille was a French state prison stormed by an armed mob of Parisians in the opening days of the French Revolution.

[e] See above, p. 588, n. 33

[f] Ovid (see above, p. 535, n. 43), *Metamorphoses*, I. 85-6: 'os homini sublime dedit caelumque videre / iussit et erectos ad sidera tollere vultus'.]

262.4–8 **would *they*, would these poor Scotch....conditions that new combinations of society would bring forward**; endless would *MS A, SGG conform, with the exception of one significant deletion in MS A given here in angle brackets* Would these poor Pariahs, Scotch and English, have stood within the benefit of any scriptural privilege, had the New Testament legislated in their behalf, and contented itself with the mere verbal *letter* of their description as Δουλοι (slaves)? Ten thousand evasions, distinctions, and <subdivisions> subdistinctions, would have neutralised the intended relief; and a verbal refinement would for ever have defeated a merely verbal concession. Endless would

262.9–10 **restorations of slavery that would take place under a Mahometan literality: endless** *SGG* restorations to slavery under a Mahometan appeal to the *letter* of the scriptural command: endless

262.10–13 **defeats that such restorations must sustain under...secret admonitions of the heart. Meantime,** *SGG* defeats of these restorations under a Christian appeal to the pervading *spirit* of God's revealed command, and under an appeal to the direct voice of God, ventriloquising through the secret whispers of man's conscience. Meantime,

262.14 **is not a light that Scripture** *SGG* is not so much a light which Scripture

262.14–15 **life so much as a light that human life and its development throw** *SGG* life, as inversely a light which human life and its eternal evolutions throw

262.16–19 **True; but then how was it possible that...some truth widely applicable to society. This truth is caught** *SGG* True: but then the very possibility of such developments for life, and for the deciphering intellect of man, was first of all opened by the spirit of Christianity. Christianity, for instance, brings to bear seasonably upon some opening, offered by a new phasis in the aspects of society, a new and kindling truth. This truth, caught

262.19 **truth is caught** *SGG* truth, caught

262.20–23 **life – is expanded prodigiously...made up, in all its details, of** *SGG* life, is prodigiously expanded by human experience; and subsequently, when travelling back to the Bible as an improved or illustrated text, is found to be made up in its details of

262.23 **argue anything disparaging to** *SGG* argue any disparagement to

262.25–263.23 **that *nucleus* by which Christianity started....house of Timour,** *MS A, SGG conform, with the exception of five significant deletions in MS A given here in angle brackets* that first elementary impulse by which Christianity awakened man's attention to the slumbering instincts of truth, started man's movement in the new direction, and moulded man's regenerated principles. To give one instance: Public charity, the charity that grows out of tender and apprehensive sympathy with human sufferings – when did it commence, and where? Who first thought of it as a paramount duty for all who had any available power – as an awful right, clamorously pleading its pangs night and day in the ear of God and man? What voice, melodious as the harps of Paradise – voice which 'all the company of heaven'[a] must have echoed with a choral antiphony, first of all insisted on cold and hunger as dreadful realities afflicting poor women and innocent children? It was the voice of one that sat upon a throne; and he was the first man, having power to realise his benign purposes, that read in the rubric of man's duties any call for such purposes. But why it was that he first read the secret writing which the whole pagan world, Rome, and insolent Greece, had so obstinately ignored, suddenly becomes clear as daylight, when we learn that he – the inaugurator of eleemosynary aid to the afflictions of man – was the first son of Christianity that sat upon a throne. Yes, Constantine[b] it was, earliest of Christian princes, that first* of all invested Pauperism with the majesty of an organ amongst political forces, on the scriptural warrant that the poor should never cease out of the land[c] – Constantine that conferred upon misery, as a mighty potentate dwelling for ever in the skirts of populous cities, the privilege of appearing by a representative and a spokesman in the <imperial> council-chamber of the Empire.

Had, then, the Pagans of all generations before Constantine, or more strictly before the Christian era, no charity, no pity, neither money nor verbal sympathy at the service of despairing poverty? No, none at all. Supposing, for instance, any Gentile establishments to have existed up and down Greece, or Egypt, or the Grecianised regions of Asia Minor and Syria, at the Apostolic era, these would undoubtedly have been referred to by the apostles as furnishing models to emulate, or to copy with improvements, or utterly and earnestly to ignore, under terror of contagion from some of those fundamental errors in their plan theoretically, or in their administration practically, which might be counted on as pretty certain to pollute the executive details, however decent in their first originating purpose. Upon any one of some half-dozen motives, St Paul,[d] in his boundless activity of inquiry and comparison, would have found cause to mention such institutions. And again, in the next generation, under the Emperor Trajan, Pliny[e] would have had abundant ground for dwelling on this early *communism* and system of reciprocal charity established amongst the Christians, had he not recoiled from thus emblazoning the beneficence of an obnoxious sect, when conscious that no parallel public bounty could be pleaded as a set-off on the side of those who desired to persecute this new-born sect. There remains, moreover, a damnatory evidence on this point, much more unequivocal and direct, in the formal systems of ethics still surviving from the Pagan world under the noonday splendour of its civilisation: Aristotle's, for example, at the epoch of Alexander the Great; and Cicero's,[f] at a corresponding period of refinement three centuries later in Rome. Now, in these elaborate systems, which have come down to us unmutilated, no traces are to be found of any recognised duty moving in the direction of public aid and relief to the sufferers from poverty. Our wicked friend Kikero,* for instance, who *was* so bad, <and> but *wrote* so well, who *did* such naughty things, but *said* such pretty things, has himself noticed in one of his letters, with petrifying coolness, that he knew of destitute old women in Rome, who went without tasting food for one, two, or even three days.[g] After making such a statement, did Kikero not tumble down-stairs, and break at least three of his legs, in his hurry to call a public meeting for the redressing of so cruel a grievance? Not he: the man continued to strut up and down his library, in a toga as big as the 'Times' newspaper, singing out –

'Cedant arma togae; concedat laurea laudi.'[h]

And, if Kikero noticed the case at all, it was only as a fact that might be interesting to natural philosophers, or to speculators on the theories of a *plenum* and a *vacuum*, or to Greek physicians investigating the powers of the human stomach, or to connoisseurs in old women. No drachma or denarius, be well assured, ever left the secret lockers or hidden fobs of this discreet barrister upon so blind a commission as that of carrying consolation to a superfluous old woman – not enjoying so much as the *jus suffragii*.[i] By a thousand indirect notices, it might be shown that an act of charity would, in the eyes of Pagan moralists, have taken rank as an act of drunkenness.

Yes, the great planetary orb of charity in its most comprehensive range – not that charity only which interprets for the best all doubtful symptoms, not that charity only which 'hopeth all things,'[j] and which, even to the relenting criminal, gives back an opening for recovering his lost position by showing that for *him* also there is shining in the distance a reversionary hope – but that charity also which brings aid that is effectual, and sympathy that is unaffected, to the households sitting in darkness – this great diffusive orb, and magnetic centre of every perfect social system, first wheeled into its place and functions on that day when Christianity shot above the horizon. But the idea, but the principle, but the great revolutionary fountain of benediction, was all that Christianity furnished, or needed to furnish. The executive arrangements, the endless machinery, for diffusing, regulating, multiplying, exalting this fountain – all this belongs no longer to the Bible, but to man. And why not? What blindness to imagine that revelation would have promoted its own purposes by exonerating man from *his* share in the total work. So far from *that*, thus and no otherwise it was – viz., by laying upon man a necessity for co-operating with heaven – that the compound object of this great revolution had any chance of being accomplished. It was as much the object of Christianity that he who exercised charity should be bettered, as he that benefited by charity – the agent equally with the object. Only in that way is Shakspere's fine anticipation realised of a two-fold harvest, and a double moral won; for the fountain itself

Is twice blessed:
It blesseth him that gives, and him that takes.'[k]

But if Providence had reserved to itself the whole of the work – not merely the first suggestion of a new and divine magnetism for interlinking reciprocally all members of the human family, but had also appropriated the whole process of deducing and distributing into separate rills the irrigation of God's garden upon earth, in that act it would have defeated on the largest scale its own scheme of training for man; just as much as if (according to a former speculation of mine) God, by condescending to teach science in the Bible (astronomy suppose, chronology, or geology), had thus at one blow, besides defrauding the true and avowed mission of the Bible, self-counteractingly stepped in to solve his own problems, and thus had violently intercepted those very difficulties which had been strewed in man's path *seriatim*,[l] and so as to advance by measured increments of difficulty, for the specific purpose of applying graduated irritations to the stimulation of man's intellect. Equally in the training of his moral habits, and in the development by successive steps of his intellect, man and the religion of man must move by co-operation; and it cannot be the policy or the true meaning of revelation to work towards any great purpose in man's destiny otherwise than through the co-agency of man's faculties, improved in the whole extent of their capacities. This case, therefore (of charity arising suddenly as a new command to man), teaches three great inferences: –

First, the power of a religion to stimulate vast developments in man, when itself stimulated by a social condition not sleeping and passive, but in a vigilant state of healthy activity.

Secondly, that if all continued cases of interchangeable development – that is, of the Bible downwards upon man, or reversely of man upwards upon the Bible and its interpretation – may be presumed to argue a concurrent action between Providence and man, it follows that the *human* element in the co-agency will always account for any admixture of evil or error, without impeaching in any degree the doctrine of a general overriding inspiration. For instance, I see little reason to doubt that economically the apostles had erred, and through their very simplicity of heart had erred, as to that joint-stock company which they, so ignorant of the world, had formed in an early stage of the infant church; and that Ananias and Sapphira[m] had fallen victims to a perplexity and a collision between their engagements and their natural rights, such as overthrew their too delicate sensibilities. But, if this were really so, the human element carries away from the divine all taint of reproach. There lies one mode of benefit from this joint agency of man and Providence.

Thirdly, we see here illustrated one amongst innumerable cases of development applicable to the Bible. And this power of development in general proves one other thing of the last importance to prove – viz., the power of Christianity to work in co-operation with time and social progress – to work variably, according to the endless variation of time and place. And this is the exact *shibboleth* of a spiritual religion.

For, in conclusion, here lies a consideration of deadliest importance. On reviewing the history of false religions, and inquiring what it was that ruined them, or caused them to tremble, or to exhibit premonitory signs of coming declension, rarely or never amongst such causes has been found any open exhibition of violence. The gay mythologic religion of Greece melted away in silence; that of Egypt, more revolting to unfamilarised sensibilities, more gloomy, and apparently reposing on some basis of more solemn and less allegoric reality, exhaled like a dream – *i.e.*, without violence, by *internal* decay. I mean, that no violence existed where the religion fell, and there *was* violence where it did *not*. For even the dreadful fanaticism of the early Mahometan sultans in Hindostan, before the accession of Baber[n] and his Mogul successors from the house of Timour,

SGG appends footnote 'Constantine that first:' – But let me warn the reader not to fancy that the public largesses of corn to the humbler citizens of Rome had intercepted the possibility of this precedency for Constantine by many generations before he was known, or even before Christianity was revealed. There was no vestige of charity in the Roman distributions of grain. These distributions moved upon the same impulse as the *sportulae*[o] of the great oligarchic houses, and the *donatives* of princely officers to their victorious soldiery upon great anniversaries, or upon accessions to the throne, or upon adoptions of successors, &c. All were political, oftentimes rolling through the narrowest grooves of intrigue; and so far from contemplating any collateral or secondary purpose of charity, that the most earnest inquiry on such occasions was – to find pretexts for excluding men from the benefit of the bounty. The primary thought was – who should *not* be admitted to participate in the dole. And at any rate none <were admissible> *were* admitted but citizens in the most rigorous and the narrowest sense. *Constantine* it was: I do not certainly know that I have anywhere called the reader's attention to another great monument which connected the name of Constantine by a separate and hardly noticed tie with the propagation of Christianity. What name is it that, being still verdant and most interesting to all the nations of Christendom, serves as a daily memorial to refresh our reverence for the emperor Constantine? What but his immortal foundation of *Constantinople*, imposed upon the ruins of the elder city Byzantium,[p] in the year of Christ 313, now therefore in the 1565th year of its age; which city of Constantinople is usually regarded, by those who have science comprehensive enough for valuing its various merits, as enjoying the most august site and circumstantial advantages, in reference to climate, commerce, navigation, sovereign policy, and centralisation, on this planet – with the doubtful reservation of one single South American station, viz., that of the Brazilian city Rio Janeiro (or, as we usually call it, Rio). Doubtless these magnificent natural endowments did much to influence the choice of Constantine; and yet I believe that no economic advantages, even though greater and more palpable, would have been sufficient to disengage his affections from a scene so consecrated by grand historical recollections as Rome, had not one overwhelming repulsion, ineradicably Roman, violently disenchanted him for ever. This turned upon religion. *Rome*, it was found, *could not be depaganised*. Too profound, too inveterately entangled with the very soil and deep substructions of Latium[q] were the old traditional records, promises, auguries, and mysterious splendours of concentrated Heathenism *in*, and *on*, and nine times *round about*, and 50 fathoms *below*, and countless fathoms <*overhead* above> in upper air *above* this most memorable of capital cities. Jupiter Capitolinus, the Sybil's Books, which for Roman minds were authentic, the dread cloister of Vestal Virgins, Jupiter Stator, and the undeniable omen of the Twelve Vultures* – centuries of mysterious sympathy between dim records and dim inquiries, could no more be washed away from the credulous heart of the Roman *plebs*, that the predictions of Nostradamus from the expecting and listening faith of Catherine de' Medici[r] and her superstitious court. In short, fifty baptisms could not have washed away the deep-seated scrofula of Paganism in Rome. Constantine therefore wisely drew away a select section of the population to the quiet waters of the Propontis (the *Sea of Marmara*,[s] which oblige me by pronouncing as if an imperfect rhyme to *armoury*, not as if the *o* in the penult. were accented). And thus, by a double service to Christianity – viz., by a solemn institution of charitable contributions to the poor, as their absolute right under the Christian law, and by a wise shepherd's segregation of diseased members from his flock – he earned meritoriously, and did not win by luck, that fortunate destiny which has locked up his name into that of the regenerated Rome – the earliest Christian city – and the mother of the Second, or the Oriental Roman Empire. *SGG appends footnote to footnote 'Omen of the twelve vultures:'*[t] – The reader must not allow himself to be repelled from the plain historic truth by foolish reproaches of superstition or credulity. The fact of twelve vultures having appeared under ceremonial circumstances, at what may be considered the inauguration of Rome, and was so understood at the time, is as certain as any fact the best attested in the history of Rome. And as it repeatedly announced itself during the lapse of these twelve centuries, when as yet they were far from being completed, there cannot be a reasonable doubt that a most impressive coincidence did occur between the early prophesy and its extraordinary fulfilment. In a gross general statement, such as *can* be made in a single sentence, we may describe the duration of Rome, from Romulus to Christ, as 750 years, which leaves about 450 to be accounted for, in order to make up the tale of <1200 years> the twelve vultures. And pretty exactly that number of 450, plus 2 or 3 suppose, measures the interval between Christ and Augustulus.[u]

SGG appends footnote It is interesting to observe, at this moment, how the proofs accumulate from the ends of the earth that the Roman C was always in value equal to K. The imperial name of Caesar has survived in two separate functions. It is found as a family name rooted amongst oriental peoples, and is always Keyser. But also it has survived as an official title, indicating the sovereign ruler. At this moment, from Milan, under the shadow of the Alps, to Lucknow,[v] under the shadow of the Himalayas, this immortal Roman name popularly expresses the office of the supreme magistrate. *Keyser* is the current titular designation of the king who till lately reigned over Oude;[w] and *der Kayser*, on the fiction which made the Empire of Germany a true lineal successor to the Western Roman Empire, has always indicated the Emperor – once German, now simply Austrian.

SGG appends footnote Coleridge, as may be seen in his 'Notes on English Divines,'[x] though free in a remarkable degree, for one so cloudy in his speculative flights, from any spirit of licentious tampering with the text of the New Testament, or with its orthodox explanation, was yet deeply impressed with the belief that the apostles had gone far astray in their first provision for the pecuniary necessities of the infant Church; and he went so far as to think that they had even seriously crippled its movements, by accumulations of debt that might have been evaded.

[[a] The Holy Eucharist: 'Joining our voices with Angels and Archangels and with all the company of heaven'.

[b] See above, p. 588, n. 39

[c] See above, p. 589, n. 11

[d] For St Paul, see above, p. 565, n. 27

[e] Pliny the Younger (*c.* AD 61–*c.* 113), Roman administrator and letter writer. He worked for the emperor Trajan (see above, p. 567, n. 54), and addressed a series of letters to him.

[f] For Aristotle, see above, p. 535, n. 38. Alexander the Great (356–23 BC), King of Macedonia. For Cicero, see above, p. 530, n. 47.

[g] See above, p. 589, n. 42.

[h] Cicero, *De Officiis*, I. 22: 'Yield, ye arms, to the toga; to civic praises, ye laurels'.

[i] 'Jus suffragii' is 'right to vote'.

[j] See above, p. 626, n. 2.

[k] Shakespeare, *The Merchant of Venice*, IV.i.186–7.

[l] 'Seriatim' is 'in a series'.

[m] See Acts 5: 1–11.

[n] More commonly, 'Babur' (1483-1530), emperor (1526-30) and founder of the Mughal dynasty of India.

[o] 'Sportulae' is, literally, 'little basket', in which it was customary for a patron to distribute presents of food or money.

[p] Byzantium (modern Istanbul) is an ancient Greek city on the shore of the Bosporus.

[q] Latium is an ancient area in west-central Italy.

[r] Nostradamus (1503-66), French astrologer and physician. He was invited to the court of Catherine de Médicis (1519-89), queen consort of Henry II of France, and subsequently regent of France, 1560-74.

[s] The Sea of Marmara partly separates the Asiatic and European parts of Turkey.

[t] Twelve vultures were said to have appeared to Romulus when he founded the city of Rome.

[u] Romulus Augustulus (*fl.* last quarter of the fifth century AD), the last of the Western Roman emperors (475-6).

[v] Lucknow is the capital of Uttar Pradesh state, northern India, on the Gomati River.

[w] More commonly, 'Oudh', historic region of north-central India. The British annexation of Oudh in 1856 was a contributing cause of the Indian Mutiny. Cf. De Quincey in *The Logic of Political Economy* (1844), where he describes the 'king of Oude' as 'a petty

Indian prince' (Vol. 14, p. 239).

[x] Samuel Taylor Coleridge, *Notes on English Divines*, ed. Derwent Coleridge, 2 vols (London: Moxon, 1853).]

263.13 **carrying** *Editorial; 1848* carrrying

263.20 **false religions** *Editorial; 1848* false reigions

263.24–6 **hollowness, under that searching trial....they have sunk away, as by palsy, from new** *SGG* hollowness, and by internal decay, under the searching trials applied by life and the changes of life, by social mechanism and the changes of social mechanism, which wait in ambush upon *every* mode of religion. False modes of religion could not respond to the demands exacted from them, or the questions emerging. One after one they have collapsed, as if by palsy, and have sunk away under new

263.29 **sank uniformly** *SGG* sank instinctively

263.30 **of accommodation.** *SGG* of plastic self-accommodation.

263.30–1 **furnished a key** *SGG* furnished always a key

263.32 **principle, by** *SGG* principle, through

263.33 **climate,* from century** *SGG* climate,* from land to land, from century

263.n.1 **Mahometans have been often scandalised and troubled by** *SGG* Mahometans are often troubled and scandalized by

263.n.2 **ignorant fellow. It** *SGG* ignorant man. It

263.n.3–4 **one had been conceived most narrowly. Many** *SGG* one was conceived by him under conditions too palpably limited. Many

263.n.4–6 **ablutions not adapted to their waterless condition. These evidences of oversight would have been fatal to Islamism, had Islamism produced a** *SGG* ablutions incompatible with their half-waterless position. Mahomet coming from Hedjas, a rich tract, and through that benefit the fruitful mother of noble horses, knew no more of the arid desert and Zaarahs than do I. These oversights of its founder would have proved fatal to Islamism, had Islamism succeeded in producing a

263.33 **from century** *SGG* from land to land, from

263.35–6 **a necessity, corresponding to such infinite flexibility of endless development.** *SGG* a corresponding necessity (corresponding, I mean, to such infinite flexibility) of an infinite development. The paganism of Rome, so flattering and so sustaining to the Roman nationality and pride, satisfied no spiritual necessity: dear to the Romans as citizens, it was at last killing to them as men.

War

Title **WAR, BY THOMAS DE QUINCEY** *F, SGG* ON WAR

269.3 **war, so ubiquitous, so ancient, and** *SGG* war, so ancient, so ubiquitous, and

269.5–6 **most highly civilized, may be looked on as tending** *SGG* most civilized, is tending

269.8 **execute that sentence.** *SGG* execute the sentence.

269.8–10 **views. The project seems to me the most romantic of all romances in the course of publication. Consequently,** *SGG* views. Of all romances, this seems to me the most romantic. Consequently,

269.10 **member in any** *SGG* member of any

269.13–14 **half a crown to the chief association for** *MS C* <to a {stain} ong to be recommended> foundation-stone of a Fund for *SGG* half-a-crown as the foundation-stone of a fund for

269.15 **the association, under** *SGG* the aforesaid fund, under

269.16 **Africa. I** *MS C* Africa. <And why not of Africa>? I

269.17 **money, she is not able** *SGG* money, so little is she able

269.20–1 **easily make good** *SGG* easily compensate

269.22–3 **be soon understood from the following explanation, by any gentleman that hopes to draw upon it.** *SGG* be readily understood by any gentleman that hopes to draw upon the fund, when he has read the following explanation.

269.26 **flat tablet of its horizontal** *SGG* flat quadrangular tablet of its upper horizontal

269.27 **height several *riyanas*, (which** *SGG* height the pillar measures several *riyanas* (which

269.31 **count your expectations** *SGG* count those expectations

269.33–4 **and the wealth of the human race in time, depend** *SGG* and the immeasurability of time, depend

269.36–7 **behind riches so appallingly too rich, that everybody is careless** *SGG* behind a time-fund so appallingly inexhaustible, that everybody becomes careless

270.1 **any private consumption of your own, you** *SGG* any consumption of your own, naturally you

270.5 **once in** *SGG* once, and *only* once, in

270.6 **visits this granite pillar. He is** *SGG* visits the granite pillar. This angel is

270.11–12 **as softly as** *SGG* as dreamily as

270.16 **we, the poor** *SGG* we, poor

270.17 **our earthly imprisonment. But** *SGG* our prison-period. But

270.19–20 **atom (no matter that it is an invisible atom) of** *SGG* atom of

270.23–4 **total funded debt of man's race to** *SGG* total arrearage of man's race, as debtors to

270.25–6 **our representatives** *SGG* our posterity

270.27–8 **angel, (who, if he were a good fellow, might just as well give a sly kick with his heel to the granite,) before** *SGG* angel, before

270.29 **accomplished. But you hear it expressed in** *MS C* accomplished. Some sceptics in Ceylon offer bets upon the granite against the muslin; conceiving that the attrition of the second by the first will far outrun the counter {↑ <of the> or inverse} or inverse attrition. But <they ought to fact that> {↑ at any rate} the muslin, being worn by an Angel, will never need washing. And the <orthodox> local *SGG* accomplished. Some sceptics in Ceylon offer bets upon the granite against the muslin; conceiving that the attrition of the second by the first will far outrun the inverse attrition. But, at any rate, the muslin, being worn by an angel, will never need washing; which, in oriental lands, is the capital mode of attrition – human or angelic. And the local

270.31–2 **quantity equal to a pinch of snuff. Despair** *SGG* quantity that is barely visible under a powerful lens. Despair

270.35 **accomplished, thank heaven, our** *SGG* accomplished, our

270.36–8 **a visiting card, which the meagre shadow cannot refuse to take, though he will sicken at seeing it; viz., a P.P.C.** *SGG* a P.P.C.

270.38–9 **the old thief is bound to give receipt** *SGG* the meagre shadow is bound to give a receipt

270.39 **and pretended arrears.** *SGG* and arrears.

270.43–44 **The reader perhaps knows of** *SGG omits paragraph break* Perhaps the reader and I know of

270.41 **off sooner than this** *SGG* off much before this

270.42 **And naturally, to** *SGG* Naturally, to

270.43–4 **slowly. My own** *MS B* <In fact> My <fund> own

270.43– 4 **an illustration. The half-crown will travel in the inverse** *MS B* an illustration <fine specimen of the class>. The half-crown {↑ will} travel<s and> in the <very> inverse

270.44 **pillar. The pillar** *MS B* pillar. <They me> The

271.1 **the half-crown move** *MS B* the <fund> {↑ half-crown} move

271.2 **(which it is for Algebra to investigate) when** *MS B* (which {↑ it is for} <I request that> Algebra to investigate <with apron>) when

271.3 **their several bisections – my** *SGG* their punctual decussation, as you see it expressed in a St Andrew's Cross, or letter X. From this half-way point of intersection, my

271.3 **my aspiring** *MS B* my <ambitious> aspiring

271.3 **half-crown tending** *SGG* half-crown will tend

271.4 **gradually towards** *MS B* gradually <(*very* gradually)> towards

271.6–7 **pillar is constantly unweaving its** *SGG* pillar will constantly unweave its

271.7 **dwindling earthwards. It** *MS B* dwindling {↑ earthwards.} <and groveling into low tendencies toward {↑ shameful} harkenings after mustard seeds> It *SGG* dwindle earthwards. It

271.8 **each of the parties will have reached its** *MS B* each <will> of the parties <the English half crown and the Ceylon pillar> will have reach<ed> its *SGG* each process will have reached its

271.10 **surplus, no body can** *MS B* surplus, nobody <that xx goes to the Doctors' Commons with a shilling for> can

271.12 **for any** *MS B* for <this> any

271.13–14 **to observe, that,** *MS B* to <say> observe – that,

271.14 **is reported to** *SGG* is proved to

271.16–17 **Service, including the** *SGG* Service, not excepting even the

271.17–18 **more half-pay; and even more clearly, there is an end to full-pay. Pensions** *MS B* more Half-Pay; and even more clearly, there is an end <at once> to Full-Pay. Pensions *SGG* more half-pay. Pensions

271.18–19 **service.' Allowances** *MS B* service.' <sincere service {↑ of any kind being} itself i at {↑ an} end. Allowances *MS C* service,' <or worth little more than Greek bonds> or fetch little more than Spanish and Greek bonds. Allowances. *SGG* service,' or fetch little more than Spanish and Greek bonds. Allowances

271.19 **wounds cannot** *MS B* wounds <are> cannot

271.19 **wounds shall have** *MS B* wounds <have themselves {↑ shall} have

271.21 **make any allowance at all. Bargains** *MS B* make any <reaction to> allowances at all. <These> Bargains *SGG* make much allowance. Bargains

271.23 **of it, as depended on rifles.** *SGG* of Birmingham as depended upon rifles.

271.24 **be hungering for beef, so** *SGG* be ruined for want of beef-steaks, so

271.25 **stretch after** *SGG* stretch out endlessly after

271.26 **war.** *MS C* war, <and would be ruinous, were they not all charged upon the huge sinking-fund of my half-crown.> and would tend to general bankruptcy, were they not all charged upon the interminable sinking-fund of my half-crown. *SGG* war, and would tend to general bankruptcy, were they not all charged upon the interminable sinking-fund of my half-crown.

271.27–8 **Now upon my half-crown fund (which will be equal to any thing by the time it is wanted) I** *SGG* Upon this fund it is (a fund able to meet anything by the time it is wanted) that I

271.28–30 **all these arrears – of the poverty, the loss, the bankruptcy, arising by reason of this *quietus* or final extinction applied to war. I** *SGG* all debts, deficiencies, or burdens incident to the final extinction of war. I

271.33 **unsocial lip** *SGG* unsocial life

271.36–8 **inexhaustible, because the period of its growth will be measured by the concurrent deposition of the Ceylon mustard-seed from the everlasting pillar.** *SGG* inexhaustible, seeing that it cannot cease growing so long as war continues to exist. Of necessity, therefore, the inexhaustibility of my provisional fund is concurrent with that of the granite pillar in Ceylon.

271.39 **see, or imagine that I see, a** *SGG* see a

271.40 **war – a necessity in two different senses – 1st,** *SGG* war: – 1st,

271.41–3 **situation; a necessity under which war...circumstances essential to human frailty. 2dly,** *SGG* situation; 2dly,

272.3–4 **spoliation; war is a scourge of God – granted:** *SGG* spoliation: granted

272.5 **itself in its character of a** *SGG* itself when viewed as a

272.8–10 **against, though all good men mourn over its existence and view it as an unconditional evil; or** *SGG* against; or

271.11–16 **man is nevertheless invoked....so that what separately** *SGG* man, that separately

271.13–14 **one only remedy** *MS C* one sole remedy

271.14 **evil and woe of** *MS C* evil <and woe> of

271.15–16 **other woe as** *MS C* other <woe> evil as

271.17 **hateful for itself, passes** *SGG* hateful, passes

271.19 **man.** *Editorial; 1848* man,

271.19–34 **instance, is in both senses necessary for man....labours for its mitigation. War** *MS C* instance, both senses necessary for man. It is necessary in the same sense as thirst is necessary (*i.e.* inevitable) in a fever – necessary as one corollary amongst <many> others, from <the eternal hollowness of all> human <efforts for organizing any perfect model of society> imbecility – a corollary which, how gladly would all of us unite to cancel, but which our hearts suggest, which Scripture <solemnly> proclaims, to be ineradicable from the land. In this sense, poverty is a necessity over which we *mourn*, – as one of the dark phases that sadden the vision of human life. But far differently, and with a stern gratitude, we recognize another mode of necessity for this gloomy distinction – a high moral call for poverty, when seen in relation to the manifold agencies by which it developes human energies, when seen in relation to the trials by which it searches the power of patience and religion, – seen in relation to the struggles by which it evokes the nobilities of fortitude; or again, amongst those who are not sharers in these trials and struggles, but sympathizing spectators, – when seen in relation to the stimulation by which it quickens the wisdom that watches over the causes of this evil, or <by which it> vivifies the spirit of love that labours for its mitigation. War *SGG* instance, stands in both categories of this twofold necessity. As a growth of physical necessity, it forms part of the primal curse; and the Scriptures warn us that it will never cease out of the land.[a] But, by the grandeur of man's nature, it is disarmed of its sting; and acting as a *moral* coercion upon the human will, it extorts innumerable graces of patience, of heroic resistance, of heaven-born energy, that would else have languished. War

[[a] See above, p. 589, n. 11.]

272.37 **impassioned exaltations.** *SGG* impassioned grandeurs.

272.38 **these. *First*, that** *SGG* these: 1st, that

272.41–4 **power is, though sincerely I grieve in avowing...weakness, to blush – not** *SGG* power is – not

272.44 **curse, no not at all, but** *SGG* curse, but

273.3 **me. I believe that's** *SGG* me. That's

273.5 **admirals. '*Pereant*** *MS C* admirals. I protest that I should have used these words even if Themistocles[a] had <broken his backbone in his 14th year, died of pulmonary consumption in his 10th year> absconded into Scythia in his boyhood. '*Pereant SGG* admirals. I protest that I should have used these words even if Themistocles had absconded into Scythia in his boyhood. '*Pereant*

[[a] See above, p. 589, n.12.]

273.7 **abolished. The** *SGG* abolished; the

273.9 **first. One at a time. Sufficient for the page is the evil thereof! How** *SGG* first. How

273.16 **by innumerable books,)** *SGG* by books)

273.18 **them. If** *SGG* them. The one mistake might authorise the other. If

273.22–4 **resistance, supposing such forces...to be permanently disposable for action, might** *SGG* resistance, might

273.24–5 **against a few personal authors of war, so presumably weak,** *SGG* against personal and casual authors of war, so weak

273.26 **supposed, whose wars argued** *SGG* presumed, whose wars had argued

273.33–5 **mendacity. Where is the Scotchman, said Dr Johnson, who does not prefer Scotland to truth? but, however this may be, rarer such a Scotchman, rarer** *SGG* mendacity. Rarer

273.39 **tissue of lies.** *SGG* tissue of falsehoods.

273.42 **is all that remains of** *MS C* is the main record of *SGG* is the main relique of

273.44–274.10 **Are these words then...or as vouchers for a fact.** *SGG omits*

274.11 **rule of unlimited application, – that, when** *SGG* rule, that, when

274.14 **false to a certainty. One** *SGG* false. One

274.17–18 **ascribed at Vienna, 90 years ago, to the Prince de Ligne, and 30 years previously to Voltaire,** *MS C* ascribed <in the> in the year 1814-15 at the Congress of Vienna <at Vienna, ninety years ago> to the Prince of de Ligne; <and thirty years previously> about 50 years earlier many of the {↑ same *mots* were} ascribed to the same Prince de Ligne,[a] then a young man: <oh de Ligne> 20 or 30 years earlier still they had been ascribed <to> to Voltaire, *SGG* ascribed in the year 1814-15, at the Congress of Vienna, to the Prince of Ligne; about fifty years earlier, many of the same *mots* were ascribed to that same Prince de Ligne, then a young man; twenty or thirty years earlier still, they had been ascribed to Voltaire,

[[a] See above, p. 590, n. 19.]

274.n.18 **that his Excellency, the diplomatist, had** *SGG* that the Right Reverend French Knave had

274.n.20 **his innocent childhood** *SGG* his childhood

274.n.20–1 **was in** *SGG* was yet in

274.n.21 **almost before he** *SGG* almost as soon as he

274.23 **thing you know claimed** *SGG* thing, claimed

274.24 **them could** *SGG* them, you know, could

275.3 **Christians, they being** *SGG* Christians, these ancients being

275.n.7–11 **Simply to have been previously unpublished...could be openly affirmed.** *SGG omits*

275.20–7 **false, (a thing that hereafter I shall...their circumstantial relations. For** *MS C* false, more especially <pro> such are all those anecdotes which <trace> for the sake of raising wonderment, trace great wars to trivial domestic brawls. For *SGG* false, more especially such are all those anecdotes which, for the sake of raising wonderment, trace great wars to trivial domestic brawls. For

275.32–276.1 **ladies, and that feud, (if I remember) tracing** *SGG* ladies, tracing

276.4–5 **of 100,000 men each, and with** *SGG* of fifty thousand men each, with

276.6 **industrious artist** *SGG* mendacious artists

276.7–22 **This man knows how to group his figures....which they will sustain.** *SGG omits*

276.23 **Louvois,** *F, SGG* Luvois,

276.26 **suddenly a task so delicate as that of** *SGG* suddenly the task of

276.27 **in a Council Chamber with** *SGG* in council with

276.33–5 **Let us see. What *was* the logic....traveled in the following channel.** *SGG omits*

276.38 **ancient, and apparently so** *SGG* ancient, or so

277.4–5 **war. / If** *SGG omits paragraph break*

277.5 **accidents could,** *SGG* accidents, and accidents so trivial, could,

277.6 **to combine personal influences that** *SGG* to preconcert personal combinations that

277.9–10 **the whole fountains** *SGG* the fountains

277.13 **enough or steady enough to merit that name. Multitudes** *SGG* enough to face and control them. Multitudes

277.14 **system, simply because** *SGG* system, merely because

277.17 **commence in new views upon war; and** *SGG* commence from the moment when the true sources of the evil were detected; and

277.21 **might be true, but were delusive. The** *SGG* might tell the truth, but not the whole truth. The

277.21–2 **they substituted an occasion for a cause.** *SGG* they confounded an occasion with a cause.

277.24–5 **true permanent causes** *SGG* true and ultimate causes

277.29 **adjacent nations,** *SGG* rival nations,

277.30 **no supreme *Areopagus*, or court of appeal, for** *SGG* no Council of Amphictions[a] for

[[a] 'Amphictyons...Deputies from the different states of ancient Greece composing an assembly or council' (*OED*).]

277.31–2 **war, because an external matrix of disputes lies in** *SGG* war – viz., in

277.32 **continually the same,** *SGG* dangerously the same,

277.33 **too close, that are continually different, and so far the** *SGG* too keen; that are dangerously different, and therefore the

277.37 **continual (because insensible) losses** *SGG* continual losses

277.42–4 **and sad it is to think that at intervals the acts and the temper suitable to those glaring eyes *must*** *SGG* and at intervals the acts suitable to such a temper *must*

278.7–8 **rest; not an enmity that belongs to** *SGG* rest; an enmity that does not belong to

278.9 **its right hand upon the hilt of its sword,** *SGG* her right hand upon the hilt of her sword,

278.15–16 **be relied on during** *SGG* be looked for during

278.16 **war, to tranquillize its wounds. Consequently** *SGG* war. Consequently

278.19–21 **time. Really, says he, I must find out some little war to exhaust the *surplus* irritability of this person, or he'll be the death of me. But irritable** *SGG* time. Irritable

278.22 **naturally have** *SGG* naturally, within a year or two, have

278.23 **Europe, within a very few months. So** *SGG* Europe. So

278.27–8 **and prolonged it, was sure to be angrily reviewed by** *SGG* and what prolonged it – were sure to be sternly scrutinized by

278.28–9 **annual exposition of the Finance Minister's Budget. These ladies, and the** *SGG* annual revision of the national finances. These ladies, and even the

278.29–30 **could at the utmost have** *SGG* could not have *caused* a war; they at the utmost might have

278.31 **gunner, the captain of a gun at** *SGG* gunner at

278.32–3 **fact) let loose and unmuzzle** *SGG* fact) unmuzzle

278.35 **longer, whether** *SGG* longer (such was the temper of the Turkish forces), whether

278.35–6 **fired the unauthorized gun or not.** *SGG* fired, or had forborne to fire, the unauthorised shot.

278.37–279.8 **But now, let me speak...its rapid degradation.** *SGG omits paragraph*

279.9 **One, in fact, of** *MS C* <In orde If therefore it is war is to exist in a high, regular, controllable, and authentic shape, amenable to principles of reinforced self-restraint> *SGG* One of

279.15 **under the national laws.** *SGG* under municipal laws.

279.18 **inverse course** *SGG* inverted course

279.20–5 **community. If again it is attempted...national police, administered** *MS C* community; from the lawless guerrilla state which <belongs If again it is attempted...national> police, administered *MS E* community; from the lawless *guerilla* <state which police> to the state of national war administered *SGG* community; from the lawless *guerilla*, to the state of national war administered

279.25 **the dignified responsibility** *SGG* the responsibility

279.28 **in warfare, which in the war of** *SGG* in human conflicts, which in a warfare of

279.29 **instantly decay,** *SGG* rapidly decay,

279.31 **run along side by side with the** *SGG* run alongside the

279.31 **civilization; look** *SGG* civilisation. Look

279.36 **nobility: and** *SGG* nobility. Look back, I say, to this, and

279.38 **ghastly ruin of his own right arm, so** *SGG* ghastly ruins worked by his own separate arm; so

279.39 **brutality is losing half of its demoralization.** *SGG* brutality, has lost half of its demoralising power.

280.9–10 **But mark, such** *SGG* But such

280.12–13 **become more perilously** *MS C* become so much <more> perilous *SGG* become perilously

280.14 **become the** *SGG* become so much the

280.15–16 **agents. However, at length, we will suppose the impossible problem solved – war, we will assume, is at last put down.** *SGG* agents.

280.17–282.14 **At length there is no more war....homage to Christianity will answer.** *SGG omits four paragraphs and a footnote*

282.15 **improve!** *F, SGG* improve?

282.22 **as the last resource, this** *SGG* as our last resource in the prosecution of national disputes, this

282.28–9 **developed. A** *MS C* developed. <But> But the cause of {↑ this} insufficient development lies in our defective civilisation, and <xxx> in {↑ explanatory} <our> intercourse {↑ between nations} too humid and passionate. *SGG* developed. A

282.33 **its system.** *SGG* its comprehension.

282.35 ***Consolato del Mare* had** *SGG* 'Consolato del Mare,' the 'Laws of Oleron,'[a] &c., had

[[a] The 'Rolls of Oléron' apparently date from the twelfth century, and became the nucleus of maritime law in England and France.]

283.1 **again will the** *SGG* again, would the

283.3 **it, will but** *SGG* it, does but

283.7–8 **poltroon (and moreover you *invite* injuries from every neighbour) if** *SGG* poltroon (and you *invite* injuries), if

283.8 **pocket your** *MS E* pocket what <are> you think your *SGG* pocket what you think your

283.12 **regimen. But mark, even** *SGG* regimen. Yet, even

283.17 **limit itself.** *SGG* narrow itself.

283.17–18 **war becomes** *MS C* war, the very admission of the truth that war cannot be dispensed with as our <final> ultimate appeal, becomes *SGG* war, the very admission of the truth that war cannot be dispensed with as our ultimate appeal, becomes

283.19 **its sole limitation. But all war whatsoever stands in those circumstances. It** *MS C* its <sole> final limitation. <At this moment no state, not even France in whose national mind war stands at the most childish that confine Sparta in holding war to be the sup. ob. of m But all war whatsoever stands in those circumstances>. It *SGG* its final limitation. It

283.21 **warfare,** *MS E appends footnote 'Spartan warfare':* – It was a tradition in Greece, that about seven centuries Before Christ the Iliad was carried into Sparta;[a] some said, by Lycurgus the lawgiver[b] when returning from his travels. But the tradition added that the {↑ importer} <importer let him have been he who he might deliberately refused to import> {↑ excluded} the Odyssey; {↑ not as being *non*-Homeric – for which objection that age was not critical enough – but as tending <and upon this argument – that it tended> to cherish <domestic> ideas of happiness derived from <the dom peace> {↑ peace} and the domestic affections; whereas the Iliad {↑ exhibited} <taught men to regard> war as the final object for which man {↑ existed} <was created>. Whether this tradition were well-founded or not, it shews <no> us in either case what was the reputed character {↑ through Greece} of the Spartan <dog>. No <nation> tribe of semi savages <that ever existed di> on record ever labored so effectually {↑ as the Spartans} to strip war of all its grandeur by clothing it with ungenerous arrogance; and the consequence is – that all readers {↑ to this day} rejoice <when the> in every defeat and humiliation which this kennel of hounds sustained. *SGG revises footnote 'Spartan warfare:'* – It was a tradition in Greece, that about seven centuries before Christ the 'Iliad' was carried into Sparta; some said, by Lycurgus the lawgiver when returning from his travels. But the tradition added, that the importer excluded the 'Odyssey;' not as being non-Homeric – for which objection that age was not critical enough; but as tending to cherish ideas of happiness derived from peace and the domestic affections; whereas the 'Iliad' exhibited war as the final object for which man existed. Whether this tradition were well-founded or not, it shows us in either case what was the reputed character through Greece of the Spartan. No tribe of semi-savages on record ever laboured so effectually as the Spartans to strip war of all its grandeur by clothing it with ungenerous arrogance; and the consequence is, that all readers to this day rejoice in every defeat and humiliation which this kennel of hounds sustained.

[[a] Sparta is the ancient capital of the Laconia district of the southeastern Peloponnese. A military oligarchy ruled the Spartan city-state from the sixth to the second century BC.

[b] Lycurgus (*fl.* seventh century BC), traditionally, the lawgiver who founded most of the institutions of ancient Sparta. De Quincey draws on Plutarch, *Lives*, Lycurgus, IV. 3-4: Lycurgus 'made his first acquaintance with the poems of Homer…and when he saw that the political and disciplinary lessons contained in them were worthy of no less serious attention than the incentives to pleasure and license which they supplied, he eagerly copied and compiled them in order to take them home with him'.]

283.22 **bounty offered to men upon** *SGG* bounty or premium upon

283.22–3 **and final adjudication** *SGG* and adjudication

283.23 **which war** *SGG* which it is that war

283.24–284.23 **Hence it is, viz., because the true….then we'll turn rebels. / Now** *MS C* Hence it is, viz., because the true boundaries of reciprocal rights are for ever ascertaining themselves more clearly, that war is growing less frequent. The fields open to injustice (which originally from pure ignorance were so vast) continually (through deeper and more expansive surveys by man's intellect – searching – reflecting – comparing) are contracting themselves. The causes of war that still remain, are causes on which international law happens <to be> hitherto to have been silent, or not to have spoken with an authentic voice <but which>. Such cases are continually withdrawing themselves, from that state of imperfect development which encouraged <dispute and x an> war, to a higher state in which they allowed of an amicable decision. All this we may see <peacefully a> mirrored in <the> a class in a class of cases that powerfully illustrate the good and bad in war, viz viz. in those cases of domestic life which <fall un> continually arise under the law of neighbourhood. This law / Now *SGG* Such cases are continually withdrawing themselves, from that state of imperfect development which enforced a warlike appeal, to a state in which they allow of an amicable solution. All this we may see mirrored in a class of cases that powerfully illustrate the good and the bad in war – viz., those cases of domestic dispute which continually arise under the law of neighbourhood. / Now

284.24 **itself and settled itself, as** *SGG* itself, as

284.25 **actions or legal suits. If** *SGG* actions at law. If

284.26 **to eat** *SGG* to consume

284.26 **smoke, or (if he chooses) to make his chimnies eat it. Here you see is a** *SGG* smoke. Here is beheld a

284.27 **war; in** *SGG* war. In

284.28–9 **men, paper bullets in the form of *Qui tam* and *Scire facias*, beat** *SGG* men, judicial investigations beat

284.32 **national attornies, *i.e.*, diplomatists.** *SGG* national attorneys – that is, through diplomatists.

284.33 **For instance, now I have myself seen a** *SGG* I have myself witnessed a

284.36–8 **flower-garden. I, a chance spectator…so it would have** *SGG* flower-garden. This wrong might have

284.41–2 **as the natural remedy for his own wrong, that** *SGG* as an obvious remedy for his own outrage, that

284.43 **forward on** *SGG* forward indefinitely on

284.44 **passing it back, without** *SGG* passing back the rubbish, without

285.1 **now, is a** *SGG* now was a

285.6 **this, does** *SGG* this distressing fact, does

285.7 **of Hampshire, Dorset, &c.,** *SGG* of Dorset, Devon, &c.,

285.9 **cannot summarily send back to self-support, at each jail-delivery. 'What** *SGG* cannot otherwise dispose of at each jail delivery. 'What

285.12 **dukes, to the** *SGG* dukes for the

285.19 **system. But, in a quiet way Jersey** *MS C* system; though in a quiet way Jersey, *SGG* system; though, by the way, Jersey
285.20 **been engaged** *MS E* been <quietly> engaged *SGG* been engaged
285.20 **rarely fails** *SGG* rarely, I am told, fails
285.21–2 **season. What amuses one besides, in** *MS C* But what <What> amuses <one besides>, in *SGG* season. But what amuses one, in
285.n.1 ***euphuismus*; but** *MS D, SGG euphemismus*, the sweet, caressing mode of expressing the case; but
285.n.2 **English soil,** *SGG* English border,
285.24 **ripe enough for** *SGG* ripe for
285.25–6 **wilderness, saying – Now, boys, shift for yourselves, and** *SGG* wilderness of Northumberland, saying, Now, boys, shift for yourselves; repent; and
285.26 **Englishmen.** *MS C* Even before the Union with Scotland, this was a public wrong. It is a literal fact – that long and long after the
285.28 **to a hostile** *SGG* to an increasing hostile
285.38 **arisen under the** *SGG* arisen during the
285.39 **and gradually** *SGG* and will gradually
286.3 **the particular statute** *SGG* the generalities of the statute
286.6 **erect a real Areopagus, or central congress for** *SGG* erect an operative tribunal, or central Amphictionic Council for
286.7–8 **would neutralize itself by re-acting as** *SGG* would re-act as
286.9 **such decrees; but** *SGG* such arrogant decrees – but
286.12 **of retiring from war. Not** *SGG* of making concessions. Not
286.13–14 **of congress,** *SGG* of a congress,
286.20 **war, which, for** *SGG* war (which
286.24–5 **the possibilities of** *SGG* the continued duration of
286.25–6 **being certainly in** *SGG* being to a certainty in
286.26–7 **tolerable certainty** *SGG* tolerable guarantee
286.28–9 **on Perpetual Peace, and with great sagacity, though otherwise that little work is not free from visionary self-delusions: and** *SGG* on a Perpetual Peace; and
286.30 **are so** *SGG* are at present so
286.31–2 **wars. This seems to the inexperienced reader a** *SGG* wars. To the inexperienced this seems a
286.33 **it may have been so; but** *SGG* it may be so;
286.33–4 **been done under the secret dictation of powerful** *MS E* been <under the> secret dictation <of> from powerful *SGG* been the result of secret dictation from powerful
286.36–7 **but the very worst: because** *MS C* but amongst the <very> worst: because *SGG* but the worst; because
287.1 **arise. Now, this** *MS E* arise. And yet <since now> how easily might this *SGG* arise. And yet how easily might this
287.1 **war could and would be** *MS C* war might be *MS E* war <might> be *SGG* war be
287.2 **an easy reform** *SGG* a reform
286.n.2 **Kant, from brevity, has** *SGG* Kant has
286n.2–287.n.1 **provision for** *SGG* provision at all for
287.n.1 **are likely enough to rise. A** *SGG* are inevitable. A
287.n.3 **desperately and equally pacific,** *SGG* desperately pacific,
287.n.5 **so, but** *SGG* so! but
287.n.5 **must, for what says the treaty?** *MS C* must, for {stain} the {↑ the} treaty <has> makes no provision for keeping the peace. <The very same evil with corre-

sponding consequences, is exhibited daily in domestic life> in the particular case before us. The very same evil, <arise> from the <same> very same neglect of provi<sion>ding for cases sure to arise, <is the> forms the most extensive source of disputes in domestic life. <what says the treaty?> *SGG* must, because the treaty makes no provision for keeping the peace in the particular case before us. The very same evil, from the very same neglect of providing for cases sure to arise, forms the most extensive source of disputes arising upon contracts in domestic life.

287.18 **had emanated** *SGG* had originally emanated

287.19–20 **which originally commenced** *SGG* which had commenced

287.20 **convenience. A Roman** *SGG* convenience. For instance, a Roman

287.21 **rank, out** *SGG* rank, as luxury advanced, out

287.23 **her; gradually** *MS C* her; this {↑ love} <reacted> by <thos gro> natural reaction {↑ <the lady's>} <upon her own sensibilities>, awakened her <most> own benevolent <capacities> sensibilities; gradually *SGG* her; this love, by natural reaction, awakened her own benevolent sensibilities; gradually

287.25 **to the sympathies with cruelty,** *SGG* to cruelty,

287.26 **purpose had** *SGG* purpose originally had

287.38 **pomp. Splendour** *SGG* pomp. Martial music, splendour

288.3–4 **war into connexion with modes of intellectual grandeur, and with the endless restraints of superstition or scrupulous religion, – a permanent** *SGG* war, a

288.8 **though merely** *SGG* though still

288.10 **scientific arts,** *SGG* subordinate arts,

288.13 **resources of science. War** *MS C* resources, mathematic and philosophic a <highly intellectual> complex science. War *SGG* resources, mathematic and philosophic, of a complex science. War

288.15 **self-preservation, became continually more** *SGG* self-preservation, becomes, continually, and must become, more

288.18–19 **impulses of self-conservation, and when searching with a view to more effectual destructiveness, war did and must refine itself** *SGG* impulses of self-defence, and with a view to more effectual destructiveness) war exalted itself

288.26–34 **Meantime a more circumstantial review of war....who (like myself) deny it.** *MS C* <But> Thus far {↑ meantime} war {↑ <at as at present existing>} has been <is> palliated merely by its relation to <its own elder stages is> something else; viz. to its own other stages as {↑ trespassing <less> much more upon human happiness and progress; <much less humanized> and <to> secondly by its relation to <the> any conceivable state <that could be so of things that social arrangement> that could take place <in the event> on the assumption that war <at a recognized and authorized state> were abolished {↑ by a Pan-christian compact.} <Thus far {↑ on this view} war is too flagrantly Argued {↑ treated} from this station, war is too palpably and redundantly defensible. It trespasses upon human happiness and {↑ upon} human progress by many degrees less than it did in its elder and {↑ ruder} <ruder> stages, and by degrees incalculably less than would attend the {↑ any such} lawless guerrilla state ↑ as} that must succeed to the {↑ supposed} abolition of {↑ regular} war xxx legalized and rational – public, answered {↑ authorized and and} rational and systematized. On this mode of treat dealing with the question war is justified as the lesser of two evils; and certainly as the lesser by {↑ increasing} immeasurably degrees.> But is this all that can be pleaded {↑ on behalf of} <for> war? Is it good only in so far as it stands opposed to something worse? No. War Under circumstances that may exist and have existed, {↑ War} is a *positive* good; not relative merely or negative but positive. <amongst the agencies that silently mold the gran-

deur of man is war ranks with the noblest, and keeps open a spiracle or organ of respiration for {↑ utter human tendencies} celestial purposes in man that except by in that last extremity cannot, except by war, be fixed {↑ that}cannot, by any {↑ other} language {↑ than that} but that of the sword, find utterances or expression all – He did Wordsworth.> A great truth it was, which Wordsworth uttered, whatever might be the {↑ <range of> expansion} which he allowed to it, <expansion which grounds on which he held it> when he said that

'God's most perfect instrument,
In working out a pure intent,
Is Man – arrayed for mutual slaughter:
Yea, Carnage is his Daughter?'[a]

There is a mystery in <the> approach<ed>{↑ ing} <to> this aspect of the case which no man {↑ has} <had> read fully <or perhaps ever *will* read>. War has a deeper and more ineffable relation to hidden <sanctities> {↑ grandeurs} in men, <nature>, than has <ever> {↑ yet} been deciphered. To execute judgements {↑ of retributions} upon <the last> outrages offered to human rights {↑ or to} <and> human dignity, to vindicate the sanctities of the altar and the sanctities of the heart, – there ↑ functions of human greatness which} <offices which> war has many times assumed, and {↑ many times} <gloriously discharged> faithfully {↑ discharged} <fulfilled>. But behind all these, there <is another. The great phenomenon of War> towers dimly a greater. The great phenomenon of War it is, this and this only, which keeps open {↑ in man} a spiracle <or as> – an organ of respiration – for <dealing> breathing a transcendent atmosphere, and dealing with <a> an idea that else would perish, viz., the idea of mixed {↑ Crusade and martyrdom, <and Crusade> doing and suffering, that finds its realisation in a battle such as that of Waterloo;[b] <that is> viz. a battle <that for> {↑ fought} for interests of the human *race*, felt even where they are not understood; so that the tutelary angel of man, when he traverses such a dreadful field, <when read> {↑ when he} reads the distorted features, counts the ghastly ruins, sums the hidden anguish, and the harvests

'Of horror breathing from the silent ground,'[c]

nevertheless, <as> speaking as God's messenger, 'blesses it, and calls it very good.'[d] *MS F, SGG conform, with the exception of ten significant variants in MS F given here in angle brackets* What opening is there for complaint? If the object is, to diminish the frequency of war, this is, at any rate, secured by the enormous and growing costliness of war. In these days of accountability on the part of governments, and of jealous vigilance on the part of tax-payers, we may safely leave it to the main interests of almost every European population not to allow of idle or frivolous wars. Merely the public debts of Christendom form a pledge, were there no other, that superfluous war will no longer be tolerated <either> by those who pay for them, <or by those who> and whose children inherit their consequences. The same cause, which makes war continually rarer, will tend to make each separate war shorter. There will, therefore, in the coming generations, be less of war; and what there is will, by expanding civilisation, and, indirectly, through <the> science continually more exquisite* <required in their> applied to its administration, be indefinitely humanised and refined.

It is sufficient, therefore, as an apology for war, that it is – 1st, systematically improving <the> in temper (privateering, for instance, at sea, sacking of cities by land, are in a course of abolition); 2dly, that it is under a necessity of becoming less frequent; 3dly, that on any attempt to abolish it, the result would be something very much worse.

Thus far, meantime, war has been palliated merely by its relation to something else – viz., to its own elder stages as trespassing much more upon human happiness and progress; and, secondly, by its relation to any conceivable state that could take place on the assumption that war were abolished by a Pan-Christian compact. But is this all that can be pleaded on behalf of war? Is it good only in so far as it stands opposed to something worse? No. Under circumstances that may exist, and have existed, war is a *positive* good; not relative merely, or negative, but positive. A great truth it was which Wordsworth uttered, whatever might be the expansion which he allowed to it, when he said that

'God's most perfect instrument,
In working out a pure intent,
Is man – array'd for mutual slaughter:
Yea, Carnage is his daughter.'

There is a mystery in approaching this aspect of the case, which no man has read fully. War has a deeper and more ineffable relation to hidden grandeurs in man, than has yet been deciphered. To execute judgments of retribution upon outrages offered to human rights or to human dignity, to vindicate the sanctities of the altar and the sanctities of the hearth – these are functions of human greatness which war has many times assumed, and many times faithfully discharged. But, behind all these, there towers dimly a greater. The great phenomenon of war it is, this and this only, which keeps open in man a spiracle – an organ of respiration – for breathing a transcendent atmosphere, and dealing with an idea that else would perish – viz., the idea of mixed crusade and martyrdom, doing and suffering, that finds its realisation in a battle such as that of Waterloo – viz., a battle fought for interests of the human *race*, felt even where they are not understood; so that the tutelary angel of man, when he traverses such a dreadful field, when he reads the distorted features, counts the ghastly ruins, sums the hidden anguish, and the harvests

'Of horror breathing from the silent ground,'

nevertheless, speaking as God's messenger, 'blesses it, and calls it very good.' *SGG appends footnote 'Science more exquisite:'* – How inadequately this is appreciated, may be seen in the popular opinion applied to our wars with the Chinese and Burmese – viz., that gradually we <should> shall teach those semi-barbarous peoples to fight. Some obvious improvements, purchasable with money, it is probable enough, will be adopted from us. But as to any general improvement of their military system, this is not of a nature to be transferred. The science, for instance, applied to our artillery and engineering systems, presupposes a total change of education, and the establishment of new institutions. <For instance, not only> It will not be sufficient to have institutions for teaching mathematics; <but> these must be supported by <calls for> a demand for mathematic knowledge <in others quarters not so fluctuating as the momentary calls of a war-office> in every quarter of public industry, in civil engineering, in nautical commerce, in mining, &c. Moreover, the manufacturing establishments that would be required as a basis of support for the improved science, such as cannon foundries, manufactories of philosophical instruments, &c., presuppose a concurrent expansion in many other directions, so as to furnish not only new means, but also new motives, and, in short, presuppose an entire new civilisation.

[[a] See above, p. 591, n. 38.

[b] Cf. De Quincey in 'The English Mail-Coach': 'We waited for a secret word, that should bear witness to the hope of nations, as now accomplished for ever. At midnight the secret word arrived; which word was – Waterloo and Recovered Christendom! (see

above, pp. 445–6).
[c] Wordsworth, 'After Visiting the Field of Waterloo', l. 14: 'And horror breathing from the silent ground!'
[d] Coleridge, 'Religious Musings', l. 113: 'And blesses it, and calls it very good. Cf. Genesis 1: 31: 'God saw everything that he had made: and behold, it was very good'.]

Sortilege on Behalf of the Glasgow Athenaeum

Title: **SORTILEGE ON BEHALF OF THE GLASGOW ATHENAEUM** *SGG* SORTILEGE ON BEHALF OF A LITERARY INSTITUTION
291.2–3 **of the Glasgow Athenaeum. What** *SGG* of a new Literary Institution, called the Athenaeum, in a great western city. What
291.7–8 **respect to bread,** *SGG* respect of bread,
291.7 **allowance of Paris; but,** *SGG* allowance (*pain à discrétion*) of Paris *restaurants*; but,
291.7–292.3 ***discrétion.* In this case, now, all....but one; and it was** *SGG discrétion.* And thus it happened that there was no resource available but one; which was
292.5 **six inches** *SGG* three inches
292.6 **by another mode of bathing, has** *SGG* by a better, has
292.14 **too ardent.** *SGG* too jealous.
292.19–20 **post. What the deuce! one can't answer *every*body by return post. – Now,** *SGG* post. – Now
292.27 **for this allegation, I** *SGG* for such allegations, I
292.28 **female attorneys,** *SGG* female lawyers,
292.40–1 **overlooking the movements of the young man and myself, the** *SGG* overlooking any irregular movements, the
292.44 **ineffectually. This angered me, and I** *SGG* ineffectually. I
293.2 **my kingdom; 'but for** *SGG* my possessions: 'But for
293.6 **to Glasgow this** *SGG* to the Athenaeum this
293.8 **Shakspere,** *SGG appends footnote Merchant of Venice.*
293.10 **to Glasgow, she** *SGG* to the Athenaeum, she
293.32 **for Glasgow, there** *SGG* for the Athenaeum, there
293.34 **under the corresponding** *SGG* under corresponding
293.37–8 **for, though twenty days after date, it** *SGG* for it
293.42 ***To eat*** *MS A appends footnote Esse* to eat: – The reader, who may chance to be no great scholar {↑ as regards Latin} will yet perhaps be aware of this meaning attached {↑ of old} to the verb {↑ *Esse*} <seem> <xxxx> <to most ancient use> from a Latin enigma current amongst schoolboys, viz. *Pes est caput*, which at first sight seems to say that *the foot is the head*: but in the true version means – *Pes* [<which> in its secondary sense <is> the same as *Pediculus* – an insect not to be named] *est* eats – *caput* the head. *SGG revises footnote Esse*, to eat: – The reader, who may chance to be no great scholar as regards Latin, will yet perhaps be aware of this meaning attached of old to the verb *Esse*, from a Latin enigma current amongst schoolboys, viz., *Pes est caput*, which at first sight seems to say that the *foot is the head:* but in the true version means – *Pes* [in its secondary sense, the same as *Pediculus* – an insect not to be named] *est*, eats – *caput*, the head.
293.43 **at ball suppers or Barmecide** *SGG* at Barmecide
294.9–17 **Portia parried this objection...I replied with equal sternness.** *SGG omits*
294.18–21 **concerning that rather visionary...with his aerial essence** *SGG omits*
294.27–8 **15th; '*Prepare to ...Dine*!' – only, by** *SGG* 15th. Only, by

294.34 **like an air-bubble;** *SGG* like a soap-bubble;
295.3 **eternal specimens** *SGG* eternal varieties
295.9–11 **I therefore became as anxious...the dipper's arm was working.** *SGG omits*
295.44 **that Glasgow had** *SGG* that a great city had
296.8 **you'll founder!'** *SGG* you'll founder.'
296.14–15 **personal, besides being founded in error from first to last. I** *SGG* personal. I
296.20–1 **body, in fee simple and not in fee conditional,' (mark Portia's learning as an attorney,) 'then** *SGG* body, then
296.23–4 **along.' Tears rushed to my eyes....my friend Potato-sack! will** *SGG* along.' In the tone of an injured man I cried out, 'friend Potato-sack! will
296.25 **me, that am as innocent as the child unborn? If** *SGG* me? If
296.28 **motion for a fresh trial. I** *SGG* motion. I
296.29 **more readily, because** *SGG* more because
296.35 **female address, that** *SGG* female art and readiness, that,
296.36 **they'll swear it's a** *SGG* they'll proclaim it a
296.37 **may seem to justify this application for a new trial.'** *SGG* may place *us* in the wrong.'
296.38 **Awful and thrilling were** *SGG* Thrilling, therefore, were
297.3 **prize?' we demanded, all** *SGG* prize?' one and all
297.4 **Portia. Guess, reader; – it** *SGG* Portia. Oh Gemini! my sympathizing reader; – it
297.5 **I, for my part, was afraid either to laugh or cry. I** *SGG* Did we laugh, or did we cry? I, for my part, was afraid to do either. I
297.6–7 **Athenaeum. Yet I had a monstrous desire to laugh horribly. But,** *SGG* Athenaeum. But,
297.8 **said, 'Oh! here is** *SGG* said, so ready were *her* wits for facing any issue, 'Oh! this is
297.16–17 **sate down** *SGG* sat down
297.18 **saying only** *SGG* whispering only
297.35 **Welch.** *SGG* Welsh.
297.36 **Welch** *SGG* Welsh
297.37–298.4 **Welch orthography? I am sure that...possibility wrong! But** *SGG* Welsh orthorgraphy? which at that time was, and (I believe) still is, a very rare accomplishment in the six counties of North Wales. But
298.6 **so shocking** *SGG* so torturing
298.6 **so agonising** *SGG* so impossible
298.20–1 ***Pig-in-a-dingle*! – why,** *SGG Pig-in-a-dingle*; why,
298.26 **torment!'** *SGG* torment.'
298.29 **Glasgow post,** *SGG* village post,
299.13 **there sate** *SGG* there sat
299.20 **pig is not necessarily rude;** *SGG* pig, if by accident dirty, is not therefore rude;
299.34–5 **which of course contained some** *SGG* which was suppose to contain some
302.5 **word answering** *SGG* word belonging
302.7 **legion. We** *SGG* legion. For the female mind is naturally but too prone to laughter. We
302.10 **mention it, I** *SGG* mention that thought, I
302.16 **as it then was. By this moment** *SGG* as in 1802 it was. By that moment
302.18 **book. It** *SGG* book. This
302.19 **book, printed in** *SGG* book, in
303.13 **then, as** *SGG* then, because
303.22 **divide that 8th** *SGG* divide the eighth

303.42 **to one of** *SGG* to a case of
303.40–3 **corolla or calyx of** *SGG* corolla of
304.17 **behind him!** *SGG* behind him?
304.27 **of the Glasgow Athenaeum.** *SGG* of a new-born Athenaeum.
304.28 **But the Glasgow post is mounting, and this paper will be lost; a** *SGG* But our village post (a boy, in fact, who rides a pony) is mounting; and the chances are that this letter of mine will be too late:[a] – a
[[a] Cf. De Quincey in 'The English Mail-Coach': 'And suddenly we upon the mail are pulled up by a mighty dial, sculptured with the hours, and with the dreadful legend of TOO LATE' (see above, p. 421).]

The Life and Adventures of Oliver Goldsmith

Title **ART. VI. – *The Life and Adventures of Oliver Goldsmith. A Biography.* In Four Books. By JOHN FORSTER. London, 1848.** *SGG* OLIVER GOLDSMITH.* *SGG appends footnote* The Life and Adventures of Goldsmith. By John Forster.
309.4 **through seventy and odd years.** *SGG* through more than seventy years.
309.5 **welcome** *Editorial; 1848* weleome
309.6 **favourite once wickedly exaggerated** *SGG* favourite long systematically exaggerated
309.7 **the powers** *SGG* the genial powers
309.7 **favourite once maliciously** *SGG* favourite too often maliciously
309.10–11 **for sympathy, two** *SGG* for such revelations, two
309.12 **together; and** *SGG* concurrently: and
309.28–9 **yet always with more peril to the accomplishment of their earthly mission.** *SGG* yet more perilously as regards the fulfilment of their intellectual mission.
309.30–1 **children too tremulously associated to the fluctuations of** *SGG* children, too sympathetically linked to the trembling impulses of
309.33 **constitutionally flexible to** *SGG* constitutionally more flexible than others to
309.33 **of sorrow and adversity, in** *SGG* of calamity, in
309.34 **really *had* more** *SGG* really met with more
309.35 **We are** *SGG* I am
309.35 **Our trust** *SGG* My trust
310.1 **midnight, and in** *SGG* midnight, in
310.2 **reached, this** *SGG* reached by one whole generation, this
310.2–3 **one so amiable, so** *SGG* one so
310.3 **otherwise for a moment only** *SGG* otherwise only
310.9 **tears one sheds at** *SGG* tears fall from every eye at
310.10 **he stood under unresistingly** *SGG* he faced unresistingly
310.n.1 **We do** *SGG* I do
310.n.2 **butt of mockery** *SGG* butt of ridicule
310.n.4 **We allude** *SGG* I allude
310.19 **and *have* happened to** *SGG* and will happen for ever, to
310.20–1 **commemoration, but not until** *SGG* commemoration, yet seldom until
310.23 **bread, we do** *SGG* bread – I do
310.31 **he would** *SGG* Charles would
310.33 **yet our persuasion is,** *SGG* yet my own belief is,
311.1 **farther** *F, SGG* further
311.2 **ladies in this** *SGG* ladies of this

311.n.1 **We point** *SGG* I point
311.n.1 **our opinion** *SGG* my opinion
311.n.3–4 **constitutional settlement? We are inclined** *SGG* consitutional root or lodgment? I am inclined
311.24 **his biographers, viz.** *SGG* its biographers – viz.,
311.40 **burthen** *F, SGG* burden
312.7 **proofs, a good Latin** *SGG* proofs, any decent Latin
312.8–9 **we presume,** *SGG* I presume,
312.12 **privileges, one subjective – the** *SGG* privileges – the one subjective, the
312.n.1 **tar-barrel: if** *SGG* tar barrel; but, if
312.n.4 **earthen ware, and once** *SGG* earthenware, and, therefore, once
312.n.4–5 **fact, it was** *SGG* fact, the home of Diogenes was
312.27 **than in ours.** *F, SGG* than ours.
312.33 **reading public** *SGG* 'reading public'
313.1 **we steadfastly resist. No** *SGG* I steadfastly deny. No
313.5 **viz., using influence** *SGG* viz., the use of influence
313.9 **we believe,** *SGG* I believe
313.11 **sum were** *SGG* sum was
313.12–13 **publisher, (a nuisance, we dare say, in all stages of his Natural History,)** ***he*** *SGG* publisher, *he*
312.21–3 **big, and would have engaged to drive the bankrupt publisher into a madhouse for twopence. Now,** *SGG* big, at the small cost of threepence; *i.e.,* six cents. Now,
313.27 **have presided over the** *SGG* have constituted the
313.42 **on a title-page** *F, SGG* on the title-page
314.n.6 **him, *In-I-go*** *SGG* him by the name of the great architect as *In-I-go*
314.23 **We are not therefore of Mr** *SGG* I am not, therefore, of Mr
314.26 **a prophecy.** *SGG* a bare prophecy.
314.33 **which (taken generally) was** *SGG* which working class was
314.37 **disadvantage. But** *SGG* disadvantage; but
315.2 **main stream** *SGG* main river
315.9 **We do** *SGG* I do
315.n.3 **however, (even in Sir Walter Scott,) are** *SGG* however, even in Sir Walter Scott, are
315.n.9 **apprehension, have** *SGG* comprehension, have
315.18 **generation that is not their** *SGG* generation other than their
315.18–19 **novels belonging to an obsolete** *SGG* novels that belong to any obsolete
315.23 **impression, or is** *SGG* impression; or he is
315.26 **Squire** *Editorial; 1848* Squoire
315.27 **Jones.** *F, SGG* Jones!
315.27 **of histrionic** *SGG* of faded histrionic
315.29 **earth.** *SGG appends footnote 'By the two leading nations of the earth:'* – viz., our own and the French. It was little known at any time, and is now forgotten, that Rousseau, Diderot,[a] and all leading minds in France, made an idol of Richardson, even more consecrated than amongst ourselves.

[[a] For Jean-Jacques Rousseau, see above, p. 579, n. 11. Denis Diderot (1713-84), French man of letters and philosopher who served as chief editor of the *Encyclopédie* (see above, p. 560, n. 14).]

316.10 **curiosity that is to** *SGG* curiosity, destined to
316.10–11 **and of a** *SGG* and the interest of a

316.12 **meaner offices** *SGG* meaner functions
316.31 **sensibilities – in** *SGG* sensibilities. In
317.8 **excuse us** *SGG* excuse me
317.10 **upon our attention** *SGG* upon attention
317.12 **our literary body** *SGG* our own literary body
317.14 **therefore we shall stir** *SGG* therefore I will stir
317.17 **of literature or literary gossip, viz.,** *SGG* of any literary anecdotage – viz.,
317.24 ***we* believe** *SGG* I believe
317.34 **behold! he** *SGG* behold, he
317.35 **almost silent.** *SGG* almost silent!
317.43 **instantly sketch** *SGG* instantly suggest
318.7 ***malis.*' Unless** *SGG malis.*' (*We are sick – but by maladies that are curable.*) Unless
318.8–9 **justify clamorous complaints;** *SGG* justify complaints;
318.13 **Mr C. might** *SGG* Mr Carlyle might
318.20 **mysterious *right:* which,** *SGG* mysterious correction of the wrong; which,
318.n.4 **Mr C., whose** *SGG* Mr Carlyle, whose
318.25 **we beg** *SGG* I beg
318.26 **our wish** *SGG* my wish
318.27 **our literary** *SGG* my literary
318.27 **We grudge** *SGG* I grudge
318.28 **We wish** *SGG* I wish
318.28–9 **creating *majorats* in** *SGG* creating state benefices in
318.29–319.1 **all; only whispering in the ear...parties who suggested the idea. But** *SGG* all. But
319.3 **bequest? We shall discuss** *SGG* bequest? Suffer me to discuss
319.5 **our own** *SGG* my own
319.6 **Mr F.** *SGG* Mr Forster
319.10 **themselves, (p. 70) Not** *SGG* themselves. Not
319.12 **We are** *SGG* I am
319.13 **we have** *SGG* I have
319.16 **might be** *SGG* might often be
319.18 **allow us** *SGG* allow me
319.20 **it. 2. Upon** *SGG* it; 2. upon
319.20 **that body** *SGG* that same body
319.20–1 **with that of the** *SGG* with the
319.21 **France. 3. Upon** *SGG* France; 3. upon
319.26 **notion we ourselves remember; viz.** *SGG* notion I myself remember – viz.,
319.n.1 **passage, we were not aware (as we now are) that** *SGG* I was not aware that
319.29 **we cannot** *SGG* I cannot
319.35 **bookseller saw** *SGG* publisher saw
320.4 **disposal. We suspect** *SGG* disposal. I suspect
320.8 ***not* bad.** *SGG less* bad.
320.9 **small, we suspect;** *SGG* small, I suspect;
320.15 **Dr G.** *SGG* Dr Griffiths
320.15 **Mrs *Dr* G. surmounting** *SGG* Mrs *Dr* Griffiths surmounting
320.20 **Mrs Dr G. off** *SGG* Mrs Dr Griffiths
320.23 **Mrs Dr G. might** *SGG* Mrs Dr Griffiths might
320.n.1–2 **His name began with A...we shall publish them** *SGG omits footnote*
320.33 **the attic story before** *SGG* the garrets before
320.36 **Mr F.'s** *SGG* Mr Forster's

321.8 **year spent** *F, SGG* year he spent
321.39 **Mrs Dr G.,** *SGG* Mrs Dr Griffiths,
322.n.1 **we think** *SGG* I think
322.n.3–4 **difference would** *SGG* difference between their eras would
322.19 **not as a pedestrian mendicant,** *SGG* not (like Goldsmith) as a mendicant,
322.20–1 **with the appointments** *SGG* with appointments
322.21 **introductions of** *SGG* introductions equal to those of
322.24 **back.' His** *SGG* back.' He was *backed* by the Whig party. His
322.27 **flattery** *F, SGG* flatteries
323.1 **because his capital was next** *SGG* because he started with a capital next
324.14 **except through casts** *F, SGG* except to casts
324.15 **We infer** *SGG* I infer
324.20 **our notice;** *SGG* my notice;
324.21 **we have** *SGG* I have
325.27 **to the nation** *SGG* to that nation
325.27 **nation that,** *SGG* nation which,
325.40 **tie, he would** *SGG* tie, this grandee would
326.23 **favour; once,** *SGG* favour. Once,
326.24 **sure to** *SGG* sure either to
326.33 **We have** *SGG* I have
326.39–40 **in society** *SGG* in Parisian society
326.40–1 **a literary scrub or mechanic** *SGG* a mere mechanic
326.43–4 **enjoyed, in right of his book, the** *SGG* enjoyed the
327.8 **Our space will not allow us to** *SGG* My space will not allow me to
327.9 **We confine ourselves to** *SGG* I confine myself to
327.29 **free discussion.** *SGG* political discussion.
327.30 **laws, or with government, or with** *SGG* laws, with government, with
327.34 **festive discussion.** *SGG social* discussion.
327.34–5 **That open area was found in** *SGG* That free area was found only in
328.2 **the system,** *SGG* the social system,
328.3–4 **therefore – is our prayer – cleanse,** *SGG* therefore – should be our general prayer – cleanse,
328.9 **of Lethe,** *SGG* of political Lethe,
328.11–12 **tastes; yes, but they did this** *SGG* tastes; but they did all this by
328.13 **of all which commanded** *SGG* of whatsoever commanded
328.18 **twenty years,** *SGG* thirty years,
328.25–6 **appropriate duties, whilst some** *F* appropriate duties, while some *SGG* appropriate functions, while some
328.28 **our residuum** *SGG* my residuum
328.28 **we first** *SGG* I first
328.29 **we have** *SGG* I have
328.30 **our paper** *SGG* my paper
328.30 **and thus we have left ourselves but** *SGG* and have thus left to myself but
328.31–2 **purpose (to which our other purpose of 'argle-bargling' was altogether subordinate) of** *SGG* purpose of
328.32 **our thanks** *SGG* public thanks
328.34 **We are** *SGG* I am
328.35 **him, with equal fervour and with** *SGG* him, with
328.38 **that exquisite** *SGG* that Goldsmith's exquisite
328.41–2 **all that sickly scorn** *SGG* all which affected scorn

328.42 **could avail** *SGG* could effect
328.44 **influences.** *SGG* influence.
329.4 **malicious constructions** *SGG* malicious interpretations
329.5 **levity** *SGG* buoyant
329.7 **with the misgiving** *SGG* with a misgiving
329.19 **an idiot to** *SGG* an *idiot* (as Dr Johnson styled him) to
329.40–1 **to kiss his hand. Yet this** *SGG* to bend reverentially. Yet even this
330.22 **he had himself made** *SGG* he himself had made
330.30–1 **writer – qualified** *SGG* writer like Mr Forster – qualified
330.38 **precedency. But,** *SGG* precedencey; but,
330.43 **name.' Be** SGG name:' – be

The Works of Alexander Pope, Esquire

Title **ART. I. – *The Works of Alexander Pope, Esquire*. By W. Roscoe, Esq. A New Edition. In eight vols. London, 1847.** *F* ALEXANDER POPE* *F appends footnote* The Works of Pope, by Roscoe. *SGG* ALEXANDER POPE
334.15 ***idola*** *F, SGG* eidola
334.34 **shewn)** *F, SGG* shown)
335.8 **crying** *MS A* <crying> <urgent> pressing *SGG* pressing
335.18 **whether it was at all *worth*** *SGG* whether, in fact, it is *worth*
336.8 **interest.** *MS A, SGG append footnote and conform, with the exception of five significant deletions in MS A given here in angle brackets* What are called *The Blue Books*, by which title are understood the folio Reports issued every session of <the> Parliament by committees of the two Houses, and stitched into <a> blue covers, – though often sneered at by the ignorant as so much waste paper, will be acknowledged gratefully by those <all> who have used them diligently, as the main well-heads of all accurate information as to the <true> Great Britain of this day. As an immense depository of faithful (*and not superannuated*) statistics, they are indispensable to the honest student. But no man would therefore class <them> the *Blue Books* as literature.
337.17 **ascending into** *SGG* ascending movement into
337.23 **droop** *SGG* drop
337.26 **condescend** *F, SGG* condescended
338.13–14 **combat is over** *SGG* combat was over
338.27 **are not separated by** *SGG* are separated not by
338.29 **differing** *F, SGG* different
338.29 **and as equal** *SGG* and if otherwise equal, as equal
338.34 **mimicries, nor be** *SGG* mimicries, that cannot be
338.34–5 **copies, nor become** *SGG* copies, that cannot become
339.21 **the *rest* of** *SGG* the repose if
339.28 **exercises** *F, SGG* exercise
339.29 **when seen stretching** *F, SGG* when stretching
340.2 **of childhood.** *SGG* of his childhood.
340.23 **earlier** *F, SGG* earliest
340.25 **struggles** *F, SGG* struggle
340.28 **We have** *SGG* We then have
341.7–8 **was influenced** *SGG* was even slightly influenced
341.9 **Dryden ridiculed** *SGG* Dryden openly ridiculed

341.37 ***correctness* is** *SGG correctness*, for elliptical it must be until its subject of control is assigned, is
341.38 **complementary** *F, SGG* complimentary
341.43 **expression.** *SGG* expressions.
342.2 **society which he** *F, SGG* society he
343.20 **after his fall,** *SGG* after that minister's fall
343.23 ***him*, *i.e.* on his behalf, thou** *SGG him* thou
343.25 **attentively; whereas** *SGG* attentively, or to look attentively; whereas
343.28 **human race. This** *SGG* British nation. This
343.30–1 **polished** *SGG* finished
343.41 **upon Robert Harley, was** *SGG* upon Harley Lord Oxford, was
343.43 **ears, when descending** *SGG* ears, from descending
345.3 **many that had** *SGG* many who had
345.20 **Quincey** *SGG* Quincy
345.28 **now, our hope is, reunited** *SGG* now (our hope is) reunited
346.2 **of glorifying his satiric** *F* of glorying his satiric *SGG* of glorying in his satiric
346.23 **steam-engine** *SGG* locomotive-engine
347.12–13 **fraud: for / 'Wherever** *SGG* fraud; no anger or displeasure attends their continual buccaneering expeditions, on the contrary, 'Wherever
348.2–3 **worse are** *SGG* worse by far are
348.4 **expose the false principles** *SGG* expose more brightly the
348.5 **worked more brightly, and** *SGG* worked, and
348.9 **of vulgarities sometimes** *SGG* of vulgar fictions sometimes
349.2 **have*** *F, SGG move footnote to* all;'*
349.2 **all;'** *F, SGG move footnote from* have
349.5–6 **theme concerning which,** *SGG* theme, he had pledged himself to a chase, on which,
349.32 **the delicacy** *SGG* the merits
350.20 **vulgarities is** *SGG* vulgarities in act is
351.2 **But we must move on.** *SGG omits*
351.3 **Next, then, let us come to the** *SGG* Next comes the
351.n.1 **Parliament for** *SGG* Parliament, then recent, for
351.11 **upon her corpse** *SGG* upon the corpse
351.34 **way, stands for the** *SGG* way, represents the
351.n.3 **died, the** *SGG* died in early youth, the
351.n.5 ***Spencer* (until lately) displaced the** *SGG Spencer*, the name of Lord Sunderland, displaced, until lately, the
352.8 **attaching** *F, SGG* attached
352.8 **so eminent,** *SGG* so illustrious,
352.n.3 **1746.** *SGG* 1746, when their hour of hope passed away for ever.
352.33 **subsequently Horace** *SGG* subsequently, next in the succession to *him*, Horace
352.38 **which of** *SGG* which pocketing of a bribe of
353.6 **cared less for** *SGG* cared nothing at all for
353.19 **valuation.** *F* valuation! *SGG* valuation?
354.16 **his repulsions** *SGG* or repulsions
354.27 **human eye.** *F, SGG* human eye!
354.29 **might be exhausted.** *SGG* might in time be exhausted.
354.31 **palsy for its billows, as** *SGG* palsy, as
354.32 **wrinkles for itself. But** *SGG* wrinkles. But
354.33 **world by comparison** *SGG* world in comparison

355.7 **ideals deposited** *SGG* ideas deposited
355.35–6 **forgiveness to man,** *F, SGG* forgiveness of man,
355.39 **Jove!** *SGG* Jove?
356.7–8 **forces that acted *in*** *F* forces that act *in* *SGG* forces acting *in*
356.30 **some people** *F, SGG* some persons
358.9 **heart, which is a deep** *SGG* heart, an unfathomed deep
358.23 **Pope's situation,** *SGG* Pope's position,
358.30 **not, with a** *SGG* not, supposing a
358.36–7 **religion confessedly as** *SGG* religion too certainly as
359.36 **which in the** *F, SGG* which is the
359.38 **variety or species** *F, SGG* variety of species
360.5 **announced: but** *SGG* announced, viz., *to justify the ways of God to man*;[a] but
[[a] Milton, *Paradise Lost,* I. 26: 'And justify the ways of God to men'.]
360.40 ***Fleece* of Dyer,** *SGG Fleece* by Dyer,
360.40 **which is** *SGG* which of the two is
361.10 **leaving** *SGG* leaves
361.12 **showing** *SGG* shows
361.27 **shewing** *F, SGG* showing
362.24 **vast, indeed so inexhaustible, as man, this** *SGG* vast as that which Pope chose for his Essay, viz., *man*, this
362.33 ***every* thing** *F, SGG everything*
363.1 **Essay** *SGG* essay
363.26 **Crousaz with** *SGG* Crousaz sometimes with
363.43 **interests** *SGG* interest

Final Memorials of Charles Lamb

Title **ART. IV. – *Final memorials of Charles Lamb* By THOMAS NOON TALFOURD. 2 vols. London: 1848.** *F, SGG* CHARLES LAMB
367.n.4–5 **It is disgraceful that more reflection...so pregnant a truth.** *SGG omits*
367.7 ***worldly*** *SGG* world
368.16–17 **peculiar bias** *SGG* particular bias
368.34 **enjoy that product** *F, SGG* enjoy the product
368.43 **Sir Thomas Brown,** *SGG* Sir Thomas Browne,
369.1 **Hamann** *F, SGG* Harmann
369.3 **writings,** *F, SGG* writing,
370.25 **engulfed** *F, SGG* ingulfed
370.36 **bondage:** *SGG appends footnote* Lamb was himself confined for six weeks at one period of his life in a lunatic asylum.[a]
[[a] See above, p. 606, n. 11.]
371.13 **which he seems** *SGG* which Mr S. seems
371.37 **the muses – he** *SGG* the graces, he
372.3 **seem** *F, SGG* seems
372.13 **Kinsale.** *SGG appends footnote* Whom, by the way, a modern Peerage tells us that, strictly speaking (or rather strictly spelling), we ought to call *Kingsale*. Very possibly. But, if so, we have been wrong throughout our whole erroneous life; and it is too late now to correct our spelling.
372.27 **interest, Charles** *SGG* interest it was that Charles

372.33–4 **wanting, and supposing the school of sufficient magnitude, it** *SGG* wanting, it
372.36 **connecting the school** *SGG* connecting every important school
372.44 **boy-king – innocent,** *SGG* boy-king (Edward VI.) – a king innocent,
373.5 **cloisteral character** *SGG* cloistral character
373.11 **for the Latin** *SGG* for his Latin
373.20 **literatures** *F, SGG* literature
373.30–1 **a 'Grecian' from the house of Christchurch. That** *SGG* a privileged 'Grecian' from Christ's Hospital. That
374.3 **Hoxton: she** *F, SGG* Hoxton. She
374.5–6 **seclusion, this house of wo. This** *SGG* seclusion, that house of wo. This
374.10 **years in age** *F, SGG* years of age
374.23 **years more** *F, SGG* years and more
374.24 **Henceforwards,** *F, SGG* Henceforward,
375.7 **scoundrel reviewers?** *SGG* merciless reviewers?
375.22 **engrafted** *F, SGG* ingrafted
375.23–4 **exertion. Let us consider what this exertion really amounted to. Holidays** *F, SGG omit*
375.31 **day. Only that, as** *SGG* day. But, as
375.32 **makes six** *SGG* makes only six
376.14–15 **admirably illustrates** *SGG* humorously illustrates
376.37 **in literature may** *SGG* in the full delight of literature, may
376.39 **Lamb's feelings** *SGG* Lamb's sincere feelings
376.43 **day, and courted** *SGG* day; they courted
377.7–8 **Sergeant Talfourd's** *SGG* Sergeant (since Mr Justice) Talfourd's
377.14 **he been** *MS A* had eve<r>n *SGG* he even been
377.36 **last sixty** *SGG* last seventy
378.4 **different. Hazlitt** *F, SGG* different, Hazlitt
378.19 **Sir Thomas Brown,** *SGG* Sir Thomas Browne,
378.24–5 **necessity fugacious,** *SGG* necessity fugitive,
379.5 **intention. All** *SGG* intention. What was the consequence? All
379.12 **Chesterfield himself, so** *SGG* Chesterfield, so
379.16 **hair-dresser: compelled** *MS A* hairdresser, who, in that age, or even thirty years later, was an artist <who> that, more even that a tailor, ministered to respectability. Compelled *SGG* hairdresser, who, in that age, or even thirty years later, was an artist that, more even that a tailor, ministered to respectability. Compelled
379.17 **naturally he demanded** *SGG* naturally Lord Chesterfield demanded
379.27 **dismissing the** *SGG* dismissing all the
379.29–30 ***pensée*, which, coming last in the succession, might oftentimes be calculated to lie deepest on the mind. To** *SGG pensée*. To
379.34 **is more dangerous** *SGG* is not less dangerous
380.18 **itself, and it** *SGG* itself – it
380.18 **itself. But** *SGG* itself – it does not propagate itself. But
381.2 **restored,' Surely** *F, SGG* restored' – surely
381.14 **exceeding our limits.** *SGG* exceeding the just limits.
381.32 **2dly, because the practice involves** *SGG* 2dly, Because sometimes it involves
382.2 **great talents,** *SGG* splendid talents,
382.3 **without any** *MS* A without <any> <high> known *SGG* without known
382.26 **signally dishonest.** *SGG* sometimes dishonest.
382.29–30 **lamp-light. / But** *SGG omits paragraph break*

382.31 **robbery. And** *F, SGG* robbery; and
382.32 **a work,** *SGG* a biographical work,
383.n.4 **the answer is – first, that** *SGG* the answers are as follows: – First, That
383.n.5 **ascertained. Secondly, that** *SGG* ascertained; not *so* nicely as to warrant the founding upon it of any solemn accusation. Secondly, That
383.n.9 **these glories. Besides** *SGG* these popular traditions. Besides
383.n.12 **particular class** *SGG* particular choice
383.n.17 **her, unless indeed by** *SGG* her, not even by
384.n.2 **But what *is*** *SGG* But that, which *is*
384.n.5 **not? That** *SGG* not? was his name Voltaire, Arouet de Voltaire,[a] or was it not? That
[[a] See above, p. 570, n. 56.]
384.19 **marriage, so** *SGG* marriage, a marriage so
385.24 **last** *SGG appends footnote* 'Last year' – This was written in 1848.
386.12 **being dull** *SGG* being, or for seeming, dull
386.19 **member. Our translation is** *SGG* member. The English version is
386.23 **memorandum!** *F, SGG* memorandum:
386.24 ***October*** *Editorial; 1848 'October*
386.34 **Mr Stuart** *SGG* Mr Daniel Stewart
387.22 **dipped.' What** *SGG* dipped. But – ' What
387.23 **sea or bathing machines; for** *SGG* sea: for
387.25 **men, rather tired** *SGG* men, tired
387.27 **'operative' clause** *SGG* 'operative clause'
387.27–8 **exclaiming at once, 'Oh yes, Sir,** *SGG* exclaiming, 'Oh yes, sir,
387.36 **wrath, once more Lamb** *SGG* wrath, for a third time Lamb
387.38 **I'm to** *SGG* I am to
387.42 ***was* – to** *SGG was* – by medical direction – to
388.6 **aerially elevated** *SGG* joyously elevated
388.8 **converting oneself:** *SGG* converting one's-self;
388.15 **until many years** *SGG* until some years
388.15–16 **murderer, and** *SGG* murderer, such he proved to be upon later discoveries, but even then looking prospectively towards that object, and
388.17–18 **unsuspecting domestic confidence** *SGG* unsuspecting confidence
388.20–1 **by Sergeant Talfourd, in the second volume of these 'Final Memoirs,' and** *SGG* by Judge Talfourd, and
388.23 **but we know** *SGG* but I know
388.27 **murderer's appearance** *SGG* murderer's dandy appearance,
388.35–6 ***Weathercock*, *Vinkbooms*, &c.) were** *SGG Weathercock* or else *Vinkbooms*), were
389.1 **spoke from himself** *SGG* spoke for himself
389.7–8 **sister had a deep feeling for what was excellent in painting.** *SGG* sister having no sensibility for music, had the deepest for painting.
389.20–1 **of that party! Trivial** *SGG* of the scene! Trivial
389.24 **have accomplished** *SGG* have founded,
389.24–5 **wickedness? In a few words I will say.** *SGG* wickedness? Here is its outline; but his murders were more than were ever made known judicially.
389.26 **1848),** *SGG appends footnote* This was written ten years ago; and doubtless I had ground sufficient for what I then said. At present, however, I have entirely forgotten the particular case alluded to, unless (as I rather believe) it was a case of infant funerals
[[a] See above, p. 611, n. 106.]

389.29–30 **toxicology, not in the mere management of poisons, was the audacity of their genius displayed. No; but** *SGG* toxicology; but

389.43 **child died!** *SGG* child dies!

390.26 **family, to** *SGG* family, and nearly related to his wife, to

390.30 **period; and then, having previously** *MS E* period. <xxx> I never saw either of the young <ladies> {↑ women} myself; but I have been assured that one of them at least was memorably distinguished by her personal attractions. <On the> In the middle of the day which Mr Wainwright had fixed for their murder, he framed a pretence for drawing his wife out of doors upon a very long walk. <He had> His fear was that *she* might have <experience> and penetration enough to notice and report the <x> agonizing spasms caused by the poison, whereas two young servant girls totally <uncertain> inexperienced were easily persuaded to believe it a case of cholera. On returning after a three hours' walk, Mr and Mrs W. found the two <victims> {↑ young ladies} dead. Having previously *SGG* period. I never saw either of the young women myself; but I have been assured that one of them at least was memorably distinguished by her personal attractions. In the middle of the day which Mr Wainwright had fixed for their murder, he framed a pretence for drawing his wife out of doors upon a very long walk. His fear was that *she* might have penetration enough to notice and report the agonizing spasms caused by the poison, whereas two young servant girls, totally inexperienced, were easily persuaded to believe it a case of cholera. On returning, after a three hours' walk, Mr and Mrs W. found the two young ladies dead. Having previously

390.31 **of this claim,** *SGG* of their claim,

390.44 **and I greatly** *F, SGG* and greatly

391.10–15 **Both Lamb and myself had a furious love…moments of relaxation.** *SGG omits*

393.1 **On awakening from his brief slumber…to patronize shoes.'** *SGG omits*

394.5 **On the table lay** *MS A* On the tea-table

394.5 **two volumes; it** *MS A* 2 vol^{s}. <from>; it

394.6 **about the** *MS A* about <18> the

394.6 **Waterloo. Wordsworth was held** *MS A* Waterloo. <and miser> Wordsworth was <no favourite> held

394.7 **house of Longman; at amy rate, *their* editions of his works were got** *MS A* house of <Longmans (as Southey> Longman; any any rate, <it was to> *their* <xxx> editions {↑ of his work} were <most> got

394.8 **manner. In** *MS A* manner. <Sheets were left out in every presentation copy that I ever saw; the printing was careless; and the very ind Table> In

394.13 **entered with** entered <in the m> with

394.15 **Lamb, reading this entry** Lamb, <'he may well say that> reading <x> this <title> entry

394.16 **like blotting** *MS A* like <paper> blotting

394.20 **uttered in** *MS A* uttered <with> in

394.22 **his spirits from** *MS A* his {↑ spirits} <conscience> from

394.23 **one instant to** *MS A* one minute to

394.25 **so mediocre as to extort high** *MS A* so <b bad> mediocre as <th> to extort <the> high

394.25 **indignation from a** *MS A* indignation <of> from a

394.26 **his collection** *MS A* his <insert any pun x or jest in his> collection

394.27 **not felicitously** *MS A* not <unless> felicitously

394.29 **a blank** *MS A* a <Folio lays> blank

394.31 **sonnet from** *MS A* sonnet <of Lord> from

394.32 **by Lord** *MS A* by <the you> Lord

394.33 **upon it, I** *SGG* upon which, I

394.35 **only twelve lines more. Now** *MS B* only 12 of <x> lines more, <How xxxxx It was there that Now

394.36 **world knows** *MS B* world <it is too notorious> knows

394.36–8 **lines; but take fourteen from twelve, and there remains very little, I fear; besides which, I am afraid two of my twelve are** *MS B* lines, leaving me absolutely on the debtor side of the account by 8 lines. <Bes A> Besides which, I am afraid 2 of my 6 lines are

394.38 **to interrupt** *MS B* to <conclude> interrupt

394.39 **of Lamb's** *MS B* of <the evening by the brief fact that did at>

394.39 **by reporting** *MS B* by <the very> reporting

394.39 **accident that** *MS B* accident <fact> that

394.40 ***that* no less characteristically expressed Lamb's peculiar spirit** *MS B that* <for that fact it was was that as happened *that* as much served as char> no less characteristically <to towards an> express<ion>ed of Lamb's peculiar<ly> spirit

394.41 **quickening itself** *MS B* quickening <traveling in its quickening its motions to meet> itself towards

394.42 **obscure readings.** *MS B* obscure <papers> readings.

395.2 **not have found** *MS B* not <particularly> have <xxxxd> found

395.3 **depressed. On** *MS B* depressed. <Lamb> On

395.5 **from himself but** *MS B* from him but

395.5 **to impress** to <be> impress

395.7–8 **We have left ourselves no room for a special examination of Lamb's writings, some of which were failures,** *SGG* Of Lamb's writings, some were confessedly failures,

395.8 **memorably beautiful** *MS C* memorably <good as to> beautiful

395.10 **many, even** *MS C* many <that even> even

395.12 **impress many** *MS C* impress <themsel> many

395.12–13 **writings. Even** *MS C* writing. <But they> Even

395.14 **value; but** *MS C* value. But

395.27 **cheerfully, and without** *F, SGG* cheerfully, without

395.36 **sister lasted through a period** *MS C* sister <in her {↑ long} in long intermitting complaint> lasted through <a life of> period

395.38 **House, by** *MS C* House {↑ <by} had all granted him a placed his own pecuniary interests by volunteering a> by

395.39 **But this** *MS C* But <he and> this

395.40 **event of his own death, the** *MS C* event <upon> of his own death <with the same nobility of feeling>, the

395.41 **the same allowance** *MS C* the <all> same allowance

395.41–2 **custom is granted** *MS C* custom *would* have been granted

395.42 **This they did; but not** *MS C* This they did; but, <on the assumption> not *SGG* This, however, they did; but Lamb not

395.43 **patronage, Lamb had** *SGG* patronage, had

396.2 **persevering prudence, so little, so little known in the literary class, amongst** *MS C* persever<ance>ing prudence {↑ so} <as> little <a> known {↑ in} <amongst> {↑ the} literary {↑ class} <men>, amongst *SGG* persevering prudence, but little known in the literary class, amongst

396.3 **generosities, often so princely as to be scarcely known in** *MS C* generosities <ev> often {↑ so} princely as to be scarcely <almost entirely un>known in
396.5 **so memorably good by** *MS C* so <x> memorably <a> good <man> by
396.10 **were united with the deepest piety)** *MS C* were <colored> united with <fervent piety feeling> the deepest <impression> piety)
396.11 **the opinions** *MS C* the <his final> opinions
396.15 **example, beginning** *MS D* example <instance> beginning
396.16 **order: and** *MS D* order. And
396.17 **Lamb is supposed simply to have obeyed** *MS D* Lamb <in this instance at least> is supposed <to> simply to have <followed the> obeyed
396.21–2 **subject, firmly** *MS D* subject <only he ventured> firmly
396.24–5 **his first great affliction, he** *SGG* his sister's first attack of lunacy, he
396.29 **religion is not** *F, SGG* religion was not
397.4 **His character.'** *F, SGG* his character.'
397.9 **that at a maturer period, when** *MS D* that {↑ at a} in maturer <life> period,
397.10 **year, no** *MS D* year <he had> no
397.11 **point; and, on the other hand, that** *MS D* point. And <the even history of his life bears witness that domestic sorrow had left him no with no intermission reasons for interup {↑ on the other hand,} that
397.11–12 **occurred in his needs for consolation,** *MS D* occurred <to diminish> in his needs for <continual> consolation,
397.12 **alas! In** *MS D* alas! <too clearly> in
397.12–14 **life. Whither, indeed, could he fly for comfort, if not to his Bible? And to whom was the Bible an indispensable resource, if not to Lamb?** *MS D* life. Whither indeed <should> {↑ could} he fly for comfort, if not to his bible? And to whom was his Bible an indispensable resource, if not to <Charles> Lamb> *SGG* life. We
397.14 **say, that** *MS D* say <of> that,
397.16 **after its** *MS D* after <the Truth, and had> its
397.19 **purest, and within** *MS D* purest <lay through stormy times, and was itself a continued storm that could not was a fine {↑ continued} drama of continued energy and unabated loss {↑ and within}
397.19–20 **little of contemporary applause. Even** *MS D* little {↑ of contemporary} public splendour of> applause. <In his own time he was> Even
397.20 **won but** *MS D* won <little> but
397.21 **with positive** *MS D* with <positive contemptuous disdain> {↑ positive <derision> derision}
397.23 **neglect. But slowly all things** *MS D* neglect. <Slowly> But slowly all <merit, which is pure and genuine in its class, reaches by its exhalations the higher> things
397.26–7 **thwarted Lamb's just estimation in** *SGG* thwarted all just estimation of Lamb in
397.27 **will continue to thwart its popular** *MS D* will <still> continue to <dispute his> thwarts its <dif> popular
397.28 **hostility. And** *SGG* hostility, and the old unmitigated scorn. And
397.30 **strains of** *MS D* strains <ascending as> of
397.32 **side, seemed to hear ascending** *MS D* side we {↑ seemed to} hear<d>, <as in the> ascending
397.32–3 **of an anthem – 'This** *SGG* of a saintly requiem – 'This
397.34 **buried; his** *MS D* buried <and> his
397.34 **memory is hallowed** *MS D* memory {↑ is} <is will be> hallowed

The English Mail-Coach, or The Glory of Motion

Title **THE ENGLISH MAIL-COACH, OR THE GLORY OF MOTION** *MS GM A, MS GM B, MS GM B, SGG* THE ENGLISH MAIL-COACH

Subtitle MS GM A, MS GM B, SGG SECTION THE FIRST. – THE GLORY OF MOTION.

408.1–2 **Palmer, M.P.** *MS GM A, MS GM B, SGG* Palmer, at that time M.P.

408.3 **may happen to be** *MS GM A, MS GM B, SGG* may be

408.3 **by the eccentric** *MS GM A, MS GM B, SGG* by eccentric

409.3 **who certainly invented (or *discovered*) the** *MS GM A* who did certainly invent (or, which is the same thing,† discover) the *MS GM A appends footnote 'The same thing:'* – Thus, in the calendar of the <xx> Church Festivals, the discovery of the true Cross (by Helen the mother of Constantine)[a] is technically called the *Invention* of the Cross. *MS GM B revises footnote* by Helen, the mother of Constantine) is recorded (and one might think – with the express consciousness of (<xxxxx sati> sarcasm) as <the *Invention*> <and one might think, satiric> the *Invention* of the Cross. *SGG revises footnote* Helen, the mother of Constantine) is recorded (and one might think – with the express consciousness of sarcasm) as the *Invention* of the Cross.

[[a] Constantine (see above, p. 588, n. 39) was the son of Flavius Valerius Constantius and his wife (or concubine) Helena.]

409.4 **points** *MS GM A, MS GM B, SGG* pretensions

409.5 **but who** *MS GM A, MS GM B, SGG* but, on the other hand, who

409.8 **dreams, an** *MS GM A, MS GM B, SGG* dreams; an

409.9 **unprecedented, they** *MS GM A, MS GM B, SGG* unprecedented – for they

409.10–11 **motion: suggesting, at the same time, an under-scene, not unpleasurable, of possible though indefinite danger; secondly, through** *MS GM A* motion: secondly, through *MS GM B, SGG* motion; 2dly, through

409.n.4 **which exactly bisected** *MS GM B, SGG* which bisected

409.16 **of night, overruled** *MS GM A* of danger, overruled *MS GM B, SGG* of danger – overruled

409.16 **co-operation in** *F* coöperation in *MS GM A, MS GM B, SGG* co-operation to

409.17 **To my** *MS GM A, MS GM B, SGG* For my

409.17 **service recalled some** *MS GM A, MS GM B, SGG* service spoke as by some

409.20–1 **heart, veins, and arteries, in** *MS GM A, MS GM B, SGG* heart, brain and lungs, in

409.21 **that particular** *MS GM* A that particular *MS GM B* that <most> particular *SGG* that particular

409.23–4 **tyrannises by terror and terrific beauty over my dreams, lay** *MS GM A, MS GM B, SGG* tyrannises over my dreams by terror and terrific beauty, lay

409.24 **political** *MS GM A, MS GM B, SGG political*

409.25 **mail-coaches** *MS GM A, MS GM B, SGG* mail-coach

409.30 **confound these battles, which** *MS GM A, MS GM B, SGG* confound battles such as these, which

409.32 **warfare, which are oftentimes but gladiatorial** *MS GM A, MS GM B, SGG* warfare, so often no more than gladiatorial

409.36 **France, and** *MS GM A* France <herself> our enemy, and *MS GM B, SGG* France, our enemy, and

409.36–7 **of western and central** *MS GM A, MS GM B, SGG* of all western or central

409.39–40 **events, became** *MS GM A* events, thus diffusely influential became *MS GM B, SGG* events thus diffusely influential, became

410.1–3 **day, all hearts were awakened. There were, perhaps, of us gownsmen, two thousand *resident** in Oxford, and dispersed through five-and-twenty colleges. In some of these the** *MS GM A* day, *all* hearts were impassioned, as being all (or nearly all) in early manhood. In most universities there <was> is one single college; in Oxford there were five-and-twenty, <in> <the> all of <them> {↑ which} were {↑ peopled} by young men, the *élite* of <the rising> {↑ their own} generation; not boys, but men; none under 18. In some of these many colleges the *MS GM B, SGG* day, *all* hearts were impassioned, as being all (or nearly all) in early manhood. In most universities there is one single college; in Oxford there were five-and-twenty, all of which were peopled by young men, the *élite* of their own generation; not boys, but men; none under eighteen. In some of these many colleges, the

410.5 **kept severally by** *MS GM A, MS GM B, SGG* kept by

410.6–7 **residence, accordingly, it** *MS GM A, MS GM B, SGG* residence, it

410.9 **fro. And as** *MS GM A* fro. <And> But as *MS GM B, SGG* fro. But, as

410.12 **Oxford. Naturally,** *MS GM A* Oxford. Three mails at the least I remember as passing every day through {↑ Oxford}, and benefiting by my personal patronage, viz. the Worcester, <mail,> the Gloucester, and the Holyhead mail. Naturally, *MS GM B, SGG* Oxford. Three mails, at the least, I remember as passing every day through Oxford, and benefiting by my personal patronage – viz., the Worcester, the Gloucester, and the Holyhead mail. Naturally,

410.15 **bye-laws not unreasonable, enacted** *MS GM A, MS GM B, SGG* bye-laws enacted

410.16 **others equally** *MS GM A* other bye-laws equally *MS GM B, SGG* other bye-laws, equally

410.17 **own exclusiveness.** *MS GM A, MS GM B, SGG* own haughty exclusiveness.

410.18–19 **not *very long* to mutiny.** *MS GM A* not very long to downright mutiny. *MS GM B, SGG* not very long to systematic mutiny.

410.19 **time, it** *MS GM A* time, say <x> 1804, or 1805 (the year of Trafalgar) it *MS GM B, SGG* time, say 1804, or 1805 (the year of Trafalgar), it

410.20 **carriages from** *MS GM A, MS GM B, SGG* carriages derived from

410.27 **which *had*** *MS GM A* which <to my knowledge> *had*

410.35 **composition. I** *MS GM A* composition when pulling against her strong democracy. I *MS GM B, SGG* composition, when pulling against her strong democracy. I

410.35 **sometimes it** *MS GM A* sometimes undoubtedly it *MS GM B, SGG* sometimes, undoubtedly, it

410.36 **extravagant** *MS GM A, MS GM B, SGG* comic

410.39 **enticed them away off to** *MS GM A, MS GM B, SGG* enticed these good men away to

410.40 **though very rarely,** *MS GM A* <though very> <however> though rarely, *MS GM B, SGG* though rarely,

411.2 **move,** *MS GM A, MS GM B, SGG* budge,

411.3 **the room.** *MS GM A, MS GM B, SGG* the general room.

411.8 **construction.** *MS GM A, MS GM B, SGG append footnote De non apparentibus, &c.*[a] [[a] See above, p. 614, 20.]

411.9 **Such now being,** *MS GM A,* Such <now> being *MS GM B, SGG* Such being,

411.12 **suspicious** *MS GM A, MS GM B, SGG* questionable

411.12 **characters, were we voluntarily to** *MS GM A* characters, were we by voluntarily going outside to *MS GM B, SGG* characters – were we, by voluntarily going outside, to

411.17 **urged** *MS GM A, MS GM B, SGG* valid

411.21 **pit suits the purpose of the** *MS GM A* pit <suits the purpose of> may be supposed to have an advantage for the <xxx> purposes of the critic or the *SGG* pit may be supposed to have an advantage for the purposes of the critic or the

411.22 **the reporter or critic is** *MS GM A, MS GM B, SGG* the critic or reporter is

411.23 **Whereas, on** *MS GM A, MS GM B, SGG* Now,

411.23–4 **incommunicable advantages** *MS GM A* incommunicable advantages *MS GM B* incommunicable <and priceless> advantages *SGG* incommunicable advantages

411.25 **should willingly** *MS GM A, MS GM B, SGG* would willingly

411.25 **but *that* was connected** *MS GM A* but the price connected *MS GM B, SGG* but not the price connected

411.26 **inside, which was insufferable.** *MS GM A* inside, which condition we pronounced was to us insufferable. *MS GM B, SGG* inside; which condition we pronounced insufferable.

411.27 **what we desired;** *MS GM A, MS GM B, SGG* what we required;

411.30 **Under coercion of this great practical difficulty,** *MS GM A, MS GM B, SGG* Such was the difficulty which pressed us; and under the coercion of this difficulty,

411.33–4 **which some had affected to call the attics, and some** *MS GM A, MS GM B, SGG* which by some weak men had been called the attics, and by some

411.34 **was really the drawing-room, and the** *MS GM A, MS GM B, SGG* was in reality the drawing-room; in which drawing-room the

411.35 **sofa in that drawing-room; whilst** *MS GM A, MS GM B, SGG* sofa; whilst

411.36 **inside,** *MS GM A, MS GM B, SGG inside*,

411.39–40 **our first embassy** *MS GM A appends footnote which is struck out* <we sent> Great Britain sent at different periods, two separate embassies to the country of China; the earliest under lord Macartney in the time of the kind-hearted old blockhead Kein Long. But the second, under lord Amherst,[a] in a very literal sense caught a Tartar:
[[a] For Lord Macartney, see above, p. 614, 26. For the Chinese emperor Qianlong, see above, p. 615, n. 27. William Pitt Amherst, first Earl Amherst (1773-1857; *DNB*) was sent to China in 1816 to negotiate commercial matters, and in 1823 became governor-general of India.]

412.1 **was a mystery** *MS GM A, MS GM B, SGG* was an intense mystery

412.2–3 **some dim and imperfect** *MS GM A, MS GM B, SGG* some imperfect

412.3 **the point;** *MS GM A, MS GM B, SGG* this point;

412.4–5 **celestial mind** *MS GM A, MS GM B, SGG* celestial intellect

412.8 **seat, and** *MS GM A, MS GM B, SGG* seat, was nearest to the moon, and

412.10 **imperial place,** *MS GM A* imperial <place> throne – *MS GM B, SGG* throne,

412.11–13 **harnessed, under a flourish of music and a salute of guns, solemnly his imperial majesty ascended his new English throne, having** *MS GM A, MS GM B, SGG* harnessed, solemnly his imperial majesty ascended his new English throne under a flourish of trumpets, having

412.16 **person, which was** *MS GM A, MS GM B, SGG* person, and *that* was

412.16–17 **individual, looking as blackhearted as he really was, audaciously** *MS GM A, MS GM B, SGG* individual audaciously

412.21 **through a window, 'how** *F* through the window, 'how *MS GM A* through the window, 'I say, how *MS GM B, SGG* through the window – 'I say, how

412.22 **the answer;** *MS GM A, MS GM B, SGG* the imperial answer;

412.23 **glory; through** *MS GM A* glory. How catch the reins? Why through *MS GM B, SGG* glory. How catch the reins? Why, through

412.23–4 **key-holes – how you please.'** *MS GM A, MS GM B, SGG* key-holes – *any*how.'

412.26 **as may be supposed.** *MS GM A* as Pekin <may be supposed.> had any right <could> to expect. *MS GM B, SGG* as Pekin had any right to expect.

412.29 **prosperous escape** *MS GM A, MS GM B, SGG* happy escape

412.29 **of a broken** *MS GM A, MS GM B, SGG* of broken

412.30 **dedicated for ever as** *MS GM A, MS GM B, SGG* dedicated thenceforward as

412.37 **when all opposition** *F, MS GM A, MS GM B, SGG* when the opposition

412.39–40 **usually above 30, (say generally from 30 to 50 years old,) naturally** *MS GM A, MS GM B, SGG* usually from thirty to fifty years old, naturally

412.43 **to our moral** *MS GM A, MS GM B, SGG* to all moral

412.44 **bribery, we observed, and** *MS GM A, MS GM B, SGG* bribery, said we, and

413.1 **Aristotle's, Cicero's,** *MS GM A, MS GM B, SGG* Aristotle's, Zeno's,[a] Cicero's,
[[a] For Zeno, see above, p. 562, n. 60.]

413.2–3 **public being demonstrated out of Euclid to be as** *MS GM A, MS GM B, SGG* public were as

413.4–5 **the stable-establishments about the mails. The whole** *MS GM A, MS GM B, SGG* the stables connected with the mails. This whole

413.6 **sur-rebribed; so that a** *MS GM A* sur-rebribed; <so that a> a mail-coach yard was like a {↑ the hustings in a} contested election; and a *MS GM B, SGG* sur-rebribed; a mail-coach yard was like the hustings in a contested election; and a

413.14 **I go for** *MS GM A, MS GM B, SGG* I fly for

413.21 **sheriff in** *MS GM A, MS GM B, SGG* sheriff and under-sheriff in

413.23 **It's** *SGG* It is

413.24–5 ***extra* (no great matter if it grazes the sheriff) touch** *MS GM A, MS GM B, SGG extra* touch

413.25 **leaders at** *MS GM A, MS GM B, SGG* leaders (no great matter if it grazes the sheriff) at

413.30–1 **Iceland;** *MS GM A appends footnote <in> Von Troil's Iceland*: – The allusion is to {↑ a} <a the> well-known chapter in Von Troil's work entitled – *Concerning the Snakes of Iceland*: The entire chapter consists of these 6 words – *There are no snakes in Iceland. SGG revises footnote 'Von Troil's Iceland:'* – The allusion is to a well-known chapter in Von Troil's work entitled, 'Concerning the Snakes of Iceland.' The entire chapter consists of these six words – '*There are no snakes in Iceland*.'[a]
[[a] See above, p. 602, n. 68.]

413.32 **in the 'coal-cellar.'** *MS GM A, MS GM B, SGG* in what I have shown to be the 'coal cellar.'

413.35 **against** *MS GM A appends partial footnote which is struck out 'set their faces against'* &c. Such was the political importance of the mail, that <all> none of the arrangements

413.35 **forbidden seat** *MS GM A* forbidden seat *MS GM B, SGG conform, with the exception of several significant deletions in MS GM B given here in angle brackets: 'forbidden seat:'* – The very sternest code of rules was enforced upon the mails by the Post-Office. Throughout England, only three outsides were allowed, of whom one was to sit on the box, and the other two immediately behind the box; none, under any pretext, to come near the guard; an indispensable caution; since else, under the guise of a passenger, a robber might by any one of a thousand advantages – which <if sudden> sometimes are created, but always <preconcerted> are favoured – by the animation of frank social intercourse, have disarmed the guard. Beyond the Scottish border, the regulation was so far relaxed as to allow of *four* outsides, but not relaxed at all as to the mode of placing them. One, as before, was seated on the box, and the other three <The> on the front of the roof, with a <broad> determinate and ample separation from the little insulated chair of the guard. This relaxation was conceded by way of compensating to

Scotland her disadvantages in point of population. England, by the superior density of her population, might always count upon a large fund of profits in the fractional trips of chance passengers riding for short distances of two or three stages. <This> In Scotland, this <brought> chance counted for much less. And therefore, to make good <this> the deficiency, Scotland was allowed <the permanent chance of> a compensatory profit upon one *extra* passenger.

413.41 **But even this left the** *MS GM A* <But even this left> Yet even <in> this <was> left the *MS GM B, SGG* Yet even this left

414.1–3 **ourselves. With a quotation rather too trite, I remarked to the coachman, – 'Jam** *MS GM A* ourselves. <With a quotation rather too trite>, I remarked to the coachman, with a quotation from Virgil's <A> Aeneid really too hackneyed, – 'Jam *MS GM B, SGG* ourselves. I remarked to the coachman, with a quotation from Virgil's 'Æneid' really too hackneyed – 'Jam

414.5 **of his education** *MS GM A, MS GM B, SGG* of the coachman's education

414.6 **interpreted so far as to say, that** *MS GM A* interpreted say, that *MS GM B, SGG* interpreted so far as to say, that

414.7–8 **and next-door neighbour Ucalegon.** *MS GM A* and next-door neighbour Ucalegon. *MS GM B, SGG* and inside passenger, Ucalegon.

414.8 **coachman said nothing, but** *MS GM A* coachman <said nothing, but, by his> made no answer, which is my own way when a stranger addresses me <in> either in Syriac or in Coptic, but *MS GM B, SGG* coachman made no answer, which is my own way when a stranger addresses me either in Syriac or in Coptic, but

414.9 **to be thinking that** *MS GM A, MS GM B, SGG* to insinuate that

414.9 **that in fact, Ucalegon,** *MS GM A, MS GM B, SGG* that Ucalegon,

414.10 **was not in the way-bill.** *MS GM A* was not booked, and therefore not in the way-bill. *MS GM B, SGG* was not in the way-bill, and therefore could not have been booked.

414.11–12 **the indeterminate and mysterious.** *MS GM A, MS GM B, SGG* the mysterious.

414.14–15 **establishment a grandeur and an official authority which** *MS GM A, MS GM B, SGG* establishment an official grandeur which

414.15–16 **terrors. But perhaps these terrors were not the less impressive, because their exact legal** *MS GM A, MS GM B, SGG* terrors. Not the less impressive were those terrors, because their legal

414.20 **road: ah!** *F, MS GM A, MS GM B, SGG* road. Ah!

414.21 **with the proclamation** *MS GM A, MS GM B, SGG* with proclamation

414.29 **ebb or flood, of** *MS GM A* ebb or flood, of *MS GM B, SGG* ebb and flood, *systole* and *diastole*, of

414.29 **intercourse –** *MS GM A* intercourse – *MS GM B, SGG* intercourse? –

414.38–9 **power, haughtily dispensing with** *MS GM A, MS GM B* power, that haughtily dispensed with *SGG* power that haughtily dispensed with

415.2–3 **smash, though, after all, I believe that damage might be levied upon the hundred. I,** *MS GM A, MS GM B, SGG* smash. I,

415.3 **as was possible,** *F, MS GM A, MS GM B, SGG* as possible,

415.6–7 **celebrated in those days from** *MS GM A* celebrated at that time from *MS GM B, SGG* celebrated at that time, from

415.7 **false*** *MS GM A, MS GM B* false *SGG moves footnote to* echoes*

415.7 **echoes** *MS GM A, MS GM B* echoes *SGG moves footnote from* false

415.n.1 **echoes' – yes,** *MS GM B, SGG echoes:'* – Yes,

415.n.2 **theatrical inventions** *MS GM B, SGG* theatrical fictions

415.n.3 **foundering *Vengeur,*** *MS GM B, SGG* foundering line-of-battle ship Vengeur,

415.n.4 ***pas,'* as** *MS GM B, SGG pas,'* or as

415.8 **was quite impossible, for in** *MS GM A, MS GM B, SGG* was evidently impossible, since in

415.8 **not even time** *MS GM A, MS GM B, SGG* not time

415.9 **post-office time, with an allowance in** *MS GM A* post-office <time, with an> allowance in *MS GM B* post-office allowance in *SGG* post-office allowance, in

415.13 **I contended,** *MS GM A, MS GM B, SGG* I felt,

415.14 ***à fortiori* I upheld its** *MS GM A* <*à fortiori* I upheld>

415.14 **rights, I** *MS GM A* rights <and I felt it> {↑ as} a {↑ matter of} duty <to assert its precedency and heraldic I *MS GM B, SGG* rights; as a matter of duty, I

415.21 **colour is this** *MS GM A* color in this *MS GM B, SGG* colour in this

415.25 **the state;** *MS GM A, MS GM B, SGG* the mighty state;

415.25 **Birmingham had** *MS GM A* Birmingham, our green-and-gold friend from false <deluding> fleeting perjured Brummagem, <whom designat<ing>ed from his hinder quarter of might rather call <xxx> cerulean-friend-and-saffron friend> *MS GM B, SGG* Birmingham, our green-and-gold friend from false, fleeting, perjured Brummagem,[a] had

[[a] Shakespeare, *Richard III*, I.iv.55: 'False, fleeting, perjur'd Clarence'.]

415.28–9 **that seemed to us sufficiently** *MS GM A, MS GM B, SGG* that already of itself seemed to me sufficiently

415.31 **was awake,** *MS GM A, MS GM B, SGG* was wide awake,

415.35 **ripe,** *F, MS GM A, MS GM B, SGG* right,

415.35 **stronger image,** *MS GM A, MS GM B, SGG* stronger word,

415.36 **resources, he** *MS GM A* resources <against the Bromicham>[a]; he *MS GM B, SGG* resources: he

[[a] An obsolete form of Brummagem (*OED*).]

415.39 **of strength,** *MS GM A, MS GM B, SGG* of moral strength,

416.5–6 **A Welshman, sitting** *MS GM A, MS GM B, SGG* A Welsh rustic, sitting

416.7 **continuance** *MS GM A, MS GM B, SGG* progress

416.7 **said – No;** *MS GM A* said with philosophic<ally> calmness – *No*; *MS GM B, SGG* said, with philosophic calmness, *No*;

416.11–12 **us perhaps,' I** *MS GM A, MS GM B, SGG* us, if you like,' I

416.14–15 **opinion, that** *MS GM A* opinion <grounding its entirely on the laws of Edward Longshanks>, that *MS GM B, SGG* opinion, that

416.16 **some Oriental region, when the prince of** *MS GM A* some <oriental region, when the prince> far {↑ oriental} <distant> kingdom, when the sultan {↑ of all the land} <and in contempt of his royalty> *MS GM B, SGG* some far oriental kingdom, when the sultan of

416.17 **his splendid court, were** *MS GM A, MS GM B, SGG* his princes, ladies, and chief omrahs, were

416.18 **prodigious** *MS GM A, MS GM B, SGG* natural

416.19–20 **in sight also of all the astonished field sportsmen, spectators, and followers, killed him on the spot. The prince was struck with amazement at** *MS GM A, MS GM B, SGG* in contempt also of the eagle's traditional royalty, and before the whole assembled field of astonished spectators from Agra and Lahore,[a] killed the eagle on the spot. Amazement seized the sultan at

[[a] Cf. Wordsworth, *The Prelude* (1850), X. 18-20: 'the Great Mogul, when He / Ere while went forth from Agra or Lahor, / Rajas and Omras in his train'.]

416.21 **and with burning** *MS GM A, MS GM B, SGG* and burning

416.22 **him; caressed** *MS GM A, MS GM B, SGG* him; he caressed

416.23 **and ordered** *MS GM A, MS GM B, SGG* and he ordered

416.24 **a crown of gold should** *MS GM A* a crown of gold should *MS GM B, SGG* a diadem of gold and rubies should

416.25 **this coronation,** *MS GM A, MS GM B, SGG* this solemn coronation,

416.26–7 **traitor that had dared to rise in rebellion against his liege lord the** *MS GM A* traitor as having dared to rise rebelliously against his liege lord and anointed sovereign the *MS GM B, SGG* traitor, as having dared to rise rebelliously against his liege lord and anointed sovereign, the

416.28–9 **Welshman,'how painful it would have been to you and me as men of refined feelings, that this poor brute,** *MS GM A* Welshman, '<how painful it would have been> to you and me, as men of refined <feelings> sensibilities, how painful it would have been that this poor Brummagem brute, *MS GM B, SGG* Welshman, 'to you and me, as men of refined sensibilities, how painful it would have been that this poor Brummagem brute,

416.30–1 **with jewellery, gold, with Birmingham ware, or paste diamonds, and** *MS GM A* with <jewellery, gold, with> Birmingham tinsel, with paste diamonds <x> and Roman pearls <ware, or paste diamond>s, and *MS GM B, SGG* with Birmingham tinsel, with paste diamonds, and Roman pearls, and

416.32–3 **the 10th of Edward III. chap. 15, for** *MS GM A, MS GM B, SGG* the 6th of Edward Longshanks,[a] chap. 18, for
[[a] Edward I, (1239–1307) King of England, 1272-1307.]

416.35–6 **mail was really treasonable,** *MS GM A, MS GM B, SGG* mail really were treasonable,

416.38–417.2 **These were among the gaieties...the mail system.** *MS GM A, MS GM B, SGG omit paragraph*

417.3 **the mail-coach** *MS GM A, MS GM B, SGG* the old mail-coach

417.4 **velocity, but not however as** *MS GM A* velocity, <but> not however as *MS GM B, SGG* velocity, not, however, as

417.7 **hour, or** *MS GM A* hour, though we are far from feeling it as a personal experiences, or *MS GM B, SGG* hour, though we are far from feeling it as a personal experience, or

417.9 **I am** *MS GM A, MS GM B, SGG* I myself am

417.11 **but *magna vivimus*. The** *MS GM A* but *vivimus*. Yes, 'magna *vivimus:*' we do not {↑ make verbal ostentation of} <assert> our grandeurs {↑ <in big wording>} <as verbally>, we realize our grandeurs in act <deed> and in the very experience of <xxx> life. The *MS GM B, SGG* but *vivimus*. Yes, 'magna *vivimus:*' we do not make verbal ostentation of our grandeurs, we realise our grandeurs in act, and in the very experience of life. The

417.15–16 **of an animal, in** *MS GM A, MS GM B, SGG* of the noblest amongst brutes, in

417.16–18 **and echoing hoofs. This speed was incarnated in the *visible* contagion amongst brutes of some impulse, that, radiating into their natures, had yet its centre and beginning in man. The** *MS GM A, MS GM B, SGG* and thunder-beating hoofs. The

417.20–21 **first – but** *MS GM A, MS GM B, SGG* first. But

417.21 **link** *MS GM A, MS GM B, SGG* links

417.21–2 **of the battle** *MS GM A, MS GM B, SGG* of battle

417.22 **horse, was the** *MS GM A, MS GM B, SGG* horse, were

417.22 **man – kindling** *MS GM A, MS GM B, SGG* man and its electric thrillings – kindling

417.23–4 **by motions and gestures to the sympathies, more or less dim, in his** *MS GM A* by <motions and> contagious <kindlings> gestures to the heart of <the sympathies, more or less dim, in> his *MS GM B, SGG* by contagious shouts and gestures to the heart of his

417.27 **power any more to** *MS GM A, MS GM B, SGG* power to

417.34–5 **afar the laurelled** *MS GM A* afar <to worry> the laurelled *MS GM B, SGG* afar the laurelled

417.35–6 **and advancing through** *MS GM A, MS GM B, SGG* and proclaiming itself through

417.38–40 **for sublime effects, for interesting personal communications, for revelations of impressive faces that could not have offered themselves amongst the hurried and fluctuating groups of** *MS GM A* for sublime effects, for interesting personal communications, for revelations of impressive faces that could not have offered themselves amongst the hurried and fluctuating groups of *MS GM B* for <sublime effects, for> public expressions of interest, scenical yet natural, in great <xx> national tidings; for revelations of <impressive> faces and groups that could not <have> offer<ed> themselves amongst the <hurried and> fluctuating mobs of *SGG* for public expressions of interest, scenical yet natural, in great national tidings; for revelations of faces and groups that could not offer themselves amongst the fluctuating mobs of

417.41 **a mail-coach had** *MS GM A* a mail-coach had *MS GM B, SGG* a laurelled mail had

417.42 **acknowledged only one interest.** *MS GM A* acknowledged only one interest. *MS GM B, SGG* acknowledged one sole interest.

418.2 **about dawn into the** *MS GM A* about dawn into the *MS GM B* about <dawn into> day-break amongst the *SGG* about daybreak amongst the

418.4 **become known to myself? Yet** *MS GM A* become <known to myself?> a memorable inmate of my dreams? Yet *MS GM B, SGG* become <a memorable> the glorified inmate of my dreams? Yet

418.6–7 **which even *her* I could not willingly have spared; yet (thirty-five years later) she** *MS GM A* which <even *her* I could not willingly have spared; yet (thirty-five years later) still> {↑ even <yet> now} from a distance of forty years she *MS GM B, SGG* which even now, from a distance of forty years, she

418.7–8 **dreams; and though, by an accident of fanciful caprice, she brought along with her into those dreams a troop** *MS GM A* dreams; and though, by an accident of fanciful caprice, she brought along with her into those dreams a troop *MS GM B* dreams; yes <and> though, by <an accident of fanciful caprice,> links of natural association she <brought> brings along with her <into those dreams> a troop *SGG* dreams; yes, though by links of natural association she brings along with her a

418.9 **that were more** *MS GM A* that were more *MS GM B, SGG* that are more

418.9 **to a human heart than** *MS GM A* to a human heart than *MS GM B* to <a human> the heart than *SGG* to the heart, than

418.10 **dawn were delightful** *MS GM A* dawn were delightful *MS GM B* dawn <were> are *SGG* dawn are delightful

418.13 **name** *MS GM A* name *MS GM B, SGG* image

418.14 **where I saw her; I do not exactly know, but** *MS GM A, MS GM B, SGG* where only I had ever seen her. Why she came so punctually, I do not exactly know; but

418.15–16 **Bath, her own residence being probably the centre to which these commissions gathered. The** *MS GM A* Bath, <her own residence being probably the centre to which these commissions gathered.> which had gathered to her own residence as a {↑ central} <natural> rendezvous for <collect> converging them. The *MS GM B, SGG* Bath, which had gathered to her own residence as a central rendezvous for converging them. The

418.17 **who wore** *MS GM A* who wore *MS GM B* who drove the Bath mail and wore *SGG* who drove the Bath mail, and wore

418.17–18 **royal livery, being one amongst the privileged few,* happened** *MS GM A* royal livery, being one amongst the privileged few,* happened *MS GM B, SGG revise sentence and move footnote* royal livery,* happened

418.n.1 **'Privileged few.'** – *MS GM B '<Privileged few>'* wore the royal livery – *SGG 'Wore the royal livery:'* –

418.n.1 **that this splendid costume belonged** *MS GM B, SGG* that the royal livery belonged

418.n.3 **belong as a matter of course, and was essential** *MS GM B, SGG* belong, I believe, and was obviously essential

418.n.3 **warrant, and a** *MS GM B, SGG* warrant, and as a

418.n.6–7 **long or special service.** *MS GM B* long (<but>, if not long, <after difficult> trying and special) service. *SGG* long (or, if not long, trying and special) service.

418.20–1 **concerned. Was I then vain enough to imagine that I myself individually could** *MS GM A* concerned. Was I then vain enough to imagine that I myself individually could *MS GM B* concerned. <Was I then vain enough to imagine> Did my vanity then suggest that I myself, individually, could *SGG* Did my vanity then suggest that I myself, individually, could

418.32 **yes; *mais oui donc;* as much love as one *can* make** *MS GM A* yes; *mais oui donc;* as much love as one *can* make *MS GM B* yes; <*mais oui donc;*> about as much love as one *could* make *SGG* yes; about as much love as one *could* make

418.32 **mail is changing** *MS GM A* mail is changing *MS GM B, SGG* mail was changing

419.5–6 **Yet he was still active; he was still blooming. Blooming** *MS GM A* Yet why not? He was still active; he was still blooming. Blooming *MS GM B* Yet, why not? <He was still> Was he not active? <he was still> Was he not blooming? Blooming *SGG* Yet, why not? Was he not active? Was he not blooming? Blooming

419.8 **No, that's** *MS GM A, MS GM B, SGG* Stop, that's

419.8 **line:** *F, MS GM A, MS GM B, SGG* line.

419.11–12 **from youth and innocence, and from the fountains** *MS GM A* from youth and <innocence, and> from the fountains *MS GM B* from <youth, and from> the fountains *SGG* from the fountains

419.13–14 **particularly (I am very sure, no *more* than one,) in** *MS GM A, MS GM B, SGG* particularly in

419.17 **probably,** *MS GM A, MS GM B, SGG* possibly,

419.19 **planted an easy opportunity for** *MS GM A* planted an easy opportunity for *MS GM B* planted <an easy opportunity> a human advantage for *SGG* planted a human advantage for

419.22 **silver** *MS GM A* silver *MS GM B, SGG* silvery

419.22 **turrets** *MS GM A appends footnote* 'turrets' – As one who <xx>loves and venerates Chaucer, <I> for his unrivalled merits of tenderness, <and> {↑ of picturesque characterization, {↑ and of <inimitable> narrative skill,} I noticed with great pleasure that the word *torrettes* is used by him to designate the little devices through which the reins are made to pass.[a] This same word <is used by uniformly and applied> in the same exact sense I heard <the word> uniformly used by many scores of <mail coachmen> illustrious mail coachmen, to whose confidential friendship I had the honour of being admitted in my younger days. *MS GM B, SGG revise footnote 'Turrets:'* – As one who loves and venerates Chaucer for his unrivalled merits of tenderness, of picturesque characterisation, and of narrative skill, I noticed with great pleasure that the word *torrettes* is used by him to designate the little devices through which the reins are made to pass. This same word, in the same exact sense, I heard uniformly used by many scores of illustrious mail-coachmen, to whose confidential friendship I had the honour of being admitted in my younger days.

[[a] De Quincey seems to have in mind Chaucer, 'The Knight's Tale', l. 2152: 'Colered of gold, and tourettes fyled rounde'. The Chaucerian term, however, is applied to a dog's collar, not to the trappings of a horse.]

419.25 **would have made me** *MS GM A, MS GM B, SGG* would make me

419.28–9 **acquiesced in her allotment, supposing that she had seen reason to plant** *MS GM A, MS GM B, SGG* acquiesced by anticipation in her award, supposing that she should plant

419.30–3 **It must not be supposed...regarded my own feelings.** *MS GM A, MS GM B, SGG omit*

419.33–41 **In fact, the utter shadowyness...as regarded hers.** *MS GM B, SGG omit*

419.42–420.1 **Bath and Bristol mail, heaven** *MS GM A* Bath and Bristol mail, heaven *MS GM B* Bath <and Bristol> mail, timing all courtships by Post-Office allowance, heaven *SGG* Bath mail, timing all courtships by post-office allowance, heaven

420.4–11 **I have...fifty years' repentance.** *MS GM A, MS GM B, SGG omit*

420.13–16 **change or perish. Even thunder and lightning, it pains me to say, are not the thunder and lightning which I seem to remember about the time of Waterloo. Roses, I fear, are degenerating, and, without a Red revolution, must come to dust. The** *MS GM A* change <or perish> – all things perish. Perish the roses and the crowns of kings: even thunder and lightning <it pains me to say> are not the thunder and lightning which I <seem to> remember <about> in the time of Waterloo. Roses, I fear, are degenerating, and, without a Red revolution, must come to dust. The *MS GM B* change – all things perish. 'Perish the roses and the <crowns> palms of kings;' <even the> perish even the crowns and trophies of Waterloo: thunder and lightning are not the thunder and lightning which I remember <in the time of Waterloo.> Roses <I fear,> are degenerating <and, without a Red revolution, must come to dust.> The *SGG* change – all things perish. 'perish the roses and the palms of kings:'[a] perish even the crowns and trophies of Waterloo: thunder and lightning are not the thunder and lightning which I remember. Roses are degenerating. The

[[a] Wordsworth, *The Excursion*, VII. 980-1: 'Perish the roses and the flowers of kings, / Princes, and emperors, and the crowns and palms'.]

420.17 **not improving;** *MS GM A, MS GM B, SGG* not visibly improving;

420.17–18 **superannuated. Mr** *MS GM A* superannuated. Crocodiles, it is possible, are stationary. Mr *MS GM B* superannuated. Crocodiles, <it is possible,> you will {[↑ say,} are stationary. Mr *SGG* Crocodiles, you will say, are stationary. Mr *SGG*

420.24 **prevailed on** *MS GM A, MS GM B, SGG* prevailed through innumerable generations on

420.29 **Waterton** *MS GM A, MS GM B, SGG append footnote; the three texts conform, with the exception of one substantive deletion in MS GM A given here in angle brackets: 'Mr Waterton:'* – Had the reader lived through the last generation, he would not need to be told that some thirty or thirty-five years back, Mr Waterton, a distinguished country gentleman of ancient family in Northumberland, publicly mounted and rode in top-boots a savage

old crocodile, that was restive <mutinous> and very impertinent, but all to no purpose. The crocodile jibbed and tried to kick, but vainly. He was no more able to throw the squire, than Sinbad was to throw the old scoundrel who used his back without paying for it,[a] until he discovered a mode (slightly immoral, perhaps, though some think not) of murdering the old fraudulent jockey, and so circuitously of unhorsing him.
[[a] See above, p. 597, n. 53]

420.33 **up – it is to be ridden; and the use of** *MS GM A* up – it is to be ridden; and the use of *MS GM B* up – <it is> viz., to be ridden; and the final cause of *SGG* up – viz., to be ridden; and the final cause of

420.38 **Perhaps,** *MS GM A* Perhaps, *MS GM B* <Perhaps>, *SGG* If,

420.38 **change, but all things else *do:*** *MS GM A* change, but all things else *do: MS GM B* change, <but> all things else undeniably *do: SGG* change, all things else undeniably *do:*

420.41 **call up** *MS GM A* call up *MS GM B* call <up> back *SGG* call back

420.41–42 **Fanny from thirty-five years back, arises suddenly a** *MS GM A* Fanny from <thirty five> forty years back, <arises> rises suddenly a *MS GM B* Fanny <from forty years back, rises suddenly a>, – up rises {↑ suddenly} from a gulph of forty years a *SGG* Fanny, up rises suddenly from a gulf of forty years a

420.44 **in a choral service, rises Fanny** *F* in the choral service, rises Fanny *MS GM A, MS GM B, SGG* in the choral service, rise Fanny

421.4 **gold, or in a coat with** *MS GM A, MS GM B, SGG* gold, with

421.6–7 **hours, and with the dreadful legend of TOO LATE. Then** *MS GM A* hours, and with the dreadful legend of TOO LATE. Then *MS GM B* hours, <and> that mingle with the <dreadful legend of TOO LATE.> heavens and the {↑ heavenly host}. The *SGG* hours, that mingle with the heavens and the heavenly host. Then

421.7 **arrived in** *F, MS GM A, MS GM B, SGG* arrive at

421.n.4–5 **of a peculiarly tender character, if less dignified by the grandeurs of savage and forest life.** *MS GM B* of peculiar tenderness, supposing even that this beautiful creature is less characteristically impressed with the grandeurs of savage and forest life. <By the way, I take this opportunity of noticing a signal blunder as to the English deer in the 'Illustrated News.' That journal speaks of the *red* deer as rarely, if ever, seen in England.[a] Now, it is clear that the habits of the red deer and their <dangerous> power, must in all civilised regions limit their expansion. But, notwithstanding this, these deer are found in *many* parts of England; in <in> at one at least, of the southernmost counties, (Devon and Exmoor) a and in one, at least, of the two northernmost counties, (viz., on the borders of Cumberland and Westmorland, over Martindale forest,[b] &c.), they are regularly hunted, and sometimes intrude upon the fallow deer in Gobarrow Park, by swimming across the Lake of Ulleswater. The red-deer are found also in the midland counties, of which fact some gentleman, personally unknown to me, took the trouble, <some> a few months ago, most obligingly to furnish me with illustrative details. I have no doubt that they exist also in Northumberland, though I cannot vouch for them, as I can in Martindale, upon direct personal observation. *SGG* of peculiar tenderness, supposing even that this beautiful creature is less characteristically impressed with the grandeurs of savage and forest life.
[[a] The *London Illustrated News* was founded by Herbert Ingram (1811-60; *DNB*) in 1842. De Quincey's reference to its discussion of roe-deer has not been traced.
[b] See above, p. 537, n. 75.]

421.8 **roe-deer: these retire** *MS GM A* roe-deer: these retire *MS GM B* roe-deer; <these> the deer and their fawns retire *SGG* roe-deer; the deer and their fawns retire

421.9–10 **roses; the roses call up (as ever) the sweet countenance of Fanny, who, being** *MS GM A* roses; the roses call up (as ever) the sweet countenance of Fanny; <who> and she, being *MS GM B* roses; once again the roses call up <(as ever)> the sweet countenance of Fanny; and she, being *SGG* roses; once again the roses call up the sweet countenance of Fanny; and she, being

421.11 **of wild semi-legendary** *MS GM A* of wild semi-legendary *MS GM B* of <wild> semi-legendary *SGG* of semi-legendary

421.14–15 **unutterable horrors of monstrous and** *MS GM A* unutterable <horrors of monstrous> and *MS GM B, SGG* unutterable and

421.17–21 **heaven, and having power (which, without experience, I never could have believed) to awaken the pathos that kills in the very bosom of the horrors that madden the grief that gnaws at the heart, together with the monstrous creations of darkness that shock the belief, and make dizzy the reason of man.** *MS GM A* heaven, when <the> is sculptured the eternal writing <which> which proclaims the frailty of Earth and <the Children of Earth> her Children. <and having power (which, without experience, I never could have believed) to awaken the pathos that kills in the very bosom of the horrors that madden the grief that gnaws at the heart, together with the monstrous creations of darkness that shock the belief, and make dizzy the reason of man.> *MS GM B, SGG* heaven, where is sculptured the eternal writing which proclaims the frailty of Earth and her children.

421.21–423.11 **This is the peculiarity...transfigured coachman of the Bath mail.** *MS GM A, MS GM B, SGG omit*

423.17 **the rest, from 1805 to 1815 inclusively, furnished** *MS GM A* the rest, from 1805 to 1815 inclusively, furnished *MS GM B* the <rest> other nine, from 1805 to 1815 inclusively, furnished *SGG* the other nine (from 1805 to 1815 inclusively) furnished

423.18–19 **in a contest of that portentous nature, had** *MS GM A* in a contest of that portentous nature, had *MS GM B* in such a contest of <that portentous nature> Titans, had *SGG* in such a contest of Titans, had

423.20–1 **alive in central** *MS GM* A alive in central *MS GM B* alive <in> through central *SGG* alive through central

423.25 **in a quarter** *MS GM A, MS GM B, SGG* in one quarter

423.n.5 **said more than once – 'Here** *MS GM B* said <more than once> in more notes than one, dated from two to four P.M. on the field of Waterloo, 'Here *SGG* said in more notes than one, dated from two to four P.M. on the field of Waterloo, 'Here

423.n.7–8 **in the north of Portugal, during his flight from an English army, and subsequently** *MS GM B* in <the north of Portugal, during his flight from an English army, and> 1809, when <x> ejected by us with headlong violence from Oporto,[a] and pursued through <Portugal> a long line of wrecks to the frontier line of Spain: subsequently *SGG* in 1809, when ejected by us with headlong violence from Oporto, and pursued through <Portugal> a long line of wrecks to the frontier of Spain: subsequently *SGG* in 1809, when ejected by us with headlong violence from Oporto, and pursued through a long line of wrecks to the frontier of Spain; subsequently

[[a] Oporto, or 'Porto', is a port city in northern Portugal. It was a key location in the Peninsular War. The city was captured by British forces under the Duke of Wellington (see above, p. 542, n. 86) on 12 May 1809.]

423.n.9 **battles.** *MS GM B, SGG* battles, to say nothing of Toulouse,[a] he should have learned our pretensions.

[[a] Marshal Soult (see above, p. 618, n. 97) unsuccessfully fought the last battle of the Peninsular War against the Duke of Wellington outside Toulouse on 10 April 1814.]

423.32 **the aroma** *MS GM A* the aroma *MS GM B, SGG* the first aroma

424.1–2 **government official news was generally the first news.** *MS GM A* government <official> news was generally the first news. *MS GM B, SGG* government news was generally the <first> earliest news. *SGG* government news was generally the earliest news.

424.4 **time, was** *MS GM A, MS GM B, SGG* time* and not in St Martin's-le-Grand,[a] was *MS GM A, MS GM B, SGG append footnote 'At that time:'* – I speak of the era previous to Waterloo.

[[a] See above, p. 619, n. 100.]

424.9 **harness, and the magnificence** *MS GM A* harness, <and the> their strength, their {↑ brilliant} cleanliness, their beautiful simplicity, – but, more than all, the royal magnificence *MS GM B, SGG* harness, their strength, their brilliant cleanliness, their beautiful simplicity – but, more than all, the royal magnificence

424.11 **an inspector** *MS GM A, MS GM B, SGG* an official inspector

424.12 **glasses, &c., were** *MS GM A, MS GM B, SGG* glasses, lamps, were

424.18 **guards, who are his Majesty's servants, and the coachmen, who are** *MS GM A* guards, <who are> as being officially his majesty's servants, and <the coachmen, who are> of the coachmen such as are *MS GM B, SGG* guards, as being officially his Majesty's servants, and of the coachmen such as are

424.20 **were won** *MS GM A, MS GM B, SGG* were naturally won

424.23 **dilated** *MS GM A, MS GM B, SGG* dilate

424.23 **openly an *official* connection** *MS GM A* openly <an *official*> a personal connection *MS GM B, SGG* openly a personal connection

424.27 **dress. The usual** *MS GM A, MS GM B, SGG* dress; for the usual

424.29–30 **English blood.** *MS GM A, MS GM B, SGG* national blood.

424.32 **servants the** *MS GM A* servants and summoned to draw up the *MS GM B SGG* servants, and summoned to draw up, the

424.35 **Edinburgh, Perth, Glasgow – expressing** *MS GM A* Edinburgh, <Perth,> Glasgow, Perth Sterling Aberdeen, – expressing *MS GM B, SGG* Edinburgh, Glasgow, Perth, Stirling, Aberdeen – expressing

424.40 **play; – horses!** *MS GM A* play – <horses> Horses! *MS GM B, SGG* play. Horses!

424.40–1 **that (unless powerfully reined in) would bound** *MS GM A, MS GM B, SGG* that bound

424.42–3 **thundering of wheels, what a trampling of horses! – what** *MS GM A* thundering of wheels, what a trampling of horses! – what a sounding of trumpets! – what *MS GM B, SGG* thundering of wheels! – what a trampling of hoofs! – what a sounding of trumpets! – what

425.8 **travel, almost without** *MS GM A, MS GM B, SGG* travel, without

425.11–12 **the approaching sympathies, yet unborn, which we were going to evoke.** *F* the approaching sympathies, yet unborn, which we are going to evoke. *MS GM A* the <approaching> yet slumbering sympathies, <yet unborn,> which in so <long> vast a succession we are going to awake. we are going to evoke. *MS GM B, SGG* the yet slumbering sympathies which in so vast a succession we are going to awake.

425.n.3 **lying,** *MS GM B, SGG* fibbing,

425.n.8 **falsehood** *MS GM B, SGG* fiction

425.n.14–15 **reached, nor likely to be reached very soon, by** *MS GM B* reached, <nor likely to be reached very soon, by> as yet by *SGG* reached as yet by

425.n.21 **'Those rascals,** *F* 'These rascals, *MS GM B* 'These <rascals> wretches, *SGG* 'These wretches,

425.n.23 **engage a** *MS GM B, SGG* engage that a

425.14 **we begin** *MS GM A, MS GM B, SGG* we soon begin

425.19 **along behind and before our course. The** *MS GM A* along us, behind us, and before us. <behind and before our course>. The *MS GM B, SGG* along us, behind us, and before us. The

425.23 **cellars, look** *MS GM A* cellars, through {↑ infinite} <endless> London, look *MS GM B, SGG* cellars, through infinite London, look

426.2 **that lies ready to their hands. On** *MS GM A* that <and which>, by catching the summer {↑ breezes} <wind>, will express an aerial jubilation (lies ready to their hands>. On *MS GM B, SGG* that, by catching the summer breezes, will express an aerial jubilation. On

426.6 **within the carriage. It** *MS GM A, MS GM B, SGG* within. It

426.13 **laurels.** *MS GM A* laurels. *MS GM B, SGG* laurels!

426.16 **hats, the** *MS GM A, MS GM B, SGG* hats to the ladies; the

426.28–9 **mistaken; they are nothing of the kind. I** *MS GM A* mistaken; they are nothing of the kind. I *MS GM B* mistaken<; they are nothing of the kind>. I *SGG* mistaken. I

426.29 **a higher rank: for** *MS GM A* a higher rank; for *MS GM B, SGG* a far higher rank; for

426.36 **two amiable daughters** *MS GM A, MS GM B, SGG* two daughters

427.16–17 **town, I forget what, where we happened to change horses near midnight.** *MS GM A* town, <I forget what,> where we <happened to change horses near midnight.> changed horses an hour or two after midnight. *MS GM B, SGG* town where we changed horses an hour or two after midnight.

427.17 **beds. We** *MS GM A* beds, and had occasioned a <beautiful> partial illumination <in the a principal street of> of the stalls and booths presenting an unusual but very impressive effect. We *MS GM B, SGG* beds, and had occasioned a partial illumination of the stalls and booths, presenting an unusual but very impressive effect. We

427.18–19 **most impressive scene on our route** *MS GM A* most <impressive> striking scene on <our> the whole route *MS GM B, SGG* most striking scene on the whole route

427.22 **upon flowers** *MS GM A* upon flowers *MS GM B, SGG* upon our flowers

427.22 **laurels.** *MS GM A appends footnote 'glittering laurels:'* – I must observe that the colour of *green* suffers almost a <ghostly> spiritual change and exaltation under the effect of Bengal lights. *MS GM B, SGG revise footnote 'Glittering laurels:'* – I must observe, that the colour of *green* suffers almost a spiritual change and exaltation under the effect of Bengal lights.

427.22–3 **around the massy darkness seemed to invest us with walls of impenetrable blackness, together** *MS GM A* around ourselves, <that for> that formed a centre of light, the darkness gathered <in> on the rear and flanks in massy blackness, – <the massy darkness seemed to invest us with walls of impenetrable blackness, these>; these optical splendors, <together> together *MS GM B* around ourselves, that formed a centre of light, the darkness gathered on the rear and flanks in massy blackness; these optical splendours, together

427.25 **affecting. As** *MS GM A, MS GM B, SGG* affecting, theatrical and holy. As

427.25 **alighted. And** *MS GM A* alighted. And *MS GM B, SGG* alighted; and

427.26 **where perhaps she** *MS GM A, MS GM B, SGG* where no doubt she

427.27 **presiding at some part of the evening,** *MS GM A* presiding through the earlier part of the night, <at some part of the evening>, *MS GM B, SGG* presiding through the earlier part of the night,

427.30 **Talavera. I** *MS GM A* Talavera <but not imperfect in bloodshed and savagery> – imperfect for its results, such was the {↑ virtual} <virtual> treachery of the Spanish general, Cuesta,[a] but not imperfect in its ever-memorable heroism. I *MS GM B, SGG* Talavera – imperfect for its results, such was the virtual treachery of the Spanish general, Cuesta, but not imperfect in its ever-memorable heroism. I
[[a] Gregorio Garcia de la Cuesta (1740-1812) was made Captain-General of Old Castile in 1809. In the Peninsular War, his forces united with those of the Duke of Wellington, but he proved a highly unreliable ally.]

427.31–2 **battle. But her agitation, though not the agitation of fear, but of exultation rather, and enthusiasm, had** *MS GM A* battle. <But her> The agitation<, though not the agitation of fear, but of exultation rather, and> of her enthusiasm<,> had *MS GM B, SGG* battle. The agitation of her enthusiasm had

427.34 **relation** *MS GM* A relation *MS GM B, SGG* relative

428.2 **then ascending** *MS GM B* then ascending *SGG* then ascended

428.4 **been all but annihilated;** *MS GM B* been <all but> barely not annihilated; *SGG* been barely not annihilated;

428.4–5 **believe, not so many as one in four survived.** *MS GM B* believe, about one in <four> <five> survived. *SGG* believe, about one in four survived.

428.6 **hours known to myself and all** *MS GM B* hours gloried and hallowed to the ear of <all London known to myself and> all *SGG* hours glorified and hallowed to the ear of all

428.6 **as stretched** *MS GM B, SGG* as lying stretched

428.8 **talking with myself in** *MS GM B, SGG* talking in

428.8 **hopeful** *MS GM B, SGG* joyous

428.9 **dream?** *MS GM B, SGG* dreams?

428.9–11 **No. I said to myself, To-morrow, or the next day, she will hear the worst. For this night, wherefore** *MS GM B* No. To-morrow, said I to myself – to-morrow, or the next day, <she> will <hear> publish the worst. For <this> one night more, wherefore *SGG* No. To-morrow, said I to myself – to-morrow, or the next day, will publish the worst. For one night more, wherefore

428.12 **respite, let** *MS GM B, SGG* respite, then, let

428.12–13 **owe this to** *MS GM B, SGG* owe to

428.14 **paid, there was no reason for suppressing the** *MS GM B, SGG* paid, not, therefore, was I silent on the

428.15–16 **to the service and glory of the day. For the very few words I had time for speaking, I governed myself accordingly. I** *MS GM B, SGG* to that day's <the> service and glory <of the day.> *SGG* that day's service and glory. I

428.20 **England, privates and officers, had** *MS GM B, SGG* England, officers and privates, had

428.22 ***her*), and** *MS GM B her*) <yes, rode into those mists, and laid> and *SGG her*), and

428.25 **mothers'** *F, MS GM B, SGG* mother's

428.26 **arms. It is singular that** *MS GM B, SGG* arms. Strange it is, yet true, that

428.26 **fears, even** *MS GM B, SGG* fears for her son's safety, even

428.27 **been conspicuously engaged, for her son's safety: but** *MS GM B* been <conspicuously> memorably engaged; but *SGG* been memorably engaged; but

428.29 **therefore *he*,** *MS GM B, SGG* therefore that *he*,

428.29 **rendered eminent service in the trying conflict** *MS GM B* rendered <personal> conspicuous service in the dreadful conflict *SGG* rendered conspicuous service in the dreadful conflict

428.30 **them the** *MS GM B* them within the last 12 hours the *SGG* them, within the last twelve hours, the

428.31 **London – that in** *MS GM B* London – so absolutely <did> was fear swallowed up in <sudden> joy – that, in *SGG* London – so absolutely was fear swallowed up in joy – that, in

428.31 **nature, she threw** *MS GM B, SGG* nature, the poor woman threw

428.32 **neck, and, poor woman, kissed me.** *MS GM B, SGG* neck, as she thought of her son, and gave to *me* the kiss which secretly was meant for *him*.

The Vision of Sudden Death

Title **THE VISION OF SUDDEN DEATH** *MS VSD F, SGG* THE ENGLISH MAIL-COACH SECTION THE SECOND. – THE VISION OF SUDDEN DEATH.

430.1–20 **[The reader is to understand...the principal image.]** *MS VSD F, SGG omit*

430.21 **be thought of sudden death?** *MS VSD F, SGG* be taken as the predominant opinion of man, reflective and philosophic, upon SUDDEN DEATH?

430.22 **society it has** *MS VSD F, SGG* society, sudden death has

430.23 **desired, and, on the other hand, as** *MS VSD F, SGG* desired, or, again, as

430.24 **is most of all to** *MS VSD F, SGG* is with most horror to

430.25 **and the very** *MS VSD F, SGG* on the very

430.25–6 **assassination, being questioned as to the mode of death which, in *his* opinion, might seem the** *MS VSD F, SGG* assassination, when the minutes of his earthly career were numbered, being asked what death, in *his* judgment, might be pronounced the

430.30 **horrors. 'From** *MS VSD F, SGG* horrors: – 'From

430.33 **it is the last** *MS VSD F, SGG* it is ranked among the last

430.34 **treated** *MS VSD F, SGG* ranked

430.35 **the difference** *MS VSD F, SGG* the essential difference

430.36 **But there I hesitate. The** *MS VSD F, SGG* But this, on consideration, I doubt. The

431.1 **Litany. It seems rather a petition indulged to** *MS VSD F, SGG* Litany, unless under a special construction of the word 'sudden.' It seems a petition – indulged rather and conceded to

431.2 **piety. And, however, *that* may be, two** *MS VSD F* piety. It is not so much a doctrine built upon the eternities of the Christian system, as a plausible opinion built upon <a> special variet<y>ies of physical temperament. Let that, however, be as it may, two *SGG* piety. It is not so much a doctrine built upon the eternities of the Christian system, as a plausible opinion built upon special varieties of physical temperament. Let that, however, be as it may, two

431.5–7 **death, (I mean the *objective* horror to him who contemplates such a death, not the *subjective* horror to him who suffers it) from the false disposition to lay a stress** *MS VSD F* death, from the <false> disposition to lay a false stress *SGG* death, from the disposition to lay a false stress

431.8 **become words** *MS VSD F, SGG* become *final* words

431.13 **reason at all for** *MS VSD F, SGG* reason for

431.18 **one?** *MS VSD F, SGG* one.

431.20–1 **that by possibility felt himself** *MS VSD F* that, having <felt> known himself *SGG* that having known himself

431.21 **God. But** *MS VSD F, SGG* God, should have suited his demeanour to an expectation so awful. But

431.23 **extra** *MS VSD F, SGG* special

431.24–6 ***sudden*. And it is a strong illustration of the duty which for ever calls us to the stern valuation of words – that very possibly** *MS VSD F, SGG sudden.* Very possibly

431.29 **but that they** *MS VSD F, SGG* but perhaps they

431.30 **Βιαιος: but the difference is – that** *MS VSD F* Βιαιος, or, in other words, death that is brought about – not by internal and <passive chance> spontaneous change, but by active force having its origin from without. In this meaning the two authorities agree. Thus far they are in harmony. But the difference is, that *SGG* Βιαιος, or, in other words, death that is brought about, not by internal and spontaneous change, but by active force having its origin from without. In this meaning the two authorities agree. Thus far they are in harmony. But the difference is, that

431.31 **means an *unlingering* death: whereas** *MS VSD F, SGG* means *unlingering*; whereas

431.32 **by 'sudden' means** *MS VSD F, SGG* by 'sudden death' means

431.37 **Litany, his death** *MS VSD F, SGG* Litany, the mutineer's death

431.41 **Meantime, whatever may be thought of a sudden death as a mere** *MS VSD F, SGG* Here at once, in this sharp verbal distinction, we comprehend the faithful earnestness with which a holy Christian Church pleads on behalf of her poor departing children, that God would vouchsafe to them the last great privilege and distinction possible on a death-bed – viz., the opportunity of untroubled preparation for facing this mighty trial. Sudden death, as a mere

431.42–3 **inevitable – a question which,** *MS VSD F* inevitable, sudden death <expresses a choice> proposes a question of choice <a question> which, *SGG* inevitable, proposes a question of choice which,

431.44–432.1 **temperament – certainly, upon one aspect** *MS VSD F, SGG* temperament < – certainly upon>. Meantime, one aspect *SGG* temperament. Meantime, one aspect

432.1–2 **there can be no opening for doubt, that of all agonies incident to man it is the most frightful, that** *MS VSD F* there <can be no doubt, that of all agonies incident to man it is the most trying,> is, one modification, upon which no doubt can arise <that> that *SGG* there is, one modification, upon which no doubt can arise, that

432.3 **most freezing to human sensibilities – namely, where it** *MS VSD F* most <freezing to human sensibilities> agitating viz. where it *SGG* most agitating – viz., where it

432.4–5 **some hurried and inappreciable chance** *MS VSD F, SGG* some hurrying, flying, inappreciably minute chance

432.5–6 **it. Any effort, by which such an evasion can be accomplished, must be as sudden as the danger which it affronts. Even** *MS VSD F* it. <Any effort by which such an evasion can be accomplished, must be as sudden as the danger which it affronts.> Sudden as the danger which it affronts, <x> must be any effort by which such an evasion can be accomplished. Even *SGG* Sudden as the danger which it affronts, must be any effort by which such an evasion can be accomplished. Even

432.8–9 **vain, self-baffled, and where the dreadful knell of *too* late is already sounding in the ears by anticipation – even** *MS VSD F, SGG* vain, even

432.10 **case, namely, where** *MS VSD F, SGG* case – viz., where

432.10–11 **the agonising appeal** *MS VSD F, SGG* the appeal

432.12 **of another life** *MS VSD F, SGG* of some other life

432.12 **cast** *MS VSD F, SGG* thrown

432.16 **another – of a** *MS VSD F, SGG* another – a

432.18–19 **The man is called upon, too probably, to die; but** *MS VSD F* You are <The man is> called upon, by the case supposed <too probably>, possibly to die; but *SGG* You are called upon, by the case supposed, possibly to die; but

432.19–20 **any momentary collapse, he is self-denounced** *MS VSD F* any <momentary> even partial failure, or effeminate collapse, of <his> your energies, <he is> you will be self-denounced *SGG* any even partial failure, or effeminate collapse of your energies, you will be self-denounced

432.20 **He had** *MS VSD F, SGG* You had

432.21 **his effort** *MS VSD F, SGG* your effort

432.21–2 **might, at the best, have been unavailing;** *MS VSD F* might have been <without hope> unavailing; *SGG* might have been unavailing;

432.22–5 **but from this shadow of a chance, small or great, how if he has recoiled by a treasonable *lâcheté?* The effort *might* have been without hope; but to have risen to the level of that effort – would have rescued him, though not from dying, yet from dying as a traitor to his duties.** *MS VSD F, SGG* but to have risen to the level of such an effort, would have rescued you, though not from dying, yet from dying as a traitor to your final and farewell duty.

432.29–30 **natures – muttering under ground in one world, to be realised perhaps in some other. Upon** *MS VSD F, SGG* natures. Upon

432.31 **projected at intervals, perhaps,** *MS VSD F, SGG* projected, perhaps,

432.33 **from languishing prostration in hope and vital energy, that** *MS VSD F* through languishing prostration in hope and <hopeful energy in> the energies <exertions *duty*> of hope, that *SGG* through languishing prostration in hope and the energies of hope, that

432.34 **before him, publishes** *MS VSD F, SGG* before the lion, publishes

432.35 **Pariah falsehood** *MS VSD F, SGG* falsehood

432.40 **is made ready for leading him** *MS VSD F, SGG* is presented for tempting him

432.40 **ruin; again,** *MS VSD F, SGG* ruin; once again,

432.41 **falls from innocence; once again, by** *MS VSD F, SGG* falls by his own choice; again, by

432.42 **God,** *MS VSD F, SGG* Heaven,

433.1 **heavens of the** *MS VSD F, SGG* heavens for the

433.1–4 **God. Many people think that one man, the patriarch of our race, could not in his single person execute this rebellion for all his race. Perhaps they are wrong. But, even if not, perhaps in** *MS VSD F, SGG* God. It is not without probability that in

433.5–14 **original act. Our English rite. . . .Even so in dreams,** *MS VSD F, SGG* original transgression. In dreams,

433.17 **the aboriginal fall.** *MS VSD F* the treason of the aboriginal fall. <But in this reverie I am anticipating and shall seem to be wandering. Let me return to my narrative.> *SGG* the treason of the aboriginal fall.

433.18–19 **As I drew near to the Manchester post-office, I found that it was considerably past midnight;** *MS VSD F* <As I drew near to the Manchester post-office, I found that> The <memorable> incident so memorable {↑ in itself by <xxxxx> its features of horror,} <to myself, and to myself and> {↑ and} so scenical {↑ by its grouping} for the eye, <and so in its circumstances so impassioned {↑ in its composition with other ongoing scenery,>} which furnished the test for this <almo> reverie upon *Sudden Death*, occurred <on> to myself {↑ in the dead of night} <in the > as a solitary spectator, when {↑ seated} <sitting> on the box of the <outside particular mail which took the name of> Manchester {↑ <mail>} <mail, or Carlisle> and {↑ Glasgow} <Carlisle> mail <or Glasgow mail, according to the section of the road with which the speaker of the moment happened to be connected. And The circumstances are taken three years after> in the second or third summer after Waterloo. <The circumstances> I find it necessary to relate the circumstances because they are <by accident> such as could not have occurred {↑ unless} under a <xxxx> singular combination<s> of accidents. – <I was a one had> In those days the oblique and lateral {↑ communications <any rural> with many rural post offices <post and county stations> were so arranged {↑ either through necessity or defect of system} as to make it <x> requisite for the <xx London> {↑ main north western mail [i..e the *down* mail]} mail, on reaching <Carli> Manchester, to halt for a number of hours; how many, I do not remember; {↑ six or seven, I think;} but the result was that, {↑ in the} <xx> ordinary course, the mail <proceeded north xxxx> recommenced its journey northwards about midnight. Wearied with the long detention at a gloomy hotel, I walked out about 11 <o'clock> at night for the sake of fresh air; <and, having lost my way in the parts of Manchester that were newly built, and at and that night> meaning to <xx> fall in with the mail {↑ and resume my seat} at the Post-Office. The night however being <and> yet dark, as the moon {↑ had scarcely risen↑ not} already now {↑ (by an hour or so)}> and the streets being <empty> at that hour {↑ empty <offering> so as to offer} <so that I> few opportunities <offered> for asking {↑ the} <my> road, I lost my way; and did not reach the P. Office until it was considerably past midnight ; *SGG* The incident, so memorable in itself by its features of horror, and so scenical by its grouping for the eye, which furnished the text for this reverie upon *Sudden Death*, occurred to myself in the dead of night, as a solitary spectator, when seated on the box of the Manchester and Glasgow mail, in the second or third summer after Waterloo. I find it necessary to relate the circumstances, because they are such as could not have occurred unless under a singular combination of accidents. In those days, the oblique and lateral communications with many rural post-offices were so arranged, either through necessity or through defect of system, as to make it requisite for the main north-western mail (*i.e.*, the *down* mail), on reaching Manchester, to halt for a number of hours; how many, I do not remember; six or seven, I think; but the result was, that, in the ordinary course, the mail recommenced its journey northwards about midnight. Wearied with the long detention at a gloomy hotel, I walked out about eleven o'clock at night for the sake of fresh air; meaning to fall in with the mail and resume my seat at the post-office. The night, however, being yet dark, as the moon had scarcely risen, and the streets being at that hour empty, so as to offer no opportunities for asking the road, I lost my way; and did not reach the post-office until it was considerably past midnight;

433.20 **saw by** *MS VSD F, SGG* saw in

433.21 **gloom of overhanging houses, that my chance** *MS VSD F* gloom <of overhanging houses>, an evidence that my chance *SGG* gloom, an evidence that my chance

433.22–3 **but by some luck, very unusual in my experience, the** *MS VSD F,* but, by some <luck> rare accident, the *SGG* but, by some rare accident, the

433.27 **signalising** *MS VSD F, SGG* notifying

433.28 **has planted his throne for ever** *SGG* has hoisted his pocket-handkerchief once and for ever

433.29 **henceforward** *MS VSD F, SGG* thenceforward

433.31–2 **either aloft in the atmosphere, or in the shafts, or squatting on the** *MS VSD F* either <aspiringly> aloft in the upper chambers of the atmosphere, or <in> groping in <grop> subterraneous shafts, or squatting audaciously on the surface of the *SGG* in upper chambers of the atmosphere, or groping in subterraneous shafts, or squatting audaciously on the surface of the

433.32–3 **trespassers – that is, decapitated by their very faithful and obedient servant** *MS VSD F* trespassers – kicked, that is to say, or decapitated, as circumstances may suggest, by their <the public's>very faithful servant *SGG* trespassers – kicked, that is to say, or decapitated, as circumstances may suggest, by their very faithful servant

433.33–4 **said bunting. Possibly my** *MS VSD F* said pocket-handerchief. <It> In the present case it is <highly> probable that my *SGG* said pocket-handkerchief. In the present case, it is probable that my

433.37 **passenger; and the** *MS VSD F* passenger to violate the ninth commandment by coveting my seat on the box, or the seventh by stealing it, was not possible under the circumstances; and thus the *SGG* passenger; and thus the

433.38–9 **criminal. By the way, I may** *MS VSD F* criminal. I may *SGG omits*

433.39–40 **point, since a circumstantial accuracy is essential to the effect of my narrative, that** *MS VSD F* point (since a circumstantial accuracy becomes of critical importance further one), that *SGG omits*

433.41 **mail – the guard, the coachman, and myself being allowed for – except** *MS VDS F* mail – over and above the guard, the coachman and myself – except *SGG omits*

433.43 **insiders, but** *MS VSD F* insiders; viz., a tenant of the coal-cellar, but *SGG omits*

433.43 **Oxford called** *MS VSD F* Oxford in these days called *SGG omits*

434.2 **pig. Yet** *MS VSD F* pig. He calls it always <it> *that other creature*> Yet *SGG omits*

434.5–6 **is always careful, out of respect to the company he is dining with, to suppress** *MS VSD F* is careful to suppress *SGG omits*

434.7 **group, and this odious beast (to** *MS VSD F* group, whilst that 'other creature,' with all its odious generations (to *SGG omits*

434.16 **the story,** *MS VSD F* the crisis of the story,

434.16–17 ***not;* or more correctly, perhaps, *it* was not. We** *MS VSD F not*. We *SGG omits*

434.18 **ten miles** *MS VSD F* ten or twelve miles *SGG omits*

434.19 **remark of a** *MS VSD F* remark having a *SGG omits*

434.20 **dies, and be repute suppose of fever,** *MS VSD F* dies (dying suppose, by repute, of fever), *SGG omits*

434.23 **consequently he will enjoy an** *MS VSD F* consequently <he will enjoy> an *SGG omits*

434.23–4 **it, that the verdict** *MS VSD F* it, an idea which perhaps never occurred to the reader, that the verdict *SGG omits*

434.25–6 **it; it is pithy, so that the surviving friends (if any *can* survive such a loss) remember** *MS VSD F* it; the surviving friends remember *SGG omits*

434.27 **that rascals and Dr Johnsons cannot pick holes in it. 'Died** *MS VSD F* that <rascals and> Dr Johnsons, <the sort of verm>in that prey upon <all> other epitaphs, cannot pick holes in this – 'Died *SGG omits*

434.29 **the said wheel** *MS VSD F* the wheel *SGG omits*

434.30–2 **What a simple lapidary inscription! Nobody much in the wrong but an off-wheel; and with few acquaintances; and if it were but rendered into choice Latin, though there would be** *MS VSD F* What a striking inscription, if it were but thrown by the coroner into lapidiary Latin, though there <would> might be *SGG omits*

434.33 **'off-wheel,' Morcellus himself, that great master of sepulchral eloquence, could** *MS VSD F* 'off-wheel,' else Morcellus* himself could *MS VSD F appends footnote Morcellus* [a] – This man was an Italian. His book, a collection (I believe) of formulae and traditional precedents, for clothing in classical Latinity all conceivable cases likely to need expression upon a sepulchral monuments was by Dr Parr[b] much lauded and cited as an authority – dull, dry, dusty, and dreary, upon all questions which have arisen, shall arise, or might have arisen, had it pleased Heaven, within the lugubrious field of epitaphial Latin. *SGG omits*

[[a] See above, p. 621, n. 26.

[b] Samuel Parr (1747-1825; *DNB*), Whig clergyman, schoolmaster and disputatious scholar.]

434.38 **But why linger on the subject of vermin? Having** *MS VSD F* But let us push on. Having *SGG* Having

434.40 **London, upon a simple breakfast. In** *MS VSD F* London < – upon a simple breakfast'. In *SGG* London. In

434.43 ***that* there** *MS VSD F, SGG that* also there

434.44 **my attention** *MS VSD F, SGG* my own attention

435.1 **size,** *MS VSD F, SGG* bulk,

435.4 **He** *MS VSD F, SGG insert paragraph break*

435.4–5 **answered in every point – a monster he was – dreadful, shapeless, huge, who had lost an eye. But** *MS VSD F* he answered <in every point:> to the conditions in <each> {↑ every one} of the <5> items: – 1. a monster he was; 2. dreadful; 3. shapeless; 4. huge; 5. who had lost an eye. But *SGG* answered to the conditions in every one of the items: – 1. a monster he was; 2. dreadful; 3. shapeless; 4. huge; 5. who had lost an eye. But

435.9 **distinctions identified** *MS VSD F, SGG* distinctions (Nos. 1, 2, 3, 4, 5) identified

435.11–12 **could best have undertaken to drive six-in-hand** *MS VSD F, SGG* could (if *any* could) have driven six-in-hand

435.12–17 **that famous bridge of Mahomet across the bottomless gulf, backing himself against the Prophet and twenty such fellows....(Cyclops the charioter.) I,** *MS VSD F* that <famous> dreadful bridge of Mahomet, with no side battlements, and of *extra* room not enough for a razor's edge – leading right across the bottomless gulf. Under this eminent man, whom in Greek I cognominated[a] <backing himself against the Prophet and twenty such fellows: – I xxx I called him *Cyclops mastigophorus*, Cyclops the whip-bearer, until I observed that his skill made whips useless, except to fetch off an impertinent fly from a leader's head; upon which I changed his Grecian name to Cyclops *diphrēlates*> (Cyclops the charioter.) I, *SGG* that dreadful bridge of Mahomet, with no side battlements, and of *extra* room not enough for a razor's edge – leading right across the bottomless gulf. Under this eminent man, whom in Greek I cognominated Cyclops *diphrēlates* (Cyclops the charioteer) I,

[[a] 'Name, style, call' (*OED*, which cites this example from De Quincey).]

435.18 **studied under him the** *MS VSD F, SGG* studied the

435.19–22 **pedantic. And...chasm for the understanding. As** *MS VSD F, SGG* pedantic. As

435.22 **fees, I cannot say that I stood high** *MS VSD F* fees, <I cannot say that I stood> it is to be lamented that I did not stand high *SGG* fees, it is to be lamented that I did not stand high

435.24 **merits. Perhaps we ought to excuse** *MS VSD F* merits. <Perhaps we ought to> Let us excuse *SGG* merits. Let us excuse

435.25 **eye. *That* made** *MS VSD F, SGG* eye. Doubtless *that* made

435.26–7 **merits. Irritating as this blindness was, (surely it could not be envy?) he always courted my conversation, in which art I certainly had** *MS VSD F, SGG* merits. In the art of conversation, however, he admitted that I had

435.28 **this occasion,** *MS VSD F, SGG* this present occasion,

435.31 **in a suit-at-law pending** *MS VSD F, SGG* in some suit-at-law now pending

435.34 **Surely we've been waiting long** *MS VSD F* Surely we<'ve been> have wait<ing>ed long *SGG* Surely we have now waited long

435.35 **and oh this** *MS VSD F, SGG* and this

435.37 **Now you** *MS VSD F, SGG* Yet you

435.37–40 **was in time for *them*. But can *they* lay their hands on their hearts, and say that they were in time for me? I, during my life, have often had to wait for the post-office: the post-office never waited a minute for me. What** *MS VSD FSGG* was here kept waiting for the post-office. Will the post-office lay its hand on its heart, in its <xx> <hours> {↑ moments}of sobriety, and assert that ever it waited <a moment> for me? What *SGG* was here kept waiting for the post-office. Will the post-office lay its hand on its heart, in its moments of sobriety, and assert that ever it waited for me? What

435.42–3 **war and by the packet-service, when as yet nothing is done by** *MS VSD F* war <and by the packet-service, when as yet nothing is done> by wind, by weather, in the packet-service, which as yet does not benefit at all by steam. *SGG* war, by wind, by weather, in the packet-service, which as yet does not benefit at all by

436.2–3 **towns. We can hear the flails going at this moment. But** *MS VSD F, SGG* towns. But

436.7–8 **to recover this last hour amongst the next eight or nine. Off** *MS VSD F* to look sharply for this lost hour amongst the next eight or nine, and to recover it (if we can) at the rate of one mile extra <in every> per hour. Off *SGG* to look sharply for this lost hour amongst the next eight or nine, and to recover it (if we can) at the rate of one mile extra per hour. Off

436.8–9 **and at first I** *MS VSD F, SGG* and for the moment I

436.11 **Westmoreland, were** *MS VSD F, SGG* Westmoreland, there were

436.12 **dated** *MS VSD F, SGG* counting

436.12 **terminated** *MS VSD F, SGG* terminate

436.12–13 **which was** *MS VSD F, SGG* which is

436.14 **three terminated in** *MS VSD F, SGG* three stages terminate in

436.15–16 **place it was** *MS VSD F, SGG* place it is

436.17 **became** *MS VSD F, SGG* become

436.17 **confluent.** *MS VSD F, SGG append footnote; the two texts conform, with the exception of two substantive deletions in MS VSD F given here in angle brackets: 'Confluent:'* – Suppose <the> a capital Y (the Pythagorean letter): Lancaster is at the foot of this letter; Liverpool at the top of the *right* branch; Manchester at the top of the *left;* proud Preston at the centre, where the two branches unite. It is thirty-three miles <It is 33 miles> along either of the two branches; it is twenty-two miles along the stem – viz., from Preston in the middle, to Lancaster at the root. There's <the reader's xx> a lesson in geography for the reader.

436.20 **which I had never previously suspected.** *MS VSD F, SGG* which previously I had never suspected.

436.20–1 **man is addicted to the** *MS VSD F, SGG* man indulges in the

436.22 **execute the motions of his will, avail** *MS VSD F, SGG* execute his notions, avail

436.23–4 **exclaimed more than once, 'Cyclops, my friend; thou art mortal. Thou snorest.'** *MS VSD F, SGG* exclaimed, 'thou are mortal. My friend, thou snorest.'

436.24 **Through this first** *MS VSD F, SGG* Through the first

436.24–5 **however, he betrayed his infirmity** *MSD VSD F, SGG* however, this infirmity

436.25 **say he** *MS VSD F, SGG* say that he

436.25–6 **Pantheon – only by short stretches.** *MS VSD F, SGG* Pantheon – betrayed itself only by brief snatches.

436.27 **mending the matter, laid an ominous foundation for coming** *MS VSD F* mending <the> matters, <laid an ominous foundation for worse> laid open a gloomy vista of <probable> coming *SGG* mending matters, laid open a gloomy vista of coming

436.28 **assizes were now proceeding at** *MS VSD F, SGG* assizes, he reminded me, were now going on at

436.30 **his uncertain summons** *MS VSD F, SGG* his own summons

436.31 **or he was drinking** *MS VSD F, SGG* or else, lest he should be missing at the critical moment, was drinking

436.32 **vigilant** *MS VSD F, SGG* pastoral

436.33–4 **it when the least temptations existed to conviviality, he was driving. Throughout** *MS VSD F,* it which at sea would form the middle watch, he was driving. This explanation certainly accounted for his drowsiness, but in a way which made it much more alarming. <After> since now <after> after several days' resistance to this infirmity, at length he <had begun to give> way. Throughout. *SGG* it which at sea would form the middle watch, he was driving. This explanation certainly accounted for his drowsiness, but in a way which made it much more alarming; since now, after several days' resistance to this infirmity, at length he was steadily giving way. Throughout

436.37–8 **sleep seemed resting upon** *MS VSD F* sleep <weighed> rest upon *SGG* sleep rested upon

436.39–41 **Roses,' for the fiftieth or sixtieth time, without any invitation from Cyclops or myself, and without applause for his poor labours, had moodily resigned** *MS VSD F, SGG* Roses' for perhaps thirty times, without invitation, and without applause, had in revenge moodily resigned

436.42 **mischief; and having, probably, no similar excuse. And** *MS VSD F, SGG* mischief. And

436.43 **Preston, I** *MS VSD F, SGG* Preston, it came about that I

437.1 **running about eleven miles** *MS VSD F, SGG* running at the least twelve miles

437.5 **and of populous** *MS VSD F, SGG* and also of populous

437.8 **required a conflict** *MS VSD F, SGG* required, 1. a conflict

437.8 **interests, a large** *MS VSD F, SGG* interests; 2. a large

437.9 **arrangements, and a** *MS VSD F, SGG* arrangements; and 3. a

437.9 **statute. As** *MS VSD F, SGG* statute. But as yet this change was merely in contemplation. As

437.10 **year** *MS VSD F, SGG append footnote 'Twice in the year:'* – There were at that time only two assizes even in the most populous counties – viz., the Lent Assizes, and the Summer Assizes.

437.11 **that a fortnight** *MS VSD F, SGG* that for a fortnight

437.11 **least occupied** *MS VSD F, SGG* least it occupied

437.12 **two judges for** *MS VSD F, SGG* two judges in

437.16–17 **roads were all silent. Except exhaustion** *MS VSD F* roads sank into <utter> profound silence. Except the exhaustion *SGG* roads sank into profound silence. Except the exhaustion

437.17–18 **election, nothing like it was ordinarily witnessed** *MS VSD F, SGG* election, no such silence succeeding to no such fiery uproar was ever witnessed
437.22 **peace. I myself, though** *MS VSD F, SGG* peace. For my own part, though
437.23 **peril, had** *MS VSD F, SGG* peril, I had
437.24 **in which** *MS VSD F, SGG* in the middle of which
437.25–6 **sigh-born** *MS VSD F* sigh-born *SGG moves footnote from* thoughts.
437.26 **thoughts.*** *MS VSD F* thoughts.* *SGG moves footnote to* sigh-born
437.29 **bodies of men only as** *MS VSD F, SGG* bodies only of men as
437.33 **stranger, that swept** *MS VSD F, SGG* stranger, which swept
437.34–6 **subsiding about sunset, united with the permanent distinction of Lancashire as the very metropolis and citadel of labour, to point** *MS VSD F* subsiding into <deep> silences back into silence about sunset, could not fail (when united with this permanent distinction of Lancashire as the very metropolis and citadel of labour) to point <united had that factor united> with this permanent distinction of Lancashire <at the very metropolis and citadel of labour> to point *SGG* subsiding back into silence about sunset, could not fail (when united with this permanent distinction of Lancashire as the very metropolis and citadel of labour) to point
437.38 **are continually** *MS VSD F, SGG* are in solitude continually
437.39 **Obliquely we were nearing the sea upon our left, which** *MS VSD F, SGG* Obliquely upon our left we were nearing the sea, which
437.41 **bore an** *MS VSD F, SGG* bore each an
438.1–2 **were now blending;** *MS VSD F, SGG* were by this time blending;
438.5 **made little** *SGG* made but little
438.28 **radix, I** *MS VSD F, SGG* radix of the series I
438.29 **in the first syllable of the** *MS VSD F* in the cruel beginning already the *SGG* in the first syllable of the
438.30 **ourselves. What could injure *us?* Our** *MS VSD F, SGG* ourselves. *Us*, our
438.31 **charmed us against** *MS VSD F, SGG* charmed against
438.31 **rode** *MS VSD F, SGG* ridden
438.33 **laughter as we looked back upon them, for** *MS VSD F* the approach to which was through tumults of horror *SGG* laughter to look back upon, the first face of which was horror – the parting face a jest, for
438.38 **then the** *MS VSD F, SGG* then, it may be said, the
438.40 **road, viz., the soft** *MS VSD F, SGG* road – viz., the luxury of the soft
438.41 **others. Our** *MS VSD F, SGG* others. The two adverse carriages would therefore, to a certainty, be travelling on the same side; and from this side, as not being ours in law, the crossing over to the other would, of course, be looked for from *us*.* Our *MS VSD F appends footnote* It is true that by the custom and even by <by precedent> legal precedents all carriages were required to give way before <a> Royal equipages, and therefore before the mail as one of them. But this only increased the danger, as <as> being a regulation <xx> very imperfectly made known, and therefore often embarrassing the movements on both sides. *SGG revises footnote* It is true that, according to the law of the case as established by legal precedents, all carriages were required to give way before Royal equipages, and therefore before the mail as one of them. But this only increased the danger, as being a regulation very imperfectly made known, very unequally enforced, and therefore often embarrassing the movements on both sides.
439.3 **effort – but as by** *MS VSD F, SGG* effort, or by succession, but by
439.3 **horrid intuition.** *SGG* horrid simultaneous intuition.
439.5 **ah reader! what** *SGG* ah! what
439.5–6 **woe, seemed to steal upon** *SGG* wo, was that which stole upon

439.8 **inevitable. What** *MS VSD F, SGG* inevitable; that, being known, was not, therefore, healed. What

439.10 **horses? What! Could I** *MS VSD F* horses> <What!> could I *SGG* horses? Could I

439.14–16 **impossible. The guard subsequently found it impossible, after this danger had passed. Not the grasp only, but also the position of this Polyphemus, made the attempt impossible. You still think otherwise. See, then, that** *MS VSD F* impossible <The guard subsequently found it impossible, after this danger had passed. Not the grasp only, but also the position of this Polyphemus, made the attempt impossible. You still think otherwise.> See<, then,> that *SGG* impossible. Easy, was it? See, then, that

439.19 **water. Or stay, reader, unhorse me that marble emperor: knock** *MS VSD F* water. Or stay, <reader,> unhorse me that Imperial rider: <unhorse me that marble emperor>: knock *SGG* water. Easy, was it? Unhorse me, then, that imperial rider; knock

439.23 **gig? Whoever it was, something** *MS VSD F* gig? Was it sorrow that loitered <heavily>, or joy {↑ that raced?} <that in a headlong career> For as yet the snatches of sound were too intermitting {↑ from distance <the duty of action>} to decipher the character of motion. Whoever it was, something *SGG* gig? Was it sorrow that loitered, or joy that raced? For as yet the snatches of sound were too intermitting, from distance, to decipher the character of the motion. Whoever were the travellers, something

439.23 **be attempted** *MS VSD F* be attempted *SGG* be done

439.25 **was my single self – rests** *MS VSD F* was reduced to my opium-shattered <my single> self – rests *SGG* was reduced to my frail opium-shattered self – rests

439.26 **not seize** *MS VSD F* not seize *SGG* not sound

439.28 **from the foreign mails being** *MS VSD F* from the accident which I have mentioned of foreign mail's being *SGG* from the accident which I have mentioned, of the foreign mails' being

439.32 **us the stage where** *MS VSD F* us the stage where *SGG* us that final stage where

439.32–4 **accomplished, the parties that seemed summoned to the trial, and the impossibility of saving them by any communication with the guard.** *MS VSD F* accomplished<, the parties that seemed summoned to the trial, and the impossibility of saving them by any communication with the guard. when the apparent> {↑ and the} catast{↑ rophe} <must be> sealed: all was apparently finished. The court was sitting; the case was heard; the judge had finished; and only the verdict was to be delivered. *SGG* accomplished, and the catastrophe sealed. All was apparently finished. The court was sitting; the case was heard; the judge had finished; and only the verdict was yet in arrear.

439.39 **a light, reedy gig** *MS VSD F* a <light> frail reedy gig *SGG* a frail reedy gig

439.41 **necessary** *MS VSD F, SGG* requisite

440.1 **nobody at this hour, and on this solitary road, likely to overhear your conversation – is it, therefore, necessary that** *MS VSD F* nobody at an hour and on a road so solitary <at this hour, and on this solitary road>, likely to overhear your conversation – is it therefore, <necessary> requisite that *SGG* nobody, at an hour and on a road so solitary, likely to overhear you – is it therefore requisite that

440.6 **a half. What** *MS VSD F, SGG* a-half. Oh heavens! what

440.7 **do? Strange** *MS VSD F, SGG* do? Speaking or acting, what help can I offer? Strange

440.8 **recourse** *SGG* resource

440.9 **But so** *SGG* Yet so
440.11 **No, certainly: but** *SGG* No: but
440.12 **militant; a shout would suffice, such as should carry** *SGG* militant; such a shout would suffice as might carry
440.18 **the stranger** *SGG* this stranger
440.38 **crisis** *SGG* summons
440.40–1 **some mountainous wave, from which accordingly as he chooses his course, he descries two courses, and** *SGG* some tumultuous crisis, from which lie two courses, and
440.41–2 **audibly – 'This way** *SGG* audibly, 'One way
440.42 **other way and** *SGG* other, and
440.42 **ever!' Yet, even** *SGG* ever!' How grand a triumph, if, even
440.43 **of the seas and** *SGG* of all around him and
441.1 **seek all his** *SGG* seek his
441.1 ***him!*** *SGG inserts paragraph break*
441.3–4 **more he sate immovably,** *SGG* more of his seventy he sat immovably,
441.4–5 **five he sate with** *SGG* five more, perhaps, he sat with
441.6 **for wisdom to guide him towards the** *SGG* for light that should guide him to the
441.7 **sudden** *SGG* powerful
441.14 **twenty** *SGG* seventy
441.14–15 **bound forward may** *SGG* bound may
441.18 **Fear not** *SGG* But fear not
441.36–7 **art above, do thou finish in heaven what** *SGG* art in heaven, do thou finish above what
441.37–8 **attempted.' We ran past them faster than ever mill-race in** *SGG* attempted.' Faster than ever mill-race we ran past them in
441.40 **transit! Either** *SGG* transit! Even in that moment the thunder of collision spoke aloud. Either
441.44 **look** *SGG* gaze
442.1 **its tale,** *SGG* its own tale,
442.3 **The horse** *SGG* Here was the map of the passion that now had finished. The horse
442.4 **party was alone untouched** *SGG* party might be supposed untouched
442.5 **dreadful** *SGG* violent
442.8–9 **man sat like a rock. He stirred not at all. But** *SGG* man trembled not, nor shivered. He sat like a rock. But
442.16 **despairing!** *SGG* despairing?
442.17 **of the unparalleled** *SGG* of that unparalleled
442.23 **crownèd** *SGG* crownéd
442.25 **numbered. In** *SGG* numbered; the strife was finished; the vision was closed. In
442.29 **DREAM FUGUE.** *SGG* THE ENGLISH MAIL-COACH / SECTION THE THIRD. – DREAM-FUGUE.
442.30 **ON THE ABOVE THEME OF SUDDEN DEATH** *SGG* FOUNDED ON THE PRECEDING THEME OF SUDDEN DEATH
443.3 **averted*** *SGG moves footnote to* signs!
443.n.2 **but let it be** *SGG* but it must be
443.3 **signs;** *SGG moves footnote from* averted
443.3 **signs; – Rapture** *F* signs! – Rapture *SGG* signs! – rapture
443.6–7 **ever; – Ah** *F* ever! – Ah, *SGG* ever! Ah,
443.7–8 **of abysses! vision** *SGG* of almighty abysses! – vision
443.9 **back – that didst reel away – like** *SGG* back, that didst reel away, like

443.13 **stern,** *SGG* passionate,
443.15 **thirty years** *SGG* forty years,
443.21 **three-decker. But both** *SGG* three-decker. Both
443.23 **chase where** *SGG* chase of ocean, where
443.24–5 **summer, and which stretches from** *SGG* summer, from
443.25 **Ah! what** *SGG* Ah, what
443.27 **moved.** *SGG* moved!
443.29 **slowly** *SGG* silently
444.2 **the forest was left without a witness to its beauty upon** *SGG* the forests with their beauty were left without a witness upon
444.3 **our own crew** *SGG* our crew
444.7 **cried aloud – 'Sail** *SGG* cried out, 'Sail
444.8 **she will founder!'** *F* she will founder.' *SGG* she also will founder.'
444.11 **sate** *SGG* sat
444.15 **deck. 'Are they blind? Do** *SGG* deck. 'Do
444.16 **sudden** *SGG* local
444.23 **us, amongst** *SGG* us, standing amongst
444.30 **not, and how I know not,** *SGG* not, nor how,
444.37 **with extremity** *SGG* in extremity
445.4 **rock** *SGG* rocks
445.8 **one marble** *SGG* one white marble
445.12 **then her** *SGG* then uttering her
445.18 **sate,** *SGG* sat,
445.20 **But the** *SGG* But suddenly the
445.20 **hushed suddenly by** *SGG* hushed by
445.22 **by its echoes among the** *SGG* by echoes from the
445.23 **said** *SGG* whispered
445.25 ***victory* that swallows** *SGG victory* that is final, victory that swallows
445.30–1 **about our carriage as** *SGG* about ourselves as
445.31 **but we saw** *SGG* but saw
445.33 **joy that acknowledged no fountain but God, to** *SGG* joy, to
445.34–5 **anthems, by reverberations rising from every choir, of the *Gloria in excelsis*. These** *SGG* anthems, and *Te Deums* reverberated from the choirs and orchestras of earth. These
445.36 **sate** *SGG* sat
446.5 **gates to receive us. The** *SGG* gates. The
446.5 **silent** *SGG* conscious
446.6 **the infinite forests,** *SGG* the forests,
446.8 **reached** *SGG* approached
446.16–17 **when we saw before us the aërial galleries of the organ and the choir.** *SGG* when before us we saw the aerial galleries of organ and choir.
446.25 **remission.** *SGG* slackening
446.n.2 **Santo at Pisa – composed** *SGG* Santo (or cemetery) at Pisa, composed
446.n.3–5 **imagine. There is another Campo Santo at Naples, formed, however, (I presume,) on the example given by Pisa. Possibly the idea may have been more extensively copied. To** *SGG* Imagine. To
446.n.8 **horses might roll; and** *SGG* horses *might* run; and
446.n.9 **carried, may** *SGG* carried, as about two centuries back they were through the middle of St Paul's in London, may

447.5 **battles – bas-reliefs of battle-fields; of battles** *SGG* battles and of battle-fields; battles

447.6 **ages – of battles from yesterday – of battle-fields** *SGG* ages – battles from yesterday – battle-fields

447.7–8 **flowers – of battle-fields** *SGG* flowers – battle-fields

447.18 **beheld a female infant that** *SGG* beheld afar off a female child, that

447.22 **topmost** *SGG* mighty

447.25 **thee?'** *SGG* thee!'

447.27 **on the bas-relief** *SGG* on a bas-relief

447.30 **baby! must have spoken from** *SGG* baby! spoke from

447.32–3 **the rattling of our harness, alarmed** *SGG* the dreadful rattle of our harness, the groaning of our wheels, alarmed

448.1 **glory. Whence came *that?* Was it from** *SGG* glory. A glory was it from

448.3 **martyrs that were painted** *SGG* martyrs painted

448.4–6 **earth? Whencesoever it were – there, within that crimson radiance, suddenly appeared a female head, and then a female figure. It was the child – now grown** *SGG* earth? There, suddenly, within that crimson radiance, rose the apparition of a woman's head, and then of a woman's figure. The child it was – grown

448.6 **altar, there she** *SGG* altar, voiceless she

448.7 **rising, trembling, fainting – raving,** *SGG* rising, raving,

448.9–10 **altar, was seen the fiery font, and dimly was descried the outline of the dreadful being that should baptise her** *SGG* altar, dimly was seen the fiery font, and the shadow of that dreadful being who should have baptised her

448.14 **that he** *SGG* that from Heaven he

448.16 **Then rose the agitation spreading through the infinite cathedral, to its agony; then was** *SGG* Then was

448.18 **but sobbed and muttered** *SGG* but muttered

448.24–8 **We, that spread flight...whence were *they?*** *SGG omits*

448.28 **'Oh,** *SGG* Oh,

448.28 **grave!' I exclaimed, 'that** *SGG* grave! that

448.29–30 **visited with secret light – that wert searched** *SGG* visited and searched

448.32–8 **joy, could it be *ye* that...though all men should rejoice? Lo!** *SGG* joy, did ye indeed mingle with the festivals of Death? Lo!

448.39 **cathedral, and saw** *SGG* cathedral, I saw

449.1 **man – ah! raving, as of torrents...children of the grave. All** *SGG* man. All

449.6 **jubilation made ready to move. Like armies** *SGG* jubilation, like armies

449.7 **pursuit, they moved** *SGG* pursuit, moved

449.8 **cathedral through its eastern gates, they** *SGG* cathedral, they

449.9–10 **thunders that overpowered our** *SGG* thunders greater than our

449.10 **together; to the skies we rose – to the dawn** *SGG* together; to the dawn

449.13 **ascending – was ascending from Waterloo – in** *SGG* ascending – from the Campo Santo of Waterloo was ascending – in

449.15 **Death – suddenly** *SGG* death, suddenly

449.18–20 **sleep, has he shown thee to me, standing before the golden dawn, and ready to enter its gates – with the dreadful Word going before thee – with the** *SGG* sleep, have I seen thee entering the gates of the golden dawn – with the secret word riding before thee – with the

449.20–3 **thee; shown thee to me, sinking, rising, fluttering, fainting, but then suddenly reconciled, adoring: a thousand times has he followed thee in the worlds**

of sleep – through *SGG* thee; seen thee sinking, rising, raving, despairing; a thousand times in the worlds of sleep have seen thee followed by God's angel through

449.24 **quicksands; through fugues and the persecution of fugues; through dreams,** *SGG* quicksands; through dreams,

449.25 **resurrections** *SGG* revelations

449.26 **motion** *SGG* sling

449.26 **might record and emblazon the** *SGG* might snatch thee back from ruin, and might emblazon in thy deliverance the

Ollscoil na hÉireann, Gaillimh
3 1111 40113 0537